MW00862275

"Seminary-level New Testament introductions are plentiful. But this one provides what others do not: a consistent hermeneutical orientation as articulated by a top-tier roster of nine different scholars associated with Reformed Theological Seminary throughout its history. In addition to chapters covering all the New Testament books, valuable appendices treat canon, text, the synoptic problem, and more. Addressing both spiritual and academic issues with a view to pastoral equipping and biblical exposition, this wide-ranging compendium will benefit readers in both classroom and personal settings."

Robert W. Yarbrough, Professor of New Testament, Covenant Theological Seminary

"With the right mix of academic integrity and purposeful accessibility, this New Testament introduction will serve time-crunched pastors, ministry-minded students, and church members looking to better understand their Bibles. What makes this new volume unique is the emphasis on examining the theological themes in each book of the New Testament, rather than focusing on arcane debates prompted by liberal scholarship. The result is an insightful and impressive resource, one I will use in my own studies and often recommend to others."

Kevin DeYoung, Senior Pastor, University Reformed Church, East Lansing, Michigan

"While introductions to the New Testament abound, this volume is a rare gem. It admirably combines depth of scholarship and theological exegesis within a biblical-theological framework—all couched in highly readable prose, offered for the sake of the church. It will no doubt instruct *and* edify. Well done."

Constantine R. Campbell, Associate Professor of New Testament, Trinity Evangelical Divinity School

"This biblical-theological introduction walks readers through key biblical themes and issues concerning the backdrop to the 27 books of the New Testament. It is judicious, informative, and also quite accessible, making it profitable for students and pastors alike."

Darrell L. Bock, Executive Director of Cultural Engagement, Hendricks Center, and Senior Research Professor of New Testament Studies, Dallas Theological Seminary

"Aimed at pastors and interested Christian readers, this biblical-theological introduction to the New Testament is a welcome addition to the introductory literature on the New Testament. The volume, a collaborative effort by nine different authors, is written within a framework of biblical theology and based on a commitment to biblical inerrancy and Reformed theology. Highly recommended!"

Andreas J. Köstenberger, Senior Research Professor of New Testament and Biblical Theology, Southeastern Baptist Theological Seminary

"Students and pastors, not to mention laypeople, usually find introductions to the New Testament writings to be rather dry and sterile. But this introduction by RTS authors has a different quality since it focuses on the theology and content of the New Testament. Those who study the New Testament want to gain a better understanding of its message, and thus this volume will prove to be an immense help for pastors, students, laypeople, and even scholars."

Thomas R. Schreiner, James Buchanan Harrison Professor of New Testament Interpretation and Associate Dean of the School of Theology, The Southern Baptist Theological Seminary

"Solid authors construct a biblical theology by providing thematic summaries of each book of the New Testament. While I would not agree with every point made by the authors, many readers will find this an extremely helpful and useful introduction to the teaching of the New Testament."

Peter J. Gentry, Professor of Old Testament Interpretation, The Southern Baptist Theological Seminary; Director, the Hexapla Institute

A Biblical-Theological Introduction to the New Testament

A Biblical-Theological Introduction to the New Testament

The Gospel Realized

Edited by Michael J. Kruger

Foreword by J. Ligon Duncan III

WHEATON, ILLINOIS

A Biblical-Theological Introduction to the New Testament: The Gospel Realized

Published by Crossway
1300 Crescent Street
Wheaton, Illinois 60187

Cover design: Studio Gearbox

First printing 2016

Printed in the United States of America

For other Scripture versions cited, see appendix E.

All emphases in Scripture quotations have been added by the authors.

Hardcover ISBN: 978-1-4335-3676-2
ePub ISBN: 978-1-4335-3679-3
PDF ISBN: 978-1-4335-3677-9
Mobipocket ISBN: 978-1-4335-3678-6

Library of Congress Cataloging-in-Publication Data

A biblical-theological introduction to the New Testament: the gospel realized / edited by Michael J. Kruger; foreword by J. Ligon Duncan III.
pages cm
Includes bibliographical references and index.
ISBN 978-1-4335-3676-2 (hc)
1. Bible. New Testament—Introductions. I. Kruger, Michael J., editor.
BS2330.3.B525 2016
225.06'1—dc23 2015032925

Crossway is a publishing ministry of Good News Publishers.

SH 26 25 24 23 22 21 20 19 18 17 16
15 14 13 12 11 10 9 8 7 6 5 4 3 2 1

Contents

Foreword

As we approach the five hundredth anniversary of the beginning of the Protestant Reformation of the Christian church, Reformed Theological Seminary (RTS) is entering its fiftieth year. The seminary has existed for only a small fraction of the time of this important quarter of Christian history, but RTS has had and continues to have a significant role in this era in which Reformed theology has enjoyed a widely recognized renewal and influence in the global Christian world.

RTS came into being in a time when the mainline denominations and seminaries were administratively in the hands of theological moderates, neoorthodox, and liberals, but the growth curve was already with the evangelicals, both inside and outside the mainline. While denominational apparatchiks were trying to maintain a status quo that was already on the wane, growing numbers of Christians were becoming frustrated with theological educators who were indifferent to or hostile toward historic Christian confessional orthodoxy and unconcerned for the gospel work of the church. RTS was created to provide a robust, reverent, and rigorous theological education for pastors and church leaders, particularly in Presbyterian and Reformed churches yet also more broadly in the larger evangelical family, coming from the standpoint of a commitment to biblical inerrancy, Reformed theology, and the Great Commission.

Because RTS was confessionally defined but not denominationally controlled, the seminary could exercise influence in numerous denominational settings and in a variety of church traditions. Also, since the founders of RTS were connected to a global evangelical network, the seminary was able to have a worldwide reach from the beginning. Over the years, RTS has served over eleven thousand students from some fifty denominations: Presbyterian, Reformed, Baptist, Anglican, Congregational, and more. A seminary that began with fourteen students from one denomination in 1966 now has about two thousand students annually in eight cities in the United States, in its global distance education, and in a doctoral program in São Paulo, Brazil, with students from every continent representing dozens of denominations, and it is the largest Reformed evangelical seminary in the world.

During that time, the academic reputation and contributions of Reformed Theological Seminary faculty have grown. In biblical studies, the RTS faculty has established a pattern of widely appreciated excellence in the fields of the Old and New

Testaments. To give only a few examples, consider former RTS Old Testament professor O. Palmer Robertson, who played a significant role in the contemporary resurgence of covenant theology through his book *The Christ of the Covenants*. Former RTS-Jackson and current RTS-Charlotte Old Testament professor John Currid has produced a complete commentary on the Pentateuch and has done important work in archaeology and ancient Near Eastern studies. Longtime RTS-Orlando Old Testament professor Richard Pratt not only is a prolific author regarded for his excellent Old Testament scholarship, single-handedly producing topical articles for an entire study Bible, but also is known for his work on apologetics and prayer. Miles Van Pelt of RTS-Jackson may be the best biblical languages professor I have ever known, with an infectious passion for canonical, Christ-centered biblical theology. Former RTS-Jackson and current RTS-Orlando New Testament professor Simon Kistemaker served as the longtime secretary of the Evangelical Theology Society and completed the multivolume New Testament commentary begun by William Hendriksen. RTS-Orlando professor Charles Hill is not only an acclaimed New Testament specialist but also one of the world's top scholars in the eschatology of early Christianity. In addition, RTS-Charlotte president and professor of New Testament Michael Kruger is a recognized scholar of early Christianity and has made major contributions to recent discussions of the canon of Scripture. Indeed, Kruger and Hill, along with RTS-Orlando professor John Frame, were cited by D. A. Carson in a recent plenary address at the Evangelical Theology Society as having made outstanding contributions in the field of the doctrine of Scripture. RTS-Jackson New Testament scholar Guy Waters has published prolifically on various topics including ecclesiology and has helped reshape the current debates on the theology of Paul.

In an effort to pass along this world-class, faithful, consecrated scholarship to the next generation, the Old and New Testament professors at RTS—both past and present—have put together two new volumes: *A Biblical-Theological Introduction to the Old Testament: The Gospel Promised* (edited by Miles V. Van Pelt), and *A Biblical-Theological Introduction to the New Testament: The Gospel Realized* (edited by Michael J. Kruger). There are several unique features and aspirations of these volumes. First, they are aimed at pastors and interested Christian readers, rather than fellow scholars. We at RTS value and produce resources intended for a scholarly audience, but the aim of these volumes is churchly edification, hence they are designed for accessibility. Second, they are written by scholars of biblical studies who are unafraid of and indeed very much appreciative of dogmatics. In many seminaries, even evangelical seminaries, there exists an unhealthy relationship between biblical theology and systematic theology, but at RTS we value both and want our students to understand their necessary and complementary value. To understand the Bible, and the Christian faith, one needs both the insights of a redemptive-historical approach and those of topical-doctrinal study. Third, these volumes unashamedly come from the standpoint of biblical inerrancy and Reformed theology. A high view of Scripture and a warm embrace of confessional Reformed theology are hallmarks of RTS, and these ideals shine through these books. Fourth, these introductions are designed to be pastoral and helpful. Preachers, ministry leaders, Bible teachers, students, and others engaged in Christian discipleship are in view. We want to edify you and help you edify others.

May these volumes bless the church of Jesus Christ for generations to come as it seeks to know his Word better and to proclaim it to the nations.

J. Ligon Duncan III
Chancellor and CEO
John E. Richards Professor of Systematic and Historical Theology
Reformed Theological Seminary

Acknowledgments

A project such as this one is certainly not an individual affair. As the editor, I am grateful for the help I have received from a number of sources. Certainly the contributors themselves deserve a word of thanks. It has been a privilege to work with such a fine collection of scholars, all exceptional professors and experts in their respective fields. Since they are routinely swamped with other teaching and writing responsibilities, I am grateful they have carved out the time to contribute to this volume. I am confident that their work here will leave a legacy of truth for future generations of pastors, Bible teachers, and seminary students.

Let me also express my appreciation for Justin Taylor and the team at Crossway. They are, as always, a delight to work with, and their keen interest in this project was a great encouragement. Guy Waters deserves a special word of thanks for his willingness to provide input and feedback at a number of critical junctures. His generous spirit and sharp intellect were a great help to me. My teaching assistants Aaron Gray and Aaron Ingle were indispensable as they spent many hours editing and proofing the manuscript of this volume. And, of course, Reformed Theological Seminary itself deserves a word of thanks as this volume is being published in honor of its fiftieth anniversary. It is a privilege to serve at an institution so committed to the authority of Scripture and the supremacy of Christ in all things. May those traits remain true for another fifty years and beyond.

Most of all, I want to thank my wife, Melissa, and my three children, Emma, John, and Kate. As with each of my prior books, they have sacrificed much as I have labored on this project, but they have always done so with joy and thankfulness. My prayer is that this volume would be a blessing to each of them as they study the Scriptures in the years to come.

Michael J. Kruger

Abbreviations

1 Apol.	*First Apology* (Justin Martyr)
1 Clem.	1 Clement
1 QS	Serek Hayahad or Rule of the Community
1–2 Macc.	1–2 Maccabees
2 Bar.	2 Baruch (Syriac Apocalypse)
3–4 Macc.	3–4 Maccabees
AB	Anchor Bible
ABD	*Anchor Bible Dictionary.* Edited by David Noel Freedman. 6 vols. New York: Doubleday, 1992
Abr.	*De Abrahamo* (*On the Life of Abraham*, Philo)
ABRL	Anchor Bible Reference Library
ACCS	Ancient Christian Commentary on Scripture
ACNT	Augsburg Commentary on the New Testament
AGJU	Arbeiten zur Geschichte des antiken Judentums und des Urchristentums
AJT	*American Journal of Theology*
An.	*De anima* (*The Soul*, Tertullian)
ANF	*The Ante-Nicene Fathers*. Edited by Alexander Roberts and James Donaldson. 1885–1887. 10 vols. Repr., Peabody, MA: Hendrickson, 1994
Ant.	*Jewish Antiquities* (Josephus)
ANTC	Abingdon New Testament Commentaries
Antichr.	*De antichristo* (*On Christ and the Antichrist*, Hippolytus)
Ant. rom.	*Antiquitates romanae* (*Roman Antiquities*, Dionysius of Halicarnassus)
Att.	*Epistulae ad Atticum* (*Letters to Atticus*, Cicero)
AYB	Anchor Yale Bible
Barn.	Epistle of Barnabas

BBR *Bulletin for Biblical Research*

BDAG Bauer, Walter, Frederick W. Danker, William F. Arndt, and F. Wilbur Gingrich. *Greek-English Lexicon of the New Testament and Other Early Christian Literature*. 3rd ed. Chicago: University of Chicago Press, 2000

BECNT Baker Exegetical Commentary on the New Testament

BETL Bibliotheca Ephemeridum Theologicarum Lovaniensium

Bib *Biblica*

BJRL *Bulletin of the John Rylands University Library of Manchester*

BNTC Black's New Testament Commentaries

BR *Biblical Research*

BST Bible Speaks Today

BTNT Biblical Theology of the New Testament

BZNW Beihefte zur Zeitschrift für die neutestamentliche Wissenschaft

Cass. *Cassiodorus*

CBET Contributions to Biblical Exegesis and Theology

CBQMS Catholic Biblical Quarterly Monograph Series

Cher. *De cherubim* (*On the Cherubim*, Philo)

Comm. Apoc. *Commentary on the Apocalypse* (Victorinus)

Comm. Jo. *Commentarii in evangelium Joannis* (*Commentary on the Gospel of John*, Origen)

ConcC Concordia Commentary

Conf. *Confessions* (Augustine)

CTR *Criswell Theological Review*

Cult. fem. *De cultu feminarum* (*The Apparel of Women*, Tertullian)

CurBS *Currents in Research: Biblical Studies*

Dial. *Dialogue with Trypho* (Justin Martyr)

DJG *Dictionary of Jesus and the Gospels*. Edited by Joel B. Green and Scot McKnight. Downers Grove, IL: InterVarsity Press, 1992

DJG[2] *Dictionary of Jesus and the Gospels*. Edited by Joel B. Green, Jeannine K. Brown, and Nicholas Perrin. 2nd ed. Downers Grove, IL: IVP Academic, 2013

DPL *Dictionary of Paul and His Letters*. Edited by G. F. Hawthorne and R. P. Martin. Downers Grove, IL: InterVarsity Press, 1993

ECC Eerdmans Critical Commentary

EDNT *Exegetical Dictionary of the New Testament*. Edited by Horst Balz and Gerhard Schneider. ET. 3 vols. Grand Rapids, MI: Eerdmans, 1990–1993

EGGNT Exegetical Guide to the Greek New Testament

EKKNT	Evangelisch-katholischer Kommentar zum Neuen Testament
Ep.	*Epistulae morales* (*Moral Epistles*, Seneca)
Eph.	*To the Ephesians* (Ignatius)
EPSC	EP Study Commentary
EvQ	*Evangelical Quarterly*
ExAud	*Ex Auditu*
FB	Focus on the Bible
fr.	*fragmentum*, *fragmenta*
Fug.	*De fuga in persecutione* (*Flight in Persecution*, Tertullian)
GCS	Die griechischen christlichen Schriftsteller der ersten [drei] Jahrhunderte
Haer. (Hippolytus)	*Refutatio omnium haeresium* (*Refutation of All Heresies*, Hippolytus)
Haer. (Irenaeus)	*Adversus haereses* (*Against Heresies*, Irenaeus)
Hist. eccl.	*Historia ecclesiastica* (*Ecclesiastical History*, various authors)
HNTC	Harper's New Testament Commentaries
Hom. Gen.	*Homilies on Genesis* (Origen)
Hom. Jos.	*Homilies on Joshua* (Origen)
Hom. Num.	*Homilies on Numbers* (Origen)
HTR	*Harvard Theological Review*
ICC	International Critical Commentary
Inv.	*De inventione rhetorica* (Cicero)
IVPNTC	IVP New Testament Commentary
JBL	*Journal of Biblical Literature*
JETS	*Journal of the Evangelical Theological Society*
JSJ	*Journal for the Study of Judaism in the Persian, Hellenistic and Roman Periods*
JSNT	*Journal for the Study of the New Testament*
JSNTSup	Journal for the Study of the New Testament: Supplement Series
JTS	*Journal of Theological Studies*
Jub.	Jubilees
J.W.	*Jewish War* (Josephus)
LCL	Loeb Classical Library
LEC	Library of Early Christianity
Leg.	*De legibus* (*On the Laws*, Cicero)

LSJ Liddell, Henry George, Robert Scott, Henry Stuart Jones. *A Greek-English Lexicon.* 9th ed. with revised supplement. Oxford: Clarendon, 1996

LTPM Louvain Theological and Pastoral Monographs

LXX Septuagint

Marc. *Against Marcion* (Tertullian)

MNTC Moffatt New Testament Commentary

Mos. *De vita Mosis* (*On the Life of Moses*, Philo)

MSS manuscripts

NAC New American Commentary

NCB New Century Bible

NCBC New Cambridge Bible Commentaries

Neot *Neotestamentica*

NICNT New International Commentary on the New Testament

NIDNTT *New International Dictionary of New Testament Theology.* Edited by Colin Brown. 4 vols. Grand Rapids, MI: Zondervan, 1975–1985

NIDNTTE *New International Dictionary of New Testament Theology and Exegesis.* Edited by Moisés Silva. 5 vols. Grand Rapids, MI: Zondervan, 2014

NIGTC New International Greek Testament Commentary

NIVAC New International Version Application Commentary

NovT *Novum Testamentum*

NovTSup Supplements to Novum Testamentum

NPNF[1] *Nicene and Post-Nicene Fathers*, Series 1. Edited by Philip Schaff. 1886–1889. 14 vols. Repr., Peabody, MA: Hendrickson, 1994

NPNF[2] *Nicene and Post-Nicene Fathers*, Series 2. Edited by Philip Schaff. 1886–1889. 14 vols. Repr., Peabody, MA: Hendrickson, 1994

NSBT New Studies in Biblical Theology

NTC New Testament Commentary

NTL New Testament Library

NTOA Novum Testamentum et Orbis Antiquus

NTS *New Testament Studies*

NTT New Testament Theology (series from Cambridge University Press)

NTTS New Testament Tools and Studies

NTTSD New Testament Tools, Studies, and Documents

Od. *Odyssey* (Homer)

Opif.	*De opificio mundi* (*On the Creation of the World*, Philo)
OTL	Old Testament Library
Phil.	*To the Philippians* (Polycarp)
Phld.	*To the Philadelphians* (Ignatius)
PNTC	Pillar New Testament Commentary
Praescr.	*De praescriptione haereticorum* (*Prescription against Heretics*, Tertullian)
Princ.	*First Principles* (Origen)
Pss. Sol.	Psalms of Solomon
RBL	*Review of Biblical Literature*
Rhet. Her.	*Rhetorica ad Herennium*
Rom.	*To the Romans* (Ignatius)
SBLECL	Society of Biblical Literature Early Christianity and Its Literature
SBLMS	Society of Biblical Literature Monograph Series
SBLStBL	Society of Biblical Literature Studies in Biblical Literature
SBLSymS	Society of Biblical Literature Symposium Series
Scorp.	*Antidote for the Scorpion's Sting* (Tertullian)
SD	Studies and Documents
Smyrn.	*To the Smyrnaeans* (Ignatius)
SNTSMS	Society for New Testament Studies Monograph Series
SOTBT	Studies in Old Testament Biblical Theology
SP	Sacra Pagina
SUNT	Studien zur Umwelt des Neuen Testaments
SWBA	Social World of Biblical Antiquity
T. 12 Patr.	Testaments of the Twelve Patriarchs
T. Ash.	Testament of Asher
T. Benj.	Testament of Benjamin
T. Dan	Testament of Dan
T. Gad	Testament of Gad
T. Isaac	Testament of Isaac
T. Iss.	Testament of Issachar
T. Jac.	Testament of Jacob
T. Job	Testament of Job
T. Jos.	Testament of Joseph
T. Jud.	Testament of Judah

T. Levi — Testament of Levi

T. Mos. — Testament of Moses

T. Naph. — Testament of Naphtali

T. Reu. — Testament of Reuben

T. Sim. — Testament of Simeon

T. Zeb. — Testament of Zebulun

TBC — Torch Bible Commentaries

TDNT — *Theological Dictionary of the New Testament*. Edited by Gerhard Kittel and Gerhard Friedrich. Translated by Geoffrey W. Bromiley. 10 vols. Grand Rapids, MI: Eerdmans, 1964–1976

Them — *Themelios*

TNTC — Tyndale New Testament Commentaries

TPINTC — TPI New Testament Commentaries

TrinJ — *Trinity Journal*

TynBul — *Tyndale Bulletin*

VC — *Vigiliae Christianae*

VTSup — Supplements to Vetus Testamentum

WBC — Word Biblical Commentary

WCF — Westminster Confession of Faith

WLC — Westminster Larger Catechism

WSC — Westminster Shorter Catechism

WTJ — *Westminster Theological Journal*

WUNT — Wissenschaftliche Untersuchungen zum Neuen Testament

ZECNT — Zondervan Exegetical Commentary on the New Testament

ZNW — *Zeitschrift für die neutestamentliche Wissenschaft und die Kunde der älteren Kirche*

Introduction

Michael J. Kruger

As professors at Reformed Theological Seminary (both past and present), all the contributors to this volume have devoted the bulk of their scholarly efforts, over the course of many years, to the study of the twenty-seven books that form this corpus we call the New Testament. This study has been motivated not simply by a desire to advance our personal knowledge of God's Word (though that is important in its own right), but it has been motivated primarily by the commitment to pass along the fruits of that study to the next generation of pastors, leaders, missionaries, and Christian thinkers. The future of the church depends on her knowledge of, and commitment to, the teachings of God's Word.

This "passing along" of what we have learned takes place primarily in the classroom setting. Our New Testament classes are designed to introduce students to these books from a variety of angles—historical, exegetical, theological—and to help students teach, preach, and apply these books to their respective audiences.

But the classroom setting has its limitations. Not all have the opportunity to be in a seminary class. And not all are in a position to study the material at the depth seminary requires. The present volume, therefore, is simply an attempt to take the core material from these courses and put it into a different medium—the medium of a book. Our goal is to produce a New Testament introduction that captures the foundational material in our classes and presents it in a way that could be readily accessible to ministry leaders, preachers, Bible study teachers, and, of course, seminary students.

Needless to say, there have been many New Testament introductions prior to this one—from Theodor Zahn's massive two-volume *Einleitung in das Neue Testament* (Leipzig, 1897) to D. A. Carson and Douglas Moo's very popular *An Introduction to the New Testament*, 2nd ed. (Grand Rapids, MI: Zondervan, 2005).[1] So the reader may wonder whether we really need another one. What is distinctive about

[1] For an overview of the history of research on the New Testament, including the many introductions, see William Baird, *History of New Testament Research*, 3 vols. (Minneapolis: Augsburg Fortress, 1992–2013).

this particular volume? In many ways, of course, this new volume is not distinctive. Like many of the volumes that have come before, it is designed to accomplish the same basic task: namely, to introduce the reader to the major historical, exegetical, and theological issues within each of the twenty-seven books.

In other ways, however, this volume is distinctive. Here are some noteworthy features that set this introduction apart from some others that have gone before:

It is accessible. Generally speaking, New Testament introductions have tended to focus primarily on historical-critical issues related to the background of each of the twenty-seven books. While many introductions spend considerable time engaging in highly technical discussions about dating, authorship, and textual history, they often devote comparably little space to the theological, doctrinal, and practical aspects of these books.

Now, it should be noted that these background issue are very important in their own right; and the authors of this volume have dealt with many of them in other places (e.g., see Charles Hill's highly technical monograph on the origins of the Johannine corpus).[2] However, for the average Bible study leader or local pastor, such discussions are not always their primary need as they prepare their lessons or sermons. Sure, they need to be introduced to the major background issues, but not in such a way that they get mired in overly technical discussions. For these reasons, the present volume has attempted to make the discussion of background issues more streamlined and more accessible.

By way of example, some of the more technical discussions that normally appear at the beginning of New Testament introductions—discussions related to the New Testament text, the New Testament canon, and the synoptic problem—now appear at the end of this one. Thus, these important appendixes are available if and when they are needed, but they are not, if you will, the lead story. And they are targeted not to the scholar but to the average pastor or student.

It is theological. In addition to spending less time on historical background issues, this volume is consciously committed to spending (comparably) more time on theological and doctrinal issues. Because this volume is designed primarily to help pastors and Bible study leaders prepare their sermons or lessons, a higher priority is placed on exploring the *message* of each New Testament book. It is this priority that has led to the title *A Biblical-Theological Introduction to the New Testament*.

Of course, the term *biblical theology* conjures up a variety of thoughts in people's minds.[3] Historically, some advocates of biblical theology viewed the New Testament as filled with diverse and contradictory theologies that merely reflect the different factions in the early church.[4] According to such an approach, there is no such thing as New

[2] Charles E. Hill, *The Johannine Corpus in the Early Church* (Oxford: Oxford University Press, 2004).

[3] For an overview of the state of the discipline of biblical theology, see Scott J. Hafemann, ed., *Biblical Theology: Retrospect and Prospect* (Downers Grove, IL: InterVarsity Press, 2002); and D. A. Carson, "Current Issues in Biblical Theology: A New Testament Perspective," *BBR* 5 (1995): 17–41.

[4] J. D. G. Dunn, *Unity and Diversity in the New Testament: An Inquiry into the Character of Early Christianity*, 3rd ed. (London: SCM, 2006); Ernst Käsemann, "The Problem of a New Testament Theology," *NTS* 19 (1973): 235–45.

Testament theology, but only, say, the theology of Paul or John or the Synoptics—and these different theologies are often at odds with one another. Such a view of biblical theology is not the one advocated in this volume. The contributors acknowledge that each biblical author makes his own distinctive contribution, but, at the same time, they acknowledge that these different contributions are consistent with one another and can still be viewed as a unified whole. Because God is the ultimate author of the New Testament writings, the distinctive theologies of individual books and the overall theology of the New Testament are fully harmonious.[5]

Others view biblical theology as a corrective to (and replacement of) systematic theology. Traditional dogmatics, some would argue, is an illegitimate enterprise that forces Scripture into artificial and man-made categories. Biblical theology, on the other hand, is presented as something that preserves, with greater integrity, the message of the Bible. Such an approach is, again, not shared by the contributors to this volume. We recognize that systematic theology can be misused; some have developed systematic systems that are, in fact, contrary to Scripture. But such misuse does not make the enterprise itself illegitimate. There are many positive examples of systematic theologies that faithfully reflect the teaching of Scripture rather than overriding it. In addition, the contributors to this volume have a deep appreciation for the value and insights of biblical theology. The message of each book can (and should) be studied within the context of the author's own historical situation. But biblical theology and systematic theology should not be pitted against each other. Both play a critical role and should not be viewed as mutually exclusive.[6] As Geerhardus Vos observed, "Biblical Theology . . . differs from Systematic Theology, not in being more Biblical, or adhering more closely to the truths of Scripture, but in that its principle of organizing the Biblical material is historical rather than logical."[7]

As an example of how this volume seeks to develop the rich theology of the New Testament authors, see the excellent chapter on Ephesians by Guy Waters. Noting how Ephesians is centrally focused on the gospel message, Waters first explores the gospel "indicatives" by highlighting how Paul uncovers the redemptive work of each member of the Trinity, Father, Son, and Holy Spirit. Then he explores the gospel "imperatives," namely, Paul's argument that, in light of the grace of Christ, we are to walk in a manner worthy of our calling (Eph. 4:1). Such a life worthy of our calling includes a commitment to serving the church, putting off the old self and putting on the new self, and submitting to the various authorities in our lives. Thus, when the chapter is finished, the reader leaves with more than just an understanding of the controversy over whether Paul wrote Ephesians (though one does leave with an

[5] Some authors express their commitment to the overall unity and coherence of the New Testament by arranging their New Testament theologies *thematically* rather than according to each individual book. E.g., Thomas Schreiner, *New Testament Theology: Magnifying God in Christ* (Grand Rapids, MI: Baker Academic, 2008).

[6] The harmony between the two can be demonstrated by the fact that Geerhardus Vos, who is mainly celebrated for his work in biblical theology (*Biblical Theology* [Edinburgh: Banner of Truth, 1975]) also wrote a systematic theology (*Reformed Dogmatics*, vol. 1, *Theology Proper* [Bellingham, WA: Lexham, 2014]). See also the balanced and helpful discussion by Robert J. Cara, "Redemptive-Historical Themes in the Westminster Larger Catechism," in *The Westminster Confession into the 21st Century: Essays in Remembrance of the 350th Anniversary of the Westminster Assembly*, ed. J. Ligon Duncan, vol. 3 (Fearn: Mentor, 2009), 55–76.

[7] Vos, *Biblical Theology*, v.

understanding of that). The reader leaves also with a deep, thorough, and full-orbed grasp of the gospel of Jesus Christ and its implications for everyday life.

It is redemptive-historical. This volume is committed not only to exploring the theological message of individual New Testament books, but also to placing the message of each book within God's unfolding redemptive plan. The goal is more than extracting timeless truths from these books. We also want to discover how these books functioned within the timeline of the larger canonical story—how an author's message contributes to our overall understanding of the work of Christ.

While many scholars would still describe this approach as an aspect of biblical theology,[8] it might be simpler to say, for the sake of terminological clarity, that we are interested in looking at each of the New Testament books through the lens of *redemptive history*.[9] We want to show how each book contributes to the fulfillment of God's salvific plan. In particular, such an approach would focus on how Old Testament history, types, and shadows all find their fulfillment in the person and work of Christ.[10]

To be sure, some contributors in this volume focus on these redemptive-historical themes more than others. Some are content to observe the theological themes of their particular book in traditional systematic categories, while others are more interested in how that book fits into the timeline of the larger biblical story. An excellent example of the latter is the chapter by Benjamin Gladd on the Gospel of Mark. Gladd explores how the redemptive activity of Jesus is really a fulfillment of a "second exodus" motif from the book of Isaiah. He demonstrates how the author Mark constructs portions of his narrative around the exodus theme to highlight Jesus as the great deliverer who brings final redemption to his people Israel. By doing so, Gladd helps the reader see how Jesus completes the story of the Old Testament narrative and how Mark's Gospel makes a key contribution to our understanding of God's plan of salvation.

Another example of a helpful focus on redemptive-historical themes is the chapter on Matthew by Reggie Kidd. Since Matthew is a Gospel steeped in the Old Testament, a Gospel likely written for a Jewish-Christian audience, Kidd helps the reader see how Matthew presents Jesus as the fulfillment of Old Testament types and the superior (and final) stage of God's redemptive activity. In particular, Kidd highlights how Jesus is presented as the new Moses (since Matthew's Gospel is presented in five sections), as greater than the temple, as greater than Jonah, and as greater than Solomon.

---

[8] Vos uses the phrase *biblical theology* in this fashion, but he admits it is "really unsatisfactory because of its liability to misconstruction" (ibid.).

[9] The terms *biblical-theological* and *redemptive-historical* are seen by many as virtually synonymous: e.g., Edmund P. Clowney, *Preaching and Biblical Theology* (Nutley, NJ: P&R, 1975), 16; and R. B. Gaffin, "Biblical Theology and the Westminster Standards," in *The Practical Calvinist: An Introduction to the Presbyterian and Reformed Heritage*, ed. Peter A. Lillback (Fearn: Mentor, 2002), 425–42, esp. 425. For additional use of the phrase *redemptive-historical*, see Herman Ridderbos, *Paul: An Outline of His Theology*, trans. John Richard de Witt (Grand Rapids, MI: Eerdmans, 1975), 39, 45.

[10] For a helpful example of such an approach, see G. K. Beale, *A New Testament Biblical Theology: The Unfolding of the Old Testament in the New* (Grand Rapids, MI: Baker Academic, 2011).

It is Reformed. For any New Testament introduction—particularly one that focuses largely on the theology and message of each book—it is important that the authors be theologically and doctrinally sound. While a number of available introductions are written by highly capable authors (academically speaking), many of these lack the doctrinal integrity one might need to prepare sermons or Bible studies. Such introductions often have a low view of the authority of Scripture and are quite content to affirm many higher-critical views, such as the belief that many of the New Testament books are forgeries and not written by the individuals to whom they are ascribed.

In contrast, the contributors to this volume, all current or past professors of New Testament at Reformed Theological Seminary, have a high view of the authority of Scripture and are all committed to the foundational doctrines born out of the Reformation. These truths are embodied in the Westminster Confession of Faith and in the five *solas* of the Reformation:

- *Sola Scriptura* (Scripture alone): the Bible alone is the highest authority.
- *Sola fide* (faith alone): faith is the sole instrument of our justification.
- *Sola gratia* (grace alone): we are saved by the grace of God alone, not by works.
- *Solus Christus* (Christ alone): Christ is the only Mediator between God and man.
- *Soli Deo gloria* (to the glory of God alone): all of life is lived for the glory of God alone.

The commitment of each of the contributors to the authority of Scripture means (among other things) that they affirm and uphold the traditional authorship of these books. By way of example, see Simon J. Kistemaker's excellent chapter on 2 Peter—a book that critical scholars roundly regard as forged by a later author pretending to be Peter. Dr. Kistemaker rejects this approach and offers a robust defense of the apostle Peter as the author. The authorial claim of the letter, he points out, goes well beyond the opening line. The author actually presents himself as Peter by recalling his presence at the transfiguration of Jesus (2 Pet. 1:16–18). To suggest that the author is *not* Peter would mean the text is making a false claim—and that would be inconsistent with a high view of Scripture.

For another example of how the contributors come from a consistently Reformed perspective, see Robert Cara's excellent chapter on 1 Thessalonians. There he covers three critical theological issues: the lordship of Christ, eschatology, and election/calling. Each of these issues is controversial in its own right and has occasioned much discussion and disagreement. But with both charity and clarity, Cara sorts through the complex issues and points the reader back to a view that is consistent not only with the text but also with the historical Reformed perspective on each of these important issues.

It is important to note, however, that these theological commitments do not come at the expense of academic competence. Some assume that any given scholar must choose between the two. However, the goal of this volume is to join together high-quality scholarship with a deep commitment to the authority of Scripture and the distinctives of Reformed theology. The modern academy will insist that these two characteristics cannot be combined. We would disagree.

It is multiauthored. Most New Testament introductions are written by a single author. And even if some introductions have multiple authors, rarely are their contributions identified by author.[11] This volume is distinctive because of the quantity of individual authors (nine) and because the reader is told which authors composed which portions.

Of course, books with multiple contributors have a number of potential (and real) weaknesses. There is the danger of disparate writing styles, inconsistency of approach, and differing academic and theological interests. We have tried to minimize some of these dangers by having every chapter follow the same fivefold structure: Introduction, Background Issues, Structure and Outline, Message and Theology, and Select Bibliography. But even within this structure, we have tried to allow each other some freedom in terms of how we approach each book. For instance, under the Message and Theology section some authors have preferred to describe the message under major theological headings, whereas others have described the message of the book chapter by chapter—almost like a commentary. So even a formal structure cannot make all chapters look exactly the same. As a result, and despite our best efforts, this volume still runs the danger of feeling like a collection of chapters lacking the consistency of a single-authored volume. With this many different writers, a level of diversity and multiplicity is simply inevitable.

But it is our hope that the weaknesses of a multiauthored volume are outweighed by its strengths. A multiauthored volume allows the reader to be exposed to a variety of different perspectives and backgrounds—something that single-authored volumes are unable to achieve. The reader is not bound to just a single voice, but is able to hear a range of voices. And certain readers will resonate with some voices more than others. In addition, a multiplicity of contributors allows for each one to home in on his particular area of expertise. Such specificity gives the reader an opportunity to hear from a scholar whose research specializes in the very area about which he is writing.

Two good examples of how such a volume allows for scholarly specialization are Charles Hill's chapters on the Johannine letters and the book of Revelation. In addition to Hill's extensive research into the Johannine corpus (see again *The Johannine Corpus in the Early Church*), he also has done intensive primary research into early Christian eschatological views in his book Regnum Caelorum*: Patterns of Millennial Thought in Early Christianity*, 2nd ed. (Grand Rapids, MI: Eerdmans, 2001). This latter volume helps Hill sift through the various views on Revelation from the perspective of the history of the church.

In addition, it should be noted that the multiauthored nature of the volume is driven

[11] Examples of well-known introductions with multiple authors are D. A. Carson and Douglas J. Moo, *An Introduction to the New Testament* (Grand Rapids, MI: Zondervan, 2005); Paul J. Achtemeier, Joel B. Green, and Marianne Meye Thompson, eds., *Introducing the New Testament and Its Literature* (Grand Rapids, MI: Eerdmans, 2001); and Andreas J. Köstenberger, L. Scott Kellum, and Charles L. Quarles, *The Cradle, the Cross, and the Crown: An Introduction to the New Testament* (Nashville: B&H Academic, 2009).

by the occasion for which it was written. As Ligon Duncan notes in the foreword, the volume is being written in commemoration of Reformed Theological Seminary's fiftieth anniversary in 2016. For this reason, nearly all New Testament professors throughout the seminary's history were included. As a result, this volume not only provides a glimpse into the thinking of individual scholars; it provides a glimpse into the ministry of Reformed Theological Seminary as a whole and its commitment to the authority of the Bible, Reformed theology, and a love for the church.

It is pastoral. As noted above, the very real purpose of this volume is to help Bible study leaders, pastors, and Christian leaders to teach and apply the Word of God to their respective audiences. This is, of course, the reason for the emphasis on the message of these books (and not just technical background issues). Moreover, this volume has sought to take the message of these books and apply it to the issues before the church in a practical and pastoral manner.

By way of example, William Barcley's chapter on 1 Peter takes the discussion of life as a foreigner and alien and, with a pastoral touch, encourages readers to keep their eyes fixed on the New Jerusalem and our eternal inheritance. Bruce Lowe, in his chapter on James, does an excellent job taking James's discussion of faith and works and applying it to the practical day-to-day struggle that Christians face over sanctification. And in my own chapter on the Gospel of John, I lay out practical ways that John's message can be applied to an audience in a sermon or Bible study series.

This pastoral dimension to this New Testament introduction is driven by two factors. First, almost all of the contributors are also ordained ministers, and many of them have years of pastoral experience. Consequently, there is a natural inclination within these scholars to teach the biblical text in a manner that is practical and pastoral. Second, all of the contributors are committed to the idea that the primary purpose of biblical scholarship is to teach and bless the *church*. This does not mean, of course, that one is forbidden from doing scholarship geared toward one's academic peers. Indeed, many of the contributors have written impressive scholarly works interacting with the broader academic guild. But those same scholars recognize that this is not the only purpose of their scholarship. Ultimately, God's Word has been given for the edification and development of God's people. A scholar can make a meaningful contribution to his field and, at the same time, apply his scholarly efforts to the local church setting. This volume (we hope) is a demonstration that the two are not mutually exclusive. In this sense, its contributors really are pastor-scholars.

With these distinctives in mind, we can now turn our attention to the individual books of the New Testament. Our hope, in the words of the apostle Paul, is that "the Word of the Lord may speed ahead and be honored" (2 Thess. 3:1) as a result of the content of this volume. *Soli Deo gloria.*

1

Matthew

Reggie M. Kidd

Introduction

Of the four canonical Gospels, Matthew's is the only one to use the term *church* (ἐκκλησία, 16:18; 18:17). For this and other reasons, Matthew's account has always commended itself as being especially useful to the "church" that Jesus founds in this Gospel. One reason is that as a master artisan—or in his own terms, a steward of old and new (13:52)—Matthew structures his Gospel in a way that ties the Old and New Testaments together as Israel's story and the continuation of Israel's story in the newly emergent church. To that end, Matthew provides richly suggestive patterns for teaching (see below, for his five teaching blocks: the Sermon on the Mount [chaps. 5–7], the mission to Israel [chap. 10], parables of the kingdom [chap. 13], life in the church [chap. 18], and preparation for judgment [chaps. 23–25]).

Another reason that Matthew's Gospel has proved so serviceable for the church's teaching and preaching is its finely balanced sense of Jesus's mission—its sense that God has come among us, first to forgive and heal, and then to remake and refashion. Immanuel has come to take our sin to the cross and then to work in us so that, at the core of our being, we reflect the character of our heavenly Father in what we do. Accordingly, beginning as early as Irenaeus in the second century, Christians have associated Matthew's Gospel with the figure of the "man" in Ezekiel 1 and Revelation 4.[1] This profound intuition takes its point of departure from the fact that Matthew begins with Jesus's human genealogy. Matthew's first words in Greek—literally, "A book of genesis"—indicate that he would have us understand that the human race's new genesis takes place now in Jesus. And in the end, there is nothing that makes human beings more radiantly alive than reflecting the character of the God whose image they bear.

[1] Irenaeus, *Haer.* 3.11.8.

Background Issues

Authorship

The "Gospel according to Matthew" never circulated without that title, and has long been believed to have been written by the apostle Matthew. According to Eusebius (fourth century), Papias (second century) received from John the elder (first century) the understanding that Mark wrote his Gospel as "Peter's interpreter" (ἑρμενευτὴς Πέτρου) and that Mark did so "not in ordered form"; then Matthew "gathered together the *logia* [a term which can refer both to words and to deeds] in an ordered arrangement in the Hebrew dialect" (Ἑβραΐδι διαλέκτῳ τὰ λόγια συνετάξατο).[2] Early church writers and modern scholars thought that by "Hebrew *dialect*" Papias meant the Hebrew or Aramaic language. But Matthew's Greek is some of the smoothest in the New Testament; more likely, Papias meant that Matthew's "ordered arrangement" was according to Hebrew sense of style.[3] Thus, for instance, his arrangement (see below) of the deeds and words of Jesus into five blocks that recall the structure of the Torah.

Additionally, Origen (third century) understood Matthew to be "once a tax collector, but later an apostle of Jesus Christ; he published it for those who came to faith from Judaism."[4] It is difficult to know by what authority Origen identifies Matthew as the tax collector—whether he has an external authority, or whether he infers it by observing (as many have since) that Matthew's Gospel alone calls him "the tax collector" when listing him as one of the twelve apostles (Matt. 10:3).[5] Regardless, early church tradition assigned Matthew the symbol of three purses.

C. F. D. Moule's suggestion that Matthew 13:52 is autobiographical is attractive: "Therefore every scribe who has been trained [μαθητεύεσθαι here is cognate both with the word "disciple" (μαθητής) and with Matthew's name (Μαθθαῖος)] for the kingdom of heaven is like a master of a house, who brings out of his treasure what is new and what is old." It is impossible to prove, despite E. J. Goodspeed's proposal, that Matthew is pointing to the sort of note taking or secretarial skills that his craft would have required, now brought into the service of Jesus. Nonetheless, it is just as plausible as (and I suggest more so than) modern theories that bypass historical Matthew—for example, "Matthew" as a written project by a collaborative group (similar to the writings of the Essene community)[6] or a work produced by "a second-generation (Hellenized) Jew."[7] Moreover, if the intention in these theoretical instances was to appropriate the name of one of the Twelve as the author to lend legitimacy to the teaching, one might have expected the use of the name of a more illustrious apostle.[8]

---

[2] Eusebius, *Hist. eccl.* 3.39.14–17 (my trans.).
[3] Or, per Craig Evans, "a Hebrew (or Jewish) way of presenting material or making an argument" (*Matthew* [Cambridge: Cambridge University Press, 2012], 2). See G. Scott Gleaves, *Did Jesus Speak Greek? The Emerging Evidence of Greek Dominance in First-Century Palestine* (Eugene, OR: Pickwick, 2015), for a persuasive argument that Matthew's Gospel is likely an originally Greek composition, and not a translation from the Aramaic.
[4] According to Eusebius, *Hist. eccl.* 6.25.3–6 (my trans.).
[5] Compare Mark 2:14 and Luke 5:27, which name "Levi" as the tax collector whom Jesus calls; the parallel story in Matthew calls him "Matthew" (Matt. 9:9–13). All three Synoptics and Acts (see Acts 1:13) list Matthew among the apostles; the Gospel according to Matthew, alone, calls him "the tax collector."
[6] Krister Stendahl, *The School of St. Matthew, and Its Use of the Old Testament* (Uppsala: Gleerup, 1954).
[7] Rudolf Schnackenburg, *The Gospel of Matthew*, trans. Robert R. Barr (Grand Rapids, MI: Eerdmans, 2002), 6.
[8] Evans, *Matthew*, 4.

Audience

Because of this Gospel's familiarity with the Jewish world of its day, the scholarly consensus is that Matthew is written to a Greek-speaking Jewish Christian community, one that is grappling with Israel's mission to the nations through Jesus the Messiah. This could be one of any number of churches, from Alexandria, to Jerusalem, to Antioch, Sidon, Tyre, or beyond. Matthew's Gospel itself does not yield many clues, except perhaps that when Matthew notes the spread of Jesus's fame early in his ministry, the Gospel writer notes his fame extending beyond Mark's Galilee (Mark 1:39) or even Luke's Judea (Luke 4:44) to include, of all places, Syria (Matt. 4:23–24). It was there, according to the book of Acts (see esp. Acts 11:19–30; 13–14), that the early church first learned how to bridge the gulf between its Jewish roots and the Gentile mission, and where "the church" was gaining an independent identity as being made up of "Christians." It was there that Matthew's Gospel is first cited, and heavily so, by a postbiblical church leader, to wit, Ignatius (second century), Bishop of Syrian Antioch (e.g., using Matt. 3:15, "to fulfill all righteousness," when describing Jesus's baptism).[9]

Date

Most modern scholars are quite certain that Matthew was written after AD 70, that is, after the Jewish war that led to the destruction of Jerusalem and the temple in AD 70. Matthew 22:7 presumably forecasts Jerusalem's destruction after the fact: "The king was angry, and he sent his troops and destroyed those murderers and burned their city." And there is the fact that of all four Gospels, Matthew alone uses the word *church* to refer to Jesus's followers. That fact in combination with the indication of the destruction of Jerusalem is thought to be decisive in a post–AD 70 dating of Matthew. Only then, so it is assumed, does "the church" come into self-consciousness for Jewish Christians as an entity distinct from synagogue and temple.

To the contrary, contends J. A. T. Robinson, Matthew's (and the other Gospels' as well) references to the destruction of Jerusalem are restrained enough to make us wonder if they are not read better as coming before the events. Matthew 22:7, says Robinson, could presuppose, but does not require, a post–AD 70 dating, especially when compared with references, say, in the Sibylline Oracles that clearly are after AD 70.[10] And the prophecies in Matthew's Olivet Discourse (chap. 24) are decidedly forward looking; especially telling is the inclusion of an "immediately" between the destruction (24:29) and "the end [consummation] of the age" (24:3) to follow. And, as Robinson contends, from "references to conditions in Jerusalem 'to this day' (27:8; cf. 28:15), one would have expected him of all people to draw attention to the present devastation of the site."[11]

These considerations, along with other indications that temple practice continues in Matthew's day (e.g., leaving your gift at the altar, paying the temple tax, swearing

[9] Ignatius, *Smyrn.* 1.1.

[10] John A. T. Robinson, *Redating the New Testament* (Philadelphia: Westminster Press, 1976), esp. 19–26.

[11] Ibid., 23. See also the very fine defense of the authenticity of Jesus's prophecies against the temple in Craig S. Keener, *The Historical Jesus of the Gospels* (Grand Rapids, MI: Eerdmans, 2009), 250–53.

by the gift on the altar—Matt. 5:23–24; 17:24–27; 23:16–22), suggest that Irenaeus got it right: Matthew wrote "at the time when Peter and Paul were preaching the gospel and founding the church in Rome."[12]

It is indeed true that one of the most distinctive things about Matthew's Gospel is that his is the only one to use the word *church*. For that reason, many scholars wrongly assume that this Gospel has read back into Jesus's ministry a teaching that could not possibly have come from him but must have been attributed to him after his death and (supposed) resurrection.[13] To the contrary, if the New Testament's unanimous sense of Jesus's mission is correct (death and resurrection, followed by ascension and the proclamation of the gospel), it is altogether reasonable to see him anticipating a communal embodiment of his work in the wake of his death, resurrection, and ascension. Moreover, Jesus's preparing of his followers for the rise of the "church" reckons most satisfactorily with the profound Jewishness of his sense of the corporate nature of God's self-expression in human history. God images his life into the world through the dyad of male and female, through the family of Abraham, through the "peculiar possession" of the children of Israel, through the nation that comes together under David and Solomon, and through the "remnant" through whom he works even in exile. That Matthew has Jesus talking about the "church" is no argument for a late date.

Purpose

Regardless of the precise location of the audience and date of composition, the purpose of Matthew's Gospel seems to be at least threefold:

1. to demonstrate that the Hebrew Scriptures have all along been pointing to Jesus as Messiah and inaugurator of God's kingdom "now and not yet";
2. to show that Jesus has brought forgiveness and personal renewal, enabling a true understanding and keeping of the Torah's intent; and
3. to explain how Jesus, who is "with you to the end of the age," is forming a community—that is, the "church"—of Jewish and Gentile followers to model the presence of God's kingdom in the present age and to take God's mission to the nations.

It is in this instruction, showing Jewish and non-Jewish believers how to live together, through lives transformed from the inside out, that the Gospel of Matthew provides deep, rich preaching material for the pastor who desires to help a congregation develop an authentic and loving witness to a skeptical world.

Historicity

To most scholars, that the Gospel of Matthew relies heavily on Mark is beyond debate: at least 90 percent of Mark shows up here, but in Matthew the stories are compressed

[12] Irenaeus, *Haer.* 3.1.1 (my trans.).

[13] See the defense of the authenticity of Matthew's ἐκκλησία sayings (16:18; 18:17) in K. L. Schmidt, "ἐκκλησία," *TDNT*, 3:518–26.

and cleaner. Consistently, Matthew displays a clearer, more concise and correct use of Greek than does Mark. Events are usually recounted in Mark's sequence—but not always. Where Matthew departs from Mark in chronology, Luke tends to agree with Mark. In fact, it is generally agreed by conservative and liberal scholars alike that Mark and Luke are more governed by chronology, while Matthew is more interested in thematic development. Regardless, it is easier for most who look into the matter to assume that if there is a literary relationship, it is more likely that Matthew is using Mark as part of his framework than that Mark works off of Matthew. This is especially so since otherwise Mark "drops" 50 percent of the material in Matthew overall and yet expands, without literary elegance, Matthew's tightly crafted stories and sayings. Worth a mention is that, in modern scholarship, there has always been a minority report arguing that if there is a literary relationship, Matthew came first, and Mark adapted his material. However, we note, with Leon Morris, "It is not easy to understand why Mark in abbreviating Matthew should so consistently come up with narratives that are longer as well as more lifelike."[14]

Scholars have offered various scenarios to account for the differences between Matthew, Mark, and Luke. Many speculate as to the existence of a separate additional writing, the "Q" document ("Q" is short for the German *Quelle*, or "source"), as the underlying source for teaching material shared by Matthew and Luke (e.g., Matthew's Sermon on the Mount and Luke's Sermon on the Plain). Along with a hypothesized "M" document to account for material unique to Matthew (e.g., the sheep and the goats) and a hypothesized "L" document to account for material unique to Luke (e.g., the good Samaritan), Mark and "Q" form the elements of the "four document" theory by which majority scholarship proposes to account for the three Synoptic Gospels. I must take issue with how easily modern scholarship insists that the relationships among the Gospels have to be accounted for by appeal to mere documents (whether actual, like Mark's, or hypothesized, like "M" and "L" and "Q"). There is every reason to think that each of the four Gospels is directly (for Matthew, see 13:52; for Mark, see 14:51–52; and for John, see 19:35; 21:24–25) or indirectly (for Luke, see 1:1–4) a product of eyewitness accounts—and, moreover, eyewitnesses who participated in a complex relational network of shared experiences and varying perspectives.

Some of the differences between the Gospels concern sequence (the order of the temptations of Christ) or timing (did Jesus cleanse the temple at the beginning of his ministry, at the end, or both?). For this particular overview of Matthew, what matters is to recognize that Matthew has, for his own reasons, arranged his material thematically. As John H. Walton and D. Brent Sandy point out, "The evangelists felt free to rearrange the order of events to suit the points they were making."[15] And, just to clarify, it is only under the most questionable of assumptions that thematic arrangement and historicity are deemed to be incompatible.

[14] Leon Morris, *The Gospel according to Matthew*, PNTC (Grand Rapids, MI: Eerdmans, 1992), 16.
[15] John H. Walton and D. Brent Sandy, *The Lost World of Scripture: Ancient Literary Culture and Biblical Authority* (Downers Grove, IL: InterVarsity Press, 2013), 148.

Structure and Outline

Matthew is "the architect among the Evangelists," says Herman Ridderbos.[16] With consummate artistry, Matthew alternates the words and deeds of Jesus. In fact, he frames the whole of his portrait of Christ around five series of narratives, each culminating in one of five respective great discourses. He ends each narrative-plus-discourse section with the identical formula, nicely preserved in the ASV: "And it came to pass when Jesus finished . . ." (7:28; 11:1; 13:53; 19:1; 26:1).

I. Genealogy, Birth, and Infancy Narratives (1:1–2:23)
II. Series 1: From Coronation to Keynote (3:1–7:29)
  A. Narrative (3:1–4:25)
  B. Discourse: Beatitudes and Sermon on the Mount (5:1–7:27)
  C. Bridge: "When Jesus had finished these words" (7:28–29)
III. Series 2: Call to Discipleship and Mission (8:1–11:1)
  A. Narrative (8:1–10:4)
  B. Discourse: Mission of the Disciples (10:5–42)
  C. Bridge: "When Jesus had finished commanding" (11:1)
IV. Series 3: The Wisdom of the Kingdom of Heaven (11:2–13:53)
  A. Narrative (11:2–12:50)
  B. Discourse: Parables of the Kingdom (13:1–52)
  C. Bridge: "When Jesus had finished these parables" (13:53)
V. Series 4: The Shape of the Church (13:54–19:2)
  A. Narrative (13:54–17:27)
  B. Discourse: Living in the Kingdom/Church (18:1–35)
  C. Bridge: "When Jesus had finished these words" (19:1–2)
VI. Series 5: Preparation for Judgment (19:3–26:1)
  A. Narrative (19:3–22:46)
  B. Discourse: Woes and the Peril and Judgment to Come (23:1–25:46)
  C. Bridge: "When Jesus had finished all these words" (26:1)
VII. Crucifixion, Resurrection, and Commissioning (26:2–28:20)

The birth and death-resurrection narratives, along with the five series between them, form a chiasm.

a Genealogy, birth, and infancy narratives (1:1–2:23)
  b Series 1: From coronation to keynote (3:1–7:29)
    c Series 2: Call to discipleship and mission (8:1–11:1)
      d Series 3: The wisdom of the kingdom of heaven (11:2–13:53)
    c' Series 4: The shape of the church (13:54–19:2)
  b' Series 5: Preparation for judgment (19:3–26:1)
a' Crucifixion, resurrection, and commissioning (26:2–28:20)

The first portion of Matthew (chaps. 1–7: lineage, birth, and infancy narratives, plus series 1) consists of a movement from the genealogy of Jesus through his birth

[16] Herman Ridderbos, *Matthew's Witness to Jesus Christ: The King and the Kingdom*, World Christian Books (New York: Association Press, 1958), 19. Ridderbos follows a widely accepted and, to my mind, eminently satisfying schema, notwithstanding the objections of Werner Georg Kümmel, *Introduction to the New Testament*, rev. ed., trans. Howard Clark Kee (Nashville: Abingdon, 1973), 106.

and rescue from Herod, followed by his baptism by John the Baptist and the beginnings of his public ministry (chaps. 1–4). The climax of the opening section is the Sermon on the Mount (chaps. 5–7), the keynote to Jesus's teaching ministry.

Matthew begins the second portion (8:1–11:1, series 2) by clustering in chapters 8–9 several power (and healing) miracle stories that are otherwise scattered throughout Mark. Here is featured the call of Matthew the tax collector (Matt. 9:9–13, which is thought by many to be Matthew's authorial signature). The twelve disciples are named in a single paragraph before Jesus commissions them all for the mission to Israel (chap. 10), the climax of the second section.

In the third section (11:2–13:53, series 3), Matthew provides narrative illustrations of the peculiar nature and timing of the kingdom of heaven—from John the Baptist's question about Jesus's identity (11:2–19), to the disciples' plucking of grain on the Sabbath (12:1–8), to Jesus's conflict with Beelzebul (12:22–32). Then he draws together parables—with a focus on the parable of the sower (13:1–9, 36–43)—in which Jesus teaches that the kingdom is "already and not yet," and also hidden and revealed.

The fourth section (13:54–19:2, series 4) marks Jesus's preparation for the cross and for the creation of the church. Appropriately, the narrative portion begins with the rejection of Jesus at Nazareth (13:54–58) and the death of John the Baptist at the hand of Herod the tetrarch (14:1–12). The section takes in the full sweep of Jesus's intention:

1. to provide heavenly food for Israel (14:13–21), the feeding of the five thousand in Israel;
2. to reshape God's people by making faith the boundary marker between "clean" and "unclean" (15:1–28); and
3. to provide bread for the nations as well as for Israel (15:32–39), the feeding of the four thousand, following Jesus's ministry in the Decapolis and before his return to Israel.

Peter's confession at Philippi (deep in Gentile Lebanon) becomes the occasion for Jesus to explain the ironic way in which he will save his people and build his church. The section culminates with what Frederick Dale Bruner aptly calls "The Sermon on the Congregation."[17] Here is Jesus's teaching on the shape of the church, the community his cross will create, marked as it will be by humility, mutual care, and forgiveness (Matthew 18).

The fifth section (19:3–28:20, series 5 and the Passion and Resurrection Narratives) begins with Jesus moving closer to Jerusalem and into deeper and deeper conflict with "the chief priests and the Pharisees" (e.g., 21:45). The narrative of his Triumphal Entry (21:1–17) as well as the accounts of his actions (like the cursing of the fig tree, 21:18–22) and teachings around the temple precincts (like the parable of the wicked tenants [21:33–45] and of the wedding banquet [22:1–14]) make it clear that the prophecy must come true:

[17] Frederick Dale Bruner, *Matthew: A Commentary: The Churchbook, Matthew 13–28*, rev. ed. (Grand Rapids, MI: Eerdmans, 2007), Kindle ed., ad loc.

The stone that the builders rejected
has become the cornerstone. (21:42)

The section climaxes with a long discourse that mirrors in many ways the Sermon on the Mount: the blessings of the kingdom (5:1–12) give way to the "woes" of the counter-kingdom (23:1–36). The city on a hill that makes God's light visible (5:14–16) gives way to a city doomed for having extinguished God's light (chap. 24). The choice to build on rock or sand (7:24–27) will prove to have been made by those who have unknowingly served or not served the King by caring for "the least of these my brothers" (25:31–46). There follow Jesus's trial, death, resurrection, and mission to the nations. Particular Matthean features include Judas's hanging himself, the rising of "many . . . of the saints who had fallen asleep" at Jesus's death (27:52), the conspiracy to cover up Jesus's resurrection, and the giving of the Great Commission.

Message and Theology

Theological Themes

Immanuel, "God with Us"

In Matthew's account of Jesus's "genesis," we meet the line of Abraham, in whom, God promised, all the families of the earth would find themselves blessed. God directs his re-creative purposes for the human race through this family—and then through the kingdom that God establishes through one of Abraham's progeny, David. Abraham's and David's stories were not told in a vacuum, nor were they intended to serve ethnic and national pride. They were told for "all the families of the earth" (Gen. 12:3; cf. Ps. 22:27, one of the most Davidic psalms). It is in this human line—even through, *precisely* through, the torturous path of exile (Matt. 1:11–12)—that Jesus, human himself and humanity's singular hope, appears.

After Matthew anchors Jesus's life in the stuff of our humanity, Matthew turns to Jesus's divinity. The Christ's name is Jesus, which means "Yah saves." And while the name Jesus served (and still does) as a normal human name, Matthew insists that for this child it means more. First, Jesus's origin (his "genesis") is not merely human, but divine as well: "she [Mary] was found to be with child from the Holy Spirit" (1:18). Second, the reason he bears the name "Yah saves" is that his mission is to "save his people from their sins" (1:21), a task only God himself can perform. Third, his name is also "Immanuel (which means, God with us)" (1:23). Nor is the title "God with us" to be taken merely metaphorically, for Matthew's Jesus maintains

1. that when his followers gather, "there am I among them" (18:20);
2. that when his followers baptize, they do so in his name as well as the Father's and the Holy Spirit's; and
3. that wherever they may go to make disciples, "I am with you always, to the end of the age" (28:20).

Some things are hard to put on *one* side of the divine-human ledger. Though Matthew is profoundly interested in Jesus's authority (7:29; 8:9; 9:6; 10:1; 21:23;

28:18), he also embraces the complementary truth: Jesus's true humanity, pointedly expressed in the "ignorance" passages: (1) the Father decides who will be on the right and on the left of the Son of Man (20:23); (2) Jesus does not know the timing of the world's end (24:36); and (3) he dies with the question "why" on his lips (27:46).

Then there is Jesus's sonship: To the extent that he is the focus of the statement "Out of Egypt I called my son" (2:15), Jesus is the personification of Israel, humanity in right relation to divinity. To the extent that he lives the wilderness-obedience that counters Israel's wilderness rebellion, he shows what it is for "man" (ὁ ἄνθρωπος) to live by more than mere bread. And, of course, the genealogy goes to some lengths to show human descent. Then again, the final puzzle Jesus poses to his interlocutors hinges upon the (scripturally derived!) conundrum of the Messiah being both David's Son and David's Lord (22:41–46)—that is to say, Jesus understands himself to be God's divine Son.

In his view of Christ as God-man, Matthew joins the other New Testament voices that stand out as christological theologians:

- John: "In the beginning was the Word, and the Word was with God, and the Word was God" (John 1:1); and note John's seven "I am" statements;
- Hebrews: "He is the radiance of the glory of God and the exact imprint of his nature, and he upholds the universe by the word of his power" (Heb. 1:3); and
- Paul: "Though he was in the form of God . . ." (Phil. 2:6).

It is not difficult to understand why the church's consensus came to be that Jesus is fully divine and fully human—or as Christian artist Shai Linne expresses it, "Jesus both God and man, two hundred percent."

What marks Matthew's christology as special is the way he organically unfolds Jesus Christ's humanity and divinity for a Jewish Christian readership. He does so in terms of Israel's story. That is to say, Jesus is the new Torah; "greater than the temple" (12:6); "greater than Jonah" (12:41); "greater than Solomon" (12:42); the one in whom God's kingdom has come and is coming; Israel's one teacher; and, finally, "God with us," who is fully known, ironically, in "the least of these" (25:45).

Jesus as the New Torah

Matthew renders the life and ministry of Jesus in five discrete sections of material, recalling the five books of Moses, the Torah or Pentateuch. Thematically, Matthew's Gospel follows the arc of Torah. No less than the book of Genesis, Matthew's account is one of "beginnings." Matthew's narrative of Jesus's birth and early ministry echoes Exodus's story of deliverance (see below). Leviticus is dominated by the theme of "holiness," both by way of sanctifying sacrifices (e.g., Lev. 16:30) and by way of instruction (e.g., Lev. 19:2, "You shall be holy, for I the Lord your God am holy"). Just so, in Matthew's account Jesus offers his own "blood of the covenant . . . for the forgiveness of sins" (Matt. 26:28) and teaches his followers to be "perfect, as your heavenly Father is perfect" (Matt. 5:48). If the book of Numbers is the story of God's people becoming a community on the journey to the Promised Land, Matthew undertakes instructions on how to be the "church" while "going and making disciples." And just as the book of Deuteronomy places a life and death choice before God's people at Mount Gerizim and Mount Ebal, so Jesus pronounces beatitudes (Matthew 5) and woes (Matthew 23),[18] and says, in effect, "Build wisely" (Matt. 7:24); in other words, "Choose life" (Deut. 30:19).

Indeed, Matthew implies that Jesus corrects wrong ideas about what the Torah was supposed to do and be. Jews contemporary to Jesus thought of the Torah as "the yoke of the Kingdom of Heaven."[19] Thus, as Simon the Just maintained, "Upon three things the world rests: upon the Torah, upon the temple service, and upon the doing of acts of kindness."[20]

Extraordinarily—and imperiously if he is not indeed divine—Jesus claims that what people sought in Torah they will instead find in him. "Come to me, all who labor and are heavy laden, and I will give you rest. Take my yoke upon you, and learn from me, for I am gentle and lowly in heart, and you will find rest for your souls. For my yoke is easy, and my burden is light" (Matt. 11:28–30). Thus, with the nine beatitudes, Jesus stands as covenant Lord, pronouncing promissory blessings as though standing on Deuteronomy's Mount Gerizim. With the seven woes, Jesus pronounces warning woes as though standing on Deuteronomy's Mount Ebal.

What the Torah was, Jesus is. Yet there are two big differences: First, to worship the Torah is idolatry at worst, or bibliolatry at best; to worship Jesus is not idolatrous, for he is "God with us" (Matt. 1:23). Second, Jesus can "save his people from their sins" (1:21); the Torah cannot. The Torah can provide what Paul will call a provisional "pass[ing] over" (Rom. 3:25) of sins through promissory "blood of the covenant" (Ex. 24:8); now Jesus provides "my blood of the covenant" (Matt. 26:28). The God-breathed book Torah can anticipate forgiveness; the God-man Jesus can provide forgiveness.

Matthew wants readers to know that the Torah is being fulfilled in Jesus. Holy Scripture was always about something and Someone beyond itself. Again and again, Matthew quotes scriptural formulas to let his readers know that Jesus is updating Israel's story.

- *Matthew 1:23*. Jesus's birth fulfills the promise that God would be Immanuel, "God with us" (cf. Isa. 7:14).
- *Matthew 2:15*. Jesus is the obedient and faithful Son Israel was supposed to have been (Hos. 11:1). Thus, his life, especially the early events, are a telling of Israel's exodus story: miraculous birth, rescue from the plot of an evil king, sojourn to and calling out from Egypt, passing through baptismal waters and reception of the Holy Spirit, temptation for forty days (instead of forty years) in the wilderness, obedience when Israel has not obeyed (thus the quotes from Deuteronomy when Jesus confronts the Devil), and the beginning of the con-

[18] N. T. Wright, *The New Testament and the People of God* (Minneapolis: Fortress, 1992), 386–87.
[19] Sifra, Kedoshim on Lev. 20:26.
[20] Pirke Aboth 1:2.

quest of God's enemies (exorcisms, healings, confrontation with maleficent and confused spiritual authorities).

- *Matthew 8:16–17.* Jesus's healings fulfill the suffering servant prophecy (Isa. 53:5).
- *Matthew 12:6.* Jesus is greater than the temple, the place where God lived (even if, for the time being, Jesus accepts the provisional arrangement—17:24–27).
- *Matthew 12:41.* Jesus is greater than Jonah (the one who was "dead" three days and nights and who went on a reluctant mission to pagans).
- *Matthew 12:42.* Jesus is greater than Solomon (the first son of David's line to inherit the throne).
- *Matthew 12:15–21.* Jesus's silence fulfills the prophecy concerning the servant who will not break a bruised reed (Isa. 42:1–4).
- *Matthew 13:10–17.* Jesus's parables fulfill Isaiah's commission to confound as well as instruct (Isa. 6:9–10 LXX).
- *Matthew 21:10–17.* Jesus cleanses the temple as part of the restoration of the Psalm 8 vision of the restoration of humankind's role to bear God's glory and lead God's creation in praise (Ps. 8:3 LXX).

By quoting Jesus as claiming to be greater than the temple (Matt. 12:6), greater than Jonah (12:41), and greater than Solomon (12:42), Matthew forces the question, is this not *the* Priest, Prophet, and King toward whom everything in Israel's history has been oriented?

"Greater Than the Temple"

Under Moses's administration, God established his presence among his people. He did so by rescuing them not just from their enemies, the Egyptians, but also from the angel of death that they, no less than the Egyptians, deserved. God established his presence by "cutting a covenant" with them, whereby he became their God, and they his people. The Ten Commandments formed the germ of a covenant document binding the Lord and his covenant people together. The Torah—the five books of Moses—served as the amplification and explication of that covenant relationship.

God established his presence among his people by providing sacrifices of atonement and fellowship, by giving oracles that revealed his character and described what it meant to bear his likeness, and by constituting them as his "peculiar people"—that is, as a showcase for what a redeemed community was to look like. The symbolic place of covenant life under Moses was the tabernacle; under Solomon, the tabernacle yielded to the temple. Matthew describes the yielding of both Torah and temple to Immanuel.

The reason that Jesus is "greater than the temple" (Matt. 12:6) is that he transforms two things: first, the sacrificial system, and second, the place of meeting.

Alone among the Gospels, Matthew cites Isaiah 53:4, "He took our illnesses and bore our diseases" (Matt. 8:17). Also alone among the Gospels, at the institution of the Last Supper, Matthew's Jesus uses Moses's language of the "blood of the covenant" (Matt. 26:28; cf. Ex. 24:8), with two startling additions: (1) the pronoun "my" to qualify the blood; and (2) the explanatory "poured out for many for the forgiveness of sins." The verb "poured out" is also a uniquely Matthean appeal to Isaiah 53—in this case, an echo of Isaiah's anticipation of the hope that the suffering servant will have "poured out his self to death" (Isa. 53:12). Almost as if to provide a bookend to the explanation that Jesus's name indicates "he will save his people from their sins" (Matt. 1:21), Matthew says that upon Jesus's death, "behold, the curtain of the temple was torn in two, from top to bottom" (27:51). The death of the Sin-Bearer marks the end of the separation between a holy God and his people. The temporary halt to sacrifices that Jesus forced when he cleansed the temple turns out to be a promise of their permanent end by means of his atoning sacrifice. As he says, "the Son of man came not to be served but to serve, and to give his life as a ransom for many" (20:28).

With the fulfillment of the temple's housing of sacrifice comes the fulfillment of the temple's role as place of meeting. What the sacrifices once provided in merely anticipatory fashion—mediation for sinners—Jesus now provides finally and fully. What the temple once was—a place of meeting for God's people—Jesus now is in himself as he gathers his own into his church.

When Jesus cleanses the temple, he objects that the building has been hijacked from its original intent: to be a "house of prayer" (Matt. 21:13). That is to say, the temple is the place for God and humans to meet together, the place of concourse between the Redeemer Lord and his redeemed people. During the consecration of Solomon's temple, the *shekinah* presence of God was so intense it was unbearable (2 Chronicles 6). Now the *shekinah* presence is Jesus himself: "Where two or three are gathered in my name, there am I among them" (Matt. 18:20). The temple, in turn, was the centerpiece of a city in which God intended to showcase his character, his holiness, and his love for the human race:

> Great is the Lord and greatly to be praised
> in the city of our God!
> His holy mountain, beautiful in elevation,
> is the joy of all the earth,
> Mount Zion, in the far north,
> the city of the great King. (Ps. 48:1–2)

Now, that city is Christ's followers: "You are the light of the world. A city set on a hill cannot be hidden" (Matt. 5:14). Immanuel, "God with us," once lived among us in flesh and blood. Now in the great period between his earthly ministry and the restoration of all things, Immanuel lives among us in the church.

"Greater Than Jonah"

In Jesus Christ, Israel's prophetic mission to the nations comes to life—literally—following the Son of Man's three days and nights "in the heart of the earth" (Matt. 12:40).

Of the four canonical Gospel writers, it is Luke who is known for his attention to the Gentile mission. Luke frames the larger corpus of Luke-Acts by beginning with the promise of John the Baptist's birth in the Jewish temple and by ending with Paul's ministering from a Roman prison. Within that larger framework itself, Luke brackets his Gospel, at one end, with Isaianic allusions to the Gentile mission in Simeon's canticle ("a light for revelation to the Gentiles," Luke 2:32; see Isa. 42:6) and the prologue to John the Baptist's ministry ("and all flesh shall see the salvation of God," Luke 3:6; see Isa. 40:5) and, at the other end, with the resurrected Jesus sending the disciples to Jerusalem to await the outpouring of the Holy Spirit so that in his name they could proclaim repentance and forgiveness of sins "to all nations" (Luke 24:47). Luke alone names Roman officials other than Pilate (e.g., Luke 2:1–2; 3:1), and Luke's Jesus provokes his fellow Galileans by reminding them of the Lord's interest in Gentiles during the ministries of the two great prophets Elijah and Elisha (Luke 4:25–27).

Conversely, Matthew strikes many as the most Jewish of the Gospels. In chapter 10, for instance, Jesus sends the disciples not "among the Gentiles" but rather to "the lost sheep of the house of Israel" (10:5–6), and in chapter 15, he maintains (if ironically) that he was sent "only to the lost sheep of the house of Israel" (15:24).

Even so, Matthew's understanding of the Gentile mission is especially noteworthy. Matthew includes pagan women in Jesus's genealogy. He recounts the homage that the pagan magi pay Israel's newborn King (Matthew 2). He notes how the Galilee of Jesus's ministry is "Galilee of the Gentiles" (Matt. 4:15; from Isa. 9:1). He maintains that Jesus's healings bear the mark of Isaiah's servant, who "will proclaim justice to the Gentiles" and in whose "name the Gentiles will hope" (Matt. 12:15–21, esp. 18, 21; from Isa. 42:1–4). Matthew attributes to the pagan Syrophoenician woman the faith to ask mercy from Jesus as "Son of David" (15:22), while the disciples show themselves abjectly obtuse about what Jesus has brought them into pagan territory to learn. Matthew foresees the "end of the age" culminating in the angels bringing cleansing fire to the whole world (13:38–39) and the Son of Man gathering "all the nations" to separate sheep from goats (25:31–46). Most strikingly, Matthew closes his Gospel with Jesus's commission to make disciples of all the (pagan) nations, baptizing them and teaching them all that he had commanded.

Matthew shares the "greater than Jonah" saying with Luke (Matt. 12:41 // Luke 11:32), as well as Jesus's protest that the only sign that will be given is "the sign of the prophet Jonah" (Matt. 12:39). Perhaps it seems like a small thing; nonetheless, only Matthew makes of the saying a duplet, specifying that Jonah was a "prophet" who "was three days and three nights in the belly of the great fish." Just so, Jesus maintains, "will the Son of Man be three days and three nights in the heart of the earth" (12:39–40). God had called Jonah to die to lovelessness for pagans. When Jonah refused that death, God gave him another—a symbolic death in the belly of the great fish. Even following his symbolic resurrection, Jonah prophesied only reluctantly. Jesus takes Jonah's place (and, I expect, would call all his fellow Israelites to do so as well) in life and in death, so that Israel's mission to tell the nations of God's mercy can be lived out in and through him (and them also).

"Greater Than Solomon"

Jesus is Israel's true King. Clearly and specifically, Matthew's Jesus is Israel's *royal* Son. Calling Joseph David's son (1:20), Matthew's genealogy stresses Jesus's belonging to the Davidic line (1:6). It is Israel's new King the magi seek, and indeed Micah says that it is from Bethlehem, city of David, that Israel's ruler is to be born (Mic. 5:2). Jesus's Davidic identity is stated in several distinctly Matthean passages (9:27; 12:3, 23; 15:22; 20:30–31). Most pointedly, on Palm Sunday his being hailed as Son of David is occasioned by a most literal of fulfillments of Zechariah 9:9: Jesus rides *both* colt and donkey (Matt. 21:2, 7). But he is also more than Israel's ultimate human king. He shuts down the inquisition of 22:15–38 by asking how, in Psalm 110, David's "Lord" could also be his Son. Here stands God himself, come to shepherd his flock, as the prophet Ezekiel promised he would (see Ezek. 34:11–16). Precisely here lies the christological mystery that theologians and hymn writers have been exploring for two thousand years.

> Thus have ye heard that Christ is both David's Son, and David's Lord:
> David's Lord always, David's Son in time:
> David's Lord, born of the substance of His Father,
> David's Son, born of the Virgin Mary, conceived by the Holy Ghost.
> Let us hold fast both. . . .
> He was made that which He made,
> that what He made might not perish.
> Very Man, Very God;
> God and man whole Christ.
> This is the Catholic faith.[21]

Finally, at his rising from the grave as David's Son and Lord, Jesus receives "all authority in heaven and on earth" (Matt. 28:18). He is thus "Christus Victor," the world's rightful, divine-human sovereign, and he has sent his followers to the ends of the earth to proclaim his lordship and to enlist in his service.

The Mystery of Kingdom Come and Coming

King Jesus proclaims and embodies a kingdom that is both "already" and "not yet"—a kingdom that is both "come" and "coming." Albert Schweitzer believed that the kingdom was entirely futuristic. He imagined Jesus dying as a failed prophet who sought to force its coming.[22] C. H. Dodd believed that the kingdom was entirely present.[23] He envisioned Jesus living, ministering, and teaching in such a way as to make the kingdom totally present in the ethic of forgiveness lived out by his followers. Each was right, and each was wrong.

Matthew's shorthand would be to say that Jesus's life, death, and resurrection have effected in the present the kingdom of the Son of Man (Matt. 13:41), and that in the

---

[21] Augustine, *Sermons* 42 (*NPNF*[1] 3:401).
[22] See especially, Albert Schweitzer, *The Quest of the Historical Jesus* (London: Adam and Charles Black, 1911).
[23] See especially, C. H. Dodd, *The Parables of the Kingdom*, rev. ed. (New York: Charles Scribner's Sons, 1961).

future the Son of Man will effect a consummation that will culminate in the kingdom of the Father (Matt. 13:43). Oscar Cullmann offers a compelling analogy for the dual nature of Jesus's perspective on the kingdom: what Christ has already effected is like the Allies' establishment of a beachhead in Normandy during World War II. D-Day meant that V-Day was assured, even though there was still much fighting left to do.[24] Through the Son, God's rule has been inaugurated even in the midst of "this age," and it will see consummation in "the age to come" (12:32). During the present kingdom of the Son of Man, Jesus's followers experience the simultaneous realities of suffering and victory, and they reject the dead-end alternatives of resignation and triumphalism.

Perhaps nowhere else does the fine nuance of Jesus's sense of the kingdom as "come and coming" take center stage than in his so-called kingdom parables of Matthew 13 (with some parallels in Mark and Luke). What George Eldon Ladd says of the parables in general is especially true of Matthew's kingdom parables:

> Our central thesis is that the Kingdom of God is the redemptive reign of God dynamically active to establish his rule among human beings, and that this Kingdom, which will appear as an apocalyptic act at the end of the age, has already come into human history in the person and mission of Jesus to overcome evil, to deliver people from its power, and to bring them into the blessings of God's reign. The Kingdom of God involves two great moments: fulfillment within history, and consummation at the end of history. It is precisely this background which provides the setting for the parables of the Kingdom.[25]

What we see in the parable of the sower is that the kingdom works quietly and secretly; because it does not force itself upon people, it must be received willingly (Matt. 13:1–9, 18–23).[26] The parable of the weeds puts us on notice that even though evil has not yet been apocalyptically expunged from society, God's kingdom has nonetheless irrevocably taken root (13:24–28, 36–42). The parables of the mustard seed and of leaven communicate to us that though the kingdom is present in the world in what seems to be a tiny and significant form, one day the kingdom will be a large and dominant presence (13:31–33).[27] The parables of the hidden treasure and the pearl of great price challenge us not to fail to see the worth of this kingdom, though it shows up in a remarkably unexpected way—whether it seems to just come up out of the ground or it somehow calls to you like a Stradivarius mistakenly hung on the wall of a pawn shop (13:44–46). And the parable of the net (13:47–50) informs us that one important aspect of the kingdom of God in its "already and not yet" form is that, despite our best and most faithful efforts, "even the community created by the working of the Kingdom in the world is not to be a pure community until the eschatological separation."[28]

[24] Oscar Cullmann, *Christ and Time: The Primitive Christian Conception of Time and History*, rev. ed., trans. Floyd B. Filson (Philadelphia: Westminster Press, 1964).

[25] George Eldon Ladd, *A Theology of the New Testament*, ed. Donald A. Hagner, rev. ed. (Grand Rapids, MI: Eerdmans, 1993), 89–90; and for the following paragraph, see Ladd's cogent section, "The Mystery of the Kingdom," 89–102.

[26] With parallels at Mark 4:1–9, 13–20 and Luke 8:4–8, 11–15.

[27] The parable of the mustard seed is paralleled at Mark 4:30–32 and Luke 13:18–19; the parable of the leaven, at Luke 13:20–21.

[28] Ladd, *Theology of the New Testament*, 99.

"You Have One Teacher"

Matthew portrays Jesus as the "one teacher" (Matt. 23:8) to whom his disciples should look. In Mark, with significantly less teaching material than in Matthew, Jesus calls us to a focused, relatively unembellished lifestyle: taking up our cross (Mark 8:34). In John, Jesus calls us to a similarly focused kind of community: loving one another as we have been loved. In Matthew, Jesus calls us to a fuller identity as community, putting feet on Mark's demands for discipleship and John's call for self-sacrificial love for one another.

The dimensions of the full-orbed discipleship that Jesus teaches in Matthew can fall under several headings: (1) Inwardness, (2) Forgiveness, (3) Rigor and elasticity in discernment, and (4) Faith and works.

Inwardness. In the first place, Jesus the teacher, while in no way backing off the normativity of God's commands, manifests the law written in hearts.[29] In the beatitudes, notes Thomas W. Ogletree, "Matthew is expressing in the language of law and commandment what might more appropriately be stated in the language of virtues."[30] Matthew's Jesus is concerned, first, with who we are and, second, with what we do. For "the good person out of his good treasure brings forth good" (Matt. 12:35). There is no need to be squeamish about affirming that Jesus's redemptive purpose for us is to make us good. He came that our lives might bear the impress of his humility, his mourning, his meekness, his hunger and thirst for righteousness, his mercifulness, his purity of heart, and his peaceableness (5:3–9)—and to the end that our lives might be the apologetic for his rule and reign (5:14–16).

Forgiveness. In the second place, the linchpin for the life that Jesus teaches is forgiveness. That is why Jesus anchors his extended teaching on the shape of the church (Matt. 13:54–20:34) with the parable of the unforgiving servant (18:21–35). Though the parable puts the matter in negative terms ("So also my heavenly Father will do to every one of you, if you do not forgive your brother from your heart," 18:35), its thrust is to teach something positive: the logic of redemption. Put simply, forgiven people forgive. More expansively, loved people love.

Matthew's approach to ethics is not often likened to Paul's. But inasmuch as both Matthew and Paul promote ethical discernment based on the logic of redemption, their thinking is strikingly similar. Clearly, they learned it from their common Savior. Paul tells the eschatologically over-realized antinomians in Corinth that the only thing that counts is "keeping the commandments" (1 Cor. 7:19).[31] But instead of illustrating his point with a list of casuistries or behavioral applications, Paul appeals to their sense of what it is to be redeemed: "You were bought with a price; do not become bondservants of men" (1 Cor. 7:23). Out of this new self-understanding,

[29] See Matthew 5–7 as illustrative of "the law fulfilled, not abolished" and "a righteousness that exceeds . . ."; see, in particular, 5:17, 20 with a view to 15:1–28.
[30] Thomas W. Ogletree, *The Use of the Bible in Christian Ethics* (Philadelphia: Fortress, 1983), 111.
[31] Hardly something he would have said to the eschatologically under-realized legalists in Galatia, by the way! Paul wants the Galatians to understand that the only thing that counts is "faith working through love" (Gal. 5:6).

they are to discern how to live as Christ's own, whether free or not, circumcised or not, married or not.

Likewise, Matthew calls for an "exceeding rightliness" (if I may adjust the language slightly to make a point), but it is not a "rightliness" of merit. Instead it is a hunger and thirst for being "rightly" synced with the mercy that has come from heaven. It is "rightly" taking the measure of forgiveness that is on offer in the blood of the new covenant. It is "rightly" reckoning the cost of one's own unpayable debt that has been written off, and "rightly" writing off the always lesser debts owed by others.

Rigor and elasticity in discernment. For the very reason that he addresses people who know that Christ's own "blood of the covenant" (Matt. 26:28) has secured their forgiveness, Matthew can portray a Jesus intent not just upon taking the commandments into the deeper places of their lives, but also upon shepherding people in the hard places of life—places that require less mechanical application of truths and more Spirit-led discernment of wisdom. "Learn from me" (11:29), says Jesus, who was anointed with the Spirit of God in his baptism (3:16; and see 12:18–20; from Isa. 42:1–4) and who accordingly promises us, "The Spirit of your Father [will be] speaking through you" (Matt. 10:20; compare 11:25).

Thus, throughout Matthew, Jesus shows how redeemed people, by the Spirit of God, learn to relate to God's commandments. For instance, demonstrates Frederick Dale Bruner, Matthew 18's instructions on love in the community should be seen as an extended treatment of the sixth commandment ("Do not murder"). Matthew 19:1–15's instructions on divorce should be seen as an extended treatment of the seventh commandment ("Do not commit adultery"). And Matthew 19:16–30's account of the rich young man should be seen as an extended treatment of the eighth and tenth commandments ("Do not steal" and "Do not covet").[32]

Jesus warns us not to present our offering when our brother has something against us, but first to seek reconciliation. Matthew would have us understand that this is what people who have been reconciled to God do. Jesus prescribes what to do when relationships break down. While, in the end, Matthew's Jesus calls upon individuals to forgive seventy times seven (18:22), he also exhorts the community not to just let the irresponsible run riot over everybody else (18:15–18). Everybody is given the procedure for handling broken relationships (chap. 18). And leaders are called upon to be stewards of a treasure (13:52) and to be gatekeepers for the integrity of the community. They are there to protect "the little ones" (e.g., 18:6). Even the proscription of divorce is spoken of in a more mitigating—less romantic and perfectionistic—fashion than in Mark or Luke. In Matthew, Jesus addresses the question, what about when *porneia* has violated the relationship?

There is an extraordinary social realism—or better, a combination of rigor and realism—that underlies Jesus's teaching in Matthew. The coming of a kingdom that is "now and not yet" calls for the utmost of wisdom—here exactitude, there elasticity. In

[32] Bruner, *Matthew 13–28*, ad loc.

the midst of a world that goes on as though nothing has happened, Christ's disciples live as "a city set on a hill" and "the light of the world" (Matt. 5:14). At the same time, they continue to show respect both to civil authorities ("render to Caesar," 22:21) and even to religious authorities who may not be completely worthy, who may in fact be anachronistic ("take that and give it [payment of the temple tax] to them for me and for yourself," 17:27).

They can do so because they know "the new world, when the Son of Man will sit on his glorious throne," is coming in due time (19:28). Meanwhile, as Bruner notes, Matthew 7 stands against a *censorious* Christianity ("Judge not, that you be not judged," 7:1), and Matthew 13 stands against a *coercive* Christianity ("Let both [weeds and wheat] grow together until the harvest," 13:30), on the one hand. On the other hand, Matthew 18 stands for a *conscientious* Christianity ("If your brother sins against you . . . ," 18:15), ensuring that the church of Matthew 7's and13's accommodation does not wink at sin. Matthew 7 and 13 keep the church from being *puritanical*, notes Bruner, while Matthew 18 keeps the church from being *epicurean*.[33]

And for Matthew, there is much at stake in our learning from Jesus both how to believe and how to live well.

Faith and works. As noted above, Matthew joins his voice to those of the other great New Testament voices that attest to the dual identity of Jesus as being both God and man. Another striking feature of Matthew's Gospel is the way he also joins other New Testament voices proclaiming the great "both–and" of faith and works.

Various New Testament writers use their own terms and nuance the relationship between faith and works uniquely. Paul writes of "faith working through love" (Gal. 5:6) and an "obedience of faith" (Rom. 1:5; 16:26). He eschews works as contributing to salvation, but insists on "good works" as constitutive of the life to which we have been saved (Eph. 2:10). Accordingly, Paul proclaims a "grace" that brings the gift of righteousness and forgiveness (Rom. 5:15, 17; Eph. 1:7; Titus 3:7); and he proclaims a "grace" that teaches a new way of living (Titus 2:11–14)—consoling and transforming grace, if you will. Congruently (though not always appreciated as such), James writes of faith and works belonging together, like body and spirit (James 2:26). John says it is vital to "confess the coming of Jesus Christ in the flesh" (2 John 7) and to keep the commandment(s) (2 John 5–6). The writer to the Hebrews calls for us to "draw near with a true heart in full assurance of faith," and for us to "stir up one another to love and good works" (Heb. 10:22, 24). In his first epistle, Peter promises us that we "are being guarded through faith for a salvation ready to be revealed in the last time" (1 Pet. 1:5). At the same time, Peter urges us to understand that when people see our "good deeds," they will "glorify God on the day of visitation" (1 Pet. 2:12). Thus, Peter calls on us to sanctify Christ in our hearts and be ready to offer an *apologia*—a reason for belief—when people ask about the hope they see within us (1 Pet. 3:15).

[33] Ibid.

In Matthew's Gospel, pointedly, it is this same Peter who confesses, "You are the Christ, the Son of the living God" (16:16), embodying the kind of faith that saves. This is a confession that can come only as blessing from above and that alone can serve as a foundation for the church which Christ himself will build (Matt. 16:18); and that would prompt Peter to write later of faith's preservative power (again, 1 Pet. 1:5). And, intriguingly, it is Peter who recalls the way the church's "good deeds" will vindicate God's character, as Jesus had taught, again in Matthew: "In the same way, let your light shine before others, so that they may see your good works and give glory to your Father who is in heaven" (Matt. 5:16).

Perhaps nowhere else in the New Testament is there such an unabashed affirmation of the need for the both–and of faith and works as in Matthew's Gospel. Two Matthean parables sum the concern. In the parable of the two sons we learn that it is not as important that you say the right words ("'I go, sir,' but [he] did not go"), as it is that you do the right thing regardless of whether you give the right words ("'I will not,' but afterward he changed his mind and went," Matt. 21:28–32). And in the parable of the wedding banquet we see the King graciously instructing his servants virtually to drag everybody to the feast, "all whom they found, both bad and good" (22:10); but then we note he expects them to have clothes for the occasion: "Friend, how did you get in here without a wedding garment?" (22:12). God expects of us faith to accept the gracious invitation to the King's feast, and readiness to learn how to carry oneself at the King's feast—a "faith and works" combination seen in the examples below.

Faith: Matthew's Sermon on the Mount begins by telling us that the first thing we must do is acknowledge the poverty and emptiness of our spirit (the first beatitude, 5:3). We are to believe in one who came "not to be served, but to serve, and to give his life as a ransom for many" (20:28). *And works:* The sermon's preamble concludes, "You are . . . a city on a hill" for the world to see who God is, and "the salt of the earth," that through our lives dissolution and decay might not have the last say in the human story (compare Matt. 5:3, the first beatitude, with 5:13–14).

Faith: The second and third beatitudes call upon us to mourn as we acknowledge the awfulness of the world and our lot in it, to do so meekly and thus without bitterness, and to submit to realities that are beyond our ability to control. All of this is the posture taken by those who believe that Christ "came not to call the righteous, but sinners" (Matt. 5:4–5; 9:9–13). *And works:* The fourth beatitude changes direction quickly by urging us to "hunger and thirst for righteousness" (5:6). It promises satisfaction for those who lean into God's plan to restore all "rightness"—personally, socially, cosmically (see Isa. 42:1–4; Hos. 12:6; Amos 5:24; Mic. 6:8). Likewise, the seventh beatitude ("Blessed are the peacemakers," Matt. 5:9) calls for us to seek to restore broken relationships. We thereby show ourselves to be offspring of the God of peace, and people who both pray and actually live congruently with the prayer that God's will be done "on earth as it is in heaven" (compare 5:6, 9 with 6:10).

Faith: We acknowledge, as the rich young ruler should have, that our goods can own us, instead of the reverse (19:16–22). We believe Jesus came to bring us in the "already" into the kingdom of heaven, which he compares to a "treasure hidden in a field" and a "pearl of great value" (13:44–46). We believe that the banquet of the kingdom of the Father is prefigured every time we partake of the bread and the "fruit of the vine" (26:26–29). *And works:* We learn the way of mercy: of unabashed care for the poor, of not just tithing our garden spices, but practicing justice, mercy, and faithfulness—"the weightier matters of the law" (compare 5:7, the fifth beatitude, with 23:23).

Faith: We confess, like the leper who cries, "Make me clean!" that we are unclean. We believe that Jesus's "blood of the covenant" (Matt. 26:28) restores innocence to the fallen. *And works:* We pursue purity of heart (compare 8:2 with 5:8, the sixth beatitude).

Faith: We believe that Jesus is the very presence of God among us, that he offers us rest from all weariness of striving—of moralism, of works-righteousness, of self- or "my people" vindication (11:28). We believe that the One who has saved us from our sins is straightforwardly with us when we gather in worship and prayer (18:8–20). *And works:* We also believe that he is with us when we go and make disciples (28:18–20), and when we give food and drink to the hungry and thirsty, when we welcome the stranger, clothe the naked, care for the sick, and visit the imprisoned who are "the least of these"; especially, perhaps, when the least of these are those who are "persecuted for righteousness' sake." For when we have done so, Jesus, "God with us," says, "You did it to me" (compare 25:31–46 with 5:10–11, the eighth and ninth beatitudes).

Chronological Overview

Genealogy, Birth, and Infancy Narratives (Matthew 1–2)

Matthew 1. One factor in the placement of Matthew at the head of the New Testament canon is the appearance of the Greek word γένεσις, "beginning" or "origin," twice in the opening chapter. Matthew begins with "The book of the genealogy [γένεσις] of Jesus" (1:1) and follows the genealogy with an account of "the birth [γένεσις] of Jesus" (1:18). The origin of Jesus lies, first, in the paternal lineage of Joseph and, second, in the heavenly word that comes to Joseph about the child within Mary being "from the Holy Spirit" (1:18).

So, in a sense, Matthew is the New Testament's book of Genesis, its book of beginnings. The church's "beginnings" lie in God's faithfulness to undo the curse of Genesis's garden of Eden through the line of Abraham, as channeled through the line of David—with the following two provisos: First, just as the original call to Abraham came while he was a pagan in the land of the Chaldees, and just as that call had in view the eventual blessing of all the nations, so the line of the Messiah has included four women of pagan background or marriage: Tamar of Canaan, Rahab of Jericho, Ruth of Moab, and "the wife of Uriah" the Hittite (Matt. 1:3, 5, 6). Second, God's undoing of the mess of the garden does not run in a straight line from Abraham through David; it takes the detour of exile for sin, "the deportation to Babylon" (1:17). Thus, the explanation of the naming of Joseph's adopted son as "Jesus" (from the Hebrew meaning "Yah saves"), "for he will save his people from their sins" (1:21).

Matthew 2. Pagan astronomers perceive what King Herod does not: Israel's Messiah-King has been born, and he merits tribute from Gentile as well as Jew. Ever envious of rival claimants to his throne (sources tell us that Herod killed his own sons to protect his rule), Herod pretends he too wishes to honor the newborn King. The magi present gifts worthy of the child's divinity (frankincense) and royalty (gold), and (whether they realize it or not) prophetic of his sacrificial death (myrrh).

God's hand is evident in his use of dreams (1) to warn the magi not to return to Herod before returning home and (2) to send the holy family into Egypt. God's hand is evident as well in the fact that all is prophesied: from Bethlehem as the birthplace of Israel's Shepherd-King, to Egypt as the place from which God, as he did earlier with Israel, would call his Son, and even to the lamentation for the innocents.

Series 1: From Coronation to Keynote (Matthew 3–7)

Matthew 3. In the Judean desert, John the Baptist prepares a way for the coming of the kingdom of heaven. That preparation is one of repentance in anticipation of judgment. John calls a circumcised nation, who already consider themselves God's people, to a humble confession of their sin and need for cleansing. Surprisingly, when the King comes, he comes to be baptized in the waters of repentance, not (yet!) to bring the baptism of judgment. As Herman Ridderbos says, "Jesus will not baptize by fire until he has himself first stood with all sinners in the waters of Jordan."[34] In order "to fulfill all righteousness" (Matt. 3:15) and thus, maintains Ridderbos, enable the kingdom to come in blessing and not in curse, Jesus will take the sins of the people upon himself as the servant of the Lord (Isaiah 53). Once Jesus has identified himself with sinners at his baptism, the Holy Spirit falls upon him to anoint him as King and to empower him to conquer sin, death, evil, and the Devil. The Father pronounces Jesus's royal sonship (see Ps. 2:7).

Matthew 4. Israel was called "out of Egypt" as God's son (Hos. 11:1). In the wilderness, the people of Israel placed their bellies above God's word, tested the Lord at the waters of Meribah, and worshiped a golden calf. Jesus, the greater Son called out of Egypt, goes into the wilderness under the Spirit's guidance to reverse Israel's failure.

The Devil tries to derail Jesus from his mission of obedient suffering-unto-glory. Jesus refuses to put his hunger ahead of his Father's voice. Jesus will not test the Lord by throwing himself off the temple wall. For the very sake of "the kingdoms of the world" (Matt. 4:8) Jesus will not worship any but the Father. His obedience signals the Devil's demise.

Jesus steps forward now to undertake his mission to save the world. Prophetically,

[34] Ridderbos, *Matthew's Witness to Jesus Christ*, 26.

he centers his mission in "Galilee of the Gentiles" (4:15), where Israel abuts the nations. He gathers disciples and names them apostles, something like ambassadors in training. In Jesus's preaching and healing, the great future of the fullness of the kingdom begins to break into the world.

Matthew 5–7. Jesus's Sermon on the Mount (Matthew 5–7) provides the crispest of summaries of the promises and demands of the coming kingdom. Keynoting the sermon are the Beatitudes (5:1–11). Jesus's statements about what makes for happiness should be taken, at one and the same time, as biddings to repentance, as sketches of Jesus's own character, and as promises of his transforming work in his disciples. The King declares his people to be "salt of the earth" and a "city on a hill," and announces that in him and his teaching "not an iota, not a dot" of the law will be lost; all of it will be fulfilled (5:13–18). Indeed, his people—the people of the kingdom—will be marked by a righteousness that exceeds the highest standards (5:19–20). By way of illustration, he points to a deeper reading of the requirements of the ethical commandments about anger, lust, divorce, oaths, retaliation, and enemies (5:21–48).

Then in chapter 6, Jesus takes up practices more commonly thought of as "religious." Almsgiving ("practicing . . . righteousness") is about giving to the needy, not about building one's spiritual portfolio (6:1–4). Prayer is neither about conjuring dead deities nor about building one's reputation for piety; it is about recalling the Father's character and name, and about succinctly stating one's need for sustenance, forgiveness, and protection (6:5–13).

The sort of faith that prays for forgiveness will be quick to forgive (6:12, 14–15). The sort of faith that asks for daily provision (6:11) will be ready to practice self-denial—not publicly for show, but privately before the Father (presumably in quest of a closer relation with the Father or for the sake of supplication for others—6:16–18; compare Isa. 58:6–8). Faith that knows each day's bread to come from God also understands that true treasures are heavenly (Matt. 6:11, 19–24). And the faith that calls upon heavenly protection (6:13) knows freedom from anxiety and freedom to "seek first the kingdom of God and his righteousness" (6:25–34).

In the concluding section of the Sermon on the Mount, Jesus commands generosity in judgment of others from those who know God's generous forgiveness for themselves (7:1–5). He assures his followers that they need not—indeed, should not—force "what is holy" on those who would not know what to do with it (7:6). He promises his disciples that their Father will respond more generously to their prayers than they do to their own children's requests (7:7–11). He sums up for them the Law and the Prophets: doing for others what you would have them do for you (7:12). And he cautions his followers against blithely assuming that everybody will want to follow the same path as they (7:13–14). Further, he cautions them against being overly impressed by prophets and exorcists who claim Jesus's name and power but who will be shown in the end not to have been his at all (7:21–23). His followers' task is quite simple: build your life wisely, on the "rock" of hearing

Jesus's words and doing them, instead of the "sand" of hearing his words and not doing them (7:24–27).

Series 2: Call to Discipleship and Mission (Matt. 8:1–11:1)

Matthew 8–9. Over the next two chapters and at a breakneck narrative pace, Matthew provides nine miracle narratives that illustrate Jesus's power over leprosy (8:1–4), sickness (8:14), the demonic (8:16, 28–34; 9:32–34), nature (8:23–28), paralysis (9:1–8), sin (9:5–8), feminine chronic "discharge of blood" (9:20–22), death (9:18–19, 23–26), and blindness (9:27–31).

Responses to Jesus vary widely: from the disciples' "little faith" (8:26) to the centurion's "great faith" (8:10 NASB); from a scribe's bloviating bluster and a would-be disciple's feeble deflection (8:19–22) to Matthew's ready acceptance of the call "Follow me" (9:9); from a city's polite request that Jesus leave town (8:34) to a crowd's fearing and glorifying God, "who had given such authority to men" (9:8).

Perhaps most intriguing is the range of responses from Jesus's enemies: scribes write him off as a blasphemer (9:3), while Pharisees smugly judge him for consorting with sinners (9:11). But the demons know exactly who he is and why he has come: "What have you to do with us, O Son of God?" And they know his coming means their doom. What confuses them is that they think he has come "before the time" (8:29).

Indeed, it is this question of timing that Jesus's coming makes most pressing. Matthew has told his readers that Immanuel is his name, God with us. We're seeing what the fact of God's being with us in human form brings. That nature's Master has come with power to still storms (8:23–28) means that finally there's hope that Genesis 3's surrender of nature to corruption can be reversed. The promised suffering servant has come to take his people's illnesses and bear their diseases (Matt. 8:17); that is why unclean lepers can be made clean again (8:1–4). One now walks on the earth with the divine prerogative to make the last day's putting away of sin a present reality (9:2–8). A merciful physician has come for the sick who know their own sacrifices can never heal (9:12–13).

Matthew 10:1–11:1. Jesus designates twelve disciples to send on a mission to "the lost sheep of the house of Israel" (Matt. 10:6). Their ministry is precisely to mirror his: proclaim the nearness of the kingdom and manifest God's power over sickness, death, leprosy, and the demonic (10:7–8). At first, Jesus appears to be talking about a mission that is extremely limited both geographically and temporally (10:5, 23). However, verses 17 and 18 imply that he expects this mission to be a prelude to a wider and longer mission: "You will be dragged before governors and kings for my sake, to bear witness before them and the Gentiles."

Because "a disciple is not above his teacher" (10:24), the Twelve (and we who follow after them) can expect to experience what Jesus experienced: resistance both from authorities and from family, empowerment by the Spirit, and a cross-shaped life. Congruently, we should also expect to see God rewarding those who receive us the way they receive his Son (10:40–42).

Series 3: The Wisdom of the Kingdom of Heaven (Matt. 11:2–13:53)

Matthew 11:2–30. John the Baptist is now in prison. He has enunciated fiery expectations for Jesus and is puzzled that Jesus's deeds are not bringing about the deliverance he envisioned. Jesus responds to emissaries from John by pointing to the ways his deeds fulfill Isaiah's prophecies about the day of salvation (Matt. 11:2–6).

But Jesus's path to kingship will take him through the valley of suffering. Before he brings the fire of judgment, he will endure the fire of suffering and sin bearing. John's confusion over the shape of Jesus's messianic ministry does not reverse the fact that John's message is the most important a prophet has ever borne: "Prepare your way" (11:7–11).

John's imprisonment at Herod's hands is the next example of satanic resistance to the coming of the kingdom (11:12). Moreover, the saving signs of Jesus's messianic identity meet an astonishing spiritual lethargy in the Galilee of Jesus's upbringing (11:20–24). Nonetheless, the kingdom is advancing, for "God with us" is among us. Thus, Jesus opens a window on his divine majesty by declaring his relationship with his heavenly Father (11:25–26) and by inviting the weary and heavy laden to come to him (11:28–29).

Matthew 12. Matthew continues to unfold Jesus's identity as Immanuel, "God with us" (1:23). Jesus's freedom with Sabbath laws shows him to be "greater than" the temple (12:6). His impending death and resurrection will show him to be "greater than" Jonah (Matt. 12:41). His wisdom shows him to be "greater than" Solomon (Matt. 12:42). The offices of priest, prophet, and king converge in him. Moreover, he is the servant whom Isaiah promised, anointed by the Spirit of God to bring healing to the broken, justice to the Gentiles, and deliverance to all from the dominion of Satan (12:15–21; see Isa. 42:1–4). His miracles are a sign that "the kingdom of God has come upon you" (Matt. 12:28). Failure to recognize the Spirit's work in him is the worst of blasphemies (12:31–32). And failure to recognize the way Jesus reconfigures family membership is to leave oneself in the loneliest of places (12:46–50).

Matthew 13:1–53. In seven parables, Jesus presents the wisdom of the kingdom: the parables of the sower (with explanation), the wheat and weeds (with explanation), the yeast, the mustard seed, the hidden treasure, the pearl of great price, and the net.

Two Old Testament passages provide the rationale for Jesus's teaching in parables: Isaiah 6's sobering message to the prophet that his words would only confirm many in their rebellion, and Psalm 78's saying about the way parables express hidden truths.

The parable of the sower is prominent, and it highlights the irresistibility of the kingdom, despite apparent failure. To be sure, of the four different kinds of soil, only one produces fruit. In the end, however, there will be a field full of plants that have produced a large amount of fruit (Matt. 13:8, 23).

That gives some perspective to the second-most-prominent parable, that of the wheat and the weeds. The master of the field is perfectly willing to allow weeds to get as much care as the wheat until the appointed time for making all things right.

When the time for final judgment comes, the angels, not the workers, will do the final sorting.

Series 4: The Shape of the Church (Matt. 13:54–19:2)

Matthew 13:54–14:36. There follow powerful signs of the hiddenness of the kingdom of heaven: Jesus experiences rejection in Nazareth, the town of his upbringing (Matt. 13:54–58); and Herod the tetrarch beheads John the Baptist, prompting Jesus to seek solitude in "a desolate place" (14:1–13a).

When the crowds pursue Jesus, reports Matthew, "he had compassion on them and healed their sick" (14:13b–14). In fact, what emerges in this and the following three chapters is a sustained unfolding of his divine mission of redemptive compassion. He feeds the five thousand (14:14–21), with a return of twelve baskets (and he will repeat the identical fourfold actions of taking, blessing, breaking, and giving the bread at the Lord's Supper—26:26). While the disciples are crossing the Sea of Galilee by boat during a storm, he walks to them on water, allows Peter to join him on the water, and rescues Peter when doubt overcomes him; the storm ceases at Jesus's command, the first occasion on which his disciples confess, "Truly you are the Son of God" (14:22–33).

Matthew 15. Sick people flock to Jesus in Galilee, but religious leaders come from Jerusalem and question him on his laxity in traditional purity customs at meals. He counters with an accusation that they substitute self-serving traditions for God-given decrees (e.g., saying that giving to God trumps providing for aging parents). It is the wickedness of the heart that defiles a person, Jesus explains, not eating with unwashed hands (Matt. 15:1–9).

Immediately—as if to extend the point about things unwashed—Jesus takes the disciples to Tyre and Sidon (classical Philistia, northwest of Galilee), populated by people whom Jews would consider unclean. A Canaanite woman there hails him as "Son of David," recognizes his power over the demonic, and begs the mercy of a healing for her daughter. In a tacit and ironic rebuke of his disciples, who would send her away, Jesus commends her great faith and heals her daughter (15:21–28).

Next Jesus teaches and heals on the east side of the Sea of Galilee (largely populated by Gentiles—see the parallel in Mark 7:31). Here he feeds the four thousand (anticipating again the Lord's Supper, with his taking, giving thanks, and breaking and giving the loaves and fishes), with a return of seven baskets (some commentators suggest that the previous twelve baskets symbolized the twelve tribes of Israel, while these seven baskets symbolize the seven nations displaced during the conquest—see Deut. 7:1b; Acts 13:19). Then Jesus returns to Magadan in Galilee proper (Matt. 15:29–39).

Matthew 16. The doctrinally driven Pharisees and the liturgically minded Sadducees are united in this: nothing that Jesus has done or taught is impressive enough to establish his credibility (Matt. 16:1). Jesus responds that the only further credential he is willing to provide will be his resurrection from the dead (16:4). Meanwhile, he warns his disciples against the toxic cynicism of his opponents' disbelief (16:5–12).

At Caesarea Philippi, Jesus finally asks the disciples about their own faith (16:13–15). By God's grace, Peter gets the right answer about *who* Jesus is: "the Christ, the Son of the living God" (16:16–17). While Peter gets the wrong answer about *what* the Messiah has come to do, Jesus will nonetheless make Peter's confession of his messianic identity the foundation of the church he has come to establish. At the same time, Jesus begins to reinform Peter and the disciples as to the cross-shaped ministry of their Messiah-King (16:21–23)—and the cruciform shape their own lives must assume (16:24–28).

Matthew 17:1–21. Six days later on the Mount of Transfiguration, three of the disciples taste the glory of "the Son of Man coming in his kingdom" (Matt. 16:28) and see proof that there is one dispensation of grace uniting old covenant (Moses and Elijah) and new covenant; Jesus experiences a luminous transformation that anticipates the fruit of his suffering; and the Father reaffirms (recalling the baptism) the Son's identity and mission.

On the way down the mount, Jesus restates the hard truth that the path to glory will involve rejection and suffering, and he urges silence about the transfiguration until the resurrection makes the whole message comprehensible (17:9–13). At the foot of the mount, Jesus heals a demon-possessed boy—something the disciples could have done themselves had they but had sufficient faith (17:14–21).

Matthew 17:22–19:2. In his "Sermon on the Congregation," Jesus sketches his mandate for life in the church. He tells his disciples he does not want a boycott of the temple tax, indicating that the church is to show a measure of flexibility to outsiders. Turning to the inner life of the church, he calls for self-denial: refusal to exalt self (Matt. 18:1–5), refusal to be hurtful to little ones (18:5–6), and refusal of personal laxity toward sin (18:7–9). Then he calls for positive acts of love: seeking out brothers and sisters who wander off (18:10–14), holding one another to account for egregious sins (18:15–17), and, aptly enough for people who understand how lavishly their heavenly Father has forgiven them, readily forgiving one another when there is sorrow for sins (18:23–35).

At the heart of his teaching about the shape of church life, Jesus promises his own presence (reminiscent of the Old Testament's promise of the presence of the *shekinah* glory; recall, for example, the dedication of the temple in 2 Chronicles 6). However, now, remarkably, he promises to be present even in the smallest prayer-filled gatherings of believers (18:19–20).

Series 5: Preparation for Judgment (Matt. 19:3–26:1)

Matthew 19:3–30. Intriguingly, as Jesus travels toward Jerusalem and his final conflict with his enemies, his teaching turns from the Christian congregation to the Christian home, specifically to marriage and finances. In answer to a question about divorce, Jesus affirms the sanctity of monogamous marriage between "male and female"

(Matt. 19:1–8), and limits the permission of divorce to matters of sexual impropriety (19:9). In the same breath, he also ennobles a call to singleness (19:10–12). When his disciples try to prevent people from bringing little children to him, he insists that it is precisely to such little ones that the kingdom of heaven belongs (19:13–15).

A rich young man asks what he must do to possess eternal life. Jesus responds by pointing him to the commandments. The young man claims he has kept the commandments but senses that he still lacks something. Jesus tells him to sell all, give to the poor, and follow him. The young man leaves in sorrow. We may infer that he does not in fact love God or neighbor more than his "great [lit. "many"] possessions" (19:22).

Matthew 20. The two main stories of Matthew 20 address two principal temptations of Christian leaders: envy and pride. Vineyard day laborers who have worked through the day resent the fact that laborers who work a short day receive equal pay. The antidote to such envy is to acknowledge the master's sovereign generosity (20:1–16). Appropriately bridging this story about envy and the next story about pride is Jesus's third prediction of his death and resurrection (20:17–19).

No doubt recalling that Jesus has spoken of "twelve thrones" for his disciples (19:28), the mother of the Zebedee brothers asks for a promise of pride of place for her sons when the kingdom comes. First, Jesus counters with a humbling question to James and John: "Are you able to drink the cup that I am to drink?" (20:22). Second, Jesus reminds them that kingdom rewards are the Father's to give, not his. Third, seeing the envy the Zebedees' ambition has stirred among the other disciples, Jesus points to the servile, "table waiting" shape of his mission and tells his disciples that his pattern is to be theirs. He explains for the first time the *meaning* of his upcoming death: it is a "ransom for many" (20:28).

Jesus concludes his journey to Jerusalem by healing two blind men outside Jericho and allowing them (unlike a pair at the beginning of his journey—see 9:27–31) to follow him (20:29–34).

Matthew 21:1–27. Three events shed further light on Jesus's person and work as King, Prophet, and Priest. First, he enters Jerusalem mounted on a foal-accompanied donkey, accepting acknowledgment as Israel's prophesied servant-King (Matt. 21:1–9). Second, he prophetically proclaims and symbolically enacts the Father's displeasure at the corruption of the temple (21:10–13). And third, he purifies the worship of the temple, healing the blind and the lame who are there, and defending the praise of children (21:14–16). His cursing of the fig tree is a rebuke of faithless Israel for not recognizing her King-Prophet-Priest (21:18–21). Jesus exposes the craven cynicism of the chief priests and elders who ask him about the authority behind his actions (21:23–27).

Matthew 21:28–22:14. In three parables, Jesus presses the question of faith. During John the Baptist's ministry, the tax collectors and prostitutes believed John the Baptist. Jesus likens them to a son who first refuses but then obeys his father's instructions.

Meanwhile the chief priests and elders rejected John's "way of righteousness." In the parable of the two sons, Jesus likens them to a son who claims he will do his father's will, but whose actions belie that commitment (Matt. 21:28–32). Faith is in the doing, more than in the saying.

The parable of the wicked tenants is virtually a recapitulation of the entire Bible's storyline. God carefully prepares his vineyard Israel. Majority Israel rejects one God-sent delegation after another, finally killing God's Son in a vain attempt to win autonomy from him. (Mercifully, the previous parable reminds us that there has always been a believing "minority report.") Ironically, God will nonetheless fulfill his intention of blessing the world through (to change the metaphor) the builders' rejection of the cornerstone (21:33–46; esp. 42).

The parable of the wedding feast looks ahead to the weighty twofold responsibility of the church: first, to invite everybody to the union of God with his people; second, to make sure that those who accept the invitation don proper wedding garments (presumably, by becoming disciples, being baptized, and learning to observe Christ's commands—see Matt. 28:16–20).

Matthew 22:15–46. Four questions (three posed by others, one posed by Jesus) frame four of the most critical matters for which his followers will have to contend.

First, when asked about paying taxes to Caesar, Jesus insists that because God is the preeminent authority in the universe, we owe him primary obedience; nonetheless, we have a secondary obligation to support and obey governing authorities (Matt. 22:15–22).

Second, when asked about resurrection, Jesus asserts that death is not the end for us, nor is it merely the portal to a permanent nonphysical consciousness. Our final state will indeed be resurrection, that is, renewed bodies, with a physicality that is unlike anything we have yet experienced and where there is neither marrying nor giving in marriage (22:23–33).

Third, when asked about which is the great commandment, Jesus acknowledges that there is one great commandment under which all others can be subsumed, and it is twofold: love God and love neighbor (22:34–40—see Lev. 19:18; Deut. 6:5).

Fourth, Jesus asks how, in Psalm 110, David could have referred to One who was both his Lord and his Son. Israel, Jesus implies, should have been expecting a messianic Son of David that was more than merely human. As Bruner (ad loc.) summarizes: "More than David is here . . . David's son as man, David's Lord as God" (22:41–46).

Matthew 23. Matthew closes Jesus's teaching ministry with three chapters (Matthew 23–25) that mirror the Sermon on the Mount (Matthew 5–7), beginning with seven woes—strikingly reminiscent of the Beatitudes—by which Jesus illustrates what he does not want from his followers.[35] He castigates those who do not mourn others' failings with respect to the law, but instead pour on more demands (23:4),

[35] For the pairing of the woes with the Beatitudes, see Reggie M. Kidd, "Tithing in the New Covenant? 'Yes' as Principle, 'No' as Casuistry," in *Perspectives on Tithing: Four Views*, ed. David Croteau (Nashville: B&H Academic, 2011), 97–121.

and whose religion is about prestige instead of poverty of spirit (23:5–12). "Woe," he pronounces, to those who do not tell God's story in meekness, but instead make proselytes "twice as much a child of hell as [themselves]" (23:13–15). "Woe" to those whose über-scrupulous giving betrays a slothful disengagement from that justice, mercy, and faith which the tithe had been instituted to promote. "Woe" to teachers who should be models of purity of heart, but are corrupt to the core of their being. "Woe" to those whose pretense at being sons of peace belies their hostility to God's true prophets—those who, when called to stand with prophets whose truth telling brings persecution, instead join the murderers.

Matthew 24. Matthew 6 dealt with the disciplines of religion: prayer, fasting, and trust. Matthew 24 deals with the housing of religion: for Jewish people, the temple. In 24:1–26, 29–35 (where the language of "coming" [ἔρχεσθαι] evokes the image of the Son of Man coming before the "Ancient of Days" in Daniel 7), Jesus explains the significance of the destruction of Jerusalem and the temple. The heavenly conferral of authority to Jesus by virtue of his baptism, death, and resurrection will have earthly consequences for the old administration: the destruction of the temple. The disciples will see this "coming" to his heavenly authority happening because it will take some development; the disciples will have opportunity to prepare (Matt. 24:15–26). In other verses, Jesus uses the language of "presence" (παρουσία, which the ESV unfortunately also translates "coming"—24:27, 36–41) to refer to his (and still to us) future return at the consummation of the ages. His παρουσία, he asserts, nobody will see in advance (24:27). The job is simple—be ready (24:36–51).

Matthew 25. Matthew 7 crowned the Sermon on the Mount with a challenge to faithfulness and fruitfulness, to living according to the so-called Golden Rule (7:12) rather than with a judgmental spirit (7:1–5), and—by hearing and doing "these words of mine" (7:24)—to building wisely rather than foolishly. Correspondingly, in Matthew 25 Jesus now provides one parable that underscores the need for faithfulness in awaiting the παρουσία (25:1–13, ten virgins) and another that underlines the need for fruitfulness during the wait (25:14–30, the talents). In his final teaching he reasserts the need to decide how to live—in service to him, or not (25:31–46, the sheep and the goats). Ironically, though, the reality is that all will find that the way they serve or do not serve the hungry, thirsty, estranged, naked, sick, and imprisoned "brother" (25:34–40, 41–46) will be the proof of whether they have served Jesus himself, and therefore of whether their lives have been built on rock or sand (recalling 7:24–27).

Crucifixion, Resurrection, and Commissioning Narratives (26:2–28:20)

Matthew 26:2–75. While a woman anoints Jesus with costly ointment (Matt. 26:6–12), Judas agrees to betray him for thirty pieces of silver (26:14–16). Jesus converts the Passover observance into a thanksgiving meal that celebrates his self-outpouring "for the forgiveness of sins" (26:28) and that anticipates the eschatological day when he will "drink it new with you in my Father's kingdom" (26:29; see also 13:43). While

Jesus prays in Gethsemane, Peter and the brothers Zebedee sleep. Judas betrays with a kiss, and an unnamed disciple cuts off the ear of the servant of the high priest. Jesus responds, "All who take the sword will perish by the sword" (26:52). Though his disciples desert him, though Peter denies him, and though false witnesses accuse him of blasphemy, Jesus promises members of the Jewish high court that Scripture will be fulfilled: his death will result in his being enthroned as the Son of Man "seated at the right hand of Power and coming on the clouds of heaven" (26:64).

Matthew 27. Jesus appears before Pontius Pilate, the Roman governor (Matthew stresses Jesus's absolute silence—recall Matt. 12:19), while Judas hangs himself in remorse for his betrayal. Despite a dream by Pilate's wife, Pilate releases Barabbas instead of Jesus and protests his own innocence of Jesus's blood (27:15–26). Following Jesus's death on the cross (Matthew's account of which is especially shaped by Psalm 22—see Matt. 27:37, 43), not only is the curtain of the temple torn (as with Mark and Luke) but "the earth shook, and the rocks were split. The tombs also were opened" (Matt. 27:51–52). We are led to understand that death has met its match in Jesus's death, and the cover-up by the chief priests and the Pharisees cannot disprove this new reality. Joseph of Arimathea (simply called "a rich man . . . who also was a disciple") buries Jesus in his own tomb, with three of Jesus's female disciples looking on—and with a guard unit from the temple there to make sure Jesus's disciples commit no mischief with the body (27:57–61).

Matthew 28. The two Marys come to the tomb on Sunday before dawn. There they find an angel. He has moved the stone covering the tomb and is sitting on it. The guards lie on the ground "like dead men" (Matt. 28:4). The angel informs the women that Jesus has been raised from the dead and that he has gone before them to Galilee, where he wants his disciples to assemble. On their way to tell the disciples, the women are met by Jesus himself. Meanwhile, the temple leaders conspire with the revived guards to blame the missing body on the disciples, who allegedly have stolen it in the middle of the night while the guards have slept. Finally, Jesus meets with his eleven remaining disciples in Galilee. There he announces his lordship over heaven and earth and instructs his disciples to go "and make disciples of all nations, baptizing them in the name of the Father and of the Son and of the Holy Spirit, teaching them to observe all that I have commanded you," promising his own presence with them "to the end of the age" (28:19–20).

Select Bibliography

Allison, Dale C. *The Sermon on the Mount: Inspiring the Moral Imagination.* New York: Crossroad, 1999.

———. *Studies in Matthew: Interpretation Past and Present.* Grand Rapids, MI: Baker Academic, 2012.

Blomberg, Craig. *Interpreting the Parables*. 2nd ed. Downers Grove, IL: IVP Academic, 2012.

Brown, Jeanine K. "Matthew." In *The Baker Illustrated Bible Commentary*, edited by Gary M. Burge and Andrew E. Hill, 950–1006. Grand Rapids, MI: Baker, 2012.

Bruner, Frederick Dale. *Matthew: A Commentary*. Vol. 1, *The Christbook, Matthew 1–12*. Rev. ed. Grand Rapids, MI: Eerdmans, 2007.

———. *Matthew: A Commentary*, vol. 2, *The Churchbook, Matthew 13–28*. Rev. ed. Grand Rapids, MI: Eerdmans, 2007.

Davies, W. D., and Dale C. Allison. *Matthew 1–7*. Vol. 1. ICC. Bloomsbury: T&T Clark, 2004.

———. *Matthew 8–18*. Vol. 2. ICC. Bloomsbury: T&T Clark, 2004.

———. *Matthew 19–28*. Vol. 3. ICC. Bloomsbury: T&T Clark, 2004.

Evans, Craig. *Matthew*. Cambridge: Cambridge University Press, 2012.

Ferguson, Sinclair. *The Sermon on the Mount: Kingdom Life in a Fallen World*. Carlisle, PA: Banner of Truth, 1988.

France, R. T. *The Gospel of Matthew*. NICNT. Grand Rapids, MI: Eerdmans, 2007.

———. *Matthew: Evangelist and Teacher*. Grand Rapids, MI: Zondervan, 1989.

Gleaves, G. Scott. *Did Jesus Speak Greek? The Emerging Evidence of Greek Dominance in First-Century Palestine*. Eugene, OR: Pickwick, 2015.

Greenman, Jeffrey P., Timothy Larsen, and Stephen R. Spencer, eds. *The Sermon on the Mount through the Centuries: From the Early Church to John Paul II*. Grand Rapids, MI: Brazos, 2007.

Hauerwas, Stanley. *Matthew*. Grand Rapids, MI: Brazos, 2006.

Jeremias, Joachim. *The Parables of Jesus*. 2nd ed. New York: Scribner's, 1972.

Keener, Craig S. *A Commentary on the Gospel of Matthew*. Grand Rapids, MI: Eerdmans, 1999.

———. *The Historical Jesus of the Gospels*. Grand Rapids, MI: Eerdmans, 2009.

———. "Matthew." In *The IVP Bible Background Commentary: New Testament*. 2nd ed., 44–125. Downers Grove, IL: InterVarsity Press, 2014.

Kidd, Reggie M. "Tithing in the New Covenant? 'Yes' as Principle, 'No' as Casuistry." In *Perspectives on Tithing: Four Views*, edited by David Croteau, 97–121. Nashville: B&H Academic, 2011.

Ladd, George Eldon. *A Theology of the New Testament*. Rev. ed. Grand Rapids, MI: Eerdmans, 1993.

Morris, Leon. *The Gospel according to Matthew*. PNTC. Grand Rapids, MI: Eerdmans, 1992.

Murray, John. *Principles of Conduct: Aspects of Biblical Ethics*. Grand Rapids, MI: Eerdmans, 1957.

Newport, Kenneth G. C. *The Sources and* Sitz im Leben *of Matthew 23*. JSNTSup 117. Sheffield: Sheffield Academic Press, 1995.

Oden, Thomas C. *The Good Works Reader*. Grand Rapids, MI: Eerdmans, 2007.

Osborne, Grant R. *Matthew*. ZECNT. Grand Rapids, MI: Zondervan, 2010.

Ridderbos, Herman. *The Coming of the Kingdom*. Philadelphia: Presbyterian and Reformed, 1973.

———. *Matthew's Witness to Jesus Christ: The King and the Kingdom*. World Christian Books. New York: Association Press, 1958.

Robinson, John A. T. *Redating the New Testament*. Philadelphia: Westminster Press, 1976.

Schnackenburg, Rudolf. *The Gospel of Matthew*. Translated by Robert R. Barr. Grand Rapids, MI: Eerdmans, 2002.

Stanton, Graham N. *A Gospel for a New People: Studies in Matthew*. Louisville: Westminster John Knox, 1992.

Talbert, Charles T. *Reading the Sermon on the Mount: Character Formation and Decision Making in Matthew 5–7*. Grand Rapids, MI: Baker Academic, 2006.

Wright, N. T. *The New Testament and the People of God*. Minneapolis: Fortress, 1992.

2

Mark

Benjamin Gladd

Introduction

The early church, taking cues from Ezekiel 1 and Revelation 4, depicted Mark's Gospel as a fierce lion. But why would the early readers of the Second Gospel choose such an image? As Richard Burridge points out, the imagery of a lion can be "uncomfortable,"[1] since lions in the Old Testament are viewed negatively and often found as vehicles for God's judgment and for enemies of Israel (Num. 23:24; Ps. 22:13; Isa. 5:29; etc.). Upon opening the Gospel of Mark, we are immediately struck with the sobering reality that Israel's God has come to judge those who are unwilling to repent. Lions are also known for their agility and action. One of the most remarkable features of Mark is his fast-paced, at times unrelenting, narrative. Lastly, lions in the Old Testament are often associated with royalty and Israel's end-time King (Gen. 49:9; Num. 24:9). The Gospel of Mark plucks at this string from beginning to end; Israel's long-awaited King has arrived on the scene. But as Mark makes clear, Israel's King differs somewhat from expectations. His rule is not confined to a plot of land but pushes the boundaries of the cosmos, and his rule is marked not by military triumph but by physical defeat.

Background Issues

The Genre of the Gospels

Imagine reading Harry Potter like *USA Today*. We would attempt to enroll immediately at Hogwarts and begin training for quidditch tryouts. We scoff at such a prospect, but why is that? How do we know Harry Potter and similar books are fiction? It doesn't claim to be fiction on the front or back cover. It is fiction because

[1] Richard A. Burridge, *Four Gospels, One Jesus? A Symbolic Reading*, 2nd ed. (Grand Rapids, MI: Eerdmans, 2005), 36.

we instinctively and unconsciously discern it. By picking up the book and flipping through the pages, our brains gather data and signals, telling us that the book is purely fictional. So by the time we begin reading the book, we understand the nature of the book and, therefore, how to read it.

The same could be said of Mark (as well as the other three Gospels). If we do not place Mark in the right literary category, we will fail to read the narrative correctly. Before any interpretation can take place, the book's genre must be determined. Burridge explains,

> Genre forms a kind of "contract" or agreement, often unspoken or unwritten, or even unconscious, between an author and a reader, by which the author sets out to write according to a whole set of expectations and conventions and we agree to read or to interpret the work using the same conventions, giving us an initial idea of what we might expect to find.[2]

In the last few decades, New Testament scholars are now categorizing the four Gospels as Greco-Roman biography. In the ancient world, there existed a genre known as "lives." A Greco-Roman biography or "lives" is a flexible genre and incorporates a variety of literary characteristics (history, praise, moral philosophy, story, etc.). The point of this type of literature is to *inform the readers of the hero or protagonist and invite the readers to believe that same message.* The Gospels, as with Greco-Roman biography, primarily narrate the story of a protagonist. In short, each chapter and literary unit in the Gospels somehow informs us of Jesus and his message.

If the Gospels are deemed to be Greco-Roman biographies, then we must keep one point uppermost in mind when reading them: the four narratives are primarily about Jesus, the protagonist of the narrative. We must continually ask ourselves, what do we learn about Jesus in light of the present passage? As an example, let us consider Mark's account of the stilling of the storm (4:35–41). This event details Jesus's sovereign power over the chaotic waters and the failure of the disciples to believe. Once the storm arises on the sea, the disciples cry out in fear, "Teacher, do you not care that we are perishing?" (4:38). Many highlight the disciples' lack of faith in Jesus's power, and rightly so, but that is not the main point of the passage. The disciples' lack of faith is secondary to Jesus's identity. The narrative connects Jesus to Yahweh in the Old Testament, who sovereignly reigns over chaotic waters. This explains why the disciples ask, "Who then is this, that even the wind and the sea obey him?" (4:41). As we progress through Mark's narrative, we must stay attuned to how each section relates to Jesus of Nazareth.

Eyewitness Testimony

Exactly how the four Gospels came about has been the focus of much scholarship for approximately the past two centuries. As one can imagine, every conceivable

[2] Richard Burridge, "Gospel Genre and Audiences," in *The Gospels for All Christians: Rethinking the Gospel Audiences*, ed. Richard Bauckham (Grand Rapids, MI: Eerdmans, 1998), 114. See also his larger volume, *What Are the Gospels? A Comparison with Graeco-Roman Biography*, 2nd ed. (Grand Rapids, MI: Eerdmans, 2004).

hypothesis has been offered to explain the creation and publication of the four Gospels, particularly the relationship between the Gospels and the historical figure of Jesus who stands behind them. The quest for the historical Jesus has, unfortunately, concerned itself with critically investigating the Jesus *behind* the Gospels. The Gospels are not taken at face value but viewed as the product of early Christian beliefs and ideologies. In order to apprehend the Jesus of history, scholars have been preoccupied with stripping away the layers of theology and ideology. The net result is a reconstructed Jesus, who looks nothing like the Jesus of Matthew, Mark, Luke, and John.

A far better way of establishing the "historical Jesus," though, is to allow the Gospels to present the figure of Jesus in their own words. Let's allow the Gospel writers to tell their story of Jesus. For nearly two thousand years, Christians have taken the Gospels at face value and believed that the Jesus of the Gospels is one and the same with the Jesus of history. Bridging the gap between the historical Jesus and the Gospel narratives is the category of eyewitness testimony. In recent years, this aspect of early Christianity has undergone considerable development, strengthening the long-held view.

Richard Bauckham's book *Jesus and the Eyewitnesses* is a most insightful book in this regard.[3] The crux of his argument is that in the ancient world, living testimony is to be preferred to secondhand tradition. In other words, the authors of the Gospels were primarily concerned with gathering content about Jesus *from those who had personally listened to, seen, and experienced Jesus.* Bauckham builds upon Samuel Byrskog's work *Story as History—History as Story.*[4] Byrskog argues that Greco-Roman historiography makes extensive use of a category known as eyewitness testimony, which preferred a witness who participated in the events. In our modern world, we prefer "objective" testimony in an attempt to get at the bare facts. We prefer a neutral observer to a prejudicial one. In disputations involving car accidents or criminal activity, the neutral observer is held in high regard. But in the ancient world, historiographers actually preferred to interview those who were active participants.

The Gospels, form critics claim, came into existence through several stages: Jesus's actual words, the apostolic proclamation, and the written Gospels. The Gospel writers, they argued, should be understood primarily as collectors of "forms" or literary units that were created by a specific community in order to meet a specific need within that same community. The task therefore is to get back to the original words of Jesus by cutting through all the ideological layers. But eyewitness testimony questions much of what form criticism seeks to accomplish. Instead of determining how a particular form evolved and developed within a community over decades, the category of eyewitness testimony cuts through the presupposition of a long oral development of the Gospels without the control of the eyewitness.

[3] Richard Bauckham, *Jesus and the Eyewitnesses: The Gospels as Eyewitness Testimony* (Grand Rapids, MI: Eerdmans, 2006).
[4] Samuel Byrskog, *Story as History—History as Story: The Gospel Tradition in the Context of Ancient Oral History* (Leiden: Brill, 2002).

The category of eyewitness testimony is particularly important for Mark's Gospel, as he was not one of the twelve disciples. Since, as we will see below, Mark relies on Peter's eyewitness testimony, his Gospel remains a trustworthy account. In other words, Mark tells the story of Jesus through St. Peter's firsthand experiences as an eyewitness to Jesus's ministry.

Audience of the Gospels

When we turn to the Epistles of the New Testament, the audience is typically mentioned at the beginning of the letter. For example, Paul says in 1 Corinthians 1:2, "To the church of God that is in Corinth"; and Peter in 1 Peter 1:1, "To those who are elect exiles of the Dispersion in Pontus, Galatia, Cappadocia, Asia, and Bithynia." But when we examine the four Gospels, the audience is never mentioned. We are left, then, to determine the audience through a different avenue of inquiry.

For the past several decades, it has been quite popular to view the audience of each Gospel as a specific community. According to many scholars, each Gospel was written *in* a particular community and *for* that same community. This approach to the Gospels has been popular for quite a while, and until recently, a better proposal has not been offered. For instance, several prominent scholars claim that the book of John was written to a specific community, most likely in Ephesus. The high christology and other particular emphases in John's Gospel were included to address specific problems *within the community*. Each Evangelist wrote his Gospel to suit the needs of *his* community.

This line of argumentation has considerable problems and lacks historical evidence. Much of the problem rests upon how we read the Gospels. The Gospels are oftentimes read as epistles—letters written to specific churches with particular sets of problems. But the Gospels are not the genre that Paul employs. The Gospels fall, as I argued above, into the category of Greco-Roman biography, whereas Paul's letters are part of the epistolary genre. With epistles, we do our best to re-create the occasion of the letter. We study the geographic location of its recipients, the history, the culture, the reason(s) why the letter was sent, and so on. But Gospels are noticeably different from letters, and therefore we need to treat them as such.

Bauckham proposes that each of the four Gospels has an "open" audience; that is, it is not intended for one specific community or communities, but each was written for *all* Christians.[5] For example, Mark may very well have been written in Rome, and Mark's Roman congregation would certainly have obtained a copy of his Gospel, but once the Gospel had been copied, it would quickly have spread throughout the eastern Mediterranean, moving from one congregation to another. In a few short years, the majority of Christians would have access to Mark's Gospel. If Bauckham is right, then the audience of each Gospel spans the entire Christian spectrum, from Jewish Christians, to Christian Jewish proselytes, to converted pagan Gentiles.

[5] Richard Bauckham, "For Whom Were Gospels Written?," in *The Gospels for All Christians*, ed. Richard Bauckham (Grand Rapids, MI: Eerdmans, 1998), 9–48.

Authorship

Our Bibles bear the name Mark at the heading of this Gospel, yet, as mentioned above, Mark was not one of the original twelve disciples. The problem especially comes to a head when we consider the Gospels as eyewitness testimony. How could Mark write a Gospel if he did not bear witness to Jesus's earthly ministry (cf. Acts 1:21–22)? The answer probably lies in the comment made by the early church leader Papias when he recollected comments made by John the presbyter:

> This also the presbyter [John] said,
>
> "Mark, having become the interpreter of Peter, wrote down accurately, though not indeed in order, whatsoever he remembered of the things said or done by Christ. For he neither heard the Lord nor followed him, but afterward, as I said, he followed Peter, who adapted his teaching to the needs of his hearers, but with no intention of giving a connected account of the Lord's discourses, so that Mark committed no error while he thus wrote some things as he remembered them. For he was careful of one thing, not to omit any of the things which he had heard, and not to state any of them falsely."[6]

From this quotation, we gain two key insights: (1) an individual named Mark wrote this Gospel; (2) Mark did not witness these events firsthand but received eyewitness testimony through the apostle Peter. Though Mark was not part of the Twelve, he was a companion of Paul and Peter. It is likely that this Mark is John Mark in the book of Acts (12:12, 25; 13:5, 13; 15:37), who had close interaction with several apostles (Col. 4:10; Philem. 24; 2 Tim. 4:11; 1 Pet. 5:13). Though many modern scholars doubt that John Mark authored the Second Gospel, there is simply not enough evidence to overthrow a few internal hints within Mark's Gospel and the external witness of the early church.[7]

Date

The dating of Mark hinges on how we understand the relationship between the Synoptic Gospels, the nature of prophecy, and so on. Several scholars date Mark in the late 50s and early 60s, allowing enough time for Matthew and Luke to use Mark in their composition of their Gospels and for the fall of Jerusalem (which all three Synoptics predict and which took place in AD 70). Keeping in mind Nero's persecution in the mid-60s, it is quite possible that Mark was written around that time, since this Gospel particularly highlights suffering and persecution. A date in the early 60s is to be preferred since Matthew and Luke depend upon Mark and publish their Gospels before the fall of Jerusalem.

Text

The ending of Mark is remarkably complex, since we have inherited four different endings; we will entertain only two of these. In modern English translations of the

---

[6] Eusebius, *Hist. eccl.* 3.39.15 (*NPNF*[2] 1:172).

[7] For a succinct overview of the debate and defense of Markan authorship, see R. T. France, *The Gospel of Mark*, NIGTC (Grand Rapids, MI: Eerdmans, 2002), 35–41.

Gospel of Mark, the translators typically set off Mark 16:9–20 with an editorial comment about how the earliest manuscripts do not contain that section. This is a particularly thorny issue, but, given the constraints of this essay, my comments must be brief. The manuscript evidence of the shorter ending (those manuscripts that omit 16:9–20) is particularly early and strong (א B). Second, scribes have a tendency to expand, elaborate, and smooth out difficulties. The rather abrupt ending of Mark's Gospel in 16:8 ("And they went out and fled from the tomb, for trembling and astonishment had seized them, and they said nothing to anyone, for they were afraid") certainly lends itself to further elaboration and clarification. Moreover, within the expanded ending of Mark (16:9–20), several words and themes are peculiar and do not resonate within Mark's Gospel. For these reasons and others, the vast majority of scholars strongly doubt the authenticity of 16:9–20.[8]

Purpose

Mark's Gospel reworks Old Testament and Jewish messianic expectations: *the Messiah's reign and his kingdom are marked not by political and physical triumph but by suffering and defeat.* Those who follow him will follow in the Messiah's footsteps. Jesus has come to liberate his people from their sins and bring them into the new creation.

Structure and Outline

Generally speaking, the Synoptics move geographically from Jesus's baptism in the Jordan to his ministry in Galilee and then on to Jerusalem. In Galilee, Jesus is welcomed by the populace, both Jews and Gentiles. Jerusalem, though, is ironically the place of suffering and death. Instead of the city of David embracing her Messiah, she scorns him, eventually nailing him to a cross. One of the most distinctive features of Mark is his three-part "drama." R. T. France persuasively argues that Mark's Gospel falls into three "dramatic acts"[9]:

- I. Introduction to Jesus and His Galilean Ministry (1:1–8:26)
  - A. Prologue (1:1–13)
  - B. Beginning of Jesus's Galilean ministry (1:14–3:6)
  - C. Second phase of Jesus's Galilean ministry (3:7–6:6)
  - D. Last phase of Jesus's Galilean ministry (6:7–8:26)
- II. The Road to Jerusalem (8:27–10:52)
  - A. Peter's confession and the transfiguration (8:27–9:13)
  - B. Instruction concerning the kingdom and further healing (9:14–10:52)
- III. The Passion and Empty Tomb (11:1–16:8)
  - A. Temple judgment, prediction of the fall of Jerusalem, and Passover (11:1–14:31)
  - B. Betrayal, crucifixion, and resurrection of the Messiah (14:32–16:8)

---

[8] See, for example, Bruce Metzger, *A Textual Commentary on the Greek New Testament*, 2nd ed. (Stuttgart: Deutsche Bibelgesellschaft, 1994), 102–6.

[9] France, *Gospel of Mark*, 11–15.

Message and Theology

Key Themes in Mark

The "Messianic Secret"

Highlighted in Mark's Gospel is Jesus's insistence that his disciples and others conceal his identity. Commentators label this Markan phenomenon the "messianic secret," and a considerable amount of scholarly effort has been expended attempting to explain Jesus's seemingly bizarre behavior.[10] For example, in Mark 1:34 Jesus exorcises demons but prohibits them from divulging his identity: "And he healed many who were sick with various diseases, and cast out many demons. And he would not permit the demons to speak, because they knew him." Again, we can make a similar observation in Mark 8:30, which immediately follows Peter's (and the disciples') accurate confession that Jesus is indeed "the Christ" (i.e., the Messiah): "And he strictly charged them to tell no one about him" (cf. Mark 9:9). Why would Jesus forbid his disciples from telling others his identity as Israel's long-awaited King? Doesn't Jesus want Israel to know that he's their Savior who has come to liberate them from political and spiritual oppression? The answer, it seems, rests on Jesus's reworking of Israel's expectations of the long-awaited Messiah. In order for us to grasp the significance of the "messianic secret," we must briefly survey a few key Old Testament texts that describe the coming Messiah.[11]

Many Old Testament passages speak of or at least hint at a coming messianic figure who will deliver Israel and redeem her from her plight. Since this theme is essential to understanding Jesus's ministry, I will develop it in more detail. The term *messiah* (Heb. מָשִׁיחַ; Gk. Χριστός) means "anointed one." The verb "anoint" connotes being set apart for a distinct purpose. We find this word used in contexts such as the tabernacle and the altar (Ex. 40:9–11). The noun form is applied to priests (Lev. 4:3; 1 Sam. 2:35) and kings (1 Sam. 24:6; 26:11; etc.) and even Cyrus, a pagan ruler (Isa. 45:1). The Old Testament speaks of an individual who is "anointed" for a specific purpose—ruling over Israel and the nations and redeeming all of creation.

Genesis 3:15 sets the stage for a development of a messianic figure, albeit in seed form:

> I will put enmity between you and the woman,
> and between your offspring and her offspring;

[10] Wilhelm Wrede contended that the Gospels are shaped by early church dogma, and he attempted to demonstrate this through Mark's Gospel (*The Messianic Secret*, trans. J. C. Greig [Cambridge: James Clark, 1971]). He claims that Mark's "messianic secret" was the early church's attempt to portray Jesus as the long-awaited Messiah. In reality, according to Wrede, Jesus had no consciousness of his messianic status. The implications of Wrede's studies were staggering. Mark's Gospel was no longer seen as "primitive" and nontheological, as was traditionally thought. If Mark's Gospel is thoroughly theological, accompanied by an agenda, how much more are Matthew, Luke, and John? The upshot is that, according to Wrede, much of the Second Gospel cannot be deemed historical. Wrede certainly put his finger on a peculiar issue in Mark's Gospel and did indeed demonstrate that Mark is robustly theological. But we must not bifurcate history and theology. Each of the four Gospels is highly theological *and* historical. In examining Mark's "messianic secret" we must uncover why Mark highlights this theme of secrecy.

[11] For more detailed surveys of the Messiah, consult Michael F. Bird, *Are You the One Who Is to Come? The Historical Jesus and the Messianic Question* (Grand Rapids, MI: Baker Academic, 2009), 31–62; John J. Collins, *The Scepter and the Star: The Messiahs of the Dead Sea Scrolls and Other Ancient Literature*, ABRL (New York: Doubleday, 1995); N. T. Wright, *The New Testament and the People of God* (Philadelphia: Fortress, 1992), 307–20.

he shall bruise your head,
and you shall bruise his heel.

One of the promises God makes to the original couple is that their descendants will form two lines of progeny, a godly and an ungodly seed, and these two will continually wage war with one another. One of their descendants, though, will eventually "bruise" (or "crush") the "head" of the Serpent.

At the end of Genesis, Jacob blesses his twelve sons, and Judah receives a particular special blessing:

Judah . . .
your hand shall be on the neck of your enemies; . . .
The scepter shall not depart from Judah,
nor the ruler's staff from between his feet,
until tribute comes to him;
and to him shall be the obedience of the peoples. (Gen. 49:8, 10)

According to this passage, in the "latter days" (49:1) a future ruler will descend from the tribe of Judah and conquer Israel's enemies. The result of this decisive victory is that the nations and Israel will pay obeisance to him. In Numbers 24:17, a "star" will come from Jacob in the "latter days" (24:14) who will "crush the forehead of Moab"—a longtime enemy of Israel.

God makes a covenant with David in 2 Samuel 7, wherein he promises to maintain a Davidic ruler in Jerusalem: "I will raise up your offspring after you, . . . and I will establish his kingdom. He shall build a house for my name, and I will establish the throne of his kingdom forever" (7:12–13). This ruler will not only establish God's eternal kingdom; he will also build God's temple or "house."

The book of Isaiah, perhaps more than any other Old Testament book, prophesies that a latter-day ruler of Israel will eliminate Israel's enemies and rule with righteousness and wisdom. Isaiah describes this messianic figure, the "branch," in some detail:

There shall come forth a shoot from the stump of Jesse,
and a branch from his roots shall bear fruit. . . .
. . . with righteousness he shall judge the poor, . . .
and he shall strike the earth with the rod of his mouth,
and with the breath of his lips he shall kill the wicked. (11:1, 4; cf. 9:6–7)

It is likely that this ruler should be identified with the suffering servant in the later portions of Isaiah, who brings about the release of Israel from Babylonian captivity and restores the righteous remnant (42:1–9; 49:1–6; 50:4–9; 52:13–53:12).

That the Messiah should suffer persecution, in some capacity, is mentioned once more. Daniel 9:25–26 seems to suggest that the Messiah will eventually be put to death: "From the going out of the word to restore and build Jerusalem to the coming of an anointed one, a prince, there shall be seven weeks. Then for sixty-two weeks. . . . And after the sixty-two weeks, an anointed one shall be cut off and shall have nothing" (cf. Zech. 12:10). In summary, the Messiah will be instrumental in the destruction of Israel's enemies, the new exodus, the forgiveness of sins, the pouring out of the Spirit, and the dawn of the new creation.

According to the Old Testament and early Judaism, the Messiah refers above all to the coming "king of Israel." The Lord promises to restore and reign over his people through his Messiah. In 2 Samuel 7, God promised David that his descendants would rule over Israel. The Old Testament traces this promise and its fulfillment in the former and latter prophets. *The Messiah, a descendant of David, will be instrumental in bringing about the establishment of God's eternal kingdom and the destruction of Israel's enemies*. That much is clear. Bound up with this phenomenon is the arrival of the new exodus, making possible the forgiveness of sins, the pouring out of the Spirit, the dawn of the new creation, and so on. Regarding the suffering aspect of the Messiah, a few passages seem to hint that the Messiah will suffer to some extent, but this suffering is not a cardinal aspect of his ministry. Messianic suffering is the means by which God will restore his people.[12]

We are now in a better position to answer why in Mark's Gospel Jesus commands individuals to stay quiet. *Jesus must rework their understanding of the Messiah* (and the kingdom he establishes). The end-time kingdom and Jesus's messiahship are marked not by political triumph but by suffering and death. The disciples will be able to grasp this truth only *after* the crucifixion and the resurrection. Only then will they understand the nature of Jesus's identity and the nature of the kingdom. This is not to say that the Old Testament lacks a conception of a suffering Messiah; throughout the Old Testament Israel's ruler is often associated with suffering (the "bruising" of the heel of God's end-time deliverer [Gen. 3:15], David fleeing persecution from Absalom [2 Samuel 17], the Son of Man's identification with the persecuted Israelites [Dan. 7:25], and so on).[13]

Jesus and Isaiah's Second Exodus

In the last few decades, commentators have made great strides in understanding Mark's carefully crafted narrative. This is largely due to the influence of the author of the Gospels in the field of redaction criticism and the meticulous analysis of narrative criticism. Adding to this helpful dimension is a considerable effort to understand the New Testament authors' use of the Old Testament. Scholars have been systematically investigating how each New Testament author employs the Old Testament. Though

[12]The New Testament writers express a clear understanding that the Old Testament conceives of a suffering Messiah: e.g., see Luke 24:25–27: "And he [Jesus] said to them, 'O foolish ones, and slow of heart to believe all that the prophets have spoken! Was it not necessary that the Christ should suffer these things and enter into his glory?' And beginning with Moses and with all the Prophets, he interpreted to them in all the Scriptures the things concerning himself" (cf. John 5:39–47); 1 Cor. 15:3–4 likewise affirms that the Old Testament anticipated a suffering Messiah: "For I delivered to you as of first importance what I also received: that Christ died for our sins in accordance with the Scriptures, that he was buried, that he was raised on the third day in accordance with the Scriptures." Likewise, 1 Pet. 1:10–11 says, "Concerning this salvation, the prophets who prophesied about the grace that was to be yours searched and inquired carefully, inquiring what person or time the Spirit of Christ in them was indicating when he predicted the sufferings of Christ and the subsequent glories."

[13]For further discussion on how the Old Testament and Judaism explicitly expect a conquering Messiah and hint at a suffering one, see G. K. Beale and Benjamin Gladd, *Hidden but Now Revealed: A Biblical Theology of Mystery* (Downers Grove, IL: InterVarsity Press, 2014), 118–23, 136–44.

scholars, including evangelicals, disagree on the particulars, hardly anyone can deny the importance of the Old Testament upon the New Testament writers.

One noteworthy feature of Mark's narrative is his use of the book of Isaiah. Rikki Watts's seminal work *Isaiah's New Exodus in Mark* convincingly argues that the book of Isaiah—particularly, Isaiah's new exodus theme—is determinative for understanding Mark's Gospel.[14] Isaiah, like other Old Testament books, looks back at Israel's exodus from Egypt and recasts the event as a prophecy.

The exodus from Egypt is of considerable importance to Israel. It was the defining moment in the nation's history. It was when the Lord brought glory to himself, redeemed Israel from bondage, vanquished their enemies, and covenanted with his people. He safely led them to the Promised Land. Not only were the Israelites to gain comfort from Yahweh's past dealings with them in the exodus; they were also to look expectantly that he would one day in the future repeat that momentous event. Throughout the Old Testament, especially in the prophets, God promised to deliver Israel out of bondage once more and bring them to the Promised Land.

One example from Isaiah is worth mentioning. Portraying Israel's return to the Promised Land, Isaiah 43 uses language from Israel's first exodus:

> When you pass through the waters, I will be with you. (43:2)
>
> I give Egypt as your ransom. (43:3)
>
> Thus says the Lord,
> who makes a way in the sea,
> a path in the mighty waters,
> who brings forth chariot and horse,
> army and warrior;
> they lie down, they cannot rise,
> they are extinguished, quenched like a wick. (43:16–17)
>
> I am doing a new thing;
> now it springs forth, do you not perceive it?
> I will make a way in the wilderness
> and rivers in the desert. (43:19)[15]

One major difference remains between the first exodus and the second: the Old Testament expects the second exodus to be a final, consummate event. The Lord will, once for all, deal with sin, forge a remnant, and usher in the new heavens and new earth (65:17; 66:22).

This Isaianic framework explains several unique features of Mark and offers a more nuanced understanding of the Second Gospel. Though Israel in the first century AD has relocated back to the Promised Land, she remains in spiritual exile

[14] Rikki Watts, *Isaiah's New Exodus in Mark*, WUNT 88 (Tübingen: Mohr Siebeck, 1997; repr., Grand Rapids, MI: Baker, 2000).

[15] For a wonderful overview of the exodus theme in the canon, see Rikki Watts, "Exodus," in *New Dictionary of Biblical Theology*, ed. T. Desmond Alexander and Brian S. Rosner (Downers Grove, IL: InterVarsity Press, 2000), 478–87.

and enjoys limited political independence.[16] Many of Jesus's actions fit nicely with Isaiah's expectations of a second exodus. As we will see throughout Mark's Gospel, Jesus has come to deliver Israel from spiritual bondage in a new exodus of sorts and usher in the new creation. Jesus has come to deliver Israel from Babylonian captivity, a captivity marked not by physical bondage but by spiritual bondage. As a mighty warrior, even one who is identified with the God of Israel, he will vanquish Israel's true enemy—Satan. Jesus has come to guide his people through the wilderness and into the Promised Land. Upon Israel's arrival into the Promised Land, Yahweh will dwell with his people in a far more glorious way—not in a man-made tabernacle or temple, but richly in the covenant community.

At this juncture, it is important for us to put things into the proper perspective, especially in light of current debate. Jesus came primarily to deliver people from their sins and reconcile them to God. The *result* of this spiritual deliverance is the establishment of the kingdom, the beginning of the new creation, the ushering of God's people into the Promised Land, and so on. In other words, we need to distinguish between the gospel proper (Christ's death and resurrection), and the effects or implications of the gospel (the kingdom, the new creation, etc.).[17]

Chronological Overview of Mark's Gospel

Introduction to Jesus and His Galilean Ministry (Mark 1:1–8:26)

Mark begins his Gospel with John the Baptist calling for Israel to repent of her sins and identify with a renewed covenant community (1:1–6). Unlike Matthew and Luke, Mark introduces Jesus as a full-grown man, perhaps reflecting the creation of Adam in the garden. Once Jesus has identified with John's renewal and is installed as King (Mark 1:9–11; cf. Ps. 2:7), the Spirit propels Jesus into the wilderness to conquer Satan (Mark 1:12–13). At the end of the temptation, only Mark mentions Jesus being with "the wild animals," perhaps recalling Adam's fellowship with the animals in the garden (Gen. 2:18–20).[18] God is thus restoring not only humanity but also creation. Mark's fast-paced narrative portrays Jesus as bounding from one event to the next. As the long-awaited Messiah, Jesus ushers in God's long-awaited kingdom (1:14–15). The series of miracles and teaching episodes demonstrates that the long-awaited kingdom has indeed arrived (1:21–34, 40–45; 2:1–13; etc.). Now that the new creation has dawned through the Messiah, demons are exorcised, lepers

---

[16] The most robust defense of Israel's continuing state of exile in the first century is N. T. Wright's multivolume work on the origins of Christianity: *The New Testament and the People of God* and *Jesus and the Victory of God* (Philadelphia: Fortress, 1996). Though he probably pushes the evidence too far (see Carey C. Newman, ed., *Jesus and the Restoration of Israel: Critical Assessment of N. T. Wright's "Jesus and the Victory of God"* [Downers Grove, IL: InterVarsity Press, 1999]), he rightly sees the importance of this theme in the New Testament and Jewish literature.

[17] See D. A. Carson, "What Is the Gospel?—Revisited," in *For the Fame of God's Name: Essays in Honor of John Piper*, ed. Sam Storms and Justin Taylor (Wheaton, IL: Crossway, 2010), 147–70. A few prominent scholars are confusing the gospel (Christ's death and resurrection) with the results of the gospel (e.g., the kingdom: N. T. Wright, *How God Became King: The Forgotten Story of the Gospels* [New York: HarperOne, 2012]; Scot McKnight, *The King Jesus Gospel: The Original Good New Revisited* [Grand Rapids, MI: Zondervan, 2011]).

[18] France, *Gospel of Mark*, 86–87, suggests that the "wild animals" here in 1:13 are inimical and hostile toward God and creation (e.g., Isa. 13:21–22; 34:13–14). In other words, the angels are protecting Jesus from antagonistic forces. On the other hand, this enigmatic verse could be saying the opposite: Jesus has begun to bring reconciliation between God and creation, and Jesus is thus seen as an Adamic figure of sorts who has begun to recapture what was lost in the fall (see G. K. Beale, *New Testament Biblical Theology: The Unfolding of the Old Testament in the New* [Grand Rapids, MI: Baker, 2011], 419).

are healed, the blind receive sight, the lame walk, and sins are forgiven. The first half of Mark's Gospel largely takes place in Galilee, where Jesus is generally successful in his proclamation of the kingdom. Yet, his message remains scandalous to some. As the paradigmatic parable of the sower clearly demonstrates, his message will be accepted by some but rejected by others (4:1–25). Near and around Galilee, the kingdom grows as many Gentiles respond to Jesus's kingdom pronouncement. Yet Jesus's identity remains veiled. Who is this Jesus of Nazareth?

Prologue (Mark 1:1–13). Mark's Gospel begins with "the beginning of the gospel of Jesus Christ" (1:1). Here the "gospel" highlights the role of the prophet, John the Baptist, and Jesus's temptation in the wilderness (1:1–13). Mark quotes from two Old Testament texts—Malachi 3:1 and Isaiah 40:3—yet mentions only "Isaiah the prophet" (Mark 1:2b–3). This literary technique is a Jewish way of citing the Old Testament. Old Testament texts can be grouped together under one specific theme (see, e.g., Romans 3; Hebrews 1). Mark strategically pairs these two Old Testament quotations, whereas Matthew and Luke separate them, placing them in different contexts (Matt. 3:3; 11:10; Luke 3:4; 7:27). The prominence of these two quotations in Mark's Gospel is remarkable in that they both set the tone for his narrative. Moreover, as mentioned above, one unique feature of Mark's Gospel is his tendency to sandwich events together. This technique appears to be employed here with the Isaiah quotation.[19] Notice how Mark first mentions "Isaiah" and then cites Isaiah 40:3:

> As it is written in *Isaiah the prophet*,
>
> "Behold, I send my messenger before your face,
> who will prepare your way [cf. Mal. 3:1],
> *the voice of one crying in the wilderness:*
> *'Prepare the way of the Lord,*
> *make his paths straight* [cf. Isa. 40:3].'" (Mark 1:2–3)

The significance of this "Isaiah sandwich" is that the reader ought to understand Exodus 23:20/Malachi 3:1 *through the lens of Isaiah 40:3*.

According to Exodus 23:20–33, the "messenger" will protect Israel along the way to the Promised Land. The messenger promises to wage war against the pagan nations, as they are idolatrous and wicked. If Israel obeys the covenant, God promises to bless them, but if they commit idolatry by conforming to pagan practices, they will be punished. Malachi 3 reworks the messenger of Exodus 23 in its application. Israel has not maintained justice within the community and has broken God's law. Malachi declares that a messenger figure will again arise and prepare the way for Yahweh to judge his people: "Behold, I send my messenger, and he will prepare the way before me" (Mal. 3:1). In Exodus 23, Israel's enemies, the idolatrous nations, are on the receiving end of judgment. According to Malachi 3:1–6, however, the messenger is paving the way for Yahweh to wage war against Israel! Like their neighbors,

[19] Watts, *Isaiah's New Exodus in Mark*, 89.

Israel has become entrenched in idolatry and social injustice (1:6–10, 12–14, etc.). Those idolatrous Israelites who refuse to repent are judged by Yahweh (3:5; 4:1–4), yet those within Israel who do turn to the Lord will escape this coming judgment. Malachi's messenger must "prepare" Israel for Yahweh's coming judgment by sparking repentance among the remnant within Israel. Those who repent will avoid God's judgment and be restored (4:6).

Isaiah 40 serves as a transitional point in the book of Isaiah. Anticipated in the first half of the book (e.g., 2:2–5; 24:1–25:12), chapters 40–66 describe Israel's release from Babylonian captivity as a second exodus (40:10–11; 51:9; 52:10), the journey to the Promised Land (49:9), and the creation of the new heavens and new earth (65:17–25; 66:22–23). All of this will take place through the Isaianic servant (42:1–9; 49:1–6; 50:4–9; 52:13–53:12). Isaiah 40:3 describes God restoring his people from Babylonian captivity by leading them through the desert to the Promised Land. Isaiah 40:3 is a significant text, as it summarizes Israel's return from Babylon to the Promised land:

> A voice cries:
> "In the wilderness prepare the way of the LORD;
> make straight in the desert a highway for our God."

Two verses later, Isaiah provides the result of Israel's return to her land:

> And the glory of the LORD shall be revealed,
> and all flesh shall see it together,
> for the mouth of the LORD has spoken. (40:5)

The return to the Promised Land will eventually give way to God's decisive act of the destruction of evil and the consummate restoration of all things. Those redeemed from Israel and the nations will *dwell* fully with God in the new creation (65:17; 66:22).

The twin quotation of Exodus 23/Malachi 3 and Isaiah 40 in Mark 1:2b–3 is explicitly applied to John the Baptist. He is *both* the "messenger" of judgment (Mal. 3:1) and the "voice" that announces the arrival of Israel's restoration from captivity (Isa. 40:3). The messenger, therefore, has a twofold agenda: (1) he must prepare rebellious Israel, lest they be annihilated at God's coming; (2) he summons Israel to repent and become part of the new covenant community through baptism. John also announces the end of Israel's spiritual captivity by heralding the fulfillment of Isaiah's long-awaited new exodus of God's people. Israel's history is on the brink of reaching its climax: John, as the end-time "messenger," announces that God is coming to judge those who have broken the covenant but to restore those who trust in his promises.

In addition to John the Baptist's identification with Malachi and Isaiah's messenger, Jesus's role in Mark 1 must be appreciated as it pertains to Malachi 3 and Isaiah 40. Yahweh, in Malachi 3, follows the messenger and judges Israel: "The *Lord* whom you seek will suddenly come to his temple" (3:1b). According to Mark 1, it is *Jesus* who comes on the heels of the messenger—a clear identification with

Yahweh. The same can be said for the Isaiah text. Isaiah 40:3 is an announcement that Yahweh has come to redeem his people from captivity and begin the process of the new creation, whereas in Mark 1 Jesus serves in this identical capacity. In other words, Mark, from the very beginning of his Gospel, identifies the role of Jesus with Yahweh, indirectly suggesting that Jesus is divine.[20]

Mark records that John's ministry was somewhat successful according to 1:5: "And all the country of Judea and all Jerusalem were going out to him and were being baptized by him in the river Jordan, confessing their sins." This tidbit is highly significant in that some Israelites were attaching themselves to John's baptism and turning their backs on Israel's long-standing (and now idolatrous) institutions, such as the temple and its sacrifices. By offering baptism for renewal, John the Baptist was indirectly challenging Israel's identity and structure. In other words, John was laying the foundation for Israel to be reconstituted according to different terms, particularly, Israel's temple.[21]

Beginning of Jesus's Galilean ministry (Mark 1:14–3:6). The first phase of Jesus's ministry in Galilee sets the tone for the remainder of the book. Immediately after John is imprisoned, Jesus flees north to Galilee, probably avoiding persecution in Judea. Jesus proclaims the arrival of the kingdom of God (Mark 1:14–15) and begins his successful public ministry by calling four disciples, three of whom form the "inner three"—Peter, James, and John (1:16–20; cf. 3:13–19). A series of exorcisms and healings punctuates Mark's fast-paced narrative, leaving no doubt that the long-awaited kingdom has indeed arrived in and through Jesus. This initial phase culminates in the dispute between Jesus and the Jewish leaders (3:1–6), an ominous sign of things to come.

Jesus summons Simon (Peter), Andrew, James, and John to follow him at the beginning of his public ministry (1:16–20). The theme of discipleship plays a key role in this Gospel, as Mark seeks to answer the all-important question, what does it take to follow the Messiah? The unequivocal answer, according to the New Testament, is that disciples must be willing to sacrifice their lives and ambitions for the sake of the kingdom. Uniquely, Old Testament prophets never called others to follow them; instead, prophets charged others to follow Yahweh. Jesus may, therefore, be acknowledging divine prerogative by commanding others to follow *him*.

Jesus confronts the disciples while they are fishing in the Sea of Galilee. His statement about becoming "fishers of men" may be more than simply a pithy statement about discipleship. The book of Jeremiah may be the background behind Jesus's summons. In Jeremiah 16:16–18, the immediate context is charged with both the

[20] Some opt for a developmental view that sees Christ's divinity as a later phenomenon in the New Testament, whereas others argue that such a perspective arose in earliest Christianity, indeed with Jesus's own self-proclamation. Richard Bauckham has cast light on this issue, arguing that Jesus fits marvelously into Jewish monotheism. He argues that, contrary to several scholars, the Old Testament and early Judaism leave no ambiguity between God and angels or exalted patriarchs; the relevant literature overwhelmingly makes no room for semidivine beings. Instead, Bauckham argues, the background to Jesus's divinity is rooted in Jewish monotheism; Jesus is to be identified with the unique person and actions of Israel's God (*Jesus and the God of Israel: God Crucified and Other Studies on the New Testament's Christology and Divine Identity* [Grand Rapids, MI: Eerdmans, 2008]).

[21] See Nicholas Perrin, *Jesus the Temple* (Grand Rapids, MI: Baker Academic, 2010), 17–45.

restoration and judgment of Israel. Verse 16 says, "Behold, I am sending for many fishers, declares the Lord, *and they shall catch them [Israelites in exile]*." On the one hand, the fishermen are to search out the scattered Israelites who are in Babylonian exile. God, in verse 15, promises to restore captive Israel and bring them back to the Promised Land. Yet God will also send "hunters," who will seek out the exiles and judge the wicked Israelites (16:16b–18). Consequently, a large part of the mission of the twelve disciples, like Jeremiah's hunters, is to pronounce judgment upon rebellious Israel. They are God's emissaries who herald judgment to those who reject the kingdom message. On the other hand, the Twelve bring mercy and restoration to those who believe in Jesus. Jesus promises to deliver those Israelites, who, despite their dwelling in the Promised Land, still remain in spiritual captivity to sin.

Second phase of Jesus's Galilean ministry (Mark 3:7–6:6). As Mark goes on to make clear, Jesus's ministry continues to gain popularity around Galilee (Mark 3:7–12). He finally assembles all twelve disciples, having already summoned four in 1:16–20. Symbolically, the Twelve constitute true Israel and not only follow their rabbi, Jesus, but are even charged with the authority to proclaim the kingdom message and cast out demons (3:14–15). As they identify themselves with Jesus, their ministry is inextricably bound up with his authority over evil. The parable of the sower explains why not all are able to accept the kingdom message (4:1–20), and the parables of the sower and the mustard seed explain how the end-time kingdom radically differs from expectations. The presence of the kingdom mysteriously overlaps with wickedness. With the kingdom message flourishing in Galilee, opposition grows against Jesus (3:20–34). This phase climaxes with four miracles that encapsulate the totality of Jesus's miracles: a nature miracle (4:35–41), an exorcism (5:1–20), a healing (5:25–34), and a resurrection (5:21–24, 35–43).

The Twelve as true Israel. Jesus, in Mark 3:13–19, officially assembles the twelve disciples "on the mountain." Several unique features of this passage are worthy of note. The first concerns the number of the disciples. Why twelve? A first-century Jew would immediately make the connection between the number of the disciples and the twelve tribes of Israel. In nucleus form, the twelve disciples symbolize the twelve tribes.[22] This explains why the apostles are so intent on preserving the number twelve in Acts 1:15–26 and elect Matthias to replace Judas Iscariot. The twelve tribes are derivative of Jacob's twelve sons (Gen. 29:32–30:24; 35:18). Each tribe was apportioned a plot of land in Canaan (save the tribe of Levi—Deut. 18:1–2; Josh. 13:14, 33) and was to adhere to the covenant stipulations made at Sinai. Moses charged the twelve tribes to function as priests to the pagan nations by converting them and bringing them into the covenant community. This charge corresponds to Adam and Eve's commission to be "fruitful" and "multiply" (Gen. 1:28), thus extending God's

[22] Thomas Schreiner likewise concludes on this passage that "the Twelve [disciples] represent the new nucleus of the people of God. They are the true Israel, and those who listen to the message proclaimed by Jesus and the Twelve become members of the new Israel" (*New Testament Theology: Magnifying God in Christ* [Grand Rapids, MI: Baker Academic, 2008], 683–84).

glory to the ends of the earth. Exodus 19:5–6 is explicit in this regard: "Now therefore, if you [Israel] will indeed obey my voice and keep my covenant, you shall be my treasured possession among all peoples, for all the earth is mine; and you shall be to me a kingdom of priests and a holy nation." Yet, Israel failed on both counts: not only did Israel repeatedly break the covenant; they also refused to bring the nations into the covenant community. The stage was set for the arrival of One who would fulfill both of these obligations.

We must deem Jesus as true Israel. He recapitulates Israel's story (baptism, wilderness temptation, etc.) and succeeds where they failed. In addition to Jesus's locating true Israel in himself, he also reconstitutes Israel by assembling the twelve disciples. Just as Moses gathered Israel on Sinai and commissioned them, so Jesus draws together the Twelve and charges them to spread the message of the kingdom and God's glory. The twelve disciples are given "authority to cast out the demons" (Mark 3:15; see 6:7–13) because they corporately identify with Jesus, who has conquered Satan at his wilderness temptation.

Jesus, the strong man of Israel. The scribes are said to be "from Jerusalem" (Mark 3:22). Mark mentions this location so that the reader may anticipate Jesus's utter rejection and suffering in Jerusalem. The scribes make a strong accusation that Jesus is possessed by the spirit of Beelzebul (3:22). This name is different from Baalzebub (Lord of the Flies), and we are unsure what exactly it means, but what we do know is that he is to be identified with Satan. Thus, not only do the scribes reject Jesus and his message, but they also attribute his miraculous power to Satan! They conclude that the only one capable of such exorcisms is someone "on the inside."

Jesus gives the parable as follows: he first asks, "How can Satan cast out Satan?" (3:23). He begins with the imagery of a kingdom. If the kingdom is divided, then it will not last, because of internal strife (3:24). The kingdom must be unified in order to withstand an attack. Second, a house must be unified in its objective as well or it will not be able to stand. Jesus then uses the analogy of the famous strong man parable (3:27). It is a rather simple analogy: one must first defeat the guardian of the house in order to pillage it.

The clearest Old Testament example of the strong man is found in Isaiah 49:24–26:[23]

> Can the prey be taken from the mighty,
> or the captives of a tyrant be rescued?
> For thus says the LORD:
> "Even the captives of the mighty shall be taken,
> and the prey of the tyrant be rescued,
> for I will contend with those who contend with you,
> and I will save your children.
> I will make your oppressors eat their own flesh,
> and they shall be drunk with their own blood as with wine.

[23] Watts, *Isaiah's New Exodus in Mark*, 146–52.

> Then all flesh shall know
> that I am the Lord your Savior,
> and your Redeemer, the Mighty One of Jacob."

In this passage, Isaiah describes the return from exile because God has not forgotten Zion, so he will inhabit her once again. Verses 22–23 speak of the exiles returning with the help of the foreign nations, which will submit. Then verse 24 begins with the question,

> Can the prey be taken from the mighty,
> or the captives of a tyrant be rescued?

The obvious answer is an emphatic no! There is no way the captives can be released, because they would have to vanquish the tyrant and the mighty man. But the text responds to this situation:

> Surely . . .
>
> Even the captives of the mighty shall be taken,
> and the prey of the tyrant be rescued. (49:25)

Here, Yahweh as the divine warrior, will fight for his people once again and bring them out of the possession of the tyrant. By the time we get to the New Testament, we discover that the true tyrant, the strong man, is not Babylon but Satan. He has held the people in spiritual exile for long enough. Now Jesus comes and "binds" the strong man, releasing his prisoners. In the context of Isaiah 49, Babylon is the strong man, and Yahweh delivers Israel from this nefarious enemy, but Jesus identifies himself as Yahweh by "binding" the strong man, namely Satan, in Mark 3. Therefore, *Jesus is Israel's Lord incarnate who has come to release Israel from spiritual slavery.*

The Old Testament background and function of parables. Chapter 4 signals an important turn in Mark's narrative. Here we encounter our first major block of teaching, yet we are immediately confronted with a substantial amount of parabolic teaching.[24] Why doesn't Jesus speak plainly? Are parables merely "heavenly stories with an earthly meaning"? Can they be categorized as simply proverbial sayings undergirded with moralism?

To grasp the nature and function of parables is to understand them in light of their Old Testament backdrop. Old Testament prophets (e.g., Moses, Elijah) originally ministered to Israel by speaking plainly in the form of sermons. Yet Israel refused to listen, so later prophets were instructed to use a different modus operandi.[25] Yahweh commanded them to begin using forms of prophetic communication such as parables and symbolic actions. For example, in Ezekiel 24:3, Yahweh commands the prophet Ezekiel to relay a "parable" to the wicked Israelites:

[24] For a general survey of parables, the history of interpretation, and their background and function, see Klyne R. Snodgrass, *Stories with Intent: A Comprehensive Guide to the Parables of Jesus* (Grand Rapids, MI: Eerdmans, 2008).
[25] David Jeffrey, "Literature in an Apocalyptic Age: or, How to End a Romance," *Dalhousie Review* 61 (1981): 426–46.

> Utter a *parable* [מָשָׁל] to the rebellious house and say to them, Thus says the Lord GOD:
>
> "Set on the pot, set it on;
> pour in water also."

The passage goes on to describe a boiled lamb in detail (24:4–5). This act thus symbolizes God's judgment upon Israel in taking her to Babylon (24:6–13; cf. 2 Sam. 12:1–15).

Symbolic actions and oracles have a twofold effect upon the audience: (1) those hardened toward God's commandments will be further hardened and ultimately judged; (2) those righteous, but complacent, will respond appropriately by obeying the prophet's actions and words. For example, Yahweh, in Isaiah 6:9–10, commands Isaiah the prophet to further *harden* Israel:

> He said, "Go, and say to this people:
>
> "'Keep on hearing, *but* do not understand;
> keep on seeing, but do not perceive.'
> Make the heart of this people dull,
> and their ears heavy,
> and blind their eyes;
> lest they see with their eyes,
> and hear with their ears,
> and understand with their hearts,
> and turn and be healed."

A few verses later, in 7:3–9 and 8:1–4, Isaiah performs several symbolic acts that further harden Israel (a fulfillment of 6:9–10). An example of a positive effect upon the righteous remnant is Nathan's confrontation of David's sin in 2 Samuel 12, resulting in David's response of contrition.

Parables in the Gospels, therefore, function as a form of riddles. If the listener is unmotivated and impassive, the parable is meaningless. But if the listener vigorously pursues the meaning of the parable and responds appropriately, then the meaning of the symbolism is unlocked.

The parable of the sower: "outsiders" and "insiders." Mark 4 is critical to our understanding of the nature of Jesus's teaching on the kingdom and how his disciples and others receive his message. Functioning paradigmatically, the parable of the sower (4:1–20) answers a pressing question: If Jesus is the long-awaited Messiah and his kingdom is the fulfillment of Old Testament expectations, then why do most reject Jesus? In the immediate context, even Jesus's own family lacks understanding (3:20–35)!

After Jesus delivers the parable, "the Twelve and others" come to him privately and ask if he can give them the meaning or interpretation of the parable. Jesus responds cryptically: "The mystery of the kingdom of God has been given to you. But to those on the outside everything is said in parables" (4:11, my trans.). Here Jesus claims that he will indeed give the meaning of the parable to the disciples (4:13–20) but not to "those on the outside." In Mark's Gospel, there is a distinction between what we may call the "outsiders" and the "insiders." Those on the inside have grasped Jesus's kingdom message and, by all appearances, will continue in their faith. The outsiders, however, lack insight and the willingness to embrace Jesus's message.

The Isaiah 6 quotation in Mark 4:12 begins with a strong purpose conjunction (ἵνα), making the readers pause and think deeply about Isaiah 6 and its immediate context. In its original context, God commands Isaiah to prophesy to Israel, but, unfortunately, Israel will not listen. In fact, *Isaiah's message will further harden the people*:

> Make the heart of this people dull,
> and their ears heavy,
> and blind their eyes. (Isa. 6:10)

The prophet Isaiah cries out in response to the fateful news, "How long, O Lord?" (6:11). God then responds and proclaims that Isaiah must continue to prophesy until Judah is completely destroyed. Verse 13 even suggests that "a tenth" of Israel that remains will be destroyed:

> "And though a tenth remain in it,
> it will be burned again,
> like a terebinth or an oak,
> whose stump remains
> when it is felled."
> The holy seed is its stump.

God's judgment is so thorough that it is even possible to understand the "holy seed" here as corrupt and idolatrous.[26] The upshot of Isaiah's message to unfaithful Israel is that God's judgment upon Israel (and even the remnant) will continue into Israel's exile and beyond. When Israel returns from exile and back to the Promised Land, she will be reconstituted under different terms.[27]

In Isaiah 6:9–10, Israel is said to be blind and deaf, which is a reflection of their idolatrous practices. *Israel has become like the objects they worship*. Recall that in 1:29 Israel is portrayed as an idolatrous tree:

> For you shall be ashamed of the oaks
> that you desired;
> and you shall blush for the gardens
> that you have chosen.
> For you shall be like an oak

[26] For a discussion of Isa. 6:9–10 and its relationship to idolatry, see G. K. Beale, *We Become What We Worship: A Biblical Theology of Idolatry* (Downers Grove, IL: IVP Academic, 2008), 2–70; Michael Daling, "Idolatry and Reversal: Isaiah 6:9–10 and Matthew's Use of an Isaianic Theme" (PhD diss., Wheaton College, 2012).

[27] Beale, *We Become What We Worship*, 60.

whose leaf withers,
and like a garden without water. (Isa. 1:29–30 ESV mg.)

The Old Testament elsewhere states that individuals become like the very objects they worship and adore.[28] For example, Psalm 115:4–8 says:

Their idols are silver and gold,
the work of human hands.
They have mouths, but do not speak;
eyes, but do not see.
They have ears, but do not hear;
noses, but do not smell.
They have hands, but do not feel;
feet, but do not walk;
and they do not make a sound in their throat.
Those who make them become like them;
so do all who trust in them. (cf. Deut. 29:3–4; Jer. 5:21; Ezek. 12:2)

To summarize, Yahweh commissions Isaiah to pronounce judgment upon Israel for her repeated acts of idolatry. Israel cherishes her idols, so God promises to transform Israel into the very thing she adores—an idol!

How does Isaiah's prominent quotation function in Mark's Gospel? The quotation is explicitly directed toward the outsiders of Mark 4:11. This includes the Jewish leaders, who represent the nation of Israel, Jesus's family (for the time being), and generally those who have rejected Jesus's message. If we keep the context of Isaiah 6 in mind, we are probably right to claim that since the outsiders have rejected Jesus's message, especially Israel's leaders (which Isaiah prophesied would happen), they are now on the receiving end of God's long-awaited judgment. The nation of Israel, as represented by the Jewish leaders, has rejected Jesus's message because they, like their ancestors in Isaiah's day, have committed idolatry, probably by worshiping the Torah and the oral tradition (Mark 7). Jesus stands in continuity with Isaiah by reiterating the prophet's words. Isaiah's prophetic act remains valid into the first century!

Recall too that, according to Isaiah 6, Israel is corrupt at its very core. Since Israel is on the receiving end of God's latter-day judgment, she will now be reconstituted around Jesus. Those who rally around Jesus separate themselves from idolatrous Israel and become part of true Israel, Jesus.

Virtually all of Jesus's parables and deeds are veiled or characterized by some form of hiddenness or inability to understand. Those who have "eyes to see" comprehend Jesus's message, but those who are "blind" are unable ever to penetrate the full meaning of the revelation. In the Gospels, the disciples oscillate between comprehension and inability to perceive. At times they understand, if not fully, Jesus's identity and mission (e.g., Mark 8:29), and at other times they lack insight (e.g., Mark 8:17). Like the disciples, the crowds are often viewed as unable to comprehend Jesus's

[28] For a biblical-theological discussion of this line of argumentation, see ibid.

mission, though occasionally they have insight. The Jewish leadership, however, appears hardened and unable to perceive. Consequently, for some the revelation is only temporarily hidden, while for others it is permanently hidden.

The "mystery" of the kingdom. Immediately following the parable of the sower, Jesus claims that the disciples have been "given the mystery of the kingdom" (Mark 4:11, my trans.). The expression "the mystery of the kingdom of God" is especially important in the immediate and broad context of Mark's Gospel. The term *mystery* (μυστήριον) originates in the book of Daniel, especially chapters 2 and 4. The content of the term in Daniel concerns primarily God's end-time kingdom. The initial revelation to Nebuchadnezzar *and* its subsequent interpretation given to Daniel are deemed a mystery. The divine revelation is thus hidden but later revealed.[29]

To get to the heart of the matter, what does Jesus mean by "mystery of the kingdom of God"? In the immediate context, the revealed mystery is directly related to the parable of the sower and the following parables concerning the kingdom. The Old Testament prophecies appear to view the establishment of the end-time kingdom as a decisive overthrow of God's enemies at one consummate point at the very end of world history (e.g., Gen. 49:9–10; Num. 24:14–19; Dan. 2:35, 44–45).

What makes Jesus's teaching about the kingdom a "mystery" is the contrast with the Old Testament and Jewish expectation of the kingdom. One of the main tenets of the prophesied latter-day kingdom is the consummate establishment of God's kingdom directly preceded by the ultimate destruction of unrighteousness and foreign oppression. The advent of the Messiah would signal the death knell of evil empires. Pagan kings and their kingdoms were to be destroyed (or "crushed") (Dan. 2:44), and the Messiah would "shatter all their substance with an iron rod" (Pss. Sol. 17:24). Such a defeat and judgment would be decisive and happen all at once at the end of history.

But here Jesus claims that the advent of the Messiah and the latter-day kingdom does not happen all at once, since a complete defeat and judgment of the wicked do not occur. Paradoxically, two realms coexist—those who belong to the kingdom and those who belong to the Evil One. The kingdom has been inaugurated but remains to be consummately fulfilled. Scholars label this framework the "already and not yet," and it is commonly referred to as "inaugurated eschatology." George E. Ladd gets to the nub of the issue: "This is indeed a mystery, a new revelation. That there should be a coming of God's kingdom in the way Jesus proclaimed, in a hidden, secret form, working quietly among men, was utterly novel to Jesus' contemporaries."[30]

Last phase of Jesus's Galilean ministry (Mark 6:7–8:26). The last portion of Jesus's ministry in Galilee further amplifies the first two phases, involving more miracles and

[29] Importantly, the mystery in Daniel is not *radically* hidden. Nebuchadnezzar appears to display some insight into the vision before the dream is fully interpreted by Daniel. The same could be said for Daniel's initial revelation later interpreted by an angel. The upshot is that when we apply this concept to the New Testament, we must keep in mind that mystery contains subtle hints in the Old Testament that were discernible to the original audience. With regard to Mark 4:11 and the "secret [or mystery] of the kingdom," the Old Testament itself contained some insight into how the kingdom would eventually unfold. That is, though dim, the Old Testament does hint at an already–not yet conception of the kingdom (e.g., Ps. 110:1).

[30] George Eldon Ladd, *The Presence of the Future: The Eschatology of Biblical Realism* (Grand Rapids, MI: Eerdmans, 1974), 225. See also the chapter on the use of "mystery" in Matthew in Beale and Gladd, *Hidden but Now Revealed*, 56–83.

greater opposition. It begins with the commissioning of the Twelve and their authority over the demonic forces (Mark 6:7–13, 30–32). John's fate is recalled, perhaps in anticipation of Jesus's eventual death. Beginning in 6:45, Jesus makes a concerted effort to reach the Gentiles. To the east of the Jordan River lay Decapolis, a region entrenched with Greco-Roman culture. Jesus's engagement with the Gentiles climaxes with the faith of the Syrophoenician woman in 7:24–30. The dispute between Jesus and the Jewish leaders reaches a boiling point in 7:1–23, especially when he declares "all foods clean" (7:19). It appears that the Jewish leaders have, ironically, made the Torah an idol. This phase of his career sounds off with the obstinacy of the disciples (8:11–21). Their continual lack of understanding is symbolized in the miracle of the blind man at Bethsaida (8:22–26). Like this blind man, the disciples will be cured of their blindness in two stages: Peter finally acknowledges that Jesus is indeed the Messiah in 8:29, but full understanding of Jesus's identity will not manifest itself until after his resurrection.

The Road to Jerusalem (Mark 8:27–10:52)

Once Jesus and the disciples turn toward Jerusalem, Jesus's identity begins to become clearer. "You are the Christ [Messiah]," Peter declares in Mark 8:29. Mark 8:27–10:52 comprises the "road to Jerusalem." It is a time of preparation and further revelation of Jesus's identity. The narrative progresses to a heightened level: the Messiah will indeed suffer and die. This is apparent from the second and third passion prediction in 9:31 and 10:33. As Jesus approaches Jerusalem, Jewish opposition will intensify and will eventually culminate in his death.

Peter's confession and the transfiguration (Mark 8:27–9:13). Mark's Gospel strikes a high note in Peter's confession that Jesus is indeed the long-awaited Messiah: "He [Jesus] asked his disciples, 'Who do people say that I am?'" (8:27). After the disciples offer their list of prime candidates, Jesus pointedly asks Peter, "But who do you say that I am?" Peter hits the nail on the head when he says, "You are the *Christ*" (8:29). As noted above, the word for "Christ" is the Greek term Χριστός, meaning "anointed one," or "Messiah." Peter is therefore claiming that Jesus is indeed the highly anticipated Messiah who has come to liberate Israel. But Jesus's messiahship breaks the mold, as he is a *suffering* Messiah who ushers in a kingdom filled with persecution and suffering (8:31–9:1). Jesus is then remarkably transformed or "transfigured" before the disciples' eyes. This event demonstrates, above all, that Jesus is the long-awaited Messiah and the *divine* Son of God. The disciples, therefore, must obey King Jesus (9:2–13).

Instruction concerning the kingdom and further healing (Mark 9:14–10:52). Immediately following the transfiguration, Jesus makes final preparation before entering Jerusalem. Many of Mark's themes continue to progress, particularly Jesus's frustration with the disciples and their lack of understanding (9:18–19; 10:35–45), and his impending death (9:30–32; 10:32–34). The healing of blind Bartimaeus does, though, receive prominence in Mark's drama (10:46–52). The healing immediately precedes Jesus's march into Jerusalem (11:1), and Bartimaeus's words are especially insightful when he declares, "Son of David, have mercy on me!" (10:48). Even before Bartimaeus is healed, he affirms what has been moving in and out of the background for several chapters—Jesus is the long-awaited Messiah. Bartimaeus's declaration sets the stage for Jesus's entrance into Jerusalem in the following chapter.

Unlike the other three Gospels, Mark alone describes the healing of two blind men: Bartimaeus here in Mark 10 and an unnamed blind man in Mark 8. In chapter 8, the blind man plays an important role in Mark's narrative as he symbolizes the two-staged healing of the disciples' blindness. Mark's (and Matthew's) inclusion of the healing of Bartimaeus is hugely important to his narrative. This is the final event before Jesus's entrance into Jerusalem. So why would Mark use a healing episode before the Triumphal Entry? And why would he use the healing of a blind man? Why not a lame or mute person? The answer probably lies in its symbolic value.

The Old Testament often uses blindness to describe Israel's inability to discern God's revelation. That is, the Israelites were unable to grasp God's actions and verbal revelation. For example, Deuteronomy 29:4 says, "But to this day the Lord has not given you a heart to understand or eyes to see or ears to hear." Israel became blind, because they turned into the very objects they worshiped (Pss. 115:5–8; 135:16–18).

When we come to the Gospels, we learn that Israel is still in a state of blindness. We already discerned this principle in Mark 4:11–12. Why would Israel be in a state of blindness? Are they still bowing down to idols? Physically, no. By the first century, Israel knows better than to make and worship idols. They paid dearly for that mistake. Instead of manufacturing physical idols, they have manufactured figurative ones. They bow down not to golden images but to oral tradition; they are guilty of worshiping human traditions and law instead of the Lawgiver.

Jesus's identity as King is central to our passage, since Bartimaeus twice exclaims "Son of David" (10:47–48). But why is Jesus's kingdom on display here? To ask the question another way, what is the relationship between healing the blind and the in-breaking of the kingdom? Matthew 11:2–5 is particularly helpful in this regard:

> Now when John heard in prison about the deeds of the Christ [lit. the Messiah], he sent word by his disciples and said to him, "Are you the one who is to come, or shall we look for another?" And Jesus answered them, "Go and tell John what you hear and see: *the blind receive their sight* and the lame walk, lepers are cleansed and the deaf hear, and the dead are raised up, and the poor have good news preached to them."

Here Jesus reveals his *kingly* or messianic identity by healing the disabled. Jesus partially quotes two Old Testament texts—Isaiah 35:5–6 and 61:1–2. In 35:5–6, the blind, the deaf, and the lame are restored because they are citizens now in God's end-time kingdom; they have been brought out of Babylonian captivity and restored through a second exodus. Importantly, only those who are restored physically are able to journey to the Promised Land (Isa. 35:8). The restored people of God will thus be spiritually and physically whole. They will be new creational beings, fit for the new heavens and earth.

By healing Bartimaeus, Jesus is demonstrating the in-breaking of the new heavens and earth. Jesus, the end-time King, is healing one of his kingdom citizens! But Bartimaeus's restoration carries significance for not only himself but also a corporate body. Blind Bartimaeus embodies blind and hardened Israel. Recall that in Mark 8 Jesus's two-staged healing of the blind man symbolized the healing of the disciples' blindness (8:18, 21, 29). In the same way, Bartimaeus's blindness here in Mark 10 likely symbolizes Israel's blindness. But why is the event placed before Passion Week? Apparently, the crucifixion and resurrection are the *means* by which Jesus will heal the blind remnant of Israel. At the crucifixion, we see nearly identical words that Bartimaeus utters but on the lips of a Roman centurion, of all people: "And when the centurion, who stood facing him, saw that in this way he breathed his last, he said, 'Truly this man was the Son of God!'" (15:39).

In the Old Testament, one of Yahweh's central attributes is his ability to heal and restore (Ex. 4:11; Ps. 146:8; Hos. 6:1–2; etc.). He created Israel, and he promises to restore her. It is important for us to keep the Old Testament texts in mind when we see Jesus healing the blind, the lame, and the mute. Jesus acts not like Old Testament prophets who, on occasion, were able to mediate God's healing power (see, e.g., 2 Kings 5), but as Yahweh himself. Jesus is the very source of healing because he is God incarnate.[31]

The Passion and the Empty Tomb (Mark 11:1–16:8)

This final act of Mark's three-part drama leaves the reader with a clearly defined portrait of Jesus. He is the *suffering* Messiah. Jesus can be known only through the cross (15:21–47) and the resurrection (16:1–8). All the events of his career must be interpreted through these two great events. It is as though Mark wishes his readers to finish the book and then immediately begin reading it all over again. Knowing the end of the story brings clarity to the beginning and middle portions. The series of Jewish confrontations in act 1 climaxes with one ultimate confrontation. Through suffering and defeat, Jesus is, in reality, executing his messianic rule. There is victory in the midst of defeat, glory in the midst of suffering, and power in the midst of weakness.

Temple judgment, prediction of the fall of Jerusalem, and Passover (Mark 11:1–14:31). Mark 11 begins with Jesus entering into the place of suffering and death. Knowing that full well, Jesus still travels to Jerusalem and performs one of the most public displays of his messiahship—riding on a donkey (11:1–10). The Gospels could not be any clearer—the Messiah has indeed arrived! The first course of business for Israel's King is to judge the fig tree. The fig tree symbolizes the nation of Israel, much as it did in the Old Testament (Jer. 24:5; Hos. 9:10). By cursing the fig tree, Jesus is, in effect, saying that the nation of Israel has come under God's wrath. Mark splits the

[31] Note the biblical-theological unpacking of this theme by Michael L. Brown, *Israel's Divine Healer* (Grand Rapids, MI: Zondervan, 1995).

cursing of the fig tree with the temple judgment (11:15–19), desiring that his audience would connect the two events. Jesus curses the nation of Israel because they have abused the temple (11:17; cf. Isa. 56:7; Jer. 7:11). Mark 11:27–33 is the beginning of a lengthy interaction with the Jewish leaders that takes place in the temple complex.

Chapters 11–12 are pivotal during Passion Week. The Jewish leaders have been scheming for quite some time to put Jesus to death, but here their scheming intensifies; the leaders are now ready to put their plan into action. Chapter 13 largely concerns God's impending judgment upon Jerusalem, an event fulfilled in AD 70. Since Israel has continually rejected the prophetic voices through the centuries, culminating in Jesus, and abused the temple on a number of levels, God promises to pour out his judgment upon Israel and Jerusalem. The mood grows darker in chapter 14 when an unnamed woman prepares Jesus for burial and anoints him with expensive perfume (14:1–9). This section ends with Jesus and his disciples celebrating Passover (14:12–26) in anticipation of Jesus's upcoming death as the Passover sacrifice. As God redeemed Israel from Egyptian bondage, Jesus's death will release those in spiritual exile.

Taking place on Sunday of Passion Week, the event commonly called the Triumphal Entry is one of the more public demonstrations in Jesus's ministry. In preparation for his entry into Jerusalem, Jesus commands his disciples to find him a specific colt, an unbroken colt that has one mission only—to carry the kingly Messiah (11:2–3).

Jesus also claims that the unbroken colt will be "tied." Surprisingly, the Old Testament speaks of a tethered colt being tied up:

> The scepter shall not depart from Judah,
>   nor the ruler's staff from between his feet,
> until tribute comes to him;
>   and to him shall be the obedience of the peoples.
> Binding his foal to the vine
>   and his donkey's colt to the choice vine. (Gen. 49:10–11)

Jacob's prophecy over his son Judah finds its ultimate fulfillment in Jesus, particularly at the Triumphal Entry. Jesus is publicly announcing his messianic prerogative to rule over Israel, just as Genesis 49:10–11 predicted. In addition to Genesis 49, Matthew even links the Triumphal Entry to his "fulfillment formula": "This took place to fulfill what was spoken by the prophet [Zechariah]" (Matt. 21:4). Jesus's abnormal request that the colt remain unbroken tightens the connection to the Greek translation of the Old Testament in Zechariah 9:9, which states that the latter-day King will come on a "foal of a donkey."

Zechariah 9 marks a new section in the book of Zechariah that pertains to God's sovereignty over the nations, thus giving hope to the captive Israelites. Verses 1–7 are a judgment oracle against the pagan nations that have continually threatened Israel's existence. Yet God promises to protect his people, Israel, from the surrounding nations. Verse 9 continues this theme of a secure and sovereign rule:

Rejoice greatly, O daughter of Zion! . . .
Behold, your king is coming to you;
  righteous and having salvation is he,
humble and mounted on a donkey,
  on a colt, the foal of a donkey.

The manner in which this King arrives in Jerusalem is unique: "humble and mounted on a donkey." Though seemingly odd, a similar event occurs in 1 Kings 1:32–33: "So they [Zadok, Nathan, and Benaiah] came before the king. And the king said to them, 'Take with you the servants of your lord and have Solomon my son ride on my own mule.'" In both contexts (Zechariah 9 and 1 Kings 1), "riding/mounted on a mule/donkey" refers not to a weak or incompetent ruler but to a peaceful ruler. Zechariah 9:10 explains,

  He shall speak peace to the nations;
his rule shall be from sea to sea,
  and from the River to the ends of the earth.

Jesus's identification with the messianic King of Zechariah 9 is particularly important to his career: Jesus has come to destroy Israel's enemy—not Rome but Satan—and lead his people out of spiritual exile (Zech. 9:16). Even the laying of palm branches and garments before Jesus (Mark 11:8) recalls previous instances of Jewish behavior in the presence of royalty (2 Kings 9:13; 1 Macc. 13:51; 2 Macc. 10:7).

Betrayal, crucifixion, and resurrection of the Messiah (Mark 14:32–16:8). On the heels of celebrating the Passover meal (Mark 14:12–31), Jesus and the disciples travel to Gethsemane, where Jesus dramatically struggles with his destiny on the cross (14:32–42). Even here, the disciples once again fail to display a robust faith in Jesus (14:34, 37, 40). Jesus is arrested at the hands of Judas and taken before the Sanhedrin—Israel's political body of representatives (14:53–65). This trial before the Sanhedrin (which only Mark and Matthew report, Matt. 26:57–68) was most likely illegal in its proceedings. Notably, during the interrogation, Jesus claims to be the Son of Man, a divine figure from Daniel 7 that represents Israel (Mark 14:62; Dan. 7:13). The Jewish leaders then accuse Jesus of blasphemy and deem him "deserving death" (Mark 14:64). The next morning the Jewish leaders take Jesus before Pilate and attempt to have him put to death for sedition against Rome, though at the core of their accusation was Jesus's claim to be divine (cf. John 19:7). Despite Pilate's ambivalence, the Jewish leaders remain steeled in their resolve to put Jesus to death (Mark 15:1–15).

Mark highlights Jesus's identity as Israel's long-awaited King by mentioning several royal features during his mocking and crucifixion: a purple robe, a crown of thorns, the Roman soldiers' taunt "Hail, King of the Jews," and the soldiers' sarcastic genuflecting (15:16–20). Taking these together, a careful reader of Mark's narrative is left with a poignant irony: in mocking Jesus, the soldiers acknowledged his true identity as King. The crucifixion occupies a central place in Mark's Gospel in that the entire narrative has anticipated this event from the very beginning. Jesus's identity as God's royal Son is on display at the crucifixion (15:21–41). It is here that Jesus refashions Israel's expectations of a coming Messiah. Jesus executes his kingly rule, not by conquering the Romans with a sword, but by dying on a cross—the symbol of bearing God's covenant curse and sedition against the Roman government.

Jesus's death may occupy the focal point of Mark's narrative, but it is certainly not its climax. Though Mark's resurrection account is relatively brief (16:1–8), the account pulls a considerable amount of theological freight. Jesus's resurrection constitutes the dawn of the new heavens and earth. By rising from the dead, Jesus demonstrates that his kingship and resurrection are indeed true. Though many, including the nation of Israel as represented by its leaders, deemed Jesus's message as scandalous, the resurrection vindicates Jesus's identity and message.

Psalm 22 in Mark 15: David's prophetic experiences. Psalm 22 plays a central role during the events leading up to the crucifixion and at the crucifixion itself.[32] Within a span of one chapter, Mark quotes Psalm 22 at least three times (see table 1).

Mark 15	Psalm 22
15:24: "And they crucified him and *divided his garments* among them, *casting lots for them*, to decide what each should take."	22:18: "They *divide my garments* among them, / *and for my clothing they cast lots.*"
15:29: "And those who passed by *derided him, wagging their heads* and saying, 'Aha! You who would destroy the temple and rebuild it in three days . . .'"	22:7: "All who see me *mock me*; / they make mouths at me; *they wag their heads.*"
15:34: "And at the ninth hour Jesus cried out with a loud voice, *'Eloi, Eloi, lema sabachthani?'* which means, *'My God, my God, why have you forsaken me?'*"	22:1: "*My God, my God, why have you forsaken me?* / Why are you so far from saving me, from the words of my groaning?"

Table 1

Matthew and Mark record Jesus citing Psalm 22:1 while on the cross: "My God, my God, why have you forsaken me?" Matthew and Mark spell Jesus's words (most likely in Aramaic) slightly differently. We are unsure if the quotation is taken from the Targum (the Aramaic translation of the Old Testament) or the Masoretic Text.

The immediate context of Psalm 22 is helpful in understanding Jesus's cry of dereliction. The Psalm claims to be written by David (which is important to note, given its notoriety in the Passion Narrative). What makes this psalm peculiar is the various genres contained within. The first part of the psalm is "prayer song," a genre in which the speaker "I" is distressed and pleads with God to intervene. What ought to be kept in mind is the relationship between the speaker ("I") and the Israelite community.

[32] On the use of the Old Testament in the Passion Narratives, particularly the typological significance of the Psalms, see Douglas J. Moo, *The Old Testament in the Gospel Passion Narratives* (Sheffield: Almond, 1983; repr., Eugene, OR: Wipf & Stock, 2007).

The speaker often represents the community in his song. Moreover, the community will repeat the speaker's "prayer," thereby becoming a participant in it.

If verses 1–21 are the prayer song, verses 22–31 represent a "thanksgiving" for what the Lord has accomplished. In verse 2 David says, "You do not answer," but in verse 21 he says, "You answer me" (NASB). In other words, verse 22 marks the hinge at which God has answered David's cry for help by acting decisively. (Notice that all three allusions in Mark 15 come from the first part of the psalm.)

Psalm 22:1 describes David's frustration with his predicament. In his moment of greatest need, God remains distant. David thus feels as if God has abandoned him. Though God does not "answer," David remains steadfast in his trust (22:4–5) and knows that God still reigns over the cosmos (22:3). Verse 8 describes the attitudes of David's enemies. They mock him by saying,

> Let him [the LORD] deliver him [David];
> let him [the LORD] rescue him [David], for he [David] delights in him
> [the LORD]!"

Verses 17–18 describe David's enemies as treating him as though he were already dead.

In the latter portion of the psalm, there is something of a prophecy or expectation describing the conversion of the pagan nations:

> All the ends of the earth shall remember
> and turn to the LORD,
> and all the families of the nations
> shall worship before you.
> For kingship belongs to the LORD,
> and he rules over the nations. (22:27–28)

Two elements are worth mentioning: (1) the conversion of the nations; (2) the cosmic rule of the Lord.

Since all three quotations of Psalm 22 take place in Mark 15, it is likely that Psalm 22 plays a central role in Mark's depiction of Passion Week, particularly, Jesus's crucifixion. The use of Psalm 22, a prominent Davidic psalm, is by no means coincidental. By quoting it three times (Mark 15:24, 29, 34), Mark explicitly connects Jesus's actions to David's.

It appears that David's enemies in Psalm 22, whoever they might be precisely in the historical context, prophetically correspond to the Roman soldiers (Mark 15:24) and "those who pass by" (Mark 15:29). The former are obviously pagan Gentiles, whereas the latter probably include some Jews, even Jewish leaders. Moreover, Jesus's cry of abandonment corresponds to David's cry. David's feeling of abandonment typologically anticipates the same feeling that Jesus experienced in a deeper and more significant way.

In the overall context of Psalm 22, David's suffering is somehow linked to the Israelites suffering (present or future). In other words, David, as an individual, suffers on behalf of or at least identifies with the righteous, suffering Israelites. Much in the same way, Jesus suffers on behalf of his people. His suffering is vicarious for those who have faith in him and his message. The emphasis in Psalm 22 on God's supreme rule continues in Mark 15. This time, however, the focus has shifted to Jesus's supreme rule on the cross. Lastly, Psalm 22 predicts the conversion of the nations (22:27–28). It, therefore, may not be a coincidence that a pagan, a Roman soldier nonetheless, makes a confession of faith at the cross following Jesus's quotation of Psalm 22:1.

The upshot of Mark's use of Psalm 22 is significant, particularly for this overall purpose of his Gospel. Mark intends to inform his readers that this Jesus of Nazareth is indeed the long-awaited King of Israel. In the throes of death and defeat, Jesus is simultaneously the supreme ruler over all expressions of authority, both physical and spiritual. David's experiences prophetically anticipate Jesus's own experiences throughout his earthly ministry, especially, here at the crucifixion. As David ruled over Israel while undergoing persecution from those around him, so too Jesus rules in the midst of defeat and despair on the part of his own countrymen. Though faint and generally undeveloped, David's actions pave the way for Christ's experience on the cross. Indeed, it is surprising that Jesus, as Israel's Messiah, should be marked by suffering and death, but it is not without an Old Testament precedent.

The resurrection of Israel's Messiah. Mark closes his Gospel with a brief account of Jesus's resurrection (16:1–8). I argued at the beginning of this essay that Mark's Gospel probably ends at 16:8 and that 16:9–20 is a later addition. Though spanning only eight verses, this concluding material is crucial for Mark's overall narrative.

The two Mary's, Mary Magdalene and Mary the mother of James, and Salome intend to anoint the body of Jesus once the Sabbath has ended (16:1), yet they find the stone rolled away (16:4), and they are unexpectedly greeted by an angel "dressed in a white robe" (16:5). The angel's words surprise them: "You seek Jesus of Nazareth, who was crucified. He has risen; he is not here" (16:6). Two points are worth mentioning: First, Jesus's death and resurrection, seemingly aberrations of God's intention, are very much in keeping with the divine design. Even within Mark's Gospel, Jesus repeatedly warns his disciples that he will eventually be put to death and then subsequently rise from the dead three days later (8:31; 9:31; 10:33–34). Yet, at the crucifixion, the majority of the disciples flee in disbelief; they cannot comprehend how Israel's King, the long-awaited deliverer of the covenant community, could fall into the hands of the Jewish and Roman authorities.

Second, Jesus's resurrection is clearly a fulfillment of Old Testament expectations (1 Cor. 15:4), yet it contains some remarkable "new" elements.[33] The Old Testament affirms that the resurrection will occur at the very end of history, when wickedness is abolished and the new creation has dawned. The righteous individuals will be physically restored in the new creation, and the unrighteous will be consummately punished (Job 19:26–27; Isa. 25:7–8; 26:19; Ezek. 37:1–14; Dan. 12:2–3). Unlike

[33] For further discussion of some "new" elements of Christ's resurrection in light of the Old Testament, see Beale and Gladd, *Hidden but Now Revealed*, 289–91.

the Old Testament, the New Testament proposes a somewhat radical idea—the resurrection of the saints takes places in generally two stages. Jesus's own resurrection is the beginning fulfillment ("the firstfruits") and the subsequent physical resurrection of all saints at the end of history is the final fulfillment (1 Cor. 15:22–23). (Keep in mind, though, that the New Testament also claims that believers have *already* been spiritually resurrected at their conversion—John 5; Ephesians 3; etc.) Jesus is physically raised first, and then later believers are raised physically. The Old Testament appeared to prophesy that all of God's people together were to be resurrected as part of one event (e.g., Dan. 12:2–3). This may explain the "astonishment" of the women at the tomb (Mark 16:8) and the disciples' slowness to believe.

By ending his Gospel with the resurrection, Mark deems Jesus's ministry victorious over Satan, sin, and the "world." Jesus's life, death, and resurrection have liberated the covenant community from sin and estrangement from God. Mark beckons his readers to believe this message, and thereby to join the redeemed.

Select Bibliography

Alexander, T. Desmond, and Brian S. Rosner, eds. *New Dictionary of Biblical Theology: Exploring the Unity and Diversity of Scripture*. Downers Grove, IL: InterVarsity Press, 2000.

Bauckham, Richard, ed. *The Gospels for All Christians: Rethinking the Gospel Audiences*. Grand Rapids, MI: Eerdmans, 1998.

———. *Jesus and the Eyewitnesses: The Gospels as Eyewitness Testimony*. Grand Rapids, MI: Eerdmans, 2006.

———. *Jesus and the God of Israel: God Crucified and Other Studies on the New Testament's Christology and Divine Identity*. Grand Rapids, MI: Eerdmans, 2008.

Bayer, Hans F. *A Theology of Mark: The Dynamic between Christology and Authentic Discipleship*. Phillipsburg, NJ: P&R, 2012.

Beale, G. K. *A New Testament Biblical Theology: The Unfolding of the Old Testament in the New*. Grand Rapids, MI: Baker Academic, 2011.

———. *The Temple and the Church's Mission: A Biblical Theology of the Dwelling Place of God*. NSBT 17. Downers Grove, IL: InterVarsity Press, 2004.

———. *We Become What We Worship: A Biblical Theology of Idolatry*. Downers Grove, IL: IVP Academic, 2008.

Beale, G. K., and Benjamin Gladd. *Hidden but Now Revealed: A Biblical Theology of Mystery*. Downers Grove, IL: InterVarsity Press, 2014.

Beale, G. K., and D. A. Carson, eds. *Commentary on the New Testament Use of the Old Testament*. Grand Rapids, MI: Baker Academic, 2007.

Bird, Michael F. *Are You the One Who Is to Come? The Historical Jesus and the Messianic Question*. Grand Rapids, MI: Baker Academic, 2009.

Brown, Michael L. *Israel's Divine Healer*. SOTBT. Grand Rapids, MI: Zondervan, 1995.

Burridge, Richard A. *Four Gospels, One Jesus? A Symbolic Reading*. 2nd ed. Grand Rapids, MI: Eerdmans, 2005.

———. *What Are the Gospels? A Comparison with Graeco-Roman Biography.* 2nd ed. Grand Rapids, MI: Eerdmans, 2004.

Byrskog, Samuel. *Story as History—History as Story: The Gospel Tradition in the Context of Ancient Oral History.* Leiden: Brill, 2002.

Collins, John J. *The Scepter and the Star: The Messiahs of the Dead Sea Scrolls and Other Ancient Literature.* ABRL. New York: Doubleday, 1995.

Daling, Michael. "Idolatry and Reversal: Isaiah 6:9–10 and Matthew's Use of an Isaianic Theme." PhD diss., Wheaton College, 2012.

Eusebius. *Ecclesiastical History.* In vol. 1 of *NPNF*[2].

France, R. T. *The Gospel of Mark.* NIGTC. Grand Rapids, MI: Eerdmans, 2002.

Garland, David E. *Mark.* NIVAC. Grand Rapids, MI: Zondervan, 1996.

Jeffrey, David. "Literature in an Apocalyptic Age: or, How to End a Romance." *Dalhousie Review* 61 (1981): 426–46.

Ladd, George Eldon. *The Presence of the Future: The Eschatology of Biblical Realism.* Grand Rapids, MI: Eerdmans, 1974.

McKnight, Scot. *The King Jesus Gospel: The Original Good News Revisited.* Grand Rapids, MI: Zondervan, 2011.

Metzger, Bruce. *A Textual Commentary on the Greek New Testament.* 2nd ed. Stuttgart: Deutsche Bibelgesellschaft, 1998.

Moo, Douglas J. *The Old Testament in the Gospel Passion Narratives.* Sheffield: Almond, 1983. Repr., Eugene, OR: Wipf & Stock, 2007.

Newman, Carey C., ed. *Jesus and the Restoration of Israel: Critical Assessment of N. T. Wright's "Jesus and the Victory of God."* Downers Grove, IL: InterVarsity Press, 1999.

Pennington, Jonathan T. *Reading the Gospels Wisely: A Narrative and Theological Introduction.* Grand Rapids, MI: Baker Academic, 2012.

Perrin, Nicholas. *Jesus the Temple.* Grand Rapids, MI: Baker Academic, 2010.

Schreiner, Thomas R. *New Testament Theology: Magnifying God in Christ.* Grand Rapids, MI: Baker Academic, 2008.

Snodgrass, Klyne R. *Stories with Intent: A Comprehensive Guide to the Parables of Jesus.* Grand Rapids, MI: Eerdmans, 2008.

Stein, Robert H. *Mark.* BECNT. Grand Rapids, MI: Baker Academic, 2008.

Storms, Sam, and Justin Taylor, eds. *For the Fame of God's Name: Essays in Honor of John Piper.* Wheaton, IL: Crossway, 2010.

Strauss, Mark L. *Four Portraits, One Jesus: A Survey of Jesus and the Gospels.* Grand Rapids, MI: Zondervan, 2007.

Watts, Rikki. *Isaiah's New Exodus and Mark.* WUNT 88. Tübingen: Mohr Siebeck, 1997. Repr., Grand Rapids, MI: Baker, 2000.

Wrede, Wilhelm. *The Messianic Secret.* Translated by J. C. Greig. Cambridge: James Clark, 1971.

Wright, N. T. *How God Became King: The Forgotten Story of the Gospels.* New York: HarperOne, 2012.

———. *Jesus and the Victory of God.* Philadelphia: Fortress, 1996.

———. *The New Testament and the People of God.* Philadelphia: Fortress, 1992.

3

Luke

Robert J. Cara

Introduction

Like the other three canonical Gospels, the Gospel of Luke presents the person and work of the Lord Jesus Christ and highlights the last week of his earthly life.

Given the similarities of the four Gospels, what are some *unique* characteristics and *relative* differences/emphases of Luke when compared with the other Gospels? Before I answer, allow me a caveat. Sometimes concentrating on the unique characteristics and relative differences is misleading. The author Luke may not have been especially emphasizing one of these differences; and conversely, Luke includes a pericope that the other writers also include because they all regard it as very important. Taking into account this caveat, it is useful to know what are the unique aspects of a Gospel and relative emphases as one evaluates it.

What are some unique aspects of the Gospel of Luke? The most noticeably different aspect from the other Gospels is that Luke has an explicit sequel, Acts. In addition, Luke includes several unique parables that are well known (e.g., good Samaritan, prodigal son, rich man and Lazarus, Pharisee and the tax collector). There are explicit literary parallels between John the Baptist and Jesus concerning their younger years that are not matched by any other Gospel (Luke 1:5–2:52). These include Mary's Magnificat and Zechariah's Benedictus.

Other, more relative differences include a much longer "travel narrative" from Galilee to Jerusalem (Luke 9:51–19:27); an emphasis on Jesus's being the rejected suffering Prophet, which then moves toward a rejected suffering Messiah; an emphasis on "salvation"; an emphasis on the redemptive-historical plan of God that is in continuity with the Old Testament and includes the salvation of the Gentiles; and an emphasis on the poor. Again, although these emphases are more pronounced in Luke, they are included in other Gospels.

Of course, Luke wrote not only the Gospel of Luke, but also Acts.[1] The Gospel of Luke is the longest book in the New Testament, and Acts is the second longest. Hence, Luke made a substantial contribution to the New Testament (27.5 percent of the New Testament by Greek word count). In fact, Luke wrote more of the New Testament than anyone else.[2]

Background Issues

Authorship and Date

I hold to the traditional view that "Luke the beloved physician" (Col. 4:14), who accompanied Paul on portions of his missionary journeys, wrote Luke and Acts.[3] Luke is explicitly mentioned in three New Testament verses (Col. 4:14; Philem. 24; 2 Tim. 4:11) and implicitly in the numerous "we" passages in Acts (e.g., Acts 16:10). Colossians 4:10–14 strongly implies that Luke was a Gentile.[4]

Luke's authorship of the Third Gospel was the unanimous view of the early church. For example, the Muratorian Canon (ca. 180) states, "The third book of the Gospel, that according to Luke, the well-known physician Luke wrote in his own name. . . . Moreover, the Acts of the Apostles are comprised by Luke in one book."[5]

Of course, the Gospel of Luke (and Acts) is technically anonymous. As noted above, the external evidence of church tradition points only to Luke. The internal evidence dovetails well with the external. (Since most of the internal evidence relates to Acts, see the Acts chapter.) Internal evidence that relates specifically to the Gospel of Luke primarily focuses on the Greek-language style. The prologue (Luke 1:1–4) is written in an elevated style, most of Luke 1–2 has a heavy Semitic sense, and the rest of Luke is written in language similar to the Septuagint, which has less of a Semitic sense. This points to an educated person. Also, the Gospel has an emphasis on Gentiles, and Luke was most likely a Gentile with knowledge of the Old Testament. Luke's association with Paul, among other factors (e.g., was he a God-fearer? [Acts 13:16]), could explain the Old Testament knowledge.

Virtually all conservative and critical scholars agree that the same author wrote Luke and Acts; however, the vast majority of critical scholars do not agree that the

[1] Virtually all scholars agree that the same author (or final editor) wrote both Luke and Acts. Conservatives see the author as Luke the physician (Col. 4:14); critical scholars see him as an unnamed Gentile who was *not* a companion of Paul. See the "Authorship and Date" section below.

[2] Matthew is the third-longest book. The Gospel of Luke is 6 percent longer by Greek word count than Matthew; and Acts is only 0.5 percent longer than Matthew. The thirteen Pauline Epistles are 23.5 percent of the New Testament by Greek word count.

[3] So also, e.g., D. A. Carson and Douglas J. Moo, *An Introduction to the New Testament*, 2nd ed. (Grand Rapids, MI: Zondervan, 2005), 203; Donald Guthrie, *New Testament Introduction*, 3rd ed. (Downers Grove, IL: InterVarsity Press, 1970), 109; Darrell L. Bock, *Luke*, vol. 1, *1:1–9:50*, BECNT (Grand Rapids, MI: Baker, 1994), 4; David E. Garland, *Luke*, ZECNT (Grand Rapids, MI: Zondervan, 2011), 21–24; Alfred Plummer, *The Gospel according to S. Luke*, 5th ed., ICC (Edinburgh: T&T Clark, 1922), xvii; and Joseph A. Fitzmyer, *The Gospel according to Luke (I–IX): Introduction, Translation, and Notes*, AB 28 (New York: Doubleday, 1970), 35–53.

[4] While referring to Aristarchus, Mark, and Jesus/Justus, Paul calls them men of the circumcision, that is, Jewish Christians (Col. 4:10–11). Paul goes on to mention Epaphras and Luke (Col. 4:12–14). Since Epaphras is from Colossae and presumably a Gentile, Luke is then assumed to be one also. So also Robert McL. Wilson, *A Critical and Exegetical Commentary on Colossians and Philemon*, ICC (London: T&T Clark, 2005), 301; *pace* David E. Garland, who takes "circumcision" in Col. 4:11 to refer to those of the circumcision party, not Jewish Christians per se (*Colossians, Philemon*, NIVAC [Grand Rapids, MI: Zondervan, 1998], 278).

[5] *ANF* 5:603.

author was actually Luke the physician who traveled with Paul. Werner Georg Kümmel boldly declares, "The author [of the Gospel of Luke] is obviously a total stranger to the theology of Paul."[6] This conclusion is based primarily on comparing Acts and the "authentic" Pauline epistles, and on broad assumptions of the compatibility of the Synoptic Gospels and Paul. Therefore, the argument goes, the author could not have been a companion of Paul. For critical scholars, the standard conclusion is that the author is unknown except to say that he was a Gentile with a good education and could not have been Paul's companion.[7]

Concerning the dating of the Gospel of Luke, given that I hold that Luke the physician is the author, I place the date in the AD 50s or early 60s. This is based primarily on Luke's having also written Acts and the assumption that Acts was written before Paul died.

For critical scholars, the initial question for the dating of Luke (and Acts) is whether it is possible for the Gospel of Luke to be dated before the destruction of Jerusalem in AD 70. This initial question revolves around two other issues: (1) the solution of the "synoptic problem" and (2) the interpretation of the destruction of Jerusalem in the Olivet Discourse (Luke 21:20–24).

Concerning the first issue: If one agrees to the standard "two-source" solution to the synoptic problem, then Mark is written first in the AD 50s or 60s. Matthew and Luke, who both used Mark and the so-called "Q" document, were written in at least the 70s or much later. My solution to the synoptic problem is different. I believe that the Synoptic Gospels were in *final form* written independently in the 50–60s with no "Q" or wholesale copying.[8]

Concerning the second issue: Most critical scholars believe that the description of the destruction of Jerusalem in Luke 21:20–24 closely matches the actual events. Also, they do not believe in Jesus's predictive abilities. Hence, they conclude, the Gospel of Luke must have been written after the destruction of Jerusalem.[9] I do believe in Jesus's predictive abilities, and so this is not decisive for me.

Critical scholars date Luke between AD 80 and 125, although 80–90 is more typical.[10] Among conservatives who accept some form of the standard "two-source"

---

[6] Werner Georg Kümmel, *Introduction to the New Testament*, rev. ed., trans. Howard Clark Kee (Nashville: Abingdon, 1975), 149. Philipp Vielhauer's famous article "On the 'Paulinism' of Acts" argued strongly that the author of Acts and Paul had different theological ideas. The article was published in German in 1951. It is included in Leander E. Keck and J. Louis Martyn, eds., *Studies in Luke-Acts* (Philadelphia: Fortress, 1980), 33–50. For a rebuttal to Vielhauer, see Carson and Moo, *Introduction to the New Testament*, 293–95.

[7] For example, Helmut Koester, *History and Literature of Early Christianity*, vol. 2 of *Introduction to the New Testament* (New York: de Gruyter, 1982), 310.

[8] Of course, this is not the place to present a defense. The primary problem is how to explain both the differences and the similarities of the Synoptic Gospels. I simply note that the *differences* between the Synoptics are best explained in that (1) different authors have different perspectives and writing styles, (2) most of the pericopes are summaries of longer events, and (3) Jesus's traveling ministry fostered repetitious teaching and healing situations. The *similarities* are best explained by (1) the true historical order of events, (2) the synoptic writers' personal knowledge of each other and their close friends in common, (3) the likelihood of written notes by eyewitnesses and others, along with the Evangelists' possibly reading portions of another Gospel, and (4) the likelihood of a fairly fixed oral tradition emanating from the apostles.

[9] Kümmel is typical: "Decisive against the early date is the fact that Lk looks back on the fall of Jerusalem" (*Introduction to the New Testament*, 150).

[10] For example, M. Eugene Boring, *An Introduction to the New Testament: History, Literature, Theology* (Louisville: Westminster John Knox, 2012), 587; Koester, *History and Literature of Early Christianity*, 310; and John T. Carroll, *Luke: A Commentary*, NTL (Louisville: Westminster John Knox, 2012), 4. All three of these acknowledge that AD 80–90 is more typical, but they prefer to extend the date to AD 125.

synoptic solution, the date of Luke fluctuates between the AD 60s and 75–85.[11] As mentioned above, I prefer a date of the 50s or early 60s. This then dovetails well with the ending of Acts, which has Paul still alive.

Addressee(s), Occasion, and Purpose

The prologues to Luke and Acts both mention that the addressee is Theophilus (Luke 1:3; Acts 1:1). Theophilus is addressed as "most excellent" (κράτιστος). Since this term is also used in Acts by Paul addressing Felix (Acts 23:26; 24:3) and Festus (Acts 26:25), it is a reasonable assumption that Theophilus is some type of Roman official, although he also could have been a good friend of Luke.[12] Based on Luke's comment that part of the purpose of the book was to confirm Theophilus in "the things [he has] been taught" (Luke 1:4), Theophilus was a Christian, maybe a recent convert.

It is assumed that Luke knew his Gospel would be circulated more widely than just to Theophilus. Based on the emphases in Luke (and Acts) concerning Gentiles, it is further assumed that the wider audience was primarily Gentile but would also include, secondarily, Jews. Because Theophilus was a Christian, Luke was certainly writing to Christians, but probably also expected nonbelievers would read his Gospel.

Virtually nothing specific is known concerning the occasion that prompted the writing of this Gospel. There are limited comments in church history that the provenance was Rome, Achaia (Greece), or Antioch.[13] Luke does mention that others also compiled narratives related to Jesus (Luke 1:1), but this is so general that it does not help us with a specific occasion. However, as with the other Gospels, we may conclude that the specific historical occasion that prompted the writing of Luke is not known, other than that Luke felt it was good for Theophilus to have this Gospel.

As mentioned above, Luke's explicit purpose is that Theophilus would "have certainty concerning the things [he has] been taught" (Luke 1:4). The content of the book relates primarily to the person and work of Jesus from his incarnation to his ascension.[14] Hence, the explicit purpose is to confirm Theophilus and others in their Christian faith by presenting a historical account of Jesus. This account is presented with the realization that the readers are aware of other Greco-Roman religions and philosophies, along with traditional Judaism(s). (For a discussion of how the explicit purpose of Luke's Gospel dovetails with the purpose of Acts, see the chapter on Acts.)

Given the explicit and primary purpose of the Gospel of Luke, one could envision many secondary and implicit purposes. These secondary purposes are normally associated with perceived theological emphases. For example, Donald A. Hagner connects the purpose to Luke's emphasis on the "first stage of the fulfillment of Sal-

[11] For an example favoring the AD 60s, see Carson and Moo, *Introduction to the New Testament*, 208; and an example favoring AD 75–85, see Garland, *Luke*, 34.

[12] Some see "Theophilus," which etymologically means "lover/beloved of God," as a code name for Christians generally. Hence, Theophilus is not a real person. See discussion in Bart D. Ehrman, *The New Testament: A Historical Introduction to the Early Christian Writings*, 4th ed. (New York: Oxford University Press, 2008), 124–26.

[13] See Carson and Moo, *Introduction to the New Testament*, 206–7.

[14] Similarly, but related to both Luke and Acts, Darrell L. Bock states, "Luke-Acts as well as Luke and Acts is intended to set forth the program of God as delivered through Jesus" (*A Theology of Luke and Acts: God's Promised Program, Realized for All Nations*, BTNT [Grand Rapids, MI: Zondervan, 2012], 60).

vation History."[15] Seeing theological emphases as secondary purposes is legitimate. For convenience, see my summary of theological emphases below in the section "Message and Theology."

Some scholars see a nontheological secondary purpose for Luke. Although I do not agree, many find in this Gospel an attempt to show that Christianity is not subversive to the Roman Empire. This conclusion is tied closely to one's view of the purposes of Acts.[16] I do not regard this as a purpose for either Luke or Acts. (See discussion in Acts chapter.)

Luke and Acts or Luke-Acts?

Given that all acknowledge that the same author wrote both Luke and Acts, should we consider them to have different purposes, themes, and emphases or the same purposes, themes, and emphases? That is, should the two books be considered separately, as Luke *and* Acts? Or should they be seen as one book, Luke-Acts? Or are there other options that combine these two?

In the scholarly world, there is a significant emphasis on seeing them as one book, Luke-Acts. Hence, separating Luke for evaluation from Luke-Acts, as I do in this chapter, would be improper. This Luke-Acts thesis began in earnest with H. J. Cadbury in 1927.[17] One of the primary arguments was that Luke-Acts was originally written as a two-volume work and was only separated for pragmatic reasons; one scroll could not hold the entire work. This view was confirmed in the 1950s with the movement, especially in critical scholarship, to see the author/editor of Luke-Acts as a "theologian," as opposed to an inconsistent historian.[18] The Luke-Acts thesis was further confirmed in the 1980s by the scholarly emphasis on "narrative criticism," which explored the many connections between the two books, resulting in the interpretation of Luke-Acts as one continuous narrative.[19] Many conservative scholars agree with the Luke-Acts thesis.[20]

There has been some resistance to this in the critical-scholarly world, however. Mikeal Parsons and Richard Pervo argue that "Acts is best understood as a sequel rather than a second chapter or simple continuation."[21] They recommend the terminology "Luke *and* Acts" and want scholars to consider the two books as having "two very distinct narratives embodying different literary devices, generic conventions, and

---

[15] Donald A. Hagner, *The New Testament: A Historical and Theological Introduction* (Grand Rapids, MI: Baker, 2012), 228.
[16] For example, Guthrie, *New Testament Introduction*, 95.
[17] H. J. Cadbury, *The Making of Luke-Acts* (London: Macmillan, 1927).
[18] W. C. van Unnik's article is commonly cited in this regard, "Luke-Acts, A Storm Center in Contemporary Scholarship," in Keck and Martyn, *Studies in Luke-Acts*, 15–32. Hans Conzelmann is normally cited as the leading scholar in this regard; see his *The Theology of St. Luke*, trans. Geoffrey Buswell (London: Faber & Faber, 1960). From a conservative perspective, I. Howard Marshall responded to the either–or critical assumption and affirmed the traditional view that Luke the author is both a historian and theologian. See *Luke: Historian and Theologian*, rev. ed. (Grand Rapids, MI: Zondervan, 1989).
[19] The leader of this emphasis is Robert C. Tannehill, *The Narrative Unity of Luke-Acts: A Literary Interpretation*, 2 vols. (Philadelphia: Fortress, 1986–1990).
[20] Prominently in favor would be Joel B. Green. See his *The Gospel of Luke*, NICNT (Grand Rapids, MI: Eerdmans, 1997); and *The Theology of the Gospel of Luke*, NTT (Cambridge: Cambridge University Press, 1995).
[21] Mikeal C. Parsons and Richard I. Pervo, *Rethinking the Unity of Luke and Acts* (Minneapolis: Fortress, 1993), 123, emphasis theirs. Also see Richard I. Pervo, "Fourteen Years After: Revisiting *Rethinking the Unity of Luke and Acts*" and Mikeal C. Parsons, "Hearing Acts as Sequel to a Multiform Gospel: Historical and Hermeneutical Reflections on Acts, Luke, and the ΠΟΛΛΟΙ," both in *Rethinking the Unity and Reception of Luke and Acts*, ed. Andrew F. Gregory and C. Kavin Rowe (Columbia, SC: University of South Carolina Press, 2010), 23–40, 128–52, respectively.

perhaps even theological concerns."[22] Parsons and Pervo acknowledge that at the "story" level there is significant unity, but they complain that other scholars also see unity at the "discourse" level (of manner and literary devices in telling the story), where they do not.[23] Also, they note theological differences such as less forgiveness in Acts.[24] A 2003 study by Andrew Gregory noted that the early church before Irenaeus rarely read Luke and Acts as a two-volume work.[25] Some have used this to support Parsons and Pervo, although Gregory himself does not.[26]

I believe that the Gospel of Luke was originally a separate book written several months or years before Acts. The Gospel was intended initially to circulate on its own. Further, it clearly has genre connections with the other three Gospels and emphasizes Jesus's person and work while on earth. Hence, it is proper to separate the Gospel of Luke from Acts in determining purposes, genre, emphases, and so on. Thus the canonical status of Luke as a separate book is legitimate.

One advantage of the separation is that emphases in only one of the books may tend to be muted if one insists on the full-blown Luke-Acts thesis. For example, the Gospel of Luke has a significant concern for the disadvantaged, but this concern is reduced in Acts, at least statistically speaking. If Luke-Acts is to be considered one, would this not reduce our interest in and affect our conclusions about this emphasis?[27] Conversely, within the Luke-Acts thesis, one may have a tendency to overemphasize a theme because it appears in both books. I tend to believe this occurs with scholars who overstress the plan-of-God theme in Luke-Acts to the slight downplaying of Jesus's person and work.[28]

On the other hand, Acts was written to Theophilus and explicitly references Luke (Acts 1:1). Hence, although Acts may be read on its own, it must be read with a very real awareness of Luke's Gospel. Also, once Acts was written, the Gospel of Luke needed to be read in close association with Acts, even though Acts would potentially have its own purposes and so forth. D. A. Carson and Douglas Moo well note, "The upshot is that we should probably consider Luke and Acts to be two separate books that stand in close relationship to each other . . . and consider each on its own when it comes to the question of genre, structure, purpose, and, to some extent, theology."[29]

In sum, I am in the "Luke *and* Acts" camp, but a camp that sees very strong

---

[22] Parsons and Pervo, *Rethinking the Unity of Luke and Acts*, 18.
[23] Ibid., 77–83.
[24] Ibid., 38–39. I do not accept this as a true difference.
[25] Andrew F. Gregory, *The Reception of Luke and Acts in the Period before Irenaeus: Looking for Luke in the Second Century*, WUNT 169 (Tübingen: Mohr Siebeck, 2003).
[26] In favor of Parsons and Pervo is C. Kavin Rowe ("History, Hermeneutics, and the Unity of Luke-Acts," in Gregory and Rowe, *Rethinking the Unity and Reception of Luke and Acts*, 43–65). *Pace* Andrew F. Gregory, "The Reception of Luke and Acts and the Unity of Luke-Acts," in Gregory and Rowe, *Rethinking the Unity and Reception of Luke and Acts*, 82–93.
[27] Within a view of the unity of Luke-Acts, S. John Roth tries to answer why the concern-for-the-disadvantaged emphasis is "so prominent in the Gospel of Luke and all but absent in the Acts of the Apostles." His conclusion is that "the christological function of these character types in the Gospel does not fit the status of Jesus in Acts" (*The Blind, the Lame, and the Poor: Character Types in Luke-Acts*, JSNTSup 144 [Sheffield: Sheffield Academic, 1997], 11, 220).
[28] For example, Green states, "Luke's agenda is not to write the story of Jesus, followed by the story of the early church. Rather, his design is to write a story of the continuation and fulfillment of God's project—a story that embraces both the work of Jesus and the followers of Jesus after his ascension. From start to finish, Luke-Acts brings to the fore one narrative aim, the one aim of God" (*Theology of the Gospel of Luke*, 47).
[29] Carson and Moo, *Introduction to the New Testament*, 203.

connections and no contradictions between the two books. Also, I conclude that it is legitimate canonically to separate the two books. If one affirms the divine inspiration of Scripture, the "heat" generated by this topic is somewhat tempered. Every book of the Bible has the same divine author and is useful for interpreting every other book. That is, whether to consider Luke alone, or Luke-Acts as one book, or Luke tightly connected to the other three Gospels, or Acts tightly connected to the Pauline Epistles is less important hermeneutically if one ultimately affirms that the Bible is a coherent whole written by a divine author.

Structure and Outline

The broad outline of Luke is generally agreed on by all and is as follows.[30] Excepting the first section, the outline is geographical.

I. John the Baptist and Jesus Parallels (1:1–4:13)
II. Galilean Ministry (4:14–9:50)
III. Journey to Jerusalem (9:51–19:27)
IV. Triumphal Entry through Ascension (19:28–24:53)

The geographical sequence of the Galilean ministry, journey to Jerusalem, and Triumphal Entry through ascension matches the same sequence in Matthew and Mark. As to broad outline, the three Synoptic Gospels differ only in the opening sections.

Dovetailing with the geographical outline above, some believe that the opening pericope of the Galilean ministry, Jesus's rejection at Nazareth (Luke 4:14–30), is especially programmatic for Luke to highlight various themes in his Gospel.[31] This pericope includes a fair amount of unique material, and the "triple tradition" material is not in the same order as the parallels in Matthew and Mark. It appears that Luke "moved" this passage to the beginning of the Galilean ministry section because of its importance.[32] This account contains important emphases from the Lucan Gospel such as Jesus's fulfillment of the Old Testament (Luke 4:18–21 related to Isa. 61:1–2) and Jesus's being a rejected Prophet (Luke 4:24). Also, Jesus's response to John the Baptist's disciples in Luke 7:18–23 alludes to the Isaiah quote in Luke 4:18. I would not go so far as seeing this passage as *the* programmatic pericope, but it is certainly an important pericope.

Luke the author is usually praised for his artistry in arranging material in his

[30] For example, in general agreement are Boring, *Introduction to the New Testament*, 568; Kümmel, *Introduction to the New Testament*, 125; and Bock, *Luke*, 1:20.

[31] For example, I. Howard Marshall: "The narrative [Luke 4:16–30] is placed here, then, for its programmatic significance, and it contains many of the main themes of Lk-Acts *in nuce*" (*The Gospel of Luke: A Commentary on the Greek Text*, NIGTC [Grand Rapids, MI: Eerdmans, 1978], 177–78); also Rebecca I. Donova, *The Things Accomplished among Us: Prophetic Tradition in the Structural Pattern of Luke-Acts*, JSNTSup 141 (Sheffield: Sheffield Academic, 1997), 126–54.

[32] Matt. 13:53–58 parallels Mark 6:1–6 in order, which is in the middle of the Galilean ministry sections for these two Gospels. The Luke text does not state that the rejection of Jesus at Nazareth was the chronologically first event in his Galilean ministry (Luke 4:14–16). The Galilean ministry was an itinerant ministry, and when appropriate, the Gospel writers apparently arranged the material to better group the events for the reader. In these situations, chronological order was not implied or required.

Gospel. Examples include the John/Jesus parallels in Luke 1–3; the "Word of God" in Luke 8:1–21; and the "lost" sheep, coin, and son parables in Luke 15.

John the Baptist and Jesus Parallels (Luke 1:1–4:13)

As does Acts, Luke opens with a statement to Theophilus giving the purpose of the book. Luke is writing an "orderly account" so that, again, Theophilus "may have certainty concerning the things [he has] been taught" (Luke 1:3–4).

Luke then begins the narrative by artfully paralleling and intertwining the events related to John the Baptist and Jesus:

- prophecy of John (1:5–25)
- prophecy of Jesus (1:26–38)
- Mary visits Elizabeth (1:39–45)
- Mary's song (Magnificat) (1:46–56)
- John's birth and circumcision (1:57–66)
- Zechariah's song (Benedictus) (1:67–79)
- summary of John's growth (1:80)
- Jesus's birth and circumcision (2:1–21)
- Jesus's dedication, Simeon (Nunc Dimittis), Anna (2:22–39)
- summary of Jesus's growth (2:40)
- Jesus at the temple (2:41–51)
- second summary of Jesus's growth (2:52)
- John in the wilderness baptizing (3:1–17)
- summary of John's ministry (3:18–20)
- Jesus's baptism (3:21–22)
- Jesus's genealogy (3:23–38)
- Jesus in the wilderness and temptation (4:1–13)
- summary of Jesus's ministry (4:14–15)

In addition to the above parallels at the pericope level, there are more parallels at the detail level. For example, Gabriel is sent to Zechariah and Mary; both Zechariah and Mary are "troubled"; Gabriel says to both, "Fear not," and furnishes the names of John and Jesus. Both Zechariah and Mary are told that their children will be "great" (μέγας, Luke 1:15, 32). John is to be a Prophet; and Jesus, a King and "Son." Both Zechariah and Mary question the announced pregnancies, with both births being miraculous, but not equally miraculous. The lineages of parents are given, although with significantly more detail for Jesus's. John will baptize with water, and Jesus will baptize with the Holy Spirit (Luke 3:16).

The opening section of this Gospel clearly presents both John (Luke 3:4–6) and Jesus (Luke 3:22) as participants in God's plan. However, Jesus is obviously portrayed as superior.[33] John is the forerunner to point toward Jesus. Yes, there are parallels, but the parallels by contrast show the superiority of Jesus.

John the Baptist will appear again in Luke only as a character in the significant

[33] For further discussion of the parallels and how they show the superiority of Jesus, see Tannehill, *Narrative Unity of Luke-Acts*, 1:15–20.

7:18–35 passage, although he is mentioned in 5:33; 9:7–9; 9:19; 11:1; and 16:16. In Luke 16:16 ("the Law and the Prophets were until John"), Jesus includes John the Baptist as an important marker of the redemptive-historical time line. This emphasis is confirmed by all the references to John the Baptist in Acts.[34]

Galilean Ministry (Luke 4:14–9:50)

The Galilean ministry section presents Jesus as a preacher, healer, and Prophet.[35] Relative to the following two sections of Luke, Jesus faces less opposition in this section as the goal that he will go to Jerusalem to die is not revealed until the end of the section. Hence, there is a generally more positive tone to Jesus's Galilean ministry.

This section begins with a summary statement that Jesus's fame was spreading throughout Galilee (Luke 4:14–15), and the first narrative is Jesus's rejection at Nazareth (4:16–30). This section ends with the fourfold complex of (1) the high point of Peter's confession (9:18–20), (2) Jesus's first of many statements that he must suffer and be killed (9:21–22), (3) Jesus's teaching on denying oneself (9:23–27), and (4) the transfiguration (9:28–36).[36] This combination forms the turning point of the book as now Jesus will be traveling to Jerusalem to die. Luke 9:51, "he set his face to go to Jerusalem," provides the literary marker to emphasize this turning point.[37]

Jesus's quote of Isaiah 61:1–2 (Luke 4:18–19)[38] at the Nazareth synagogue emphasizes, among other things, that he is a preacher, healer, and Prophet.[39] As a preacher, Jesus will "proclaim good news," "proclaim liberty to the captives," and "proclaim the year of the Lord's favor." Luke does present Jesus's teaching fairly consistently throughout the Gospel, not just in the Galilean ministry section.

Jesus's healings are connected to Luke 4:18 by "recovery of sight to the blind." This is then strongly connected to Luke 7:22. The verb σῴζω, which has a semantic range of physical healing to spiritual saving, is used often in Luke with one or the other nuance (e.g., 6:9; 7:50; 8:36, 48, 50; 17:19).[40] This furthers the connections between preaching and healing and shows the healings as part of God's redemptive purposes.

Luke 4:17–18 also emphasizes that Jesus is a Prophet. The quote itself is from Isaiah, a prophetic book, and more specifically, Isaiah 61, which is one of the suffering servant songs.[41] In fact, the suffering/rejected prophet motif, which then moves

[34] In Acts, John and/or his followers are mentioned several times; see 1:5, 22; 10:37; 11:16; 13:24–25; 18:25; 19:4.

[35] See summary verses, Luke 4:15; 5:15, 17; 6:18; 7:22; 8:1; 9:11; also Acts 10:37–38. For discussion of these three themes, see Tannehill, *Narrative Unity of Luke-Acts*, 1:77–99.

[36] Matthew and Mark also have the same complex as the turning point of their narratives (Matt. 16:13–17:13; Mark 8:27–9:13).

[37] This statement is not in the other Gospels. From a narrative plot-flow perspective, the Galilean ministry section could be viewed as ending with the high point of Peter's confession that Jesus is the Christ (Luke 9:20). Immediately after this confession, the plot takes a negative tone as Jesus informs the disciples for the first time he must suffer and die. From a literary-maker perspective, Luke 9:51 (and 9:53), a few pericopes later, confirms the negative plot twist and is considered the beginning of the next section, owing to its explicitness.

[38] "To set at liberty those who are oppressed" is probably a quote from a portion of Isa. 58:6. Compare the LXX, ἀπόστελλε τεθραυσμένους ἐν ἀφέσει, with Luke 4:18, ἀποστεῖλαι τεθραυσμένους ἐν ἀφέσει. The only difference is the grammatical change of an imperative to an infinitive to dovetail with the grammar of Isa. 61:1. Also note that the themes in Isa. 61:1–2 are paralleled in Lev. 25:8–17.

[39] Other themes from this quote are Luke's emphasis on the poor and on Jesus as the deliverer. For an extended discussion of this quote and its connections to Luke, see Bock, *Luke*, 1:394–411.

[40] The more specific "heal" verbs θεραπεύω (e.g., 5:15; 6:18; 7:21) and ἰάομαι (e.g., 5:17; 6:19; 8:47) are also used often in Luke.

[41] The suffering servant songs are Isa. 42:1–7; 49:1–9a; 50:4–9; 52:13–53:12; 61:1–11.

to the suffering/rejected Messiah, is a significant theme in Luke.[42] The prophet motif connects to Jesus's rejection in that many Old Testament prophets suffered and were rejected (e.g., Luke 4:24; 13:33; 24:19–20). Luke often emphasizes that this rejection was according to God's will and matches what the Old Testament taught (e.g., Luke 2:34–35; 16:31; 17:25; 24:26–27, 44–47). The prophet motif also connects the healing and preaching motifs through the Old Testament prophets Elijah and Elisha (Luke 4:25–26; 9:8, 19, 30).

Journey to Jerusalem (Luke 9:51–19:27)

The journey to Jerusalem section is also commonly called the travel narrative. This section in Luke is much longer than its parallels in Matthew and Mark (Luke 9:51–19:27; cf. Matt. 16:21–20:34; Mark 8:31–10:52). That is primarily because it presents more of Jesus's teaching. There are several unique and well-known parables in this section, including the good Samaritan (Luke 10:25–37), the prodigal son (15:11–32), the rich man and Lazarus (16:19–31), the widow and the unjust judge (18:1–8), and the Pharisee and the publican (18:9–14). There are also unique narratives in this section, including the ten lepers (17:11–19) and Zacchaeus (19:1–10).

The travel narrative presents Jesus's going from Galilee to Jerusalem. However, there are not many geographical markers showing exactly where Jesus and his followers are at most points during the trip. The overall point is simply that Jesus is going to Jerusalem to complete his work, which includes his rejection (e.g., Luke 13:33–34; 18:31). Along the way, this section presents a significant amount of Jesus's interaction with both his followers and his opponents. These interactions are not focused on a single theme but present a wide variety of Jesus's teachings.

Triumphal Entry through Ascension (Luke 19:28–24:53)

As in the other three Gospels, a large percentage of Luke's Gospel narrates Jesus's last week, which is the climax of his work.

This section begins with the Triumphal Entry and Jesus's weeping over Jerusalem. He then cleanses the temple (Luke 19:28–48). After this, Jesus is shown teaching in the temple for several days (20:1–21:38). As in the other Synoptic Gospels, this teaching includes several confrontations with Jesus's opponents. These confrontations include the question about Jesus's authority and his question in reply concerning John the Baptist (20:2–4), the parable of the wicked tenants (20:9–18), paying taxes to Caesar (20:19–26), the Sadducees' question about the resurrection (20:27–40), Psalm 110 and whether the Messiah is David's Son (Luke 20:41–44), and Jesus's warning to beware of the scribes (20:45–47).

Luke 21 primarily includes Jesus's discussion related to the destruction of the temple and his second coming. This is also known as the Olivet Discourse.

The passion narrative per se is included in Luke 22–23. This begins with a com-

[42] See, for example, Luke 4:24; 6:22–23; 7:11–17; 9:7–8; 13:33; 24:19; Acts 3:23. See discussions of the prophet motif in Green, *Theology of the Gospel of Luke*, 61–63; Marshall, *Luke: Historian and Theologian*, 126–28; and Bock, *A Theology of Luke and Acts*, 189–93.

ment about the Passover and the chief priests and scribes' wanting to put Jesus to death (22:1–2). It ends with Jesus's burial.

The final chapter of Luke presents the resurrection; Jesus's discussion on the road to Emmaus, which is unique material; Jesus's appearance with the disciples; and finally the ascension, at which Jesus gives a priestly benediction. Within this chapter, Jesus's two comments that his humiliation and exaltation were predicted in the Scriptures are often noted: "Thus it is written, that the Christ should suffer and on the third day rise from the dead" (24:46; see also 24:26). Also, important hermeneutical statements are included; for example, "And beginning with Moses and all the Prophets, [Jesus] interpreted to them in all the Scriptures the things concerning himself" (24:27; see also 24:44).

The book ends with several themes that will be prominent in Acts (Luke 24:44–49): Jesus's humiliation and exaltation were according to the Scriptures (e.g., Acts 2:23–24; 4:10–12; 5:30–31); the disciples are to be witnesses and preach to all nations, beginning in Jerusalem (Acts 1:8); and the "promise of the Father," that is, the Holy Spirit, will be given to the disciples (Acts 2).

Message and Theology

Although included in the other Synoptic Gospels, several theological themes are highlighted in Luke. Of course, several of them overlap. From my perspective, these emphasized themes are (1) Jesus's being the rejected suffering Prophet, which then moves toward his being the rejected suffering Messiah; (2) "salvation"; (3) the redemptive-historical plan of God that is in continuity with the Old Testament and includes the salvation of the Gentiles; and (4) the poor.[43]

To some degree, I have already discussed aspects of these four themes, especially the rejected Prophet. For this section, I will discuss the other three, along with the Lord's Supper and parables.

Salvation

At the end of the Zacchaeus account, which is unique to Luke, Jesus declares about himself, "The Son of Man came to seek and to save [σῴζω] the lost" (Luke 19:10). I. Howard Marshall is known for his "thesis that the idea of salvation supplies the key to the theology of Luke" and that this verse is the "epitome of the message of this Gospel."[44] Although I think Marshall is slightly overstating the issue, I agree that salvation and Jesus as Savior are important themes in Luke.[45]

[43] For comparison purposes, the critical scholar Ehrman notes Lucan emphases as temple orientation, Gentile and whole-world salvation, Jesus as the rejected Prophet, Gentile mission, divine plan, delay of the end of time, Jesus's death, and social implications (*The New Testament: A Historical Introduction*, 129–38). Evangelical scholars Carson and Moo include God's plan, "salvation," Gentiles, and outcasts (*Introduction to the New Testament*, 219–21).

[44] The "thesis" quote is found in Marshall, *Luke: Historian and Theologian*, 92; also see 9, 93–119. The "epitome" quote is from Marshall, *Gospel of Luke*, 695. Elsewhere, Marshall notes that Luke does not have the ransom sayings (Matt. 20:28; Mark 10:45) and surmises that Luke 19:10 may be a "replacement" in a "different idiom" (*New Testament Theology: Many Witnesses, One Gospel* [Downers Grove, IL: InterVarsity Press, 2004], 148).

[45] Our differences are partly due to Marshall's more favorable use of redaction criticism and the two-source hypothesis. But Marshall does see Luke as being faithful to his sources; that is, Marshall uses a modified version of redaction criticism. See his methodological discussion in *Luke: Historian and Theologian*, 16–20, 216–19.

Luke uses the verb σῴζω, "save," seventeen times in the Gospel of Luke, although this is not significantly out of proportion compared with Matthew and Mark.[46] Also, since σῴζω can be used for "heal" and "rescue," this statistic is not very informative on the surface. However, Luke does use σωτήρ, "savior," two times and σωτηρία/σωτήριον, "salvation," six times, and these terms are not used by Matthew or Mark.[47] Hence, it is Luke's use of σῴζω combined with these other cognate terms that shows his emphasis. This is confirmed by a similar emphasis in Acts.[48]

As one would expect, Luke centers "salvation" upon the "Savior," Jesus. The angel tells the shepherds that born in "the city of David, [is] a Savior, who is Christ the Lord" (Luke 2:11).[49] Zechariah refers to Jesus as the "horn of salvation" (Luke 1:69). In the Zacchaeus incident, Jesus notes that "salvation" has come and that he "came to seek and to save the lost" (Luke 19:9–10). Acts 4:12, a classic passage, declares that "salvation is [found] in no one else."

What is salvation in Luke? It is a broad word that assumes difficulties and sin, and asserts deliverance and restoration through Christ.[50] It has both present (e.g., Luke 7:50) and future/eschatological (e.g., 13:23) aspects.[51] Salvation is part of God's plan; it often has Davidic covenant overtones and is promised to all groups, including the Gentiles (1:69; 2:30–32). Forgiveness of sins is the central component (e.g., 1:77; 7:50; 18:26; Acts 5:31), but healings (Luke 8:48),[52] demon suppression (8:36), personal and social role reversals (1:71; 19:9), personal sanctification (9:24), and the joys of the new heavens and earth (3:6; 23:39–43) are also included.[53]

In sum, "salvation" in Luke does include the traditional Reformed personal and "spiritual" dimensions of justification, sanctification, and glorification; but as Reformed theology also teaches, God's work of salvation is broader.[54] This salvation is brought about by the triune God with the emphasis on the "Savior," the Lord Jesus Christ.

God's Plan

Many scholars note that the plan of God is a consistent theme in both Luke and Acts.[55] Of course, every New Testament book has this same theme to one degree or another. In Luke, God is orchestrating his plan, which matches predictions from an-

[46] Σῴζω occurs 15 times in Matthew, 15 times in Mark (including Mark 16:16), 6 times in John, and 13 times in Acts.

[47] Σωτήρ is used twice in Acts; σωτηρία, seven times; σωτήριον, once (Acts 28:28). Σωτηρία is included in the textual variant/addition (conclusion *brevior*) added to Mark 16:8.

[48] See Joel B. Green, "'Salvation to the End of the Earth' (Acts 13:47): God as Saviour in the Acts of the Apostles," in *Witness to the Gospel: The Theology of Acts*, ed. I. Howard Marshall and David Peterson (Grand Rapids, MI: Eerdmans, 1998), 83–106.

[49] Acts 5:31 and 13:23 explicitly refer to Jesus as "Savior." Note that in the Magnificat, Mary refers to "God" as "Savior" (Luke 1:47).

[50] See the well-balanced discussion in Bock, *A Theology of Luke and Acts*, 227–47.

[51] See E. Earle Ellis, *Eschatology in Luke* (Philadelphia: Fortress, 1972).

[52] See previous discussion of the relationship between healing and "salvation" in the section "Galilean Ministry (Luke 4:14–9:50)."

[53] Green puts the central emphasis elsewhere: "Salvation is, preeminently, status reversal" (*Theology of the Gospel*, 94).

[54] Marshall summarizes salvation by observing that "the deliverance brought by Jesus is basically spiritual with wider effects" (*New Testament Theology*, 144).

[55] See Green, *Theology of the Gospel of Luke*, 28–35, 47–49; Bock, *Theology of Luke and Acts*, 99–148; and John T. Squires, *The Plan of God in Luke-Acts*, SNTSMS 76 (Cambridge: Cambridge University Press, 1993).

gels, Jesus, and the Old Testament. The plan and events related to it are "necessary" (Gk. δεῖ, sometimes translated "must"), implying a *divine* necessity.

Luke begins with an angel telling Zechariah about his son, John, and his ministry of preparation (1:13–17). Similarly, an angel tells Mary about Jesus's kingdom (1:30–33). Mary's Magnificat and Zechariah's Benedictus use Old Testament language and allusions to foretell the coming salvation (Luke 1:46–55, 68–79). Jesus predicts his death and resurrection (e.g., 9:22; 13:33). Various Old Testament quotes are used to show that God's plan is being accomplished (e.g., Luke 3:4–6 // Isa. 40:3–5; Luke 4:18–19 // Isa. 61:1–2; Luke 20:17 // Ps. 118:22), along with the general statements that Christ's humiliation and exaltation match the Old Testament (Luke 24:26–27, 44–47). It is "necessary" for Jesus to be at his Father's house (2:49), preach the good news (4:43), die as a Prophet in Jerusalem (13:33), meet Zacchaeus (19:5), be rejected by this generation (17:25), be numbered with transgressors (22:37), die and rise again (9:22; 24:7), and fulfill Scripture (24:26, 44).

In addition to Jews (19:9), God's plan relates to the Gentiles/nations, who will also receive salvation.[56] The Gentiles are emphasized in Luke relatively but more significantly in Acts (see the chapter on Acts). Luke's relative emphasis on Gentiles is clearly expressed in Simon's Nunc Dimittis ("light for revelation to the Gentiles," Luke 2:32), in John the Baptist's mission as quoted in Isaiah 40:5 ("all flesh shall see the salvation of God," Luke 3:6),[57] and in Jesus's departing statement ("repentance and forgiveness of sins should be proclaimed in his name to all nations," Luke 24:47).

Hints of the Gentile emphasis in Luke include, for example, the genealogy of Jesus going back to Adam (3:38), not Abraham as in Matthew;[58] at the Nazareth synagogue, Jesus's reference to the widow of Zarephath and Naaman as the final straw (Luke 4:26–28); and Jesus's commending of the centurion's faith (7:9), the queen of the South, and Nineveh (11:31–32). Not all references to Gentiles are positive; for example, Tyre and Sidon are paragons of evil (10:14), and the Gentiles will be partially responsible for Jesus's death (18:32).

Of course, the Old Testament itself looks forward to all nations, Jew and Gentile, being part of God's salvation (Gen. 12:3; Isa. 49:6). Therefore, all of the Gospels indicate that the Gentiles will be part of God's people. But relatively speaking, Luke has more of this emphasis.

In scholarship, when one speaks of the plan of God, this invokes Luke's redemptive-historical scheme and Hans Conzelmann's theory.[59] Conzelmann was a redaction critic who wanted to answer why only Luke among the Gospels has a sequel. He concluded that Luke's redemptive history is separated into three phases: (1) Israel up to John the Baptist; (2) the time of Jesus, also called the "middle of time"; and (3) the time of the church. Conzelmann based the first two time periods on Luke

[56] See Bock, *A Theology of Luke and Acts*, 291–301; and Stephen G. Wilson, *The Gentiles and the Gentile Mission in Luke-Acts*, SNTSMS 23 (Cambridge: Cambridge University Press, 1973).
[57] Luke is the only one of the four Gospels that includes this portion of the Isaiah 40 quote.
[58] On the other hand, Matthew's genealogy includes four Gentile women, and an Abraham emphasis could be related to Abraham's Gentile promise (Gen. 12:3).
[59] Conzelmann, *The Theology of St. Luke*.

16:16. He further assumed that most in the early church thought that Jesus would immediately return and there would be no "time of the church." When Jesus did not return immediately, Luke alone added the "time of the church" to the early church's theology by writing Acts to make up for this "delay in the parousia."[60] Also, Luke added the "now" component of the "now and not yet" to make up for the delay.

This is not the place for a detailed response to Conzelmann, who includes many historical-critical assumptions with which I differ.[61] I simply note that all New Testament writers work with a redemptive-historical scheme that includes creation, the Old Testament, Jesus's earthly life, his church, and the new heavens and earth. Hence, Luke's scheme is consistent with them. Also, all New Testament writers work with a "now and not yet" scheme, with varying degrees of emphasis. Hence, again, Luke's emphasis on "now" aspects of eschatology, while also including "not yet," is not unusual. Finally, I note that if the ascension of Jesus and Pentecost occurred historically, then the "time of the church" was a reality and known in the early church along with the "now" benefits of the *eschaton*.

The Poor

Luke's Gospel is known for its greater emphasis on the poor than that of other Gospels.[62] But this emphasis does not continue into Acts.[63] Luke does include more women and uses "sinners" more often than do the other Gospels. These two, women and "sinners," could be combined with the poor to form a larger "outcasts" emphasis.

The poor (πτωχός), often mentioned in Luke,[64] are highlighted in the quasi-programmatic verse Luke 4:18 (with 7:22), which announces that Jesus has come to proclaim the "good news to the poor." The poor are contrasted with the rich in the Lucan Beatitudes (6:20, 24–25). Three unique Lucan parables relate rich and poor themes: the rich fool (12:13–21), the unjust steward (16:1–13), and the rich man and Lazarus (16:19–31).[65] The actions of the poor widow with two copper coins are praised (21:1–4). Mary's Magnificat praises God as he has "filled the hungry" (1:53).

The "poor" are the head of an apparent category that includes others at the margins of society. Two sample lists are the poor, crippled, lame, and blind of Luke 14:13 and the blind, lame, lepers, deaf, dead, and poor of Luke 7:22. However, it is clear that Jesus does not simply equate the poor with all who lack material goods. The "poor" are only those who depend on God and are part of his kingdom, in

---

[60] Carson and Moo remark, "In itself, this scheme is neither problematic nor particularly noteworthy. But what made Conzelmann's proposal significant was his explanation of the origin of this salvation history and its consequences" (*Introduction to the New Testament*, 217).

[61] For a fairly detailed negative response, see Marshall, *Luke: Historian and Theologian*, 77–94. For a history of the variety of critical agreement and negative responses, see François Bovon, *Luke the Theologian: Fifty-Five Years of Research (1950–2005)*, 2nd ed. (Waco, TX: Baylor University Press, 2006), 1–85.

[62] For discussions of the "poor" in Luke from differing critical viewpoints, see Tannehill, *Narrative Unity of Luke-Acts*, 1:127–32; Roth, *The Blind, the Lame, and the Poor*, 28–55; Bock, *A Theology of Luke and Acts*, 247–48, 352–57; Craig L. Blomberg, *Neither Poverty nor Riches: A Biblical Theology of Material Possessions*, NSBT 7 (Grand Rapids, MI: Eerdmans, 1999), 111–46, 160–74; and Green, *Theology of the Gospel of Luke*, 79–84, 112–17.

[63] Not that this theme is completely absent in Acts; see for example Acts 6:1.

[64] Here is an exhaustive list for πτωχός: Luke 4:18; 6:20; 7:22; 14:13, 21; 16:20, 22; 18:22; 19:8; 21:3. There is no mention in Acts. The synonym πενιχρός ("poor") is parallel to πτωχός in Luke 21:2. "Poverty" (ὑστέρημα) is used once in Luke 21:4.

[65] I take the rich man and Lazarus as a parable because it opens with typical parable wording (ἄνθρωπός τις, "a certain man").

addition to being economically deficient (e.g., 6:20; 12:34; 14:21).[66] Similarly, the "rich" are not simply those with money, but those who oppress the poor (e.g., 6:24; 16:19–31). The use of *rich* and *poor* with a social and spiritual/believing component matches the Old Testament usage of these terms.[67] In light of Luke's/Jesus's use of *rich* and *poor*, economic implications for today's world need to take this spiritual/believing component into account.

Two major thrusts for us come from the "poor" passages. First, Jesus's kingdom includes all types of people, including the poor (Luke 4:18). Hence, the church should certainly seek to evangelize the poor and appreciate the Christian poor's gifts to the church. Second, possessions/money have special temptations to inhibit one's spiritual growth; therefore, we should be wise in using worldly goods. "For where your treasure is, there will your heart be also" (12:34). "You cannot serve God and money" (16:13).

Lord's Supper

Of course, the Lord's Supper is a large and important topic in Christian theology.[68] For the purposes of this chapter, I will only briefly discuss a few issues.

As would be true of all the Gospels, the importance of the Lord's Supper is enhanced by its literary function and position in the narrative. As all of Luke's narrative is marching toward Jesus's death and resurrection, Jesus's words of institution are a (perhaps *the*) primary explanation of his death within the book (22:19–20). The new covenant was being inaugurated. As foreshadowed by the Passover Lamb, Jesus's death involved blood and was substitutionary for the sins of God's people (Luke 9:22; 19:10; 23:45; 24:46; cf. Ex. 24:8; Lev. 17:11; Jer. 31:31–34; Matt. 26:28; John 1:36; 1 Cor. 5:7; Heb. 9:22; 1 Pet. 1:19; Rev. 5:6). These emphases are clearly confirmed in Acts (e.g., Acts 2:38; 8:32–35; 20:28).

As further foreshadowed and paralleled by the Passover ceremony, the church would celebrate the Lord's Supper in remembrance. Also, the celebration would involve the special presence of God and be part of a covenant renewal ceremony.[69]

Jesus's words at the Lord's Supper relate to the sweep of redemptive history. Jesus was referring backward to the historic Passover event (Luke 22:7, 14). He was emphasizing his death and resurrection, which were to occur in the immediate future (14:22). Jesus was looking to the New Testament church age in the continued celebration of the Lord's Supper ("do this in remembrance," 22:19). Finally, he was

[66] Given that Jesus said both, the comparison of the Beatitudes "blessed are the poor" (Luke 6:20) versus "blessed are the poor in spirit" (Matt. 5:3) simply shows that the spiritual component is assumed in the Lucan version.

[67] See Roth, *The Blind, the Lame, and the Poor*, 112–34. P. H. Davids views Jesus's eschatological ethic (present and future kingdom) as explaining the usage of these terms ("Rich and Poor," in *DJG*, 701–10).

[68] Standard Reformed treatments include WCF 29; WLC 168–77; WSC 96–97; Belgic Confession 35; French Confession 36–37; Heidelberg Catechism 75–82; Thirty-Nine Articles 28–29; Francis Turretin, *Institutes of Elenctic Theology*, ed. James T. Dennison Jr., trans. George Musgrave Giger, 3 vols. (Phillipsburg, NJ: P&R, 1992–1997 [1679–1685]), 3:428–548; Herman Bavinck, *Reformed Dogmatics*, 4 vols. (Grand Rapids, MI: Baker Academic, 2003–2008 [1906–1911]), 4:540–85; and G. C. Berkouwer, *The Sacraments*, trans. Hugo Bekker (Grand Rapids, MI: Eerdmans, 1969), 188–296.

[69] See B. B. Warfield's insightful article comparing the Lord's Supper and the Passover ("The Fundamental Significance of the Lord's Supper," in *Selected Shorter Writings of Benjamin B. Warfield*, ed. John E. Meeter, 2 vols. [Nutley: Presbyterian and Reformed, 1970–1973], 1:332–38).

anticipating the new heavens and earth when he would again eat with the church at the great eschatological banquet (22:16–18).[70]

Concerning the Lord's Supper narrative itself, Luke includes a few comments not in Matthew, Mark, or John. One relates to drinking an additional cup before the formal words of institution of the bread and wine (Luke 22:17). Drinking multiple cups matches the Mishnah's discussion of the Passover as having four cups.[71] In conjunction with Matthew, Mark, and John, this confirms the impression that the Gospels give only a summary of the Passover meal highlighting Jesus's words of institution.

Luke includes Jesus's statement "I will not drink of the fruit of the vine until the kingdom of God comes" (22:18) earlier in the narrative than do Matthew and Mark. Also, he uniquely includes Jesus's words "I have earnestly desired to eat this Passover with you before I suffer. For I tell you I will not eat it until it is fulfilled in the kingdom of God" (22:15–16). As noted above, Jesus is alluding to the eschatological banquet. Luke's narrative puts more emphasis on this than do the other Gospels. Of course, the historical disciples in that context do not readily understand what he is referring to, but readers do.

One final difference relates to the words of institution of the cup. Luke has "new covenant," as opposed to simply "covenant" in Matthew and Mark, although Paul also has "new covenant" (1 Cor. 11:25). In addition, Luke simply says that the cup was poured out "for you" as opposed to Matthew's "for the forgiveness of sins" and Mark's "for many" (Luke 22:20; Matt. 26:28; Mark 14:24). From my perspective, Jesus historically spoke all of these sayings during the Lord's Supper event, and in the compressed language of each Gospel the concepts of the other Gospels are implied.

Parables

As is well known, Jesus used many parables in his teaching. Since Luke recorded the most parables, and several of the most famous parables are unique to Luke, a discussion of parables is warranted in this chapter. The comments below about parables would also apply to the parables in the other Gospels. The emphasis of this discussion will be hermeneutical, ending with some interpretive aids for the reader.

Table 2 offers a sense of the distribution of parables among the Gospels.[72] When counting parables, scholars differ at the margins as to what constitutes a parable; hence, the numbers vary slightly from scholar to scholar.

[70] So also Norval Geldenhuys, *Commentary on the Gospel of Luke: The English Text with Introduction, Exposition and Notes*, NICNT (Grand Rapids, MI: Eerdmans, 1951), 553–54; William Hendriksen, *Exposition of the Gospel according to Luke*, NTC (Grand Rapids, MI: Baker, 1978), 960; and Joseph A. Fitzmyer, *The Gospel according to Luke: (X–XXIV): Introduction, Translation, and Notes*, AB 28A (New York: Doubleday, 1985), 1398.

[71] See m. Pesahim 10:1–9. Although it includes earlier traditions, the Mishnah was written in approximately AD 200. In m. Berakhot 6:1, which is not specifically connected to the Passover, a blessing over wine would include "Creator of the fruit of the vine." Some connect this to Jesus's "fruit of the vine" comment in Luke 22:18. Also see Deut. 22:9 and Isa. 32:12.

[72] With a few differences, my numbers follow K. R. Snodgrass, "Parable," *DJG*, 591–601, esp. 595.

Gospel	Total Parables	Those Unique
Matthew	27	10
Mark	11	1
Luke	33	14
John	3	3

Table 2

As can be seen, the parables are evenly distributed in the Synoptic Gospels, given the relative lengths of the books. John, however, has few parables.

Table 3 lists the thirty-three parables in Luke. Those with an asterisk are unique to Luke.

Bridegroom and guests	Luke 5:33–34	Leaven	13:20–21
Unshrunk cloth	5:36	Narrow door	13:24–27
New wine	5:37–39	Wedding banquet	14:15–24
Wise/foolish builder	6:47–49	Tower builder*	14:28–30
Two debtors*	7:41–50	Warrior King*	14:31–33
Sower	8:4–15	Lost sheep	15:1–7
Lamp and jar	8:16–18	Lost coin*	15:8–10
Good Samaritan*	10:25–37	Prodigal son*	15:11–32
Friend at midnight*	11:5–8	Unjust manager*	16:1–8
Father and son's requests	11:11–13	Rich man and Lazarus*	16:19–31
Strong man's palace	11:21–23	Unworthy servants*	17:7–10
Rich fool and barns*	12:16–21	Unjust judge*	18:1–8
Watchman	12:35–38	Pharisee and tax collector*	18:9–14
Thief in the night	12:39–40	Servants and minas	19:11–27
Faithful/unfaithful manager	12:42–46	Wicked tenants	20:9–19
Barren fig tree*	13:6–9	Budding fig tree	21:29–33
Mustard seed	13:18–19		

* Unique to Luke

Table 3

Before continuing, we need a working definition of a parable. The English word *parable* is etymologically related to the Greek παραβολή. However, παραβολή has a broader meaning than does our English word *parable*. In the Septuagint, παραβολή (as well as παροιμία) translates the Hebrew מָשָׁל, which also has a broad range of meanings, including "proverb," "taunt," "riddle," and "allegorical story" (e.g., 1 Sam. 24:13; Ps. 49:4; Prov. 1:1; Isa. 14:3–4; Ezek. 17:2; Mic. 2:4). Similarly, in the New Testament, παραβολή (and παροιμία) has a broad range, including "proverb," "metaphor," "riddle," "figure of speech," "symbol," and "allegorical story" (παραβολή: Matt. 13:33; Mark 3:23; Luke 4:23; 15:3; Heb. 9:9; παροιμία: John 10:6; 16:25, 29; 2 Pet. 2:22). The general linguistic conclusion is that παραβολή (as well as παροιμία and מָשָׁל) is a saying/story (short or long) that has *two levels of meaning*. For most parables, the surface level is obvious, and the intended implications relate to the deeper level.

In modern English, we somewhat arbitrarily distinguish a short saying (that is, a proverb) from a longer "saying," such as the prodigal son, which we designate as a parable. Yet this distinction has its uses as the longer sayings are characteristic of Jesus's teaching. For my working definition, following most scholars and English Bible translations, I designate as parables (1) medium-length similes such as "the kingdom of heaven is like . . ." (e.g., Matt. 13:33), (2) fictional exemplary stories[73] (e.g., on the model behavior of the Good Samaritan, Luke 10:25–37), and (3) allegories (e.g., comparing lost sheep to lost men, Luke 15:3–7). I will not designate as a parable short proverbial statements such as "Physician, heal yourself," even though Luke calls this a παραβολή (Luke 4:23).

Does a parable have only one point, or is it allegorical in the sense that it has several points of connection? In the history of exegesis, many have tended toward excessive allegorizing, finding a meaning for every detail of parables. For example, in Augustine's interpretation of the wedding-banquet parable (Luke 14:15–24), he equated buying the farm with sinful ambition in life; the five oxen with the lust of the "eyes," though with all five senses; marrying a wife with lust of the flesh; and going to the streets with going to Gentiles.[74]

Beginning with Adolf Jülicher in 1888, a large portion of scholarship began interpreting parables as having only one point.[75] Parables were not considered allegorical at all. Critical scholars tended to see all parables as having the same one point. For example, some critical scholars saw "mystery" as the one point of every parable; others saw "kingdom." Despite disagreeing over the content of the one consistent point, they did agree that whatever the one point was, it was always the same. Also, they argued that the clearly allegorical parables (e.g., wheat and tares, Matt. 13:24–43) came not from Jesus but from the early church. Conservatives also tended to find one point in each parable, but that point differed among the parables. Conservatives had a more well-rounded understanding of the parables because their interpretation did not assume that all parables made the same one point. They explained the wheat-

[73] Scholars usually designate only four parables as exemplary stories, which are all in Luke: the good Samaritan, the rich fool and barns, the rich man and Lazarus, and the Pharisee and tax collector.

[74] *NPNF*[1] 6:446–49.

[75] Adolf Jülicher, *Die Gleichnisreden Jesu*, 2nd ed., 2 vols. (Tübingen: Mohr, 1899, 1910). Also influential in promoting the one-point view was C. H. Dodd, *The Parables of the Kingdom*, rev. ed. (New York: Scribner's, 1961); and Joachim Jeremias, *The Parables of Jesus*, trans. S. H. Hooke, rev. ed. (New York: Scribner's, 1963).

and-tares parable as an exception, not the rule. This one-point view was dominant from the late 1800s through the 1970s.

Currently, many scholars, both critical and conservative, have moved toward an allegorical understanding, believing that some but not all of the details in parables have meaning.[76] Arguments favoring an allegorical understanding include these: (1) Jesus's explicit interpretations of the wheat-and-tares (Matt. 13:24–43) and the sower (Luke 8:4–15) parables are allegorical in that many of the details, though not all, have meaning (cf. Matt. 15:11, 15–20). (2) It is in the context of the allegorical sower parable that Jesus gives one of the primary purposes of parables (Mark 4:11–13; Luke 8:9–11). (3) Some parables clearly have more than one point. The prodigal-son (Luke 15:11–32) parable makes a different point for the father, the prodigal son, and the older son. The parable of the Pharisee and the tax collector (Luke 18:9–14) has two primary points (the proper and improper heart motives). (4) The allegorical nature of parables fits well with the mysterious kingdom of God and the curse function of parables (Matt. 13:11–17, 34–35; Luke 8:10).

My view is that parables should be interpreted allegorically, though not every detail is to be pressed. Some in the one-point camp may not be far from this view when they take several implications from the parable and restate them as a well-rounded single point.

The following are some concluding reminders and recommendations for interpreting the parables:

1. Parables often refer to Jesus himself (Matt. 13:37; Luke 5:33–34; 20:13, 17). Whether explicitly or implicitly, parables are about the King of the kingdom of God.
2. Parables have a redemptive-historical character. They are about Jesus and often indicate that the kingdom of God is growing or advancing (Luke 5:39; 13:18–20). Jesus intended that the interpretation of some parables would become clearer later. For example, in the wicked-tenants parable (Luke 20:9–16), Jesus quotes Psalm 118:22. The first half of the quote ("The stone that the builders rejected") connects the parable (in which the vineyard owner's son is killed) to Jesus's rejection, which the historical audience would have understood to some degree. However, the second half of the quote ("has become the cornerstone") does not connect to the parable and would have been understandable only after Jesus's resurrection, which the reading audience of Luke completely understands.

[76] Standard books on parables include Robert H. Stein, *An Introduction to Parables of Jesus* (Philadelphia: Westminster Press, 1981). Stein is in the one-point camp. Madeleine Boucher's study is well known and influential as she concludes that parables are allegories (or occasionally exemplary stories) (*The Mysterious Parable*, CBQMS 6 [Washington: Catholic Biblical Association, 1977], 17–25). Brad H. Young argues that Jesus's parables need to be seen in the context of rabbinic parables (*The Parables: Jewish Tradition and Christian Interpretation* [Peabody, MA: Hendrickson, 1998]). His view has not been adopted by many. Craig L. Blomberg is in the allegory camp and, from my perspective, has produced the best work on parables (*Interpreting the Parables* [Downers Grove, IL: InterVarsity Press, 1990]). Klyne Snodgrass similarly is in the allegory camp and has also produced a very useful guidebook as he discusses virtually every parable (*Stories with Intent: A Comprehensive Guide to the Parables of Jesus* [Grand Rapids, MI: Eerdmans, 2008]). Personally, I have been most influenced by Vern S. Poythress's PhD class on parables; Poythress is also in the allegory camp. For a good popular exegesis of many parables, see Simon J. Kistemaker, *The Parables: Understanding the Stories Jesus Told* (Grand Rapids, MI: Baker, 2002).

3. While many details are true-life portrayals of first-century-AD Palestine, often the key details of parables are surprisingly unrealistic (e.g., Matt. 13:44–46; Luke 14:15–24).
4. Parables invite the audience to judge themselves. Many times the surface-level meaning of a parable is clear on who are the "good" and "bad" characters (e.g., Luke 6:46–49; 10:25–37; 13:24–30). Readers are then implicitly invited to judge at the deeper level which character they truly resemble and/or their view of Jesus.
5. Parables that begin with τίς ἐξ ὑμῶν ("which one of you") usually will make a lesser-to-greater argument (e.g., Luke 14:28–33).
6. Often parables begin with ἄνθρωπός τις ("a certain man," e.g., Luke 15:11).[77]
7. Jesus does not always use a metaphor in the same way. For example, "treasure" is something positive in Matthew 13:44 and something negative in Luke 12:21.
8. Sometimes several characters are really just one type of character. For example, consider the priest and the Levite in the parable of the good Samaritan (Luke 10:31–32), those with various excuses for not coming to the wedding banquet (Luke 14:18–20), and the "five" wise and foolish virgins (Matt. 25:2).
9. Many parables are one-, two-, or three-*character* parables.[78] The three-character parables feature a God/Jesus character, a positive person, and a negative person.

    - One-character examples: hidden treasure, pearl of great price (Matt. 13:44–46); mustard seed, leaven (Luke 13:18–21); tower builder, warrior king (Luke 14:28–30; 31–33)[79]
    - Two-character examples: unjust judge (Luke 18:1–8); rich fool and barns (Luke 12:16–21); wise and foolish builders (Luke 6:47–49); Pharisee and tax collector (Luke 18:9–14)
    - Three-character examples: ten virgins (Matt. 25:1–13); good Samaritan (Luke 10:25–37); sower (Luke 8:4–15); two sons (Matt. 21:28–32)

10. For teaching and preaching, it is best to construct a "main point" for each character. Let the context determine which of the main points should receive more emphasis and which, less emphasis.

    - The parable of the friend at midnight (Luke 11:5–8) has two characters: a man sleeping and his friend. (1) Even more than the sleeping man who first balks at a request but then gives in, God honors bold, persistent prayers abundantly. (2) Like the persistent friend, Christians should boldly and persistently offer up requests to God.
    - The parable of the prodigal son (Luke 15:11–32) has three characters: a father, a prodigal son, and an older son. (1) Like the father, God/Christ wonderfully and joyously forgives those who repent and believe. (2) As with the prodigal son, no matter the depth of sin, it is never too late to repent and believe. (3) Like the older son, some in the covenant community are trusting in their works and do not appreciate grace.

[77] One confirmation that the parable of the rich man and Lazarus is indeed a parable is that it begins with ἄνθρωπός τις.
[78] See the excellent discussion in Blomberg, *Interpreting the Parables*, 171–287.
[79] Often one-character parables are grouped together.

Select Bibliography

Augustine. *Harmony of the Gospels*. In vol. 6 of *NPNF*[1].

Blomberg, Craig L. *Interpreting the Parables*. Downers Grove, IL: InterVarsity Press, 1990.

Bock, Darrell L. *Luke*. 2 vols. BECNT. Grand Rapids, MI: Baker, 1994–1996.

———. *A Theology of Luke and Acts: God's Promised Program, Realized for All Nations*. BTNT. Grand Rapids, MI: Zondervan, 2012.

Bovon, François. *Luke*. Translated by Christine M. Thomas. Edited by Helmut Koester. 3 vols. Hermeneia. Minneapolis: Fortress, 2002–2013.

———. *Luke the Theologian: Fifty-Five Years of Research (1950–2005)*. 2nd ed. Waco, TX: Baylor University Press, 2006.

Cadbury, H. J. *The Making of Luke-Acts*. London: Macmillan, 1927.

Calvin, John. *A Harmony of the Gospels Matthew, Mark, and Luke*. Translated by A. W. Morrison. 3 vols. Calvin's Commentaries. Grand Rapids, MI: Eerdmans, 1972.

Carroll, John T. *Luke: A Commentary*. NTL. Louisville: Westminster John Knox, 2012.

Conzelmann, Hans. *The Theology of St. Luke*. Translated by Geoffrey Buswell. London: Faber & Faber, 1960.

Evans, C. F. *Saint Luke*. TPINTC. Philadelphia: Trinity Press International, 1990.

Fitzmyer, Joseph A. *The Gospel according to Luke: Introduction, Translation, and Notes*. 2 vols. AB 28, 28A. New York: Doubleday, 1970–1985.

———. *Luke the Theologian: Aspects of His Teaching*. New York: Paulist, 1989.

Garland, David E. *Luke*. ZECNT 3. Grand Rapids, MI: Zondervan, 2011.

Geldenhuys, Norval. *Commentary on the Gospel of Luke: The English Text with Introduction, Exposition, and Notes*. NICNT. Grand Rapids, MI: Eerdmans, 1951.

Green, Joel B. *The Gospel of Luke*. NICNT. Grand Rapids, MI: Eerdmans, 1997.

———. *The Theology of the Gospel of Luke*. NTT. Cambridge: Cambridge University Press, 1995.

Green, Joel B., and Michael C. McKeever. *Luke-Acts and New Testament Historiography*. IBR Bibliographies 8. Grand Rapids, MI: Baker, 1994.

Hendriksen, William. *Exposition of the Gospel according to Luke*. NTC. Grand Rapids, MI: Baker, 1978.

Johnson, L. T. *The Gospel of Luke*. SP 3. Collegeville, MN: Liturgical, 1991.

Keck, Leander E., and J. Louis Martyn, eds. *Studies in Luke-Acts*. Philadelphia: Fortress, 1980.

Marshall, I. Howard. *The Gospel of Luke: A Commentary on the Greek Text*. NIGTC. Grand Rapids, MI: Eerdmans, 1978.

———. *Luke: Historian and Theologian*. Rev. ed. Grand Rapids, MI: Zondervan, 1989.

Parsons, Mikeal C., and Richard I. Pervo. *Rethinking the Unity of Luke and Acts*. Minneapolis: Fortress, 1993.

Plummer, Alfred. *A Critical and Exegetical Commentary on the Gospel according to S. Luke*. 5th ed. ICC. Edinburgh: T&T Clark, 1922.

Snodgrass, Klyne. *Stories with Intent: A Comprehensive Guide to the Parables of Jesus*. Grand Rapids, MI: Eerdmans, 2008.

Stein, Robert H. *Luke*. NAC 24. Nashville: Broadman, 1992.

Tannehill, Robert C. *The Narrative Unity of Luke-Acts*. 2 vols. Philadelphia: Fortress, 1986–1990.

4

John

Michael J. Kruger

Introduction

While the Gospel of John tells the same basic story as the Synoptics, it offers a distinctive perspective on the person and work of Christ. John writes the story of Jesus in a unique style (leaving aside the pithy language of the Synoptics), he includes unique events (e.g., the man born blind, the raising of Lazarus from the dead), he provides some of the most beloved teachings of Jesus (e.g., the Upper Room Discourse), he highlights the divinity and preexistence of Jesus ("In the beginning was the Word"), and he presents Christ as the only path to eternal life (John 3). For these reasons, the Gospel of John has become one of the most beloved books in the New Testament, if not the whole Bible. Not only was it the most popular Gospel within early Christianity,[1] but it was enormously influential on early Christian theology.[2]

While John's unique features are no doubt part of the reason for its immense popularity, they have also raised concerns. John's discursive style, high christology, and emphasis on eternal life have been viewed by some scholars as evidence that John, unlike the Synoptics, is concerned more with theological issues than with historical ones.[3] In order to bolster this claim, appeal is often made to Clement of Alexandria's famous observation that, in contrast to the Synoptics, John is "a spiritual Gospel" (πνευματικὸν εὐαγγέλιον).[4] Aside from whether this is an accurate understanding

[1] If extant manuscripts are indication of usage, then the Gospel of John is the most popular. For a recent account of manuscripts of John, see Juan Chapa, "The Early Text of the Gospel of John," in *The Early Text of the New Testament*, ed. Charles E. Hill and Michael J. Kruger (Oxford: Oxford University Press, 2011), 140–56. For a broader account of the usage of John, see Charles E. Hill, *The Johannine Corpus in the Early Church* (Oxford: Oxford University Press, 2004).

[2] See discussions in J. N. Sanders, *The Fourth Gospel in the Early Church: Its Origin and Influence on Christian Theology up to Irenaeus* (Cambridge: Cambridge University Press, 1943); and T. E. Pollard, *Johannine Christology and the Early Church* (Cambridge: Cambridge University Press, 1970).

[3] For a survey of the history of criticism against John, see Paul Anderson, *The Fourth Gospel and the Quest for Jesus: Modern Foundations Reconsidered* (London: T&T Clark, 2006), 8–25.

[4] Eusebius records Clement's words in *Hist. eccl.* 6.14.7.

of Clement's intent,[5] it has been used to present John as a Gospel so theologically conditioned that it can tell us very little about the historical Jesus.

The purpose of this chapter is to explore more fully the nature of John's Gospel and the challenges it presents. I will argue, in contrast to much of modern scholarship, that the Gospel is based on real eyewitness history and, at the same time, presents a deep, rich theological vision for the person and work of Christ. And these two aspects are not mutually exclusive. Indeed, it is only when they are understood together, in a symbiotic relationship, that this Gospel can serve its proper function in the church of Christ. The historical dimension of the book gives us confidence that it is based on real events and therefore can be trusted. And the theological dimension provides a distinctive interpretation of those real events and a distinctive application to the life of the church. Because the Gospel of John provides such a unique contribution to the latter dimension, this chapter shall devote most of the discussion to the book's theological message—and how pastors can effectively apply that message to the modern world.

Background Issues

Authorship

As a book that is formally anonymous, John is no different from the Synoptics.[6] However, unlike the Synoptics, John's Gospel provides more direct clues about the identity of its author. In John 21:24 we are told that it is the beloved disciple "who is bearing witness [μαρτυρῶν] about these things, and who has written [γράψας] these things."[7] Of course, the identity of this mysterious "beloved disciple" has engendered much academic debate, and there are various suggestions about who he might be, ranging from John the elder[8] to Thomas,[9] to Lazarus the brother of Mary and Martha.[10] Indeed, J. H. Charlesworth has cataloged twenty-three different positions on the authorship of John![11] However, there are good reasons to think that the

[5] Andreas J. Köstenberger, *A Theology of John's Gospel and Letters*, BTNT (Grand Rapids, MI: Zondervan, 2009), 38–39, argues that Clement's use of the term "spiritual" should not be taken as evidence that he viewed it as nonhistorical.

[6] Armin D. Baum, "The Anonymity of the New Testament History Books: A Stylistic Device in the Context of Greco-Roman and Ancient Near Eastern Literature," *NovT* 50 (2008): 120–42, argues that the historical books of the New Testament (Gospels and Acts) were *intentionally* written as anonymous works in order to reflect the practice of the Old Testament historical books, which were themselves anonymous (as opposed to other Old Testament writings, like the Prophets, which included the identity of the author).

[7] J. H. Bernard, *A Critical and Exegetical Commentary on the Gospel according to St. John* (Edinburgh: T&T Clark, 1928), and a number of other scholars depending on his work, have suggested that John 21:24 means only that John is a "source" behind the Gospel, but not that he actually wrote it. However, Richard Bauckham makes a compelling argument that γράψας cannot mean that John was a "source" but must mean that he, as the author, directly wrote it or dictated it to a secretary (*Jesus and the Eyewitnesses: The Gospels as Eyewitness Testimony* [Grand Rapids, MI: Eerdmans, 2006], 358–62). Others have suggested that 21:24 means only that the beloved disciple wrote the immediately preceding verses. However, even Rudolf Bultmann, *The Gospel of John: A Commentary* (Philadelphia: Westminster Press, 1971), 717n4, acknowledges that 21:24 "looks back to the gospel" itself. See also Rudolf Schnackenburg, *The Gospel according to St. John*, 3 vols. (London: Burns and Oates, 1982), 3:373.

[8] The most developed version of this approach can be found in Martin Hengel, *Die Johanneische Frage: Ein Lösungsversuch mit einem Beitrag zur Apokalypse von Jörg Frey* (Tübingen: Mohr Siebeck, 1993). Following Hengel is Bauckham, *Jesus and the Eyewitnesses*, 358–437.

[9] James H. Charlesworth, *The Beloved Disciple: Whose Witness Validates the Gospel of John?* (Valley Forge, PA: Trinity, 1995), 225–437.

[10] Vernard Eller, *The Beloved Disciple: His Name, His Story, and His Thought* (Grand Rapids, MI: Eerdmans, 1987).

[11] Charlesworth, *The Beloved Disciple*, 127–224. The traditional view that the beloved disciple was John the apostle, son of Zebedee, is still held by a number of scholars: Craig S. Keener, *The Gospel of John* (Peabody, MA: Hendrickson, 2003), 83–104; Leon Morris, *The Gospel according to John* (Grand Rapids, MI: Eerdmans, 1995), 775–77; D. A. Carson, *The*

dominant position of the early church[12]—that the beloved disciple was John the son of Zebedee—still has the most to commend it: (1) The beloved disciple is present at the Last Supper (13:23) and thus is presented as one of the apostles;[13] (2) the beloved disciple is described as a witness (21:24) and as one present from the beginning (1:35–40[14]), both attributes that Jesus uses to expressly describe the apostles in 15:27: "you also will bear witness, because you have been with me from the beginning"; (3) this individual is clearly none of the other named disciples (Peter, Philip, Judas, Thomas, et al.); (4) the beloved disciple is often in the company of Peter (e.g., 20:2; 21:20); and (5) John the son of Zebedee, one of the most prominent disciples, is never named (and if he is not the beloved disciple, then where is he?). The best explanation for all of these factors is that the beloved disciple is John the son of Zebedee.

Occasion and Purpose

Part of understanding and interpreting a book is locating the proper historical setting in which it was written and the issues it intended to address. While there has been a long history of scholarly discussion around this question,[15] in the second half of the twentieth century a quasi consensus emerged that suggested John was written in reaction to the expulsion of Christians from the Jewish synagogue at the end of the first century.[16] According to this hypothesis, popularized by J. Louis Martyn, the Gospel of John was written not as an account of the historical Jesus, but as an account of the Johannine community. Many of the events and characters of the Gospel story, therefore, are merely representations of the events and characters of the community that wrote it. However, by the turn of the century, this consensus had begun to receive some serious and much-needed critique.[17] The critiques have been significant enough that the Johannine-community hypothesis has largely collapsed.[18]

With the Johannine-community hypothesis now in turmoil, the question of John's historical setting still remains. Andreas Köstenberger has persuasively argued that a key factor in the composition of John is the aftermath of the destruction of the temple

Gospel according to John (Grand Rapids, MI: Eerdmans, 1991), 682–85; Andreas J. Köstenberger, *John*, BECNT (Grand Rapids, MI: Baker Academic, 2004), 603–6; and Craig Blomberg, *The Historical Reliability of John's Gospel: Issues and Commentary* (Downers Grove, IL: InterVarsity Press, 2001).

[12] E.g., Irenaeus, *Haer.* 2.22.5, 3.3.4, 3.11; Eusebius, *Hist. eccl.* 3.23.3–4, 4.14.3–8, 5.8.4; Muratorian Fragment (see section on John).

[13] Some have disputed whether the Last Supper was exclusively attended by the Twelve, but the Synoptics seem quite clear that this was the case (Matt. 26:20; Mark 14:17; Luke 22:14).

[14] Although the phrase "beloved disciple" does not occur here, Bauckham makes a compelling argument that the parallels between John 1:35–40 and John 21 confirm that the "beloved disciple" is in view in both passages (*Jesus and the Eyewitnesses*, 390–93).

[15] Most notable in this regard is the suggestion that John was responding to Gnostic-type thought; e.g., Rudolf Bultmann, *Primitive Christianity in Its Contemporary Setting* (London: Thames and Hudson, 1956), 162–71. For a survey of suggestions that John was either Gnostic or Hellenistic, see S. Smalley, *John: Evangelist and Interpreter* (London: Paternoster, 1978), 45–74. Updated discussions of John's origin and purpose can also be found in Tom Thatcher, ed., *What We Have Heard from the Beginning: The Past, Present, and Future of Johannine Studies* (Waco, TX: Baylor University Press, 2007).

[16] J. L. Martyn, *History and Theology in the Fourth Gospel* (New York: Harper & Row, 1968); Oscar Cullmann, *The Johannine Circle*, trans. J. Bowden (London: SCM, 1976).

[17] For a broad critique of the Johannine community hypothesis, see Edward W. Klink, *The Sheep of the Fold: The Audience and Origin of the Gospel of John* (Cambridge: Cambridge University Press, 2007); and Richard Bauckham, ed., *The Gospel for All Christians: Rethinking the Gospel Audiences* (Grand Rapids, MI: Eerdmans, 1998). For a critique of the role of the *birkat ha-minim* (the supposed synagogue curse against Jewish Christians), see William Horbury, "The Benediction of the Minim and Early Jewish-Christian Controversy," *JTS* 33 (1982): 19–61.

[18] Köstenberger, *Theology of John's Gospel*, 52–53.

in AD 70.[19] The destruction of the temple would have been a monumental event for both Jews and Jewish Christians, raising the inevitable question of the relationship between Jesus and the temple.[20] When we look to the Gospel of John, we see that it answers this very question by describing Jesus as the *fulfillment* of the Jerusalem temple (e.g., 1:14; 2:18–22).[21] Whereas the Synoptics record Jesus's vivid predictions of the temple's destruction (Matthew 24; Mark 13; Luke 21), John focuses on the theological implications of that destruction, namely, that Jesus is the embodiment of all that the temple was intended to be. No doubt this is why John places the story of Jesus's cleansing the temple at the beginning of his Gospel (whereas it occurs at the end of the Synoptics).[22] This redemptive-historical perspective on Jesus as the new temple fits quite well with the end of the first century—80s or 90s—when Jews and Jewish Christians would have been reflecting upon the meaning of AD 70.

If Köstenberger is correct about the historical occasion for John's composition (and I think he is), then it also tells us something about John's overall purpose. John's Gospel appears to have an evangelistic goal, namely, to reach a Jewish audience struggling with the end of the temple and to give them the good news that Jesus is not only the fulfillment of the temple, but one greater than the temple.[23] Drawing near to God no longer requires an earthly location (John 4:21), but a relationship with Jesus (14:6). But John goes even further than this. In order to put Jesus in his proper redemptive-historical place, he also argues that Jesus is the fulfillment of the entire Old Testament, including Israel's festivals (e.g., 7:37) and even Israel's own history (e.g., 3:14; 6:32). This fits quite well with John's own stated evangelistic purpose for the book: "But these are written so that you may believe that Jesus is the Christ, the Son of God" (20:31). Given the Jewish audience of John's Gospel, D. A. Carson's suggestion that 20:31 should be translated as "so that you may believe that *the Christ is Jesus*" is particularly compelling.[24]

Date

When it comes to the date of John's Gospel, scholarly opinions vary widely. Some have suggested quite an early date for John, even prior to AD 70.[25] However, our discussions above suggest that John's Gospel functions largely as a response to the destruction of the temple, making such an early date unlikely. Moreover, an early date runs counter to much of the Patristic evidence that indicates John lived to be

[19] Ibid., 59–67.

[20] M. Goodman, "Diaspora Reactions to the Destruction of the Temple," in *Jews and Christians: The Parting of the Ways A.D. 70–135*, ed. J. D. G. Dunn (Tübingen: Mohr Siebeck, 1992), 27–38.

[21] For more on this theme, see Alan R. Kerr, *The Temple of Jesus' Body: The Temple Theme in the Gospel of John*, JSNTSup 220 (Sheffield: Sheffield Academic, 2002).

[22] See discussion in J. A. Draper, "Temple, Tabernacle and Mystical Experience in John," *Neot* 31 (1997): 263–88, esp. 263.

[23] For arguments that John has an evangelistic purpose, see W. C. van Unnik, "The Purpose of St. John's Gospel," *Studia Evangelica* (1959): 382–411; and J. A. T. Robinson, "The Destination and Purpose of St. John's Gospel," *NTS* 6 (1959): 117–31. For the view that John is written simply to encourage existing believers, see Keener, *Gospel of John*, 195–214.

[24] D. A. Carson, "The Purpose of the Fourth Gospel: John 20:30–31 Reconsidered," *JBL* 106 (1987): 639–51. For a response, see G. Fee, "On the Text and Meaning of John 20, 30–31," in *The Four Gospels 1992: Festschrift for Frans Neirynck*, ed. F. van Segbroeck et al. (Leuven: Leuven University Press, 1992), 3:2193–205.

[25] E.g., J. A. T. Robinson, *Redating the New Testament* (Philadelphia: Westminster Press, 1976); and F. Lamar Cribbs, "A Reassessment of the Date of Origin and the Destination of the Gospel of John," *JBL* 89 (1970): 38–55.

very old (even past the reign of Domitian, ca. 81–96),[26] and that he was the last Gospel author to write.[27]

Others scholars have suggested late dates for John, even into the middle of the second century. However, if the author was really John the son of Zebedee, as I have argued above, then such a late date is untenable. Moreover, a late date is ruled out by the fact that manuscripts of John's Gospel were already circulating (even in Egypt!) by the early second century, as indicated by the discovery of $\mathfrak{p}^{52}$, our earliest manuscript of John, dated ca. 125.[28] Moreover, Charles Hill has made convincing arguments that John was already known and used by a number of authors in the early second century, likely including Papias and Ignatius.[29]

If these considerations rule out both early and late dates, then a time period in the 80s or perhaps early 90s seems most likely. We would not expect John to have been written immediately after AD 70; it would have taken some time for the impact of the temple's destruction to be felt in the Diaspora, and for that impact to result in mature theological reflection about the relationship between Jesus and the temple.[30] In addition, John's more explicit language regarding the divinity of Jesus fits more closely with what we see in Ignatius and thus suggests a date toward the end of the first century.[31]

Historicity

When it comes to the historical nature of John's Gospel, it has received more than its share of criticism over the years.[32] As noted above, this is due not only to its mature theological reflection regarding the preexistence of Jesus, but also to the many stylistic, chronological, and content differences with the Synoptics. But do these factors mean that John is theology and not history? These are complex matters that cannot be fully addressed in this single chapter, but a few considerations can help.

First, there is the question of whether John intended to write history. In a 2007 article, Richard Bauckham has argued that John bears certain characteristics that his readers would have understood as historiographical—meaning they would have understood John to be a work of history.[33] And these characteristics are actually more prominent in John than in the Synoptics. These characteristics include

1. *Topography/geography*. John has layers of detail that regularly surpass the more vague statements in the Synoptics.

[26] Irenaeus, *Haer.* 2.22.5, 3.3.4; Eusebius, *Hist. eccl.* 3.23.1–4.

[27] Eusebius, *Hist. eccl.* 3.24.7–13, 6.14.7 (citing Clement of Alexandria).

[28] C. H. Roberts, "An Unpublished Fragment of the Fourth Gospel in the John Rylands Library," *BJRL* 20 (1936): 45–55. It should also be noted that P.Egerton 2, fragmentary remains of an apocryphal gospel, is dated ca. 150 and also shows clear dependence on the Gospel of John; see T. Kraus, Michael J. Kruger, and T. Nicklas, *Gospel Fragments* (Oxford: Oxford University Press, 2008), 11–114.

[29] Hill, *Johannine Corpus*, 360–446.

[30] Carson, *Gospel according to John*, 85.

[31] D. A. Carson and Douglas J. Moo, *An Introduction to the New Testament*, 2nd ed. (Grand Rapids, MI: Zondervan, 2005), 266–67.

[32] Recent examples include Maurice Casey, *Is John's Gospel True?* (New York: Routledge, 1996); and R. W. Funk and Roy W. Hoover, *The Five Gospels: The Search for the Authentic Words of Jesus* (New York: Macmillan, 1993).

[33] Richard Bauckham, "Historiographical Characteristics of the Gospel of John," *NTS* 53 (2007): 17–36. See also Anderson, *Fourth Gospel*, 78–84; and Keener, *Gospel of John*, 42–47.

2. *Eyewitness testimony*. More expressly than even the Synoptics, John makes it clear that his Gospel is a firsthand account.[34]
3. *Long discourses*. Contrary to the abbreviated/condensed teachings preserved by the Synoptics, John's longer discourses are, historically speaking, a more realistic account of what Jesus probably sounded like.

If Bauckham is correct about these characteristics, then we are faced with the counterintuitive reality that John, in many ways, is more like ancient historiographical literature than even the Synoptics.

Second, differences with the Synoptics can be partially explained on the premise that John knew (some of) the Synoptics but was intent on writing his own book.[35] In such a scenario, it is plausible to think that he might have intentionally omitted certain stories (already in the Synoptics), and included additional stories (omitted by the Synoptics), for his own theological purposes.[36] While C. H. Dodd's arguments that John did not know the Synoptics still hold sway among many modern scholars,[37] there is an increasing recognition that historical probabilities are in favor of John's knowing at least Mark (and perhaps even Luke and Matthew).[38]

Third, the uniform style in John's Gospel—regardless of whether the speaker in a particular narrative is John the Baptist, Jesus, or the narrator—need not imply that John's Gospel is historically untrustworthy. It was not unusual for ancient authors to record a person's speeches or words in a style that was very much their own.[39] No doubt, John has stylized Jesus's teaching in a manner that fits his own vocabulary and grammatical characteristics.[40] However, while John does not preserve the *ipsissima verba* ("very words") of Jesus, we have no reason to think that it does not preserve the *ipsissima vox* ("very voice") of Jesus.[41]

Fourth, it should be remembered that theology and history are not necessarily mutually exclusive.[42] It is certainly true that John offers a more sustained and more thorough theological reflection upon the ministry of Jesus than we find in the Synoptics. But such theological reflection can still be grounded (and should be grounded) in real historical events.

[34] On this note, see also Bauckham, *Jesus and the Eyewitnesses*, 358–83; and Samuel Byrskog, *Story as History—History as Story: The Gospel Tradition in the Context of Ancient Oral History* (Leiden: Brill, 2002).
[35] For a history of scholarship on John's use of the Synoptics, see D. Moody Smith, *John among the Synoptics*, 2nd ed. (Columbia: University of South Carolina Press, 2001); and J. D. Dvorak, "The Relationship between John and the Synoptic Gospels," *JETS* 41 (1998): 201–13.
[36] Anderson, *Fourth Gospel*, 50–51.
[37] C. H. Dodd, *Historical Tradition in the Fourth Gospel* (Cambridge: Cambridge University Press, 1963); see further discussion in D. Moody Smith, "John and the Synoptics: Some Dimensions of the Problem," *NTS* 26 (1980): 425–44; and Smith, "Jesus Tradition in the Gospel of John," in *Handbook for the Study of the Historical Jesus*, ed. Tom Holmén and Stanley E. Porter, 4 vols. (Leiden: Brill, 2010), 1997–2039.
[38] E.g., Richard Bauckham, "John for Readers of Mark," in *The Gospels for All Christians: Rethinking the Gospel Audiences*, ed. Richard Bauckham (Grand Rapids, MI: Eerdmans, 1998), 147–71; F. Neirynck, "John and the Synoptics," in *L'évangile de Jean*, ed. M. de Jonge (Leuven: Leuven University Press, 1977), 73–106; C. Kingsley Barrett, *The Gospel according to John* (London: SPCK, 1978); R. H. Lightfoot, *St. John's Gospel: A Commentary* (Oxford: Clarendon, 1956).
[39] Bauckham, "Historiographical Characteristics," 30–31. For more on recording speeches in the ancient world, see F. W. Walbank, *Speeches in Greek Historians* (Oxford: Holywell, 1965).
[40] See the thorough discussion in Keener, *Gospel of John*, 67–76.
[41] On this point, see the helpful discussion in Darrell L. Bock, "The Words of Jesus in the Gospels: Live, Jive, or Memorex?," in *Jesus under Fire* (Grand Rapids, MI: Zondervan, 1995), 74–99.
[42] Anderson, *Fourth Gospel*, 73–74.

Structure and Outline

It is widely acknowledged that John's Gospel can be divided into four sections:

I. Prologue (1:1–18)
II. "Book of Signs"[43] (1:19–12:50)
III. "Book of the Passion"[44] (13:1–20:31)
IV. Epilogue (21:1–25)

There is little doubt that the prologue is the most famous section of the Gospel of John, if not the entire New Testament.[45] Instead of starting with birth narratives or genealogies (like Matthew or Luke), or even with the Old Testament prophecies (like Mark), John takes the reader back to the time before creation, focusing on Jesus as the preexistent "Word." The use of λόγος has occasioned much discussion, but is best understood in light of its Old Testament background—where the λόγος is God's powerful self-expression in creation, revelation, and redemption—as opposed to the background of Hellenistic philosophy.[46] Craig S. Keener even argues that "the Fourth Gospel presents the Logos of its prologue as Torah."[47] Some have suggested that the prologue was later added by a redactor and was not original to John's Gospel, but there is no extant manuscript evidence for this hypothesis. Moreover, the themes of the prologue interface quite impressively with the themes taken up in the rest of the book, suggesting that the prologue is likely a natural and original part of the Gospel's production.[48]

The "Book of Signs" (John 1:19–12:50) gets its name from the fact that Jesus performs his six (or seven)[49] key miracles in these twelve chapters—which John prefers to call "signs" (σημεῖα). Historically, scholars have argued that these signs are evidence that John used a "signs source" when he composed his Gospel,[50] but this theory is much less popular today. These six signs include turning the water into wine (2:1–11), healing of the nobleman's son (4:46–54), healing of the crippled man (5:2–15), feeding of the five thousand (6:1–15), healing the man born blind (9:1–41), and, of course, raising Lazarus from the dead (11:1–57). Unlike the Synoptics, these acts were not so much designed to display God's power (though they did), but were "prophetic-symbolic" acts designed to validate Jesus as the Messiah and Son of God.[51] This fits quite well with the purpose of John discussed above, namely, that John was written to a Jewish audience (though not exclusively) to demonstrate that the Messiah was Jesus.

[43] C. H. Dodd, *The Interpretation of the Fourth Gospel* (Cambridge: Cambridge University Press, 1968), 297–389.
[44] Dodd, *Interpretation of the Fourth Gospel*, 390–443. This section has had other names, such as the "Book of Glory" and the "Book of Exaltation" (Köstenberger, *Theology of John's Gospel*, 167–68).
[45] For further exploration of the prologue, see R. Alan Culpepper, "The Pivot of John's Gospel," *NTS* 27 (1980): 1–31; Smalley, *John*, 135–39;
[46] Köstenberger, *John*, 27.
[47] Keener, *Gospel of John*, 360.
[48] See discussion in ibid., 333–34; and Carson, *Gospel according to John*, 111–12.
[49] Köstenberger, *Theology of John's Gospel*, 329–35, argues that the cleansing of the temple (2:13–22) is also a sign, making the total seven (with the raising of Lazarus the climactic seventh). Dodd, *Interpretation of the Fourth Gospel*, 297–389, suggests that the walking on water (6:16–21) is the seventh sign, while Smalley, *John*, suggests that the seventh is the miraculous catch of fish (21:1–14).
[50] E.g., R. T. Fortna, *The Gospel of Signs* (Cambridge: Cambridge University Press, 1970); Bultmann, *Gospel of John*, 698; W. Nicole, *The Semeia in the Fourth Gospel: Tradition and Redaction* (Leiden: Brill, 1972).
[51] Köstenberger, *Theology of John's Gospel*, 326.

The "Book of the Passion" (John 13:1–20:31) focuses largely on Christ's final week and the extended teachings sections that surround it. The fact that John does not include the institution of the Lord's Supper (13:1–19) has made some scholars suggest that John has intentionally disassociated the meal from the Passover feast so that Jesus can be portrayed as dying the next day simultaneously with the Passover lambs.[52] However, John's omission need not be taken as a rejection of the Last Supper, but merely reflects a desire to focus on Jesus's act of foot washing and his distinctive teachings in the Upper Room Discourse (13:1–14:31).[53] The "Book of the Passion" also includes other cherished teachings that are distinctive to John's Gospel, including the Garden Discourse (15:1–16:33), and, of course, the High Priestly Prayer (17:1–26). As we shall see below, many of John's unique theological contributions can be found within these important blocks of teaching.

The epilogue (John 21:1–25) has occasioned an abundance of scholarly activity, particularly concerning whether this chapter was added at a later date.[54] On the surface, one can understand why it might look like John has two endings; 20:30–31 would certainly constitute a reasonable ending to the book. But it must not be forgotten that epilogues were not uncommon in antiquity, and, by definition, they were designed to look separate from the main body of the work.[55] In addition, scholars have shown that there is impressive interconnectivity between the epilogue and the rest of John, again suggesting that there is no reason to posit some later redactor as its source.[56] Indeed, the epilogue provides the proper literary balance to a book that begins with such a distinctive prologue. One should also be cautious in reading too much into the use of the first-person plural "we" in 21:24. While some have suggested it is the leaders of the Johannine community who are placing their endorsement on the book,[57] Bauckham has recently argued that this is "the 'we' of authoritative testimony," a literary device designed to bolster the authority of the speaker, and not an indication of a plurality of authors.[58]

Within this larger fourfold structure the reader quickly observes that the structure of the individual stories of Jesus is also distinctive. While the standard stories of Jesus in the Synoptics are relatively brief and often concluded by a pithy saying, John's stories are typically longer and more detailed, sometimes covering entire chapters (e.g., Jesus and the Samaritan woman [John 4]; the man born blind [John 9]; the death and resurrection of Lazarus [John 11]). Such a structural reality has implications for how John's Gospel might be preached or taught. While a sermon series in the Synoptics might naturally devote a single sermon to each brief pericope, a sermon series in John would want to consider taking larger chunks of material.

[52] Bart D. Ehrman, *The New Testament: A Historical Introduction to the Early Christian Writings*, 4th ed. (New York: Oxford University Press, 2008), 63–64.

[53] For a discussion of chronological issues regarding the time of the Last Supper, see Barry D. Smith, "The Chronology of the Last Supper," *WTJ* 53 (1991): 29–45.

[54] E.g., Raymond E. Brown, *The Gospel according to John XIII–XXI* (New York: Doubleday, 1970), 1078; C. H. Roberts, "John 20:30–31 and 21:24–25," *JTS* 38 (1987): 409–10.

[55] Köstenberger, *John*, 583.

[56] Herman Ridderbos, *The Gospel of John* (Grand Rapids, MI: Eerdmans, 1997), 656–58; Keener, *Gospel of John*, 1219–22.

[57] J. Chapman, "We Know That His Testimony Is True," *JTS* 31 (1930): 379–87.

[58] Bauckham, *Jesus and the Eyewitnesses*, 370–83.

Such an approach would allow each story to be viewed as a complete narrative and would keep the sermon series from getting bogged down in repetition.[59]

Message and Theology

John's theology is so rich and multifaceted that a brief introduction such as this could never cover all its aspects. But standing at the center of John's theology is the person of Jesus. As George Beasley-Murray put it, "The theme of the Fourth Gospel is Christ."[60] While the same certainly could be said of the Synoptic Gospels, John offers a unique and compelling vision of Jesus that can be articulated under three headings: (1) Christ as the one and only God (christology); (2) Christ as the bringer of new life (soteriology); and (3) Christ as the fulfillment of the Old Testament (biblical theology).

Christ as the One and Only God (Christology)

It has long been observed that John, even more plainly than the other Gospels, identifies Jesus with the one true God of Israel. John makes this identification in a number of different ways.

First, John affirms that Jesus is the very *Creator* of the world. This motif begins in the very opening line of the Gospel, "In the beginning was the Word" (John 1:1).[61] This language intentionally directs the reader back to the original creation account—"In the beginning, *God*" (Gen. 1:1)—but John has placed the Word (Jesus) in the role of God.[62] As such, Jesus is presented not as a creature, but as the very Creator of the world: "All things were made through him" (John 1:3). Just as God brings life and light in Genesis, Jesus is the bringer of life (John 1:4) and the one who brings light out of darkness (1:5).[63] This backdrop provided by the prologue offers the proper context for seeing how other miracles in John's Gospel—changing the water to wine (2:1–11), feeding the five thousand (6:1–14), walking on water (6:16–21), the miraculous catch of fish (21:4–8)—are reflections of Jesus as the Creator of the world. Moreover, the description from John 20:22 in which Jesus "breathed" new life into the disciples through a symbolic giving of the Spirit (more on this below) is a vivid echo of Genesis 2:7, where God initially breathed life into Adam.[64] Thus, John 1:1–4 and John 20:22 form a creation-themed *inclusio* in the Gospel of John that presents Jesus as both the Creator of physical life and the Creator of new (spiritual) life.

Second, John consistently presents Jesus as the *Son of God*[65]—so much so, that Rudolf Schnackenburg was able to declare, "The 'Father-Son' relationship is a key

[59] Carson, *Gospel according to John*, 102.
[60] George Beasley-Murray, *John*, WBC 36 (Waco, TX: Word, 1987), lxxxi.
[61] For discussion of how the *Logos* language reflects Jewish wisdom tradition, see James D. G. Dunn, "Let John Be John: A Gospel for Its Time," in *The Gospel and the Gospels*, ed. Peter Stuhlmacher (Grand Rapids, MI: Eerdmans, 1991), 293–322.
[62] Richard Bauckham, "Monotheism and Christology in the Gospel of John," in *Contours of Christology in the New Testament*, ed. Richard N. Longenecker (Grand Rapids, MI: Eerdmans, 2005), 153–63, esp. 149–51. See also Beasley-Murray, *John*, 10; Morris, *Gospel according to John*, 64–65.
[63] Morris, *Gospel according to John*, 65–66.
[64] Both John 20:22 and Gen. 2:7 use the Greek term ἐνεφύσησεν ("he breathed [up]on").
[65] See discussion of John's use of this title in Leon Morris, *New Testament Theology* (Grand Rapids, MI: Zondervan, 1990), 232–34; and Smalley, *John*, 243–44.

to the understanding of Jesus as portrayed by the Evangelist, and of his words and actions as interpreted by him."[66] The theme of Jesus as "Son" dominates the Gospel, and the term υἱός refers to Jesus forty-one times. Likewise, Jesus regularly refers to God as "Father" in the Gospel of John; indeed, the term πατήρ occurs on his lips more than one hundred times. The unique status of Jesus's sonship is emphasized in numerous ways: (1) Jesus is often referred to as the μονογενὴς υἱός or "only Son" (e.g., John 1:14, 18; 3:16, 18), showing that he has a special relationship with the Father that is not true of any other being.[67] The fact that 1:18 also refers to Jesus with the unique combination of μονογενὴς θεὸς ("the only [Son], who is God"),[68] shows that the phrases μονογενὴς θεὸς and μονογενὴς υἱός are basically interchangeable.[69] (2) Over twenty times Jesus refers to God as "*my* Father" (e.g., 2:16; 5:17, 43; 6:32, 40; 8:19, 38, 49, 54; 10:18, 25, 29), implying again a unique relationship between the two.[70] This allows Jesus to make statements about how he is working just as his Father is working (5:17), and about how he and the Father are one (10:30; cf. 10:38), both of which cause the Jews to try to kill him because he is "calling God his own Father, making himself equal with God" (5:18; cf. 10:33).[71] (3) In the High Priestly Prayer, Jesus refers to his special relationship with the Father as one that existed "before the world existed" (17:5). This passage is yet another echo of the prologue and shows that Jesus's sonship does not begin at his baptism or his resurrection, but it is an eternal sonship that goes back to the beginning of all things. Thus, Jesus's status as "Son of God" is really another way (or even the main way) of articulating his status as the Logos of God (1:1). Jesus is the "Logos-Son."[72]

Third, John presents Jesus, along with the Father, as the *sender of the Holy Spirit*. Not only does John frequently use the language of "Son" to refer to Jesus, and "Father" to refer to God; he then offers extensive teaching on the role of the Holy Spirit (see esp. John 14–16).[73] Here is where we enter into some remarkable Trinitarian themes.[74] Just as the Son and the Father are presented as fully divine, the Spirit (or "Helper," παράκλητος) also bears divine attributes. For one, he is sent by both the Son and the Father: John 14:26 tells us that "the Father will send" the Holy Spirit in Jesus's name, and in 15:26 Jesus says, "*I* will send [the Holy Spirit] to you from the Father" (cf. 16:7; 20:22).[75] Thus, there is clearly a complex, mutually interfacing

[66] Schnackenburg, *Gospel according to St. John*, 2:172.
[67] The term has engendered much debate but is best understood not as "only begotten" but as "one of a kind," or perhaps "beloved." See Keener, *Gospel of John*, 412–14; Köstenberger, *John*, 43; Carson, *Gospel according to John*, 128.
[68] There is even a text-critical debate over whether 1:18 originally read μονογενὴς υἱός ("only Son") or μονογενὴς θεὸς ("only [Son] who is God"). However, in addition to superior external support (𝔭[66] and 𝔭[75]), internal considerations also favor the latter reading, particularly the fact that it is the more difficult reading and forms a natural *inclusio* with 1:1. Köstenberger, *John*, 49, argues rightly that μονογενὴς is likely being used substantively ("only [Son]") and that θεός is in apposition ("who is God").
[69] It is worth observing that 1:18 has additional indicators of a close Father-Son relationship, as Jesus is described as being in τὸν κόλπον (literally, the "bosom") of the Father, which has connotations of being on his Father's "lap."
[70] For discussions of the Father-Son theme in John, see Thomas Schreiner, *New Testament Theology: Magnifying God in Christ* (Grand Rapids, MI: Baker Academic, 2008), 240–46; and Morris, *New Testament Theology*, 248–50.
[71] Bauckham, "Monotheism and Christology," 152–53.
[72] Dunn, "Let John Be John," 319.
[73] Morris, *New Testament Theology*, 256–65; George Eldon Ladd, *A Theology of the New Testament*, ed. Donald A Hagner, rev. ed. (Grand Rapids, MI: Eerdmans, 1993), 322–33.
[74] For more on this important issue, see Andreas J. Köstenberger and Scott R. Swain, *Father, Son, and Spirit: The Trinity and John's Gospel* (Downers Grove, IL: InterVarsity Press, 2008).
[75] Smalley, *John*, 257–62.

relationship between the Father, Son, and Holy Spirit. Moreover, the Spirit is identified with the ministry of Jesus by virtue of the fact that he is called *another* Helper like Jesus (14:16), he will be with his people forever (14:16), his presence is equivalent to the presence of Jesus (14:18), and his purpose is to bring glory to Jesus (16:14). At the end of John's Gospel, Jesus also brings a symbolic (or pre-) Pentecost when we are told that "he breathed on them and said to them, 'Receive the Holy Spirit'" (20:22; cf. 7:38–39).[76]

Fourth, John highlights the divine nature of Jesus through a series of *"I am" statements* that are unique to his writings. These statements are noteworthy because they are Jesus's own self-declarations, describing his nature and purpose. Although not all deal directly with Jesus's divinity, they all have implications for the way we understand his identity. John contains seven such statements, each followed by a predicate nominative: Jesus is the Bread of Life (6:35, 41); the Light of the World (8:12; 9:5); the gate to the sheep (10:7); the Good Shepherd (10:11); the resurrection and the life (11:25); the way, the truth, and the life (14:6); and the true Vine (15:1, 5). The number seven is certainly significant on a symbolic level and often speaks of completeness or fullness. The seven "I am" sayings can therefore be seen as a full-orbed revelation of Jesus as both God and Savior.[77] The fact that there are seven "I am" sayings is noteworthy because it forms a parallel with the (potentially) seven signs in the Gospel of John, as discussed above. Indeed, some of these signs correspond directly with some of the "I am" sayings. For instance, when Jesus feeds the five thousand, he announces, "I am the bread of life" (6:35); in the chapter when Jesus heals the man born blind, he declares, "I am the light of the world" (9:5); and when Jesus raises Lazarus from the dead, he declares, "I am the resurrection and the life" (11:25).

Of course, it should not be overlooked that John also uses the phrase "I am" (ἐγὼ εἰμί) in an absolute sense, without a predicate. There are also seven instances in which the phrase is used in this manner.[78] While some of the absolute instances of "I am" can be taken in the ordinary sense (e.g., 4:26 could simply mean "I am [he]"), there are good reasons to think that others refer quite directly to the divine identity of Jesus. This is particularly evident in John 8:58, where Jesus declares, "Before Abraham was, I am [ἐγὼ εἰμί]," and the Jews "picked up stones to throw at him" (8:59). There also appear to be implications for the divine identity of Jesus in 18:6 when Jesus says, "I am [he]," and the soldiers "drew back and fell to the ground." The Old Testament background for these absolute "I am" statements is possibly found in God's own self-declaration in Exodus 3:14 when he declares, "I AM WHO I AM." However, other passages form a more likely background, such as Deuteronomy 32:39, "See now that I, even I, am he [LXX ἐγὼ εἰμί], / and there is no god beside me," and Isaiah 41:4, "I, the LORD, the first, / and with the last; I am he [LXX ἐγὼ εἰμί]." Similar statements are found all throughout Isaiah 40–55 (e.g., 43:10, 13, 25; 46:4; 48:12; 51:12; 52:6).

[76] For discussion of the complexities of this passage, see Carson, *Gospel according to John*, 649–55.
[77] Bauckham, "Monotheism and Christology," 153–54.
[78] John 4:26; 6:20; 8:24; 8:28; 8:58; 13:19; 18:5–6, 8. There are seven "I am" sayings without a predicate if 18:5–6, 8 is taken naturally as a single unit.

For some scholars, John's christological vision stands in conflict with first-century Jewish monotheism.[79] However, there are no indications that John viewed the divine identity of Jesus as something that contradicted Judaism. On the contrary, John presents Jesus within a robust monotheistic framework. By describing Jesus as the λόγος in the opening verses (John 1:1, 14), he intentionally presents Jesus in a category already familiar to Jews, namely, God's powerful Word (Ps. 33:6).[80] Indeed, by presenting Jesus as the Creator (the "Word") in the book of Genesis, John is not contradicting Jewish monotheism, but affirming it: only the one true God created all things.[81] Moreover, as we have seen, the "I am" declarations in the Gospel of John are largely set against the backdrop of Isaiah 40–55, passages that are richly monotheistic as God asserts his unique deity over against the false gods of the nations. Even Jesus's declarations that he and the Father are "one" (John 10:30; 17:11, 22) are, according to Bauckham, an echo of the most fundamental monotheistic claims in Judaism, namely, the *Shema* in Deuteronomy 6:4: "Hear, O Israel: The LORD our God, the LORD is one."[82]

As we consider each of the major theological loci in the Gospel of John, it is worth pausing to briefly consider its implications on preaching through the book. If, as we have just seen, the Gospel of John is keen to portray Jesus as the one and only God of Israel, then there will be ample opportunity throughout a preaching series to emphasize the following:

1. *The power of Christ*. Congregations can be encouraged by the reminder that Christ—as the ruler, Creator, and Lord of the universe—is powerful enough to protect and sustain his people.
2. *The worship of Christ*. Congregations will come face-to-face with the glory, wonder, and beauty of Christ, and this can draw them into renewed worship of Christ.
3. *The lordship of Christ*. If Christ is the one true God, then he calls us to follow him as his disciples in faithful obedience.

All of this can be summarized by saying that the christological focus in the Gospel of John allows a sermon series to be characterized by (among other things) a focus on Jesus as *King*.

Christ as the Bringer of New Life (Soteriology)

Inasmuch as the prior section focused on how John presents Jesus as the Creator of life (Gen. 1:1; John 1:1), this section will focus upon how John presents Jesus as the

[79] Maurice Casey, *From Jewish Prophet to Gentile God: The Origins and Development of New Testament Christology* (Cambridge: Clarke, 1991). For more on first-century Jewish monotheism, see Larry W. Hurtado, *One God, One Lord: Early Christian Devotion and Ancient Jewish Monotheism*, 2nd ed. (Edinburgh: T&T Clark, 2003); the collection of essays in Hurtado, *How on Earth Did Jesus Become a God? Historical Questions about Earliest Devotion to Jesus* (Grand Rapids, MI: Eerdmans, 2005); and Richard Bauckham, *Jesus and the God of Israel: God Crucified and Other Studies on the New Testament's Christology of Divine Identity*, rev. ed. (Grand Rapids, MI: Eerdmans, 2009); Köstenberger and Swain, *Father, Son, and Spirit*, 27–44.
[80] Dunn, "Let John Be John," 319.
[81] Bauckham, "Monotheism and Christology," 151.
[82] Ibid.

Creator of *new* life (John 1:4; 3:16), the one who brings redemption and salvation. While the Synoptic Gospels also portray Jesus as Savior, John largely does so through a unique combination of contrasting statements, or what is often called Johannine "dualism."[83] While the contrasts in the Synoptics tend to be horizontal, a contrast between two ages (this age and the age to come), John's contrasts tend to be vertical, a contrast between the world above and the world below. Of course, this is not to suggest that John has no horizontal dualism, because it does (e.g., 5:25–29); nor does it suggest that the Synoptics entirely lack vertical dualism, because they do not (e.g., Matt. 19:29). It merely suggests that John's dualism is decidedly on the vertical side of the spectrum. This sort of dualism has been regarded by many scholars as reflective of Gnostic or Greek philosophy,[84] but the discovery of the Qumran materials has made it clear that it was not uncommon in a first-century Jewish context.[85]

The first of these Johannine contrasts is *light and darkness*. From the very beginning of John's Gospel, we are told that the mission of Jesus is to bring light to a world filled with darkness: "The light shines in the darkness, and the darkness has not overcome it" (1:5). While this passage echoes the literal creation of light and darkness in Genesis, John uses it figuratively to represent the cosmic battle in the universe between God and Satan, or between good and evil.[86] As the one who brings light into the world, Jesus is presented by John as a Redeemer and Savior who delivers his people from the darkness. The "vertical" nature of this contrast is evident from the fact that Jesus comes *into* the world (from heaven) for the purpose of bringing light (1:9). Thus, Jesus can declare about himself (and his mission), "I am the light of the world" (9:5). Whoever is a follower of truth will embrace the light that Christ brings (3:21; cf. 8:12), but whoever pursues wickedness will hate the light because it exposes their evil deeds (3:19–20). Followers of Christ are thus called "sons of light" (12:36) and "will not walk in darkness" (8:12).

A second instance of this Johannine dualism is *life and death*. In the same way that the prologue teaches that Jesus brought light into the world (1:5), it also teaches that "in him was life" (1:4). As Creator, Jesus is the consummate life giver, both physically and spiritually. John 5:21 tells us that, "as the Father raises the dead and gives them life, so also the Son gives life to whom he will" (cf. 5:26). Similarly, Jesus expresses his life-giving identity in one of his "I am" statements: "I am the way, and the truth, and the life" (14:6). Thus, in John's Gospel, Jesus is the bringer of new life, or "eternal life,"[87] to a world that is marred by death; he has come to roll back the effects of the curse. Indeed, the most well-known passage in John (and arguably the entire Bible)

[83] J. Ashton, *Understanding the Fourth Gospel* (Oxford: Clarendon, 1991), 205–37; W. Hall Harris, "Polarization in Johannine Theology," in *A Biblical Theology of the New Testament*, ed. Roy B. Zuck (Chicago: Moody Press, 1994), 203–12; Warren Carter, *John: Storyteller, Interpreter, Evangelist* (Peabody, MA: Hendrickson, 2006), 86–106.
[84] Rudolf Bultmann, *Theology of the New Testament*, trans. Kendrick Grobel, vol. 2 (New York: Charles Scribner's Sons, 1951), 17–21.
[85] See helpful discussion in Ladd, *A Theology of the New Testament*, 268–72; and David E. Aune, "Dualism in the Fourth Gospel and the Dead Sea Scrolls: A Reassessment of the Problem," in Neotestamentica et Philonica*: Studies in Honor of Peder Borgen*, ed. David E. Aune, Torrey Seland, and Jarl Henning (Leiden: Brill, 2003), 281–303.
[86] For more on light symbolism, see Dodd, *Interpretation of the Fourth Gospel*, 201–8; and Keener, *Gospel of John*, 382–85. The Old Testament often uses light in a symbolic way; e.g., Num. 24:17; Pss. 19:8; 119:105; Isa. 9:2; 42:6–7; 60:1–5; Mal. 4:2.
[87] Keener, *Gospel of John*, 328, argues that "life," for the most part, means "eternal life" in John's Gospel. See also, Dodd, *Interpretation of the Fourth Gospel*, 144–50.

contrasts life and death: "For God so loved the world, that he gave his only Son, that whoever believes in him should not perish but have eternal life" (3:16). Even the stated purpose of John's Gospel is "that you may believe that Jesus is the Christ, the Son of God, and that by believing you may have life in his name" (20:31). Thus, for John, eternal life can be a *present* reality, something the Christian can begin to enjoy here and now (10:10).[88] This stands in contrast to the popular Synoptic theme of the kingdom of God which tends to focus on a *future* divine in-breaking. John has, in some sense, replaced the focus on the kingdom of God with a focus on eternal life, though he does touch the kingdom theme on occasion (e.g., 1:49; 3:3; 6:14; 18:36).[89]

A third Johannine contrast is *earthly and heavenly*.[90] One of Jesus's favorite pedagogical techniques in John's Gospel is to take earthly realities and compare them to heavenly ones—and then to draw out a salvific message from that comparison. For instance, he calls Nicodemus not just to be born in a physical, earthly manner, but to be born again, or born from above (3:3). Similarly, Jesus asks the Samaritan woman not to be content only with earthly water from the well, but to drink "living water" that only Jesus can bring (4:10), water welling up to eternal life (4:14).[91] And, again, Jesus calls the people not to content themselves with earthly "food that perishes" (6:27), but instead to eat of the "bread that came down from heaven" (6:41, 51) so that they might "live forever" (6:51).[92] In each of these instances, Jesus reminds his listeners that eternal life is found not in earthly realities (birth, water, bread) but in heavenly ones that only he himself can provide (new birth, living water, bread of life). Jesus always presents *himself* as the means of salvation; the earth-heaven contrast is used to show how he has come down to earth to redeem those who are lost.

In the midst of many of these salvation-oriented contrasts, it should be noted that the sovereignty of God in redemption is often emphasized in John's Gospel. When Jesus mentions to Nicodemus that a person must be born of the Spirit to enter the kingdom of God, he also emphasizes that the work of the Spirit cannot be controlled or determined by men; it is like the wind and "blows where it wishes" (3:8). New birth is being born "not of blood nor of the will of the flesh nor of the will of man, but of God" (1:13). It is solely and entirely an act of God. Reminiscent of the valley of dry bones in Ezekiel 37, the lost are lifeless until God acts by his Spirit to breathe new life into them.[93] Likewise, John 5:21 highlights the sovereignty of Christ in salvation: "The Son gives life *to whom he will*." Although faith is the instrument by which new life is received, Christ "chooses those to whom he gives life."[94] As Jesus reminds his disciples elsewhere, "You did not choose me, but I chose you" (15:16).

---

[88] It should be noted, however, that John does have a future eschatology as well. See discussions in Schreiner, *New Testament Theology*, 84–90.

[89] Keener, *Gospel of John*, 328. For discussion of possible reasons for John's shift in emphasis, see Köstenberger, *Theology of John's Gospel*, 285–86.

[90] Depending how this contrast is construed, it could also be called a contrast between *flesh and spirit* (e.g., John 6:63).

[91] For more on water symbolism, see L. P. Jones, *The Symbol of Water in the Gospel of John* (Sheffield: Sheffield Academic, 1997). Other "water" passages in John include 3:5; 7:37–39; 9:6–7. The Old Testament background to many of these Johannine references can be found in passages like Ps. 78:16; Isa. 12:3; 44:3; 55:1; Ezek. 36:25–27; Joel 2:28–29; etc.

[92] For more discussion of bread imagery in the Gospel of John, see R. Alan Culpepper, *Anatomy of the Fourth Gospel* (Philadelphia: Fortress, 1983), 195–97.

[93] Carson, *Gospel according to John*, 198, argues that John 3:8 may be echoing Ezekiel 37.

[94] Ibid., 253.

This theme of Christ's sovereignty in salvation, particularly the doctrine of election, is made most explicit in the Bread of Life Discourse in John 6. Here Jesus declares that "all that the Father gives me will come to me" (6:37), implying not only that Christ has been given a distinct and particular set of people, but also that none of *those* people will be lost (cf. 6:39). Although some reject him, Jesus explains this reality not by an appeal to free will, but by stating, "No one can come to me unless the Father who sent me draws him" (6:44; cf. 6:65). Thus, Jesus affirms the foundational truth of the doctrine of election, namely, that people, on their own, are unable to choose God, and therefore God must first choose them and draw them to himself.

In regard to preaching through the Gospel of John, the truth that Jesus is Savior allows for a congregation to consider a number of key themes:

1. *The darkness of the world and our own hearts.* One of the major emphases in the Gospel of John is that we are in darkness, bound for death, and in desperate need of a Savior—without the Son, we are "condemned already" (3:18).[95]
2. *The grace of Christ.* In the midst of our rebellion, Christ was willing to leave heaven and the Father's side to enter our world as the true light, to endure rejection, and to bring us eternal life.
3. *The sufficiency of Christ.* Christ not only saves, but saves fully and to the uttermost. He is the water that leaves us without thirst; he is the bread that fully satisfies and does not leave us hungry.

All of these points can be summarized by saying that the soteriological focus in the Gospel of John allows a sermon series to be characterized by (among other things) a focus on Jesus as *Priest*.

Christ as the Fulfillment of the Old Testament (Biblical Theology)

While John is certainly concerned to proclaim the story of Jesus, he does not present that story as merely something that occurred in his own day, but he presents it as something that completes a much bigger and older story. For John, Jesus is not just a present-day means to "be saved," but the culmination and fulfillment of the long history of Israel that God began two thousand years before. Thus, John's Gospel is *redemptive-historical* in its outlook; it is always eager to place Jesus within the larger context of God's saving activity.[96] This outlook fits quite well with what is likely John's primary audience (as discussed above), namely, Jews or Jewish Christians struggling to understand the identity of the Messiah. John places the work of Jesus in its redemptive-historical context by showing that Jesus is the fulfillment of (1) the temple, (2) the festivals, and (3) Israel's history. Let us consider these one at a time.

First, Jesus presents himself as the fulfillment of the *temple itself*.[97] Raymond Collins

[95] For a discussion of sin, death, and darkness in John, see R. Alan Culpepper, *The Gospel and Letters of John*, Interpreting Biblical Texts (Nashville: Abingdon, 1998), 89–92.

[96] Oscar Cullmann, *Salvation in History* (London: SCM, 1967), 268–91.

[97] Discussions of the temple motif in John can be found in R. J. McKelvey, *The New Temple: The Church in the New Testament* (Oxford: Oxford University Press, 1969), 75–84; Paul M. Hoskins, *Jesus as the Fulfillment of the Temple in the Gospel of John* (Carlisle: Paternoster, 2007); Mark Kinzer, "Temple Christology in the Gospel of John," *SBL Seminar Papers* 37 (1998): 447–64; and Mary L. Coloe, *God Dwells with Us: Temple Symbolism in the Fourth Gospel* (Collegeville, MN: Liturgical, 2001).

observes, "That Jesus is the replacement of the Temple is, in fact, one of the principal themes in the Fourth Gospel."[98] We find the beginnings of this theme in the prologue, where John declares that the Word became flesh and "dwelt" (ἐσκήνωσεν) among us (1:14). This term literally means "pitch a tent" and is an indicator that the Word, who is God, has come to "tabernacle" with his people in such a way that they "beheld his glory."[99] This act of Jesus thus fulfills the very purpose of the tabernacle (or temple), namely, God's glory dwelling with his people (compare John 1:14 and Ex. 40:34–35).[100] This fits remarkably well with John 1:17, which contrasts the period of Moses (and the earthly temple) and the period of Jesus (the new temple). Even more explicitly, Jesus links himself with the temple when he cleanses it (2:13–17) and then declares, "Destroy this temple, and in three days I will raise it up" (2:19), clearly referring to his own body (2:21).[101] Commenting on this passage, Herman Ridderbos observes that Jesus "is also the temple that will replace the existing temple and in whom the indwelling of God among people will be truly and fully realized."[102] In both of these passages, John is highlighting the fact that in Jesus a new age of redemptive history has arrived—no longer do men draw near to God by drawing near to a physical building (which is soon to be destroyed); they now draw near to God by drawing near to Jesus. For this reason, Jesus is able to tell the Samaritan woman that the location of worship is no longer preeminent: "The hour is coming when neither on this mountain nor in Jerusalem will you worship the Father. . . . But the hour is coming, and is now here, when true worshipers will worship the Father in spirit and truth" (4:21–23).[103] This emphasis on Jesus as the new temple fits well with the suggested historical setting for the Gospel (discussed above), where Jews and Jewish Christians were struggling to understand the significance of the destruction of the temple in AD 70.

Second, and closely related to Jesus's fulfillment of the temple, is that John presents Jesus as the fulfillment of *Israel's festivals*. Such festivals prove to be more prominent in John because it focuses more on Judea and therefore records three trips to Jerusalem, whereas the Synoptics tend to focus mainly on Galilee and therefore record only one trip to Jerusalem. With such a focus on Jerusalem, there is little surprise that Jesus is seen as the fulfillment of the Passover. From the very first chapter, John the Baptist makes it plain that Jesus is "the Lamb of God, who takes away the sin of the world" (1:29), a uniquely Johannine statement that clearly refers to the lambs slaughtered during the Passover feast.[104] This connection is confirmed elsewhere when John observes that the legs of Jesus were not broken during the crucifixion, "that

[98] Raymond F. Collins, *These Things Have Been Written: Studies on the Fourth Gospel* (Grand Rapids, MI: Eerdmans, 1990), 209.
[99] Ibid., 198–209.
[100] Morris, *Gospel According to John*, 91–92.
[101] See the discussion in Köstenberger, *Theology of John's Gospel*, 427–29. The fact that John moves the temple cleansing to the front of his Gospel (cf. Matt. 21:12–17; Mark 11:15–19; Luke 19:45–48) is a further indication that the Jesus-as-the-temple theme is central.
[102] Ridderbos, *Gospel of John*, 120.
[103] Collins, *These Things Have Been Written*, 212–13. Other passages that likely portray Jesus as the fulfillment of the temple include John 10:7 (Jesus is the "door" to the temple); 11:48 (Jesus fulfills "the place" of the Jews); and 12:41 (Jesus is the glory of the temple as seen in Isa. 6:1–7).
[104] There are also possible allusions to the suffering servant in Isaiah 53, which describes "a lamb that is led to the slaughter" (53:7).

the Scripture might be fulfilled: 'Not one of his bones will be broken'" (19:36)—a quotation from Exodus 12:46 regarding the preparation of the Passover lamb. The fact that Jesus refers to his own sacrificial death while standing in the temple during the Passover feast (John 2:19–21) is another inescapable allusion to Jesus as the Passover Lamb. In addition, Jesus is also presented by John as fulfilling the Feast of Tabernacles (or Booths). During each day of this feast, the high priest led a procession from the Pool of Siloam to the temple, carrying a golden flagon of water, which was then poured out in celebration and in hope of the future blessings of God.[105] John tells us that on the last day of this feast, Jesus stood and declared, "If anyone thirsts, let him come to me and drink. Whoever believes in me, as the Scripture has said, 'Out of his heart will flow rivers of living water'" (7:37–38). In this stunning statement, Jesus indicates that he is the fulfillment and completion of the Feast of Tabernacles—only through him can a person have rivers of living water flowing through him or her, a clear reference to the promise of the Holy Spirit (7:39). Regardless of which feasts Jesus fulfilled (and there were others[106]), the message of John is the same: all of these Old Testament institutions pointed toward, and find their realization in, the person of Jesus.

Third, John presents Jesus as the fulfillment of *Israel's history*. In a remarkable hermeneutical move, John makes it clear that even historical events within the nation of Israel, and not just explicit prophecies, pointed toward the coming Messiah. Jesus tells the skeptical Nathanael, "You will see heaven opened, and the angels of God ascending and descending on the Son of Man" (1:51), a vivid allusion to Jacob's dream of a "ladder" reaching up to heaven (Gen. 28:12). Jesus is the ultimate ladder, or connection between heaven and earth, to which Jacob's dream pointed.[107] Similarly, Jesus reminds Nicodemus of how Moses lifted up a bronze serpent so that the people might be delivered from the fiery serpents that were attacking them (Num. 21:4–10), and Jesus then declares that this historical event is fulfilled in his own life: "So must the Son of Man be lifted up, that whoever believes in him may have eternal life" (John 3:14–15). In another example, Jesus recalls Israel's desert wanderings and how Moses provided "bread from heaven" (6:32; cf. Ex. 16:15–35), but then connects this event to himself, claiming, "I am the living bread that came down from heaven" (John 6:51). More examples could be provided, but the point of all of these accounts is the same. Jesus is interpreting the Old Testament stories in such a way that all of the Old Testament speaks of him, both prophetic portions and historical portions.

In any sermon series through the Gospel of John, this redemptive-historical perspective allows for a discussion of the following implications:

---

[105] M. Sukkah 4:9–10; Lev. 23:33–43; Num. 29:12–39; Zech. 14:16–19. For more, see J. L. Rubenstein, *The History of Sukkot in the Second Temple and Rabbinic Periods* (Atlanta: Scholar's, 1995).

[106] Although not a feast, the miracle of changing the water into wine (2:1–12) is no doubt a statement that the old Jewish purification system is now obsolete and the new kingdom of the Messiah (marked by new wine) has come. For discussion, see Ladd, *Theology of the New Testament*, 267.

[107] Collins, *These Things Have Been Written*, 209–10, views this story as another instance where Jesus fulfills the temple/tabernacle, since Jacob's vision took place at Bethel, the location of Israel's primitive sanctuary.

1. *The importance of the Old Testament*. John teaches us that we cannot really understand the story of Jesus without understanding the story of Israel; Jesus is not the beginning of a new story as much as the completion of an old one.
2. *The temporary nature of Israel's infrastructure*. John reminds us that the religious infrastructure of Israel was not permanent, but merely anticipatory of a day when it would be realized; thus we should not seek a return to the time of the temple and festivals, but we should now find the reality in Jesus himself.
3. *Christ in the Old Testament*. John reminds us that *all* the Old Testament, and not just the prophetic portions, is ultimately about Jesus. As Jesus declared elsewhere, "Everything written about me in the Law of Moses and the Prophets and the Psalms must be fulfilled" (Luke 24:44).

All of these implications, inasmuch as they are about Jesus pronouncing the fulfillment of God's word, can be summarized by saying that Jesus is our great *Prophet*. He is the full and final revealer of God's redemptive plan.

When these theological themes—Christ as the one and only God, Christ as the bringer of new life, and Christ as the fulfillment of the Old Testament—are viewed in tandem, we recognize that they capture the three offices of Christ as Prophet, Priest, and King. Thus, if one preaches the main themes of John's Gospel, then that sermon series will capture all of Christ's offices in a balanced and multifaceted manner.

Select Bibliography

Anderson, Paul. *The Fourth Gospel and the Quest for Jesus: Modern Foundations Reconsidered*. London: T&T Clark, 2006.

Ashton, J. *Understanding the Fourth Gospel*. Oxford: Clarendon, 1991.

Aune, David E. "Dualism in the Fourth Gospel and the Dead Sea Scrolls: A Reassessment of the Problem." In Neotestamentica et Philonica: *Studies in Honor of Peder Borgen*, edited by David E. Aune, Torrey Seland, and Jarl Henning, 281–303. Leiden: Brill, 2003.

Barrett, C. Kingsley. *The Gospel according to John*. London: SPCK, 1978.

Bauckham, Richard, ed. *The Gospels for All Christians: Rethinking the Gospel Audiences*. Grand Rapids, MI: Eerdmans, 1998.

———. "Historiographical Characteristics of the Gospel of John." *NTS* 53 (2007): 17–36.

———. *Jesus and the Eyewitnesses: The Gospels as Eyewitness Testimony*. Grand Rapids, MI: Eerdmans, 2006.

———. *Jesus and the God of Israel: God Crucified and Other Studies on the New Testament's Christology of Divine Identity*. Rev. ed. Grand Rapids, MI: Eerdmans, 2009.

———. "John for Readers of Mark." In *The Gospels for All Christians: Rethinking the Gospel Audiences*, edited by Richard Bauckham, 147–71. Grand Rapids, MI: Eerdmans, 1998.

———. "Monotheism and Christology in the Gospel of John." In *Contours of Christology in the New Testament*, edited by Richard N. Longenecker, 153–63. Grand Rapids, MI: Eerdmans, 2005.

Baum, Armin D. "The Anonymity of the New Testament History Books: A Stylistic Device in the Context of Greco-Roman and Ancient Near Eastern Literature." *NovT* 50 (2008): 120–42.

Beasley-Murray, George. *John*. WBC 36. Waco, TX: Word, 1987.

Bernard, J. H. *A Critical and Exegetical Commentary on the Gospel according to St. John*. Edinburgh: T&T Clark, 1928.

Blomberg, Craig. *The Historical Reliability of John's Gospel: Issues and Commentary*. Downers Grove, IL: InterVarsity Press, 2001.

Bock, Darrell L. "The Words of Jesus in the Gospels: Live, Jive, or Memorex?" In *Jesus under Fire*, edited by Michael J. Wilkins and J. P. Moreland, 74–99. Grand Rapids, MI: Zondervan, 1995.

Brown, Raymond E. *The Gospel according to John XIII–XXI*. AB 29. New York: Doubleday, 1970.

Bultmann, Rudolf. *The Gospel of John: A Commentary*. Philadelphia: Westminster Press, 1971.

———. *Primitive Christianity in Its Contemporary Setting*. London: Thames and Hudson, 1956.

———. *Theology of the New Testament*. Translated by Kendrick Grobel. Vol. 2. New York: Charles Scribner's Sons, 1951.

Byrskog, Samuel. *Story as History—History as Story: The Gospel Tradition in the Context of Ancient Oral History*. Leiden: Brill, 2002.

Carson, D. A. *The Gospel according to John*. PNTC. Grand Rapids, MI: Eerdmans, 1991.

———. "The Purpose of the Fourth Gospel: John 20:30–31 Reconsidered." *JBL* 106 (1987): 639–51.

Carson, D. A., and Douglas J. Moo. *An Introduction to the New Testament*. 2nd ed. Grand Rapids, MI: Zondervan, 2005.

Carter, Warren. *John: Storyteller, Interpreter, Evangelist*. Peabody, MA: Hendrickson, 2006.

Casey, Maurice. *From Jewish Prophet to Gentile God: The Origins and Development of New Testament Christology*. Cambridge: Clarke, 1991.

———. *Is John's Gospel True?* New York: Routledge, 1996.

Chapa, Juan. "The Early Text of the Gospel of John." In *The Early Text of the New Testament*, edited by Charles E. Hill and Michael J. Kruger, 140–56. Oxford: Oxford University Press, 2011.

Chapman, J. "We Know That His Testimony Is True." *JTS* 31 (1930): 379–87.

Charlesworth, James H. *The Beloved Disciple: Whose Witness Validates the Gospel of John?* Valley Forge, PA: Trinity, 1995.

Collins, Raymond F. *These Things Have Been Written: Studies on the Fourth Gospel*. Grand Rapids, MI: Eerdmans, 1990.

Coloe, Mary L. *God Dwells with Us: Temple Symbolism in the Fourth Gospel*. Collegeville, MN: Liturgical, 2001.

Cullmann, Oscar. *The Johannine Circle*. Translated by J. Bowden. London: SCM, 1976.

———. *Salvation in History*. London: SCM, 1967.

Culpepper, R. Alan. *Anatomy of the Fourth Gospel*. Philadelphia: Fortress, 1983.

———. *The Gospel and Letters of John*. Interpreting Biblical Texts. Nashville: Abingdon, 1998.

———. "The Pivot of John's Gospel." *NTS* 27 (1980): 1–31.

Cribbs, F. Lamar. "A Reassessment of the Date of Origin and the Destination of the Gospel of John." *JBL* 89 (1970): 38–55.

Dodd, C. H. *Historical Tradition in the Fourth Gospel*. Cambridge: Cambridge University Press, 1963.

———. *The Interpretation of the Fourth Gospel*. Cambridge: Cambridge University Press, 1968.

Draper, J. A. "Temple, Tabernacle and Mystical Experience in John." *Neot* 31 (1997): 263–88.

Dunn, James D. G. "Let John Be John: A Gospel for Its Time." In *The Gospel and the Gospels*, edited by Peter Stuhlmacher, 293–322. Grand Rapids, MI: Eerdmans, 1991.

Dvorak, J. D. "The Relationship between John and the Synoptic Gospels." *JETS* 41 (1998): 201–13.

Ehrman, Bart D. *The New Testament: A Historical Introduction to the Early Christian Writings*. 4th ed. New York: Oxford University Press, 2008.

Eller, Vernard. *The Beloved Disciple: His Name, His Story, and His Thought*. Grand Rapids, MI: Eerdmans, 1987.

Fee, G. "On the Text and Meaning of John 20, 30–31." In *The Four Gospels 1992: Festschrift for Frans Neirynck*, edited by F. van Segbroeck, et al., 2193–205. Leuven: Leuven University Press, 1992.

Fortna, R. T. *The Gospel of Signs*. Cambridge: Cambridge University Press, 1970.

Funk, R. W., and Roy W. Hoover. *The Five Gospels: The Search for the Authentic Words of Jesus*. New York: Macmillan, 1993.

Goodman, M. "Diaspora Reactions to the Destruction of the Temple." In *Jews and Christians: The Parting of the Ways A.D. 70–135*, edited by J. D. G. Dunn, 27–38. Tübingen: Mohr Siebeck, 1992.

Harris, W. Hall. "Polarization in Johannine Theology." In *A Biblical Theology of the New Testament*, edited by Roy B. Zuck, 203–12. Chicago: Moody Press, 1994.

Hengel, Martin. *Die Johanneische Frage: Ein Lösungsversuch mit einem Beitrag zur Apokalypse von Jörg Frey*. Tübingen: Mohr Siebeck, 1993.

Hill, Charles E. *The Johannine Corpus in the Early Church*. Oxford: Oxford University Press, 2004.

Horbury, William. "The Benediction of the Minim and Early Jewish-Christian Controversy." *JTS* 33 (1982): 19–61.

Hoskins, Paul M. *Jesus as the Fulfillment of the Temple in the Gospel of John*. Carlisle: Paternoster, 2007.

Hurtado, Larry W. *How on Earth Did Jesus Become a God? Historical Questions about Earliest Devotion to Jesus*. Grand Rapids, MI: Eerdmans, 2005.

———. *One God, One Lord: Early Christian Devotion and Ancient Jewish Monotheism*. 2nd ed. Edinburgh: T&T Clark, 2003.

Jones, L. P. *The Symbol of Water in the Gospel of John*. Sheffield: Sheffield Academic, 1997.

Keener, Craig S. *The Gospel of John*. 2 vols. Peabody, MA: Hendrickson, 2003.

Kerr, Alan R. *The Temple of Jesus' Body: The Temple Theme in the Gospel of John*. JSNTSup 220. Sheffield: Sheffield Academic, 2002.

Kinzer, Mark. "Temple Christology in the Gospel of John." *Society of Biblical Literature Seminar Papers* 37 (1998): 447–64.

Klink, Edward W. *The Sheep of the Fold: The Audience and Origin of the Gospel of John*. Cambridge: Cambridge University Press, 2007.

Köstenberger, Andreas J. *John*. BECNT. Grand Rapids, MI: Baker Academic, 2004.
———. *A Theology of John's Gospel and Letters*. BTNT. Grand Rapids, MI: Zondervan, 2009.
Köstenberger, Andreas J., and Scott R. Swain. *Father, Son, and Spirit: The Trinity and John's Gospel*. Downers Grove, IL: InterVarsity Press, 2008.
Kraus, T., Michael J. Kruger, and T. Nicklas. *Gospel Fragments*. Oxford: Oxford University Press, 2008.
Ladd, George Eldon. *A Theology of the New Testament*. Rev. ed. Grand Rapids, MI: Eerdmans, 1993.
Lightfoot, R. H. *St. John's Gospel: A Commentary*. Oxford: Clarendon, 1956.
Martyn, J. L. *History and Theology in the Fourth Gospel*. New York: Harper & Row, 1968.
McKelvey, R. J. *The New Temple: The Church in the New Testament*. Oxford: Oxford University Press, 1969.
Morris, Leon. *The Gospel according to John*. NICNT. Grand Rapids, MI: Eerdmans, 1995.
———. *New Testament Theology*. Grand Rapids, MI: Zondervan, 1990.
Neirynck, F. "John and the Synoptics." In *L'évangile de Jean*, edited by M. de Jonge, 73–106. Leuven: Leuven University Press, 1977.
Nicole, W. *The Semeia in the Fourth Gospel: Tradition and Redaction*. Leiden: Brill, 1972.
Pollard, T. E. *Johannine Christology and the Early Church*. Cambridge: Cambridge University Press, 1970.
Ridderbos, Herman. *The Gospel of John: A Theological Commentary*. Grand Rapids, MI: Eerdmans, 1997.
Roberts, C. H. "John 20:30–31 and 21:24–25." *JTS* 38 (1987): 409–10.
———. "An Unpublished Fragment of the Fourth Gospel in the John Rylands Library." *BJRL* 20 (1936): 45–55.
Robinson, J. A. T. "The Destination and Purpose of St. John's Gospel." *NTS* 6 (1959): 117–31.
———. *Redating the New Testament*. Philadelphia: Westminster Press, 1976.
Rubenstein, J. L. *The History of Sukkot in the Second Temple and Rabbinic Periods*. Atlanta: Scholar's, 1995.
Sanders, J. N. *The Fourth Gospel in the Early Church: Its Origin and Influence on Christian Theology up to Irenaeus*. Cambridge: Cambridge University Press, 1943.
Schnackenburg, R. *The Gospel according to St. John*. 3 vols. London: Burns and Oates, 1982.
Schreiner, Thomas. *New Testament Theology: Magnifying God in Christ*. Grand Rapids, MI: Baker Academic, 2008.
Smalley, S. *John: Evangelist and Interpreter*. London: Paternoster, 1978.
Smith, Barry D. "The Chronology of the Last Supper." *WTJ* 53 (1991): 29–45.
Smith, D. Moody. "Jesus Tradition in the Gospel of John." In *Handbook for the Study of the Historical Jesus*. 4 vols., edited by Tom Holmén and Stanley E. Porter, 1990–2039. Leiden: Brill, 2010.
———. *John among the Synoptics*. 2nd ed. Columbia: University of South Carolina Press, 2001.
———. "John and the Synoptics: Some Dimensions of the Problem." *NTS* 26 (1980): 425–44.
Thatcher, Tom, ed. *What We Have Heard from the Beginning: The Past, Present, and Future of Johannine Studies*. Waco, TX: Baylor University Press, 2007.
van Unnik, W. C. "The Purpose of St. John's Gospel." *Studia Evangelica* (1959): 382–411.
Walbank, F. W. *Speeches in Greek Historians*. Oxford: Holywell, 1965.

5

Acts

Robert J. Cara

Introduction

The book of Acts is a theological interpretation of the history of the first three decades of the early church. It begins with the ascension of Jesus from the Mount of Olives and ends with Paul in Rome under house arrest preaching the kingdom of God. In addition to the breadth of geography, the narrative includes many miraculous and "exciting" events, including healings, speaking in tongues, prison breaks, mass conversions, martyrdom, riots, persecutions, shipwrecks, and appearances before high officials. Behind and orchestrating all these events is the triune God who is "gathering and perfecting" the church.[1]

Acts is closely related to both the Gospels and the New Testament Epistles, especially Paul's. In connection with the Gospels, Acts continues the story of Jesus by including the apostles in a postresurrection world. Of course, Acts is explicitly connected to one of the Gospels, Luke. Acts is also closely related to the New Testament Epistles as it provides a historical framework to put these letters in context. For example, without Acts, it would be difficult to construct a coherent "life of Paul's ministry" using only the Pauline Epistles. Acts provides the information for Paul's persecution of the church and his wonderful conversion, Paul's three missionary journeys, his journey to Rome, his various companions, and more. Interestingly, in early canonical lists, Acts sometimes followed the Gospels (e.g., Muratorian Fragment, second century) and sometimes followed the Pauline Epistles (Sinaiticus, fourth century).[2]

[1] "Gathering and perfecting" comes from WCF 25.3.

[2] See the convenient table in Paul J. Achtemeier, Joel B. Green, Marianne Meye Thompson, *Introducing the New Testament: Its Literature and Theology* (Grand Rapids, MI: Eerdmans, 2001), 246. In lists given in Reformation creeds, Acts follows John (e.g., Belgic Confession 4; Irish Articles of Religion 2; WCF 1.2). The French Confession 3 explicitly mentions that Luke is the author of Acts: "the Holy Gospel . . . according to St. Luke; according to St. John; then the second book of St. Luke, otherwise called the Acts of the Apostles."

In addition to providing a historical framework for many of the New Testament epistles, Acts provides us other basic information about early Christianity. For example, we learn about Pentecost, Stephen's martyrdom, the joys and difficulties of the early church, the content of sermons, and various events related to solidifying the church's mission to the Gentile lands.

Background Issues

Since Acts is a sequel to the Gospel of Luke written by the same author, many issues in this section are related to and overlap with those in the parallel section in the Luke chapter. Hence, the reader is encouraged to review the section "Authorship and Date," under "Background Issues," in the Luke chapter.

Historical Background

The book of Acts covers a wide area geographically. The narrative includes Palestine, Syria, "Asia" (modern western Turkey), the east and west shores of the Aegean Sea, Rome, and the islands of Cyprus, Crete, and Malta. The "intellectual" background is equally broad and includes Jewish Palestinian and Diaspora views along with the many Greco-Roman religions and philosophies.

Because of the wide geographical area and broad intellectual views, any substantive discussion of the historical background is beyond the scope of this chapter. The best place to begin is the five-volume work *The Book of Acts in Its First Century Setting*, which covers Greco-Roman setting, Paul in Roman custody, Palestinian setting, Jewish Diaspora setting, and the ancient literary setting.[3]

Historical Accuracy

The author, Luke, in both the Gospel of Luke and Acts begins with comments to Theophilus about the historical reality of the events that these books narrate. In Luke, he mentions eyewitnesses and that he "has followed all things closely" (Luke 1:2–3). In Acts, he comments on the "many proofs" of Jesus's postresurrection appearances (Acts 1:3). Within the Acts narrative, Luke connects some events to the explicit fulfillment of Old Testament Scripture (e.g., Peter's Pentecost sermon, Acts 2:14–41) and connects all events to the providence of God (e.g., Acts 1:8 and 9:15 with later events in Acts). In addition to this and preeminently, the books of Luke and Acts are Holy Scripture. Hence, I consider all of Acts, the miraculous events and the travel details, historically accurate. Secondarily, in support of this view, many have confirmed through historical investigation, at least at the travel-detail level, the historical accuracy of Acts.[4]

---

[3] Bruce W. Winter, ed., *The Book of Acts in Its First Century Setting*, 5 vols. (Grand Rapids, MI: Eerdmans, 1993–1996). The authors in this multivolume work have generally conservative conclusions.

[4] Famously, the archaeologist William M. Ramsey was skeptical of the historical accuracy of Acts but changed his mind after extensive field research. See the updated version with useful photographs in his classic *St. Paul: The Traveler and Roman Citizen*, ed. Mark Wilson, rev. ed. (Grand Rapids, MI: Kregel, 2001). Also see Colin J. Hemer's impressive defense of the historical accuracy of Acts (*The Book of Acts in the Setting of Hellenistic History*, ed. Conrad H. Gempf [Winona Lake, IN: Eisenbrauns, 1990]).

However, even when bracketing out the miraculous aspects of Acts, critical scholarship has a negative view of much of the historicity of Acts.[5] In the mid-1800s, F. C. Baur argued widely that the author of Acts played loose with the historical facts to promote his theological "tendency."[6] Similarly, in the twentieth century, three influential scholars, Martin Dibelius, Hans Conzelmann, and Ernst Haenchen, all believed that the theological tendency trumped the author of Acts's concern for historical accuracy, although they did not all see the same tendency.[7] In addition to the "tendency" problem, critical scholars complained that the Paul of Acts and the Paul of his letters were not the same, that Palestinian geography was especially suspect, and that the speeches in Acts were too uniform.

Given the limited scope of this chapter, the following simply refers to other scholars' work to answer the complaints above. The "tendency" problem reduces down to the claim that one cannot be both biased and accurate, that is, both a theologian and a historian. I. Howard Marshall responded to this either–or assumption by critical scholarship to affirm that Luke was both a theologian and a historian.[8]

Concerning the two "Pauls," Philipp Vielhauer wrote a famous article where he compared the *theological* ideas of Paul in his letters with the ideas presented in speeches attributed to him in Acts. He looked at four categories, "natural theology, law, christology, and eschatology," and concluded that the Paul of Acts could not be the historical Paul.[9] For a good, brief response to Vielhauer, see D. A. Carson and Douglas Moo.[10]

Critical scholars will generally admit that many, although not all, of the geographical details and titles for rulers in Acts within the Aegean Sea lands are fairly accurate. However, it is often remarked that there are significant errors in Palestinian geography in both Luke and Acts. For a response, see Martin Hengel's long article.[11]

Large sections of Acts contain, as scholarship terms it, "speeches" (e.g., Acts 2:14–40; 7:2–53; 13:16–41; 17:22–31; 20:18–35; 22:3–21; 26:2–23). Most of critical scholarship considers these Lucan inventions inserted into the mouths of Peter, Stephen, and Paul. This is based on the perceived similarities of the speeches and comments made by the ancient historian Thucydides, who admitted that he judiciously

[5] Of course, there are exceptions. See Adolf von Harnack, *Luke the Physician* (New York: Putman, 1907).

[6] Baur believed that the early church had degenerated into two factions, one pro-Paul and one pro-Peter. The "tendency" in Acts was to show, contrary to historical fact, that Paul and Peter were united. "[Acts's] chief tendency is to represent the difference between Peter and Paul as unessential and trifling" (*Paul the Apostle of Jesus Christ: His Life and Works, His Epistles and Teachings*, 2 vols. [Peabody, MA: Hendrickson, 2003], 1:6).

[7] Martin Dibelius, *Studies in the Book of Acts of the Apostles*, trans. Mary Ling (London: SCM, 1973); Hans Conzelmann, *The Theology of St. Luke*, trans. Geoffrey Buswell (London: Faber & Faber, 1960); Ernst Haenchen, *The Acts of the Apostles: A Commentary*, trans. Bernard Noble and Gerald Shinn (Philadelphia: Westminster Press, 1971). Also see W. C. van Unnik, "Luke-Acts, A Storm Center in Contemporary Scholarship," in *Studies in Luke-Acts*, ed. Leander E. Keck and J. Louis Martyn (Philadelphia: Fortress, 1980), 15–32.

[8] I. Howard Marshall, *Luke: Historian and Theologian*, rev. ed. (Grand Rapids, MI: Zondervan, 1989). Somewhat related, Cornelius Van Til argued that it is impossible to be neutral as one comes to Scripture. In fact, one is morally required to come to Scripture with the only true bias that God is speaking through the human authors. See Van Til, *The Defense of the Faith* (Philadelphia: Presbyterian and Reformed, 1967). Or to put it in my own jargon, "Biases are not bad; bad biases are bad."

[9] Philipp Vielhauer, "On the 'Paulinism' of Acts," in Keck and Martyn, *Studies in Luke-Acts*, 33–50, esp. 34.

[10] D. A. Carson and Douglas J. Moo, *An Introduction to the New Testament*, 2nd ed. (Grand Rapids, MI: Zondervan, 2005), 293–95. Also see F. F. Bruce, "Is the Paul of Acts the Real Paul?," *BJRL* 58 (1975–1976): 282–305.

[11] Martin Hengel, "The Geography of Palestine in Acts," in *The Book of Acts in Its Palestinian Setting*, ed. Richard Bauckham, vol. 4 of *The Book of Acts in Its First Century Setting* (Grand Rapids, MI: Eerdmans, 1995), 27–78.

invented speeches when he did not have adequate information.[12] A brief response is to first note that there are differences between the speeches that do seem to match the situations. The similarities are primarily explained by the similar contexts of speeches given to non-Christians.[13] The fact that portions of the speeches may be summaries may secondarily explain the data.[14] Finally, although Thucydides thought it was proper to invent speeches, other ancient historians did not (e.g., Polybius, *The Histories* 2.56.10).[15] Moreover, Luke was more likely following Old Testament historiography that, from his perspective, would not have countenanced the invention of speeches, since for him it was the Word of God.

Authorship and Date

See, again, the Luke chapter, "Authorship and Date" (under "Background Issues"), for a more substantive discussion than is presented here. To summarize that discussion as to author, I hold to the traditional view that "Luke the beloved physician" (Col. 4:14), who accompanied Paul on portions of his missionary journeys and was a Gentile, wrote both Luke and Acts.[16] Critical scholars agree that the same author (or final editor) wrote both Luke and Acts, but that person is said to have been an unnamed Gentile who was *not* a companion of Paul.[17] The traditional view is based on (1) the external evidence of church tradition that points only to Luke the physician and (2) the internal evidence of both Luke and Acts that dovetails with this. For purposes of this chapter, only the internal evidence of Acts is presented.

Luke is mentioned by name in only three passages in the New Testament: Colossians 4:14; Philemon 24; and 2 Timothy 4:11. In Colossians 4:14, Luke is called "the beloved physician," and the context implies that he is a Gentile.[18] In Philemon

[12] Well-known critical studies on the speeches include H. J. Cadbury, "The Speeches in Acts," in *The Beginnings of Christianity*, ed. F. J. Foakes-Jackson and Kirsopp Lake, 5 vols. (London: Macmillan, 1922–1933), 5:405–27; Martin Dibelius, "The Speeches of Acts and Ancient Historiography," in *Studies in the Acts of the Apostles*, 138–85; Eduard Schweizer, "Concerning the Speeches in Acts," in Keck and Martyn, *Studies in Luke-Acts*, 208–16. For Thucydides's view, see his *History of the Peloponnesian War* 1.22.

[13] Paul's speech to the Ephesian elders (Acts 20:18–35) is different from the other Pauline speeches in content and word choice. This makes sense as this is the only recorded speech to Christians by Paul in Acts.

[14] For an argument that relies heavily, too heavily in my view, on justifying the historical accuracy of the speeches as "summaries of actual speeches," see Hemer, *The Book of Acts in the Setting of Hellenistic History*, 415–27, esp. 421.

[15] For a discussion of the methodologies of various ancient historians, see Conrad Gempf, "Public Speaking and Published Accounts," in *The Book of Acts in Its Ancient Literary Setting*, ed. Bruce W. Winter and Andrew D. Clarke, vol. 1 of *The Book of Acts in Its First Century Setting* (Grand Rapids, MI: Eerdmans, 1993), 259–303.

[16] So also, e.g., Carson and Moo, *Introduction to the New Testament*, 290–96; J. A. Alexander, *A Commentary on the Acts of the Apostles*, 2 vols., Geneva (Carlisle, PA: Banner of Truth, 1963), 1:iv–viii; F. F. Bruce, *The Book of Acts*, rev. ed., NICNT (Grand Rapids, MI: Eerdmans, 1988), 6–7; Simon J. Kistemaker, *Exposition of the Acts of the Apostles*, NTC (Grand Rapids, MI: Baker, 1990), 20–21; John B. Polhill, *Acts*, NAC 26 (Nashville: Broadman, 1992), 27; Joseph A. Fitzmyer, *The Acts of the Apostles: A New Translation with Introduction and Commentary*, AB 31 (New York: Doubleday, 1998), 49–51; and Ben Witherington III, *The Acts of the Apostles: A Socio-Rhetorical Commentary* (Grand Rapids, MI: Eerdmans, 1998), 51–60. For a weak vote for possible Lucan authorship, see Raymond E. Brown, *An Introduction to the New Testament*, ABRL (New York: Doubleday, 1997), 322–27; and Luke Timothy Johnson, *The Acts of the Apostles*, SP 5 (Collegeville, MN: Liturgical, 1992), 1.

[17] For typical discussions, see Werner Georg Kümmel, *Introduction to the New Testament*, rev. ed., trans. Howard Clark Kee (Nashville: Abingdon, 1975), 147–50, 176–80; and Richard I. Pervo, *Acts: A Commentary*, Hermeneia (Minneapolis: Fortress, 2009), 5–7.

[18] While referring to Aristarchus, Mark, and Jesus/Justus, Paul calls them men of the circumcision, that is, Jewish Christians (Col. 4:10–11). Paul goes on to mention Epaphras and Luke (Col. 4:12–14). Since Epaphras is from Colossae and presumably a Gentile, Luke is then assumed to be one also. So also R. McL. Wilson, *A Critical and Exegetical Commentary on Colossians and Philemon*, ICC (London: T&T Clark, 2005), 301; *pace* David E. Garland, who takes "circumcision" in Col. 4:11 to refer to those of the circumcision party, not Jewish Christians per se (*Colossians, Philemon*, NIVAC [Grand Rapids, MI: Zondervan, 1998], 278).

24, Luke is called one of Paul's "fellow workers." Both of these comments are in the greetings section, indicating that Luke was with Paul at the time of the writing of these letters. Also, it is assumed that the Colossian church and Philemon, who was at the Colossian church, knew Luke to some degree. Assuming a traditional, conservative chronology of Paul, both of these letters were written while Paul was under house arrest in Rome. This would then relate to Acts 28:16–31. In 2 Timothy 4:11, Paul comments to Timothy, "Luke alone is with me." Again, assuming a traditional, conservative chronology, 2 Timothy is Paul's last canonical letter and written while he was under arrest in Rome for a second time. This second imprisonment occurred after the final events in Acts. This comment in 2 Timothy 4:11 also indicates that Timothy knew Luke. To summarize, Luke was a physician, a fellow worker and companion of Paul, and a Gentile. Also, he was with Paul at least in both his first and second Roman imprisonments. Finally, the Colossian church, Philemon, and Timothy knew Luke at least to some degree.

Is Acts compatible with the above information about Luke? For brevity, I will address only the "we" passages. The famous "we" passages in Acts confirm that (1) Luke was a fellow worker and companion of Paul, (2) Luke was with Paul during his first imprisonment, and (3) the Colossian church and Timothy knew Luke. The explicit "we" passages are Acts 16:10–17; 20:5–15; 21:1–18; and 27:1–28:16.[19] Taking these passages in a straightforward manner produces the conclusion that the author of Acts was with Paul during at least portions of Paul's second and third missionary journeys, along with his trip from Jerusalem to Rome.[20] Obviously, the author was a companion of Paul. The author also says, "God had called us to preach" (Acts 16:10). This indicates that the author was part of the ministry team. Acts clearly portrays him as being with Paul during his first Roman imprisonment (Acts 28:16). Finally, the author had personal knowledge of Aristarchus, Tychicus, and Timothy, along with the Ephesian church and its elders. All of these have connections with the Colossian church (Acts 16:3, 10; 20:4, 15–17; 27:2; Eph. 6:21; Col. 4:7, 10; 2 Tim. 4:12; Philem. 24). Hence, the internal evidence of Acts matches what we know of Luke from other New Testament books.

Critical scholars do not take the "we" passages as autobiographical. This is based on their prior assumption that the Paul of Acts and the Paul of his letters are so different that no true traveling companion of Paul could have written Acts.[21] Many believe that the author intended the "we" passages to appear as a diary; that is, the

[19] For a wide variety of views of the "we" passages, see Donald Guthrie, *New Testament Introduction*, 3rd ed. (Downers Grove: InterVarsity, 1970), 101–7, 367–68; Kümmel, *Introduction to the New Testament*, 176–80; V. K. Robbins, "The We-Passages in Acts and Ancient Sea Voyages," *BR* 20 (1975): 5–18; Joseph A. Fitzmyer, *Luke the Theologian: Aspects of His Teaching* (New York: Paulist, 1989), 16–22; Hemer, *The Book of Acts in the Setting of Hellenistic History*, 308–64; and Stanley E. Porter, "The 'We' Passages," in *The Book of Acts in Its Graeco-Roman Setting*, ed. David W. J. Gill and Conrad Gempf, vol. 2 of *The Book of Acts in Its First Century Setting* (Grand Rapids, MI: Eerdmans, 1994), 545–74. The "Western Text" (Codex Bezae, D) has the first "we" passage at Acts 11:28, which has Barnabas and Paul in Antioch with the author.

[20] Of course, Luke may have been with Paul for more than the explicit "we" sections. For example, Luke may have been present at Paul's defense at the temple (Acts 22:3–21), as he has already indicated that he was in Jerusalem with Paul (Acts 21:17).

[21] Kümmel states, "The author of Acts is so misinformed that he can scarcely have been a companion of Paul on his missionary journeys" (*Introduction to the New Testament*, 181).

author invented scenes and used the literary device of diary to give the narrative a realistic feel.[22]

Concerning the dating of Acts, the discussion hinges on the prior conclusion concerning the dating of Luke. It is assumed that Acts was written a few months or years after Luke. I have previously argued in the Luke chapter that Luke was written in the AD 50s or early 60s. There I noted that most critical scholars date Luke somewhere in AD 80–125 and conservatives date Luke either in the 50s–60s or in 75–85.

The concluding event in Acts is Paul's two-year stay during his first Roman imprisonment/house arrest, which would be AD 62. Hence, AD 62 is the earliest Acts could have been written. According to the traditional chronology, Paul is then set free and travels for several more years, writing 1 Timothy and Titus. He is rearrested and in a Roman prison for a second time, where he writes 2 Timothy. He is executed in AD 65. My view is that Acts was written at the end of Paul's first imprisonment in 62. This is based on the assumptions that (1) the Gospel of Luke was already written and (2) the author Luke would have included more of Paul's life and ministry if it had already occurred.[23]

Addressee(s), Occasion, and Purposes

As discussed in more detail in the Luke chapter (second section under "Background Issues"), the named addressee for both Luke and Acts is Theophilus (Luke 1:3; Acts 1:1). It is reasonable to conclude that he is some type of Roman official, although he might also be a good friend of Luke's. Theophilus is a Gentile Christian, maybe a recent convert.

It is assumed that Luke knew that the Gospel of Luke and Acts would be circulated more widely than to just Theophilus. Based on the emphasis in both Luke and Acts concerning Gentiles, it is further assumed that Luke knew the reading audience would be primarily Gentiles but would also include, secondarily, Jews.[24] Because Theophilus was a Christian, Luke was certainly writing to Christians, but he probably also expected that non-Christians would read his Gospel and Acts. Given my view that Acts was written toward the end of Paul's first imprisonment, the provenance of Acts was most likely Rome.

Again, all agree that the same author wrote Luke and Acts. However, before discussing the occasion and purpose of Acts, the issue needs to be resolved as to literary relationship between Luke and Acts. Should they be considered one book, termed Luke-Acts? Or should they be considered separately with Acts being a sequel, thus

[22] So, for example, William S. Campbell, *The "We" Passages in the Acts of the Apostles: The Narrator as Narrative Character*, SBLStBL 14 (Atlanta: SBL, 2007). For a summary of various critical views, see M. Eugene Boring, *An Introduction to the New Testament: History, Literature, Theology* (Louisville: Westminster John Knox, 2012), 573–75.

[23] F. F. Bruce, a conservative, does not agree with me. He believes that the omission of Paul's execution is not decisive for the dating of Acts as he dates Acts between AD 69 and 96. According to Bruce, Luke's presentation of Paul and other Roman authorities may have "intended to suggest that Nero's anti-Christian activity was an irresponsible and criminal attack" (*Book of Acts*, 11–12).

[24] *Pace* the majority of critical and conservative scholars, Jacob Jervell sees the readers as Hellenistic-Jewish Christians who are being told by their Jewish countrymen that the church is not a continuation of Old Testament Israel. Also, they are hearing rumors that Paul is not observing the law. Acts is written to confirm that the church is the true Israel and that Jewish Christians should still follow the ceremonial aspects of the law. See Jacob Jervell, *The Theology of the Acts of the Apostles*, NTT (Cambridge: Cambridge University Press, 1996), 12–15, 82–94, and my review of this book in *WTJ* 58 (1996): 333–35.

Luke *and* Acts? The Luke-Acts thesis would have a singular occasion and unified purpose(s) and emphases. The Luke-*and*-Acts thesis would allow differing occasions, purposes, and emphases for the two books, in addition to overlapping purposes and emphases. This issue is discussed in detail in the Luke chapter. There I opt for the Luke-*and*-Acts thesis, but I also conclude that there are very strong connections and no contradictions between the two books.

Although there is potentially a significantly different purpose for Luke as compared with Acts, I do believe that the purposes of the two books are very similar. The explicit purpose given in the Gospel of Luke is that Theophilus would "have certainty concerning the things [he has] been taught" (Luke 1:4). The content of the book relates primarily to the person and work of Jesus. Hence, the explicit purpose of Luke is to confirm Theophilus and others in their Christian faith by presenting a historical account of Jesus. Theophilus, the Gospel of Luke ("first book," Acts 1:1), and Jesus are all referenced in the prologue to Acts (1:1–3). This strongly implies that Acts is also designed to produce "certainty concerning the things [Theophilus has] been taught" (Luke 1:4). It is further said about Jesus in the Acts prologue that he presented himself alive after his resurrection and would send the Holy Spirit to aid the early church (Acts 1:3–5). Hence, I conclude that the primary purpose of Acts is to confirm Theophilus and others in the Christian faith by presenting a historical account of the triune God's special providence[25] over the early church.[26]

Given this primary purpose of Acts, one could envision many secondary purposes. These secondary purposes are normally associated with perceived theological emphases within Acts. In addition, nontheological secondary purposes are also considered by some. For example, many believe that Acts is an attempt to influence Roman authorities by showing that Christianity is not subversive to the Roman Empire.[27] The following is a list of purposes proposed by various scholars. For brevity, I will simply list them and indicate whether or not I agree.[28] For me, these are possible secondary purposes under the one primary purpose mentioned above. Many scholars see some of the below as the primary purpose:

- To show the relationship between Christ and the Holy Spirit as Christ rules the church (Agree)
- To confirm that the church is for Gentiles (Agree)

[25] I use the expression "special providence" purposely, alluding to its use in the Westminster Standards: "As the *providence* of God doth, in general, reach to all creatures, so, after a most *special* manner, it taketh care of his church, and disposeth all things to the good thereof" (WCF 5.7, emphasis mine).

[26] Dennis E. Johnson emphasizes that the starting point for understanding Acts's purpose is to see the primary emphasis on God's saving acts. One will be frustrated if Acts is turned preeminently into a "manual of church polity or mission policies." In Acts, "God's Spirit unveils the identity of the church between Jesus' two comings, the divine power at work in this church, the results of that powerful Presence, and the environment in which we are to pursue our mission until 'this same Jesus, who has been taken from you into heaven, will come back in the same way you have seen him go into heaven' (Acts 1:11)" (*The Message of Acts in the History of Redemption* [Phillipsburg, NJ: P&R, 1997], 5).

[27] For example, Guthrie, *New Testament Introduction*, 95. I do not agree. Admittedly, there are many comments showing Christians as innocent with respect to Roman law, but the many comments about God's salvation and providence would not fit with an apologetic to Roman authorities.

[28] For other lists of purposes of Acts proposed by scholars, see Jervell, *Theology of the Acts of the Apostles*, 11; and David Peterson, "Luke's Theological Enterprise: Integration and Intent," in *Witness to the Gospel: The Theology of Acts*, ed. I. Howard Marshall and David Peterson (Grand Rapids, MI: Eerdmans, 1998), 521–44, esp. 532–44.

- To confirm that the church is one and expands across geographical boundaries (Jerusalem to Rome), ethnic boundaries (Jewish, Samaritan, Gentile), and redemptive-historical boundaries (Old Testament, John the Baptist) (Agree)
- To defend Paul to Jewish Christians (Disagree)
- To defend Paul to Roman authorities (Disagree)
- To show Roman authorities that Christianity is different from Judaism and not responsible for disturbances (Disagree)
- To show that Christianity is a continuation of Old Testament Israel within God's overall redemptive-historical plan (Agree)
- To confirm and bring the good news of salvation to all (Agree)
- To show that the Word of God spreads despite opposition (Agree)
- To encourage Christians to spread the gospel (Agree)
- To give examples of how the present church is to act by imitating the early church (Agree)
- To explain the delay in the second coming (Disagree)
- To encourage the Peter and Paul parties to get together (Disagree)
- To show God's divine guidance over history (Agree)
- To show that the promises in Scripture about Jesus and the church are fulfilled (Agree)

Of these secondary purposes, my combination view would hold that the most prominent is Luke's wish to emphasize the one, unified church that, by God's Word, expands geographically, ethnically, and redemptive-historically. This secondary purpose is a subset of the primary purpose to confirm Theophilus and others in the Christian faith by presenting a historical account of the triune God's special providence over the early church.

The Greek Text

The Greek text of Acts has a complication that no other New Testament book has. There is a recension of the text that is approximately 8.5 percent longer than the traditional text of Acts.[29] This longer text is called the "Western Text,"[30] and the most famous manuscript is Codex D, which is also called Codex Beza or Codex Cantabrigiensis.[31] Bible translations of Acts do not follow the Western Text.

Interesting additions by the Western Text include a "we" passage while Paul and Luke are in Antioch (Acts 11:28). This would be the first "we" passage and is taken by some to imply that Luke's home was Antioch. In the letter produced by the Jerusalem Council, the Western Text adds "whatever you do not wish to come about to yourself, do not do to others" (Acts 15:29). As Peter is escaping from prison and going down to the street, it is added that he "went down seven steps" to get to the street (Acts 12:10).

In the history of scholarship, some have thought that Luke produced two ver-

[29] The most extensive attempt to provide a full Western Text, more than simply Codex D, is by M. E. Boismard and A. Lamouille, *Le texte occidental des Actes des Apôtres: Reconstitution et rehabilitation*, 2 vols. (Paris: Editions recherche sur les civilisations, 1984).

[30] Now considered a misnomer, as some manuscripts have been found that originated in the east. Also, it is noted that the Western Text is not a monolith. Maybe one should speak of Western *texts*.

[31] The names come from the fact that Theodore Beza gave the Codex D manuscript to the library at Cambridge University. In addition to Codex D, the Western Text is also represented by the Greek texts $\mathfrak{p}^{29}$, $\mathfrak{p}^{38}$, $\mathfrak{p}^{48}$, E, 383, and 614.

sions of Acts, and a few have thought that the Western Text was original.[32] However, the vast majority of former and current scholars have considered the Western Text a later recension by someone other than the author of Acts.[33] My functional view is that not one of the Western Text additions was part of the original inspired text, although they may preserve some historically true information.[34]

Structure and Outline

Outlines of narratives can both clarify and distort. The best of outlines emphasize what the author intended to emphasize and de-emphasize the author's tertiary issues. Therefore, a good outline clarifies the main points. However, since a good outline barely, if at all, mentions tertiary points, even a good outline distorts slightly by elevating the main points too highly and underemphasizes the tertiary points because they are not mentioned at all.

There are several reasonable ways to outline Acts. One's conclusion about the best outline is related to one's view of Luke's primary and secondary purposes. I will present several outline options below and conclude that the "geographical" outline of Acts is the most useful.

Peter-and-Paul Biographical Outline

I. Peter (1–12)
II. Paul (13–28)

As Guthrie notes, "It is one of the most striking features about Acts that it says so little about the other apostles and so much about Peter and Paul."[35] Also, there are many parallels between Peter and Paul. Examples include their both healing cripples (Acts 3:7–8 // 14:8–10), both preaching (2:14–40 // 13:26–41), and both miraculously being released from prisons (12:7–10 // 16:25–30).[36] Although Peter is primarily associated with Jews, and Paul with Gentiles, both apostles interact with both Jews and Gentiles.[37] One could argue that Peter takes the narrative from Jerusalem to

[32] Two versions: e.g., Eb. Nestle, "Some Observations on the Codex Bezae," *Expositor* 5 (1895): 235–40. Western original: e.g., A. C. Clark, *The Acts of the Apostles: A Critical Edition with Introduction and Notes on Selected Passages* (Oxford: Clarendon, 1933); and Boismard and Lamouille, *Le texte occidental des Actes des Apôtres*. Jaroslav Pelikan opts for using the Western Text, which he terms *textus a patribus receptus* ("text accepted by the church fathers"), throughout his commentary (*Acts*, Brazos Theological Commentary on the Bible [Grand Rapids, MI: Brazos, 2005], 33). For a good summary of the history of scholarship on these questions, see Bruce M. Metzger, *A Textual Commentary on the Greek New Testament*, 2nd ed. (Stuttgart: Deutsche Bibelgesellschaft, 1994), 222–36.

[33] E.g., Haenchen, *Acts of the Apostles*, 50–60; Fitzmyer, *Acts of the Apostles*, 66–79; Guthrie, *New Testament Introduction*, 377–78; Metzger, *Textual Commentary on the Greek New Testament*, 235–36; and Carson and Moo, *Introduction to the New Testament*, 309–10.

[34] So also Metzger, *Textual Commentary on the Greek New Testament*, 235. Carson and Moo see as a "whole" that the Western Text is not original, but do note that the Western Text "may . . . at points preserve the original reading" (*Introduction to the New Testament*, 310). C. K. Barrett's view is similar to Carson and Moo's (*A Critical and Exegetical Commentary on the Acts of the Apostles*, 2 vols., ICC [Edinburgh: T&T Clark, 1994–1998], 2:xix).

[35] Guthrie, *New Testament Introduction*, 338.

[36] James D. G. Dunn gives the following complete list of Peter/Paul parallels in Acts: 2:22–39 // 13:26–41; 3:1–10 // 14:8–11; 4:8 // 13:9; 5:15 // 19:12; 8:17 // 19:6; 8:18–24 // 13:6–11; 9:36–41 // 20:9–12; 12:6–11 // 16:25–34. In addition to the Peter/Paul parallels, there are parallels between Jesus in the Gospel of Luke and Peter/Paul (and Stephen) from Acts. Dunn lists the Luke/Acts parallels as 3:21–22 // 2:1–4; 4:14–21 // 2:14–39 and 13:16–41; 4:40 // 28:9; 5:17–26 // 3:1–10 and 14:8–11; 8:40–56 // 9:36–41 and 20:9–12; 22:66–71 // 6:8–15; 22:69 // 7:56; 23:34, 46 // 7:59–60. See *Acts of the Apostles*, Narrative Commentaries (Valley Forge, PA: Trinity Press International, 1996), xiv.

[37] Peter is associated with the Gentile Cornelius (Acts 10:1–11:18), and Paul, in his travels to the Gentile lands, went to Jewish synagogues (e.g., Acts 17:2; 18:4; Rom. 1:16).

Antioch (Acts 1–12), and Paul from Antioch to Rome (Acts 13–28). All of these considerations confirm a unified church.

Some scholars favor this biographical outline in relation to the Baur thesis that Acts is an attempt to get the Peter and Paul parties together.[38] Others simply see the emphasis on Peter and Paul as a way to stress the unity of the church, especially concerning the Gentile mission.[39] Werner Georg Kümmel complains that this outline "is scarcely the intention of the author, who pursues no biographical aims."[40] Also, this outline seems to ignore the importance of Acts 1:8 and the Jerusalem Council (Acts 15:1–35).

Holy Spirit–Events Outline

I. Jerusalem, Judea, Samaria, the Ends of the Earth (1:8)
II. Pentecost, Jews (Hellenistic and Palestinian) (2:1–4)
III. Samaritans Converted, Connection to the Jerusalem Church (8:14–17)
IV. Paul and Ananias, Connection to the Gentiles (9:15–19)
V. Cornelius and Peter, Gentiles, Peter Reports to the Jerusalem Church (10:44–46)
VI. The Jerusalem Council, Gentiles and Jews (15:8)
VII. John the Baptist's Disciples and Paul (19:1–7)

This is not an outline per se; however, it is worth noting that the occurrences of the Holy Spirit "events"[41] do dovetail with some of the major themes in Acts. Some scholars see the Holy Spirit itself as a major theme in the book.[42] As can be seen from the above, the Holy Spirit events are related to Acts 1:8, Pentecost, solving intra-Jewish divisions, the Samaritans, Gentiles, the Jerusalem Council, and John the Baptist's converts. This emphasizes the unity and expansion of the church ethnically and redemptive-historically.

Six-Summary-Statements Outline

I. Acts 1:1–6:7
Summary: "The word of God continued to increase [αὐξάνω], and the number of the disciples multiplied [πληθύνω] greatly in Jerusalem, and a great many of the priests became obedient to the faith" (Acts 6:7). This follows Hellenistic and Palestinian Jews' disagreement and the apostles commissioned to preach.

II. Acts 6:8–9:31
Summary: "So the church throughout all Judea and Galilee and Samaria had peace and was being built up. And walking in the fear of the Lord and in the comfort of the Holy Spirit, it multiplied [πληθύνω]" (Acts 9:31). This

[38] See discussion in Kümmel, *Introduction to the New Testament*, 160–61.
[39] E.g., Boring, *Introduction to the New Testament*, 569; and Charles H. Talbert, *Reading Acts: A Literary and Theological Commentary on the Acts of the Apostles*, Reading the New Testament (New York: Crossroad, 1997), 93–94. Carson and Moo have a modified version of this (*Introduction to the New Testament*, 286).
[40] Kümmel, *Introduction to the New Testament*, 154.
[41] I am using "events" as a purposely neutral term.
[42] E.g., Helmut Koester, *History and Literature of Early Christianity*, vol. 2 of *Introduction to the New Testament* (New York: de Gruyter, 1982), 319–22.

summary follows Paul's conversion and confirmation that he is no longer persecuting the church.

III. Acts 9:32–12:24
Summary: "But the word of God increased [αὐξάνω] and multiplied [πληθύνω]" (Acts 12:24). This follows Herod's death.

IV. Acts 12:25–16:5
Summary: "So the churches were strengthened in the faith, and they increased [περισσεύω] in numbers daily" (Acts 16:5). This comes after the Jerusalem Council and the deliverance of the letter to unify Christian Jews and Gentiles.

V. Acts 16:6–19:20
Summary: "So the word of the Lord continued to increase [αὐξάνω] and prevail mightily" (Acts 19:20). This summary follows the planting of the Ephesian church, which is the final one in Acts.

VI. Acts 19:21–28:31
Summary: Paul for two years was "proclaiming the kingdom of God and teaching about the Lord Jesus Christ with all boldness and without hindrance" (Acts 28:31). This follows Paul's arrival in Rome and his preaching while under house arrest.

The above summary statements occur at major points in Acts.[43] Note the parallel statements of the "word of God/the Lord" and "churches" growing. Ben Witherington uses these six summary statements not to determine an outline per se, but to "provide reasonable clues to the development and subsectioning by Luke of his material" and concludes with the following:[44]

I. Primitive Church in Jerusalem (1:1–6:7)
II. Judea and Samaria (6:8–9:31)
III. Gospel to the Gentiles (Ethnic, Non-geographical) (9:32–12:24)
IV. Asia and Shift to Gentile Missions (12:25–16:5)
V. Europe (but with a Return to Ephesus) (16:6–19:20)
VI. To Rome (19:21–28:31)

These summary statements emphasize key themes in Acts. The church is unified across ethnic and geographic differences and grows by the Word of God despite opposition and problems.

Geographic Outline

I. The Church in Jerusalem (1:1–7:60)
II. The Church in Judea, Samaria, and Antioch (8:1–12:25)
III. The First Missionary Journey of Paul (Northeast Mediterranean) (13:1–14:28)
IV. The Jerusalem Council (15:1–35)

[43] Secondary summary verses that use "word of God/the Lord" are Acts 8:25; 11:1; 13:49; 18:11; 19:10.

[44] Witherington, *Acts of the Apostles*, 74; also see 157–59. A "classic" discussion of the summaries in Acts is provided by Cadbury, who also concludes that these summaries should not be considered the outline per se ("The Summaries in Acts," in Foakes-Jackson and Lake, *The Beginnings of Christianity*, 5:392–402).

V. The Second Missionary Journey of Paul (Aegean Sea) (15:36–18:22)
VI. The Third Missionary Journey of Paul (Aegean Sea) (18:23–21:16)
VII. From Jerusalem to Rome (21:17–28:31)

As stated above, the primary purpose of Acts is to confirm Theophilus and others in the Christian faith by presenting a historical account of the triune God's special providence over the early church. A prominent secondary purpose is that there is one, unified church that, by the Word of God, expands geographically, ethnically, and redemptive-historically. No one outline can show all of this, but the geographical one best shows the expanding unified church. Also it dovetails well with the other outline options.[45]

The geographical outline seems to be supported by Acts 1:8, "You will be my witnesses in Jerusalem and in all Judea and Samaria, and to the end of the earth." As David Peterson comments, "Acts 1:8 is a prediction and promise of the way this divine plan will be fulfilled, rather than a command. The rest of [Acts] shows how it happened."[46]

The above distinction between the second and third missionary journeys, although true, is not especially emphasized by Luke. The transition between Acts 18:22 and 18:23, that is, between the second and third journeys, is not highlighted at that point in the text, and Paul travels to the same basic Aegean Sea location. On the other hand, there is some emphasis on the third missionary journey because Acts 19:20 is a summary verse, and one of the Holy Spirit "events" occurs in Acts 19:1–7.

Message and Theology

Overview of Acts

The Church in Jerusalem (Acts 1:1–7:60)

The first seven chapters of Acts recount the church's history in Jerusalem and match the Jerusalem portion of Acts 1:8, "You will be my witnesses in Jerusalem and in all Judea and Samaria, and to the ends of the earth."

Paralleling the beginning of Luke, Acts opens with a statement or prologue to Theophilus (Acts 1:1–3). In this prologue, Luke references his first book and summarizes the content in it, which was "all that Jesus began to do and teach," including his "sufferings" and subsequent resurrection appearances.

Without any significant literary markers, Luke moves out of the prologue and begins his long historical account by expanding on the brief ascension scene presented in the Gospel (Luke 24:50–53).[47] His emphasis in Acts 1:4–11 is clearly on the Holy Spirit. Luke recalls Jesus's statements that (1) the apostles are to "wait for the promise [Holy Spirit] of the Father," (2) they will be "baptized with the Holy

[45] Many scholars prefer a geographical outline for Acts; for example, Kümmel, *Introduction to the New Testament*, 154–55; Kistemaker, *Acts*, 36; David G. Peterson, *The Acts of the Apostles*, PNTC (Grand Rapids, MI: Eerdmans, 2009), 35–36; and Rudolf Pesch, *Die Apostelgeschichte*, 2 vols., EKKNT 5 (Düsseldorf: Benziger, 1986), 1:41.
[46] Peterson, *Acts of the Apostles*, 112.
[47] As to no literary markers, so also Robert C. Tannehill, *The Narrative Unity of Luke-Acts*, 2 vols. (Philadelphia: Fortress, 1986–1990), 2:9.

Spirit not many days from now [by Jesus]," and (3) they "will receive power when the Holy Spirit has come upon [them], and [they] will be [his] witnesses" (Acts 1:4–8; cf. Luke 3:16; 24:49; Acts 2:33, 38). Hence, the beginning of Acts makes explicit the connection between the Holy Spirit and Jesus. In conjunction with the Father, Jesus will pour out the Holy Spirit (Acts 2:33) and guide the church corporately (Acts 1:8) and individually (Acts 1:5; 16:7). The Holy Spirit will be a gift (Acts 2:38), and in Acts, the emphasis of this gift will be on the ability to witness/preach (Acts 1:8). The messianic age that started with Jesus's coming has not ended because he is not here. The messianic age continues through the special outpouring of the Holy Spirit.[48]

Following the ascension, the disciples cast lots to choose Matthias to replace Judas as the twelfth apostle (Acts 1:15–26). Peter notes that the defection of Judas does not spoil God's plan; in fact, the defection and his subsequent death "fulfilled" (πληρόω, Acts 1:16) Old Testament Scripture.[49] Peter quotes from Psalm 69:25 (Ps. 69:26 Heb.; Ps. 68:26 LXX) and Psalm 109:8 (Ps. 108:8 LXX) to prove his point and justify that a replacement is needed (Acts 1:20).[50] As part of the qualification of an apostle, one needs to be a "witness" (μάρτυς). As used in Acts, "witness" is given a technical meaning and clearly defined as one who has seen the resurrected Jesus (Acts 1:22).[51]

The Pentecost event of Acts 2 is part of the grand redemptive-historical change initiated by Jesus's coming. Now the "last days" of the church begin (Acts 2:17). On Pentecost, the Holy Spirit comes upon the Christians in a special way, fulfilling Jesus's promise that "you will receive power when the Holy Spirit has come upon you" (Acts 1:8) and confirming various Old Testament Scriptures. Part of the miracle of Pentecost is that other Jews from all over the Greco-Roman world hear the disciples speak in their own languages.[52] Following this event, Peter delivers a sermon that connects Pentecost to Jesus, with the theological conclusion that Jesus is "both Lord and Christ" (Acts 2:36). Peter then encourages all to "repent and be baptized . . . in the name of Jesus Christ" (Acts 2:38), and three thousand are baptized.[53]

In the sermon, Peter uses three Old Testament texts: Joel 2:28–32 (Heb./LXX 3:1–5) // Acts 2:17–21; Psalm 16:8–11 (LXX 15:8–11) // Acts 2:25–28; and Psalm 110:1 (LXX 109:1) // Acts 2:24–25. There are several interesting aspects. From

[48] See Darrell L. Bock's discussion of the Holy Spirit in both Luke and Acts (*A Theology of Luke and Acts: God's Promised Program, Realized for All Nations*, BTNT [Grand Rapids, MI: Zondervan, 2012], 211–26).

[49] In Acts 1:16, Luke through Peter presents a high view of God speaking in Scripture. It is "the Holy Spirit [that] spoke beforehand by the mouth of David concerning Judas." Even critical scholars readily admit this, although they generally do not like Peter's exegesis (e.g., Barrett, *Acts of the Apostles*, 1:100; and Pervo, *Acts*, 50, 53–54).

[50] Also related to Old Testament quotes about Judas's death, see John 13:18 // Ps. 41:9 and Matt. 27:9–10 related to Zech. 11:13 and possibly Jeremiah 19.

[51] See Acts 1:8, 22; 2:32; 3:15; 5:32; 10:39, 41; 13:31; 22:15, 20; 26:16. Note that in addition to the apostles, Paul and Stephen are included as "witnesses." See discussions in Peter Bolt, "Mission and Witness," in Marshall and Peterson, *Witness to the Gospel*, 215–34; and Robert J. Cara, "The Ambiguous Characterization of Barnabas in Acts 15:36–41" (PhD diss., Westminster Theological Seminary, 2001), 122–27.

[52] This seems to allude to the reversal of the multiple-language curse at Babel (Gen. 11:1–9; cf. Zeph. 3:9). As Peterson points out, however: "Communication actually took place through the diversity of languages represented there. God was expressing his ultimate intention to unite people 'from every tribe and language and people and nation'" (*Acts of the Apostles*, 136).

[53] Many critics do not take these speeches at face value. C. H. Dodd says of the speeches in Acts 2–4, "We may with some confidence take these speeches to represent, not indeed what Peter said upon this or that occasion, but the *kerygma* of the Church at Jerusalem at an early period" (*The Apostolic Preaching and Its Developments* [New York: Harper & Brothers, 1960], 21).

Joel's perspective, the pouring out of the Holy Spirit will be in the future, and Peter interprets Pentecost as the beginning of the events described in Joel. Therefore, for obvious redemptive-historical reasons, Peter intentionally changes the Joel 2:28 wording of "afterward" (אחרי־כן, μετὰ ταῦτα) to "in the last days" (ἐν ταῖς ἐσχάταις ἡμέραις) to reflect the God-intended meaning of the Joel text as Peter quoted it post-Pentecost.[54] Another interesting feature of these quotes is that the Hebrew names in the Old Testament texts that are used to prove that Jesus is "Lord" are Yahweh (יהוה, Joel 2:32 // Acts 2:21) and Adonai (אדני, Ps. 110:1 // Acts 2:34), although in the same sermon other texts are used where Jesus is contrasted with Yahweh (Ps. 16:8 // Acts 2:25; Ps. 110:1 // Acts 2:34). Thus, Jesus is referred to as Yahweh from Joel, implied as Christ and contrasted with Yahweh from Psalm 16, and referred to as Adonai and implied as Christ from Psalm 110. It is because of the Trinity that New Testament writers can use some Old Testament Yahweh texts to refer to the Father, others to refer to the Son, and others to refer to the one God.[55]

Acts 2:42–7:60 narrates several stories that present the church as unified and growing despite opposition. The unity is shown in the believers' "breaking bread in their homes" (2:46), praying together following the arrest of Peter and John (4:24), gathering at "Solomon's Portico" (5:12), and reaching agreement following the widow dispute between the Hellenistic and Palestinian Jewish Christians (6:5). Opposition to the gospel comes from the arrest of Peter and John (4:3), the deception of Ananias and Sapphira (5:1–11), another arrest of the apostles (5:17–18), and the arrest and stoning of Stephen (6:9–7:60). At this point in Acts, the gospel has been primarily confined to ethnic Jews, and the preaching has been confined to areas near Jerusalem.

The Church in Judea, Samaria, and Antioch (Acts 8:1–12:25)

Following the stoning of Stephen, "there arose on that day a great persecution against the church in Jerusalem, and they [Christians] were all scattered throughout the regions of Judea and Samaria, except the apostles" (Acts 8:1). In addition to Judea and Samaria, both of which during this time extended west to the Mediterranean Sea, this section of Acts also includes the gospel spreading north to Phoenicia, Cyprus, and Antioch (11:19).

In Samaria, Philip preaches and baptizes. The Samaritans "believed" and "received the word of God," but they did not "receive the Holy Spirit" (8:12–16). The apostles in Jerusalem send Peter and John to Samaria to pray and lay hands on them. Then the Samaritans do receive the Holy Spirit by a visible sign (8:17–18). Although it is not explicitly stated, I interpret this as the Samaritans speaking in tongues. Apparently, because the Samaritans are not fully ethnic Jews, God through the visible manifestation of the Holy Spirit is confirming that the Samaritans are also part of the church. This pattern will be repeated for the inclusion of the Gentiles (10:44–46) and John

[54] Often New Testament writers slightly change the grammar of an Old Testament quote to blend the grammar of the Old Testament text into the New Testament sentence. Much more interesting is when the New Testament writer changes the Old Testament quote for redemptive-historical reasons.

[55] See L. W. Hurtado's excellent discussion of Paul's use of Old Testament texts that connect Jesus as "Lord" to Yahweh ("Lord," in *DPL*, 560–69).

the Baptist's disciples (19:6).[56] (See more discussion in the section "Tongues," under "Theology," below.)

Paul is minimally introduced to the reader with a brief comment that he approved of Stephen's stoning (Acts 8:1).[57] Later, Paul is traveling to Damascus to harm believers there, but he is wonderfully converted by a personal encounter with Jesus (9:1–7).[58] The Lord tells the disciple Ananias, "[Paul] is a chosen instrument of mine to carry my name before the Gentiles and kings and the children of Israel. For I will show him how much he must suffer for the sake of my name" (9:15–16). These verses clearly indicate Paul's future, which unfolds in the remainder of Acts.[59] Note that God will use Paul to bring the gospel to both Jews and Gentiles, although Gentiles are the key audience, a point that anticipates the Peter-and-Cornelius episode in Acts 10–11.

Peter's interaction with Cornelius, the Gentile centurion, and subsequently Peter's interaction with church leaders about this are important for the message of Acts as it deals directly with the Gentile "problem" (10:1–11:18; 15:8).[60] There were actually two problems, although not of equal importance: (1) the difficulty of Jewish Christians interacting with Gentiles, given the Jewish food and hospitality laws/mores (10:13–14, 28; 11:3); (2) many Jewish Christians were not convinced that Gentiles were part of God's plan for the church, or at least part of the plan without first obeying Jewish ceremonial laws (10:45; 11:18; 15:8). The importance of this episode is shown not only by the topic of the Gentiles, but also by the length and repetition of the narrative itself.[61]

Cornelius, who is in Caesarea, is told by an angel to send to Joppa to get Peter. While Cornelius's men are on their way to Joppa, Peter has the vision of unclean or common animals. He is told, "What God has made clean, do not call common" (10:15). Peter is escorted to Cornelius in Caesarea, where Peter interprets his animal vision as indicating that he may show hospitality to Gentiles and that, he says, "I should not call any person common or unclean" (10:28). Peter then preaches the gospel, and Cornelius and others are converted, which includes their receiving the Holy Spirit, speaking in tongues, and being baptized. Also, the Jewish Christians "with

---

[56] Similarly, Kistemaker says, "The outpouring of the Spirit occurred in Jerusalem (2:1–4) and was repeated when the church added new groups: Samaritans (8:11–17), the Gentiles (10:44–47), and the disciples of John the Baptist (19:1–7)" (*Acts*, 302).

[57] As is well known, Paul is called "Saul" in Acts until the "first missionary journey," where the reader is told that Saul is "also called Paul" (13:9). From that point on in Acts, the name "Paul" is always used, except when Paul recounts his conversion (22:7; 26:14).

[58] Acts includes the conversion of Paul three times. Here it is historically narrated (9:1–19), and Paul twice recounts this experience (22:1–16; 26:12–18).

[59] For a summary of all the connections between Acts 9:15–16 and the rest of Acts, see Tannehill, *Narrative Unity of Luke-Acts*, 2:119–20.

[60] Previously, Philip presented the gospel to an Ethiopian. Apparently, although ethnically Gentile, the Ethiopian was a converted Jew (Acts 8:27).

[61] Cornelius's encounter with the angel is described four times (Acts 10:1–6, 17–23a, 27–29; 11:11–14). Peter's vision is described three times (Acts 10:9–16, 27–29; 11:5–9). The pouring out of the Holy Spirit on the Gentiles is described three times (10:44–48; 11:15–17; 15:8). There is also significant repetition in Paul's Damascus Road experience, as it is included three times (9:1–18; 22:4–16; 26:11–18). Robert C. Newman has an excellent article noting the parallels in Acts and how in the repeated incidents Luke does not feel the need to repeat every detail. In fact, often details are added in subsequent retellings. Newman then compares this to Synoptic Gospel parallels and critics' conclusions about conservatives' attempts at harmonization. He concludes, "I suggest that we here have a precedent in a single author [Luke] for many phenomena occurring in parallel passages of the synoptic Gospels, features which liberals regularly take as evidence of error, ignorance, bias, or suppression in the Gospel authors and from which they conclude that these accounts cannot be inerrant. Nothing of the sort is necessary" ("Parallel Narratives in Acts: A Case Study for Synoptic Harmonization," in *The Gospels Today: A Guide to Some Recent Developments*, ed. John H. Skilton [Philadelphia: Skilton House, 1990], 150–65, esp. 163).

Peter were amazed, because the gift of the Holy Spirit was poured out even on the Gentiles" (10:45). Peter returns to the Jerusalem church and responds to complaints that he has interacted with Gentiles. Upon his recounting of the events, the church concludes that "to the Gentiles also God has granted repentance that leads to life" (11:18). Clearly, the reader is to see that Gentiles are to be part of the church and, in addition, I argue, that the speaking in tongues in Acts 10:46 confirms this by a sign.

The Acts narrative now turns to several instances of persecution and its effect on the church. The previously described persecution of Stephen drove men bearing the gospel to Jews in Phoenicia, Cyprus, and Antioch (11:19–20), but some of those men spoke, as well, to Gentiles ("Hellenists," Ἑλληνιστής) in Antioch.[62] This prompts the Jerusalem church to send Barnabas and Paul to Antioch, which becomes a center of missionary activity.[63] Herod persecutes the church by killing James the brother of John and imprisoning Peter (12:1–3). Peter miraculously escapes from prison (12:7–11), and Herod dies a horrible death (12:23). In conclusion, despite the persecutions, "the word of God increased and multiplied" (12:24).

The First Missionary Journey of Paul: Northeast Mediterranean (Acts 13:1–14:28)

From Acts 13 through the remainder of Acts, Paul becomes the central human character.[64] He is included in every pericope except Acts 18:24–28 (Apollos in Ephesus). This emphasis on Paul further reinforces the emphasis on the Gentiles.

Acts 13–14, which narrates Paul's first missionary journey, is a clear unit. It begins at Antioch with the Holy Spirit and the church commissioning and calling Paul and Barnabas for a particular "work" (ἔργον) (13:2). It ends with Paul and Barnabas returning to Antioch and being commended for the "work [ἔργον] that they had fulfilled" (14:26; cf. 13:41).[65]

Geographically, this missionary journey is confined to the area of the northeastern Mediterranean Sea. From Antioch, Paul and Barnabas travel to the island of Cyprus, then on to the mainland areas of Pamphylia, Pisidia, and "South Galatia" (modern south-central Turkey), and back by sea to Antioch. Paul and Barnabas encounter persecution but also see many converts among both Jews and Gentiles.[66] In addition to their going to Gentile lands, the mission to Gentiles is emphasized by Paul's quote

[62]The context demands that Ἑλληνιστής is Greek-speaking non-Christian Gentiles. Thus in Acts Ἑλληνιστής has three slightly different meanings (1) Greek-speaking Jewish Christians (6:1), (2) Greek-speaking Jewish non-Christians (9:29), and (3) Greek-speaking non-Christian Gentiles (11:20). So also Barrett, *Acts of the Apostles*, 1:550. Note that many manuscripts have Ἕλλην ("Greeks") instead of Ἑλληνιστής; see Metzger's extended discussion (*Textual Commentary on the Greek New Testament*, 340–42).

[63]Hans Conzelmann provocatively notes, "[Antioch] appears as the *historical* center for the expansion of Christianity into Gentile territory. It is subordinate to the *dogmatic* center (Jerusalem), and in this way the unity of the church, made up of Jews and Gentiles, is portrayed" (*Commentary on the Acts of the Apostles*, trans. James Limburg, A. Thomas Kraabel, and Donald H. Juel, Hermeneia [Philadelphia: Fortress, 1987], 98, emphasis his).

[64]Paul's life will fulfill the Lord's statement about him in Acts 9:15–16.

[65]"Work" here, and in Acts 15:38, is being used in a semi-technical manner to refer to the work that Paul and Barnabas did on the first missionary journey. So also Pesch, *Die Apostelgeschichte*, 2:93, and Haenchen, *Acts of the Apostles*, 474.

[66]The persecution comes primarily from Jews (Acts 13:6, 50; 14:19), but it does include Gentiles (14:5). Strictly adhering to the Greek construction of Acts 14:19, the Jews, and not the crowd, stoned Paul. See Haenchen, *Acts of the Apostles*, 434; and Fitzmyer, *Acts of the Apostles*, 532–33.

of Isaiah 49:6 (Acts 13:46–47) and Paul and Barnabas's post-journey report to the Antioch church that God has "opened a door of faith to the Gentiles" (Acts 14:27).

While he is at the synagogue in Antioch of Pisidia, Paul's fairly long redemptive-historical sermon is recorded (Acts 13:16–47).[67] This is one of three somewhat lengthy redemptive-historical sermons in Acts, the other two being Peter's (2:17–40) and Stephen's (7:2–53).

Within Acts 13–14, there are several parallels to Jesus and Peter that tend to highlight Paul and show his continuity with Jesus and Peter.[68] All three at the beginning of their ministries have similar sermons, heal a lame man, and experience partial rejection (Luke 4:16–30; 5:17–26; Acts 2:5–3:10).[69] Paul's punitive miracle toward Bar-Jesus (Acts 13:6–11) may parallel Peter's episode with Ananias and Sapphira (Acts 5:1–10).

The Jerusalem Council (Acts 15:1–35)

The Jerusalem Council is prompted by some Christians "from Judea" who come to Antioch and are teaching that one must be circumcised in order to be "saved" (Acts 15:1). Not all in the church, especially some in Jerusalem, agree on all aspects of the Gentile question. Apparently, Acts 10–11 solves the food/hospitality question and whether Gentiles could be saved. But for some, the remaining question of whether Gentiles are required to observe the ceremonial law, especially circumcision, is not clear. The council concludes that Gentiles do not need to be circumcised or follow the ceremonial demands of the law but are "saved through the grace of the Lord Jesus" and "faith," as are Jews (15:9, 11, 19; cf. 13:38–39).

At the council, three arguments are made to support this conclusion: (1) Peter recalls the events related to Cornelius (Acts 15:7–11); (2) Barnabas and Paul recall their experiences with the Gentiles (Acts 15:12); and (3) James, the brother of Jesus, quotes Amos 9:11–12 and concludes that Gentiles are part of the church (Acts 15:13–19).

Many scholars see the Jerusalem Council as the center and turning point of Acts. Marshall declares, "Luke's account [in Acts 15] of the discussion regarding the relations of the Gentiles to the law of Moses forms the centre of Acts both structurally and theologically."[70] Another argument for seeing the Jerusalem Council as the center is that Peter makes his last appearance in Acts at the council, and Paul is clearly the main human figure after the council.[71] While I agree that Acts 15 is fairly important in Acts, I do not agree that it is *the* center of Acts.

---

[67] Of course, the actual historical sermon was probably much longer. Luke records a truncated, but accurate, version of it.

[68] See Tannehill, *Narrative Unity of Luke-Acts*, 2:161–63; and Charles Talbert, *Literary Patterns, Theological Themes, and the Genre of Luke-Acts*, SBLMS 20 (Missoula, MT: Scholars, 1974), 16–19, 23–26.

[69] Some additional Peter/Paul parallels include that both heal by strange means (Acts 5:15; 19:12), both encounter sorcerers (8:18; 13:8), and both are miraculously freed from prison (12:7; 16:26).

[70] I. Howard Marshall, *The Acts of the Apostles: An Introduction and Commentary*, TNTC (Grand Rapids, MI: Eerdmans, 1980), 242. Howard Clark Kee says, "Acts 15 is literarily, conceptually, and theologically the midpoint of the book" (*Good News to the Ends of the Earth: The Theology of Acts* [Philadelphia: Trinity Press International, 1990], 57). Pervo disagrees that Acts 15 is the "pivot" as this seems to ignore the major break between Acts 12 and 13. Chapter 13 "inaugurates the Diaspora mission that quickly brings Paul to leadership" (*Acts*, 20–21, 367–68, esp. 21).

[71] Haenchen states, "Now in this connection Chapter 15 marks the turning-point. Not only does Peter make his last appearance here, the Apostles also are mentioned for the last time in reference to the decree at 16:4. . . . So far Paul has been only one among many secondary figures in the history of the primitive mission. From Chapter 15 onward he becomes the dominant figure" (*Acts of the Apostles*, 461–62).

Most critical scholars believe that Acts 15 is Luke's version of what happened in Galatians 2:1–10 and that Luke's version has major historical errors where the two accounts differ.[72] As most conservatives point out, the critics simply assume that there could only have been one such meeting in Jerusalem. The problem is solved by equating Galatians 2:1–10 with the Acts 11:29–30 Jerusalem trip, not the Acts 15 trip. This solution assumes that Galatians was written in AD 48 and the Jerusalem Council occurred after that in AD 49.

Using this chronology also helps to explain the differences between Paul's actions regarding Titus and Timothy. In Galatians 2:1–5, Paul vehemently refuses to have Titus circumcised. However, in Acts 16:3, Paul encourages Timothy to be circumcised. The reason for the difference is that before the Jerusalem Council, there are some who still in principle want Gentiles circumcised relative to their justification. Paul does not bend to having Titus circumcised for that rationale. However, after the Jerusalem Council, when the principle has been decided, it is acceptable to have Timothy circumcised to avert a potential "stumbling block" to some. In stumbling-block situations, Christians forgo some of their rights for the good of others. I equate the "stumbling block" theology of Romans 14 and 1 Corinthians 8, 10 to Paul's "becoming all things to all people" of 1 Corinthians 9:22.

This stumbling-block theology also applies to the letter that the council writes to the churches in Antioch, Syria, and Cilicia concerning the Christian Gentiles' voluntarily agreeing, at least for the time being, to adhere to some ceremonial food laws and not eat food previously sacrificed to idols (Acts 15:20, 29).[73] Calvin also calls this a "stumbling-block" situation and notes that Paul himself, who delivered the letter, later clearly says that all foods are clean, but in some cases one might refrain from eating food sacrificed to idols (Rom. 14:14–15; 1 Cor. 10:23–30).[74]

The Second Missionary Journey of Paul (Aegean Sea) (Acts 15:36–18:22)

This section opens with Paul and Barnabas separating (Acts 15:36–41). Paul's second missionary journey begins in Antioch and quickly takes him and his various intermittent companions across modern-day Turkey to Troas on the coast of the Aegean Sea. This is orchestrated by the "Spirit of Jesus" (16:7). In Troas, Paul has a vision and hears the "Macedonian call" to travel from "Asia" across the Aegean to the European continent.[75] He and his companions obey the call. They minister in various cities in Macedonia and then south to Achaia (16:11–18:17). Notable conversions and various persecutions occur in Philippi, Thessalonica, Berea, Athens, and Corinth. From Cenchreae (near Corinth), Paul's group crosses back over the Aegean Sea to Ephesus

[72] E.g., Pervo, *Acts*, 369; and Barrett, *Acts of the Apostles*, 2:xxxvi–xl, 696–97.

[73] A difficulty for all interpreters is that "sexual immorality" (πορνεία) is included, which on the surface appears to be a moral law not in the category of the other ceremonial laws (Acts 15:20, 29; 21:25). John Calvin surmises that it is the pagan practice of taking a common-law wife (*The Acts of the Apostles*, trans. John W. Fraser and W. J. G. McDonald, 2 vols., Calvin's Commentaries [Grand Rapids, MI: Eerdmans, 1965–1966], 2:50–51). Witherington connects πορνεία and the other prohibitions to the debauchery related to pagan temple feasts and temple prostitution (*Acts of the Apostles*, 460–64).

[74] Calvin, *Acts of the Apostles*, 2:55–57. Marshall makes the same connections between the letter, 1 Corinthians 8–10, and Romans 14 (*Luke: Historian and Theologian*, 185).

[75] In the geographical terms of Acts, "Macedonia" is modern-day northern Greece and southern Macedonia; "Achaia" is southern Greece.

(Acts 18:21). From there, Paul travels across the Mediterranean Sea to Caesarea and then back home to Antioch (18:22).

The separation of Paul and Barnabas is due to a "sharp disagreement" (παροξυσμός) over Mark, who departed from the "work" (ἔργον) during the first missionary journey (Acts 15:36–41). This results in two missionary teams. Throughout church history, there has been disagreement as to who, if anyone, is wrong in this split, which affects one's interpretation of who is exemplary.[76]

Chrysostom believes that the different character traits of Paul and Barnabas explain the split and that neither sinned. He further argues that they purposely separated for the advantage of two preaching teams.[77] In popular literature, Acts 15:36–41 is commonly used to justify a church split.[78] On the other hand, many argue (including me) that Paul is portrayed as correct and Barnabas wrong.[79] Acts 15:36–41 notes that Paul was "commended" for his future trip, which resulted in "strengthening the churches," that is, those addressed by the apostolic letter. The passage also gives Paul's rationale for not taking Mark. None of these references has an equivalent for Barnabas. In addition, Barnabas is never again mentioned in Acts. Therefore, I conclude that Paul is to be imitated here, and not Barnabas (although, the previous actions and traits of Barnabas in Acts are exemplary).

No, this pericope should not be used to justify church splits, even though God in his providence used this separation for good. Wonderfully, elsewhere the New Testament indicates that Paul, Barnabas, and Mark are again on good terms, and Mark is again involved in ministry (1 Cor. 9:6; Col. 4:10; 2 Tim. 4:11; Philem. 24; 1 Pet. 5:13). Derek Thomas uses this to conclude, rightly I believe, that as Mark was given a second chance in ministry, so should others be.[80]

Paul's Areopagus address (Acts 17:22–31) in Athens is his second of six major speeches in Acts.[81] It is an evangelistic speech to Gentiles. Paul notes the idols in

[76] As I have written elsewhere:

> "Exemplary" interpretation notes character's actions and traits. It then concludes that the author intended that the reader should see those as exemplars, with the intention of imitating them. The reader is to distinguish between "good" examples, which are to be imitated, and "bad" examples, which show the reader what not to do. Further, and more difficult, the reader also needs to distinguish between those actions and traits that the author intended as an example (either good or bad), and those that are simply miscellaneous details of the narrative.

(Cara, "The Ambiguous Characterization of Barnabas in Acts 15:36–41," 154–55). Richard L. Pratt Jr. sees exemplary interpretation as legitimate, but notes that it can be abused and is usually "secondary to the main purpose of the book" (*He Gave Us Stories: The Bible Students' Guide to Interpreting Old Testament Narratives* [Brentwood, TN: Wolgemuth & Hyatt, 1990], 91). Some who emphasize "redemptive-historical" interpretation question the legitimacy of any exemplary interpretation (e.g., Sidney Greidanus, *The Modern Preacher and the Ancient Text: Interpreting and Preaching Biblical Literature* [Grand Rapids, MI: Eerdmans, 1988], 116–18, 161–63, 305).

[77] Chrysostom, *Acts* 34 (*NPNF*[1] 11:214).

[78] "There is biblical precedent for Christians deciding to separate because they could not agree. Paul and Barnabas had different agendas in Acts 15. Separation allowed them each to fulfill what they believed God was calling them to do. History affirms that the separation was wise, enabling ministry to happen" (Alan Reutter, "Let's Divide," *Monday Morning*, 4 October 1993, 6). In a different situation, the separation of Paul and Barnabas was used to justify splitting a contentious presbytery ("Westminster Presbytery Votes to Divide," *Presbyterian & Reformed News*, January–February 2000, 6–7).

[79] For example, Cara, "The Ambiguous Characterization of Barnabas in Acts 15:36–41"; Calvin, *Acts of the Apostles*, 2:59–62; and Johnson, *Message of Acts*, 282–88.

[80] Derek W. H. Thomas, *Acts*, Reformed Expository Commentary (Phillipsburg: P&R, 2011), 444–46. Thomas notes that Mark's ministry failure was not a "moral failure." It was a "ministerial failure" because of "inexperience and timidity."

[81] His first speech is an evangelistic and redemptive-historical speech to Jews (Acts 13:16–41). This, his second one, is an evangelistic speech to Gentiles. Previously, Paul did have a brief evangelistic speech to Gentiles (14:15–17). The third major one is a farewell speech to the Ephesian elders (Acts 20:18–35). His fourth and sixth major speeches relate to Paul's recounting of his Damascus Road experience given at the temple (22:3–21) and before Agrippa (26:2–29). His fifth major speech is before Felix (24:10–21).

Athens. One has an inscription "to the unknown God" (17:23), which Paul uses as his talking point to move from an unknown to the known God. Instead of rehearsing the history of Israel, he emphasizes God as Creator and providential controller of all things, including mankind. In fact, Paul quotes two Greek poets who, at least on the word level, agree with him that God providentially controls humans (17:28).[82] Given that God and humans are related and that God made everything, idols of stone do not make sense for God. Further, this Creator God requires that all repent, and he will one day judge the world by a man who has been raised from the dead.

While the Areopagus address is different from others in Acts, it does have similarities to the other speeches. For example, God as Creator is discussed in Acts 4:24 and 14:15; Stephen also notes that God does not live in a temple (7:48); and Peter notes that Jesus will be Judge (10:42).[83]

Two brief theological issues confront us. First, Paul states that God "made from one man every nation of mankind" (Acts 17:26). This dovetails with Luke's genealogy, which traces Jesus's line back to Adam, implying that all men came from Adam (Luke 3:38). Currently, some movements within "evangelicalism" deny that Adam and Eve are the parents of all humans, despite the clear teaching of Acts 17:26.[84] This denial, among other problems, destroys the parallelism of Adam and Christ related to our salvation (Rom. 5:12–21). Second, Paul refers to Jesus as a "man" who will come to judge at the second coming (Acts 17:31). This verse reminds us that even after the resurrection, and forever, Jesus is the God-man (cf. 1 Cor. 15:45–49; 1 Tim. 2:5). His human nature did not cease to exist after the resurrection or ascension.[85]

The Third Missionary Journey of Paul (Aegean Sea) (Acts 18:23–21:16)

The third missionary journey begins, as the other two did, in Antioch. Paul travels across modern-day Turkey as he did before, but now he goes into the heart of Asia (modern-day western Turkey), the city of Ephesus. He ministers there for three years (Acts 19:8, 10; 20:31), and Luke records several incidents related to Ephesus (Acts 19). From Ephesus, Paul crosses the Aegean Sea and goes to Macedonia. He continues south to Achaia and back north again through Macedonia. Little is said of this portion of the journey except that Paul is strengthening churches as he goes (Acts 20:1–2). Although not stated in Acts, this portion of the trip takes about two years. Paul crosses back over the Aegean Sea to Troas, where the incident with Eutychus takes place (20:7–12). Paul continues south along the coast of Asia and comes to Miletus. There the elders from Ephesus visit him, and Luke records Paul's farewell

[82] All agree that the second quote, "for we are indeed his offspring" (17:28), is from Aratus's poem *Phaenomena*. The first quote, "in him we live and move and have our being" (17:28), is less certain. The most common option is Epimenides. In favor of Epimenides is Kirsopp Lake, "The Unknown God" and "Your Own Poets," in Foakes-Jackson and Lake, *The Beginnings of Christianity*, 5:240–51, esp. 5:245; against Epimenides, Pervo, *Acts*, 438–39.

[83] Tannehill lists five similarities (*Narrative Unity of Luke-Acts*, 2:211–12).

[84] For example, the Biologos Foundation.

[85] WSC 21 famously makes this point. "The only Redeemer of God's elect is the Lord Jesus Christ, who, being the eternal Son of God, became man, and so was, and *continueth to be*, God and man in two distinct natures, and one person, *for ever*" (emphasis mine).

speech to them (Acts 20:18–38). From Miletus, Paul sails across the Mediterranean Sea to the coast of Palestine and eventually to Jerusalem.

The first and second missionary journeys emphasize the founding of new churches. The Acts narrative of the third journey emphasizes the founding of the Ephesian church and simply reports the strengthening of the other existing churches. Concerning the Ephesian church, although Paul previously visited Ephesus briefly at the end of his second journey (Acts 18:19–21) and Apollos was there before Paul's arrival (18:24–26), it is during the third missionary journey that the Ephesian church is founded. Acts 18:10 implies that other areas in Asia are also evangelized during his stay at Ephesus. Probably, during this time, the relatively nearby churches in Colossae, Laodicea, and Hierapolis are evangelized by Paul's companions (cf. Acts 20:4; Eph. 6:21; Col. 1:7–8; 2:1; 4:7, 12–13; 2 Tim. 4:12).[86]

As Paul first comes to Ephesus, he interacts with disciples of John the Baptist (Acts 19:1–7).[87] Paul inquires as to whether they received "the Holy Spirit when [they] believed." They answer that they have "not even heard that there is a Holy Spirit" (Acts 19:2). Paul thus realizes that they do not have the normal Christian baptism (and do not fully understand John the Baptist's teaching, Luke 3:16). He asks, "Into what then were you baptized?" (Acts 19:3). For Paul to question their baptism because these disciples have not heard of the Holy Spirit implies that Paul's understanding of Christian baptism is Trinitarian.[88] Interestingly, in Acts Luke uses the wording "baptized in the name of the Lord Jesus" (see Acts 2:38; 8:16; 10:48; 19:5). Apparently, Luke's wording is shorthand technical language for the full Trinitarian formula.

Paul then explains Jesus to the disciples of John the Baptist. They believe, are baptized, receive the Holy Spirit, and speak in tongues (Acts 19:4–6). By the visible sign of tongues, God confirms that John the Baptist's disciples are also now part of the church and included in the grand redemptive-historical change effected by Jesus's life and death and by Pentecost. This event is similar to the only other two tongues episodes following Pentecost: with the Samaritans (8:17–18) and with the Gentiles (10:44–46). (See more discussion in the section "Tongues," under "Theology," below.)

Paul's farewell address to the Ephesian elders while at Miletus is his third major speech recorded in Acts. Although Acts often characterizes Paul as teaching Christians, this address to Christians is the only one recorded. Many critical scholars view this address as the separation of the apostolic age from the post-apostolic age and the establishment of "Christendom." That is, according to the critics, the writer of Acts is now directly addressing the church of his day by putting his ideas into Paul's mouth.[89] Although this is not the place for a detailed response, I would contend that

---

[86] Bruce agrees and adds, "Perhaps all seven of the churches of Asia addressed in the Revelation of John were also founded about this time" (*Acts*, 366).

[87] The previous pericope related to Apollos, who properly applied John the Baptist's teaching to Jesus (Acts 18:24–28).

[88] So also Alexander, *Commentary on the Acts of the Apostles*, 2:187–88.

[89] For example, Brevard S. Childs:

> Paul has been faithful to the ministry which he received from the Lord Jesus (20:20) in testifying to the gospel. The issue is of continuity of the tradition. Paul has declared "the whole counsel of God." The issue is of completeness. . . . Paul is not sketched from a historical reconstruction, but his role has been gathered, universalized, and made repre-

the differences noted in this address compared with others in Acts are simply due to Paul's audience.

Within the address, Paul remarks that he declares "the whole counsel of God" (Acts 20:27). This expression is often used in Reformed theology circles to emphasize that all of the Bible is to be taught, not just one's favorite sections.[90] Paul parallels this comment with others: "to testify to the gospel of the grace of God" (20:24) and "proclaiming the kingdom" (20:25).[91] As least in this context, "the gospel" broadly parallels "the whole counsel of God."[92] Elsewhere in the New Testament, "gospel" many times has a slightly more truncated or core meaning focusing on salvation through the work of Christ (e.g., Rom. 1:16–17; 1 Cor. 15:1–4). The New Testament also includes the broader meaning (e.g., Mark 14:9; Rom 1:1; 2:16; 1 Pet. 1:24–25), matching Acts 20:24.[93] Of course, the core and broad meanings of the "gospel" are related (as everything is related) to the triune God's person and work (Rom. 11:36; Col. 1:15–20).

From Jerusalem to Rome (Acts 21:17–28:31)

The last section of Acts is the intriguing story of how Paul gets from Jerusalem to Rome. Except for the beginning of this section, Paul is under various levels of arrest/custody/imprisonment for the whole section (e.g., Acts 21:33; 22:30; 23:10; 24:23; 27:3; 28:30).

Jews are primarily responsible for Paul's arrest and continued imprisonment in Palestine (e.g., 21:27–28; 22:30; 23:12; 24:9; 25:15; 28:17–20). Governor Felix is also partially to blame, as he keeps Paul in prison for two years, hoping to receive a bribe and do favors for the Jews (24:25–27); and the subsequent governor, Festus, also tries to do favors for the Jews (25:9). A turning point in the custody story is Paul's statement before Festus "I appeal to Caesar" (25:11–12; see also 25:25; 26:32; 28:19; cf. 22:25–28; 23:27). This then sets in motion his long journey to Rome, including the exciting trip across the Mediterranean Sea (Acts 27:1–28:14). The book of Acts ends with Paul under house arrest for two years in Rome awaiting trial. To "all who came to him [he was] proclaiming the kingdom of God and teaching about the Lord Jesus Christ with all boldness and without hindrance" (Acts 28:30–31).

The emphasis on getting to Rome and eventually before Caesar is important in Acts because it dovetails with the book's overall purpose to show God's providence over the expanding church despite opposition, with an emphasis on Gentiles. More

---

sentative. . . . The canonical Paul is, thus, a theological composite, at least one stage removed from the Paul of the letters, who now addressed the future needs of the Christian Church (Acts 20).

(*The New Testament as Canon: An Introduction* [Philadelphia: Fortress, 1985], 226, 233).

[90] See WCF 1.6 and WLC 159. This expression is included in many ordination vows; e.g., "Do you promise to preach the gospel in its purity and simplicity, declaring the whole counsel of God, and to perform all your official duties with zeal and faithfulness, seeking the salvation of sinners?" (Associate Reformed Presbyterian Church Form of Government, 9.30, Q. 8). The original seal of Westminster Theological Seminary includes this expression in Greek.

[91] See, for example, Luke 16:16 and Acts 8:12 for the connection of gospel (verb form) and kingdom.

[92] The noun "gospel" (εὐαγγέλιον) is used only twice in Luke and Acts: Acts 15:7 and 20:24. However, the verb "preach the good news" (εὐαγγελίζομαι) is used ten times in Luke and fifteen times in Acts.

[93] For standard discussions of "gospel" in the New Testament, see A. B. Luter Jr., "Gospel," *DPL*, 369–72; and Moisés Silva, ed., "Εὐαγγέλιον," *NIDNTTE*, 2:306–13.

specifically, the Rome/Caesar emphasis is connected to Jesus's pronouncement that the good news of him will go "to the end of the earth" (Acts 1:8) and that Paul will be brought before "kings" (9:15). Also, while under arrest in Jerusalem, Paul is explicitly told by the Lord, "Take courage" as "you must testify [about me] also in Rome" (23:11). Later, while the ship is floundering, an angel of God tells Paul, "Do not be afraid, Paul; you must stand before Caesar" (27:24). Yes, Acts ends with Paul under house arrest, but the reader is to rejoice that this is God's providential way of expanding the church.

Within this section, Paul has three major speeches in which he defends himself. The first is his recounting of the Damascus Road experience at the temple complex (22:3–21). The Jews are upset because Paul has indicated that God wanted him to go to the Gentiles with the message (22:21–23). As Simon Kistemaker remarks, "This one word, Gentiles, was sufficient for [the Jews] to condemn Paul as a desecrator of the temple."[94] The Roman authorities therefore take Paul away.

Paul's second major speech is his defense before Felix at Caesarea (24:10–21). Here Paul emphasizes that his disagreement with the Jews is simply over the "resurrection of the dead" (24:21). Previously, in the context of the Jewish Council (Sanhedrin), Paul deftly used the difference between the Sadducees and Pharisees over the possibility of resurrection to his advantage (23:6–9; 24:20). Paul assumes that Felix will see that believing in the doctrine of resurrection is no crime because one of the major Jewish parties, the Pharisees, also believes this. Of course, Paul's view and the Pharisees' view of a future resurrection are similar only at a surface level; Paul believes that Jesus has already been raised, and it is through Jesus that the future resurrection will occur (13:37–39; 21:13; 24:24; 26:23). Felix makes no decision concerning Paul.

Paul's third major speech in this section is his defense in Caesarea before King Agrippa, his wife, Bernice, and Governor Festus (Acts 26:2–29). Again Paul recounts his Damascus Road experience. He highlights that he has a mission to the Gentiles (26:17–18, 23) and that he is preaching "nothing but what the prophets and Moses said would come to pass: that the Christ must suffer and . . . [be] the first to rise from the dead" (26:22–23). Agrippa, Bernice, and Festus conclude that if Paul had not appealed to Caesar, he would have been set free (26:30–32).

Theology

Several theological themes in Acts clearly overlap with the Gospel of Luke. The themes of salvation and the plan of God are most often noted. These two themes are discussed in the Luke chapter, under "Message and Theology." Carson and Moo suggest six themes for the theology of Acts: (1) the plan of God, (2) the presence of the future (the "last days" have dawned), (3) salvation, (4) the Word of God, (5) the Holy Spirit, and (6) the people of God.[95] While these are all legitimate themes, for

[94] Kistemaker, *Acts*, 796.

[95] *Introduction to the New Testament*, 322–25. For broad discussions of the theology of Acts, see Marshall, *Luke: Historian and Theologian*, 157–215; I. Howard Marshall, *New Testament Theology: Many Witnesses, One Gospel* (Downers Grove, IL: InterVarsity Press, 2004), 155–83; Bock, *Theology of Luke and Acts*; Mark Allan Powell, *What Are They Saying about Acts?* (New York: Paulist, 1991); Kee, *Good News to the Ends of the Earth*; Jervell, *Theology of the Acts of the Apostles*;

purposes of this chapter I will include only two discussions. The first will consider portions of several of the above themes as I will try to coordinate the gift of the Holy Spirit, baptism, belief/conversion, and tongues. The second discussion will focus on the preached Word of God.

The Gift of the Holy Spirit, Baptism, Belief/Conversion, and Tongues[96]

In Acts, there are obviously strong connections between the gift of the Holy Spirit, baptism, belief/conversion, and tongues, but on the surface, no consistent pattern of how they relate to each other. Indeed, many scholars see ultimately no pattern among them.[97] I do believe, however, that there is a theological consistency. I will offer an explanation for the occurrence of tongues, previously mentioned, and will also recommend three overlapping categories that explain various other "irregularities" related to the gift of the Holy Spirit in Acts.[98] Finally, I will note the relationship between baptism and ministry gifts.

What are the surface irregularities? In several instances many are baptized with no mention of speaking in tongues (Acts 2:41; 8:38–39; 9:18; 16:15, 32). Sometimes conversion is mentioned, but without reference to the Holy Spirit (8:39; 13:48; 16:34), and sometimes conversion is mentioned but baptism is not (4:4; 6:7; 9:42; 11:21–24; 13:48; 14:1, 21; 17:34). The temporal relationship between receiving the Holy Spirit and being baptized differs: sometimes the Holy Spirit comes before baptism (10:47); sometimes the Spirit comes at approximately the same time (2:38); and sometimes the Spirit comes after baptism (8:15; 19:6). In some instances men and women are filled with the Holy Spirit at conversion (2:38), and at other times they are filled on special occasions for particular tasks (4:8; 6:3; 7:55; 13:9; etc.).

Tongues. The gift of tongues occurs in only four situations in Acts: Pentecost (2:3, 4, 11); Peter and John's visit with the Samaritan converts (8:15–18);[99] the gathering of Cornelius and friends (10:46); and Paul's visit with the Ephesian disciples of John the Baptist (19:6). In all four events, tongues is considered part of the gift of the Holy Spirit. What connects these four examples? *All four events involve important new groups that are added to the church.*

In Acts there occurs a great turning point in the history of God's redemption. The long-awaited Messiah has lived, died, been resurrected, and ascended. God is about to give the Holy Spirit and additional gifts, benefits, and sacraments to the new covenant community (the New Testament church). The covenant people are changing from an Israel-based group to an international community.

George Eldon Ladd, *A Theology of the New Testament*, ed. Donald A. Hagner, rev. ed. (Grand Rapids, MI: Eerdmans, 1993), 347–93; Thomas R. Schreiner, *New Testament Theology: Magnifying God in Christ* (Grand Rapids, MI: Baker Academic, 2008), 289–304; and Marshall and Peterson, *Witness to the Gospel*.

[96] Some of this discussion is included in Robert J. Cara, "In Acts: Baptism Signifies Ministry Gifts," *Faith and Practice* 1 (1996): 27–32.

[97] Marshall says, "It is clear that Luke had received several varying accounts of how the Spirit was received by men, but he has not tried to harmonize them and impose a pattern on them" (*Luke: Historian and Theologian*, 199).

[98] Portions of this discussion will parallel my article "In Acts: Baptism Signifies Ministry Gifts."

[99] As argued previously, tongues is included in Acts 8:15–18. See the above section "The Church in Judea, Samaria, and Antioch."

Through a visible, audible sign (tongues), God shows the early church and the readers of Acts that all these once-separate groups are included in the new covenant community. Let us look briefly at each of these four events.

Pentecost (Acts 2:1–12) is the first occurrence with tongues and is the important beginning of the new covenant change that involves a special outpouring of the Holy Spirit. It also includes both Palestinian and Hellenistic Jews.

The second tongues occurrence is in Samaria (Acts 8:9–25). The Samaritans (partially Jewish, see 11:19) are converted and baptized but have not yet received the Holy Spirit. They receive the Holy Spirit when representative apostles (Peter and John) from Jerusalem place their hands on the converts. This fits well with the expectation of Acts 1:8, "in Jerusalem and in all Judea and *Samaria*." Even those hated Samaritans are to be part of the church.

The third occurrence involves Peter and the Gentile Cornelius. The entire episode is very important to Acts as the story is repeated again and again (10:1–48; 11:1–18; 15:7–11). The key theme in these sections is that Gentiles are indeed part of the new church. Peter reasons with Jewish Christians in Jerusalem based on the evidence of the Holy Spirit, tongues: "If then God gave the same gift to them [Gentiles] as he gave to us [Jewish Christians] . . . who was I that I could stand in God's way?" (11:17). Note the emphasis of Peter's argument: speaking in tongues proves that the new church should include the Gentiles. In this new era, God is including the Gentiles in the new covenant community, Peter argues in both Acts 11 and 15. Therefore, a new major ethnic group is included in the church.

The fourth tongues event revolves around the disciples of John the Baptist who have not yet heard the full Christian message (Acts 19:1–7). This time it is Paul who is the church's representative to clarify the relationship between John the Baptist's disciples and the church. In light of new realities based on Christ's death and resurrection, the followers of John are now absorbed into the church and no longer exist as a separate entity.

Clearly, the primary purpose of the gift of tongues in Acts is to show that these groups are to be included in the new covenant community. Tongues serve as an outward visible sign that the various groups have received the Holy Spirit and are to be incorporated into this new covenant community. I regard this as strong *supporting* evidence that tongues are not normative for today because the foundational purpose of tongues was fulfilled by the end of the first century.[100]

The gift of the Holy Spirit. I will recommend three overlapping categories related to the gift of the Holy Spirit in Acts to explain the irregularities mentioned above. These categories follow Calvin's distinction in Acts between the "Spirit of regeneration" and the Spirit of "special gifts,"[101] which in turn matches well Paul's distinction between the possession of the Spirit (Rom. 8:1–17) and the gifts of the Spirit

[100] Similarly, Richard B. Gaffin Jr., *Perspectives on Pentecost: Studies in New Testament Teaching on the Gifts of the Holy Spirit* (Phillipsburg, NJ: P&R, 1979).
[101] Calvin, *Acts of the Apostles*, 2:148.

(1 Corinthians 12 [χάρισμα]; Eph. 4:1–16 [δωρεά, δόμα]). The three categories are (1) regeneration by the Holy Spirit, (2) *miraculous*-sign ministry gifts given by the Holy Spirit (foundational gifts), and (3) *non*-miraculous ministry gifts given by the Holy Spirit. The Holy Spirit's coming upon someone in Acts may include one or all three of these categories. In the book of Acts, the third category is most often in view. We will look briefly at each.

Regeneration by the Holy Spirit. Here I am following the traditional Reformed understanding that, whether in the Old Testament or in the New, all people need the Holy Spirit "before" (logical/causal priority) they are able to believe.[102] This regeneration is described in Acts 10:43–47, is implied in Acts 13:48 and 28:25–28, and is also implied in the connection of the Holy Spirit to the preached Word.[103] But often this gift of regeneration is not included in the "gift of the Holy Spirit" in Acts. Why? People who believe have received the Holy Spirit for regeneration but (1) have not yet received the Holy Spirit *as a ministry gift* due to the redemptive-historical stage in which they live (e.g., 8:14–17) or (2) have already received the Holy Spirit as a ministry gift but have had a post-conversion *"filling" for a special task* (e.g., 4:8; 7:55). These other senses of the "gift of the Holy Spirit" explain why the Samaritans are converted and yet have not received the gift of the Spirit (8:4–17). That is, the Samaritans *have* received the Holy Spirit in the sense of conversion but have *not* received the new "last days" giving of the Spirit that includes the new ministry gifts. All true believers in the Old Testament required the Holy Spirit for conversion, but few had any Spirit-ministry gifts.

Miraculous-sign ministry gifts given by the Holy Spirit (foundational gifts). As shown above, in Acts, tongues relates to the foundation and redemptive-historical expansion of the church. I assume that the ability to perform miraculous healings is from the Holy Spirit (e.g., 5:12–16; 19:11). Hence, I see these aspects of the gift of the Holy Spirit as related to the grand redemptive-historical event of the founding of the New Testament church (cf. Eph. 2:20).

Non-miraculous ministry gifts given by the Holy Spirit. Ministry gifts that are *not* miraculous are probably the main emphasis of the giving of the Holy Spirit in Acts. New Testament believers will have "more fulness" and more "spiritual efficacy" for giftedness than Old Testament believers had, because of the new redemptive-historical realities.[104] This is probably the "center of the circle" for Acts 2:38, though the expression "gift of the Holy Spirit" does sometimes include the miraculous sign gifts. In Acts, the non-miraculous gift is primarily related to witnessing for Christ (e.g., 1:4, 8; 4:31; 9:17–20), although it is also related to other activities (e.g., 6:3; 11:24; maybe 20:28). The gift of the Holy Spirit is also related to post-conversion "fillings," which are organically related to the initial

[102] See WCF 10.1–2, 11.4, 6; and Louis Berkhof, *Systematic Theology*, 4th ed. (Grand Rapids, MI: Eerdmans, 1986), 465–79.
[103] Also see John 3; Eph. 2:8; Phil. 1:29; and Titus 3:5.
[104] WCF 7.6.

receiving of the gift. Of course, various other New Testament ministry gifts are discussed elsewhere in the New Testament (e.g., Rom. 12:3–8; 1 Corinthians 12–14), along with the sanctifying work of the Holy Spirit in the sense of personal ethical holiness (e.g., Rom. 8:9; Gal. 5:22). In the present age, because the founding of the new covenant church has been completed, there is no time gap between the Spirit's work of conversion and the Spirit's bestowal of ministry gifts. Today, if one is converted, then one has the Spirit's ministry gifts and also will experience post-conversion fillings of the Holy Spirit.

Baptism and ministry gifts. In Acts, baptism is strongly connected to the Holy Spirit. "Repent and be baptized . . . and you will receive the gift of the Holy Spirit" (Acts 2:38; also see 10:47; 11:16–17; 19:4–6). As the functions of the Holy Spirit have several aspects in Acts, so does baptism. Given its associations with the Holy Spirit, baptism in Acts is connected with conversion, being incorporated into the church, and receiving ministry gifts.

In Acts, the list of ministry gifts that one might receive is not very large. As we saw above, the primary ministry gift is related to preaching and witnessing—which makes sense, given one of the main themes of the book. However, from Paul and elsewhere in the New Testament, we discover that there are many more ministry gifts.

If one looks at the Westminster Confession or any other historic Protestant creed, the ministry-gifts aspect of baptism is not emphasized.[105] To be sure, it is implied. For example, WCF 27.1 says that the sacraments "represent Christ and his benefits." The Heidelberg Catechism connects Christ's "treasures and gifts" to us with the doctrine of the "communion of saints" (Q. 55). Consequently, we ought to make explicit another aspect of baptism: ministry gifts through the power of the Holy Spirit are endowed to all who are Christians.

Preached Word of God

All scholars see the preaching of the "word of God" as an important theme in Acts. Some even consider it the main theme. Haenchen states, "The real subject of Acts is the *logos tou theou* and its growth."[106] Although not going that far, I do consider the preaching of the Word of God to be an important secondary theme in Acts (see "Addressee[s], Occasion, and Purposes," above).

The importance of this theme is shown by its inclusion in three of the six main summary verses (Acts 6:7; 12:24; 19:20) and five of the secondary summary verses (8:25; 11:1; 13:49; 18:11; 19:10).[107] By my count, the expression "word of God" and its shorthand forms (see below) are used thirty times in Acts. The pericope concerning the choosing of deacons to attend to the widows so that the apostles can "devote [them]selves to prayer and the ministry of the word" highlights the importance of

[105] The Catechism of the Catholic Church 1266 does connect baptism directly with the gifts of the Holy Spirit and justification.
[106] Haenchen, *Acts of the Apostles*, 49. Peterson sees the main theme as "A reassurance about the triumph of the word through suffering" ("Luke's Theological Enterprise," 540).
[107] See F. V. Filson, "Live Issues in Acts," *BR* 9 (1964): 25–42.

word ministry (Acts 6:4). Most significantly, the primary method by which the church grows in Acts is through the preaching of the word.[108]

The expression "word of God" is never used in Acts to refer directly to Scripture but always refers to some type of preaching or teaching.

Data concerning "word of God." First, a few surface-level observations concerning the expression "word of God." Although I am not primarily discussing the Gospel of Luke, I will include information from Luke for completeness.

In the Greek LXX and New Testament, the term translated "word" is either ῥῆμα or λόγος. In Luke and Acts, the expression ῥῆμα τοῦ θεοῦ/κυρίου occurs only in Luke 3:2; 22:61; and Acts 11:16.[109] The first passage refers to a statement by God to John the Baptist, and the latter two texts refer to a specific statement by Jesus in his earthly existence. Hence, ῥῆμα does not relate to this discussion, as it is not directly associated with preaching.

In Luke, the expression λόγος τοῦ θεοῦ occurs four times (Luke 5:1; 8:11, 21; 11:28). The first is a summary statement related to Jesus's preaching, and the others are direct quotes of Jesus referring to his preaching or teaching as the word of God.

In Acts, κυρίου ("of the Lord") is used several times with λόγος as opposed to θεοῦ ("of God"). In addition, many textual variants use κυρίου and θεοῦ interchangeably. Therefore, for this discussion, λόγος τοῦ θεοῦ and λόγος τοῦ κυρίου will be considered equivalent.[110] I will not continue to distinguish them but will simply refer to both as "word of God."

Many times in Acts λόγος τοῦ θεοῦ is shortened to simply λόγος , especially when used with λαλέω ("speak").[111] When I refer to "word of God" in this discussion, I will be including these instances.

All the instances of "word of God" with the above nuances are grouped in table 4, more or less on a pericope basis.

"Word of God" in Acts		
4:29, 31	12:24	16:6
6:2, 4	13:5, 7, 44, 46, 48	16:32
6:7	13:49	17:11, 13
8:4, 14, 25	14:25	18:5, 11
10:36, 44; 11:1	15:35	19:10
11:19	15:36	19:20

Table 4

[108] For significant articles on this topic, see Jerome Kodell, "'The Word of God Grew': The Ecclesial Tendency of Λόγος in Acts 1:7, 12:24, 19:20," *Bib* 55 (1974): 505–19; and Brian S. Rosner, "The Progress of the Word," in Marshall and Peterson, *Witness to the Gospel: The Theology of Acts*, 215–33.

[109] The majority text includes ῥῆμα in Luke 4:4 and λόγος in Luke 22:61.

[110] Occasionally the context provides a possible clue to why κυρίου is used. For example, κυρίου appears in Acts 16:32 where the previous verse uses κύριος in referring to Jesus. However, I am still not able to discern any difference in meaning.

[111] Acts 4:29; 11:19; 14:25; 16:6; cf. 18:5; 20:7. Haenchen believes that this expression is a technical term for missionary preaching (*Acts of the Apostles*, 227).

Propositional content of the word of God. Of course, when the expression "word of God" is used, there is not *necessarily* an even brief description of its propositional content. But often there is.

Generally in Acts, the propositional content of the word of God is closely associated with the message to potential converts. For example, the long redemptive-historical speeches are to be seen as the word of God (e.g., Acts 13:46). These speeches include Old Testament information, facts about Jesus's person, death, and resurrection, and a call for conversion. The verb εὐαγγελίζομαι ("preach the good news") is often associated with the word of God.[112] In addition, the message of the word of God in Acts is directly connected with the "proclaimed . . . Christ" (8:5), "the kingdom of God and the name of Jesus Christ" (8:12), "peace through Jesus Christ" (10:36), the need to "believe in the Lord Jesus, and you will be saved" (16:31), "testifying to the Jews that the Christ was Jesus" (18:5), and "the kingdom of God" (19:8). All of these may be termed the "core" of the gospel.

However, several factors indicate that the word of God is more than the "core" of the gospel. Although the word of God is spoken primarily to those who are not converted in Acts, there are instances where it is spoken to those who already believe (14:25; 15:35). Also, the extended length of time Paul spends in Corinth (Acts 18:11) and the hall of Tyrannus (Acts 19:9–10) speaking the word of God argues for a broad view of the content of the word of God. Finally, the verbs διδάσκω ("teach"), διαλογίζομαι ("argue"), and ἐπιστηρίζω ("strengthen"), used with the word of God, point toward a broader content (14:22; 15:35, 41; 18:11; 19:9).

Calvin notes that "the Word of God is said to grow in a twofold way, either when new disciples are added to its obedience [Acts 6:7], or in proportion as each one of us makes progress in it [Acts 19:10]."[113] Here Calvin confirms that the content of the word of God is more than that spoken to potential converts.

In summary, the propositional content of the word of God is most often associated with the message to potential converts, but it does have a broader meaning. This broader meaning includes the Old Testament and the apostolic tradition with all applications to potential converts and believers. Or we may conveniently summarize this broad meaning as "the whole counsel of God" (Acts 20:27).

Dynamic aspect of the word of God. In Acts, the preached word of God is more than propositional content. One factor that gives the reader this impression is its use in three of the main summary verses (6:7; 12:24; 19:20). In all three, the word of God "increased" (αὐξάνω). Also, the word of God "multiplied" (12:24), was "received" (8:14), "prevail[ed] mightily" (19:20), and "spread" (13:49). Obviously, there is some level of figurative linguistic use here, but the impression is still given as to the dynamic qualities of the word of God.

In addition, the extent to which "God" in the phrase "word of God" is a subjective genitive (meaning "word spoken by God") adds to the dynamic impression.

---

[112] Acts 8:4, 12, 25; 10:36; 11:19–20; 13:32; 14:7, 21; 15:35; 16:10. Also note 15:7, "word of the gospel."
[113] Calvin, *Acts of the Apostles*, 1:164.

Of course, all must admit that Acts presents God as the root of all preaching and teaching. But is not the subjective genitive stronger than this? That is, Acts presents the triune God as actively speaking with power when a human proclaims the word of God (cf. 14:3).

Finally, and most significantly, is the relationship between Jesus, the Holy Spirit, the preacher, and those converted. Jesus sends out the preachers as his witnesses with the power of the Holy Spirit (Acts 1:8). The Holy Spirit is involved with those who preach (2:4; 4:8, 31; 5:32; 6:3, 10; 7:55; 11:24; 13:9). The Holy Spirit is also involved with those who hear the message (8:15; 9:31; 10:45; 11:15; 13:52; 19:6). Hence, in addition to propositional content, the word of God has a dynamic component of God actively involved in both the preacher and those converted when the word is preached. This dynamic aspect of the word of God is elsewhere in the New Testament (e.g., Rom. 1:16–17; 10:13–17; 1 Thess. 1:8; 2:13; Titus 1:3; 1 Pet. 1:24–25).

Relationship to Reformed theology. The emphasis in Acts on the preached word of God as a primary "outward and ordinary" means of grace matches the historic Protestant emphasis on preaching.[114]

Acts connects preaching to the Old Testament and the apostolic tradition—that is, at the time, the entire Bible. Hence, the preached (and read) "word of God" is truly the word spoken by God as it is properly *derivative* of the written Word of God (see 1 Thess. 2:13). Reformed creeds, therefore, following biblical language, make a distinction between the "written Word of God" (i.e., the Bible) and the "preached Word of God" (i.e., preaching properly derivative of the Bible).[115] (Yes, preachers say things that are not always properly derivative of the Bible!)

The dynamic aspect of the word of God in Acts well matches the Reformed emphasis on "Word and Spirit."[116] Calvin said, "The Spirit wills to be conjoined with God's Word by an indissoluble bond."[117] That is, it is not the bare propositional content of the Bible that is the only cause when one is regenerated. Charles Hodge well said,

> Christians then do not refer the saving and sanctifying power of the Scriptures to the moral power of the truths which they contain; or to the mere cooperation of the Spirit in a manner analogous to the way in which God cooperates with all second causes, but to the power of the Spirit as a divine Person acting with and by the truth, or without it, as in his sovereign pleasure He sees fit.[118]

---

[114] WLC 154.

[115] Second Helvetic Confession 1; WCF 1.2; WLC 155.

[116] There are many uses of this phrase in the Westminster Standards; e.g., WCF 1.5, 1.6, 8.8, 10.1; WLC 2, 43, 155, 159; WSC 24, 89. Also see the Second Helvetic Confession 13 and the Heidelberg Catechism 54. Donald G. Bloesch entitled the opening volume of his seven-volume systematic theology *A Theology of Word and Spirit: Authority and Method in Theology*, Christian Foundations (Downers Grove, IL: InterVarsity Press, 1992).

[117] John Calvin, *Institutes of the Christian Religion*, ed. John T. McNeill, trans. Ford Lewis Battles, 2 vols. (Philadelphia: Westminster Press, 1960), 4.8.13.

[118] Charles Hodge, *Systematic Theology*, 3 vols. (Grand Rapids, MI: Eerdmans, 1952), 3:476.

Select Bibliography

Many books and articles combine Luke and Acts as well as a few commentaries. See the bibliography in the Luke chapter for additional sources, as I will not include them again here.

Alexander, J. A. *A Commentary on the Acts of the Apostles*. Geneva. Carlisle, PA: Banner of Truth, 1963.

Barrett, C. K. *A Critical and Exegetical Commentary on the Acts of the Apostles*. 2 vols. ICC. Edinburgh: T&T Clark, 1994–1998.

Bauckham, Richard, ed. *The Book of Acts in Its Palestinian Setting*. Vol. 4 of *The Book of Acts in Its First Century Setting*. Grand Rapids, MI: Eerdmans, 1995.

Bruce, F. F. *The Book of Acts*. Rev. ed. NICNT. Grand Rapids, MI: Eerdmans, 1988.

Calvin, John. *The Acts of the Apostles*. Translated by John W. Fraser and W. J. G. McDonald. 2 vols. Calvin's Commentaries. Grand Rapids, MI: Eerdmans, 1965–1966.

Chrysostom, John. *Homilies of St. John Chrysostom on the Acts of the Apostles*. In vol. 11 of *NPNF*[1].

Conzelmann, Hans. *A Commentary on the Acts of the Apostles*. Translated by James Limburg, A. Thomas Kraabel, and Donald H. Juel. Hermeneia. Philadelphia: Fortress, 1987.

Dibelius, Martin. *Studies in the Acts of the Apostles*. Edited by Heinrich Greeven. New York: Scribner's, 1956.

Dodd, C. H. *Apostolic Preaching and Its Developments*. New York: Harper, 1960.

Dunn, James D. G. *The Acts of the Apostles*. Narrative Commentaries. Valley Forge, PA: Trinity, 1996.

Fitzmyer, Joseph A. *The Acts of the Apostles: A New Translation with Introduction and Commentary*. AB 31. New York: Doubleday, 1998.

Foakes-Jackson, F. J., and Kirsopp Lake, eds. *The Beginnings of Christianity*. 5 vols. London: Macmillan, 1922–1933.

Gasque, W. Ward. *A History of the Interpretation of the Acts of the Apostles*. 2nd ed. Peabody, MA: Hendrickson, 1987.

Gill, David W. J., and Conrad Gempf, eds. *The Book of Acts in Its Graeco-Roman Setting*. Vol. 2 of *The Book of Acts in Its First Century Setting*. Grand Rapids, MI: Eerdmans, 1994.

Haenchen, Ernst. *The Acts of the Apostles: A Commentary*. Translated by Bernard Noble and Gerald Shinn. Philadelphia: Westminster Press, 1971.

Hemer, Colin J. *The Book of Acts in the Setting of Hellenistic History*. Edited by Conrad H. Gempf. Winona Lake, IN: Eisenbrauns, 1990.

Jervell, Jacob. *The Theology of the Acts of the Apostles*. NTT. Cambridge: Cambridge University Press, 1996.

Johnson, Dennis E. *The Message of Acts in the History of Redemption*. Phillipsburg, NJ: P&R, 1997.

Johnson, Luke Timothy. *The Acts of the Apostles*. SP 5. Collegeville, MN: Liturgical, 1992.

Kee, Howard Clark. *Good News to the Ends of the Earth: A Theology of Acts*. Philadelphia: Trinity, 1990.

Kistemaker, Simon J. *Exposition of the Acts of the Apostles*. NTC. Grand Rapids, MI: Baker, 1990.

Levinskaya, Irina. *The Book of Acts in Its Diaspora Setting*. Vol. 5 of *The Book of Acts in Its First Century Setting*. Grand Rapids, MI: Eerdmans, 1996.

Marshall, I. Howard. *The Acts of the Apostles: An Introduction and Commentary*. TNTC. Grand Rapids, MI: Eerdmans, 1980.

Marshall, I. Howard, and David Peterson, eds. *Witness to the Gospel: The Theology of Acts*. Grand Rapids, MI: Eerdmans, 1998.

Pelikan, Jaroslav. *Acts*. Brazos Theological Commentary on the Bible. Grand Rapids, MI: Brazos, 2005.

Pervo, Richard I. *Acts: A Commentary*. Hermeneia. Minneapolis: Fortress, 2009.

Pesch, Rudolf. *Die Apostelgeschichte*. 2 vols. EKKNT 5. Düsseldorf: Benziger, 1986.

Peterson, David G. *The Acts of the Apostles*. PNTC. Grand Rapids, MI: Eerdmans, 2009.

Polhill, John B. *Acts*. NAC 26. Nashville: Broadman, 1992.

Powell, Mark Allan. *What Are They Saying about Acts?* New York: Paulist, 1991.

Ramsay, William M. *St. Paul: The Traveler and Roman Citizen*. Edited by Mark Wilson. Rev. ed. Grand Rapids, MI: Kregel, 2001.

Rapske, Brian. *The Book of Acts and Paul in Roman Custody*. Vol. 3 of *The Book of Acts in Its First Century Setting*. Grand Rapids, MI: Eerdmans, 1994.

Thomas, Derek W. H. *Acts*. Reformed Expository Commentary. Phillipsburg, NJ: P&R, 2011.

Waters, Guy Prentiss. *Acts*. EPSC. Darlington: Evangelical Press, 2015.

Winter, Bruce W., and Andrew D. Clarke. *The Book of Acts in Its Ancient Literary Setting*. Vol. 1 of *The Book of Acts in Its First Century Setting*. Grand Rapids, MI: Eerdmans, 1993.

Witherington, Ben, III. *The Acts of the Apostles: A Socio-Rhetorical Commentary*. Grand Rapids, MI: Eerdmans, 1998.

6

Romans

Guy Prentiss Waters

> [Romans] is worthy not only that every Christian should know it word for word, by heart, but also that he should occupy himself with it every day, as the daily bread of the soul. We can never read it or ponder over it too much; for the more we deal with it, the more precious it becomes, and the better it tastes.
>
> *Martin Luther, "Preface to the Epistle to the Romans" (1522)*[1]

Introduction

The epistle to the Romans is one of the most beloved and prized possessions of the Christian church. It has played a central role in the Christian experience of some of the greatest leaders in the church. Augustine relates in his *Confessions* how a child uttering the words *tolle lege* ("take and read") prompted him to turn to Romans 13:14: "But put on the Lord Jesus Christ, and make no provision for the flesh, to gratify its desires." It was through reading that verse in Romans that Augustine was converted.

Martin Luther's famous *Turmereignis* (tower experience) centers on Romans 1:16–17. After reading these verses as a young monk with a burdened conscience, Luther testified, "Here I felt that I was altogether born again and had entered paradise itself through open gates."[2] A couple of centuries later, John Wesley attended "a society in Aldersgate Street, where one was reading Luther's preface to the Epistle to the Romans." It was then, Wesley testifies, that "I felt my heart strangely warmed. I felt I

[1] Cited in Timothy F. Lull and William R. Russell, eds., *Martin Luther's Basic Theological Writings*, 3rd ed. (Philadelphia: Fortress, 2012), 76.
[2] Cited in ibid., 497.

did trust in Christ, Christ alone for salvation; and an assurance was given me that He had taken away my sins, even mine, and saved me from the law of sin and death."[3]

It is not difficult to understand why Romans has featured so prominently in the history and life of the church. It is the fullest summary and most comprehensive exposition of Paul's gospel that we have. The academic study of Paul, especially in the last generation, has raised some pointed questions relating to the study of Romans along just these lines. What is Paul's gospel? What does it mean to be justified by faith and not by works of the law? Why does Paul spend so much time in Romans talking about Jews and Gentiles?

To answer these questions is not simply to resolve an academic debate about the meaning of Romans. It is to touch on the heart of the Christian gospel itself. In order to appreciate and better grasp Paul's message, however, we first need to understand something of the background of the letter. When did Paul write it? To whom did he write it? Why did he write it?

Background Issues

When Did Paul Write Romans?

Paul's Christian life spanned from his conversion sometime in the mid–AD 30s to what reliable ecclesiastical tradition places as his martyrdom in Rome, ca. AD 67.[4] Paul's public ministry filled approximately two-thirds of that three-decade span. At what point in this window did Paul write the epistle to the Romans?

Paul's closing salutations in Romans 16 provide some valuable information in dating the letter. As was customary in ancient epistles, writers concluded their letters with greetings (16:1–23) and well-wishing (16:20; cf. 16:25–27).[5] The letters of the New Testament, in particular, frequently convey greetings from one quarter of the church to another and pronounce divine blessing on the recipients. Romans concludes not only with a benediction (16:20), that is, a word of blessing from God, but also with a doxology, a word of praise to God (16:25–27).[6]

Before he pens that benediction and doxology, Paul sends greetings. These greetings help to pinpoint his whereabouts at the time of writing. Paul initially commends to the Romans "Phoebe, a servant of the church at Cenchreae, that you may welcome her in the Lord in a way worthy of the saints, and help her in whatever she may need from you, for she has been a patron of many and of myself as well" (16:1–2). Paul first mentions and commends Phoebe likely because she is the one entrusted

[3] John Wesley, *The Journal of the Rev. John Wesley, A.M. (enlarged from original mss. with notes from unpublished diaries, annotations, maps, and illustrations)*, vol. 1, ed. Nehemiah Curnock (London: Culley, 1909), 475–76. Wesley's journal entry is dated May 24, 1738. I am grateful to Nathan Lee for this reference.

[4] For a readable survey of the life and ministry of Paul, see Paul Barnett, *Paul: Missionary of Jesus* (Grand Rapids, MI: Eerdmans, 2008).

[5] On ancient letter writing and the New Testament, see E. Randolph Richards, *Paul and First-Century Letter Writing: Secretaries, Composition, and Collection* (Downers Grove, IL: InterVarsity Press, 2004).

[6] Some critical scholars have challenged "the integrity of the doxology" of Rom. 16:25–27 "and its placement at 16:25–27" (Richard N. Longenecker, *Introducing Romans: Critical Issues in Paul's Most Famous Letter* [Grand Rapids, MI: Eerdmans, 2011], 35). For a helpful survey of the discussion and a defense both of the authenticity of the closing doxology at Rom. 16:25–27 and of its location at the close of the letter, see Longenecker, *Introducing Romans*, 34–38. Against the proposal that Romans 16 as a whole is not original to Paul's letter, see Thomas R. Schreiner, *Romans*, BECNT (Grand Rapids, MI: Baker, 1998), 7–10.

with carrying this epistle to Rome.[7] She is part of the church in Cenchreae, one of the two port cities of Corinth. This detail suggests that Paul is in Corinth at the time he drafts this letter. If the "Gaius, who is host to [Paul]" (16:23) is the "same Gaius whom Paul baptized at Corinth (1 Cor. 1:14)," as Douglas Moo argues, then we have further confirmation of this conclusion.[8]

The New Testament tells us that Paul made more than one visit to Corinth. His first recorded visit is the eighteen-month stay in which the church was founded (Acts 18:1–18). Luke also documents a subsequent three-month stay in Corinth (Acts 20:1–3). This latter stay was part of a longer journey in which Paul had purposed to go to Rome by way of Corinth and Jerusalem (Acts 19:21). It is on this itinerary that we should locate Paul's writing of the epistle to the Romans. He tells the Romans that he plans to travel to Spain, but he first intends to go to Jerusalem and then to Rome (Rom. 15:24–25, 28). Putting the pieces together, Paul is in Corinth when he writes this letter (Acts 20:1–3). He intends to travel, first to Jerusalem, then to Rome, and finally to Spain (Rom. 15:24–25). We may therefore reliably date the letter to the "winter of [AD] 57–58."[9]

To Whom Did Paul Write Romans?

Paul addresses the epistle "to all those in Rome who are loved by God and called to be saints" (Rom. 1:7). Some scholars are reticent to say that Roman Christians were formally gathered into local churches.[10] There is, however, no compelling reason to infer from the absence of the word *church* in Romans 1:7 that Paul did not regard the Roman Christians as members of Christian congregations. Other scholars hesitate to claim that believers in Rome were deemed "a single entity."[11] Given the way Paul addresses the Roman Christians as a single audience, however, it is unlikely that the Roman believers had sequestered themselves into separate groups.[12]

What may we say of the founding and subsequent history of the church at Rome? Given the presence of "visitors from Rome" at Peter's Pentecost sermon (Acts 2:10), it is a reasonable supposition that some of those individuals returned to Rome bearing their new-found faith in the crucified and risen Savior.[13] These Jewish believers likely shared the gospel with other Roman Jews in the context of the "strong Jewish community" already in place in the imperial capital.[14]

If Roman synagogues were analogous to synagogues in other ancient cities, they were populated with "God-fearers" or "proselytes," Gentile adherents to Judaism.

[7] C. E. B. Cranfield, *Romans 9–16*, ICC (Edinburgh: T&T Clark, 1979), 780.
[8] Douglas J. Moo, *The Epistle to the Romans*, NICNT (Grand Rapids, MI: Eerdmans, 1999), 3.
[9] Longenecker, *Introducing Romans*, 49–50. Longenecker notes that a "majority of NT scholars" embrace this date (ibid.).
[10] See Günther Klein, "Paul's Purpose in Writing the Epistle to the Romans," in *The Romans Debate*, rev. ed., ed. K. P. Donfried (Peabody, MA: Hendrickson, 1991), 29–43.
[11] On which, see James D. G. Dunn, *Romans 1–8*, WBC 38A (Nashville: Thomas Nelson, 1988), lii.
[12] So, rightly Moo, *Epistle to the Romans*, 12, responding to the proposal of Paul Minear, *The Obedience of Faith: The Purposes of Paul in the Epistle to the Romans* (London: SCM, 1971).
[13] The New Testament affords no evidence that Peter was involved in the founding of the church at Rome, much less that he was its head.
[14] Dunn, *Romans 1–8*, xlv. For a concise history of Jews in Rome prior to the mid–first century AD, see Dunn, *Romans 1–8*, xlv–xlvi. Compare Wolfgang Wiefel, "The Jewish Community in Ancient Rome and the Origins of Roman Christianity," in Donfried, *The Romans Debate*, 85–101; and Longenecker, *Introducing Romans*, 60–69.

If the progress of the gospel in Rome was analogous to its progress as documented by Luke in the Acts of the Apostles, these Gentiles were likely some of the first non-Jewish adherents to the Christian faith.[15] Through these new God-fearing believers, the gospel likely spread further to Gentiles who had no prior acquaintance with the synagogue or the Old Testament.[16]

The ethnic composition of the church at Rome is a matter of disagreement among scholars.[17] Was the church at Rome a predominantly Jewish congregation or a Gentile congregation? At first glance, there is evidence in Romans to support both positions. The extensive quotations from and interpretations of the Old Testament throughout Romans; the concern for Israel "according to the flesh" (9:3) in Romans 9–11; and the denomination of certain Christians in Rome as "kinsmen," that is, fellow Jews (16:7, 11) commend an understanding of the Roman church as a Jewish church. On the other hand, Paul twice addresses his readers as "Gentiles" (see 1:13; 11:13; cf.15:15–16). In particular, Paul appears to have crafted the olive-tree metaphor of Romans 11:16b–24 with a Gentile readership in mind.[18]

How, then, are we to reconcile indications in Romans that Paul's readers were Jewish with Paul's occasional descriptions of the church as Gentile? Even if we conclude that the church was "a mixed group of Jewish and Gentile Christians," we must still find some way to explain the shape of these data.[19]

A solution to this difficulty lies in the history of the church at Rome antecedent to Paul's composition of this epistle. While this church's origins and progress in the first century are shrouded in mystery, one event from the AD 40s sheds light on an important chapter in the Roman church's history. In the late 40s, the Roman emperor Claudius issued a decree, in the words of the Roman historian Suetonius, "expel[ling] Jews from Rome because of their constant disturbances at the instigation of Chrestus."[20] Luke tells us that this expulsion included Jewish Christians as well as non-Christian Jews; at this early date, Rome did not distinguish or discriminate the two (cf. Acts 18:2). Suetonius's explanation for the riots ("at the instigation of Chrestus") may be his garbled accounting of Jewish public disturbances occasioned by Christians' proclamation of the gospel. Acts certainly tells us of many other such disturbances in cities across the Eastern Mediterranean basin.

Overnight, the decree effectively transformed the church at Rome into a Gentile congregation. But when the emperor Claudius died in AD 54, his decree died with him. Under Nero's reign, Jewish Christians (and non-Christian Jews) were thus free to return to Rome. In the three or four years preceding Paul's letter, the church at Rome witnessed a considerable influx of Jewish Christians.

---

[15] Moo, *Epistle to the Romans*, 9. If the phrase "both Jews and proselytes" in Acts 2:11a modifies "visitors from Rome," then Acts affords support for the position that some of the earliest Roman Christians were both Jewish and Gentile.
[16] The lines of the above reconstruction roughly follow those in Longenecker, *Introducing Romans*, 71–72.
[17] For a concise survey of this question in historical critical interpretation, see ibid., 75–77.
[18] The same may be said, arguably, of Rom. 14:1–15:13, if the "strong" and "weak" correspond to two differing positions on the ongoing observance of Jewish ceremonial laws.
[19] Moo, *Epistle to the Romans*, 12. Compare the classic formulation of Sanday and Headlam, cited in Longenecker, *Introducing Romans*, 78.
[20] Suetonius, *Claudius* 25.4, cited in Dunn, *Romans 1–8*, xlviii.

These circumstances help to explain and synthesize some of the details we have noted above. They suggest three observations that have bearing on our reading of the letter. First, Paul addresses the Roman church as Gentiles in light of its de facto Gentile identity until the few years prior to the letter's composition (Rom. 1:13; 11:13). For Paul, those Gentile Christians whose residency in the Roman church was uninterrupted by Claudius's edict bear particular responsibilities toward their returning brethren. Second, there is no need to conclude that the church did not contain Jewish Christians at the time of writing. That Paul does not address Jewish Christians in the way he addresses Gentile Christians may simply reflect their recent restoration to the church in Rome. Third, this background provides context for the predominance in Romans of concerns with the relationship between Jew and Gentile in redemptive history and between Jewish and Gentile believers in the new covenant church.

Why Did Paul Write Romans?

What were Paul's purpose(s) in drafting this letter? One recent commentator has wisely noted that "Romans has several purposes."[21] One ought not, then, urge one purpose to the exclusion of others. If Paul had a multiplicity of purposes, what were they, and how do they complement one another?[22]

One of Paul's purposes surely was to provide a personal and theological introduction of himself to the church at Rome. Paul twice tells the church that his desires to visit them have been hitherto thwarted (Rom. 1:13; 15:22–23). That he is not wholly unacquainted with believers in Rome is clear from the greetings he conveys in Romans 16:1–15. Prisca and Aquila (16:3) we know to be close associates of Paul in gospel endeavor. Paul's other greetings suggest that he both knew and worked with a number of Christians who were by this time in Rome. Even so, Paul had neither founded nor visited the Roman church. He declared his eagerness "to preach the gospel to you also who are in Rome" (1:15). For Paul, preaching the gospel "involved more than initial conversion."[23] It entailed "the ongoing work of teaching and discipleship that builds on initial evangelization."[24]

The fact that Paul periodically addresses objections to his argument in Romans suggests a concerted effort to clear his gospel of misconception ("And why not do evil that good may come?—as some people slanderously charge us with saying," 3:8; "Do we then overthrow the law by this faith? By no means!" 3:31; "What shall we say then? Are we to continue in sin that grace may abound? By no means!" 6:1–2; "What then? Are we to sin because we are not under law but under grace? By no means!" 6:15). Many of these objections suggest that Paul was being accused of undermining the law and promoting sinful license (cf. Acts 21:20–21). Paul fears that these slanders have reached the Roman Christians. In providing the Roman

[21] Moo, *Epistle to the Romans*, 20.

[22] The following three purposes correspond to those identified in Dunn, *Romans 1–8*, liv-lviii.

[23] Schreiner, *Romans*, 53, cited in Colin G. Kruse, *Paul's Letter to the Romans*, PNTC (Grand Rapids, MI: Eerdmans, 2012), 66.

[24] Moo, *Epistle to the Romans*, 63; cf. Kruse, *Paul's Letter to the Romans*, 66.

Christians a summary of his gospel, he is at the same time responding to objections that have been raised against that gospel over the course of his ministry.

A second purpose is related to Paul's apostolic calling. He tells the Romans that he has "fulfilled the ministry of the gospel of Christ" (Rom. 15:19), at least "in the northeastern quadrant of the Mediterranean."[25] As John Murray summarizes Paul's point, "Paul had discharged his commission and fulfilled the design of his ministry within the wide area specified."[26] Paul is therefore turning his attention to another sphere of ministry altogether, a place where no gospel foundation has yet been laid (15:20). Spain, on the western edge of Roman civilization, would be Paul's desired point of entry into this new sphere. As the church at Antioch had supported Paul in the course of his three missionary campaigns, so Paul sought a strong regional church to support him in his anticipated Spanish mission. The apostle expresses his desire to the Romans that they "help" him on his "journey there" (15:24). Paul is surely soliciting the Romans' prayers and financial support.[27]

Paul solicits the help of the Romans in another area relating to his apostolic calling. Before he goes to Rome and thence to Spain, he intends to go to Jerusalem for the purpose of "bringing aid to the saints" (15:25). In view is the collection that Paul has been gathering from Gentile churches in Galatia, Macedonia, and Achaia (cf. 1 Cor. 16:1–4; 2 Corinthians 8–9) for their poorer Jewish brethren in Jerusalem (Rom. 15:26). Paul understands this offering to be a display of the unity of the church, Jew and Gentile, and therefore a matter of tremendous importance for the church and for his apostolic ministry (Rom. 15:27). Paul wants the Romans to pray, first, that he would be "delivered from the unbelievers in Judea" and, second, that his "service for Jerusalem may be acceptable to the saints" (15:31). Both prayers, Luke tells us in Acts 21–28, were granted, although in ways that the apostle likely could not have foreseen.[28] His offering accepted in Jerusalem, Paul was delivered from a riot of unbelieving Jews by the Roman authorities. Incarceration was the means by which, in God's providence, Paul would be "delivered from the unbelievers in Judea." Paul did make it to Rome, but as a prisoner of the Roman emperor and in Roman custody. Whether Paul ever made it to Spain is a matter about which we must be content to be uncertain.[29]

A third and final purpose for which Paul wrote the epistle to the Romans was to address and resolve a pastoral problem that had arisen within the Roman church. This pastoral problem surfaces most explicitly in Romans 14:1–15:13 and entails a disagreement among two groups in the church, the "strong" and the "weak" (cf. 15:1). The disagreement likely centers on the insistence of the "weak" upon "observ[ing] certain requirements of the Mosaic law," particularly those relating to food, drink, and "special religious days."[30] The disagreement has proved divisive

[25] Dunn, *Romans 1–8*, lv.
[26] Murray, *Epistle to the Romans*, 2 vols. (Grand Rapids, MI: Eerdmans, 1959, 1965), 2:214.
[27] Kruse, *Paul's Letter to the Romans*, 545; Robert Jewett, *Romans*, Hermeneia (Minneapolis: Fortress, 2006), 923–26.
[28] On which, see Kruse, *Paul's Letter to the Romans*, 550–51.
[29] Arland J. Hultgren, *Paul's Letter to the Romans* (Grand Rapids, MI: Eerdmans, 2011), 553.
[30] Moo, *Epistle to the Romans*, 830–31.

within the church, even to the point of generating quarrels (14:1). Paul's exhortation to the church, therefore, begins (14:1) and concludes (15:7) with an appeal to unity and mutual forbearance.

The theological and specifically christological shape of Paul's argument demonstrates that the unity for which the apostle pleads is not a pragmatic one but a principled one. Specifically, it is an application to the church in Rome of the gospel that Paul has devoted the previous thirteen chapters to expounding. Paul appeals to the lordship of the risen Christ (14:8–9) and the corresponding ultimate accountability of every Christian to his Lord (14:5–7). The lordship of Christ underscores the sinfulness of "pass[ing] judgment" on or "despis[ing]" one's brother (14:10–12). It also prompts believers to "pursue what makes for peace and mutual upbuilding" (14:19). Paul appeals to the example of Christ who "did not please himself" but made himself a "servant" to Jew and Gentile alike (15:3, 8–9). Paul furthermore stresses that the way in which Christ has "welcomed" believers through the gospel provides the pattern according to which believers ought to "welcome one another" (15:7; cf. 14:3).

These three purposes are not independent of one another. Rather, they "hang together and . . . reinforce each other when taken as a whole."[31] Paul's exposition and defense of his gospel bolster his desire that the church in Rome provide support for him in his anticipated Spanish mission. They furthermore provide both the foundation and structure for his resolution of the pastoral problem plaguing the Roman Christians. A unified church, moreover, will provide a more desirable missionary base for Paul's western travels than would a divided one. Paul can conceive, as well, a church that is both well informed about the gospel *and* committed to supporting its extension with its finances and prayers to be a church prepared to resolve the specter of internal division in principled fashion.

Structure and Outline

Key Introductory Verses

Paul's purposes in Romans converge upon his exposition of the gospel he preaches. While Romans may not be a "compendium of Christian doctrine" (Philip Melanchthon), it certainly is a comprehensive *summa* of Paul's gospel. Two important passages at the outset of Romans (Rom. 1:1–7, 16–17) have a twofold function in the epistle as a whole. First, each passage supplies the content of Paul's gospel. Second, each passage signals the shape and structure of Paul's argument in Romans.

Romans 1:1–7

Romans 1:1–7 is Paul's opening salutation to the church at Rome. Ancient epistles conventionally began with the author's self-identification, the author's identification of the recipients, and a word of greeting. Each of these elements is present in the first seven verses of Romans. The apostle identifies himself ("Paul," 1:1), identifies the

[31] Dunn, *Romans 1–8*, lviii. What follows differs from the way in which Dunn understands these three purposes to cohere.

recipients ("to all those in Rome," 1:7a), and extends greetings ("Grace to you and peace from God our Father and the Lord Jesus Christ," 1:7b).

By the standards of the day, Paul's introduction "was . . . extraordinarily long."[32] In comparison with Paul's other epistolary greetings, it is remarkably "theologically complex."[33] This length and complexity were not required by literary convention. They are Paul's way of signaling important concepts and themes that will surface throughout Romans. Paul first describes himself as "a servant of Christ Jesus, called to be an apostle" (1:1). The way in which Paul serves Christ Jesus is as his apostle. Apostles were "called," that is specially chosen by Jesus Christ as his eyewitnesses. What follows in this letter, then, are not the musings of "a private individual" or "even . . . a gifted teacher," but the greetings and instructions of one "whose words bear the authority of God himself."[34]

As an apostle of Christ Jesus, Paul has been "set apart for the gospel of God" (1:1). What that gospel is, Paul proceeds to elaborate in the next five verses. Of this gospel, Paul makes three fundamental points. First, he relates the gospel of Christ to what has preceded Christ in redemptive history. The gospel, he affirms, was "promised beforehand through his prophets in the Holy Scriptures" (1:2). The gospel neither departs from nor contradicts what God has spoken under the old covenant.[35] On the contrary, the gospel that Paul preaches is the fulfillment of God's promises in the Old Testament. Paul is therefore concerned to show in Romans how "the Law and the Prophets bear witness to" the "righteousness of God" (3:21). He will endeavor to show in Romans 9–11 that "the word of God has [not] failed" (9:6). At critical junctures in his argument, Paul will introduce strings or clusters of Old Testament citations in support of his argument for the gospel (e.g., Rom. 3:10–18; 9:1–11:36; 15:8–13). The exposition of the Abraham narrative in Genesis dominates Paul's argument in Romans 4:1–25 as he shows that the believing Abraham is the "father of us all" (4:16).

The second fundamental point that Paul makes about the gospel concerns its content. The gospel's center and focus is Jesus Christ. The gospel "concern[s] [God's] Son" (Rom. 1:3). Paul then proceeds to make several important claims about the person and work of Jesus Christ in Romans 1:3b–4: "[He] was descended from David according to the flesh and was declared to be the Son of God in power according to the Spirit of holiness by his resurrection from the dead, Jesus Christ our Lord." Scholars have noted in the Greek text a parallel structure to these verses (see table 5).[36]

---

[32] Kruse, *Paul's Letter to the Romans*, 37.
[33] Schreiner, *Romans*, 31.
[34] Moo, *Epistle to the Romans*, 42.
[35] Murray, *Epistle to the Romans*, 1:3–4.
[36] For what follows, see Geerhardus Vos, *The Pauline Eschatology* (1930; repr., Phillipsburg, NJ: P&R, 1994), 155n10; Vos, "The Eschatological Aspect of the Pauline Conception of the Spirit," in *Redemptive History and Biblical Interpretation: The Shorter Writings of Geerhardus Vos*, ed. Richard B. Gaffin Jr. (Phillipsburg, NJ: P&R, 1980), 91–125, esp. 103–5; Herman N. Ridderbos, *Paul: An Outline of His Theology*, trans. John Richard de Witt (Grand Rapids, MI: Eerdmans, 1975), 66–67; Ridderbos, *Aan de Romeinen* (Kampen: Kok, 1959), 24–26; Murray, *Epistle to the Romans*, 1:5–12; Richard B. Gaffin Jr., *Resurrection and Redemption: A Study in Paul's Soteriology*, 2nd ed. (Phillipsburg, NJ: P&R, 1987), 98–113. See the helpful chart in Vos, "Eschatological Aspect," 104.

Romans 1:3	Romans 1:4
"was descended"	"was declared"
"from David"	"by his resurrection from the dead"
"according to the flesh"	"according to the Spirit of holiness"

Table 5

Commentators have recognized that Paul is making a fundamental contrast with respect to Jesus Christ. Some have argued that the contrast concerns Christ's two natures.[37] In verse 3, Paul is said to be speaking about the human nature of Christ; in verse 4, about the divine nature of Christ. One of the main liabilities of this reading of the text is that it requires the phrase "the Spirit of holiness" to denote Christ's divine nature. It almost certainly is a reference, however, to the person of the Holy Spirit.[38]

While Paul unequivocally affirms both the deity and the humanity of Jesus Christ, that is not what Paul has in view in this contrast.[39] The contrast in Romans 1:3–4 does not concern the two natures of Christ. It concerns the two states of Christ. That is to say, Paul in 1:3 is describing Christ in his estate of humiliation, the period between his incarnation and burial. Romans 1:4, then, describes Christ in his estate of exaltation, the period beginning with his resurrection and continuing through his glorious return at the end of the age.

With respect to Christ's humiliation, Paul stresses that the "Son," that is, the eternal Son of God, "was descended from David according to the flesh." Paul is not simply saying that Christ assumed our humanity in the virgin's womb. He is saying two further things. First, he is a Davidic descendant and therefore David's Son. Paul here "had a view to Old Testament prophecy and to its vindication in the fulfillment of its promises."[40] Second, Paul characterizes Christ's human existence between the incarnation and before the resurrection as "according to the flesh." When Paul pairs the two terms "flesh" and "Spirit," as he does in Romans 1:3–4, he denotes "two modes of existence" corresponding to two epochs of history.[41] "Flesh" is characterized by "the creaturely in its weakness"; "Spirit," by "power, imperishableness and glory."[42] In this period of his human existence, Christ was "a man subject to transitoriness, dishonor, [and] frailty," but not sin (so Rom. 8:3).[43]

With respect to Christ's exaltation, Paul highlights in 1:4 Christ's resurrection as the point of transition from weakness to glory, from "flesh" to "Spirit." Paul stresses here that Jesus was raised from the dead by the Holy Spirit (cf. 8:11). At

[37] Representatives of this position include John Calvin, Charles Hodge, and B. B. Warfield.
[38] Dunn, *Romans 1–8*, 15; Gaffin, *Resurrection and Redemption*, 103–4.
[39] That said, Paul almost certainly has in mind Jesus's eternal sonship when he calls him "Son" in 1:3; and his messianic sonship when he calls him "Son of God" in 1:4 (Murray, *Epistle to the Romans*, 1:5, 9–10). In this respect, Paul is affirming the two natures of Christ in Rom. 1:3–4. This understanding is the only way to avoid taking Paul's statement ("his *Son* . . . was appointed the Son," NIV 2011) tautologically (Moo, *Epistle to the Romans*, 48).
[40] Murray, *Epistle to the Romans*, 1:8.
[41] Ridderbos, *Paul*, 66.
[42] Ibid.
[43] Ibid.

his resurrection, Jesus was "declared to be the Son of God in power" (1:4). That is to say, the resurrection ushered Jesus into a new and powerful phase of his Davidic sonship.[44] At Jesus's resurrection, the humanity of the Son of God was raised, transformed, and empowered by the Spirit of God. This present phase of his sonship is characterized by the power and life of the Holy Spirit.[45] It is precisely these resources that the crucified and risen Christ graciously bestows upon and shares with his people for their salvation. He shares them with us by his Spirit, the "Spirit of Christ" (8:9).

Paul, then, is stating critical, foundational matters concerning the gospel in these two verses. The gospel finds its center in the person and work of Jesus Christ. Our Savior is the eternal Son who assumed our humanity and, in our humanity, accomplished our redemption. In our nature, he died and rose again from the dead by the power of the Holy Spirit. Raised and seated in glory (8:34), Jesus now ministers to his people the resources he secured by his death and resurrection. Our salvation is, therefore, a gift and all of grace. We have in no way earned or merited it. The beneficiaries of Christ's work are weak, helpless, and dead in their sins. Salvation does not come from within. It comes from without, from "Jesus Christ our Lord" (1:4; cf. 14:9).

The third and final fundamental point that Paul makes about the gospel in Romans 1:1–7 is found in verses 5–6, where he speaks of "[Jesus Christ our Lord], through whom we have received grace and apostleship to bring about the obedience of faith for the sake of his name among all the nations, including you who are called to belong to Jesus Christ." Paul returns to a point he made in the opening verse: his apostleship has come from Jesus Christ. The goal of his apostleship is what he calls the "obedience of faith."[46] Paul concludes this epistle with the same phrase in Romans 16:25–26. The fact that Paul begins and ends the letter by saying that the goal of his apostolic ministry and gospel is to "bring about the obedience of faith" (16:26) suggests the importance of "the obedience of faith" to the letter as a whole.

What, then, is the "obedience of faith"? Some commentators have taken the phrase to mean "the obedience that consists of faith." On this reading, Paul aims in his gospel to see people responding to the gospel with the faith that the gospel commands and the Spirit supplies. Others have taken the phrase to mean "the obedience that is the fruit of faith." On this reading, Paul seeks not only the response of faith to the gospel, but also the good works that a living faith necessarily produces. Both readings have support in other statements of Paul. To "believe" the gospel, Paul stresses in Romans 10:16, is parallel with "obeying" the gospel. In 1–2 Thessalonians, Paul speaks of the "work of faith," that is, the good works or obedience that is the fruit of saving faith in Christ (1 Thess. 1:3; 2 Thess. 1:11). It is difficult to decide between these two options, but given the importance of "faith" to this epistle,

[44] Taking the phrase "in power" to modify the noun clause, "the Son of God" (Moo, *Epistle to the Romans*, 48). The verb translated "declared" is better translated "appointed" (Ridderbos, *Aan de Romeinen*, 26; C. E. B. Cranfield, *Romans 1–8*, ICC [Edinburgh: T&T Clark, 1975], 61–62).

[45] For further reflection on the relationship between Jesus and the Holy Spirit in light of Jesus's resurrection from the dead, see the chapter on 1–2 Corinthians.

[46] Moo, *Epistle to the Romans*, 51.

the first reading is likely what Paul has in mind here: "the obedience that consists of faith." As John Murray paraphrases Paul's point, "Faith is regarded as an act of obedience, of commitment to the gospel of Christ. . . . [It] was not an evanescent act of emotion but [a] commitment of wholehearted devotion to Christ and to the truth of his gospel."[47] This faith, as Paul will argue throughout Romans, is one that is fruitful and abundant in well doing.

In both Romans 1:5–6 and 16:25–26, Paul conjoins the phrase "the obedience of faith" with the phrase "all nations." In this way, he sounds a note that will reverberate throughout the epistle—the universal reach of the gospel. The gospel is for both Jew and Gentile. That is to say, the gospel is not restricted to a single ethnicity or people group. God has purposed it to extend to all kinds of people. The Roman Christians, "called to belong to Jesus Christ," are but a portion or subset of "all the nations" (1:5–6). Paul will devote much of this letter not only to underscoring a common human problem (our sin in Adam), but also to highlighting a solution adapted to that shared human plight (redemption in Jesus Christ).

Romans 1:16–17

Although Romans 1:16–17 is several verses removed from Romans 1:1–7, Paul intends for us to read these two sections closely together. The intervening verses (1:8–15) are an extended thanksgiving section. Romans 1:1–7 has broached some of the themes and concerns that will dominate the letter. It falls to Romans 1:16–17 to concentrate those themes and concerns into a pithy formulation that is widely recognized as the thesis of the epistle.[48]

Paul begins these verses by a declaration that he is "not ashamed of the gospel." What might occasion the "shame" that Paul eschews? The explanatory particle "for" refers back to Romans 1:14–15, in which Paul declares his "obligation" to preach the gospel "both to Greeks and to barbarians, both to the wise and to the foolish." To the Gentile world, the gospel of a crucified Savior is "folly" (1 Cor. 1:23), but to Paul there is no shame in preaching for the salvation of Jews and Gentiles.[49]

The reason ("for") that there is no such shame for Paul is that the gospel "is the power of God for salvation to everyone who believes, to the Jew first and also to the Greek" (Rom. 1:16). Paul here makes several important points about the gospel he preaches. First, it is a message that has in view the "salvation" of human beings, their rescue and deliverance from a plight in which they presently are and, Paul will go on to argue, their "restoration . . . to a share of the 'glory of God.'"[50] Second, Paul speaks of the gospel in terms of the "*power of God* for salvation." The word "power" is the same word that Paul has used in Romans 1:4. He therefore has in view in 1:16 the resurrecting power of the Spirit of Christ. It is this power that makes

[47] Murray, *Epistle to the Romans*, 1:13–14.
[48] Note the way in which the word "gospel" unites both the opening verses (1:1–7; cf. 1:1), the thanksgiving section (1:8–15; cf. 1:9, 15), and the thesis statement (1:16–17) (Schreiner, *Romans*, 59).
[49] Ridderbos, *Aan de Romeinen*, 32.
[50] Moo, *Epistle to the Romans*, 67. Moo notes the way in which Paul uses the word "save" in precisely this context at Rom. 8:24.

the gospel an effective and saving message. Third, the gospel is for "everyone who believes." By faith a person responds to the gospel, and through faith he receives Christ and his benefits held out in the gospel. It is the Spirit who makes the dead sinner alive. It is faith, the gift of the Spirit, that is the first conscious indication of this new life in a person's experience. The glory of faith is that it utterly excludes merit on our part (cf. 4:4–5), but it does not thereby render us "a totally passive instrument."[51] Fourth, picking up the word "everyone," Paul again underscores the fact that the gospel is "to the Jew first and also to the Greek" (1:16). The gospel is for all kinds of people. As Paul will explain in Romans 9–11, there is a kind of redemptive-historical priority to the Jew ("first") in God's unfolding plan of redemption. This fact underscores what Paul will later argue are the privileges and dangers attending membership in God's people.

Paul then declares in 1:17 that "in [the gospel] the righteousness of God is revealed from faith for faith, as it is written, 'The righteous shall live by faith.'" The heart of Paul's gospel is what he calls "the righteousness of God." This phrase will resurface at important junctures in the opening chapters of Romans (cf. 3:21, 22, 25; cf. 3:5; 3:26), and again in Romans 10:3. What then is "the righteousness of God"?

There have been several proposals. Some have argued that Paul is referring to an attribute of God. Within this group, some argue that what Paul has in mind is the justice or uprightness of God. Others within this group contend that Paul is referring to God's covenantal faithfulness, his fidelity to his promises to Israel. A second understanding of "the righteousness of God" is a dynamic one. The phrase, it is argued, refers to the saving power or action of God for his people. "God's righteousness is manifested, apart from the law, by providing redemption through Christ's death, so making possible a righteousness (a right standing before God) to be received by faith."[52] A third understanding of this phrase sees the "righteousness" in view as the gift of God to undeserving sinners, a gift that provides the sinner what he needs "in order to be able to stand in the divine judgment."[53]

Each of these positions has been defended in the history of interpretation, and each makes plausible claims. With respect to what Paul is saying in Romans 1:17, however, the third position makes best contextual sense. The "righteousness" of which Paul speaks here is not an attribute (as it is in 3:5, 25–26). Neither does it denote here God's saving action that has yielded or produced this righteousness. The "righteousness of God" here is the provision of God to sinners. God is its "author," and this righteousness not only meets with the "divine approval," but also "meets all the demands of his justice and therefore avails before God."[54] The "righteousness of God" is the "righteousness that God attributes to man as opposed to [man's]

[51] Ibid. Moo proceeds to cite Calvin: "Faith is 'a kind of vessel' with which we 'come empty and with the mouth of our soul open to seek Christ's grace'" (John Calvin, *Institutes of the Christian Religion*, ed. John T. McNeill, trans. Ford Lewis Battles [Philadelphia: Westminster Press, 1960], 3.11.7). Murray notes the importance of the conjunction of "power" and "faith": "salvation is not accomplished irrespective of faith" (*Epistle to the Romans*, 1:27).
[52] Kruse, *Paul's Letter to the Romans*, 79.
[53] Ridderbos, *Paul*, 163; cf. Ridderbos, *Aan de Romeinen*, 35–38.
[54] Murray, *Epistle to the Romans*, 1:31.

own righteousness."[55] It is what God gives to the sinner in the divine courtroom and thereby alone grounds God's legal or forensic declaring the sinner to be "righteous" (see 3:21–24).

Paul says three more things in verse 17 about the "righteousness of God." First, it is "revealed." By affirming the "righteousness of God" to be "revealed" in the gospel, Paul attributes the disclosure of this righteousness to God's initiative, not humanity's. Further, the verb "reveal" is here a historical term. In other words, it refers to the "righteousness of God" as "the becoming historical reality of that which until now did not exist as such, but was kept by God, hidden, held back" (cf.16:25–26).[56] As Paul will argue in Romans 3:21, the "righteousness of God" has become a historical reality in the finished, saving work of Jesus Christ.

Second, Paul says that in the gospel, "the righteousness of God is revealed *from faith for faith*" (1:17). The phrase "from faith for [or "to"] faith" has perplexed commentators, but it likely means "from faith from first to last."[57] Paul is once again saying that the gift of righteousness is received through faith alone.

Third, Paul illustrates his point in 1:1–2 ("the gospel of God, which he promised beforehand through his prophets in the holy Scriptures . . .") with a citation from Habakkuk 2:4, "As it is written, 'The righteous shall live by faith'" (Rom. 1:17). Paul appeals to the prophet to prove that "righteousness is to be attained only [through] faith."[58] In light of Paul's appeals to Abraham and David in Romans 4, it is clear that Paul is saying more than that the prophets anticipated "the righteousness of God." Paul is saying that God's people in all ages have, through faith, received the righteousness of God that Christ accomplished in history through his death and resurrection.

A Brief Outline of Romans

Paul's thesis statement in Romans 1:16–17 provides the main point in the letter—the "righteousness of God." From this vantage point, we may discern a fourfold structure to the remainder of the epistle. In 1:18–3:20, Paul demonstrates that the "righteousness of God" is something that humanity, Jew and Gentile, needs but lacks. In 3:21–8:39, Paul details how it is that God has given the "righteousness of God" to undeserving sinners. Much of this section is devoted to detailing the gift of the imputed righteousness of God to sinners, a gift that is received through faith alone (3:21–4:25; 5:12–21). Paul also details the assurance that Christians have in light of our possession of this gift (5:1–11; 8:1–39). He is also concerned to show that this gift of righteousness does not undermine but undergirds the believer's call to holiness (6:1–7:25). Imputed righteousness is always accompanied and followed by imparted righteousness in the life of the justified person.

Paul then addresses a powerful objection against what he has been arguing in the preceding chapters. In light of the unbelief of so many Jews, Paul asks, has the

[55] Ridderbos, *Paul*, 163.
[56] Ibid., 47.
[57] The phrase is that of Schreiner, *Romans*, 73. See the discussions in Kruse, *Paul's Letter to the Romans*, 75–78; Moo, *Epistle to the Romans*, 76. The NIV has "by faith from first to last."
[58] Moo, *Epistle to the Romans*, 76.

"word of God failed" (9:6)? Is God's word of promise reliable and trustworthy? Does the gospel "fulfill" or "betray" what God said in the Old Testament?[59] In Romans 9:1–11:36, Paul defends the trustworthiness of God's Word, and upholds the gospel as the fulfillment of what God spoke in the Old Testament.

In the closing section of the book (Rom. 12:1–16:27), Paul explains what the lives of those who have received the gift of righteousness should look like. Appealing to God's mercies in Christ (12:1), Paul presents a comprehensive platform of Christian living, one that encompasses both body (12:1) and mind (12:2). The following chapters detail this pattern of Christian living across a variety of circumstances (12:1–13:14) before proceeding to address a difficult situation facing the Roman Christians in their own church (14:1–15:13). Before giving final greetings in Romans 16, Paul "returns to where he began, speaking of the Roman Christians and of his own ministry and plans (cf. 1:1–15)" in Romans 15:14–33.[60]

We have, then, the following outline of Romans:

I. Introduction and Thesis: The Righteousness of God (1:1–17)
II. The Lack of and Need for the Righteousness of God (1:18–3:20)
III. The Gift of the Righteousness of God (3:21–8:39)
IV. A Challenge to the Righteousness of God (9:1–11:36)
V. The Moral Demands of the Righteousness of God (12:1–16:27)

Message and Theology

The Lack of and Need for the Righteousness of God (Rom. 1:18–3:20)

In Romans 1:18–3:20, Paul establishes the universal human lack of and need for the gift of righteousness of which he has spoken in 1:1–17. This portion of Romans is in three parts: Paul's indictment of humanity, particularly Gentiles (1:18–32), Paul's indictment of Jewish humanity (2:1–3:8), and Paul's concluding verdict on all humanity (3:9–20).

In 1:18–32, he indicts all humanity by stating, first, that "the wrath of God is revealed from heaven against all ungodliness and unrighteousness of men, who by their unrighteousness suppress the truth" (1:18). Paul is saying that human beings are ungodly and unrighteous. They know God but suppress the truth of the God they know. God is presently manifesting his just displeasure toward humans who are in rebellion against him.

Throughout Romans 1:18–32, Paul emphasizes that people, far from being ignorant of God, know him from the created order (1:19, 20, 21, 25, 28, 32). In 2:14–15, Paul will stress that the "conscience" of every human being "bears witness" to the universally binding standards of God's righteous law.[61] People are therefore responsible to God and culpable for their sinful thoughts and behavior. Their knowledge

[59] Ibid., 553.
[60] Ibid., 884.
[61] Some commentators have argued that Paul has Gentile Christians in view in Rom. 2:14–15. It is unlikely, however, that Paul would begin to discuss Christians at this juncture in his argument. It is furthermore unlikely that Paul would describe any Christian (Jew or Gentile) as "a law to themselves" (2:14).

of God from the creation has not led them to worship and to glorify God (1:21). On the contrary, "they became futile in their thinking, and their foolish hearts were darkened" (1:21). They turned their worship to the creature instead of the Creator (1:23, 25). God therefore has justly given human beings over to the sins they love and desire (1:24, 26–27).[62] It is this divine abandonment that helps us to understand the way in which God's wrath is presently and provisionally being revealed from heaven.

Paul underscores in this section the fact that the human condition, so described, is beyond mere human remedy. So committed to sin are human beings that they devote their talents and energies to "invent[ing] evil" (1:30). So hardened are they in sin that "though they know God's righteous decree that those who practice such things deserve to die, they not only do them but give approval to those who practice them" (1:32).

Although Paul does not mention the Jew until Romans 2:17, many commentators rightly understand the apostle to turn his attention to the Jew at Romans 2:1.[63] Why does Paul discuss Jews at this juncture of his argument? Certainly his prior division of humanity along the lines of Jew and Gentile in the letter's thesis gives a partial reason (1:16; cf. 2:9–10; 3:9). But why does Paul single out Jews from the rest of humanity? We find the answer in the way he describes Jews in 2:1–3:8. Jews, Paul argues, have an "advantage" that is unique to them. They "were entrusted with the oracles of God" (3:2). As Paul goes on to say of the Jews later in this letter: "To them belong the adoption, the glory, the covenants, the giving of the law, the worship, and the promises. To them belong the patriarchs, and from their race, according to the flesh, is the Christ" (9:4–5).

Paul highlights two Jewish privileges in particular in Romans 2:1–3:8. The first is the possession of the Torah, the law of Moses (2:12–24). The second is "circumcision," the sign and seal of God's covenant with the descendants of Abraham (2:25–29). These privileges do not automatically convey salvation, Paul argues. God is an impartial Judge and his judgment is just (2:1–5, 11). God "will render to each one according to his works" (2:6), whether "tribulation and distress" to the evildoer (2:9) or "glory and honor and peace" for the one who "does good" (2:10). Therefore, if one is relying on his performance to render himself acceptable to God, then he must not merely possess the law but also do all that the law requires (2:13; cf. 2:14).[64] The problem is that no Jew meets this standard. On the contrary, Jews violate the very standards they accuse Gentiles of transgressing (2:1–3, 17–24). Consequently, Paul reasons, physical "circumcision" is only "of value if you obey the law" (2:25). Were

[62] Note the way in which Paul establishes a relationship between the sin of idolatry and the sin of same-sex relations by the use of the verb "exchanged" at Rom. 1:23, 25, 26. Both sins, for Paul, involve a fundamental corruption of the creation order and an upending of the good purposes for which God has created the world. Idolatry corrupts the creature into an object of worship. Same-sex relations reject the created ordinance of marriage and God's purposes for human sexuality. See further Moo, *Epistle to the Romans*, 114–15.

[63] Hultgren, *Paul's Letter to the Romans*, 111; Dunn, *Romans 1–8*, 78–79.

[64] Some commentators have taken this statement to refer to Christians. Of those who do, some argue that Paul is teaching here that the Christian will be justified at the last day on the basis of his life lived. One problem with this understanding of Rom. 2:13 is that Paul denies this very possibility later in Romans (see 3:21–26; 4:4–5). Others argue that Paul is saying that Christians' good works will evidence their (present) justification by faith alone. This interpretation is true to Paul's teaching elsewhere in Romans, but it requires a definition of the verb "justify" ("to evidence that one is justified") that does not surface elsewhere in Paul's letters. It is preferable to take Paul's statement in Rom. 2:13 to refer to a person who is seeking to be justified on the basis of his performance. The same such person is in view at Rom. 2:9, on which see the survey of scholarly opinion in Moo, *Epistle to the Romans*, 140–41.

an uncircumcised person to keep the law perfectly, God would regard that person as though he were circumcised (2:26). When a circumcised person violates the law, his "circumcision becomes uncircumcision" (2:25).

Anticipating concerns that he will address more fully in Romans 9–11, Paul concludes in Romans 3:1–8 that Israel's "faithlessness" does not "nullify the faithfulness of God" (3:3). Paul, furthermore, affirms God's prerogative to judge not only the "world" but also his covenant people (3:5b–6). In asserting this claim, Paul brings his argument full circle: God is an impartial Judge who requires righteousness of any and all human beings in order for them to stand and to be vindicated in the final judgment.

The provisional but palpable expressions of divine wrath upon human unrighteousness (1:18) and the failure of Israel to live in keeping with their covenant privileges and responsibilities (3:1–3) prepare the reader for Paul's sweeping and concluding statement of universal human condemnation for sin in Romans 3:9–20. In 3:9, Paul declares, "We have already charged that all, both Jews and Greeks, are under sin." Here, Paul underscores the twofold dilemma of humanity with respect to sin. First, in speaking of this assessment in terms of a "charge," he highlights the judicial or forensic character of humanity's plight.[65] In speaking of humanity as "under sin," he "personifi[es]" sin as an enslaving, dominating power.[66]

In support of this assessment, Paul proceeds to cite the Old Testament (3:10–18). These citations are drawn primarily from the Psalms, but also from the Proverbs and Isaiah.[67] They stress the comprehensive reach of sin within human experience. In Romans 3:10–12, Paul highlights the universality of sin ("none is righteous . . . all have turned aside . . . no one does good"). In 3:13–18, he shows how human speech ("throat," "tongues," "lips," "mouth") and human behavior ("feet," "paths") are thoroughly committed to the service of sin. What is striking about his use of these passages is that "Paul . . . merges the prophetic charge against the people of God with the complaint of the psalmists against their enemies."[68] Israel stands among the number of those subject to God's just judgment.

For this reason, Paul concludes, the law plays the indispensable function of "stopp[ing] . . . every mouth [that] the whole world may be held accountable to God" (3:19). To the sinner, the law brings "knowledge of sin" (3:20). Thus, by the "works of the law"—that is, human efforts to perform the duties required by God's law—"no human being will be justified in his sight"—that is, declared righteous in the presence of God (3:20).[69] All human beings stand as unrighteous persons before

[65] Mark Seifrid, "Romans," in *Commentary on the New Testament Use of the Old Testament*, ed. G. K. Beale and D. A. Carson (Grand Rapids, MI: Baker Academic, 2007), 615.

[66] Jewett, *Romans*, 258–59. "To be 'under sin' is to be under the dominion of sin" (Murray, *Epistle to the Romans*, 1:102).

[67] See further Seifrid, "Romans," 616–18.

[68] Ibid., 617. Compare Moo, *Epistle to the Romans*, 202–3.

[69] Both of these definitions have been contested within recent New Testament scholarship. Some scholars, such as James D. G. Dunn and N. T. Wright, have argued that "works of the law" should be taken in a predominantly sociological sense. That is to say, they serve as boundary-marking devices to demarcate Jew from Gentile. Paul is therefore said to be attacking ethnocentric pride and to be contrasting that pride with the inclusivity of the gospel. Wright in particular has argued that the verb *justify* for Paul has the primary signification of God's declaring a covenant member to be a member of God's people. To be "justified by faith," for Wright, means in the first instance to be declared a covenant member on the basis of the badge of covenant membership, faith. For a fuller treatment of and response to what has been called the "New Perspec-

a righteous God. The law provides no resources to recover them from their lost condition. It serves only to underscore their plight.

The Gift of the Righteousness of God (Rom. 3:21–8:39)

Having shown that all human beings both lack and need righteousness, Paul proceeds to show where and how that righteousness may be obtained. It does not come from within humanity ("apart from the law," Rom. 3:21), but it is "of God" (3:21). This righteousness has appeared on the plane of history in Jesus Christ ("But now," 3:21; cf. "the Law and the Prophets bear witness to it," 3:21).[70]

Paul devotes Romans 3:21–31 to explaining the content and significance of this "righteousness of God." First, he locates it firmly in the death (and resurrection, 4:25) of Christ. Jesus's death ("blood," 3:25), Paul claims, is explained in terms of "redemption" (3:24) and "propitiation" (3:25). In dying on the cross for his sinful people (cf. 3:23, "For all have sinned and fall short of the glory of God"), Jesus redeemed them from the guilt of sin by bearing in his body the penalty for their sins. He also propitiated, or turned away, the wrath of God on their behalf by enduring the divine wrath for them on Calvary. Second, one receives Christ and the benefits of his death through "faith in Jesus Christ" (3:22; cf. 3:25).[71] Faith is the sole instrument of receiving Christ and his work for sinners. Because it is appropriated by faith, Christ's work is therefore available "for all who believe" (3:22), a point that Paul expands at length in 3:27–31. Third, this "righteousness of God" is "by his grace as a gift" (3:24). Sinful human beings have not merited or qualified for it (cf. 4:4–5). It is the free and undeserved gift of the righteous God to unrighteous people. Fourth, this gift of righteousness demonstrates God's upright character (3:25–26). In forgiving sins past and present, God does not neglect the just demands of his own character. Rather, he is both "just and the justifier of the one who has faith in Jesus" (3:26).

In Romans 4:1–25, Paul summons both Abraham and David as Old Testament witnesses in support of justification by faith alone (cf. 3:31, "On the contrary, we uphold the law"). In Romans 4:1–8, Paul appeals to both Genesis 15:6 and Psalm 32:1–2 to show that Abraham and David were justified by faith alone, apart from works of the law. In the remainder of Romans 4, he dwells on Abraham's justifying faith (cf. 4:22, "That is why his faith was 'counted to him as righteousness'") as pattern and paradigm for all who, following Abraham, look to God by faith for justification (4:23).

In the course of chapter 4, Paul makes two fundamental points about Abraham in

---

tive on Paul," see Stephen Westerholm, *Perspectives Old and New on Paul: The "Lutheran" Paul and His Critics* (Grand Rapids, MI: Eerdmans, 2004); Westerholm, *Justification Reconsidered: A Pauline Theme* (Grand Rapids, MI: Eerdmans, 2013); John Piper, *The Future of Justification: A Response to N. T. Wright* (Wheaton, IL: Crossway, 2007); Guy Prentiss Waters, *Justification and the New Perspectives on Paul* (Phillipsburg, NJ: P&R, 2004).

[70] On the redemptive-historical meaning of the phrase "but now," see Ridderbos, *Aan de Romeinen*, 82.

[71] Some have argued that the phrase "faith in Jesus Christ" should be rendered "the faithfulness of Jesus Christ." On this reading of the verse, Paul would be claiming here that it was Jesus's faithfulness to his Father's commission that secured the righteousness of God for his people. Conceptually this is true to Paul. It is doubtful, however, that this is what Paul means by the Greek expression (πίστεως Ἰησοῦ Χριστοῦ) underlying the ESV translation "faith in Jesus Christ." On this question, see Moisés Silva, "Faith versus Works of Law in Galatians," in *Justification and Variegated Nomism*, vol. 2, *The Paradoxes of Paul*, ed. D. A. Carson, Peter T. O'Brien, and Mark Seifrid (Grand Rapids, MI: Baker Academic, 2004), 217–48.

relation to believers today. First, Paul stresses that Abraham received the "blessing" of justification by faith alone while he was yet "uncircumcised" (4:9). Circumcision therefore did not justify him, but it was a "sign" and "seal" of the righteousness that he had already received from God through faith in God's promise (4:11). Abraham, therefore, is the "father" of those uncircumcised persons who "walk in the footsteps of [Abraham's] faith" (4:12). Second, Paul stresses that Abraham's faith is a faith in God's resurrection promise (4:13–25). It is in Romans 4:25 that Paul explicitly ties our justification to Christ's resurrection. Paul is saying here that "Christ's resurrection was the *de facto* declaration of God in regard to his being just. . . . Resurrection had annulled the sentence of [the] condemnation" that he had borne on behalf of his people.[72] Jesus's resurrection therefore "was the demonstration and proof of the acquitting righteousness of God, revelation thus of righteousness in the sense of Rom 1:17; 3:21."[73]

The structure of Paul's argument in the remainder of this section has posed a formidable challenge to commentators. Some have argued that Romans 5:1–21 concludes the material that precedes it (3:21–4:25), while others have argued that Paul begins a fresh line of thought at Romans 5:1.[74] Douglas Moo has proposed understanding Romans 5:1–8:39 chiastically.[75] In 5:1–11 and 8:18–39, Paul's concern is assurance of future glory. In 5:12–21 and 8:1–17, Paul provides the basis for this assurance in the work of Christ and the work of Christ mediated by the Spirit, respectively. In the two innermost sections, 6:1–23 and 7:1–25, Paul deals with the problem of sin and the law, respectively. The unifying theme of this section, then, is the assurance that God's presently justified people may now have that they will persevere to, and certainly attain, future glory.[76]

In Romans 5:1–11, Paul affirms that, "justified by faith," believers now "rejoice in hope of the glory of God" (5:1–2). Paradoxically, we also "rejoice in our sufferings" because God is at work in and by them to nurture that "hope" (5:3–4). Furthermore, believers will never be disappointed in this hope because "God's love has been poured into our hearts through the Holy Spirit who has been given to us" (5:5). The love of God, supplied by the indwelling Holy Spirit, both sustains us and assures us of glory to come.

Paul then turns to the ground or basis of this assurance in Romans 5:12–21, the work of Christ. Here, Paul sets in antithetical parallel the two Adams—the first Adam, who is "a type of the one who was to come" (5:14), and Christ. By the one trespass (5:16, 18; cf. 5:14) of the one man Adam (5:12, 15–17, 19) have come "condemnation" (5:16, 18) and "death" (5:17; cf. 5:21). By the "one act of righteous-

[72] Vos, *Pauline Eschatology*, 151.
[73] Ridderbos, *Paul*, 167. See further Gaffin, *Resurrection and Redemption*, 121–24.
[74] On which see Moo, *Epistle to the Romans*, 290–95.
[75] For what follows, see ibid., esp. 294.
[76] For proposals that see these chapters as retellings of Israel's narrative history, see N. T. Wright, "The Letter to the Romans: Introduction, Commentary, and Reflections," in *The New Interpreter's Bible*, vol. 10, *Acts; Introduction to Epistolary Literature; Romans; 1 Corinthians*, ed. Leander E. Keck (Nashville: Abingdon, 2002), 508–619, esp. 508–14; and, more concisely, Frank Thielman, "The Story of Israel and the Theology of Romans 5–8," in *Pauline Theology*, vol. 3, *Romans*, ed. David M. Hay and E. Elizabeth Johnson (Minneapolis: Fortress, 1995), 169–75, and N. T. Wright, "Romans and the Theology of Paul," also in Hay and Johnson, *Romans*, 30–67.

ness" or "obedience" (5:18–19) of the "one man Jesus Christ" (5:15, 17) have come "justification" (5:16, 18) and "life" (5:17–18, 21). The work of each representative head has been imputed or reckoned to those whom each represents.[77] As Adam's sin has been imputed to his posterity for their condemnation, Paul argues, Christ's righteousness has been imputed to believers for their justification. But Christ's work differs from Adam's. It differs not only in its outcome but also in its scope ("much more," 5:17; "all the more," 5:20). Paul's main point comes in verse 21. Because it is Christ's righteousness and only Christ's righteousness that has secured "life" for those united with Christ, we may be assured that we will "reign in life"—that is, "eternal life"—"through Jesus Christ our Lord" (5:17, 21).

In Romans 6:1–23, Paul addresses one problem or threat to this assurance—indwelling or remaining sin. Paul has, in fact, more than one objective in chapter 6. He wants to demonstrate that grace is no license to sin (6:1–2). He wants believers to understand that, united to Christ, they have a new relationship with sin and with righteousness. This new relationship therefore obligates them to a new lifestyle—one of "righteousness leading to sanctification" (6:19). The righteousness of which Paul speaks throughout this chapter (6:13, 16, 18–20) is not the imputed righteousness of Christ on the basis of which we are justified through faith alone (cf. 3:21–26). It refers, rather, to one's inward and outward conformity to God's righteous standards. "Sanctification," or the process by which believers become more and more righteous in this latter sense of the word, has as its "end" the "free gift" of "eternal life" (6:19, 22–23).

How is it that believers are to pursue sanctification? Paul here reminds us that every believer is united to Christ in his death and resurrection (6:1–14). This reality carries with it certain obligations and responsibilities (6:15–23). What does our union with Christ mean for sanctification? In Christ, "sin" no longer has "dominion" over believers (6:14; cf. 6:9). They have "died with Christ" and are therefore "dead to sin" (6:8, 11). They are united to Christ in his resurrection and therefore may now "walk in newness of life" (6:4; cf. 6:10–11). In light of this reality, Paul commands believers to "consider [them]selves dead to sin and alive to God in Christ Jesus" (6:11). They are, furthermore, to live not as the "slaves of sin" they once were but as the "slaves of righteousness" they now are (6:17–18). This reality means that they must submit themselves to biblical teaching (6:17), refuse to "obey" remaining sinful "passions" (6:12; cf. 6:13, 19), and present their whole selves to "God" in the service of "righteousness" (6:13; cf. 6:19). The gracious outcome of such a pattern of living, Paul argues, is "sanctification" and "eternal life" (6:22–23).

In Romans 7:1–25, Paul addresses a second problem or threat to the assurance he has described—the law of God. In 7:1–6, Paul explains what he meant when he said earlier that believers are "not under law but under grace" (6:14). He meant that they are no longer under the dominion of sin, a condition that the law is powerless to

[77] For an exegetical defense of the imputation of Adam's sin and Christ's righteousness to their respective posterities, see John Murray, *The Imputation of Adam's Sin* (Phillipsburg, NJ: P&R, 1992); and John Piper, *Counted Righteous in Christ: Should We Abandon the Imputation of Christ's Righteousness?* (Wheaton, IL: Crossway, 2002).

remedy (7:5). On the contrary, sin only makes the law the occasion of more sinning (7:5; cf. 5:20). In union with Jesus Christ and by the power of the indwelling Spirit (7:6), we now have at our disposal all the resources of grace and are free from the old enslaving "regime."[78]

In Romans 7:7–25, Paul proceeds to speak of himself ("I") in relation to the law. While some modern interpreters have questioned this conclusion, Paul is speaking autobiographically in these verses.[79] And yet, his main interest in these verses is not himself, but the law. Paul wishes to defend the law. Far from being "sin" (7:7), the law is "spiritual" (7:14), that is, produced by the Holy Spirit. As such, "the law is holy, and the commandment is holy and righteous and good" (7:12). In Romans 7:7–13, Paul views the law in relation to himself as an unbeliever. In doing so, he vindicates the law from blame (7:12) and lays all culpability upon himself (see references to his "sin" in 7:8–9, 11).

Paul's argument in Romans 7:14–25 has garnered considerable attention. Is he still speaking of himself as an unbeliever, or is he now speaking of himself as a believer? The latter is surely the case, and that for at least three reasons. First, Paul has consistently used the past tense in 7:7–13. Now, in 7:14–25, he consistently uses the present tense. Second, Paul refers to what he calls his "inner being" (7:22), something that he elsewhere predicates only of the believer (2 Cor. 4:16; Eph. 3:16). Third, Paul declares a consent to (Rom. 7:16), delight in (7:22), and service of (7:25a) the law of God that he later affirms is categorically impossible for the unbeliever (8:7).[80] Paul's point in these verses is that, even as the law continues to serve as a mirror reflecting remaining sin within the believer, the law remains good and holy. To the genuine believer, indwelling sin is a grave burden and a matter of great grief. It is not, however, a matter for despair, as Paul triumphantly declares in Romans 7:24–8:1. The work of sanctification that Paul has earlier outlined is an imperfect one in the believer's present experience. That imperfection is a constant reminder to ground our assurance of future glory in the justifying work of Christ.

Paul returns to that work in Romans 8:1 ("There is therefore now no condemnation for those who are in Christ Jesus"). In 8:1–17, Paul comprehensively addresses the work of Christ in conjunction with the ministry of the Spirit (cf. 1:4; 5:5). The law is powerless to deliver us from our plight, which Paul describes using the word "flesh" (8:3; cf. 1:3–4). That deliverance has come through Christ, who assumed sinless humanity (8:3), and in our nature not only was "condemned" for our sin (8:3), but also "fulfilled" on our behalf the "righteous requirement of the law" (8:4).[81] It is the Holy Spirit, Paul argues, who has effectually applied this work of Christ

[78] The word is that of Moo, *Epistle to the Romans*, 421.

[79] For surveys of the issues, see J. Lambrecht, *The Wretched "I" and Its Liberation: Paul in Romans 7 and 8*, LTPM 14 (Louvain: Peeters, 1992); Michael Paul Middendorf, *The "I" in the Storm: A Study of Romans 7* (St. Louis, MO: Concordia Academic, 1997); Schreiner, *Romans*, 359–65; and Moo, *Epistle to the Romans*, 423–28.

[80] Paul's statements in Rom. 7:14 ("of the flesh, sold under sin") and 7:25 ("with my flesh I serve the law of sin") are sometimes invoked as evidence that Paul is still speaking of himself as an unbeliever (7:23). While these statements evidence the power and reach of indwelling sin in believers, they are not inconsistent with Paul's statements elsewhere that believers are no longer under sin's dominion.

[81] Paul's point here is not that our law keeping as Christians is the way in which the law is brought to fulfillment. His point, rather, is that Christ has fulfilled all the requirements of the law for life and blessing in reference to us, his people.

to us (8:2). The Spirit of the risen Christ has delivered us from the realm of "flesh," which is this present evil age (cf. Gal. 1:4; Eph. 1:21). He has transferred us into the realm of "Spirit," that is, the age to come (cf. Eph. 1:21; Col. 1:13). Now united to Christ by the Holy Spirit and through faith, we share in all that Christ has won for us as our representative head.

It is in the remainder of this section (Rom. 8:4b–17) that Paul details the ministry of the Spirit in the lives of those who now belong to Christ. We have a new lifestyle; we "walk not according to the flesh but according to the Spirit" (8:4). So closely united are the Spirit and Christ in their saving activity that it is impossible to "belong to [Christ]" without also "hav[ing] the Spirit of Christ" (8:9). For the Spirit to dwell in us (8:11) is for Christ to dwell in us (8:10). The fruit and evidence of the Spirit's indwelling is a new "mind" (8:5–7), a new "walk" (8:4), and the "put[ting] to death the deeds of the body" (8:13). The Spirit, Paul continues, assures us that we who belong to the Son of God (Rom. 1:3–4) are "sons of God" (8:14–17). He presently testifies to our sonship (8:16) and to our being "heirs of God and fellow heirs with Christ" (8:17). This ministry of the Spirit assures us, amid present suffering, that we will be "glorified with [Christ]" (8:17).

In Romans 8:18–39, Paul concludes where he began—the assurance of future glory, our unseen but certain "hope" (8:24–25). This glory will encompass our resurrected bodies (8:23), which Paul takes to be the consummation of our present adoption (8:18, 23). But it will also encompass the whole of the creation (8:20–22). Steeled in the knowledge of God's eternal and unchangeable purpose (8:28–30), the ongoing "help" and intercession of the Spirit in the present (8:26–27), and the finished work of the crucified, risen, and interceding Christ (8:31–34), believers face their glorious future in the knowledge that no created thing can separate them from God's love in Christ (8:35–39).

A Challenge to the Righteousness of God (Rom. 9:1–11:36)

Romans 9–11 begins in "great sorrow and unceasing anguish" (9:2) and concludes with exultation in the "depth of the riches and wisdom and knowledge of God" (11:33). This conclusion reflects the resolution that the argument of Romans 9–11 brings to the problem with which Paul wrestles in the opening verses of Romans 9—Israel's unbelief. To appreciate the argument of these chapters, it is important to understand why the gospel's rejection by so many Israelites burdened Paul. Were there a *Sonderweg*—another way of salvation—for Jews, Paul's anguish would be incomprehensible.[82] Paul's conviction that there is no salvation outside of Jesus Christ, however, means that his unbelieving "kinsmen according to the flesh" are "accursed" (9:3).

There are, however, further dimensions to Paul's anguish. He has insisted that the gospel is "to the Jew first and also to the Greek" (1:16; cf. 2:9–10). There is

[82] For a survey and analysis of this position, see Terence L. Donaldson, "Jewish Christianity, Israel's Stumbling, and the *Sonderweg* Reading of Paul," *JSNT* 29 (2006): 27–54. See also the helpful treatment of Scott J. Hafemann, "The Salvation of Israel in Romans 11:25–32: A Response to Krister Stendahl," *ExAud* 4 (1988): 38–58.

a redemptive-historical priority of the Jew to the Greek. Now that the gospel has gone to the nations, what are we to make of the fact that this same gospel has been rejected by so many Jews? This redemptive-historical "priority . . . appears to be contradicted by the large-scale unbelief and apostasy of Israel."[83] Is this state of affairs not a blemish on the gospel? Furthermore, Paul has triumphantly ended Romans 5:1–8:39 with the declaration that nothing "in all creation, will be able to separate us from the love of God in Christ Jesus our Lord" (8:39). On the face of it, Jewish rejection of the gospel calls that proposition into question. If believers are to trust this promise, they must also know that God has proved himself utterly trustworthy in his dealings with Israel.

How, then, does Paul's argument progress toward its doxological conclusion in 11:33–36? His argument unfolds in four stages. First, in Romans 9:1–29, Paul defends the thesis that "the word of God has [not] failed" (9:6a). The first reason that Paul gives in support of this thesis ("for," 9:6b) is that "not all who are descended from Israel belong to Israel." Paul shows from the Old Testament itself that individuals' reception of spiritual blessing is not a function of genealogical descent (9:6–13). God is sovereign in both giving to and withholding mercy from undeserving sinners (9:14–29).[84]

Second, in Romans 9:30–10:21, Paul sets Israel's rejection of the gospel in the context of God's broader purposes in redemptive history. Returning to concerns addressed earlier in the letter, Paul stresses that unbelieving Israel has sought to "establish their own" righteousness by the works of the law and "did not submit to God's righteousness" that comes through faith in Christ alone (10:3; cf. 9:30–33; 10:4). The righteousness of God comes not by striving but through faith in Christ (10:5–13). It is therefore available to all kinds of people, whether "Jew [or] Greek" (10:12). Paul concludes this section by citing representative portions of the Old Testament (Psalm 19 in Rom. 10:18; Deuteronomy 32 in Rom. 10:19; Isa. 65:1–2 in Rom. 10:20–21). He does so in order to prove at least two points: (1) Israel is responsible and culpable for her unbelief. (2) God has brought the gospel to the Gentiles in order to provoke Israel to jealousy. Israel's unbelief, therefore, is not the last word about Israel in God's saving purposes.

Third, in Romans 11:1–10, Paul proceeds to show that Israel's fall is not complete. There are Israelites in Paul's day who have responded to the gospel in faith. "So too at the present time there is a remnant, chosen by grace" (11:5). God has "by no means . . . rejected his people" (11:1–2), and Paul can point to himself as modest proof of the fact. What of nonelect Israelites? While "the elect obtained" the righteousness of God, "the rest were hardened," futilely seeking it by works (11:7).[85] This hardening Paul ascribes to the counsel and purpose of God (11:8–10). In his sovereign mercy,

[83] Murray, *Epistle to the Romans*, 2:xiii.

[84] Some interpreters have argued that in Romans 9 Paul has in view the nation of Israel and not individual Israelites (see Ridderbos, *Aan de Romeinen*, 227–31). In other words, it is said, Paul's interests in addressing election are national or corporate, not individual. But throughout Romans 1–8, Paul has been concerned with the individual. It is unlikely that he would set aside that concern in Romans 9–11. Furthermore, the noun "election" at Romans 9:11 must refer to God's eternal election of individuals to salvation, on which see further and decisively Murray, *Epistle to the Romans*, 2:15–20.

[85] Murray, *Epistle to the Romans*, 2:72.

God has chosen some to salvation. In his sovereign power and by the unsearchable counsel of his own will, God has passed by the rest and left them to their desert.[86]

Fourth, in Romans 11:11–36, Paul shows that Israel's fall is not "final."[87] These verses, particularly 11:25–27, raise some difficult issues about which Reformed interpreters are not altogether agreed.[88] Paul's basic point, however, is clear. As Israel's "trespass" has occasioned "salvation" for "the Gentiles, so as to make Israel jealous," so there is a further chapter for Israel in God's unfolding saving purposes (11:11–12). Likening the people of God to an olive tree, and God to that tree's cultivator, Paul asserts the sovereignty of God in grafting back into the tree its branches that were formerly broken off for unbelief (11:16b–24). For now, there is a "partial hardening . . . upon Israel," one that will last "until the fullness of the Gentiles has come in" (11:25). What will happen at this future time when this hardening is lifted? Paul's answer is that "all Israel will be saved" (11:26). What does Paul mean by "all Israel"? Likely what he has meant by "Israel" throughout Romans 9–11, not least in 11:25—"ethnic Israel."[89] Paul has in view here the nation and is not therefore making a pronouncement about how many ethnic Israelites will or will not be saved.[90] He may even envision this large-scale conversion of ethnic Israelites as the occasion of even further "gospel blessing" for Gentiles (11:12).[91]

Paul concludes this section of his argument in two ways. One is to remind the Roman Christians that "God has consigned all to disobedience, that he may have mercy on all" (11:32). They ought not, therefore, look upon unbelieving Israelites in pride and contempt. Second, Paul ascribes all that he has written of God's ways in redemptive history to the "riches" of his grace in Christ, his "unsearchable . . . judgments," and his "inscrutable . . . ways" (11:33). Indeed, God is he "from" whom, "through" whom, and "to [whom] are all things," and "to him" alone belongs the "glory forever" (11:36).

The Moral Demands of the Righteousness of God (Rom. 12:1–16:27)

In Romans 6 and 8, Paul described the dynamics of Christian living in terms of union with Christ in his death and resurrection, on the one hand, and the ministry of the Spirit of Christ, on the other. Paul is no mystic and has reminded the Romans that

---

[86] See WLC 13.

[87] Murray, *Epistle to the Romans*, 2:xiv. Compare the judgment of Charles Hodge, *Commentary on the Epistle to the Romans* (New York: A. C. Armstrong and Son, 1896), 567: "As there [11:1] the apostle wished to have it understood that the rejection of God's ancient people was not entire, so here [11:11a], he teaches that this rejection is not final."

[88] In addition to those in the commentaries, see the helpful discussions of Anthony A. Hoekema, *The Bible and the Future* (Grand Rapids, MI: Eerdmans, 1979), 139–47; and Cornelis P. Venema, *The Promise of the Future* (Edinburgh: Banner of Truth, 2000), 127–39.

[89] Murray, *Epistle to the Romans*, 2:96.

[90] Ibid., 2:98. We may note two other interpretations of Paul's statement "and in this way all Israel will be saved" that Reformed interpreters have adopted. The first, as summarized by Hoekema and as embraced by John Calvin, sees this statement "as referring to the salvation of all the elect, not only from the Jews, but also from the Gentiles, throughout history" (*The Bible and the Future*, 140). The second view, held by such prominent Dutch Reformed theologians as Herman Bavinck and Herman Ridderbos, sees Paul's statement as "describing the bringing to salvation throughout history of the total number of the elect from among the Jews" (ibid.).

[91] As Murray, *Epistle to the Romans*, 2:78–79, 93–96. It is worth remembering that Paul terms the content of Rom. 11:25f. a "mystery," that is, a matter that God has only now revealed under the new covenant (cf. Rom. 16:25; Eph. 3:3–6). It is also worth remembering the caution of Charles Hodge that "Paul is here speaking as a prophet . . . and therefore his language must be interpreted by the rules of prophetic interpretation. Prophecy is not proleptic history" (*Commentary on the Epistle to the Romans*, 588, cited in Murray, *Epistle to the Romans*, 2:96n48).

they now have become "obedient from the heart to the standard of teaching to which [they] were committed" (6:17). While the law of God plays a vital role in exposing the ongoing sin of the believer (7:14–25), it also plays a positive and necessary role in guiding the steps and directing the life of the believer.

In Romans 12–16, Paul outlines the contours of the moral demands that rest upon those who have received "righteousness of God" by faith alone. This is not the way in which they are justified. It is, rather, the way in which justified persons must live. It is the way in which they are to pursue "sanctification" (6:19) in the power of the Spirit who indwells them (cf. Rom. 8:4b–11). Above, we have reflected on Paul's specific applications of this gospel-informed lifestyle to the church in 14:1–15:7. We have also touched on how, in Romans 15:8–16:27, Paul stresses the critical social component of the Christian life. Believers are to be actively engaged in supporting those who are called to preach the gospel (15:22–33), and to live and serve Christ in the context of a fellowship of believers (16:1–23).

In Romans 12:1–13:14, Paul addresses some of the specific details of Christian living. In 12:1–2, he provides initial orienting principles before he proceeds to particular commands. First, he underscores the fact that Christian obedience entails the whole person, body (12:1) and mind (12:2). We are to present our "bodies as a living sacrifice, holy and acceptable to God, which is [our] spiritual worship" (12:1). Under the new covenant, God's people no longer offer animal sacrifices. Now that Christ has come, the purpose of those sacrifices has been served. But believers are to count themselves "living sacrifice[s]," committing and consecrating their whole selves to God and to his service. Believers are also not to be "conformed to this world ["age," ESV mg.]." Rather, we are "transformed by the renewal of [our] mind," with the goal of discerning and applying God's will (12:2). Second, Paul stresses that Christian obedience is lived in grateful response to the "mercies of God" (12:1), likely the mercies that Paul has devoted the whole of the letter to expounding. Obedience is the response of the Christian to God's goodness in Christ. Third, Paul defines Christian obedience in terms of God's "will." Paul describes God's will here as "good and acceptable and perfect" (12:2), terms that recall his prior description of God's law (7:12).[92] The "will" of God that Christians are to learn and "discern" is God's law. In Romans 13:8–10, Paul will define that law in explicit terms as the Decalogue, or the Ten Commandments.

How may we characterize the imperatives of Romans 12:3–13:14? First, in pointing believers to the Ten Commandments (13:8–10), Paul directs us to understand the whole of this section (12:3–13:14) as an application of the Decalogue to the life of the believer. Since "love is the fulfilling of the law" (13:10), these commands detail the life of love (cf. 12:9). Second, recognizing that there is a diversity of gifts represented in each congregation (12:3–8), Paul stresses that those who have gifts should use them (12:6) for the good of the body (12:5) and in humility (12:3). Third, believers have obligations to the civil magistrate (13:1–7). We must conscientiously

[92] Murray, *Epistle to the Romans*, 2:115.

submit (13:5) to temporal rulers in the knowledge that they are God's "servant[s]" (13:4) who rule by God's appointment (13:2). Our obedience to these rulers is not implicit. Both they and we stand under God, and we may never obey human authority when that means disobedience to God. Fourth, Paul reminds us that "salvation is nearer to us now than when we first believed" (13:11). We must live as those who know that the imminent return of Christ will bring this present age to a close.[93] That knowledge prompts us to put away those evil deeds that are characteristic of this present evil age, and to live in this age as those who belong to Christ (13:13–14).

How may one summarize a letter as grand as the epistle of Paul to the Romans? Perhaps one word that ties together many of the letter's leading themes and concerns is *glory*. God made human beings to worship him, but, in Adam, people have universally "exchanged the glory of the immortal God" for the worship of the creature (1:23). Indeed "all have sinned and fall short of the glory of God" (3:23), by which Paul likely means a failure to "reflect the glory of God, that is, [to be] conform[ed] to his image."[94] The "glory" held out to "everyone who does good" is unavailable to sinners bent on doing evil (2:10).

But God is glorifying his name through the redemption of sinners. He has purposed to "make known the riches of his glory for vessels of mercy, which he has prepared beforehand for glory" (9:23). Christ, "raised from the dead by the glory of the Father," has "welcomed" us in the gospel of grace "for the glory of God" (6:4; 15:7). In Christ, we bring glory to God now by trusting in his promises (4:20). What's more, we rejoice in the hope of the glory of God (5:2), a glory that will be given to us with the redemption of the body, and a glory that is nothing less than cosmic in scope (8:18, 21; cf. 8:23). Indeed, Paul can exult in the God from whom, through whom, and to whom are "all things," and ascribe to him "glory forever" "through Jesus Christ" (11:36; 16:27). And having surveyed with Paul the breadth and depth of God's glorious purposes in redemption, we join the apostle in saying, "Amen" (11:36; 16:27).

Select Bibliography

Barnett, Paul. *Romans: The Revelation of God's Righteousness*. FB. Fearn: Christian Focus, 2003.

Cranfield, C. E. B. *Romans 1–8*. ICC. Edinburgh: T&T Clark, 1975.

———. *Romans 9–16*. ICC. Edinburgh: T&T Clark, 1979.

Donfried, Karl P., ed. *The Romans Debate*. Rev. and exp. Peabody, MA: Hendrickson, 1991.

[93] The nearness of Christ's return is "the nearness of prophetic perspective and not that of chronological calculations" (Murray, *Epistle to the Romans*, 2:168). The next and last event in redemptive history is Christ's glorious return at the end of the age. It is in that sense that Paul speaks of the nearness of the consummation of our salvation in 13:11. See the perceptive discussion in Ridderbos, *Paul*, 487–97.

[94] Murray, *Epistle to the Romans*, 1:113.

Dunn, James D. G. *Romans 1–8*. WBC 38A. Nashville: Thomas Nelson, 1988.
———. *Romans 9–16*. WBC 38B. Nashville: Thomas Nelson, 1988.
Fitzmyer, Joseph A. *Romans: A New Translation with Introduction and Commentary*. AB 33. New Haven, CT: Yale University Press, 1993.
Gaffin, Richard B., Jr. *By Faith, Not by Sight: Paul and the Order of Salvation*. 2nd ed. Phillipsburg, NJ: P&R, 2013.
———. *Resurrection and Redemption: A Study in Paul's Soteriology*. 2nd ed. Phillipsburg, NJ: P&R, 1987.
Hay, David M., and E. Elizabeth Johnson, eds. *Pauline Theology*. Vol. 3, *Romans*. Minneapolis: Fortress, 1995.
Hodge, Charles. *Commentary on the Epistle to the Romans*. Rev. ed. New York: A. C. Armstrong and Son, 1896.
Jewett, Robert. *Romans*. Hermeneia. Minneapolis: Fortress, 2006.
Kruse, Colin G. *Paul's Letter to the Romans*. PNTC. Grand Rapids, MI: Eerdmans, 2012.
Longenecker, Richard N. *Introducing Romans: Critical Issues in Paul's Most Famous Letter*. Grand Rapids, MI: Eerdmans, 2011.
Moo, Douglas. *The Epistle to the Romans*. NICNT. Grand Rapids, MI: Eerdmans, 1996.
Murray, John, *The Epistle to the Romans*. 2 vols. Grand Rapids, MI: Eerdmans, 1959, 1965.
Ridderbos, Herman N. *Aan de Romeinen*. Kampen: Kok, 1959.
———. *Paul: An Outline of His Theology*. Translated by John Richard de Witt. Grand Rapids, MI: Eerdmans, 1975.
Schreiner, Thomas R. *Romans*. BECNT. Grand Rapids, MI: Baker, 1998.
Stott, John. *Romans: God's Good News for the World*. BST. Downers Grove, IL: InterVarsity Press, 2004.
Thielman, Frank. *Paul and the Law: A Contextual Approach*. Downers Grove, IL: InterVarsity Press, 1994.
Vos, Geerhardus. "The Eschatological Aspect of the Pauline Conception of the Spirit." In *Redemptive History and Biblical Interpretation: The Shorter Writings of Geerhardus Vos*, edited by Richard B. Gaffin Jr., 91–125. Phillipsburg, NJ: P&R, 1980.
———. *The Pauline Eschatology*. 1930. Repr., Phillipsburg, NJ: P&R, 1994.
Waters, Guy Prentiss. *Justification and the New Perspectives on Paul*. Phillipsburg, NJ: P&R, 2004.
Westerholm, Stephen. *Justification Reconsidered: A Pauline Theme*. Grand Rapids, MI: Eerdmans, 2013.
———. *Perspectives Old and New on Paul: The "Lutheran" Paul and His Critics*. Grand Rapids, MI: Eerdmans, 2004.
Wright, N. T. "The Letter to the Romans: Introduction, Commentary, and Reflections." In *The New Interpreter's Bible*. Vol. 10, *Acts; Introduction to Epistolary Literature; Romans; 1 Corinthians*, edited by Leander E. Keck, 393–770. Nashville: Abingdon, 2002.
———. *Paul and the Faithfulness of God*. Minneapolis: Fortress, 2013.

7

1–2 Corinthians

Guy Prentiss Waters

[First Corinthians is] an Epistle not less obscure than useful.

John Calvin, "First Epistle Dedicatory" (1546)[1]

More than any other of Paul's epistles, [2 Corinthians] bears the impress of the strong feelings under the influence of which it was written.

Charles Hodge (1859)[2]

Introduction

Passionate. Imposing. These are two words that aptly describe the two epistles of Paul to the church in Corinth. First and Second Corinthians are attractive and winning. But they are also formidable and even foreign.

First and Second Corinthians are paradoxically two of Paul's most accessible and most distant letters. A survey of some of the issues that Paul addresses in these two letters explains their accessibility to modern readers: ecclesiastical politics (1 Corinthians 1–4), gross and scandalous sexual immorality (1 Corinthians 5), professing believers suing each other in courts of law (1 Corinthians 6), confusion about divorce and remarriage (1 Corinthians 7), serving Christ in the world without compromise (1 Corinthians 8–10), worship wars (1 Corinthians 11–14), denial of the bodily resurrection (1 Corinthians 15), and celebrity leadership in

[1] Cited in Roy E. Ciampa and Brian S. Rosner, *The First Letter to the Corinthians*, PNTC (Grand Rapids, MI: Eerdmans, 2010), 1.

[2] Charles Hodge, *An Exposition of the Second Epistle to the Corinthians* (New York: A. C. Armstrong and Son, 1891), 1.

the church (2 Corinthians). The church in Corinth might very well be the church down the street.

But these letters also seem quite distant from modern readers. At points, readers cannot help but feel dropped into the middle of an ongoing conversation between Paul and the Corinthian church. Interpreters are compelled to engage in what has been called "mirror reading"—"try[ing] to reconstruct what [the Corinthians] were thinking so as to better understand his responses."[3] Add to this difficulty the fact that modern readers simply do not inhabit the world that Paul and his Corinthian audience did. Speaking with reference to 1 Corinthians, Roy E. Ciampa and Brian S. Rosner have noted that "it is far removed from our world in terms of language, geography, economics, social customs, and religious practice. It talks with little or no explanation of human wisdom, law courts, prostitution, meat markets, and pagan worship, not to mention head coverings and baptism for the dead."[4] Compounding this particular difficulty is that both letters move—sometimes briskly, sometimes abruptly—from one issue to the next. Even sympathetic and thoughtful readers can struggle to discern what unifies the array of topics broached in each letter.

Studying these two letters is difficult but rewarding. The rewards well repay the ardor of the undertaking. In what follows, I will first attempt to place these two letters in the context of Paul's unfolding and sometimes stormy relationship with the church in Corinth. For all the variety of problems and difficulties in the life of this church that Paul labors to document and redress in these two letters, we will see that these problems, for Paul, all stem from a common root—the failure of Christians to relate properly to the world around them.[5] The Corinthian Christians exhibit in their beliefs, attitudes, choices, and behaviors a worldview that at many points is insufficiently formed by, and at points even antithetical to, the gospel. No small part of these letters, we will see, is Paul's providing the church with the vocabulary and grammar of the gospel in order to meet the challenges of living in our world.

Part of this project is Paul's helping the Corinthians to understand their place in redemptive history. As Richard B. Hays has noted, "In 1 Corinthians we find Paul calling his readers and hearers to a *conversion of the imagination.* He was calling Gentiles to understand their identity anew in light of the gospel of Jesus Christ—a gospel message comprehensible only in relation to the larger narrative of God's dealing with Israel."[6] Consequently, we find Paul appealing to the Old Testament at crucial junctures in both these letters to assist his readers in understanding the fabric and flow of redemptive history and their place in it. We will need to devote concerted attention to the way in which Paul does just that in 1–2 Corinthians.

Once these foundations have been laid, we will then be in a position to explore the outline and structure of each letter. If we understand Paul's intentions in forming

[3] David E. Garland, *1 Corinthians*, BECNT (Grand Rapids, MI: Baker Academic, 2003), 13.
[4] Ciampa and Rosner, *First Letter to the Corinthians*, 1.
[5] Noted perceptively by Charles Hodge, *An Exposition of the First Epistle to the Corinthians* (New York: Robert Carter, 1866), xx–xxi.
[6] Richard B. Hays, *The Conversion of the Imagination: Paul as Interpreter of Israel's Scripture* (Grand Rapids, MI: Eerdmans, 2005), 5, emphasis his.

the sensibilities of the Corinthian Christians, then we will be able to appreciate the genuine unity of each letter and be poised to survey the contents of the Corinthian correspondence.

Background Issues

Paul and the Church in Corinth

According to Luke, the church in Corinth was established on Paul's second missionary campaign (Acts 18:1–18). Paul spent eighteen months on this founding visit (Acts 18:11), and his time there fell during Gallio's proconsulship of the Roman province of Achaia. Inscriptional evidence sets the scene of Acts 18:12–17 firmly in AD 51.[7] Paul thus arrived in Corinth in 49 or 50, ministered there for a year and a half, and then departed in 51 or 52, bringing his second missionary campaign to a close shortly thereafter in Antioch (Acts 18:22).

Luke's account of the founding of the church in Corinth helps us to understand some of the features of Paul's subsequent correspondence with that church. The city of Corinth was located on the isthmus that joins the mainland of Greece and the Peloponnesian Peninsula.[8] Served by two port cities, Cenchreae and Lechaeum, it was a crossroads of both land and sea trade. Destroyed by the Romans in 146 BC, the city was rebuilt as a modern, planned community in 44 BC under Julius Caesar. It served as the capital of the Roman province of Achaia and was, therefore, a center of government as well as commerce.

The city was characterized by the wealth that trade brought and by the power that the Roman presence represented. As is often the case with commercial centers, Corinth was a cosmopolitan community. Persons from all over the Roman Empire settled there, including "veterans," "freedmen," and Jews.[9] Greco-Roman religion was well represented, as were religions that had been imported from the East.[10] Corinth was also a town frequented by "impressive, traveling public speakers" who dispensed their oratorical services to adherents who financially supported their work.[11]

Socially and ethnically, the church in Corinth reflects this background.[12] Some of the Corinthians were highborn and powerful, but most were not (1 Cor. 1:26; cf. 1:27–31). Luke tells us that the foundation of the Corinthian church consisted of Jews from the local synagogue who had come to faith in Christ (Acts 18:4–8). Among these Jews was "Crispus, the ruler of the synagogue" (Acts 18:8), whom Paul mentions at 1 Corinthians 1:14. The church also included certain Gentiles who had

---

[7] On which, see the discussion at F. F. Bruce, *The Acts of the Apostles: Greek Text with Introduction and Commentary*, 3rd ed. (Grand Rapids, MI: Eerdmans, 1990), 394–95.

[8] For surveys of the location and history of Corinth, see Scott J. Hafemann, "Corinthians, Letters to the," *DPL*, 172–73; D. A. Carson and Douglas J. Moo, *Introduction to the New Testament*, 2nd ed. (Grand Rapids, MI: Zondervan, 2005), 419–20; Ben Witherington III, *Conflict and Community in Corinth: A Socio-Rhetorical Commentary on 1 and 2 Corinthians* (Grand Rapids, MI: Eerdmans, 1995), 5–12.

[9] Hafemann, "Corinthians, Letters to the," 173.

[10] Carson and Moo, *Introduction to the New Testament*, 420. See further Witherington, *Conflict and Community in Corinth*, 12–18.

[11] Ciampa and Rosner, *First Letter to the Corinthians*, 3.

[12] A standard study for the degree to which Greco-Roman culture influenced the beliefs and practices in view in 1 Corinthians is Bruce W. Winter, *After Paul Left Corinth: The Influence of Secular Ethics and Social Change* (Grand Rapids, MI: Eerdmans, 2001).

been attached to the synagogue in Corinth (Acts 18:4, 7), as well as other Gentiles with no such previous attachment (Acts 18:6; cf. 18:8). Judging from some of the pastoral difficulties that Paul addresses in the Corinthian letters, the church seems to have been overwhelmingly composed of Gentiles.[13]

Many of the difficulties that Paul addresses are explicable against this background. At any number of points, he reckons with the way in which the Greco-Roman values of wealth, wisdom, and power have surfaced in the Corinthians' beliefs and behaviors (cf. 1 Corinthians 1–4). The sexual immorality for which centers of trade are often known and attending confusion about marriage, divorce, and singleness emerge in Corinthian thought and life (cf. 1 Corinthians 5–7).[14] The religious pluralism of the city raises questions of conscience for the young church, and Paul has to help the Corinthians understand what Christian liberty means and does not mean in that setting (1 Corinthians 8–10). The city's social and economic stratification have likely influenced the way in which the church observes the Lord's Supper (1 Corinthians 11). Such stratification has also influenced the way in which the Corinthians have viewed, valued, and exercised spiritual gifts within the church (1 Corinthians 12–14). Hellenistic philosophical speculation undoubtedly plays a role in the heresy about the resurrection that Paul combats in 1 Corinthians 15. Much of 2 Corinthians is devoted to Paul directly challenging the values system of Greco-Roman rhetoric.

How may we characterize Paul's history with the Corinthians? What interactions did Paul have with the Corinthians after he left Corinth in AD 51 or 52? Where do the letters, presumably written after this initial visit, fall in that history? After Paul left Corinth, he returned to his sending church of Antioch (cf. Acts 13:1–3; 14:24–28; 18:22). Departing from Antioch, Paul commenced a third round of missionary travels and labors. Unlike his two previous campaigns, this third campaign was largely centered in the western Asia Minor city of Ephesus (Acts 19:1–41), where Paul was based and was ministering for three years (Acts 20:31).

It is certain that Paul wrote 1 Corinthians from Ephesus at this time (ca. AD 52–55). He tells the Corinthians in 1 Corinthians 16:8–9, "I will stay in Ephesus until Pentecost, for a wide door for effective work has opened to me, and there are many adversaries." In 1 Corinthians 16:19, he sends "greetings" from the "churches of Asia" and from "Aquila and Prisca" (cf. Acts 18:24–28).

First Corinthians was not the first letter that Paul had written the Corinthians. In 1 Corinthians 5:9 he mentions a previous letter, not extant ("I wrote to you in my letter not to associate with sexually immoral people"). He mentions this letter in order to clear up a misconception about its contents (cf. 1 Cor. 5:10–11).[15] What Paul's reference to this lost letter indicates is that the apostle maintained an epistolary correspondence with the Corinthians even as he was ministering in residency in Asia

[13] Hafemann, "Corinthians, Letters to the," 173. Hafemann here notes 1 Cor. 6:1–6, 10–20; 7:1–40; 8:1–11:1; and 12:2 as proof.
[14] Commentators frequently note that the oft-cited proliferation of temple prostitutes in Corinth dates from the period prior to 146 BC and may not necessarily reflect practice in Corinth in Paul's day. Even so, there is ample evidence from within and outside the New Testament that sexual immorality was a prominent feature of the city's life.
[15] Garland notes a pattern throughout 1 Corinthians: Paul pauses to ensure that the Corinthians do not misunderstand or misconstrue what he has just said (4:14; 9:15; 10:19) (*1 Corinthians*, 20).

Minor. This reference is also suggestive of the way in which Paul's written words were misconstrued by the Corinthians. Such misunderstanding would only resurface subsequently in the Corinthians' relationship with Paul.

Much of 1 Corinthians appears to reflect prior communication with Paul by diverse quarters within the church.[16] Paul mentions in 1:11 that he has received a report "by Chloe's people" concerning "quarreling" or "strifes," the subject of the opening chapters of the letter.[17] He mentions the anonymous report of the gross sexual immorality that occasions Paul's words in chapter 5 ("it is actually reported . . . ," 5:1). Without specifying the source, he says, "I hear that there are divisions among you" in connection with the observance of the Lord's Supper (11:18). Some of these concerns may have been raised in a letter or letters that the Corinthians sent Paul ("now concerning the matters about which you wrote," 7:1).[18] The presence of a Corinthian delegation consisting of "Stephanas and Fortunatus and Achaicus" (16:17) with Paul in Ephesus raises further possibilities. These three men may have "carried" the Corinthians' letter, provided commentary on the contents of the letter, or reported matters to Paul that have found their way into 1 Corinthians.[19]

Paul signals intentions about his future plans at the close of 1 Corinthians. After leaving Ephesus (1 Cor. 16:8–9), he plans to come to Corinth prior to a planned visit to Jerusalem (16:3). His plans about this Corinthian stay are to some degree indefinite: "Perhaps I will stay with you or even spend the winter, so that you may help me on my journey, wherever I go" (16:6; cf. 16:9). First, however, Paul will "pass through Macedonia" (16:5). In the meantime, Paul is sending Timothy to Corinth and urges the Corinthians to give him a warm reception (16:10–11).

What happened after Paul wrote 1 Corinthians and before he wrote 2 Corinthians is difficult to reconstruct and a matter of some debate. In 2 Corinthians, Paul characterizes a previous visit to the Corinthians as a "painful visit" (2 Cor. 2:1). Since nothing in Luke's account suggests that this "painful visit" is Paul's "original visit" to Corinth, it must be a subsequent one, likely during Paul's three-year stay in Ephesus.[20] It was likely "occasioned by the arrival of news, possibly brought by Timothy, to the effect that there had been a revolt against the Apostle's authority in Corinth."[21] Many scholars before the twentieth century placed this painful visit prior to the composition of 1 Corinthians.[22] Consequently, such scholars have identified the "painful letter" of 2 Corinthians 7:8 with 1 Corinthians. On this reconstruction, then, Paul wrote three letters to the Corinthians, the latter two of which are extant—1 Corinthians (i.e., "the painful letter") and 2 Corinthians.

Contemporary New Testament scholars, however, generally and plausibly identify

---

[16] In what follows, I am dependent on the discussion in ibid., 20–21.

[17] The Greek word that Paul uses (ἔρις) has more in view than disagreement. It denotes strife and dissension.

[18] Although certainty is impossible, some of the statements in 1 Cor. 6:12–20 may be Paul's quotations of prior Corinthian correspondence, as the ESV indicates (cf. 6:12–13).

[19] Garland, *1 Corinthians*, 21. Garland (ibid.) notes R. B. Terry's proposal that 1 Corinthians consists of an alternating pattern: Paul addresses matters raised by oral reports (1:10–4:17; 4:18–6:20; 11:2–34; 15:1–58) followed by matters raised by the Corinthian letter (7:1–40; 8:1–11:1; 12:1–14:40; 16:1–12).

[20] Philip Edgcumbe Hughes, *Paul's Second Epistle to the Corinthians*, NICNT (Grand Rapids, MI: Eerdmans, 1962), 51–52.

[21] Hughes, *Second Epistle to the Corinthians*, 52.

[22] Ibid. Cf. 31–33.

the "painful visit" of 2 Corinthians 2:1 with a visit subsequent to the composition of 1 Corinthians.[23] Distressing news about the church, conveyed to Paul in Ephesus by Timothy, prompted the apostle to travel to Corinth and confront the Corinthians about the matters that Timothy had reported to him.[24] That visit did not conclude well. Scholars identify the "painful letter" of 2 Corinthians 7:8 with a lost letter that Paul drafted after 1 Corinthians, after the painful visit, but before 2 Corinthians. Paul likely wrote this letter after he had returned to Ephesus from Corinth, and Titus is probably the individual who delivered that letter.[25]

Also at some point between the composition of 1 Corinthians and 2 Corinthians, false teachers who claimed to be apostles arrived at the church in Corinth (2 Cor. 11:1–6, 12–15).[26] They appear to have attacked not only Paul's doctrine but also his apostolic credentials (cf. 2 Cor. 12:11–13). They capitalized on the fact that, whereas Paul had earlier told the Corinthians that he would visit them once more, he, after the "painful visit," determined for pastoral reasons not to make an additional visit to the church (2 Cor. 1:15–16).[27] Paul's opponents pounced on this change of plans and accused Paul of duplicity (cf. 2 Cor. 1:17–2:4).

Paul had hoped to meet Titus in Troas in order to find out how this "painful letter" had been received in Corinth (2 Cor. 2:12). It was not until Paul traveled to Macedonia, however, that he met Titus and received the news for which he was looking (2 Cor. 7:5–6; cf. Acts 20:1–2). Paul's concerns were put to rest by Titus's report. Titus himself had been spiritually "refreshed" by his time in Corinth (2 Cor. 7:13–16). The offender had expressed his repentance publicly, and the congregation had repented of its sin in the matter (2 Cor. 7:8). Paul's "painful letter" had in fact done its work (2 Cor. 7:8–9).

It is at this point, while Paul is in Macedonia (Acts 20:1–2), that he writes 2 Corinthians (AD 55 or 56). Paul has at least three aims in this letter. First, he writes in relief and joy that the previous difficulties between him and the Corinthians are now settled and concluded. The letter rehearses, to some degree, the painful history between the composition of the two extant Corinthian letters. It does so not to reopen freshly healed wounds, but to express Paul's joy and confidence in the church (2 Cor. 7:16). Second, Paul writes the Corinthians to stir them up to contribute to the offering for believers in Jerusalem (2 Corinthians 8–9). The Corinthians earlier expressed their desire to do so, and their poorer Macedonian brothers have already given quite generously. The intervening difficulties that the Corinthians had with Paul surely delayed the collection in Corinth. Now is the time, Paul writes, for the Corinthians to bring their intention to give to fruition. Third, Paul writes

[23] See the discussion at Carson and Moo, *Introduction to the New Testament*, 422–23.

[24] It is impossible to be certain what those matters were. See the discussion at Paul Barnett, *The Second Epistle to the Corinthians*, NICNT (Grand Rapids, MI: Eerdmans, 1997), 12. If the penitent man of 2 Cor. 2:5–8; 7:11–12 is not the offender of 1 Corinthians 5 but an individual who had personally harmed Paul, then part of what rendered this particular visit "painful" may have been this man's activities (ibid., 12; David E. Garland, *2 Corinthians*, NAC 29 [Nashville: Broadman & Holman, 1999], 27).

[25] Garland, *2 Corinthians*, 27.

[26] The identification of these opponents is a long and vexed question within critical scholarship. For a survey of representative positions, see Hafemann, "Corinthians, Letters to the," 177–78.

[27] Barnett, *Second Epistle to the Corinthians*, 12.

the Corinthians to defend his ministry against the attacks by apostolic pretenders who have taken up residence in Corinth (2 Corinthians 10–13). For Paul's joy in the Corinthians to continue, and for the offering to be gathered and delivered on schedule, Paul must respond to the criticisms that these opponents have been circulating about him in Corinth.

We have been assuming throughout this discussion that both 1 and 2 Corinthians are unified letters, each written on a single occasion by a single author, Paul. Since the eighteenth century, scholars, particularly in the critical tradition, have questioned the unity of both epistles, especially 2 Corinthians.[28] Some evangelical scholars have suggested that 2 Corinthians 1–9 and 2 Corinthians 10–13 are separate Pauline letters, the latter having been composed after the former.[29]

The strongest argument for the unity of 2 Corinthians comes from the New Testament manuscript tradition. As Colin Kruse—an evangelical proponent of understanding 2 Corinthians 1–9 and 2 Corinthians 10–13 as separate letters—concedes, "There are no extant manuscripts supporting the division of the letter as [Kruse himself has] suggested."[30] Why then have scholars proposed two letters (2 Corinthians 1–9 and 10–13)?[31] They plausibly argue that the considerable difference in tone between these two portions of 2 Corinthians invites us to understand them as two originally separate and independent letters.[32] This difference, however, may be pressed too far. David Garland has noted the way in which 2 Corinthians 6:14–7:1 anticipates the tone of 2 Corinthians 10–13, thus easing the transition from 2 Corinthians 1–9 to 2 Corinthians 10–13.[33] Ben Witherington has argued on literary grounds that the tone of 2 Corinthians 10–13 is appropriate to the "forensic rhetoric" that Paul employs in 2 Corinthians.[34] Paul Barnett concludes that the variations in tone between 2 Corinthians 7, 8–9, and 10–13 reflect Paul's deft "pastoral method."[35] In conclusion, then, the absence of supporting external evidence and alternative ways of explaining the internal evidence together support understanding 2 Corinthians as a single letter authored on a single occasion by a single author, Paul.

---

[28] See the survey discussions in Carson and Moo, *Introduction to the New Testament*, 430–42; Barnett, *Second Epistle to the Corinthians*, 17–25; Garland, *2 Corinthians*, 33–44; Murray J. Harris, *The Second Epistle to the Corinthians*, NIGTC (Grand Rapids, MI: Eerdmans, 2005), 8–51.

[29] F. F. Bruce, *1 and 2 Corinthians* (London: Oliphants, 1971), 166–70; Colin G. Kruse, *2 Corinthians*, TNTC (Grand Rapids, MI: Eerdmans, 1987), 29–35. Other scholars have argued that 2 Corinthians 10–13 is the "painful letter" mentioned in 2 Cor. 2:3–4; 7:8, for which see Garland, *2 Corinthians*, 36n42.

[30] Kruse, *2 Corinthians*, 33. Kruse accounts for this fact by suggesting that the letters were "copied on to one scroll very early in the history of the transmission of the text" (ibid.). Kruse's suggestion, however, is neither verifiable nor falsifiable.

[31] In this discussion, we will leave aside the welter of other interpolation theories circulating in the literature, on which see the discussions cited above in note 28.

[32] Some hypothesize that, after a lapse of time following the composition of the initial letter (2 Corinthians 1–9), Paul learned of the activity of the apostolic pretenders and proceeded to draft another letter (2 Corinthians 10–13). Carson and Moo, who adopt a version of this hypothesis, suggest that Paul took "weeks, or even longer" to draft and complete a single letter (2 Corinthians 1–13) (*Introduction to the New Testament*, 434). That is to say, in the course of this protracted span of time, having already drafted 2 Corinthians 1–9, Paul learned of the apostolic pretenders and thereupon composed 2 Corinthians 10–13.

[33] Garland, *2 Corinthians*, 40–41.

[34] Witherington, *Conflict and Community in Corinth*, summarized in Garland, *2 Corinthians*, 41–42. Compare the independent but corroborating rhetorical argument of Barnett, *Second Epistle to the Corinthians*, 17–19. Barnett also argues for the unity of the epistle on the basis of similarities in concept and wording between 2 Corinthians 1–9 and 2 Corinthians 10–13 (pp. 19–21).

[35] Barnett, *Second Epistle to the Corinthians*, 22.

The Problems in Corinth

Among Paul's thirteen letters, 1–2 Corinthians most vividly and transparently reflect the particular circumstances and issues that have occasioned their composition. In 1 Corinthians particularly, Paul appears to be breathlessly moving from one brushfire to the next, hoping to extinguish the one before the other gets out of control. The welter of issues that Paul addresses in both letters poses a question: Do they have a common denominator? Is there any thread uniting the apparently disparate matters that Paul raises in both letters?

In offering an affirmative answer to these questions, we may begin by considering what constitutes the first main section of 1 Corinthians, namely, 1:10–4:21. Not only does this section address the first issue to which Paul turns his attention in this letter, but it is also one of the epistle's largest sections. The topic of "divisions" (1:10) dominates this portion of 1 Corinthians, and Paul begins by making a strong appeal to "be united in the same mind and the same judgment" (1:10).

Paul does more, however, than simply isolate the problem and prescribe the solution. He analyzes the Corinthians' sin of disunity and factionalism in order to help the church understand this sin's deep structure and inner working. Paul begins 1 Corinthians 1:10–4:21 by contrasting the divisions at work in the church with the "gospel," or what Paul later calls the "word of the cross" (1:17–18), the "wisdom of God" (1:21, 24). This wisdom, Paul goes on to explain, is "not a wisdom of this age or of the rulers of this age" (2:6).[36] It is, rather, "a secret and hidden wisdom of God, which God decreed before the ages for our glory" (2:7). This wisdom has been "revealed" to the church "through the Spirit" (2:10; cf. 2:12). The apostles communicate "spiritual truths" in "words not taught by human wisdom but taught by the Spirit" (2:13). They communicate them to "those who are spiritual" (2:13). Those who are "natural," however, do not "accept the things of the Spirit of God" (2:14). The church's divisions, Paul argues in 1 Corinthians 3:1–3, evidence not a "spiritual" mind-set but a "flesh[ly]" and "human" one (3:1, 3; cf. Gal. 5:20–21).[37] The Corinthians need to understand that they are "God's temple and that God's Spirit dwells in [them]" (1 Cor. 3:16). They need to grasp that "the wisdom of this world is folly with God" (3:19). Each needs to be willing to "become a fool that he may become wise" (3:18).

In 1:10–4:21, Paul is pivoting back and forth between two mutually exclusive realities vying for the loyalties of the Corinthians. On the one hand, there is the "wisdom of the world," the "wisdom of this age," which Paul describes using the adjectives "natural," "fleshly," and "human." On the other hand, there is the "gospel," the "wisdom of God," which is not only "spiritual" but has been uniquely conveyed to the church by the "Spirit," through the apostles.

[36] Paul's argument in 1 Cor. 2:6–16 "expands on but does not contradict 'the word of the cross' in 1:18ff." (Richard B. Gaffin Jr., "Some Epistemological Reflections on 1 Corinthians 2:6–16," in *Revelation and Reason: New Essays in Reformed Apologetics*, ed. Scott Oliphint and Lane Tipton [Phillipsburg, NJ: P&R, 2007], 21).

[37] Gordon Fee notes, "With this paragraph [i.e., 1 Cor. 3:1–4], therefore, Paul makes the transition from the one argument (over the nature of the gospel and the meaning of true 'wisdom') to the other (about division in the name of their leaders)" (*The First Epistle to the Corinthians*, NICNT [Grand Rapids, MI: Eerdmans, 1987], 121–22). In this respect, then, 1 Cor. 3:1–4 unites 1 Cor. 2:6–16 not only with 3:5–17 but also with 1:17–2:16.

The contrast between "flesh" and "Spirit" is both significant and oft-repeated in Paul's letters. In Romans 1:3–4, it expresses the aeonic, eschatological, or redemptive-historical contrast between two orders or ages.[38] As Herman Ridderbos has observed, "flesh" and "Spirit" "represent two modes of existence, on the one hand that of the old aeon which is characterized and determined by the flesh, on the other that of the new creation which is of the Spirit of God."[39] How does Paul understand these two aeons or ages? There is, on the one hand, this present age, or what Paul calls "the present evil age" (Gal. 1:4). For Paul, this age is spatiotemporal. It is a span of time, but more than a span of time. It is a moral order that characterizes and defines the world of humanity untouched by the saving grace of God in Christ.[40] It is for this reason that Paul can use the terms "age" and "world" synonymously in 1 Corinthians 1:20 and 2:6.[41] This age stands in systemic and concerted rebellion against and hostility toward God and Christ. Thus, it is "the rulers of this age" who "crucified the Lord of glory" (1 Cor. 2:8).

Paul, however, defines the age to come, inaugurated in history by the resurrection of Christ from the dead, in terms of the activity of the Spirit who raised Christ from the dead. In a word, Paul can speak of this order in terms of the "life" that Christ has secured by his death and resurrection, the "life" that the Spirit is now applying to his people (Rom. 8:10). This application begins when the Spirit unites a sinner to Christ in his death and resurrection and when, by the Spirit, that sinner lays hold of Christ by faith (Eph. 2:5–6; Col. 2:12). This dynamic helps to explain why Paul identifies the gospel of the cross of Christ with a wisdom that he proceeds to define explicitly in terms of the revelatory activity of the Holy Spirit (1 Cor. 2:12–14).

For Paul, it is not simply that Christians have been translated from this present evil age and brought into the age to come. They certainly have experienced that transfer (Gal. 1:4; Col. 1:13). But they have not altogether left this present age. As Paul tells the Corinthians in 1 Corinthians 5:10, Christians have not presently left the "world." Having been delivered from this age, we yet continue to live within this age, even as we no longer belong to this age. Negotiating life in the overlap of the ages is not always easy. It poses certain challenges and opportunities for believers.

It is this challenge that shapes Paul's discussion in 1 Corinthians 1:10–4:21. Here Paul is contrasting two antithetical orders—that of "flesh," and that of the "Spirit." The wisdom of which Paul speaks and to which Paul directs the Corinthians is an "eschatological" wisdom.[42] Seen in this light, the problem of divisions and factions in the church at Corinth is symptomatic of a deeper and more fundamental problem among the Corinthians. Their divisiveness, Paul argues, is characteristic of an order

[38] See the chapter on Romans for further discussion of Rom. 1:3–4. Note Eph. 1:21, where Paul mentions both ages together, "not only in this age but also in the one to come."

[39] Herman Ridderbos, *Paul: An Outline of His Theology*, trans. John Richard de Witt (Grand Rapids, MI: Eerdmans, 1975), 66.

[40] In speaking of this age in terms of the "world," Paul is not suggesting that the creation is anything other than fundamentally good. In this context, Paul speaks of the world in terms of "the human situation qualified by sin, or mankind itself. [It] is the world turned away from God, rebellious and hostile toward him . . . depraved mankind that is headed for judgment" (ibid., 92).

[41] In 1 Cor. 1:20, "the debater of *this age* . . . the wisdom of *this world*"; in 2:6, "a wisdom of *this age*."

[42] So, rightly, Gaffin, "Epistemological Reflections on 1 Corinthians 2:6–16," 21; cf. 21–30.

from which they profess to have been delivered (Gal. 1:4) and to which they have professed not to belong (cf. 1 Cor. 1:1–9).

When we read the remainder of the Corinthian correspondence, we see that the problems that Paul identifies and addresses in these letters are ones that need to be understood in terms of the two-age contrast introduced in 1 Corinthians 1:10–4:21.[43] In 1 Corinthians 5, Paul is appalled that the Corinthians have failed to address a moral infraction that "is not tolerated even among pagans" (lit. "Gentiles," 5:1), that is to say, the denizens of this present evil age. The Corinthians, furthermore, are "arrogant" (lit. "puffed up," 1 Cor. 5:2). The verb translated "puffed up" is the same verb that Paul earlier used to describe the Corinthians in 1 Corinthians 4:6, thereby linking the problem addressed in 1 Corinthians 5 to that in 1:10–4:21. In 1 Corinthians 6, Paul admonishes the Corinthians for taking their disputes to the Roman courts, reminding them that "the saints will judge the world" (6:2) and that believers will inherit the "kingdom of God" (6:9–10).[44] In 1 Corinthians 7, Paul reminds the Corinthians that "the present form of this world is passing away" (7:31). In 1 Corinthians 8–10, he begins by warning the Corinthians of a "knowledge" that "puffs up" (cf. 4:6; 5:2), that is, a knowledge that is characteristic of this present age (8:1). He reminds the Corinthians in 1 Corinthians 10:11 that upon them "the end of the ages has come." In connection with his discussion of the Lord's Supper, Paul reminds the Corinthians that God is disciplining them "so that [they] may not be condemned along with the world" (11:32). At the heart of Paul's discussion of spiritual gifts in the Corinthian church (1 Corinthians 12–14) is his conviction that the Corinthians have yet to grasp adequately the nature, exercise, and purpose of those gifts that the "Spirit" has given the church (12:4). In 1 Corinthians 15, Paul defends the bodily resurrection, in part by setting the resurrection within the context of the two-age framework of history (15:42–49).

The same dynamic is present in 2 Corinthians. In this letter, Paul is reaffirming his integrity as an apostle of Christ in light of the painful and recently concluded history of his relationship with the Corinthians. Further, Paul's conflict with the apostolic pretenders, or the "super-apostles" (2 Cor. 12:11), amounts to disagreement about the criteria of a true apostle. In each case, Paul defines his apostleship and defends his conduct in terms of the two-age (flesh-Spirit) dichotomy. He does so in order to provide the Corinthians with the resources to recognize the legitimacy of his apostleship and to reject the counterfeit apostles who have taken up residence in Corinth.

In 2 Corinthians, Paul repeatedly denies that his apostolic office and conduct are "according to the flesh" (1:17; 5:16; 10:2–4).[45] As Garland has noted, the "subject of boasting (1:12, 14) appears as a central theme in the letter (see 5:12; 10:8, 13, 15–16, 18; 11:10, 12, 16–18, 30; 12:1, 5–6, 9)."[46] In 1 Corinthians, Paul explicitly tied "boasting" to this present age—to the flesh and to the world (1 Cor. 1:29, 31; 3:21;

[43] In what follows, I am indebted to the textual list in Garland, *1 Corinthians*, 17.
[44] Compare Col. 1:13, where Paul speaks of the two ages in terms of two domains or dominions: "He has delivered us from the domain of darkness and transferred us to the kingdom of his beloved Son."
[45] Garland, *2 Corinthians*, 43.
[46] Ibid.

4:7; 5:6). In 2 Corinthians, Paul uses this motif of boasting not only to characterize his opponents' labors in terms of this present age, but also to characterize his own ministry in terms of the Spirit. The evidence of the Spirit's "power" in his apostolic ministry (2 Cor. 13:4; cf. 12:12) is, paradoxically, Paul's weakness (12:9–10). And it is precisely in this "weakness" that Paul will "boast" (12:5).

Paul, furthermore, attributes the efforts of the apostolic pretenders to Satan (2 Cor. 11:3, 13–14). And it is Satan who is, Paul writes, the "god of this world" (2 Cor. 4:4). But Paul's ministry belongs to the age to come. In more than one place in 2 Corinthians, Paul explains what it means that his ministry is part of the age to come (3:1–4:6; 5:11–6:2), explicitly setting his ministry in the context of such realities of that age as the "new covenant" (3:6), the Spirit of the risen Christ (3:3, 6, 8, 17–18), the "glory" of Christ (3:18) and of the Spirit (3:8), and the "new creation" (5:17; cf. 4:1–6).

Structure and Outline

Before I sketch this argument through the two Corinthian letters, it will be helpful to have a sense of each letter's outline or structure. Between the salutation and thanksgiving of 1 Corinthians 1:1–9 and the sundry concluding matters of 1 Corinthians 16:1–24, the body of Paul's argument in 1 Corinthians falls in five sections.[47] First, in 1:10–4:21, Paul takes up the problem of divisions and factions in the Corinthian church. Second, in 5:1–7:40, he addresses a variety of problems relating to sexual integrity. Third, in 8:1–11:1, Paul handles the complex pastoral issues relating to "food offered to idols" (8:1). Fourth, in 11:2–14:40, he looks at several issues pertaining to the public worship of the church. Fifth and finally, in 15:1–58, Paul responds to a serious error circulating in the Corinthian church concerning the bodily resurrection. While this is not the only possible outline, it does serve to highlight the epistle's focus—the problems within the Corinthian church that have come to Paul's attention.[48]

Assuming our previous conclusion that 2 Corinthians is a literary unity and the production of a single author, Paul, we may divide the body of the letter into three parts corresponding to the three purposes we above identified.[49] In 2 Corinthians 1–7, Paul, in the course of rehearsing the painful history between himself and the Corinthian church, explains and defends his apostolic ministry. In 2 Corinthians 8–9, he encourages the Corinthians to bring to fruition their prior commitment to contribute to the Judean offering. In 2 Corinthians 10–13, Paul defends his ministry against the criticisms of the "super-apostles." In doing so, he underscores and glories in the characteristics of an authentic new covenant apostolic ministry.

[47] Paul Barnett, *1 Corinthians*, FB (Fearn: Christian Focus, 2000), 16. Barnett labels each of these sections "pastoral sermons." Whether or not these five portions of the letter's body are properly sermonic, Barnett has accurately described the major divisions of the epistle. Compare the similar outlines of Leon Morris, *1 Corinthians*, rev. ed., TNTC (Grand Rapids, MI: Eerdmans, 1985), 32–34; Anthony C. Thiselton, *The First Epistle to the Corinthians*, NIGTC (Grand Rapids, MI: Eerdmans, 2000), vi–xiii; Ciampa and Rosner, *First Letter to the Corinthians*, v–xii.

[48] Some commentators divide the epistle's body along formal lines: the reports that Paul received from Corinth (1:10–6:20); the letter that Paul received from Corinth (7:1–16:4) (C. K. Barrett, *First Epistle to the Corinthians*, HNTC [New York: Harper & Row, 1968], 28–29; Fee, *First Epistle to the Corinthians*, 21–23).

[49] See now the comprehensive survey of proposed outlines of this epistle at Harris, *Second Epistle to the Corinthians*, 105–12.

Outline of 1 Corinthians

I. Salutation and Thanksgiving (1:1–9)
II. First Set of Problems: Divisions and Factions (1:10–4:21)
III. Second Set of Problems: Sexual Integrity (5:1–7:40)
IV. Third Set of Problems: Food Offered to Idols (8:1–11:1)
V. Fourth Set of Problems: Public Worship in the Church (11:2–14:40)
VI. Fifth Problem: The Bodily Resurrection (15:1–58)
VII. Concluding Matters (16:1–24)

Outline of 2 Corinthians

I. Paul's Defense of His Apostolic Ministry: A Historical Account (1–7)
II. The Gentile Churches' Offering (8–9)
III. Paul's Defense of His Apostolic Ministry: Response to the "Super-apostles" (10–13)

Message and Theology

Paul's Redemptive-Historical Framework

In both Corinthian letters, then, Paul is not content simply to name problems and to propose solutions. He sets those problems in redemptive-historical context. He wants the Corinthians to understand their sins and difficulties in terms of negotiating life as those who belong to the age to come but also continue to live in this present age, an age to which they no longer belong, since Christ has delivered them from it by the Spirit.[50]

The Gospel

For Paul, the "gospel" characterizes and defines his apostolic ministry (1 Cor. 1:17). It stands in eschatological antithesis to the wisdom of "this age" or "this world" (1:20; 2:6). Exploring the content of this gospel will help us better to appreciate the character of this antithesis. It will also help us understand with more specificity and clarity the way in which Paul is guiding the Corinthians to negotiate their place and position in redemptive history, and to live in and for Jesus Christ.

It is in 1 Corinthians 15:1–4 that Paul gives one of his clearest and crispest definitions of the gospel he preached. Before he describes its content in verses 3–4, Paul makes four important preliminary comments about the gospel in verses 1–2. First, the gospel is a message that he "preached" (15:1). It is a propositional message that is verbally and publicly proclaimed. Earlier in the letter, Paul made the same point.

---

[50] Some scholars have argued that the Corinthians suffered from what has come to be called an "over-realized eschatology." See Anthony Thiselton, "Realized Eschatology at Corinth" *NTS* 24 (1978): 510–26; Thiselton, *First Epistle to the Corinthians*, 40; and Fee, *First Epistle to the Corinthians*, 12 (Fee prefers the term "spiritualized eschatology"). "Over-realized eschatology" refers to a failure to balance the dawn of the age to come with its unrealized consummation, on the one hand, and with the continuation of this present age, on the other. For criticisms of over-realized eschatology in relation to the Corinthians, see Hays, *Conversion of the Imagination*, 6–7, and Ciampa and Rosner, *First Letter to the Corinthians*, 4–5, 179. Note the judicious comments of Garland, who dissents from the over-realized eschatology hypothesis but notes, "The Corinthians' problems are more attributable to a *lack* of a clear eschatological vision of the defeat of the powers of this age and the final judgment of God looming on the horizon. They did not view this world as decisively evil and consequently were ready to make compromises with it" (*1 Corinthians*, 14, emphasis his).

There, he sharply distinguished preaching from baptism, defining his ministry not in terms of sacramental administration but in terms of evangelical proclamation (1 Cor. 1:17).[51] Second, the gospel is a message of salvation "by which you are being saved" (15:2; cf. Eph. 1:13, "the gospel of your salvation"). Its aim is the salvation of the hearer.[52] That from which the gospel saves a person Paul will make clear in 15:3–4. Third, the gospel is a message that must be "received" (15:1). It is not automatically effective. Any benefit that the gospel brings, it brings when it is appropriated by the hearer. Fourth, Paul addresses the mode of appropriation in verse 2, "unless you believed in vain." A believing response to the gospel is the way in which it is properly "received," and the way in which it becomes effective in the life of an individual. This faith, Paul stresses, is not ephemeral or passing. It entails "hold[ing] fast to the word" preached (15:2). Perseverance in believing distinguishes true faith from what Paul calls "vain" faith (15:2: cf. 15:14, 58).[53]

With these dynamics of the gospel's transmission in place, Paul proceeds in verses 3–4 to reflect on the content and significance of the gospel.[54] First, he addresses the origins of the gospel in verse 3: "For I delivered to you . . . what I also received." Paul's formulation is "nearly identical to that in 11:23."[55] It denotes the passing down of tradition from person to person. Paul elsewhere tells the Galatians, "I did not receive [the gospel] from any man, nor was I taught it, but I received it through a revelation of Jesus Christ" (Gal. 1:12). How are we to reconcile these two statements? In Galatians, Paul insists that he "received" the gospel, immediately, from Christ.[56] He means that what "convinced" him of the "decisive fact" of the resurrection and of the "way of salvation" was "the divine interposition on the road to Damascus."[57] That is to say, these fundamental convictions came from God and not man. Paul's point in 1 Corinthians 15:3 is that the contents of the gospel he preaches are neither idiosyncratic to Paul nor his private possession.[58] They "are the common teaching of the early church."[59] These Paul has received and has passed on to the Corinthians. His statements in Galatians 1:12 and 1 Corinthians 15:3, far from being mutually exclusive, are altogether complementary.[60] The gospel originates exclusively from God, by divine revelation. It is also the common property of the church.[61]

---

[51] Paul, of course, rejects neither baptism nor his role in administering baptism. Paul is concerned here to respond to individuals who are conscripting baptism in the service of factionalism.

[52] As Paul stresses in Rom. 10:14–17, the preaching of the gospel of Jesus Christ is the God-appointed means by which people are saved.

[53] Barrett, *First Epistle to the Corinthians*, 337, citing Origen.

[54] The explanatory particle "for" (γάρ) indicates that 15:3–4 will provide the content of "the word I preached to you" (Fee, *First Epistle to the Corinthians*, 721). The following discussion is particularly indebted to Richard B. Gaffin Jr., *By Faith, Not by Sight: Paul and the Order of Salvation*, 2nd ed. (Phillipsburg, NJ: P&R, 2013), 26–34.

[55] Fee, *First Epistle to the Corinthians*, 721.

[56] Hodge, *First Epistle to the Corinthians*, 312.

[57] J. Gresham Machen, *The Origin of Paul's Religion* (New York: Macmillan, 1921), 146.

[58] "The point is that St Paul did not invent what he communicated to them" (Archibald Robertson and Alfred Plummer, *A Critical and Exegetical Commentary on the First Epistle of St. Paul to the Corinthians*, 2nd ed., ICC [Edinburgh: T&T Clark, 1914], 333).

[59] Douglas J. Moo, *Galatians*, BECNT (Grand Rapids, MI: Baker Academic, 2013), 94.

[60] Ibid.

[61] This explanation is preferable to that of, for example, Ciampa and Rosner, who argue that Paul received from Christ a skeletal gospel, and that Christians provided him additional "elements" reflected in the formulation of vv. 3–4 (*First Letter to the Corinthians*, 745).

Second, Paul stresses in verse 3 that what Paul has passed down to the Corinthians is "of first importance."[62] This phrase signals what is, for Paul, of central importance to his gospel. To be sure, Paul's gospel is broader than what he will proceed to outline in verses 3b–4.[63] At the same time, Paul insists that what he is about to describe sits not at the periphery but at the core of his preaching and teaching (cf. 2:2; 1:17–18).[64]

Third, Paul in verses 3b–5 presents in parallel fashion the core of his gospel:

Christ died for our sins
    in accordance with the Scriptures,
        . . . he was buried,
. . . he was raised on the third day
    in accordance with the Scriptures,
        . . . he appeared to Cephas, then to the twelve.

To reformat Paul's summary in this fashion is to draw out some of its most prominent features. Paul's gospel centers upon the historical person and historical activity of Jesus Christ. Christ ("Messiah") is the one who "died," who "was buried" and "was raised," and who subsequently "appeared" to Cephas, to the Twelve, to "more than five hundred brothers at one time," to James, to "all the apostles," and finally to Paul.[65] The gospel centers not simply upon Christ's person, but upon his person and work. Paul brings this work to a twofold focus—Christ's death and resurrection in history (cf. 1 Thess. 4:14, "we believe that Jesus died and rose again"). Paul does not invoke Jesus's burial and his appearances as saving actions parallel with his death and resurrection. They are, rather, ancillary and supporting. Burial confirms that Christ did in fact die. The multiple appearances that Paul recounts confirm that Christ did in fact rise from the dead.[66]

Paul's interest in Christ's death and resurrection is in reference to "our sins." The apostle does not specify here a specific way in which Christ's death and resurrection address human sin. Paul must, then, be thinking of Christ's saving work as providing a "comprehensive" solution to the human plight of "sin."[67] In other words, he is thinking of Christ's death and resurrection as dealing with sin not only in its forensic dimensions (guilt, wrath), but also as "enslaving and corrupting power."[68] To borrow two terms that Paul has used earlier in the letter, and that he develops more fully in Romans 1–8, Paul has in mind here Christ's death and resurrection for the sinner's justification and sanctification.[69] What is clear from Paul's formulation is that the resources for solving the human plight of sin are to be found exclusively

[62] As the ESV properly renders the Greek construction, ἐν πρώτοις (Paul Barnett, *1 Corinthians*, FB [Fearn: Christian Focus, 2000], 271; Fee, *First Epistle to the Corinthians*, 722).
[63] So, rightly, Gaffin, *By Faith, Not by Sight*, 27.
[64] In light of this conclusion Fee's observation "Here is the 'bare bones' content of the gospel that saves" is a puzzling one (*First Epistle to the Corinthians*, 722).
[65] Ciampa and Rosner, *First Letter to the Corinthians*, 744–45.
[66] Fee, *First Epistle to the Corinthians*, 8, 725; Ciampa and Rosner, *First Letter to the Corinthians*, 746, citing G. Schneider, "Thaptō," *EDNT*, 2:134.
[67] Gaffin, *By Faith, Not by Sight*, 33.
[68] Ibid., 37; cf. 38.
[69] Ibid., 39.

and comprehensively in the death and resurrection of Jesus Christ. Paul does not look outside of Christ, much less his saving work for sinners, to point us to the way in which a sinner may be delivered from his sin.

Paul's emphasis that Christ died for "*our* sins" indicates the personal character of Jesus's work. Christ did not die and rise to deal with sin as some cosmic abstraction. He accomplished his saving work for sinners, for persons who were guilty of, under the dominion of, and corrupted by their sin (cf. 1 Cor. 8:11, "the brother for whom Christ died"). Paul has earlier in the letter stressed the personal substitutionary character of Christ's death, declaring him to be the new covenant Passover sacrifice for believers (11:23–26; cf. 5:7).[70] Paul will dwell on the character of this exchange in 2 Corinthians 5:19–21 in equally personal terms.

Finally, Paul qualifies both the death and resurrection of Christ with the important phrase "according to the Scriptures." While the apostle may have particular passages from the Old Testament in mind, he is likely referring to the entirety of the Old Testament Scripture.[71] Paul is saying more, however, than that particular prophecies have found their fulfillment in the person and work of Christ. He is accenting the eschatological nature of the death and resurrection of Christ.[72] Redemptive history, Paul insists, has its *telos* in Christ's saving work for sinners. The "fulfillment" represented by the phrase "according to the Scriptures" "is not relative but absolute—consummate."[73] That Paul understands Christ's death in such terms is evident from the fact that he uses the identical phrase "for our sins" at Galatians 1:4: "who gave himself for our sins to deliver us from the present evil age."[74] It is Christ's death that, in the "fullness of time" (Gal. 4:4), has rescued us from, or brought us out of, this "present evil age" (cf. Col. 1:13–14).

For Paul, then, Christ's death and resurrection are the heart, center, or core of his gospel. They are historical, saving acts, and Paul proclaims them in order that hearers, through faith in Christ, may be saved from their sins. With respect to the sinner's salvation, Christ's death and resurrection are comprehensive in their saving scope. All the resources for delivering a person from the plight of his sin Paul traces to these two works of Christ. Christ's death and resurrection, furthermore, are eschatological. They represent the consummation of redemptive history. They are the foundation upon which a sinner is delivered from "this present evil age" and, we shall see, brought into the age to come. How, then, does Paul point the Corinthians to the death and resurrection of Christ in order to direct them how to think and live as those who have experienced this decisive transition? We may answer this question by surveying some of Paul's statements in the Corinthian correspondence about Christ's death and resurrection.

---

[70] The fuller phrase "for our sins" is pregnant with meaning. Its pattern of use in the Septuagint suggests that Paul is framing Christ's death here in explicitly sacrificial terms (Thiselton, *First Epistle to the Corinthians*, 1191; cf. Fee, *First Epistle to the Corinthians*, 725–26).

[71] Fee, *First Epistle to the Corinthians*, 724–25; Thiselton, *First Epistle to the Corinthians*, 1190–91.

[72] Gaffin, *By Faith, Not by Sight*, 30.

[73] Ibid.

[74] Thiselton, *First Epistle to the Corinthians*, 1191; Gaffin, *By Faith, Not by Sight*, 31.

The Death of Christ

In addressing the problems and challenges that he does in 1–2 Corinthians, Paul frequently brings the cross to bear upon them.[75] The cross is on fullest display in 1 Corinthians 1:10–4:21. Here Paul challenges the priorities and values of the "world" or "this age" that are manifesting themselves in the divisions and factions in the Corinthian church. The "word of the cross," as Paul develops it in 1:18–2:5, stands in the sharpest antithesis to what Paul calls "the wisdom of the world" (1:20). It is through this word that "Spirit" and "power," that is, the powers of the age to come, were brought to bear on the lives of the Corinthian believers (2:4; cf. 2:5). In 1 Corinthians 5, Paul appeals to the sacrificial death of Christ as "Passover lamb" to ground the command "Cleanse out the old leaven that you may be a new lump, as you really are unleavened" (5:7). In 1 Corinthians 6, Paul exhorts the Corinthians to "flee from sexual immorality" (6:18) by reminding them, "You are not your own, for you were bought with a price. So glorify God in your body" (6:19c–20).

Similarly, Paul reminds the Corinthians that they were "bought with a price" (7:23). They are therefore, paradoxically, both enslaved and free (7:22), and ought not "become bondservants of men" (7:23). Paul's counsel to the Corinthians in negotiating the question of eating food offered to idols hinges on prioritizing the well-being of the "weak person," lest "the brother for whom Christ died" be "destroyed" (8:11). The Lord's Supper not only commemorates the death of Christ for sin (11:23–26), but also provides a clear alternative to the idolatrous feasting of pagan Corinth (10:14–22). Paul's closing malediction ("If anyone has no love for the Lord, let him be accursed," 16:22) assumes that Christ's death for believers was curse-bearing.

Christ's death is no less important to Paul's argument in 2 Corinthians. He appeals to Christ's death in conjunction with his explication and defense of his apostolic ministry (2 Corinthians 1–7). Broaching a theme that he will develop throughout the letter, Paul tells the Corinthians, "We share abundantly in Christ's sufferings" (2 Cor. 1:5; cf. 4:10, "always carrying in the body the death of Jesus").[76] Echoing his earlier statement that Christ's death (and resurrection) were "in accordance with the Scriptures" (1 Cor. 15:3), Paul declares that "all the promises of God find their Yes in [Christ]" (2 Cor. 1:20). In his defense of his apostolic ministry in 2 Corinthians 3:1–4:6, Paul denominates his work as not a ministry of "condemnation" but a ministry of "righteousness" (3:9). Given the pairing of the two terms "condemnation" and "righteousness," Paul must be thinking of "righteousness" forensically, that is, in terms of the imputed righteousness of Christ to the believer for justification. In other words, Paul defines his apostolic ministry in terms of the justifying death of Christ. In 2 Corinthians 5:11–6:2, Paul terms his ministry "the message of reconcili-

[75] In most of the texts that follow, I am indebted to Garland, *1 Corinthians*, 17.

[76] Scholars differ on precisely what connection Paul has in mind here between "Christ's sufferings" and the believer's own sufferings; see the seven positions outlined by Margaret Thrall, *A Critical and Exegetical Commentary on the Second Epistle to the Corinthians*, 2 vols., ICC (Edinburgh: T&T Clark, 1994), 1:107–10. Likely Paul is saying that "the solidarity between Christ and his followers applies also to his sufferings" (Garland, *2 Corinthians*, 66; cf. Barnett, *Second Epistle to the Corinthians*, 75, cited in Garland, *2 Corinthians*, 66).

ation" (5:19), by which he has in mind the reconciliation grounded in Christ's death on the cross (5:20–21).

Paul explicitly points to Christ's death to motivate the Corinthians' giving to the Jerusalem offering (2 Corinthians 8–9). He reminds the Corinthians, "You know the grace of our Lord Jesus Christ, that though he was rich, yet for your sake he became poor, so that you by his poverty might become rich" (8:9). In this way, the Corinthians' giving is an act of "submission that comes from [their] confession of the gospel of Christ" (9:13).

In defending his ministry against the criticisms of the "super-apostles," Paul once again defines his ministry in relation to the death of Christ (2 Corinthians 10–13). It is Paul's "weakness" that credentials him as a servant of Christ (11:23, 30; cf. 12:9–10). Why is weakness a matter of boasting for Paul? Why does he stake his whole apostleship upon this point? It is because Christ "was crucified in weakness, but lives by the power of God." Therefore, Paul reasons, "we also are weak in him, but in dealing with you we will live with him by the power of God" (13:4). Paul is saying that "his weakness is a direct consequence of his union with Christ in his weakness in crucifixion."[77] It is in that present context of weakness that Paul goes on to speak of the power of God at work in his own apostolic ministry.

The Resurrection of Christ

In bringing the death of Christ to bear on the matters facing him in the church of Corinth, Paul does not view the death of Christ in isolation from his resurrection. In fact, very often when Paul mentions Christ's death, explicit mention of Jesus's resurrection is not far behind (cf. 1 Cor. 2:1–5; 2 Cor. 3:9, 17–18; 4:10–11; 13:4). This raises the question of how Paul understands the resurrection of Christ. What saving significance does it have for the believer? How does it relate to the two-age understanding of history in which Paul locates the problems facing the church in Corinth? How does Paul appeal to the resurrection in the Corinthian correspondence to address these problems?

The foundational passage for Paul's understanding of the resurrection and, therefore, for the beginnings of an answer to these questions is 1 Corinthians 15:1–58. Paul develops at least two important points in 1 Corinthians 15. He first describes Jesus as the firstfruits of the resurrection harvest. Second, Paul compares and contrasts Christ with Adam in order to explain the meaning and significance of the resurrection. The first point comes in 1 Corinthians 15:20. In saying that Jesus "has been raised from the dead," Paul describes Christ as "the firstfruits of those who have fallen asleep." As Ridderbos notes, "Here the picture of the harvest is in the background."[78] The background to this image is the considerable number of laws in the Old Testament governing the ingathering of the firstfruits of the harvest.[79] The idea in 1 Corinthians

[77] Sinclair B. Ferguson, *The Holy Spirit* (Downers Grove, IL: InterVarsity Press, 1996), 171.
[78] Ridderbos, *Paul*, 56.
[79] See G. Delling, ἀπαρχή, *TDNT*, 1:485; G. M. Burge, "First Fruits, Down Payment," *DPL*, 300–301.

is at least twofold.[80] First, in his resurrection, Christ has begun the resurrection harvest of the age to come.[81] His resurrection "means the breakthrough of the new aeon in the real, redemptive-historical sense of the word."[82] Paul is thereby calling attention to the temporal priority of Christ's resurrection to believers' resurrection, as he goes on to explain in 15:23 ("But each in his own order: Christ the firstfruits, then at his coming those who belong to Christ").[83] The in-breaking of the age to come, therefore, has already begun but is not yet consummated.

This observation hardly exhausts the significance of Christ as "firstfruits" of the resurrection harvest of the age to come. There is a second and equally important point that Paul is making in reference to Christ as "firstfruits." The "firstfruits" bear an "organic connection and unity" with the remaining harvest, such that there is an "inseparability of the initial quantity with the whole."[84] Paul would have us understand Christ's resurrection and believers' resurrections on precisely these terms. "In the firstfruits, the whole harvest becomes visible. . . . In [Christ] the resurrection of the dead dawns, his resurrection represents the commencement of the new world of God."[85] For this reason, Richard B. Gaffin concludes, "Paul views the two resurrections not so much as two events but as two episodes of the same event," even as Paul makes a "temporal distinction" between them.[86]

Paul expands these observations in a second important point that he develops later in the argument of 1 Corinthians 15. In 15:42–49, he compares and contrasts Adam and Christ. As in Romans 5:12–21, they are both representative figures. Adam is "the first man Adam" (1 Cor. 15:45), "the first man" (15:47). Jesus is "the last Adam" (15:45), "the second man" (15:47). This framework helps us to understand Paul's comparing and contrasting the "dead body of the believer and his resurrection body" in 1 Corinthians 15:42–44a.[87] These two bodies correspond to the two ages overseen by the two representative men, Adam and Christ, and the "two different modes of existence pertaining to them."[88]

What is striking is that Adam is in view in Paul's argument not primarily as the one through whom sin entered the world, but as the one whom God created in uprightness and integrity.[89] This perspective is evident from the fact that Paul quotes Genesis 2:7 in 1 Corinthians 15:45 regarding Adam's (pre-fall) body: "Thus it is written, 'the first man Adam became a living being.'" The Adamic order, in our experience of it, is indelibly characterized by sin, corruption, and death. Paul looks in 1 Corinthians 15:44b–49, however, to the Adamic order prior to the fall, in its "original state."[90]

[80] Ridderbos, *Paul*, 56.
[81] "Paul regards the resurrection of Jesus the actual beginning of this general epochal event" (Geerhardus Vos, *The Pauline Eschatology* [1930; repr., Phillipsburg, NJ: P&R, 1994], 45).
[82] Ridderbos, *Paul*, 55.
[83] Delling, ἀπαρχή, 1:486.
[84] Richard B. Gaffin Jr., *Resurrection and Redemption: A Study in Paul's Soteriology*, 2nd ed. (Phillipsburg, NJ: P&R, 1987), 34.
[85] Ridderbos, *Paul*, 56.
[86] Gaffin, *Resurrection and Redemption*, 35.
[87] Ibid., 78.
[88] Ridderbos, *Paul*, 542.
[89] Vos, *Pauline Eschatology*, 167.
[90] Ridderbos, *Paul*, 542n152; cf. Vos, who notes that Paul "widens . . . the representation . . . out to a far more general, even cosmical, one" (*Pauline Eschatology*, 167).

What, then, characterizes or distinguishes the eschatological order inaugurated by Christ's resurrection from the pre-eschatological order inaugurated by the creation of Adam? In 1 Corinthians 15:45b, Paul affirms that whereas Adam "became a living being," the "last Adam became life-giving Spirit" (my trans.; ESV, "a life-giving spirit"). The two words translated "being" (ψυχή) and "Spirit" (πνεῦμα) in verse 45 are cognate with the adjectives translated "natural" (ψυχικόν) and "spiritual" (πνευματικόν) in verses 44 and 46. These two words in verse 45 therefore capture the difference between the two Adamic orders that Paul is contrasting in 15:42–49.

What does Paul mean when he says that Christ at his resurrection "became life-giving Spirit"? I have capitalized the noun "Spirit" in my translation because Paul is surely speaking here of the Holy Spirit.[91] The adjective "spiritual" (πνευματικόν) invariably refers, in Paul, to the Holy Spirit.[92] Since two uses of the adjective "spiritual" (πνευματικόν) bracket the cognate noun in verse 45 (πνεῦμα), we should understand that noun to refer to the third person of the Godhead, the Holy Spirit.

That conclusion raises yet another question: What does Paul mean when he says that Christ "became life-giving Spirit"? He cannot be confusing or mixing Christ and Spirit as two distinct persons, since elsewhere in his letters he takes care to make personal distinctions between the two (cf. Rom. 8:9–11). In other words, Paul is not erasing the distinction between the person of the Son and the person of the Spirit. He is, however, making an economical or functional identification of Christ and the Spirit (cf. 2 Cor. 3:17). This identification took place at the resurrection, when Christ was raised from the dead by the power of the Holy Spirit (cf. Rom. 8:11; Eph. 1:19–20). Gaffin explains the significance of what transpired at the resurrection.

> At his resurrection the personal mode of Jesus' existence as the last Adam was . . . decisively transformed by the Holy Spirit. The Spirit, who raised him up as the firstfruits, indwells him so completely and in such a fashion that in their functioning he *is* the Spirit who will be instrumental in the resurrection of the full harvest. . . . Only by virtue of the functional identity of the Spirit and Christ, effected redemptive-historically in his resurrection, is Christ the communicator of life.[93]

In light of what Paul has argued earlier in 1 Corinthians 15, and in light of what Paul goes on to say in 15:46–49, we may bring this discussion of 15:45b and of 15:42–49 to a close with three concluding considerations. First, Paul's concern in verse 45 is Christ as the second Adam, the representative of his people. By virtue of his resurrection, Christ has secured the Spirit and bestows him upon his people. At the very least, we may say that what happened to Christ's body at his resurrection will happen for believers' bodies at their resurrection (1 Cor. 15:49; cf. Phil. 3:21). But that hardly exhausts the significance of Paul's point. Although Paul's focus in this chapter is the future bodily resurrection of believers, Paul elsewhere argues, in Ephesians 2:5–6 and Colossians 3:1–4, that believers are presently raised with Christ.

[91] For the argument that follows, see Gaffin, *Resurrection and Redemption*, 86–87.
[92] See ibid.
[93] Ibid., 89.

Paul surely understands an "organic" connection among (1) the resurrection of Jesus from the dead, (2) the "initial soteric experience in the life of the believer," which Paul characterizes in explicit resurrection terms, and (3) "the future bodily resurrection of the believer."[94] The entirety of the believer's salvation, from its beginning to its completion, is as a tributary running from the fountain, the risen Christ.

Second, in 1 Corinthians 15, Paul is underscoring the aeonic significance of the resurrection of Christ.[95] Jesus's resurrection has inaugurated the age to come, an order whose counterpart is the order standing under Adam (15:46–48). What characterizes and even denominates this age to come is the activity of the Spirit of the risen and exalted Christ. As Paul argues in verse 50, the resources of this present age are categorically insufficient and inadequate to enable one to "inherit the kingdom of God" or to "inherit the imperishable." The necessary resources are found only in the second Adam, who at his resurrection became life-giving Spirit.[96]

Third, Paul has charted a sweeping representation of redemptive history. The age to come, defined by the second man and last Adam, stands in contrast with the present age, defined by the first man, Adam. That Christ is the "second man" indicates that there is no representative figure or age that stands between Adam and Christ. That Christ is the "last Adam" indicates that there is no representative figure or age that will follow Christ. The "contrast between Adam and Christ" here "is not only pointed but also comprehensive and exclusive."[97]

With this sketch in place, we are better positioned to see how Paul brings Christ's resurrection to bear on the problems he is addressing in Corinth. Critical to understanding Paul's pastoral application of the resurrection is his aforementioned conviction that, at his resurrection, Christ and the Spirit became economically or functionally one. A reference to the activity of the "Spirit," therefore, is necessarily a reference to the risen and exalted Christ. The power of the Spirit, for Paul, is the resurrection power of Christ at work in the life of the believer.

In the opening verses of 1 Corinthians, Paul reminds the church in Corinth of the various spiritual gifts that they have received (1:7; cf. 4:7; 12:1). The adjective "spiritual," as we have seen, refers to the Holy Spirit. Paul has in view the gifts that the Holy Spirit has supplied the church, gifts in which they are "not lacking" (1:7). Paul refers to two of these gifts ("speech," "knowledge"), indicating that these, like all such gifts, have been supplied to them by Christ (1:4–5). Although it is difficult to identify precisely what Paul has in mind by these gifts, they certainly anticipate the discussion that follows in 1:10–4:21.[98] The word "speech" (1:5) appears subsequently in Paul's phrases "the word of the cross" (1:18) and "lofty speech" (2:1).[99]

---

[94] Ibid., 60.
[95] Ibid., 89–90.
[96] In light of Paul's emphasis in this chapter on Adam in his prelapsarian condition, it is fair to conclude, with both Vos and Gaffin, that Paul is "correlat[ing] protology and eschatology," *not* soteriology and eschatology (Vos, *Pauline Eschatology*, 169n19; Gaffin, *Resurrection and Redemption*, 82n14). See especially the important qualifications and caveat raised in this connection by Gaffin.
[97] Gaffin, *Resurrection and Redemption*, 85.
[98] See the discussion in Fee, *First Epistle to the Corinthians*, 38–40.
[99] "Knowledge" appears later in the letter, both positively (1 Corinthians 12–14) and negatively (1 Corinthians 8) (Ciampa and Rosner, *First Letter to the Corinthians*, 64; Fee, *First Epistle to the Corinthians*, 40).

What is Paul doing here? To prepare to address the *fleshly* divisions and factions at work in Corinth, Paul reminds the Corinthians of the sufficiency of their *spiritual* gifting in Christ. Not only do these gifts stand antithetically against the worldly wisdom in play in Corinth, but they also provide the resources, through the gospel, to combat that wisdom (cf. 2:1–5).

In at least two additional critical places in the argument of 1 Corinthians 1:10–4:21, Paul calls the Corinthians' attention to the Spirit. In 2:10–15, he stresses that all apostolic teaching has been "revealed . . . through the Spirit" (2:10).[100] Thus, "we have received not the spirit of the world, but the Spirit who is from God, that we might understand the things freely given us by God" (2:12). The Spirit "is not only the principle of knowledge in God but also . . . the principle and means for communicating that knowledge."[101] Critical to Paul's argument here is the antithesis between "the Spirit who is from God" and "the spirit of the world" (2:12), the latter likely providing a metaphorical reference to this present evil age.[102] The Spirit, to whose person and work Paul links the age to come, provides a wisdom that not only belongs to the age to come but also stands opposed to the wisdom of this present evil age. This Spirit-wisdom of the age to come finds its center and focus in the gospel that Paul preached (1:17–18; 2:1–5). What's more, Paul argues in 2:14–16 to the effect that the "believer's . . . reception of the apostle's Spirit-taught words" is a "Spirit-worked" reception.[103] By contrast, "the natural person does not accept the things of the Spirit of God, for they are folly to him, and he is not able to understand them because they are spiritually discerned" (2:14). Paul is, therefore, pressing the Corinthians to see the sheer incompatibility between the Spirit-wisdom of the age to come, a wisdom they profess to have (cf. 2:5), and the worldly or fleshly divisions that have taken root in the Corinthian church. It is the Spirit of the risen Christ, Paul argues, who alone provides the Corinthians an exit from their self-inflicted fleshly crisis.

A second place in Paul's argument in 1 Corinthians 1:10–4:21 where he invokes the Spirit of the resurrected Christ is 1 Corinthians 3:16–17. There Paul reminds the Corinthians of something they should already know—that they are "God's temple," and "God's Spirit dwells in" them (3:16). They are therefore a "holy" people (cf. 1:2, "sanctified in Christ Jesus"). The Spirit of the risen Christ has uniquely taken up residence in their midst. Not only is Paul saying that the Spirit is the church's "key to unity," but Paul is also warning the Corinthians against the destructive, fleshly influences of "boastful arrogance, . . . eagerness to appraise others, and . . . competitive partnership," as Garland summarizes.[104]

In 1 Corinthians 5, Paul commands the church to remove the immoral offender from their midst (5:5, 13). They are to do so when they are assembled "in the name

---

[100] Following Gaffin, 2:10 and 2:12 refer to all believers, while 2:13 refers specifically to the apostles (Gaffin, "Some Epistemological Reflections," 26).
[101] Ibid., 25–26.
[102] Ibid., 26.
[103] Ibid., 27.
[104] Garland, *1 Corinthians*, 120–21.

of the Lord Jesus . . . with the power of our Lord Jesus" (5:4), that is, the resurrection power of Christ. In 1 Corinthians 6:11, Paul reminds the Corinthians that they were "washed . . . sanctified . . . justified in the name of the Lord Jesus Christ and by the Spirit of our God." Paul relates "regeneration, sanctification, and justification" to the "work of the Spirit," whom Paul understands as "the means whereby God in the new age effects the work of Christ in the believer's life."[105] It is this reality that grounds the moral exhortation of 1 Corinthians 6:1–8. In the immediately following argument (1 Cor. 6:12–20), it is the believer's union with the risen Christ (6:17) and the believer's body as a "temple of the Holy Spirit within you, whom you have from God" (6:19) that grounds Paul's argument to "flee from sexual immorality" (6:18). In 1 Corinthians 7:40, Paul concludes his counsel on marriage, divorce, engagement, and widowhood by reminding his readers, "I too have the Spirit of God." The apostle Paul speaks here words of Spirit-wisdom that belong to the age to come.

In the midst of his comments on the gifts of the Spirit (1 Corinthians 12–14), Paul reminds the Corinthians, "In one Spirit we were all baptized into one body—Jews or Greeks, slaves or free—and all were made to drink of one Spirit" (12:13). This reality explains how the church has become "one body" (12:12), that is, the "body of Christ" (cf. 12:27). To belong to the body of Christ is necessarily to share in the *one* Spirit.[106] Such is the economical identity between Christ and the Spirit that to possess one is to possess the other. It was this reality that Paul thought critical for the Corinthians to grasp if they were rightly to understand the nature and exercise of the gifts of the Spirit in their midst.

When Paul brings the resurrection to bear on his argument in 2 Corinthians, he does so in a striking way. His opponents have insisted that Paul is contemptible and weak in person (10:10). Paul inverts this criticism by stressing that his weakness, far from disqualifying him as an apostle, serves to credential him as an apostle (cf. 11:30; 12:5). It is insufficient to say, however, that Paul views "weakness" by itself as vindicating his apostleship. For Paul, his "weaknesses" are a matter of boasting in order that "the power of Christ may rest upon [him]" (12:9).

We have already seen how Paul understands his weaknesses in relation to his union and communion with the crucified Christ. Paul paradoxically understands weakness and power to characterize his apostolic ministry because he is in union and communion with the Christ who both has been crucified and is risen. In 2 Corinthians 13:4, Paul says of Christ that "he was crucified in weakness, but lives by the power of God." This pattern of Christ's ministry—his humiliation and his subsequent exaltation—provides a template for Paul's own ministry: "For we also are weak in him, but in dealing with you we will live with him by the power of God" (13:4). For Paul, weakness and power are *simultaneously* at work in his present ministry.[107] In the

[105] Fee, *First Epistle to the Corinthians*, 247.

[106] Richard B. Gaffin Jr., *Perspectives on Pentecost: New Testament Teaching on the Gifts of the Holy Spirit* (Phillipsburg, NJ: P&R, 1979), 29.

[107] Note Kruse's comments in relation to Paul's words in 2 Cor. 1:5: "While Paul and his co-workers *share abundantly in Christ's sufferings* because the old age still persists, they *share abundantly in comfort too* because the new messianic age has already begun" (*2 Corinthians*, 62, emphasis his).

context of his weakness in Christ, "the power of God" is manifest.[108] This power, of course, is the resurrection power of the risen Christ, which Paul experiences by the indwelling Spirit of Christ. United to Christ, we share in his weakness and thereby share in his resurrection power by the Holy Spirit.

It is on precisely this note that Paul begins 2 Corinthians. If, he says, "we share abundantly in Christ's sufferings," then "so through Christ we share abundantly in comfort too" (1:5). This comfort comes from "God," the "God of all comfort" (1:3–4), even as it comes "through Christ" (1:5). Paul likely has in mind the ministry of the Spirit in this connection, since "it is God who establishes us with you in Christ, and has anointed us, and who has also put his seal on us and given us his Spirit in our hearts as a guarantee" (1:21–22).[109] "Suffering" and "comfort" are likely reflective of Jesus's death and resurrection, respectively.[110] The comfort of which Paul speaks, then, is tied to Jesus's resurrection and is experienced by the working of the Spirit of the risen Christ. The affliction and comfort that Paul experiences is for the Corinthians' comfort (1:6–7; cf. 4:7–12).[111] This is so because believers, united with Jesus Christ, are in communion with one another.

The Relationship between the Old and New Covenants

We have witnessed the degree to which Paul's understanding of the two ages permeates his reflections in the Corinthian correspondence, as in all his letters. We have also seen how he argues in 1 Corinthians 15:42–49 that this present age was inaugurated at the creation, and that the age to come was inaugurated at the resurrection of Christ. And we have seen how Paul identifies so many of the Corinthians' problems with a failure to break with the patterns of this present evil age and to apprehend the new mind-set and life-patterns of the age to come. For Paul, the gospel of the crucified and risen Christ was critical to redressing this failure. He brings both the death and the resurrection of Christ to bear on the matters before him in Corinth. In both letters, Paul points the Corinthians to the resources that are found only in Christ, crucified and risen, and in the Spirit of Christ (1 Cor. 15:45; 2 Cor. 3:17) to live lives fitting those who are "called" and "bought with a price" (1 Cor. 1:2; 6:20).

Given Paul's keen eschatological awareness of the work of Christ in history (cf. 1 Cor. 15:3, "in accordance with the Scriptures"), we may pose a question that Paul does not formally raise but that nevertheless emerges from his writings: Where does the Old Testament belong in Paul's understanding of the history of redemption? Does Paul in fact restrict the operations of the grace of Christ and of the Spirit to the period of time beginning with the inauguration of the age to come? If he does not, then how does Paul articulate the differences between what he calls the "old covenant" and the "new covenant"? To put the question another way, what is it that

[108] Ferguson rightly notes that Paul is striking a different note here than in 2 Cor. 12:10 ("For when I am weak, then I am strong"). Paul's point in 2 Cor. 12:10 is that the weakness is his own. His point in 2 Cor. 13:4 is that the weakness is his-in-Christ (Ferguson, *Holy Spirit*, 171).

[109] Cf. Ibid., 172.

[110] Barnett, *Second Epistle to the Corinthians*, 75.

[111] Ibid., 78–79. For Paul's argument in 2 Cor. 4:7–12, see Ferguson, *Holy Spirit*, 171–72.

makes the new covenant "new"? To answer these questions, we will turn to what Paul has to say in 1 Corinthians 10:1–13 and 2 Corinthians 3:1–4:6.

1 Corinthians 10:1–13

First Corinthians 10:1–13 falls in a larger section (1 Corinthians 8–10) in which Paul addresses a host of issues relating to the Corinthians' life in and engagement with the culture around them. Paul is concerned that the Corinthians have failed to grasp the threat of paganism to their faith. Their posture, as he summarizes it, is represented in the slogan "all things are lawful" (10:23).

To address this problem, Paul goes to what at first glance seems an unlikely place—Israel in the wilderness between Egypt and Canaan. The fact that Paul can guide the Corinthians through the intricacies of the Pentateuchal wilderness narrative in 1 Corinthians 10 testifies to his readers' competence as students of the Old Testament.[112] This competence surely owes to the fact that Paul's gospel proclaimed Christ as the fulfillment of Old Testament expectation (cf. 15:3). Even though the Corinthians had formerly been Gentiles ("you know that when you were pagans . . . ," 12:2), Paul from the beginning immersed them in the Old Testament.

One reason why the Old Testament is so important to Paul's preaching and teaching becomes evident in these verses. Paul tells the Corinthians that the Israelites of the wilderness generation were "our fathers" (10:1). He clearly does not have in mind biological descent, since he is able elsewhere to characterize the congregation as Gentile (cf. 12:2). This paternity is a spiritual paternity, along the lines of the way Paul elsewhere calls all true believers the sons of Abraham (Galatians 3; Romans 4).[113] That Paul is thinking along these lines is evident from how he addresses the Corinthians as "brothers" (1 Cor. 10:1). This familial term is not a biological one but a spiritual one. They call God "father," and one another "brothers," by virtue of their adoption in Jesus Christ and by the Holy Spirit.[114]

Paul does more, however, than establish a spiritually lineal descent. The experiences of the wilderness generation that Paul relays in 1 Corinthians 10:1–5 "took place as examples for us, that we might not desire evil as they did" (10:6). The meaning of the Greek word translated "examples" (τύποι) is debated among commentators, but "examples" is an appropriate translation. Thiselton has rendered this word even more precisely as "formative model."[115] It is important to remember, however, that the wilderness generation served as formative models for the Corinthians precisely by virtue of the relationship Paul has articulated in verse 1 ("our fathers").

Paul makes a similar point in verse 11: "Now these things happened to them as an example, but they were written down for our instruction, on whom the end of

[112] Navigating the complexities of which particular portions of the Pentateuch Paul is engaging at any given point in his argument is beyond the scope of my present work. See the helpful discussion at Ciampa and Rosner, *First Letter to the Corinthians*, 455–64.
[113] Garland, *1 Corinthians*, 448.
[114] Ciampa and Rosner, *First Letter to the Corinthians*, 446. That Paul is thereby thinking of the Israelites as the Corinthian believers' "adopted 'fathers,'" as Ciampa and Rosner go on to say, may press the point too much.
[115] Thiselton, *First Epistle to the Corinthians*, 730–33.

the ages has come."[116] The Greek word translated "as an example" is cognate with the word translated "example" in verse 6.[117] What befell the wilderness generation (10:7–10) provides a formative example for the church. This was why these events were "written down for our instruction."[118] God committed these matters to writing precisely for the benefit of the new covenant church ("on whom the end of the ages has come").[119] The fact that the Corinthians are God's new covenant people does not mean that either the Old Testament Scriptures or the experiences of their spiritual fathers are of no concern to them. On the contrary, it is precisely as they are the people who live at the dawn of the age to come that the Old Testament and the experiences of the pre-eschatological people of God concern them.

This relationship is not a purely theoretical one for Paul. In verses 7–10, it assumes concrete form as he draws connections between the failings of the Israelites in the wilderness and the temptations that lie before the Corinthians in the first century. In these verses, Paul delivers four grammatically parallel imperatives: "do not be idolaters" (10:7); "we must not indulge in sexual immorality" (10:8); "we must not put Christ to the test" (10:9); "nor grumble" (10:10).[120] Each of these four imperatives is followed by a negative reference to the wilderness generation.[121] Paul does not fault the whole number of the Israelites with the sins in view; "some of them" sinned and suffered the divine consequences of their actions. The consequences are dire: "twenty-three thousand fell in a single day" (10:8); some "were destroyed by serpents" (10:9); they "were destroyed by the Destroyer" (10:10). Although the forms of death and destruction vary, each is appointed by the God whom the Corinthians worship and serve (cf. 8:4–6).

What of the sins themselves? Paul summarizes them in 10:6 as "desir[ing] evil." Each of the behaviors that follow in verses 7–10 are expressions of this more basic sin. As Ciampa and Rosner have aptly summarized the matter,

> The "evil things" which the Israelites craved and which led them to test the Lord and grumble when their cravings were not satisfied tended to be based on a willingness to gratify appetites (either sex or food) in ways prohibited by the Lord or an insubordinate attitude toward the Lord arising from his failure to gratify those appetites as they wanted.[122]

The idolatry of verse 7 has the clearest connection with Paul's argument in these chapters (cf. 10:14, "Therefore, my beloved, flee from idolatry"). Sexual immorality

---

[116] So Fee, *First Epistle to the Corinthians*, 458.
[117] In 10:6, the Greek noun is τύπος; in 10:11, the Greek adverb is τυπικῶς.
[118] The Greek construction suggests divine purpose or intent (Fee, *First Epistle to the Corinthians*, 458n43).
[119] Commentators dispute the meaning of the phrase translated "the end of the ages" (τὰ τέλη τῶν αἰώνων). Part of the difficulty is that the word translated "end" (ESV) is a plural in the Greek ("the ends"), bringing more than one "age" into view. Paul, however, does not view the present evil age to have been brought to an absolute end, and he certainly does not view the age to come as presently consummate (cf. 1 Cor. 15:24). Paul may mean, then, that the Corinthians (like all new covenant Christians) inhabit the overlap of the ages—the era when the age to come has been inaugurated but the present age has not yet come to a complete end.
[120] The ESV obscures the parallelism. In the Greek, Paul joins the particle μηδὲ either with the present active imperative (10:7, 10) or with the hortative subjunctive (10:8–9).
[121] Again, Paul crafts a deliberate grammatical parallelism. Each reference is introduced by the particle καθώς (except 10:10, καθάπερ). The phrase "some of them" follows (τινες αὐτῶν). Paul then repeats the verb of the initial imperatival construction (except for 10:7, where it is implied, and 10:9b, where Paul uses the uncompounded form of the verb used in 10:9a).
[122] Ciampa and Rosner, *First Letter to the Corinthians*, 454–55.

(10:8) may have in view a "metaphorical harlotry."[123] But Paul may also "suggest that [the Corinthians'] feasting in the idol temples also at times involved sexual play."[124] As the mention of "serpents" indicates, the "testing" that Paul has in view in verse 9 is that of Numbers 21. The "testing" entailed Israel's "complain[ing] about a lack of *food and water* (ironically mentioning that they detested the food they had)."[125] The "grumbl[ing]" of 1 Corinthians 10:10 does not appear, in Paul's mind, to be directly related to food or idolatry. Mention of this Israelite sin and its consequences may be Paul's way of warning the Corinthians against resisting his divinely appointed apostolic authority.[126]

For all these correspondences, Paul is not oblivious to the historical distance between the Israelites and the Corinthians. For all the moral thrust of his argument, Paul is not engaging in timeless moralizing. Nor is he unaware of the fact that the Corinthians stand at a place in redemptive-history that the Israelites did not; the Corinthians are a people "on whom the end of the ages has come" (10:11).

In light of these matters, what are we to make of a curious statement within the imperatival section (10:7–10)? Paul exhorts the Corinthians not to "put Christ to the test, as some of them did and were destroyed by serpents" (10:9). Some manuscripts read "the Lord" instead of "Christ," but "Christ" is almost certainly the original reading.[127] The one whom the Israelites put to the test, Paul claims, was none other than Christ.

This raises the question of how the Israelites could have put Christ to the test. Paul provides the resources to answer that question in 1 Corinthians 10:1–5. His focus in verses 7–10 has been on what "some" of the Israelites did. In verses 1–5, his emphasis is on the whole people: "our fathers were all under the cloud" (10:1); "all were baptized into Moses in the cloud and in the sea" (10:2); "all ate the same spiritual food" (10:3); "all drank the same spiritual drink" (10:4). Paul is enumerating blessings and privileges that were the possession of the Israelite covenant community as a whole. To possess these privileges did not safeguard one against the kinds of destruction that Paul subsequently enumerates (10:8–10). That was true for Israel, Paul argues, and it remains true for Corinth.

Even so, these blessings were not inconsequential. Their importance explains why Paul takes the time to enumerate them. In verses 1–2, Paul describes the Israelites' blessings under the banner of baptism: "All were baptized into Moses in the cloud and in the sea" (10:2). Paul is undoubtedly thinking of Moses's leading the nation of Israel through the parted waters of the Red Sea, followed by the "pillar of cloud" (Ex. 14:19–22). Paul describes this experience in terms of the nation having been "baptized into Moses." The phrase translated "baptized into" appears only in a couple of other places in Paul (Rom. 6:3, "baptized into his death"; Gal. 3:27, "baptized into Christ"). In each case, the phrase denotes an identification with the

[123] Garland, *1 Corinthians*, 461.
[124] Fee, *First Epistle to the Corinthians*, 455.
[125] Ciampa and Rosner, *First Letter to the Corinthians*, 462.
[126] Fee, *First Epistle to the Corinthians*, 458.
[127] Ibid., 457. See Fee's discussion of the textual evidence at 457n34.

one into whom the individual or individuals are said to be baptized. Here, "cloud" and "sea" stand for "the redemptive event by which Israel escaped the tyranny of Pharaoh and the life of slavery in Egypt."[128] Israel's redemption is tied to Moses; she had "received Moses as leader and head and was contained in Moses," that is, was "incorporate[d]" into Moses.[129] Paul is not thinking here of a baptismal ceremony that God had instituted for Israel.[130] He employs baptismal language to express, on the one hand, the relationship between Moses and Israel as that of mediator and redeemed and, on the other hand, the corporate benefits that Israel experienced in connection with that relationship.[131]

In 1 Corinthians 10:3–4, Paul turns from the Exodus proper to the wilderness sojourning. Here he enumerates Israel's blessings in terms of "food" and "drink." This food and drink were "spiritual," Paul says, and "all" partook the "same" "spiritual food" and "spiritual drink." To define the adjective "spiritual" as simply "supernatural" is not so much inaccurate as imprecise.[132] The adjective denotes, we have seen, the person and activity of the Holy Spirit. The food and drink that Israel enjoyed in the wilderness, Paul is saying, was not only divinely supplied, but the particular provision of God the Spirit.

Paul specifies the source of this Spirit-provided "drink" in verse 4b: "They drank from the spiritual Rock that followed them, and the Rock was Christ." Understandably, much attention has been devoted to Paul's statement that this "spiritual Rock" "followed" Israel in the wilderness.[133] What should not be overlooked is Paul's identification of this "Rock" with "Christ." As Charles Hodge has rightly noted, "The expression is simply figurative. . . . [Christ] was the source of all the support which the Israelites enjoyed during their journey in the wilderness."[134] Paul is, therefore, identifying Christ with the God who delivered and sustained Israel in the wilderness.[135]

Paul, then, understands the God who delivered Israel from bondage in Egypt in clearly Trinitarian terms. That is to say, the one God who rescued Israel is triune, or hypostatically three. What is furthermore striking is the precise way in which Paul relates Christ and the Spirit in his telling of the wilderness narrative. The "Rock was Christ" (10:4), but the Rock is also said to be "spiritual," that is, of or pertaining to the Holy Spirit. Paul therefore conjoins the activity of the pre-incarnate Christ and the Spirit with respect to the provision of Israel in the wilderness. Paul, we have

[128] Ridderbos, *Paul*, 405.

[129] Ibid.

[130] Interpretations that understand Paul to be speaking with reference to the Corinthians' mistaken understandings of sacramental efficacy are, while adopted by many scholars, foreign to Paul's concern here, as Garland rightly observes (*1 Corinthians*, 453–54).

[131] In this sense, Paul is speaking with an eye to the sacrament of Christian baptism. Christian baptism signifies and seals to the believer the reality of which Paul is speaking here—union with or incorporation into a mediatorial Head.

[132] See Garland, *1 Corinthians*, 454.

[133] Some have argued that Paul is interpreting Exodus through the mediation of intertestamental Jewish tradition (Peter Enns, "The 'Moveable Well,' in 1 Cor. 10:4: An Extrabiblical Tradition in an Apostolic Text," *BBR* 6 [1996]: 23–38). There is no clear and compelling evidence that Paul is aware of, much less indebted to, such a tradition. Paul is only speaking metaphorically of the fact that God never failed to provide water to his people during their sojourning. See further G. K. Beale, *The Erosion of Inerrancy in Evangelicalism: Responding to New Challenges to Biblical Authority* (Wheaton, IL: Crossway, 2008), 97–101, 118–20.

[134] Hodge, *First Epistle to the Corinthians*, 175.

[135] Ibid. See further Ciampa and Rosner, *First Letter to the Corinthians*, 451; Garland, *1 Corinthians*, 457–58; Fee, *First Epistle to the Corinthians*, 448–49.

seen, argues that a relationship was established between Christ and the Spirit at his resurrection (15:42–49) such that Paul can say that Christ "became life-giving Spirit" (15:45, my trans.). What Paul is indicating in 1 Corinthians 10 is a foreshadowing of this economic identification that took place at Christ's resurrection.[136]

What, then, is Paul saying about the work of redemption in the period before the death and resurrection of Christ? We may answer this question by drawing several conclusions about Paul's statements in 1 Corinthians 10:1–13. First, Paul understands Israel and the church to be a single people. To state the matter using Paul's own terminology, Israel and the church are members of the same family ("brothers," "our fathers," 10:1). What distinguishes the Corinthian church from the ancient Israelites is not ultimately ethnicity but its place or standing in redemptive history. Believers in Corinth are those "on whom the end of the ages has come" (10:11). Second, Paul understands the God of Abraham, Isaac, and Jacob to be one and the same with the God and Father of our Lord Jesus Christ. From the vantage point of new covenant revelation, Paul highlights the workings of the triune God during the exodus and wilderness periods (10:1–4, 9).

Third, Paul underscores the privileges that belonged to each Israelite by virtue of Israel's redemption from Egypt. They include a baptism (10:2) and divinely provided food and drink (10:3–4). While it may be too much to term these "sacraments," they nevertheless are analogous to the spiritual signs that the Corinthian believers themselves enjoy—baptism (1:14–15; cf. 12:13) and the Lord's Supper (10:14–22). These are privileges common to all professing believers.[137] Fourth, with these spiritual privileges come spiritual responsibilities. As in Israel of old, so in Corinth of Paul's day (10:11)—God's people are not to "desire evil" (10:6) with all the manifestations such a desire may assume (10:7–10; cf. 10:14–22). Paul does not shirk from apprising the Corinthians of the spiritual dangers that attend their wilderness sojourn: "Nevertheless, with most of them God was not pleased, for they were overthrown in the wilderness" (10:5). Such attendant dangers call for humility and ongoing self-examination (10:12), as well as dependence on the God who will not let one of his elect fall into apostasy (10:13).

Paul's concern in this passage, then, is to accent the continuity between the privileges that Israel and believers enjoy, and the continuity between the dangers that face both Israel and believers. Paul's deliberately chosen language indicates that even the common benefits that Israel enjoyed were bestowed by Christ, through the Holy Spirit. The very way in which the pre-incarnate Christ grants these benefits to Israel is patterned after the way in which the resurrected Christ grants redemptive benefits to his people now—by the Holy Spirit (cf. 1 Cor. 15:42–49). This pattern suggests two related conclusions. First, the benefits that Israel received from the triune God were bestowed by virtue of Christ's coming death and resurrection. Second, these

[136] I owe this observation to Richard B. Gaffin Jr., who has termed what Paul describes in 1 Cor. 10:4 a "sync" between the pre-incarnate Christ and the Holy Spirit.

[137] These common benefits must be distinguished from the saving benefits that Christ provides his people. While common benefits are the possession of every professing believer (even nonelect persons), saving benefits belong to the elect and to the elect only. Unlike common benefits, saving benefits may not be lost or forfeited.

benefits, received by believers prior to the death and resurrection of Christ, were received, as it were, "out of time."[138]

2 Corinthians 3:1–4:6

It is these two latter points that Paul develops at some length in 2 Corinthians 3:1–4:6.[139] In this portion of the letter, in which he anticipates some of what will follow in 2 Corinthians 10–13, Paul defends his ministry to the Corinthians.[140] The course of the argument is set by his statement in 2:17, "For we are not, like so many, peddlers of God's word, but as men of sincerity, as commissioned by God, in the sight of God we speak in Christ." Garland has noted four specific claims in this verse that Paul will develop in the following chapter.[141] First, Paul defends his "sincerity" against those who were accusing him of deceitfulness. Second, Paul insists that he is "commissioned by God." Third, Paul labors "in the sight of God," that is, as one who "know[s] that he will be judged by God."[142] Fourth, Paul "speak[s] in Christ," which is "synonymous with being taught by the Spirit."[143]

Second Corinthians 3:1–4:6 is a running contrast between Paul's new covenant ministry and the old covenant ministry of Moses. Why Paul has chosen to provide this here in his letter is a matter of dispute. Some see Paul already addressing the Judaizing "super-apostles," whom he will critique more directly in 2 Corinthians 10–13.[144] Others see Paul responding to a different set of opponents' criticisms of his ministry.[145] Still others see Paul responding only to the Corinthians directly and not to any opponents' criticisms.[146] In any case, Paul defends his apostolic ministry by distinguishing it from that of Moses. What becomes clear from this defense is that the contrast between his ministry and that of Moses reflects fundamental differences between the new covenant and the old.

So what are those differences? Paul outlines at least four in this section. First, he associates the "new covenant" with the "Spirit," and the old covenant with the "letter" (2 Cor. 3:6). Explaining the distinction, the apostle claims that "the letter kills, but the Spirit gives life" (3:6). What precisely does Paul have in view in denominating the difference between these two covenants along the lines of letter and Spirit?[147] Paul's statement has been the subject of reflection among Christian theologians since

[138] Compare the similar reasoning of Paul in Rom. 3:25: old covenant believers genuinely experienced the forgiveness of sins (cf. 4:7), and that benefit was granted to them on the sole basis of the decreed but, as yet, historically unachieved death of Christ.

[139] As commentators recognize, 2 Cor. 3:1–4:6 is a substantial portion of a much larger section in the letter (2:14–7:4) in which Paul defines and defends his apostolic ministry. Murray Harris notes that in 2 Cor. 2:14–7:4, Paul "lays bare successively [his ministry's] grandeur and superiority (2:14–4:6), its suffering and glory (4:7–5:10), and its essence and exercise (5:11–6:10) [followed by] exhortation and ethical injunction (6:11–7:4)," whereupon Paul resumes his "travel narrative" in 7:5–16, picking up where 2:13 left off (Harris, *Second Epistle to the Corinthians*, 240–41).

[140] Kruse, *2 Corinthians*, 87–88. This is not to say, of course, that the opponents in view in this portion of the letter are necessarily those to whom Paul responds later in the letter. See further the discussion in Barnett, *Second Epistle to the Corinthians*, 141–42.

[141] Garland, *2 Corinthians*, 153–54.

[142] Ibid., 154.

[143] Ibid.

[144] Kruse, *2 Corinthians*, 93.

[145] Barnett, *Second Epistle to the Corinthians*, 142–44.

[146] Garland, *2 Corinthians*, 167–68.

[147] The following discussion is indebted to Garland, *2 Corinthians*, 163–67.

at least the time of Origen.[148] Many in the history of interpretation have divined from these words a cardinal hermeneutical principle. Origen saw in them Paul's preference for what was said to be the "spiritual, internal sense of Scripture" over "the literal, external sense of Scripture."[149] Paul's interests, however, surely lie elsewhere. He is helping us to see how the Mosaic and the new covenants differ.

Others have understood the letter-Spirit disjunction to express Paul's critique of legalism, that is, the corruption or perversion of the Mosaic covenant into a system by which one tries to merit righteousness and acceptance with God by keeping the Mosaic law.[150] To be sure, Paul critiques legalism throughout his letters and even characterizes his own former life in Judaism precisely along those lines (see Phil. 3:1–11). It is doubtful that this is Paul's concern here in 2 Corinthians 3:1–4:6, however. His concern, after all, is the law, not the corruption of the law.[151]

When we consider what Paul contrasts with "letter," we are in a better position to understand what Paul means by that term. Paul sets "letter" against "Spirit," surely a reference to the Holy Spirit.[152] It is the Spirit whom Paul identifies with the risen Lord (2 Cor. 3:17), and to whose operations Paul ascribes the transformation of the believer after the image of Christ "from one degree of glory to another" (3:18). Paul's interest in the Spirit, then, is as he brings transformation and the life of the age to come to sinners. By way of contrast, the Mosaic covenant has no such inherent or intrinsic power. It has no power to enable a person to keep its requirements. Paul's criticism of the Mosaic covenant is not that it is an "external code" or "what is merely written" *simpliciter.*[153] It is that, as such, it has no ability to transform or change a person so that the person might meet the law's demands.

It is important, at this juncture, to be clear what Paul is not saying. He is not saying that the Spirit was inoperative under the old covenant. Paul has, after all, argued the contrary in 1 Corinthians 10:1–13. Nor is he saying that the written Word or the law of God has no claim on the believer under the new covenant. Paul points believers to the Old Testament Scripture as continuing to regulate our belief and practice (2 Tim. 3:16–17). What Paul is saying, rather, is that the law, "as a piece of writing and consisting in letters of stone . . . cannot touch the heart."[154] The Spirit, on the other hand, "is mighty to give what he demands, because he is capable of writing on the heart."[155] The law has no "principle of life."[156] In every age of redemptive history, life has come only from Christ by the Spirit.[157]

The second point that Paul makes in distinguishing these two covenants follows

[148] See Hughes, *Second Epistle to the Corinthians*, 96–102; Richard B. Hays, *Echoes of Scripture in the Letters of Paul* (New Haven, CT: Yale University Press, 1989), 123–25.
[149] Garland, *2 Corinthians*, 163–64.
[150] So Kruse, *2 Corinthians*, 92; cf. C. K. Barrett, *The Second Epistle to the Corinthians*, HNTC (New York: Harper & Row, 1973), 113, cited in Garland, *2 Corinthians*, 164.
[151] Hays, *Echoes of Scripture*, 131.
[152] *Pace* Hughes, *Second Epistle to the Corinthians*, 101. Hughes sees "spirit" as "what is internal."
[153] *Pace* Garland, *2 Corinthians*, 165.
[154] Ridderbos, *Paul*, 219.
[155] Ibid.
[156] Ibid., 217.
[157] Were a person bereft of the Spirit's work, as Paul describes it here, the new covenant would be to that person precisely what Paul describes as the old covenant here in 2 Cor. 3:1–4:6. Paul, in other words, is not advocating a form of redemptive-historical universalism!

on the heels of the first point. Given the letter-Spirit distinction, Paul goes on to say that "the letter kills, but the Spirit gives life" (2 Cor. 3:6). Paul develops this difference in the verses that follow. The law is a "ministry of death" (3:7), a "ministry of condemnation" (3:9). Paul's ministry under the new covenant, however, is "a ministry of righteousness" (3:9). How is it that the law is a ministry of death and of condemnation? To sinners who are "in the flesh," that is, under the dominion of and in bondage to sin, the law serves to arouse "our sinful passions . . . at work in our members to bear fruit for death" (Rom. 7:5).[158] This is not the law's fault (Rom. 7:14). It is entirely the sinner's fault. The law serves only to accentuate the sinner's plight. It has no resources to deliver him from that plight (cf. Gal. 3:21). In the hands of the flesh, the law is an instrument by which the sinner only sins more. In that respect, Paul highlights the law as a "ministry of condemnation" (2 Cor. 3:9). The law "can only condemn those who fail to meet its demands."[159] It pronounces a curse on those who fail to meet its perfect requirements and who transgress its demands (cf. Gal. 3:10–13).[160] Paul's new covenant ministry, however, is a ministry of "righteousness" (2 Cor. 3:9). It proclaims that, in Christ, one may be declared righteous in the courtroom of God. As Paul will go on to explain, the sinner is accepted and accounted righteous solely because of the imputed righteousness of Christ, received through faith alone (2 Cor. 5:21). And this too is the work of the Spirit (cf. Rom. 8:2, "For the law of the Spirit of life has set you free in Christ Jesus from the law of sin and death").[161]

Once again, it is important to remember that Paul is not saying that this righteousness was unavailable to persons who lived under the old covenant. He strenuously argues the contrary in Romans 4. Paul's point is that at no point in redemptive history has this righteousness ever been secured by sinners' efforts to keep God's commands. It is the provision of Christ by the Spirit. It is, therefore, and in this respect, a new-creation reality (2 Cor. 5:17). Even under the new covenant, however, those who refuse the gospel in unbelief experience Christ as "a fragrance from death to death" (2:16) and perish in their sins (2:15).[162]

The third difference between these two covenants and, correspondingly, the two ministries of Moses and Paul concerns their "glory." Paul does not say what one might have expected him to say—that the old covenant lacked glory and the new covenant alone has glory. On the contrary, Paul insists that Moses's ministry was attended "with such glory that the Israelites could not gaze at Moses' face because of its glory, which was being brought to an end" (2 Cor. 3:7). Paul reasons, then, "Will not the ministry of the Spirit have even more glory?" (3:8; cf. 3:9). In fact, in light of the "surpass[ing]" glory of the new covenant, "what once had glory has come to have no glory at all" (3:10). In the light of the new covenant, the old covenant "ceased to be glorious . . .

[158] Note that Rom. 7:6 ("we serve in the new way of the Spirit and not in the old way of the written code") is formally parallel to 2 Cor. 3:6. Since Rom. 7:6 concludes Rom. 7:1–6, these six verses may fairly be taken as Paul's own gloss on his earlier statement in 2 Cor. 3:6.

[159] Kruse, *2 Corinthians*, 95.

[160] Harris, *Second Epistle to the Corinthians*, 287.

[161] Garland, *2 Corinthians*, 177.

[162] Ibid. In this respect, Paul can conceive of his own ministry, bereft of the Spirit's saving operations, as a ministry of death.

as the moon loses its brightness in the presence of the sun."[163] If we inquire what accounts for this difference in glory, one answer Paul gives is that the old administration was transitory ("being brought to an end," 3:7), whereas the new administration is "permanent" (3:11). By design, the old covenant was temporary and intended to yield to the coming new covenant (cf. Rom. 10:4). The new covenant, however, is the final installment in God's plan and yields to no successive administration.[164] That Paul uses the same word ("glory") of both covenants suggests not only a progressive but also an organic relationship between them. Each covenant, "coming *from God*, was necessarily glorious."[165] Each played a distinct role in God's unfolding plan of redemption, but, in that particular role, each displayed the glory of God.

The fourth distinction that Paul draws between these two covenants is found in 2 Corinthians 3:12–18. The former administration, he argues, was veiled and relatively obscure (3:13). The new covenant, however, is unveiled and clear (3:16, 18). To illustrate and to explain the difference, Paul references the account of Moses's veiling his face before the people of Israel (Exodus 34). "The text in Exodus does not reveal explicitly why Moses donned the veil, and what follows in [2 Corinthians] 3:13b–14 is Paul's explanation for the action."[166] The details of Paul's explanation are difficult, but he seems to be making two basic points.[167] First, the old covenant, by comparison with the new covenant, is objectively "veiled." Moses veiled to the Israelites "the outcome of what was being brought to an end" (3:13). That is to say, the transitory and impermanent nature of the Mosaic covenant was veiled to Israel.[168] Second, notwithstanding the foregoing ("but," 3:14), Israel suffered a subjective problem or failing. Their "minds were hardened" (3:14). In 3:15–16, Paul extends the image of the "veil" (3:13) to include the hardness of which he speaks in 3:14.[169] He does so, in part, to say that the Mosaic covenant cannot alleviate or remedy that state of inner hardness. Rather, "only through Christ is it [i.e., the veil] taken away" (3:14); "when one turns to the Lord, the veil is removed" (3:16). When a person is renewed by the Spirit and, by the faith supplied by the Spirit, receives and rests upon the Christ whom he hears preached in the Word, this veil is gone. It is Christ, who is the Spirit (3:17), who removes the veil, who brings "freedom" (3:17) and enables one with "unveiled face" to behold "the glory of the Lord" (3:18). In the succeeding verses (4:1–6), Paul explains in practical terms what his unveiled new covenant ministry of openness, boldness, and glory looks like.[170]

Once again, it is important to note an important qualification that Paul adds in his argument. The subjective "veil" of which Paul speaks in 2 Corinthians 3:12–18

[163] Hodge, *Second Epistle to the Corinthians*, 62. This illustration dates back at least as far as Theodoret.
[164] Kruse, *2 Corinthians*, 96.
[165] Hughes, *Second Epistle to the Corinthians*, 103.
[166] Garland, *2 Corinthians*, 183.
[167] For the details of Paul's argument, see especially Scott Hafemann, *Paul, Moses, and the History of Israel: The Letter/Spirit Contrast and the Argument from Scripture in 2 Corinthians*, WUNT 81 (Tübingen: Mohr Siebeck, 1995).
[168] Kruse, *2 Corinthians*, 97, esp. note 2; cf. Hodge, *Second Epistle to the Corinthians*, 66–67.
[169] Paul "finds in the veil a way of describing Israel's hardness" (Kruse, *2 Corinthians*, 97). As Garland properly observes, the "veil" does not simply denote a failure of the intellect to grasp the transitory character of the old covenant. It also denotes a moral failure, the hardness of willful unbelief (*2 Corinthians*, 191).
[170] On the numerous verbal and thematic connections between 3:1–18 and 4:1–6, see the helpful summary at Garland, *2 Corinthians*, 203.

is not a reality that the historical dawning of the new covenant has now brought to an end. In fact, Paul notes that, to some, "our gospel is veiled" (2 Cor. 4:3). "Those who are perishing" cannot see "the light of the gospel of the glory of Christ, who is the image of God" because "the god of this world has blinded the minds of the unbelievers" (4:3–4). Nothing short of a new creation work of the Spirit can lift this veil and restore the capacity to see the glory of God aright (cf. 4:6).

Paul's argument in 2 Corinthians 3:1–4:6, then, complements and reinforces his argument in 1 Corinthians 10:1–13. In the latter passage, Paul argues that Christ, by the Spirit, was at work in the lives of God's people under the old covenant. In 2 Corinthians 3:1–4:6, Paul underscores this argument by stressing that the old covenant ("letter") had no power to convey what it required. Only the Spirit can bring "life" and "righteousness" (3:6, 9). We have also observed the nuances of Paul's argument in 2 Corinthians 3:1–4:6. The apostle in no way denies that old covenant believers had access to life and righteousness, and in no way affirms that every person living after the resurrection of Christ possesses Christ and the Spirit. That nuance, however, raises the question of why Paul so weds the Spirit and the new covenant, on the one hand, and "death," "condemnation," and the old covenant, on the other (3:7, 9). The answer is likely found in 3:17. What marked the termination of the old covenant and the inauguration of the new covenant was the resurrection of Christ. In light of the resurrection, Paul may now say that "the Lord is the Spirit" (3:17a), because "the last Adam became life-giving Spirit" (1 Cor. 15:45a, my trans.). The new covenant, then, historically coincides with the ministry of the Spirit of the risen Christ. Paul's delineation of the old and new covenants in 2 Corinthians 3:1–4:6 is not, in the first instance, an experiential or existential one. It is an eschatological or a redemptive-historical one.[171]

Chronological Overview of Paul's Corinthian Letters

I have spent some time demonstrating the way in which Paul labors to help the Corinthians understand the structure and progress of the history of redemption. He does so along the lines of the "two ages" (this present age and the age to come), which Paul will sometimes denominate "flesh" and "Spirit." For Paul, the death and resurrection of Christ marked the historical inauguration of the age to come, its in-breaking into human history. This basic structure shapes the argument of the Corinthian correspondence in two profound ways. First, Paul traces the problems within the church at Corinth to the abiding sinful influences of this present evil age in the lives of believers. Second, to resolve these problems, Paul directs the church to the resources of the age to come, namely, Christ crucified and raised from the dead, and the Spirit of Christ.

1 Corinthians 1:1–9

Following ancient epistolary convention, Paul begins 1 Corinthians by identifying himself (1:1) and his audience (1:2), and by extending a word of blessing to them

[171] Ridderbos, *Paul*, 218.

(1:3). Also in keeping with literary convention, Paul follows his opening salutation with a thanksgiving section (1:4–9). Since each of these four opening components is fuller and lengthier than custom required, it is reasonable to conclude that Paul is "signal[ing] in his opening words an important theme or themes which will be developed throughout the letter."[172] First, he identifies himself as "called by the will of God to be an apostle of Christ Jesus" (1:1). Although Paul identifies himself as an apostle in most of his thirteen letters, this occasion is particularly significant. The divisions and factions within the church indicate to Paul a profound misapprehension of the nature of his apostolic office (cf. 1:12, "each one of you says, 'I follow Paul,' or 'I follow Apollos,' or 'I follow Cephas,' or 'I follow Christ'"). Paul reminds them that he is *Christ's* apostle and has been "called by the will of God" to that office, matters to which Paul will return in the first main section of the epistle (1:10–4:21).

Second, Paul identifies the Corinthians as "the church of God that is in Corinth, sanctified in Christ Jesus, called to be saints together with all those who in every place call upon the name of our Lord Jesus Christ, both their Lord and ours" (1:2). This description of the Corinthians signals two points that will surface often in the letter. The first is that the Corinthians are "sanctified in Christ Jesus" and "called to be saints" (1:2). By God's calling, they are set apart from the world and for God.[173] They have an identity, beliefs, and practices that God has laid upon them and called them to take up in their lives. The second point is that not only are the Corinthians a single "church" belonging to God ("of God"), but they are one with "all those who in every place call upon the name of our Lord Jesus Christ, both their Lord and ours." In light of the divisions threatening the church in Corinth, Paul wants the Corinthians to understand the unity of the church of Jesus Christ—in Corinth and around the world.[174]

Third, Paul's benediction wishes "grace to you and peace from God our Father and the Lord Jesus Christ" (1:3). Since this is Paul's customary opening to his epistles, it is easy to pass over it as though it were a merely formulaic introduction. In fact, Paul is summarizing here the two chief benefits of the believer's salvation, "grace" and "peace." He is also highlighting the sole source of these benefits—"God our Father and the Lord Jesus Christ." The titles "Father," "Lord," and "Christ" lend "eschatological" specification to the Corinthians' salvation.[175] That is to say, the grace and peace that the Corinthians enjoy are blessings of the age to come, proceeding from the Father through the risen and exalted Lord Jesus Christ.

Fourth, Paul's thanksgiving (1:4–9) signals these and additional motifs to come in the letter. The overwhelming focus of the thanksgiving is Christ himself. "Christ or the pronoun referring to him is repeated in every verse of the thanksgiving."[176] Paul first points the Corinthians to their past. He reminds them that "the grace of God" was "given" them "in Christ Jesus" (1:4; cf. 4:7). They therefore have no ground

[172] Barnett, *1 Corinthians*, 18.
[173] Morris, *1 Corinthians*, 36.
[174] Ciampa and Rosner, *First Letter to the Corinthians*, 56–57.
[175] Ibid., 57–58.
[176] Garland, *1 Corinthians*, 33.

for boasting, much less rendering "Christ divided" (1:13). Further, Christ has gifted them sufficiently: "You were enriched in him with all speech and all knowledge . . . so that you are not lacking in any gift" (1:5, 7a). Rather than valuing worldly wisdom, wealth, and status (cf. 1:26–31), the Corinthians are urged to prize the riches they already possess in Christ. Paul is furthermore anticipating his later discussion of spiritual gifts (1 Corinthians 12–14), in which he will remind them that "gifts come from God for the upbuilding of the community" and that "all Christians are gifted, and no one gift makes one greater than another."[177] Paul also ties the bestowal and exercise of the gifts to the gospel ("even as the testimony about Christ was confirmed among you," 1:6). If gifts in any way come to cloud, distort, or trump the gospel, then both those gifts and the gospel have been misunderstood and misapplied.

Paul then points the Corinthians to the future, specifically to the sure return of Christ (1:7b–8). For all that the Corinthians now possess in Christ and have experienced at the inauguration of the age to come, they still await the consummation of the age to come.[178] But if the Corinthians have not yet arrived, Paul is sure that their faithful God will sustain them to "the end"(1:8–9a).[179] On that day they will stand before God blameless, that is, acquitted, righteous, and free from condemnation (cf. 1:30; 6:11; 2 Cor. 5:19–21), because now, in Christ, they already stand justified before God. But because this is God's work, "there will be no room for Corinthian boasting on that day."[180] In the meantime, God has "called [them] into the fellowship of his Son, Jesus Christ our Lord" (1 Cor. 1:9). This fellowship entails breaking from communion with pagan temples (1 Corinthians 8–10) and pursuing unity in the context of the life and worship of the church (1 Cor. 1:10–4:21; 11:17–34; 12–14).

1 Corinthians 1:10–4:21

The problem that dominates 1 Corinthians 1:10–4:21 is the divisions and factions that have taken root in the church in Corinth. After noting the nature and extent of these divisions, and clearing himself of any involvement in them (1:10–17), Paul turns in 1 Corinthians 1:18–2:5 to diagnose and to treat this problem. The divisions in Corinth reflect the "wisdom of the world" and of this "age" (1:20). This world's wisdom stands diametrically opposed to what Paul calls "the word of the cross" (1:18), the "wisdom of God" (1:21), or "the weakness of God" (1:25).

From the standpoint of God's wisdom, this world's values of worldly wisdom, power, and noble birth are null (1:26). God's wisdom exalts what is weak and despised in order to nullify human boasting (1:27–29) and to direct all boasting to God himself (1:31). These principles are nowhere more clearly on display than in the sufficiency of Christ for the believer's salvation (1:30). Furthermore, the preaching of the cross of Christ illustrates these same principles (2:1–5). Paul reminds the Corinthians that he preached only "Christ and him crucified," and that he did so "in weakness and

[177] Ibid., 34.
[178] Fee, *First Epistle to the Corinthians*, 36, referencing 1 Cor. 4:8–13; 13:8–13.
[179] Ibid., 44.
[180] Ciampa and Rosner, *First Letter to the Corinthians*, 67.

in fear and much trembling," not in the world's wisdom but "in demonstration of the Spirit and of power" (2:2–4). The work of Christ for salvation, the preaching of Christ to sinners, and the conversion of the Corinthians (2:5) all concur in their setting aside the wisdom of the world and in their exalting the wisdom of God.

In 1 Corinthians 2:6–16 we find a meditation upon the "wisdom" that the apostle Paul has brought the Corinthians, that is, the gospel through which they were saved. This wisdom is a "secret and hidden wisdom of God, which God decreed before the ages for our glory" (2:7). It is a "revealed" wisdom (2:10), and we understand this wisdom by the same Spirit who has revealed it (2:12). As such, this wisdom stands diametrically opposed to "human wisdom" in two respects. First, the wisdom of God did not derive from human wisdom (2:13). Second, the "natural person," that is, the person who belongs to this age, does not receive or accept God's wisdom (2:14; cf. 2:8, "none of the rulers of this age understood this), as the apostles have committed that wisdom to writing by the inspiration of the Holy Spirit (2:13).

In 1 Corinthians 3:1–23, Paul returns to the problem of divisions in the church at Corinth. Employing terminology that he elsewhere uses of each of the two ages ("flesh," "Spirit"), the apostle accuses the Corinthians of behaving like "people of the flesh" not "spiritual people" (3:1). These words have sometimes been misunderstood. Paul is not establishing here two tiers of Christianity, one lower ("carnal") and one higher ("Spirit-filled"). He is saying not that the Corinthians "are acting like young, low-level Christians, but that they are not acting like Christians at all."[181] These divisions and their fruit (3:4) are simply the "flesh" at work (3:3).

Paul then turns to correct this way of thinking. He reminds the Corinthians of the true nature of Apollos and Paul, whom the Corinthians have appointed heads of their factions (cf. 1:12). They are, in fact, "servants through whom you believed, as the Lord assigned to each" (3:5; cf. 3:6–9). In 1 Corinthians 3:10–15, Paul cautions ministers to take heed how they build on the apostolic foundation that has been laid for the church of Jesus Christ. In 3:16–17, he reminds the church that they are "God's temple," indwelt by the Holy Spirit. In both exhortations, he reminds the Corinthians that there is coming a day of judgment when all will have to give account for their conduct within the church (3:15, 17). God will hold promoters of division to account. In 3:18–23, Paul ventures an "interim conclusion" to 1 Corinthians 1:10–4:21, underscoring the radical and antithetical difference between the "wisdom of this world" (3:19) and the wisdom of the age to come (3:21b–23).[182]

In 1 Corinthians 4:1–21, Paul returns to the way in which the Corinthians should regard the apostles, that is, as "servants of Christ and stewards of the mysteries of God" (4:1). In doing so, he brings 1:10–4:21 to a close by drawing together many of the points he has earlier raised. In 1 Corinthians 4:1–5, Paul stresses that the one who will judge and assess his ministry is God himself. Paul labors, therefore, not

[181] Gaffin, "Some Epistemological Reflections," 27n26. Gaffin notes that "jealousy and strife" (3:3) are, in Gal. 5:19, specified as "works of the flesh" and, in Rom. 13:12–13, as "the works of darkness." Gaffin rightly concludes, "Sin is sin wherever it is found, even in God's people."

[182] Barnett, *1 Corinthians*, 58.

with a view to winning the approval of the Corinthians, "any human court," or even himself (4:3), but with a view to pleasing God (4:5). In fact, part of Paul's ministry in Corinth has been to impress these principles upon the Corinthians "for [their] benefit" (4:6; cf. 4:7). Anticipating what he will argue at greater length in 2 Corinthians, Paul next sharply contrasts the worldly values and ideals of the Corinthians with the apostles' own lives and ministries (4:8–13).[183] In a section (4:14–21) rich with familial language ("beloved children," 4:14; "fathers," "father," 4:15; "faithful child," 4:17), Paul urges the Corinthians to "be imitators of me" (4:16). The apostles have not only lived before and served God according to the values of the wisdom of God, but they have done so in order to model such a life to the church (cf. 11:1).

1 Corinthians 5:1–7:40

In the next three chapters, Paul takes up a set of issues relating to sexual integrity in the church. In 1 Corinthians 5:1–13, he cannot conceal his shock at the report of "sexual immorality among you, and of a kind that is not tolerated even among pagans, for a man has his father's wife" (5:1). This sexual sin is in violation of God's moral law, a fact known not only from the written law of God, but also from the moral sensibilities of the world around them.[184] What is especially disconcerting to Paul is that the Corinthians have handled this circumstance in a way that mirrors this present evil age; they are "arrogant" and have failed to "mourn" (5:2; cf. 5:6, "your boasting is not good").[185] They have failed to exercise church discipline in "remov[ing]" the offender "from among [them]" (5:2).

Paul commands the church, "Cleanse out the old leaven that you may be a new lump, as you really are unleavened." He grounds this command in the fact that "Christ, our Passover lamb, has been sacrificed" (5:7; cf. 5:8). The realities of the age to come, which the Corinthians enjoy by virtue of their union with the crucified and risen Christ, are the resources with which the Corinthians must combat such expressions of the present evil age. Paul reminds the Corinthians that God has not called them to depart from the world (5:10), nor to pronounce ecclesiastical judgment on individuals who are not part of the church (5:12). Rather, they are to pronounce such judgment on those who profess to belong to the age to come but whose lives betray that profession (5:11). Paul presses the Corinthians to exercise discipline (5:13) "in the name of the Lord Jesus" and "with the power of our Lord Jesus" (5:4), in the hopes that the offender may be found in the "Spirit" (my trans.) and "saved in the day of the Lord" (5:5).[186]

At first glance, 1 Corinthians 6:1–11 seems to be something of a thematic

[183] In 1 Cor. 4:18–19, Paul hints that there are "ringleaders" at Corinth who are fomenting opposition in the church against him (Fee, *First Epistle to the Corinthians*, 190). On the identity of these opponents, see ibid., 7–15, although Fee may see more of a coordinated opposition at this stage of Paul's dealings with the Corinthians than the text warrants.

[184] On the Old Testament background not only of this verse but of this entire section, see Brian S. Rosner, *Paul, Scripture, and Ethics: A Study of 1 Corinthians 5–7* (Grand Rapids, MI: Baker, 1999).

[185] The word translated "arrogant" (πεφυσιωμένοι) is the same Greek verb translated "puffed up" in 1 Cor. 4:6 and "arrogant" in 4:18–19 (see Thiselton, *First Epistle to the Corinthians*, 387–88).

[186] The translation "that his spirit" (ESV) is misleading in its suggestion that the offender's human soul is in view, rather than the Holy Spirit (see Fee, *First Epistle to the Corinthians*, 212; Thiselton, *First Epistle to the Corinthians*, 390–400).

interruption. In a section dealing with issues of sexual morality, Paul takes up the problem of professing Christians suing one another in Roman courts. The disjunction with what precedes, however, is more apparent than real.[187] Paul has been speaking of no fewer than three judgments in 1 Corinthians 5:9–13: the church's judgment of unbelievers (which they are not to do), the church's judgment of its own membership (which they are to do), and God's final and eschatological judgment at the end of the age (5:5, 13). In 6:1–11 Paul takes up an unacceptable forum of judgment to which professing believers have been submitting themselves—the courts of unbelievers. While he does not categorically forbid believers' appearing in such courts of law, he urges Christians to try to settle disputes among themselves within the church (6:5) and to put the reputation of Christ and his church before their own private interests (6:7–8). He therefore pauses to remind them of who they are in Christ and what Christ, by his Spirit, has done for them (6:11). He also warns them of the outcome of the "unrighteous" (6:1), whom God, along with his saints, will judge (6:2), and who will not inherit God's "kingdom" (cf. 4:20). The age to come has been inaugurated by the work of Christ through his Spirit (6:11), but the eschatological judgment of the world has not yet occurred (6:10). Paul is reminding the Corinthians that to live in this period of redemptive history, in the overlap of the ages, carries tremendous privileges and bears great responsibilities.[188]

In 1 Corinthians 6:12–20, Paul resumes addressing problems of sexual morality among the Corinthians.[189] Taking up the specific problem of Corinthians who are consorting with prostitutes (6:15), and the theological slogans that the Corinthians used to justify such behavior ("all things are lawful for me," 6:12; "food is meant for the stomach and the stomach for food," 6:13), Paul argues that the human body is not to be indulged, and that it is not a matter of indifference to Christ. On the contrary, our bodies belong to God and their use matters to God. We were "bought with a price" and must therefore "glorify God in [our] body" (6:20). Our bodies are now united to Christ (6:15) and will be raised up in "power," just as Jesus's body was raised by God (6:14). We are indwelt by the Holy Spirit, as his "temple" (6:19). In light of these realities, then, one must never join his body to a prostitute (6:16), but must "flee from sexual immorality" (6:18).

In 1 Corinthians 7:1–40, Paul continues to address matters pertaining to sexual integrity. Here, he explicitly addresses "the matters about which you wrote" (7:1).[190] In 7:1–24, he addresses questions mostly relating to married Christians; in 7:25–40, questions mostly relating to unmarried Christians.[191] With Jesus (cf. 7:10), Paul affirms marriage as a created good that believers will ordinarily pursue (cf. Eph. 5:31).

[187] Barnett, *1 Corinthians*, 88.

[188] Fee, *First Epistle to the Corinthians*, 242. Fee also notes how Paul invokes the kingdom in 1 Cor. 4:20 as "already" present and, in 6:9–10, as "not yet" consummated (ibid.).

[189] On the interpretative difficulties of this passage, see especially Ciampa and Rosner, *First Letter to the Corinthians*, 245–51.

[190] Fee notes that the phrase "now about" is a recurring one in this portion of the letter: 7:1, 25; 8:1; 12:1; 16:1, 12 (*First Epistle to the Corinthians*, 267).

[191] Note the outline of Fee: 7:1–7 addresses the married; 7:8–9, "the unmarried and the widows"; 7:10–11, two married believers; 7:12–16, a believer married to an unbeliever; 7:25–38, "the virgins" (ESV mg.); 7:39–40, married women (and widows) (*First Epistle to the Corinthians*, 268).

Marriage is, therefore, an ordinance of this present age (cf. 1 Cor. 15:42–49) to which God continues to call those who belong to the age to come (cf. 1 Cor. 7:17–24). The calling of marriage is in this respect evidence of the overlap of the ages.

In this chapter Paul lays down principles for believers' negotiating life in this overlap of the ages. First, he affirms the goodness of marriage and of sexual relations within marriage (7:1–5). Paul is no ascetic and does not deem wholesale withdrawal from marriage or marital responsibilities to be a Christian duty. Second, he recognizes that God calls some Christians to serve him as single persons (7:6–9, 32–35). Such a calling does not render one superior to other believers who are called to marriage. The call to singleness does, however, provide unique opportunities to serve the Lord. Third, Paul lays down rules governing divorce and remarriage (7:10–16).[192] Believing spouses should not divorce but remain married (7:10).[193] If one spouse does leave the other, the leaving spouse should "remain unmarried or else be reconciled to her husband" (7:11). If a believer is married to an unbeliever, the one spouse's unbelief does not of itself warrant divorce (7:12–13). If the unbelieving spouse abandons the believing spouse, then the believer is free to pursue a divorce and remarry a believer in good conscience (7:15).

Fourth, Paul lays down a "rule" for all callings, whether marital or occupational: "Only let each person lead the life that the Lord has assigned to him, and to which God has called him" (7:17; cf. 7:24). This assigned life is one in which a person finds himself when he becomes a believer (7:18–20). Paul is not opposed to social mobility, and he encourages slaves who are able to do so to pursue their freedom (7:21–23). By the same token, Christians are to have a holy indifference regarding their particular callings. The important thing is "keeping the commandments of God" wherever God has stationed them (7:19).

Fifth, Paul addresses fathers whose daughters are engaged to be married (7:25–36). Shall they permit their daughters to marry or not?[194] Since the question involves movement from one calling to another, it follows nicely on the heels of the previous section (7:17–24). As he has done at 7:12, Paul distinguishes, in 7:25, his authoritative and apostolic "judgment" from the "command from the Lord" during his earthly ministry.[195] He does not recommend breaking existing engagements, but he advises caution in pursuing marriage in light of what he calls the "present distress" (7:26–27). Paul likely has in mind not the entirety of the overlap of the ages, but a particular (and, to us, obscure) set of circumstances facing the first-century Corin-

[192] For biblical, practical guidance concerning divorce and remarriage, see especially John Murray, *Divorce* (Phillipsburg, NJ: P&R, 1987).

[193] The phrase "I, not the Lord" (7:12) is not Paul disagreeing with Jesus. On the contrary, Paul is conscious that he is writing the Lord's command (14:37). Paul, rather, having restated Jesus's teaching concerning marriage and divorce in his earthly ministry (7:10–11), now proceeds to address a set of circumstances that Jesus never addressed on earth (7:12–16). Paul's qualification, then, is an expression of respect for the historical integrity of Jesus's words.

[194] This portion of the chapter is notoriously difficult to translate. Some translations (e.g., the ESV) follow the approach charted above. Others (e.g., the NIV) translate Paul's words to refer to an engaged person pondering whether or not to continue his engagement to his betrothed. On the translational and interpretative difficulties, see Fee, *First Epistle to the Corinthians*, 325–27.

[195] Barnett, *1 Corinthians*, 124–25. Paul's words, then, are not pious but dispensable thoughts. They are apostolic counsel, diplomatically and sensitively stated. See also Hodge, *First Epistle to the Corinthians*, 126–27.

thian church.[196] Even so, and in addition to this local and temporary set of difficulties, Paul recognizes the fleeting duration of this present age and the eschatological nearness of Christ's return (7:29–31). On this basis, Paul counsels, Christians should think twice before pursuing the estate of marriage (7:32–35). But, he hastens to say, marriage and the pursuit of marriage are not sinful but are good for those called to them (7:36–38).[197]

Sixth and finally, Paul addresses "widows," those who find their marriages dissolved by the deaths of their spouses and, in the providence of God, become newly single. They may remarry, but "only in the Lord" (7:39; cf. 7:8–9). Even so, Paul counsels them to consider serving the Lord as single persons (7:40; 7:8).

In summary, Paul's approach to sexuality reflects well-formed principles. These principles are eschatological in nature, that is, they imply that believers belong to the age to come but continue to live in this present age. Life in this overlap presents temptations of many kinds, and professing believers are not immune to the sexual sins that characterize the world around them. In light of these dangers, Paul reminds believers of who they are in Christ, the resources of grace that are theirs by the Spirit, and the glorious destiny that God has prepared for them, body and soul.

1 Corinthians 8:1–11:1

In these chapters, Paul turns to another problem in the Corinthian church occasioned by the overlap of the ages—"food offered to idols" (8:1).[198] He quotes another of the Corinthians' slogans—"all of us possess knowledge" (8:1). As with the previous slogans (cf. 6:12–13), this one betrays a misplaced spiritual confidence that threatens to lead the Corinthians into sin.

What is the issue that Paul addresses here? He is in fact dealing with a host of questions of conscience. He first tackles the common practice of purchasing meat "in the marketplace that," says Garland, "may or may not have been sacrificed in a pagan temple."[199] Paul furthermore explores whether a Christian may also eat that food in an "idol's temple" (8:10), and goes on to ask whether believers may eat "pagan sacrificial meals" (see 10:14–22).[200] What about dining with an unbeliever who serves food that may or may not have been "offered in sacrifice" (10:28)?

Paul is concerned that the Corinthians embrace the principles that they need to negotiate this casuistic thicket in which they find themselves. So he returns to first principles in the opening verses of 1 Corinthians 8. He reminds them of the importance of "love." What distinguishes love from the sort of "knowledge" that some of the Corinthians were vaunting is that this "knowledge" (so-called) "puffs up," while "love builds up" (8:1). Paul then reminds them of the doctrine of creation. "There

---

[196] Garland, *1 Corinthians*, 324.

[197] Part of discerning this calling, Paul reasons, is gauging one's own sexual continence (7:36; cf. 7:9).

[198] For a survey of these chapters and some of the problems attending their interpretation, see Garland, *1 Corinthians*, 347–62. Some recent interpreters, such as Fee, argue that Paul does not have in mind primarily the eating of food, sold in the marketplace, that had formerly been offered to idols; he rather addresses the practice of "eating . . . sacrificial food at the cultic meals in the pagan temples" (Fee, *First Epistle to the Corinthians*, 359).

[199] Garland, *1 Corinthians*, 362.

[200] Ibid., 473.

is no God but one," and idols are nothing (8:4). This one God has made all things through our Lord Jesus Christ (8:6).

There are, however, Corinthian brothers whose "conscience . . . is weak" (8:12; cf. 8:9–11). Should they see their fellow Christians "eating in an idol's temple," they are tempted to do the same, to commit idolatry, and risk destroying their souls (8:7, 10–11). In light of this reality, Paul gives two directives in 1 Corinthians 8. First, he affirms that Christians are at liberty to eat food that has been offered to an idol. (He defers judgment on the practice of eating in an idol's temple until 1 Corinthians 10). Idols are nonentities, and Christians are freed from the burden of the belief that any created matter is irredeemably corrupted by contact with pagan idols. Second, Paul also affirms the power and pull of some Christians' former associations with idolatry. Those whose consciences are informed and strong should put the good of their brother over their permissible desire for meat (8:9, 13). Food, after all, "will not commend us to God," and we are not "better" or "worse" for eating or not eating (8:8). To harm our weak brother is, Paul affirms, to "sin against Christ" (8:12).

In 1 Corinthians 9, Paul proceeds to present himself as an example (cf. 11:1) of how Christian liberty is properly to be exercised. He insists throughout the first half of the chapter that "those who proclaim the gospel should get their living by the gospel" (9:14). This is what the "Lord commanded" (9:14). But Paul is willing to suspend this "right" for the sake of the "gospel of Christ" (9:12; cf. 9:15–18). Paul is "free from all," but makes himself a "servant to all" for the gospel's sake (9:19; cf. 9:20–23). This self-suspension of rights requires the equivalent of athletic discipline but is necessary, he says, "lest after preaching to others I myself should be disqualified" (9:27b).

Paul's argument in 1 Corinthians 10:1–13, which we have surveyed above, presses home upon the Corinthians (especially those professing to have "knowledge") the danger of idolatry. The church stands between Egypt and Canaan, and exists in the threatening environment of the wilderness. He who "thinks that he stands" must "take heed lest he fall" (10:12); he must depend upon the preserving grace of God (10:13).

In 1 Corinthians 10:14–22, Paul exhorts the church to "flee from idolatry," an exhortation that Ciampa and Rosner properly call "the main point" of these three chapters.[201] Paul categorically forbids Christians from eating sacrificial meals offered in the context of idol worship (10:20). Their exclusive commitment to Christ (10:21) and the holy jealousy of the God they serve (10:22) ground this prohibition.

In the closing verses of 1 Corinthians 10, Paul addresses more systematically the propriety of eating food offered to idols. Appealing once again to the doctrine of creation (10:26; cf. 8:4–6), he says that believers may eat such food sold in the marketplace and are under no obligation to "rais[e] any question on the ground of conscience" (10:25). Similarly, a believer may enjoy a meal with an unbeliever without asking him about the food's origins (10:27).

[201] Ciampa and Rosner, *First Letter to the Corinthians*, 469.

If, however, the believer is informed that the food in question "has been offered in sacrifice" (10:28), Paul instructs him not to eat it. Paul takes care to deny that the unbeliever's conscience is in any way binding the believer's conscience (10:29). The apostle's concern is that, if the unbeliever sees the believer eating that meat, he will interpret that act as the believer's "sanctioning his idolatry."[202] Whether in the company of believers or unbelievers, the Christian is to exercise his liberty with a view to the spiritual well-being of those around him. He is, Paul concludes, to "do all to the glory of God" (10:31). This means that one will not be "seeking [his] own advantage, but that of many, that they may be saved" (10:33).

In summary, Paul highlights in these chapters the dangers and opportunities that come from living in the overlap of the ages. On the one hand, idolatry remains a threat. It threatens "weak" Christians who continue to associate certain foods with their former life in paganism. It equally threatens Christians who, professing their "knowledge," place themselves in positions of serious spiritual danger (8:8–13; 9:24–27; 10:1–13, 21–22). On the other hand, the believer's liberty is an opportunity to do much good to others. Since eschatological judgment has not yet arrived, the proper exercise of Christian liberty should have in view the salvation of sinners (9:19–23; 10:31–33) and the preservation of weak brothers (8:11–12). Even in something as seemingly trivial as eating and drinking, nothing less than the glory of God is in the balance (10:31).

1 Corinthians 11–14

The next four chapters all deal with the subject of the public worship of the Christian church. In 1 Corinthians 11:2–16, Paul takes up the matter of head coverings in the church. Women, it appears, were engaged in "pray[ing] or prophes[ying]" in the public assembly with "head[s] uncovered" (11:5; cf. 11:13). This practice, Paul insists, is a matter of dishonor (11:5) and unacceptable in the church (11:16).

Why does Paul insist on women wearing head coverings in the Corinthian assemblies? A partial answer comes from the fact that for a woman's head to be uncovered in public was a matter of disgrace and shame in first-century culture (Jewish and Greco-Roman).[203] Covered heads were a sign of female chastity; uncovered heads were a sign of female immodesty and sexual availability.[204]

Paul wants the married women of the Corinthian church to embrace their calling as wives (11:2–3). When a woman wears a head covering, she is signaling her acceptance of her husband's domestic authority and her God-appointed role in the home (11:3, 7–10).[205] Men and women, Paul is quick to say, are ontologically equal (11:11–12). They are, however, functionally different. Just as the incarnate Christ

[202] Morris, *1 Corinthians*, 147.
[203] See Garland, *1 Corinthians*, 520–21.
[204] Since covered heads no longer denote such virtues in contemporary Western society, head coverings are not mandatory for women during public worship. The principle that Paul articulates is unchanging, but the expression and application of that principle will change from time to time, place to place, and culture to culture.
[205] Paul uses the term "head" in these verses in two senses. In some places, it refers to one's physical head. In others, it refers metaphorically to one who has authority over another; see Wayne Grudem, "Does *kephalē* ('Head') Mean 'Source' or 'Authority Over' in Greek Literature? A Survey of 2,336 Examples," *TrinJ* 6 (1985): 38–59.

embraced the call to submit to his heavenly Father (11:3), so also wives should embrace the call to submit to their earthly husbands.[206]

Paul's frequent appeals to the created order in these verses (11:7–9, 14–15) underscore an important point. The dawn of the age to come does not mean that Christians are free to transcend or transgress the created order and the ordinances of creation (cf. 7:17–24).[207] On the contrary, the life of the age to come is lived out in the context of that order and those ordinances.

In 1 Corinthians 11:17–34, Paul addresses another problem of public worship. The Corinthians' "divisions" have spilled over into their observance of the Lord's Supper (11:18–19). Some eat and drink to excess; others are forced to watch and go hungry (11:21). The Corinthians' conduct is so egregious that Paul questions whether they are even observing the sacrament at all (11:20). Paul reminds them of what the Supper is—the covenantal remembrance of the death of Christ and the public proclamation of Christ's sure return (11:23–26). In light of these realities, the Corinthians should engage in self-examination before they approach the Lord's Table (11:28), lest they profane the body and blood of the Lord (11:27) and invite his severe discipline (11:29–32).

In 1 Corinthians 12–14, Paul turns to a related but distinct topic ("now concerning . . . ," 12:1)—spiritual gifts in the Corinthian church. In these chapters, Paul makes six points regarding the nature and exercise of these gifts. First, prior to the gifts is the giver, the Holy Spirit. In 12:12–13, Paul argues that all believers ("we . . . all," "Jews or Greeks, slaves or free," "all") "were made to drink of one Spirit," and "in one Spirit we were all baptized into one body." Far from advocating a second-blessing theology, Paul stresses here that "all believers share in the gift of the Spirit" and "that they do so from the time of their incorporation into the body of Christ."[208] It is in the context of this common possession of the Spirit that Paul addresses the subject of the Spirit's gifts to the church.

Second, the gifts proceed from the triune God and are his sovereign grant to the church. In three successive verses, Paul identifies Father (12:6), Son (12:5), and Spirit (12:4) as the author and source of the gifts. Paul, however, particularly identifies God the Spirit in connection with the bestowal of the gifts (12:11). The Spirit distributes them sovereignly ("as he wills," 12:11). In 1 Corinthians 12:8–10, Paul highlights the breadth and comprehensive character of the gifts that the Spirit has given the church. The gifts therefore afford no room for boasting or posturing in the church (cf. 4:7).

Third, the purpose for which the Spirit has so gifted the church is "the common good" (12:7), that is, the edification of the body of Christ (12:14–31). If this is the Spirit's intention, then it should be our intention as well. The desire for edification should inform the particular gifts for which we strive (14:1) as well as the way in which we exercise our gifts in the church (14:12).

---

[206] For a more thorough examination and treatment of this subject, see the essays in John Piper and Wayne Grudem, *Recovering Biblical Manhood and Womanhood* (Wheaton, IL: Crossway, 1991).

[207] This may be an instance of what has been termed "over-realized eschatology" (Barnett, *1 Corinthians*, 203; cf. Barnett's reference to "eschatological madness," 198).

[208] Gaffin, *Perspectives on Pentecost*, 31. For an exegetical defense and elaboration of these conclusions, see ibid., 28–32. Compare the similar comments in Ridderbos, *Paul*, 372–73.

Fourth, Paul emphasizes in 1 Corinthians 12:14–31 that every Christian needs the others' gifts (cf. 12:25–26). No Christian, therefore, is self-sufficient. In these verses, Paul stresses that God has set each believer in his place in the body of Christ (12:18). Every believer plays a God-assigned and therefore indispensable role in the whole body's well-being and growth (12:21). Believers should therefore go out of their way to esteem those gifts that are "less honorable" (12:23).

Fifth, Paul maintains that not all gifts are equal. There are "greater gifts" (12:31 NASB, NIV; "higher gifts," ESV). What makes a gift "greater" is its capacity to edify ("the one who prophesies is greater than the one who speaks in tongues, unless someone interprets, so that the church may be built up," 14:5). It is this criterion of edification that likely informs Paul's ranking of gifts in 12:28 ("first . . . second . . . third . . . then . . ."), and his preference of prophecy to tongues in 14:1–25. But greater than even the greatest gifts are Christian graces, "faith, hope, and love," of which "love" is the greatest (13:13). It is possible to exercise even the greatest of gifts in the most extraordinary of ways and yet, without love, be "nothing" (13:1–3).

Sixth, Paul insists in 1 Corinthians 14:26–33 that the gifts must be exercised in a proper order. The gifts' author is a God of order, not of confusion but of peace (14:33). Therefore, all things must be "done decently and in order" (14:40). What does an orderly exercise of the gifts look like? In Paul's guidelines, edification is the primary concern: "Let all things be done for building up" (14:26).

The focus of these chapters is the so-called "sign gifts" of tongues and prophecy. All Christians agree that the Spirit continues to indwell and to gift the church today. Christians disagree, however, whether these particular sign gifts continue in the life of the church or have ceased with the passing of the apostolic age.[209]

What are the nature and purpose of tongues and prophecy? Biblically, a tongue has two distinct but inseparable components. First, it is a recognized foreign language, unstudied by and unknown to the one exercising the tongue (Acts 2:8, 11b; 1 Cor. 14:10–11, 21a). Second, it is a revelatory gift. An interpreted tongue is the functional equivalent of prophecy (14:5).[210] By a tongue, Paul argues, one utters "mysteries in the Spirit" (14:2), and a mystery is, for Paul, revelatory in nature (Rom. 16:25–26; Eph. 3:4–6).

What of prophecy? While some have tried to argue for a category of New Testament prophecy distinct from prophecy in the Old Testament and elsewhere in the New Testament, there is no compelling biblical reason to draw such a distinction. In both Testaments, prophecy is revelatory. The prophet is the mouthpiece of the Lord.

The question, then, is whether these revelatory gifts have ceased or continue in the life of the church.[211] The answer to that question will be found in a consideration of their function and purpose.[212] In the Acts of the Apostles, tongues mark the

[209] For more extensive treatment of these questions, see especially Gaffin, *Perspectives on Pentecost*, 89–116; Ferguson, *Holy Spirit*, 207–39; Edmund P. Clowney, *The Church* (Downers Grove, IL: InterVarsity Press, 1995), 237–68; O. Palmer Robertson, *The Final Word: A Biblical Response to the Case for Tongues and Prophecy Today* (Edinburgh: Banner of Truth, 1993).
[210] Ferguson, *Holy Spirit*, 214.
[211] I leave to the side the question whether the gifts, as I have defined them, are one and the same with what modern proponents claim to be exercising in the contemporary church.
[212] Ferguson, *Holy Spirit*, 229.

once-for-all redemptive-historical progression of the gospel from Jew to Samaritan to Gentile (Acts 2:17a, 33; cf. Acts 8, 10). In 1 Corinthians, tongues have a similar but distinct role. In 14:21–25, tongues "are the sign of God's judgment at the inauguration of the new covenant and founding of the church."[213] In the New Testament, there is no provision for the continuation of prophets and prophecy in the way that the Pastoral Epistles make provision for the continuation of elders and deacons in the post-apostolic church. Furthermore, Paul stresses that the church is built on the foundation of the apostles and the prophets (Eph. 2:20). This metaphor suggests that prophecy is peculiar to the foundation of the new covenant church. The foundation having already been laid, there is no reason to expect its continuation in subsequent generations of the church.

In conclusion, the overlap of the ages shapes and colors Paul's argument about the nature and exercise of the gifts. On the one hand, the gifts are the gifts of the Spirit of Christ. Their very existence testifies to the exaltation and reign of the risen Christ. In particular, tongues and prophecy mark the inauguration of the age to come. They are, therefore, provisional and not intended to abide with the church indefinitely. On the other hand, the graces of faith, hope, and love have an importance that the gifts do not. It is possible to exercise extraordinary gifts and not be a genuine Christian. One's gifts may be deemed modest or spectacular, but what will "abide" and not "pass away" when "the perfect comes" is "love" (13:10, 13).

1 Corinthians 15

In 1 Corinthians 15, Paul defends the bodily resurrection of the Christian at the end of the age against "some" in the Corinthian church who "say that there is no resurrection of the dead" (15:12). Some scholars have pointed to this belief as evidence that these Corinthians thought the age to come was already consummated. Others argue that it indicates that the common Greek rejection of an embodied immortality persisted in these Corinthians' minds. Whatever the reason behind this "denial of the bodily resurrection," Paul treats it with utmost seriousness (cf. 15:33–34) and as a threat to the Christian gospel (15:1–11).[214]

Paul begins this chapter by arguing that the resurrection is an indispensable and necessary component of the Christian gospel (15:1–11). The remainder of the chapter consists of two parts. In 15:12–34, Paul treats the "that" of the bodily resurrection; in 15:35–58, the "how" of the bodily resurrection.[215] He argues in 15:12–34 the necessity of the resurrection. Such is the organic union between Christ and believers, between his resurrection and theirs, that to deny believers' bodily resurrection from the dead is to deny Christ's bodily resurrection from the dead (15:12–19). Paul can reason this way because Christ is "the firstfruits of those who have fallen asleep" (15:20; cf. 15:23).

In 1 Corinthians 15:35–58, Paul addresses the nature of the resurrection body

[213] Gaffin, *Perspectives on Pentecost*, 108.
[214] Ridderbos, *Paul*, 539.
[215] Ibid., 540.

and the way we will receive the resurrection body at Christ's return. He is responding to incredulous opponents who cannot conceive how the body will be raised or "with what kind of body . . . they [will] come" (15:35). With respect to the first objection, Paul appeals to God's "irresistible power."[216] With respect to the second objection, Paul first appeals to analogies from the created order (15:36–41) before he says that our resurrection body will be "spiritual" (15:44b), that is, transformed by and indwelt by the Holy Spirit.[217] As such, it is patterned after Christ's resurrection body and altogether suited to the age to come (15:47–49). Our bodies will be "imperishable," immortal, "raised in glory" and "power" (15:42–43, 53–54). Although we have not yet experienced this final deliverance from death, we may be certain that we will, since God "gives us the victory through our Lord Jesus Christ" (15:57). This assurance of a certain future gives us the confidence to serve God in the present—steadfastly, immovably, and abundantly (15:58).

Conclusion to 1 Corinthians

For Paul, believers live in the overlap of the ages; the age to come has already been inaugurated in history with the death and resurrection of Christ, and with the outpouring of his Spirit. It has not yet, however, been consummated in history. Believers continue to live "in" but are not "of" this present age.

At a number of points in this letter, Paul indicates that this present evil age has manifested itself in the lives of the Corinthians. One of the most serious of these manifestations, for Paul, was the trend of divisions that racked the church (1 Corinthians 1–4; cf. 1 Cor. 11:17–34). But this was hardly all. Sexual confusion (1 Corinthians 5–7), blurry lines between the church and the world (1 Corinthians 8–10), disorderly public worship (1 Corinthians 11–14), and skepticism about the bodily resurrection (1 Corinthians 15) were all manifestations of the evil of this age in the lives of the Corinthians. In each case, Paul brings the gospel of the death and resurrection of Christ to bear on these issues. In doing so, he repeatedly upholds the goodness of the created order and the creation ordinances (cf. 1 Cor. 7:17–24; 8:4–6; 10:26; 11:7–9, 14–15) and points believers to their future hope in Christ (the "kingdom of God," 6:10; 15:24; the glorious resurrection body, 15:1–58). As Paul moves from issue to issue, he again and again demonstrates the symmetry, the versatility, and the broad reach of the grace of God in the lives of Christ's people.

2 Corinthians 1:1–7:16

In the first and longest portion of 2 Corinthians, Paul reflects on his past and troubled interactions with the church at Corinth. He concludes by saying, "I rejoice, because I have complete confidence in you" (7:16). There is something of a sandwiched structure (A-B-A) to these chapters. In the outer sections, 2 Corinthians 1:1–2:13 and 7:5–16, Paul rehearses his travels since the time he wrote 1 Corinthians. In the

---

[216] Barnett, *1 Corinthians*, 292.

[217] As Barnett notes, it is the idea of "continuity and transformation" that unites the agricultural analogy of 15:36–39 with Paul's teaching about the resurrection body in 15:42–49 (*1 Corinthians*, 293). See, further, Garland, *1 Corinthians*, 729–32.

middle section, 2 Corinthians 2:14–7:4, Paul gives particular attention to his apostolic ministry—its new covenant character and its purpose and fruits. While some scholars understand 2:14–7:4 to be an interpolation, disruptive of the portions of the letter surrounding it, there is no good or necessary reason to question the letter's unity on this account.[218] We may preferably characterize this middle portion as a "digression" from Paul's "personal travel narrative," which he resumes and brings to conclusion at 7:5–16.[219] In exploring these three portions of this first part of 2 Corinthians, we may better understand why Paul opted to digress from his travel narrative, and to do so where he did.

In 2 Corinthians 1:1–2:13, Paul rehearses his comings and goings with the church in Corinth since the composition of 1 Corinthians. In doing so, he establishes at least two of the main lines of reflection that will characterize this epistle. First, in 2 Corinthians 1:3–11, he highlights the degree to which God has called him, an apostle, to suffer. Paul begins by reflecting on the affliction he has experienced as an apostle (1:3–7; cf. 1:1). He pauses to convey to the Corinthians how seriously this affliction has affected him, such that he and his colleagues "despaired of life itself" (1:8).[220] Even so, it was in the crucible of this affliction that God drew his servants to place their hope in him (1:9–10) and provided comfort for the church (1:4–7).

Second, in 2 Corinthians 1:12–2:4, Paul turns from his apostolic affliction to his apostolic sincerity. The report that Timothy brought from Corinth to Paul in Ephesus occasioned a change in the plans Paul had earlier drafted and shared with the Corinthians in 1 Corinthians 16:5–9.[221] This change in plans resulted in the charge of double-mindedness that Paul expressly refutes in these verses. After a general statement defending his sincerity (2 Cor. 1:12–14), Paul proceeds to handle specific accusations relating to his apostolic conduct. In 1:15–2:4, he defends his integrity with respect to his change of plans. He had not "vacillat[ed]" (1:17). On the contrary, his change in plans was designed to "spare" the Corinthians (1:23). The so-called "painful letter" that Paul wrote after this painful visit (2:3–4) was written out of Paul's "love" for the Corinthians, to ensure that any subsequent visit by Paul to the Corinthians was not painful to him but joyful—for him and for them (2:3).

In 2 Corinthians 2:5–11, Paul turns to the individual whose conduct toward Paul on that previous visit "caused pain" (2:5). Paul pleads that the church would not deal with him too severely. His desire is that this individual, who appears to have professed penitence over his actions, be restored to the love and fellowship of the church (2:7–8).

Paul, in 2 Corinthians 2:12–13 and 7:5–16, provides the rest of the story. He went

---

[218] For a survey of interpolation theories with respect to 2 Cor. 2:14–7:4, see Harris, *Second Epistle to the Corinthians*, 11–14. For Harris's defense of the letter's unity and integrity, see ibid., 8–51.

[219] Ibid., 14. Harris notes that the "recapitulative character of 7:5" with respect to 2:13 "suggests that what intervenes . . . was recognized by Paul as a digression" (ibid., 240). For various proposals accounting for the apparently abrupt transition from 2:13 to 2:14, and for specific literary connections among and commending the unity of 2 Cor. 1:1–2:13; 2:14–7:4; and 7:5–16, see Kruse, *2 Corinthians*, 36–37.

[220] Scholars have been unable successfully to identify the nature and timing of the afflictions "in Asia" that Paul describes here (1:8). For discussion, see Kruse, *2 Corinthians*, 68–69.

[221] Ibid., 21–22. See further Harris, *Second Epistle to the Corinthians*, 194–95; cf. 59–64.

from Ephesus to Troas, hoping to meet Titus there with some news from Corinth about the effect of the "painful letter." Not finding Titus there, Paul went on to Macedonia (2:13), where Titus did meet him and brought him the glad report of the Corinthians' repentance (7:9). It was through this news that Paul received "comfort" (7:13) and joy (7:13, 16).

Why, then, does Paul pause his narrative to provide the extensive meditation on his apostolic ministry in 2 Corinthians 2:14–7:4? When he pauses his account at 2:13, he does so at a low point in that account. At this juncture, Paul has already completed the painful visit and sent the painful letter. He does not yet know whether that letter has had its desired effect on the Corinthian church. His hopes to meet Titus in Troas and receive that news were unfulfilled, and Paul felt that disappointment keenly ("my spirit was not at rest," 2:13). He proceeds to reflect on his apostolic ministry (2:14–7:4) to share with the Corinthians how "God had enabled him to carry on an effective ministry despite many difficulties and criticisms."[222]

Second Corinthians 2:14–7:4 is, we have seen, in four parts.[223] First, in 2:14–4:6, much of which we have surveyed above, Paul "lays bare successively" his apostolic, new covenant ministry's "grandeur and superiority."[224] Second, in 4:7–5:10, he describes his ministry in terms of "suffering" and glory."[225] He makes clear that power and glory belong to God and his gospel, not to those called to preach the gospel. God has committed the treasure of the gospel to "jars of clay" (4:7). Returning to a line of thought introduced at the letter's beginning, Paul stresses that out of the "death" that the apostles carry and experience (4:10–11) comes "life" for not only the apostles (4:11) but also the Corinthians (4:12). Although Paul's present "outer self is wasting away," God is at work to renew him from within (4:16). This present "affliction" will issue in and is presently preparing an "eternal weight of glory beyond all comparison" (4:17), even as Paul by faith "look[s] . . . to the things that are unseen" (4:18). No small part of Paul's glorious hope is the hope of the resurrection body (cf. 4:14). It is that hope which occasions the meditation on that body in 5:1–10.

Third, in 2 Corinthians 5:11–6:10, Paul relates his apostolic ministry as a "ministry of reconciliation" (5:18). Compelled by Christ's love for him, and persuaded that Christ by his death and resurrection (5:14–15) brings sinners into the "new creation" (5:17), Paul proclaims a "message of reconciliation" (5:19), making urgent "appeal" to people (6:1). Those who respond to the preached Christ "in him" by faith "become the righteousness of God" (5:21). By the imputed righteousness of Christ, received through faith alone, the sinner is fully pardoned, accepted, and accounted righteous in the sight of God (cf. 5:19). United to Christ, forgiven, and having entered into the new creation, new believers "no longer live for themselves but for him who for their sake died and was raised" (5:15). So important is this message and ministry that Paul is willing to go to extraordinary lengths to be faithful to his charge (6:3–10).

---

[222] Kruse, *2 Corinthians*, 35.
[223] Following, again, Harris, *Second Epistle to the Corinthians*, 240–41.
[224] Ibid., 240.
[225] Ibid., 241.

Fourth, in 2 Corinthians 6:11–7:4, Paul identifies for the Corinthians areas where Christ calls them to live "for him who for their sake died and was raised" (5:15).[226] He first appeals to the Corinthians to "convert [their] partial reconciliation with himself into full reconciliation."[227] Paul then returns to a theme broached in 1 Corinthians, the integrity of the believer in the midst of his daily interactions with the unbelieving world (2 Cor. 6:14–7:1).[228] There can be no full reconciliation within the church in the absence of a commitment to personal holiness.[229] Having turned from personal reconciliation (6:11–13) to personal holiness (6:14–7:1), Paul then returns to make a final plea for personal reconciliation in 7:2–4. He fittingly concludes this section of the letter on the notes of comfort and joy he has already experienced with the Corinthians (7:5–13). In making appeal for full reconciliation (6:11–13; 7:2–4), Paul hopes to experience these fruits in even greater measure once any remaining barriers between him and the Corinthian church are removed.[230]

2 Corinthians 8–9

Having concluded the previous section on a note of comfort, joy, and "confidence" (2 Cor. 7:16), Paul proceeds on that foundation to make a renewed appeal to the Corinthians to join their Macedonian brothers in giving to the Jerusalem collection.[231] He reminds the Corinthians that the Macedonians have given not out of plenty and generosity but out of "affliction," "poverty," and "beyond their means" (8:2–3). Yet they have given in "their abundance of joy" (8:2). In this respect, the Macedonians' giving serves to model the pattern of apostolic ministry that Paul outlined in 2 Corinthians 1:1–7:16. Paul mentions this example precisely because he is confident that the Corinthians will follow suit and "excel in this act of grace also" (8:7).

While Paul does not issue the call to participate in the offering as a "command," he nevertheless "outline[s] the reasons why [the Corinthians] should participate," lest they give "for the wrong reasons."[232] In 2 Corinthians 8:8–15, Paul appeals to the example of Christ (8:9), the Corinthians' earlier stated intentions to contribute (8:10–11), God's willingness to accept even a small offering (8:12), and the way in which the Corinthians are poised to meet the needs of their Christian brothers (8:13–15).

Paul then proceeds to commend Titus and other unnamed "brothers" (8:18, 22–23) to the Corinthians as reliable stewards of whatever gifts they choose to send to Paul. He does so in order that this offering might reflect the kind of apostolic sincerity of which he spoke earlier in the letter (8:20–21). In light of that delegation's imminent

[226] For a recent response to proposals that these verses are an interpolation, a defense of 2 Corinthians' integrity at this point, and the structure of Paul's argument in these verses, see Garland, *2 Corinthians*, 314–28, and Barnett, *Second Epistle to the Corinthians*, 337–41. For the way in which 2 Cor. 6:14–7:1 sits comfortably in Paul's larger argument, see also Hughes, *Second Epistle to the Corinthians*, 243–44.

[227] Harris, *Second Epistle to the Corinthians*, 487.

[228] That he does so suggests that Paul judged that some of the concerns broached in 1 Corinthians 8–10 needed revisiting (see Garland, *2 Corinthians*, 323–24).

[229] Kruse, *2 Corinthians*, 140.

[230] Barnett, *Second Epistle to the Corinthians*, 364–67. Barnett notes how "joy" links 7:4 and 7:16.

[231] Ibid., 388; Kruse, *2 Corinthians*, 149–50.

[232] Garland, *2 Corinthians*, 375.

arrival in Corinth, Paul appeals to the Corinthians in 9:1–5 to "arrange in advance for the gift [they] have promised" (9:5), and thus spare them "humiliat[ion]" (9:4), especially before the Macedonian Christians to whom Paul has already "boast[ed]" of Corinthian readiness to give (9:3). Paul closes his appeal (9:6–15) by exhorting the Corinthians to give "bountifully" (9:6), willingly (9:7), abundantly (9:8), in reliance on the surpassing grace of God (9:8–11), with longing for God to be thanked and glorified through their gift (9:12–13), and in anticipation of the grace-filled affection that the Judean churches would express for their gift (9:14–15).

2 Corinthians 10–13

In the closing chapters of the letter, Paul addresses opponents ("super-apostles") who have taken up residence in Corinth. These opponents not only differ sharply from Paul in method and message, but have set themselves against Paul. While there is a palpable difference in tone moving from 2 Corinthians 8–9 to 2 Corinthians 10–13, this movement, Paul Barnett has observed, is an entirely understandable one. First, there is a natural thematic connection between the two sections. Paul's "exposition of divine grace in those chapters forms a fitting prelude to his exposition of power in weakness as opposed to triumphalism in 10:12–12:13."[233] Second, in keeping with ancient rhetorical convention, Paul reserves "the most urgent and controversial matters until the end and deal[s] with them passionately so that his last words make their greatest impact on the Corinthians."[234] Second Corinthians, a passionate letter from the start, reaches its passionate crescendo in these four chapters.

In this concluding section, Paul takes up his earlier, positive statements of his apostolic ministry (2 Cor. 1:1–7:16) and applies them polemically to the false teachers in Corinth.[235] He does this because he is preparing to make one more visit to Corinth (10:2). He wants this upcoming visit to continue the progress he and the Corinthians have made (cf. 7:5–16). For that to happen, Paul will have to deal with the super-apostles directly.

Paul's opening salvo is in 2 Corinthians 10:3: "For though we walk in the flesh, we are not waging war according to the flesh." Paul ministers in this age, but his ministry and his ministerial resources are of the age to come. That he does not wage war according to the world's standards does not mean that his ministry is not eschatologically martial (10:3–6). Paul illustrates this by advancing a defensive maneuver (10:7–11) and an offensive strike (10:12–18). Against criticisms that he is "weighty and strong" in his letters, but "weak" and "of no account" in person (10:10), Paul maintains his consistency in letter and in person (10:11). The super-apostles may not understand how Paul is exercising his apostolic authority, but he wants the Corinthians to know that he is exercising it for the church's edification, not destruction (10:8). Paul then accuses the super-apostles of "commending themselves" (10:12)

[233] Barnett, *Second Epistle to the Corinthians*, 451n6.
[234] Ibid., 452.
[235] On the internal structure of 2 Corinthians 10–13, see Garland, *2 Corinthians*, 422–23. On literary grounds, he argues for the following divisions: 10:1–11; 10:12–18; 11:1–21a; 11:21b–12:13; 12:14–21; 13:1–10.

and "trespassing into Paul's 'field' of labor" (cf. 10:13–16).[236] Paul, however, has been faithful to "the area of influence God assigned to [him]" (10:13). His boast is in the Lord, and it is the Lord's commendation that he seeks (10:18).

Second Corinthians 11:1–12:13 has been called "The Fool's Speech."[237] Forms of the word "fool" predominate in this section (11:1, 16, 17, 19, 21; 12:6, 11).[238] In 11:1–6, Paul outlines in starkest terms the differences between his apostolic ministry and that of the "super-apostles" (11:5). Not only are they radically different in method, but they are radically different in message as well (11:3–4). Illustrating the difference between the two ministries, Paul, in 11:7–15, defends himself for having "preached God's gospel . . . free of charge" to the Corinthians (11:7). Paul's opponents have represented this decision as evidencing a lack of love for the Corinthians (11:11). On the contrary, Paul does love them, and it is his "boast" that he preached without soliciting payment from the Corinthians (11:9–10). In the closing verses of this section (11:13–15), Paul returns to his earlier point that his opponents are "false apostles" (11:13). He has more than strategic differences with these teachers. They are simply not serving the same master. The super-apostles are "servants" of "Satan" (11:14–15).

It is in 2 Corinthians 11:16–12:13 that Paul conjoins the ideas of "boasting" (10:12–18; cf. 11:10, 12) and "foolishness" (11:1).[239] He recognizes that the super-apostles' boasting is characteristic of this present age, life "according to the flesh" (11:18; cf. 10:3). Paul inverts and upends their boasting by boasting "as a fool." Like the super-apostles, Paul has "impeccable Jewish ancestry" (see 11:22).[240] The real and deciding difference between the super-apostles and Paul, however, is that he is a genuine servant of Christ (11:23). What qualifies Paul as a servant of Christ, however, is his suffering (11:23b–12:10). Even his having received "visions and revelations of the Lord" (12:1) was tempered by the gift of a "thorn . . . in the flesh" (12:7). The Lord gave Paul this thorn, a "messenger of Satan," to keep him humble (12:7). When Paul asked Jesus to remove it, the Lord refused, saying, "My grace is sufficient for you, for my power is made perfect in weakness" (12:9). In Paul both the "power of Christ" (cf. 12:1–4, 12) and "weaknesses" reside together (12:9) and thereby legitimate his ministry. The super-apostles, however, possessed neither "the signs of a *true* apostle" (12:12) nor the concomitant weaknesses of which Paul was prepared to boast (12:10).

In the remainder of this section (12:14–13:14), Paul readies the Corinthians for what he calls his "third" visit (12:14). He reiterates his desire not to burden them (12:14–18), and reminds them why he has taken the time to defend his apostolic

[236] Barnett, *Second Epistle to the Corinthians*, 481.
[237] See, for example, Jerome Murphy-O'Connor, *The Theology of the Second Letter to the Corinthians* (Cambridge: Cambridge University Press, 1991), 107. For background to this phrase and history of scholarship, see Barnett, *Second Epistle to the Corinthians*, 494, esp. 494n1. Kruse places the beginning of the speech at 11:16 (*2 Corinthians*, 191). Garland argues that the "fool's discourse begins in 11:1, but Paul does not start speaking as a fool until 11:21" (*2 Corinthians*, 459); compare the concurring comments of Barnett, *Second Epistle to the Corinthians*, 495.
[238] Texts cited by Murphy-O'Connor, *Theology of the Second Letter to the Corinthians*, 107.
[239] Harris, *Second Epistle to the Corinthians*, 777.
[240] Kruse, *2 Corinthians*, 193.

ministry (12:19–21). He raises, again, his concerns about persistent divisions and sexual immorality within the church (12:20–21), and warns them that he will need to deal decisively with these on his upcoming visit (13:1–10).[241] Paul's aim, however, is nothing less than the Corinthians' "restoration" (13:9), that they would "do what is right" (13:7). It was in order that this upcoming visit not be a "severe" one that Paul has written 2 Corinthians beforehand (13:10). To that end, the apostle closes his letter affectionately and with a word of blessing (13:11–14).[242]

Conclusion to 2 Corinthians

Second Corinthians puts on vivid display church life and ministry in the overlap of the ages. Not only is Paul "weak in [himself] but . . . strong in Christ," but he is also "weak *in Christ*, as well as powerful in him."[243] Because he is united to Christ in his death and resurrection, Paul's ministry assumes a form of weakness and power, suffering and glory (13:4). It is precisely through Paul's suffering that "glory" is being wrought (4:17). For the Corinthians, Paul's afflictions meant comfort (1:3–7), life (4:12), the extension of grace, and the increasing of thanksgiving (4:15).

Paul's ministry was one that was unreservedly committed to the gospel of the death and resurrection of Jesus Christ (5:14–15). It was a "ministry of reconciliation" (5:18). This gospel promotes the holiness of God's people (6:14–7:1) and prompts us to sacrificial generosity (2 Corinthians 8–9).

On the other hand, the "super-apostles'" credentials were "according to the flesh" (11:18). They were promoting a "different gospel," that is, "another Jesus" (11:3–4; cf. 11:13–15). Their ministry had power as the world counts power, but in fact lacked the power of Christ and his Spirit, the power of the age to come.

For Paul, the gospel has far-reaching implications for the way in which the church sees itself, and for the way in which Christian leaders undertake their work. Neither the Christian life nor Christian ministry is easy. What's more, the stakes are high. But, Paul stresses again and again, the reward is great, surpassing anything this age can offer or provide, even an "eternal weight of glory beyond all comparison" (2 Cor. 4:17).

For all the differences between the Corinthian church and the contemporary church, Paul underscores one fundamental similarity—we live in the overlap of the ages. The age to come has dawned in human history with the death and resurrection of Christ and the outpouring of his Spirit on all flesh. Believers have been delivered from the age to come and await its conclusion with the consummation of the age to come at Christ's return. In the meantime, we live *in* this present age, even as we are not *of* this present age. We belong to another age, because we belong to the Christ who died and was raised for us. To this Christ we are presently united, and his Spirit now indwells us.

It is this framework that Paul brings to bear on the host of pastoral issues that

[241] Garland, *2 Corinthians*, 531.
[242] Hughes, *Second Epistle to the Corinthians*, 486.
[243] Ferguson, *Holy Spirit*, 171, emphasis his.

surface in 1–2 Corinthians. Whether we can relate to some of the problems that the Corinthians were facing or those problems seem foreign and distant to us, Paul pursues the same strategy relentlessly. Specific problems and challenges may vary from church to church, place to place, and time to time, but there is a glorious simplicity and constancy in the way the gospel works itself out in the lives of believers and Christian congregations. That this gospel is in fact adapted to meet all the needs of every believer until Christ returns is the glory of these two letters.

Select Bibliography

Barnett, Paul. *1 Corinthians*. FB. Fearn: Christian Focus, 2000.

———. *The Second Epistle to the Corinthians*. NICNT. Grand Rapids, MI: Eerdmans, 1997.

Barrett, C. K. *The First Epistle to the Corinthians*. HNTC. New York: Harper & Row, 1968.

———. *The Second Epistle to the Corinthians*. HNTC. New York: Harper & Row, 1973.

Ciampa, Roy E., and Brian S. Rosner. *The First Letter to the Corinthians*. PNTC. Grand Rapids, MI: Eerdmans, 2010.

Fee, Gordon D. *The First Epistle to the Corinthians*. NICNT. Grand Rapids, MI: Eerdmans, 1987.

Fitzmyer, Joseph A. *First Corinthians*. AB 32. New Haven, CT: Yale University Press, 2008.

Gaffin, Richard B., Jr. *By Faith, Not by Sight: Paul and the Order of Salvation*. 2nd ed. Phillipsburg, NJ: P&R, 2013.

———. *Perspectives on Pentecost: New Testament Teaching on the Gifts of the Holy Spirit*. Phillipsburg, NJ: P&R, 1979.

———. *Resurrection and Redemption: A Study in Paul's Soteriology*. 2nd ed. Phillipsburg, NJ: P&R, 1987.

Garland, David E. *1 Corinthians*. BECNT. Grand Rapids, MI: Baker Academic, 2003.

———. *2 Corinthians*. NAC 29. Nashville: Broadman & Holman, 1999.

Grosheide, F. W. *De eerste brief aan de kerk te Korinthe*. Kampen: Kok, 1957.

———. *De tweede brief aan de kerk te Korinthe*. Kampen: Kok, 1959.

———. *The First Epistle to the Corinthians*. NICNT. Grand Rapids, MI: Eerdmans, 1953.

Harris, Murray J. *The Second Epistle to the Corinthians*. NIGTC. Grand Rapids, MI: Eerdmans, 2005.

Hays, Richard B. *The Conversion of the Imagination: Paul as Interpreter of Israel's Scripture*. Grand Rapids, MI: Eerdmans, 2005.

———. *First Corinthians*. Interpretation. Louisville: John Knox, 1997.

Heil, John Paul. *The Rhetorical Role of Scripture in 1 Corinthians*. SBLMS 15. Leiden: Brill, 2005.

Hodge, Charles. *An Exposition of the First Epistle to the Corinthians*. New York: Robert Carter, 1866.

———. *An Exposition of the Second Epistle to the Corinthians*. New York: A. C. Armstrong and Son, 1891.

Hughes, Philip Edgcumbe. *The Second Epistle to the Corinthians*. Grand Rapids, MI: Eerdmans, 1962.

Kruse, Colin G. *2 Corinthians*. TNTC. Grand Rapids, MI: Eerdmans, 1987.
Morris, Leon. *1 Corinthians*. Rev. ed. TNTC. Grand Rapids, MI: Eerdmans, 1985.
Murphy-O'Connor, Jerome. *The Theology of the Second Letter to the Corinthians*. Cambridge: Cambridge University Press, 1991.
Plummer, Alfred. *A Critical and Exegetical Commentary on the Second Epistle of St. Paul to the Corinthians*. ICC. Edinburgh: T&T Clark, 1915.
Prior, David. *The Message of 1 Corinthians: Life in the Local Church*. BST. Downers Grove, IL: InterVarsity Press, 1985.
Ridderbos, Herman N. *Paul: An Outline of His Theology*. Translated by John Richard de Witt. Grand Rapids, MI: Eerdmans, 1975.
Robertson, Archibald, and Alfred Plummer. *A Critical and Exegetical Commentary on the First Epistle of St. Paul to the Corinthians*. 2nd ed. ICC. Edinburgh: T&T Clark, 1914.
Talbert, Charles H. *Reading Corinthians: A Literary and Theological Commentary on 1 and 2 Corinthians*. New York: Crossroad, 1987.
Thiselton, Anthony C. *The First Epistle to the Corinthians*. NIGTC. Grand Rapids, MI: Eerdmans, 2000.
Vos, Geerhardus. "The Eschatological Aspect of the Pauline Conception of the Spirit." In *Redemptive History and Biblical Interpretation: The Shorter Writings of Geerhardus Vos*, edited by Richard B. Gaffin Jr., 91–125. Phillipsburg, NJ: P&R, 1980.
———. *The Pauline Eschatology*. 1930. Repr., Phillipsburg, NJ: P&R, 2004.
Winter, Bruce W. *After Paul Left Corinth: The Influence of Secular Ethics and Social Change*. Grand Rapids, MI: Eerdmans, 2001.
Witherington, Ben, III. *Conflict and Community in Corinth: A Socio-Rhetorical Commentary on 1 and 2 Corinthians*. Grand Rapids, MI: Eerdmans, 1995.

8

Galatians

Guy Prentiss Waters

> The Epistle to the Galatians is my own epistle to which I am betrothed. It is my Katie von Bora.
>
> *Martin Luther (1535)*[1]

Introduction

Paul's letter to the Galatians is a passionate production. False teachers have entered the churches in Galatia and are actively promoting what Paul calls a "different gospel" (1:6).[2] Those who propagate this gospel stand "accursed" (1:8–9; cf. 5:10b). That the Galatians have entertained these teachers prompts Paul to pronounce the Galatians "foolish" and "bewitched" (3:1).

But this epistle is no less rigorously reasoned than it is passionate. Paul declares his "confidence in the Lord that [the Galatians] will take no other view" than his (5:10a). The Galatians earlier heard and embraced the gospel that Paul preached to them (3:1–5; 4:13–15). In this letter, Paul seeks to persuade them to embrace decisively the gospel of grace and to reject no less decisively the false teachers in their midst.

Galatians, then, is a vigorous defense of the biblical gospel. The letter poses a number of questions to the reader. What precisely is the complex of errors that was assaulting the gospel in Galatia? How was it that these errors fundamentally challenged the gospel? How does Paul's extended defense of his apostleship in the

[1] Martin Luther, *Luther's Works*, vol. 26, *Lectures on Galatians 1535: Chapters 1–4*, ed. Jaroslav Pelikan (St. Louis, MO: Concordia, 1963), ix. Katie von Bora was Luther's beloved wife.

[2] That these teachers have entered the church from without is evident from the fact that, while Paul addresses the Galatians in the second person ("you"), he consistently speaks of these teachers in the third person ("they") (James D. G. Dunn, *The Theology of Paul's Letter to the Galatians* [Cambridge: Cambridge University Press, 1993], 8, cited by Ben Witherington III, *Grace in Galatia: A Commentary on Paul's Letter to the Galatians* [Grand Rapids, MI: Eerdmans, 1998], 23).

opening chapters of Galatians relate to the gospel and its defense? In answering these questions, we will better understand not only this epistle, but also the gospel that Paul was so concerned to defend and to preserve in the church.

Background Issues

Location and Date

Scholars debate both the location of "the churches of Galatia" (1:2) and the date when Paul wrote this letter to them.[3] These two questions, furthermore, have proved interrelated. The way in which one resolves the destination of this letter can have implications for how one settles the date.

Complicating the question of the location of "Galatia" is the term's breadth of denotation in antiquity. Galatia was the name of a Roman province in central Asia Minor (modern Turkey) that stretched from near the coast of the Black Sea in the north to near the Mediterranean coast in the south.[4] The province of Galatia in the first century was far from homogenous. The northern portion was mountainous and sparsely populated, while its southern portion was urban and populous. The northern part of the province was inhabited by the "Galatians," Celtic peoples who had settled in that area in the third century BC. The southern part of the province had substantial Jewish populations in such cities as Pisidian Antioch and Iconium (see Acts 13–14).

"Galatian," therefore, could refer to any inhabitant of the Roman province Galatia, or more specifically to the ethnic Galatians who resided in the northern part of the province. Some commentators argue that Paul wrote this letter to churches comprising these ethnic Galatians (the North Galatian theory).[5] Many contemporary commentators believe that the Galatian churches were located in the southern part of the province (the South Galatian theory).[6]

The South Galatian theory allows for an early date for this letter. Since Paul established churches in South Galatia on his first missionary journey in the AD 40s, he could have written this epistle any time afterward. The North Galatian theory, however, requires a later date. We have no record of Paul visiting this northern region before his second missionary journey (see Acts 16:6). If the churches to which Paul wrote this letter were located in North Galatia, then he would likely not have written Galatians before the mid-50s.

One further matter that must be taken into consideration concerns the identity and the date of the meeting that Paul records in Galatians 2:1–10. Some have argued that the gathering that Paul records in 2:1–10 is identical with that of Acts 15. Paul, in other words, offers an independent account of the Jerusalem Council. Others have

[3] For recent and representative surveys, see D. A. Carson and Douglas J. Moo, *An Introduction to the New Testament*, 2nd ed. (Grand Rapids, MI: Zondervan, 2005), 458–65; and Moisés Silva, *Interpreting Galatians: Explorations in Exegetical Method*, 2nd ed. (Grand Rapids, MI: Baker Academic, 2001), 129–39.
[4] On the changing boundaries of the province both before and after the first century, see Witherington, *Grace in Galatia*, 2–5.
[5] J. B. Lightfoot, *St. Paul's Epistle to the Galatians: A Revised Text with Introduction, Notes, and Dissertations* (1881; repr., Peabody, MA: Hendrickson, 1995), 1–35; Hans Dieter Betz, *Galatians: A Commentary on Paul's Letter to the Churches in Galatia*, Hermeneia (Philadelphia: Fortress, 1979), 1–5.
[6] See a partial listing in Thomas R. Schreiner, *Galatians*, ZECNT (Grand Rapids, MI: Zondervan, 2010), 23n8.

alleged that the differences between these two accounts are too stark for them to be records of the same meeting. Paul's account in Galatians 2:1–10 better aligns, it is argued, with the Jerusalem meeting documented in Acts 11:27–30.[7]

These data admit of no fewer than six proposals concerning when and to whom Paul wrote this epistle.[8] It is fair to say that reasonable cases may be made for both the North and South Galatian theories.[9] It is also fair to say that this complex of questions has more importance for the chronology of Paul's life and ministry than for the interpretation of Galatians.[10]

Recognizing these difficulties, how may we settle these questions? The similarities between Luke's account of the Jerusalem Council in Acts 15 and Paul's account in Galatians 2:1–10 are too numerous to be incidental.[11] Paul is likely writing about the Jerusalem Council and, therefore, writing after the council, which took place at about AD 49.[12] At the same time, the data of Acts better suits the South Galatian theory than the North Galatian theory. Luke documents an extensive Pauline ministry in southern Galatia but is silent about any such missionary activity in northern Galatia. That southern Galatia was both urban and populated with Jews and Gentiles better suits the situation of the churches reflected in this letter. The churches that Luke records Paul establishing in Acts 13–14 are the best candidates for the recipients of this letter. We may conclude, then, that Paul wrote Galatians to churches in southern Galatia sometime after the Jerusalem Council.

Paul's Opponents

There is no question that Paul is responding to a well-defined set of opponents who have made their way into the churches in Galatia. What did they believe and teach? In what ways were they criticizing the apostle Paul? Part of the difficulty in answering these questions is that we do not have these opponents' beliefs, practices, and criticisms of Paul in their own words. We must infer them from Paul's statements in this letter. This process of inference, often termed "mirror reading," is a challenging but necessary part of studying this letter.[13]

---

[7] For a listing of arguments and counterarguments for each position, see Richard N. Longenecker, *Galatians*, WBC 41 (Dallas: Word, 1990), lxi–lxxxviii; Schreiner, *Galatians*, 24–29.

[8] See Douglas J. Moo, *Galatians*, BECNT (Grand Rapids, MI: Baker Academic, 2013), 9.

[9] As Carson and Moo rightly note, neither theory approaches "complete demonstration" (*Introduction to the New Testament*, 461).

[10] Schreiner, *Galatians*, 24.

[11] Lightfoot, cited by Silva, *Interpreting Galatians*, 135. For a helpful harmonization of what are sometimes alleged to be irreconcilable discrepancies between Luke's and Paul's accounts, see Silva, *Interpreting Galatians*, 132–36.

[12] The objection often arises as to why Paul did not simply cite the Jerusalem decree of Acts 15:19–21, a decree that was materially pertinent to the Galatian controversy. We may first note that Paul also does not cite the decree in addressing subsequent controversies in Corinth (1 Corinthians 8–10) and Rome (Romans 14–15)—controversies to which the decree is also relevant. It is not necessary to conclude, then, that Galatians could not have been written after the Jerusalem Council. In the second place, Paul is defending his apostolic credentials in this part of Galatians (1:1–2:14). Without denying the legitimacy of his fellow apostles or slighting their approbation of his own apostolic ministry (cf. Gal. 2:1–10), Paul is concerned both to show that he is an apostle "not from men nor through man, but through Jesus Christ and God the Father" (1:1), and to resolve the Galatian controversy by his own apostolic authority. Direct appeal to the decree would have, at the very least, proved a distraction from this objective.

[13] For a helpful overview of the pitfalls and opportunities attending "mirror reading," see John M. G. Barclay, "Mirror-Reading a Polemical Letter: Galatians as a Test Case," in *The Galatians Debate: Contemporary Issues in Rhetorical and Historical Interpretation*, ed. Mark D. Nanos (Peabody, MA: Hendrickson, 2002), 367–821; Witherington, *Grace in Galatia*, 21–23; and D. A. Carson, "Mirror-Reading with Paul and against Paul: Galatians 2:11–14 as a Test Case," in *Studies in the Pauline Epistles: Essays in Honor of Douglas J. Moo*, ed. Matthew S. Harmon and Jay E. Smith (Grand Rapids, MI: Zondervan, 2014), 99–112.

Paul's opponents have been termed "Judaizers," a label drawn from the Greek verb that Paul uses at Galatians 2:14 (Ἰουδαΐζειν, "to live like Jews").[14] What may we safely predicate of this group of opponents from Paul's statements in Galatians? At least four defining traits of the Judaizers emerge. First, the Judaizers appear to be professing Jewish Christians (cf. 2:4) who claim some kind of adherence to the church in Jerusalem (2:12).[15] The conflict reflected in Galatians, then, transpires within the bounds of the Christian church. Second, these Judaizers teach that Gentiles cannot be justified persons unless they receive circumcision according to the Mosaic law (2:3–5; 5:1–6; 6:11–16). Likely these opponents have pressed circumcision as the gateway ordinance to a whole lifestyle characterized by observance of the Mosaic law for justification (4:10, 21; 5:3–4).[16]

Third, these Judaizers have made appeal to the Old Testament in an effort to substantiate their teaching. Paul's extensive treatment of the Abrahamic narrative in Galatians 3–4 suggests that this portion of Genesis is a favorite of the Judaizers. Likely they have argued that since circumcision was an ordinance indispensable to the Abrahamic covenant, one could not experience the blessing held out in that covenant apart from reception of circumcision. How, then, could one accept Paul's gospel if it repudiated the settled teaching of the Old Testament?

Fourth, these Judaizers have discredited Paul's apostleship. They portray his authority as derivative of the Jerusalem apostles and his teaching as a corruption of the same (1:1, 12, 17–21).[17] Thus, the Judaizers have attacked Paul both materially and formally. They have portrayed Paul's gospel as unfaithful to the Old Testament and to the Jerusalem apostles. They have represented Paul as an untrustworthy delegate of the Jerusalem authorities. The Judaizers, however, argue that they have not only unimpeachable biblical argument but also sterling credentials as teachers in the Christian church.

We have noted that Paul's differences with the Judaizers centers on what Paul calls the "works of the law" (Gal. 2:16; 3:10). Paul denies that one is "justified by works of the law," but affirms that one is justified "through faith in Christ Jesus" (2:16). Protestant interpreters have historically taken these words to mean that a person is declared righteous solely on the basis of the imputed righteousness of Christ, received through faith alone. A person is not accounted righteous on the basis of anything that he or she has done, is doing, or will do.

In the last forty years, an influential wing of academic scholarship, the "New Perspective on Paul," has challenged this interpretation.[18] In doing so, New Perspec-

[14] Some prefer to employ a form of the participle that Paul uses of his opponents at Gal. 1:7—agitators (ESV, "some who trouble you"). For a recent defense of the label "Judaizers," see Schreiner, *Galatians*, 39–51.

[15] We may assume that Paul's narrative at Gal. 2:1–14, on these points at least, parallels the situation in Galatia. The precise connection between these opponents and Jerusalem is unclear, although Paul makes clear that the opponents did not have the sanction or blessing of the Jerusalem apostles (2:1–10).

[16] Carson and Moo, *Introduction to the New Testament*, 466.

[17] "It is probable that the opponents considered Paul to be an unreliable delegate of the Jerusalem church" (Barclay, "Mirror-Reading," 379).

[18] For surveys and critical engagements of the so-called "New Perspective on Paul," see Guy Prentiss Waters, *Justification and the New Perspectives on Paul* (Phillipsburg, NJ: P&R, 2004); Stephen Westerholm, *Perspectives Old and New on Paul: The "Lutheran" Paul and His Critics* (Grand Rapids, MI: Eerdmans, 2004); John Piper, *The Future of Justification: A Response to N. T. Wright* (Wheaton, IL: Crossway, 2007); and D. A. Carson, Peter T. O'Brien, and Mark Seifrid, eds.,

tive proponents have affected the recent study of Galatians in at least two ways. First, New Perspective proponents have challenged conventional understandings of first-century Judaism.[19] Judaism, they argue, is not a religion of merit, but a religion of grace. Consequently, Paul does not oppose Judaism because he perceives it to be a performance-based religion. Neither, then, should we understand the Judaizers to have corrupted a wholly gracious justification by the introduction of human merit.

Second, the reason that Paul is said to have opposed Judaism primarily concerns ecclesiology or identity.[20] That opposition does not, in the first instance, concern the salvation of the sinner. Paul's disagreement with the Judaizers addresses the way in which one defines the boundaries of God's people. For Paul, "faith" alone serves as the identifying badge of membership in the people of God. For the Judaizers, "the works of the law," that is, the practices required by Torah, are necessary markers of belonging to the church. Circumcision and other distinctively Jewish ordinances required by the Torah are the flash point of the Galatian controversy. The Judaizers insist that one be circumcised and observe the Torah in order to be "justified," that is, declared to be a true member of the church. Paul argues, to the contrary, that faith is a sufficient badge of identity in the new covenant people of God. To be "justified by faith in Christ and not by works of the law" (Gal. 2:16), then, means that one's membership in God's people is reckoned by the identity marker of faith, not the identity markers of law observance. Such an understanding of the controversy in Galatia has thoroughgoing implications for how one reads this letter. New Perspective proponents do not argue that Paul has nothing to say about personal salvation—only that personal salvation is not the main concern of Galatians.

The New Perspective is correct to remind us that the Jew/Gentile question lies in the foreground and not the background of Paul's troubles in Galatia. After all, circumcision (2:3; 5:2, 11; 6:12–13, 15) and the Jewish dietary laws (2:11–14) figure prominently in the letter. It is also correct to point out that questions of Christian identity are certainly in play in the Galatian controversy.

The problem, however, comes in the denial of the fundamentally soteriological character of the Galatian controversy. The "works of the law" in Galatians are things done or performed in order to be justified (3:10b, 12).[21] The law requires that one keep all of its commands perfectly and continually (3:10; 5:3). No one, Paul reasons, is able to meet that standard.[22] To fail to perform all that the law requires is to subject

Justification and Variegated Nomism, vol. 2, *The Paradoxes of Paul* (Grand Rapids, MI: Baker Academic, 2004). For a concise introduction to the issues in the debate, see Carson and Moo, *Introduction to the New Testament*, 375–85.

[19] Beginning with the work of E. P. Sanders, *Paul and Palestinian Judaism: A Comparison of Patterns of Religion* (Philadelphia: Fortress, 1977), and *Paul, the Law, and the Jewish People* (Philadelphia: Fortress, 1983), whose conclusions have been accepted, with some modification, by J. D. G. Dunn, "The New Perspective on Paul," *BJRL* 65 (1983): 95–122; and N. T. Wright, *What Saint Paul Really Said: Was Paul of Tarsus the Real Founder of Christianity?* (Grand Rapids, MI: Eerdmans, 1997).

[20] This second point finds particular emphasis and development in the work of Dunn and Wright.

[21] On the phrase "the works of the law" in Galatians, see further Moisés Silva, "Faith versus Works of the Law in Galatians," in Carson, O'Brien, and Seifrid, *The Paradoxes of Paul*, 217–48.

[22] Both this and the preceding proposition are controverted within New Testament scholarship. For a discussion and defense, see Thomas R. Schreiner, "Paul and Perfect Obedience to the Law: An Evaluation of the View of E. P. Sanders," *WTJ* 47 (1985): 245–78; and, more recently, Schreiner, *Galatians*, 204–5.

oneself to the law's "curse" (3:10a). But when Christ died on the cross, he "redeemed us from the curse of the law by becoming a curse for us" (3:13). He not only has delivered us from the law's curse but also has won for us the Abrahamic "blessing" that God promised to Gentiles (3:14). This "blessing" includes our justification.

To be "justified" (2:16) is to be declared righteous (3:11) solely because of the "righteousness" (2:21; 3:21) that Christ won for his people in his death and resurrection.[23] This righteousness is imputed to the sinner (3:6) and received through faith alone (2:16).[24] The righteousness by which we are justified is not achieved, merited, or otherwise secured by things we do in obedience to God's law, "because by works of the law no one will be justified" (2:16).

"Circumcision," while a matter of indifference in itself (5:6; 6:15), carries in Galatia the freight of the Judaizers' gospel-denying teachings (5:2–4). Whatever role that circumcision and other ordinances of the Mosaic law may play in marking out the identity of believers in Galatia, deeper questions relating to salvation are at stake. Paul's opponents are pressing law keeping on the Galatians—not merely as a means of covenant identification, but as the basis upon which the Galatians are to be declared righteous before God. Paul insists that there is only one way in which the sinner may be justified by God—through faith in the Son of God, crucified and raised from the dead. The obedience and death of Christ alone are our righteousness for justification. The gospel that Paul preaches and his opponents' teachings are mutually exclusive (2:16). There is no third way, neither is there room for compromise or rapprochement (1:6–9). It is to the defense and exposition of this gospel that Paul dedicates his energies in the epistle to the Galatians.

Structure and Outline

What form does Paul's defense and exposition of the biblical gospel assume in this letter? There are at least two complementary ways in which one may understand the structure of this letter. The first is that of a conventional Hellenistic letter.[25] Paul begins the letter with a salutation in standard form: identification of the author (Gal. 1:1–2a) and of the recipients (1:2b), and an opening greeting (1:3–5).[26] Paul closes the letter with concluding exhortations centering on circumcision and the cross (6:11–17), and a benediction (6:18). The body of the letter (1:6–6:10) comprises three main parts: narrative (1:6–2:15), argument (2:16–4:31), and exhortation (5:1–6:10). The broad movement from argument to exhortation finds parallel in several other New Testament letters.

---

[23] On the liability of understanding the verb "justified" in Gal. 2:16 primarily in terms of covenant membership, see Moo, *Galatians*, 161–62. Moo's survey of justification and righteousness in Galatians is a concise introduction to the discussion and issues at stake (ibid., 48–62).

[24] On the way in which Gen. 15:6, as Paul reads it in Romans 4, yields what has come to be known as the imputed righteousness of Christ, see D. A. Carson, "The Vindication of Imputation: On Fields of Discourse and Semantic Fields," in *Justification: What's at Stake in Current Debates*, ed. Mark Husbands and Daniel J. Treier (Downers Grove, IL: InterVarsity Press, 2004), 46–78.

[25] An outline followed, for example, by F. F. Bruce, *The Epistle to the Galatians: A Commentary on the Greek Text*, NIGTC (Grand Rapids, MI: Eerdmans, 1982); Ronald Y. K. Fung, *The Epistle to the Galatians*, NICNT (Grand Rapids, MI: Eerdmans, 1988); Schreiner, *Galatians*; and Moo, *Galatians*.

[26] Tellingly omitted after the salutation is a feature common in most of Paul's other letters—a section of thanksgiving. As Bruce rightly notes, "Paul was impelled by a sense of overmastering urgency to come straight to the point" (*Galatians*, 80).

In the last forty years, scholars have begun to consider the way in which the structure of Galatians reflects the conventions of Hellenistic rhetoric.[27] Hans Dieter Betz, for instance, argues for the following outline: prescript (1:1–5), *exordium* (1:6–11), *narratio* (1:12–2:14), *propositio* (2:15–21), *probatio* (3:1–4:31), *exhortatio* (5:1–6:10), and postscript (6:11–18).[28]

Not all scholars agree that Galatians proceeds along these lines, and even students of rhetoric disagree about what particular rhetorical model Galatians may reflect.[29] It is conceivable that Galatians is a blend of more than one rhetorical model.[30] It is also possible that the influence of ancient rhetoric on Galatians may have been, at most, indirect.[31]

It is best, then, to be wary of insisting on one particular outline to the letter to the exclusion of others. Galatians reflects clear epistolary structure and, likely, the influence of the rhetorical modes of persuasion to which formally educated persons such as Paul would have been exposed. We may proceed, then, with the following blended outline consisting of eight sections:

I. Opening Salutation (1:1–5)
II. Statement of the Issues (1:6–10)
III. Defense of Paul's Apostleship (1:11–2:14)
IV. Thesis (2:15–21)
V. Argument (3:1–4:11)
VI. Appeal and Illustration (4:12–31)
VII. Exhortation (5:1–6:10)
VIII. Closing Words (6:11–18)

Message and Theology

Opening Salutation (Gal. 1:1–5)

In the opening salutation of the letter, Paul identifies himself as the author and the Galatians as recipients (1:1–2). He then pronounces a blessing upon them (1:3–5). It is what Paul adds to these conventional elements of the salutation that signals the concerns of the letter to follow. First, Paul not only identifies himself as "an apostle" but also specifies the origin of his apostleship—"not from men nor through man, but through Jesus Christ and God the Father" (1:1). Paul "denies that [his] apostleship had a human source" and "that it had come to him through a human channel, by

[27] See the landmark work of H. D. Betz, *Galatians: A Commentary on Paul's Letter to the Galatians*, Hermeneia (Philadelphia: Fortress, 1979). See, further, Witherington, *Grace in Galatia*, and Longenecker, *Galatians*.

[28] As summarized by Bruce, *Epistle to the Galatians*, 58. The *exordium* in ancient rhetoric served to identify the leading issues that would occupy the remainder of the discourse. The *narratio* was a narrative recounting of the facts and circumstances pertinent to the point that the speaker was going to argue. The *propositio* was the thesis that the speaker intended to prove. The *probatio* was the proof of the thesis. The *exhortatio* drew out the implications of the proven thesis for the hearers' lives.

[29] Betz insists that Paul has followed the conventions of "forensic rhetoric." On this reading, Galatians is akin to a legal brief. Witherington has argued that Galatians follows the conventions of "deliberative rhetoric." On this reading, Galatians is less a formal legal argument than an effort "to convince the audience by various means to take a particular course of action in the near future, and it argues on the basis of what will be the possible, expedient, useful, and honorable course for them to follow" (*Grace in Galatia*, 27).

[30] Longenecker, *Galatians*, cix.

[31] "In Galatians . . . Paul seems to have availed himself almost unconsciously of the rhetorical forms at hand, fitting them into his inherited epistolary structures and filling them out with such Jewish theological motifs and exegetical methods as would be particularly significant in countering what the Judaizers were telling the converts" (ibid.).

human agency."[32] His apostleship proceeds directly and immediately from "Jesus Christ and God the Father." This assertion is one that Paul will demonstrate in the verses that follow (1:11–2:14). It serves as a direct refutation of the Judaizers, who have called Paul's apostleship into question on this very point.

Second, Paul details the saving work of Jesus Christ for his people. Christ "gave himself for our sins to deliver us from the present evil age, according to the will of our God and Father" (1:4). The Father has "raised him from the dead" (1:1). Why does Paul mention the death and resurrection of Christ at the outset of the letter? In verse 4, Paul stresses that it is the work of Christ that has rescued us "from the present evil age." The phrase "present evil age" denotes the condition of Adamic humanity under the dominion of sin and Satan.[33] Outside of Christ, people belong to an order that is defined and determined by sin, corruption, curse, and death. Only in Christ may one be rescued from that order and be brought into the "age to come" or the "new creation"—the order inaugurated in history by the death and resurrection of Christ, and characterized by the Spirit, blessing, life, and glory (see 6:14–15). There are, then, no resources in the law by which a sinner may be translated from "the present evil age" into "new creation." Paul thereby counters the Judaizers' insistence that one must obey the law of God to be justified, to secure the blessing held out by the law.

Paul, then, introduces the two great concerns of the letter in these opening verses: his apostleship and the gospel. Paul's apostleship comes directly from God. As an apostle of Christ, Paul bears Christ's authority in the church. Paul exercises that authority to uphold the gospel of grace and to unmask the "different gospel" on offer in Galatia (1:6). Law keeping can in no way justify the sinner. Only the death and resurrection of Christ can rescue sinners from their plight.

Statement of the Issues (Gal. 1:6–10)

In the next section (1:6–10), Paul proceeds to state the leading issue that will define the remainder of the letter—the fact that the Galatians "are so quickly deserting him who called [them] in the grace of Christ and are turning to a different gospel" (1:6). The Galatians earlier "received" the gospel that Paul preaches (1:9). Now, however, they appear to be turning from it.

Paul is insistent that there is only one true gospel, and that the "different gospel" is in fact a corruption of that one true gospel (1:6–7). He twice says that to preach "a gospel contrary to" the true gospel is to subject oneself to the curse of God ("let him be accursed," 1:8–9). The idea of curse has its background in the life of Israel under the old covenant (see Ex. 22:20; Num. 21:3; Deut. 7:26; Josh. 6:17).[34] To be "accursed" is to be set apart or devoted to destruction. In the context of Galatians,

[32] Ernest De Witt Burton, *A Critical and Exegetical Commentary on the Epistle to the Galatians*, ICC (Edinburgh: T&T Clark, 1921), 3.

[33] See Herman N. Ridderbos, *The Epistle of Paul to the Churches of Galatia*, NICNT (Grand Rapids, MI: Eerdmans, 1953), 43–44, and, further, Ridderbos, *Paul: An Outline of His Theology*, trans. John Richard de Witt (Grand Rapids, MI: Eerdmans, 1975), 91–93.

[34] See Burton, *Epistle to the Galatians*, 28; Dunn, *The Epistle to the Galatians*, BNTC (Peabody, MA: Hendrickson, 1993), 46.

it is to be subjected to "God's own curse," that is, the "judicial wrath of God."[35] The gospel that Paul preaches alone brings blessing (Gal. 3:8–9, 14). The "different gospel" carries with it only "curse."

In the last verse of this section, Paul pleads the sincerity of his motives. As a "servant of Christ," he seeks only to "please God," and not to "please man" (1:10). This assertion may well be in response to the Judaizers' claims that Paul was crafting his message—justification by faith apart from the works of the law—to court Gentiles.[36] Paul, however, once did please men ("still"), but he does so no longer ("now") (1:10). In the section that follows, Paul will defend his apostleship, in part by demonstrating that very point. God, in calling Paul to be his apostle, also changed Paul from a man-pleaser to a God-pleaser.

Defense of Paul's Apostleship (Gal. 1:11–2:14)

In Galatians 1:11–2:14, Paul defends his apostleship as having proceeded immediately and directly from God (cf. 1:1).[37] One reason why Paul is so adamant in establishing this point emerges in verses 11–12. Like his apostleship, Paul's gospel did not come to Paul "from any man"; nor was Paul "taught it" (1:12). It is not "man's gospel" (1:11). On the contrary, Paul "received [his gospel] through a revelation of Jesus Christ" (1:12). Paul not only received his apostleship and gospel at the same time, but his apostleship and gospel alike trace their origin to God, apart from any human cause or instrumentality.[38]

Paul vindicates this claim in five stages. In the first (1:13–14), he demonstrates that he did not receive the gospel in his life in Judaism. Not only was Paul a vehement persecutor of the church (1:13), but his zeal was oriented toward, he says, "the traditions of my fathers" (1:14), that is, the extra-biblical, authoritative teachings and practices of first-century Pharisaical Judaism (cf. Matt. 15:2–3, 6).[39]

In the second stage (Gal. 1:15–16a), Paul recounts his calling and conversion. It was God who both "was pleased to reveal his Son to [Paul]" and commissioned him to "preach [his Son] among the Gentiles" (1:16). The God who so acted in Paul's life had "set [him] apart before [he] was born" (lit. "from the womb of my mother," 1:15) and "called [him] by his grace." Paul's call and conversion were entirely the work of the sovereign grace of God.[40] Paul played no part in securing either his apostleship or his gospel.

In the third stage (1:16b–24), Paul recounts his early movements in the church

---

[35] Moisés Silva, "Galatians," in *New Bible Commentary: 21st Century Edition*, ed. G. J. Wenham, J. A. Motyer, D. A. Carson, and R. T. France (Downers Grove, IL: InterVarsity Press, 1994), 1209.

[36] Dunn, *Epistle to the Galatians*, 48–49.

[37] One measure of this section's importance is the fact that it constitutes "nearly one-fifth of the whole letter" (Bruce, *Epistle to the Galatians*, 87).

[38] Ibid., 88.

[39] Lightfoot, *Paul's Epistle to the Galatians*, 82; Silva, "Galatians," in Wenham et al., *New Bible Commentary*, 1210.

[40] Paul's words here echo Jer. 1:5 and Isa. 49:1, in which the calls of the prophet Jeremiah and of the servant are described, respectively. Paul is, at the very least, aligning his apostolic call with that of the Old Testament prophets. The gracious "call" of Gal. 1:15, furthermore, echoes Paul's words in 1:6 ("him who called [the Galatians] in the grace of Christ") and therefore must encompass the gracious, salvific call of God to Paul in the gospel (cf. Rom. 8:29–30). See Moisés Silva, "Galatians," in *Commentary on the New Testament Use of the Old Testament*, ed. G. K. Beale and D. A. Carson (Grand Rapids, MI: Baker Academic, 2007), 786–87.

after his call and conversion. He stresses that he "did not immediately consult with anyone" (lit. "with flesh and blood," 1:16b). It was only after "three years" that he "went up to Jerusalem" (1:18). Even then, the only contact with the apostles that he had was with Peter and James (1:18–19), and that for a short window of time (1:18). Paul had spent so little time in Judea that Christians, although they had heard reports about him, could not have recognized him (1:22–24). In short, "during the first fourteen (possibly seventeen) years of his ministry, when the character of his preaching was established, [Paul] did not have the opportunity to be trained by a human source."[41]

In the fourth and fifth stages, Paul takes up two specific events in which he did have contact with the Jerusalem apostles (2:1–10) and with Peter specifically (2:11–14). In the Jerusalem meeting that Paul describes in Galatians 2:1–10, he further tells of his ongoing relationship with the Jerusalem apostles. He again emphasizes his independence from the other apostles. He went to Jerusalem, after all, "because of a revelation," that is, from God (2:2). Even when he was there, he says, these apostles "added nothing to me" (2:6).

Paul's primary concern in this portion of his argument, however, is to show that he and the Jerusalem apostles were united in message and mission. Once he presented his message to the other apostles (2:2), they confirmed Paul by extending to him "the right hand of fellowship" (2:9). Furthermore, when "false brothers" attempted to circumcise Paul's Gentile co-laborer Titus, neither Paul nor the other apostles permitted them to do so (2:3–5). The apostles' united purpose was that "the truth of the gospel might be preserved for you [i.e., Gentile Christians]" (2:5b).

The only difference that surfaces in this meeting concerns the destination to which the ministry of each is directed. Paul and Barnabas will continue to minister to the "Gentiles"; James, Peter, and John, to the "circumcised" (Gal. 2:9). Each acknowledges the other to be a true apostle and a preacher of the one true gospel (2:7–8). Without yielding what he has argued about the divine origin of his apostleship and call, Paul has expressed the mutual confidence and esteem in which he and his fellow apostles held one another as fellow servants of Christ.

Paul's account of his confrontation with Peter in Antioch (Gal. 2:11–14) serves at least two purposes. First, it shows that the confidence and unity expressed in Jerusalem (2:1–10) did not trump the gospel. When a fellow apostle bore uncertain witness to the gospel, Paul did not shrink from admonishing him publicly. Paul's ultimate allegiance was not to other people, even the apostles in Jerusalem, but to the God who called and commissioned him to preach the gospel.[42]

Second, the Antioch incident brought to the surface the very issues that would later agitate the church in Galatia. It is these issues that occasion the thesis statement (2:15–21) that follows. What exactly happened in Antioch? Why did Paul rebuke Peter? How did Paul see Peter's actions as compromising the gospel (2:14)?

[41] Silva, "Galatians," in Wenham et al., *New Bible Commentary*, 1211.
[42] Lightfoot, *Paul's Epistle to the Galatians*, 111.

The triggering event in Antioch was the arrival of "certain men . . . from James" (2:12). Before their arrival in Antioch, Peter had enjoyed table fellowship with Gentile Christians; after their arrival, "he drew back and separated himself" (2:12). The reason that Peter withdrew was that he "fear[ed] the men of the circumcision" (2:12, my trans.).[43] Peter likely feared negative repercussions from Jewish persons in Jerusalem once reports of his eating with Gentiles surfaced there.

Why does Paul interpret Peter's withdrawal as "not in step with the truth of the gospel" (Gal. 2:14)? Paul accuses Peter of hypocrisy (2:13). That is to say, Peter's actions did not align with Peter's gospel principles. His actions suggested that Gentiles were not genuine Christians and that, in order to be regarded as true, justified Christians, they had to observe the Mosaic law. In the context of a church where the Judaizers' teachings were being industriously spread, Peter's withdrawal was as much to say that one must perform the works of the law in order to be justified.[44] Fundamentally at issue was not merely the unity of the church.[45] At issue was the integrity of the gospel of grace—that a person, whether Jew or Gentile, is justified by faith alone apart from works of the law.[46]

Thesis (Gal. 2:15–21)

The Antioch incident provides a natural segue to the situation in Galatia.[47] Paul is now prepared to advance the thesis that much of the remainder of the epistle will argue. He first declares that a person is justified, or declared righteous, through faith in Christ and not because of deeds that one does in obedience to the law (2:15–16). This principle holds true for all people, whether Jew or Gentile ("no one," 2:16).[48]

Second, Paul stresses that justification by faith alone in no way promotes sin (2:17–18). While it is true that Christ justifies the sinner, Christ is in no way the "servant" or promoter "of sin" (2:17).[49] On the contrary, to abandon justification by faith alone and to return to the law for justification necessarily entails a "renewed surrender to" sin.[50]

[43] *Pace* ESV, "the circumcision party." The ESV's translation is possible, but the word "party" suggests a degree of organization and theological self-consciousness that may not have been true of this group of people. It is preferable to translate the phrase as "Jews," as does Longenecker, *Galatians*, 74. Paul does not explicitly identify this group with the "certain men . . . from James." Neither does Paul specify the relationship that the "certain men" had with James, although the previous section (2:1–10) safely eliminates any tacit or express approval on the part of James for individuals who are pressing law-observance for justification.

[44] The context afforded by the previously reported controversy in Jerusalem (2:1–10, esp. 2:1–5) and the present controversy in Galatia supports this understanding of Paul's perception of Peter's actions.

[45] Burton, *Epistle to the Galatians*, 112–13. To be sure, Peter's action did have significant ecclesiological repercussions. It established, at the very least, a two-tiered membership within the church along the lines of Jew and Gentile.

[46] J. Gresham Machen, *Notes on Galatians: Notes on Biblical Exposition and Other Aids to the Interpretation of the Epistle to the Galatians*, ed. John H. Skilton (1972; repr., Birmingham, AL: Solid Ground Christian Books, 2002), 142–44.

[47] Scholars debate whether Paul uttered these words in Antioch (2:11–14) or they were crafted by Paul after the fact. It is impossible to be certain, but the context of this epistle requires that we interpret them not only in light of what follows (3:1–4:11), but also in light of what precedes (2:11–14).

[48] The phrase translated "faith in Jesus Christ" (Gk. πίστεως Χριστοῦ Ἰησοῦ) has received considerable attention in recent years. Some commentators have argued that the phrase should be translated "the faithfulness of Jesus Christ." This is a syntactically possible translation, but the traditional translation ("faith in Jesus Christ") is preferable (see Moo, *Galatians*, 38–48, and Silva, "Faith Versus Works of the Law in Galatians"). Paul's leading concern in this passage, as well as in the argument that follows, is the receptive faith of the believer in distinction from any works that he might do in obedience to the law's commands.

[49] Ridderbos, *Epistle of Paul to the Churches of Galatia*, 101. On the complexities of this and the following verse, see Schreiner, *Galatians*, 167–70.

[50] Ridderbos, *Epistle of Paul to the Churches of Galatia*, 103, summarizing Gal. 2:18.

Third, Paul shows the inseparability of justification and holy living. Each Christian is united with Jesus Christ, sharing in both his sacrificial death ("crucified with Christ," 2:20) and his resurrection life ("Christ who lives in me," 2:20). By virtue of Christ's death, Paul has "through the law . . . died to the law" (2:19). That is to say, Christ has satisfied all that the law demanded of Paul for justification. Paul, therefore, now "live[s] to God" (2:19) as a brand-new person.[51] This life is lived by the power of Jesus's resurrection and through "faith in the Son of God" (2:20). The prevailing motive to living this new life is Christ's self-giving love for Paul at the cross (2:20). In summary, Paul concludes, to render justification in any other way than through faith alone in Christ alone is to "nullify the grace of God" (2:21).

Argument (Gal. 3:1–4:11)

Paul next argues this thesis. Paul's argument proceeds in threefold fashion. There is an argument from the Galatians' experience of the Spirit (3:1–5), from the testimony of the Old Testament Scripture (3:6–14), and from the covenants that God made with his people (3:15–4:11).

Paul first appeals to the Galatians' experiences of the Holy Spirit when Paul initially preached Christ to them (3:1). The powerful working of the Holy Spirit accompanied their believing reception of the gospel (3:2). Why then, Paul reasons, would one seek to complete in the "flesh" a work "begun by the Spirit" (3:3)? In other words, why would the Galatians revert to the "works of the law," that is, the resources of the "present evil age" (1:4), if they have already entered into all that Christ has won for them and shares with them by the Spirit?[52]

Paul then appeals to the express testimony of the Old Testament in support of his gospel (3:6–14). His justifying gospel is one and the same with that preached to Abraham in Genesis 12 (Gal. 3:8). Through faith in that gospel, people are both "blessed along with Abraham, the man of faith" and, through faith, true "sons of Abraham" (3:7, 9). The law, however, testifies that "all who rely on works of the law are under a curse" (Gal. 3:10; cf. Deut. 27:26). The law cannot supply the righteousness that the sinner needs for justification (Gal. 3:11; cf. Hab. 2:4). The only way that one may pass from "curse" to "blessing" is through faith in Christ, who bore the curse of God on the cross (Gal. 3:13) in order to secure "the blessing of Abraham," that is, "the promised Spirit through faith," for "Gentiles" (3:14).[53]

Finally, Paul appeals to the succession of covenants that God has made with his people (3:15–4:11). He denominates the Abrahamic covenant one of "promise"; the Mosaic covenant, "law"; and the new covenant, "faith." Paul first insists that the Mosaic covenant in no way modified or annulled the promise that God made to Abraham (3:15–18). That promise, furthermore, has always had reference to

[51] "It is no longer I who live" (2:20); "and the life I now live in the flesh I live by faith in the Son of God" (2:20).

[52] Ridderbos, *Epistle of Paul to the Churches of Galatia*, 114; Silva, "Galatians," in Wenham et al., *New Bible Commentary*, 1213. Silva notes the way in which "flesh" and "Spirit," eschatologically understood, resurface throughout the letter in 4:23, 29; 5:13, 16–26; 6:8, 12.

[53] On the particular ways in which Paul cites and interprets the Old Testament in Gal. 3:10–14, see Silva, "Galatians," in Beale and Carson, *Commentary on the New Testament Use of the Old Testament*, 795–804.

Christ, the "offspring" of Abraham (3:16). In Christ, furthermore, that promise is the concern and possession of all believers (3:29).

Paul then asks why God gave the law (3:19). The Mosaic covenant was never intended to be a permanent administration. It had a definite beginning (3:17, 19) and a definite end (3:19). Furthermore, the Mosaic covenant "was added because of transgressions" (3:19). Paul likely means that the purpose of the law was to identify and to "define" sin as sin, that is, as "transgression in its proper and terrible character."[54] God never gave the law so that people could merit blessing by obedience to its demands. The Judaizers have fundamentally misunderstood the nature and purpose of the Mosaic law.

Paul proceeds to insist that the Mosaic and Abrahamic covenants were fully complementary (3:21). God intended the Mosaic covenant to be a custodian or "guardian" of God's people until Christ should come (3:25).[55] The law was never designed to supply "righteousness" or "life" (3:21), but was given to prepare God's people for the promised offspring of Abraham, in whom, by faith, they had and have righteousness and life.

In Galatians 3:21–4:7, Paul develops a relative contrast between the condition of God's people "until Christ came" and after "faith has come" (3:24–25), that is, under the Mosaic and new covenants, respectively. From the vantage point of the finished work of Christ, life under the law was a life in bondage, under the strictures and regimen appropriate to a child, even a child who is an heir (3:23, 25; 4:1–3). But now that Christ has come (4:4–5), God's people have fully entered, in Christ, into all that our sonship and inheritance entails (4:6). Why, then, Paul asks, would the Galatians want to revert to an immature state that, in light of the finished work of Christ, is one of slavery (4:9)?[56]

Appeal and Illustration (Gal. 4:12–31)

Commentators have struggled to account for the place of Galatians 4:12–31 in Paul's letter. Are they a continuation of Paul's argument, the formal beginning of his exhortation, or something else?[57] Likely, they serve as something of a bridge between Paul's now concluded argument and the body of exhortations with which he will conclude the epistle. In 4:12–20, Paul makes a personal appeal to the Galatians. Speaking

[54] Schreiner, *Galatians*, 240; Ridderbos, *Epistle of Paul to the Churches of Galatia*, 138.

[55] On the background to this term (Gk. παιδαγωγός), see Longenecker, *Galatians*, 146–48. The "custodian" in antiquity was a household slave who ensured that a young person heeded the directives of his or her father. Paul is emphasizing the way in which the law served to discipline and oversee Israel until the time of her maturity, that is, the time when Christ would come.

[56] Paul in this section says that the Galatians were "enslaved" to the "elementary principles of the world" (4:3; cf. 4:9). This reality was true not only of the Jewish but also of the Gentile Christians in Galatians (so 4:9). The meaning of the phrase translated "elementary principles" (στοιχεῖα) is debated (see Moo, *Galatians*, 260–63). The reference to bondage in 4:3 and to Jewish calendrical observance in 4:10 suggests that Paul understands the στοιχεῖα in terms of the Mosaic law. Because the Gentiles have been under the στοιχεῖα, however, the στοιχεῖα must encompass more than the Mosaic law. It must embrace the religions out of which the Gentile Galatians were converted (4:8–9a). Paul is likely saying here that the law, "while quite different in basic ways from the pagan religions under which the Galatians once lived, . . . like those religions, belongs to a stage of religious experience that has been brought to an end with the coming of Christ" (Moo, *Galatians*, 263; compare the concurring conclusion of John Eadie, *A Commentary on the Greek Text of the Epistle of Paul to the Galatians* [Edinburgh: T&T Clark, 1869], 311–13).

[57] See the survey of opinion at Frank J. Matera, "The Culmination of Paul's Argument to the Galatians: Gal. 5:1–6:17," *JSNT* 32 (1988): 79–91, as cited at Schreiner, *Galatians*, 283n8.

to them parentally (4:19), he reminds them of their concern for him when he first preached the gospel to them (4:13). They showed concern for Paul in his bodily weakness (4:13–14) and received the blessing of the Holy Spirit attending Paul's ministry of the gospel among them (4:15).[58] In contrast, the Judaizers, who cannot bring such gospel blessing to the Galatians, do not have good intentions toward them (4:17). Paul's abiding desire, however, is that "Christ [be] formed" in the Galatians (4:19).

Paul follows this personal appeal with an illustration drawn from Genesis 21—the account of Hagar and Sarah (Gal. 4:21–31). What is unusual about this passage is Paul's statement that the two sons of Sarah and Hagar "may be interpreted allegorically" (4:24). This description, unique in Paul's letters, suggests that Paul is distinguishing his reading of this text from his other readings of Old Testament passages (cf. 3:6–14). The Greek term rendered "allegorical" by the ESV is better translated "figurative," since the term does "not have the technical sense often associated with the word in later centuries."[59] What Paul intends by this word is best gleaned from observing the way in which he here handles the text of Genesis.

Paul relates Hagar and Sarah to "two covenants" (4:24), that is, the Mosaic covenant and the new covenant, respectively. To Hagar correspond "slavery," "flesh," and the "present Jerusalem"; to Sarah correspond "freedom," "Spirit," "the Jerusalem above," and inheritance (4:23, 25–26, 29–30). New covenant believers are "not children of the slave but of the free woman" (4:31; cf. 4:1–7). With the assistance of Isaiah 54:1, which Paul quotes at Galatians 4:27, and in light of Christ's finished work, Paul employs the text of the historical narrative of Genesis 21 in order to reinforce the redemptive-historical argumentation of Galatians 3:1–4:7 and to apply it to the circumstances in Galatia.[60]

Exhortation (Gal. 5:1–6:10)

Paul formally takes up the task of exhortation in Galatians 5:1–6:10. In 5:1–15, he cautions against the misuse of the law and urges its proper use. Paul warns the Galatians not to submit themselves to the law for justification (5:1–4). To do so is to take on "a yoke of slavery" (5:1). But the "righteousness" bestowed in justification necessarily carries with it a "hope" that we eagerly and certainly anticipate.[61] Between now and the time we enter into "future blessedness and glorification," our lives are characterized by the "Spirit" and "faith," that is, "faith working through love" (5:5–6).[62] The life of "love" is a life of "freedom" and "serv[ing] one another" (5:13). Christian freedom is in no way "an opportunity for the flesh" (5:13).

Believers, then, are no longer to live according to the "flesh," that is, the old

[58] Schreiner, *Galatians*, 287.
[59] Moo, *Galatians*, 295.
[60] See Silva, "Galatians," in Wenham et al., *New Bible Commentary*, 1217; Moo, *Galatians*, 295–96; Matthew S. Harmon, "Allegory, Typology, or Something Else? Revisiting Galatians 4:21–5:1," in *Studies in the Pauline Epistles: Essays in Honor of Douglas J. Moo*, ed. Matthew S. Harmon and Jay E. Smith (Grand Rapids, MI: Zondervan, 2014), 144–58. It is important to note, with Moo, that even as Paul "gives to the narrative before him in Genesis . . . an additional or added meaning in light of [his] hermeneutical axioms," he does so "without denying its intended historical sense" (ibid., 296).
[61] Geerhardus Vos, *The Pauline Eschatology* (1930; repr., Phillipsburg, NJ: P&R, 1994), 30.
[62] Eadie, *Galatians*, 387.

Adamic, sinful patterns of thinking, choosing, and behaving. We are to live according to the "Spirit." This life is characterized by faith and love. In practical terms, love is the fulfillment of the law (5:14), that is, the "law of Christ" (6:2). The law of Christ is the law of God as Christ has put that law into the hands of believers. It is the law having undergone redemptive-historical transformation in light of the finished work of Jesus Christ.[63] Specifically, that law consists of the moral core of the Mosaic law, or the Decalogue (5:14). Life in the Spirit is marked by keeping the demands of the moral law, not for justification but as the necessary fruit and evidence of justifying faith.

In Galatians 5:16–26, Paul commands believers to "walk by the Spirit" and "keep in step with the Spirit" (5:16, 25). Negatively, this is a life that does not "gratify the desires of the flesh" (5:16). In this context, as throughout Paul's correspondence, "flesh" and "Spirit" denote the two ages—the "present evil age" from which believers have been rescued, and the "new creation" into which believers have been placed by the work of Christ. The "desires" and "works" of the flesh and the "desires" and "fruit" of the Spirit stand in utter antithesis (5:17, 19, 22). The old Adamic ways ("flesh") remain a constant threat to believers, who must resolutely refrain from them (5:19–21).

Positively, this is a life in which believers, who are "led by the Spirit" (5:18), want to do the things that are pleasing to the Spirit (cf. 5:17). Since we now "live by the Spirit," we must also "keep in step with the Spirit" (5:25). Furthermore, those "who belong to Christ Jesus have crucified the flesh with its passions and desires" (5:24). This is not a command but a statement of fact; united to Jesus Christ in his death, we have a brand-new relationship with sin. While sin remains in us (5:17), sin no longer reigns over us (5:24).[64] This fact carries with it the obligation to think, purpose, and behave conformably to the mind of the Spirit.

Paul, however, is no "mere idealis[t]" and proceeds to "address the very real possibility of sin" in 6:1–5.[65] He reminds believers that they are "spiritual," that is, indwelt and governed by the Holy Spirit (6:1; cf. 5:18). This fact means that they should have a genuine concern for the spiritual welfare of fellow believers (6:2; cf. 5:26). It also means that they should take care not to "boast" in themselves, as the Judaizers do (6:4; cf. 6:14).

The concern for others that characterizes the "spiritual" new covenant community extends to providing for ministers (6:6) and to "do[ing] good" not only to the church ("the household of faith") but also to "everyone" (6:10). This other-centered concern is the responsibility of each individual Christian. Paul warns believers that those who live according to the "flesh" will "reap corruption" as its eternal consequence (6:8). We should aspire, rather, to live according to the "Spirit" by "do[ing] good"

[63] See Ridderbos, *Epistle of Paul to the Churches of Galatia*, 200–201, 213; *Paul*, 278–88.

[64] In the context of this passage, Paul's statement in Gal. 5:18 that believers are not "under the law" does not mean that believers have no obligation to the law of God. It refers, rather, to "the condition of impotence and condemnation to which man is subjected outside faith and the life-giving power of the Spirit" (Ridderbos, *Paul*, 283; cf. Ridderbos, *Epistle of Paul to the Churches of Galatia*, 204).

[65] Silva, "Galatians," in Wenham et al., *New Bible Commentary*, 1219.

(6:10) and so "reap eternal life" (6:8). Once again, Paul insists that good works are not optional in the Christian life. While they in no way justify anyone, good works are the way that God has appointed for justified persons to enter into "eternal life."

Closing Words (Gal. 6:11–18)

In the final section of the letter, Paul underscores two realities that have dominated this epistle: "circumcision" (6:12–13, 15) and the "cross" (6:12, 14). He again associates circumcision with the "flesh" (6:12; cf. 6:13), and he stresses that the Judaizers do not keep the law they press on the Galatians for their justification (6:13). Circumcision is in itself a matter of indifference (6:15). It utterly lacks the significance that Paul's opponents have placed upon it.

It is in the cross alone that one may truly "boast," that is, "in the cross of our Lord Jesus Christ" (6:14). By the cross, we have died to the "world," that is, the "present evil age" (6:14; cf. 1:4). In Christ, we have been brought into the "new creation" and, by the Spirit, enjoy all the resources of the age to come (6:15). Such persons ("all who walk by this rule") are "the Israel of God" and "brothers." They therefore may be assured of the "peace," "mercy," and "grace" that come alone from the Father and the Son (6:16, 18).[66]

Galatians is one of Paul's most passionate and exhaustively reasoned defenses of the gospel. Against opponents who challenge his apostolic credentials and the content of his gospel, Paul mounts a twofold response. He defends his apostleship as coming directly and immediately from God. He further defends his gospel as having proceeded from God and not from man. Paul, furthermore, mounts a counteroffensive against the Judaizers. They do not understand justification. The imputed righteousness of Christ, received by faith alone, alone justifies a sinner. Neither do they understand the law that they promote for justification. God never gave the Mosaic law so that people could be justified by it. It cannot provide the sinner what it demands. God gave the Mosaic law, rather, to prepare his people for Christ, who has now come. Justified people gladly and necessarily take up God's law, not for justification but in grateful response to the Savior who has already justified them.

Paul exerts himself in this letter because, apart from Christ, no person can see righteousness and life. He deeply loves the Galatians and wants them to return to their first love. We may be grateful for this labor of Paul's love for the church. In Galatians, the beauty, glory, and sufficiency of Christ as Savior and Lord are on full display. May this reality fill the horizon of our lives no less than it did the life of the apostle Paul.

---

[66] The "Israel of God" must refer to the church, inclusive of Jews and Gentiles. Were this phrase to refer to unbelieving Israel, it would contradict Paul's argument throughout this letter that these blessings are enjoyed only in Christ and through faith. See, further, Schreiner, *Galatians*, 381–83. The word translated "and" (ESV) is better rendered epexegetically ("even," NIV) according to Lightfoot, *Paul's Epistle to the Galatians*, 225.

Select Bibliography

Betz, Hans Dieter. *Galatians: A Commentary on Paul's Letter to the Churches in Galatia.* Hermeneia. Philadelphia: Fortress, 1979.

Brown, John. *An Exposition of the Epistle of Paul the Apostle to the Galatians.* 1853. Repr., Evansville, IN: Sovereign Grace, 1957.

Bruce, F. F. *The Epistle to the Galatians: A Commentary on the Greek Text.* NIGTC. Grand Rapids, MI: Eerdmans, 1982.

Burton, Ernest De Witt. *A Critical and Exegetical Commentary on the Epistle to the Galatians.* ICC. Edinburgh: T&T Clark, 1921.

Dunn, James D. G. *The Theology of Paul's Letter to the Galatians.* Cambridge: Cambridge University Press, 1993.

Elliott, Mark W., Scott J. Hafemann, N. T. Wright, and John Frederick, eds. *Galatians and Christian Theology: Justification, the Gospel, and Ethics in Paul's Letter.* Grand Rapids, MI: Baker Academic, 2014.

Gaffin, Richard B., Jr. *By Faith, Not by Sight: Paul and the Order of Salvation.* 2nd ed. Phillipsburg, NJ: P&R, 2013.

George, Timothy. *Galatians.* NAC 30. Nashville: Broadman & Holman, 1994.

Hays, Richard B. "The Letter to the Galatians: Introduction, Commentary, and Reflections." In *The New Interpreter's Bible*, edited by Leander E. Keck et al., 181–348. Nashville: Abingdon, 2000.

Lightfoot, J. B. *St. Paul's Epistle to the Galatians: A Revised Text with Introduction, Notes, and Dissertations.* 1881. Repr., Peabody, MA: Hendrickson, 1995.

Longenecker, Richard N. *Galatians.* WBC 41. Dallas: Word, 1990.

Machen, J. Gresham. *Notes on Galatians: Notes on Biblical Exposition and Other Aids to the Interpretation of the Epistle to the Galatians.* Edited by John H. Skilton. 1972. Repr., Birmingham, AL: Solid Ground Christian Books, 2002.

Martyn, J. Louis. *Galatians.* AB 33A. New York: Doubleday, 1997.

Moo, Douglas J. *Galatians.* BECNT. Grand Rapids, MI: Baker Academic, 2013.

Morris, Leon. *Galatians: Paul's Charter of Christian Freedom.* Downers Grove, IL: InterVarsity Press, 1996.

Nanos, Mark D., ed. *The Galatians Debate: Contemporary Issues in Rhetorical and Historical Interpretation.* Peabody, MA: Hendrickson, 2002.

Ridderbos, Herman N. *The Epistle of Paul to the Churches in Galatia.* Translated by Henry Zylstra. NICNT. Grand Rapids, MI: Eerdmans, 1953.

———. *Paul: An Outline of His Theology.* Translated by John Richard de Witt. Grand Rapids, MI: Eerdmans, 1975.

Schreiner, Thomas R. *Galatians.* ZECNT. Grand Rapids, MI: Zondervan, 2010.

Silva, Moisés. "Galatians." In *New Bible Commentary: 21st Century Edition*, edited by G. J. Wenham, J. A. Motyer, D. A. Carson, and R. T. France, 1206–21. Downers Grove, IL: InterVarsity Press, 1994.

———. *Interpreting Galatians: Explorations in Exegetical Method.* 2nd ed. Grand Rapids, MI: Baker Academic, 2001.

Stott, John R. W. *The Message of Galatians.* BST. Downers Grove, IL: InterVarsity Press, 1968.

Westerholm, Stephen. *Perspectives Old and New on Paul: The "Lutheran" Paul and His Critics.* Grand Rapids, MI: Eerdmans, 2004.

Witherington, Ben, III. *Grace in Galatia: A Commentary on Paul's Letter to the Galatians.* Grand Rapids, MI: Eerdmans, 1998.

9

Ephesians

Guy Prentiss Waters

> [Paul] is said indeed to have entrusted [the Ephesians], as being persons already well-instructed, with his profoundest conceptions; and the Epistle itself is full of sublime thoughts and doctrines.
>
> *John Chrysostom, "The Argument"*[1]

Introduction

Paul's letter to the Ephesians is a remarkable accomplishment. More than any other epistle that he wrote, Ephesians draws together in short compass many of the leading themes of the apostle's teaching. At the heart of the letter's message is the work of the triune God to save his people. At more than one point in Ephesians, Paul invokes the three persons of the Godhead in quick succession (1:3; 2:18, 20; 3:14–17, 20–21; 4:4–6). Paul also dwells at greater length upon the saving works that are particular to each person of the Trinity.[2]

Since the centerpiece of the divine purpose is the exaltation of Jesus Christ at "the fullness of time, to unite all things in him, things in heaven and things on earth" (1:10), it is no surprise that the saving work of Jesus Christ dominates Paul's message in this letter. Jesus took on our flesh in time (4:9).[3] In love for his people, he shed his blood on the cross to atone for their sins (1:7; 5:2, 25) and to reconcile them to God (2:13). He rose from the dead that we might share in his resurrection life, the life of

[1] In *Homilies on Ephesians* (*NPNF*[1] 13:49).
[2] See, for example, the way in which Paul reflects on the work of the Father (1:4–6), of the Son (1:7–12), and of the Spirit (1:13–14) (Harold E. Hoehner, *Ephesians: An Exegetical Commentary* [Grand Rapids, MI: Baker Academic, 2002], 153–60).
[3] Taking the "descent" of this verse to refer to the incarnation, as does Peter T. O'Brien, *The Letter to the Ephesians*, PNTC (Grand Rapids, MI: Eerdmans, 1999), 295. For a fuller survey of the interpretative options, see W. Hall Harris II, *The Descent of Christ: Ephesians 4:7–11 and Traditional Hebrew Imagery*, AGJU 32 (Leiden: Brill, 1996).

the age to come (2:4–10). He is seated in glory over "all things" (1:22; cf. 1:19–23). Having ascended on high, he labors in glory even now to build his church (4:7–16) until he presents the church to himself in mature perfection (5:25–27).

Paul in Ephesians sets forth the Christian life in its personal, corporate, and cosmic dimensions. He reminds believers of who they used to be apart from Jesus Christ (2:1–3; 4:17–19). He helps us to understand that we have been brought from death to life (2:5)—nothing less than a work of new creation whose ultimate outcome is our moral conformity to the glorious image of Jesus Christ (4:24). United with Jesus Christ, we share in all that he has won for us as our Savior (1:3–4, 7, 11; 2:4–6). The Holy Spirit is the bond of our union with Christ and powerfully preserves us in fellowship with the Savior (3:16–17). In view of these resources, Paul calls us to put off the "old self," the remains of who we once were in Adam, and to put on the "new self," the kind of person that each believer is becoming in Jesus Christ (4:22, 24). This dynamic requires a life of observing the law of God (6:1–3; cf. 4:25–32) that extends to the motions of our hearts (5:3), our speech (4:29), and our behaviors (4:28; 5:18). It is a life lived in relation to other people—fellow believers (4:32), spouses (5:22–33), parents and children (6:1–3), employers and employees (6:5–9). It is also a life lived in conscious struggle with unseen and hostile "cosmic powers" (6:12).[4]

All the major lines of Paul's teaching about the accomplishment and application of redemption in Jesus Christ, therefore, coalesce in Ephesians. It is, in this respect, distinctive among Paul's letters. But Ephesians is distinctive in another respect. Compared with Paul's other letters, Ephesians has very few details about the church in Ephesus and its circumstances. It lacks the list of personal greetings that concludes many of Paul's other letters. There is no overwhelming evidence of a presenting crisis in the church that has occasioned this epistle.

The letter's magisterial scope and generality are closely related. The church in Ephesus, Luke tells us, was one that Paul had served for three years (Acts 20:31). During those three years, Paul had devoted hours of public instruction to the church (see Acts 19:9–10).[5] The congregation at Ephesus, then, was one of the best taught bodies that Paul had served. This background helps us to understand what this letter is. It is a summary or digest of that gospel instruction.

It would be a mistake, however, to characterize this epistle as lacking any particular reference to the circumstances of the church at Ephesus.[6] In this letter, Paul devotes considerable attention to the "power[s]" that Christ subjugated in his death and resurrection (Eph. 1:19–23).[7] Paul, furthermore, explicitly places the church at

[4] On the "powers" in Ephesians, see especially Clinton E. Arnold, *Power and Magic: The Concept of Power in Ephesians in Light of Its Historical Setting* (Cambridge: Cambridge University Press, 1989); and Arnold, *Powers of Darkness: Principalities and Powers in Paul's Letters* (Downers Grove, IL: IVP Academic, 1992).

[5] The Western text of Acts indicates that Paul taught "from the fifth hour until the tenth" hour of the day. If this variant reflects an accurate memory of Paul's labors in Ephesus, then his two-year tenure at the Tyrannus Hall conceivably yielded thousands of hours of public teaching.

[6] *Pace* John Eadie, who concludes that "the epistle before us may therefore be regarded as prophylactic more than corrective in its nature. What the immediate occasion was, we know not" (*A Commentary on the Greek Text of the Epistle of Paul to the Ephesians* [Edinburgh: T&T Clark, 1891], li).

[7] A feature of this letter noted by recent commentators, such as Clinton E. Arnold, *Ephesians*, ZECNT (Grand Rapids, MI: Zondervan, 2010), 41–46; Frank Thielman, *Ephesians*, BECNT (Grand Rapids, MI: Baker Academic, 2010); O'Brien, *Letter to the Ephesians*, 61–62.

the heart of the letter's message.[8] One scholar has gone so far as to characterize the church as "the primary motif of the letter."[9] Paul likely emphasized these two areas for a reason. The apostle addressed these two areas to help the church in Ephesus meet certain challenges in precisely these two areas.

Paul's main concern in Ephesians, then, is to reiterate and to reinforce the gospel instruction that this church had enjoyed under his ministry to them. He accents certain dimensions of that instruction for the pastoral upbuilding of the church. These two areas of emphasis, we will see, resonate powerfully in the modern world. The letter to the Ephesians, then, helps the contemporary church not only to grasp better the "gospel of [our] salvation" (1:13), but also to bring that gospel to bear on matters that jeopardize the church's life and witness.

Background Issues

Authorship

The epistle to the Ephesians claims to have been written by "Paul, an apostle of Christ Jesus" (1:1). For nearly eighteen centuries, no reader of this letter seriously questioned that Paul was its author.[10] In the last two centuries, however, the tide of historical critical scholarship has shifted in favor of the letter's pseudonymity.[11] That is to say, many scholars believe that the author of Ephesians is not Paul, but nevertheless represented himself to his readership as Paul. Such scholarship has often objected to Pauline authorship of Ephesians for three general reasons.[12] First, some scholars claim that the vocabulary, syntax, and style of Ephesians are sufficiently different from Paul's undisputed letters to warrant the conclusion that Paul did not author the letter.[13] Second, scholars point to the many verbal, structural, and conceptual similarities between Ephesians and Colossians.[14] The similarities not only between these two epistles but also between Ephesians and the undisputed letters of Paul have aroused suspicions that Ephesians is a post-Pauline compendium of Pauline phrases and ideas.[15] Third, some scholars perceive the themes and motifs of Ephesians to be sufficiently distinct from those of the undisputed Pauline letters as to preclude Pauline authorship.[16]

[8] See the thematic surveys of the church in Ephesians in O'Brien, *Letter to the Ephesians*, 25–29; and Hoehner, *Ephesians*, 111–12.

[9] H. Chadwick, "Die Absicht des Epheserbriefes," *ZNW* 51 (1960): 146, cited by O'Brien, *Letter to the Ephesians*, 25.

[10] A point sometimes acknowledged by scholars who question its Pauline authorship, such as C. Leslie Mitton, *Ephesians*, NCB (London: Oliphants, 1976), 3. For acknowledgment of the reception of this letter in the early church as Pauline, see T. K. Abbott, *A Critical and Exegetical Commentary on the Epistles to the Ephesians and to the Colossians*, ICC (Edinburgh: T&T Clark, 1897), xiii; Werner Georg Kümmel, *Introduction to the New Testament*, rev. ed., trans. Howard Clark Kee (Nashville: Abingdon, 1975), 357; and Stephen E. Fowl, *Ephesians: A Commentary*, NTL (Louisville: Westminster John Knox, 2012), 9nn6, 18.

[11] Kümmel estimated over forty years ago that the number of those defending the letter's authenticity was "equally high" as that of those questioning it (*Introduction to the New Testament*, 357). More recently, Raymond E. Brown estimated that "about 80 percent of critical scholarship holds that Paul did not write Eph[esians]" (*An Introduction to the New Testament*, ABRL [New York: Doubleday, 1997], 620). Hoehner has challenged Brown's assessment on statistical grounds (*Ephesians*, 19).

[12] For recent cases against full Pauline authorship of Ephesians, see Ernest Best, *A Critical and Exegetical Commentary on Ephesians* (Edinburgh: T&T Clark, 1998), 6–36; and John Muddiman, *The Epistle to the Ephesians*, BNTC (New York: Continuum, 2001), 2–24.

[13] An important discussion of the lexical and stylistic data pertaining to this question remains that of Abbott, *Epistles to the Ephesians and to the Colossians*, xiv–xix, xxxi–xxxii.

[14] See Ernest Best, "Who Used Whom? The Relationship of Ephesians and Colossians," *NTS* 43 (1997): 72–96. For a chart comparing "parallel passages" between the two letters, see that of DeWette, reproduced in Abbott, *Epistles to the Ephesians and to the Colossians*, xxiii; see also the chart in Andrew T. Lincoln, *Ephesians*, WBC 42 (Dallas: Word, 1990), xlix.

[15] On the similarities between Ephesians and the undisputed letters of Paul, see Lincoln, *Ephesians*, lvi–lviii; and Best, *Commentary on Ephesians*, 25–27.

[16] See Lincoln, *Ephesians*, lxxxviii–xcvii; Best, *Commentary on Ephesians*, 46–59; Fowl, *Ephesians*, 21–27.

Many scholars, however, rightly continue to adhere to the letter's claim to have been authored by the apostle Paul.[17] How have such scholars responded to the above arguments and defended Pauline authorship of Ephesians?[18] First, they have observed that arguments from vocabulary, syntax, and style fail to establish that Paul did not write Ephesians. The incidence of unique vocabulary, phrases, and syntactical constructions in Ephesians parallels that of other Pauline letters.[19] Furthermore, such arguments frequently overlook the fact that the letter's themes and the circumstances that occasioned the letter are factors determinative of which words and grammatical constructions will or will not appear in any given text.[20]

Second, the similarities between Ephesians and Colossians do not of themselves militate against Pauline authorship of Ephesians. These similarities are consistent with a single author drafting both letters "within a short time of each other, perhaps no more than a year or two apart."[21] One expects, furthermore, that any author will return to phrases and ideas that he has used in his earlier writings. Third, while some themes and motifs are characteristic of Ephesians, none contradicts anything that Paul has written elsewhere in his letters.[22] They are best seen, rather, as the apostle's "refine[ments] or develop[ments]" of what he wrote earlier.[23]

Defenders of Pauline authorship of Ephesians return to two leading considerations in support of this traditional position. First, there is the letter's claim to Pauline authorship and the univocal acceptance of this claim in the early church. The individuals closest to the circumstances of the letter's composition concurred that Ephesians was a genuine production of Paul. Second, the early church declined on moral grounds to accept pseudonymous compositions as canonical.[24] In the case of Ephesians in particular, it is impossible morally to reconcile its particular commands and claims with pseudonymous authorship.[25] There is no evidence from antiquity that Ephesians was so much as suspected of pseudonymous composition. This serves only to confirm our confidence in Ephesians as a genuine letter of the apostle Paul.

"To the Ephesians"?

Scholars have questioned whether this letter was written to the church in Ephesus. They note that the phrase "who are in Ephesus" (1:1b) is missing from some important, early manuscripts, as well as from some of the church fathers' references to this

[17] O'Brien rightly notes that "we should hold anyone who claims to be the author of any letter coming to us from antiquity to be just that unless there is very strong evidence to the contrary" (*Letter to the Ephesians*, 4).

[18] For representative recent defenses of Pauline authorship of Ephesians, see D. A. Carson and Douglas J. Moo, *An Introduction to the New Testament*, 2nd ed. (Grand Rapids, MI: Zondervan, 2005), 480–86; O'Brien, *Letter to the Ephesians*, 4–47; Hoehner, *Ephesians*, 1–61. See also the classic study of A. van Roon, *The Authenticity of Ephesians*, NovTSup 39 (Leiden: Brill, 1974).

[19] See especially Hoehner, *Ephesians*, 24–28.

[20] Thielman, *Ephesians*, 11; O'Brien, *Letter to the Ephesians*, 6–7; Hoehner, *Ephesians*, 28–29.

[21] O'Brien, *Letter to the Ephesians*, 20–21. See the concurring judgment of Thielman, *Ephesians*, 10.

[22] See the especially helpful survey of O'Brien, *Letter to the Ephesians*, 21–33.

[23] Hoehner, *Ephesians*, 106.

[24] O'Brien, *Letter to the Ephesians*, 40.

[25] Thielman notes the incompatibility of the command to "put away falsehood" and "speak truth with his neighbor" (4:25) with the author's alleged underlying deceit regarding his own identity (*Ephesians*, 5). O'Brien notes the moral incongruity of the "request that the readers pray specifically for Paul's needs (6:19–20)" with "the author . . . know[ing] that the apostle is already dead!" (*Letter to the Ephesians*, 43).

letter.[26] Some scholars have therefore suggested that this document "was originally meant as a circular letter" and ultimately came to be associated with the church in Ephesus.[27] When the textual evidence is considered as a whole, however, one may fairly conclude that the phrase "who are in Ephesus" is part of the original letter.[28] Such a conclusion need not militate against the understanding of Ephesians as an encyclical letter.[29] It does, however, point to the church in Ephesus as the intended recipients of this letter.

Purpose of Letter

What was Paul's purpose in writing the Ephesian church? We have already observed that this epistle serves as a sweeping survey of the gospel instruction this church had received during Paul's three-year ministry in Ephesus. We have also noted that, while this epistle gives no indication of a pressing pastoral crisis within the church at Ephesus, two motifs are prominent. The first motif is that of the "powers." The second motif is that of the church. As we will see below, Paul's attention to these two concerns illumine the purposes for which he may have written this letter.

Structure and Outline

Paul wrote the letter to the Ephesians as a summary of his three-year gospel instruction in Ephesus. Out of pastoral concern for the Ephesian church, the apostle placed particular emphasis upon the subjugation of the "powers" to Christ and the nature, calling, and destiny of the church of Jesus Christ. Before we turn to further consideration of Paul's message in Ephesians, we may give some attention to the form and outline of the letter.

Although some scholars have questioned whether Ephesians may properly be called a letter, Ephesians is recognizably an ancient epistle.[30] Apart from a brief opening salutation (1:1–2) and concise closing greetings (6:21–24), the letter consists of a substantial body (1:3–6:20). Commentators have proposed different ways to reflect the structure of this body. Some understand the letter's outline in terms of the conventions of ancient rhetoric.[31] Others adopt a more conventional understanding of the letter's body as consisting of two proportioned halves, 1:3–3:21 and 4:1–6:20. These two halves are often characterized as doctrinal and applicatory, respectively.[32]

[26] See the concise overview in Bruce M. Metzger, *A Textual Commentary on the Greek New Testament*, 2nd ed. (Stuttgart: Deutsche Bibelgesellschaft, 1994), 532. These manuscripts include 𝔓[46], א, and B. The fathers include Basil, Origen, Marcion, Tertullian, and Ephraem. For a recent discussion of this question that doubts the authenticity of this phrase, see Ernest Best, *Essays on Ephesians* (Edinburgh: T&T Clark, 1997), 1–24.
[27] Carson and Moo, *Introduction to the New Testament*, 488.
[28] See Hoehner, *Ephesians*, 144–48; Thielman, *Ephesians*, 11–16; and Arnold, *Ephesians*, 23–29. Yet note the skepticism of Carson and Moo, *Introduction to the New Testament*, 490, and the defense of the absence of the phrase in O'Brien, *Letter to the Ephesians*, 47–49.
[29] Arnold, *Ephesians*, 28–29.
[30] See the concise treatments of the question in Hoehner, *Ephesians*, 69–77; and Best, *Commentary on Ephesians*, 59–63. Best concludes that Ephesians is "of mixed genre," a "homily . . . disguis[ed] . . . as a letter" (62). Lincoln, however, sees Ephesians as "in the form of a letter" with the "bulk of it equivalent to a sermon" (*Ephesians*, xli). Hoehner helpfully reminds us that the epistolary genre in the first century was a plastic one and that Ephesians sits comfortably within that genre (*Ephesians*, 75–76). Note the way in which Arnold identifies "discrete literary units" within Ephesians (*Ephesians*, 55–56).
[31] Lincoln, *Ephesians*, xliii. Lincoln structures the letter as follows: *Exordium* (1:1–23); *Narratio* (2:1–3:21); *Exhortatio* (4:1–6:9); *Peroratio* (6:10–24). See further on the rhetorical analysis of this letter in O'Brien, *Letter to the Ephesians*, 73–82.
[32] And yet not exclusively so. Note F. W. Grosheide's helpful delineation of "het meer theoretische deel van den brief" and "het meer practische" (*De brief van Paulus aan de Efiziërs* [Kampen: Kok, 1960], 60).

Since Ephesians is a summation of Paul's gospel instruction in Ephesus, we may fairly characterize the first half as rehearsing the great indicatives of the gospel, and the second half as rehearsing the great gospel imperatives.[33] The indicatives denote "the salvation accomplished once-for-all in Christ and received in being united to him by faith." The collection of imperatives "has in view the law of God, with the Ten Commandments at its core."[34] Each is "the object of faith. . . . Faith in its *receptivity* answers to the indicative . . . faith in its *activity* answers to the imperative."[35]

One word that structures the second half of the letter's body and also integrates the letter's two halves is the term "walk." Many of the main divisions of the letter's second half begin with an exhortation to "walk" (4:1, 17; 5:2, 8, 15).[36] The call to "walk" is expressly grounded in Paul's description of the origin and nature of the Christian life in 2:1–10. Before we were believers, we used to "walk" in "trespasses and sins" in keeping with the dictates of the world, the flesh, and the Devil (2:1–3). Now we have been united with Christ (2:5), "by grace . . . saved through faith . . . not a result of works" (2:8–9). We are, therefore, "his [God's} workmanship, created in Christ Jesus for good works, which God prepared beforehand, that we should walk in them" (2:10). We were not saved by good works, but we are saved for good works. It is the second half of Ephesians that helps us to understand those good works in which we are called to "walk."

Message and Theology

We may approach the message and theology of Ephesians in two complementary ways. First, we will explore the motifs of the "powers" and the church in this letter. These motifs are closely related to Paul's purposes for writing Ephesians. Second, we will consider how the two halves of the epistle accent the indicatives and imperatives of the gospel, respectively.

The Powers

What does Paul understand the "powers" to be in Ephesians? He has several ways of describing them. They are "the rulers, . . . the authorities, . . . the cosmic powers over this present darkness, . . . the spiritual forces of evil in the heavenly places" (6:12). Paul mentions them in the same breath as "the devil" (6:11; cf. 4:27) and expressly sets them apart from "flesh and blood" (6:12), that is, human beings (cf. Gal. 1:16). We are therefore to regard these powers as unseen and angelic beings in league with and under the authority of Satan (cf. Eph. 2:2). They are not impersonal but personal.[37] Paul locates them and their activities "in the heavenly places" (6:12; cf. 3:10), even as he documents their unceasing activity in the affairs of humanity.

[33] Note O'Brien's characterization of the two halves of the letter's body: "The New Humanity a Divine Creation" and "The New Humanity in Earthly Life" (*Letter to the Ephesians*, vi–vii).
[34] Richard B. Gaffin Jr., *By Faith, Not by Sight*, 2nd ed. (Phillipsburg, NJ: P&R, 2013), 81.
[35] Ibid., 82. Note as well the fuller discussion on pp. 79–85 and in Herman N. Ridderbos, *Paul: An Outline of His Theology*, trans. John Richard de Witt (Grand Rapids, MI: Eerdmans, 1975), 253–58.
[36] Hoehner, *Ephesians*, 66–69.
[37] Lincoln, *Ephesians*, 443.

Paul describes these powers in three ways. First, they are malevolent ("evil") and therefore hostile to Christ and his people. Second, they possess an authority or power that is not localized but is universal ("cosmic"). The word "darkness" indicates a demonic authority that extends to all unbelieving persons, whether Jew or Gentile. "'Darkness' is the sphere in which these believers formerly belonged (Eph. 5:8) . . . and from which they were rescued by the Lord (Col 1:13)."[38] It is, therefore, an authority that Paul associates with "this age" (Eph. 1:21; cf. 5:16; 6:13), the present Adamic order characterized by sin, corruption, curse, and death.[39]

Third, the plurality of these demonic powers and their designation by terms of rank ("rulers," "authorities") suggests a gradation within their numbers. Earlier in the letter, Paul stresses that the "prince of the power of the air" is "the spirit that is now at work in the sons of disobedience—among whom we all once lived in the passions of our flesh" (Eph. 2:2–3). Satan therefore stands at the head of a host of demonic powers who govern and influence all those who are in Adam (cf. 2 Cor. 4:4).

The "powers" constitute a genuine threat to believers' well-being (Eph. 6:11–12). Even so, Paul is insistent that the Ephesians understand that these demonic authorities have been brought into subjugation to Jesus Christ. In his exaltation, the second Adam, Jesus Christ, was "seated . . . far above all rule and authority and power and dominion, and above every name that is named, not only in this age but also in the one to come. And he put all things under his feet" (1:20–22).[40] The cosmic, mediatorial dominion of Jesus Christ encompasses "all things," even the Devil and his angelic allies.

The "rulers and authorities in the heavenly places," furthermore, are perpetually reminded of their defeat and subjugation (3:10). The "manifold wisdom of God," which denotes the eternal purpose of God to redeem sinners by the death and resurrection of Christ and to gather the redeemed into a united people under the benevolent reign of the Lord Jesus, is ever proclaimed to them.[41] The instrument through which God makes this wisdom known to the powers is "the church." The very existence of the church, in other words, is standing testimony to the powers' defeat and subjugation to the Lord Jesus Christ.[42]

Why would Paul emphasize this dimension of the work of Christ to the Ephesians? Luke's account of Paul's ministry in Acts offers an explanation. Luke stresses that Paul ministered in Ephesus in the power of the Holy Spirit. Paul's labors there were prefaced by an encounter with twelve disciples who had an imperfect knowledge of Jesus (Acts 19:1–7). It was through the laying on of Paul's hands that "the Holy Spirit came on them" (19:6). Once Paul began to preach boldly in Ephesus (19:8–10), Luke notes, "God was doing extraordinary miracles by the hands of Paul" (19:11). This activity occasioned the brazen efforts of the seven sons of Sceva to "invoke the

[38] Arnold, *Ephesians*, 448; cf. Charles Hodge, *A Commentary on the Epistle to the Ephesians* (1856; repr., New York: A. C. Armstrong and Son, 1891), 378–79.
[39] For a brief survey of Paul's teaching on this present age, see Ridderbos, *Paul*, 91–93.
[40] Notice how Paul elsewhere ties the defeat and subjugation of the demonic powers to Christ's death on the cross (Col. 1:13).
[41] O'Brien, *Letter to the Ephesians*, 245. What Paul says in the following verse (3:11) clarifies that the "wisdom" in view in 3:10 includes the saving work of Jesus Christ (Grosheide, *De brief van Paulus aan de Efeziërs*, 55).
[42] Paul is not saying that the church has a mission to preach to the demonic powers, Hoehner rightly observes (*Ephesians*, 462).

name of the Lord Jesus over those who had evil spirits, saying 'I adjure you by the Jesus whom Paul proclaims'" (19:13). These spirits acknowledged the authority of Jesus and Paul, but fell upon these seven pretenders, "master[ing] all of them and overpower[ing] them" (19:16).

Luke then notes that many professing "believers" came forward, repenting of having "practiced magic arts" (19:18–19). They proceeded publicly to burn their valuable magical books (19:19). These believers recognized, in other words, that consulting the help of unseen powers through magical arts was inconsistent with living under the lordship of Jesus Christ.

The concluding and lengthiest account from Paul's Ephesian ministry is that of the riot at Ephesus. Incensed that Paul's evangelical labors had resulted in a noticeable dent in the once-lucrative sale of "silver shrines of Artemis" (Acts 19:24; cf. 19:26), a leading Ephesian silversmith, Demetrius, stirred his fellow tradesmen to passionate anger. This frenzy proved infectious, and ultimately all of Ephesus "was filled with the confusion" (Acts 19:29). The cry that defined the riot was one of professed devotion to the local deity, Artemis of Ephesians (Acts 19:34).

Paul's ministry in Ephesus, then, was not only conducted in the power of the Spirit, but also marked by conflict with the demonic powers.[43] The Ephesian Christians themselves had been rescued from a lifestyle of seeking protection and assistance from demonic powers. They continued, however, to live in a culture marked by the presence and activity of the "rulers . . . and authorities." They were to continue to "wrestle" with these spiritual forces (Eph. 6:12). For these reasons, in the course of reminding the Ephesians of the gospel instruction that he shared with them, Paul accents the powers' subjugation to the Lord Jesus Christ. He wants to reassure the church that these demonic powers are in fact defeated. He also wants the church to look to the Lord Jesus Christ alone for protection and provision, and to grasp the powerful work of the Spirit of Christ in their lives (cf. 1:19–23; 3:14–21; 6:10–20).

The Church

The conflict with the powers is an important part of the message of Ephesians. It does not suffice, however, as a comprehensive explanation of the letter's contents.[44] One other leading motif in Ephesians is the nature and mission of the church. Paul has a number of ways of describing the church in Ephesians. The church is the "body" of Christ and Jesus Christ is her "head" (1:22).[45] As such she grows to maturity, that is, "to the measure of the stature of the fullness of Christ" (4:13; cf. 4:15–16). Paul also represents the church as the bride of Christ (5:23–24), for whom Christ died and whom Christ will "present . . . to himself in splendor" (5:27). The church

[43] Recall the way in which Paul identifies pagan gods with "demons" in 1 Cor. 10:20. One may fairly understand the genesis of the Ephesian riot, therefore, as a conflict between Paul, apostle of Jesus, and Ephesians devoted to the service of demons.

[44] As recognized by Arnold, who has especially stressed the importance of the "powers" to this letter (*Ephesians*, 43; cf. O'Brien, *Letter to the Ephesians*, 55).

[45] For the ways in which Paul's description of the church as "body" in Ephesians (and Colossians) differs from his prior characterizations of the church as "body" in 1 Corinthians and Romans, see the discussion in Ridderbos, *Paul*, 369–87. These differences do not amount, however, to contradictions. Ridderbos aptly characterizes the image of the body in these later letters as "a still further unfolding and elaboration" (ibid., 376).

is "one new man" comprising Jew and Gentile (2:15) and the "household of God" (2:19). Paul likens the church to a house "built on the foundation of the apostles and prophets, Christ Jesus himself being the cornerstone" (2:20). Specifically, the church is "grow[ing] into a holy temple in the Lord," a "dwelling place for God by the Spirit" (2:21–22).

In Ephesians, Paul stresses two dimensions of the church's existence and work. The first dimension is christological. As many of Paul's descriptions of the church indicate, the church draws her origin, identity, and calling from Jesus Christ, with whom she is united as his body, bride, and building. Paul explicitly relates the church to the historical work of Christ, that is, his death, resurrection, ascension, session, and glorious return. Paul speaks of Jesus's death as an act of Christ's love for the church (5:25), that he "might reconcile us both to God in one body through the cross, thereby killing the hostility" (2:16).[46] Not only is the Spirit who raised Jesus from the dead presently at work in the lives of believers (1:19–20), but believers passed from death to life when they were united with the risen Christ (2:5–6). The ascended Christ has furnished the church with both grace (4:7) and gifts (4:11), by means of which the "body of Christ" is built up to maturity (4:12–13, 16). In view of Christ's having been seated at the right hand of the Father (1:20), the Father "put all things under his feet and gave him as head over all things to the church" (1:22). That is to say, "all the supremacy and power God has given to Christ he has given to be used on behalf of the Church."[47] When he returns at the end of the age, Christ will "present the church to himself" in glorious perfection (5:27).

The second dimension of the church in Ephesians is eschatological. That is to say, Paul is concerned that the church understand her place and role in redemptive history. For Paul, the historical ministry of Christ transpired, in God's plan, at "the fullness of time" (1:10; cf. Gal. 4:4). God's intention was, through Christ's finished work in history, "to unite all things in him, things in heaven and things on earth" (Eph. 1:10). This intent has found partial realization in the subjection of the entire creation to the second Adam (1:21–23) and will find full and consummate realization when Christ returns, fully establishes his messianic reign (cf. 1 Cor. 15:24), and renews the creation (cf. Rom. 8:18–25).[48] For the present, Paul stresses, the church is the single locus in the creation where the reconciling work of Christ is on clearest and fullest display.[49]

The church therefore occupies a unique role within the creation. She is the instrument whose very existence as a body of people reconciled to God in Christ declares

---

[46] As O'Brien rightly notes, Paul says here not only that "the rift between Jews and Gentiles" has been removed, but also that "the hostility between both of them and God" has been removed (*Letter to the Ephesians*, 205); cf. John R. W. Stott, *The Message of Ephesians: God's New Society*, BST (Downers Grove, IL: InterVarsity Press, 1984), 102.

[47] Lincoln, *Ephesians*, 70. Lincoln takes the word "church" to be the indirect object of the verb "give" (ibid., 66); cf. Hoehner, *Ephesians*, 289.

[48] Stott, *Message of Ephesians*, 44; O'Brien, *Letter to the Ephesians*, 113–14; Hoehner, *Ephesians*, 224–25. Paul is not saying here that all human beings (much less nonhumans) have been, are, or will be saved. The uniting in view in Eph. 1:10 (cf. Col. 1:20) entails the setting of the universe to rights, that is, under the dominion of the second Adam. Some people, saved by the grace of Christ, will gladly embrace this reign. Other people, left in their sins, will be compelled to submit themselves unwillingly to this reign. See further the helpful comments in O'Brien, *Letter to the Ephesians*, 60–63.

[49] It goes beyond Paul's argument in Ephesians, however, to claim that the church thereby is "designed by [God] to be his agency . . . for the bringing about of the ultimate reconciliation," as does F. F. Bruce, *Ephesians*, 322.

to the "rulers and authorities" their defeat and subjugation at the hands of Christ (Eph. 3:9–10). It is in light of the church's identity as a reconciled body that Paul emphatically stresses the church's unity throughout Ephesians. Christ, in his death and resurrection, has "made us both [i.e., Jew and Gentile] one," and has created "one new man in place of the two" (2:14–15). Consequently, both Jew and Gentile "through [Christ] . . . have access in one Spirit to the Father" (2:18). Believers are intimately "joined together" in one "structure" or "body" (2:21; 4:15–16). They therefore have an obligation to "maintain the unity of the Spirit in the bond of peace" (4:3).[50]

The uniting of Jew and Gentile in "one new man" is significant in another regard. It represents the outworking of God's purposes in redemptive history leading up to the accomplished work of Jesus Christ. Formerly, Gentiles were "separated from Christ, alienated from the commonwealth of Israel and strangers to the covenants of promise" (2:12). But by the "blood of Christ," those once "far off have been brought near" (2:13). Not only have these Gentiles, through faith in Christ, been introduced into the people of God, but the very shape and composition of the people of God have been transformed. Believing Gentiles are now "fellow citizens with the saints and members of the household of God" (2:19).[51] This household of God is now "built on the foundation of the apostles and prophets" (2:20), that is, the apostles and prophets of the apostolic age (cf. 3:5–6).[52] In Christ and under the new covenant, "Gentiles are fellow heirs, members of the same body, and partakers of the promise in Christ Jesus through the gospel" (3:6).[53] The church is, therefore, both new and old. It stands in decided continuity with God's people of old. It is the same entity as God's people under the old covenant (2:12–13). Even so, the form of the people of God has undergone decisive transformation in the wake of the finished work of Jesus Christ (2:14–15). All that once served to define the people of God in terms of the ceremonial and civil provisions of the Mosaic law has been "abolish[ed]" (2:15). Jew and Gentile stand as spiritual equals in the body of Christ (3:5–6).

Paul, then, paints a grand vision of the church in Ephesians. Why would he emphasize this dimension of his gospel instruction in Ephesus? Some have posited a rift within the Ephesian church along the lines of Jew and Gentile.[54] The letter, however, gives no indication of such a crisis.[55] A better reason presents itself. Paul's

[50] Note the sevenfold repetition of the word "one" that follows in 4:4–6, verses that are likely the ground for the exhortation of 4:3 (Hoehner, *Ephesians*, 514).

[51] Notice how, in the Greek text, Paul three times uses the Greek prefix *syn* (σύν, "with") to indicate how Jewish and Gentile believers stand, through faith in Christ, on equal footing in the church.

[52] William J. Larkin, *Ephesians: A Handbook on the Greek Text* (Waco, TX: Baylor University Press, 2009), 44–45; Thielman, *Ephesians*, 180–81. Compare Richard B. Gaffin Jr., *Perspectives on Pentecost: New Testament Teaching on the Gifts of the Holy Spirit* (Phillipsburg, NJ: P&R, 1979), 92–95.

[53] Paul describes this reality as the "mystery of Christ" (3:4). The word "mystery," which surfaces at important junctures in this letter (1:9; 3:3, 4, 9; 5:32; 6:19) does not denote an arcane secret known to a select body of initiates. It is a redemptive-historical term denoting "that which has not yet appeared, that which still exists in the counsel of God and has not yet been realized in history as fulfillment of that counsel" (Ridderbos, *Paul*, 47). Gentile incorporation into the church on terms equal with that of the church's Jewish membership, Paul is saying, is a fundamentally redemptive-historical reality.

[54] See the arguments surveyed by Best, *Commentary on Ephesians*, 68–69. Mitton speculates that the author writes Ephesians out of a fear that "the Gentiles would impatiently disown their Jewish origins as of no importance and, following Gnostic counsels, depend wholly on the spiritual truth within their hearts" (*Ephesians*, 30–31).

[55] Fowl, *Ephesians*, 29.

readers are overwhelmingly Gentile (2:11) and, according to Luke, have experienced rejection not only by the synagogue but also by their pagan townsmen. Paul wants these believers to understand that they belong to a people unlike any other in the world. This people has privileges, a mission, and a destiny shared by no other entity in the world. They have been brought into this body by the purpose of the Father, the redeeming work of the Son, and the saving power of the Holy Spirit, and will be preserved in this body by the same.[56] Paul, in other words, is undertaking the work of "identity formation," or identity confirmation, in this letter.[57] He wants the Ephesian Christians to have a clearer grasp of who they are in relation to Christ, the church, and the world. They need this grasp if they are to live as befits the "one new man" that they are (2:15; cf. 4:20–21), those who have been "created in Christ Jesus for good works, which God prepared beforehand, that we should walk in them" (2:10).

The Indicatives of the Gospel (Ephesians 1–3)

How does Paul describe the great indicatives of Christian salvation? We have already noted the way in which Paul relates the gospel to the working of the triune God. We may therefore give further attention to the specific work that Paul ascribes in Ephesians to each person of the Godhead.

God the Father

God the Father is the great source of the believer's salvation. It is from the Father that the panoply of "blessing" enjoyed by every Christian proceeds (1:3). The Father has "chose[n] us in [Christ]" (Eph. 1:4). Christ is in view here as his people's "head and representative," such that the believer's "exalted privileges" that Paul enumerates in this chapter are theirs "through a Redeemer."[58] This election is eternal ("before the foundation of the world," 1:4; cf. 1:11), is rooted "in love" toward us (1:4), and has as its goal "that we should be holy and blameless before him" (1:4). This "predestin[ation]" (1:5), therefore, is wholly gracious. We are not chosen because we are holy. We are chosen so that we might become holy. We are chosen "according to the purpose of him who works all things according to the counsel of his will" (1:11). The listing of the benefits that Paul relates to the purpose of the Father is staggering: holiness (1:4), adoption (1:5), forgiveness (1:7), an inheritance (1:11), and the gift of the Holy Spirit (1:13). In fact, in 3:11, Paul can ascribe the entirety of the believer's salvation in Christ to "the eternal purpose" of the Father. For this reason variants of the refrain "to the praise of his glorious grace" (1:6; cf. 1:12, 14) appear three times in this opening section (1:3–14). The gratuity of our salvation is evident from its origins in the eternal, sovereign counsel of God.

Paul underscores the love of the Father as the font of this purposed salvation. Although we were "dead in our trespasses," God "made us alive together with Christ"

[56] O'Brien, *Letter to the Ephesians*, 29.
[57] Ibid., 57, citing Klyne Snodgrass, *Ephesians*, NIVAC (Grand Rapids, MI: Zondervan, 1996), 23.
[58] Hodge, *Epistle to the Ephesians*, 31. Hodge proceeds to relate the election of God's people to the eternal covenant of redemption between the Father and the Son.

(2:5). He did this because he is "rich in mercy" and "because of the great love with which he loved us" (2:4). Therefore, Paul reasons, "by grace you have been saved" (2:5; cf. 2:8).[59] The Father's objective in lavishing such grace upon us is that "in the coming ages he might show the immeasurable riches of his grace in kindness toward us in Christ Jesus" (2:7). We are eternal trophies or monuments of the Father's steadfastly gracious purpose and activity toward the unworthy.

The Father does not save individual persons in isolation, but he incorporates them into the church, "a dwelling place for God" (2:22). As we have seen above, those who once "ha[d] no hope and [were] without God in the world" have been brought near to God through Christ (2:12–13). Consequently, every Christian has, in Christ and by the one Spirit, "access . . . to the Father" (2:18).[60]

God the Son

God the Son has accomplished the salvation of all those whom the Father has chosen in eternity. We have reflected, above, how Paul highlights the death, resurrection, ascension, session, and glorious return of Christ as works that Christ undertakes for the redemption of those whom the Father has chosen before the foundation of the world. The various benefits of our salvation proceed from the Lord Jesus Christ. One of the characteristic ways in which Paul expresses this reality in Ephesians is union with Jesus Christ.[61] We are chosen "in him" (1:4) and adopted "through Jesus Christ" (1:5). In Christ we have "redemption through his blood, the forgiveness of our trespasses" (1:7). Our inheritance is possessed in Christ (1:11), and in Christ we "were sealed with the promised Holy Spirit" (1:13). In summary, the Father has "blessed us in Christ with every spiritual blessing in the heavenly places" (1:3).

The inception of our Christian lives is owing to our union with Christ. We who were "dead in trespasses" were "made . . . alive together with Christ" (2:5). We have not only shared in the benefits of Jesus's death for us (1:7). We are also expressly said to share in his resurrection and in his session (2:6; cf. 1:19–20). This work is nothing less than a work of new creation. We have been "created in Christ Jesus" (2:10).

Now united with Christ, we have been brought near to God (2:13) and engrafted into his body (2:14–16). In the body of Christ, the wall between Jew and Gentile has been broken down (2:14), and the barrier between the sinner and God has been removed (2:16).[62] This reality, brought into historical existence by the death and resurrection of Christ, is no small part of the "mystery of Christ" that Paul now proclaims (3:4–5).

[59] Commentators debate Paul's meaning in 2:8. What precisely is the "gift of God"? Some object to identifying faith as that "gift" because the demonstrative pronoun ("this") antecedent to "gift" is not the same gender as "faith." Likely Paul is identifying as the antecedent of the demonstrative the whole complex of 2:8a, "for by grace you have been saved through faith" (Hoehner, *Ephesians*, 342–43). The whole of our salvation, inclusive of its parts, is therefore the "gift of God" to the unworthy.

[60] In light of this access, believers pray to the Father. See two such specimens of prayer in the first half of the letter: 1:15–23 and 3:14–21.

[61] For a recent survey of the approximately two hundred texts in Paul that speak of the believer's union with Christ, see Constantine Campbell, *Paul and Union with Christ: An Exegetical and Theological Study* (Grand Rapids, MI: Zondervan, 2012).

[62] Taking the "hostility" in 2:14 to refer to that which divided Jew and Gentile under the Mosaic economy, and "hostility" in 2:16 to refer to the enmity between the unreconciled sinner and God (O'Brien, *Letter to the Ephesians*, 204–5; Arnold, *Ephesians*, 160, 166).

Paul can comprehensively describe the "gospel" he preaches in terms of the "unsearchable riches of Christ" (3:6–8). In possession of such riches, every believer has "boldness and access with confidence through our faith in him" (3:12). The way in which believers mature, Paul emphasizes, is by experiential appropriation of Christ's incomprehensible and unfailing love for them (3:17–19).

God the Spirit

God the Spirit applies in time the redemption accomplished by Christ to those whom the Father chose in eternity. Paul can characterize every blessing that we have received in Christ as "spiritual," that is, "as resulting from the presence and work of the Holy Spirit" (see Eph. 1:3).[63] Consequently each benefit enumerated by Paul in Ephesians 1:3–14 must be understood in terms of the Spirit's ministry of conveying to each believer what the Father has purposed and the Son has accomplished for him or her.

Paul stresses that the Spirit plays a critical role in the preservation of each believer. From the moment a person believes in Christ (and so is united to Jesus Christ), that person is "sealed with the promised Holy Spirit" (1:13). This person, in other words, receives and possesses the indwelling Holy Spirit.[64] The believer in turn is marked out by the Spirit as God's own possession. But more than possession is in view. Paul goes on to describe the indwelling Spirit as "the guarantee of our inheritance until we acquire possession of it" (1:14).[65] The Spirit himself serves as the "down payment" on the fullness of all that Christ has won for us.[66] Although we do not yet fully experience all that Christ has purchased for us, we nevertheless have title to it and are assured that we shall consummately experience it at Christ's return. The Spirit's indwelling and ongoing ministry in the life of the believer assures the believer that he will "acquire [full] possession" of the "inheritance" that is his in Christ (1:14).

In his prayers, Paul highlights the ministry of the Spirit in preserving and maturing the believer. Not only has the Spirit revealed to people the "mystery of Christ" under the new covenant (3:4), but he makes effectual both the knowledge of Christ (1:17–18) and the surpassing love of Christ (3:17–19) in each believer's life. We have, furthermore, access to the Father "in one Spirit" (2:18). The Spirit ensures that we remain in fellowship and communion with both the Father and the Son.

In Ephesians the apostle frequently speaks of the Spirit's work in terms of "power." The powerful working of the Spirit is responsible for the beginning of the Christian life. It is this spiritual power that not only raised Jesus from the dead (1:19–20), but also united us to the risen Christ and in this way brought us from death to life (2:4–5). The powerful working of the Spirit is also responsible for the continuation of the Christian life. Paul prays that believers would be "strengthened with power through his Spirit in [their] inner being" (3:16). In each case, the Spirit's ministry is one of ensuring that those whom the Father has eternally chosen and for whom the

[63] Lincoln, *Ephesians*, 19–20.
[64] Ibid., 40.
[65] On the difficulties of translating this verse, see Hoehner, *Ephesians*, 241–45.
[66] As the word translated "guarantee" may be translated (see Hoehner, *Ephesians*, 241–42).

Son died and was raised are irrevocably brought into saving union with Jesus Christ (2:4–5; 3:17). This ministry of the Spirit, Paul stresses, not only exalts the Son, but also redounds to the glory of the Father (3:20–21).

The Imperatives of the Gospel (Ephesians 4–6)

In the second half of Ephesians, Paul accents the obligation that corresponds to the privileges that the triune God in his grace has showered upon his people. We are to "walk in a manner worthy of the calling to which [we] have been called" (4:1). The last three chapters of this letter help us to see what this "worthy walking" looks like in concrete detail.

Paul first stresses both the unity and the upbuilding of the church (4:1–16). The command to "maintain the unity of the Spirit in the bond of peace" (4:3) is grounded in the fact that Paul calls believers to preserve an already existing unity; "it is a unity which arises from the fact—there is and can be but one body, one Spirit, one hope, one Lord, one faith, one baptism, and one God" (4:4–6).[67] If Paul stresses unity in 4:1–6, he accents the diversity that exists within that unity in 4:7–16.[68] Christ has given "grace" to each believer (4:7), but he has distributed a diversity of gifts within the church (4:11). The gifts that Paul enumerates here are all people whose calling it is to minister the Word of God in the church. The purpose of these gifts, Paul stresses, is to "equip the saints for the work of ministry" (4:12). The resultant goal of this equipping action is that "of preparing [the saints] for the work of . . . ministry, which in turn has the final goal of building up the body of Christ."[69] As elders in the church minister the Word of God to the whole people of God, the church matures and is built up toward the goal of "the unity of the faith and of the knowledge of the Son of God, to mature manhood, to the measure of the stature of the fullness of Christ" (4:13).[70]

In Ephesians 4:17–32, Paul calls the church "no longer [to] walk as the Gentiles do" (4:17). Paul highlights the stark differences between the walk of unbelief and that of faith. The life of unbelief is characterized by thinking that is "futil[e]," "darkened" and "ignoran[t]" (4:17–18). Such a mind stems from the unbelievers' "hardness of heart" (4:18). Their lives are "callous" and characterized by "sensuality" and "impurity" (4:19).

The gospel (4:21–22), however, has taught the Ephesians that they have "put off the old self"—the patterns of thinking and living that characterized their Adamic existence. They have "put on the new self," a reality that Paul terms a work of new "creat[ion]" (4:24). These gospel realities carry with them an obligation to rid their lives of any remains of those old sinful patterns, and to live as the new people that they are in Christ.[71] In this way, they are being transformed after the "likeness of

[67] Hodge, *Epistle to the Ephesians*, 203.
[68] O'Brien, *Letter to the Ephesians*, 273.
[69] Hoehner, *Ephesians*, 549.
[70] Paul stressed in Eph. 1:23 that the church is Christ's "body, the fullness of him who fills all in all." Here, Paul represents "fullness" as something that the church strives to attain (cf. 3:19; 4:10). There is, therefore, a sense in which the church is, in Christ, already his "fullness," and a distinct sense in which the church has not yet consummately appropriated in its experience that "fullness" (O'Brien, *Letter to the Ephesians*, 307).
[71] Ibid., 326–27.

God"—a reality that reaches their thinking (4:23) and their whole lives (4:24). In the remaining verses of this section, Paul concretely spells out what this putting off and putting on look like—in our speech, our emotions, and our behaviors (4:25–32).

In the next section (5:1–14), Paul calls the Ephesians to "be imitators of God" (5:1; cf. 4:24) and, therefore, to "walk in love" (5:2), with the love of Christ as the "reason and pattern" for such a walk.[72] Such a walk in love means that believers must have nothing to do with "love's perversion in adultery and sexual abuse."[73] Similarly, he calls believers to "walk as children of light" since we are now "light in the Lord" (5:8). This walk entails a break from the "darkness" that once characterized their lives (5:8).The light that emanates from such a walk will even serve to "expose" the furtive and "unfruitful works of darkness" that unbelievers commit (5:10–14).

Paul then calls believers to "walk, not as unwise but as wise" (5:15). In 5:16–21, he defines this wise walk in terms of adherence to the revealed "will of the Lord" (5:17). Believers are not to be under the intoxicating influence of wine, but to "be filled with the Spirit" (5:18). To be Spirit filled is, as the parallel text in Colossians states, for "the word of Christ to dwell in you richly" (Col. 3:16). A life filled with the Holy Spirit is one marked by public praise (Eph. 5:19), constant and wide-ranging thanksgiving (5:20), and submission to others for Christ's sake (5:21).

In 5:22–6:9, Paul helps different groups in the church understand what the call to submission entails. He addresses people according to their various relations within the ancient household: wives and husbands, children and parents, slaves and masters.[74] Paul does not say that any person or group is inherently inferior to another. He has stressed throughout this letter that no believer has preeminence over another with respect to his or her standing and privileges in Jesus Christ. He emphatically affirms the inherent dignity and equality of every human being, made in the image of God (see 1 Cor. 11:1–16). Without compromising these core convictions, Paul recognizes that believers may find themselves called to positions of authority or called to be under authority. In either case, the believer must yield obedience preeminently to Jesus Christ (cf. Eph. 6:6, 9), whose command, example, and reward govern every Christian's life.

In the final section of the body of the letter (6:10–20), Paul tells the Ephesians not to "walk" but to "stand" (6:11). This portion of the epistle "catches up many of the theological and ethical concerns of the letter" and therefore serves as a fitting conclusion to Paul's argument.[75] Believers struggle against the "powers" (6:12), but do so as those who are "in the Lord" Jesus and are equipped with the "strength of his might" (6:10; cf. 1:19–20; 3:20). They have been endowed with the "whole armor of God" (6:11, 13). Each element of this armor captures a dimension of the

[72] Arnold, *Ephesians*, 310.
[73] Francis Foulkes, *The Epistle of Paul to the Ephesians*, TNTC (Grand Rapids, MI: Eerdmans, 1956), 141.
[74] On the relation of this "household code" to similar texts in the New Testament and to Hellenistic understandings of household relations and responsibilities, see Hoehner, *Ephesians*, 720–29. See, as well, Hoehner's careful discussion distinguishing slavery in antiquity from nineteenth-century chattel slavery (*Ephesians*, 800–804).
[75] O'Brien, *Letter to the Ephesians*, 490.

gospel that the Ephesians have embraced for their salvation.[76] Furnished with both the indicatives and imperatives of the gospel, believers will be able, "having done all, to stand firm" until Christ returns (6:13).

The epistle to the Ephesians provides the church with one of the richest summaries of the "gospel of salvation" that survives from Paul's pen (cf. 1:13). Ephesians reminds us that it is the triune God who has saved his people, and that our salvation is entirely of grace. The indicatives of the gospel are inseparably tied to and mandate our embrace of the imperatives of the gospel. In this way, we are increasingly conformed after the image of the Christ who loved us and gave himself for us. But Paul's vision for the glory of Christ transcends the individual. God's gracious purposes extend to Christ's bride, body, and building—the church. And it is in the church that even the subjugated powers can see the outworking of the divine purpose at the "fullness of time, to unite all things in him, things in heaven and things on earth" (1:10). Paul has written this letter so that the Ephesians will have a clearer grasp of who they are—in relation to God, to themselves, to the church, to unbelievers, and to the "powers." Confirmed in the identity that the gospel alone affords, they and we stand equipped to live to the glory of God in Jesus Christ.

Select Bibliography

Abbott, T. K. *A Critical and Exegetical Commentary on the Epistles to the Ephesians and to the Colossians*. ICC. Edinburgh: T&T Clark, 1897.

Arnold, Clinton E. *Ephesians*. ZECNT. Grand Rapids, MI: Zondervan, 2010.

———. *Power and Magic: The Concept of Power in Ephesians in Light of Its Historical Setting*. Cambridge: Cambridge University Press, 1989.

———. *Powers of Darkness: Principalities and Powers in Paul's Letters*. Downers Grove, IL: IVP Academic, 1992.

Best, Ernest. *A Critical and Exegetical Commentary on Ephesians*. ICC. Edinburgh: T&T Clark, 1998.

———. *Essays on Ephesians*. Edinburgh: T&T Clark, 1997.

Bruce, F. F. *The Epistles to the Colossians, to Philemon, and to the Ephesians*. NICNT. Grand Rapids, MI: Eerdmans, 1984.

Calvin, John. *Sermons on the Epistle to the Ephesians*. Translated by Arthur Golding. 1577. Repr., Edinburgh: Banner of Truth, 1974.

Eadie, John. *A Commentary on the Greek Text of the Epistle of Paul to the Ephesians*. Edinburgh: T&T Clark, 1891.

Foulkes, Francis. *The Epistle of Paul to the Ephesians*. TNTC. Grand Rapids, MI: Eerdmans, 1956.

Fowl, Stephen E. *Ephesians: A Commentary*. NTL. Louisville: Westminster John Knox, 2012.

[76] For elaboration, see the admirable discussion in Lincoln, *Ephesians*, 439–40.

Gaffin, Richard B., Jr. *By Faith, Not by Sight: Paul and the Order of Salvation*. 2nd ed. Phillipsburg, NJ: P&R, 2013.

———. *Perspectives on Pentecost: New Testament Teaching on the Gifts of the Holy Spirit*. Phillipsburg, NJ: P&R, 1979.

———. *Resurrection and Redemption: A Study in Paul's Soteriology*. 2nd ed. Phillipsburg, NJ: P&R, 1987.

Grosheide, F. W. *De brief van Paulus aan de Efeziërs*. Kampen: Kok, 1960.

Hodge, Charles. *A Commentary on the Epistle to the Ephesians*. 1856. Repr., New York: A. C. Armstrong and Son, 1891.

Hoehner, Harold W. *Ephesians: An Exegetical Commentary*. Grand Rapids, MI: Baker Academic, 2002.

Lincoln, Andrew T. *Ephesians*. WBC 42. Dallas: Word, 1990.

Mitton, C. Leslie. *Ephesians*. NCB. London: Oliphants, 1976.

Muddiman, John. *The Epistle to the Ephesians*. BNTC. New York: Continuum, 2001.

O'Brien, Peter T. *The Letter to the Ephesians*. PNTC. Grand Rapids, MI: Eerdmans, 1999.

Ridderbos, Herman N. *Paul: An Outline of His Theology*. Translated by John Richard de Witt. Grand Rapids, MI: Eerdmans, 1975.

Stott, John R. W. *The Message of Ephesians: God's New Society*. BST. Downers Grove, IL: InterVarsity Press, 1984.

Thielman, Frank. *Ephesians*. BECNT. Grand Rapids, MI: Baker Academic, 2010.

10

Philippians

Bruce A. Lowe

Introduction

Philippians is a letter of friendship, that is, partnership/brotherhood.[1] But it is also about bereavement. How so? The answer is found in reading this letter in light of Paul's circumstances. The apostle does not know if he will live or die (1:27). So he writes to prepare his partnering church for either extreme. It is in Philippians 1 and 4 (the framing chapters) that Paul focuses on friendship/partnership/brotherhood, arguing that the Philippians should not shift their support to anyone else. Paul is not dead yet. He is alive and serving the Lord in prison (1:12–14). They should not give up partnering with him.

But even as Paul encourages friendship/partnership/brotherhood, he also seeks to prepare his readers for a bleaker result. In ancient times a responsible leader who knew he might leave his post would stitch stability into the social fabric of his followers in places where he thought tears might occur because of his departure (Deuteronomy 31–34; Joshua 23–24; John 13–17; Acts 20). This meant presenting a farewell speech for the gathered community and family leaders,[2] in which the bonds of relationship were reiterated,[3] a pointed prayer might be offered,[4] the need for humble other-centered thinking was expounded,[5] the prospect of a social tear was announced[6]

[1] S. K. Stowers, "Friends, Enemies and the Politics of Heaven: Reading Theology in Philippians," in *Pauline Theology*, vol. 1, ed. Jouette M. Bassler, David M. Hay, and E. Elizabeth Johnson, SBLSymS 4 (Minneapolis: Fortress, 1991), 107; Gordon D. Fee, *Paul's Letter to the Philippians*, NICNT (Grand Rapids, MI: Eerdmans, 1995), 12.

[2] Gen. 27:1; 49:1; Josh. 23:2; 1 Sam. 11:14; John 13:1; Acts 20:1; cf. T. Job 1:2–3; T. Reu. 1:1; T. Sim. 1:2; T. Levi 1:1–2; T. Jud. 1:1; T. Iss. 1:1; T. Dan 1:1–2 (note esp. "clan"); T. Naph. 1:2. Others could also be present: Deut. 31:7; T. Jos. 1:1.

[3] Gen. 27:1; 49:2; Josh. 23:4; 1 Kings 2:4; John 15:1–17; Acts 20:18; 2 Tim. 1:2; 2 Pet. 1:1; cf. T. Reu. 1:3; T. Sim. 2:1; T. Jud. 1:2; T. Iss. 1:1; T. Zeb. 1:2; T. Dan 1:2; T. Naph. 1:5; T. Ash. 1:2; T. Jos. 1:2.

[4] Gen. 27:28; Deut. 33:6–11; John 17; Acts 20:36.

[5] John 13:1–20; Acts 20:18–24; 2 Tim. 2:24–25; cf. T. Jud. 21:7; T. Zeb. 5:1; 8:1; T. Dan 2:1–4.7.

[6] Gen. 27:2; 48:21; Josh. 23:2; Deut. 31:2; 1 Kings 2:2; Acts 20:22–25; 2 Tim. 4:6–8; 2 Pet. 1:14; cf. T. Job 45:1; T. Isaac 3:7; T. Jac. 4:1–6; T. Zeb. 10:1; T. Dan 2:1; T. Naph. 1:3; Josephus, *Ant.* 12.279. Note MacDonald has complained that a speech like Acts 20 cannot be a farewell testament because this is not in anticipation of immediate death (D. R. MacDonald, *Does the New Testament Imitate Homer? Four Cases from the Acts of the Apostles* [New Haven, CT: Yale University Press, 2003], 70). But cf. Gen. 27:1/35:29; Josh. 23:2/24:28; T. Levi 1:2; T. Ash. 1:2.

(along with reminders that death might be best),[7] emotions were managed,[8] and love and unity for the community's future were urged;[9] also, examples to follow were given,[10] successors were anointed,[11] a drastic warning against false teachers[12] (even in their midst)[13] might be issued, there was often urging toward moral virtue,[14] and people were directed to hope in the Lord.[15]

As a responsible leader, Paul weaves exactly the same elements into Philippians.[16] In the opening verse he explicitly includes other leaders (Phil. 1:1). He reiterates his own relational bond toward them (1:3–11, 12–18). He spends significant time wrestling with whether he will live or die (1:19–27; 2:12, 17–18, 24). He even wrestles with whether his death might be best (1:23–24; 2:17–18). Paul manages their emotions by reassuring them of his current well-being. In addition, he seeks to stabilize the community by focusing on love and unity—so much so that many commentators label this Paul's primary purpose for writing.[17] Paul sets out examples to follow (e.g. 3:4–17). Timothy is anointed as successor (2:19–24), and a drastic warning is given against false teachers (3:2) and divisive people already present (1:15–17; 2:18–19). Paul echoes his "be who you are" ethic of Romans 6, reflecting new covenant realities,[18] and the Philippians are repeatedly pointed to the Lord.

But how does Paul hold these opposite themes (partnership and farewell) together in one coherent letter? Interestingly, many commentators have struggled with this question,[19] leading to the extreme notion that Philippians was originally multiple letters, later edited into a single text.[20] But there is a theme, which Paul has woven into the text to unify the two poles presented in this letter. This theme is "joy."

"Joy" (χαῖρε/χαίροις/χαίρειν) is an extraordinarily prominent theme in Philippians,[21] even as it was an extraordinarily common word in daily interaction

[7] John 14:28; Acts 21:13.

[8] Josh. 24:19–22; 1 Sam. 12:20; John 14:1, 21; 16:20–24; Acts 20:37; 21:13; 2 Tim. 1:3–8; cf. T. Isaac 3:8–14; 6.29–31.

[9] John 15:12–17; 17:20–24; Acts 20:17–37; 2 Tim. 2:14; 2 Pet. 1:7; cf. Josephus, *Ant.* 12.283; T. Reu. 6:9; T. Sim. 3:1–6; T. Jud. 25:3; T. Gad 6:1; 7:7; T. Jos. 17:2–3; T. Benj. 3:3–6.

[10] John 13:1–20; Acts 20:34–35; 2 Tim. 1:13; 2:1; 3:10–16; T. Reu. 1:5–10; T. Sim. 2:1–3.1; T. Levi 2:1–3:1; T. Jud. 1:2–12:12; T. Iss. 1:1–4:1; T. Zeb. 1:2–5:1; T. Dan 1:2–2:1; T. Naph. 1:5–4:1; T. Gad 1:2–3:1; T. Ash. 7:1; T. Jos. 1:2–17:2; 18:4; T. Benj. 1:2–3.1; 4:1.

[11] Deut. 31:7; John 14:15–31; 19:26–27; 2 Tim. 2:1–7; cf. Josephus, *Ant.* 12.284; T. Reu. 6:8–12; T. Sim. 5:4–6; 7.1–3; T. Levi 5:2; 18:1–14; T. Jud. 24:1–6; T. Iss. 5:6–8; T. Dan 5:4, 7–11; T. Naph. 6:6–10; 8:2; T. Gad 8:1; T. Jos. 19:11; T. Benj. 4:1.

[12] Josh. 23:11–13; Acts 20:29–30; 2 Tim. 2:25; 3:1–8; 4:1–4; 2 Pet. 2:1–22; 3:3; cf. T. Jud. 25:3; T. Gad 4:1; T. Ash. 2:1–3:2; T. Ben. 7:1.

[13] Josh. 23:7, 12; John 13:21–30; Acts 20:30; 2 Tim. 2:16–18; 2 Pet. 2:1.

[14] Deut. 31:9–13; Josh. 24:14–17; 1 Kings 2:3–4; John 13:31–35; 14:15–24; 2 Tim. 2:20–26; 2 Pet. 3:11–14; cf. T. Job 45:1; Josephus, *Ant.* 12.279–81; T. Isaac 4:12–22; T. Reu. 1:3; 6:1–12; T. Jud. 14–20; T. Iss. 4–5; T. Dan 5:1–4; T. Ash. 3:1–6:5; T. Jos. 17:1–18:4; T. Benj. 3:1–10:11.

[15] Deut. 31:5–6, 8; 32:1–52; Josh. 24:14–17; John 14:1–14; Acts 20:24, 35; 2 Tim. 2:1–13; 2 Pet. 3:18; cf. T. Job 45:1; T. Sim. 5:2; 6:3; T. Levi 18; T. Jud. 24:1–6; T. Dan 6:1; T. Gad 7:6; T. Jos. 6:5–8; 11:6–7; T. Benj. 3:1–8.

[16] For a different list of characteristics, see E. Stauffer, *New Testament Theology* (London: SCM, 1955), 344–47.

[17] Cf. Bonnie B. Thurston and Judith M. Ryan, *Philippians and Philemon*, ed. Daniel J. Harrington, SP 10 (Collegeville, MN: Liturgical, 2009), 35–37.

[18] Extra-biblical examples: T. Job 45:1; Josephus, *Ant.* 12.279–81; T. Isaac 4:12–22; T. Reu. 1:3.

[19] "The prevailing view of Philippians today is that it contains several heterogeneous themes, and that there is no central idea which is being addressed and discussed throughout the letter. Hence the letter is perceived as a collection of only loosely related themes with no specific single purpose. He simply wanted to write to them so that when an occasion for sending a letter presented itself, Paul took it" (Davorin Peterlin, *Paul's Letter to the Philippians in the Light of Disunity in the Church*, NovTSup 79 [Leiden: Brill, 1995], 1–2).

[20] E.g., B. D. Rahtjen, "The Three Letters of Paul to the Philippians," *NTS* 6 (1959): 167–73.

[21] Moisés Silva, *Philippians* (Grand Rapids, MI: Baker Academic, 2005), 10. "Very noticeable is the frequency of 'joy' terminology, namely, the verb (χαίρω) and the noun (χαρά): these terms occur fourteen times (3.5 times per chapter) in Philippians, while the total for the rest of Paul's letters is thirty-six times (less than 0.5 times per chapter)."

between people. It was used as both a greeting and final farewell. And within this it was essentially a word implying *a wish/prayer for well-being*. The wish/prayer for joy expressed in a greeting (or farewell) conveyed the desire for health and good circumstances upon an associate or friend.[22] Thus, when Paul is interested in assuring the Philippians of his current well-being he (very logically) tells them he is rejoicing. This is a resonant theme throughout the letter. Currently, things are well with Paul, and the Philippians should remember this when deciding on their partnership together. But Paul also cleverly employs the word "rejoice" near the end of the letter, this time where a reader might expect it to mean "Farewell!" (3:1; 4:4). Paul also captures the other side of the tension of this letter, showing the Philippians they must be prepared for a more sober result. In this sense, "joy" is a thread, used by Paul, by which he cleverly holds the polar opposites of this letter together.

But how might this reading of Philippians benefit a modern Christian? The question may be answered by asking a series of other questions. Do we face uncertainty over death? Do we face tensions over the loss of a loved one? Are we afraid of becoming redundant as we get older, or of losing a sense of usefulness in the kingdom? Do we need to think what it means to transition better? And on the other side, do we feel tension in saying good-bye? Do we long for a word from a godly Christian that might help put our own future in perspective? Do we need to be reminded of what matters most as we have one foot in this world and one in eternity? If we answer yes to any of these questions, we must acknowledge the power this letter still has for today. Here is a letter for the twenty-first century as much as it was for the first century.

Background Issues

In what follows I will devote attention to what *can* be known, as opposed to what is uncertain about the historical background of Philippians. The tendency has sometimes been to dig for controversy and division in the church at Philippi and to make these the basis for the historical background. As noted above, however, the prospect of Paul's death is enough to drive him to offer warnings without any such controversies being immediately present. Therefore, I will focus more on cultural elements (e.g., imprisonment, the nature of farewells, and the city of Philippi) that should prove more helpful.

Exile, Prison, and Death

Death is a topic certainly not avoided and, in fact, regularly highlighted in Philippians. Paul openly discusses his imprisonment and whether or not he might survive (1:19–27; 2:17). Then, using the example of Christ, he highlights Jesus's shameful death as an apparent parallel to what could happen (2:8). When mentioning Epaphroditus's stay in prison, Paul seems to parade (not hide) his near-death experience (2:27, 30). Death is a highlighted theme, not one avoided in Philippians.

[22] B. A. Lowe, "From G'Day to Bless You: An Australian-American Reflects on Paul's 'Greetings' and 'Farewells' in Philippians" (paper presented at the annual meeting of the Society of Biblical Literature, Baltimore, November 24, 2013).

Why? Because everyone knew that people die in Roman prisons. Seneca (a contemporary of Paul) speaks of humanity's "fear of two most grievous things, death and imprisonment" (*Ep*. 29.4–5). In the context of Seneca's letter, imprisonment, exile, and death become near synonyms. A major reason for being imprisoned was to await death. Convicted criminals were kept until they were sent as slaves to public works or to be gladiators—both of which equated to death. Alternatively the convict might be left to starve or else (in due course) be executed.[23] In theory, the Roman prison was not a place of remediation or punishment (as with modern prisons), but rather a place to hold someone awaiting death or another judicial decision. This may have meant freedom, but in many cases the result was torture and execution. So death was a common and realistic outcome to imprisonment.[24]

It also appears that prisoners were often allowed to receive sustenance from others. This was their lifeblood (2 Tim. 4:9–11), which explains why it was so important that the Philippians sent Epaphroditus (Phil. 2:30). Note carefully then, the stark and sobering picture Epaphroditus must have painted, walking back into Philippi. Word gets out—"Epaphroditus has returned!" But all looks grim for Paul.

Ancient Farewells

So Paul is in prison, which is bad. Epaphroditus has returned, which is ominous. And now Paul's letter begins by gathering leaders (Phil. 1:1). This sounds like a final farewell (cf. John 13–17; Acts 20).[25] In both the Old and New Testaments we find many lengthy farewell speeches indicating just how important a leader's words were near his departure; examples come from Isaac (Genesis 27), Jacob (Genesis 49), Moses (Deuteronomy 31–33), Joshua (Joshua 23–24), Samuel (1 Samuel 12), David (1 Kings 2), Jesus (John 13–17), Paul (Acts 20; 2 Timothy), and Peter (2 Peter). Besides these, Jews near Paul's day were so keen to hear these kinds of testimonies that they invented farewell speeches where Bible characters left none; examples are attributed to Adam (*Life of Adam and Eve*), Job (*Testimony of Job*), and Jacob's sons (*Testimony of the Twelve Patriarchs*). A popular explanation for this propensity is Jewish minority status. Farewells were a chance to remind everyone of their hope.[26]

Yet we must realize it was not only Jews who were keen about farewells. In Homer's *Iliad* a long farewell account by Hector became a template for other farewells. Plato's *Phaedo*, Virgil's *Aeneid*, Seneca's *Troades*, and Ovid's *Heroides* are all based on this.[27] In a text written not long before Paul, the widow of King Tarquinius describes the

---

[23] Cf. Plato, *Phaedo* 57–58 on the possibility of delay even when a person was condemned; and Cicero, *Att.* 6.2, on the possibility of being left to starve.

[24] See especially E. Peters, "Prison before the Prison: The Ancient and Medieval Worlds," in *The Oxford History of Prison: Practice and Punishment in Western Society*, ed. N. Morris and D. J. Rothman (Oxford: Oxford University Press, 1998), 13–21. For the social shame of prison, see Bruce J. Malina and John J. Pilch, *Social-Science Commentary on the Letters of Paul* (Minneapolis: Fortress, 2006), 301–2. Cf. Dionysius of Halicarnassus, *Ant. rom.* 4.11.2.

[25] "The most striking feature of the salutation, is the addition of the phrase, 'with the overseers and deacons.' Surprisingly, this is the first designation of its kind in Paul's letters; even more surprisingly, after being thus singled out in the address, they are not hereafter spoken to" (Fee, *Paul's Letter to the Philippians*, 66–67, 69). The explanation here clarifies why Paul would mention them immediately, only in this letter.

[26] A. B. Kolenkow, "The Genre Testament and Forecasts of the Future in the Hellenistic Jewish Milieu," *JSJ* 6 (1975): 65.

[27] MacDonald, *Does the New Testament Imitate Homer?*, 73.

great tragedy of her husband dying "without having either made any disposition by will of his private interests or left injunctions concerning *the public business of the commonwealth*, and without having had it in his power even to embrace any of us and *utter his last farewells.*"[28]

So why were farewells important to everyone of that day? Bruce Malina and Richard Rohrbaugh offer an insightful explanation:

> In the United States, with economics as the focal social institution, final words and testaments deal with the disposition of goods. In Mediterranean antiquity, however, with kinship institutions being focal, final words deal with concern for the tear in the social fabric resulting from the dying person's departure. Hence, the dying person will be deeply concerned about what will happen to his or her kin (or fictive kin) group.[29]

In a Christian context today this is a helpful challenge. How might we think to farewell people when we are near our own deaths? Materially or relationally? We live in a society where death is something simply to be awaited or (by many) feared, and if any provision is made, it is usually material. But what about calling those who are left behind to the Lord? What about the relational side of leaving this world well? This is an important theme in Scripture, which is also a challenge in Philippians. Here is a theme to be explored.

Philippi

But further to the last point, there were locational and circumstantial reasons for Paul to give the Philippians (in particular) a proper "good-bye." At a minimum, Paul's uncertain situation would have led him to be prepared. We know from both Acts (16:11–38) and Philippians (1:5; 4:10–20) that a close partnership existed. Within a highly Romanized colony like Philippi, partnerships were the life-blood of people's existences and taken extremely seriously.

The lower Manhattan area of New York known as Little Italy received its name because it was once seen as a slice of Italy—a Rome away from Rome.[30] This description could readily have been given to the colony of Philippi. A famous sea battle took place just off the coast in 42 BC wherein the forces of Octavian and Antony defeated the republican forces of Brutus and Cassius. Two major battles in the space of less than a month decided the fate of the Roman Republic. During these battles Octavian (who later became Emperor Augustus) realized the strategic nature of this city. So afterward, veteran soldiers were retired here, and Philippi joined other Roman colonies (*coloniae*) with the special status of functioning under Roman law (*jus Italicum*). The colony was a Rome away from Rome.[31]

[28] Dionysius of Halicarnassus, *Ant. rom.* 4.4.4 (trans. Earnest Cary, LCL).

[29] Bruce J. Malina and Richard L. Rohrbaugh, *Social-Science Commentary on the Gospel of John* (Minneapolis: Fortress, 1998), 222.

[30] Bill Tonelli, "Arrivederci, Little Italy," *New York*, September 27, 2004, 1.

[31] Cf. Marvin Richardson Vincent, *A Critical and Exegetical Commentary on the Epistles to the Philippians and to Philemon*, ICC (New York: C. Scribner's Sons, 1911), xvii.

What followed from this, we must then comprehend, was a Roman person's overwhelming sense of social connectedness. Seneca, in his book *On Benefits*, speaks of the worst people in society as those who had no regard for social obligation. In fact, the very definition of "righteousness" (*iustitia*) for a Roman amounted largely to doing what was socially appropriate in terms of relational obligations.[32] It is not hard to understand why this was so. Many may remember the iconic movie *The Godfather* and the way "family" spread beyond blood ties to social connection throughout the community; Corleone was God*father* to many.[33] This is how a place like Philippi would have functioned, with powerful family groups dominating the landscape.[34] So as Paul speaks of his relational bond with his Philippian partners (1:5; 4:10–20), it would be doubly true for converts like Lydia, the jailer, and others who see Paul as part of the fabric of their worlds.[35]

Perhaps there is a word for us here too. What sense of our relational responsibility toward others do we have today? How much obligation does a pastor feel in leaving his flock well? How much sense of commitment does the average Christian have toward other Christians when they fall on hard times? The Bible describes us as brothers and sisters—family—and perhaps we do well to consider what this means in terms of our common bond together.

Literary Unity

Bishop Polycarp of Smyrna, less than a century after Paul, said to the Philippians, "Paul . . . also when he was absent wrote *letters* to you" (Polycarp, *Phil.* 3.2). Particularly in the late 1800s to mid-1900s, Polycarp's reference to "letters" (plural) inspired commentators struggling to understand the flow of Paul's argument.[36] They noted how Philippians 3:1f. seems to take a dramatic turn (in both tone and topic) toward something resembling Paul's letter to the Galatians. They also observed how Paul's apparent "thank you" in Philippians 4:10–20 seems strangely formulated and out of place near the end. As a result, some writers pressed a case that Philippians was a collage of three letters covering a scenario climaxing in a Galatian-type crisis: Letter A: Letter of Thanks (4:10–20); Letter B: Letter of Imprisonment (1:1–3:1a; 4:2–7, 21–23); Letter C: Letter of Battle (3:1b–4:1, 8–9).[37] With no textual evidence for this snip-and-paste job, few English commentaries today follow this line.[38] Yet

[32] Cf. *Rhet. Her.* 3.3.4; Cicero, *Inv.* 2.160–61; *Leg.* 1.42–43.

[33] See especially R. P. Saller, *Personal Patronage under the Early Empire* (Cambridge: Cambridge University Press, 2002); P. Veyne, *Bread and Circuses: Historical Sociology and Political Pluralism*, trans. B. Pearce (London: Penguin, 1990). At a more popular level, David A. deSilva, *Honor, Patronage, Kinship and Purity: Unlocking New Testament Culture* (Downers Grove, IL: InterVarsity Press, 2000).

[34] My sense is that Sampley goes too far in claiming that there was actually a legal arrangement binding the two parties (J. P. Sampley, *Pauline Partnership in Christ: Christian Community and Commitment in Light of Roman Law* [Philadelphia: Fortress, 1980], 51–77).

[35] So while other letters like Philemon, Colossians, and Ephesians also indicate a prison context, there is not the same partnership with them (cf. Phil. 4:15–16).

[36] John Reumann, *Philippians: A New Translation with Introduction and Commentary*, AYB 33B (New Haven, CT: Yale University Press, 2008), 9.

[37] See especially Rahtjen, "Three Letters of Paul to the Philippians"; Jean-François Collange, *The Epistle of Paul to the Philippians*, trans. A. W. Heathcote (London: Epworth, 1979), 1–21; Reumann, *Philippians*, 1–20. For an excellent history of discussion, see Ralph P. Martin, *Philippians*, NCB (Grand Rapids, MI: Eerdmans, 1980), 10–22.

[38] Note, though, Reumann, *Philippians*.

what such a move exposed was the presence of key points of dissonance needing explanation.[39]

I suggest that reading Philippians in light of Paul's possible death and well-being helps explain the rather abrupt transition between 3:1 and 3:2. Paul's call to "rejoice" in 3:1 echoes a Greek deathbed farewell.[40] This was a call to hope and hopefulness even within the acknowledgment of the emotion of looming loss. As noted, warning against false leaders was a recognized theme in farewell speeches (see esp. Acts 20:29–30). The emotional overtone of an abrupt "good-bye" in Philippians 3:1 suitably matches Paul's dire change in tone as he begins to discuss false teachers in 3:2f.[41]

Reading Philippians in light of Paul's friendship/partnership with the Philippians also helps explain the rather odd position of 4:10–20. This is not a "thankless thanks," ill placed (as some have seen it).[42] It is the reiteration (at the center of his tension) of Paul's optimism that he will yet see the Philippians again.[43]

Place and Date of Writing

Where determines *when*, with possible locations of Paul's imprisonment being Ephesus (AD 54–55), Caesarea (57–59), Rome (60–62), and, less likely, Corinth.[44] Issues for deciding include (1) distance and travel time from Philippi, (2) the meaning of the Praetorium and "the emperor's household" (1:13), (3) the serious nature of Paul's imprisonment (1:20–23), (4) the identity of brothers and sisters with Paul (4:21), and (5) reference to his movements elsewhere, such as 1 Corinthians 4:17.[45] In the end, however, location and date change little in how we interpret Philippians.

Opponent(s)

Much ink has also been spilled over "the opponents" in Philippi with the impression sometimes given that this apparently positive letter has very dark waters of conflict flowing beneath. Robert Jewett, for example, makes much of an Ephesians location to argue that there were three sets of issues present.[46] But again, if we understand that a leader would feel responsible to prepare those left behind, it would make sense (in the midst of uncertainty) that Paul would warn the Philippians of the kinds of false teachers he knew were lurking. There is no need to make too much of "opponents" behind this letter.

---

[39] Still, today the shift in Phil. 3:1 is recognized as one of the major anomalies of New Testament studies: "As is well known, the crux in the analyses of Philippians comes at 3.1, where Paul, after apparently winding down towards the close, takes off again into a polemical passage combining exhortation with an impassioned warning about false teaching" (Loveday Alexander, "Hellenistic Letter-Forms and the Structure of Philippians," *JSNT* 37 [1989]: 89). Engberg-Pedersen speaks of 3:1 as "exactly where the letter structure begins to crack up" (T. Engberg-Pedersen, *Paul and the Stoics* [Edinburgh: T&T Clark, 2000], 83).

[40] When Odysseus gives permanent leave to Arete, he says, "My farewell, oh queen" (χαῖρέ μοι, ὦ βασίλεια; *Od.* 13.59). When Heracles is about to go off to the world of the dead, he says to his brother, "And farewell my brother" (καὶ χαῖρε πόλλ' ὦδελφέ; Aristophanes, *Frogs* 164). See further, LSJ, χαίρω, III.2.

[41] See Lowe, "From G'Day to Bless You."

[42] G. W. Peterman, "'Thankless Thanks': The Epistolary Social Convention in Philippians 4:10–20," *TynBul* 42 (1991): 261–70.

[43] This is yet another example of the backward and forward tension of this letter. He has played on "farewell" in 3:1; now he rebounds with optimism.

[44] Martin, *Philippians*, 36.

[45] See Reumann, *Philippians*, 14.

[46] Robert Jewett, "Conflicting Movements in the Early Church as Reflected in Philippians," *NovT* 12 (1970): 363–90.

Structure and Outline

Genre

Whatever else, Philippians is a letter. And this is helpful when we see that Philippians 1:12 contains a disclosure formula: "I want you to know, brothers . . ." This ought to be where the author states the purpose for what follows. But what Paul wants them to know about is his well-being—that is, his imprisonment, its present character, and its final outcome in terms of death or otherwise. This only reinforces what we have been saying.[47]

The other thing to note is the popularity of rhetorical studies today.[48] But should letters be read as speeches?[49] Some think not.[50] Certain classicists are more moderating.[51] Most proponents conclude that Paul is writing Philippians as a deliberative argument on the advantages of unity over against disunity.[52] Epideictic rhetoric tended to use numerous historical examples and amplification through repetition.[53] Perhaps, then, if rhetoric is important for appreciating the structure of Philippians, it is in terms of Paul's moving to commend himself and others through examples (see the structure, below).

Outline

As noted above, if Philippians is about Paul's well-being, we should expect a looser structure, hinging on *examples* of people by way of urging them to prepare for the future. Everyone agrees that this is a difficult letter to outline. My outline is based on letter structure, combined with the idea that certain aspects of farewell will be brought out most clearly through the *example* of others: introduction (1:1–2), thanksgiving (1:3–11), disclosure of purpose for the letter body (1:12), letter body (1:13–4:7), letter close (4:8–23), and the idea of amplification through repetition:[54]

I. Introduction (1:1–2)
II. Thanksgiving (1:3–11)
III. Disclosure of Purpose (1:12)

[47] This reinforces why Paul A. Holloway, *Consolation in Philippians: Philosophical Sources and Rhetorical Strategy*, SNTSMS 112 (Cambridge: Cambridge University Press, 2001), 45–48, goes too far in then trying to place on equal footing with this theme the conflict between Euodia and Syntyche (4:2–3). Epistolography is most often used further to draw attention to different types of letters (as noted above), and commonly Philippians is viewed as a "family" or "friendship letter." See Alexander, "Hellenistic Letter-Forms and the Structure of Philippians." Note that "farewell" is also a type of letter category, as indicated by 2 Bar. 77:11–26 (L. Doering, *Ancient Jewish Letters and the Beginnings of Christian Epistolography*, WUNT 298 [Tübingen: Mohr Siebeck, 2012], 241–53).

[48] For the beginnings of all this, see the famous essay H. D. Betz, "The Literary Composition and Function of Paul's Letter to the Galatians," *NTS* 21 (1975): 352–79.

[49] Demetrios, *De elocutione* 225; Seneca, *Ep.* 75.1–4; but see C. Julius Victor, *Ars rhetorica* 27.

[50] P. H. Kern, *Rhetoric and Galatians: Assessing an Approach to Paul's Epistle*, SNTSMS 101 (Cambridge: Cambridge University Press, 1998). R. D. Anderson, *Ancient Rhetorical Theory and Paul*, rev. ed., CBET 18 (Leuven: Peeters, 1999).

[51] C. J. Classen, *Rhetorical Criticism of the New Testament* (Boston: Brill Academic, 2002). J. Fairweather, "The Epistle to the Galatians and Classical Rhetoric: Parts 1 & 2," *TynBul* 45 (1994): 1–38. Fairweather, "The Epistle to the Galatians and Classical Rhetoric: Part 3," *TynBul* 45 (1994): 213–43.

[52] Duane F. Watson, "A Rhetorical Analysis of Philippians and Its Implications for the Unity Question," *NovT* 30 (1988): 57–88. Ben Witherington III, *Friendship and Finances in Philippi: The Letter of Paul to the Philippians*, The New Testament in Context (Valley Forge, PA: Trinity, 1994), 11–20.

[53] See especially Y. L. Too, "Epideictic Genre," in *Encyclopedia of Rhetoric*, ed. T. O. Sloane (Oxford: Oxford University Press, 2001).

[54] Note that this kind of structuring around examples is followed by Stowers, "Friends, Enemies and the Politics of Heaven"; and Thurston and Ryan, *Philippians and Philemon*, 37–38.

- IV. Letter Body (1:13–4:7)
  - A. Example: Paul (1:13–26)
    Instruction (1:27–30)
  - B. Example: Christ (2:1–11)
    Instruction (2:12–18)
  - C. Example: Timothy and Epaphroditus (2:19–30)
  - D. Example: Paul and others (3:1–17)
    Instruction (3:18–4:1)
  - E. Example: true companions (4:2–3)
    Instruction (4:4–7)
- V. Letter Close (4:8–23) Including Example 6: Don't Forget Paul (4:10–20)

Message and Theology

Brief Commentary

Although the opening line of Philippians is fairly typical, Paul does add some unexpected components:

> Paul *and Timothy*, servants of Christ Jesus,
> To all the saints in Christ Jesus who are at Philippi, *with the overseers and deacons*:
> Grace to you and peace from God our Father and the Lord Jesus Christ. (1:1–2)

Note how Paul's inclusion of Timothy on equal footing with himself foreshadows 2:19–24 and Timothy's potential appointment as successor. This, together with the mention of "overseers and deacons," aligns nicely with the theme that Paul is offering a possible "farewell."

Paul then proceeds to thank God for the Philippians' partnership (1:3–11) in the gospel. The "remembrance" in verse 3 is likely their remembering Paul in support.[55] The "good work" that God has begun (1:6) then relates to the gospel ministry, and he will continue to work among them (cf. 1:9–11). So this is less likely about general perseverance and more about endurance in ministry. The Christian life is not just about "making it"; it is about triumphing and making a positive impact for the Lord (cf. 2:14–16). Thus we find the theme of the Philippians' friendship/partnership in the gospel.

This theme of partnership continues into the disclosure of 1:12, where Paul begins talking of his imprisonment and how it is for the best (1:13–20), before closely discussing whether he will live or die (1:21–26). These again are themes consistent with partnership but also the tension over whether this may be "farewell." In 1:27, just after saying how confident he is of returning, Paul adds "whatever happens" (NIV). The Philippians' hope must not be in him but in the Lord. The tension over ongoing friendship and his possible farewell is strong here. What has been an explanation of

[55] P. T. O'Brien, *The Epistle to the Philippians: A Commentary on the Greek Text*, NIGTC (Grand Rapids, MI: Eerdmans, 1991), 59–61.

his circumstances now becomes something of an *example* to follow as he urges them to unity for the sake of each other and their endurance (1:27–30). Paul is fortifying them together in case he will be taken from them.

But even as he has tightened then loosened the strings of their shared bond (like working shoelaces), he will now point them to the example of Christ as the one who gives context to self-sacrificial unity (2:1–11). There is much theological richness here (see below).

Paul again reminds his readers of his absence (2:12), which also reminds them that his future is uncertain. He then repeats the call for unity and endurance (2:12–18), which he rounds out with a shocking turnaround on whether he may actually die (2:17–18). It is as if Paul is gradually working the laces back and forth by moving from himself to their interaction with each other and ultimately to the Lord in fortifying endurance. What would be a logical next step? In terms of a more obvious farewell tone, it would be to add another party (or two)—his successor and Epaphroditus, who has just returned (2:19–29).

There is, by Philippians 3:1, a sense in which all necessary matters of "farewell" have been covered—except one (cf. Acts 20:29–30), that is, a warning against false teachers. This, as we see from Acts 20, is a very sobering topic, and so a way to strike the right tone is to announce, in effect, an abrupt "finally brothers, 'deathbed farewells to you!'" Debate on whether "rejoice" should be translated "farewell" has often been marred by (1) the failure to realize that "Rejoice!" was a well-known deathbed farewell; (2) this argument's use by "three-letter theory" scholars, which then tars and feathers the concept for others; and (3) the tendency to read it as either–or, whereas a deathbed "Rejoice!" had genuine content, as well as social cueing. The starkness of this statement matches the growing uncertainty from Philippians 1:25–26 to 1:27 to 2:17–18, and its trajectory continues into 4:3–4.

Paul now warns of Judaizers (3:2), but then quickly shifts this discussion to his own *example* of hoping in Christ alone and looking toward enduring to the end (3:3–16). It is this example (and others like it) that they should look to rather than those caught in the world (3:17–21).

Philippians 4:1 is a telling verse because it is all about Paul's hope to see the Philippians, yet the need for endurance, which must be found completely in the Lord: "Therefore, my brothers, whom I love and long for, my joy and crown, stand firm thus in the Lord, my beloved." This sounds like "farewell" and the felt tension of weaning them from himself to Christ, for endurance's sake.

But where does Paul go next? In something of a confidence vote for an "*example* structure," he turns in 4:2–3 to speak of fellow leaders, but this time in light of the tone set in 3:1–2. This is the perfect place to deal with a leadership example, coming as a kind of repetition of 2:19–30, but in light of the warnings against false individuals in 3:2–4:1.

In 4:4 he will repeat the emotional cry of 3:1 again—and yet again! Yes, they will have issues to sort out even in their midst (4:2–3)—Why can't we just have our old senior pastor back!—but their hope must not be in people, Paul says; it must be in the Lord (4:5–7).

One last matter remains (note again, "finally," 4:8). In what is a close to the letter frame,[56] Paul urges his readers to do right, even as he has given *examples* (4:8–9), knowing that even if Paul is not there, "the God of peace will be with you." This rings of a final push away from the pier as Paul leaves them to God. And yet this reminder of what he has been saying all along provides a perfect foil so that he may finish with the reminder that he is not fully gone just yet (4:10–20). This section is less about thanking the Philippians for past gifts as it is a reminder about partnership. Paul has made the sacrificial move of pointing them away from himself. But now, in closing, it is appropriate to remind them (one last time) that he is actually still alive and that they should act in light of his current well-being. Final greetings round out the letter (4:21–23).

Major Themes

Though much more could be included, we have space for two theological matters: Jesus in Philippians 2, and the justification debate as related to Philippians 3.

The Preexistent Jesus

Throughout history people have been excited by Philippians 2:5–11, "one of the most theologically significant passages in the New Testament."[57] Why? It shows that Paul believed in the preexistence and divinity of Christ. Moreover, the possibility emerges that Paul is quoting an older traditional hymn, which would imply that the early church was persuaded of Christ's preexistence from almost the beginning. What reasons are given for this earlier tradition? First,[58] there are structural reasons. Its rhythm, parallelism, and arrangement suggest that it was a hymn, perhaps even originally composed in Aramaic or Hebrew.[59] Second, this passage contains unusual vocabulary:

> So μορφή turns up in the NT only at Phil. 2:6, 7 (apart from the longer ending of Mk. 16:12); in fact, μορφῇ θεοῦ, ἴσα θεῷ, and δοῦλος are not elsewhere used of Christ in Paul's writings. Κενόω occurs on four other occasions in the literal sense of annihilating or emptying (Rom. 4:14; 1 Cor. 1:17; 9:15; 2 Cor. 9:3), but is used metaphorically of Christ at Phil. 2:7. Ὑπερυψόω is a *hapax legomenon* in the NT, and its cognate ὑψόω, which is used for ascension of the risen Christ in Acts 2:33; 5:31 and for the Johannine glorification of Jesus at his death (Jn. 3:14; 8:28; 12:32, 34) is not found in Paul. Χαρίζομαι is normally used of people as recipients, but at Phil. 2:9 it is Christ who is the indirect object of this verb. Ἁρπαγμὸν ἡγέομαι is a *hapax legomenon* in the entire Greek Bible, while καταχθόνιος is a *hapax* in the NT.[60]

---

[56] Jeffrey A. D. Weima, *Neglected Endings: The Significance of the Pauline Letter Closings*, JSNTSup 101 (Sheffield: Sheffield Academic, 1994), 191–201.
[57] Stephen E. Fowl, *Philippians* (Grand Rapids, MI: Eerdmans, 2005), 89.
[58] For an excellent summary of all evidence, see O'Brien, *Epistle to the Philippians*, 198–202.
[59] See especially E. Lohmeyer, *Kyrios Jesus: Eine Untersuchung zu Phil. 2,5–11* (Heidelberg: Carl Winter, 1927).
[60] O'Brien, *Epistle to the Philippians*, 199.

Third, it is argued on theological grounds that if Paul had composed this hymn, he would probably have included the crucifixion and resurrection. Such arguments, I believe, are sufficient to conclude that this text existed before Paul and as such reflects a much earlier tradition of Christ's preexistent divinity.

But to turn to the christology itself,[61] Ambrosiaster, who wrote right around the time of serious christological controversies, brought out the significance of this passage in the fourth century.[62] We can do no better than to trace what Ambrosiaster said.

Did the early church believe that Jesus, before his birth, was God? Yes. As Ambrosiaster says in interpreting Philippians 2, "Christ was always in the form of God because he was the image of the invisible God. . . . He knew he was the Father's equal, but rather than claim that equality he submitted himself" (68–69). "Although he is not God the Father, he is what God is" (69). "Paul says 'in the likeness' in order to indicate that Christ was also God" (70). Ambrosiaster derives this from thoughtful analysis. Speaking of verse 7 he observes, "Why would he be said to have become like a man, if he were no more than a man? And by what logic would he have been found in the likeness of a man, if he were not also God?" (69). Ambrosiaster then ponders at length the complaint that because God later gave Christ a glorious name, Christ was somehow lacking before (70). Others might say, "Perhaps he was God by adoption. . . . Christ would then start off being part God and part adopted, or else being two gods" (71). But Ambrosiaster responds, "What would there be to praise by saying that he was made in the likeness of a man, when every man is made in that likeness. . . . Nor would creation bow the knee to an adopted God, but only to one who was not a fellow creature" (71).

Someone once said that you should always ask, what would be lost if this part of the Bible were not there? The answer for Philippians 2:5–11 is clear. We would be lacking one of the most significant theological passages in the New Testament, one which gives us the clearest sense that Christ was always "God of God, Light of Light, Very God of Very God, begotten, not made" (Nicene Creed).

But note too, with Gordon Fee, how this passage reveals even more about the character of God:

> For in "pouring himself out" and "humbling himself to death on the cross," Christ Jesus has revealed the character of God himself. Here is the epitome of God-likeness: the pre-existent Christ was not a "grasping, selfish" being, but one whose love for others found its consummate expression in "pouring himself out," in taking the role of a slave, in humbling himself to the point of death on behalf of those so loved. No wonder Paul cannot abide triumphalism. . . . It goes against everything God is and that God is about.[63]

Paul's own selflessness throughout this letter models well the selflessness he sees in his Savior.

[61] But see ibid., 108–17 on this and other alternate foci (e.g., possible Christ-Adam comparisons).

[62] Ambrosiaster, *Commentaries on Galatians–Philemon*, trans. G. L. Bray, Ancient Christian Texts (Downers Grove, IL: IVP Academic, 2009). Subsequent quotations are cited parenthetically by page numbers.

[63] Fee, *Paul's Letter to the Philippians*, 197.

Justification and Judaizers

Is Paul's language of justification and righteousness primarily about covenant faithfulness or a legal judgment of God? Historically Protestants have believed the latter. But in recent years the former has gained a strong following, prominently through the work of E. P. Sanders and suggestions that Judaism always saw salvation as being about grace: get in by grace, and stay in by repentance and avoiding gross sin. Also, because Paul's discussion of justification is largely limited to Romans, Galatians, and Philippians 3 (all in the context of Judaizers), it is sometimes argued that this must be read as a doctrine countering Judaizers. Readers are directed to several books that argue for a traditional Protestant response.[64] Here though I will add some observations about Greeks and Romans, in the context of Philippians 3.

In the view of Sanders and others, the most important question is What did a Jew think about God and his law? But with Paul as the apostle of the Gentiles, an equally important question must be What would a pagan have heard when confronted with Israel's God? Greeks and Romans (who filled Philippi and the surrounding area) believed in righteousness. Pagans believed God (or the gods) could be placated (i.e. kept from meddling) if humans gave him (or them) honor, and provided humans *maintained reasonable standards of righteousness.* What then would pagans have thought when they heard from Jews that God had stipulated (in writing) a universal expression of his requirements? They would have thought these were the standards to be centralized and kept. This describes well the issue in Romans 2:17–24, where the Gentiles end up blaspheming God because of the Jews' hypocrisy. It also captures some of what Paul says in Romans 3:2–4 about what the Jewish relationship with God becomes when the written law is wrongly centralized. What then would pagans have heard in the words "Unless you are circumcised according to the custom of Moses, you cannot be saved" (Acts 15:1), or "It is necessary to circumcise them and to order them to keep the law of Moses" (Acts 15:5)? First, they would have looked at the Jews/Jewish Christians as hypocritical for parading this law and then claiming God did not require 100 percent obedience (cf. Rom. 2:24; Gal. 3:10). They themselves would have been inclined to think of 100 percent fulfillment. Second, they would have been inclined toward their old *distant* view of God or the gods who stand aloof and would only have worried the average person when they broke the laws of nature. In short they would have heard "works salvation" and *a relational distance from God.*

With the words "those who mutilate the flesh" (Phil. 3:2), Paul starts off by echoing a Greco-Roman perspective on circumcision as immoral and unrighteous. Then he proceeds to speak not only about righteousness apart from personal law keeping, but also about how true Christianity is *personal, not distant* (Phil. 3:7–11). Finally (as if to show that this really is a general issue of morality), Paul finishes by speaking of those who have played fast and loose with righteousness. This section reads well when read in light of Greco-Roman perspectives, but in light of those perspectives it reads best as a response to "works salvation."

---

[64] See discussion in Romans.

Something extra must be added here on the subject of imputation. N. T. Wright sees the idea that Christ's righteousness has been imputed to sinful humans as highly problematic because "to think that way is to concede, after all, that 'legalism' was true after all—with Jesus as the ultimate legalist."[65] The first part here is problematic for Wright's scheme, while the second part (he claims) is a problem for traditional Reformed theology. This discussion is relevant to Philippians because John Piper (for one) uses Philippians 3:9 as a key place for arguing a traditional imputation perspective in Paul's writings. Paul counted all things as rubbish, he says, "that I may be found in [Christ], not having my righteousness, which is from law, but rather which is through the faithfulness of Christ, which is a *from-God* righteousness on the basis of faith" (my trans. of καὶ εὑρεθῶ ἐν αὐτῷ, μὴ ἔχων ἐμὴν δικαιοσύνην τὴν ἐκ νόμου ἀλλὰ τὴν διὰ πίστεως Χριστοῦ, τὴν ἐκ θεοῦ δικαιοσύνην ἐπὶ τῇ πίστει).[66] As can be seen from the translation above, much more is involved in this discussion than union with Christ. The "faith in Christ" versus "faithfulness of Christ" debate is front and center of what this verse must mean. But to bring in again what has just been said about *pagan perspectives*, it must be repeated that a pagan would have naturally resonated with the "my righteousness" (ἐμὴν δικαιοσύνην) theme—which controls all the "which" phrases that follow (τὴν . . . τὴν . . . τὴν). In this way, righteousness *from* law (τὴν ἐκ νόμου) would make sense to a pagan as a way of earning God's favor through moral obedience. Paul's answer, however, involves Christ (ἀλλὰ τὴν διὰ πίστεως Χριστοῦ), which is then interpreted in terms of righteousness *from* God (τὴν ἐκ θεοῦ δικαιοσύνην).

Two things noteworthy about the Greek phrase here are (1) that "from God" is pushed into an emphatic position, and (2) that "righteousness" is repeated again for good measure. Paul's subject all along has been "my righteousness," which a pagan would have naturally interpreted as moral standing. Now he speaks emphatically of this as righteousness from God. Whether the mediation of this (through Christ) is best thought of in terms of "imputation" or somehow participatory through our union with Christ, this text still sounds remarkably like a righteous status, alien to us, being counted to us by God. Piper's interpretation seems well founded.

Select Bibliography

Alexander, Loveday. "Hellenistic Letter-Forms and the Structure of Philippians." *JSNT* 37 (1989): 87–101.

Ambrosiaster. *Commentaries on Galatians–Philemon*. Translated by G. L. Bray. Ancient Christian Texts. Downers Grove, IL: IVP Academic, 2009.

[65] N. T. Wright, *Justification: God's Plan and Paul's Vision* (Downers Grove, IL: InterVarsity Press, 2009), 214.

[66] Besides engaging with Wright on this topic, Piper has also exchanged blows with Don Garlington, who seemingly affirms the substance of imputation, but claims it should be seen more in terms of union with Christ (Don Garlington, "Imputation or Union with Christ," *Reformation & Revival* 12 [2003]: 45–113; John Piper, "A Response to Don Garlington on Imputation," *Reformation & Revival* 12 [2003]: 121–28).

Collange, Jean-François. *The Epistle of Paul to the Philippians*. Translated by A. W. Heathcote. London: Epworth, 1979.

Fee, Gordon D. *Paul's Letter to the Philippians*. NICNT. Grand Rapids, MI: Eerdmans, 1995.

Fowl, Stephen E. *Philippians*. Grand Rapids, MI: Eerdmans, 2005.

Hansen, G. Walter. *The Letter to the Philippians*. Grand Rapids, MI: Eerdmans, 2009.

Holloway, Paul A. *Consolation in Philippians: Philosophical Sources and Rhetorical Strategy*. SNTSMS 112. Cambridge: Cambridge University Press, 2001.

Jewett, Robert. "Conflicting Movements in the Early Church as Reflected in Philippians." *NovT* 12 (1970): 363–90.

Malina, Bruce J., and John J. Pilch. *Social-Science Commentary on the Letters of Paul*. Minneapolis: Fortress, 2006.

Martin, Ralph P. *Philippians*. NCB. Grand Rapids, MI: Eerdmans, 1980.

O'Brien, Peter T. *The Epistle to the Philippians: A Commentary on the Greek Text*. NIGTC. Grand Rapids, MI: Eerdmans, 1991.

Peterlin, Davorin. *Paul's Letter to the Philippians in the Light of Disunity in the Church*. NovTSup 79. Leiden: Brill, 1995.

Peterman, G. W. "'Thankless Thanks': The Epistolary Social Convention in Philippians 4:10–20." *TynBul* 42 (1991): 261–70.

Piper, John. "A Response to Don Garlington on Imputation." *Reformation and Revival* 12 (2003): 121–28.

Rahtjen, B. D. "The Three Letters of Paul to the Philippians." *NTS* 6 (1959): 167–73.

Reumann, John. *Philippians: A New Translation with Introduction and Commentary*. AYB 33B. New Haven, CT: Yale University Press, 2008.

Silva, Moisés. *Philippians*. BECNT. Grand Rapids, MI: Baker Academic, 2005.

Thurston, Bonnie B., and Judith M. Ryan. *Philippians and Philemon*. Edited by Daniel J. Harrington. SP 10. Collegeville, MN: Liturgical, 2009.

Vincent, Marvin Richardson. *A Critical and Exegetical Commentary on the Epistles to the Philippians and to Philemon*. ICC. New York: C. Scribner's Sons, 1911.

Watson, Duane F. "A Rhetorical Analysis of Philippians and Its Implications for the Unity Question." *NovT* 30 (1988): 57–88.

Witherington, Ben, III. *Friendship and Finances in Philippi: The Letter of Paul to the Philippians*. The New Testament in Context. Valley Forge, PA: Trinity, 1994.

11

Colossians

Benjamin Gladd

Introduction

Though only four chapters long, Colossians packs enough theological sophistication for the most learned pastors and scholars. Yet, its message remains simple and clear: Christ is better—better than all forms of human teaching, and better than outdated Jewish regulations. If Christ doesn't occupy the center of one's entire existence and worldview, Paul argues, something has gone awry. Colossians is one of Paul's most elegant yet compact epistles in the New Testament.

A prominent thread woven throughout the entire Old Testament is God's unrivaled sovereign rule over the cosmos. Adam and Eve were created to mediate this rule over the earth and extend it to the ends of the earth. Though the fall marred the first couple's capacity to rule, God overcame this dilemma by restoring humanity's "image." This deliverance culminated in the life, death, and resurrection of his Son. Since Christ is in the perfect image of his Father, he rules at his right hand over the cosmos. In Christ, believers enjoy a restored image so that they may join in Christ's reign and mediate that rule on earth. The book of Colossians strikes this chord loudly, reverberating in nearly every passage. With the bombardment of corrupt teaching in the world today and its ease of accessibility, Christians would do well to take Paul's message to heart.

Background Issues

Occasion

Paul most likely wrote Colossians, Philemon, Ephesians, and Philippians from the same place, hence their designation as the "Prison Epistles." The close relationship between Colossians and Philemon, based on the named individuals in the letters, is readily affirmed. The textual similarities between Colossians and Ephesians are also striking.

Epaphras apparently planted the congregation at Colossae (1:7–8): "You learned it [the gospel] from Epaphras our beloved fellow servant. He is a faithful minister of Christ on your behalf and has made known to us your love in the Spirit." Yet, Paul takes it upon himself to communicate with this church. Many within the church at Colossae have fallen prey to false teaching, a teaching that incorporates aspects of Judaism and paganism (see discussion below). Though we cannot reconstruct the precise details of this heresy, we can be confident in Paul's response to it. The Colossians struggled in their identity within the physical and spiritual world around them. In response to this dilemma, much of Paul's letter to the Colossians centers on their identity in Christ and the new creation.

Authorship

The letter claims to have been written by Paul (Col. 1:1, 23; 4:18), and, until recently, there had been little doubt that the letter was written by the apostle. Those who argue against Pauline authorship claim that the letter differs significantly from Paul's other epistles, particularly in its theology and language. Its relationship to Ephesians has also engendered serious doubt. Here the issue of pseudonymity comes to the fore.

It has been fashionable in recent years to argue that someone under the guise of Paul penned Colossians. (The same argument is applied to other New Testament letters, such as Ephesians, 2 Thessalonians, 1–2 Peter, and Jude.) Paul himself did not write the letter, but an individual (or more than one) deliberately imitated him. Certainly, within the Second Temple Judaism pseudonymity existed (e.g., 1 Enoch, 2 Baruch, 4 Ezra), but the question remains whether or not the early church embraced this literary technique, especially, pseudonymous *letters*. A detailed survey of this problem is beyond the scope of this essay, but the facts seem clear enough.[1] Little evidence exists that the early church condoned pseudonymity. Indeed, the early church explicitly denounced it.

The theology contained in Colossians comports well with Paul's other letters when this epistle is understood correctly.[2] The grammar, syntax, and vocabulary, though different in some portions of Colossians, are not enough to debunk the traditional view. Since Paul combated a specific heresy at a specific time and place, he probably tailored the letter accordingly.

Date

That Paul writes Colossians in prison is clear enough (4:18), but *which* imprisonment is in mind? Acts mentions a few imprisonments: Philippi (16:22–40), Caesarea

[1] For a wonderful discussion of this thorny issue, consult D. A. Carson and Douglas J. Moo, *An Introduction to the New Testament*, 2nd ed. (Grand Rapids, MI: Zondervan, 2005), 337–50.

[2] N. T. Wright argues that authorship of this letter ultimately turns on the theology of Colossians itself (*Colossians and Philemon*, TNTC [Downers Grove, IL: InterVarsity Press, 1986], 35).

(23:23–26:32), and Rome (27:1–28:31). But in 2 Corinthians 11:23 (which was probably written before Paul's trip to Jerusalem to deliver the famine relief), Paul claims to have endured "far more imprisonments." In other words, Luke has not furnished a complete list of Paul's imprisonments in the book of Acts. So this letter may have been written from an unknown imprisonment. A few commentators suggest Ephesus, as Paul remained there for a few years and was greatly persecuted there (Acts 19:1–41). Nevertheless, for a variety of reasons, a Roman imprisonment is preferred.[3] If Paul wrote from a prison in Rome, then it is likely that Colossians was written sometime around AD 60–61. There was a severe earthquake in Colossae shortly thereafter, and it seems unlikely that Paul would not have mentioned such a catastrophe.

Purpose

The church at Colossae wanted more. They desired to know not only the crucified Christ, but also deeper spiritual truths. They believed in Christ and in the gospel, yet they found themselves looking for something else. They dabbled in Jewish philosophy and pagan magical practices. In their eyes, the gospel was not sufficient to meet all their needs—some, perhaps, but not all. Paul therefore writes Colossians to correct the Greco-Roman/Jewish heresy and affirm the priority of Christ and the gospel.

Structure and Outline

I. Letter Opening (1:1–2)
II. Thanksgiving (1:3–14)
    A. Fulfillment of the Adamic commission (1:3–12)
    B. Christ and the new creation (1:13–14)
III. The Exalted Christ (1:15–23)
    A. Christ's supremacy over the first creation (1:15–18a)
    B. Christ's supremacy over the new creation (1:18b–20)
    C. Christ's work of reconciliation (1:21–23)
IV. Christ and the Unveiled Mystery (1:24–29)
    A. Sharing in Christ's suffering (1:24)
    B. The union of Jew and Gentile in Christ (1:25–29)
V. Admonition to Denounce False Teaching (2:1–23)
    A. The superiority of Christ (2:1–15)
    B. The folly of wisdom outside of Christ (2:16–23)
VI. Life as Resurrected Beings (3:1–4:1)
    A. The believers' identification with the risen Christ (3:1–11)
    B. Living in light of the believers' resurrection (3:12–4:1)
VII. Gospel Proclamation and the Letter Closing (4:2–18)
    A. Paul's request for evangelism (4:2–6)
    B. Personal requests and the letter closing (4:7–18)

[3] See Carson and Moo, *Introduction to the New Testament*, 521–22; David W. Pao, *Colossians and Philemon*, ZECNT (Grand Rapids, MI: Zondervan, 2012), 23–24.

Message and Theology

Key Themes in Colossians

Jews and Gentiles and the Unveiled "Mystery" of Christ

The key term "mystery" in Colossians originates in the book of Daniel, especially chapters 2 and 4. Mystery in Daniel concerns God's end-time kingdom and related events. It can be defined roughly as God's disclosure of end-time wisdom, knowledge that was largely hidden but has been subsequently revealed (Dan. 2:20–23). God primarily communicates his wisdom through dreams and visions mediated by either an individual person or an angel. The structure of mystery is a bit peculiar: an individual (Nebuchadnezzar) receives a cryptic dream followed by an interpretation (Daniel). In the book of Daniel, this structure is found in dreams (chaps. 2, 4), visions (chaps. 7–8, 10–12), writing (chap. 5), and previous prophecy (chap. 9). The two-tiered component of mystery (cryptic vision followed by interpretation) signals its hidden nature and subsequent revelation—at first hidden but then revealed.

The New Testament picks up and applies this word and concept to a number of prominent themes: kingdom (Matt. 13:11), the crucifixion (1 Cor. 2:1, 7), resurrection (1 Cor. 15:51), Christ's cosmic rule (Eph. 1:9), and the nature of the Antichrist (2 Thess. 2:7). One prominent theme that is tied to "mystery" is the relationship between Jewish Christians and Gentile Christians (Rom. 11:25).

Though occurring only four times in the letter, the word "mystery" (μυστήριον) takes on special significance, particularly for how Jews and Gentiles relate to one another (Col. 1:26–27; 2:2; 4:3). This ethnic relationship is pronounced in the book of Ephesians, where Paul devotes a considerable amount of space to the subject (Eph. 3:1–13). Paul generally employs the term "mystery" throughout his letters to refer to a particular end-time doctrine that was largely hidden in the Old Testament but has been revealed fully in the New (Rom. 11:25; 1 Cor. 2:7; etc.). Here in the book of Colossians, Paul broaches the topic of the Jew-Gentile relationship through his use of mystery. Why does Paul contend that the way in which Jews and Gentiles relate to one another at Colossae was generally hidden in the Old Testament? The answer probably lies in the general expectation of *how* Gentiles would become part of Israel in the "latter days."

According to the Old Testament, Gentiles became members of true Israel through their adherence to the Torah (e.g., Rahab, Ruth, Uriah).[4] They were to conform to Israelite culture in all aspects of life by taking on national distinctives such as circumcision, food laws, living in Israel's land, and honoring Sabbath rest, which were required by Israel's law for one to be a legitimate citizen of Israel. The Old Testament also prophesied that when Gentiles would become Israelites in the latter days, they also would adhere to the same nationalistic tags that identified one as an Israelite (Isa. 56:3–8; 66:18–21; Zech. 14:16–19).

[4] Consult G. K. Beale and Benjamin L. Gladd, *Hidden but Now Revealed: A Biblical Theology of Mystery* (Downers Grove, IL: InterVarsity Press, 2014), 186–97, for a brief survey of Old Testament and Jewish passages that describe the conversion of Gentiles in the "latter days."

Surprisingly, Paul claims that the Colossian Gentiles, together with Jewish believers, have now become true Israelites through faith in Christ, the embodiment of true Israel, without having to identify themselves with the various nationalistic distinctives formerly required by Israel's law.[5] Simply put, the mystery in Colossians generally comprises *how Gentiles become true Israelites in the end-time without taking on the physical, covenantal markers of Israel.* The only tag or marker now required is identification with Christ.

This theme is particularly important in Colossians, where the largely Gentile audience struggles with their relationship to the Torah. Instead of finding their identity in their adherence to external prescriptions of the Torah, they must rest in their identity in Christ.

Colossian Heresy

Paul somehow has learned that the church at Colossae is under the threat of false teaching. Nuancing the precise content of the heresy is notoriously difficult, so our conclusions are tenuous at best. It seems that the heresy is a blend of Greco-Roman and Jewish beliefs.[6] The stress on wisdom, knowledge, and "elemental spirits of the world" indicates a Greco-Roman belief system (Col. 2:8, 18–19), and the tenets of Sabbath observance and possibly religious festivals and food regulations may indicate a Jewish side of the heresy (2:11, 20–23). Whatever the case may be, the stakes are quite high. The Colossians are in danger of polluting the gospel and skewing their view of Christ. It seems that the Colossians are being led astray by a syncretistic belief system, a system that incorporates Greco-Roman philosophy and Jewish commandments.

A key tenet to this false teaching is the strong belief in evil spirits and their interaction in the world. "The advocates of the new teaching . . . emphasized a rigorous asceticism with a variety of taboos, ritual observances, and dietary regulations. These practices were motivated at least in part by a desire to gain ritual power over the harmful and malignant forces."[7] In other words, *the Colossians have performed various rituals in order to gain power over these spiritual forces.*

Paul therefore combats this belief system by arguing, first, that Christ is not just a powerful being but also completely supreme over spiritual forces. Second, Christ has defeated these cosmic forces, so there is no need to fear them or perform magic for personal deliverance. These inimical forces were defeated at the cross! Third, the Colossians are free from demonic bondage and are raised with Christ and identified with his authority and image (3:1–10). Fourth, Sabbath and dietary observance is part of the "old" age and has therefore been deemed a "shadow." The new age has

[5] Keep in mind, though, that the Old Testament contained hints that Gentiles would one day join themselves to Israel apart from external markers (e.g., Gen. 15:6). For further discussion of the complex relationship of the Old Testament to the New on this issue, see Beale and Gladd, *Hidden but Now Revealed*, 169–72.

[6] See Douglas J. Moo, *The Letters to the Colossians and to Philemon*, PNTC (Grand Rapids, MI: Eerdmans, 2008), 46–60, for a well-balanced understanding of the Colossian heresy.

[7] Clinton E. Arnold, *The Colossian Syncretism: The Interface between Christianity and Folk Belief at Colossae*, WUNT 77 (Tübingen: Mohr Siebeck, 1995; repr., Grand Rapids, MI: Baker, 1996).

dawned in Christ, so to continue to affirm such practices is to participate in the old age. Lastly, the Colossians must cease all attempts at philosophizing outside of Christ. Their hunger for "knowledge" and "wisdom" is in vain. True wisdom and knowledge stem from Christ alone. Whatever the nuances of the Colossian heresy may be, the core issue is that some leaders at Colossae are "adding" to Christ. Paul counters this belief by proclaiming the centrality of Christ and the centrality of the gospel.

Overview of Colossians

Letter Opening (Col. 1:1–2)

Paul begins this epistle with his standard introductory features; he identifies himself (and his coworker) and the audience of the letter (cf. Gal. 1:1–2; Eph. 1:1–2; Phil. 1:1).[8] Paul anchors his apostleship in the "will of God," which provides the basis for his authority to write the letter. The audience is identified as "the saints and faithful brothers in Christ at Colossae." Though Paul did not establish the church at Colossae (Col. 1:7), he possesses the authority to admonish and encourage this "faithful" church.

Thanksgiving (Col. 1:3–14)

In typical Pauline fashion, the "thanksgiving" section comes on the heels of the letter's opening. This section, like most of Colossians, is laced with Old Testament themes and concepts. Paul subtly places the Colossian church in God's overarching storyline of the Bible and reveals how they are playing a crucial role within it. The divine commission that Adam and Eve were given (Gen. 1:28) has blossomed in Christ (Col. 1:6).

Since the gospel is "bearing fruit" and "growing" at Colossae (1:6), Paul has been fervently praying that the church would persevere and reach a state of maturity (1:9–12). Paul's thankful spirit is also rooted in Christ's work on the Colossians' behalf: "He has delivered us from the domain of darkness and transferred us to the kingdom of his beloved Son, in whom we have redemption, the forgiveness of sins" (1:13–14).

Fulfillment of the Adamic commission (Col. 1:3–12). Paul gives thanks for the church's reception of the gospel. He further claims that the gospel was "bearing fruit and increasing" "in the whole world" (Col. 1:6). Many suggest that Paul alludes to a notable Old Testament passage, Genesis 1:28: "God blessed them and said to them, '*Be fruitful and multiply* and fill the *earth* and subdue it.'"[9] Adam and Eve are commanded to have children, forming a community that enjoys perfect fellowship with God and keeps the created order under their subjection and dominion (Gen. 1:28b). Not only were Adam and Eve to bring the earth under their subjection, but they were also to extend God's presence that was originally limited to the garden of Eden to

[8] For a brief introduction to the genre and structure of Paul's letters, see Patrick Gray, *Opening Paul's Letters: A Reader's Guide to Genre and Interpretation* (Grand Rapids, MI: Baker Academic, 2012).

[9] G. K. Beale, "Colossians," in *Commentary on the New Testament Use of the Old Testament*, ed. G. K. Beale and D. A. Carson (Grand Rapids, MI: Baker Academic, 2007), 842; Christopher A. Beetham, *Echoes of Scripture in the Letter of Paul to the Colossians* (Boston: Brill, 2008), 41–59.

the ends of the earth.[10] Adam and Eve failed to obey God, so their commission was passed on to succeeding generations: Seth, Noah, the patriarchs, and, finally, Israel. But Israel, like the original couple, failed to bring the earth under subjection and extend God's glory to the ends of the earth.

God's plan to fill the earth with his glorious presence and subject it to his rule reaches a decisive point of fulfillment during Jesus's ministry. God's glorious presence has begun to descend from heaven to earth. By alluding to Genesis 1:28, Paul claims that the promise/command to Adam has now begun to be fulfilled in Christ. *God is now beginning to dwell with his people in a new way, and God's glory is indeed beginning to fill the earth.* The church at Colossae plays a key role in the expansion of God's glory!

Since Paul has heard that the Colossians have received the gospel, he encourages them to press on in their faith "bearing fruit" while "increasing in the knowledge of God" (1:10). In other words, they are to continue to live, propagate, and be filled with the gospel.

Christ and the new creation (Col. 1:13–14). The last bit of the thanksgiving section ends on a high note. The focus lands not so much on who Christ is (that will come later) but on what he has accomplished. Verse 13 describes, in graphic detail, the believers' transfer from one realm to another: "He [God] has delivered us from the domain of darkness and transferred us to the kingdom of his beloved Son." Through Christ's work during his life, death, and resurrection (1:14), Christians are no longer held captive to the "domain of darkness" but participate in the "kingdom of his beloved Son." This transfer entails the forgiveness of sin and the new life that is found only in Christ, a new creational existence that is nothing short of astounding. If believers have robust faith in Christ's work (1:10–11), they are assured of a present and future existence in the new heavens and earth.

The Exalted Christ (Col. 1:15–23)

What follows is one of the most treasured portions of Colossians. This unit is typically referred to as a "hymn," since it is a distinct unit and poetically arranged.[11] We aren't sure whether Paul authored this hymn or simply adapted it for his purposes. Whatever the case may be, Paul has tailored it to fit his purpose here in the immediate context.

The hymn focuses on the person and work of Christ and primarily develops two facets: (1) the chronological priority of Christ (his preexistence)—Christ's supremacy over the first creation (1:15–17); (2) the creational priority of Christ—his supremacy over the new creation (1:18–20).

Christ's supremacy over the first creation (Col. 1:15–18a). Within the first portion of the hymn (1:15–18a), Christ is viewed as an Adamic figure who has regained

[10] For a biblical-theological discussion of the temple and God's intention to dwell with creation and humanity, see G. K. Beale, *The Temple and the Church's Mission: A Biblical Theology of the Dwelling Place of God*, NSBT 17 (Downers Grove, IL: InterVarsity Press, 2004), and the abridged volume G. K. Beale and Mitchell Kim, *God Dwells among Us: Expanding Eden to the Ends of the Earth* (Downers Grove, IL: InterVarsity Press, 2014).

[11] See Ralph P. Martin, "Hymns, Hymn Fragments, Songs, Spiritual Songs," in *DPL*, 419–23, for a general overview of hymns in the Pauline literature.

control over the universe, including both physical and spiritual beings. Colossians 1:15 recalls Genesis 1:27:

> So God created man *in his own image*,
> *in the image of God* he created him;
> male and female he created them. (cf. 1 Cor. 11:7; 2 Cor. 4:4)

Sonship is intimately tethered to existing in one's "image." God's relationship to Adam illustrates this. Since Adam is created in God's "image," he is deemed God's "son." Adam's son, Seth, was said to be in Adam's image: "When Adam had lived 130 years, he fathered a *son* in his own likeness, *after his image*, and named him Seth" (Gen. 5:3). The first Adam, being in the image of God, was to rule over the created order on behalf of God. But as we know all too well, Adam failed. So God raised up others and made them "in his image" (Seth, Noah, Abraham, Isaac, et al.). They were fashioned to rule over the created order and spread God's glorious presence. Finally, God sent his Son to earth, who was also in his image. Jesus is God's "Son," which means that he is also in the "image" of his Father (Col. 1:13, 15). Jesus, as God's pristine image, fulfilled the original Adamic commission by faithfully bringing all of creation under God's subjection.

Paul also calls Christ "the firstborn": "He is the image of the invisible God, *the firstborn* of all creation" (1:15). Though some argue that Christ as the "firstborn" reflects a creaturely state, this is both theologically and exegetically problematic. Christ's status as the "firstborn" is to be taken not as a literal depiction (i.e., Christ is literally the first one *born*) but as a figurative expression. This particular concept is rooted in the Old Testament.[12] "Then you shall say to Pharaoh, 'Thus says the LORD, Israel is my *firstborn* son'" (Ex. 4:22; cf. Ps. 89:27; Heb. 1:6). These texts refer not to a literal or physical "firstborn" but to relational priority. In other words, Christ is the "firstborn" because he is the *most supreme* being (not because he is created). Paul's point in Colossians 1:15 is quite clear: Christ is preexistent and sovereign over the created order.

Christ's supremacy over the new creation (Col. 1:18b–20). The second portion of Paul's hymn is stunningly majestic and focused on Christ (1:18b–20). It centers on how Christ relates to the new order of creation. First, Christ, as a resurrected being, has begun the end-time renewal of the cosmos ("and through him to reconcile to himself all things," 1:20). Second, Christ embodies God's glorious presence, as the end-time temple. This is the same divine presence that was promised to Adam and Eve and was partially housed in the tabernacle/temple. Now, God's unfettered presence has descended to earth in Christ (cf. Matt. 1:22–23).

Christ's work of reconciliation (Col. 1:21–23). Following hard on the heels of Paul's description of Christ as the supreme ruler and God's divine, preexistent Son, the

[12] See Craig S. Keener, *The IVP Bible Background Commentary: New Testament*, 2nd ed. (Downers Grove, IL: InterVarsity Press, 2014), 571.

apostle highlights his role as the great reconciler: "You, who *once were alienated and hostile in mind*, doing evil deeds, *he has now reconciled* in his body of flesh by his death" (Col. 1:21–22a). Here is the very heart of the gospel: God choosing to accept wretched sinners through the death of his righteous Son (cf. 2 Cor. 5:21). Paul carefully discloses the intended *effect* of God's great act of reconciling sinners: "to present you holy and blameless and above reproach before him" (Col. 1:22b). God desires that humanity exist in a restored condition, a condition that was initially promised to Adam and Eve if they obeyed perfectly (Gen. 1:28; 2:15).

Christ and the Unveiled Mystery (Col. 1:24–29)

The last portion of Colossians 1 largely entails Paul's relationship to the gospel and his role in promulgating it. The thrust of this section is that Paul endures great personal suffering for the sake of converting unbelievers, particularly the Gentiles.

Sharing in Christ's suffering (Col. 1:24). Verse 24 is notoriously difficult to understand on several levels: "Now I rejoice in my sufferings for your sake, and *in my flesh I am filling up what is lacking in Christ's afflictions* for the sake of his body, that is, the church." Is Paul suggesting that Christ's work on the cross was somehow incomplete? Does Paul suffer the same way as Christ suffered on the cross?

Paul's language here generally refers to Paul's "cruciform lifestyle" (cf. 2 Cor. 4:7–12; 12:9–10). That is, the apostle embodies the paradox of the cross: strength in weakness, victory in defeat, and wisdom in foolishness. Paul's discussion of wisdom in 1 Corinthians 1–2 is his longest exposition of the nature of the cross and the believer's understanding of it. At the heart of those two chapters is this concept of power in weakness. To state it succinctly, while Jesus is suffering a shameful death on the cross, he is simultaneously the supreme ruler. He rules while undergoing defeat. Mysteriously, Jesus is King at the very moment he is accursed (cf. John 3:14; 12:32).

Therefore, when Paul states that he "fill[s] up" Christ's "afflictions," he refers to living a cruciform lifestyle, a life that embodies the cross. A key Old Testament background probably lies in Isaiah's conception of the suffering servant (42:1–9; 49:1–6; 50:4–9; 52:13–53:12). Jesus fulfills this Isaianic expectation, and, by implication, so too does Paul (and all believers). When Paul suffers for the sake of Christ, he's conforming to the pattern of the Christ. Just as Christ displayed power in the midst of defeat, so too Paul displays power in the midst of defeat. Christ executes his messianic prerogative to rule while dying, and Paul rules alongside Christ when he suffers. Paul's ministry is, therefore, brought into conformity with Christ's work on the cross, not with reference to sin but with reference to ruling.

A question still remains, however: What is the nature of the intimate relationship between suffering and the expansion of the gospel? Paul acknowledges this connection when he claims that he "fill[s] up" Christ's "afflictions." This is not solely a New Testament phenomenon, but a redemptive-historical relationship that has been established from the beginning.

Part of the curse that Eve receives in light of the fall demonstrates the organic relationship between suffering and multiplication:

> To the woman he said,
>
> "I will surely multiply your pain in childbearing;
> *in pain you shall bring forth children.*
> Your desire shall be for your husband,
> and he shall rule over you." (Gen. 3:16)[13]

The curse recalls Adam and Eve's commission to fill the earth with godly individuals who will subdue it and spread God's glory (Gen. 1:28). Within the curse, this commission is reaffirmed; God will ensure that Adam and Eve will have progeny, but this process strangely entails great pain and suffering.

We see the twin themes of suffering and multiplication crop up once more in Israel's career in Egypt: "But the more they [the Israelites] were oppressed, *the more they multiplied and the more they spread abroad*" (Ex. 1:12; cf. 1:7). The Israelites have come under the Egyptian hand of slavery, yet, paradoxically, the more the Israelites suffer, the more they multiply.

As we make our way into the New Testament, we can trace this theme through the book of Acts. The narrative of Acts carefully weaves together suffering and the expansion of the gospel. For example, in Acts 6:7 we see that "the word of God continued to increase, and the number of the disciples multiplied greatly in Jerusalem, and a great many of the priests became obedient to the faith." Immediately following this episode is the first martyr of Acts—Stephen (Acts 6:8–7:60; cf. 9:31; 12:24; 16:5; 19:20).

When we view Colossians 1:24 through this biblical-theological lens, we can grasp the significance of Paul's enigmatic words. As Paul and the saints suffer, the gospel ever increases.

The union of Jew and Gentile in Christ (Col. 1:25–29). Paul shifts his attention to the content of his message to the Gentiles:

> I have become its servant by the commission God gave me to present to you the word of God in its fullness—*the mystery that has been kept hidden for ages and generations, but is now disclosed to the Lord's people.* To them God has chosen to make known *among the Gentiles* the glorious riches of *this mystery*, which is Christ in you, the hope of glory. (1:25–27 NIV 2011)

Though only a few verses, this section is packed with great significance. Why would Paul claim that a particular aspect of the relationship between Jews and Gentiles was previously "hidden"? In other words, there's something about the way in which Jews and Gentiles relate to one another in the New Testament age that was not perfectly clear in the Old Testament.

[13] For a biblical-theological study of this theme, see Mitchell Kim. "The Blessing of the Curse: Fulfilling Genesis 1:28 in a Context of Suffering" (PhD diss., Wheaton College, 2011).

When we examine Colossians 1:25–27 in light of Ephesians 3, we conclude that both passages are remarkably similar. Helpfully, Paul's discussion of the relationship between Jews and Gentiles is far more developed in Ephesians 3 than in his brief words in Colossians 1:25–27. What remains implicit in Colossians 1:27 ("Christ in you") becomes explicit in Ephesians 3:6 ("Gentiles are fellow heirs, members of the same body, and partakers of the promise in Christ Jesus").

The mystery is not that these two groups are merely one covenant community, since that was already clearly prophesied in the Old Testament (Psalm 87; Isa. 19:18–24; 49:3–6; 66:18–21; etc.); rather, they are one in the person of Christ. Paul claims that Gentiles have now become true Israelites through faith in Christ, the embodiment of true Israel, without having to identify themselves with the various nationalistic distinctives formerly required by Israel's law. Simply put, the mystery comprises how Gentiles become true Israelites in the end-time without taking on the covenantal markers of Israel.

Admonition to Denounce False Teaching (Col. 2:1–23)

Colossians 2 is largely a confrontation with the Colossian heresy. Most of what we know about this false teaching stems from this chapter. The first half of the chapter (2:1–15) generally entails Christ's work on behalf of believers, that is, his victory over the inimical spirits and his great act of spiritually resurrecting believers. The second half of chapter 2 confronts the false teaching more or less head-on (2:16–23). Christ is far better than any shred of Jewish or pagan ritual.

The superiority of Christ (Col. 2:1–15). Paul admits that though he's never met the Colossians personally (Epaphras founded the church—1:7; 4:12–13), he strives earnestly for them and holds a special place in his heart for this congregation. The main point of Colossians 2:1–5 occurs in 2:4: "I say this in order that no one may delude you with plausible arguments." I mentioned in the introductory portion of this study that one of the reasons why Paul penned this letter is because of the false teaching in Colossae. It appears that some at Colossae were advocating the use of pagan rituals alongside a belief in the gospel. Not only were rituals a part of this false teaching, but so too was some form of Jewish philosophy. Though we are unable to reconstruct this false teaching with great precision, we can nevertheless grasp Paul's reaction to it: the Colossians were to embrace Christ without wavering. Apparently these false teachers were quite skilled in their delivery; hence their "plausible arguments" (2:4). The false teachers were apparently so persuasive that they managed to convince some of the Colossians to abandon aspects of the apostolic teaching.

Colossians 2:6 moves the argument along by further unpacking the thrust of 2:1–5. The main point of the previous section (2:1–5) is "that no one may delude you with plausible arguments" (2:4). Here in the following section, the main point exposes the problem with the false teaching—it is "philosophy and empty deceit, according to human tradition, according to the elemental spirits of the world, and *not according to Christ*" (2:8). Instead of embracing a teaching that is Christ-focused, the Colossians have believed a message that is void of the gospel and Christ.

Paul's imperative to "walk in him [Christ]" (2:6a) is spelled out in the following verses. In the immediate context, the primary way the Colossians must conduct themselves is to resist false teaching and be "rooted and built up in him" as they "were taught" (2:7). Colossians 2:8a further unpacks Paul's statement in 2:6a, that the church must "walk" in Christ, by first telling them what *not* to do: "See to it that no one takes you captive by philosophy and empty deceit" (2:8a). In other words, the spiritual health of the Colossians hinges on their denial of false teaching and their embrace of sound doctrine.

The second part of 2:8b gives us the specifics of the false doctrine: it is "according to human tradition, according to the elemental spirits of the world." The first part of this description ("according to human tradition") probably describes the origin of the false teaching. Instead of having its origin in the triune God, the false teaching is, from start to finish, characterized by a human worldview (whether Jewish or pagan). That is, the Colossians are confronted with a teaching that is opposed to the worldview of God as it is manifested in the apostolic teaching. The second part ("according to the elemental spirits of the world" [κατὰ τὰ στοιχεῖα τοῦ κόσμου]) is most peculiar here in 2:8b (and, in part, 2:20) and not easy to understand.

The phrase "elemental spirits" is the plural of one Greek word (στοιχεῖον) which generally refers to a "principle," or something "basic."[14] It describes the most basic structure of a given topic. For example, the term can mean a letter of the alphabet or elementary teachings. But Paul provides some help in this regard, as he contextualizes the term with the key term "world" (κόσμος). Some scholars argue that "elemental spiritual forces of this world" refers to "basic teaching" of the Torah, and others argue that the phrase refers exclusively to spiritual beings or angelic forces (ESV, HCSB, NIV). Both of these views fail to reckon with the word "world." The most natural interpretation of the τὰ στοιχεῖα τοῦ κόσμου is the *basic elements of the cosmos*. The combination of στοιχεῖον and κόσμος appears several times in Greek literature, most of which come from a first-century-AD Jewish author Philo. One of his most pertinent texts comes from *On the Life of Moses* 1.96.3: "The chastisement was different from the usual kind, for *the elements* [στοιχεῖα] of the universe—earth, fire, air, water—carried out the assault. God's judgment was that the materials which had served to produce *the world* [κόσμος] should serve also to destroy the land of the impious."[15]

Yet, the phrase in 2:8b and 2:20 may also *include* a "spiritual" or demonic element, since angels are intertwined with this physical cosmos. This spiritual and physical dimension to the phrase makes much sense in light of Paul's use of the term "world" elsewhere (e.g., Rom. 3:6, 19; 5:12–13; 11:12, 15). According to the New

[14] For a brief taxonomy of options for evaluating τὰ στοιχεῖα τοῦ κόσμου, consult Murray J. Harris, *Colossians and Philemon*, EGGNT (Nashville: B&H, 2010), 84–85. One of the most detailed analyses of this phrase is furnished by G. Delling, "στοιχεῖον," in *TDNT*, 7:670–87.

[15] See also *Mos.* I, 155.5; II, 267.4; *Abr.* 162.6; *Opif.* 52.5; *Cher.* 127.3; cf. 2 Pet. 3:10, 12.

Testament, the "world" is part of the two-aged schema, whereby the "old age" has begun to be destroyed and the "new age" has broken in. When we define "world" according to this pervasive New Testament framework, we learn that the term encompasses not only the physical particulars but also the spiritual. In other words, "elemental things" consist of demonic forces that are intertwined with the fallen physical cosmos (cf. Gal. 4:3, 9).

Therefore, when Paul states that the heresy is "according to human tradition, according to the elemental spirits of the world," he claims that the false teaching is the product of and aligned with the fallen angels and cosmos.[16] Simply put, the false teaching at Colossae is the product of an "old-age" worldview, a corrupt worldview that has come under divine judgment.

The folly of wisdom outside of Christ (Col. 2:16–23). Colossians 2:16 and 2:21 describe what appears to be a Jewish teaching: "Therefore let no one pass judgment on you in questions of *food and drink*, or with regard to a *festival or a new moon or a Sabbath*. . . . '*Do not handle, Do not taste, Do not touch*.'" In the Old Testament, the Israelites were forbidden to eat certain types of food, as they were associated with the pagan nations and idolatry (Leviticus 11; Deuteronomy 14). The Israelites were also required to celebrate several annual feasts and rest on the Sabbath (Ex. 10:9; 12:14, 17; 20:8; Lev. 23:34; etc.). The point of these requirements is that they demarcated the Israelites from the surrounding pagan nations. God is "holy," void of sin, and he requires his people to act accordingly (Lev. 11:44–45; 20:26; etc.). Apparently, some of the false teachers at Colossae were requiring the church to keep portions of the Mosaic law.

Paul responds vigorously to this teaching and labels these Jewish regulations a "shadow": "These [Jewish laws] are a *shadow* of the things to come" (Col. 2:17a). The point is that these Jewish rules were not an end in and of themselves. They pointed beyond themselves and expected something greater and more permanent.

Paul then discloses the very object to which these pointed: "The substance belongs to *Christ*" (2:17b). In other words, these Jewish rules that were being required by the false teachers find their fulfillment in Christ, nothing more and nothing less. Now that Christ has come, why are they continuing to embrace a "shadow" (cf. Heb. 10:1a)?

Life as Resurrected Beings (Col. 3:1–4:1)

After confronting the Colossians' heresy, Paul unveils the key motivation for Christian living: the initial, spiritual resurrection of the saints. The resurrection not only imparts new life to believers; it also serves as the basis for Christian ethics.[17] A guiding principle to this section is found in Colossians 3:14: "And above all these put

[16] See Moo, *Letters to the Colossians and to Philemon*, 191–92.

[17] For further discussion of the believer's already–not yet resurrected status, see G. K. Beale, *A New Testament Biblical Theology: The Unfolding of the Old Testament in the New* (Grand Rapids, MI: Baker Academic, 2011), 131–36, 234–38; and Benjamin L. Gladd and Matthew Harmon, *Making All Things New: Eschatology in the Life of the Church* (Grand Rapids, MI: Baker Academic, 2016).

on love, which binds everything together in perfect harmony." Unity between all personal relationships (3:18–4:1) is the climax of this chapter and the entire book, but this can be achieved only by identifying with the risen Christ.

The believers' identification with the risen Christ (Col. 3:1–11). In Greek, Colossians 3:1 begins with a conditional term "if." But this condition assumes the reality. We could thus rephrase Paul's words: "If, then, you have been raised with Christ (which you have), seek the things that are above." This is why some translations use the word "since" at the beginning of verse 1 (NIV, NLT). In other words, *because* Colossians have been "raised with" Christ, they must "seek the things that are above."

The language used here in 3:1 ("raised with") is specific; Paul has in mind none other than the resurrected status of believers.[18] It is tempting to view the wording here as purely figurative (Christians are *like* resurrected saints), but that does not reckon with the seriousness of Paul's claims here and in the rest of the New Testament (see John 5; Eph. 2:5–6).

Paul views the resurrection to have begun in the souls of believers. He even roots Christian ethics in the believers' resurrected status. Note Colossians 3:1–2: "Since, then, *you have been raised with Christ*, set your hearts on things above, where Christ is seated at the right hand of God. *Set your minds on things above, not on earthly things*" (NIV). Believers are to adopt a heavenly mind-set *because* they have been spiritually raised with Christ. Though believers still wrestle with indwelling sin, they enjoy an inaugurated resurrected status with the risen Christ.

Colossians 3:5–11 is the natural implication of the believers' current and future resurrected status: "Put to death *therefore* what is earthly in you: sexual immorality, impurity, passion, evil desire, and covetousness, which is idolatry" (3:5). In typical fashion, Paul refrains from naming every single sin under the sun but simply mentions a smattering of sins (cf. Gal. 5:19–20). Intriguingly, the imperative in Colossians 3:9a receives quite a bit of emphasis in this section: "Do not lie to one another." It is unclear why Paul lands on this theme. Perhaps there is a specific problem with the members at Colossae lying to each other, or perhaps Paul wants to speak to the church very generally here.

Colossians 3:9–10 details why Paul's readers must not lie: "Do not lie to one another, *seeing that you have put off the old self* with its practices and *have put on the new self*, which is being renewed in knowledge after the image of its creator." The wording here in Greek is, on the surface, most peculiar. A literal translation would be "Do not lie to one another, because you have taken off *the old man* . . . and have put on *the new man*." English translations render "man" here as "self," which misses a crucial biblical-theological link. Paul's wording reflects the believers' identity as fashioned in the image of Christ, the "last Adam" or "man" (1 Cor. 15:45).

Notice how Paul taps into this biblical-theological theme through the use of a clothing metaphor: "you have *put off* the old man . . . and have *put on* the new man"

[18] See also Peter T. O'Brien, *Colossians–Philemon*, WBC 44 (Nashville: Thomas Nelson, 1982), 119–21, 159.

(cf. Col. 3:12–13).[19] But why would Paul make use of this clothing metaphor? Judaism appropriates this metaphor in a considerable number of texts similar to Paul's imagery. For example, 1 Enoch 62:15–16 states, "The righteous and elect ones shall rise from the earth and shall cease being of downcast face. *They shall wear the garments of glory. These garments of yours shall become the garments of life from the Lord of the Spirits. Neither shall your garments wear out.*" Again, in the Ascension of Isaiah 4:16 we read, "But the saints will come with the Lord *with their robes* which are stored up in the seventh heaven above." These Jewish texts clearly indicate that righteous individuals will don heavenly garments. Judaism speculated about Adam and Eve's garments. Adam was first created in an exalted position, but as a result of the fall, he was stripped of his glorious "robe" (cf. Gen. 3:21).

Paul's teaching on the resurrection body, corresponding to the image of the last Adam, generally differs from the Jewish conception of resurrection. According to the Jewish position, Adam was created in a glorious state and, after the fall, lost that glory. The righteous saints are, therefore, to return to Adam's pre-fall state and become like the original Adam. When Paul touches on this issue here in Colossians 3 and elsewhere, he claims that believers conform not to the image of the first Adam but to the image of the last Adam. Christ (along with believers in him) differs from the first Adam; his new body is not a return to the pre-fall body but an entirely different body, re-created by the Spirit (1 Cor. 15:45–49).

In Colossians 3:11, Paul lists a concrete example of how his readers are to live this Adamic life: "Here there is not Greek and Jew, circumcised and uncircumcised, barbarian, Scythian, slave, free; but Christ is all, and in all." In other words, an effect of resurrection life is the complete equality between all members of the church. Division and fracture characterize "first-Adam" living, whereas life according to the "last Adam" entails genuine unity.

Living in light of the believers' resurrection (Col. 3:12–4:1). The last half of Colossians 3 details how the resurrection life in Christ operates within the body of Christ. As is typical of Paul, he moves from the indicative (the believers' position in Christ) into the imperative (how believers are to function now that they have been united to Christ). The second half of chapter 3 continues the imperative of the Christian life. Believers must never attempt to "do" the Christian life outside of a robust faith in Christ. With this in mind, Paul will now detail how Christians ought to relate to one another within the body of Christ.

The beginning of verse 12 is crucial to the entire section of 3:12–17: "Put on then, *as God's chosen ones*, holy and beloved, compassionate hearts, kindness, humility, meekness, and patience." The command to "put on" is rooted in the Colossians status "as God's chosen ones." This expression is reminiscent of 1 Peter 2:9: "But you are a *chosen race*, a royal priesthood, a *holy* nation." Interestingly, in the immediate context of this verse, Peter alludes to an Old Testament text that establishes Israel's

[19] For a discussion of clothing in the Old Testament, see Gordon P. Hugenberger, *Marriage as a Covenant: Biblical Law and Ethics as Developed from Malachi*, VTSup 52 (Boston: Brill, 1994; repr., Grand Rapids, MI: Baker, 1998), 198–99n129.

status and mission before God: "Now therefore, if you will indeed obey my voice and keep my covenant, you shall be my treasured possession among all peoples, for all the earth is mine; and *you shall be to me a kingdom of priests and a holy nation*" (Ex. 19:5–6). This Old Testament text and others like it remind the Israelites of their commission to be a godly community that evangelizes the surrounding nations, so that the entire earth would be filled with God's glory (cf. Gen. 1:26–28; Psalm 8). This commission was originally given to Adam and Eve, but they failed. It was then passed down to the patriarchs and Israel, but they, like the original couple, failed. Jesus, as the "last Adam" and true Israel, obeyed where his predecessors failed. He subdued God's enemies, began the process of building a godly community, and initiated the descent of God's glory on the earth.

All believers who identify with Christ through faith participate in God's end-time people group (i.e., "true Israel"). As the end-time people of God, the Colossians can rightly be called "chosen . . . holy and beloved" (3:12). The same Christ who spiritually resurrected this community has also formed them into the end-time covenant community.

Colossians 3:14–15 is wonderfully important to this section, as Paul gets to the core issue at stake: "And above all these *put on love, which binds everything together in perfect harmony*. And let the *peace* of Christ rule in your hearts, to which indeed you were called in one body." Love is the key characteristic of Christian conduct within the covenant community (cf. Mark 12:31; Rom. 13:9). But love is a means to an end in this context. The purpose of love between covenant members is "perfect harmony." Unity between people groups, families, and all other communities can be achieved and maintained only if all parties earnestly love one another.

This section in Colossians 3:18–21 is known as the "household codes" and is nearly identical to the codes found in Ephesians 5:22–6:9. Many scholars believe that these codes stem from the wider Greco-Roman world, wherein codes were given concerning the relationship between husband and wife, master and slave, and fathers and children. What must be kept in mind, though, is the codes' relationship to the end-time people of God as a new creational community.[20] The household codes are intimately bound up with the gospel and the believer's relationship to them. In Colossians 3:1, Paul rehearses the believers' identification with Christ, the last Adam. Verse 10 also mentions that believers are participating in the last Adam's image ("put on the new [man]"). Note that immediately following both of these new creational indicatives stand two sets of new creational imperatives (3:2–9, 11–17). The household codes in 3:18–4:1 are the functional outworking of being in the image of the last Adam.

The codes progress from the relationship between husband and wife, to children and their parents, and then to slaves and masters:

> *Wives*, submit to your husbands, as is fitting in the Lord. *Husbands*, love your wives, and do not be harsh with them. *Children*, obey your parents in everything, for this pleases the Lord. *Fathers*, do not provoke your children, lest they become

[20] See Philip H. Towner's balanced essay, "Households and Household Codes," in *DPL*, 417–19.

> discouraged. *Bondservants*, obey in everything those who are your earthly masters. (3:18–22)

It is not clear why Paul proceeds in this manner. It could be that the husband and wife form the ultimate relational nucleus, and all other relationships flow from that first grouping.

Gospel Proclamation and the Letter Closing (Col. 4:2–18)

Paul urgently requests that he may have an opportunity to spread the gospel (4:2–6) and then relates several personal requests (4:7–17). He finishes this letter intent on reminding the Colossians how much he and his friends care for them. They are to take comfort knowing that Paul's words, as contained in this epistle, are meant for their spiritual health. This letter stems from Paul's love and concern.

Paul's request for evangelism (Col. 4:2–6). Following the household codes, the apostle turns his attention once more to conduct within the covenant community, but this time with an eye on their vertical relationship with God: "Continue steadfastly in prayer, being watchful in it with thanksgiving" (Col. 4:2). Colossians 4:2–4 is a concluding subsection of 3:5–4:6, which is tied to Paul's concern for the gospel message to be communicated to unbelievers. Paul asks the Colossian congregation to pray earnestly for their own lives and his (4:2). Specifically, when the Colossians pray for Paul, they are to ask that God would "open" a "door for the word" (4:3a). This opportunity will enable Paul to "declare the mystery of Christ." Here the "mystery of Christ" appears to be synonymous with the "word" or "message." In other words, Paul pleads with the Colossians that they pray for the proclamation of the disclosed mystery that incorporates the Torah-free message to Gentiles (see discussion above). According to verse 3b, Paul was imprisoned for preaching the "mystery of Christ": "on account of which I am in prison." Paul's personal insight betrays the significance of the "mystery of Christ" and the urgency of his request; he remains imprisoned because of the proclamation of this unveiled mystery.

Personal requests and the letter closing (Col. 4:7–18). After finishing the body of the letter (4:6), Paul begins the formal "closing" section. Two individuals will accompany the epistle to the church at Colossae: Tychicus and Onesimus. Though we are unsure whether these two are the epistle's official letter couriers, it seems likely they are.

According to Colossians 4:7–8, Tychicus and Onesimus will perform two duties: (1) inform the Colossians of Paul's Roman imprisonment; (2) "encourage" the "hearts" of the Colossians. This probably entails worshiping with the church and also some form of teaching. This latter component is crucial for a variety of reasons. The letter couriers will be able to explain and perhaps supplement the epistle. Tychicus and Onesimus are no doubt familiar with its contents by the time they are sent to the church. Though there are no formal quotations from the Old Testament, as we have seen, Colossians is rich with Old Testament allusions and concepts. The Gentiles at

Colossae have varying degrees of Old Testament knowledge, some understanding most, if not all, of the Old Testament allusions. Others, though, might not be able to perceive Paul's subtle references. The letter couriers can fill this gap and inform the members of the Old Testament texts or concepts Paul has in mind.

In 4:10–11, Paul highlights three key individuals who are with him in Rome:

> *Aristarchus* my fellow prisoner greets you, and *Mark* the cousin of Barnabas (concerning whom you have received instructions—if he comes to you, welcome him), and *Jesus who is called Justus*. These are the only men of the circumcision among my fellow workers for the kingdom of God, and they have been a comfort to me.

Aristarchus is described as Paul's "fellow prisoner." The second prominent individual is named Mark. This is the same Mark that would write a gospel bearing his name (see Acts 12:25; 13:4–12; Philem. 24; 2 Tim. 4:11; 1 Pet. 5:13). The last person that Paul mentions is an individual named "Jesus Justus." He is mentioned only here in Colossians 4, so we know little about him.

Epaphras, the founder of the church in Colossae, sends his greetings back to the church. Paul and his coworkers learned about the Colossians and the false teaching from him (Col. 1:4). Apparently, Epaphras does not embark on the journey back to Colossae from Rome. Mark is not the only person in Rome who will write a Gospel on the life of Jesus. Luke, too, is with Paul and his coworkers. Paul describes Luke only as "the beloved physician" (4:14). When Paul is once again imprisoned in Rome, Luke stays by his side. Taken together, Mark, Luke, and Paul will write a considerable amount of the literature in the New Testament. Their theology is the result of years of ministry, personal interaction, and hardship.

Select Bibliography

Alexander, T. Desmond, and Brian S. Rosner, eds. *New Dictionary of Biblical Theology: Exploring the Unity and Diversity of Scripture*. Downers Grove, IL: InterVarsity Press, 2000.

Arnold, Clinton E. *The Colossian Syncretism: The Interface between Christianity and Folk Belief at Colossae*. WUNT 77. Tübingen: Mohr Siebeck, 1995. Repr., Grand Rapids, MI: Baker, 1996.

Beale, G. K. "Colossians and Philemon." In *Commentary on the New Testament Use of the Old Testament*, edited by G. K. Beale and D. A. Carson, 841–70. Grand Rapids, MI: Baker Academic, 2007.

———. *A New Testament Biblical Theology: The Unfolding of the Old Testament in the New*. Grand Rapids, MI: Baker Academic, 2011.

———. *The Temple and the Church's Mission: A Biblical Theology of the Dwelling Place of God*. NSBT 17. Downers Grove, IL: InterVarsity Press, 2004.

Beale, G. K., and Benjamin Gladd. *Hidden but Now Revealed: A Biblical Theology of Mystery*. Downers Grove, IL: InterVarsity Press, 2014.

Beale, G. K., and Mitchell Kim, *God Dwells among Us: Expanding Eden to the Ends of the Earth*. Downers Grove, IL: InterVarsity Press, 2014.

Beetham, Christopher A. *Echoes of Scripture in the Letter of Paul to the Colossians*. Boston: Brill, 2008.

Bruce, F. F. *The Epistles to the Colossians, to Philemon, and to the Ephesians*. NICNT. Grand Rapids, MI: Eerdmans, 1984.

Carson, D. A., and Douglas J. Moo. *An Introduction to the New Testament*. 2nd ed. Grand Rapids, MI: Zondervan, 2005.

Delling, Gerhard. "στοιχεῖον." *TDNT* 7:670–87.

Garland, David E. *Colossians, Philemon*. NIVAC. Grand Rapids, MI: Zondervan, 1998.

Gladd, Benjamin L., and Matthew Harmon, *Making All Things New: Inaugurated Eschatology in the Life of the Church*. Grand Rapids, MI: Baker Academic, 2016.

Gray, Patrick. *Opening Paul's Letters: A Reader's Guide to Genre and Interpretation*. Grand Rapids, MI: Baker Academic, 2012.

Harris, Murray J. *Colossians and Philemon*. EGGNT. Nashville: B&H, 2010.

Hugenberger, Gordon P. *Marriage as a Covenant: Biblical Law and Ethics as Developed from Malachi*. VTSup 52. Boston: Brill, 1994. Repr., Grand Rapids, MI: Baker, 1998.

Keener, Craig S. *The IVP Bible Background Commentary: New Testament*. 2nd ed. Downers Grove, IL: InterVarsity Press, 2014.

Kim, Mitchell. "The Blessing of the Curse: Fulfilling Genesis 1:28 in a Context of Suffering." PhD diss., Wheaton College, 2011.

Martin, Ralph P. "Hymns, Hymn Fragments, Songs, Spiritual Songs." In *Dictionary of Paul and His Letters*, edited by Gerald F. Hawthorne, Ralph P. Martin, and Daniel G. Reid, 419–23. Downers Grove, IL: InterVarsity Press, 1993.

Moo, Douglas J. *The Letters to the Colossians and to Philemon*. PNTC. Grand Rapids, MI: Eerdmans, 2008.

O'Brien, Peter T. *Colossians–Philemon*. WBC 44; Nashville: Thomas Nelson, 1982.

Pao, David W. *Colossians and Philemon*. ZECNT. Grand Rapids, MI: Zondervan, 2012.

Towner, Philip H. "Households and Household Codes." In *Dictionary of Paul and His Letters*, edited by Gerald F. Hawthorne, Ralph P. Martin, and Daniel G. Reid, 417–19. Downers Grove, IL: InterVarsity Press, 1993.

Wright, N. T. *Colossians and Philemon*. TNTC. Downers Grove, IL: InterVarsity Press, 1986.

12

1 Thessalonians

Robert J. Cara

Introduction

For many Christians, 1 Thessalonians (along with 2 Thessalonians) is known primarily as the book that has several somewhat difficult second coming passages (1 Thess. 4:13–18; 5:1–11; also 2 Thess. 1:5–10; 2:1–12).[1] And it does. Some in the young Thessalonian church had questions or were confused about aspects of the second coming. Thankfully, Paul's central points in these passages are clear, even if not all the details are.

In the scholarly world, 1 Thessalonians is similarly known for its eschatological aspects, but also its early date. Scholars of all stripes assign it a date of approximately AD 50. Depending on one's dating of Galatians, all agree that 1 Thessalonians is Paul's first or second canonical letter.[2] By studying 1 Thessalonians, we see some of Paul's earliest statements about the glories of Christ (e.g., 1:10) and his love for the young Thessalonian church (e.g., 2:20).[3]

Background Issues

Thessalonica

Ancient Thessalonica was an important and prosperous city. At the time of Paul's writing, it was the capital city of the Roman Macedonian province (modern-day northern

[1] If one is especially interested in debates about dispensational theology, 1 Thessalonians takes on even more notoriety for this topic, as 1 Thess. 4:17 is the classic "rapture" passage.

[2] Depending on one's dating of James and Galatians, 1 Thessalonians may be the first, second, or third earliest New Testament canonical book. According to my chronology, James was the first book written (mid–AD 40s), then Galatians (AD 48), and then 1 Thessalonians (AD 50). Raymond E. Brown believes 1 Thessalonians is "the oldest preserved Christian writing" (*An Introduction to the New Testament*, ABRL [New York: Doubleday, 1997], 456).

[3] From my perspective, some critical scholars overemphasize the importance of the early date of 1 Thessalonians. Many semantic differences with later Pauline letters are viewed as contradictions based on the assumption that Paul changed his theology in contradictory ways through time. Yes, Paul did learn through time, but this is not always the explanation for his semantic differences. Sometimes, for example, it is related to the specific problem at the church to which he is writing. As far as contradictions are concerned, my view of the Word of God would not concede that any of these differences are contradictions.

Greece, the southern portion of modern-day Macedonia, and modern-day Albania). The economy was aided by its being a major harbor on the Aegean Sea and a major stop on the Via Egnatia, an important east-west road connecting Dyrrhachium in western Macedonia (modern-day Albania) with Byzantium (modern-day Istanbul).

Thessalonica had good relations with Rome. At the time that 1 Thessalonians was written, Thessalonica was a senatorial province under the direct control of the Roman senate, and Claudius was the Roman emperor (AD 41–54). Because of the good relations with Rome, it is assumed that the imperial cult was strong in Thessalonica and may explain at least in part the hostility toward the Thessalonian Christians (Acts 17:7–8; 1 Thess. 2:14; also 2 Thess. 1:6).[4]

Besides 1–2 Thessalonians, "Thessalonica" and "Thessalonians" are mentioned in the New Testament in Acts 17:1–9, 13; 20:4; Philippians 4:16; and 2 Timothy 4:10.

Since the provenance of 1–2 Thessalonians is Corinth, information about Corinth may, in theory, also be valuable for the interpretation of 1 Thessalonians. (For information on Corinth, see the discussion in the 1 Corinthians chapter.)

Authorship and Date

First Thessalonians 1:1 states that this letter is from Paul, Silvanus (Silas), and Timothy. There is clear indication that Paul is the real author and that Silvanus and Timothy endorse what he writes (i.e., Paul primarily uses "we" as an editorial "we").[5]

As will be discussed in the chapter on 2 Thessalonians, much of critical scholarship does not accept the Pauline authorship of 2 Thessalonians. However, there is no debate about 1 Thessalonians. Virtually all agree that the historical Paul is the real author.[6]

Some critical scholars see 1 Thessalonians 2:13–16 (or 2 Thess. 2:14–16) as a later interpolation, however, and not written by Paul.[7] Arguments favoring the non-Pauline authorship of the interpolation include the belief that (1) the statement "[God's] wrath has come upon them [Jews]" (1 Thess. 2:16) is based on the AD 70 destruction of Jerusalem, (2) the charge that Jews killed Jesus (1 Thess. 2:15) is unique in Paul, and (3) the overall negative tone toward Jews does not match Romans 9:4 and 11:26.[8] A response, in brief, would include the following: (1) Paul and the New Testament have a multifaceted understanding of the relationship between present and future wrath that does not necessitate that this refers only to the AD 70 events (see Matt.

[4] For a good summary of the history and culture of Thessalonica, see Gene L. Green, *The Letters to the Thessalonians*, PNTC (Grand Rapids, MI: Eerdmans, 2002), 1–47. For information on extant archaeological evidence, see Holland L. Hendrix, "Thessalonica," *ABD*, 6:523–27.

[5] Related to the editorial "we," see comments on 1 Thess. 2:18 and 2 Thess. 3:17 in Robert J. Cara, *A Study Commentary on 1 and 2 Thessalonians*, EPSC (Darlington: Evangelical Press, 2009), 78, 247–48.

[6] See, for example, the standard critical work of Werner Georg Kümmel, *Introduction to the New Testament*, rev. ed., trans. Howard Clark Kee (Nashville: Abingdon, 1975), 260–62, and the standard evangelical work of D. A. Carson and Douglas J. Moo, *An Introduction to the New Testament*, 2nd ed. (Grand Rapids, MI: Zondervan, 2005), 534–36. Although he has no substantive followers, the famous German radical critic F. C. Baur argued in 1845 that the historical Paul did not write either 1 or 2 Thessalonians (*Paul, the Apostle of Jesus Christ: His Life and Works, His Epistles and Teachings*, 2 vols. [Peabody, MA: Hendrickson, 2003], 2:85–97, 314–40).

[7] For a listing of critical scholars both for and against, see Robert Jewett, *The Thessalonian Correspondence: Pauline Rhetoric and Millenarian Piety* (Philadelphia: Fortress, 1986), 36–42. Surprisingly, the conservative scholar F. F. Bruce is noncommittal concerning whether 1 Thess. 2:14–16 was written by Paul (*1 & 2 Thessalonians*, WBC 45 [Waco, TX: Word, 1982], 47–51).

[8] The best pro-interpolation arguments are presented by Birger A. Pearson, "1 Thessalonians 2:13–16: A Deutero-Pauline Interpolation," *HTR* 64 (1971): 79–94. Daryl Schmidt adds linguistic arguments to Pearson's ("1 Thess 2:13–16: Linguistic Evidence for an Interpolation," *JBL* 103 [1983]: 269–79).

23:37–39; Rom. 1:18; 3:5; 4:15; Eph. 2:3; Heb. 3:11). (2) Other New Testament texts also place blame on Jews for Jesus's death (e.g., Acts 7:51–52). (3) Paul's view that "not all who are descended from Israel belong to Israel" (Rom. 9:6) explains the tensions between negative and positive texts related to Jews.[9] Also, there is no textual evidence of an interpolation. It is safe to conclude, then, that 1 Thessalonians 2:13–16 is not an interpolation but was written by Paul.

The date of 1 Thessalonians is generally not in question.[10] The epistle was written while Paul was in Corinth (Acts 18:1) shortly after his founding of the Thessalonian church (Acts 17:1–9) during his "second missionary journey" (Acts 15:36–18:22). Paul was in Corinth at least partly while Gallio was proconsul (Acts 18:12). Scholars are fairly certain that Gallio's stay in Corinth was only from midsummer of 51 to midsummer of 52.[11] Acts 18:11 states that Paul was in Corinth eighteen months. It is implied that the eighteen months occurred before Gallio arrived, although some take this to mean that Paul's stay partially overlapped with Gallio's.[12] Acts 18:18 indicates that Paul left Corinth before Gallio did. The excited tone of 1 Thessalonians 2:17–3:6 implies that Paul would have written as soon as Timothy returned from Thessalonica to him in Corinth, which would have been early in Paul's stay at Corinth. Putting all this together produces a date of approximately AD 50 for Paul's writing of 1 Thessalonians.

Occasion and Purpose[13]

Regarding the occasion, the majority of scholars agree, even many who generally have a low view of the historicity of Acts.

During Paul's "second missionary journey" (AD 49–52, Acts 15:36–18:22), he comes to Thessalonica and founds the church (Acts 17:1–4). Silas (Silvanus) and Timothy are with him (Acts 17:14–15). As a result of disturbances over Paul and his teachings, the apostle is forced by those outside the church to leave Thessalonica earlier than he wanted to (Acts 17:5–10). Paul's stay in Thessalonica may have been only a month ("three Sabbath days," Acts 17:2) or perhaps a few months.[14] Silas and Timothy leave Thessalonica after Paul does (Acts 17:15).

---

[9] For a detailed response to Pearson's article, see Charles A. Wanamaker, *The Epistles to the Thessalonians: A Commentary on the Greek Text*, NIGTC (Grand Rapids, MI: Eerdmans, 1990), 29–33. Also see Jeffrey A. D. Weima as he responds to Pearson and Schmidt (*1–2 Thessalonians*, BECNT [Grand Rapids, MI: Baker Academic, 2014], 41–46).

[10] Of course, there are exceptions. Paul J. Achtemeier, Joel B. Green, and Marianne Meye Thompson opt for no conclusion as to date; it could have been early or late in Paul's ministry (*Introducing the New Testament: Its Literature and Theology* [Grand Rapids, MI: Eerdmans, 2001], 437–39). Karl P. Donfried argues for a very early date of AD 41–44 ("The Theology of I Thessalonians," in *The Theology of the Shorter Pauline Letters*, NTT [Cambridge: Cambridge University Press, 1993], 9–12), as does Earl Richard, "Early Pauline Thought," in *Pauline Theology*, vol. 1, *Thessalonians, Philippians, Galatians, Philemon* (Minneapolis: Fortress, 1991), 39–51, esp. 40.

[11] For explanation and bibliography related to this dating, see F. F. Bruce, *The Book of Acts*, rev. ed., NICNT (Grand Rapids, MI: Eerdmans, 1988), 351–53.

[12] Barrett views Gallio's arrival as after the eighteen months; and Bruce, as overlapping. See C. K. Barrett, *A Critical and Exegetical Commentary on The Acts of the Apostles*, 2 vols., ICC (Edinburgh: T&T Clark, 1994–1998), 2:870–72; and F. F. Bruce, *New Testament History* (Garden City: Doubleday, 1980), 315–17.

[13] Much of this section is taken directly from my previous work, Cara, *Study Commentary on 1 and 2 Thessalonians*, 21–23.

[14] Possibly the "three Sabbath days" refer only to Paul's direct interaction with the synagogue. After this, he may have moved his teaching ministry elsewhere in the city. The emphasis on Gentile converts from paganism in 1 Thessalonians suggests this (e.g., 1 Thess. 1:9). Philippians 4:16 might also imply a longer period than one month. For a brief summary of the arguments on both sides, with the conclusion that Paul was in Thessalonica for only a month, see Donald Guthrie, *New Testament Introduction*, 3rd ed. (Downers Grove, IL: InterVarsity Press, 1970), 568.

Later, while in Athens with Timothy, Paul longs to know how the young Thessalonian church is faring and to encourage her. He decides to send Timothy back to Thessalonica (1 Thess. 3:1–2). In the meantime, Paul goes to Corinth, and eventually Silas arrives there also. Timothy does indeed go to Thessalonica and subsequently returns to Paul and Silas in Corinth (1 Thess. 3:6; cf. Acts 18:1, 5). Timothy gives a report to Paul, who then writes 1 Thessalonians (1 Thess. 3:6). Given this scenario, 1 Thessalonians may have been written only six months after Paul first went to Thessalonica. We do not know who delivered 1 Thessalonians to the church.

More specifically, what was in Timothy's report? Its content was primarily positive. Two positive aspects are summarized in 1 Thessalonians 3:6: (1) the church was spiritually healthy despite outside opposition (cf. 2:14); and (2) the Thessalonians still appreciated Paul. However, Timothy also reports that people outside the church have accused Paul of being a conniving traveling teacher (1 Thess. 2:1–12). In addition, Timothy relays several questions from church members about the second coming (1 Thess. 4:13–5:10). And Timothy brings news that some members are lazy, idle, and unruly and do not want to work (1 Thess. 4:11–12; 5:14).

Given this mixed report, the purpose of 1 Thessalonians is for Paul to convey to the Thessalonians his encouragement from the good news about them (3:7) and to encourage them by dealing with other news brought by Timothy. Of course, not everything in the letter is directly related to this report. Paul includes teachings (e.g., 1 Thess. 5:16–17) as well as personal information and/or requests (e.g., 1 Thess. 5:25) that might relate to any church in the Greco-Roman world.

1 Thessalonians 2:1–12: A Facile Apostolic Defense?[15]

First Thessalonians 2:1–12 is Paul's defense of his apostolic ministry. Until the 1970s, most scholars assumed that real charges were leveled against Paul by actual opponents and that 2:1–12 was an authentic defense against those charges.[16] Since then, however, many scholars have assumed that Paul is not arguing against specific charges, but is following a typical rhetorical format that includes a facile defense.[17] The sole purpose of 2:1–12, according to this newer view, is for Paul to present himself as a good example to follow. To overgeneralize, those in favor of the newer view usually combine the following three elements: (1) a very high regard for the influence of ancient oratory-rhetoric upon Paul's writing style; (2) an assumption that Paul and his audience were significantly influenced by traditions of the traveling philosophers; and (3) some degree of doubt as to the historicity of the account of Paul in Thessalonica recorded in Acts 17:1–9. Although this is not the place to argue these issues, I will just state that I am methodologically opposed to an overuse of rhetorical criticism and against a low estimate of the historicity of Acts.

[15] Much of this section is taken directly from my previous work, Cara, *Study Commentary on 1 and 2 Thessalonians*, 51–52.
[16] Abraham Malherbe's denial of real charges was very influential ("'Gentle as a Nurse': The Cynic Background to 1 Thess. 2," *Nov T* 12 [1970]: 203–17). For a good summary of the history of scholarship and a strong argument in favor of a real defense, see Jeffrey A. D. Weima, "An Apology for the Apologetic Function of 1 Thessalonians 2:1–12," *JNST* 68 (1997): 73–79.
[17] Dio Chrysostom's *Discourse 32* (written ca. AD 110) is usually presented as the best example of a philosopher defending himself against nonpersonal and generic charges.

I firmly believe that 1 Thessalonians 2:1–12 is a defense against specific charges made by some outside the church. Clearly Acts 17:1–9 indicates that Jews, and subsequently Gentiles, in Thessalonica were opposed to Paul. The reference in 1 Thessalonians 2:2 to Paul's troubles in Philippi argues for the existence of real opponents in Thessalonica. First Thessalonians 2:14 shows that Gentiles were still harassing the Thessalonian church. Finally, it is not unusual for Paul to present some kind of defense in his letters (e.g., 2 Corinthians 10–13; Gal. 1:6–2:21).

There are, however, some kernels of truth in the newer view. Parts of the defense do appear similar to charges that traveling philosophers also had to refute. It is most likely that, in addition to truths of the gospel that upset the opponents and gave them ammunition against Paul, he was also accused of well-known sins committed by many traveling philosophers, such as greediness and flattery.[18] It was simply convenient to paint Paul with the same broad brush (cf. 2 Cor. 2:17; 1 Tim. 6:5).

As mentioned previously, the newer view states that in 1 Thessalonians 2:1–12, Paul is merely portraying himself as an example to follow. I disagree, but I would grant that Paul is *secondarily* presenting himself as an example to follow. This would then explain the connections between several aspects of Paul's behavior, as described in the defense, and his advice to his readers elsewhere in 1 Thessalonians to do the same (e.g., 2:3 with 4:7; 2:4 with 4:1; 2:8 with 4:9; 2:9 with 4:11; 2:10 with 5:23). It would also be consistent with Paul's general theology of imitation (1 Cor. 11:1; 1 Thess. 1:6).

Structure and Outline

The outline for 1 Thessalonians is straightforward:[19]

- I. Opening (1:1)
- II. Thanksgiving (1:2–10)
- III. Body (2:1–5:22)
  - A. Apostolic defense (2:1–12)
  - B. Thanksgiving (2:13–16)
  - C. Timothy's mission (2:17–3:13)
  - D. Hortatory words (4:1–5:22)
- IV. Closing (5:23–28)

Note that the two eschatological sections, 1 Thessalonians 4:13–18 and 5:1–11, are included in the hortatory section. They both end with similar exhortations for the Thessalonians to encourage (παρακαλέω) each other.

The outline of 1 Thessalonians matches well Paul's other letters. The most generic Pauline outline would be (1) opening, (2) thanksgiving, (3) body (often doctrinal then hortatory, but occasionally including travel plans and defenses), and (4) closing. The

[18] For example, see Theophrastus, *Characters* 2.1–13, written in approximately 320 BC. Theophrastus gives several comical examples of flatterers.

[19] For a discussion of first-century AD Hellenistic and Jewish letters and their relationship to New Testament letters, see David E. Aune, *The New Testament in Its Literary Environment*, LEC 8 (Philadelphia: Westminster Press, 1987). Although I do not think it helpful, some are especially interested in connecting Greco-Roman oral-rhetoric categories to Paul's epistles. For an example of this using 1 Thessalonians, see Robert Jewett, *Thessalonian Correspondence*, 63–78.

1 Thessalonians outline differs in that it has no clear doctrinal section, and there is a second thanksgiving section.[20]

The opening section (1 Thess. 1:1) follows Paul's normal format of "[from whom], [to whom], grace and peace." Many times Paul elaborates upon these elements. First (along with Second) Thessalonians has minimal elaboration, although Paul does include that the church is "in God the Father and the Lord Jesus Christ," instead of using his more common and shorter phrase "in Christ." Combining the Father and Christ into Paul's traditional union-with-Christ phraseology shows his high view of the divinity of Christ.[21]

In the thanksgiving (εὐχαριστέω) section (1 Thess. 1:2–10), Paul tells the Thessalonian Christians that he thanks God for their good works. He summarizes this as their "work of faith," "labor of love," and "steadfastness of hope" (1:3). The triad of faith, hope, and love is also in 5:8. The Thessalonians are further commended for being examples to others in the way they have spread the gospel (1:7–8). Upon noting that others positively characterized the Thessalonians, Paul summarizes a believer as one who has "turned to God from idols" with the double result being that the believer "serve[s] the living and true God" and "wait[s] for his Son from heaven" (1:9–10). Because this is not a common summary of a believer by Paul, there is a lot of scholarly interest in this.[22]

As discussed previously, 1 Thessalonians 2:1–12 is Paul's defense against outside opponents who are questioning his integrity. Paul asks the Thessalonians to remember the boldness with which he has preached the gospel (2:2). This boldness proves Paul's integrity. He is not a man-pleaser, nor a deceiver, nor greedy for money, nor a glory seeker (2:3–6). On the contrary, Paul is concerned for them as a parent is for his children (2:7, 11).

In the second thanksgiving (εὐχαριστέω) section (1 Thess. 2:13–16), Paul thanks God that the Thessalonians accepted and were changed by the preached Word of God. One aspect of this change was their positive response to suffering, which paralleled the suffering by Christians in Judea.

First Thessalonians 2:17–3:13 presents in chronological order the events related to Timothy's mission to Thessalonica. Paul's primary point is to pour out his heart concerning the good news he received from Timothy about the church.[23] This sec-

[20] Only 1 and 2 Thessalonians have two thanksgiving sections.

[21] See B. B. Warfield, "God Our Father and the Lord Jesus Christ," in *Biblical Doctrines* (Carlisle, PA: Banner of Truth, 1988), 213–31; and Larry Hurtado, "Lord," *DPL*, 560–69.

[22] Many assume that this type of summary is the outline for Paul's sermons to (nonbelieving) Gentiles. Hence, this contrasts with the typical Pauline phrases in the epistles (e.g., "in Christ") that are for believers. See Abraham J. Malherbe, *Paul and the Thessalonians: The Philosophic Tradition of Pastoral Care* (Mifflintown, PA: Sigler, 2000), 30–33. Some explain this as related to the eschatological emphasis of the letter; e.g., see Colin R. Nicholl, *From Hope to Despair in Thessalonica: Situating 1 and 2 Thessalonians*, SNTSMS 126 (Cambridge: Cambridge University Press, 2004), 80–82. Others see this summary as a pre-Pauline formula; e.g., see Ernest Best, *The First and Second Epistles to the Thessalonians*, BNTC (Peabody, MA: Hendrickson, 1986), 81–87. Although this description *may* be pre-Pauline, many of those in favor of this view erroneously assume that Paul has a limited vocabulary and rarely adds nuances while discussing Christianity.

[23] Some argue that this section partially continues Paul's defense. Paul's enemies were telling the Thessalonians that Paul's departure and continued absence showed he had no concern for them. So say John Calvin, *The Epistles of Paul the Apostle to the Romans and to the Thessalonians*, trans. Ross Mackenzie (Grand Rapids, MI: Eerdmans, 1960), 350; James Everett Frame, *A Critical and Exegetical Commentary on the Epistles of St. Paul to the Thessalonians*, ICC (Edinburgh: T&T Clark, 1912), 116–17; and Leon Morris, *The First and Second Epistles to the Thessalonians: The English Text with Introduction, Exposition and Notes*, NICNT (Grand Rapids, MI: Eerdmans, 1959), 93.

tion is written in joyous, emotional language (e.g., 1 Thess. 2:20; 3:1, 8) and ends with a benediction (3:11–13). Paul recounts that he was "torn away" from the Thessalonians (2:17). "When [he] could bear it no longer," he sent Timothy to them (1 Thess. 3:1). Eventually, Timothy returned with the good report, and "now we live" (1 Thess. 3:8). Paul's benediction partially includes that both God the Father and our Lord Christ "may . . . direct our way to you" (3:11), and that the "Lord," that is, Christ, may aid them to love one another (3:12). Appealing to Christ shows a high view of his divinity.[24]

Paul often included large hortatory sections toward the end of his letters (e.g., Rom. 12:1–15:21; Gal. 5:13–6:10; Eph. 4:1–6:20). Hence, the large section of 1 Thessalonians 4:1–5:22 is not unusual. Paul introduces this section by asking the Thessalonians to abound more in their walking and pleasing God (4:1). In 4:3, he connects the "will of God" to their "sanctification," which in context is to be understood as progressive sanctification.[25] As mentioned above, Paul's topics are not necessarily related to specific problems at or questions from the Thessalonian church; some may be more general to any church in the Greco-Roman culture.[26]

The following is the list of topics covered in the hortatory section:

- Introduction (4:1–2)
- Abstain from sexual immorality (4:3–8).
- Continue brotherly love (4:9–12).
- Do not grieve as the dead in Christ will rise first (4:13–18).
- Be awake for the day of the Lord (5:1–11).
- Respect[27] your rulers (5:12–13).
- Admonish the unruly/idle (5:14).
- Do not repay evil for evil (5:15).
- Always rejoice (5:16).
- Unceasingly pray (5:17).
- In everything give thanks (5:18).
- Test all things (5:19–22).

The closing section (1 Thess. 5:23–28) reasonably matches the closings in Paul's other letters. Paul often includes—in order—a peace benediction, greetings, and a

[24] Francis Turretin summarizes the case for Christ's divinity under (1) divine names, (2) the divine attributes, (3) the divine works, and (4) divine worship. Concerning worship and Christ's divinity, he notes that it "is proved from invocation, because grace and peace and other spiritual blessings (which can be expected from God alone) are sought from Christ no less than from the Father in the epistles of Paul" (see *Institutes of Elenctic Theology*, ed. James T. Dennison Jr., trans. George Musgrave Giger, 3 vols. [Phillipsburg, NJ: P&R, 1992–1997], 1:282–92, esp. 289).

[25] Paul uses "sanctification" and its cognates in two ways. The first, often called "definitive sanctification," indicates the existential state of a Christian in which there has been a radical break from his non-Christian past and he is now deemed "holy" (see, e.g., 1 Cor. 6:11; Eph. 5:26; Phil. 1:1). The second sense denotes the process of becoming more and more holy throughout the Christian life, commonly referred to either as "sanctification" or "progressive sanctification" (see, e.g., Rom. 6:19–22; 2 Cor. 7:1; 1 Thess. 5:23). See Robert L. Reymond, *A New Systematic Theology of the Christian Faith* (Nashville: Thomas Nelson, 1998), 756–59; John Murray, *Redemption Accomplished and Applied* (Grand Rapids, MI: Eerdmans, 1955), 141–50; Thomas R. Schreiner, *Paul: Apostle of God's Glory in Christ* (Downers Grove, IL: InterVarsity Press, 2001), 219–22; and Cara, *Study Commentary on 1 and 2 Thessalonians*, 107.

[26] Because of the brevity of the commands in 1 Thess. 5:12–22 and the similarities between Rom. 12:3–21 and 1 Thess. 5:12–22, most likely the commands in 1 Thess. 5:12–22 are not specifically related to the Thessalonians. "Admonish the idle" in 1 Thess. 5:14 is a clear exception.

[27] The Greek is οἶδα, which is the generic verb "know." Here it has the sense of "know, and therefore recognize the merit of." See BDAG, 694.

grace benediction. The order does not vary even if some items are omitted.[28] Here Paul includes a peace benediction (5:23–24), a greeting (5:26), and a grace benediction (5:28). Also included are two exhortations: prayer (5:25) and the public reading of the letter (5:27).

Message and Theology

Below are discussions of several theological topics emanating from 1 Thessalonians. These discussions are necessarily truncated in that all of Paul and all of the Bible should ultimately be considered.

Be Imitators

Paul famously says in 1 Corinthians 11:1, "Be imitators [μιμηταί, from μιμητής] of me, as I am of Christ." What does 1 Thessalonians add to or confirm about our understanding of Paul's doctrine of imitation?[29]

Paul uses μιμητής and its cognates (συμμιμητής, μιμέομαι) in 1 Thessalonians 1:6; 2:14; and 2 Thessalonians 3:7, 9; as well as 1 Corinthians 4:16; 11:1; Ephesians 5:1; and Philippians 3:17. In addition, many other passages include the imitation idea at the conceptual level (e.g., Phil. 4:9). In these passages, Paul portrays *himself* as the one to be imitated.[30] Contexts vary as to what specific character traits or actions Paul wants his readers to imitate.

In Paul's view, this imitation of him is related to his imitation of Christ. Is Paul thinking of imitating specific situations in Christ's earthly life? W. Bauder answers no. Paul is thinking "of the kind of behavior that would be consistent with existence in the sphere of the Lordship of Christ."[31] (That is, a believer is to act as Christ would want one to act through the power of the Holy Spirit.) In general, I agree that Paul is not thinking primarily of specific events in Christ's life that we are to imitate, but Paul does occasionally use specific events in Christ's life as ethical examples (e.g., Rom. 15:3; 2 Cor. 8:9; 10:1; Eph. 5:2, 25; Phil. 2:3–8; 2 Thess. 3:5; 1 Tim. 6:12–13). Even though none of these texts is an explicit μιμητής passage, Paul probably is including them in the exhortation to imitate Christ. Hence, the phraseology about imitating Christ is related primarily to behavior in the sphere of the lordship of Christ, but it might secondarily include examples from Christ's earthly life.

In 1 Thessalonians 1:6, Paul gives as a proof of the Thessalonians' election that they "became imitators [μιμηταί] of us and of the Lord." Paul commends them for receiving the preached Word joyfully amid much tribulation. It is not clear how

[28] See Jeffrey A. D. Weima, *Neglected Endings: The Significance of the Pauline Letter Closings*, JSNTSup 101 (Sheffield: Sheffield Academic, 1994), 28–76; and Andrew T. Lincoln, *Ephesians*, WBC 42 (Dallas: Word, 1990), 462–64.

[29] For a variety of views of Paul's imitation doctrine, see Malherbe, *Paul and the Thessalonians*, 52–60; Mary Ann Getty, "The Imitation of Paul in the Letters of the Thessalonians," in *The Thessalonian Correspondence*, ed. Raymond F. Collins (Leuven: Leuven University Press, 1990), 277–83; W. P. DeBoer, *The Imitation of Paul* (Kampen: Kok, 1962); and S. E. Fowl, "Imitation of Paul/of Christ," *DPL*, 428–31. Malherbe connects Paul's exhortations to imitation to a similar practice of Greek moral philosophers. Fowl connects the imitation language to Paul's view of the cross. I tend to connect it, at least conceptually, to *imago Dei* ("Be holy for I am holy," Lev. 11:44; 1 Pet. 1:16).

[30] Exceptions are Eph. 5:1 (imitate God) and 1 Thess. 2:14 (imitate other churches).

[31] W. Bauder, "*mimeomai*," *NIDNTT*, 1:490–92.

this is an active imitation of Paul. Probably he is referring to the general theme of responding to difficult circumstances positively, as Paul did during his difficulties in Thessalonica (3:3).[32]

In the benediction at the end of the section on Timothy's mission, Paul uses his love for the Thessalonians as an explicit paradigm of how they are to love others (1 Thess. 3:12).

As mentioned above, several of Paul's actions noted in his defense section are closely tied to exhortations in the hortatory section. Hence, there is an implicit exhortation for the Thessalonians to imitate him. These include avoiding impurity (1 Thess. 2:3 with 4:7), acting to please God (2:4 with 4:1), loving others (2:8 with 4:9), working (2:9 with 4:11), and blameless conduct (2:10 with 5:23).

In 1 Thessalonians 1:7–8, Paul commends the Thessalonians for being an example (τύπος) to other believers outside their church.[33] More specifically, as individuals and as a church, they are examples by sending out preachers. Here is an example of Paul extending the imitation exhortation beyond himself to others who are also to be imitated.

In 1 Thessalonians 2:14, Paul commends the Thessalonians for becoming imitators (μιμηταί) of the churches in Judea in that both Thessalonian and Judean churches responded appropriately to suffering inflicted by their own countrymen. Again, Paul uses others (Judean church) besides himself as the ones to be imitated.

In sum, Paul's imitation doctrine is asking others to behave within the sphere of the lordship of Christ. In addition to occasionally referring to imitating aspects of Christ's earthly life, this includes imitating specific character traits and actions of Paul. Further, as 1 Thessalonians shows us, it is not only Paul but others who are appropriately to be imitated. Hence, all Christians, and especially leaders, should be models for others.[34]

"Consistent" Eschatology[35]

As is well known, a significant portion of 1 Thessalonians relates to the second coming of Christ and associated events.[36] Passages that pertain to these events include brief comments in 1:3, 10; 2:12; and 3:13 and extended comments in 4:13–18 and 5:1–11.[37] Although this emphasis is in the forefront of Paul's thought, it must be said

[32]See Cara for arguments that 1 Thess. 3:3 refers to Paul's tribulations and not the Thessalonians' (*Study Commentary on 1 and 2 Thessalonians*, 83–84).

[33]Note 2 Thess. 3:9 and Phil. 3:17, where μιμητής cognates and τύπος are in the same context.

[34]Concerning leaders being examples, Calvin in his Catechism of 1538 (sec. 30) included within the responsibility of pastors that they are to be examples. "Pastors had to be set over churches both to instruct the people publicly and privately in pure doctrine, to administer the sacraments and *to teach them by the best example concerning holiness and purity of life*" (emphasis added). This translation by Ford Lewis Battles may be found in I. John Hesselink, *Calvin's First Catechism: A Commentary*, Columbia Series in Reformed Theology (Louisville: Westminster John Knox, 1997), 35–36.

[35]For purposes of this section, I will not include the "now" portion of Paul's "now and not yet" full-orbed eschatology. Scholars often use "inaugurated eschatology" to refer to the "now" aspect of Christ's kingdom, which started at his first coming. They use "consistent eschatology" to refer to the "not yet" aspect of Christ's kingdom, which focuses on the second coming and associated events, along with the eternal new heavens and new earth.

[36]For an overview of eschatology in 1 Thessalonians, see the conservative Leon Morris, *1, 2 Thessalonians*, Word Biblical Themes (Dallas: Word, 1989), 41–62, and the critical Donfried, "Theology of 1 Thessalonians," 31–51.

[37]I did not include 1 Thess. 2:16 as I view "[the] wrath has come upon them [Jews] at last" as referring to a present wrath, although one that is related to a future wrath. See Cara, *Study Commentary on 1 and 2 Thessalonians*, 74.

that these discussions arise somewhat naturally as Paul encourages the Thessalonians and/or answers their questions.[38]

In the triad of faith, hope, and love (1 Thess. 1:3), Paul mentions "hope in [or "of," genitive case] our Lord Jesus Christ." As most commentators interpret this, it is hope in the second coming of Christ.[39] In context, the belief in the second coming aids the Thessalonians in their enduring trials now.

In 1 Thessalonians 1:9–10, two eschatological phrases are included. Paul summarizes the double result of a believer's turning to God as one that "serve[s] the living and true God" and "wait[s] for his Son from heaven." Then in two clauses Paul summarizes the "Son" as the one who was "raised from the dead" and "delivers us from the wrath to come." Believers' "waiting" includes an ethical component as it encourages them to lead holy lives with the motivation being to honor Christ at his return.[40] One aspect of the second coming is that it will include wrath, but believers will be delivered from it. Obviously, deliverance from wrath is a comforting thought.

At the end of 1 Thessalonians 2:12, God is described as one "who calls you into his own kingdom and glory." Paul's writings do not often use "kingdom."[41] His overall usage of "kingdom" includes that Christ is the King of the kingdom (e.g., Eph. 5:5; Col. 1:13), and the one kingdom has both a present aspect (e.g., Rom. 14:17; 1 Cor. 4:20) and a future aspect (e.g., 1 Cor. 6:9–10; Gal. 5:21). Paul is speaking here of the future aspect of the kingdom;[42] "kingdom" is closely associated grammatically with "glory," as one article controls both substantives.[43] Hence, to state the obvious, the future kingdom is characterized by God's glory. In the context of 1 Thessalonians 2:12, Paul is adding encouragement to "walk in a manner worthy of God" in that the God who calls us to future glory will also call and enable us to live for him now.

As part of the benediction at the end of the section on Timothy's mission, Paul asks that the Thessalonians abound in love so that at the second coming their hearts would be "blameless in holiness" (1 Thess. 3:13). Most likely the word "blameless" here refers to the combination of (1) the forgiveness of believers' sins based on Christ's work, (2) the progressive change in believers during their lives, and (3) an instantaneous change of their sinful nature occurring at their death or at the second coming. Although

---

[38] On the contrary, some in the history of scholarship have seen this consistent eschatological emphasis as an aspect of the "early Paul," who later moved to other emphases, which is a mistaken view from my perspective. Supporting my view, see Richard N. Longenecker, "The Nature of Paul's Early Eschatology," *NTS* 31 (1985): 85–95.

[39] The genitive case is taken as an objective genitive. An argument for this exegesis is that normally in the triad "hope" is related to eschatology (e.g., Col. 1:4–5; 1 Thess. 5:8). Also, the third item of the triad is the one emphasized to fit the context, which in this case is a letter with a general eschatological emphasis. In agreement, see Calvin, *To the Romans and to the Thessalonians*, 335; William Hendriksen, *Exposition of I and II Thessalonians*, NTC (Grand Rapids, MI: Baker, 1955), 47–48; and J. B. Lightfoot, *Notes on the Epistles of St. Paul* (Peabody, MA: Hendrickson, 1995), 10–11.

[40] Bruce, *1 & 2 Thessalonians*, 19; and Hendriksen, *I and II Thessalonians*, 57.

[41] Exhaustive list: Rom. 14:17; 1 Cor. 4:20; 6:9–10; 15:24, 50; Gal. 5:21; Eph. 5:5; Col. 1:13; 4:11; 1 Thess. 2:12; 2 Thess. 1:5; 2 Tim. 4:1, 18; also Acts 14:22; 19:8; 20:25; 28:23–31.

[42] Arguments include the close grammatical association with the term "glory" and the conceptual similarity to 1 Thess. 3:13 and 2 Thess. 1:5. In agreement are Geerhardus Vos, *The Pauline Eschatology* (Phillipsburg, NJ: P&R, 1986), 259; Best, *First and Second Epistles to the Thessalonians*, 108–9; and Bruce, *1 & 2 Thessalonians*, 38. Others see "kingdom" as including both present and future aspects. See Karl Paul Donfried, "The Kingdom of God in Paul," in *The Kingdom of God in 20th-Century Interpretation*, ed. Wendell Willis (Peabody, MA: Hendrickson, 1987), 175–90, esp. 181–83, 188; and Abraham J. Malherbe, *The Letters to the Thessalonians: A New Translation with Introduction and Commentary*, AB 32B (New York: Doubleday, 2000), 153.

[43] For a discussion of the article-substantive-καί-substantive form, see Daniel B. Wallace, *Greek Grammar beyond the Basics: An Exegetical Syntax of the New Testament* (Grand Rapids, MI: Zondervan, 1996), 270–90.

including all three, the emphasis is on the second—progressive change.[44] As can also be seen from 1 Thessalonians 3:13, both the Father and the Lord Jesus are involved in the judgment. This is another sign of the divinity of Christ. Finally, the second coming is described here as the "coming of our Lord Jesus with all his saints." As can be seen from other biblical passages, Christ will come with both humans (1 Thess. 4:14) and angels (2 Thess. 1:7; see also Matt. 25:31). Which of these (or both) is this passage referring to? If Paul is alluding to Zechariah 14:5, here it is angels.[45]

The two longer eschatological passages, 1 Thessalonians 4:13–18 and 5:1–11, are intentionally grouped together and probably are related to some aspects of Timothy's news. Paul includes facts about the second coming and implications for one's life *now*. He ends each section with an exhortation toward comfort (1 Thess. 4:18; 5:11). Although conservative scholars may disagree over some of the details of the passage, owing partially to varying millennial views, the central aspects of these two passages are fairly clear.[46]

In 1 Thessalonians 4:13–18, some Thessalonian Christians have died, and confusion exists as to whether the dead will be resurrected. Although this pericope does not directly concern the intermediate state, once there is doubt about the future resurrection, this produces (1) doubt about the current status of souls of dead Christians (i.e., the intermediate state) and (2) doubt and confusion about the sequence of second coming events and realities of the new heavens and new earth.[47]

Paul famously states that the Thessalonians "may not grieve as others do who have no hope" (1 Thess. 4:13). Calvin notes that Paul "does not forbid us to express any grief at all, but calls for restraint in our sorrow."[48] In context, Paul's antidote to excessive grieving is union with Christ (4:14). If Christ died and rose, all those connected to him will also die and be raised.[49] Hence, if one believes in Christ, one also believes that those currently "sleeping" (souls with Christ) are currently connected to Christ and will also be bodily raised at the second coming.[50]

The remainder of the 1 Thessalonians 4:15–18 pericope is a subset of 4:14. It

[44] Cara, *Study Commentary on 1 and 2 Thessalonians*, 97. Herman Ridderbos explains these types of passages in Paul's writings concerning the "perfection of believers [to] refer above all to the totalitarian character of the fullness of the redemption in Christ" (*Paul: An Outline of His Theology*, trans. John Richard de Witt [Grand Rapids, MI: Eerdmans, 1975], 262–72, esp. 270). I. Howard Marshall comments that the "blameless" passages at first glance may create a tension with Paul's doctrine of justification. He solves this by noting that "the tension disappears when we note that Paul appears to believe that God will achieve this blamelessness in the lives of his people" (*New Testament Theology: Many Witnesses, One Gospel* [Downers Grove, IL: InterVarsity Press, 2004], 358–59). See also 1 Cor. 1:8; Phil. 1:6; 3:21; 1 Thess. 5:23; cf. 1 Cor. 3:10–15.

[45] Vos, *Pauline Eschatology*, 136–38; Green, *Letters to the Thessalonians*, 181; and Wanamaker, *Epistles to the Thessalonians*, 145. If this is an allusion to Zech. 14:5, it is another indication of the divinity of Christ because Paul has taken a verse that explicitly refers to Yahweh God and interpreted it as applying to Christ. See Hurtado, "Lord," 560–69, esp. 563.

[46] My personal view is amillennialism.

[47] There is a trend among scholars to see the grief of the Thessalonians as being related only to the sequence in which dead Christians would be resurrected and how they would fare in comparison with Christians who were alive at the second coming. For example, see Best, *First and Second Epistles to the Thessalonians*, 181; Bruce, *1 & 2 Thessalonians*, 99–100; James D. G. Dunn, *The Theology of Paul the Apostle* (Grand Rapids, MI: Eerdmans, 1998), 299; Helmut Koester, "From Paul's Eschatology to the Apocalyptic Schemata of 2 Thessalonians," in Collins, *The Thessalonian Correspondence*, 441–58, esp. 447. Against this view, Green aptly states that this "does not [explain] the overwhelming grief the church experienced as they struggled to cope with the death of some members" (*Letters to the Thessalonians*, 214). Also see Cara, *Study Commentary on 1 and 2 Thessalonians*, 123–27.

[48] Calvin, *To the Romans and to the Thessalonians*, 363.

[49] 1 Thess. 4:14 has the parallel between Christ "died" and Christians "have fallen asleep"; also Christ "rose" and Christ "will bring" resurrected Christians.

[50] WLC 86 correctly notes that "even in death [we] continue united to Christ."

gives the sequence of events at the second coming with the comforting conclusion that all believers will be bodily with Christ forever. The sequence begins with the Lord's command, the voice of an archangel, and a trumpet; the relationship between these three is not clear. Then dead believers will rise and be caught in the air with the "alive" and "meet" all together with the Lord (4:17). The text does not say where the group goes from there. This has generated considerable disagreement among scholars.[51] I see the meeting in the air as similar to a people coming outside their city to greet an approaching king. Hence, as Christ comes toward the earth (the city), but before he reaches it, his people come out to greet him as they meet in the air. Then Christ leads the procession to the earth (into the city) with the people to effect the final judgment and set up the new heavens and new earth.[52]

In addition to being concerned about dead loved ones (1 Thess. 4:13–18), the Thessalonians apparently want to know when the second coming will occur (5:1–11). Paul answers that he already told them that, although no one knows the time of Christ's return, it *will* occur (5:1–2). This not-knowing and sudden ("thief in the night," 5:2) aspect should produce vigilance *now* (5:6). Finally, Christ's work produces the ("destined") reality and the confidence that Christians will continue being vigilant (5:9–10). This work of Christ ultimately results in "salvation"[53] and not "wrath." Again, these results are given in consistent eschatological terms.

Within 1 Thessalonians 5:1–11 are many of Christ's earthly expressions, including "times and the seasons" (1 Thess. 5:1; cf. Acts 1:7), "thief" (1 Thess. 5:2; cf. Matt. 24:23), "awake" (1 Thess. 5:6; cf. Matt. 24:42). Also, the not-knowing aspect related to being vigilant is prevalent in Christ's eschatological parables of Matthew 25. Given Paul's comment in 1 Thessalonians 4:15, it is probable that much of 1 Thessalonians 5:1–11 is taken directly from the sayings of the earthly Christ.[54]

In sum, 1 Thessalonians has a considerable number of texts related to consistent eschatology. Aspects of the second coming—Christ's bodily return, all believers having resurrected bodies, the judgment, the new heavens and new earth ("kingdom and glory," 2:12)—are all wonderful and amazing future realities. Not surprisingly, Paul explicitly uses these as motivations for proper Christian living *now*.

Election and Calling

The closely associated concepts of election and calling are a key theological theme in 1 Thessalonians (see 1:4; 2:12; 4:7; 5:9; 5:24).[55] This theme emphasizes God's initiative and grace in salvation.

[51] My dispensational brethren, although agreeing that union with Christ is the primary antidote to grieving, see 1 Thess. 4:13–18 as specifically discussing the "rapture" of the church, which is to occur seven years before Christ's return to set up the earthly millennial kingdom. Christ meets the church in the air and immediately returns to heaven. For a classic statement of this view, see John F. Walvoord, *The Rapture Question*, rev. ed. (Grand Rapids, MI: Zondervan, 1979), 197–210.

[52] Cara, *Study Commentary on 1 and 2 Thessalonians*, 131–33. In addition to dispensationalists, those who see Christ returning to heaven include Vos, *The Pauline Eschatology*, 138; and Wanamaker, *Epistles to the Thessalonians*, 175.

[53] Here the future eschatological aspect of "salvation" is emphasized as it is connected to the "hope of salvation" in 1 Thess. 5:8.

[54] So also Lightfoot, *Notes on the Epistles of St. Paul*, 71; Frame, *Epistles of St. Paul to the Thessalonians*, 181; and Bruce, *1 & 2 Thessalonians*, 109.

[55] Statistically speaking, 1 Thessalonians has the highest concentration of election/calling language among Paul's letters. Use of this language is significant also in 2 Thessalonians; see 2 Thess. 1:11; 2:13–14.

Several times in 1 Thessalonians Paul uses election/calling as the basis for commands to lead holy lives (sanctification).[56] This reflects what scholars refer to as Paul's "indicative and imperative" pattern.[57] Paul declares some aspect of our gracious salvation that has been and/or will be accomplished by God (indicative), and this then forms the basis for commands to further our sanctification (imperative). This pattern of election/calling and sanctification in 1 Thessalonians matches well Paul's pattern of justification and sanctification in Romans and Galatians. This may partially explain why the word *justification* is not in 1 Thessalonians. It is subsumed within the larger concept of election/calling.[58]

Virtually always in the New Testament, God's "call," when used to refer to an aspect of salvation, produces the intended effect and thus is known in Reformed theology as the "effectual call."[59] The New Testament often uses the "call" to emphasize the initial act of bringing a believer to Christ (e.g., 1 Cor. 1:23–24; Gal. 1:6; 2 Pet. 1:10). However, "call" is also used to show that this initial act includes progressive sanctification and eventually being with Christ in glory (e.g., Eph. 1:18; 2 Thess. 2:14). In 1 Thessalonians, multiple aspects of our full-orbed salvation are shown by the election/calling word group. Our initial salvation is shown in 1 Thessalonians 1:4. Our progressive sanctification is shown in 4:7 ("For God has not called us for impurity, but in holiness [sanctification]"). Here Paul emphasizes that God's calling of believers will have the intended effect of sanctification, which in context relates to sexual purity. First Thessalonians 5:24, "He who calls you is faithful; he will surely do it," relates to the second coming (5:23) and God's faithfulness to keep his promises/callings to ensure our final salvation.

Select Bibliography

Aune, David E. *The New Testament in Its Literary Environment*. LEC 8. Philadelphia: Westminster Press, 1987.

Bassler, Jouette M., ed. *Pauline Theology*. Vol. 1, *Thessalonians, Philippians, Galatians, Philemon*. Minneapolis: Fortress, 1991.

Beale, G. K. *1–2 Thessalonians*. IVPNTC. Downers Grove, IL: InterVarsity Press, 2003.

[56] Although the following do not fully agree on a definition of election, they do agree that there is a pattern of election leading to sanctification in 1 (and 2) Thessalonians. See Morris, *1 & 2 Thessalonians*, 15–17; Donfried, "The Theology of I Thessalonians," 28–30, 60–66; I. Howard Marshall, "Election and Calling to Salvation in 1 and 2 Thessalonians," in Collins, *The Thessalonian Correspondence*, 259–76; and Frank J. Matera, *New Testament Ethics: The Legacies of Jesus and Paul* (Louisville: Westminster John Knox, 1996), 123–37.

[57] For an excellent discussion, see Ridderbos, *Paul*, 253–58.

[58] That is not to say that significant aspects of the concept of justification are not in 1 Thessalonians. The pronouncement now that Christians will be delivered from the wrath to come related to Christ's death and our faith, and all by grace, is in 1 Thessalonians (1 Thess. 1:10; 4:14; 5:9–10). For a discussion defending the notion that 1 Thessalonians contains the traditional view of justification against "New Perspective on Paul" authors, see Seyoon Kim, *Paul and the New Perspective: Second Thoughts on the Origin of Paul's Gospel* (Grand Rapids, MI: Eerdmans, 2002), 85–100; Stephen Westerholm, *Justification Reconsidered: Rethinking a Pauline Theme* (Grand Rapids, MI: Eerdmans, 2013), 5–11; and Westerholm, *Perspectives Old and New on Paul: The "Lutheran" Paul and His Critics* (Grand Rapids, MI: Eerdmans, 2004), 353–61.

[59] See for example Rom. 8:28–30; 11:29; 1 Thess. 5:24; 2 Tim. 1:9. Matthew 22:14 ("Many are called, but few are chosen") is a rare example of the general/universal call. For a discussion of effectual and general calling, see Murray, *Redemption Accomplished and Applied*, 88.

Best, Ernest, *The First and Second Epistles to the Thessalonians*. BNTC. Peabody, MA: Hendrickson, 1986.

Bruce, F. F. *1 & 2 Thessalonians*. WBC 45. Waco, TX: Word, 1982.

Burke, Trevor J. *Family Matters: A Socio-Historical Study of Kinship Metaphors in 1 Thessalonians*. JSNTSup 247. London: T&T Clark, 2003.

Calvin, John. *The Epistles of Paul the Apostle to the Romans and Thessalonians*. Translated by Ross Mackenzie. Calvin's Commentaries. Grand Rapids, MI: Eerdmans, 1960.

Cara, Robert J. *A Study Commentary on 1 and 2 Thessalonians*. EPSC. Darlington: Evangelical Press, 2009.

Chrysostom, John. *Homilies of St. John Chrysostom on the First Epistle of St. Paul the Apostle to the Thessalonians*. In vol. 13 of *NPNF*[1].

Collins, Raymond F., ed. *The Thessalonian Correspondence*. BETL 87. Leuven: Leuven University Press, 1990.

DeBoer, W. P. *The Imitation of Paul*. Kampen: Kok, 1962.

Donfried, Karl P. *Paul, Thessalonica, and Early Christianity*. Grand Rapids, MI: Eerdmans, 2002.

———. "The Theology of I Thessalonians." In *The Theology of the Shorter Pauline Letters*, by Karl P. Donfried and I. Howard Marshall, 1–79. NTT. Cambridge: Cambridge University Press, 1993.

Donfried, Karl Paul, and Johannes Beutler, eds. *The Thessalonians Debate: Methodological Discord or Methodological Synthesis?* Grand Rapids, MI: Eerdmans, 2000.

Frame, James Everett. *A Critical and Exegetical Commentary of the Epistles of St. Paul to the Thessalonians*. ICC. Edinburgh: T&T Clark, 1912.

Furnish, Victor Paul. *1 Thessalonians, 2 Thessalonians*. ANTC. Nashville: Abingdon, 2007.

Green, Gene L. *The Letters to the Thessalonians*. PNTC. Grand Rapids, MI: Eerdmans, 2002.

Hendriksen, William. *Exposition of I and II Thessalonians*. NTC. Grand Rapids, MI: Baker, 1955.

Holtz, Traugott. *Der erste Brief an die Thessalonicher*. EKKNT 13. Zurich: Benziger, 1998.

Jewett, Robert. *The Thessalonian Correspondence: Pauline Rhetoric and Millenarian Piety*. Philadelphia: Fortress, 1986.

Lightfoot, J. B. *Notes on the Epistles of St. Paul*. Peabody, MA: Hendrickson, 1995.

Longenecker, Richard N. "The Nature of Paul's Early Eschatology." *NTS* 31 (1985): 85–95.

Luckensmeyer, David. *The Eschatology of First Thessalonians*. NTOA / SUNT 71. Göttingen: Vandenhoeck & Ruprecht, 2009.

Malherbe, Abraham J. "'Gentle as a Nurse': The Cynic Background to 1 Thess. 2." *NovT* 12 (1970): 203–17.

———. *The Letters to the Thessalonians: A New Translation with Introduction and Commentary*. AB 32B. New York: Doubleday, 2000.

———. *Paul and the Thessalonians: The Philosophic Tradition of Pastoral Care*. Mifflintown, PA: Sigler, 2000.

Martin, D. Michael. *1, 2 Thessalonians*. NAC 33. Nashville: Broadman & Holman, 1995.

Morris, Leon. *The First and Second Epistles to the Thessalonians: The English Text with Introduction, Exposition and Notes*. NICNT. Grand Rapids, MI: Eerdmans, 1959.

———. *1, 2 Thessalonians*. Word Biblical Themes. Dallas: Word, 1989.

Nicholl, Colin R. *From Hope to Despair in Thessalonica: Situating 1 and 2 Thessalonians*. SNTSMS 126. Cambridge: Cambridge University Press, 2004.

Pearson, Birger A. "1 Thessalonians 2:13–16: A Deutero-Pauline Interpolation." *HTR* 64 (1971): 79–94.
Richard, Earl J. *First and Second Thessalonians*. SP 11. Collegeville, MN: Liturgical, 1995.
Shogren, Gary S. *1 & 2 Thessalonians*. ZECNT. Grand Rapids, MI: Zondervan, 2012.
Vos, Geerhardus. *The Pauline Eschatology*. Phillipsburg, NJ: P&R, 1986.
Wanamaker, Charles A. *The Epistles to the Thessalonians: A Commentary on the Greek Text*. NIGTC. Grand Rapids, MI: Eerdmans, 1990.
Warfield, B. B. "God Our Father and the Lord Jesus Christ." In *Biblical Doctrines*, by B. B. Warfield, 213–31. Carlisle, PA: Banner of Truth, 1988.
Weima, Jeffery A. D. "An Apology for the Apologetic Function of 1 Thessalonians 2:1–12." *JSNT* 68 (1997): 73–79.
———. *1–2 Thessalonians*. BECNT. Grand Rapids, MI: Baker Academic, 2014.
———. *Neglected Endings: The Significance of the Pauline Letter Closings*. JSNTSup 101. Sheffield: Sheffield Academic, 1994.
Weima, Jeffrey A. D., and Stanley E. Porter. *An Annotated Bibliography of 1 and 2 Thessalonians*. NTTS 26. Leiden: Brill, 1998.
Witherington, Ben, III. *1 and 2 Thessalonians: A Socio-Rhetorical Commentary*. Grand Rapids, MI: Eerdmans, 2006.

13

2 Thessalonians

Robert J. Cara

Introduction

Second Thessalonians is best known for the difficult second coming passage that includes the man of lawlessness, a restrainer, and Satan (2:1–12). Second Thessalonians 1:7–10 also discusses the second coming. There is an emphasis on Christ as the divine warrior, and this passage includes some of the most explicit comments about eternal judgment in the Bible (1:9).

Another fairly well-known passage concerns those in the church who are idle and do not want to work (2 Thess. 3:6–12). Paul gives the command, "If anyone is not willing to work, let him not eat" (3:10).

Unfortunately, in the critical/liberal scholarly world, many believe that 2 Thessalonians was not written by the historical Paul, that is, it is pseudepigraphical. It is considered one of the six deutero-Pauline letters.[1] Hence, less attention is paid to 2 Thessalonians than would be expected. For example, many modern books on Pauline theology base their analysis on only the seven "authentic" Pauline letters and do not include 2 Thessalonians.[2]

Background Issues[3]

Authorship and Date

As does the opening verse of 1 Thessalonians, 2 Thessalonians 1:1 states that the letter is from Paul, Silvanus (Silas), and Timothy.[4] Conservative scholars believe that the

[1] The standard list of deutero-Pauline letters is Ephesians, Colossians, 2 Thessalonians, 1–2 Timothy, and Titus. The "authentic" letters are Romans, 1–2 Corinthians, Galatians, Philippians, 1 Thessalonians, and Philemon.
[2] E.g., J. Christian Beker, *Paul the Apostle: The Triumph of God in Life and Thought* (Philadelphia: Fortress, 1980), 3.
[3] For historical background concerning the city of Thessalonica, see "Background Issues," "Thessalonica," in the 1 Thessalonians chapter.
[4] Scholars agree that an editorial "we" is being used.

historical Paul did write 2 Thessalonians.[5] However, as noted above, many critical/liberal scholars do not concur, although there are notable exceptions.[6]

I firmly believe that the historical Paul wrote 2 Thessalonians.[7] My primary, and indeed ultimate, argument is that the Scripture, the Word of God, says so (2 Thess. 1:1). However, there are also secondary arguments that dovetail with this primary one.

In the following, I will present three of the standard arguments against Pauline authorship and then respond with my "secondary" counterarguments.[8]

> *Argument 1.* Second Thessalonians is too closely patterned after 1 Thessalonians to have been written by Paul.
>
> *Response.* Yes, some sections are parallel (e.g., 1 Thess. 1:1 with 2 Thess. 1:1; 1 Thess. 2:9 with 2 Thess. 3:8; 1 Thess. 2:13 with 2 Thess. 2:13), but many are not. It is not so unusual that Paul, when writing a second letter from the same location to the same church at about the same time, should use similar phrases as in the first letter.
>
> *Argument 2.* Second Thessalonians is more formal in tone than 1 Thessalonians.
>
> *Response*: Yes, this is true, but it is also to be expected. Paul was obviously thrilled about the health of the Thessalonian church when Timothy gave him the first report. When the second report arrives, Paul has already indicated his love for the church and does not need to repeat all of the emotional language.
>
> *Argument 3.* There are two differing views of "signs" related to the second coming. First Thessalonians expects that the end will come suddenly (1 Thess. 5:2, "like a thief in the night"). Second Thessalonians expects anticipatory signs/events before the end ("rebellion comes first," 2 Thess. 2:3). Paul would not have contradicted himself in such a short space of time.
>
> *Response.* As many have noted, "both conceptions—the End is coming suddenly, and it has historical antecedents—occur together in the apocalyptic of Judaism

[5] E.g., Leon Morris, *The First and Second Epistles to the Thessalonians: The English Text with Introduction, Exposition and Notes*, NICNT (Grand Rapids, MI: Eerdmans, 1959), 29–34; and G. K. Beale, *1–2 Thessalonians*, IVPNTC (Downers Grove, IL: InterVarsity Press, 2003), 14–18. Charles A. Wanamaker also sees Paul as the author of 2 Thessalonians, but with the twist that 2 Thessalonians was written first, then 1 Thessalonians (*The Epistles to the Thessalonians: A Commentary on the Greek Text*, NIGTC [Grand Rapids, MI: Eerdmans, 1990], 37–45).

[6] Those against Pauline authorship include M. Eugene Boring, *An Introduction to the New Testament: History, Literature, Theology* (Louisville: Westminster John Knox, 2012), 360–66; Bart D. Ehrman, *The New Testament: A Historical Introduction to the Early Christian Writings*, 4th ed. (New York: Oxford, 2008), 384–86; Wolfgang Trilling, *Die zweite Brief an die Thessalonicher*, EKKNT 14 (Zurich: Benziger, 1980), 21–28; and Earl J. Richard, *First and Second Thessalonians*, SP 11 (Collegeville, MN: Liturgical, 1995), 19–30. Critical scholars who favor authentic Pauline authorship include Abraham J. Malherbe, *The Letters to the Thessalonians: A New Translation with Introduction and Commentary*, AB 32B (New York: Doubleday, 2000), 349–75; and Werner Georg Kümmel, *Introduction to the New Testament*, rev. ed., trans. Howard Clark Kee (Nashville: Abingdon, 1975), 260–69. Raymond E. Brown concludes, "Looking at the argument for and against Paul's writing 2 Thess., personally I cannot decide with certitude" (*An Introduction to the New Testament*, ABRL [New York: Doubleday, 1997], 596). Jeffrey A. D. Weima complains that some exaggerate the number of scholars opposed to Pauline authorship and concludes that the Pauline-authorship view "is still the widespread view held today" (*1–2 Thessalonians*, BECNT [Grand Rapids, MI: Baker Academic, 2014], 46).

[7] Much of this section is taken from my previous work, Robert J. Cara, *A Study Commentary on 1 and 2 Thessalonians*, EPSC (Darlington: Evangelical Press, 2009), 24–26.

[8] For a good summary of arguments in favor of Pauline authorship, see D. A. Carson and Douglas J. Moo, *An Introduction to the New Testament*, 2nd ed. (Grand Rapids, MI: Zondervan, 2005), 534–42. For standard arguments against Pauline authorship, see Helmut Koester, *History and Literature of Early Christianity*, vol. 2 of *Introduction to the New Testament* (New York: de Gruyter, 1982), 242–46.

> and early Christianity, and lie within the same perspective."[9] Also, many Old Testament prophecies about Christ's first coming seemed contradictory until the actual fulfillment came. Will not aspects of the second coming that appear contradictory be consistent when the events occur? Finally, I believe that anticipatory signs mentioned in 2 Thessalonians 2 will occur at basically the same time as the second coming; hence, the dilemma is solved.[10]

Another secondary argument favoring Pauline authorship is that the early church universally attributed 2 Thessalonians to Paul. This was despite knowing that there may have been a pseudonymous letter in Paul's name associated with Thessalonica (2 Thess. 2:2; 3:17).

For those who see Paul as the true author, it is assumed that 2 Thessalonians was written several weeks or a few months after 1 Thessalonians, which places the date at approximately AD 50.[11] For those who see 2 Thessalonians as pseudonymous, a date of AD 80–100 is common.[12]

Occasion and Purpose[13]

We do not know who delivered 1 Thessalonians to the Thessalonian church. But apparently, after delivering the letter, this person (or persons) returns to Paul with more-recent news about the church and her reception of 1 Thessalonians.

Paul is evidently still in Corinth when he receives the report. This assumption is based on both 1 and 2 Thessalonians having the same opening words, "Paul, Silvanus, and Timothy" (1 Thess. 1:1; 2 Thess. 1:1), and because Paul stayed eighteen months in Corinth according to Acts 18:11. It is further assumed that Paul wrote 2 Thessalonians several weeks or a few months after 1 Thessalonians. This puts the date at AD 50.

Paul received a report from Timothy that prompted his writing of 1 Thessalonians. Similarly, this second report that Paul receives prompts his writing of 2 Thessalonians. This second report is primarily positive but does contain two negatives. The positive aspects are that the church is spiritually healthy (1:3–4) despite continued outside persecution (1:5–6), and that the Thessalonians still have a high regard for Paul, which is implied by the fact that he no longer has to defend himself. The negative aspects are that the Thessalonians have received false information about the second coming (2:2), and that the problem of idleness, mentioned in 1 Thessalonians (1 Thess. 4:11–12; 5:14), has not been solved or may have worsened (2 Thess. 3:6–15).

Hence, Paul's purpose for writing 2 Thessalonians includes (1) commending the Thessalonians for their continued spiritual growth despite persecution and encouraging them to progress further (1:3–4; 2:13–17; 3:4), (2) dealing with the false information

---

[9] Kümmel, *Introduction to the New Testament*, 266.

[10] That is, the fullness of the appearing of the Antichrist ("man of lawlessness") and Christ's battle with him will essentially take place at the same time. See Cara, *Study Commentary on 1 and 2 Thessalonians*, 206–7. Although I do not agree, Weima solves the dilemma by restricting the "thief in the night" (1 Thess. 5:2) scenario to unbelievers (*1–2 Thessalonians*, 51).

[11] See the discussion under "Background Issues," "Authorship and Date," in the 1 Thessalonians chapter.

[12] E.g., Edgar M. Krentz, "Thessalonians, First and Second Epistles to the," *ABD*, 6:517–23.

[13] Much of this section is taken from my previous work, Cara, *Study Commentary on 1 and 2 Thessalonians*, 22–23, 171.

about the second coming (2:1–12), and (3) giving an extended discussion concerning the idleness problem (3:6–15).[14] Not everything in 2 Thessalonians is directly related to the report, and thus Paul includes comments that are more general in their application (e.g., 3:16).[15]

Structure and Outline

The outline for 2 Thessalonians is straightforward:

I. Opening (1:1–2)
II. Thanksgiving (1:3–12)
III. Body (2:1–3:15)
   A. Man of lawlessness (2:1–12)
   B. Thanksgiving (2:13–17)
   C. Prayer request (3:1–5)
   D. Idleness (3:6–15)
IV. Closing (3:16–18)

The outline matches Paul's other letters reasonably well. The major exception is that 2 Thessalonians has two thanksgiving sections. The first thanksgiving section immediately after the opening is standard, but having a second thanksgiving section within the body is not. (First and Second Thessalonians are the only two Pauline letters with two thanksgiving sections.) Also, 2 Thessalonians differs from 1 Thessalonians and several other Pauline letters in that it does not have an extended hortatory section.

The opening section (2 Thess. 1:1–2) is very similar to the beginning of 1 Thessalonians. (See comments concerning the opening section under "Structure and Outline" in the 1 Thessalonians chapter.)

In the initial thanksgiving (εὐχαριστέω) section (2 Thess. 1:3–12), Paul tells the Thessalonian Christians that he thanks God for their faith and love and boasts about them to other churches (1:3–4).[16] Paul is impressed with their faith and perseverance especially in light of their being persecuted. The mention of persecution prompts Paul to comment on the eschatological "righteous judgment of God" that will have a positive result for the Thessalonian Christians and a negative one for their persecutors (2 Thess. 1:5–12). Within this section are strong statements about Christ being a divine warrior, "in flaming fire, inflicting vengeance," and hell as "eternal destruction" (1:8–9). (See more discussion below, under the heading "Divine Warrior.")

Following the thanksgiving section, Paul begins the body section with a discussion of the second coming (2 Thess. 2:1–12). Apparently, because of false information proffered in Paul's name, some of the Thessalonians are confused and are tempted to

[14] My summary of the purpose substantially matches Carson and Moo, although they see more of a focus on the persecution as occasioning all aspects of the letter, including the false information about the second coming and the idleness problem (*Introduction to the New Testament*, 546).

[15] For those who see 2 Thessalonians as pseudonymous and written toward the end of the first century AD, M. Eugene Boring is typical as to the occasion and purpose. He sees three issues: (1) "persecution of Christians," (2) "the delay of the parousia," and (3) "changes in church leadership and structure" (*Introduction to the New Testament*, 366).

[16] We have a specific example of this boasting. Paul boasts about the Macedonians, which includes the Thessalonians, to the Corinthians concerning their generosity (2 Cor. 8:1–5).

believe that the second coming has already occurred or is just about to occur (2:2–3).[17] Paul answers that, no, the second coming has not taken place. At minimum, the "man of lawlessness" (2:3) needs to be revealed before or in association with the second coming. Since that has not happened, the second coming has not occurred (2:4). This central point of the passage is clear. However, as is well known, other aspects of this passage are difficult and have generated many views down through church history to the present. Paul gives more details about events associated with the second coming that include the man of lawlessness, a temple, a restrainer, Satan, Christ's divine warrior activity (he "will kill with the breath of his mouth"), and God the Father's activity (he "sends them a strong delusion") (2:6–12). In brief, I regard the "man of lawlessness" as the future Antichrist (Mark 13:22; 1 John 2:18; 4:3).[18] The "temple" (2 Thess. 2:4) may allude to a well-known religious center, but it emphasizes the man of lawlessness's perverse view of his own deity. The "restrainer" is an evil force ultimately related to Satan that is working to reveal the man of lawlessness at the correct time.[19] When the man of lawlessness is *fully* revealed, Christ will destroy him. (See, again, discussion under the heading "Divine Warrior.")

The second thanksgiving (εὐχαριστέω) section (2 Thess. 2:13–17) includes a thanksgiving statement per se, a command to "stand firm," and a closing benediction that Christ and God the Father would "comfort your hearts and establish them in every good work and word." In addition to being the second in the letter, this thanksgiving is unusual in another way. In most cases Paul thanks God for the specific *good works of the Christians* to whom he is writing; here, however, Paul gives thanks to God for *God's works* that relate to Christians.[20] God has chosen and called the Thessalonians.

Paul begins 2 Thessalonians 3:1–5 by requesting prayer "for us, that the word of the Lord may speed ahead and be honored" and "we may be delivered from wicked and evil men" (3:1–2). Given the reality of evil, Paul turns away from himself and offers encouragement to the Thessalonians that the Lord will establish them and thereby guard them against the "evil one"[21] (3:3–4). He then ends with another benediction (3:5).

As noted above, one of the main purposes of the letter was to address the conduct of some in the church who were living in "idleness" and did not want to work. Paul has an extended discussion of this in 2 Thessalonians 3:6–16. He uses himself as an example and also gives the command, "If anyone is not willing to work, let him not eat" (3:10). (For more discussion, see "Idleness," below.)

The closing section of 2 Thessalonians is typical of Pauline letters and contains

[17] Cf. 2 Tim. 2:18; 2 Pet. 3:4–10.

[18] For my detailed exegesis of 2 Thess. 2:1–12, see Cara, *Study Commentary on 1 and 2 Thessalonians*, 195–214. Also see Herman Ridderbos's long discussion of this passage (*Paul: An Outline of His Theology*, trans. John Richard de Witt [Grand Rapids, MI: Eerdmans, 1975], 508–28).

[19] Augustine famously said about the restrainer, "I frankly confess I do not know what he means" (*The City of God*, trans. Marcus Dods [New York: Random House, 1950], 739 [20.19]).

[20] Cara, *Study Commentary on 1 and 2 Thessalonians*, 217–19.

[21] Grammatically, the Greek adjective form τοῦ πονηροῦ could be either masculine ("evil one"—that is, Satan) or neuter ("evil"—that is, generic evil). The KJV opts for "evil," and most modern translations, "evil one."

a peace benediction (3:16), a greeting (3:17), and a grace benediction (3:18). Paul's greeting notes that it is in his "own hand" and that "this is the sign of genuineness in every letter of mine" (3:17). He wrote such greetings in his own handwriting, and an amanuensis wrote the rest of each letter.[22] Why does Paul call attention to his handwriting here? He may simply be following standard Greco-Roman format for authenticating a letter.[23] A stronger possibility, which dovetails with the first, is that he is intentionally guarding against forgeries, as alluded to in 2 Thessalonians 2:2.[24]

Message and Theology

Second Thessalonians contributes in important ways to our overall understanding of two topics in particular. Obviously, discussions of these two topics are necessarily truncated below, and connections with all of Paul and all of the Bible could ultimately be considered.

Divine Warrior

In the Old Testament, God and the Messiah are depicted as warriors (e.g., Ex. 15:3; Pss. 110; 136:4–12; Isa. 11:1–4; 42:13; 66:15–16; Mal. 4:1).[25] Scholars often point to Exodus 15:1–18 as an important text showing God as a divine warrior.[26] Exodus 15:1–18 is the song of Moses immediately following God's victory over Egypt at the sea.

> The Lord is a man of war;
> the Lord is his name. (Ex. 15:3)

Building on the Old Testament, Christ is portrayed as a divine warrior in the New Testament. He fights for and wins the victory at the cross and at the second coming (e.g., Matt. 24:30; 1 Cor. 15:24–28; Col. 2:14–15; Rev. 1:16; 19:11–21). Revelation 19:11 declares that Christ "judges and makes war" as the rider on the white horse. New Testament scholars combine many New Testament motifs under the divine warrior theme. These include Christ's triumph over death, sin, flesh, Satan, and all evil powers; Christ's protection of his church; Christ's righteous judgment at the second coming; aspects of Christ's kingship; and all warfare and military imagery.[27] (Another aspect of this theme is that Christians are warriors patterned after the divine

---

[22] The amanuensis Tertius sends his own greeting in Rom. 16:22. Paul explicitly mentions his own handwriting in 1 Cor. 16:21; Gal. 6:11; Col. 4:18; 2 Thess. 3:17; and Philem. 19.

[23] See Richard N. Longenecker, "Ancient Amanuenses and the Pauline Epistles," in *New Dimensions in New Testament Study*, ed. Richard N. Longenecker and Merrill C. Tenney (Grand Rapids, MI: Zondervan, 1974), 282–97; and Stanley K. Stowers, *Letter Writing in Greco-Roman Antiquity*, LEC 5 (Philadelphia: Westminster Press, 1986), 60–61.

[24] Chrysostom, "Homily 5 on Second Thessalonians" (*NPNF*[1] 13:395); F. F. Bruce, *1 & 2 Thessalonians*, WBC 45 (Waco, TX: Word, 1982), 216; and Malherbe, *Letters to the Thessalonians*, 463.

[25] Walther Eichrodt notes, "The God of Israel is praised in hymns as a warrior-hero, powerful and highly exalted, terrible and glorious in holiness, mighty and a doer of wonders. The title 'Yahweh of Hosts' very specially refers to this demonstration of his power in war" (*Theology of the Old Testament*, trans. J. A. Baker, 2 vols., OTL [Philadelphia: Westminster Press, 1961, 1967], 1:229).

[26] Tremper Longman III and Daniel G. Reid, *God Is a Warrior*, SOTBT (Grand Rapids, MI: Zondervan, 1995), 31.

[27] For a discussion of the divine warrior in Paul, see D. G. Reid, "Triumph," *DPL*, 946–54. N. T. Wright has especially highlighted that the cross of Christ was a victory over evil; Wright maintains a somewhat unusual view of the Old Testament background to this (*Jesus and the Victory of God* [London: SPCK, 2004], 607–10).

warrior—cf. Eph. 6:10–20 and 1 Thess. 5:8 with Isa. 59:17.)[28] Systematic theologians usually include divine warrior themes within the *Christus Victor* theme.[29]

Concerning 2 Thessalonians and the divine warrior theme, two passages are in view: 1:5–10 and 2:8. In 1:5–7a, Paul notes that Christ's coming will grant the Thessalonians "relief" from suffering as the evildoers will be punished. There are many advantages for Christians in the new heavens and new earth; here one of them is "relief" from suffering caused by those opposed to Christ. Paul then describes in divine warrior language that Christ will be revealed "with his mighty angels in flaming fire, inflicting vengeance" (2 Thess. 1:7–8). Christ's divinity is on display in that the Bible often presents God as a flaming fire who inflicts vengeance (e.g., Ex. 3:2; 13:21; Ps. 94:1; Isa. 66:15; Nah. 1:2; Rom. 12:19).

Christ's punishment of the wicked will be "eternal destruction, away from the presence of the Lord" (2 Thess. 1:9). In my view, as with most major commentaries and the majority of the historic Christian church, "eternal destruction" refers to eternal and *conscious* punishment.[30] The primary argument in context is that "away from the presence of the Lord" assumes that the evil ones have ongoing existence.[31] However, Anabaptist traditions have favored, instead, annihilation (the view that God will annihilate the wicked so that they have no more consciousness or existence). In the latter years of the twentieth century, annihilationism gained favor even among some evangelical theologians.[32]

In 2 Thessalonians 2:8, concerning Satan's man of lawlessness, Christ "will kill [him] with the breath of his mouth." Behind this expression is wording from Isaiah 11:4, which is part of the messianic passage that emphasizes the shoot coming forth from the stump of Jesse (Isa. 11:1–9).[33] Here it is Christ's "mouth" that will kill. As elsewhere in Scripture, God's "mouth" or words are not simply words but also his power (e.g., Gen. 1:3; Ps. 29:4; Isa. 55:11; Rom. 1:16; 1 Thess. 1:5; 2:13; Heb. 1:3;

---

[28] Thomas R. Yoder Neufeld notes, "In 1 Thessalonians 5 Paul takes the breathtaking step of placing the confused and even fearful Thessalonians into God's armour, thereby implicating them in the invasion of the Divine Warrior" (*'Put on the Armour of God': The Divine Warrior from Isaiah to Ephesians*, JSNTSup 140 [Sheffield: Sheffield Academic, 1997], 154).

[29] For example, G. C. Berkouwer, *The Work of Christ*, trans. Cornelius Lambregtse, Studies in Dogmatics (Grand Rapids, MI: Eerdmans, 1965), 327–42; J. van Genderen and W. H. Velema, *Concise Reformed Dogmatics*, trans. Gerrit Bilkes and Ed M. van der Maas (Phillipsburg, NJ: P&R, 2008), 531–36; and G. Aulen, *Christus Victor: An Historical Study of the Three Main Types of the Idea of the Atonement* (London: SPCK, 1931). For a critique of Aulen and his reading of the church fathers, see Douglas F. Kelly, *The Beauty of Christ: A Trinitarian Vision* , vol. 2 of *Systematic Theology: Grounded in Holy Scripture and Understood in the Light of the Church* (Fearn: Christian Focus, 2014), 437–39.

[30] See John Calvin, *The Epistles of Paul the Apostle to the Romans and to the Thessalonians*, trans. Ross Mackenzie, Calvin's Commentaries (Grand Rapids, MI: Eerdmans, 1960), 392; James Everett Frame, *A Critical and Exegetical Commentary on the Epistles of St. Paul to the Thessalonians*, ICC (Edinburgh: T&T Clark; 1912), 234; Ernest Best, *The First and Second Epistles to the Thessalonians*, BNTC (Peabody, MA: Hendrickson, 1986), 261–62; Malherbe, *Letters to the Thessalonians*, 402; Cara, *Study Commentary on 1 and 2 Thessalonians*, 185–86; Weima, *1–2 Thessalonians*, 474; Baltimore Catechism 3.185; Catechism of the Catholic Church 1035, 1861; Orthodox Confession of the Catholic and Apostolic Eastern Church 68; Augsburg Confession 17; Belgic Confession 37; WCF 33.3; WLC 29, 89.

[31] In addition, other biblical texts confirm this eternal, frightening reality (e.g., Isa. 33:14; Dan. 12:2; Matt. 3:12; 18:8; 25:41, 46; Mark 9:43, 48; Luke 16:26; Jude 6–7; Rev. 14:11; 20:10).

[32] Evangelical theologians in favor of annihilation include Philip E. Hughes, *The True Image: The Origin and Destiny of Man in Christ* (Grand Rapids, MI: Eerdmans, 1989), 405–7; Clark H. Pinnock, "The Destruction of the Finally Impenitent," *CTR* 4 (1990): 246–47; and John R. W. Stott and David L. Edwards, *Evangelical Essentials: A Liberal-Evangelical Dialogue* (Downers Grove, IL: InterVarsity Press, 1989), 275–76, 312–21. For a defense of the traditional view along with interaction with some of the newer evangelical views, see Robert A. Peterson, *Hell on Trial: The Case for Eternal Punishment* (Phillipsburg, NJ: P&R, 1995).

[33] For more New Testament connections to Isa. 11:1–9, see Matt. 3:16; Rom. 15:12; Eph. 6:14; 1 Pet. 4:14; Rev. 1:16; 19:15; cf. 4 Ezra 13:10–11.

1 Pet. 1:23–25). Interestingly, Revelation has several judgment passages that connect "mouth" to a "sword" (Rev. 1:16; 2:16; 19:15).

What does 2 Thessalonians emphasize relative to the divine warrior theme from 1:5–10 and 2:8? Both of these passages emphasize Christ as a divine warrior coming in judgment to punish evil and thereby protect and vindicate the persecuted church.[34] At the imagery level, it is Christ's ability to fight and destroy as a divine warrior that is emphasized. Also, 1:9 confirms the traditional view of hell as eternal punishment.

Idleness

In 2 Thessalonians 3:6, Paul says, "Keep away from any brother who is walking in idleness [ἀτάκτως]." The Greek adverb ἀτάκτως and its cognates (1 Thess. 5:14; 2 Thess. 3:7, 11) are sometimes translated in terms of "idleness/idle" (e.g., ESV, NIV, NRSV) or a "disorderly" manner (e.g., KJV, NJB) or, as I prefer, "in an unruly manner."[35] Although, technically, "unruly" is the best translation, it is obvious from the context that the sinning Christians were unruly by being idle and lazy and not submitting to leaders. Hence, "in idleness" is a reasonable translation. Jeffrey Weima notes well that these Christians were "'rebellious idlers'—those who were not merely lazy but who compounded their sin by rebelliously refusing to obey the command of both their congregational leaders and even Paul himself."[36]

Second Thessalonians 3:6–15 is an extended discussion of the idleness problem. The Thessalonian church corporately or its wealthier members individually (Acts 17:4) were supporting the physical needs of those in the church who were idle and did not want to work. First Thessalonians also mentions the idleness problem (1 Thess. 4:11–12; 5:14). Apparently, it was growing worse or no action was taken; hence, an extended discussion is warranted in 2 Thessalonians.

Although all agree that the idle brothers did not want to work, scholars disagree concerning the reasons and motivations for their behavior as Paul did not discuss this directly. Concerning the reasons and motivations, scholars propose three scenarios:[37]

1. Some Thessalonians did not want to work because of their wrong view of the second coming. If Christ was coming very soon, or if he had already come in a secret way, they thought that Christians did not need to work.[38]

---

[34] Karl P. Donfried argues that the "primary image of Jesus in 2 Thessalonians is that of a judge, a judge who will be extolled and celebrated by his saints for his exercise of power on the last day" ("The Theology of 2 Thessalonians," in *The Theology of the Shorter Pauline Letters*, NTT [Cambridge: Cambridge University Press, 1993], 96). Edgar Krentz agrees; Christ is "the future judge *par excellence*, who will destroy the persecutors of the suffering community" ("Traditions Held Fast: Theology and Fidelity in 2 Thessalonians," in *The Thessalonian Correspondence*, ed. Raymond F. Collins [Leuven: Leuven University Press, 1990], 509, emphasis his).

[35] Cara, *Study Commentary on 1 and 2 Thessalonians*, 233. For ἀτάκτως, BDAG prefers "disorderly," although it is noted that in 2 Thessalonians 3 the negative behavior is "freeloading, sponging" (BDAG, 148).

[36] Weima, *1–2 Thessalonians*, 600.

[37] Much of the following is from my commentary, Cara, *Study Commentary on 1 and 2 Thessalonians*, 231–44.

[38] For example, M. J. J. Menken, "Paradise Regained or Still Lost? Eschatology and Disorderly Behaviour in 2 Thessalonians," *NTS* 38 (1992): 271–89; Robert Jewett, *The Thessalonian Correspondence: Pauline Rhetoric and Millenarian Piety* (Philadelphia: Fortress, 1986), 105, 173; Morris, *First and Second Epistles to the Thessalonians*, 251; G. K. Beale, *1–2 Thessalonians*, IVPNTC (Downers Grove, IL: InterVarsity Press, 2003), 249.

2. Some Thessalonians did not want to work as a result of various Greco-Roman social forces.[39]
3. Some Thessalonians did not want to work because of the sin of laziness.

My own view is that the sin of laziness was at the heart of the problem. My primary arguments are that (1) idleness persisted in both Thessalonian letters notwithstanding their differing views and discussions of the second coming; and (2) laziness with regard to work is a very common human problem. Of course, there may have been other aggravating factors. In the end, Paul's argument that Christians should work applies no matter the motivations for not wanting to.

The passage may be outlined as follows: In 2 Thessalonians 3:6, Paul tells the church to keep away from the idle brothers. He then gives two reasons why Christians ought not to be idle. First, they should follow his *example* (2 Thess. 3:7–9; cf. 1 Cor. 9:6–15; 1 Tim. 5:17–18). Second, he has given the *command* not to be idle (2 Thess. 3:10; cf. Eph. 4:28; 1 Tim. 5:8). In 2 Thessalonians 3:11, Paul recounts that he has heard that there were idle brothers, and then he addresses them directly in verse 12. Paul again speaks to the rest of the brothers and exhorts them about dealing with difficulties in the church (3:13–15). Second Thessalonians 3:15 clearly considers the idle members "brother[s]."

Paul's command is "If anyone is not willing to work, let him not eat" (2 Thess. 3:10). By using "not willing" (οὐ θέλω), he emphasizes the ethical component. Paul is, therefore, not speaking of situations in which someone is willing to work but cannot find a job, or has a job but it pays very little, or is physically or mentally not able to work. These situations may require alms. Paul is speaking of those who intentionally decide not to work. "As for you, brothers, do not grow weary in doing good," he says (3:13). Here, Paul's exhortation does not directly reference idleness, but dealing with the idle is obviously a subset of this general proverb. In context, this exhortation would be an encouragement to those who were helping the poor and were possibly "burned" by some of them. Despite this, they should continue to help the poor, except the completely idle.

A theology of the church's responsibility toward the materially poor is an important topic, but it is significantly beyond the scope of this discussion.[40] However, 2 Thessalonians 3:6–15 does add two important points: (1) If a church member is not *willing* to work, he should not receive alms from the church. (2) Working with poor church members is sometimes difficult; however, the church should continue this work and not grow weary.

[39] R. Russell sees poor workers "caught up as beneficiaries of Christian love" ("The Idle in 2 Thess 3:6–12: An Eschatological or a Social Problem?," *NTS* 34 [1988]: 113). A more recent view is that the patron-client relationship of Greco-Roman culture was infiltrating the Thessalonian church (e.g., Bruce W. Winter, "'If a Man Does Not Wish to Work . . .': A Cultural and Historical Setting for 2 Thessalonians 3:6–16," *TynBul* 40 [1989]: 303–15; Wanamaker, *Epistles to the Thessalonians*, 282; Gene L. Green, *The Letters to the Thessalonians*, PNTC [Grand Rapids, MI: Eerdmans, 2002]). Malherbe sees these Thessalonians as imitating certain philosophical groups that disliked labor (Abraham J. Malherbe, *Paul and the Thessalonians: The Philosophic Tradition of Pastoral Care* [Mifflintown, PA: Sigler, 2000], 100–101).

[40] A good place to start on this significant topic is Craig L. Blomberg, *Neither Poverty nor Riches: A Biblical Theology of Material Possessions*, NSBT 7 (Grand Rapids, MI: Eerdmans, 1999). Also see Abraham Kuyper's interesting political address in *The Problem of Poverty*, ed. James W. Skillen (Grand Rapids, MI: Baker, 1991).

Select Bibliography[41]

Augustine, *The City of God*. Translated by Marcus Dods. Modern Library. New York: Random House, 1950.

Aulen, G. *Christus Victor: An Historical Study of the Three Main Types of the Idea of the Atonement*. London: SPCK, 1931.

Beker, J. Christian. *Paul the Apostle: The Triumph of God in Life and Thought*. Philadelphia: Fortress, 1980.

Berkouwer, G. C. *The Work of Christ*. Translated by Cornelius Lambregtse. Studies in Dogmatics. Grand Rapids, MI: Eerdmans, 1965.

Blomberg, Craig L. *Neither Poverty nor Riches: A Biblical Theology of Material Possessions*. NSBT 7. Grand Rapids, MI: Eerdmans, 1999.

Boring, M. Eugene. *An Introduction to the New Testament: History, Literature, Theology*. Louisville: Westminster John Knox, 2012.

Chrysostom, John. *Homilies of St. John Chrysostom on the Second Epistle of St. Paul the Apostle to the Thessalonians*. In vol. 13 of *NPNF*[1].

Donfried, Karl Paul. "The Theology of 2 Thessalonians." In *The Theology of the Shorter Pauline Letters*, by Karl P. Donfried and I. Howard Marshall, 81–113. NTT. Cambridge: Cambridge University Press, 1993.

Ehrman, Bart D. *The New Testament: A Historical Introduction to the Early Christian Writings*. 4th ed. New York: Oxford, 2008.

Eichrodt, Walther. *Theology of the Old Testament*. Translated by J. A. Baker. 2 vols. OTL. Philadelphia: Westminster Press, 1961, 1967.

Genderen, J. van, and W. H. Velema. *Concise Reformed Dogmatics*. Translated by Gerrit Bilkes and Ed M. van der Maas. Phillipsburg, NJ: P&R, 2008.

Hughes, Philip E. *The True Image: The Origin and Destiny of Man in Christ*. Grand Rapids, MI: Eerdmans, 1989.

Kelly, Douglas F. *The Beauty of Christ: A Trinitarian Vision*. Vol. 2 of *Systematic Theology: Grounded in Holy Scripture and Understood in the Light of the Church*. Fearn: Christian Focus, 2014.

Koester, Helmut. *History and Literature of Early Christianity*. Vol. 2 of *Introduction to the New Testament*. New York: de Gruyter, 1982.

Krentz, Edgar. "Traditions Held Fast: Theology and Fidelity in 2 Thessalonians." In *The Thessalonian Correspondence*, edited by Raymond F. Collins, 505–15. Leuven: Leuven University Press, 1990.

Kuyper, Abraham. *The Problem of Poverty*. Edited by James W. Skillen. Grand Rapids, MI: Baker, 1991.

Longenecker, Richard N. "Ancient Amanuenses and the Pauline Epistles." In *New Dimensions in New Testament Study*, edited by Richard N. Longenecker and Merrill C. Tenney, 282–97. Grand Rapids, MI: Zondervan, 1974.

Longman, Tremper, III, and Daniel G. Reid. *God Is a Warrior*. SOTBT. Grand Rapids, MI: Zondervan, 1995.

[41] Many commentaries, books, and articles on 2 Thessalonians and Paul are already listed in the bibliography for the chapter on 1 Thessalonians. Below are only those not listed there.

Menken, M. J. J. "Paradise Regained or Still Lost? Eschatology and Disorderly Behaviour in 2 Thessalonians." *NTS* 38 (1992): 271–89.

Neufeld, Thomas R. Yoder. *'Put on the Armour of God': The Divine Warrior from Isaiah to Ephesians*. JSNTSup 140. Sheffield: Sheffield Academic, 1997.

Peterson, Robert A. *Hell on Trial: The Case for Eternal Punishment*. Phillipsburg, NJ: P&R, 1995.

Pinnock, Clark H. "The Destruction of the Finally Impenitent." *CTR* 4 (1990): 246–47.

Plummer, Alfred. *A Commentary on St. Paul's Second Epistle to the Thessalonians*. 1918. Repr., Eugene, OR: Wipf & Stock, 2001.

Russell, R. "The Idle in 2 Thess 3:6–12: An Eschatological or a Social Problem?" *NTS* 34 (1988): 113.

Stott, John R. W., and David L. Edwards. *Evangelical Essentials: A Liberal-Evangelical Dialogue*. Downers Grove, IL: InterVarsity Press, 1989.

Stowers, Stanley K. *Letter Writing in Greco-Roman Antiquity*. LEC 5. Philadelphia: Westminster Press, 1986.

Trilling, Wolfgang. *Der zweite Brief an die Thessalonicher*. EKKNT 14. Zurich: Benziger, 1980.

Winter, Bruce W. "'If a Man Does Not Wish to Work . . .': A Cultural and Historical Setting for 2 Thessalonians 3:6–16." *TynBul* 40 (1989): 303–15.

Wright, N. T. *Jesus and the Victory of God*. London: SPCK, 2004.

14

Introduction to the Pastoral Epistles

William B. Barcley

Introduction

The Pastoral Epistles are unique among Paul's letters in that they are addressed to individuals with specific instructions for ordering the affairs of local churches. Timothy and Titus have been given pastoral oversight of the churches in Ephesus and Crete, respectively. Both need encouragement in the face of false teachers and other opposition. And Paul gives both of them basic instructions regarding their primary duties as spiritual leaders, as well as the proper functioning of their churches.

The Pastoral Epistles speak to many questions that are relevant to churches and their leaders today. For example:

- What is at the heart of the ministry of the church?
- How should women participate in the church?
- How important is the preaching ministry of the church, and what should the church's preaching look like?
- How much diversity can we allow in the teaching and preaching ministry of the church?
- What is the church's responsibility to the poor?
- What type of leadership should the church have?
- Who should occupy positions of leadership?
- What should the worship of the church entail?

Paul certainly does not deal with each of these questions as exhaustively as we might like. He does not give specific answers to all of our modern questions. But the Pastoral Epistles guide our wrestling with many of the problems and struggles that the church faces today. In this sense, they are just as important and relevant for Christians in the twenty-first century as they were in the first century.

Background Issues

Scholars generally group the Pastoral Epistles together and look at them as a unit. There are good reasons to do this. They are similar in many ways: all are written to encourage Paul's colleagues to be faithful in ministry, all address false teaching and false teachers, and all at some level speak to proper ministry in local churches. But we also need to recognize the many differences between the individual letters. First Timothy and Titus, for instance, deal more with the proper ordering of the church than does 2 Timothy, which is a more intimate and personal letter to Paul's "beloved child" (1:2) in the faith. In addition, while all three letters address false teaching, and we can detect some similarities in the false teaching that is addressed in these letters, it is not clear that the false teaching is exactly the same in all three.[1]

Nevertheless, there are enough similarities between the letters to enable us to deal with many of the background questions together in this single chapter (which will also include a combined bibliography). Some of the distinctive features of the letters will come out in subsequent chapters when we examine the content and themes of each one individually.

Authorship

As we have seen in this volume, Pauline authorship of many of the letters that bear Paul's name is debated among many New Testament scholars. Of the six most debated letters (Ephesians, Colossians, 2 Thessalonians, 1–2 Timothy, and Titus), Pauline authorship of the Pastoral Epistles is denied most frequently and most adamantly. Even many scholars who believe that Paul wrote or probably wrote Ephesians, Colossians, and 2 Thessalonians deny Pauline authorship of the Pastorals (though some of these scholars believe that he wrote 2 Timothy, because of its intensely personal nature). But by and large, Pauline authorship of the Pastorals is denied by a large portion of New Testament scholars today.[2]

[1] As Carson and Moo point out, it is usually assumed that the false teaching is the same in all of the letters (D. A. Carson and Douglas J. Moo, *An Introduction to the New Testament*, 2nd ed. [Grand Rapids, MI: Zondervan, 2005], 563). One issue of debate is that Paul seems to address what we might call an "over-realized eschatology" in 2 Tim. 2:17–18, in which two men, Hymenaeus and Philetus, are teaching that "the resurrection has already happened." Hymenaeus is also mentioned as a false teacher in 1 Tim. 1:20. Philip Towner sees an over-realized eschatology, similar to what Paul addresses in 1 Corinthians, as the root of the Ephesian false teaching. See Towner, "Gnosis and Realized Eschatology in Ephesus (of the Pastoral Epistles) and the Corinthian Enthusiasm," *JSNT* 31 (1987): 95–124; and Towner, *The Goal of Our Instruction: The Structure of Theology and Ethics in the Pastoral Epistles* (Sheffield: JSOT, 1989). But it is not entirely clear that the false teaching Paul interacts with in 1 Timothy has this same exact component. Compare William B. Barcley, *1 & 2 Timothy*, EPSC (Darlington: Evangelical Press, 2005), 17–18.

[2] Carson and Moo write, "Contemporary critical orthodoxy insists that the Pastorals were all written by someone other than Paul and at a time considerably later than that of the apostle" (*Introduction to the New Testament*, 555). Pauline authorship of the Pastorals has been affirmed by the church and was rarely questioned by anyone for 1900 years. Irenaeus first quotes the Pastorals as Pauline in *Against Heresies* 2.14.7 and 3.3.3 around AD 180. From the late second century onward they are treated as Pauline and listed with the Pauline Epistles in every list of canonical writings, including the Muratorian Canon. The classic work refuting Pauline authorship of the Pastorals, the one that almost all critical scholars point to, is that of P. N. Harrison, *The Problem of the Pastoral Epistles* (London: Oxford University Press, 1921). C. F. D. Moule alternatively suggests that the Pastorals were written by Luke, but for Paul during Paul's lifetime ("The Problem of the Pastoral Epistles: A Reappraisal," *BJRL* 47 [1965]: 430–52).

Most of the arguments against Pauline authorship come down to four categories: vocabulary, style, theology, and ecclesiology. About a century ago, P. N. Harrison made an impressive case against Pauline authorship based on vocabulary, as well as certain stylistic features.[3] Harrison showed that of the approximately nine hundred words that Paul uses in the Pastoral Epistles, more than one-third of them do not appear anywhere else in Paul's letters. Furthermore, of these 306 unique words, 175 are not found anywhere else in the New Testament, but 211 of the 306 are found in Christian writings from the early second century. This has led many to assert that the Pastoral Epistles were written by a devoted follower of Paul in the late first century, or early second, in an attempt to apply Paul's thought to particular problems in his own day.[4] In addition, many of the connecting words (about half of them) that give Paul's earlier letters their stylistic feel are missing from the Pastoral Epistles.[5]

But these kinds of statistics are by no means conclusive—or convincing. Paul's letters are certainly but a snapshot of the total vocabulary he used in his life. There is no reason to believe that he was limited by what he said elsewhere. Furthermore, some of Paul's other letters also have a high degree of unique vocabulary, though admittedly not as high as the Pastorals. Yet his vocabulary and style often reflect the particular situation he was addressing and arise out of that historical context. William Mounce takes Harrison's 306 "non-Pauline" words and breaks them down by category, showing that the vast majority of them can be explained historically within the setting of Paul's life and the issues he was addressing.[6]

Arguments against Pauline authorship based on theology deal with the strength and style of Paul's opposition to false teaching, reflecting (the argument goes) a later stage in the church's history when theology was more developed.[7] Similarly, arguments based on ecclesiology also assert that the church structure Paul lays down in the Pastorals (such as, elders who rule, deacons) reflects a more developed church formation than would have been present in Paul's day.[8] But from the beginning of his ministry, Paul opposed false teaching (see 1 Corinthians and Galatians), and one would expect that in letters addressed to individual colleagues (as opposed to whole churches) instructing them in how to deal with false teaching, Paul's approach might be a little different. Furthermore, on his first missionary journey, Paul made sure that elders were put in place in all the churches he founded (Acts 14:23), and there

[3] Harrison, *Problem of the Pastoral Epistles*.

[4] Harrison (ibid., 115–35), however, does argue that the Pastorals contain genuine fragments from letters written by Paul that were incorporated by a later writer into these letters. For other arguments supporting a late date of the Pastorals, see below.

[5] Cf. ibid., 36f. A. M. Hunter wrote, "How are we to explain the fact that 'the connective tissue' (particles, etc.—a very subtle test of style) is clearly not Paul's?" (*Interpreting the New Testament: 1900–1950* [London: SCM, 1951], 64).

[6] William Mounce, *Pastoral Epistles*, WBC 46 (Nashville: Thomas Nelson, 2000), civ–cxiii. Mounce's entire discussion of Pauline authorship is very helpful.

[7] See the arguments of Anthony T. Hanson, *The Pastoral Epistles*, NCBC (Grand Rapids, MI: Eerdmans, 1982), who believes that Paul did not write the Pastorals. Hanson states, "Editors [with whom Hanson agrees] have also observed that the author of the Pastorals does not argue with his theological opponents as Paul does" (ibid., 4). He goes on to state, "The author of the Pastorals seems to have an attitude toward doctrine that is not Paul's. For [the author of the Pastorals] Christian doctrine is *paratheke*, 'what has been entrusted to you' (1 Tim. 6:20). This deposit of faith has been delivered by Paul to Timothy and must be in turn handed on by Timothy to trustworthy successors. . . . This is not the way the historical Paul handles Christian doctrine" (ibid., 5–6).

[8] See the discussion of Knight, who favors the historical Christian view supporting Pauline authorship (*The Pastoral Epistles*, NIGTC [Grand Rapids, MI: Eerdmans, 1992], 28–32). Cf. also, concisely, Carson and Moo, *Introduction to the New Testament*, 564.

is nothing in the Pastorals that reflects a church structure that could not have been in place in Paul's day.

We know that Paul used a scribe when he wrote his letters (cf. Rom. 16:22). Some of the vocabulary and stylistic differences between the Pastoral Epistles and other letters may reflect a certain amount of freedom that Paul gave his scribe in writing his letters.[9] But on the whole, the clear personal touches in the Pastorals (e.g. 1 Tim. 1:3, 18–20; 5:23; 2 Tim. 1:3–7; 4:9–13), as well as the almost universal testimony of the church from the early second century onward, point to Paul as the author of these letters.

Date and Occasion

When and why were these letters written? It is difficult to be certain about the date of 1 Timothy and Titus. Most likely Paul wrote both of them during a time of active ministry after release from his first Roman imprisonment, dating them in the early to mid-60s.[10] Paul begins his instructions to Timothy, "As I urged you when I was going to Macedonia, remain at Ephesus so that you may charge certain persons not to teach any different doctrine" (1 Tim. 1:3). But neither Acts nor Paul's other letters make reference to this event. So it is difficult to date it with certainty.

The final chapters of Acts detail for us the events that led to Paul's first Roman imprisonment, beginning with an arrest in Jerusalem, a transfer to Caesarea, and Paul's appeal to Caesar that finally landed him in house arrest in Rome (cf. Acts 21–28). During Paul's trip to Jerusalem that ended with his arrest, he met with the Ephesian elders and had a tearful farewell with them (cf. Acts 20:17–38). Significantly, he warned them about false teachers who would arise, "fierce wolves" who would not "spar[e] the flock" (Acts 20:28–31). The most likely scenario is that, within a few years, Paul's prediction has come true and Paul has commissioned Timothy to deal with the problem. His first letter to Timothy, then, is to encourage him and to instruct him how to battle the false teachers and how to conduct the life of the church in light of this threat to the church's unity and purity.

The problems in dating Titus are similar. Paul writes, "This is why I left you in Crete, so that you might put what remained into order, and appoint elders in every town as I directed you" (Titus 1:5). The only other New Testament reference to Crete is in Acts 27, which tells of a brief stop there on the journey to Rome. But Acts and Paul's other letters do not tell of missionary activity there, or of the planting of churches there. Again, the most likely scenario is that this took place during a time of active ministry after Paul's release from prison, thus in the early to mid-60s. Like 1 Timothy, Titus is a letter of encouragement and instruction in ordering the affairs of the church, the nature of Titus's ministry in Crete, defending against false teaching, and dealing with the difficult people of Crete.

Paul wrote 2 Timothy a few years later, during his second Roman imprisonment (mid-60s, if the traditional date of Paul's death around 67 is correct). He knows

[9] Fee argues that the best solution for the linguistic and stylistic differences is that Paul used a different amanuensis for these letters than for his earlier ones (Gordon D. Fee, *1 and 2 Timothy, Titus* [San Francisco: Harper & Row, 1984], xxxvi–xxxvii).
[10] For a discussion on the dating of the Pastorals, see Knight, *Pastoral Epistles*, 53–54.

his present trials will lead to his death (2 Tim. 4:6–8). The false teachers remain a problem in Ephesus (cf. 2 Tim. 2:14–3:9).[11] But Paul's tone in this letter changes. As his life and ministry are coming to an end, he wants to see his longtime friend and fellow worker, both to encourage him and to be encouraged by him. The work of the gospel must continue after Paul has departed this life. Timothy needs to be strengthened for this task, and he needs to make plans to train others to carry on the teaching and preaching ministry of the church (2:1–2). Given the circumstances surrounding the letter, 2 Timothy is more personal and more poignant than the rest of Paul's letters. It gives us a glimpse into the heart and soul of the apostle. It is a letter to be treasured, stamped with Paul's legacy.

False Teaching

What is the nature of the false teaching that Paul addresses in the Pastorals? Many commentators write with more confidence about this matter than is warranted by the sketchy nature of what Paul says in these letters. Nevertheless, we can make some general comments about the false teaching, and interestingly, there are some striking similarities in what Paul says, whether he is addressing the false teaching in Ephesus or the false teaching in Crete. We will look at more of the details when we study the individual letters, but we can sketch out some basic facts.

First, the false teaching that Paul addresses in the Pastorals appears to be Jewish in its orientation, with the false teachers using the law as a springboard for extra-biblical speculation (cf. 1 Tim. 1:3–7; Titus 1:10; 3:9). They have promoted certain "myths" and "genealogies" supposedly based on the law but clearly not rooted in it (cf. 1 Tim. 1:4; Titus 1:14; 3:9). This has led to controversies and quarrels that Paul exhorts both Timothy and Titus to avoid (1 Tim. 6:20–21; 2 Tim. 2:14, 23; Titus 3:9; cf. 1 Tim. 6:3–5). This speculative teaching is dangerous because it actually causes people to fall away from the faith (1 Tim. 6:20–21).

In 1 Timothy 1:3 Paul refers to the false teaching as "different doctrine" (ἑτεροδιδασκαλεῖν), which seems to be a term coined by Paul himself.[12] We can compare this to the false teaching that he addresses in Galatians. In Galatians 1:6, Paul refers to the Galatian heresy as a "different" (ἕτερον) gospel, which, he goes on to say, is no gospel at all (1:7). The similarity in language suggests that Paul takes both forms of teaching seriously, even though they seem to be of a different nature. The Galatian heresy was in direct opposition to Paul's gospel. The false teaching in 1 Timothy seems to be of a more speculative nature. Paul sees both of them as a direct threat to the health and purity of the church. He uses the word "different doctrine" again in 1 Timothy 6:3, where he essentially defines it by its opposite: the different teaching "does not agree with the sound words of our Lord Jesus Christ and the teaching that accords with godliness." Calvin captures Paul's thought well:

---

[11] Timothy's exact location is debated, since the text of 2 Timothy does not specifically mention Ephesus. But the signs all point to Timothy still laboring at Ephesus when Paul wrote this second letter to him, including reference to the same opponents, Hymenaeus (2:17) and Alexander (4:14), of whom Paul speaks in 1 Timothy (1:20).

[12] See Fee, *1&2 Timothy*, 6; Mounce, *Pastoral Epistles*, 19.

> It is worth noting that by new doctrine is meant not only teaching that is in open conflict with the pure doctrine of the Gospel, but anything that either corrupts the pure Gospel by new and adventitious inventions or obscures it by unholy speculations. All the imaginings of men are so many corruptions of the Gospel, and those who put the Scriptures to frivolous uses in an ungodly way, so as to make Christianity a clever display, darken the Gospel. All teaching of that kind is opposed to God's Word and to that purity of doctrine in which Paul enjoins the Ephesians to remain.[13]

Paul calls both Timothy and Titus not only to avoid foolish controversies, but also to oppose the false teachers themselves. Timothy is to "charge" or command them not to teach falsely (1 Tim. 1:3). Titus is to "silence" them (Titus 1:11). In addition to this, however, Paul exhorts both Timothy and Titus to teach the opposite—namely, "sound" or healthy doctrine (1 Tim. 1:10; Titus 2:1). The Greek word meaning "be sound or healthy" is one from which we get our word *hygiene* (ὑγιαίνω). Paul uses this verb eight times in the Pastorals (mostly as an adjectival participle: 1 Tim. 1:10; 6:3; 2 Tim. 1:13; 4:3; Titus 1:9, 13; 2:1, 2). Interestingly, the desire to be healthy sounds very modern in our therapeutic age. But what is put forward as "healthy" teaching in churches today is often at odds with biblical truth. Furthermore, in Titus 2:1–2, Paul links "healthy" doctrine to "healthy" living. Theology and ethics, what we believe and what we do, are directly tied to one another. Theology is for living.[14]

For Paul, this false teaching is deadly serious. He dispatches his most trusted companions and coworkers to deal with it.

Recipients

What, then, do we know about Timothy and Titus? Timothy was arguably Paul's closest companion and a prominent figure in his ministry. In six of Paul's thirteen letters, he links himself with Timothy in the opening greeting section, as if Timothy has coauthored the letters (2 Corinthians, Philippians, Colossians, 1–2 Thessalonians, and Philemon). Timothy is mentioned in two other letters (Romans and 1 Corinthians). Two letters are addressed to him. So, of the thirteen Pauline letters, Timothy shows up in ten.

We also see, both in Acts and in Paul's letters, Timothy's active involvement in a number of churches, including Philippi, Thessalonica, and Corinth. Timothy's ministry in Corinth is significant (cf. 1 Cor. 4:17) because of the difficulties Paul experienced with the believers there. Timothy appears to have been Paul's most trusted helper, a faithful servant of Christ, whose ministry of the Word of God was vital in helping the early churches become established, grow, and avoid falsehood.

The fact that Paul trusted Timothy so much and that Timothy appears to have been so effective in ministry is striking, given the fact that Timothy did not appear to be personally impressive. First, we know that he was relatively young. Paul in-

[13] John Calvin, *The Second Epistle of Paul the Apostle to the Corinthians and the Epistles to Timothy, Titus and Philemon*, trans. T. A. Small, Calvin's Commentaries (Grand Rapids, MI: Eerdmans, 1964), 189.

[14] See chap. 1 of Sinclair Ferguson, *The Christian Life: A Doctrinal Introduction* (Edinburgh: Banner of Truth, 1989).

structs him not to let others look down on him because of his youth (1 Tim. 4:12). Second, Timothy was relatively timid, which is implied both in 2 Timothy 1:6–7 and in 1 Corinthians 16:10. Third, Timothy was relatively sick. Paul instructs him to drink a little wine "for the sake of [his] stomach and . . . frequent ailments" (1 Tim. 5:23). These are not the characteristics of someone we would typically consider to be a strong, forceful leader. But we know one final thing about Timothy—namely, that he knew and was rooted in the Word of God (2 Tim. 3:14–17). It was precisely this knowledge and commitment to God's Word that made Timothy an effective minister of Jesus Christ, one who was used mightily of God, and one in whom Paul had complete confidence.

Titus is not mentioned in the book of Acts. But he does show up in several places in Paul's letters. In Galatians 2 we read that Titus accompanied Paul and Barnabas to Jerusalem. Titus is also mentioned nine times in 2 Corinthians (2:13; 7:6, 13, 14; 8:6, 16, 23; and 12:18 twice). Second Corinthians 8:23 is striking because Paul refers to Titus as "my partner and fellow worker for your benefit." In 2 Corinthians in particular, Titus is linked to the collection that Paul was taking up from the Gentile churches for the church in Jerusalem. This collection was important for Paul and shows up in several of his letters. The fact that Titus was involved in this indicates that he was one of Paul's most faithful and trusted associates.

Titus's latest assignment, the place where he was when Paul wrote him, was on the island of Crete. This would have been a very difficult assignment for two reasons. First, if our historical reconstruction above is correct, the church would have been a new church. And, second, the citizens of Crete did not have a very good reputation: "One of the Cretans, a prophet of their own, said, 'Cretans are always liars, evil beasts, lazy gluttons'" (Titus 1:12). Serving in Crete would have been hard work among difficult people. Yet Paul assigns it to his trusted associate Titus.

Select Bibliography for the Pastoral Epistles

Barcley, William B. *1 & 2 Timothy*. EPSC. Darlington: Evangelical Press, 2005.

Bauer, Walter. *Greek-English Lexicon of the New Testament and Other Early Christian Literature*. 3rd ed. Edited by Frederick W. Danker. Translated by William F. Arndt and F. Wilbur Gingrich. Chicago: University of Chicago Press, 2000.

Blass, F., and A. Debrunner. *A Greek Grammar of the New Testament and Other Early Christian Literature*. Edited and translated by Robert W. Funk. Chicago: University of Chicago Press, 1961.

Calvin, John. *The Second Epistle of Paul the Apostle to the Corinthians and the Epistles to Timothy, Titus and Philemon*. Translated by T. A. Small. Calvin's Commentaries. Grand Rapids, MI: Eerdmans, 1964.

Carson, D. A., and Douglas J. Moo. *An Introduction to the New Testament*. 2nd ed. Grand Rapids, MI: Zondervan, 2005.

Chrysostom, John. *Homilies on the Epistles of St. Paul the Apostle to Timothy, Titus, and Philemon*. In vol. 13 of *NPNF*[1].

Fee, Gordon D. *1 and 2 Timothy, Titus*. San Francisco: Harper & Row, 1984.

Guthrie, Donald. *The Pastoral Epistles*. TNTC. Grand Rapids, MI: Eerdmans, 1990.

Hanson, Anthony T. *The Pastoral Epistles*. NCBC. Grand Rapids, MI: Eerdmans, 1982.

Harris, M. J. "Titus 2:13 and the Deity of Christ." In *Pauline Studies: Essays Presented to Professor F. F. Bruce on His 70th Birthday*, edited by Donald A. Hagner and Murray J. Harris, 262–77. Grand Rapids, MI: Eerdmans, 1980.

Harrison, P. N. *The Problem of the Pastoral Epistles*. London: Oxford University Press, 1921.

Hendriksen, William. *Exposition of the Pastoral Epistles*. NTC. Grand Rapids, MI: Baker, 1957.

Hunter, A. M. *Interpreting the New Testament: 1900–1950*. London: SCM, 1951.

Kelly, J. N. D. *A Commentary on the Pastoral Epistles*. New York: Harper & Row, 1963.

Kidd, Reggie M. *Wealth and Beneficence in the Pastoral Epistles*. Atlanta: Scholars, 1990.

Knight, George W. *The Faithful Sayings in the Pastoral Letters*. Grand Rapids, MI: Baker, 1979.

———. *The Pastoral Epistles*. NIGTC. Grand Rapids, MI: Eerdmans, 1992.

Köstenberger, Andreas J., Thomas R. Schreiner, and H. Scott Baldwin, eds. *Women in the Church: A Fresh Analysis of 1 Timothy 2:9–15*. Grand Rapids, MI: Baker, 1995.

Lea, Thomas D., and Hayne P. Griffin. *1, 2 Timothy, Titus*. NAC 34. Grand Rapids, MI: Zondervan, 1999.

Liefeld, Walter L. *1 and 2 Timothy, Titus*. NIVAC. Grand Rapids, MI: Zondervan, 1999.

Louw, Johannes P., and Eugene A. Nida, eds. *Greek-English Lexicon of the New Testament: Based on Semantic Domains*. New York: United Bible Societies, 1988.

Marshall, I. Howard. *A Critical and Exegetical Commentary on the Pastoral Epistles*. In collaboration with Philip H. Towner. Edinburgh: T&T Clark, 1999.

Moule, C. F. D. "The Problem of the Pastoral Epistles: A Reappraisal." *BJRL* 47 (1965): 430–52.

Mounce, William D. *Pastoral Epistles*. WBC 46. Nashville: Thomas Nelson, 2000.

Piper, John, and Wayne Grudem, eds. *Recovering Biblical Manhood and Womanhood: A Response to Evangelical Feminism*. Wheaton, IL: Crossway, 1991.

Simpson, E. K. *The Pastoral Epistles*. Grand Rapids, MI: Eerdmans, 1954.

Stott, John R. W. *Guard the Gospel: The Message of 2 Timothy*. Downers Grove, IL: InterVarsity Press, 1973.

———. *The Message of 1 Timothy and Titus*. BST. Downers Grove, IL: InterVarsity Press, 1996.

Towner, Philip. "Gnosis and Realized Eschatology in Ephesus (of the Pastoral Epistles) and the Corinthian Enthusiasm." *JSNT* 31 (1987): 95–124.

———. *The Goal of Our Instruction: The Structure of Theology and Ethics in the Pastoral Epistles*. Sheffield: JSOT, 1989.

Wilson, Geoffrey B. *The Pastoral Epistles*. Carlisle, PA: Banner of Truth, 1982.

15

1 Timothy

William B. Barcley

Structure and Outline[1]

Paul's primary concern in 1 Timothy is the false teaching at Ephesus. He begins by telling Timothy how to handle the false teachers, he comes back to the false teaching in the middle of the letter, and he ends the letter by returning to it one last time. A broad outline of 1 Timothy is as follows:[2]

I. Timothy and the False Teachers, 1 (1:1–20)
II. Proper Conduct in the Household of God, 1 (2:1–3:16)
III. Timothy and the False Teachers, 2 (4:1–16)
IV. Proper Conduct in the Household of God, 2 (5:1–6:2)
V. Timothy and the False Teachers, 3 (6:3–21)

Essentially, 1 Timothy is made up of two broad, repeating themes: Timothy and the false teachers, and proper conduct in the household of God. This highlights for us Paul's focus and emphasis on the false teachers and his instructions to Timothy for how to handle them. But Paul also tells Timothy that, while he hopes to come see him, he is writing so that "if I delay, you may know how one ought to behave in the household of God" (3:15). This proper behavior includes Paul's instructions about some important topics, including prayer, the role of women, and requirements for church officers. I will touch on each of these but will organize the following discussion around the two broad, repeating themes in the outline above.

[1] For background material on 1 Timothy, see the chapter "Introduction to the Pastoral Epistles."
[2] On the structure of 1 Timothy, see the discussion of I. Howard Marshall, *A Critical and Exegetical Commentary on the Pastoral Epistles*, in collaboration with Philip H. Towner (Edinburgh: T&T Clark, 1999), 25–33. Marshall sees two main sections in 1 Timothy, chaps. 1–3 and 4–6, with each section having similar themes and patterns (see esp. 30–31). But, contrary to many scholars who attempt to see an overall chiastic structure in 1 Timothy, Marshall asserts that "no chiastic structure so far proposed appears to be cogent" (ibid., 33).

Message and Theology

Timothy and the False Teachers

The opening verses of Paul's letters are always important because they give clues to what he is attempting to say and accomplish in them. The opening verses of 1 Timothy are slightly unusual in a couple of different ways. First, Paul's standard greeting in his letters includes the words "grace and peace." Grace (χάρις) is a Pauline, Christianized adaptation of the standard greeting in Greco-Roman letters (χαίρειν). To this Paul adds the word "peace," which reflects the Jewish greeting *shalom*. Here, for the first time in Paul's letters, he adds the word "mercy" (1 Tim. 1:2; he will use it again in 2 Tim. 1:2).

What do we make of the addition of "mercy" to Paul's well-established formula? Later in chapter 1, Paul is going to dwell on the mercy that God has shown him, undeserving though he is. Paul anticipates this discussion by inserting this atypical word into his greeting. "Mercy" carries the idea of compassion to the needy,[3] but in Hebrew usage and in Paul's writings it is more specific than that. The Greek word used here, ἔλεος, often translated the Hebrew word *hesed*, which referred to God's loving-kindness to Israel, especially in his entering and keeping a covenant relationship with them. In Paul's writings, both the noun form, *mercy* (ἔλεος), and the verb form, *to be shown mercy* (ἐλεέω), consistently appear in contexts that emphasize the election and salvation of God to those who are undeserving. But these contexts, furthermore, are discussing God's mercy to Israel, or individual Jews, or those under the law. It is fitting, then, in 1 Timothy 1, where Paul goes on to deal with a false teaching that is Jewish in origin, that he alters his typical greeting with the addition of "mercy." It is not national Israel who is the recipient of God's mercy (or *hesed*), but it is God's new covenant people, the believing church, "the Israel of God" (cf. Gal. 6:16), who are shown the undeserved compassion of God.

The other unusual feature of the opening verses of 1 Timothy is that Paul skips the thanksgiving section that we normally find in his letters and that was a standard feature of Greco-Roman letters in general. Instead, he gets right down to business and addresses the false teachers and false teaching. The only other times Paul does this in his letters are in Galatians and Titus. It is possible, as George Knight suggests, that the lack of a thanksgiving section in 1 Timothy and Titus is due to their being "mandates" or "official letters."[4] But we also must see that in each of the three letters that lack a thanksgiving, Paul immediately moves on to address the problem of false teaching. Thus, Gordon Fee's assessment is probably more accurate in stating simply that "what is taking place in the church gives no cause for thanksgiving."[5]

Proper teaching is vital to the life, stability, and health of the church. Paul elsewhere states that the church is built on the foundation of the apostles and prophets; that is, their teaching is foundational for the church. The church stands or falls on

[3] Johannes P. Louw and Eugene A. Nida, eds., *Greek-English Lexicon of the New Testament: Based on Semantic Domains*, 2nd ed., 2 vols. (New York: United Bible Societies, 1988), 1:751.

[4] George W. Knight, *The Pastoral Epistles*, NIGTC (Grand Rapids: Eerdmans, 1992), 70.

[5] Gordon D. Fee, *1 & 2 Timothy, Titus* (San Francisco: Harper & Row, 1984), 4.

its doctrine. Later in 1 Timothy, Paul calls the church "the pillar and buttress of the truth" (3:15). So when false teaching is the problem, Paul views it as deadly serious, dispenses with social custom, and gets down to business.

In this opening section of the letter, Paul directs Timothy to "charge certain persons not to teach any different doctrine" (1:3). The word translated here "charge" also means "command" and has the sense of an army commander commanding his troops.[6] Timothy's call, like that of any ordained minister, is to act with authority. While humility and gentleness are important characteristics of any minister (cf. 2 Tim. 2:24–25), he must also act and speak with authority and boldness when needed, especially when the purity of the gospel is at stake.

What do we know about these "certain persons" who are teaching different doctrine? Fee suggests that they are elders of the church who think of themselves as teachers of the law (cf. 1 Tim. 1:7). Fee lists the following as reasons for this interpretation:[7] (1) teaching is the responsibility of the elders (3:2; 5:17); (2) elders are a prominent concern of Paul's throughout the letter, in terms of both their qualifications and their discipline (5:19–25); (3) Paul in 1:19–20 refers to two false teachers whom he, not the church, personally excommunicated, probably indicating that they were in leadership positions (cf. 1 Corinthians 5; 2 Thess. 3:14). We can add to this Paul's own words to the elders of Ephesus in Acts 20, warning them of false teachers to come. He tells them, "From among your own selves will arise men speaking twisted things, to draw away the disciples after them" (Act 20:30). The words "from among your own selves" probably mean from among your own ranks as elders. Churches must make sure that their leaders are well-trained men who know Scripture and who are sound in all areas of doctrine.

Paul asserts that these false teachers desire "to be teachers of the law" (1 Tim. 1:7). The problem, however, is not that they teach the law, but that they don't know what they are talking about (1:7) and are using the law as a springboard for all kinds of questionable speculation (1:4). In fact, Paul maintains that there is a proper use for the law (1:8) that is fully in line with the gospel of Jesus Christ (1:11). Scripture never puts law and gospel in opposition to one another. While it condemns wrong uses of the law, such as making it a means to justification (Galatians) or, as here, a means to improper speculation, the Bible affirms that the law is "holy and righteous and good" (Rom. 7:12). It reveals God's holy character and his holy will for those created in his image. It also reveals, as Paul says in this passage in 1 Timothy, what is "contrary to sound doctrine" (1:10), another reminder that doctrine and life, theology and ethics, can never be separated but always go hand in hand.

The law reveals God's proper way for his people to live. But the law can also be twisted to teach a wrong set of ethics. This comes out when Paul returns to the false teaching in chapter 4. This teaching, Paul says, comes from "deceitful spirits and teachings of demons," so its origin is hell itself. But it is passed on by human

[6] Marshall, *Pastoral Epistles*, 364.
[7] Fee, *1 & 2 Timothy*, 5–6.

teachers who are insincere liars, "whose consciences are seared" (4:1–2). These false teachers "forbid marriage and require abstinence from foods that God created to be received with thanksgiving by those who believe and know the truth" (4:3). In other words, the false teachers are imposing on people what we might call a strict asceticism.

Certain religious groups around the first century forbade marriage. The reason typically was rooted in the belief that sexual activity, even within marriage, was bad. We see evidence of this in the church in Corinth (cf. 1 Cor. 7:1–7). Paul corrects this by exhorting husbands and wives not to abstain from sexual relations, except maybe for a time, and teaching them that the norm in marriage is that husbands and wives should give themselves to one another sexually.

Questions of what to eat and what to drink were also prevalent in the church in the first century (cf. Romans 14; 1 Corinthians 8; Col. 2:16–23). Some of this stems from the fact that meat and wine were sometimes offered up to pagan gods and then later sold in local markets. Paul makes clear that Christians are free to eat anything as long as they do not participate in idol worship, do not destroy a weaker brother, and have fully resolved the issue in their own minds. The other cause for questions about eating and drinking appears to stem from a misunderstanding of the Christian's relationship to Old Testament purity laws. But Christ did away with Old Testament purity restrictions, declaring all foods clean (Mark 7:19).

A rigorous asceticism is common in many religions in the world and has even been prominent in some Christian teaching because, as Paul tells the Colossians, it has the appearance of wisdom (Col. 2:23) and godliness. Yet it promotes a false humility, fails to truly check sensual indulgence (Col. 2:23), and, most importantly, is contrary to God's revealed will in Scripture. On the contrary, Paul says that everything created by God is good (1 Tim. 4:4) and so is to be enjoyed (cf. 6:17), as long as we receive it with thanksgiving (4:4). To sum up, when eating and drinking, we need to pay attention to context and conscience. But an absolute ban on certain foods is contrary to the Word of God.

The irony in all this is that the false teachers themselves are materialistic. Paul makes this clear when he picks up the theme of the false teachers again in chapter 6. Here Paul's focus is more on their motives than on the nature of the false teaching itself, though he repeats some of the language that he used earlier. He uses, for the second time in this letter, the unfamiliar word ἑτεροδιδασκαλέω, translated "teach a different doctrine" (6:3), which occurs only here and in 1:3 in the entire New Testament. He also repeats his earlier language that the false teaching is contrary to "sound" (healthy) teaching (6:3; cf. 1:10), and that the false teachers really do not know what they are talking about (6:4; cf. 1:7).

But Paul here goes on to indicate that the motivations of these false teachers are more ominous than he earlier indicated. While he has asserted that the false teaching leads to speculations (1:4) and vain discussion (1:6), here he asserts that the false teachers themselves actually have "an unhealthy craving for controversy and for quarrels about words, which produce envy, dissension, slander, evil suspicions, and constant friction" (6:4–5). It is clear that speculative teaching easily leads to controversy and quarrels. But Paul charges that controversy is actually part of the false teachers' motivation. They love to stir up trouble and dissent among God's people.[8]

Their larger motivation, however, is the desire for material gain. They imagine that "godliness is a means of gain" (6:5). Paul has already made clear that these false teachers are not godly. So "godliness" here must mean the appearance of godliness, rather than true godliness in heart and life. In Paul's day, many philosophers and teachers of religion sought to become wealthy by their persuasive teaching, often masking greedy motivations behind the guise of sincerity and character. The same, of course, is true today. Our world is filled with preachers and teachers of religion whose primary motivation is to get rich off of God's people. Perhaps that is one reason why Paul says that an elder must be "not a lover of money" (3:3), and a deacon, "not greedy for dishonest gain" (3:8). Paul will go on in this letter to insist on the importance of being content with what we have and to highlight the dangers of the love of money (6:6–10).

First Timothy, then, ends with a final word to Timothy regarding the false teachers: "O Timothy, guard the deposit entrusted to you. Avoid the irreverent babble and contradictions of what is falsely called 'knowledge,' for by professing it some have swerved from the faith. Grace be with you" (6:20–21). This is an apt summation of the confused and confusing speculative teaching of the false teachers. "Avoid" probably has the sense both of Timothy's guarding against it in his own life and of not getting caught up in useless debates over it.

In many ways, this letter ends as it began. Paul gives no final greetings. He says nothing about his plans. And there are no other personal or social conventions that often mark the closing section of a letter. The fact that Paul abruptly begins and ends the letter with instruction about the false teachers highlights its urgency and importance in Timothy's ministry in Ephesus.

A Redemptive-Historical Perspective on False Teachers

The revelation of God and the gift of his Word are central to biblical faith. There can be no salvation without God's revelation. Salvation consists in knowing God and his Son, Jesus Christ (John 17:3). But no one can know God unless God first reveals himself to him or her. God's Word in particular teaches us who God is and what he requires of us.

God's Word is also at the heart of biblical covenants, by which God establishes a relationship with his people. This is clearly seen in the old or Mosaic covenant with the prominence of the "ark of the covenant," so named because it contained the central covenant documents, the copies of the Ten Commandments. In this light, it is significant that under the new covenant God's law will be written on the hearts of

[8] Guthrie writes that we see here "a noteworthy example of the processes by which intellectual wrangling so often ends in moral deterioration" (Donald Guthrie, *The Pastoral Epistles*, TNTC [Grand Rapids, MI: Eerdmans, 1990], 123).

his people (Jer. 31:31–34; Ezek. 36:25–27). Even under the new covenant, the law of God is a central element.

Furthermore, it is through the proclamation of God's Word that God acts in mighty ways in history. God spoke and creation came into being. Similarly, it is through his Word that God brings about a new creation. The dry bones in Ezekiel's vision become living beings only as Ezekiel "prophesie[s]" to them (Ezekiel 37). In the New Testament we consistently see the teaching and preaching of God's Word as the God-ordained means to bring men and women to saving faith in Jesus Christ.

Thus, throughout the Bible special attention is given to those who teach and preach the Word. Priests in the Old Testament not only performed sacrifices and read the Word; they also "gave the sense" so that the people would understand the reading (see Neh. 8:5–8), which in turn cut God's people to the heart and led them to confession and repentance. There is also a clear distinction in the Old Testament between true and false prophets. False prophets were those who not only prophesied the future wrongly, but also led God's people away from the purity of God's truth. And the penalty for false prophets was death.

Under the new covenant, Paul writes that God gave his church apostles, prophets, evangelists, pastors, and teachers "to equip the saints for the work of ministry, for building up the body of Christ," which will lead in turn to unity and maturity among God's people (Eph. 4:11–16). But for that unity and maturity to happen, the teaching must be sound. That's why Jesus and the apostles reserve their harshest criticisms for false teachers among God's people. Paul in particular declares that false teachers are "accursed" (Gal. 1:8–9) and specifically tells Timothy that he has handed two false teachers, Hymenaeus and Alexander, over to Satan "that they may learn not to blaspheme" (1 Tim. 1:20). The new covenant censure of false teachers, then, reflects the old covenant penalty for false prophets.

What does this mean for the church today? It emphasizes for us the primacy of the Word and the centrality of the teaching and preaching ministry in the church. It also calls the church to vigilance regarding who participates in that teaching ministry. Throughout 1 Timothy (and 2 Timothy as well), Paul continually calls Timothy back to his central task of teaching and preaching the Word. First Timothy 4:6–16 is particularly striking in its repetition of the idea that Timothy must focus his attention on the teaching ministry. Paul tells Timothy that he will be "a good servant of Christ Jesus" if he "puts . . . before" the church (i.e., teaches them) what Paul has been telling him (1 Tim. 4:6). In 4:11, he exhorts Timothy, "Command and teach these things." In 4:13, Paul tells him, "Devote yourself to the public reading of Scripture, to exhortation, to teaching." Timothy is not to neglect his gift, but to "immerse" himself in his teaching duties (4:14–15). And Paul ends this chapter by telling Timothy: "Keep a close watch on yourself and on the teaching. Persist in this, for by so doing you will save both yourself and your hearers" (4:16). Paul also highlights the centrality of Timothy's teaching ministry in 2 Timothy (2 Tim. 2:1–2, 15, 24–25; 4:2).

The Pastoral Epistles are as close as we come in the New Testament to letters directly addressed to pastors. Timothy appears to have ministered in Ephesus for several years and, in partnership with the elders, to have had spiritual oversight of the church. These letters, then, are invaluable for teaching and training pastors today. In our age, when there is much confusion over the role of a pastor (CEO? counselor? leader of church programs?), we need to return to Paul's instructions to Timothy. A pastor is first and foremost a teacher and preacher of the Word of God. And he is to devote himself to that ministry.

The second lesson that we learn for the church today is that, in addition to teaching the truth, we are to treat false teaching as deadly serious. God's Word, the revelation of himself, is one of his greatest gifts to his people. His Word is life, strength, and sustenance to them. Any distortion of his Word, then, leads to a lack of vitality and ultimately to death. Pastors must be willing to confront and tackle false teaching head-on. They must be vigilant in guarding against false teachers and false teaching (cf. Acts 20:28–31). But they also must have the proper goal in their defense of the truth.

In the midst of Paul's initial discussion of the false teachers, when he tells Timothy to "charge" them not to teach different doctrine, he says, "The aim [or goal] of our charge is love" (1 Tim. 1:5). Love is the motivation for our confronting and correcting, not an angry or selfish desire to be right and to prove others wrong. Church leaders are to oppose false teaching because the pure Word leads to life, and a distortion of that Word leads to death. So we are called to oppose false teaching because we love God's people and want to see them grow and flourish in the faith. And we confront false teachers because we love them also and desire that they turn from harmful and destructive teaching, which destroys them as well as those who are persuaded by them. Contrary to popular opinion, love and unity in the church do not spring from tolerating teaching that departs from the truth of Scripture. Rather, love and unity spring from opposing different doctrines and standing firm in the truth.

Proper Conduct in the Household of God

First Timothy contains more than instructions for combating false teaching. It is filled with positive instructions for how the church is to function and to conduct its affairs. Paul writes to Timothy, "I hope to come to you soon, but I am writing these things to you so that, if I delay, you may know how one ought to behave in the household of God, which is the church of the living God" (1 Tim. 3:14–15). Paul gives guidance on a number of different matters, including the public ministry of the church, the nature and qualifications of those who are to teach and lead God's people, proper care for the needy in their midst, especially widows, and godly attitudes toward possessions.

The Priority of Prayer

Paul has spent most of chapter 1 dealing with the false teachers. But he also presents himself as an example of God's grace reaching out to sinners, both in his conversion (1 Tim. 1:12–16) and in his being entrusted with the gospel (1:11). Likewise, Paul entrusts to Timothy the task of waging the good warfare and holding to faith and a good conscience as a minister of the gospel (1:18–19). In order for Timothy and the church to be steadfast in gospel purity and committed to gospel proclamation, they must "first of all" (2:1) devote themselves to prayer. The word "then" (or "therefore") at the beginning of 2:1 shows that Paul's instructions on prayer in this chapter are directly tied to what he has just said about Timothy's "charge" at the end of chapter 1. It is also through prayer that the church does battle against false teaching and the schemes of the Devil. The words "first of all" show that prayer is a top priority. No ministry can take place that is not first bathed in prayer.

A devotion to prayer is the mark of the people of God and is a means of God's grace to them. Before his ascension, Jesus told his disciples to "wait" for the promise of the Father (Acts 1:4). Waiting in Scripture always includes God's people giving themselves to prayer—and that is precisely what the early Christians did (cf. Acts 1:12–14). As someone has put it, the early church did not *have* a prayer meeting; the early church *was* a prayer meeting. Or as another has said, prayer was Jesus's last command and is the church's top priority.

Paul gives a partial description in 1 Timothy 2 of what this prayer entails. He says, first, that it includes "supplications, prayers, intercessions, and thanksgivings" (2:1). This list includes a general term (prayers), requests made with a sense of urgency (supplications),[9] prayers on behalf of others (intercessions), and the offering up of our praise and thanks to God (thanksgivings). In other words, we are to offer up to God *all kinds of prayers*.

Second, Paul says, we are to offer up prayers *for all kinds of people*, including "kings and all who are in high positions" (2:2). These prayers are, on the one hand, for government leaders, that they might rule wisely and for the common good ("that we may lead a peaceful and quiet life"). But these prayers also include praying for the salvation of our leaders, because God desires all kinds of people "to be saved and to come to the knowledge of the truth" (2:4). The Greek word translated "all" in verses 1, 4, and 6 clearly has the idea of "all kinds," as the tie between verses 1 and 2 indicates.[10] In other words, while we are certainly to pray for the church and for one another within the body of Christ, our prayer is also to be outwardly focused and evangelistically motivated. We are to pray for unbelievers, even government leaders, that they might come to a knowledge of the truth. God uses the prayers of the saints to bring sinners to repentance and faith in Jesus Christ.

Proper Leadership in the Church

Paul devotes much attention in this letter to leadership in the church. He gives a detailed description of the qualifications of church leaders that takes up all of 1 Timothy 3. He returns to the theme of leadership in chapter 5, discussing both elders who rule well in the church and the proper way to bring charges against an elder who sins. Proper leadership is crucial for the spiritual health of the body of Christ. Leaders

[9] For the sense of urgency carried by the Greek word δέησις, see Louw and Nida, *Greek-English Lexicon of the New Testament*, 408, and BDAG, 213.
[10] See the discussion of Knight, *Pastoral Epistles*, 115.

are to be an example to the church (4:12). In addition, as Paul earlier instructed the Ephesian elders, as shepherds they are to guard the flock against fierce wolves who, by their false teaching, will seek to destroy the church (cf. Acts 20:28–30). Thus, it is important to recognize both the types of people who are to lead in the church and those who are not to exercise authority as officers among the people of God.

Paul actually begins his discussion of leadership in 1 Timothy 2 with the negative, namely, those who are not to teach and have authority: "I do not permit a woman to teach or to exercise authority over a man" (2:12). In our egalitarian age, these words can sound harsh, even backward. Indeed, many have called Paul a misogynist (a hater of women). But Paul's letters make clear that many women ministered alongside him and that he had a tender relationship with many women (cf. Phil. 4:2–3; also Rom. 16:1–4, 6, 12–13, and the other women listed in this greeting section). But it is not clear that any of the women mentioned in Acts or in Paul's letters were involved in doing what Paul forbids in 1 Timothy 2.

Two of the biggest emphases in the Pastoral Epistles are proper leadership by the officers of the church and the public preaching and teaching of the Word of God. This is precisely what Paul is dealing with here—exercising authority and teaching. And he specifically forbids women from teaching and exercising authority over men.

This is one of the most controversial passages in the New Testament. Biblical egalitarians[11] in particular argue that, since this instruction comes in the midst of a letter that deals so heavily with false teaching, Paul's words here are directly tied to the false teachers and what they taught. Either women were being led astray by the false teachers, or some women themselves were propagating the false instruction, the argument typically goes. So Paul's prohibitions here are merely temporary until women come to see the errors of the false teaching and have learned enough to teach properly in the church. Thus, the argument goes, Paul is not forever banning women from teaching and having authority over men.

The problem with this interpretation is that Paul's argument is diametrically opposed to it.[12] First, Paul roots his argument not in the local situation, but in creation: "For Adam was formed first, then Eve" (1 Tim. 2:13). Paul's appeal to creation indicates that this is the way God intended for human beings to function all along, even before sin and the fall. If Paul had wanted us to understand that he was temporarily banning women from teaching and having authority over men, he could have easily said so. But his appeal to creation indicates that his instructions here transcend the local, temporary situation.

Second, Paul begins his instructions in this section in 2:8 with a universal appeal

[11] For the biblical egalitarian position, see, e.g., the works of Paul Jewett, *Man as Male and Female* (Grand Rapids, MI: Eerdmans, 1975); Aida Besançon Spencer, *Beyond the Curse: Women Called to Ministry* (Nashville: T. Nelson, 1985); Richard Clark and Catherine Clark Kroeger, *I Suffer Not a Woman: Rethinking 1 Timothy 2:11–15 in Light of Ancient Evidence* (Grand Rapids, MI: Baker, 1992).

[12] For an excellent collection of essays presenting the complementarian position, namely, that men and women have different roles in the church and in the home that complement one another, see John Piper and Wayne Grudem, eds., *Recovering Biblical Manhood and Womanhood: A Response to Evangelical Feminism* (Wheaton, IL: Crossway, 1991). For an in-depth discussion of this particular passage, see Andreas J. Köstenberger and Thomas R. Schreiner, eds., *Women in the Church: An Interpretation and Application of 1 Timothy 2:9–15*, 3rd ed. (Wheaton, IL: Crossway, 2016).

to proper practice in all churches: "I desire then that *in every place* the men should pray, lifting holy hands without anger or quarreling; likewise also that women . . ." In other words, Paul places his instructions regarding women leading and teaching in a universal, transcultural context. These instructions are not just for women in the churches in first-century Ephesus. They are for women in all churches everywhere.

Third, the instructions for women in the church in 1 Timothy 2 are in line with the authority structure that God sets up elsewhere in his Word.[13] In particular, Scripture makes clear that husbands are to be the head of the home, and that wives are to submit to the authority of their husbands (Eph. 5:22–33; Col. 3:18–19; 1 Pet. 3:1–7). The New Testament is filled with the language of the church as the family of God. The leadership structure of the church family, therefore, is to correspond with the leadership structure of the family in the home.

After dealing with leadership negatively, in terms of who is not to exercise leadership, Paul moves on positively to discuss the characteristics and qualifications of those men who are to lead God's people, the church. Significantly, these qualifications do *not* include things like charisma, popularity, or management style. What *is* required, rather, can be summed up as follows: purity of life and purity in doctrine.

In 1 Timothy 3, Paul lays out the qualifications for the two biblical officers: overseers and deacons. In the New Testament, the terms *overseer* and *elder* are used interchangeably to describe church officers. In Acts 20, Paul calls for the elders of Ephesus to meet him in Miletus, and he goes on to tell them, "Pay careful attention to yourselves and to all the flock, in which the Holy Spirit has made you *overseers*" (Acts 20:28). Similarly, in Titus 1, Paul tells Titus, "Appoint *elders* in every town as I directed you—if anyone is above reproach. . . . For an *overseer*, as God's steward, must be above reproach" (Titus 1:5–7). Thus, "elder" and "overseer" refer to the same office. Each word highlights different important aspects of that office. The word "elder" (πρεσβύτερος) emphasizes the importance of the maturity and wisdom that typically comes with age. The word "overseer" describes the work of an elder in providing spiritual oversight of God's people.

Elders are the spiritual shepherds of God's people. This is the language that Paul used when he addressed the Ephesian elders in Acts 20. Paul instructed them, "Pay careful attention to . . . the flock, in which the Holy Spirit has made you overseers, to care for the church of God" (Acts 20:28). The verb "to care for" literally means

[13]The Greek verb translated "exercise authority over" in 2:12 is used only here in the New Testament. Some have concluded from this and from some of the uses of this verb and its cognate noun outside the New Testament, that Paul's use of it points to an extreme situation in which women were usurping authority or exercising authority that was domineering or tyrannical. But the verb itself was not uncommon outside the New Testament, and in many of its uses it simply means "have or exercise authority." See the articles of H. Scott Baldwin, "A Difficult Word: αὐθεντέω in 1 Timothy 2:12," and "Appendix 2: αὐθεντέω in Ancient Greek Literature," in Köstenberger, Schreiner, and Baldwin, *Women in the Church*, 65–80, 269–305. Furthermore, as Köstenberger has convincingly shown, the structure of the Greek sentence in 2:12 indicates that both teaching and exercising authority are positive activities, though restricted to men. He shows that in the New Testament, the Greek word οὐδέ always joins terms both of which denote activities viewed either positively or negatively by the writer or speaker. Thus, the words "to teach" and "to have authority," connected by οὐδέ, should both be viewed either positively or negatively. Paul does talk about teaching in a negative way in 1 Timothy, i.e., when he is referring to the false teachers. But when he uses teaching negatively, he always qualifies it as such. When Paul uses the verb to teach in an unqualified way, it is always positive, as here. Thus, teaching and having authority should be seen in this verse as positive activities (Köstenberger, "A Complex Sentence Structure in 1 Timothy 2:12," in Köstenberger, Schreiner, and Baldwin, *Women in the Church*, 81–103).

"to shepherd" and is tied to Paul's reference to God's people as "the flock," that is, the sheep. One aspect of the elders' shepherding work is to guard the flock against the "fierce wolves" (Acts 20:29), that is, false teachers, who will seek to destroy the people of God. Elders have the responsibility to make sure that the teaching and preaching of God's Word in the church are pure and sound. But, of course, the work of the shepherd extends beyond protecting the flock. Elders are to guide God's people, feed them, and care for them.

Leadership of God's people by elders is the fundamental structure of biblical government from beginning to end. When Moses returned to Egypt as God's messenger and the instrument by which God would lead his people out of slavery, he went first to the elders of Israel as the leaders of God's people (Ex. 3:16, 18; 4:29). In fact, though often overlooked, Moses and the elders went together to tell Pharaoh to let the Israelites go (Ex. 3:18). Throughout the Old Testament, even with judges, kings, and prophets, elders maintain a central role of leadership among God's people (cf., e.g., Exodus 24; Numbers 11; Deuteronomy 21–22; Josh. 8:10, 33; Ruth 4; 1 Kings 8; Ezra 5; etc.). In the New Testament, at the end of their first missionary journey, Paul and Barnabas have elders appointed in each town where they have established churches (Acts 14:23). Elders play a crucial role in the first church council at Jerusalem (Acts 15). And, finally, Revelation makes repeated reference to elders who are before God's throne. From beginning to end, then, the Bible sets forth elder rule as the basic leadership structure for God's people.

Because of this, and because the office of overseer is a "noble task" (1 Tim. 3:1), elders must meet a number of qualifications with regard to personal ethics, how they lead their families, and how they treat others. Personal ethics includes things like sexual purity ("husband of one wife," 3:2)[14] and not being a drunkard (or addicted to alcohol) or greedy, as well as being someone who exercises self-control in all things. An elder must also be one whose household is in order and who manages his family well. This requirement is directly related to the New Testament language for the church as family. A man who does not lead his personal family well will not be able to lead the church family well. Elders must also be marked by godly, Christ-like treatment of others. They must not be angry and given to quarrels and arguments, but must be gentle. They must be hospitable and respected by others, both inside and outside the church. Finally, they must be able to teach. Paul says later in 1 Timothy 5:17 that some elders have a special call to give themselves to teaching and preaching. But all elders need to be able to instruct others in the basics of the faith and to help God's people apply God's Word to their lives.

Elders play a vital role in the life of God's people. For that reason, potential elders must be carefully chosen, thoroughly prepared, and closely examined (5:22). Elders can fall into sin and so at times must be properly disciplined (5:19–25). But as is the case throughout redemptive history, when godly men lead, God's people flourish.

[14] For a brief discussion of the different ways this phrase has been interpreted and problems with the alternatives, see William B. Barcley, *1 & 2 Timothy*, EPCS (Darlington: Evangelical Press, 2005), 103.

Paul next moves on to address the qualifications for deacons. The Greek word διάκονος means servant, or one who serves. Deacons, then, are in essence those who serve the church in special ways. The first deacons were most likely the seven men chosen in Acts 6 to oversee the daily distribution to the widows of the church. They are not specifically called deacons in that passage, but the related words διακονία and διακονέω are used in Acts 6:1–2. The primary task of deacons was to care for the physical and material needs of God's people, especially the most needy and vulnerable.

All of God's people are called to be servants. In Acts 6, the word for service is also used for the work of the apostles. But their work is called "the ministry of the word" (διακονίᾳ τοῦ λόγου, 6:4) and is set in contrast to ministry that focuses on physical needs. Both ministries are vital for the proper functioning of the church. Acts 6 describes an important distribution of labor. The problem of the Grecian widows who were being overlooked in the daily distribution of provisions threatened to distract the apostles from their calling to devote themselves to prayer and to the ministry of the Word (6:4). But when all faithfully carry out the work of their particular calling, the church flourishes and God's kingdom advances. At the end of the section on the choosing of the seven in Acts 6, Luke writes, "And the word of God continued to increase, and the number of the disciples multiplied greatly in Jerusalem, and a great many of the priests became obedient to the faith" (Acts 6:7). Deacons who faithfully carry out their work are central to the mission of the church.

In light of the importance and sensitive nature of the deacons' work, they too, like elders, are to have certain qualifications. In Acts 6, the apostles tell the church to pick "seven men of good repute, full of the Spirit and of wisdom" (6:3). The qualifications in 1 Timothy 3 are similar to the qualifications for elders, though not quite as exhaustive. Like elders, deacons are to be sexually pure and not addicted to alcohol. They are also to manage their households well. While both elders and deacons are to have proper attitudes toward money, Paul more specifically writes that deacons are not to be "greedy for dishonest gain" (3:8). This probably reflects the deacons' role of handling, at least in part, church financial resources. Paul also says that deacons are not to be "double-tongued" (3:8). In other words, they are to be sincere in speech and totally trustworthy. Deacons have a unique position of trust in the body of Christ, and everything about them must demonstrate that they are utterly reliable.

Unlike elders, deacons are not required to be "able to teach" (cf. 3:2). That reflects the different role and different gifts that deacons are to have. But this does not mean that deacons are exempt from doctrinal qualifications. Paul writes that deacons "must hold the mystery of the faith with a clear conscience" (3:9). In other words, they are to be theologically sound. In Paul's writings, "mystery" and gospel are often interchangeable (cf. Rom. 16:25–27). Like elders, then, deacons are to be pure in life and doctrine, though some of the qualifications reflect more specifically the unique work and gifts of deacons.

Care for the Needy

As we have seen, central to the work of deacons is caring for the material needs of God's people. This leads us to another important emphasis in 1 Timothy, namely, caring for the needy, particularly widows. Much of chapter 5 is devoted to this vital work of the church. Before turning to that chapter, however, we will briefly look at one debated verse in chapter 3. In the middle of Paul's discussion of the qualifications for deacons, he makes a reference to "wives" or "women" (3:11), saying that they "likewise must be dignified, not slanderers, but sober-minded, faithful in all things." The ESV translates the subject "their wives," but in the Greek, "their" is absent. In addition, the Greek word translated "wives" is often used generally for women.

The big question is why this reference to "wives" or "women" comes in the middle of Paul's laying out qualifications for deacons. If Paul is discussing the qualifications for deacons' wives, why would he not also be concerned about qualifications for elders' wives? Calvin believed that this verse applies to the wives of both elders and deacons.[15] But the placement of this verse, right in the middle of the qualifications for deacons, seems to refute that.

The best explanation is that Paul is referring not to wives, but more generally to women who assist the deacons in their work of mercy ministry.[16] Widows in particular in the first century were among the most vulnerable in society, often with little or no source of income. It is appropriate, then, that women of godly character and good repute be chosen to help the deacons in their work, especially when it comes to ministering to widows or other women in the church. In fact, that seems to be precisely what Paul is referring to in chapter 5 when he discusses those widows who are "enrolled" (5:9).

As we move into chapter 5, the proper care of widows becomes a central concern. Paul exhorts Timothy, and therefore the church, to "honor widows who are truly widows" (5:3). Paul uses the word "honor" again in 5:17, where the context clearly indicates that this honor includes, as one commentator puts it, "both honor and honorarium" (cf. 5:18).[17] In other words, honor means financial support, as well as proper treatment and proper respect. That is the idea in 5:3. Widows are to be treated properly, with respect. But they are also to be given the financial support they need. Jesus taught that keeping the fifth commandment to honor father and mother includes giving them proper financial support (cf. Matt. 15:5–6). Since Paul has just exhorted Timothy to treat "older women as mothers" (1 Tim. 5:2), it is likely that he has the fifth commandment in mind here.

The larger context makes clear what Paul means by honoring widows who are "truly widows." Those who are "truly widows" are those who do not have children and grandchildren to care for them (5:4). In fact, Paul makes clear that the care for

[15] John Calvin, *The Second Epistle of Paul the Apostle to the Corinthians and the Epistles to Timothy, Titus and Philemon*, trans. T. A. Small, Calvin's Commentaries (Grand Rapids, MI: Eerdmans, 1964), 229.
[16] For a fuller discussion, see Barcley, *1 & 2 Timothy*, 114–16.
[17] Knight, *Pastoral Epistles*, 232.

widows in one's own family is essential to godliness. In contrast, the widow who is "truly a widow" is one who, "left all alone, has set her hope on God and continues in supplications and prayers night and day" (5:5). The description that Paul gives here is similar to Old Testament descriptions of the godly poor who put their hope in God because they have no one else to turn to (cf., e.g., Psalm 146). Widows who had no family, especially sons or sons-in-law, had little or no means of income. Thus they were especially destitute and often exploited. The church had a responsibility to care for them and make sure their needs were met. Paul ends this section on widows by saying, "If any believing woman has relatives who are widows, let her care for them. Let the church not be burdened, so that it may care for those who are truly widows" (1 Tim. 5:16).

In 5:9ff., Paul goes on to discuss widows who are to be "enrolled." This is a particularly difficult passage to interpret. It is possible that by "enrolled" Paul simply means those widows who are to be put on the list of those to be cared for by the church. There are, however, two problems with this interpretation. The first is that Paul goes on to give qualifications for these widows who are to be enrolled that sound in many ways similar to the qualifications he gave earlier for church officers ("the wife of one husband . . . having a reputation for good works . . . has shown hospitality . . . has devoted herself to every good work," 5:9–10). The second problem is that Paul tells the church to refuse to enroll "younger widows" (5:11). It would be very strange for him to tell the church not to help younger widows financially, especially if they have no one else to care for them.

Most likely, then, Paul is referring to a special group of widows who have the responsibility to help the deacons in caring for other widows. As we have already seen, women—and widows in particular who had the time to give to this work—are especially helpful in the work of caring for (other) widows. What we seem to have here are the seeds of what would be known in the second-century church as an "order of widows," who carried on mercy ministry.[18]

Biblical religion, from beginning to end, is marked by a special concern and care for the poor and needy. The Old Testament is filled with biblical commands and instructions to care for the material needs of others (cf. e.g., Ex. 22:22–27; Deut. 10:18; 14:29; Isa. 1:17, 23; Mal. 3:5). Widows and orphans, who were especially destitute and vulnerable, are often singled out for special care. We see these same emphases in the New Testament (cf. e.g., Acts 6:1–7; James 1:27; 2:15–17). Christians demonstrate that they are disciples of Christ by their love (John 13:34–35), and giving to those in need is a tangible demonstration of that love (1 John 3:16–18). But ultimately the biblical concern for mercy and care for those unable to care for themselves is rooted in the love and mercy of God for poor and helpless sinners. Because we have been shown mercy, we are to extend mercy to others. All of this points to God, who reveals himself as, "The LORD, the LORD, a God merciful and gracious, slow to anger, and

[18] For further support for this interpretation, see the discussions in John R. W. Stott, *The Message of 1 Timothy and Titus* (Downers Grove, IL: InterVarsity Press, 1996), 132–35; Knight, *Pastoral Epistles*, 222–31; Barcley, *1 & 2 Timothy*, 151–66. For an opposing view, see Fee, *1 & 2 Timothy*, 75–84.

abounding in steadfast love and faithfulness" (Ex. 34:6). As we show mercy and grace to others, we point them to the character of God.

A Proper Attitude toward and Use of Money

We can never show this biblical mercy and generosity to others without first having a proper attitude toward our own possessions. In 1 Timothy 6, Paul describes the false teachers as being motivated by a desire for financial gain (6:5). Paul contrasts this with "godliness with contentment," which, he says, "is great gain" (6:6). Our attitude toward our money and how we use our money say a lot about the state of our hearts. Jesus said, "You cannot serve God and money" (Luke 16:13). He warns of the difficulty of the rich man to enter the kingdom of God (Luke 18:25). Money and possessions carry an inherent danger because as they increase, we can easily become attached to them and put our trust in them. Yet, as Paul indicates in 1 Timothy 6, the problem is not with money itself. The problem is with the sinful human heart.

Paul warns that those who "desire to be rich" get caught up in a downward spiral that goes from the temptations that arise from sinful desires to getting ensnared in a lifestyle of greed and the pursuit of earthly things, which in turn leads to further sensual desires, and finally to eternal ruin and destruction (6:9). As Paul says in 6:10, the love of money leads to all kinds of sins and has consequences both for this life ("pierced . . . with many pangs") and the life to come (leading people away from the faith). Christ is clear that where our treasure is, there our hearts will be also (Matt. 6:21).

In contrast, Paul asserts the importance of "godliness with contentment" (1 Tim. 6:6). Contentment is a central Christian virtue, though one that is extremely difficult for the sinful human heart. Yet, as Paul indicates in Philippians 4:11–12, he has learned to be content in any and every circumstance. This is not because of Paul's superior personal spirituality. It is rather because he "can do all things through [God] who strengthens" him (Phil. 4:13). Paul asserts that this kind of godliness with contentment is "great gain," that is, it is one of the greatest forms of spiritual riches.[19]

Ultimately, Paul says, money has no lasting eternal value—"for we brought nothing into the world, and we cannot take anything out of the world" (1 Tim. 6:7).[20] He urges Christians to "be content" with "food and clothing" (6:8). In reality, however, God often blesses faithful Christians with material wealth. Diligent Christians who live for Christ in their occupations and vocations, who are honest and seek to serve others, often become successful in what they do and so are blessed financially. The Bible makes reference to several wealthy men and women who were blessed by God in a material sense. How are these individuals to use their money? Paul goes on to give specific instructions for wealthy Christians.

---

[19]The classic work on contentment is Jeremiah Burroughs, *The Rare Jewel of Christian Contentment* (Edinburgh: Banner of Truth, 1964), first published in 1648. Cf. also William B. Barcley, *The Secret of Contentment* (Phillipsburg, NJ: P&R, 2010).

[20]The Greek of this verse is difficult because of the presence of the word ὅτι at the beginning of the second clause (translated "and" in the ESV). The Greek word ὅτι typically means "that" or "because." Knight (*Pastoral Epistles*, 254) suggests that Paul has omitted the words "it is clear" at the beginning of this clause, a reading that is found in later manuscripts to help make this verse clear. But Calvin is most likely correct that ὅτι sometimes had a weakened sense, and it is best to simply translate "and" (*Epistles to Timothy*, 343).

In 6:17–19, he gives Timothy instructions for "the rich in this present age." He first addresses their attitude. Then he discusses what they are to do. And finally he describes the motivation and outcome of proper Christian living as wealthy followers of Christ. Paul begins by addressing attitudes. Rich Christians "are not to be haughty, nor to set their hopes on the uncertainty of riches, but on God." These are the two great dangers of wealth. The first is the tendency toward pride—feeling superior to others, or perhaps being caught up with the notion that they themselves are responsible for their status in life. But Paul clearly states that God is the one "who richly provides us with everything to enjoy" (6:17). All that we *have* and all that we *are* comes from God. This should fill all, especially the wealthy, with humility.

The second danger of wealth is that the wealthy can easily "set their hopes on" their riches, rather than "on God" (6:17). The more we have, the greater the temptation to trust in those things—putting our faith in the tangible gifts, rather than the giver. In the Old Testament, God warned the Israelites about this very thing when they were about to enter the Promised Land: "Take care lest . . . when your herds and flocks multiply and your silver and gold is multiplied and all that you have is multiplied, then your heart be lifted up, and you forget the LORD your God" (Deut. 8:11–14).

At the end of 1 Timothy 6:17, Paul highlights the generosity of God. God, he says, "richly provides us with everything to enjoy." Some Christians have tended to downplay the true enjoyment that we should get from the material gifts that God gives us. Many believers have often felt guilty for enjoying this-worldly gifts. But the enjoyment of God's good gifts is good and right, especially as it points to our enjoyment of God himself. Paul's emphasis here is that God is a generous giver, and the result should be gratitude that leads to humility, as well as to trust in and devotion to God alone.

God's generosity should, in turn, lead rich Christians to act in generous ways. The rich are "to do good, to be rich in good works, to be generous and ready to share" (6:18). The wealthy are to be generous both with their time and with their money. Paul uses a wonderful play on words—"rich in good works." Instead of simply being wealthy in their possessions, the rich are to be wealthy in their devotion to serving Christ and advancing his kingdom. But they are also to be generous with their money, not hoarding their wealth, which can so easily happen, but giving to the church and to God's people.

Finally, Paul briefly mentions the motivation and outcome of this type of godly living. Those who give generously of their time, talents, and treasure to the kingdom of God will store up "treasure for themselves as a good foundation for the future" (6:19). The point here is not that the wealthy can buy or earn their way into heaven. It is, rather, as we have already stated, that our use of money is a window into our souls. Jesus said, "lay up for yourselves treasures in heaven, where neither moth nor rust destroys and where thieves do not break in and steal. For where your treasure is, there your heart will be also" (Matt. 6:20–21). While many live only for this world and what it has to offer, the Christian takes hold "of that which is truly life"

(1 Tim. 6:19), the enjoyment of God and the pleasure of living for him both now and for eternity.

John Stott beautifully sums up Paul's wise and balanced counsel on wealth and material possessions:

> Against materialism (an obsession with material possessions) he sets simplicity of lifestyle. Against asceticism (the repudiation of the material order) he sets gratitude for God's creation. Against covetousness (the lust for more possessions) he sets contentment with what we have. Against selfishness (the accumulation of goods for ourselves) he sets generosity in imitation of God. Simplicity, gratitude, contentment and generosity constitute a healthy quadrilateral of Christian living.[21]

The Importance and Centrality of the Church

A final theme in 1 Timothy is the importance and centrality of the church. We see this both implicitly and explicitly throughout the letter. Implicitly we see it in the instructions for how the church is to function and in the qualifications for leaders in the church. Explicitly we see it in the language that Paul uses to refer to the church. Paul tells Timothy, "I hope to come to you soon, but I am writing these things to you so that, if I delay, you may know how one ought to behave in the household of God, which is the church of the living God, a pillar and buttress of the truth" (1 Tim. 3:14–15). In the New Testament, sometimes biblical writers can use the word "church" to refer to the church universal. But more typically it is used of individual, local congregations. The context makes clear that Paul is using the term "church" in the latter sense here. He is writing to inform the Christians in Ephesus how that local body of believers is to function—though, of course, his instructions apply to all local churches.

In this verse, Paul refers to the church in three ways. First, he says the church is "the household of God." The word "household" can mean one of two things. It can refer to the church as *the family of God*. The New Testament often uses the language of family to refer to Christians. The term "brothers" is used over 220 times in the New Testament. While a few of these refer to biological brothers, the vast majority refer to fellow believers. Ultimately, this familial language stems from Jesus's teaching that God is our Father. The fact that the church is the family of God teaches us that there is to be a close-knit bond of love and fellowship, one that can even take precedence over biological families (Matt. 10:35–37; 19:29; Luke 12:53; 14:26; etc.). When Jesus was told that his mother and brothers were outside wanting to speak with him, he replied, "Who is my mother, and who are my brothers? . . . Here are my mother and my brothers! For whoever does the will of my Father in heaven is my brother and sister and mother" (Matt. 12:48–50).

The Greek word translated "household" can also mean *house*, in the sense of a building or a place to dwell. It was even used with reference to a palace or a temple. This interpretation fits nicely with the building imagery used later in the verse. To

[21] Stott, *Message of 1 Timothy and Titus*, 162–63.

refer to the church as the "household of God," then, could mean that it is metaphorically the house in which he dwells.

The New Testament idea of the church as a house where God dwells goes back to the Old Testament. Although God fills heaven and earth, he chose to make his home in the temple (or tabernacle), to meet there with his people, and to reveal his power and glory (cf. Ps. 63:2). In the New Testament, it is not a building that God inhabits, but he dwells in the midst of his new covenant people. As Paul says to the church in Corinth, "Do you not know that you [plural] are God's temple and that God's Spirit dwells in you [plural]?" (1 Cor. 3:16); or as we would say in the south, "God dwells among y'all." The church as the people of God is the temple or house of God, and God dwells in its midst. This says something pretty significant about the local church.

Second, in 1 Timothy 3:15, Paul calls the local congregation in Ephesus "the church of the living God." The common first-century meaning for the Greek word translated "church," ἐκκλησία, was "assembly or gathering." The first two definitions listed for ἐκκλησία in Bauer's *A Greek-English Lexicon of the New Testament and Other Early Christian Literature* are (1) "a regularly summoned legislative body, assembly," and (2) "a casual gathering of people, an assemblage, gathering."[22] The other standard Greek lexicons and dictionaries indicate the same thing; the first meaning listed is "an assembly" or "gathering." Louw and Nida's lexicon points out that ἐκκλησία "was in common usage for several hundred years before the Christian era and was used to refer to an assembly of persons constituted by well-defined membership. . . . For the New Testament, however, it is important to understand the meaning of ἐκκλησία as 'an assembly of God's people.'"[23] This is actually highlighted when we see ἐκκλησία used in the New Testament for groups that are not Christian assemblies. For instance, the angry, violent mob in Ephesus is twice called an ἐκκλησία (Acts 19:32, 40).

The very name "church," then, identifies it as a gathering or assembly of God's people. The fact that it is the church "of the living God" highlights that the living and active God is present in the midst of his people when they gather together. He is with his people. He empowers their worship and service. He equips and transforms. But the bottom line is that when God's people come together, God is there with them. The irony of this is that many Christians today are leaving the church to "find God," instead of putting themselves where God says he specially dwells and reveals himself.

Finally, Paul calls the church "a pillar and buttress of the truth" (1 Tim. 3:15). As a pillar and buttress, the church upholds the truth. Evangelical Christians often think of the church as being upheld by the truth, and that is true. Martin Luther famously said that justification by faith is the doctrine on which the church stands or falls. When the church departs from the truth of Scripture, it falls.

But it is also true that the church upholds the truth. We see this in three ways. First,

---

[22] BDAG, 303.

[23] Louw and Nida, *Greek-English Lexicon of the New Testament*, 1:126.

the church holds up the truth by proclaiming it to the world. The church is the vehicle of truth in the world. Second, the church guards and defends the truth. God has entrusted his truth to the church, and so the church must stand firm in that truth, supporting it and defending it against distortions, as Paul instructs Timothy to do. Third, the church is the pillar and buttress of the truth in that the church gives the truth stability. God has always given his revelation to his people, and then through his people to the world. As Brian Habig and Les Newsom put it, "Truth in the world and in the lives of believers has no stability if it does not have the church. The church is the support system of Truth itself."[24] Without the church, the truth is weakened and loses its force in the world.

Once again, it is vital to see that Paul is making these statements about the local church, not the church universal. How vital it is then to commit ourselves to the local church and to make sure that our local churches are healthy and flourishing.

These truths about the church are consistent with how God has worked throughout redemptive history. God's plan has always been to build a people as his own possession, not simply to save individuals. We see this in the call of Abraham; God would make of him a great nation, and in him all the families of the earth would be blessed (Gen. 12:1–3). Scripture consistently places emphasis on the importance of the covenant community, from Israel as a nation to the church as "the Israel of God" (Gal. 6:16). In fact, the continuity of the community of God's people under the old and new covenants is highlighted by Jesus's and the New Testament writers' use of the word ἐκκλησία, a term found over two hundred times in the Septuagint (the Greek translation of the Hebrew Old Testament) to refer to the assembly of Israel. Throughout redemptive history, God has chosen to dwell in a special way and to reveal himself in a special way among his people. This was symbolized by the ark of the covenant under the old covenant and repeated in the New Testament language of the church as God's temple (1 Cor. 3:16–17).

The eternal God exists in community, one God in three persons. So God has created and redeemed his people to live in community together. It is only in community that God's people grow and flourish. Paul says in Ephesians 3 that it is together "with all the saints" that we are able to know the greatness of God and the breadth and depth of the love of Christ (3:18–19). At the end of Acts 2, Luke writes that "the Lord added to their number day by day those who were being saved" (Acts 2:47). He did not add them to the church without saving them. But neither did he save them without adding them to the church. Christ builds his church. And the church is the primary means by which Christ works in the world to extend his kingdom.

Select Bibliography

Please see the bibliography at the end of chapter 14, "Introduction to the Pastoral Epistles."

[24] Brian Habig and Les Newsom, *The Enduring Community: Embracing the Priority of the Church* (Jackson, MS: Reformed University Press, 2001), 36.

16

2 Timothy

William B. Barcley

Structure and Outline[1]

If you were facing the end of your life and knew that death was coming soon, whom would you contact and what would you say? This was Paul's situation when he wrote his second letter to Timothy. Second Timothy is the last of Paul's letters that have been preserved for us. He is writing from prison in Rome awaiting execution, and he knows that the end of his earthly life is near.

Paul's primary concerns in this letter are that the Christian faith be passed on and preserved, and that Timothy persevere in that faith and in gospel ministry. Paul wants to ensure that the words of Scripture and the teaching of the apostles are passed down in the church, especially through faithful teachers and preachers. But he also writes to encourage Timothy in his own faith and ministry. This encouragement is especially timely in light of two factors. The first is that false teaching and false teachers continue to be a problem by distorting the truth of God's revelation. The second factor is that Christians, including Paul himself, are being persecuted for the faith. Paul's overriding commitment is that the pure, life-giving gospel be preserved for the coming generations after he and the other apostles are gone. This will require devotion, intentionality, and perseverance on the part of God's people.

The theme of 2 Timothy is "a call to faithfulness." Paul calls Timothy to be faithful in his ministry of preaching the gospel and teaching God's people. And Paul is seeking to ensure a faithful gospel witness after he and the other apostles are gone. We can outline 2 Timothy as follows:

I. Faithfulness in Ministry (1:1–18)
II. Faithfulness in Hardship (2:1–13)

[1] For background material on 2 Timothy, see the chapter "Introduction to the Pastoral Epistles."

III. Faithfulness in the Face of False Teaching (2:14–4:5)
IV. Paul's Faithfulness and His Faithful Lord (4:6–22)

A final reason Paul writes this letter is to express his desire to see his beloved colleague and child in the faith one last time before Paul dies. Second Timothy is perhaps the most personal of all Paul's letters. In it we see his love for people. We hear his pain at being abandoned by several friends. We learn of his delight in the faithful friends who remain committed to him and to his ministry. Paul has often been painted as a loner, as someone who cannot get along with people, who parted with Barnabas and was unwilling to be patient and forgiving of John Mark (cf. Acts 15:36ff.). But Paul's letters, and especially 2 Timothy, paint a different picture. Here we see a man who loves deeply, who is committed to others, who delights in their presence, and who desires to see them grow and flourish in the Lord. We even read in this letter that Paul and John Mark have been restored and reconciled (2 Tim. 4:11). This letter presents Paul as a tender warrior—strong in the Lord and strong in the gospel, faithful unto death, but with a tender love for his friends and a commitment to their well-being.

Second Timothy, then, is a great gift and wonderful legacy for the church. Here we see Paul's heart in all of the facets of his life and ministry.

Message and Theology

Faithfulness in Ministry (2 Tim. 1:1–18)

As in all of Paul's letters, the opening verses set the tone and introduce several key themes. In 1 Timothy 1:1, Paul called himself an apostle of Christ Jesus "by command of God our Savior." In doing this he emphasized his authority and set up a chain of command, which led to his exhortation to Timothy to "charge," or command, the false teachers not to teach false doctrine (1 Tim. 1:3). In 2 Timothy 1:1, Paul refers to himself as "an apostle of Christ Jesus by the will of God according to the promise of the life that is in Christ Jesus." The words "by the will of God" emphasize God's sovereignty in his life, while Paul's reference to "the promise of the life that is in Christ Jesus" points to the eternal life and "crown of righteousness" (4:8) that await him. In other words, the language here reflects that Paul's life is coming to an end. Eternity is in view as he writes to his beloved colleague. In addition, whereas Paul has earlier addressed Timothy as "my true child in the faith" (1 Tim. 1:2), here he addresses him as "my beloved child" (2 Tim. 1:2). This endearing address sets the tone for this very personal letter that includes Paul's stated desire to see Timothy one more time before the apostle dies.

We saw in our study of 1 Timothy that Paul omits his customary thanksgiving section, which typically follows his opening greeting, and gets right down to business regarding the danger of the false teaching in Ephesus. But here Paul returns to the conventional thanksgiving (2 Tim. 1:3–5). In this thanksgiving section, we catch a glimpse of what Paul will do in the rest of the letter.[2] He appeals to the special

[2] According to Gordon D. Fee, *1 & 2 Timothy, Titus* (San Francisco: Harper & Row, 1984), 171, "Paul is about to urge Timothy to loyalty (to himself) and perseverance (in the gospel), especially in the face of hardship. In so doing he will appeal

relationship he and Timothy have with one another. He remembers Timothy night and day in prayer. But he also remembers Timothy's "tears," most likely at their most recent parting, and tells Timothy that he longs to see him again (1:4). Paul will return to this theme at the end of the letter. But he also encourages Timothy to be faithful. He does this in two ways.

First, Paul encourages Timothy to faithfulness by setting forth his own example of faithful ministry. He begins by speaking of serving God "with a clear conscience" (1:3). He has been faithful in doing what God has called him to do, and so has no regrets in his gospel ministry. The reference to a "clear conscience" may also have to do with Paul being in prison. Those who have deserted Paul (cf. 1:15; 4:10–11) may have done so because of fear or embarrassment regarding his imprisonment (cf. also 1:8). But Paul maintains a clear conscience because he is in prison for Christ and for preaching the gospel, not because he is a wrongdoer. Paul also tells Timothy how he faithfully prays for him "constantly . . . night and day" (1:3). Paul's faithfulness thus serves as an example and encouragement for Timothy to be faithful.

Second, Paul appeals to his own and Timothy's spiritual heritage. The apostle says that he serves God "as did my ancestors" (1:3). Likewise, he writes that Timothy's "sincere faith" was present first in Timothy's grandmother Lois and mother, "Eunice" (1:5). This appeal to the faithfulness of ancestors and relatives encourages those who have this heritage to be faithful themselves. The Christian hymn "Faith of Our Fathers" serves this very function. But the appeal to spiritual heritage also serves Paul's purpose in this letter of seeking to ensure that the Christian faith and gospel be passed on from generation to generation, especially after the apostles have died.

From a redemptive-historical perspective, Paul's reference to the godly heritage of his "ancestors" ties the faith of those under the new covenant to the faith of those under the old. Paul understands the Christian faith not as a new religion that replaces Old Testament Judaism, nor as a religion that stands alongside old covenant Judaism, but as one that is in continuity with the religion of the old covenant. For Paul, under the new covenant, Gentiles are "grafted in" to the Jewish root (Rom. 11:17–24) so that there is continuity in the people of God. As Paul can say, "not all . . . Israel [is] Israel" (Rom. 9:6). There is a true Israel, a believing remnant among larger ethnic Israel. Thus, true spiritual Israel and believing Gentiles make up the one people of God.

In the rest of the chapter (2 Tim. 1:6–18), Paul moves on more directly to call Timothy to faithful ministry. In this passage, Paul returns to Timothy's ordination, when he was set apart for the gospel ministry, calling him to live up to his calling (1:6–7; cf. 1 Tim. 4:14). He also calls Timothy not to be ashamed of the gospel message, nor of Paul in his imprisonment for the Lord (2 Tim. 1:8). This is set over against Paul's example as one who is not ashamed (1:11–12), as well as the negative and positive examples of others' reactions to Paul in his gospel witness and imprison-

to his (Paul's) own example . . . to their long association . . . and to Timothy's own spiritual history. . . . These are precisely the items that dominate the thanksgiving."

ment (1:15–18). Along the way, Paul makes clear that a bold and courageous gospel witness comes only by the empowering work of the Spirit (1:7, 14), and he briefly summarizes the gospel message that Timothy is to proclaim.

In 1 Timothy, Paul encouraged Timothy to carry out his ministry in light of his ordination, when "the council of elders" laid their hands on him (1 Tim. 4:14). Here in 2 Timothy 1:6, Paul makes mention of his own participation in that ceremony. In light of that, Paul exhorts Timothy to "fan into flame" the "gift" (a term also used in 1 Tim. 4:14) that Timothy received on that occasion. The language of fanning the gift into flame expresses the idea of reviving a dying fire, or of making sure that it is fully burning all the time.[3] Paul immediately follows this exhortation with an explanatory statement: "for God gave us a spirit not of fear but of power and love and self-control" (2 Tim. 1:7). Fear or natural timidity can cause a minister to shy away from keeping his gospel ministry burning brightly. The Greek word translated "fear" in this verse is not the word normally used in the New Testament for the fear of God. The word here could mean timidity. But it was often used in the context of a battle, when some turned back in fear or cowardice in the face of the enemy.[4] Timothy—like all gospel ministers—is called to overcome this fear. But he is not on his own in this task. Ultimately, the Spirit empowers God's servants, enabling them to be bold, especially in the face of opposition. The ESV translation "spirit" is most likely a reference to the Holy Spirit, as in verse 14.[5]

The gospel minister must not only be empowered by the Spirit; he must also be gripped by the gospel message. Paul summarizes that message in verses 9–10. The gospel proclaims that God has "saved" us from sin and from his wrath, and has "called" us to himself. This salvation and "holy calling" are all of God—"not because of our works but because of his own purpose and grace" (1:9). Furthermore, this calling took place "in Christ Jesus before the ages began." This verse contains an echo of Paul's words in Ephesians 1:4 that God's people were chosen in Christ before the foundation of the world. Thus, Paul emphasizes the fact that our salvation is all of God. Sinful human beings can do nothing to save themselves. The coming of Christ to earth made clear that salvation is God's work and that only in and through Christ can human beings know God (2 Tim. 1:10). Finally the message of salvation means that death has been abolished through Christ's death and resurrection, and that those united to Christ by faith have "life and immortality" (1:10).

But while Christ's work is the ground of our salvation, it is "through the gospel" (1:10) that men and women are saved. In other words, gospel proclamation is the ordinary (and extraordinary) means by which God draws people to saving faith in Jesus Christ. For Paul, this is why the proclamation of the gospel is so vital, and why the servants of Christ must not shy away from this ministry. Paul himself was "appointed" to be a preacher of this gospel (1:11). And he has been faithful in it,

[3] See ibid., 176; Donald Guthrie, *The Pastoral Epistles*, TNTC (Grand Rapids, MI: Eerdmans, 1990), 138. According to Guthrie, the call here is to "keep the fire burning at full flame."

[4] Fee, *1 & 2 Timothy*, 177. See also William Mounce, *Pastoral Epistles*, WBC 46 (Nashville: Thomas Nelson, 2000), 478.

[5] According to John Stott, the "gift" in 1:6 is most likely a special anointing of the Holy Spirit to equip him for his work (*Guard the Gospel: The Message of 2 Timothy*, BST [Downers Grove, IL: InterVarsity Press, 1973], 29–30).

even though it has led to suffering (1:12). So, too, Timothy has been "entrusted" (1:14) with "the pattern of the sound words" (1:13) of the gospel message, and he too must be faithful in proclaiming it. The idea of suffering for the proclamation of the gospel is a major theme of 2 Timothy 2, and we will return to it shortly. But the main theme of chapter 1 is Paul's call to Timothy to follow Paul's example and be faithful in gospel ministry.

Second Timothy 1:12 is a glorious verse, but has also been the subject of much debate. Paul writes, "But I am not ashamed, for I know whom I have believed, and I am convinced that he is able to guard until that Day what has been entrusted to me." As J. I. Packer has pointed out, human beings were created to know God, and salvation at its essence means knowing God.[6] Thus, Paul's proclamation "I know whom I have believed" is a glorious one and stands at the heart of the Christian faith. But the debated words are the second half of this verse. In particular, the question comes down to whether God is able to guard what has been entrusted to Paul or what Paul has entrusted to God. The ESV and RSV read "what has been entrusted to me." The KJV, NASB, NIV, NKJV, and NRSV all read "what (or "which") I have entrusted (or committed) (un)to him." The Greek literally says, simply, "my deposit." The best way to interpret verse 12 is in light of a parallel statement in verse 14. There, Timothy is called to guard "the good deposit" that has been entrusted to him (most likely, the gospel). Since in verse 14 the one who guards is the one to whom something has been entrusted, it seems best to understand verse 12 as saying that God guards what has been entrusted to him.[7] The "deposit" may be Paul's life and ministry.[8] Or, perhaps better, it could refer to the churches and believers that are the result of Paul's gospel ministry, whom he has committed to the Lord (cf. Acts 14:23, where Paul and Barnabas "committed them to the Lord in whom they had believed").[9] Either way, the point is that God holds his saints in his hands, and he holds on to them to the end.

Faithfulness in Hardship (2 Tim. 2:1–13)

In 2 Timothy 2, Paul moves on to expound on the theme of being faithful in suffering. In verse 3, he exhorts Timothy to "share in suffering" for Christ. He uses an unusual verb here that occurs only twice in the entire New Testament. The only other occurrence is in 1:8, where Paul exhorts Timothy to share in suffering with him, as a prisoner for Christ. There is a price for being faithful in gospel ministry. Paul knows

---

[6] J. I. Packer, *Knowing God* (Downers Grove, IL: InterVarsity Press, 1973), 29.

[7] For this interpretation, that God guards what Paul has entrusted to God, see Fee, *1 & 2 Timothy*, 181; George W. Knight, *The Pastoral Epistles*, NIGTC (Grand Rapids, MI: Eerdmans, 1992), 380; Mounce, *Pastoral Epistles*, 488; I. Howard Marshall, *A Critical and Exegetical Commentary on the Pastoral Epistles*, in collaboration with Philip H. Towner (Edinburgh: T&T Clark, 1999), 711; and John Calvin, *The Second Epistle of Paul the Apostle to the Corinthians and the Epistles to Timothy, Titus and Philemon*, trans. T. A. Small, Calvin's Commentaries (Grand Rapids, MI: Eerdmans, 1964), 200–201. For the interpretation that God guards what God has entrusted to Paul, see Guthrie, *Pastoral Epistles*, 144, and J. N. D. Kelly, *A Commentary on the Pastoral Epistles* (New York: Harper & Row, 1963), 165f.

[8] Calvin (*Epistles to Timothy*, 201) believes the phrase refers to our salvation and eternal life, which are fully in the hands of God and do not depend on us.

[9] According to Mounce (*Pastoral Epistles*, 488), "Paul does not limit what he means by deposit, so there is no reason to limit it to just one item. Paul's deposit (singular) could be the sum total of all that Paul has entrusted to God, including his life, apostolic ministry, converts, etc."

and has paid that price with many hardships in this world. And he will soon pay it with his life. Now he exhorts Timothy to suffer with him.

Verses 1–2 highlight two vital truths for Timothy to keep in mind as he follows Paul's example of faithfulness, even to the point of suffering for the gospel. The first is the need to "be strengthened" by God's grace. Grace is the unmerited favor of God, but it also can refer to God's enabling power. Timothy must actively pursue this strengthening in God's grace; the verb is an imperative, a command. But the form of the verb (passive voice) also makes clear that it is God who does the strengthening. Here, then, we see the common biblical dialectic of divine sovereignty and human responsibility.

The second truth is the vital importance of the gospel message. With his death on the horizon, and perhaps the deaths of other faithful servants, Paul wants to ensure that others are trained to teach and preach the gospel. Plummer has suggested that we see here "the earliest traces of a theological school."[10] Paul's—and Timothy's—gospel ministry, then, includes three facets: evangelizing the unsaved, equipping the saints, and training future gospel ministers. The ministry of the gospel is vital. It must be preserved and passed on. Recognizing the importance of the gospel ministry encourages God's servants to suffer for it.

Paul uses three metaphors to encourage Timothy to faithful perseverance: a soldier, an athlete, and a farmer. In 2:3, he states the imperative: "Share in suffering as a good soldier of Christ Jesus." Military metaphors are common in Paul's letters, bringing out the biblical truth that Christian life and service are a difficult struggle and involve warfare. Soldiers enter into service knowing that injury or death may await them.

In 2:4–6, Paul gives three reasons why Timothy should obey the command to share in suffering. The first focuses on the soldier's desire to please his commanding officer. Because of this desire, the soldier cannot be "entangled in civilian pursuits" (2:4). In other words, a good soldier is single-minded in his devotion to his commander and does not concern himself with the worldly costs. So the soldier in Christ's army lives not for this world, but to serve his Lord.

The next two metaphors focus on the reward for faithful service. For an athlete to be "crowned" he must compete "according to the rules" (2:5). When an athlete in competition breaks the rules, he faces disqualification. For the Christian, the goal and reward is receiving the "crown of righteousness" (4:8; cf. also the "crown of life," James 1:12; Rev. 2:10) and sharing in the glory of God. But one of the rules of engagement for the Christian to be glorified with Christ is that he or she must "suffer with him" (Rom. 8:17). Similarly, in order to reap a harvest of crops, the farmer must be "hard-working," not lazy and careless (2 Tim. 2:6). All of these metaphors emphasize the struggle, pain, and toil that are required to live and serve faithfully as a servant of Christ.

In 2 Timothy 2:8–13, Paul focuses Timothy's attention on Christ himself in his

[10] Quoted in Knight, *Pastoral Epistles*, 392.

power and glorious majesty. He also highlights both the benefits of serving our great King and the dangers of failing to serve faithfully. The gospel is the good news of God's grace and salvation in Jesus Christ. But it also contains the bad news of judgment for those who reject or deny Christ as Lord. Both elements are present in this section.

Paul calls Timothy to "remember" Jesus Christ (2:8). The goal of gospel ministry is exalting Christ. This includes both leading others to Christ and extolling his greatness. These go hand in hand. The beauty, grace, and love of the Lord Jesus draw sinners to him. So the effective gospel minister must keep his eyes firmly fixed on Christ.

Paul begins this section by highlighting two truths about Christ: his resurrection and his kingship. He is "risen from the dead, the offspring of David" (2:8). Death was not the final word. Christ triumphed over sin, death, hell, and Satan. Christ is also the messianic King, great David's greater son. And his reign will be "from sea to sea, / and from the River to the ends of the earth!" (Ps. 72:8). These truths highlight Christ's power and majesty.

Paul also reminds Timothy that Christ works through his Word. Even when his servants are in chains, his Word is never bound, but will go forward with power and be effective (2 Tim. 2:9). The gospel itself is "the power of God for salvation to everyone who believes" (Rom. 1:16). Christ has been exalted, but he continues to work by his Word and Spirit, bringing all of his elect to salvation (2 Tim. 2:10).

In 2:11–13, Paul most likely quotes part of a well-known confession or hymn in the early church.[11] These verses have a distinct poetic or hymn-like structure that follows a succinct "if–then" pattern, with only the final verse adding an extra clause at the end, indicating that it is the climactic thought in this confession. The emphasis is on the Christian's endurance, in terms of both the benefits of faithfulness and the warning for unfaithfulness. Those who endure will reign with the divine Davidic King. But as Christ himself warned, he will deny those who deny him (cf. Matt. 10:32–33).

The final stanza of this confession is the most difficult to interpret and the most debated:

> If we are faithless, he remains faithful—
>
> for he cannot deny himself. (2 Tim. 2:13)

The primary question is What does God's faithfulness entail? Does God remain faithful to bring his people to salvation even when they are faithless? Or does God remain faithful to mete out judgment to those who prove faithless? Many commentators, especially most recent commentaries on 2 Timothy, opt for the first interpretation and see this confession as ending on a positive note highlighting God's sovereignty and control over his people, even when they prove temporarily faithless.[12] A strong argument in favor of this interpretation is that when we read of God's faithfulness

[11] See Guthrie, *Pastoral Epistles*, 156–58. For a helpful, extended discussion, see Knight, *Pastoral Epistles*, 400–408. For an even more extensive discussion, see George W. Knight, *The Faithful Sayings in the Pastoral Letters* (Grand Rapids, MI: Baker, 1979), 112–37.

[12] See, e.g., Fee, *1 & 2 Timothy*, 200–201; Knight, *Pastoral Epistles*, 406–7; Mounce, *Pastoral Epistles*, 517–18. For a slight variation, see Marshall, *Pastoral Epistles*, 741–42.

in the New Testament, it almost always refers to his faithfulness on behalf of and in favor of his people.

But three factors support the second interpretation.[13] The first is the structure of the confession itself, consisting of two lines highlighting positive characteristics with the fitting response, followed by two lines pointing to negative activities and God's response. The denial of Christ and faithlessness are parallel ideas. It would seem, then, that God's response of denial and faithfulness are also parallel with one another. In other words, God's denial of those who deny him is tied to his own faithfulness.

Second, the only other time Paul uses the verb "to be faithless," he links it to God's faithfulness (Rom. 3:3). There, God's faithfulness is specifically spelled out in terms of God's faithfulness in bringing judgment on the faithless (cf. Rom. 3:4–5, which speaks of the judgment and wrath of God). Third, the larger context of 2 Timothy supports this interpretation, promising blessings to those who remain faithful, but giving dire warnings to those who are faithless.

The confession ends with the assertion that God cannot deny himself. God must remain true to his character and true to his promises. Jesus has promised that he will deny those who have denied him. That clearly implies judgment. God will be faithful to that promise. In line with his own character, he must bring judgment on those who resist his will and show themselves faithless.

Thus, Paul emphasizes in this section the urgent necessity of faithfulness—both in holding to the faith and in gospel witness. Despite the threat of persecution, imprisonment, and death, Timothy must be faithful in serving Christ. Great rewards are stored up for those who endure. But judgment awaits those who fall away. Christians must live the Christian life not focused on rewards of this life, but with eternity in view. And Christian ministers must always remember that the eternal destiny of souls is at stake in their gospel ministry.

Faithfulness in the Face of False Teaching (2 Tim. 2:14–4:5)

For the next chapter and a half, Paul returns to the theme that dominated 1 Timothy, namely, false teachers and false teaching. But the focus in this section is not on the false teaching itself. Rather, it is on how Timothy is to handle it. Most gospel ministers know *that* they must defend the truth over against error. But many fail to see that equally important is *how* we are to defend the truth. In 2 Timothy 2:14–26, Paul gives special attention to the *how* question. He instructs Timothy in what he is to avoid, what the focus of his ministry should entail, and how he should specifically deal with opponents of the truth.

First, Paul tells Timothy what he should avoid. This is a theme that runs throughout this section. Paul instructs Timothy "not to quarrel about words" (2:14), to "avoid irreverent babble" (2:16), and to "have nothing to do with foolish, ignorant controversies," which only "breed quarrels" (2:23). The gospel minister must know how to pick his battles. Some discussions and controversies are fruitless and only lead

[13] On this interpretation, see Calvin, *Epistles to Timothy*, 311.

to ongoing quarrels, which are destructive to God's people ("spread like gangrene," 2:17). Pastors and elders need wisdom to know which controversies are important to engage and which ones to avoid.

Second, Paul instructs Timothy that the best response to false teaching is the patient, careful exposition of the truth. He writes, "Do your best to present yourself to God as one approved, a worker who has no need to be ashamed, rightly handling the word of truth" (2:15). The idea of "rightly handling" God's Word most likely carries with it the dual notions of correct interpretation and proper teaching.[14] This requires diligence and hard work. The minister cannot cut corners when it comes to making sure he is accurately interpreting and carefully teaching God's people. Only those rightly handling God's Word are "approved," that is, they are shown to be tested and true. As such, they need not be ashamed when they stand before God at the time of judgment. Eternal destinies, including those of both the hearers and the teachers, are at stake in careful, sound exposition (cf. 1 Tim. 4:16). It is in the faithful teaching of the Word that truth is victorious over error.

Third, when correcting false teachers is necessary, Paul tells Timothy that he must do this "with gentleness" (2 Tim. 2:25). Some false teaching is extremely dangerous. It moves some away from the truth and upsets their faith (2:18). Paul gives an example of this, namely, the teaching that the resurrection has already happened (2:18). Most likely, this teaching was a kind of "over-realized eschatology" that taught that everything believers were going to receive from God had already been received.[15] Many commentators believe that this was the root issue of the many problems Paul addressed in 1 Corinthians.[16] It can lead to a kind of triumphalism and a host of ethical problems. But in the end it only leaves believers hopeless. When we believe that this world is all we have to live for, hope soon fades.

This kind of teaching is dangerous and heretical. Paul even names two men "who have swerved from the truth" (2:18) and are promoting error. Still, he instructs Timothy that he must not be quarrelsome, but must instruct his opponents with kindness, patience, and gentleness (2:24–25). The reason for this comes out at the end of the chapter: "God may perhaps grant them repentance leading to a knowledge of the truth" (2:25). In other words, the ultimate goal is their salvation. With this in view, how we approach our opponents is just as important as what we say.

In this letter, then, Paul has moved from calling Timothy to faithfulness in suffering to urging his faithfulness in the face of false teaching. Not only are Christians to endure the persecutions and opposition of the world, but they are to remain steadfast in the face of distortions of God's Word. Ultimately, the dangers from within the church are just as destructive, if not more so, than dangers from without. Yet, crucial for Paul is how we deal with our opponents, both without and within.

[14] See Knight, *Pastoral Epistles*, 412. Fee, by contrast, sees only a reference to correctly teaching the Word (*1 & 2 Timothy*, 205). Cf. Marshall, who says that the main choice in this verse "lies between right teaching and right living," though he opts for right teaching as the correct interpretation (*Pastoral Epistles*, 749).

[15] See Philip H. Towner, "Gnosis and Realized Eschatology in Ephesus (of the Pastoral Epistles) and the Corinthian Enthusiasm," *JSNT* 31 (1987): 95–124. See also Towner, *The Goal of Our Instruction: The Structure of Theology and Ethics in the Pastoral Epistles* (Sheffield: JSOT, 1989).

[16] The seminal work on this was A. C. Thiselton, "Realized Eschatology at Corinth," *NTS* 24 (1977/78): 510–26.

The balance in this passage is striking. On the one hand, Paul does not shy away from denouncing false teaching as dangerous and heretical, or even from naming those who perpetrate it. On the other hand, he admonishes Timothy to deal with false teaching with patience and gentleness, not with an angry, bellicose spirit. The minister of Jesus Christ needs to remember that while the truth is of infinite value, so are the souls of those who oppose the gospel. Practically speaking, a gentle spirit typically is more effective than angry denouncements that antagonize and alienate. And a gentle spirit better adorns the gospel.

This leads to one final emphasis in this section: the need to pursue holiness. A proper response to opponents of the truth can only come from a sanctified life. Thus Paul exhorts Timothy, "So flee youthful passions and pursue righteousness, faith, love, and peace, along with those who call on the Lord from a pure heart" (2:22). The "youthful passions" that Timothy is to flee from may mean the sensual desires associated with youth or perhaps the youthful infatuation with what is novel and innovative. But it could very well also mean the angry passions and hotheadedness that often characterize youth, which would fit well with the present context (cf. 2:23ff.). Either way, Paul's point here is that a godly response in conflict must come from a heart and life trained in godliness.

In 2 Timothy 3, Paul highlights the deadly serious nature of false teaching and false teachers. Some might read Paul's instructions in chapter 2 concerning gentleness and patience as an indication that false teaching is not all that serious. But that would be a great mistake. In fact, Paul links the motives and characteristics of false teachers with the evils that mark the "last days" (3:1).[17] From a biblical perspective, the last days have already begun (cf. 1 Cor. 10:11; 1 Tim. 4:1). They came when Jesus arrived and proclaimed the coming of the kingdom, already here (Luke 11:20) but not yet in its fullness. But with the coming of Jesus and the kingdom, this meant an increase in demonic and Satanic activity. When God's kingdom, the age to come, broke into the present age, the forces of evil stepped up their attack on Christ and his people, seeking to destroy them.

In 2 Timothy 3:1–9, Paul shows the increased evil and immorality of the last days. But here he specifically links this to the false teachers. Their corruption is in line with the decadence that marks increased satanic opposition to God. Their motives and desires are evil. They have "the appearance of godliness, but [deny] its power" (3:5). In other words, they are pious frauds who know nothing of the true life-changing power of the gospel and of a life lived in the pursuit of God-honoring holiness. Their evil is especially seen in the fact that they take advantage of the weak and vulnerable (3:6–7). Ultimately, however, God will triumph and expose their lies and foolish ways (3:9). Far from being soft on false teaching, then, Paul calls Timothy to recognize evil for what it is and treat false teaching as a threat to the peace and purity of the church.[18]

[17] Knight (*Pastoral Epistles*, 433) points out that the present tense verbs in 3:6 ("are," "creep into," "capture") indicate clearly that the earlier future-tense verbs (see 3:1–2) that speak of the "last days" are being fulfilled in Paul's own day and do not apply to the distant future.

[18] Knight (*Pastoral Epistles*, 427) appeals to the Latin proverb "gentle in manner, resolute in purpose" as an apt summary of Paul's instructions on dealing with the false teachers.

One potential interpretive problem in this passage is the relationship of verse 9 with what Paul goes on to say in verse 13. In verse 9, he says that the false teachers "will not get very far," while in verse 13 he says "evil people and imposters will go on from bad to worse" and apparently make progress in their deception. But as Calvin helpfully points out, these are not contradictory statements; they reflect two viewpoints that the church needs to recognize. He writes:

> In order that godly pastors may not be brought to despair, as though they were carrying on a battle against errors to no effect, they are to be told about the good success that the Lord will give to His own teaching. And yet to keep them from thinking that their work is done when they have fought in one or two battles, they are to be reminded that there will always be fresh calls to fight.[19]

In light of this, Paul calls Timothy to prepare for opposition and to apply himself to the study of Scripture. Paul reminds his protégé once again of his own perseverance in the face of opposition (3:10–11), thereby setting an example for Timothy to follow, while also reminding him that it is the Lord who helps his people in times of trouble. But Paul is not alone in suffering for Christ. Indeed, "all who desire to live a godly life in Christ Jesus will be persecuted" (3:12). In spite of Paul's earlier assurance of God's ultimate triumph (cf. 3:9), evil and opposition will continue (3:13). Timothy's response must be that he remain established in the Word of God, for only then will he be equipped for the work to which God has called him (3:14–17).

The main point in the final verses of chapter 3 is found in verse 14, "continue in what you have learned and have firmly believed," the only imperatival statement found in verses 10–17. But we cannot read verse 14 in isolation from verse 10, where Paul tells Timothy that the latter *has followed* Paul's "teaching . . . conduct . . . steadfastness . . . persecutions and sufferings." In fact, the Greek text of verses 10 and 14 begins with the exact same words (lit. "but you"), indicating a link between them. In other words, Paul calls Timothy here to continue and persevere in what he has already been doing. Once more we see the call to ongoing faithfulness.

More specifically, Paul calls Timothy to "continue in" the teaching of the Word of God. He reminds him again of his godly heritage, how "from childhood" he has been taught "the sacred writings, which are able to make you wise for salvation through faith in Christ Jesus" (3:15). The term "sacred writings" is not found elsewhere in the New Testament, but was used by Greek-speaking Jews to refer to the Old Testament. Yet it is not the Old Testament alone that Timothy was taught.

Paul says that "all Scripture is breathed out by God and profitable for teaching, for reproof, for correction, and for training in righteousness" (3:16).[20] The term "all Scripture" surely includes New Testament writings that already existed, as well as apostolic proclamation that was not yet in written form.[21] In 1 Timothy 5:18, Paul

---

[19] Calvin, *Epistles to Timothy*, 326.

[20] The words πᾶσα γραφὴ θεόπνευστος at the beginning of this verse are the subject of great debate. For an extended discussion of the debate surrounding these three words, see Mounce, *Pastoral Epistles*, 565–70, and Knight, *Pastoral Epistles*, 444–48.

[21] See Knight, *Pastoral Epistles*, 448.

quoted from Luke and referred to it as "Scripture." Peter clearly refers to Paul's own writings as Scripture (2 Pet. 3:15–16). Paul's use of the word "all" at the beginning of this verse indicates that he has in mind the totality of divine revelation. Throughout 1–2 Timothy, Paul has repeated his refrain that Timothy is to remain in *his* teaching, the effect of which is to lead people to salvation, instruct them in godly living, and equip God's servants for ministry. That repeated refrain forms a clear parallel to what Paul says in 2 Timothy 3:16–17.

Thus, Paul calls Timothy to remain steadfast in the teaching of God's Word. But this is not a static task. Being "equipped for every good work" (3:17) requires the constant study, teaching, and application of God's Word. As Timothy continues in this, he remains faithful to his calling as a follower of Christ and minister of the gospel.

From a redemptive-historical perspective, Paul's linking of the "sacred writings" to "all Scripture" indicates a continuity in divine revelation. Men and women were saved under the old covenant in the same way they are saved under the new covenant, by faith in God's provision of salvation (cf. Paul's appeals to Abraham in Romans 4 and Galatians 3). The Old Testament reveals that God requires perfect obedience to his commands (Genesis 1–3), its laws show us our sin and inability to live up to that standard, and its sacrifices point to our need of an atoning sacrifice. But from beginning to end the Old Testament points us to the seed of the woman who will crush the Serpent's head (Gen. 3:15), who himself will be the suffering servant who takes on himself the sin of his people and bears the wrath of God, and who is the King who will reign over all nations. The message of all Scripture regarding salvation is one. The gospel is found in both the Old Testament and the New.

Paul brings this section to a close in 2 Timothy 4:1–5 by repeating his earlier exhortations to Timothy to remain steadfast in his ministry of preaching and teaching. He is to do this especially in light of the fact that people will grow tired of sound teaching and will surround themselves with teachers who tell them what they want to hear. The remedy to this is not to find new and innovative ways of getting the message out. It is to endure patiently in the teaching and preaching ministry.[22] This is the means that God has ordained to bring sinners to repentance and to build up the saints in the faith.

Paul's Faithfulness and His Faithful Lord (2 Tim. 4:6–22)

Paul's final letter ends with a poignant and hopeful tone. He knows that his death is near. The judicial process is underway and clearly heading in that direction. He writes, "I am already being poured out as a drink offering, and the time of my departure has come" (2 Tim. 4:6). The language of the "drink offering" is significant

[22] According to Chrysostom, the phrase "in season and out of season" (4:2) means that Timothy is to be constantly at the task (John Chrysostom, *Homilies on the Epistles of St. Paul the Apostle to Timothy, Titus, and Philemon* [*NPNF*[1] 13:510]). It is possible, in light of the reference to "time" in 4:3 (καιρός), which comes from the same Greek root as εὐκαίρως ἀκαίρως ("in season and out of season") in 4:2, that Paul is speaking of a convenient or inconvenient time for Paul's hearers. This is the interpretation of most recent commentaries; see, e.g., Marshall, *Pastoral Epistles*, 800; Fee, *1 & 2 Timothy*, 234; Knight, *Pastoral Epistles*, 453–54. Or, as Calvin (*Epistles to Timothy*, 333) suggests, perhaps both are in view.

because it reflects Old Testament sacrificial language. Paul's death, as his entire life, is one of being poured out as a sacrifice to God.

But his death is not the end. It is merely a "departure" from this life to the next. Paul earlier used similar language when he wrote to the Philippians during his first Roman imprisonment concerning his desire to "depart and be with Christ" (Phil. 1:23, using the verbal form of the noun found here). Death is not the end. For the Christian, something better awaits. In fact, Paul goes on to refer to the "crown of righteousness" that is laid up for him (2 Tim. 4:8). But, as he states, this crown is not for him only. It is for "all who have loved his appearing." Thus, this passage not only shows Paul as hopeful when facing death. It also encourages other believers of what awaits those who patiently, faithfully follow Christ and long for his final victory.

In verse 7, Paul paints a picture of what this faithfulness entails as he reflects on his own life. He says, "I have fought the good fight, I have finished the race, I have kept the faith." Here he returns to the military and athletic metaphors that he used earlier (cf. 2:3–5).[23] The emphasis is on the hard work and perseverance that have marked Paul's life. This verse reflects his life not only as a Christian but also as an apostle. He has been faithful in his calling to Christ in every sense of the word. Implicitly, Paul calls Timothy—and all believers—to do the same.

Second Timothy ends with Paul's final instructions to Timothy and final greetings. The heart of Paul's appeal, repeated twice, is that Timothy would come to see Paul as soon as possible (4:9, 21). The repetition also indicates that there is a sense of urgency to this request. There may be many reasons for this: the uncertain timing of his death, the need for Timothy to come before winter, Paul's desire to have his cloak and his books (4:13), or simply Paul's desire to see Timothy again and to have his companionship. Much of this final section details Paul's having been abandoned and wronged. So it seems that the personal side, his desire to be with his beloved companion, is at the heart of Paul's appeal.

In this final section of the letter, Paul informs Timothy of his own situation relative to other people. Demas, who appears in two other Pauline letters as one who was with Paul during his first Roman imprisonment (Col. 4:14; Philem. 24), has "deserted" Paul (2 Tim. 4:10). The fact that in Philemon 24 Paul calls Demas his "fellow worker" indicates that Demas's desertion would have been very painful, especially since his reason for leaving was that he was "in love with this present world" (2 Tim. 4:10). Causing Paul even greater pain, however, is his experience during his "first defense" when "all deserted" him (4:16). To compound Paul's suffering, he recounts for Timothy that "Alexander the coppersmith did [him] great harm," but he rests assured in the fact that God's justice will prevail ("the Lord will repay him according to his deeds," 4:14).

[23] It is possible that both clauses carry athletic overtones, since the words in the first clause can refer to the struggle of an athletic contest. See Fee, *1 & 2 Timothy*, 238; Marshall, *Pastoral Epistles*, 807. But Knight (*Pastoral Epistles*, 459) correctly points out that the language was used in both military and athletic fields. The closest parallel to this verse is 1 Tim. 1:18, where Paul specifically uses warfare language urging Timothy to "fight the good fight" (NASB) (different Greek verb and noun). Cf. 1 Tim. 6:12.

In contrast to those who have hurt or wronged Paul, he tells of others who have left seemingly for positive reasons. Crescens and Titus have both left, but the fact that Paul specifies where they have gone suggests that they have departed to do ministry. Likewise, Paul says that he has sent Tychicus to Ephesus—possibly to deliver the letter to Timothy and fill in for him when Timothy leaves to visit Paul in Rome.

Although Luke is with Paul, the discussion of those who have left suggests that Paul is experiencing loneliness and a longing for others during his imprisonment. Happily, he tells Timothy, "Get Mark and bring him with you, for he is very useful to me for ministry" (4:11). But his great desire is to see Timothy and to be united with his child in the faith, his colleague, and his friend. Paul and Timothy have had a long and fruitful ministry together that spans at least ten years. Paul mentions Timothy as a cowriter of some of his earliest letters (1–2 Thessalonians; 2 Corinthians), as well as some of his later letters (Philippians, Colossians, and Philemon, all written during Paul's first Roman imprisonment). When we combine this with the earlier mention of Timothy's "tears" (2 Tim. 1:4), it is clear that Paul and Timothy have had a deep personal and emotional bond with one another.

But in spite of the personal loneliness and loss that Paul has experienced, he exalts in his faithful Lord. When all deserted Paul at his first defense, he writes, "the Lord stood by me and strengthened me, so that through me the message might be fully proclaimed and all the Gentiles might hear it. So I was rescued from the lion's mouth" (4:17). Note here that the Lord's presence with Paul and his strengthening of Paul were so that Paul might be able to continue his gospel ministry even in the direst of circumstances. The idea of "all the Gentiles" hearing means that Paul was able to faithfully proclaim Christ in the best setting for the widest possible distribution of the gospel message. Rome was the capital of the Gentile world and a major metropolitan area. And very likely the message would have been passed on to others through those who heard. Being rescued from the lion's mouth is a metaphor for escaping extreme danger. In this context, the sense is that Paul has temporarily avoided death so that his gospel ministry might continue, at least for a short time.

Even more, Paul says, "The Lord will rescue me from every evil deed and bring me safely into his heavenly kingdom" (4:18). God's faithfulness during Paul's trial assures him that God will be faithful to the end of his life. Paul has made it clear that he expects to be martyred (cf. 4:6). When he says that the Lord will rescue him from every evil deed, he is not talking about physical deliverance from imprisonment and death. Rather, he is referring to the spiritual evils of apostasy, denying the faith, turning from the proclamation of the truth—clear temptations when faced with the choice of physical life or death.

To the very end, we see Paul's commitment to preaching the gospel and to his call as the apostle to the Gentiles. He has shared this ministry throughout his life with many friends and coworkers. Many of these have deserted Paul in his final days on earth. Yet, some faithful ones remain, who continue to support Paul and work alongside him, even while he is in prison for preaching the gospel. But most importantly, Paul has a faithful Lord who will sustain him, in faith and in ministry, even unto death, and after that receive him into glory.

Select Bibliography

Please see the bibliography at the end of chapter 14, "Introduction to the Pastoral Epistles."

17

Titus

William B. Barcley

Structure and Outline[1]

Paul writes to his close associate Titus to instruct and encourage him in his ministry on the island of Crete. He states, "This is why I left you in Crete, so that you might put what remained into order" (Titus 1:5). This verse implies that Paul has been involved in an evangelistic and church-planting ministry there.[2] The problem, however, is that we do not read of a ministry to Crete anywhere else in the New Testament. The only other place where Crete appears is in Acts 27, in the narrative description of Paul's voyage to Rome. But certainly Paul would not have been able to participate in a church-planting ministry during that voyage.

Most likely, then, Paul visited Crete and engaged in ministry after being released from his first Roman imprisonment, sometime in the early to mid-60s. This means that he wrote Titus around the same time that he wrote 1 Timothy. (See "Introduction to the Pastoral Epistles.")

The striking similarities between Titus and 1 Timothy support this date. As in 1 Timothy, Paul's central concern in Titus is false teachers whose instruction is Jewish in its orientation (Titus 1:10, 14). Paul also uses parallel language when he warns Titus to "avoid foolish controversies, genealogies, dissensions, and quarrels about the

[1] For background material on Titus, see the chapter "Introduction to the Pastoral Epistles."

[2] Most recent commentators are in agreement that the verb "left" (ἀπέλιπόν) implies that Paul was with Titus on Crete and left him behind. See, e.g., Gordon D. Fee, *1 & 2 Timothy, Titus* (San Francisco: Harper & Row, 1984), 126; George W. Knight, *The Pastoral Epistles*, NIGTC (Grand Rapids, MI: Eerdmans, 1992), 287–88; William Mounce, *Pastoral Epistles*, WBC 46 (Nashville: Thomas Nelson, 2000), 386; and Donald Guthrie, *The Pastoral Epistles*, TNTC (Grand Rapids, MI: Eerdmans, 1990), 196. Compare, however, I. Howard Marshall, *A Critical and Exegetical Commentary on the Pastoral Epistles*, in collaboration with Philip H. Towner (Edinburgh: T&T Clark, 1999), 150, who says that the verb could possibly mean "dispatched" or "deployed," which suggests that Paul himself was never actually on Crete. Knight more convincingly points out that the nuance of being left "behind" is supported by the other occurrences of this verb in the Pastoral Epistles. Another question regarding 1:5 is whether Paul actually engaged in a preaching and church-planting ministry on Crete. He may simply have visited Crete and found an already established church in disarray. See the discussion of Mounce, *Pastoral Epistles*, 386; Knight, *Pastoral Epistles*, 287–88; and Fee, *1 & 2 Timothy*, 126.

law" (3:9). Also as in 1 Timothy, Paul gives instructions regarding the qualifications of elders (Titus 1:5–9). Finally, Paul positively expounds how God's people are to live, both with one another in the body of Christ and before outsiders.

We saw in the introduction to the Pastoral Epistles that the word "sound" or "healthy" is important in the Pastorals. It occurs twice in each of 1 and 2 Timothy. But in this short letter to Titus it occurs four times. Paul in particular makes it clear that sound/healthy doctrine leads to sound/healthy living. In Titus 2:1–2, he writes, "But as for you, teach what accords with *sound* doctrine. Older men are to be sober-minded, dignified, self-controlled, *sound* in faith, in love, and in steadfastness." The repetition of the word "sound" in these verses shows a connection between them. Sound doctrine has ethical consequences, leading to qualities like being self-controlled, loving, and steadfast.

This is an important emphasis in Titus for two reasons. First, Paul describes the false teachers themselves as being involved in unethical practices (1:11, 16). He says, "They deny [God] by their works" (1:16). Second, the people of Crete do not have a very good reputation: "Cretans are always liars, evil beasts, lazy gluttons"—and this from one of the Cretans' own prophets (1:12). In fact, the people of Crete had a reputation in the ancient world for immorality.

For Paul, the gospel is not only the power of God unto salvation; it also leads to the transformation of lives: "For the grace of God has appeared, bringing salvation for all people, training us to renounce ungodliness and worldly passions, and to live self-controlled, upright, and godly lives in the present age" (Titus 2:11–12). Paul's letter to Titus is filled with ethical instruction and is heavy on the imperative. There are fourteen imperative verbs in this short letter. But it is all rooted in the truth of gospel. The true gospel transforms, leading God's people to live differently from the world. The indicative of who God's people are in Christ comes before the imperatives calling God's people to live a holy life. Paul's desire is that God's people live differently before a watching world (2:8).

We can identify three key themes in Titus:

I. The False Teachers: Sound Neither in Doctrine nor in Life
II. The Leaders of God's People Must Be Sound Both in Doctrine and in Life
III. How Sound Doctrine Works Itself Out Daily in Sound Christian Living

These three themes will be the focus of our discussion of this letter.

Message and Theology

The False Teachers: Sound Neither in Doctrine nor in Life

False teachers largely frame Paul's letter to Titus. He deals with them in 1:10–16, then returns to them, and Titus's response to them, right before his final instructions and greetings at the end of the letter (3:9–11). Significantly, the first major topic that Paul discusses after his opening greeting is the qualifications for elders. This opening section ends by stating that part of the task of elders is "to give instruction in sound doctrine and also to rebuke those who contradict it" (1:9). Thus, a major part of Titus's task of putting what remains in order and appointing elders is to uphold the purity of teaching in all the churches in Crete.[3]

In the introduction to the Pastorals I have already dealt with the nature of the false teaching that Paul confronts in these letters, and so I will not repeat that information here. In fact, Paul spends more time in Titus detailing the conduct and motivations of the false teachers than he does the nature of their teaching. In essence, Paul denounces their character. We can highlight several things that he says about their conduct and character.

First, they are lawless hypocrites. In Titus 1:10, the word translated "insubordinate" is the same word that Paul uses in 1 Timothy 1:9 for the "disobedient," those who do not submit themselves to the law of God. The irony is that these false teachers, like those at Ephesus, seem to be presenting themselves as teachers of the law (cf. Titus 3:9 with the Jewish orientation in 1:10, 14). As some suggest, "pure" and "defiled" in 1:15 may indicate that much of their teaching revolves around Jewish purity laws.[4] But, Paul says, instead of keeping that law, they are lawless and thus hypocritical.

Second, Paul points out their evil motivations. They are "deceivers" who teach for "shameful gain" (1:10–11). In other words, they have not mistakenly wandered away into error. Their intent is to deceive so that they can become rich by leading others astray. In addition to this, Paul says, "their consciences are defiled" (1:15). He makes a similar comment about the false teachers in 1 Timothy 4:2, saying that they are insincere liars "whose consciences are seared." For Paul, the conscience is the inner moral detector that indicates to us that we have broken God's law.[5] But when we allow our conscience to become defiled or seared, we sin brazenly and without guilt. These false teachers are nothing but charlatans who seek to get rich by appearing to be godly teachers of Scripture.

Third, Paul says, "they profess to know God, but they deny him by their works" (Titus 1:16). This gets at the heart of Paul's message in Titus. Those who truly know God and have been transformed by their relationship with him demonstrate that in their lives. Thus, Jesus says of false prophets, "You will recognize them by their fruits" (Matt. 7:15–16). Paul similarly writes of the "fruit of the Spirit" (Gal. 5:22). Those who hold to the true Christian gospel and have God's Spirit show that in lives of good works. And those good works are themselves a demonstration of Christian faith. This becomes the heart of Paul's teaching in Titus 2–3.

Fourth, the false teachers are divisive (Titus 3:9–11). Paul instructs Titus to warn a divisive person twice, following Jesus's teaching in Matthew 18. But if he remains divisive and unrepentant, Paul says, "have nothing more to do with him" (Titus 3:10).

---

[3] Mounce (*Pastoral Epistles*, 395–96) points out that the following section (1:10–16), dealing explicitly with the false teachers, begins with the word γάρ, showing a connection between the two sections. A major part of the duty of elders is to teach sound doctrine and correct those who teach otherwise. On the connection between these two sections, see also Fee, *1 & 2 Timothy*, 128; and Knight, *Pastoral Epistles*, 294.

[4] See, e.g., Marshall, *Pastoral Epistles*, 207–11; Thomas D. Lea and Hayne P. Griffin, *1, 2 Timothy, Titus* (Grand Rapids, MI: Zondervan, 1999), 292.

[5] See the helpful discussion in Marshall, *Pastoral Epistles*, 217–27.

This emphasis on the divisive nature of false teaching is in line with all of Scripture. In Galatians 5:19–21, for example, the majority of Paul's list of "the works of the flesh" deals with sins that bring division to the body of Christ. The issue there is not that Paul sees division as the main problem in Galatians. In the false gospel, salvation itself is at stake. But false teaching always has the negative effect of bringing division. Often we hear today that those who oppose the teaching of others and are uncompromising in their stand for truth are themselves divisive, and their posture is unloving. But just the opposite is true. Aberrant teaching is divisive, and standing firm in the truth is the best way to promote love.

The Leaders of God's People Must Be Sound Both in Doctrine and in Life

Titus begins, like all of Paul's other letters, with a salutation, but then, like only 1 Timothy and Galatians, omits the standard thanksgiving section and immediately addresses Titus's need to "put what remained into order" (Titus 1:5) by appointing elders in all the churches. The salutation (1:1–4) is longer than most of Paul's opening greetings, with only Romans and Galatians being longer.[6] In the salutation, Paul expounds on his work as servant and apostle, which is "for the sake of the faith of God's elect and their knowledge of the truth, which accords with godliness" (1:1). In the opening verse, we see the theme of the letter. The goal of God's servants is to lead God's people to knowledge of the truth. But that truth is always in accord with and leads to godliness. If we were to formulate a title for Titus, it would be "The Truth That Accords with Godliness." This of course is in contrast to the false teachers, who lacked both truth and godliness.

The salutation also introduces a few other key ideas in the letter. Gospel truth brings "hope of eternal life" (1:2), a theme that Paul returns to in two later "gospel summary"[7] portions of the letter (cf. 2:13; 3:7). "Hope" in Scripture is not a wishful uncertainty but a confidence that is rooted in God's work and his promises.[8] In addition, Paul twice uses the word "Savior"—once of "God our Savior" (1:3) and once of "Christ Jesus our Savior" (1:4). "Savior" appears four more times in the letter, each time in the gospel summary sections (2:10, 13; 3:4, 6), and each time alternately referring to God as our Savior and Christ as our Savior.[9] In keeping with this emphasis on God as Savior, Paul writes of God's "salvation" (2:11) and his having "saved us" (3:5).

[6] For helpful discussions on the significance of the extended salutation in Titus, see Fee, *1 & 2 Timothy*, 121; Knight, *Pastoral Epistles*, 281–82; and Marshall, *Pastoral Epistles*, 111–15.

[7] According to Fee (*1 & 2 Timothy*, 156), 2:11–14 and 3:4–7 set before the Cretan believers "the gospel in capsule form," both of which remind them of the "sound teaching" they are to cling to and form the theological basis for Paul's ethical exhortation.

[8] Cf., for example, Col. 1:27, "Christ in you, the hope of glory." Christ's presence in the believer leaves him not with a wistful wish of glory, but with confidence in it. On this, see William Barcley, *"Christ in You": A Study in Paul's Theology and Ethics* (Lanham, MD: University Press of America, 1999).

[9] Titus 2:13 has been the subject of significant debate with regard to whether the text is referring to one person or two. The ESV translates, "waiting for our blessed hope, the appearing of the glory of our great God and Savior Jesus Christ," which implies one person, Christ, and makes a strong affirmation of the deity of Christ. The Greek text, however, could also be translated "the great God and our Savior Jesus Christ," referring to two persons. For a discussion of this verse and support for the affirmation of the deity of Christ here, see M. J. Harris, "Titus 2:13 and the Deity of Christ," in *Pauline Studies: Essays Presented to Professor F. F. Bruce on His 70th Birthday*, ed. D. Hagner and M. J. Harris (Grand Rapids, MI: Eerdmans, 1980), 262–77. See also Knight, *Pastoral Epistles*, 322–26, and Mounce, *Pastoral Epistles*, 425–31. A third alternative, supported by Fee (*1 & 2 Timothy*, 148–49), sees two persons in this verse, but the glory of one—our God and Savior (i.e., God the Father)—is revealed in the appearing of the other, Jesus Christ.

Finally, Paul introduces the ideas that the promise of salvation in Christ comes from God, "who never lies," (1:2) and is revealed "through the preaching" (1:3) of his Word. In other words, Paul emphasizes right from the beginning the trustworthiness of the Word of God and the importance of the teaching and preaching ministry of the church. God works through the preaching and teaching of his Word, bringing sinners to repentance and building up the saints. The ministry of the Word is powerful and effective. But preachers and teachers must be faithful and proclaim only the truth. This is set over against the false teachers, who are "empty talkers," "deceivers," and "liars" (1:10–12). All teaching can have a powerful effect. But only the teaching of the truth leads to salvation and godliness. False teaching leads to destruction.

This leads directly to Paul's instructions about the qualifications for elders. The list of qualifications is similar to what Paul spells out in 1 Timothy 3, placing the emphasis on godly character. But significantly, Paul concludes by saying, "He must hold firm to the trustworthy word as taught, so that he may be able to give instruction in sound doctrine and also to rebuke those who contradict it" (Titus 1:9). Elders must be sound in doctrine and in life. But Paul emphasizes here that they must also be able to give instruction in sound doctrine (cf. "able to teach," 1 Tim. 3:2), as well as be able to call to account those who teach falsely. Strong, godly elders are vital for the spiritual health of God's people. They teach God's people the life-giving and transforming truth of the gospel. But as shepherds they also guard the flock from the wolves who seek to destroy the sheep through false teaching (see Acts 20:28–31).

One requirement for elders found in Paul's list in Titus but not in 1 Timothy 3 is that their children must be πιστός (Titus 1:6). This Greek word can mean either "believers" (ESV) or "faithful" (KJV, NKJV) in the sense of being trustworthy. Of its 67 uses in the New Testament, the vast majority have the meaning of "faithful" or "trustworthy." That is its predominant meaning in the Pastoral Epistles, including the two other instances in Titus, one in this immediate context (1:9, "the trustworthy word"; cf. 3:8).

In Paul's list in 1 Timothy 3, the requirement for elders' children is that they must be obedient and submissive, not that they must be Christians. And that seems to be the overall sense of Titus 1:6, where Paul goes on to say that the children of elders must not be "open to the charge of debauchery or insubordination." Since Paul has already referred to God's people as his "elect" (1:1), indicating that salvation is all of God and by God's choosing, it is inconceivable that Paul would hold fathers responsible for the saved state of their children. A father clearly has the responsibility to teach his children the Word of God, set before them a godly example, and hold them accountable to being obedient and submissive to his leadership while they live under his roof. But fathers cannot be held responsible for the spiritual state of the heart. Thus, "faithful" or "trustworthy" (perhaps even in the sense of "obedient," as in 1 Timothy) seems the best translation here.[10]

[10] In support of this interpretation, see Knight (*Pastoral Epistles*, 289–90), who includes several biblical and secular references. See also Walter L. Liefeld, *1 and 2 Timothy, Titus* (Grand Rapids, MI: Zondervan, 1999), 312–13. For the interpretation that the children of elders must be "believers," see Mounce, *Pastoral Epistles*, 388–89, and Marshall, *Pastoral*

How Sound Doctrine Works Itself Out Daily in Sound Christian Living

The rest of the letter instructs Titus in how he is to train all of God's people in godly Christian living. All but one of the fourteen imperatives in Titus occur in chapters 2–3. But this section is also punctuated by two gospel summary[11] sections that are especially suited to Paul's ethical instructions. The indicative of God's work of "regeneration and renewal" (3:5) is primary. But it always leads to transformed lives and to the imperative of walking in ways fitting to the gospel and to the God who has called us.

In Titus 2, Paul directs Titus how to instruct different groups in the church. These include older men (2:2), older women (2:3–5), younger men (2:6), and slaves (2:9–10). The instructions for each are suited to their particular situations in life. The instructions to older men sound like a miniature version of Paul's qualifications for elders, minus the required ability to teach and rebuke false teachers. In the first century in particular, elders for the church would primarily have been older men (as the title suggests), and the requirements for elders are in many ways no different from the requirements for all men, except that elders are to clearly meet those standards and serve as examples of godliness to the church.

While in 1 Timothy 2 Paul makes clear that women are not to teach or have authority over men, here he indicates that older women do have an important teaching ministry. Specifically, older women are to "teach" and "train" (Titus 2:3–4) younger women in godly living, especially with regard to submission to their husbands (2:4–5). The instructions to younger men and slaves also fit their stations in life. Younger men are to be "self-controlled" (2:6), while slaves are to be submissive to their masters and faithful in their work.

Paul's instructions for how these different groups are to act are punctuated by direct exhortations to Titus for his own life and ministry. This chapter begins and ends with directions concerning Titus's teaching ministry: "teach what accords with sound doctrine" (2:1); "declare these things; exhort and rebuke with all authority" (2:15). In other words, as we have seen in Paul's letters to Timothy, Paul exhorts Titus to be faithful in his primary task as a teacher and preacher of God's Word. This focus on Titus's teaching ministry serves as an *inclusio* (pair of bookends) that holds this chapter together. But right in the middle of the chapter, Paul also exhorts Titus to be a "model of good works," as well as to show "integrity" in his teaching (2:7–8). Once again, then, we see Paul's emphasis in this short letter on both proper teaching and proper Christian living.

In Titus 3:1–3, Paul gives general instructions for how to treat others. God's people are to be submissive to rulers and authorities, and they are to treat all people

Epistles, 157–59. Marshall argues that in first-century patriarchal society the children were more likely to accept their father's religion than is the case in our world today. Furthermore, he says, in the earlier context the father's reputation was at stake, both inside and outside the church, depending on whether his children embraced the Christian faith. Either way, as both Knight and Marshall point out, the participle ἔχων implies cases only in which the children are still in the home under the father's authority.

[11] Marshall (*Pastoral Epistles*, 21–24) says that these sections give the "doctrinal" basis for the exhortations in the letter. Cf. John R. W. Stott, *The Message of 1 Timothy and Titus* (Downers Grove, IL: InterVarsity Press, 1996), 192. Other writers use the terms "theology" or "theological basis." See, e.g., Guthrie, *Pastoral Epistles*, 209.

with gentleness and courtesy, speaking evil of no one. Paul gives a reason for treating others well: "For we ourselves were once foolish, disobedient, led astray, slaves to various passions and pleasures, passing our days in malice and envy, hated by others and hating one another" (3:3). Just as God's people have been shown the goodness and grace of God when they were wretched and unbelieving (3:4ff.), so they are to show goodness and grace to others.

An important emphasis in Paul's ethical instructions in chapters 2–3 is that Christians are to be evangelistically minded. His teaching about how God's people are to live includes an emphasis on being a good witness to unbelievers. So Paul tells Titus, "In your teaching show integrity, dignity, and sound speech that cannot be condemned, so that an opponent may be put to shame, having nothing evil to say about us" (2:7–8). Similarly, slaves are to act in such a way that "in everything they may adorn the doctrine of God our Savior" (2:10). Certainly Paul's instructions in 3:1–2 about treating unbelievers properly and with courtesy is to a large measure driven by evangelistic motivation. This of course reflects Paul's call and passion to do all things—even becoming all things to all people (1 Cor. 9:22)—so that they might be saved. So also Christians are called to act properly before a watching world and in a way that adorns the gospel.

Ultimately, the heavy emphasis in Titus on good works and living properly is simply because that is the outworking of the gospel's transforming work in the lives of God's people. We are called to "become who we are" in Christ. This is actually the weight of the gospel summary sections in 2:11–14 and 3:4–7. The "grace of God" that brings "salvation for all people" also "train[s] us to renounce ungodliness and worldly passions, and to live self-controlled, upright, and godly lives in the present age" (2:11–12). Christ gave himself on the cross, Paul says, "to redeem us from all lawlessness and to purify for himself a people for his own possession who are zealous for good works" (2:14). The "goodness and loving kindness of God" that has "saved us" has been through "the washing of regeneration and renewal of the Holy Spirit" (3:4–5). Believers are a new creation in Christ. Thus, Paul goes on to tell Titus, "I want you to insist on these things, so that those who have believed in God may be careful to devote themselves to good works" (3:8).

Of course, this is no different from James's teaching that faith without works is dead. But it is striking how infused the gospel summary sections are with the importance of proper Christian living and with exhortations to good works. Interpreters of Paul often rightly point out that his imperatives are rooted in and the result of the indicatives of what we are in Christ (e.g., you are holy/set apart, so be holy). The problem comes, however, when we equate only the indicatives with the gospel. The good news of God's love for sinners, of forgiveness of sins, of being clothed in Christ's righteousness, and of God's acceptance of sinners cannot be separated from the good news of God's transforming work and of the call to live holy lives to the glory of God. It is a glorious truth that we who "were once foolish, disobedient, led astray, slaves to various passions and pleasures, passing our days in malice and envy, hated by others and hating one another" (3:3) have been changed and transformed by the gospel and by the power of God so that we might live joyful lives in obedience to God's commands. And those commands themselves are a joy and delight to the people of God (cf. Psalm 119). They are especially a joy and delight because now we are able to keep them and to live the soul-satisfying life that God intended for human beings to live. For Christians, even God's commands to his people are gracious. The imperatives, then, no less than the indicatives, are for God's people—dare I say it?—good news!

Select Bibliography

Please see the bibliography at the end of chapter 14, "Introduction to the Pastoral Epistles."

18

Philemon

Benjamin Gladd

Introduction

Christ's work on the cross and his resurrection not only deliver individuals from their spiritual plight; they also restore a host of fractured relationships—cosmic, ethnic, familial, and so on. Since the church is the restored people of God, a community that finds its identity in the new heavens and earth, it must behave accordingly, especially in regard to how its members relate to one another. Recall Paul's words in Galatians 3:28: "There is neither Jew nor Greek, there is neither slave nor free, there is no male and female, *for you are all one in Christ Jesus.*" A few chapters later Paul expands upon this key declaration: "For neither circumcision counts for anything, nor uncircumcision, *but a new creation*" (Gal. 6:15). Therefore, believers must consciously recognize their position in Christ, particularly how they relate within the church. Against this background, Paul pens a brief letter to reconcile a slave with his master. Yet this reconciliation between a master and his slave flows not purely from a practical consideration but from a redemptive-historical one.

Background Issues

Occasion

Traditionally, scholars have maintained that Onesimus, a slave of Philemon, flees from his master for an unknown reason. Perhaps Onesimus has robbed his master (v. 18). Coincidentally, Philemon meets Paul in Rome and embraces the gospel (v. 10). Fortunately for Onesimus, Paul *already knows* Philemon. As it turns out, Onesimus becomes a great asset for Paul's ministry, so the apostle writes to Philemon, the owner of Onesimus, to be reconciled with the slave. Once Philemon frees his servant Onesimus, he is able to return to Paul and assist him further.

This long-standing view suffers from a few problems. How does Philemon encounter Paul in Rome, who is under house arrest? In addition, what are the chances that Paul already knows Philemon?

Another possibility is that Onesimus came to know Paul (or, at least, learn about him) through Philemon or the house church at Colossae. Onesimus, therefore, decides to flee from his master (perhaps he has stolen or mismanaged funds), seeking to find a safe haven in Rome. He purposefully journeys there and visits the famed Paul. Onesimus is converted while in Rome (v. 10) and attempts to reconcile with Philemon *through* Paul. The advantage of this view is that it makes better sense of how Onesimus met Paul. Instead of happenstance, this meeting is thoroughly intentional.

At the end of the day, it makes little interpretative difference how Paul and Onesimus meet. What remains crucial is the conversion of Onesimus and Paul's desire for him to be reconciled with his master.

Authorship

The epistle names Paul as its author (v. 1), and the early church affirmed this. Some have doubted Pauline authorship because of the letter's narrow purpose and brief remarks. Yet, nothing internally or externally overthrows the traditional view that Paul wrote this letter.

Date

Colossians and Philemon appear to be written from the same location and at approximately the same time. The appropriation of names in both letters is striking. In Colossians, Paul sends greetings from Aristarchus, Mark, Epaphras, Luke, Demas, and Justus (Col. 4:10–14), while Tychicus and Onesimus deliver the letter to the church at Colossae (4:7, 9). Philemon follows suit, mentioning greetings from Aristarchus, Mark, Epaphras, Luke, and Demas (v. 23). Onesimus and Archippus are also stated in Philemon (vv. 2, 10–16). In addition, Onesimus (Col. 4:9) and probably Philemon were residents of Colossae.

Given the epistle's close ties to Colossians, Philemon was probably written at the same time and place. Three main options exist for situating Colossians and Philemon: Ephesus (AD 55–56), Caesarea (57–59; Acts 23:23–26:32), and Rome (60–62; Acts 28:14–31). Of these three, a Roman provenance is probably the best option (see the discussion under "Date" in the chapter on Colossians). Therefore, Paul wrote Philemon at Rome in 60–61.

Purpose

Paul writes this brief letter to reconcile Onesimus and Philemon. Philemon ought to welcome Onesimus not as a slave but as a brother in Christ. Also, Paul wishes that Philemon return Onesimus to Paul so that they may continue to experience a great harvest of ministry in Rome.

Structure and Outline

I. Letter Opening (vv. 1–3)
II. Thanksgiving (vv. 4–7)
III. Paul's Request for Onesimus (vv. 8–21)
IV. Letter Closing (vv. 22–25)

Message and Theology

Key Themes in Philemon

Slavery in the Ancient World

The issue of slavery in the New Testament continues to be problematic. For example, does Paul (and do other New Testament writers) condone slavery within the church? He often makes references to "masters" and "slaves" in his letters, yet he never explicitly attempts to overturn these societal structures. It is of upmost importance to peek into the nature of slavery in the Greco-Roman world before we seek to understand Paul's discussion of it.[1]

In the Greco-Roman world, slaves were granted many rights, such as worshiping, marrying, and making money. They were artisans, architects, doctors, philosophers, teachers, and writers. Race also was not an issue.[2] It was possible for slaves to gain freedom (manumission) for a price. In other words, slavery in Paul's day looked different from its modern form. Certainly, some owners were cruel to their slaves and treated them poorly, though not all. But one key principle held true in the Greco-Roman world and continues into the present: slaves were *owned*. Murray Harris rightly explains, "At the heart of slavery, ancient or modern, are the ideas of total dependence, the forfeiture of autonomy and the sense of belonging wholly to another."[3]

By briefly examining Paul's admonitions to slaves in Colossians 3, we can generally grasp his approach in Philemon. Though Paul in Colossians 3 doesn't rail against slavery, he does tacitly undermine it. Douglas Moo points out that "Paul clearly relativizes the status of the slave's master by repeatedly reminding both slave (vv. 22, 23, 24) and master (4:1) of the ultimate 'master' to whom both are responsible: the Lord Jesus Christ."[4] Notice how Paul often appeals to Christ as the cosmic Master in contrast to the "earthly master":

> Bondservants, obey in everything those who are your *earthly masters*, not by way of eye-service, as people-pleasers, but with sincerity of heart, fearing the *Lord*. Whatever you do, work heartily, as for the *Lord* and not for *men*, knowing that from the *Lord* you will receive the inheritance as your reward. You are serving the *Lord Christ*. For the wrongdoer will be paid back for the wrong he has done, and there is no partiality. Masters, treat your bondservants justly and fairly, knowing that you also have a *Master in heaven*. (3:22–4:1)

[1] On the notoriously difficult subject of slavery in the ancient world and the New Testament, see Murray J. Harris, *Slave of Christ: A New Testament Metaphor for Total Devotion to Christ*, NSBT 8 (Downers Grove, IL: InterVarsity Press, 1999).
[2] S. Scott Bartchy, "Slavery," *ABD*, 6:65–72.
[3] Harris, *Slave of Christ*, 44–45.
[4] Douglas J. Moo, *The Letters to the Colossians and to Philemon*, PNTC (Grand Rapids, MI: Eerdmans, 2008), 308.

The Greek word here for "Lord" often carries with it the notion of "master" (e.g., Col. 4:1). Therefore, Paul is claiming, in effect, that slaves are not ultimately responsible to their "earthly" masters but to Christ, the supreme Master. Also, earthly masters must, like their servants, submit to the cosmic Master. In a real sense, all of humanity, whether masters, servants, rich, or poor, are all "servants" of the King.

The Restructuring of God's People

As mentioned above, this letter presupposes a knowledge of ancient social structures, particularly the relationship between "masters" and "slaves." But what must be kept in mind is how the New Testament, on the one hand, somewhat preserves these structures but, on the other, reconfigures them in light of Christ's work. Broaching this topic requires us to consult other New Testament letters that engage this thorny issue.

Ephesians, Colossians, and 1 Peter display some knowledge of Greco-Roman "household codes," which refer to a Greco-Roman social understanding of the ancient family structure. Proper relationships between the members of the family household order must be preserved. Scholars often find strong conceptual links between the Greco-Roman household codes and those found in Ephesians 5–6, Colossians 3–4, and 1 Peter 2–3. What must be kept in mind, however, is the codes' relationship to the end-time people of God as a new creational community. Before we consider the New Testament understanding of social structures, we must first briefly survey the Old Testament counterpart.

According to the Old Testament (and Second Temple Judaism), God appointed angels in Genesis 11 to rule over the nations on his behalf. We discern this phenomenon in Deuteronomy 32:8:

> When the Most High gave to the nations their inheritance,
> when he divided mankind,
> he fixed the borders of the peoples
> *according to the number of the sons of God.*

The last phrase of this verse is notoriously difficult to pin down, but the Septuagint (the Greek translation of the Old Testament) is explicit: "according to the number of the angels of God" (κατὰ ἀριθμὸν ἀγγέλων θεοῦ). Apparently, these angelic overseers were to report to God and manage the nations' affairs.[5] Israel, on the other hand, did not have a patron "deity" acting on behalf of God.[6] God had an intimate relationship with Israel and did not require a mediatorial ruler. Instead of ruling well

[5] An early Jewish commentary, the Targum, on Deut. 32:8–9 (Pseudo Jonathan) is explicit in this regard:

> When the Most High made allotment of the world unto the nations which proceeded from the sons of Noah, in the separation of the writings and languages of the children of men at the time of the division, He cast the lot among the *seventy angels, the princes of the nations with whom is the revelation to oversee the city*, even at that time He established the limits of the nations according to the sum of the number of the seventy souls of Israel who went down into Mizraim. When the Most High divided the nations by lot, and distinguished the languages of the children of men, He appointed the bounds of the peoples according to the number of the tribes of the Beni Israel.

[6] For a discussion of this important theme, see Daniel Block, *The Gods of the Nations: Studies in Ancient Near Eastern National Theology*, 2nd ed. (Grand Rapids, MI: Baker, 2000); and G. B. Caird, *New Testament Theology*, ed. L. D. Hurst (Oxford: Clarendon, 1995), 102–3.

on God's behalf, the angels perverted their God-given authority and sought power by attempting to be the source of power and authority (Psalm 82; cf. Deut. 4:19; Judg. 11:24; Dan. 10:13, 20; Acts 17:26). The point should not be missed: as a result of humanity's sin, humanity splintered into various people groups.

Division and fracture would not prevail, though. The Old Testament longs for the day when people groups will live in harmony (Isa. 2:3; 56:3–8; Zech. 2:11; 8:20–23; etc.). Creation, too, is expected to dwell in harmony:

> The wolf and the lamb shall graze together;
> the lion shall eat straw like the ox,
> and dust shall be the serpent's food.
> They shall not hurt or destroy
> in all my holy mountain. (Isa. 65:25)

Now that Christ has come, all of creation has found its end-time unity in him. This doctrine is most apparent in Colossians 1:19–20: "For in him all the fullness of God was pleased to dwell, and *through him to reconcile to himself all things, whether on earth or in heaven*, making peace by the blood of his cross." Unity in Christ extends to the various people groups, social structures, and angels. The household code is therefore intimately bound up with Christ's work and believers' relationship to him. Ephesians 1:10 says that Christ's "unit[ing] all things" was for a kind of household management at the "fullness of the time." Christ, as a "household manager," has come to restore fractured people groups, particularly the relationship between Jews and Gentiles. In addition to restoring people groups in God's cosmic household, Christ has come to repair the fragmented relationships of *all* individuals—husbands and wives, children and their parents, and employers and employees.

Therefore, when Paul addresses Philemon, he exhorts him *on the basis of* Christ's work in unifying people groups and existing social structures. Since Philemon and Onesimus have been unified in Christ, Paul expects them to relate to one another in accordance with this end-time reality. Philemon is not simply any "master" in the Greco-Roman society, but a citizen in Christ's cosmic house. Paul expects Philemon to conduct himself as one who identifies with the people of God in the new age. Note how Paul exhorts Philemon in verses 15–16: "For this perhaps is why he was parted from you for a while, that you might have him back forever, *no longer as a bondservant but more than a bondservant, as a beloved brother*—especially to me, but how much more to you, both in the flesh and in the Lord." Philemon and Onesimus have a complicated past concerning their master-slave relationship, yet their ultimate identity is bound up with the end-time people of God as a new creation.

Overview of Philemon

Letter Opening (Philem. 1–3)

The letter contains all the usual features (opening, thanksgiving, body, closing, etc.). Despite its brevity and somewhat narrow purpose, the epistle is coauthored by Timothy.

This is not the first time that Timothy has coauthored an epistle with Paul (see 2 Cor. 1:1; Phil. 1:1; 1 Thess. 1:1; 2 Thess. 1:1). Unfortunately, we do not know *how* Timothy played a role in the composition of this letter or any other. Perhaps he gave some input during the letter's composition with the secretary[7] or read over the various drafts. Though these details are lost to us, we must keep in mind that Timothy, a close associate of Paul (1 Cor. 4:17), plays some integral role in the contents of the letter.

Verse 1 explains that Philemon is the central target of the letter, while verse 2 adds Apphia, Archippus, and the house church ("the church in your [Philemon's] house"). By expanding his audience, we can probably conclude that Paul intends for his teachings contained within this brief letter—at least the principles contained therein—to apply to the Christians within the region at Colossae. Recall that the epistle to the Colossians was primarily directed toward those house churches in Colossae, yet it was to be circulated to the church at Laodicea: "And when this letter [Colossians] has been read among you, have it also read in the church of the Laodiceans; and see that you also read the letter from Laodicea" (Col. 4:16). Though brief, this verse gives us some insight into how Paul's letters circulated within the early church and Paul's desire for them to do so.[8] The upshot is that Paul's letter to Philemon (as well as his other epistles) contains a wider intended audience, whereby the apostle[9] communicates God's *timeless* truth to the church (cf. v. 8).

Paul calls Philemon a "beloved *fellow worker* [συνεργῷ]" (v. 1). The metaphor of being a "worker" is common in Paul's writings (Rom. 16:3, 9; 2 Cor. 1:24; etc.), and it is difficult to determine if this is a general metaphor of labor or a specific end-time designation. In 1 Corinthians 3–4, Paul argues at length how pastors/elders must minister or "work" in harmony with one another: "He who plants and he who waters are one, and each will receive his wages according to his labor. For we are God's *fellow workers* [συνεργοί]. You are God's field, God's building" (1 Cor. 3:8–9). As several commentators argue, 1 Corinthians 3 is laced with end-time language that depicts pastors as eschatological temple builders and guardians of latter-day revelation.[10] The Old Testament anticipates the day when God will dwell richly with his people (e.g., Isa. 66:1–2) and all the saints will function as priests in his new creational temple (Jer. 31:33–34). Paul exhorts the Corinthian house leaders to take seriously their role as pastors and overseers of God's flock (cf. 1 Pet. 5:1–4). Whether or not Paul has in view this rich Old Testament background in Philemon 1 is difficult to say. Since the church apparently meets in Philemon's home (v. 2), this end-time metaphor may lie in the background. If this Old Testament background applies to Philemon, then he must take his role seriously as a priest serving in God's end-time temple, the church.

[7] It is plausible that Paul penned the entire letter, though, with his own hand (Philem. 19). In either case, Timothy enjoys a significant role in the formation of the letter.

[8] Consider Paul's brief remark in 1 Cor. 1:2: "To the church of God that is in Corinth, to those sanctified in Christ Jesus, called to be saints *together with all those who in every place call upon the name of our Lord Jesus Christ*."

[9] Note two textual variants in v. 1 that follow "Paul," which read ἀπόστολος (D) and ἀπόστολος δέσμιος (629).

[10] See H. H. Drake Williams, *The Wisdom of the Wise: The Presence and Function of Scripture within 1 Cor. 1:18–3:23*, AGJU 49 (Leiden: Brill, 2000), 237–55; G. K. Beale, *The Temple and the Church's Mission: A Biblical Theology of the Dwelling Place of God*, NSBT 17 (Downers Grove, IL: InterVarsity Press, 2004), 246–52.

Thanksgiving (Philem. 4–7)

In typical fashion, Paul progresses from the letter opening to the thanksgiving section. As usual, he tells us *why* he is thankful for Philemon: "I hear of your love and of the faith that you have toward the Lord Jesus and for all the saints" (v. 5). Apparently, Philemon has fully embraced the gospel and is demonstrating his faith by "refresh[ing]" the "hearts of the saints" (v. 7) and having "love" for the "saints" (v. 5). This was probably demonstrated by Philemon's care for the local congregation. We should also keep in mind that the church in Colossae meets in Philemon's house (v. 2; cf. 1 Cor. 16:17–18; 2 Cor. 7:13).

Paul's Request for Onesimus (Philem. 8–21)

Paul appeals to Philemon out of "love" (v. 9). Paul could, because of his apostolic authority, command Philemon to be reconciled with Onesimus and send him back to Rome (v. 8). Instead, he appeals to love. He even gives a personal tidbit: "Paul, an old man and now a prisoner also for Christ Jesus" (v. 9). Paul's appeal as an "old man" imprisoned in Rome may even invoke a tinge of sympathy. When Onesimus arrived in Rome, apparently the two "hit it off." Paul goes on to comment how Onesimus became "my child" (v. 10)—a strong term of endearment, which most likely entails his conversion. Paul even labels Timothy "my child" (1 Cor. 4:17; 1 Tim. 1:2, 18; 2 Tim. 1:2; 2:1). It would have been easy for Paul to claim that Onesimus was only useful to him, but he avoids this. Instead, Paul says that he is now useful to *both* Philemon and him (v. 11).

Paul sends him, his "very heart," back to Philemon, although Paul would rather he stay in Rome (v. 12). But before Paul makes any decisions involving Onesimus, he needs Philemon's blessing. The apostle desires that Philemon act on his own accord: "I preferred to do nothing without your consent in order that your goodness might not be by compulsion but of your own accord" (v. 14). Paul explains that perhaps the reason why God intended Onesimus to flee from his master was to give him the opportunity to meet Paul and embrace the gospel (v. 15). So now, although still a slave, Onesimus is a brother in Christ. It simply will not do to continue to treat Onesimus only as a slave: "no longer as a bondservant but more than a bondservant, as a beloved brother—especially to me, but how much more to you, both in the flesh and in the Lord" (v. 16). Murray Harris gets at the heart of the matter: "Here is Paul, a highly educated Roman citizen, pleading the cause of a runaway slave whose life was potentially forfeit because of his flight and theft. This indicates that Paul believed that the same brotherly love that would be shown to a free person should be expressed to a slave."[11] Philemon is a participant in God's end-time community, and he must treat Onesimus accordingly.

Building on his previous argument, Paul now pleads that Philemon would welcome Onesimus as he would Paul himself (v. 17). Verse 18 may give us a little insight into what was causing the rift between Philemon and Onesimus: "If he has wronged you

---

[11] Harris, *Slave of Christ*, 58.

at all, or owes you anything, charge that to my account." It seems as though there is some sort of financial loss or mismanagement of funds by Onesimus. Paul therefore promises to pick up the tab and "repay it" (v. 19). Notice here the reference to Paul taking over where the secretary leaves off: "I, Paul, write this with my own hand" (v. 19; cf. 1 Cor. 16:21; Gal. 6:11; Col. 4:18; 2 Thess. 3:17). It is not clear what Paul means when he claims that Philemon owes Paul his "very self" (v. 19 NIV). Perhaps Paul's ministry directly or indirectly led to Philemon's conversion.

Paul then comments, "Yes, brother, I want some benefit from you in the Lord. Refresh my heart in Christ. Confident of your obedience, I write to you, knowing that you will do even more than I say" (vv. 20–21). If we read between the lines, it seems as though Paul wants Philemon not only to be reconciled with Onesimus but also to send Onesimus back to Rome for Paul's benefit (see v. 14). Paul asks that Philemon "refresh" his heart in the same way that he "refreshed" the hearts of the "saints" in verse 7.

Letter Closing (Philem. 22–25)

Paul's first Roman imprisonment affords him a considerable amount of flexibility.[12] In Acts 28:16–31 he was imprisoned under house arrest where he conducted a substantial amount of ministry. There he ministered to a number of people and published several letters. The last two verses of Acts explain, "He lived there two whole years at his own expense, and welcomed all who came to him, proclaiming the kingdom of God and teaching about the Lord Jesus Christ with all boldness and without hindrance" (Acts 28:30–31).

In the letter closing, Paul asks that Philemon "prepare a guest room," since he is planning on visiting Colossae once he is released from Rome (v. 22). Inasmuch as Paul is held wrongfully under house arrest, he expects that justice will prevail and he will be released.

Epaphras, the individual who started the church Paul addresses in Colossians (Col. 1:7), sends his greetings to Philemon and his house church. Recall that Paul and his coworkers probably learned about the Colossian heresy from Epaphras (Col. 1:4). Epaphras's devotion to Paul's ministry is unwavering, as he will stay with Paul in Rome. But not only is Epaphras dedicated to Paul; he remains steadfastly committed to the Colossian congregation:

> Epaphras, who is one of you, a servant of Christ Jesus, greets you [the Colossians], always struggling on your behalf in his prayers, that you may stand mature and fully assured in all the will of God. For I bear him witness that he has worked hard for you and for those in Laodicea and in Hierapolis. (Col. 4:12–13)

Two other important figures send their greetings: Mark and Luke. This is not the only time Paul has mentioned his close association with them (see Col. 4:10, 14;

[12] On the nature of Paul's Roman imprisonment, see Brian Rapske, *The Book of Acts and Paul in Roman Custody*, vol. 3 of *The Book of Acts in Its First-Century Setting* (Grand Rapids, MI: Eerdmans, 2004).

2 Tim. 4:11). If we date this epistle to the early 60s, then this same Mark's Gospel has already been or will soon be published.

We first meet Mark at the beginning of Paul's "first missionary journey." After ministering to the Jerusalem church, Paul, Barnabas, and Titus bring Mark (also known as "John Mark") with them back to Antioch (Acts 12:25). Acts 13:2–3 says: "While they were worshiping the Lord and fasting [at Antioch], the Holy Spirit said, 'Set apart for me Barnabas and Saul for the work to which I have called them.' Then after fasting and praying they laid their hands on them and sent them off." In Cyprus, Paul, Barnabas, and John Mark have a fruitful ministry and appear to have converted the proconsul Sergius Paulus (13:4–12). Paul and Barnabas venture north, evangelizing the southern portion of Galatia (Acts 13:14–14:23). Upon arriving in Perga, John Mark, for an unknown reason, abandons his comrades and heads for Jerusalem.

Later on, however, Mark reconciles with Paul. The book of Acts never mentions this reconciliation between the two, but it can be inferred from Paul's letters (Col. 4:10; Philem. 24; 2 Tim. 4:11). Not only does Mark become a traveling companion of Paul, but he also befriends the apostle Peter (1 Pet. 5:13). The point is that Mark and Paul have not always gotten along, but in the end, they work through their issues and become key players in the expansion of the early church. This principle of reconciliation that Paul and Mark demonstrate must be brought to bear on the strained relationship between Philemon and Onesimus.

As mentioned earlier in this volume, Mark is not the only person in Rome to write a Gospel on the life of Jesus. Luke, too, is with Paul and his coworkers. Paul describes Luke only as "the beloved physician" (Col. 4:14). When Paul is once again imprisoned in Rome, Luke stays by Paul's side: "Luke alone is with me" (2 Tim. 4:11). Paul is, therefore, not clueless about Jesus's life and ministry. He knows much about Jesus's life and ministry through Mark, Luke, James (Jesus's half brother), and Peter (Gal. 1:18–19). Taken together, Mark, Luke, and Paul will write a considerable amount of the literature in the New Testament. Their theology is the result of years of ministry, personal interaction, and hardship.

A person named Demas is also mentioned, but nothing more is said. Paul will, however, make reference to him at the end of his career when he's once again imprisoned: "For Demas, in love with this present world, has deserted me and gone to Thessalonica. Crescens has gone to Galatia, Titus to Dalmatia" (2 Tim. 4:10). If this is the same individual, then Demas, though at one time committed to the gospel, abandons the faith.

Select Bibliography

Alexander, T. Desmond, and Brian S. Rosner, eds. *New Dictionary of Biblical Theology: Exploring the Unity and Diversity of Scripture*. Downers Grove, IL: InterVarsity Press, 2000.

Beale, G. K. *A New Testament Biblical Theology: The Unfolding of the Old Testament in the New*. Grand Rapids, MI: Baker Academic, 2011.

———. *The Temple and the Church's Mission: A Biblical Theology of the Dwelling Place of God*. NSBT 17. Downers Grove, IL: InterVarsity Press, 2004.

Block, Daniel. *The Gods of the Nations: Studies in Ancient Near Eastern National Theology*. 2nd ed. Grand Rapids, MI: Baker, 2000.

Bruce, F. F. *The Epistles to the Colossians, to Philemon, and to the Ephesians*. NICNT. Grand Rapids, MI: Eerdmans, 1984.

Caird, G. B. *New Testament Theology*. Edited by L. D. Hurst. Oxford: Clarendon, 1995.

Carson, D. A., and Douglas J. Moo. *An Introduction to the New Testament*. 2nd ed. Grand Rapids, MI: Zondervan, 2005.

Garland, David E. *Colossians, Philemon*. NIVAC. Grand Rapids, MI: Zondervan, 1998.

Gray, Patrick. *Opening Paul's Letters: A Reader's Guide to Genre and Interpretation*. Grand Rapids, MI: Baker Academic, 2012.

Harris, Murray J. *Colossians and Philemon*. EGGNT. Nashville: B&H, 2010.

———. *Slave of Christ: A New Testament Metaphor for Total Devotion to Christ*. NSBT 8. Downers Grove, IL: InterVarsity Press, 1999.

Keener, Craig S. *The IVP Bible Background Commentary: New Testament*. 2nd ed. Downers Grove, IL: InterVarsity Press, 2014.

Longenecker, Bruce W., and Todd D. Still. *Thinking Through Paul: A Survey of His Life, Letters, and Theology*. Grand Rapids, MI: Zondervan, 2014.

Moo, Douglas J. *The Letters to the Colossians and to Philemon*. PNTC. Grand Rapids, MI: Eerdmans, 2008.

O'Brien, Peter T. *Colossians–Philemon*. WBC 44. Nashville: Thomas Nelson, 1982.

Pao, David W. *Colossians and Philemon*. ZECNT. Grand Rapids, MI: Zondervan, 2012.

Rapske, Brian. *The Book of Acts and Paul in Roman Custody*. Vol. 3 of *The Book of Acts in Its First-Century Setting*. Grand Rapids, MI: Eerdmans, 2004.

Williams, H. H. Drake. *The Wisdom of the Wise: The Presence and Function of Scripture within 1 Cor. 1:18–3:23*. AGJU 49. Leiden: Brill, 2000.

Wright, N. T. *Colossians and Philemon*. TNTC. Downers Grove, IL: InterVarsity Press, 1986.

19

Hebrews

Simon J. Kistemaker

Introduction

In the Gospels, Jesus is described as a Prophet and as a King but not as a Priest. For example, the crowds surrounding Jesus at his triumphal entrance into the city of Jerusalem said, "This is the prophet Jesus, from Nazareth of Galilee" (Matt. 21:11).[1] The magi asked Herod the Great, "Where is he who has been born king of the Jews?" (Matt. 2:2). But, except for the author of Hebrews, no writer of the New Testament speaks directly to the priesthood of Jesus.[2]

It was indeed too dangerous to even hint at his priesthood. When Paul returned to Jerusalem from his third missionary journey, the elders told him about the dangers he was facing from the Jews because of his failure to teach the Gentiles the laws and customs of Moses (Acts 21:21). Peter and John do not write anything about Jesus's priesthood either. In all of the New Testament, only the writer of the epistle to the Hebrews focuses on the priesthood of Christ. It is safe to say that without this doctrine, the canon would be incomplete.

After the temple was destroyed in AD 70 and the priesthood came to an end, it was relatively safe to teach the doctrine of Christ's priesthood in a place away from Israel. This could be safely done as long as it was based on the Old Testament:

> You are a priest forever
> after the order of Melchizedek. (Ps. 110:4)

The author was well versed in the Greek version of the Old Testament, the so-called Septuagint. To teach the people the doctrine of Christ's priesthood, he chose the

---

[1] See also Mark 6:15; Luke 7:16; 9:8, 19; 24:19; John 4:19; 6:14; 7:40; 9:17.

[2] Of course, when the Gospels portray Jesus as the perfect sacrifice on the cross, they are implicitly describing his priestly role, although they do not explicitly refer to it as such. Paul's reference to Christ as the "one mediator between God and men" (1 Tim. 2:5) could also be construed as an implicit reference to his priestly role.

Psalms because they were sung in the local synagogues. In the absence of readily available books, the worshipers had memorized the Psalms. Thus in the first chapter of Hebrews selections from the Psalter abound: Psalms 2:7; 8:6; 45:6–7; 102:25–27; 104:4. In succeeding chapters the author cites Psalms 8 and 95, after which he introduces Psalm 110:4 (quoted above) in Hebrews 5:6. Nowhere else in the New Testament is Psalm 110:4 ever discussed, perhaps because none of the apostles felt free to discuss the priesthood of Christ. Not even John mentions this subject as he composed the Fourth Gospel, three epistles, and Revelation at an advanced age. Only the writer of Hebrews, in every chapter from the beginning to the end of his epistle, speaks about Christ's priesthood. Here are the passages:

- "After making purification for sins" (1:3)
- "that he might become a merciful and faithful high priest in the service of God" (2:17)
- "consider Jesus, the apostle and high priest of our confession" (3:1)
- "Since then we have a great high priest . . . Jesus, the Son of God" (4:14)
- "So also Christ did not exalt himself to be made a high priest" (5:5)
- "[he was] designated by God a high priest" (5:10)
- "[he has] become a high priest forever after the order of Melchizedek" (6:20)
- "resembling the Son of God he continues a priest forever" (7:3)
- "we have such a high priest, one who is seated at the right hand of the throne of the Majesty" (8:1)
- "Christ appeared as a high priest of the good things that have come" (9:11)
- "since we have a great priest over the house of God" (10:21)
- "By faith he kept the Passover and sprinkled the blood" (11:28)
- "to Jesus, the mediator of a new covenant, and to the sprinkled blood" (12:24)
- "So Jesus also suffered . . . to sanctify the people through his own blood" (13:12)

Indeed Jesus fulfilled the obligations of both the Aaronic and the Melchizedekian priesthoods, as the writer indicates in all thirteen chapters. The epistle consists of two segments: 1:1–10:18 and 10:19–13:25. The writer's approach is to present instruction interspersed with exhortation throughout his epistle. By contrast, Paul in many of his epistles first sets forth doctrine and then in a practical segment writes exhortations. See, for example, the structure of Ephesians, where in the first four chapters Paul discusses the doctrine of Christ and the church, then in the concluding two chapters he applies this teaching to the readers with exhortations to Christian living. Not so in the epistle to the Hebrews, whose writer combines teaching and application in the same paragraph. And this he does with reference to the priesthood of Christ applied to the readers from beginning to end.

Background Issues

Occasion

After the destruction of Jerusalem in AD 70, the Jews lost not only the capital city but also the temple. In the course of time, no Jew was allowed to return to the city.

By comparison, when the priesthood had come to an end at the time of the exile, the Jews returned to Jerusalem under the leadership of Ezra and Nehemiah. Then the priesthood was restored and the temple rebuilt. But after the fall of Jerusalem and the dispersion of the Jewish people in AD 70, the priesthood was never reestablished. The Jews came together along the coast at Joppa, where the leaders declared that they now would be a people of the Book, that is, the Old Testament Scriptures, without the priesthood. In addition, the Jewish people faced the rise of Christianity with its New Testament canon of Gospels and Acts, Epistles and Revelation. They would never accept this literature as a sequel to the Old Testament Scriptures.

As a consequence, the rivalry between them and the Christians became contentious because of Jesus. He was mocked as the King of the Jews (Matt. 27:29); they had allowed him to be regarded as a prophet, but no one would dare to ascribe to him the rank of priesthood, and certainly not that of high priest. For the Jews, this would be not only abominable but, indeed, unspeakable blasphemy. It is therefore not surprising that the writers of the New Testament canon shied away from uttering a word about the priesthood of Jesus. It was difficult, if not nearly impossible, for a writer to state that Jesus was High Priest. But even in the midst of these challenges, the book of Hebrews, appealing to Psalm 110:4, makes the bold declaration that God made Jesus a High Priest forever in the order of Melchizedek (Heb. 5:6, 10; 6:20).

Genre

Is Hebrews an epistle or an exhortation? It could be regarded as a letter in which theology is followed by exhortation in an undulating succession.[3] For instance, after the first chapter, which is theological, the writer in the next chapter exhorts his readers to pay more careful attention to God's teaching in the Decalogue. This is followed by a theological passage on the supremacy of Christ as the Son of Man in a quotation from Psalm 8:4–6. This pattern is evident throughout the epistle and clearly demonstrates the author's intention to both teach and exhort, the one following the other.

Hebrews is definitely an epistle, even though it does not feature the name of an author. But this in itself is not to be regarded as an obstacle to canonicity. John wrote three epistles but did not affix his name to any of them. Similarly the four Gospels as such are anonymous, though the church at large added individual titles at an early stage in the development of the New Testament canon.

Authorship

Hebrews was regarded as having been written by Paul until Augustine cast doubt on Pauline authorship at the beginning of the fifth century. At that time, Jerome also expressed doubts about Pauline authorship, for in his opinion authorship was not important.[4] The epistles of Paul appear in the canon in a descending order by length,

---

[3] George H. Guthrie, *Hebrews*, NIVAC (Grand Rapids, MI: Zondervan, 1998), xxx.

[4] See Peter T. O'Brien, *The Letter to the Hebrews* (Grand Rapids, MI: Eerdmans, 2010), 3. Philip Edgcumbe Hughes, *Commentary on the Epistle to the Hebrews* (Grand Rapids, MI: Eerdmans, 1977), 26, notes that Pauline authorship was forthrightly rejected in the sixteenth century by Erasmus, Luther, and Calvin.

from Romans with sixteen chapters to Philemon with one. Similarly, the other epistles in the New Testament canon are arranged according to length. It is interesting to note that in the Chester Beatty papyrus manuscript 𝔭[46], dating from approximately AD 200, Hebrews was placed after Romans and before 1 Corinthians, even though it is shorter than 1 Corinthians.[5] It was omitted in Codex Claromontanus in 300, but about fifty years later Hilary accepted it as Pauline.[6]

Could Paul have written the epistle to the Hebrews? Although some scholars speak in the affirmative, the objections to Pauline authorship are formidable. In his epistles Paul refers to God as Father some thirty-five times; the writer of Hebrews never does this. Paul writes the combination *Jesus Christ* twenty-four times; but Hebrews, only three times (10:10; 13:8, 21). Paul pens the combination *Christ Jesus* seventy-eight times; the author of Hebrews, never. The phrase *in Christ* is common in Paul's writings but is absent in Hebrews. And last, Paul begins each of his epistles with his name, a greeting, and a prayer of thanks. Often he uses the first-person pronoun *I*, as in "I, Paul." Hebrews is anonymous and lacks an address, greetings, and thanksgiving. The author of Hebrews uses the pronoun *I* sparingly (11:32; 13:19, 22, 23). Paul was converted at the gates of Damascus, probably in AD 32, and began his ministry immediately. The author of Hebrews writes, "[This salvation] was declared at first by the Lord, and it was attested to us by those who heard" (2:3). This indicates that he was not an apostle but heard the gospel from the apostles as a second-generation Christian.

If Paul did not author the epistle to the Hebrews, then who did? In the third century, Tertullian suggested Barnabas—who grew up as a youth among Jewish people living in dispersion, was able to communicate in excellent Greek, and was knowledgeable about the priesthood. But this suggestion has garnered little support. Others have argued that Luke could be the author, but this suggestion too has lacked support throughout the centuries.[7] Luther suggested that Apollos (Acts 18:24–26) was the author of Hebrews, since he knew the Old Testament Scriptures, knew the way of the Lord, and was a learned man fluent in Greek. But Apollos as the author of Hebrews was unheard of prior to Luther.[8]

In the end, there is no certainty about the authorship of the book of Hebrews. We can agree with Origen when he declares, "But who wrote the epistle, in truth God knows."[9] However, this need not be viewed as a problem for the canonical status of the book, given that the author is apparently part of the apostolic circle (Heb. 13:23) and specifically acknowledges that the message of the book was "attested to us by those who heard" the Lord (2:3), a clear reference to the apostles. Thus, Hebrews clearly presents itself as an apostolic book.

[5] F. F. Bruce, *The Canon of Scripture* (Downers Grove, IL: InterVarsity Press, 1988), 130.
[6] Bruce M. Metzger, *The Canon of the New Testament* (New York: Oxford University Press, 1987), 232.
[7] For a recent argument that Luke wrote Hebrews, see David L. Allen, *Lukan Authorship of Hebrews* (Nashville: B&H Academic, 2010).
[8] Authors supporting this view include C. Spicq, *L'Épître aux Hébreux* (Paris: Gabalda, 1952); Harold W. Attridge, *The Epistle to the Hebrews*, Hermeneia (Philadelphia: Fortress, 1989).
[9] Origen, in *Hist. eccl.* 6.25.14 (trans. J. E. L. Oulton, LCL).

Date

We know that Hebrews was quoted by Clement of Rome[10] in AD 96; thus the epistle to the Hebrews was written earlier, probably by a decade or two. The author indicates that he belongs to a post-apostolic generation (Heb. 2:3) because he addresses people whose leaders have passed away (13:7). Many of the people he addresses no longer attend the worship services (10:25) and are weak spiritually (12:12). The epistle seems to indicate that its recipients no longer live in a time of persecution but rather enjoy a period of peace. The author reminds them of earlier days of hardship when they endured hardship and persecution (10:32–34), whereas at the time of writing, severe suffering belongs to the past.

However, the author informs the recipients that Timothy has been released and will soon come to visit them. We learn about young Timothy who, in approximately AD 50, met Paul when the apostle had begun his second missionary journey. It was in Lystra that Paul met Timothy (Acts 16:1). This young man was probably a late teenager, because in later years Paul instructed Timothy not to become distressed when people looked down on him because of his youth (1 Tim. 4:12). Paul made this comment probably in the mid 60s, which means that Timothy could have been released from prison a decade later (Heb. 13:23).

There are indications in Hebrews that the temple in Jerusalem is still standing, because sacrifices are offered by the priests. Note the present tense in 9:6–7: "the priests go regularly into the first section, performing their regular duties, but into the second only the high priest goes." And see 10:11, "And every priest stands daily at his service, offering repeatedly the same sacrifices." In these two verses the present tense points to a time when the temple is still standing. The majority of scholars therefore opt for a date shortly before AD 70. Others, such as Josephus and Clement of Rome at the end of the first century, interpret the present tense as a historical present because in the closing decades of the century both of them describe the temple services as if they are still ongoing. Although most commentators opt for an early date prior to 70, a somewhat later year is not unrealistic and may even be preferred. Undoubtedly, it would be safer for the author to write a letter on the priesthood of Jesus in a place away from Jerusalem and in a time after the demolition of the temple than in a time when it was still standing.

Provenance

The question is whether the author provides any hints as to the place of the writer or recipients. The only direct information comes from Hebrews 13:24, "Those who come from Italy send you greetings." This short sentence can mean either that residents in Italy greet the recipients of the letter living abroad or that émigrés living outside their homeland convey greetings to residents at home. Usually the preposition *from* signifies that someone is away from his or her native soil. Nonetheless, this preposition can also be used to indicate where home is located, as, for example, when John

[10] 1 Clem. 36.

writes in his Gospel that Lazarus was from Bethany (John 11:1). The question is whether the letter to the Hebrews originated in Italy or away from it. The evidence seems to point to Christians who lived abroad and now greet friends and relatives back home in Italy.

Purpose

The New Testament would be incomplete without the doctrine of the high priesthood of Jesus. Although Luke in the book of Acts quotes Stephen's portrayal of Jesus as "the Righteous One" (Acts 7:52), there is no mention of Jesus's priesthood. Even Peter, who in his first epistle refers repeatedly to the sufferings of Christ (1 Pet. 1:11; 2:21; 4:1, 13; 5:1) and calls him the "chief Shepherd" (5:4), desists from applying the concept of priesthood to Jesus. While he describes God's people as "a holy priesthood, [who are] to offer spiritual sacrifices acceptable to God through Jesus Christ" (2:5), he does not portray Jesus as Priest or High Priest. Except for a general reference to those who work in the temple (1 Cor. 9:13), Paul avoids a discussion on the priesthood altogether. John, in the book of Revelation, describes God's people as priests to serve the Father and Christ (Rev. 1:6; 5:10; 20:6).

Structure and Outline

The book of Hebrews is structured around its macro-theme, namely, the superiority of Christ. The author demonstrates how Christ is superior to the great leaders, figures, and institutions of the past. He is superior to the angels (chap. 1), to Moses (chap. 3), to Joshua (chap. 4), to Aaron (chaps. 5–7), and to the old covenant order (chaps. 8–10). Thus, Jesus is the Mediator of a new and better covenant, now that the old is obsolete. The specific outline is as follows:

- I. Jesus's Superiority and His Role as Savior and High Priest (1:1–2:18)
  - A. Introduction (1:1–4)
  - B. Jesus's superiority to angels (1:5–14)
  - C. Jesus: Savior and High Priest (2:1–18)
- II. Jesus's Superiority to Moses (3:1–4:13)
  - A. Moses (3:1–6)
  - B. A warning against unbelief (3:7–19)
  - C. Rest (4:1–13)
- III. Jesus's High Priesthood (4:14–5:10)
  - A. Encouragement for the readers (4:14–16)
  - B. Enablement of the High Priest (5:1–3)
  - C. Fulfillment of the High Priestly office (5:4–10)
- IV. Exhortations (5:11–6:20)
  - A. Do not fall away (5:11–6:12)
  - B. Hold on to God's promise (6:13–20)
- V. Jesus: A High Priest Like Melchizedek (7:1–28)
  - A. Melchizedek, King and Priest (7:1–10)
  - B. Melchizedek's superior priesthood (7:11–19)
  - C. Christ's superior priesthood (7:20–28)

VI. Jesus: High Priest and Sacrifice (8:1–10:18)
   A. The heavenly sanctuary (8:1–2)
   B. Jesus the Mediator (8:3–6)
   C. God's new covenant (8:7–13)
   D. The earthly sanctuary (9:1–10)
   E. Jesus's sacrificial blood (9:11–28)
   F. Jesus's effective sacrifice (10:1–18)
VII. More Exhortations (10:19–39)
   A. An exhortation to persevere (10:19–25)
   B. A warning to pay attention (10:26–31)
   C. A reminder to continue (10:32–39)
VIII. The Heroes of Faith (11:1–40)
   A. A definition of faith (11:1–3)
   B. Three examples of faith: Abel, Enoch, and Noah (11:4–7)
   C. The faith of Abraham (11:8–19)
   D. The faith of Isaac, Jacob, and Joseph (11:20–22)
   E. The faith of Moses (11:23–29)
   F. The faith of Jericho (11:30–31)
   G. Known and unknown heroes of faith (11:32–40)
IX. Admonitions and Exhortations (12:1–13:25)
   A. Divine discipline (12:1–13)
   B. A divine warning (12:14–29)
   C. Communal obligations (13:1–6)
   D. Ecclesiastical duties (13:7–17)
   E. Prayers and benedictions (13:18–21)
   F. Final greetings (13:22–25)

Message and Theology

The size of the epistle to the Hebrews is approximately the same as Paul's first epistle to the Corinthians. But the style of Hebrews and its content are entirely different. The writer focuses his attention on the unique office of the priesthood and, by doing so, fills in this missing part of the New Testament.

Hebrews 1

The beginning of Hebrews 1 features a section of four verses (1:1–4) that is superior in arrangement. The subject in verse 1 is God, who in Old Testament times spoke through the prophets. By implication, in the New Testament Jesus the Son of God is the speaker, as is evident from the wording of verse 2. Verse 3 reveals the Son's identity, ability, task, and honor. That is, Jesus is the radiance of God's glory, an authentic representation of God's being, and an upholder of all things by his powerful word; everything is sustained, preserved, and upheld by God's Son.

Verse 4 describes the Son's superiority over angels in both status and name. This concise segment sets the tone for the rest of the epistle because it stresses the person and work of God's Son. The paragraph consisting of these four verses is brilliant in style, alliteration, grammar, and content. It serves admirably as an introductory section to the rest of the epistle. For example, 1:1 features a series of five Greek words, all beginning with the Greek letter π (*p*), an alliteration that cannot be duplicated in any English translation.

Without a doubt, the center of the first four verses is located in verse 3, where the author describes the Son as the radiance of God's glory, depicts Jesus as the exact representation of God's being, and concludes by ascribing to him the verbal power to sustain all things. In this verse, the writer portrays the Son as Prophet who speaks a powerful word, Priest who provides purification for sins, and King who sits at God's right hand.

To prove his point, the writer calls attention to passages from the Old Testament, many of which are taken from the Psalter, which is familiar to everyone worshiping in the synagogue or church. These selections are indisputably well known because the people at worship have had to memorize them for singing psalms and hymns in their weekly services. Books are expensive and possibly unavailable to the public, except to those asked to read. Therefore, the worshipers have learned the psalms and hymns by heart and are able to recite them verbatim.

The author illustrates the relationship of Father and Son by quoting Psalm 2:7, a line from the Song of Moses (Deut. 32:43 LXX; also Dead Sea Scrolls), and quotations from Psalms 45:6–7; 102:25–27; 104:4; and 110:1.[11] These passages illustrate the close relationship between God the Father and God the Son as expressed in Psalm 45:6 and 7, and especially these words quoting verse 7:

> Therefore God, your God, has anointed you
> . . . beyond your companions. (Heb. 1:9)

This psalm clearly speaks of God the Father and God the Son and thus affirms the deity of Jesus.

The writer concludes the chapter by stating that angels are merely ministering spirits charged with serving God's people who inherit salvation. Obviously angels have no physical bodies, do not marry and multiply, were created to minister and to serve, and were not created in the image of God.[12]

Hebrews 2

After a paragraph in which the author alerts the readers to pay close attention to "the message declared by angels" (Heb. 2:2), which is a reference to God's giving Israel the Decalogue, he indirectly notes that as a writer of this epistle he is not an apostle. This becomes clear when we analyze the following three groupings:

- "salvation . . . was first declared *by the Lord*,"
- "it was attested *to us*"
- "*by those* who heard [him]."

[11] Simon J. Kistemaker, *The Psalm Citations in the Epistle to the Hebrews* (Amsterdam: Van Soest, 1961), 17–29.
[12] Herman Bavinck, *Reformed Dogmatics*, vol. 2, *God and Creation* (Grand Rapids, MI: Baker Academic, 2004), 461–63.

The sequence in these lines clearly shows that neither the readers nor the writer has received the message of salvation directly from the Lord.[13] The words *to us* exclude the possibility of direct apostolic authorship.

The quote from Psalm 8:4–6 is applied to Jesus, who suffered a shameful death to bring his people to glory. By suffering and dying he made his people holy and gathered them as his family. Quotations from Psalm 22:22 and Isaiah 8:17–18 confirm the unity between the Lord Jesus and his people.[14] The quote from the Psalter clearly indicates that Jesus sings with his people when they sing praises to God at worship: "In the midst of the congregation I will sing your praise" (Heb. 2:12).

In this chapter, and those that follow, the author of Hebrews stresses the humanity of Jesus more than any other New Testament writer does.[15] Jesus came to save those who are lost, became like them in every respect (sin excepted), was tempted, suffered, and died. The author compares him to angels (chap. 1) and points out that Jesus suffered death for all his people (chap. 2). He describes him as a merciful and faithful High Priest who made atonement for the sins of his people. Jesus suffered, was tempted for the purpose of helping his people facing temptations, and made propitiation for their sins. The writer implies the sinlessness of Jesus, who was triumphant over death and who offers sustaining care to his people.

Hebrews 3

In chapter 3 the writer begins a new section by contrasting Jesus with Moses. Among Jewish people Moses was revered as the lawgiver because through him God gave the Israelites the Ten Commandments (Exodus 20). In addition, Moses was a faithful servant to God among the people as he repeatedly reproved them when they willfully went astray. Then Moses would plead with God to grant them remission of sins and restoration. Indeed, he led the people of Israel out of Egypt and through the wilderness, but as the author of Hebrews points out, Jesus is far greater than Moses. Note the wording in verses 5 and 6 in respect to names, status, verb tenses, and prepositions:

- "*Moses* was . . . a *servant in* all God's house." (3:5 NIV)
- By contrast "*Christ* . . . is a *son over* God's house." (3:6 NIV)

The Greek word θεράπων, translated as "servant," differs from the term for "slave," δοῦλος, because Moses served as God's honored servant.[16]

In his undulating style of teaching that is followed by a lengthy psalm quotation, the writer continues to exhort the people with an extended quotation from Psalm 95:7–11. He introduces these verses with the words "the Holy Spirit says" (Heb. 3:7). With this citation the Spirit scolds the people because of a hardening of their hearts.

[13] Paul Ellingworth, *The Epistle to the Hebrews: A Commentary on the Greek Text*, NIGTC (Grand Rapids, MI: Eerdmans, 1993), 140.
[14] See George H. Guthrie, *The Structure of Hebrews: A Text-Linguistic Analysis*, NovTSup 73 (Leiden: Brill, 1994), 77–78.
[15] George Eldon Ladd, *A Theology of the New Testament*, ed. Donald A. Hagner, rev. ed. (Grand Rapids, MI: Eerdmans, 1993), 621.
[16] Leon Morris, *Hebrews*, in *Expositor's Bible Commentary*, vol. 12, *Hebrews through Revelation*, ed. Frank E. Gaebelein et al. (Grand Rapids, MI: Zondervan, 1982), 32.

Incidentally, note that in Hebrews 1, God is the speaker in the words from Deuteronomy 32:43; 2 Samuel 7:14; and Psalms 2:7; 45:6–7; 102:25–27. In Hebrews 2, it is Jesus who speaks by quoting Psalm 22:22, but in Hebrews 3, it is the Holy Spirit who speaks in the words of Psalm 95:7–11. In short, the writer of Hebrews teaches the doctrine of God Triune.

God swore an oath and said that the Israelites would never enter his rest. The gravity of the psalm citation is that though a law can be repealed, an oath remains in force forever. These Israelites who failed to listen to God's voice were cut off, hence the writer of Hebrews now pleads with his spiritual brothers and sisters not to be hardened by sin's deceitfulness, but to turn to Christ. The rebellious Israelites who had left Egypt, known to them as the land of slavery, were on their way to Canaan, which was called the Promised Land. But because of disobedience and unbelief, they faced an angry God who swore on oath that they would die in the desert and never enter Canaan (Heb. 3:16–19). The writer of Hebrews uses the verb *enter* a total of seventeen times, eleven of which appear in the sense of entering the rest in chapters 3 and 4. Entering the presence of God is devoid of fear and filled with certainty.[17] The implied spiritual message is that those who in faith hold firm to the end will share in Christ's redemptive rest and be saved.

Hebrews 4

The author continues to develop the theme of rest by discussing a Sabbath rest for God's people (Heb. 4:1–11). Though he has addressed unbelievers in chapter 3, in the next chapter he talks to believers and assures them of their entering that rest. As long as the hearers of the gospel apply its message to their hearts in faith and live by it, they enter God's rest. On the contrary, those people who do not unite the good news with faith come up short and fail to enter the presence of God.[18] On the basis of Psalm 95:11, the author writes that unbelievers are excluded from his sacred presence:

> As I swore in my wrath,
> "They shall not enter my rest." (Heb. 4:3)

In his Word, God sets the example of working six days and resting on the seventh. The writer uses the word σαββατισμός to express Sabbath rest (4:9). This word implies not idleness but rather peace of heart and mind. "It stands for consummation of a work accomplished and the joy and satisfaction attendant upon this. Such was its prototype in God."[19] Indeed this word of Hebrew origin is a reminder of the last day of the week, which connotes happiness in celebrating the Sabbath as a day of rest and gladness. There is a difference between the word "rest" in verse 8 and the expression "Sabbath" in the following verse. The context of rest relates to

[17] Ibid., 35.

[18] B. F. Westcott, *The Epistle to the Hebrews* (Grand Rapids, MI: Eerdmans, 1952), 94. In his commentary O'Brien points out that regarding the translation "*seem* to have failed" (4:1, ESV, NRSV) he prefers the reading "to be found or judged" (ibid., 160).

[19] Geerhardus Vos, *Biblical Theology* (Grand Rapids, MI: Eerdmans, 1954), 156.

Israel taking possession of the Promised Land and enjoying a rest from warfare and prefigured the Sabbath rest of God.[20] It is this peace of God that is embodied in the command to keep the Lord's Day as a day of rest. As Joshua led the Israelites into the Land of Promise, so Jesus leads us into the presence of God to enjoy a Sabbath rest that is everlasting. Fitting are the words of John Newton in the hymn "Safely through Another Week": "Day of all the week the best, emblem of eternal rest."

The writer of Hebrews concludes this passage with a reference to the Word of God, which he describes as living and active. He uses the illustration of a dreadfully sharp double-edged sword with which to divide soul and spirit, joints and marrow, and to judge thoughts and attitudes of the heart. Humanly speaking, we are unable to handle such a sword in a literal sense to bring about these divisions. Yet the Word of God can do so.

In his German translation of the New Testament, Martin Luther begins chapter 5 at 4:14, thereby indicating that the last segment (4:14–16) should be part of the author's discussion in the following chapters on the Aaronic high priest, and subsequently on the priesthood of Christ. Indeed at this point the writer introduces a new topic that constitutes the main part of the epistle and eventually comes to an end at 10:18. He describes Jesus the Son of God as the great High Priest who has gone through the heavens.

In the next segment, we read that because of his sonship, Jesus is great, but being High Priest, he is even greater. As the Son of God, he has gone through the heavens and thus excels because of his divinity. In his status of being both human and divine, Jesus has ascended and is exalted above the heavens. The writer points out that this High Priest is able to sympathize and understands our weaknesses; though he was tempted in every way just as we are, yet he remained without sin. This is the second time the author refers to Jesus's being tempted (cf. 2:18) and now he adds the qualifying phrase—he was without sin. The sinlessness of Jesus is not achieved passively but, rather, is actively demonstrated in complete obedience to the will of God. Thus we are encouraged to boldly approach the throne of God in prayer.[21]

Hebrews 5

As stated in the preceding chapter, Jesus is the one who, while totally human, experienced all our weaknesses and temptations, and yet without sin. He can empathize with us as we experience failures and flaws. This uniquely qualified High Priest differs from the Aaronic high priest, who is prone to fall into sin like his fellow man. The Aaronic high priest entered the very presence of God, first in the tabernacle and later the temple, to offer sacrifices for his own sins and then for the sins of the people (Heb. 5:3). Jesus offered himself to God both in the garden of Gethsemane and on the cross of Calvary. He assumed the position of High Priest because God called him and said,

> You are my Son;
> today I have begotten you. (Ps. 2:7)

[20] William L. Lane, *Hebrews 1–8*, WBC 47A (Dallas: Word Books, 1991), 101.
[21] Hughes, *Epistle to the Hebrews*, 173. Ellingworth, *Epistle to the Hebrews*, 271.

And

> You are a priest forever
> after the order of Melchizedek. (Ps. 110:4)

This is the only passage in the New Testament that combines the two concepts of sonship and high priesthood.[22] That is, Jesus's high priesthood is derived from his sonship, as is evident from these two successive quotations from the Psalter. The quotations first appeared in Hebrews 1:5 and 1:13 and are now repeated. Thus, they portray the two bookends of this entire series of quotations from chapters 1 through 5.[23]

The one and only reference in this epistle to Jesus's earthly life appears in 5:7, where the author speaks of "the days of his flesh." He follows this up with the words "Jesus offered up prayers and supplications, with loud cries and tears." This obviously is a reference to both Gethsemane and Calvary; tears were shed in the garden, and cries were heard from the cross. On the cross, Jesus experienced the so-called second death (Rev. 2:11; 20:6, 14; 21:8), which is an eternal death and constitutes a complete separation from God; hence he cries out, "Why have you forsaken me?" (Matt. 27:46; Mark 15:34).[24] We can only describe the significance of this horrible event but are unable to explain it fully. He endured severance from God the Father so that his followers would never have to experience eternal separation. Jesus removed the curse, fulfilled the penalty against him, and thus transferred his freedom to all the people who obey him (Heb. 5:9).

Hebrews 6

After a summary statement involving elementary teachings about repentance, the resurrection, and eternal judgment, the author writes a segment on the impossibility of bringing back to repentance people who at one time confessed belief in Jesus but then willfully fell away from the faith (Heb. 6:4–6). The writer says that it is impossible for those who have once been enlightened, have tasted the heavenly gift—that is, the goodness of God's Word—and have shared in the Holy Spirit, and then fall away, to be brought back to repentance, "since they are crucifying once again the Son of God to their own harm and holding him up to contempt."[25] In this section, the author lists five participles in the aorist tense (*be enlightened*, *taste*, *share*, *taste*, and *fall away*), followed by two participles (*crucify* and *subject*) in the present tense.

Here is the paradigm of Hebrews 6:4–6:

> It is impossible for those
> who have once been enlightened [past tense],
> who have tasted the heavenly gift [past tense],
> who have shared in the Holy Spirit [past tense],

[22] Geerhardus Vos, *The Teaching of the Epistle to the Hebrews* (Grand Rapids, MI: Eerdmans, 1956), 77.
[23] O'Brien, *Letter to the Hebrews*, 195n45.
[24] Simon J. Kistemaker, *Exposition of the Epistle to the Hebrews*, NTC (Grand Rapids, MI: Baker, 1984), 137.
[25] See Herbert W. Bateman IV, ed., *Four Views on the Warning Passages in Hebrews* (Grand Rapids, MI: Kregel, 2007), 128, 184–85, 273–76.

who have tasted the goodness of the word of God and the powers of the
coming age [past tense],
[who have fallen] away [past tense] . . . to be brought back to repentance,
because to their loss they are crucifying the Son of God all over again[26]
[present tense]
and subjecting him to public disgrace [present tense]. (NIV, reformatted)

The author begins this section with the word "impossible," which states an absolute fact that cannot be changed. It relates, for example, to the inability of Judas Iscariot, who, for betraying Jesus, cannot be saved. Whereas Simon Peter wept and returned to Jesus, who restored him to his apostleship, Judas hanged himself, and Jesus called him "the son of destruction" (John 17:12). Anyone who has come to know Jesus and his ultimate sacrifice on the cross and then purposely repudiates and subjects him to open shame is lost forever. The last two clauses are introduced by the word "because" to reinforce the impossibility stated in Hebrews 6:4. Notice that these two clauses are in the present tense, in contrast to the preceding five clauses, which are in the past tense.

Did not Jesus send out Judas with a fellow disciple on a missionary journey to "heal the sick, raise the dead, cleanse lepers, [and] cast out demons" (Matt. 10:8)? Jesus instructed him to preach the coming of the kingdom of heaven and to perform miracles. Yet this same Judas betrayed his Master and caused his cruel death on Calvary's cross. Judas had tasted the heavenly gift, had shared in the Holy Spirit, and had tasted the goodness of the Word of God and the powers of the coming age, and yet he fell away by betraying Jesus. This does not mean that Judas lost his salvation. It simply demonstrates that an individual can *seem* to be a Christian, and even participate in the blessings of the covenant community, and yet later prove to be an unbeliever.

Although the writer of Hebrews does not say that the recipients of his letter have themselves committed the sin of apostasy, in numerous places he warns against having a hard heart that can lead to a turning away from God (Heb. 3:12–15; 4:1; 6:6). He counsels them not to neglect meeting together but rather to encourage each other (10:25). He wants Christians to live by faith and continue to grow spiritually as they hear and respond to God's Word. Thus, the author repeatedly emphasizes the importance of perseverance (3:6, 14; 4:11). Those who are true followers of Christ, and not followers in name only, will make it to the end.

The next segment (6:7–8), written in the form of a parable, is applicable to the preceding section (6:4–6). It makes a comparison using land as the common denominator. In the first instance, land that regularly receives rain bears crops that hardworking farmers receive as blessings from God. By contrast, the same rain falls also on land that is not tilled but lies idle. As a result this land is filled with thorns and thistles even though there is sufficient moisture. Because there is no one to work the soil, it is of no value, and no one is interested in a worthless piece of property. Eventually the thorns and thistles will be set on fire in a scorched-earth policy. The message of

[26] Translations differ: "crucifying once again" (ESV), "crucify . . . on their own account" (RSV), and "crucify . . . afresh" (KJV).

this segment is that while we must diligently work for the coming of the kingdom and experience God's approval, unbelievers, because of their failure to work, await his curse and condemnation. The reference to the land being burned is an allusion to disciplinary action against those who have failed to work for the coming of the kingdom.[27] The Jewish historian Josephus writes that when the Roman forces surrounded Jerusalem in AD 69–70, General Vespasian told his forces to "set fire, not only to the city itself, but to all the villas and small cities that were around it." The temple hill was ablaze in a mass of flame.[28]

What does this teaching mean for the recipients of the letter to the Hebrews? The writer speaks of better things to come for those who love God and do his will, namely, things that accompany salvation. What are these things? They are the blessings that Christ's followers enjoy, namely, the surety of eternal salvation and, for this life, the daily sharing of love to one's fellow man (6:10). God forgets sin that is forgiven, but deeds of kindness extended by his people to others he remembers.

The author of Hebrews admonishes the readers of his epistle to be fully aware of sin's deceitfulness. It enters deceptively into the human mind and persuades the believer to accept the lie instead of the truth of God. Indeed, "Satan disguises himself as an angel of light," as Paul notes in 2 Corinthians 11:14. Christians must always ask themselves, what does God say in his Word? They must daily walk in the light of God's Word and claim his promises. What are these promises? The writer of Hebrews turns his attention to Abraham, to whom God swore an oath and said, "I will surely multiply your offspring" (Gen. 22:17). Indeed Abraham's descendants are as numerous as the stars in the sky and as the grains of sand on the seashore, being a blessing to many nations. God's promise to Abraham is extended to all people; that is, all those who have been redeemed by Christ Jesus are recipients of his blessings (Gal. 3:29). Because of the oath God has sworn, these blessings never fail. As the writer of Hebrews states, "It is impossible for God to lie" (Heb. 6:18). We realize all this because Jesus has entered the very presence of God for us as High Priest in the order of Melchizedek.

Jesus fulfilled the Aaronic priesthood, but in effect he belonged to another priesthood, namely, that of Melchizedek. Note that the author mentions this name twice in Hebrews 5:6 and 5:10, and once in 6:20. Thus, he sets the stage for a full explanation of this name and concept in the next chapter.

Hebrews 7

The writer of Hebrews explains the significance of Melchizedek by identifying him as king of Salem and priest of God Most High, thus reminding his readers of Genesis 14:18–20. The name in Hebrew means "my king is righteousness," and the word *Salem* is an abbreviated form of the word *Jerusalem*. This king gave Abraham bread and wine, and as priest of God Most High he blessed this patriarch. In return Abra-

[27] Buist M. Fanning, "A Classical Reformed View," in Bateman, *Four Views*, 188–89.

[28] Josephus, *J.W.*, in *The Complete Works of Josephus*, trans. William Whiston (Nashville: Thomas Nelson, 1998), 3.7.1, 6.275.

ham gave Melchizedek a tenth of everything. Of course, the name Melchizedek is mentioned once more in the Old Testament, in Psalm 110:4:

> You are a priest forever
> after the order of Melchizedek.

This king-priest worshiped Abraham's God and described him as God Most High, Creator of heaven and earth (Gen. 14:19). Thus Melchizedek, in worshiping the God of Abraham, was a monotheist.

The Jewish rabbis had neglected a study of the name Melchizedek recorded in the two Old Testament passages; and the name appears nowhere in the New Testament other than in Hebrews (5:6, 10; 6:20; 7:1, 10, 11, 15, 17). It is only the writer of Hebrews who explains the messianic significance of the two Old Testament references to Melchizedek. By doing so, he establishes the significance of Jesus as a Priest not in the Levitical order but in that of Melchizedek, and thus his presentation is irrefutable; the writer proves to be an eminent theologian.

Abraham met Melchizedek at the King's Valley, which was thought to be located near Jerusalem (Gen. 14:17; 2 Sam. 18:18; Ps. 76:2).[29] This priest blessed Abraham in the name of God Most High, whom he praises as Creator of all things. Melchizedek is the first priest mentioned in Scripture and thus transcends Jacob's son Levi. In a sense, we may say that this transcendence marks superiority over Levi's priesthood.

If anything would have upset an Israelite, it would have been statements to the effect that perfection could not have been attained through the Levitical priesthood (Heb. 7:11) and the setting aside of the ancestry regulation because "the law made nothing perfect" (7:19).

Nonetheless, the author of Hebrews convincingly points out the inadequacy of the Levitical priesthood. The priests in the Aaronic line were subject to death, for they served on average twenty-five years; in contrast, Christ Jesus lives forever. The priesthood in the line of Aaron proved to be inadequate, but the one according to Melchizedek represented by Christ is eternal. Table 6 is the paradigm in Hebrews 7:18–19:

a former commandment	a better hope
is set aside	is introduced
because of	through which
its weakness and uselessness	we draw near
(for the law made nothing perfect)	

Table 6

The introductory ruling, namely, the regulation concerning the Levitical priesthood, was temporary, while the priesthood of Melchizedek is permanent. The hope

[29] O'Brien, *Letter to the Hebrews*, 247.

of every believer is anchored in Jesus Christ (Heb. 6:19–20).[30] Consider also the repetitive offerings of animal sacrifices presented to meet the need for daily forgiveness; but this course of action demonstrated their inherent ineffectiveness (see 10:2–4). By contrast, Jesus offered himself once for all to pay for the sins of all his people (7:27). The difference between the inferiority of the Levitical priesthood and the superiority guaranteed by Jesus is indeed striking.[31]

Hebrews 8

Chapter 8, with just thirteen verses, is the shortest in the entire epistle to the Hebrews. The fact that half of it is a quote from Jeremiah 31:31–34 proves the significance of God's covenant with his people. The author of Hebrews expresses the difference between the ministry of the Levitical priesthood and that of Jesus by means of the word *mediator*. He notes that the dissimilarity is unusual because the ministry of Jesus "is enacted on better promises" (Heb. 8:6). Jesus, the sinless one, stands between God and sinful humanity, which an Aaronic high priest could not do because he himself was a sinner.

At this juncture in his instruction, the writer presents the prophecy of Jeremiah 31:31–34 to remind the people of the covenant God had made with the Israelites. God promised the people that he would regard them as his prized possession, that is, as a kingdom of priests and a holy nation (Ex. 19:5–6). But the Jews failed to keep the covenant promises, and thus, through the prophet Jeremiah, God made a new covenant with them. With this covenant he put his laws on their minds and hearts; he told his people to teach all people, from the least of them to the greatest. God promised to forgive their sins and to remember them no more.

God expects his covenant people to worship him. Note that the writer of Hebrews, in both chapters 8 and 9, consistently refers to the tabernacle (Gk. σκηνή; 8:2, 5; 9:2, 3, 6, 8, 11, 21). Yet he refers to the true tabernacle not in the order of Aaron but in that of Melchizedek. He indicates thereby that the priesthood of Jesus is superior to that of Aaron and the sons of Levi. The implication is that the old covenant is obsolete and the new is superior.

The author of Hebrews points out that the people of Israel had not kept the ordinances of the covenant given them at Mount Sinai. The wording of the covenant was not at all outdated or inadequate. It was perfect, but the people had ignored their responsibility to fulfill their part of the covenant so that, from God's perspective, the covenant became faulty; not its wording but the covenant keepers were at fault. It had to be replaced with a new covenant (8:7). Therefore, the writer quotes a lengthy segment from Jeremiah's prophecy, written about six centuries before the birth of Jesus.

The prophet used the word *new*, as in "new covenant," to indicate that God would eventually set aside the old one. Again, it was not that the old one was faulty

[30] Kistemaker, *Hebrews*, 197.
[31] Hughes, *Epistle to the Hebrews*, 267.

or outdated; rather the Jewish people's willful indifference had made the old one obsolete. As an aside, it is interesting to note that for about seven centuries, Jewish rabbis had not paid any attention to God's words in Jeremiah's prophecy (31:31–34):

> Behold, the days are coming, declares the LORD, when I will make a new covenant with the house of Israel and the house of Judah, not like the covenant that I made with their fathers on the day when I took them by the hand to bring them out of the land of Egypt, my covenant that they broke, though I was their husband, declares the LORD. For this is the covenant that I will make with the house of Israel after those days, declares the LORD: I will put my law within them, and I will write it on their hearts. And I will be their God, and they shall be my people. And no longer shall each one teach his neighbor and each his brother, saying, "Know the LORD," for they shall all know me, from the least of them to the greatest, declares the LORD. For I will forgive their iniquity, and I will remember their sin no more.

On the night before his death, Jesus spoke the words "the *new* covenant in my blood" (Luke 22:20) and thus fulfilled Jeremiah's prophecy. The author of Hebrews fully explains this point in chapter 9, where he discusses regulations for worship in an earthly sanctuary.

When the Israelites traveled to Mount Sinai, God gave them the Decalogue (Exodus 20) and then instructed Moses to build the tabernacle (Exodus 25–27). Here we see God's confirmation of the covenant he had made with his people. People at worship are guided by the teachings of the Ten Commandments as they confess their sins and are strengthened in their faith by the preaching of God's Word.

Hebrews 9

In the time of Moses, the tabernacle was divided into two rooms (Heb. 9:2–4). The first room was called the Holy Place, where the lampstand and the table for the consecrated bread were placed. The second room was called the Most Holy Place, which was separated from the first room by a curtain. Here were the altar of incense and the ark, called the covenant, which was gold covered and contained the gold jar of manna, Aaron's staff, and the stone tablets of the covenant.[32]

God made a covenant with his people, and throughout the Old Testament era the blood of animals was shed to cleanse the people from their sins. This covenant symbolized in the shedding of animal blood came to an end when Christ became a human sacrifice on the cross. With his sacrificial death he cleansed his covenant people of their sins. Thus he became the Mediator of the new covenant (9:16–22). Christ's sacrifice on the cross is for all believers, those who lived before his coming to earth and all those afterward. He died once for all his people for all times. He arose from the dead, ascended to heaven where he intercedes for us, and will come again.

Jesus came to earth to be the Mediator of a new covenant, by dying on the cross, and to redeem his people from the burden of sin. At his death, the curtain in the temple

[32] G. K. Beale, *The Temple and the Church's Mission: A Biblical Theology of the Dwelling Place of God* (Downers Grove, IL: InterVarsity Press, 2004), 236.

split from top to bottom and thus revealed the Most Holy Place.[33] He inaugurated a new covenant with them and became their Mediator. Whereas in the old covenant, the sprinkling of animal blood *signified* forgiveness of sin, in the new covenant the shedding of Christ's blood *achieved* remission of sin. Jesus, standing between God and sinful people, removed the condemnation that was due them. In short, his death ratified the new covenant.[34]

The Greek word διαθήκη is translated as either "will" or "testament." Current translations feature "will" because the context of 9:16–17 speaks of the death of a testator. "For where a will is involved, the death of the one who made it must be established. For a will takes effect only at death."[35]

Hebrews 10

The author of Hebrews emphatically states that animal blood can never perfect human beings, for the blood of bulls and goats cannot take away sins (10:4). By contrast, Christ came into this world to remove the consequences of sin. Concerning Christ's coming he writes:

> Sacrifice and offering you have not desired,
> but a body have you prepared for me. (10:5, quoting Ps. 40:6)

The second part of this text in a translation of the Hebrew reads, "But you have given me an open ear." Hermeneutically this is a case where a part of the body, the ear, represents the whole. God opened Christ's ear to make him listen obediently to the divine voice.[36]

Burnt offerings and sin offerings were substitutes with which God was not pleased; they could never atone for the sins of his people. Thus Jesus came to do God's will so that, through his sacrifice on the cross, he sanctifies them once and for all.

Jesus ended the Old Testament dispensation and inaugurated the time of the new covenant in which his people could now find remission of sin in him. The time of the Aaronic priesthood came to an end permanently in AD 70 at the destruction of the Jerusalem temple because Christ's priesthood had replaced it once for all (Heb. 10:10).

The second part of chapter 10 is an exhortation to the followers of Christ to persevere and to remain faithful. The author urges his readers to be faithful in attending the worship services and to do so in view of the Lord's inevitable return (10:25). He highlights this with a warning not to sin deliberately, that is, while fully knowing God's truth. The consequence is that there is no possibility of restoration because "there no longer remains a sacrifice for sins" (10:26). Anyone who, after coming to know the Lord, derides Jesus's sacrifice on the cross faces God's judgment and his

---

[33] Lane, *Hebrews 9–13*, WBC 47B (Dallas: Word Books, 1991), 223; Hughes, *Epistle to the Hebrews*, 322.

[34] Lane, *Hebrews 1–8*, 149. Ellingworth avers that there is no reason to adopt a single meaning for the word διαθήκη because that is not "how language works" (*Epistle to the Hebrews*, 462). There is an extended discussion on this matter in Vos, *Teaching of the Epistle to the Hebrews*, 27.

[35] The following translations have "will": ESV, JB, NAB, NEB, NIV, NRSV, TEV, and TNIV. The NASB has "covenant." See O'Brien, *Letter to the Hebrews*, 329n119.

[36] Isa. 50:5 reads, "The Lord GOD has opened my ear, / and I was not rebellious."

unmitigated anger. This person commits the sin against the Holy Spirit, an offense that can never be revoked (see Matt. 12:32).

The readers of this epistle have gone through hardship, suffering, persecution, and confiscation of property. The writer does not indicate when this took place, but he reminds them that they have "a better possession" (Heb. 10:34). They are not to be discouraged but instead should put their faith in God and thus be saved.

Hebrews 11

Hebrews 11 is known as the faith chapter because the word *faith* appears here a total of twenty-four times. The author's definition of faith consists of two phrases that display perfect balance: "the assurance of things hoped for, the conviction of things not seen."

After the writer gives a definition of faith in the first two verses, he applies it to our understanding of the creation of the universe, which came into being at God's command. God spoke six times in succession (Gen. 1:3, 6, 9, 14, 20, 24). The only way for human beings to understand the origin of the universe is by faith. No human being was present when God created the universe: light, sky, stars, water, earth, vegetation, fish, birds, animals, and man. Therefore the only way for human beings to understand the origin of the universe is to depend on what God has revealed to us in his Word. And thus we accept that information by faith. Faith then is a demonstration of the substance of things that are objects of hope and the evidence of things not seen.[37]

Accordingly, the writer of Hebrews introduces three heroes of faith (Abel, Enoch, and Noah) living in the era prior to the great flood. He does not refer to Adam as a hero of faith. In fact, it is surprising how few times the name Adam is mentioned in all of Scripture (four times in the Old Testament and six in the New). It is noteworthy, therefore, that Abel is the first one in the list of heroes. He is commended for his righteousness. The author says that Abel, though dead, still speaks, which is evident in the New Testament where his name appears four times (Matt. 23:35; Luke 11:51; Heb. 11:4; 12:24). Abel is described twice in succession as one who acted by faith (Heb. 11:4). He was the first human being whose blood was shed and whom God honored throughout Scripture.

Enoch did not die, for God translated him to glory in heaven. He walked and talked with God, and at the age of 365 years he entered the presence of God without having to experience death. That Enoch lived in a godless society is evident from his prophecy recorded in Jude 14–15: "Behold, the Lord comes with ten thousands of his holy ones, to execute judgment on all and to convict all the ungodly of all their deeds of ungodliness that they have committed in such an ungodly way, and of all the harsh things that ungodly sinners have spoken against him." Note especially the repetitive adjective "ungodly" and the noun "ungodliness."

[37] John Calvin, *Commentaries on the Epistle of Paul to the Hebrews*, Calvin's Commentaries (Grand Rapids, MI: Baker, 1999), 262.

The use of the word "impossible" in the clause "without faith it is impossible to please [God]" (Heb. 11:6) is a throwback to Hebrews 6:4, "it is impossible" to restore those who willfully abandon the faith. The word impossible means just that: it cannot be done.

Noah is the next hero of faith. He condemned the sinful world in which he lived while building the ark and thus became, through faith, the heir of righteousness. When the flood swept away all of humanity, only Noah was left and his family (Gen. 7:23). In many places of Scripture, the name of Noah appears as a model of one who had faith in God. The apostle Peter calls him "a herald of righteousness" (2 Pet. 2:5) when only eight people survived the devastating flood (Gen. 8:18; 1 Pet. 3:20). In other words, apart from his immediate family, he alone stood against the rest of humanity.

After these three pre-flood heroes of faith, the author spends considerable space on Abraham's faith (Heb. 11:8–19). In contrast, his descendants Isaac, Jacob, and Joseph receive only one verse each.

Abraham is called "a friend of God" (James 2:23) because even though his faith was tested repeatedly, he steadfastly believed in what God had said. God told him to leave his native land, Ur of the Chaldeans (Gen.11:28), because of the idolatry of the people (Josh. 24:2). Abraham and his family members went via Haran to the land of Canaan, where his name would become great (Gen. 12:1–3). He lived in tents, which is an indication of a temporary residence.[38] He was seventy-five years of age when he left his native land and came to Canaan, but he had to wait in faith for another twenty-five years to receive Isaac as the son of the promise.

When Isaac was a youth, God put Abraham to the test by telling him to offer his son as a sacrifice in the region of Moriah (Gen. 22:2), a place that later became the temple ground in Jerusalem now known as the Dome of the Rock. When Isaac asked his father about the lamb to be offered, Abraham replied that God would supply the lamb. He reasoned, so writes the author of Hebrews, that God could raise the dead (Heb. 11:19). Abraham told his servants to stay with the donkeys while he and Isaac went to the sacrifice: "I and the boy will go over there and come again to you" (Gen. 22:5). Indeed, in a manner of speaking, Abraham received Isaac back from the dead, and God rewarded his faith.

Through Abraham, together with his wife Sarah, numerous descendants were born—as many as the stars in the sky and the sand on the seashore. Nonetheless, when this hero of faith died at the age of 175 (Gen. 25:7–8), he had the one son of the promise, Isaac, and two grandsons, the twins Esau and Jacob, of which only Jacob was a believer. Yet the countless multitudes that have placed their faith in God are able to call Abraham their father. Whereas the faith of Abraham is exemplary, the writer only mentions Isaac, Jacob, and Joseph in passing. Note this interesting sequence: Isaac is Abraham's son of the promise, not Ishmael; Jacob receives the covenant blessing, not Esau, the firstborn; and it is Joseph, also not the firstborn,

[38] Ellingworth, *Epistle to the Hebrews*, 583.

who is characterized as a hero of faith because his words spoken to his brothers predicted the exodus of all the Israelites (Gen. 50:24).[39]

Moses is another hero of faith, whom God protected in a papyrus basket and caused to be raised in Pharaoh's court (Heb. 11:25). Growing up as the adopted son of Pharaoh's daughter, he refused to be known as such and at the age of forty decided to identify with his own people, Pharaoh's Hebrew slaves. The writer of Hebrews portrays Moses as choosing between the treasures of Egypt and disgrace for the sake of Christ, of which Moses chose the latter. It was a choice between falling away from God at Pharaoh's court or throwing in his lot with Pharaoh's slaves who were God's chosen people.[40] Moses wanted to be mistreated alongside the Israelites. Instead of being called the son of Pharaoh's daughter, he became known in later years as the voice of God. As an alternative to enjoying the pleasures of sin, he looked ahead to his reward, namely, the invisible Christ.

Incidentally, the life of Moses is divided into three parts, of equal duration: forty years at Pharaoh's court, forty in the wilderness in Midian, and forty leading the people of Israel to the Promised Land (see Deut. 34:7; Acts 7:23, 30).

Moses led God's people out of Egypt and kept the Passover by sprinkling blood on the doorposts. This ceremony signified that the angel of death bypassed the dwellings of the Israelites but struck the firstborn sons of the Egyptians, including the son of Pharaoh. Moses guided the people, with all their possessions, through the Red Sea (Heb. 11:29). He indeed was a man of faith. So, too, the prostitute Rahab triumphed in faith, even though she had three strikes against her: she was a woman, a prostitute, and a pagan Canaanite. But note that in his epistle, James places her on the same level as Abraham, whom he calls a friend of God (James 2:25).

These heroes of faith were victorious because they "conquered kingdoms, enforced justice, obtained promises, stopped the mouths of lions, quenched the power of fire, escaped the edge of the sword, were made strong out of weakness, became mighty in war, [and] put foreign armies to flight" (Heb. 11:33–34). There are no details of names, times, and places, but God gave them perseverance and strength.

The writer names Gideon, Barak, Samson, Jephthah, David, and Samuel and then speaks more generally of the category of prophets while omitting their names. A host of unnamed heroes of faith suffered torture, flogging, and death by the sword. The author of Hebrews concludes this chapter on faith by bringing both Old Testament and New Testament believers together as one people of God (11:40).

We as believers in Jesus Christ are privileged because, as the author of Hebrews points out, we have a better salvation (6:9), a better hope (7:19), a better covenant (7:22), better promises (8:6), and better and lasting possessions (10:34).[41] We are privileged indeed, and thus we ought to live lives of thankfulness.

---

[39] Ibid., 608; Kistemaker, *Hebrews*, 334; Hughes, *Epistle to the Hebrews*, 491.
[40] Spicq, *L'Épître aux Hébreux*, 2:357.
[41] Kistemaker, *Hebrews*, 360.

Hebrews 12

In the twelfth chapter of Hebrews, the author focuses attention on how Christians ought to live their spiritual lives. They should learn from the heroes of faith mentioned in the preceding chapter; their example offers encouragement to present-day believers. As we saw, for example, Abel still speaks even though he died (11:4).

Yet, ultimately Christians should focus their attention on Jesus. As runners in a race focus on the finish line, so the followers of Jesus must always concentrate on him, the author and perfecter of their faith, and lay aside every sin that entangles them. They should view him as their example, for he endured the cross, scorned its shame, and sat down in the seat of honor next to the Father's throne.

How do we understand the clause "who for the joy that was set before him endured the cross" (12:2)? Where is joy when the one who is crucified endures the most painful suffering imaginable? The wording appears to be a conundrum for which there is no ready answer, because joy and intense suffering just do not go together. But there is an explanation that is helpful: Jesus suffered in order to receive the status of being seated at God's right hand. The path Jesus trod was planned by God for him, and Jesus obeyed his Father because of the outcome of future joy.

The suffering of Jesus is unique; it cannot and need not be repeated by his followers. But God disciplines all those who call him Father. Through discipline he strengthens the faith of Christians and demonstrates his love to them. Human fathers restrain their children physically, but God reproves his people spiritually.[42] This discipline results in a harvest of righteousness because God's children are peacemakers who live at peace with all people as much as possible. The author mentions Esau by name, calling him godless because he hardened his heart even as he sought a blessing from his father (12:17). By despising his birthright, Esau broke his covenant relationship with God.

In a few verses the writer of Hebrews contrasts the difference between Mount Sinai and Mount Zion. God's people stood at Sinai and heard the voice of God giving them the Ten Commandments. They were filled with fear; even Moses was trembling. But Christian believers come to Zion, the heavenly Jerusalem. They are in the presence of untold thousands of angels, with all the saints whose names are recorded in heaven because of Jesus, the Mediator of a new covenant. They are cleansed through the blood of Christ—"blood that speaks a better word than the blood of Abel" (12:24).

The writer exhorts fellow Christians to worship God with reverence and awe. They should do so with thankful hearts, thus expressing their gratitude in worship by walking and talking with God. The last words in this chapter are poignant: "our God is a consuming fire." These words echo Old Testament passages (Ex. 24:17; Deut. 4:24; 9:3) and refer to unmitigated punishment.

[42] F. F. Bruce, *The Epistle to the Hebrews*, rev. ed. (Grand Rapids, MI: Eerdmans, 1990), 344.

Hebrews 13

How then ought we to live? The author of Hebrews concludes his epistle with a number of exhortations in chapter 13. He focuses attention on loving one another, offering hospitality, and visiting prisoners and those who are being mistreated. He stresses the sanctity of marriage because God condemns adultery and immorality. He wants his people not to worship the idol of monetary possessions, because the love of money is a root of all kinds of evil (see 1 Tim. 6:10). He desires them to live wholesome lives in a sexually perverted world.

Hebrews 13:1–4 features exhortations followed by instructions to show love by reaching out to others in the form of hospitality,[43] and to care for those living in poverty or abuse. Marriage should be characterized by honor and purity, and daily lives ought to demonstrate contentment that is free from the love of money. A dialogue between God and his people is instructive and should be exercised daily. God promises to stand next to his people at all times and will never forsake them. His people can fully depend on him to be their helper and protector.

Pastors who faithfully proclaim God's Word from Sunday to Sunday should be regularly remembered in prayer and receive honor and respect; and they should be models worthy of being emulated. The writer of Hebrews urges all Christians to imitate their leaders' faith and way of life. The implication is that ministers of the gospel must consistently set the example of Christian living. Even though pastors come and go, for no one's earthly stay is eternal, the principle remains intact. By contrast, whereas human life is temporal, "Jesus Christ is the same yesterday and today and forever" (13:8). He is changeless, a stay and helper to every believer.

After portraying the high priest in the wilderness, where sacrifices were offered and animal bodies were burned outside the camp, the author turns to Jesus, who suffered outside the city gate. Note the switch from the Israelites' forty years of camp life in the wilderness to the city gate of Jerusalem. The first covenant was ratified at Mount Sinai (Ex. 24:6–8); the second covenant was confirmed in the upper room in Jerusalem at the Last Supper (Luke 22:20). We as the recipients of the letter to the Hebrews are exhorted to go outside the camp; this means that we are to separate ourselves from the "fallen values of a degenerate society."[44]

Thus, in a few words the writer contrasts the old and new courses of religious conduct. The new is characterized by Christians' offering to God a continual sacrifice of praise. The author of Hebrews adds, "Do not neglect to do good and to share what you have, for such sacrifices are pleasing to God" (Heb. 13:16).

To be a pastor is a full-time calling, feeding the members of the congregation Sunday after Sunday, and often during the week at times of weddings and funerals. Pastors are in the employ of the Chief Shepherd, who has called them to be his representatives. They must watch over the spiritual lives of the members of the congregation, for

[43] 1 Clem. 35 instructs Christians to render hospitality to those who need it.
[44] Hughes, *Epistle to the Hebrews*, 580.

they must give an account to their Master. This can be effectively accomplished only when both pastor and church members have dedicated themselves to much prayer.

The benediction at the end of the epistle is classic and frequently heard as the conclusion of a worship service. God is a God of peace, Jesus is the Shepherd of the sheep, and the people are urged to do his will with everything that is good and pleasing to the Lord. He is the one who works out all things that are pleasant in the sight of God. Thus, Jesus Christ receives all the glory throughout all ages and into eternity.

Select Bibliography

Allen, David L. *Lukan Authorship of Hebrews*. New American Commentary Studies in Bible and Theology. Nashville: B&H Academic, 2010.

Attridge, Harold W. *A Commentary on the Epistle to the Hebrews*. Hermeneia. Philadelphia: Fortress, 1989.

Bateman, Herbert. *Early Jewish Hermeneutics and Hebrews 1:5–13: The Impact of Early Jewish Exegesis on the Interpretation of a Significant New Testament Passage*. New York: Lang, 1997.

———, ed. *Four Views on the Warning Passages in Hebrews*. Grand Rapids, MI: Kregel, 2007.

Bauckham, Richard. *A Cloud of Witnesses: The Theology of Hebrews in Its Ancient Contexts*. London: T&T Clark, 2008.

Bavinck, Herman. *Reformed Dogmatics*. Vol. 2, *God and Creation*. Grand Rapids, MI: Baker Academic, 2004.

Beale, G. K. *The Temple and the Church's Mission: A Biblical Theology of the Dwelling Place of God*. Downers Grove, IL: InterVarsity Press, 2004.

Bruce, F. F. *The Canon of Scripture*. Downers Grove, IL: InterVarsity Press, 1988.

———. *The Epistle to the Hebrews*. Rev. ed. Grand Rapids, MI: Eerdmans, 1990.

Calvin, John. *Commentaries on the Epistle of Paul the Apostle to the Hebrews*. Translated by John Owen. Calvin's Commentaries. Grand Rapids, MI: Baker, 1999.

Ellingworth, Paul. *The Epistle to the Hebrews: A Commentary on the Greek Text*. NIGTC. Grand Rapids, MI: Eerdmans, 1993.

Guthrie, Donald. *The Epistle to the Hebrews: An Introduction and Commentary*. TNTC. Grand Rapids, MI: Eerdmans, 2002.

———. *Hebrews: An Introduction and Commentary*. Downers Grove, IL: IVP Academic, 2008.

Guthrie, George H. *Hebrews*. NIVAC. Grand Rapids, MI: Zondervan, 1998.

———. *Hebrews: Running the Race before Us*. Bringing the Bible to Life. Grand Rapids, MI: Zondervan, 2008.

———. *The Structure of Hebrews: A Text-Linguistic Analysis*. NovTSup 73. Grand Rapids, MI: Baker, 1998.

Hughes, Philip Edgcumbe. *Commentary on the Epistle to the Hebrews*. Grand Rapids, MI: Eerdmans, 1977.

Kistemaker, Simon J. *Exposition of Thessalonians, the Pastorals, and Hebrews*. NTC. Grand Rapids, MI: Baker, 1995.

———. *The Psalm Citations in the Epistle to the Hebrews*. Amsterdam: Van Soest, 1961.
Ladd, George Eldon. *A Theology of the New Testament*. Edited by Donald A. Hagner. Rev. ed. Grand Rapids, MI: Eerdmans, 1993.
Lane, William L. *Hebrews 1–8*. WBC 47A. Nashville: Thomas Nelson, 1991.
———. *Hebrews 9–13*. WBC 47B. Waco, TX: Word, 1991.
Lenski, R. C. H. *The Interpretation of the Epistle to the Hebrews and the Epistle of James*. Minneapolis: Augsburg Fortress, 2008.
Metzger, Bruce M. *The Canon of the New Testament: Its Origin, Development, and Significance*. New York: Oxford University Press, 1987.
Morris, Leon. *Hebrews, James*. In *The Expositor's Bible Commentary*. Vol. 12, *Hebrews through Revelation*. Edited by Frank E. Gaebelein et al. Grand Rapids, MI: Zondervan, 1996.
O'Brien, Peter T. *The Letter to the Hebrews*. PNTC. Grand Rapids, MI: Eerdmans, 2010.
Vos, Geerhardus. *Biblical Theology*. Grand Rapids, MI: Eerdmans, 1954.
———. *The Teaching of the Epistle to the Hebrews*. Eugene, OR: Wipf & Stock, 1998.
Westcott, B. F. *The Epistle to the Hebrews*. Grand Rapids, MI: Eerdmans, 1952.

20

James

Bruce A. Lowe

Introduction

James is a logically cohesive letter, written (nevertheless) in a rather "stream of consciousness" kind of way. This means that while its message is discernible, it defies a strict organizational structure, making it somewhat difficult to teach or preach straight through. James's letter has a loose organic feel wherein the author tends (among other things) to repeat himself. It was written early in the history of the church to strengthen troubled Jewish Christians scattered geographically throughout the Mediterranean world.

How is James's audience troubled? They are in danger of being "polluted by the world" (1:27 NIV). What is James's approach to counter this? He presents to them "religion that is pure" (1:27). This involves reminding them of two anchors they already have—God, who is undivided, generous, and trustworthy; and his implanted Word (i.e., his law), which gives undivided moral clarity and assurance to those abiding in it.[1] Having outlined these in the first chapter, the rest of the letter simply explains the stabilizing effect of these two anchors in the face of worldly temptations.

There is something refreshingly straightforward and practical in all this, which accounts for James's being so loved by many Christians throughout history.[2] We also gain a hint here of the richness of James's theology, which complements the rest of the Bible. Sometimes people approach this letter with fear (as we will note), expecting something disturbingly "legalistic" and/or contradictory to Paul. As this chapter will seek to show, there is nothing intrinsically disturbing or contradictory

[1] On divided versus undivided, see Sophie Laws, *A Commentary on the Epistle of James*, BNTC (Peabody, MA: Hendrickson, 1980), 29–32.

[2] Luke Timothy Johnson, *The Letter of James: A New Translation with Introduction and Commentary* (New York: Doubleday, 1995), 130–40. Scot McKnight, *The Letter of James*, NICNT (Grand Rapids, MI: Eerdmans, 2011), 10–11. Illustratively so, see Gerald L. Bray, ed., *James, 1–2 Peter, 1–3 John, Jude*, ACCS 11 (Downers Grove, IL: InterVarsity Press, 2000), 3–63.

here. So to neglect James on this basis would be a travesty. James is a treasure trove for all who will stop long enough to appreciate its very practical gems for life. It is a letter to be cherished, not feared. We therefore neglect this part of God's Word to our greatest loss. Yet, what has delighted many has also disturbed others, as we must now briefly note.

Anyone knowing anything of the history of this letter will have heard Martin Luther's famous complaint that James is "an epistle of straw, compared to these others, for it has nothing of the nature of the Gospel about it."[3] One purpose in this chapter, as just indicated, must be to correct such an impression.[4] Fortunately, such a critique has recently been pushed aside by those moving to fully respect James's message on its own terms. Yet, a new danger arises here, that is, of arguing that James is promoting a different Christianity, with a different gospel than Paul's, one that must supposedly be embraced on equal terms.[5]

A complementary purpose of this chapter, therefore, will be to explore the unique texture of James, by way of addressing queries, both old and new. But more than this, we will see (positively) how James affirms the substance of Paul's gospel while offering unique insights into the workings of the human heart, the place of trials for faith, and the importance of God's wisdom and law in salvation and sanctification. If we believe Jeremiah 31—that the law is written on the hearts of every new covenant believer—and if we accept Paul's complementary discussion of law and Spirit in Romans 8, we will find no contradictory voice in James, but instead a rich and clarifying harmony of what it means to please God and live as a Christian in a fallen world.

Background Issues[6]

Authorship and Date

The author identifies himself as "James . . . a servant" (Ἰάκωβος . . . δοῦλος, James 1:1), but this statement alone does not tell us which James is in view.[7] Most obvious is James the half-brother of Jesus,[8] someone with legendary prominence in the

[3] Martin Luther, *Luther's Works*, vol. 35, *Word and Sacrament, I*, ed. Jaroslav Pelikan and Helmut T. Lehmann (St. Louis, MO: Concordia, 2002), 35:362.

[4] Some reasons for his reaction were clearly pragmatic: "The epistle of James gives us much trouble, for the Papists embrace it alone and leave out all the rest. . . . Accordingly, if they will not admit my interpretations, then I shall make rubble also of it. I almost feel like throwing Jimmy into the stove, as the priest in Kalenberg did" (ibid., 34:317). More recently Martin Dibelius, *James: A Commentary on the Epistle of James*, trans. M. A. Williams, Hermeneia (Philadelphia.: Fortress, 1976), 49–50, has bemoaned what he sees as James's "sub-Christian statements" (49), which he equates with everything Nietzsche hated about Christians.

[5] "James's soteriology is not a 'gospel' by which one can be reborn, but a logos implanted by God in all humanity at creation that finds written expression in the Torah" (Matt A. Jackson-McCabe, *Logos and Law in the Letter of James: The Law of Nature, the Law of Moses, and the Law of Freedom*, NovTSup 100 [Leiden : Brill, 2001], 243). Scholars like Hans Dieter Betz (1985), Helmut Koester (1990), and John S. Kloppenborg (1987a) suggest that in early Christianity there were Christians who did not find the significance of Jesus in (the Pauline proclamation of) his death, burial, and resurrection (1 Cor. 15.3–7). Instead some Christians appear to have found the "turning point of the ages" in Jesus' words and deeds. For these Christians "the sayings of Jesus actually constituted the message of salvation upon which they based their faith," and I think they are correct (W. H. Wachob, *The Voice of Jesus in the Social Rhetoric of James*, SNTSMS 106 [Cambridge: Cambridge University Press, 2000], 39).

[6] For a well-organized discussion of the history of recent research, see Todd C. Penner, "The Epistle of James in Current Research," *CurBS* 7 (1999): 257–308.

[7] Clearly it is not James son of Zebedee who died too early. Calvin was "inclined to the conjecture" of James son of Alphaeus, another of the Twelve (John Calvin, *Commentaries on the Catholic Epistles*, trans. John Owen, Calvin's Commentaries [Grand Rapids, MI: Eerdmans, 1948], 277).

[8] Cf. Gal. 1:19.

early church,[9] who "was remembered as a Christian loyal to the Torah" and a man of prayer.[10] On account of such piety we know him as "the Just."[11] Yet, ironically, some then use this prominence against the idea of his authorship. They propose that this letter must be a pseudonym, written by a later Christian, using James's name for credibility's sake.[12] But apart from integrity issues, would not someone writing under James's name give more, unmistakable clarity concerning his supposed identity in 1:1 if credibility were really the goal here?[13] The issue of Torah is also used against James the Just, on account of the real James having broader opinions. This is hardly convincing.[14] Another argument for a pseudonym relates to whether the son of Joseph, a Palestinian tradesman, could compose a Greek text such as this one. But even Dale Allison, who offers a detailed argument in favor of pseudonymity, does not find such a point compelling.[15] Perhaps the most controlling complaint has been that parallels between James 2:14–26 and Paul must reflect a later response, which then requires a date beyond AD 62.[16] And yet, as Romans 3:8 makes clear, Paul's detractors were already misrepresenting him on issues like the relationship between grace and works, requiring just the kind of clarity James offers.[17]

Several considerations speak directly in favor of this being James the Just: (1) the letter lacks any of the signs normally attributed to pseudonymity; (2) it contains all telltale discussions one might expect in early Christianity and few that would characterize a later text; (3) James shows great evidence of the traditional sayings of Jesus, placing it alongside other early texts of Christianity; (4) even the way James seems to respond to Paul's teaching may indicate an earlier time; and (5) there are a number of incidental details suggesting Palestinian provenance.[18] In terms of language, others have pointed to overlap between the Greek of Acts 15:13–21 (a speech of James) and this letter.[19]

It seems there is no reason to assume a late date or pseudonymity. A safe and credible conclusion is that James the Just, half-brother of Jesus and lover of piety

[9] Besides passages clearly demonstrating his prominence in the Jerusalem church (Acts 15:13; 21:18; Gal. 2:9, 12), we find Paul singling him out as receiving a resurrection appearance prior to the Twelve (1 Cor. 15:7). External to the New Testament, he is prominent enough for Josephus to mention in a passage widely accepted as original (*Ant.* 10.200), and important enough to be adopted by the later Gnostics (Apocryphon of James; First and Second Apocalypse of James).

[10] Laws, *Epistle of James*, 41.

[11] Eusebius, *Hist. eccl.* 23.

[12] D. A. Carson and Douglas J. Moo, *An Introduction to the New Testament*, 2nd ed. (Grand Rapids, MI: Zondervan, 2005), 623, counter that bloodline connection to Jesus was only later a thing of credibility.

[13] An argument noted by James Hardy Ropes, *A Critical and Exegetical Commentary on the Epistle of St. James*, ICC (Edinburgh: T&T Clark, 1916), 48.

[14] Carson and Moo, *Introduction to the New Testament*, 624–25.

[15] D. C. Allison, *James: A Critical and Exegetical Commentary* (London: T&T Clark, 2013), 25. See also J. N. Sevenster, *Do You Know Greek? How Much Greek Could the First Jewish Christians Have Known?* (Leiden: Brill, 1968), 191. P. J. Hartin, *James* (Collegeville, MN: Liturgical, 2003), 24–25, adds that a scribe may have helped, or else that the work may have been compiled by someone more competent in Greek just after James's death. Cf. Peter H. Davids, *The Epistle of James*, NICNT (Grand Rapids, MI: Eerdmans, 1982), 22, who argues for a later redaction. For more general discussion about the use of Greek in Galilee and Jesus's linguistic competence, see S. E. Porter, "Did Jesus Ever Teach in Greek?," *TynBul* 44 (1993): 199–235.

[16] This was the date when James appears to have been martyred (Hartin, *James*, 24), making him an impossible candidate for authoring a letter that such people see as being written after this time.

[17] Jackson-McCabe, *Logos and Law in the Letter of James*, 179n172.

[18] Johnson, *Letter of James*, 118–21. T. C. Penner, *The Epistle of James and Eschatology: Re-Reading an Ancient Christian Letter*, JSNTSup 121 (Sheffield: Sheffield Academic, 1996), 35–74.

[19] Joseph B. Mayor, *The Epistle of St. James* (London: Macmillan, 1910), iii–iv.

and prayer, wrote a letter displaying all these priorities early in Christian history (probably the 40s or 50s).[20]

Occasion and Purpose

Since James is written "to the twelve tribes in the Dispersion" (1:1) we can conclude three things as reasonable: (1) it is likely written to more than one Christian congregation, meaning we might expect more generalized discussion; (2) it is likely penned to Jewish Christians (cf. the twelve tribes), who see themselves as the new Israel; and (3) they are dispersed, meaning they are likely Jewish Christians living outside Palestine, that is, throughout the Mediterranean world. Our above conclusion that this is James the Just leads us to say that he wrote from Palestine.[21]

So why would James write this letter? Clearly early Christian leaders had a keen sense of their responsibility to "shepherd the flock" (1 Pet. 5:2).[22] As mentioned already, Jewish Christians (of all Christians) would also have felt a need for clarity in their newly formed identity, over against where they had come from (and perhaps were still existing) within non-Christian Judaism. In this regard it is interesting to note that James uses both the word "assembly" (or "synagogue," συναγωγή, James 2:2) and "church" (ἐκκλησία, 5:14) in this letter.[23]

Note that what was said above about the two anchors introduced in James 1 (God, who is undivided, generous, and trustworthy; and his implanted Word, the law) also fits with such circumstances. A scattered community would be facing temptations of worldliness (cf. 1:27; 4:4), and would need tangible reminders of God's character and his implanted Word in the midst of shifting situations.

James, then, is best seen as a general text written to strengthen Jewish Christians scattered throughout the world, by reminding them where they stand as a community and as individuals. They are the special people of a trustworthy God, who has implanted a sure Word within them capable of clarifying where they stand with regard to this world. Were they poorer rather than richer? Probably.[24] But beyond this, there is no need to get more specific about occasion and purpose. Indeed, to be more specific sometimes does greater harm than good by making uncertain details control how we then read the text.

Structure and Outline

Genre

In what form of artistic composition (i.e., genre) did James write? It has been common until recent times to think of James as a loose collection of wisdom sayings

[20] For discussion of an older argument (soon to be revived) that James was originally a non-Christian work, see B. A. Lowe, "James 2:1 in the Πιστίς Χριστοῦ Debate: Irrelevant or Indispensable?," in *The Faith of Jesus Christ: Exegetical, Biblical, and Theological Studies*, ed. M. F. Bird and P. M. Sprinkle (Peabody, MA: Hendrickson, 2010), 239–57.

[21] Richard Bauckham, *James: Wisdom of James, Disciple of Jesus the Sage*, New Testament Readings (London: Routledge, 1999), 16; Penner, *Epistle of James and Eschatology*, 261–63. For its placement at a later time, see D. G. Horrell, "Early Jewish Christianity," in *The Early Christian World*, ed. P. F. Esler, vols. 1–2 (London: Routledge, 2002), 136–67.

[22] Note the oft-overlooked detail that both the second and third "missionary journeys" of Paul began as pastoral follow-up (Acts 15:36; 18:23).

[23] Penner, *Epistle of James and Eschatology*, 269–70.

[24] Ibid., 271–72. See, further, "Rich and Poor," under "Message and Theology," below.

(much like Proverbs).[25] But in light of his careful repetition of themes and the neat structure of James 2:1–3:12, this is now widely rejected.[26] At the same time, attempts to make the entire letter one big rhetorical argument are forced.[27] A more obvious starting point, based on 1:1, is to see this as a letter[28] and to use this information to help with structure and argument (see below).[29] The problem is that ancient letters regularly served multiple purposes,[30] and this has led to a further reaching for parallels to discern overlap in form.[31] But as Scot McKnight wisely notes, "James is a one of a kind document. At the literary level, there is no real parallel among ancient letters, essays, and homilies."[32] We do best not to push discussion beyond what the text itself reveals by latching on to one such parallel over against others.[33]

But an additional comment must be made, not so much on literary parallels but in terms of overlapping details between James's material and that found in Matthew—particularly the Sermon on the Mount.[34] What should we make of this? This helps us see that, like Matthew, James was written to Jewish Christians who needed to distinguish themselves from surrounding Judaism, on the one hand, and the constant threat of worldliness, on the other.[35] This, then, allows us to note various prominent *themes*, such as distance from the world, single-mindedness, the law, and expectation of the *eschaton*, all within a goal of righteous living. It also allows us to note comparisons and contrasts with other writings, such as the *Community Rules* of Qumran, which also attempt to distinguish a group of Jews from mainstream practice of the time.[36] Sensible comparison with such texts should not frighten us, but only serves to clarify further the kinds of things noticed in the biblical text itself.[37]

Outline

As with some other New Testament letters, the structure of James is not easily determined. This, though, is the nature of letters, which were always more fluid and

[25] Dibelius, *James*, 1–11. Cf. Bauckham, *James*, 13, 29–35.

[26] D. A. Watson, "James 2 in Light of Greco-Roman Schemes of Argumentation," *NTS* 39 (1993): 94–121; Watson, "The Rhetoric of James 3:1–12 and a Classical Pattern of Argumentation," *NovT* 35 (1993): 48–64.

[27] L. Thurén, "Risky Rhetoric in James?," *NovT* 37 (1995): 262–84. Ben Witherington III, *Letters and Homilies for Jewish Christians: A Socio-Rhetorical Commentary on Hebrews, James and Jude* (Downers Grove, IL: IVP Academic, 2007), 388–93.

[28] The "from A to B" greetings (χαίρειν) structure is highly typical of an ancient letter. See especially F. X. J. Exler, *The Form of the Ancient Greek Letter of the Epistolary Papyri: 3rd C. B.C.–3rd C. A.D.* (Washington, DC: ARES, 1923), 60–64.

[29] F. O. Francis, "The Form and Function of the Opening and Closing Paragraphs of James and I John," *ZNW* 61 (1970): 110–26. S. R. Llewelyn, "The Prescript of James," *NovT* 39 (1997): 385–93, questions whether James is even a letter, arguing that the beginning, 1:1, is not original. But in 1:2 James is clearly basing his entire introductory discussion "count it all joy" on a pun of χαίρειν (the regular joy greeting in an ancient letter). If we remove 1:1 and claim this is not a letter, the way James begins in 1:2f. makes little sense.

[30] Stanley K. Stowers, *Letter Writing in Greco-Roman Antiquity*, LEC 5 (Philadelphia: Westminster Press, 1986).

[31] Johnson, *Letter of James*, 26–88. "Scholars today are obsessed by the 'historical James' and his place in Jewish Christianity, obsessed by Jewish and Roman and Greek parallels, and impressed by those who find the most parallels or parallels no one has noticed before" (McKnight, *Letter of James*, 1).

[32] McKnight, *Letter of James*, 2.

[33] Note Johnson, *Letter of James*, 33–34, and his sensible warning against overemphasizing wisdom.

[34] W. D. Davies, *The Setting of the Sermon on the Mount* (Cambridge: Cambridge University Press, 1966), 401–5; P. J. Hartin, *A Spirituality of Perfection: Faith in Action in the Letter of James* (Collegeville, MN: Liturgical, 1999), 129–47.

[35] "It would seem that like Matthew's Christian community, the community of the Epistle of James operates in close proximity to Judaism, but has also separated itself to the degree that it holds its own judicial assemblies" (Penner, *Epistle of James and Eschatology*, 270).

[36] No better clarity could be gained than simply to read the twenty or so pages of the English translation of *Community Rules* in G. Vermes, *The Complete Dead Sea Scrolls in English* (London: Penguin, 1998), 97–117.

[37] In this sense compare the use of Ben Sira by Bauckham, *James*, 74–93, with Seth Schwartz, *Were the Jews a Mediterranean Society? Reciprocity and Solidarity in Ancient Judaism* (Princeton, NJ: Princeton University Press, 2010), 45–79.

personal than formalized speeches.[38] Yet it is this very letter character that is used by F. O. Francis to produce the following outline:[39]

Introduction of Themes in Standard Twofold Opening (1:1–25)
Epistolary Prescript (1:1)
- A Testing/steadfastness (1:2–4)
- B Wisdom/words/reproach (prayer) (1:5–8)
- C Rich/poor and doers (1:9–11)
- A^i Testing/steadfastness (1:12–18)
- B^i Wisdom/words/reproaching (1:19–21)
- C^i Rich/poor and doer (1:22–25)

Linking Passage Summarizing and Previewing Body of Letter (1:26–27)
Main Exposition (2:1–5:6)
- A^ii (Underlying concern of testing)
- B^ii Main exposition: faith and actions vis-à-vis rich and poor (2:1–26)
- C^ii Main exposition: anger over wisdom/words/position (3:1–5:6)

Closing Remarks in Standard Form (5:7–18)
- A^iii Steadfastness/patience until the second coming (5:7–8)
- B^iii No strife (reproaching) eschatological judgment (5:9)
- A^iv Steadfastness/God's purpose (5:10–11)
- B^iv Words: no swearing (5:12)
- A^v Prayer and suffering (5:13–18)

Conclusion (5:19–20)

Helpful as this scheme is, one wonders if it is unnecessarily complicated. Richard Bauckham, noting how it has "often been observed that 1:2–17 . . . introduces virtually every topic that is expounded at greater length in chapters 2–5,"[40] gives the following rather straightforward alternative:[41]

I. Prescript (1:1)
II. Introduction (1:2–27)
III. Exposition (2–5)

My only added comment is that I believe that what Bauckham calls the introduction is a foundation for what follows in terms of two anchors, as I have briefly noted above: (1) God, who is undivided, generous, and trustworthy; and (2) his implanted Word (i.e. his law), which gives undivided clarity and assurance to those abiding in it. The "Exposition" section thereby simply applies these anchors to real-life issues, like partiality (2:1–26; which itself is a form of duplicity), the tongue (3:1–12), patience in suffering (5:7–12), and so on.

---

[38] M. B. Trapp, ed., *Greek and Latin Letters: An Anthology, with Translation*, Cambridge Greek and Latin Classics (Cambridge: Cambridge University Press, 2003), 180–93, as illustrated by the letters Trapp includes throughout.
[39] Francis, "The Form and Function of the Opening and Closing Paragraphs of James and I John," 120–21, here expressed in the simplified form; cf. Witherington, *Letters and Homilies for Jewish Christians*, 405.
[40] Bauckham, *James*, 71.
[41] Ibid., 63.

Message and Theology

While it has sometimes been suggested that James has no theology—that he was simply a creative compiler of proverbs for general consumption[42]—nothing could be further from the truth. What we find, rather, is James providing a rich array of dogmatic and practical theology. Though it cannot all be covered in this short space, in what follows I hope at least to sketch some of the major themes and to view them in the context of both their own world and the sphere of the rest of the New Testament—all for the sake of seeing instruction for today.[43]

God

As we begin, it is worth noting what the world of James's day taught about God/the gods, so that James's arguments might make sense to us at a later time and place. But more than this, it will help us see similarities with thinking in our own day and apply the text to ourselves.

The general attitude to God/the gods in the Mediterranean world was that they were there for everyone. There was normally no belonging to a particular god, which is why the Roman senate met in different pagan temples on a rotating basis.[44] When people began their letters, they would therefore commonly wish/pray joy and health upon the recipient as if God/the gods were at humans' beck and call.[45] James's letter starts differently. Having wished "joy" (χαίρειν, 1:2), he then does two subversive things in light of normal letter-writing practice: (1) rather than praying for good health and circumstances,[46] he argues that pleasant circumstances may not be God's will (1:2); and (2) he then takes aim at the presumptuous attitude to prayer reflected in how letters normally begin. "Despite God's *giving* nature . . . his granting of requests is not automatic," James would say; there must be *serious* prayer if one is to receive anything from God, and the prayer must be with faith, not doubting (1:5–8).[47] Here is an immediate challenge to us as readers today. Sometimes we don't give a second thought to the ongoing role of faith in the Christian's life. Do we actually believe what we are praying for? Are we prepared to trust God in situations we don't understand? Are we prepared to come to him seriously and seek him out? These are among the many challenges we find as we start reading the letter of James and notice some of its culturally subversive ideas.

[42] Rudolf Bultmann, *Theology of the New Testament*, trans. K. Grobel, 2 vols. (London: SCM, 1955), contains no discussion of James.

[43] Commentators cover a diverse number of topics under themes and theology. McKnight, *Letter of James*, 39–47, lists only two (God and ethics—though the latter with sub-headings). Pheme Perkins, *First and Second Peter, James, and Jude*, Interpretation (Louisville: John Knox, 1995), 88–92, lists three (God, rich and poor, and prayer), as does Ralph P. Martin, *James*, WBC 48 (Waco, TX: Word, 1988), lxxvii–lxxxvi (perfection, wisdom, and the piety of the poor). G. M. Stulac, *James*, IVPNTC (Downers Grove, IL: InterVarsity Press, 1993), 17–23, has four (christology, the law, faith and deeds, and spiritual growth). Laws, *Epistle of James*, 26–32, discusses five (rich and poor, speech, ethics, eschatological reward and punishment, and double-mindedness). Davids, *Epistle of James*, 34–57, has seven (suffering/testing, eschatology, christology, poverty-piety, law/grace/faith, wisdom, and prayer). Douglas J. Moo, *The Letter of James: An Introduction and Commentary*, PNTC (Grand Rapids, MI: Eerdmans, 2000), 27–43, also has seven (God, eschatology, the law, wisdom, poverty and wealth, the Christian life, and faith/works/justification).

[44] R. J. A. Talbert, *The Senate of Imperial Rome* (Princeton, NJ: Princeton University Press, 1984), 113–28.

[45] Exler, *Form of the Ancient Greek Letter*, 102–13. Trapp, *Greek and Latin Letters*, 34–35.

[46] J. A. Motyer, *The Message of James: The Tests of Faith* (Downers Grove, IL: InterVarsity Press, 1985), 33–35, discusses these verses in "health" terms, though without reference to letter theory.

[47] Penner, *Epistle of James and Eschatology*, 200.

James's theology (proper) is rich and robust. God is intimate and desires to be loved (1:12) and clearly he loves back with all that is good—much like a patron or benefactor of that day.[48] In this there are echoes of Jesus's words in Matthew 7:7–10:[49]

> Ask, and it will be given to you; seek, and you will find; knock, and it will be opened to you. For everyone who asks receives, and the one who seeks finds, and to the one who knocks it will be opened. Or which one of you, if his son asks him for bread, will give him a stone? Or if he asks for a fish, will give him a serpent? If you then, who are evil, know how to give good gifts to your children, how much more will your Father who is in heaven give good things to those who ask him!

As with this teaching of Jesus, therefore, James presents to us a gracious and generous God.

But God is also not to be taken for granted as if he were some cosmic Santa Claus. God is someone who must be trusted, even when circumstances do not go our way. There is also a need for humility and right motives (James 4:1–6).[50] So there is much here that needs to be preached and taught among Christians today. Here is not an oppressive picture (as some might call it), but a rich and balanced picture of God as God, which stands in contrast to the false pictures of God that we sometimes form in our minds.[51] Here again we see the richness of James in teaching us afresh what God is like!

Wisdom and Change

Receiving wisdom in James's letter does not precisely equate to receiving the Holy Spirit elsewhere in the New Testament.[52] If it did, this would simplify our interpretation of James. But then we would also lose some of the rich nuancing James adds to New Testament theology. What James has to say about wisdom is in the ballpark of what Paul does with the Holy Spirit in (for example) Romans 6–8. But as we will see, James's discussion of wisdom is more concrete and "action oriented." It is almost as if James is on a mission to make theology as "grass roots" as possible.

In line with the teaching of Proverbs, wisdom in James "is the means by which the godly can both discern and carry out the will of God (e.g. [Prov.] 2:10–19; 3:13–14; 9:1–6)."[53] James does not say what wisdom *is* in 1:5 (i.e., when he encourages us to pray for wisdom); he does outline what wisdom *means* in James 3:13–18, via the contrast between earthly wisdom and true heavenly wisdom:

> Who is wise and understanding among you? By his good conduct let him show his works in the meekness of wisdom. But if you have bitter jealousy and selfish

[48] Z. A. Crook, *Reconceptualising Conversion: Patronage, Loyalty, and Conversion in the Religions of the Ancient Mediterranean*, BZNW 130 (Berlin: de Gruyter, 2004).
[49] D. B. Deppe, "The Sayings of Jesus in the Epistle of James" (PhD diss., Free University of Amsterdam, 1989), 404, notes that this connection is the third most commonly recognized echo from the Gospels in James.
[50] See especially Jackson-McCabe, *Logos and Law in the Letter of James*, 201–6.
[51] More "legalistic" to most people is 1QS 7.
[52] J. A. Kirk, "The Meaning of Wisdom in James: Examination of a Hypothesis," *NTS* 16 (1969): 24–38. Davids, *Epistle of James*, 51–57. For example, parallels with Luke 11 do not work. Cf. W. R. Baker, "Searching for the Holy Spirit in the Epistle of James: Is 'Wisdom' Equivalent?," *TynBul* 59 (2008): 293–315.
[53] Moo, *Letter of James*, 57.

> ambition in your hearts, do not boast and be false to the truth. This is not the wisdom that comes down from above, but is earthly, unspiritual, demonic. For where jealousy and selfish ambition exist, there will be disorder and every vile practice. But the wisdom from above is first pure, then peaceable, gentle, open to reason, full of mercy and good fruits, impartial and sincere. And a harvest of righteousness is sown in peace by those who make peace.

Here we get a great sense of James's intention throughout this letter. True wisdom is not something to be explained or contemplated (like a philosophical idea). It is not something to be pondered or reveled in. True wisdom is something you have and *you know you have* by your actions! It is like "love for God" in 1 John. How do we know if we love God, whom we cannot see? John answers—if you love *your brother*, whom you *can see* (1 John 4:20).[54]

All this is powerful and applicable for today. When we talk about being godly, being holy, being righteous, we may be inclined to turn to passages like Galatians 5 and read about the fruit of the Spirit (Gal. 5:22–23), which comes by *walking in the Spirit* (Gal. 5:16). But what exactly does this mean? What does it mean to walk in the Spirit? How do we *do* this? James (all at once) pushes such discussion in an immensely practical direction by speaking in terms of wisdom:

> If any of you lacks wisdom, let him ask God, who gives generously to all without reproach, and it will be given him. But let him ask in faith, with no doubting, for the one who doubts is like a wave of the sea that is driven and tossed by the wind. For that person must not suppose that he will receive anything from the Lord; he is a double-minded man, unstable in all his ways. (James 1:5–8)

And the answer to how wisdom comes is also immensely practical—by prayer. If you lack wisdom, you need to pray for it. But because our struggle with sin can be so fierce, someone might say, "Yes I've tried asking and I didn't receive!" James challenges such a response too: "Don't doubt!" The Lord does not say when or where or how we will be changed. He only says that we should keep looking to him. This is a section that must be taken to heart. Our negative experience of change must not capsize our belief in God, who gives generously to all who ask—even wisdom to change!

But James's rich discussion of change in the Christian life does not end in 1:8. As we turn to James 1:21–25, we read the following:

> Therefore put away all filthiness and rampant wickedness and receive with meekness the implanted word, which is able to save your souls. But be doers of the word, and not hearers only, deceiving yourselves. For if anyone is a hearer of the word and not a doer, he is like a man who looks intently at his natural face in a mirror. For he looks at himself and goes away and at once forgets what he was like. But the one who looks into the perfect law, the law of liberty, and

[54] Hartin, *Spirituality of Perfection*, goes too far in emphasizing perfection in these opening verses (M. Konradt, "Review," *RBL* 06/2005).

> perseveres, being no hearer who forgets but a doer who acts, he will be blessed in his doing.

Here is a further development. If we lack wisdom, we should ask and believe we have received it (1:5). Now, as part of this belief we must also act upon it. What does it really mean to believe that God has given what we asked for? What these verses suggest is that we must step out, acting upon the wisdom of God that he has implanted within us.[55] There is something refreshingly bold and challenging to be found in this teaching from James.

Paul, Faith, and Works

James 2:14–26 reads like Paul. Here James writes of faith, works, and justification in a style that sounds like a direct interaction with verses like Galatians 2:16 and Romans 3:28. So far so good. We should expect Scripture to reiterate other parts of Scripture. The problem is that everything seems reversed. James 2:14–21 appears to be in conversation with Paul, but it seems to contradict him:

> What good is it, my brothers, if someone says he has faith but does not have works? Can that faith save him? . . . faith by itself, if it does not have works, is dead. . . . Do you want to be shown, you foolish person, that faith apart from works is useless? Was not Abraham our father justified by works when he offered up his son Isaac on the altar? . . . You see that a person is justified by works and not by faith alone. . . . For as the body apart from the spirit is dead, so also faith apart from works is dead.

What must be realized, however, is that James's allusions to Paul are not limited to 2:14–26. They extend throughout James 2, and it is in appreciating this that we gain greater clarity on what is happening in 2:14–26.

James 2:1 has the expression πίστις Χριστοῦ, which is found almost exclusively in Paul (Gal. 2:16 [2x], 20; 3:22; Rom. 3:22, 26; Phil. 3:9). It literally translates "the faith[fulness] of . . . Christ" (KJV), which can mean either "faith *in* Christ" (cf. ESV, NIV, RSV) or "Christ's faith(fulness)."[56] The meaning of this expression has been much discussed, though the details of this debate need not concern us. For our purposes, the point is that when Paul first uses πίστις Χριστοῦ in Galatians (2:16), he is in the middle of debating how Jews should not distinguish themselves from Gentiles (Gal. 2:11–14). James 2:1–7 also confirms that Jewish Christians should not exclude rich Gentile benefactors from their meetings. But they *should* distance themselves from worldly social practices that may accompany such people! Including the Gentiles does not mean including their ideas. James's readers may be inclined to "say to the poor man, 'You stand over there,' or, 'Sit down at my feet'" (2:3), and to "pay attention to the one who wears the fine clothing and say, 'You sit here in a good place'" (2:3). James says no! Certainly we must welcome Gentiles (cf. Galatians), but no,

[55] For more on the "implanted word," see Jackson-McCabe, *Logos and Law in the Letter of James*, 214–15.
[56] R. B. Hays, *The Faith of Jesus Christ: The Narrative Substructure of Galatians 3:1–4:11*, 2nd ed. (Grand Rapids, MI: Eerdmans, 2002).

you must not welcome their worldly social hierarchy! This is not a godly thing to do. Such teaching has obvious and powerful application for today, since there is always danger of worldliness entering into the church—especially when money is at stake.

James 2:8 also echoes an important theme in Paul—that the law is fulfilled in the love commandment: "If you really fulfill the royal law according to the Scripture, 'You shall love your neighbor as yourself,' you are doing well" (James 2:8; cf. Rom. 13:8–10; Gal. 5:14). James again qualifies how Paul might be interpreted on this point, and *yet again it is in the context of partiality*. The fact that love fulfills the law does not mean that the law (in all its details) can be neglected.

> But *if you show partiality*, you are committing sin and are convicted by the law as transgressors. For whoever keeps the whole law but fails in one point has become accountable for all of it. For he who said, "Do not commit adultery," also said, "Do not murder." If you do not commit adultery but do murder, you have become a transgressor of the law. (James 2:9–11)

Next we find James turning to the theme of the graciousness of God. But rather than focusing on *grace* (as Paul loves to do), James speaks of God's mercy within justice: "So speak and so act as those who are to be judged under the law of liberty. For judgment is without mercy to one who has shown no mercy. Mercy triumphs over judgment" (2:12–13). James 2:12–13, like 2:1–7 and 2:8–11, relates to the theme of social distinctions; qualifying Paul (without contradicting him), James sees the danger of his readers absorbing worldly social values to the neglect of the poor and underprivileged. The pattern emerging in James 2 is one of *agreement* with Paul, but also exploring an area where James is afraid Paul's teaching may open doors for worldly thinking. This brings us to an important but often neglected passage in discussions on the relationship between James and Paul.

In Galatians 2:6–10 Paul recounts an incident where he and Barnabas presented their gospel to James and the other leaders in Jerusalem. Wholesale approval came from this meeting. James and the others gave Paul and Barnabas "the right hand of fellowship when they recognized the grace given to [Paul]" (Gal. 2:9 NIV). So, as McKnight helpfully points out, Paul and James have a lot of history when it comes to discussing and agreeing upon the gospel.[57] But in the next verse of Galatians 2 there is a fascinating additional comment. Paul says, "Only, they asked us to remember the poor, the very thing I was eager to do" (Gal. 2:10). James heard Paul's gospel to the Gentiles and agreed with all Paul said. His *only* concern was that the poor not be neglected. Paul assured him that they would not be.

James's concern here serves to clarify what we find in James 2. James is not correcting Paul at any point. There is no indication of hostility between James and Paul in Acts, Galatians, or the letter of James. Yet James also feels the need to emphasize a point he thinks *might* be misinterpreted in Paul's teaching—the danger of worldliness and its impact on care for the poor. Thus we should not conclude that Paul and

[57] McKnight, *Letter of James*, 260–61.

James have fundamentally different beliefs. James is only concerned that care for the poor not be neglected.

So, "before looking at James 2:14–26 in relation to Galatians and Romans, we do well to pay attention to the context leading up to that passage."[58] Noting context helps us move into 2:14–26 and see what James says about faith and works and justification. James is not writing to contradict Paul. Rather we should expect that James is qualifying Paul where he fears worldly social values might lead to a neglect of the poor.

Specifically, James 2:14–26 challenges readers about how they perceive themselves as "trusters," *as opposed to* "doers."[59] The audience was in danger of drinking the worldly Kool-Aid of Greek and Roman culture, which said that certain people were the benefactors of society and the rest had no social obligation toward each other. This showed up in the somewhat "socialist" system of Rome itself, where the emperor provided food for the poor and did not expect anyone else to do anything for them.[60] This picture, James says, is not in line with God's ideals. In God's economy *everyone is a giver*; all are called to help each other as instruments through whom God himself provides.[61] Thus in 2:14–26 James must challenge his readers to understand that they (and we) are all "doers" and that *the great advantage of this is that it proves the genuineness of faith*. Assurance (among other things) is at stake here, even as we find in 1 Peter 1:6–9 and Romans 4:18–25.[62] In this sense James is not contradicting Peter or Paul, but is instead challenging Christians about how we sometimes act worldly (cf. James 4:4–12). This has immense application not only to the justification-faith debate, but also to temptation—as we will now discuss further.

Practically, this section offers a powerful challenge to Christians today. Often works can be seen as the "bad guy," something leading to pharisaism. But works are not bad. Indeed, we do well to hear what Peter has to say about the value of works in creating assurance:

> For this very reason, make every effort to supplement your faith with virtue, and virtue with knowledge, and knowledge with self-control, and self-control with steadfastness, and steadfastness with godliness, and godliness with brotherly affection, and brotherly affection with love. For if these qualities are yours and are increasing, they keep you from being ineffective or unfruitful in the knowledge of our Lord Jesus Christ. For whoever lacks these qualities is so nearsighted that he is blind, having forgotten that he was cleansed from his former sins. (2 Pet. 1:5–9)

Perhaps the struggle of many Christians today, when it comes to assurance of their salvation, is not that they are *too* focused on their works, but that they are

[58] Dan G. McCartney, *James*, BECNT (Grand Rapids, MI: Baker Academic, 2009), 273.

[59] This is what is meant by the otherwise confusing v. 18. Some benefactor will say to us: "You plebs whom James is writing to are the 'trusters' and I (James your leader) am the 'doer.' This is just how society works, some are 'trusters' and others are 'doers.'" But turning to the audience, James responds, "Show me your faith apart from your works (you plebs), and I will show you my faith by my works." All need to be "doers" lest our faith be unclear to others and ourselves.

[60] P. Veyne, *Bread and Circuses: Historical Sociology and Political Pluralism*, trans. B. Pearce (London: Penguin, 1990).

[61] Schwartz, *Were the Jews a Mediterranean Society?*; S. Sorek, *Remembered for Good: A Jewish Benefaction System in Ancient Palestine*, SWBA 2/5 (Sheffield: Sheffield Phoenix, 2010).

[62] Lowe, "Oh Διά! How Is Romans 4:25 to Be Understood?," *JTS* 57 (2006): 149–57.

not focused enough. We must not separate good works from faith, as if works are somehow contradictory to faith or (God forbid!) somehow against the Lord's will for Christians (cf. Titus 2:14). Rather, as we walk in the power of God's implanted Word, we will have confidence and affirmation that we are his. It is true that works cannot save (Gal. 3:10), but it is also true in a general sense that fruit affirms the character of the tree (Matt. 7:16).

Rich and Poor

Bridging from our last point and returning to the all-important beginning of the letter, James 2:5 reads, "Listen, my beloved brothers, has not God chosen those who are poor in the world to be rich in faith and heirs of the kingdom, which he has promised to those who love him?" Thus, James is very positive about the poor from the start.

But we must not miss his qualification, lest we misunderstand that the heirs of the kingdom are "those who love [God]" (2:5), not simply the poor per se. Sometimes liberation theologians have argued that, according to James, God loves poor people more than others. But note that the audience themselves are identified with neither the rich nor the poor in 2:1–13. They appear to be somewhere in the middle as those capable of honoring or dishonoring one or the other.

So what is James's teaching about the poor? Certainly they should *not* be treated as worthy of less honor than the rich. As a generalization (James argues), the rich around them tend to oppose the work of God (2:6–7; 5:1–6), while the poor (because of their need to trust God) are more inclined to faith. Here is the substance of why the poor should not be made less. But what does James actually say beyond equally honoring both rich and poor? He says that the poor should receive the wages they were promised by the rich (5:4); the failure of the rich to deliver in this promise explains why God (implied) is taking away their wealth (5:3), which expands on what James said earlier in 1:10–11.

How should this be applied today? Two balancing ideas are worth noting: (1) There is no call here for a social revolution. The middle-class readers are not called upon to become poor. The rich (while condemned for overindulgence) are not told to become poor. There is no suggestion that poverty is being eliminated (cf. John 12:8) or is somehow intrinsically righteous. And (2) there are hints that what Susan Sorek has labeled the Old Testament system of *hesed* ("loving-kindness") is in mind here. Everyone trusts God to provide and therefore gives and receives what he or she is moved by God to exchange in good conscience, with all trust and thankfulness directed to God (cf. 2 Cor. 9:7).[63] One comment to add is that the *hesed* system was always "in house," and likewise nothing in particular here suggests a general shift in political system. The emperor would give bread and circuses as he pleased,[64] and other patrons and benefactors would do what they did. But Christians were called to act in a way consistent with what Yahweh had said all along.[65]

[63] Sorek, *Remembered for Good*, 187.
[64] Veyne, *Bread and Circuses*.
[65] Schwartz, *Were the Jews a Mediterranean Society?*, 13–20.

This last point begs one further comment in closing. Christians (particularly in capitalist societies) must guard against a kind of worldliness that says: "People do best when having to work their way out of difficulty, without *any* help from others. Dependence is the root of laziness." While there is some truth to this in general (1 Thess. 4:11), it would be wrong to use this as a rationalization for not helping other Christians who are in need. The Bible commands us, "So then, as we have opportunity, let us do good to everyone, and especially to those who are of the household of faith" (Gal. 6:10). It seems that with this word we have both the perfect biblical challenge and the perfect biblical balance.[66]

Selected Bibliography

Bauckham, Richard. *James: Wisdom of James, Disciple of Jesus the Sage*. New Testament Readings. London: Routledge, 1999.

Bray, Gerald L., ed. *James, 1–2 Peter, 1–3 John, Jude*. ACCS 11. Downers Grove, IL: InterVarsity Press, 2000.

Calvin, John. *Commentaries on the Catholic Epistles*. Translated by John Owen. Calvin's Commentaries. Grand Rapids, MI: Eerdmans, 1948.

Davids, Peter H. *The Epistle of James*. NICNT. Grand Rapids, MI: Eerdmans, 1982.

Dibelius, Martin. *James: A Commentary on the Epistle of James*. Translated by M. A. Williams. Hermeneia. Philadelphia: Fortress, 1976.

Hartin, P. J. *James*. Collegeville, MN: Liturgical, 2003.

Jackson-McCabe, Matt A. *Logos and Law in the Letter of James: The Law of Nature, the Law of Moses, and the Law of Freedom*. NovTSup 100. Leiden: Brill, 2001.

Johnson, Luke Timothy. *The Letter of James: A New Translation with Introduction and Commentary*. AB 37A. New York: Doubleday, 1995.

Laws, Sophie. *A Commentary on the Epistle of James*. BNTC. Peabody, MA: Hendrickson, 1980.

Lowe, B. A. "James 2:1 in the Πιστίς Χριστοῦ Debate: Irrelevant or Indispensable?" In *The Faith of Jesus Christ: Exegetical, Biblical, and Theological Studies*, edited by M. F. Bird and P. M. Sprinkle, 239–57. Peabody, MA: Hendrickson, 2010.

———. "Oh Διά! How Is Romans 4:25 to Be Understood?" *JTS* 57 (2006): 149–57.

Luther, Martin. *Works of Martin Luther*. Edited by Jaroslav Pelikan and Helmut T. Lehmann. 55 vols. St. Louis, MO: Concordia; Philadelphia: Fortress, 2002.

Martin, R. P. *James*. WBC 48. Waco, TX: Word, 1988.

Mayor, Joseph B. *The Epistle of St. James*. London: Macmillan, 1910.

McCartney, Dan G. *James*. BECNT. Grand Rapids, MI: Baker Academic, 2009.

McKnight, Scot. *The Letter of James*. NICNT. Grand Rapids, MI: Eerdmans, 2011.

Moo, Douglas J. *The Letter of James: An Introduction and Commentary*. PNTC. Grand Rapids, MI: Eerdmans, 2000.

Motyer, J. A. *The Message of James: The Tests of Faith*. Downers Grove, IL: InterVarsity Press, 1985.

[66] For further practical discussion on this topic, see Stulac, *James*, 96–100.

Penner, Todd C. "The Epistle of James in Current Research." *CurBS* 7 (1999): 257–308.
Perkins, Pheme. *First and Second Peter, James, and Jude*. Interpretation. Louisville: John Knox, 1995.
Ropes, James Hardy. *A Critical and Exegetical Commentary on the Epistle of St. James*. ICC. Edinburgh: T&T Clark, 1916.
Stulac, George M. *James*. IVPNTC. Downers Grove, IL: InterVarsity Press, 1993.
Witherington, Ben, III. *Letters and Homilies for Jewish Christians: A Socio-Rhetorical Commentary on Hebrews, James and Jude*. Downers Grove, IL: IVP Academic, 2007.

21

1 Peter

William B. Barcley

Introduction

Peter wrote his first epistle to encourage Christians to stand firm in the faith in the face of suffering and in light of the glorious inheritance laid up for them. In the first sentence, Peter addresses his readers as "elect exiles," and these words encapsulate the key themes of the entire letter.[1] As "elect," God's people have been chosen by God and so are set apart and distinct from the world. Their mind-set and their behavior are to be different from the world. They belong to God, not to this world.

As "exiles," they live in a place that is not their home, and this leaves them in a vulnerable position, where they are subject to being mistreated by the world. Yet, as exiles who live away from their heavenly home, they are called to live as faithful witnesses for Christ in this world, even as they look forward to the "crown of glory" that awaits them in the world to come (1 Pet. 5:4). As witnesses for Christ, they are to look to Christ, who himself has suffered to redeem his people from this present age and has entered into glory. Christ is thus their Savior and their example.

First Peter is filled not only with encouragement, but also with ethical instruction. Peter exhorts his readers to live faithfully during the time of their exile. This includes a general call to holiness (1:15), submission to authority (2:12–25), proper roles within marriage (3:1–7), true love for one another (1:22; 4:8), abstaining from the passions of the flesh (2:11), and using what they have, including both material and spiritual gifts, for the good of others (4:9–11). This holy living, furthermore, reflects God's character (1:16), honors God (2:13), is a fitting response to Christ's death for sin (2:22ff.), and serves as a witness to the world of the grace of God in

[1] See Victor Paul Furnish, "Elect Sojourners in Christ: An Approach to the Theology of I Peter," *Perkins School of Theology Journal* 28, no. 3 (1975): 1–11.

Jesus Christ (2:12; 3:1–6, 13–17; 4:1–4). Faithful Christian living, especially in the midst of hardship, best adorns the gospel and points others to Jesus Christ.

A striking feature of 1 Peter is Peter's adopting of Old Testament language that was used of Israel and applying it to Christians.[2] The word "inheritance" is used close to two hundred times in the Old Testament, typically to refer to Israel's inheritance in the land. According to Peter, believers have an "inheritance that is imperishable, undefiled, and unfading" (1 Pet. 1:4). In 1:16, Peter cites Leviticus 11:44, quoting God's words to Israel that they are to "be holy, for I am holy," and thus applies these words to the church. Furthermore, the salvation that believers receive was foretold in the prophets (1 Pet. 1:10) and delivered through the Word of God that Isaiah spoke of (1:24–25).

Most striking, however, is the language that Peter uses in 2:9–10, a crucial transition passage in the letter: "But you are a chosen race, a royal priesthood, a holy nation, a people for his own possession" (2:9). This is Old Testament language used of Israel as God's covenant people (Ex. 19:5–6; Deut. 7:6–7). But here it is applied to Christians, most of whom are Gentiles (more on this below). The point here is not that the church replaces Israel as God's people. But neither does it mean that there are two separate entities, the church and national Israel, both of whom are the people of God. Rather, as Paul says in Romans 11:17ff., believing Gentiles are "grafted in" to the root of the historic people of God. True Israel, as Paul says in Romans 9–11, has always been only a true believing remnant within larger national Israel (cf. 9:6, 25–29; 11:1–6). Gentiles who believe now become part of God's "holy nation" (1 Pet. 2:9). Those who were not a people are now God's people (2:10). In spite of their current vulnerable state, they have an identity as those who belong to God and a secure home in God's household.[3]

Background Issues

Authorship

First Peter begins with the words, "Peter, an apostle of Jesus Christ" (1:1). Peter is one of the most prominent figures in the New Testament, mentioned over 150 times. Among the original twelve apostles, Peter stands out. He was part of Jesus's "inner circle" (with James and John), and seemingly the leader among the Twelve. When Matthew lists the apostles, he begins, "The names of the twelve apostles are these: first, Simon, who is called Peter" (Matt. 10:2). The word "first" not only emphasizes that Peter heads the list, but may also point to a position of leadership in the group (cf. Matt. 16:17–18). He clearly emerges as a leader in the early church, as his prominence in the first half of the book of Acts indicates. Paul explicitly refers to Peter as having an "apostolic ministry to the circumcised" (Gal. 2:8), in contrast to Paul's call as an apostle to the Gentiles. Apart from Jesus himself, Peter and Paul have the most prominent ministries in the New Testament.

[2] Ibid. See also D. A. Carson and Douglas J. Moo, *An Introduction to the New Testament*, 2nd ed. (Grand Rapids, MI: Zondervan, 2005), 650–51.

[3] See Carson and Moo, *Introduction to the New Testament*, 650–51.

It makes sense, then, that letters of Peter would survive and make their way into the canon. The church historically has affirmed that 1–2 Peter were written by the apostle Peter himself. Yet relatively recently many scholars have challenged this.[4] The two most important arguments against Petrine authorship are based on a discussion about the date of the letter and the style of the Greek. With regard to the date, the argument essentially is that the persecution described in the letter reflects a worldwide, government-sponsored persecution that fits a later time, after Peter's death, better than persecution going on while Peter was alive. The two most likely options, critics argue, are the persecutions under Domitian in the late first century and under Trajan in the second century. But the description of the persecution in the letter easily fits what Christians would have faced under Roman rule in the early 60s—and before. We will return to this below.

The argument from the style of the Greek is more significant and is typically the deciding factor for most scholars who deny that Peter wrote the letters. The basic argument is this: The Greek of the letters attributed to Peter is of too high a quality to be written by an "uneducated" Galilean fisherman (Acts 4:13). A closely related argument is that the Old Testament quotations in the letters closely follow the Septuagint, the Greek translation of the Hebrew Old Testament, and it is unlikely that Peter would have used the Greek version of the Old Testament.

Historians and New Testament scholars today, however, recognize that Greek was widely used in Palestine, especially for commerce. Peter would have needed to know (and use) Greek in order to operate his fishing business. Furthermore, there is no reason to assume that he was completely uneducated, nor that he could not have attained to a high degree of fluency in the Greek language. It is possible that the eloquent Greek of the letters is due to Peter's amanuensis. But there is no reason to suppose that Peter himself could not have written at such a high level. Many people throughout history with low levels of education have become beautiful writers.

Occasion and Date

As we have already seen, Peter is writing to encourage believers who are facing persecution. But what is the nature of this persecution? Peter refers to the trials and suffering of believers several times throughout the letter. In the opening thanksgiving or blessing section, he addresses his audience as those who "have been grieved by various trials" (1 Pet. 1:6). In 2:18ff., he encourages slaves to do good, even when they suffer unjustly for it. The suffering in this case appears to be beatings by their masters. Similarly, in 3:13ff., Peter promises a blessing for those who suffer for righteousness' sake (3:14) and for doing good (3:17). In this context, the mistreatment is that of being "slandered" and having "your good behavior in Christ" reviled (3:16). In 4:1–5, Peter speaks of unbelievers who are "surprised" when Christians do not

[4] See the comment of Furnish that "very few scholars still defend Petrine authorship in any direct sense" ("Elect Sojourners in Christ," 1n1). For strong arguments in favor of Petrine authorship (though possibly through an amanuensis), see Carson and Moo, *Introduction to the New Testament*, 641–46; Wayne Grudem, *1 Peter*, TNTC (Grand Rapids, MI: Eerdmans, 1988), 21–33; Karen Jobes, *1 Peter*, BECNT (Grand Rapids, MI: Baker Academic, 2005), 5–19; Thomas R. Schreiner, *1, 2 Peter, Jude*, NAC 37 (Nashville: Broadman & Holman, 2003), 21–36.

join in their debauchery and who "malign" them (4:4). Likewise, in 4:14 he encourages believers who are "insulted for the name of Christ." Yet, in this same context he also warns believers, "Do not be surprised at the fiery trial when it comes upon you to test you" (4:12). The imagery of fiery trial could refer to a more severe form of persecution leading to death. But more likely in the context the image of fire is that of a refiner's fire that purifies and that separates the silver from the dross (cf. 4:12, 17).

In light of this, we can draw a few conclusions. First, the suffering and persecution that Peter writes about is without a doubt the suffering that comes because of a commitment to Jesus Christ. Second, there does not appear to be anything about this suffering that makes it any different from what Christians experienced from the time of Christ's ascension. Peter does say that "the same kinds of suffering are being experienced by your brotherhood throughout the world" (1 Pet. 5:9). Yet nothing in the letter points to the kind of organized physical persecution that Christians experienced later during the reigns of Domitian and Trajan. It is the same kind of persecution that Christians in all places and in all times face when they seek to live for Christ and witness for the gospel in a dark and dying world. And Peter wants to encourage the believers to be steadfast.[5]

At the end of the letter, he writes, "She who is at Babylon . . . sends you greetings" (5:13). "Babylon" appears to have been a code name among first-century Christians for Rome (cf. Rev. 14:8; 17:5; 18:2, 10, 21). Reliable church tradition teaches us that Peter was martyred in Rome by Nero around 64–65. Given that Peter would have written 2 Peter (cf. the apparent reference to 1 Peter in 2 Pet. 3:1), a probable date for 1 Peter would be around 62–63. He most likely wrote before Nero's persecution of the Christians in Rome began, though perhaps with signs on the horizon that greater persecution was to come.

Audience

A final introductory matter that has been the subject of debate is the audience that Peter was addressing. Since Paul refers to Peter as having an apostolic ministry to the Jews (Gal. 2:7), many commentators have concluded that Peter was writing to Jewish Christians. This is supported by Peter's reference in 1 Peter 1:1 to "elect exiles of the Dispersion" or, literally, the "Diaspora." The term *diaspora* was commonly used to refer to Jews who lived among the Gentiles outside of Israel. In addition, the places that Peter mentions in 1:1—Pontus, Galatia, Cappadocia, Asia, and Bithynia—all had large Jewish populations. When we add to this Peter's frequent use of the Old Testament, we can make a good case that Peter is addressing Jewish believers.

But a number of other factors support at least a mixed audience, if not almost exclusively Gentile recipients. While Paul saw himself as the apostle to the Gentiles and Peter as the apostle to the Jews, this distinction was not hard and fast. During Paul's missionary journeys, he typically went first to the Jews in the synagogue, and

[5] For a good discussion of the nature of the persecution Peter was addressing in this letter, see Paul J. Achtemeier, *1 Peter*, Hermeneia (Minneapolis: Fortress, 1996), 28–36; and John H. Elliott, *1 Peter: A New Translation with Introduction and Commentary*, AB 37B (New York: Doubleday, 2000), 97–103.

only when rejected there did he turn to the Gentiles. Likewise, Peter was the first to engage in a significant Gentile mission, going to the house of Cornelius (Acts 10). Thus, the designations of apostles to the Jews and to the Gentiles are not hard and fast.

In addition, some statements in 1 Peter point directly to a Gentile audience. In 1:18, Peter speaks of "the futile ways inherited from your forefathers." This could refer to Jewish ancestors who did not believe in Christ. But it most likely points to Gentiles who lived in sin apart from God's revelation. In 2:10, Peter says to his recipients, "Once you were not a people, but now you are God's people," language that elsewhere points to the inclusion of Gentiles in the people of God (cf. Hos. 1:6, 9–10; 2:23; Rom. 9:25–26; 10:19). Finally, in 1 Peter 4:3, Peter says that his readers spent time in the past "doing what the Gentiles [or pagans] want to do," and the list of sins that follow was commonly associated with "Gentile sinners."

Most likely, then, Peter is writing to churches that are primarily Gentile in their makeup, though there may also be Jewish Christians mixed in. The reference to the Diaspora in 1:1 describes Christians living in the world away from their heavenly home. As we have seen, the theme of believers living in this world in light of the hope of glory is vital to the encouragement of this letter.[6]

Structure and Outline

First Peter is a difficult book to outline because certain themes, such as suffering, recur throughout the book (1:6; 2:12, 18–24; 3:8–17, 18; 4:1–5, 12–19; 5:8–10). In addition, as D. A. Carson and Douglas Moo point out,[7] unlike Paul, who often develops a theological point and then applies it, Peter mixes the imperative and indicative together throughout the letter. In fact, with two exceptions (1:3–9 and 2:4–10), every paragraph in the letter begins with a command. These exhortations do not seem to follow an order that gives structure to the whole letter.

Even though there may not be a clear-cut structure for outlining the entire letter, a helpful way to organize it is around the key themes from 1:1: the *elect*, who are *exiles*. From 1:3 to 2:10, Peter highlights that God's people, as his elect ones, are set apart by God and called to be separate from the world. The word "elect"/"chosen" (ἐκλεκτός) forms an *inclusio* in this opening section (1:1 and 2:9) and is found only in this section of the letter (occurring also in 2:4 and 2:6). As Wayne Grudem points out, the word ἐκλεκτός, which occurs twenty-two times in the New Testament, "always refers to persons chosen by God *from* a group of others who are not chosen, and chosen *for* inclusion among God's people, as recipients of great privilege and blessing."[8]

Of course, the language of God's chosen people is taken from the Old Testament, used there with regard to the people of Israel. As we've already seen, in 2:9–10 (at the end of this opening section), Peter emphasizes this connection with the old covenant people of God by applying Old Testament language to the church. And along

[6] On the recipients, see the discussions of Schreiner, *1, 2 Peter, Jude*, 37–41, and Jobes, *1 Peter*, 23–25.
[7] Carson and Moo, *Introduction to the New Testament*, 636.
[8] Grudem, *1 Peter*, 48, emphasis his.

the way, Peter quotes Leviticus 11:44, commanding God's new covenant people to be holy for God himself is holy.

The church, as God's elect, is to be set apart from the world, even set apart from their own past (1 Pet. 1:18), as those who belong to God. They have been rescued from God's wrath to come (the meaning of "salvation" in 1:9), having been ransomed by the blood of Christ (1:18–19). So they are called now to live in accord with their new status—loving one another (1:22), longing for the pure milk of the Word (2:2),[9] and worshiping and serving God as a spiritual house and holy priesthood (2:5, 9).

First Peter 2:9–12 is an important transition section in the letter. Here Peter returns to the two key themes from 1:1, elect (2:9) and exiles (2:11). Beginning in 2:11, he focuses more exclusively on what it means to live as exiles (or sojourners) in this world, away from our true, heavenly home. There is an interesting and important dynamic in 2:9–12. Peter has just used the language of Old Testament Israel to describe the church. Then in verse 12 he describes unbelievers as "Gentiles." Of course, Peter is mostly addressing Gentile Christians. But now they are in a transformed state and have become part of true (believing) Israel.

But there is another important theme that Peter introduces in 2:10 and develops in the following section. After describing the church using the Old Testament language for Israel in verse 9a, Peter states that their purpose as a chosen race set apart for God is "that you may proclaim the excellencies of him who called you out of darkness into his marvelous light" (2:9b). This, too, picks up on an important Old Testament theme, namely, that Israel was to be a light to the nations. Since Israel has fallen into idolatry and unbelief, this task now belongs to the church. In fact, Peter reiterates this important theme a few verses later, in 2:12: "Keep your conduct among the Gentiles honorable, so that when they speak against you as evildoers, they may see your good deeds and glorify God on the day of visitation."

First Peter 2:11, then, begins the second major section of the letter that runs through 4:11. The focus is more specifically on what it means for Christians to live as exiles, or sojourners, in a land that is not their home. We can sum it up in two words: suffering and witness. These themes are intertwined throughout this section and directly relate to one another. On the one hand, as Christians live faithfully, bearing witness to Christ, this will invite opposition and persecution. On the other hand, Peter exhorts his readers to respond properly to suffering as a way of pointing those who persecute them to Christ. The theme of suffering is found in 2:18ff.;

[9] Most modern interpreters understand the "pure spiritual milk" to be the Word of God. However, Karen Jobes argues that it may refer to "a wider view of God's life-sustaining grace in Christ" ("Got Milk? Septuagint Psalm 33 and the Interpretation of 1 Peter 2:1–3," *WTJ* 64 [2002]: 14). She appeals to Calvin, who sees a wider reference than the Word of God, though one integrally related to it:

> After having taught the faithful that they had been regenerated by the Word of God, he now exhorts them to lead a life corresponding with their birth. . . . Infancy is here set by Peter in opposition to the ancientness of the flesh, which leads to corruption; and under the word milk, he includes all the feelings of the spiritual life. . . . He then compares the vices, in which the oldness of the flesh indulges, to strong food; and milk is called that way of living suitable to innocent nature and simple infancy.

(John Calvin, *Commentaries on the Catholic Epistles*, trans. John Owen, Calvin's Commentaries [Grand Rapids, MI: Baker, 2005], 61). Jobes points out that the expression "pure milk" here does not have the negative connotation that it has in other New Testament writings. Rather, "Peter presents pure spiritual milk as that which all Christians need in order to grow up into their salvation" ("Got Milk?," 2).

3:8–18; and 4:1 (though it spills over into the next section as well, with a slightly different point, in 4:12–19). The exhortation to witness occurs in 2:15ff.; 3:1, 13–16; and 4:6. Over against all of this, Peter sets forth Christ as the example for believers to follow (2:21–25; 3:18–4:1; cf. also 4:13).

Proper living in this world also includes proper submission to those whom God has put over us: submission of all believers to governing authorities, of servants to masters, and of wives to husbands. Even though Christians are not at home in this world, this does not exempt them from fulfilling their proper duties in the world. Rather, those duties are part of the believer's proper witness. Our duties are transformed by Christ into service to Christ.

A final important aspect of living as sojourners in this world is loving one's brothers and sisters in Christ. Peter repeats this exhortation three times in this section: 2:17; 3:8; 4:8 (cf. also 1:22; 5:14). Love means not living for oneself, and it is another way that believers follow the example of Christ, who loved us and gave himself for us. It should also come as no surprise that this theme would be important in a section focusing on Christian witness (cf. John 13:35). The world knows that Jesus's disciples belong to him by the way they love one another.

The final major section of the letter is 1 Peter 4:12–5:11. Here Peter calls his readers to a living hope. Believers are to live as sojourners in this world with their eyes fixed on their heavenly home. Peter has introduced this theme in the opening "thanksgiving" or "blessing" section in 1:3–7. In some ways, 4:7–11, which begins, "The end of all things is at hand," serves as a transition section that brings the previous section to a close and introduces the final major section of the letter (cf. the earlier discussion of 2:9–10). But beginning in 4:12, Peter brings his letter to a close with a consistent focus on living in light of coming glory. The suffering of believers (4:12–19) is a hope-filled suffering they can endure with joy because of coming glory (4:13–14) and because their souls are in the hands of a faithful God (4:19). Elders are called to shepherd God's flock in light of the crown of glory that awaits them (5:1–5). Finally, all believers are called to humble themselves and live faithfully in this age, in light of coming glory (5:6–11). Peter then brings the letter to a close with a brief section of final greetings (5:12–14).

Peter has sometimes been called "the apostle of hope" because his letters, while filled with difficult truths about the Christian life, are teeming with the hope of coming glory. It is this hope that fortifies believers for the difficult days to come.

Message and Theology

Living in a World That Is Not Our Home

Peter uses several words taken from Judaism and the Old Testament (the LXX) that carry the sense of those living in a land that is not their home, and he applies them to Christians. We see two of them at the very outset of 1 Peter: "Peter, an apostle of Jesus Christ, To those who are elect exiles of the Dispersion" (1:1). BDAG defines the Greek word for "exile" (παρεπίδημος) as referring to someone "staying for a while in a strange or foreign place, sojourning, residing temporarily." Peter uses a similar word in 2:11—"sojourners," from πάροικος, which means "one who lives in a place that is not one's home," a resident foreigner, stranger, alien (BDAG).

These words are used in the Septuagint and the New Testament to refer both to Jews living in a foreign land and to foreigners living in Israel. God tells Abraham, "Know for certain that your offspring will be sojourners [πάροικοι] in a land that is not theirs and will be servants there, and they will be afflicted for four hundred years" (Gen. 15:13). Similarly, Abraham himself tells the Hittites that he is a "sojourner [πάροικος] and foreigner [παρεπίδημος] among you" (Gen. 23:4). In the New Testament, these words are used of Israel's stay in Egypt (Acts 7:6) and of Moses's time in Midian (Acts 7:29). Significantly, however, we also see παρεπίδημος used of Abel, Enoch, Noah, Abraham, and Sarah as those who did not receive the things God promised, but only saw them from afar, "having acknowledged that they were strangers and exiles on the earth" (Heb. 11:13).

More frequently, however, words for sojourners and foreigners are used in the Old Testament (and LXX) to refer to non-Israelites living in the land of Israel (Lev. 22:10; 25:6; etc.). God often gave instructions about sojourners living in the land and how they were to be treated. Most importantly, God instructs the Israelites that they are to treat foreigners well, not mistreating them (Ex. 22:21), not oppressing them (Ex. 23:9). In Leviticus 19:33–34, God says, "When a stranger sojourns with you in your land, you shall not do him wrong. You shall treat the stranger who sojourns with you as the native among you, and you shall love him as yourself, for you were strangers in the land of Egypt: I am the LORD your God." Sojourners and strangers in the ancient world were vulnerable to being mistreated, taken advantage of, oppressed. And God appeals to the fact that the Israelites themselves were oppressed and made slaves in Egypt as one reason why they are not to mistreat foreigners who live in their midst (cf. Ex. 22:21; 23:9).

Peter also begins his letter using the term "Dispersion" (διασπορά): "To those who are elect exiles of the Dispersion" (1 Pet. 1:1). The word *dispersion* means "scattered," and it was used to refer to Jews who were scattered among the nations and dispersed among the Gentiles (cf. John 7:35). They lived in a foreign land, away from their true home in Israel. Much of this dispersion of the Jews came during Old Testament times, when Israel and Judah were scattered and taken as exiles by the Assyrians and Babylonians. It is in this context that Peter writes in 1 Peter 5:13, "She who is at Babylon, who is likewise chosen, sends you greetings." This key theme of being scattered and living in a foreign land that is not one's home frames the entire letter.

It is theologically significant, on the one hand, that Peter uses this language of Israel and applies it to the church, even referring to non-Christians as "Gentiles" (2:12). On the other hand, Peter's main point is that Christians living in the world are sojourners, exiles, pilgrims away from their true heavenly home. This informs how we live in this world. We are not to live for this world, in pursuit of what this world has to offer, or for the pleasures of this world. In this sense, Christians will live differently from unbelievers (4:3–5). We live with our eyes fixed on the heavenly Jerusalem and our eternal inheritance. Believers will never be truly at home in this world.

An important implication of this is that believers are in a vulnerable position. Sojourners or "resident aliens" were strange and out of place. They did not have full rights and privileges as citizens. They experienced social and cultural alienation, and were often looked on with suspicion and disdain. They were often exploited. John Elliott writes that resident aliens were "met with the ignorance, suspicion, and verbal abuse typically directed by natives against those who do not share the history, traditions, customs, loyalties, and deities of the local populace."[10]

The Life of Suffering, Following Christ's Example

We have already looked at the nature of the suffering that Peter describes of believers. An important emphasis in 1 Peter is that as believers suffer, they follow the example of Christ. We see this in the letter both explicitly and implicitly. Explicitly, Peter links the suffering of Christians to the suffering of Christ (2:18–25; 3:18; 4:1, 13). Peter says with regard to this suffering, "For to this you have been called, because Christ also suffered for you, leaving you an example, so that you might follow in his steps" (2:21). Similarly, Peter exhorts his readers that when the "fiery trial" comes on them, they should rejoice "insofar as [they] share Christ's sufferings" (4:12–13). Believers who suffer follow the example of Christ, and in fact are to walk in Christ's path, which is itself the way that leads to suffering.

Implicitly, Peter frequently uses the verb πάσχω to refer to the suffering of believers. This verb occurs twelve times in 1 Peter (he also uses the cognate noun πάθημα four times). But it occurs only eleven times in all the rest of the New Testament epistles. The verb does occur several times in the Gospels and Acts, where it is used almost exclusively for the suffering of Christ. Thus, in striking fashion, Peter takes a verb that in the Christian tradition was commonly used for the suffering of Christ and applies it repeatedly to the suffering of Christ's followers. As Peter learned from Christ himself, if Christ the Lord suffered, so his disciples will also suffer (John 15:20). They should expect it, not run from it, and they should walk in the way that typically leads to suffering of various kinds in a world that is hostile to God and his ways.

Living as Those Set Apart from the World

It is common in evangelical circles to describe Christians as "in the world, but not of the world." This idea comes out clearly in 1 Peter. It is also closely tied to the previous themes of living as pilgrims in the world and the life of suffering. The Jews in exile, while exhorted to seek the prosperity of the place where they would go, were also called to maintain their unique identity as those who were different from the conquering nation. They were to be faithful to God's covenant and his ways. In the

[10] John H. Elliott, "The Church as Counter-Culture: A Home for the Homeless and a Sanctuary for Refugees," *Currents in Theology and Mission* 25 (1998): 178.

same way, Christians are to be different from the world around them. This in turn will lead to ridicule and persecution.

Call to Holiness

A central theme of 1 Peter is the theme of holiness, which literally means being set apart. The adjective holy, ἅγιος, is used eight times in 1 Peter. It is used once with reference to the Holy Spirit (1:12). Twice it is used of God (1:15–16). The other five times it is used of believers. In 1:15–16, Peter calls his readers to be holy (in 1:16 quoting Lev. 11:44), specifically because God himself is holy. Peter also describes believers as a "holy priesthood" (1 Pet. 2:5) and a "holy nation" (2:9). In addition, Peter presents from the Old Testament "holy women who hoped in God" as examples for wives in the church to submit to their husbands (3:5), an implicit call to holiness.

In the opening greeting section, Peter addresses his readers as "elect exiles of the Dispersion . . . according to the foreknowledge of God the Father, in the sanctification of the Spirit, for obedience to Jesus Christ and for sprinkling with his blood" (1:1–2). The Greek word translated "sanctification" is ἁγιασμός, the noun form of the adjective holy. The sanctification, or being made holy, by the Spirit, then, is emphasized as a key theme in Peter's letter. This is also evident in the two phrases that follow. Sanctification is specifically "for obedience to Jesus Christ," walking in his ways, not the ways of the world, and "for sprinkling with his blood." The imagery of something sprinkled with blood is Old Testament language for something or someone being set apart for God.

What does this holiness look like in the lives of God's people? Peter gives several examples. One is the example of slaves who are called to submit to their masters with all respect, even when they are beaten and suffer unjustly (2:18–20). In this, they are following the example of Christ (2:21–23). Peter gives another example in 4:1–6. Christians are to live differently from the world, not following the "Gentiles" in their "sensuality, passions, drunkenness, orgies, drinking parties, and lawless idolatry" (4:3). The result of living unlike the world is that unbelievers "are surprised when you do not join them in the same flood of debauchery, and they malign you" (4:4). Walking in God's ways, according to God's laws, will bring various forms of persecution. But Christians, whose home is not this world, have a higher standard and are to live in ways that show them to be set apart from this world.

Witness

A closely related theme is that of witness. Several times Peter appeals to witness as a motivation for living differently from the world. In fact, it is a central theme of the second major section of the letter, 1 Peter 2:11–4:11. It appears in 2:11–12, which, as we saw earlier, introduces this larger section. Peter then elaborates on it in 2:13–15; 3:1–2, 13–17; and 4:1–6.[11] In the middle of this larger section, in the much-debated passage 3:18–22, Peter also presents Christ not only as an example

[11] According to Thomas Schreiner, "the call to mission informs the entire section" (*1, 2 Peter, Jude*, 119).

of one who suffered, but also as one who bore witness in his proclamation "to the spirits in prison" (3:19).

Peter begins the second section of the letter with an appeal to what Karen Jobes calls "lifestyle evangelism."[12] He writes, "Keep your conduct among the Gentiles honorable, so that when they speak against you as evildoers, they may see your good deeds and glorify God on the day of visitation" (2:12). This honorable conduct seems to include that they "abstain from the passions of the flesh" (2:11), but it also most likely includes "good deeds" of kindness and love. Many pagan philosophers and moralists taught high standards of ethical conduct. So the appeal here is to live a life that even pagans would view as good and honorable, though rooted in the teaching of Scripture and the transforming power of the gospel. Since Christians did not worship the gods of first-century culture, they would have been viewed with suspicion, not only as being "godless" but also as potentially subversive ("evildoers"). So Peter calls them to live an attractive lifestyle that shows them to be good neighbors and good citizens (cf. 2:13ff.). Ultimately, however, the goal is the salvation of those who do not believe "so that . . . they may . . . glorify God on the day of visitation" (2:12).

This same theme of lifestyle evangelism is also present in 3:1–2. Peter exhorts wives to be subject to their husbands, acting in a way that draws them to the Lord by their conduct without even having to say a word. A similar idea, though without the explicit appeal to the salvation of unbelievers, appears in 2:13–15 and 4:1–6. In 2:13–15, Peter calls his readers to submit to "every human institution," with the explicit goal "that by doing good you should put to silence the ignorance of foolish people," most likely a reference to those who call Christians "evildoers." In 4:1–6, believers are to live differently than "the Gentiles" (4:3), even if it means being maligned by them, for they "will give account to him who is ready to judge the living and the dead" (4:5).

Lifestyle evangelism, however, is typically not sufficient. God's normal way of transforming sinners is through the proclamation of the gospel (cf. Rom. 10:14–17). So, in 1 Peter 3:13–17, the apostle also exhorts believers, "Always [be] prepared to make a defense to anyone who asks you for a reason for the hope that is in you." Christians need to be ready and able to share the good news of Jesus Christ when God gives them the opportunity. The Greek word translated "defense" is ἀπολογία, from which we get our word *apologetics*. Christianity is a rational religion, with firm intellectual grounds. The Holy Spirit must work through the proclamation of the Word, but the Christian faith was easily able to hold its own in the first-century world of many "gods," most of whom were nothing but glorified human beings. In the same way today, the Christian message is the only rational alternative to the prevailing irrational views of creation and the denial of a Creator-creation distinction. We contend for the gospel because it is true and because it is the power of God unto salvation (Rom. 1:16).

One of the most debated passages in 1 Peter, if not the entire New Testament,

[12] Jobes, *1 Peter*, 167.

comes immediately after 3:13–17 and is directly tied to it. In 3:13–17, Peter brings together most of the major themes of the letter: suffering (3:14), living as those set apart from the world (3:16–17), and witness (3:15). He then proceeds to tie these themes to the life of Christ:

> For Christ also suffered once for sins, the righteous for the unrighteous, that he might bring us to God, being put to death in the flesh but made alive in the spirit, in which he went and proclaimed to the spirits in prison, because they formerly did not obey, when God's patience waited in the days of Noah, while the ark was being prepared, in which a few, that is, eight persons, were brought safely through water. (3:18–20)

Martin Luther struggled with this passage and wrote, "This is a strange text and certainly a more obscure passage than any other passage in the New Testament. I still do not know for sure what the apostle meant."[13]

At the heart of the debate is Peter's statement that Christ "went and proclaimed to the spirits in prison" (3:19). Wayne Grudem[14] has helpfully summarized the key questions regarding this assertion: (1) Who are the spirits in prison? (a) Unbelievers who have died? (b) Old Testament believers who have died? (c) Fallen angels? (2) What did Christ preach? (a) A second chance for repentance? (b) The completion of his redemptive work? (c) Final condemnation? (3) When did he preach? (a) In the days of Noah? (b) Between his death and resurrection? (c) After his resurrection?

There are numerous interpretations of this text, too many to list here. But we can summarize the most commonly held views. They can be organized in three basic categories having to do with the question of *when* Christ "proclaimed to the spirits in prison":

1. Before his death, during an earthly ministry.
2. After his death, but before his resurrection. Most interpretations in this category include some kind of "descent into hell."
3. After his resurrection, typically at his ascension.

1. *Theories that Christ's proclamation took place before his death, during an earthly ministry.*

a. The first, and widely held, theory places the time of Jesus's proclamation in the days of Noah (cf. 1 Pet. 3:20). When Noah was building the ark, Christ "in the spirit" was preaching through Noah, calling his contemporaries to repentance and obedience. They did not repent and are now in prison (hell). A slight variation of this view is that the words "in prison" are not literal, but refer to those in Noah's day who were ensnared in sin.[15]

[13] Martin Luther, *Sermons on the First Epistle of St. Peter*, in *Luther's Works*, vol. 30, *The Catholic Epistles*, ed. Jaroslav J. Pelikan, trans. M. H. Bertram (St. Louis, MO: Concordia, 1967), 113.

[14] Grudem, *1 Peter*, 157–58.

[15] Augustine, *Letters of St. Augustine* 164.15–17; Thomas Aquinas, *Summa theologica* III, q. 52, art. 2, ad. 3; Grudem, *1 Peter*, 157–62; John S. Feinberg, "1 Peter 3:18–20, Ancient Mythology, and the Intermediate State," *WTJ* 48 (1986): 303–36. According to Feinberg, "the passage in question has nothing to do with [an underworld, Christ preaching in hell, or Christ transferring Old Testament saints to heaven], but should be understood as a reference to Christ preaching by

b. The second theory is that Christ himself preached by the Spirit to his own contemporaries during his earthly ministry. At the beginning of Jesus's ministry, he read from Isaiah 61:1–2 and proclaimed that the words of the prophet were fulfilled in him:

> The Spirit of the Lord is upon me,
> because he has anointed me
> . . . to proclaim liberty to the captives. . . . (Luke 4:18)[16]

In context, the point of both of these theories would be that as God vindicated Noah and Christ, he would vindicate Christians now. They need to be faithful and make Christ known in their own generation.

2. *Theories that Christ's proclamation took place after his death, but before his resurrection.*

a. After Christ died, he went and liberated Old Testament saints, setting them free to go to their heavenly home.[17]

b. After Christ died, he went into hell and preached to the sinful people who died during the flood, offering them a second chance to repent and be saved. Many who hold this view extend it by saying that Christ will offer a second chance of salvation to all who die and go to hell, especially those who have never heard the gospel.[18]

c. After Christ died, he went into hell and proclaimed his victory over all who were there, announcing to them that their condemnation was final. One version of this theory is that Christ specifically proclaimed his victory to Noah's evil contemporaries.[19]

d. After Christ died, he went into hell and declared his victory over the fallen angels (identified by many interpreters as the "sons of God" in Gen. 6:1–4) who before the flood bore children by human women and were imprisoned for their sin. This appears to be the majority view today. It fits the context by assuring Christians that Christ has triumphed over evil powers and that they do not need to be afraid (1 Pet. 3:14, 22).[20]

e. After Christ died, he went to those who had repented right before they died in the flood and proclaimed to them their release from their imprisonment in purgatory.[21]

Most of these theories essentially teach that just as Christ was vindicated after his death, so faithful believers will also be vindicated. Christ has won the victory, and he has the keys of heaven and hell.

3. *Theories that Christ's proclamation took place after his resurrection.*

There is one main theory in this category, namely, that Christ proclaimed victory over his enemies after his resurrection at his ascension.[22] This fits the context because

the Holy Spirit through Noah to the people of Noah's day." See also John H. Skilton, "A Glance at Some Old Problems in First Peter," *WTJ* 58 (1996): 1–9.

[16] R. C. Sproul, *1–2 Peter*, St. Andrews Expositional Commentary (Wheaton, IL: Crossway, 2011), 126–29.

[17] Calvin, *Catholic Epistles*, 112–16.

[18] Charles Bigg, *A Critical and Exegetical Commentary on the Epistles of St. Peter and St. Jude*, ICC (Edinburgh: T&T Clark, 1987), 162–63; C. E. B. Cranfield, *1 and 2 Peter and Jude*, TBC (London: SCM, 1960), 84–86.

[19] A popular Lutheran position. See, e.g., R. C. H. Lenski, *The Interpretation of the Epistles of St. Peter, St. John, and St. Jude* (Minneapolis: Augsburg, 1966), 160–69.

[20] Elliott, *1 Peter*, 648–50; E. G. Selwyn, *The First Epistle of St. Peter* (London: Macmillan, 1949), 197–203, 314–62.

[21] A common Roman Catholic position. See, e.g., H. Willmering, *A Catholic Commentary on Holy Scripture*, ed. B. Orchard (London: Nelson, 1953), 1179.

[22] Achtemeier, *1 Peter*, 262; W. J. Dalton, *Christ's Proclamation to the Spirits* (Rome: Pontifical Biblical Institute, 1965), 135–201; Jobes, *1 Peter*, 235–51; Schreiner, *1, 2 Peter, Jude*, 188–90. A variation of this is Peter H. Davids, *The First Epistle of Peter* (Grand Rapids, MI: Eerdmans, 1990), 138–41, who sees the proclamation as being specifically to fallen angels.

the statement in 3:19 follows Peter's declaration in 3:18 that Christ was "made alive in the spirit." It also anticipates Peter's assertion in 3:22 that Christ "has gone into heaven and is at the right hand of God, with angels, authorities, and powers having been subjected to him." The point again would be to give assurance that even though Christ was "put to death" (3:18), he was ultimately victorious. Thus, Christians who faithfully testify to Christ will be victorious in the end.

No matter what position you hold (and Reformed commentators historically have largely stayed away from any interpretation involving a literal descent into hell), Jesus's ministry of proclamation and being victorious after suffering is intended to encourage faithfulness and embolden Christian witness.

Another debated verse, one often seen to be closely related to 3:19–20, is 1 Peter 4:6: "For this is why the gospel was preached even to those who are dead, that though judged in the flesh the way people are, they might live in the spirit the way God does." The phrase "the gospel was preached even to those who are dead" has often been thought to refer to Jesus's preaching to the "spirits" in hell. More likely, however, given the immediately preceding statement in 4:5 (God will "judge the living and the dead"), it refers to those who believed the gospel when it was preached, but who are now dead.[23] Though all will die ("though judged in the flesh the way people are"), those who believe the gospel will live ("they might live in the spirit the way God does"). Here again, however, we see Peter's emphasis on proclamation within the context of being faithful witnesses for Christ (4:1–6). The ungodly will perish (4:5). So Christians must be more urgent to preach Christ so that, though dying, they will live.

One final important interpretational issue is in 1 Peter 3:21. Peter states in 3:20 that during the flood, Noah and his family "were brought safely through water." He then says, "Baptism, which corresponds to this, now saves you." Does Peter here teach baptismal regeneration? His next words make clear that baptism does not literally save. The best water can do is remove dirt from the body. The means of salvation, on the other hand, is not an external rite. Salvation comes through what baptism signifies, namely, union with Christ in his death and resurrection, and washing with his blood. We have an example here of what theologians call "sacramental union." Because of the close relationship between the sign and the thing signified, biblical writers can sometimes virtually equate the sign with what it signifies. Peter's point here is that the physical salvation of Noah and his family through the flood prefigures the waters of baptism and the salvation they signify.

The Community of Faith

An important aspect of living *set apart* from the world is living *together* in the community of faith. Peter's instructions for living together as God's people are punctuated through the entire letter. But two images in particular stand out. The first is the church as God's temple. The second is God's people as family.

[23] Compare David Horrell, "Who Are 'the Dead' and When Was the Gospel Preached to Them? The Interpretation of 1 Pet 4.6," *NTS* 49 (2003): 70–89.

In 1 Peter 2:5, Peter writes, "You yourselves like living stones are being built up as a spiritual house, to be a holy priesthood, to offer spiritual sacrifices acceptable to God through Jesus Christ." The combination of language here—"a spiritual house," "priesthood," "offer . . . sacrifices"—hearkens back to the image of the temple (or tabernacle) in the Old Testament. The temple was central to the life of God's people under the old covenant. Moses devoted twelve chapters in Exodus to the building of the tabernacle—first its description, then the actual building of it. First Kings also includes a detailed description of the temple. The temple was significant because it was the place where God chose to dwell in the midst of his people and where God met with them.

With this imagery of the physical temple in the background, Peter writes that individual Christians are the "living stones" that are used to build God's "spiritual house." Like the stones in the temple, God's people are intimately connected with one another, and each stone is vital to holding together the entire building. But the imagery is more than simply the maintenance of a static structure. It is an organic building; God's people "are being built up as a spiritual house" (1 Pet. 2:5). The picture is that of growth, which in turn requires growing through the pure milk of the Word (2:2), offering "spiritual sacrifices" (2:5) to the glory of God and the good of one another, using our gifts for building up the body (4:10), and having godly shepherds who exercise oversight over the whole (5:1–4).

An important Old Testament word for the temple was "sanctuary," which highlights two features. The first is that it is to be holy, set apart for God's use. We have already seen that important theme in 1 Peter. The second aspect of a "sanctuary" is that it is a place of safety and refuge. Paul highlights this when he tells the Corinthian church to hand the immoral brother over to Satan (1 Cor. 5:5). To be outside the church is to be in a place of spiritual danger. No one knows the importance of community better than exiles living in a foreign land. Community gives strength and a sense of identity.

A final point: this use of the Old Testament imagery for the temple is one more reminder that Peter sees the church as the true Israel, the true covenant people of God.

The second image that Peter uses for the church is that of family. Peter twice exhorts his readers to show "brotherly love" (1 Pet. 1:22; 3:8) and once to "love the brotherhood" (2:17). Just like being in a family, living together in the church is not easy. It requires hard work. That's why, for good measure, Peter returns to the exhortation to love one more time: "Above all, keep loving one another earnestly, since love covers a multitude of sins" (4:8). In the living temple of God, while united by the Spirit we remain imperfect sinners who wrong and hurt one another. That's why living together requires not only love, but also a commitment to unity (3:8), hospitality (4:9), and especially humility (3:8; 5:5).

Present Living in Light of Future Glory

A final theme that permeates the entire letter is that Christians must live in this world with their eyes and hearts fully fixed on the glory that is to come. The central theme of believers as pilgrims and sojourners is a reminder that this world is not our home. So Peter keeps his readers' eyes focused on the inheritance that awaits them in their heavenly home. In this world, for "a little while" (1 Pet. 1:6; 5:10), believers will suffer. But that is nothing compared with the hope of glory that is soon to be revealed.

The letter begins and ends with the theme that for the Christian, life in the present must be lived in light of future glory. Some have called Peter "the apostle of hope" and the word "hope" is prominent in chapter 1 (vv. 3, 13, 21). The opening thanksgiving section blesses God because the Christian has been "born again to a living hope" (1:3) and "to an inheritance that is imperishable, undefiled, and unfading, kept in heaven for you" (1:4). Christians, furthermore, are being guarded by God's power "for a salvation ready to be revealed in the last time" (1:5). This, in turn, gives them joy, even though now "for a little while" they face various trials (1:6). And it will lead to praise, glory, and "joy that is inexpressible" when Christ is revealed at his second coming and believers obtain "the salvation of [their] souls" (1:7–9).

This thanksgiving section, then, orients the entire letter, placing our focus on what is to come. It also helps us to understand the nuance in Peter's use of three key biblical words. "Salvation" in the New Testament can have both an "already" and "not yet" sense to it. While the "already" is present in 1 Peter (see 3:21), salvation is primarily future-oriented in the letter (1:5, 9–10; 2:2). The noun "glory," which appears ten times in the letter (the verb "glorify" also appears four times), can be used essentially as a synonym for giving praise (1:7). But the prominent meaning in 1 Peter is that of an "eternal glory" that is yet to be revealed (see especially 5:1, 4, 10; cf. 4:11–14). Finally, the word "hope" appears only four times in the letter. But it is consistently tied to the major themes of the letter. Believers endure suffering because they have hope of future inheritance (1:3–4). Hope forms the basis for the life of holiness, set apart from the world (1:13ff.). And even the content of the believer's witness is described by Peter as "the hope that is in you" (3:15).

Peter concludes the letter by exhorting elders in particular (5:1, 4) and all believers in general (5:10) to live in light of the glory that is to be revealed. But this is possible only because of what Jesus Christ has already accomplished. He has already accomplished the victory for his people in his death (2:21–25; 3:18), resurrection (1:3; 3:18, 21), and ascension (3:22). Not only has he "healed" us and reconciled us to God (2:24–25). He has also brought all "angels, authorities, and powers" in submission to him (3:22). Thus, the believers' hope of glory is based not on anything they have done or can do, but only on what Christ has already accomplished on their behalf.

Select Bibliography

Achtemeier, Paul J. *1 Peter.* Hermeneia. Minneapolis: Fortress, 1996.

Bigg, Charles. *A Critical and Exegetical Commentary on the Epistles of St. Peter and St. Jude*. Edinburgh: T&T Clark, 1987.

Calvin, John. *Commentaries on the Catholic Epistles*. Translated by John Owen. Calvin's Commentaries. Grand Rapids, MI: Baker, 2005.

Carson, D. A., and Douglas J. Moo. *An Introduction to the New Testament*. 2nd ed. Grand Rapids, MI: Zondervan, 2005.

Cranfield, C. E. B. *1 and 2 Peter and Jude*. London: SCM, 1960.

Dalton, W. J. *Christ's Proclamation to the Spirits*. Rome: Pontifical Biblical Institute, 1965.

Davids, Peter H. *The First Epistle of Peter*. NICNT. Grand Rapids, MI: Eerdmans, 1990.

Elliott, John H. "The Church as Counter-Culture: A Home for the Homeless and a Sanctuary for Refugees." *Currents in Theology and Mission* 25 (1998): 176–85.

———. *1 Peter: A New Translation with Introduction and Commentary*. New York: Doubleday, 2000.

———. *A Home for the Homeless: A Sociological Exegesis of 1 Peter, Its Situation and Strategy*. Philadelphia: Fortress, 1981.

Feinberg, John S. "1 Peter 3:18–20, Ancient Mythology, and the Intermediate State." *WTJ* 48 (1986): 303–36.

Furnish, Victor Paul. "Elect Sojourners in Christ: An Approach to the Theology of I Peter." *Perkins School of Theology Journal* 28, no. 3 (1975): 1–11.

Grudem, Wayne A. *1 Peter: An Introduction and Commentary*. TNTC. Grand Rapids, MI: Eerdmans, 1988.

Harrell, William W. *Let's Study 1 Peter*. Carlisle, PA: Banner of Truth, 2004.

Horrell, David. "Who Are 'the Dead' and When Was the Gospel Preached to Them? The Interpretation of 1 Pet 4.6." *NTS* 49 (2003): 70–89.

Jobes, Karen. *1 Peter*. BECNT. Grand Rapids, MI: Baker Academic, 2005.

———. "Got Milk? Septuagint Psalm 33 and the Interpretation of 1 Peter 2:1–3." *WTJ* 64 (2002): 1–14.

Lenski, R. C. H. *The Interpretation of the Epistles of St. Peter, St. John, and St. Jude*. Minneapolis: Augsburg, 1966.

Luther, Martin. *Sermons on the First Epistle of St. Peter*. In *Luther's Works*. Vol. 30, *The Catholic Epistles*. Edited by Jaroslav Pelikan. Translated by M. H. Bertram. St. Louis, MO: Concordia, 1967.

Michaels, J. Ramsey. *1 Peter*. WBC 49. Waco, TX: Word, 1988.

Schreiner, Thomas. *1, 2 Peter, Jude*. NAC 37. Nashville: Broadman & Holman, 2003.

Selwyn, E. G. *The First Epistle of St. Peter*. London: Macmillan, 1949.

Skilton, John H. "A Glance at Some Old Problems in First Peter." *WTJ* 58 (1996): 1–9.

Sproul, R. C. *1–2 Peter*. St. Andrews Expositional Commentary. Wheaton, IL: Crossway, 2011.

22

2 Peter

Simon J. Kistemaker

Introduction

Second Peter is arguably one of the most neglected books in the New Testament canon. It has lived on the margins of modern scholarship for generations, receiving substantially less academic attention than other writings of a similar length. As John Snyder has observed, "[2 Peter] has probably received the least scholarly attention in the twentieth century."[1] The situation in the church is not much different. Since the earliest stages of Christianity, 2 Peter has been largely overlooked, with no mention of it (by name) until the third century. Even in the modern day, it is preached less frequently in local churches than other biblical books and not studied (or cited) as often by individual Christians. No doubt this neglect is due to the critical issues regarding authorship and date, as well as the number of difficult and complex passages that focus on God's future destruction of the world and judgment on sin.

But God has placed the epistle of 2 Peter in the canon for a reason. Upon further examination, it becomes clear that this book provides critical guidance and encouragement to the church as it endures the hostile criticisms of skeptics, scoffers, and doubters. In response to these challenges, Peter reminds the reader that Christ is certainly coming back (2 Pet. 3:1–18), that God will hold false teachers accountable for leading people astray (2:1–22), that the testimony of the apostles and the authority of Scripture can be trusted (1:16–21), and that believers are to be diligent in making their calling and election sure (1:1–15).

The message of 2 Peter is summed up in the closing verses:

> You therefore, beloved, knowing this beforehand, take care that you are not carried away with the error of lawless people and lose your own stability. But grow

[1] John Snyder, "A 2 Peter Bibliography," *JETS* 22 (1979): 265.

in the grace and knowledge of our Lord and Savior Jesus Christ. To him be the glory both now and to the day of eternity. Amen. (3:17–18)

Background Issues

Authorship

The first impression a reader receives when reading this epistle is that both its style and wording differ noticeably from that of 1 Peter. This gives the appearance that two different authors were involved in writing these epistles. It also raises the obvious question of whether the second letter was composed by a forger who assumed the name of the chief apostle and wanted the reader to think that this epistle originated from the pen of Simon Peter. Among critical scholars today, the consensus opinion is that 2 Peter was written by someone other than the apostle and was probably composed in the late first or early second century.[2]

However, a substantial case can be made for the traditional authorship of the book, with a likely date somewhere in the 60s.[3] It is true that the writing styles in the two epistles of Peter differ from each other; to be precise, 1 Peter is smooth while in places 2 Peter is jarring. The percentage of "out-of-the-way expressions" in 2 Peter is unusually high, with about fifty-seven words that do not occur in the rest of the New Testament.[4] Yet, this unevenness does not necessarily indicate a pseudonymous author. Several other factors must be considered.

First, some stylistic changes may be attributed to the input of an individual scribe (or secretary) whose methods and work habits differed from others'.[5] The use of scribes was common in those days: Tertius tells the readers that he was Paul's scribe in writing down the letter of Romans (16:22), and Peter makes it known that he wrote his first epistle with the help of Silvanus (Silas) (1 Pet. 5:12).

Second, an author's circumstances and subject matter can affect his writing style and vocabulary. These two epistles were written at varying times and in substantially different circumstances; indeed 2 Peter was written right on the eve of Peter's death (2 Pet. 1:12–15). Moreover, 2 Peter's subject matter was distinctively darker than 1 Peter's, focusing on false teachers, the second coming, and God's impending judgment. Surely such changes would make a meaningful impact on the content of any literary production.

Third, the differences between 1 and 2 Peter should not overshadow the number of striking parallels between the two books. Table 7 shows a few examples.

---

[2] Joseph B. Mayor, *The Epistle of St. Jude and the Second Epistle of St. Peter* (Grand Rapids, MI: Baker, 1965), cxxiv; J. N. D. Kelly, *A Commentary on the Epistles of Peter and of Jude* (New York: Harper & Row, 1969), 235; Richard Bauckham, *Jude, 2 Peter*, WBC 50 (Waco, TX: Word, 1983), 157–63; and Bart D. Ehrman, *Forgery and Counterforgery: The Use of Literary Deceit in Early Christian Polemics* (New York: Oxford University Press, 2012), 222–29.

[3] E. M. B. Green, *2 Peter Reconsidered* (London: Tyndale, 1960); Donald Guthrie, *New Testament Introduction* (Downers Grove, IL: InterVarsity Press, 1990), 805–42; B. B. Warfield, "The Canonicity of 2 Peter," in *Selected Shorter Writings of Benjamin B. Warfield*, ed. John E. Meeter, vol. 2 (Phillipsburg, NJ: P&R, 1973), 49–79; Michael J. Gilmour, "Reflections on the Authorship of 2 Peter," *EvQ* 73, no. 4 (2001): 291–309; and Michael J. Kruger, "The Authenticity of 2 Peter," *JETS* 42 (1999): 645–71.

[4] Mayor, *Jude and the Second Epistle of St. Peter*, lxiv; Simon Kistemaker, *The Epistles of Peter and Jude*, NTC (Grand Rapids, MI: Baker, 1987), 217.

[5] For more on the use of secretaries in the ancient world, see E. R. Richards, *The Secretary in the Letters of Paul* (Tübingen: Mohr, 1991).

1 Peter		2 Peter
1:10–12	inspiration of the Old Testament	1:19–21
1:2	doctrine of election	1:10
1:23	doctrine of the new birth	1:4
2:11–12	need for holiness	1:5–9
3:19	sinful angels in prison	2:4
3:20	Noah and his family protected	2:5
4:2–4	immorality and judgment	2:10–22
4:7–11	exhortation to Christian living	3:14–18
4:11	doxology	3:18*

* Kistemaker, *Epistles of Peter and Jude*, 220.

Table 7

In addition, in both epistles the author identifies himself as "an apostle of Jesus Christ," and uses similar language to refer to Jesus Christ, God the Father, and the Holy Spirit. The link between the letters is also evident in that the author of the second letter refers to a prior letter he penned to the same audience (2 Pet. 3:1).

In sum, we have no reason to doubt that the apostle Peter is the author of this letter. Indeed, we should remember that the authorial claims of 2 Peter stem from more than just the title. The contents reveal a number of personal references that are presented as coming from the apostle himself. The author confirms his recollection of his presence on the Mount of Transfiguration, where the glorified Jesus appeared with Moses and Elijah (1:16–18). He remembers the words of the heavenly voice, "This is my beloved Son, with whom I am well pleased" (1:17). The author also notes his personal acquaintance with Paul (3:15) and thus places himself within the apostlic circle—something confirmed by the opening verse, which identifies him as an "apostle of Jesus Christ" (1:1).

Date

Peter tells his readers that he expects to pass away soon for he is coming to the end of his earthly life. He writes that the Lord Jesus communicated with him that he would soon depart from this life and that after his death, the readers would be able to recall the things he taught them (2 Pet. 1:14–15). Peter passed away most likely during the persecution instigated by Nero in the years 64–68. If we date 1 Peter early in that period, the second letter could have been composed a few years prior to Nero's suicidal death in 68.

Peter writes about scoffers who apparently in the second century are questioning the promise of Jesus's coming. They ask, "Where is the promise of his coming? For ever since the fathers fell asleep, all things are continuing as they were from the beginning of creation" (3:4). The critical issue in this question is the interpretation of the phrase "the fathers." Does it refer to first-generation apostles? Some commentators assert that Jesus's disciples were born in the decade before AD 10, and when 2 Peter was composed, most of the apostles had passed away.[6] However, there is no absolute certainty as to what is meant, except to say that in the New Testament this phrase usually refers to Old Testament fathers (Acts 3:13; Rom. 9:5; Heb. 1:1).[7]

The author is acquainted with Paul and his letters, for he writes "Our beloved brother Paul also wrote to you" (2 Pet. 3:15). This places him next to this apostle to the Gentiles, who wrote a number of epistles familiar to the recipients of 2 Peter. This is a clear indicator that these two were contemporaries. Peter even mentions that Paul's letters are hard to understand (3:16).

An early date for 2 Peter is also suggested by the fact that other historical documents know and use the letter. For instance, 2 Peter appears to have been known by 1 Clement (ca. 96), which has several places of overlap (e.g., 23.3 [2 Pet. 3:4]; 9.2 [2 Pet. 1:17]; 35.5 [2 Pet. 2:2]),[8] and also the Apocalypse of Peter (ca. 110), which also seems to have known the letter.[9] Richard Bauckham considers the connections to the Apocalypse of Peter to be "very good" and "sufficient to rule out a late date for 2 Peter."[10] Such considerations raise further doubts about the scholarly consensus that 2 Peter must have been authored by a second-century forger.

If we accept the apostolic authorship of 2 Peter, then the epistle was most likely written in the period of AD 64–68.[11] This fits the tone and tenor of the epistle that refers to Peter's approaching death presumably after AD 64.

Genre

Second Peter is a letter with an eschatological message that amplifies what Jesus said and Paul has written about the end of times (Matt. 24:37; 2 Thess. 1:7). Peter uses apocalyptic speech to reveal what is going to happen at the consummation when "the heavens will pass away with a roar, and the heavenly bodies will be burned up and dissolved, and the earth and the works that are done on it will be exposed" (2 Pet. 3:10). In preparation for the end of time, Peter is asking his readers what kind of people they ought to be. He tells them to speed its coming (3:12). Indeed this can be accomplished by evangelizing the world.

The fact that Peter discusses these topics on the eve of his own death (1:13–15) has led some scholars to suggest that 2 Peter is an instance of what is known as the "testamentary" genre.[12] This genre, also known as a "farewell speech," was not uncommon

[6] Compare Bauckham, *Jude, 2 Peter*, 158.

[7] Michael Green, *2 Peter and Jude* (Grand Rapids, MI: Eerdmans, 1987), 140. See Guthrie, *New Testament Introduction*, 815.

[8] Robert E. Picirilli, "Allusions to 2 Peter in the Apostolic Fathers," *JSNT* 33 (1988): 59; H. C. C. Cavallin, "The False Teachers of 2 Peter as Pseudoprophets," *NovT* 21 (1979): 268; Kruger, "The Authenticity of 2 Peter," 654–655.

[9] Mayor, *Jude and the Second Epistle of St. Peter*, cxxx–cxxxiv.

[10] Bauckham, *Jude, 2 Peter*, 162. See also T. V. Smith, *Petrine Controversies in Early Christianity* (Tübingen: Mohr, 1985), 53; and J. A. T. Robinson, *Redating the New Testament* (Philadelphia: Westminster Press, 1976), 178.

[11] Edwin A. Blum, *1, 2 Peter*, in *Expositor's Bible Commentary*, vol. 12, *Hebrews through Revelation*, ed. Frank E. Gaebelein et al. (Grand Rapids, MI: Zondervan, 1981), 262. See also Green, *2 Peter and Jude*, 16, who conditionally places the date very early, before AD 68.

[12] For broad overviews of this genre, see Eckhard von Nordheim, *Die Lehre der Alten*, vol. 1, *Das Testamente als Literaturgattung im Judentum der hellenistische-romischen Zeit* (Leiden: Brill, 1980); and O. Knoch, *Die "Testamente" des Petrus und Paulus* (Stuttgart: KBW, 1973). See also discussion in Bauckham, *Jude, 2 Peter*, 131–35, 158–62.

in the Second Temple time period and supposedly recorded the last instructions of a significant leader or teacher right before he passed away.[13] Since most known examples of testamentary texts are forgeries, scholars have suggested that 2 Peter must therefore be a forgery.[14] However, such a conclusion does not necessarily follow. Although 2 Peter certainly shares certain features with the testamentary genre, it lacks others. For instance, it does not record a "heavenly journey" of Peter—something often found in other testamentary literature.[15] But the most important difference is that 2 Peter is in the form of a *letter*—a feature lacking in all testamentary literature up to this period.[16] For these reasons, 2 Peter does not appear to be a formal instance of the testamentary genre.

Provenance

There is no indication of a place from which or to which the epistle was addressed. Peter spent time in Rome prior to his death. There he was incarcerated in the Mamertine Prison before his execution, according to medieval tradition. Oral reports relate that at his own request Peter was crucified upside down because he considered himself unworthy to be crucified in the same manner as Jesus. Because of the brevity of this epistle, there are no indications with reference to its origin.

Place in the Canon

Of all the books in the New Testament canon, 2 Peter may have had the most difficult journey. It was infrequently used in the earliest centuries—though we do have evidence that some Patristic writers were aware of it. In addition to its probable use by 1 Clement and the Apocalypse of Peter (discussed above), it also seems to have been known by Justin Martyr, Irenaeus, and Hippolytus.[17] Clement of Alexandria appears to have received it as Scripture, since he wrote a (now lost) commentary on it.[18] Likewise, Origen regarded it as Scripture even though he acknowledged that some in his day had doubts about it.[19] Eusebius regarded 2 Peter as part of the "disputed" books, along with James, Jude, and 2 and 3 John. According to Bruce Metzger, Eusebius still regarded such books as canonical, despite the opposition of some.[20] Eventually the church coalesced around 2 Peter, and it was received as authentic by such figures as Jerome, Athanasius, and Augustine, as well as the councils of Laodicea (ca. 360) and Carthage (ca. 397).

Purpose

The main purpose of the book of 2 Peter is to refute the influence of false teachers in the midst of the recipients. Knowing that he is approaching the end of his earthly

---

[13] E.g., T. Mos., T. 12 Patr., T. Job. Parts/sections of writings can also be considered testamental in nature: 1 Enoch 91–107; 4 Ezra 14:28–36; 2 Baruch 77–86; Jub. 21:1–23:7; Josephus, *Ant.* 4.309–19.

[14] Richard Bauckham, "Pseudo-Apostolic Letters," *JBL* 107 (1988): 469–94.

[15] A. B. Kolenkow, "The Genre Testament and Forecasts of the Future in the Hellenistic Jewish Milieu," *JSJ* 6 (1975): 66–67.

[16] The book of 2 Baruch seems to be a farewell speech in letter form, but it was written in the second century AD and could not have been the prototype for 2 Peter.

[17] Justin Martyr, *Dial.* 82.1; Irenaeus, *Haer.* 5.23.2; Hippolytus, *Haer.* 9.7.3.

[18] See Eusebius, *Hist. eccl.* 6.14.1, 3.25.3.

[19] *Hom. Num.* 13.8.1; *Hom. Jos.* 7.1; *Hist. eccl.* 6.25.11.

[20] B. M. Metzger, *The Canon of the New Testament: Its Origin, Development, and Significance* (Oxford: Clarendon, 1987), 205. Cf. *Hist. eccl.* 3.25.3.

life, Peter offers a final warning about the danger of these false teachers, highlighting their future destruction and even referring to them as "accursed children" (2:14). He instructs the followers of Christ Jesus to pursue holiness and godliness as they wait for the return of Christ.

There has been much scholarly discussion about the identity of these false teachers. Some have suggested that 2 Peter is responding to Gnostic teaching;[21] others have suggested Epicurean philosophy.[22] But neither of these views is wholly convincing.[23] In the end, the false teachers may not be associated with any well-known school of thought, but may be a unique local phenomenon in that time and place. Regardless, it is clear that at the heart of the false teaching is a commitment to "eschatological skepticism,"[24] denying both the return of Christ and the willingness of God to bring judgment on sin. Given that these same denials are made by many today, 2 Peter's message is immediately applicable to the modern world.

Structure and Outline

Outline

- I. Introduction (1:1–2)
  - A. Greetings (1:1)
  - B. Salutation (1:2)
- II. Promises and Virtues (1:3–11)
  - A. Promises (1:3–4)
  - B. Virtues (1:5–7)
  - C. Growth (1:8–9)
  - D. Assurance (1:10–11)
- III. Divine Revelation (1:12–21)
  - A. Memory (1:12–15)
  - B. Eyewitnesses (1:16–18)
  - C. Prophecy (1:19–21)
- IV. False Teachers (2:1–22)
  - A. Destructive heresies (2:1)
  - B. Shameful ways (2:2–3)
  - C. Condemnation (2:4–10a)
  - D. Flagrant misconduct (2:10b–16)
  - E. Inevitable doom (2:17–22)
- V. The Day of the Lord (3:1–13)
  - A. Reminder (3:1–2)
  - B. Scoffers (3:3–4)
  - C. Destruction (3:5–7)
  - D. Time (3:8–9)
  - E. Elements (3:10)
  - F. Consummation (3:11–13)

[21] C. Talbert, "2 Peter and the Delay of the Parousia," *VC* 20 (1966): 141–43.
[22] Bauckham, *Jude, 2 Peter*, 156.
[23] See discussion in Thomas R. Schreiner, *1, 2 Peter, Jude* (Nashville: Broadman & Holman, 2003), 277–80; and Gene L. Green, *Jude and 2 Peter*, BECNT (Grand Rapids, MI: Baker Academic, 2008), 150–59.
[24] Bauckham, *Jude, 2 Peter*, 154.

VI. Exhortations (3:14–18)
   A. Be blameless (3:14)
   B. Accept God's truth (3:15–16)
   C. Reject error (3:17)
   D. Grow in grace (3:18)

Arrangement

In the first two verses the author identifies himself by his double name, Simon Peter, as an apostle of Jesus Christ, whom he describes as God and Savior (2 Pet. 1:1). Indeed, he is even more precise in his salutation, where he speaks of "the knowledge of God and of Jesus our Lord" (1:2). After writing about promises and virtues, he as an eyewitness recalls the glory of Christ at the transfiguration when God spoke and identified Jesus as his Son (1:17). Peter has much to say about false teachers and their flagrant misconduct, which results in their inevitable condemnation (2:1–22). He concludes his epistle with a chapter on eschatology and exhortations (3:1–18).

Message and Theology

As noted above, the core purpose of 2 Peter is to respond to false teachers who are leading the flock astray. Although we are unable to identify these false teachers with any known group, their main error is "eschatological skepticism"; they deny the second coming of Christ. Consequently, the major theological foci of the letter, which we will examine below, are designed by Peter to respond to this false teaching and any implications that might be drawn from it. Since the root heresy (denial of the second coming) is addressed at the end of the epistle, it is more natural to start at the end and work backward.

The Return of Christ (2 Pet. 3:1–13)

Toward the end of his letter, Peter directly addresses the topic of the second coming of Christ. As he does so, he reminds his audience that they are living in the "last days" (2 Pet. 3:3) and that skepticism about the second coming is not unexpected (3:4). This eschatological language reveals that Peter views the "last days" not as something yet to come in the distant future, but as something the church currently experiences until Christ returns again (cf. 1 Pet. 1:20). Thus, for Peter, the term "last days" is not so much a reference to a quantity of time as a reference to the quality of time. The phrase speaks to the *kind* of time the church finds itself in—a time where the second coming is the next big eschatological event on the horizon.

While the scoffers say, "Where is the promise of his coming?" (3:4), Peter offers a twofold rebuttal. First, he reminds his readers of the reality of Noah's flood (3:5–7)—if God judged the whole world once before, he can and will do it again. He judged the world previously through water, and in the future he will judge it through fire (3:7; cf. Deut. 32:22; Isa. 29:6; 30:27–33; 66:15–24).[25] Second, he reminds them

[25] Schreiner, *1, 2 Peter, Jude*, 377–78.

that God's timing is not like our timing. While we might think God is late, to him "one day is as a thousand years and a thousand years as one day" (2 Pet. 3:8). But eventually Christ will return "like a thief" (3:10), a truth echoing other New Testament passages, such as Matthew 24:43–44; Mark 13:32–37; and Acts 1:7.

Then Peter proceeds to provide one of the most detailed descriptions in the New Testament of what will happen to the physical world upon Christ's return. We are told that "the heavens will pass away with a roar, and the heavenly bodies will be burned up and dissolved" (2 Pet. 3:10). This sort of cosmic-upheaval language is consistent with what we find in other eschatological passages describing the second coming (e.g., Isa. 34:4; Matt. 24:29; Mark 13:24; Rev. 6:12–17). This destructive activity, says Peter, is the precursor to God's greater and more glorious promise to remake the world into "new heavens and a new earth in which righteousness dwells" (2 Pet. 3:13).[26] Here Peter draws upon Old Testament texts where God declares that someday he will transform the world into a new creation (Isa. 65:13, 17)—a theme picked up in a variety of other New Testament passages (Matt. 19:28; Rom. 8:22; Rev. 21:1).[27]

Peter's eschatological focus has tremendous implications for present-day congregations. First, the modern church is reminded that we too live in the "last days," just like Peter, awaiting Christ's return. Thus, we should not be surprised or discouraged when skeptics and scoffers come along and question the promises of God. Second, this passage demonstrates that the ultimate Christian hope is not simply that someday we will "go to heaven," but that someday God will bring heaven to earth. The implications of the second coming are not just spiritual; they are also physical. God will remake this fallen sin-cursed world; will give his people new, imperishable bodies; and we will dwell with Christ forever, face-to-face. That is the "promise we are waiting for" (2 Pet. 3:13) during these last days.

Judgment of False Teachers (2 Pet. 2:1–22)

As Peter continues his rebuttal of the false teachers, he not only establishes the reality of the second coming, but also reassures his readers that these false teachers will be judged by God. Apparently, some had begun to doubt whether God would hold these false teachers accountable, and perhaps the false teachers themselves claimed that God would never judge them.

Peter, however, says otherwise. To prove his point, he offers a list of examples of how God has judged the wicked in the past. These examples include the judgment of rebellious angels (2 Pet. 2:4), the judgment of the flood (2:5), and the judgment on Sodom and Gomorrah (2:6–8). Then Peter draws some implications from this brief historical tour, namely, that "the Lord knows how to rescue the godly" and the Lord is able to "keep the unrighteous under punishment until the day of judgment" (2:9). Contrary to what the false teachers are saying, God is a God who protects the righteous and judges the wicked.

[26] Ibid., 384–85.

[27] D. A. Carson and Douglas J. Moo, *Introduction to the New Testament*, 2nd ed. (Grand Rapids, MI: Zondervan, 2005), 665–66.

But Peter is not finished. He makes his case that God will judge these false teachers not just by looking to the past, but also by looking to the present and showing the depth of their depravity. Here he embarks on a lengthy description of their moral corruption: they are blasphemers (2:10–12), deceivers (2:13), revelers (2:13), adulterers (2:14), greedy (2:14), seducers (2:14), boastful (2:18), and corrupt (2:19). Thus, Peter compares them to "irrational animals" (2:12), "accursed children" (2:14), "waterless springs" (2:17), "mists driven by a storm" (2:17), and a dog returning to its vomit (2:22).

What makes these false teachers particularly worthy of God's judgment is not only this list of depraved practices, but the fact that they were once part of the people of God. Peter makes it clear that, like the false prophets of the Old Testament, these false teachers "arose among the people" (2:1), were guilty of "denying the Master who bought them" (2:1), shared a "feast" (likely the Lord's Supper)[28] with the people (2:13), and at one point seemed to have "escaped the defilements of the world through the knowledge of our Lord and Savior Jesus Christ," but now "are again entangled in them and overcome" (2:20). In short, these false teachers are *apostates*; they were once part of the covenant community but have fallen away and proved to be unbelievers.[29] Thus, their judgment is even more severe than it otherwise would have been. As Peter says, "It would have been better for them never to have known the way of righteousness than after knowing it to turn back" (2:21).

This section on judgment is particularly relevant to modern-day congregations who have grown up in a world that says God does not care much about sin and certainly would never judge sin. Peter challenges this misconception and reminds us of critical attributes of God, particularly his unwavering holiness and his hatred of sin. And a deeper awareness of these attributes can drive people deeper into the arms of Jesus and to the forgiveness he offers in the cross. Moreover, this section serves as a much-needed warning about apostasy. The reality is that some people in our churches profess to be Christians when they really are not. Preaching a passage like this issues a call to a congregation, "Be all the more diligent to confirm your calling and election" (1:10).

Trustworthiness of God's Authoritative Messengers (2 Pet. 1:16–21)

Since Peter is writing to refute false teachers, it is no surprise that he devotes some space to bolstering the trustworthiness of God's genuine messengers. In order to overcome false teaching, one must be reassured of the validity of true teaching. One group of genuine messengers is the apostles themselves. Peter reassures the reader that the apostles "did not follow cleverly devised myths"—in contrast to the false teachers who "exploit you with false words" (2 Pet. 2:3)—but based their teaching about the second coming on their own eyewitness experience of the transfiguration and the accompanying voice from heaven (1:16–18). For Peter, the glory and the majesty (μεγαλειότητος) of Christ revealed at his transfiguration is evidence that he is the divine figure who will return one day to judge the world. As Gene L. Green observes,

[28] Green, *Jude and 2 Peter*, 280–81.
[29] Kistemaker, *Epistles of Peter and Jude*, 312.

"Using the word [majesty] is tantamount to acknowledging Christ's divinity."[30] Thus, the transfiguration is a prophetic anticipation of the second coming itself.[31]

The theme of Christ's divinity, so apparent in the recounting of his transfiguration, also appears elsewhere in the epistle. The opening verse affirms Christ's divinity quite plainly when it refers to "our God and Savior Jesus Christ" (1:1). The fact that *both* titles—God and Savior—apply to Jesus is evident not only from the grammar[32] of this verse but also from comparing this verse with the parallel construction in verse 11, "our Lord and Savior Jesus Christ." In addition, the closing doxology at the end of the letter, a declaration of worship applied to Christ, also is an expression of his divinity: "But grow in the grace and knowledge of our Lord and Savior Jesus Christ. To him be the glory both now and to the day of eternity. Amen" (3:18).[33] Thus, the theme of Christ's divinity appears at both the beginning and the end, forming a literary *inclusio* around the epistle of 2 Peter.

In addition to defending the authoritative eyewitness testimony of the apostles, Peter goes even further and offers a defense of the authority of Scripture itself. He tells us in 1:19 that the "prophetic word"—a clear reference to the Old Testament Scriptures—is "more fully confirmed" (βεβαιότερον). Peter may be arguing that the Scriptures are even more certain than eyewitness testimony,[34] or he may simply be stating that the eyewitness testimony confirms the Scriptures.[35] Regardless, he sees the Scriptures as bearing the very authority of God himself. He makes this point by insisting that its contents are not due to "the will of man," but that "men spoke from God as they were carried along by the Holy Spirit" (1:21). Indeed, "in the writing of Scripture, man is passive and the Spirit active."[36] Here Peter provides one of the most explicit statements regarding the inspiration of Scripture. Whereas a passage like 2 Timothy 3:16 speaks to the *product* of inspiration (a God-breathed text), 2 Peter 1:21 speaks to the *process* of inspiration (a Spirit-carried author).

The authority of the Scriptures is relevant to Peter's argument because the Scriptures, alongside the apostolic testimony, also proclaim the glory, majesty, and future coming of Christ. Thus, the Scriptures function as a "lamp shining in a dark place" (1:19), something much needed in the struggle against false teachers. And the Scriptures will function as this lamp "until the day dawns" (1:19), a clear reference to the day of the Lord, when Christ returns to judge the world.

This discussion of the authority of Scripture is certainly applicable to today's church, which also struggles against various sorts of false teaching. Perhaps more than anything else, Christians in the modern world need reassurance that the Scriptures really are the product of authors who were "carried along by the Holy Spirit" (1:21) and therefore can be fully trusted.

---

30 Green, *Jude and 2 Peter*, 221.
31 Ibid.
32 Charles Bigg, *Epistles of St. Peter and St. Jude* (Edinburgh: T&T Clark, 1961), 250–52.
33 T. Callan, "The Christology of the Second Letter of Peter," *Bib* 82 (2001): 253–63.
34 B. B. Warfield, *The Inspiration and Authority of the Bible* (Phillipsburg, NJ: P&R, 1948), 135.
35 Schreiner, *1, 2 Peter, Jude*, 320.
36 Kistemaker, *Epistles of Peter and Jude*, 273.

Pursuit of Holiness (2 Pet. 1:3–11)

Since the false teachers denied the second coming, and also denied the reality of judgment, it is no surprise that they lived in licentiousness. Why worry about holiness if there is no day of reckoning? In contrast, Peter makes it clear that the second coming of Christ should lead to a life of purity: "Since all these things are thus to be dissolved, what sort of people ought you to be in lives of holiness and godliness . . . !" (2 Pet. 3:11). So central is this theme for Peter that he begins his epistle with it: "His divine power has granted to us all things that pertain to life and godliness, through the knowledge of him who called us to his own glory and excellence" (1:3).

As this verse makes clear, the path to holiness comes through *knowledge* of God through his Son Jesus Christ.[37] Indeed, a major theme in the epistle is growing in one's knowledge of Jesus Christ. Peter mentions this theme just one verse earlier, "May grace and peace be multiplied to you in the *knowledge* of God and of Jesus our Lord" (1:2), and also mentions it at the very end of the letter, "But grow in the grace and *knowledge* of our Lord and Savior" (3:18). Peter wants his readers not just to be able to recite facts about God, but to have an intimate, personal knowledge of God—and for that personal knowledge of God to be ever growing. This is what distinguishes true believers from the false teachers. The latter have an external association with God (2:1), but not an internal, personal relationship with God. And only that internal relationship can lead to true holiness.

Peter mentions the theme of knowledge again when he offers his well-known "staircase" of Christian virtues: "Supplement your faith with virtue, and virtue with knowledge, and knowledge with self-control, and self-control with steadfastness, and steadfastness with godliness, and godliness with brotherly affection, and brotherly affection with love" (1:5–7). This list is akin to the fruit of the Spirit that we find elsewhere in the New Testament (e.g., Gal. 5:22–23).

This is a critical teaching for the modern church to hear. Many today hesitate to preach on holiness and the fruit of the Spirit for fear that it will undermine the gospel of free grace. However, Peter sees no such contradiction between the two. On the contrary, the gospel of free grace is what leads to holiness. A lack of holiness can be a sign that a person has not genuinely embraced the gospel. Thus, Peter is able to call Christians to be active in their pursuit of holiness, not passive. Effort is not inconsistent with the gospel. We are to "make every effort" (2 Pet. 1:5) and to "be all the more diligent" so that we may confirm our "calling and election" (1:10). Why? Because "we are waiting for new heavens and a new earth in which righteousness dwells" (3:13).

Select Bibliography

Please see the bibliography at the end of chapter 24, on Jude.

[37] John Calvin. *2 Peter, Jude*, Calvin's Commentaries (Grand Rapids, MI: Eerdmans, 1948), 369.

23

1–3 John

Charles E. Hill

1 JOHN

Introduction

Jesus Christ, the "word of life" (1 John 1:1), who existed eternally with the Father (John 1:1; 1 John 1:1–2), was manifested in the flesh. His coming brought light into the world. John composes his Gospel and epistles in the full and penetrating clarity of that eschatological light, bearing witness to the light and thus inviting others into fellowship with the Father and the Son (1 John 1:3). The light is now shining in the darkness and overcoming the darkness, the world, and the Devil (John 1:5; 1 John 2:8, 17; 3:8).

The progressive dawning of the light stirs up great opposition from the darkness. At the time when John wrote his epistles, recent events in Asia Minor had confirmed the advanced stage of eschatological development: false prophets, people he calls "antichrists," had appeared and were teaching a false doctrine of Christ (1 John 2:18, 22; cf. 4:1; 2 John 7–9). These antichrists, through circumstances unknown to us, had either chosen to withdraw from the community or been forced to do so. Yet, though they had departed, their deception was still a source of disruption and confusion to the community. John now writes to confirm and to restore fullness of joy to those who have remained in Christ, who have not forsaken what their anointing has taught them is true. While the specific circumstances that called forth John's response have long since passed, what John provides to the church through these circumstances remains a permanent source of theological, ethical, and devotional instruction.

A popular critical reading of the evidence advocated by Raymond Brown and many others is that the antichrists or "secessionists" in 1 John believed they were carrying on the true legacy of the Gospel of John and were claiming it as their authority. In this scenario the secessionists are often portrayed as having at least as legitimate a claim on this Gospel as had the group who remained with the author. The secessionists' "high" christology, it is thought, followed a trajectory set by the Gospel, while the author of 1 John believed that their christology had progressed too high and needed to be reined back in. But this reading of the situation can only be pulled off by assuming either, (1) that the secessionists so badly misread the Gospel that they utterly missed fundamental aspects of its teaching (like the Word becoming flesh, and Jesus thirsting, bleeding, and dying), or (2) that they were reading a hypothesized, earlier "docetic" edition of the Gospel, one that has left no trace in history. Neither option is at all probable.

The Gospel of John itself, in fact, articulates a christology profoundly at odds with that which was held by the opponents in 1 John, so much so that one could suspect that the publication of the Gospel forced the opponents to see their need to retreat from the fellowship. In any case it is clear that what the antichrists were teaching was not what the community had received "from the beginning" (1 John 2:24; cf. 2 John 9).

Background Issues

Date of Writing

The Johannine Epistles (as with all the books in the Johannine corpus) appear to occupy a place near the end of the New Testament chronology and depict the initial realization of the eschatological scenario predicted by Jesus, Paul, 2 Peter, and Jude. The most common dating places the letters in the late first century (ca. 85–100). This is most probable on the following external and internal grounds:

1. First, the testimony of several early Christian writers is that the apostle John, the assumed author of these epistles, lived to be very old. He is believed to have survived his exile on Patmos under Domitian and to have returned to Ephesus, where he ministered until the time of his death, which Irenaeus placed early in the reign of Trajan (98–117).[1]

2. Second, while nothing in the internal witness of the letters can prove a theory of composition in the last years of the first century, a few factors are consistent with it:

a. The type of heresy encountered in 1–2 John is consistent with developments that, as far as we know, occurred only late in the first century and not before. The closest analogies to the group's evident docetism are found not in any other New Testament books but in the letters of Polycarp and Ignatius written around 108, in the late first-century or early second-century heresy of Cerinthus (as described by Irenaeus, *Haer.* 1.26.1 and elsewhere),[2] and then in the teaching of the Apocryphon of James and countered in the Epistle of

[1] Irenaeus, *Haer.* 2.22.5, 3.3.4, 5.30.3; cf. Clement of Alexandria, *Who Is the Rich Man?* 42; Victorinus, *Comm. Apoc.* 10.11.
[2] See C. E. Hill, "Cerinthus, Gnostic or Chiliast? A New Solution to an Old Problem," *Journal of Early Christian Studies* 8 (2000): 135–72.

the Apostles, each written sometime in the first half of the second century. All these parties with affinities to the opponents were also active in Asia Minor.

b. The author of 1 John stresses the beginnings of the Christian movement in such a way as to give the impression that a considerable period of time has elapsed since then (2:7; 3:11). Related to this, he writes as if he has seen a great deal transpire in his lifetime, from the appearance of the "word of life" himself in the world, leading to the dispersion of the darkness, and finally to antichrists coming.

c. The author, in 2 and 3 John, refers to himself as ὁ πρεσβύτερος, "the elder." This could of course refer to the church office, but there are also reasons to think that the author is referring to his advanced age and uses the word to mean, or to include the meaning, "the old man" (e.g., Luke 15:25; Acts 2:17; 1 Tim. 5:1–2).[3] (For more on this, see the section on 2 John, "Authorship.")

While none of these factors alone is decisive, the consistency of the early external witnesses, the best historical placement of the ideas combatted in the letters, and the signs of the author's age at the time of writing all point toward a late first-century date.

Chronological Order

The relative chronological order of the Gospel and letters is unclear, and a number of plausible proposals can be made. The author of the Muratorian Fragment and Clement of Alexandria (*fr. Cass.* 3), both writing in the late second or early third century, believed that 1 John was written after the Gospel. This has probably been the dominant position of modern interpreters as well, though with many exceptions.[4] A plausible but by-no-means-provable hypothesis is as follows:

The Gospel according to John, the product of many years of preaching and teaching, was completed and sent out at a time when the false teaching known from 1–2 John was already beginning to circulate (1 John 2:19; 2 John 7).[5] This Gospel may have been distributed to churches in Asia Minor accompanied by the letter we know as 2 John as a sort of cover letter—the address to "the elect lady" (2 John 1) being a general one that would apply to any local church in the region. One leader in one congregation (house church), however, rebuffed the representatives John had sent to deliver the Gospel and letter, perhaps aligning himself instead with the "antichrists." In response, John sent a new letter to Gaius, one of the faithful of the congregation, commending his faithfulness and serving notice about Diotrephes. Finally, after John had visited "face to face" with some churches and individuals like Gaius, John wrote and sent out to the churches of Asia Minor the general "letter" we know as 1 John, to deal more explicitly and at length with the

[3] Some describe the author's style as repetitive and like that of an aged person (James Hope Moulton, *A Grammar of New Testament Greek*, vol. 4, *Style*, by Noel Turner [Edinburgh: T&T Clark, 1976], 135, cited approvingly by Martin Hengel, *The Johannine Question* [London: SCM, 1989], 47).

[4] Hengel, for instance, thinks the Gospel "was completed some years after the letters and edited after the death of the elder" (*Johannine Question*, 73); and Schuchard thinks the Gospel was the last of the apostle's five works, composed "as a last will and testament" (Bruce Schuchard, *1–3 John*, ConcC [St. Louis, MO: Concordia, 2013], 3).

[5] This might have happened either before or after John's exile on the island of Patmos. Tertullian thought 1 John, at least, was written after Revelation (*Fug.* 9; *Scorp.* 12).

issue of the false teachers and to serve as his final witness to "that which was from the beginning" (1 John 1:1).

Place of Writing

Early Christian tradition identifies John as the apostle, the evangelist, and the author of Revelation and places him in Asia Minor, associated especially with Ephesus.[6] This seems to be confirmed in that many of the earliest traces of the use of these letters are found in sources from Asia Minor or with Asian connections: Polycarp of Smyrna (1–2 John, ca. 110); Papias (1 John, along with John and Revelation, ca. 125), the *Epistle of the Apostles* (1 John, with John and Revelation, ca. 120 or 145), and Irenaeus (1–2 John, with John and Revelation, 180–190).

Authorship

Common Authorship

There is great diversity of opinion today as to the authorship of each book of the Johannine corpus, though theories of a Johannine school, at least in their most developed forms, appear to be losing some of the ground they once held. Nevertheless, both for stylistic reasons and by virtue of the early external testimony, the most likely conclusion remains that the same author wrote the three epistles and that this author is the disciple who claims responsibility for the Fourth Gospel (John 21:24), "the disciple whom Jesus loved" (21:20). One finds in these works the same theology expressed in very similar terminology, the same simplicity of construction, and a common use of Hebrew parallelism. There is the same love of contrasts: light and darkness, life and death, love and hatred, truth and falsehood, Christ and antichrist, of the world and not of the world. The Gospel and the letters often repeat and reapply concepts using slightly different expressions. Unity of authorship is not only the immediate impression of the novice reader but also the studied conclusion of the vast majority of actual students of the question, despite the present trends of scholarly opinion.

Throughout antiquity there was a clear and consistent assumption of common apostolic authorship of the Gospel and at least the first epistle, going back to sources in Asia Minor, the probable place of writing. Most often the second and third epistles, and Revelation, were included as well, though circumstances in the third century brought these last three books into question in some circles.[7]

The Author's Identity

None of the five books that make up the Johannine corpus makes any explicit claim of authorship by John the son of Zebedee. Nevertheless, the unusually strong external attestation for the Johannine authorship of these books, even as a group, is hard to dismiss if one wants to maintain any integrity with the historical sources.[8] Irenaeus

[6] Irenaeus, *Haer.* 3.1.1, 3.3.4; Clement of Alexandria, *Who Is the Rich Man?* 42; Eusebius, *Hist. eccl.* 3.20.9.
[7] See the introductions to 2 and 3 John, and Charles E. Hill, *The Johannine Corpus in the Early Church* (Oxford: Oxford University Press, 2004).
[8] See also the chapter on the Gospel of John in this volume.

and the author of the Muratorian Fragment, both writing in the last decades of the second century, identify the author of the epistles as John the apostle of Jesus. Moreover, each shows that these letters are already firmly connected to the Gospel and the Revelation, and a belief in the Johannine authorship of the Gospel is visible even earlier in Theophilus of Antioch, Ptolemy the Valentinian, the *Epistle of the Apostles*, and probably Justin Martyr (with whom the evidence is more subtle); the book of Revelation is clearly attributed to the apostle by Justin.

It is a common assumption today that the tradition of Johannine authorship arose as a deliberate fiction, invented to provide these books with an authority they lacked for the first several decades of their existence. But explanations for how, when, or by whom the myth was fabricated and then how it was so quickly adopted and so consistently maintained throughout the church are leaky at best and often turn positively conspiratorial. It has come to the point that many critical scholars simply dismiss the early external evidence as self-evidently unreliable, preferring to rely instead on their own individual construals of the internal evidence.[9] The proposal advanced by Martin Hengel and Bauckham, which attributes the Gospel and letters to the mysterious figure of John the elder mentioned obliquely by Papias of Hierapolis,[10] pays greater attention to the historical evidence, but it has to rely on several highly questionable interpretations and reconstructions.[11]

The question of the authorship of the epistles is necessarily connected to the evidence of the Fourth Gospel. But there are relatively strong reasons from the epistles themselves for affirming authorship by an apostle.

The author's eyewitness testimony. The author, in the first few verses of the first epistle, makes clear his claim to having known Jesus personally when Jesus walked this earth: "That which was from the beginning, which we have heard, which we have seen with our eyes, which we looked upon and have touched with our hands, concerning the word of life . . ." (1 John 1:1). This is a witness not only to what *was* heard, seen, and felt, though this may be the most important thing, but also to what *we* have heard, seen, and felt. The reluctance of so many contemporary scholars to admit these verses as a claim to personal knowledge of the historical Jesus of Nazareth is curious.[12]

The authority with which the author writes. About the first letter, Hengel observes, "The letter does not so much argue as decree";[13] and about the third, he says, "The elder, backed by no church institution, with an authority based only on his bare

---

[9] See in particular the critique of Hengel, *Johannine Question*, expanded in the German edition, *Die johanneische Frage: Ein Lösungsversuch*, with a contribution by J. Frey (Tübingen: Mohr Siebeck, 1993).

[10] Hengel, *Johannine Question*; Richard Bauckham, "Papias and Polycrates on the Origin of the Fourth Gospel," *JTS* 44 (1993): 24–69; Bauckham, *Jesus and the Eyewitnesses: The Gospels as Eyewitness Testimony* (Grand Rapids, MI: Eerdmans, 2006).

[11] For some of these see Andreas J. Köstenberger and Stephen O. Stout, "'The Disciple Jesus Loved': Witness, Author, Apostle—A Response to Richard Bauckham's *Jesus and the Eyewitnesses*, *BBR* 18 (2008): 209–31.

[12] Note, e.g., the treatment of Raymond E. Brown, *The Epistles of John*, AB 30 (New York: Doubleday, 1982), 158–63, who argues that the "we" in 1:1–4 refers to "a School of traditionbearers" who did not actually see, hear, or touch Jesus, "rather than to eyewitnesses" (160).

[13] Hengel, *Johannine Question*, 46.

reputation as a witness to Jesus and a teacher which had been proven over many years, has the firm intention of delivering a public rebuke to Diotrephes on his planned visit."[14] The author's confident but unpretentious assumption of authority stands in vivid contrast to the deferential attitudes of writers like Clement of Rome, a close contemporary of the author, and of Ignatius of Antioch and Polycarp of Smyrna, who wrote perhaps ten to twenty years later. All of these church leaders appeal to the greater authority of the apostles before them. The Johannine author instead appeals only to what he has seen, heard, and touched concerning the "word of life," that is, his direct connection with Jesus. And he writes as if the authorizations of the Fourth Gospel stand behind him: "And you also will bear witness, because you have been with me from the beginning" (John 15:27); "'As the Father has sent me, even so I am sending you.' And when he had said this, he breathed on them and said to them, 'Receive the Holy Spirit'" (John 20:21–22). It is a sense of this kind of special commissioning and unique authority that stands behind the author's boldness in the epistles.

Moreover, the author writes in this way not only to one but to several congregations in these three epistles. D. A. Carson and Douglas Moo conclude, "But that means that the most obvious explanation for this cross-congregational authority is that the author of these epistles was an apostle, since elders per se did not, so far as we know, enjoy such authority."[15]

The author's apostolic self-consciousness. "That which we have seen and heard we proclaim also to you, so that you too may have fellowship with us; and indeed our fellowship is with the Father and with his Son Jesus Christ" (1 John 1:3). Here the author strikingly interposes a link between his readers and the revelation of the divine majesty in Jesus Christ, and that link is none other than himself. The "us" does not include the Christian community at large, whom he is addressing; the only other members of this group would be the small band that shared the apostolic commission. In the first and third letter there is an indignation expressed against those who break fellowship not just with the church, but with the author, and with the author as representative of a group of commissioned eyewitnesses (1 John 1:1–4; 4:6; 3 John 9–10).

All this is much easier to believe about an apostle, who needed no other ecclesiastical authorization to carry out this kind of activity. Based on these indications of apostolic identity, combined with the external evidence for the attribution to John the son of Zebedee, the treatment here will refer to this John as the author.

Purpose

There are several places where John states an explicit reason for writing one or another portion of the epistle (1 John 1:4; 2:1, 12–14, 21, 26; 5:13). Based on these

[14] Ibid., 38.
[15] D. A. Carson and Douglas J. Moo, *An Introduction to the New Testament*, 2nd ed. (Grand Rapids, MI: Zondervan, 2005), 675.

and the rest of the contents, there seem to have been two main, intimately related reasons for 1 John.

To Impart True Assurance and Promote True Fellowship

One of the main purposes of 1 John is to impart true assurance to a troubled church that has recently seen the exodus of an influential group of people from its midst. While this first-century occasion has long since passed, the need for Christian assurance and true spiritual fellowship is perennial, and John's words continue to minister to Christ's people in all kinds of circumstances. The letter is full of what could be called "assurance tests," or "marks of a true Christian." These are both doctrinal and behavioral in focus and may be expressed positively or negatively. Positively, for instance, believers may be assured of the following:

Doctrinal

- "Everyone who believes that Jesus is the Christ has been born of God" (5:1).
- "You who believe in the name of the Son of God . . . may know that you have eternal life" (5:13).

Behavioral

- "Whoever loves his brother abides in the light, and in him there is no cause for stumbling" (2:10).

Conversely, the letter also contains what might be called "marks of a non-Christian (or Antichristian)" in order to dispel any lingering doubts created by those who had left:

Doctrinal

- "Who is the liar but he who denies that Jesus is the Christ? This is the antichrist, he who denies the Father and the Son" (2:22).
- "No one who denies the Son has the Father" (2:23).
- "And every spirit that does not confess Jesus is not from God" (4:3).

Behavioral

- "If we say we have fellowship with him while we walk in darkness, we lie and do not practice the truth" (1:6).
- "Whoever says 'I know him' but does not keep his commandments is a liar, and the truth is not in him" (2:4).
- "But whoever hates his brother is in the darkness and walks in the darkness, and does not know where he is going, because the darkness has blinded his eyes" (2:11).

Along with assurance goes true fellowship. John is also writing that all true believers may have fellowship with one another, with the apostles, and with the Father and his Son, Jesus Christ (1:3–4).

To Counteract False Teaching

First John was written in response to a specific form of false teaching that was afflicting a particular church or group of churches. Clearly, this was no side issue[16] for the author, but a driving motivation for his composition. Though the rupture was now in the past, the threat of deception from the opponents was still a live one when John wrote, "I write these things to you about those who are trying to deceive you" (2:26), and "Little children, let no one deceive you" (3:7). This is not to say that had there been no controversy, John would not have addressed any of the topics of the epistle. But that historical moment provided the impetus for John to deliver teaching that has become foundational for the church in all subsequent ages.

Probably the most prominent feature of the false teaching was in the area of christology (cf. 2 John 9, "the teaching of Christ"). But theological concepts are always interconnected, and this christological error had many tentacles, affecting both theology and life.

Structure and Outline

John frequently uses structuring devices as he writes, mainly parallelisms and repetitions, which are easiest to see in relatively small portions of the epistle. He often writes in an a, b, a', b' pattern or in a chiastic a, b, b', a' pattern. The first of these is epitomized in 1 John 2:12–14, where one can count nine elements from verses 12–13 that are repeated in verse 14. An example of the second is in 3:9:

a No one born of God
  b makes a practice of sinning,
    c for God's seed abides in him,
  b' and he cannot keep on sinning
a' because he has been born of God.

Also, John often arranges things in threes (three false claims, using ἐὰν εἴπωμεν, "if we say," 1 John 1:6–10; three more false claims, using ὁ λέγων, "whoever says," 2:4–9; three reasons for writing [γράφω], 2:12–13; three reasons for having written [ἔγραψα], 2:14; three witnesses, 5:7–8; three affirmations with οἴδαμεν, "we know," 5:18–20).

While such structuring devices are easily discernible on a micro level, a clear structure for the entire epistle is not as easy to discern; thus, attempts by modern interpreters to find one can vary greatly. John repeats ideas, words, or phrases in different contexts, and it is not always clear whether these have structural significance or not. One principle to keep in mind is that he often finishes one section with a key word or phrase that serves to transition to the next. This can make it hard to see

[16] Some interpreters today argue for what they call a "non-polemical" approach to 1 John, an approach that understands the polemical interests of the epistle as minimal and as restricted to the two passages that specifically mention the "antichrists," 2:18–23 and 4:1–6. As examples, see Judith M. Lieu, "'Authority to Become Children of God': A Study of 1 John," *NovT* 23 (1981): 210–28; T. Griffith, "A Non-Polemical Reading of 1 John," *TynBul* 49 (1998): 253–76; Hansjörg Schmid, "How to Read the First Epistle of John Non-Polemically," *Bib* 85 (2004): 24–41; Daniel R. Streett, *They Went Out from Us: The Identity of the Opponents in First John*, BZNW 177 (Berlin: de Gruyter, 2011).

exactly where one section ends and the next begins. With these considerations in mind, one possible outline of 1 John is as follows:

I. Prologue: The Message of the Incarnation of the Son of God (1:1–5)
  A. What was from the beginning—the word of life—we announce to you (1:1–4)
  B. What we heard from him—that God is light—we announce to you (1:5)
II. False Claims about Sin and Their Solution in the Work of Jesus Christ (1:6–2:17)
  a Three false claims (1:6–10)
    b The real solution for sin: propitiation, Jesus Christ the righteous (2:1–2)
  a' Three false claims (2:3–11)
    b' Three truths: sins forgiven, Christ known, the Evil One defeated (2:12–14)
  Summary: Love the Father, not the world (2:15–17)
III. The Last Hour (2:18–28)
  a The coming of the Antichrist and the antichrists (2:18–19)
    b The anointing distinguishes truth from lies (2:20–21)
      c The liar and Antichrist denies the Son (2:22–23)
        d Abide in what you learned from the beginning (2:24–25)
      c' The deceivers (2:26)
    b' The anointing teaches you, abide in it (2:27)
  a' The coming of the Christ (2:28)
IV. Righteousness and Sin (2:29–3:10)
  a Righteousness and purity demonstrate that we are his children (2:29–3:3)
    b Christ came to take away sin and lawlessness (3:4–5)
    b' Christ came to destroy the works of the Devil (3:6–8)
  a' Righteousness demonstrates that we are God's children, not the Devil's (3:9–10)
V. Love of One Another (3:11–18)
  a The ancient message: love one another (3:11)
    b Avoid the example of Cain, who hated his brother and killed him (3:12–15)
    b' Follow the example of Jesus, who loved us and gave his life for us (3:16–17)
  a' Make this love authentic (3:18)
VI. Confidence before God (3:19–24)
  a We shall know that we are of the truth (3:19)
    b From a clear conscience (3:20–21)
    b' From the work of the Spirit, enabling obedience in faith and love (3:22–24a)
  a' We know that we abide in him (3:24b)
VII. Knowing the Spirit of God and the Spirit of Antichrist (4:1–6)
  a Test the spirits (4:1)
    b By confession that Jesus Christ has come in the flesh (4:2–3)
    b' By hearing the apostolic witness (4:4–6)

VIII. Love One Another as God Loved Us (4:7–21)
- a Love of one another is tied to love of God (4:7–8)
  - b The essence of love: God loved us and sent his Son to save us (4:9–10)
    - c Perfect love is to follow God's example of love (4:11–12)
      - d Confessing Jesus and abiding in love mean we abide in God and he in us (4:13–16)
    - c' Perfect love conquers fear of judgment (4:17–18)
  - b' The essence of love: we love because he first loved us (4:19)
- a' Love of one another is tied to love of God (4:20–21)

IX. Belief in Jesus (5:1–13)
- A. Belief that Jesus is the Christ enables us to love God's children (5:1)
- B. Belief that Jesus is God's Son enables us to love God and keep his commandments (5:2–5)
- C. Belief in God's Son accepts God's threefold witness concerning his Son (5:6–10)
- D. Belief in the name of God's Son brings assurance of eternal life (5:11–13)

X. Boldness and Prayer (5:14–17)
- A. Assurance that God hears our requests (5:14–15)
- B. Prayer and the sin unto death (5:16–17)

XI. Final Affirmations and a Warning (5:18–21)
- A. Everyone born of God does not sin (5:18)
- B. We are of God (5:19)
- C. The Son of God has come and has given us understanding (5:20)
- D. Keep yourselves from idols (5:21)

Message and Theology

Theology Proper

The message John heard from Jesus and wants immediately to impress upon his readers is the foundational assertion that "God is light, and in him is no darkness at all" (1 John 1:5). His final assertion at the end of the epistle, "[This] is the true God and eternal life" (5:20), also comes with a warning: "Little children, keep yourselves from idols" (5:21). Clearly, John sees the true teaching about God as being of primary importance. Some have argued that John sees the false understanding of God as the root of all the false teaching addressed in the epistle.

But who would be asserting that God contains darkness? It is possible that the opponents were not claiming this, but that John only meant to teach that if we confess God as light, we ought to walk in the light. On the other hand, we know that later docetic teachers (in particular, Cerinthus, according to Irenaeus, *Haer*. 1.26.12) claimed that in fact the Creator God, the God of the Old Testament, was immoral and ignorant, and that there was another God who was high above the Creator. John might have seen that the opponents' teaching was headed in this direction and might have sought to preempt it by reasserting the pure goodness and truthfulness of the one true God.

Today, John's assertion that God is pure light is certainly no less fundamental.

It stands against any attempt to cast a shadow of reproach over scriptural morality, while favoring the shifting, self-determined morality of a self-divinizing culture.

Ethics

Connected integrally to the assertion that God is light in 1 John 1:5 are repeated points made against some who claim to be without sin, yet whose lives are characterized by darkness rather than light (1:5–10; 2:4–5; 3:7–10). The author wants to guard against any far-fetched claim that one has not sinned (1:5–2:2), any indifference to God's commands (2:3–11), any denial of the need for righteous behavior (2:15–3:18), any despising of the Christian brethren (2:9–11; 3:10c–18, 23; 4:7–12; 4:16–5:3), and any love for a world that is passing away (2:15–17; 4:5; cf. 3:17–18). Instead, he teaches that everyone who has the Christian hope will purify himself, as Christ is pure (3:3), and that the one who loves God will love those who are born of God (5:1).

That God is light means that his children must walk in the light, as Christ is in the light. That God is love means that his children too must love as he loved—that is, in a way that sacrifices self for the sake of the brotherhood, imitating the self-giving love of the God who sent his Son to be the propitiation for our sins (4:9–12).

Christology: Atonement

The ethical breaches of the antichrists imply christological errors. The immediately preceding context in 1 John 1:5–10 shows that in the controverted passage 2:1–2, John is not moving in the orbit of the modern debate over the extent of the atonement. He proclaims that Jesus Christ "*is* the propitiation"[17] for our sins and for the sins of the whole world. This is not the same as saying he "*has made* propitiation" for our sins and for the sins of the whole world. In the same way, to say that Jesus *is the Savior* of the (whole) world (John 3:17; 4:42; 1 John 4:14) does not mean that he has saved or will save every individual person in the world; it means that the whole world needs saving, and that he is the world's only Savior.[18]

It is helpful to remember that this pointed affirmation is made in the face of a particular form of false teaching that evidently promotes a type of elitism or exclusivism. The elitism in view is, however, apparently not the assumption of those who think only *their* sins will be expiated by Christ, those who would thus need chiding by John to broaden their outlook and admit that Christ died for others too. To the contrary, these people apparently do not think they *need* such sin-expiating work. If John's words in 1 John 1:5–10 are related to the teaching of the opponents, it seems

---

[17]The RSV translates ἱλασμός as "expiation"; the ESV, KJV, NASB, and NKJV, as "propitiation"; the NET, NIV, and NRSV, as "atoning sacrifice." The sense of *propitiation* surely cannot be denied, for in the previous verse Jesus is presented as our advocate with the Father. Yet there is no need to deny that *expiation* of our sins is also in view, as it is more explicitly in 4:10. See Roger Nicole, "C. H. Dodd and the Doctrine of Propitiation," *WTJ* 17 (1954–1955): 117–57; J. Ramsey Michaels, "Atonement in John's Gospel and Epistles," in *The Glory of the Atonement: Biblical, Historical and Practical Perspectives: Essays in Honor of Roger Nicole*, ed. Charles E. Hill and Frank A. James III (Downers Grove, IL: InterVarsity Press, 2004), 106–18; Robert W. Yarbrough, *1–3 John*, BECNT (Grand Rapids, MI: Baker Academic, 2008), 78.

[18]In this same sense, God *is* the God of all people, even the Buddhist and the atheist, though neither the Buddhist nor the atheist worships this God. He is their only God, because there is no other God. In 1 John 2:2, the assertion that Jesus Christ is the propitiation for the sins of the whole world certifies that the whole world needs propitiation because of its sins and that Jesus Christ is the world's only propitiation.

they are claiming (subtly or overtly) that they have no sin—even that they have never sinned. Such people would not think they need the atoning blood of Christ (1:7, 9) to turn away God's righteous judgment, even if other people do.[19] John's assertion that Jesus Christ is the propitiation for the sins of the whole world then reestablishes for his readers that *all* people, even these deceivers who might claim otherwise, *need* propitiation, the propitiation that is found in Jesus Christ alone.

There is also a christological aspect to the issue of the antichrists' lack of love for the Christian brethren. For John insists that we do not really know what love is unless we know the truest manifestation of love, namely, God's sending of his only Son into the world to save us through his propitiating work (1 John 4:9–10; cf. 3:16). Here again, ethics and theology are bound together.

Christology: Incarnation

The rest of 1 John shows that at the center of the controversy are grave and fundamental errors about the person of Christ. There are two major strands of the opponents' christological denials. First, they do not confess that Jesus Christ has come in the flesh (4:2; 2 John 7), which includes Jesus Christ's coming through and by (the) water and (the) blood (1 John 5:6). That is, they deny Jesus Christ's true humanity and suffering. Second, they do not confess that "Jesus is the Christ" (2:22; 5:1) or that "Jesus is the Son of God" (4:15; 5:5; cf. 2:23).

Regarding the first issue, it is probably significant that John never accuses them of denying that *Jesus* has come in the flesh. It is always a denial that *Jesus Christ* has come in the flesh, or in the water and in the blood (see table 8).[20] Closely related to this is John's emphasis in 1 John 1:7 on the blood of Jesus, God's Son, which cleanses from all sin.

What they deny	What they do not deny
Jesus Christ has come in flesh	(Jesus has come in flesh)

Table 8

Regarding the second, it is never framed as a denial that Christ is the Son of God, but always that Jesus is the Christ or that Jesus is the Son of God (see table 9).

What they deny	What they do not deny
Jesus is the Christ	(Christ is the Son of God)
Jesus is the Son of God	

Table 9

[19] This attitude might have an analogue today when the ideas of propitiation, expiation, or atonement are looked down on or ridiculed as "primitive" ideas unworthy of God.

[20] "It is probably for this reason that the un-Johannine (in *GJ* [Gospel of John] terms) Jesus Christ becomes characteristic in 1 John. The two names together are shorthand for Jesus is the Christ in a context where there were those who denied this" (J. Painter, "The 'Opponents' in 1 John," *NTS* 32 [1986]: 64).

We thus have a rather clear disjunction between *Jesus* and *Christ*, or between Jesus and "Jesus Christ." On the surface, this might be compatible with either of two positions. It might signify a return to a "Jewish" outlook that refused to confess Jesus's messiahship and messianic sonship to God in a typical Jewish sense. This view relies on a plausible interpretation of 2:22–23 and 5:1 and has been defended by a number of exegetes.[21] But it is much more likely that the problem is instead what could be called a "Cerinthian" docetism, which refuses to confess that the man Jesus is himself the heavenly Christ figure, claiming instead that the heavenly Christ has not (and cannot) come in the flesh.

First, although the "Jewish" view can make sense of 2:22–23 and 5:1, it has trouble accounting for John's emphasis on confessing the human, physical nature of Jesus Christ in 1 John 4:2 and 5:6. This confession is apparently so crucial to the controversy that it becomes the focal point in 2 John 7, and it soon resurfaces in Polycarp, *Phil.* 7.1, and then elsewhere in the second century. Second, people attracted to Jewish messianism might deny that Jesus is the true Messiah, but that the Messiah is a true human being who came "in the flesh" (1 John 4:2) would hardly disturb them.[22]

A third reason has to do with the way christological titles are used in the Gospel and the epistles. In the Gospel, the title "Son of God" primarily signifies Jesus's *divinity* and heavenly origin, and "Christ," because it typically is used in the narrative to depict the way Jesus's contemporaries used the term, primarily denotes a merely human, Jewish Messiah, the one Moses and the prophets wrote about (John 1:41, 45). In other words, "Christ" and "Son of God" are typically not synonymous in John.[23] But in 1 John, "Christ" and "Son of God" each seem to signify Jesus's divinity. The opponents deny both that "Jesus is the Christ" (1 John 2:2; 5:1) and that "Jesus is the Son of God" (4:15; 5:5; cf. 2:23). Therefore, the denial of unity between "Jesus" the man and a divine "Christ" would indicate a Cerinthian, docetic type of error.

Today, the greater tendency is obviously to run to the other christological extreme and to deny Jesus Christ's full deity. But maintaining the robust incarnational christology of 1 John (along with the Gospel of John and the integrated witness of the entire New Testament) is just as critical today as it was in John's day. A savior who is only human and is not also the divine Son of God cannot be a pure and sinless sacrifice for sin (John 1:29–34; 1 John 1:7; 2:1–2), and union with him could not be union with God, communicating divine life and opening up divine fellowship to God's people (John 15:4–5; 17:20–23; 1 John 2:23–25; 5:11–12).

Doctrine of Sin

Discussion has arisen over what seems to be a contradiction in 1 John's treatment of sin: in 1:8–2:2, John assumes that Christians may still sin, and in 3:4–10 he alleges

[21] Most recently and extensively by Streett, *They Went Out from Us*.

[22] As Trypho later asserts, he and his people "all expect that Christ will be a man [born] of men" (Justin, *Dialogue with Trypho the Jew* 49.1 [*ANF* 1:219]).

[23] The only exception to this is significant. "Son of God" seems to be equivalent to "Christ" in John 20:31: "that you may believe that Jesus is the Christ, the Son of God." But here John is specifically addressing his contemporary readers. This indicates then his *readers'* situation, in which it was necessary to affirm the identity that *Jesus* is the Christ, the Son of God.

that they do not and cannot. Some seek to resolve the tension by distinguishing between certain kinds of sins that Christians do commit and others that they do not (for instance, between "intentional" and "unintentional" sins or, more plausibly, between the "sin that leads to death" [5:16–17] and other sins). But there is no clear indication in the context that John has such a distinction in mind. Others see a hidden condition in John's words: believers do not sin *as long as they are abiding in Christ*. But this seems refuted by 1 John 3:9, where John sees the Christian's inability to sin as a consequence of being born of God, something one cannot fall in and out of: "for His seed remains in him; and he cannot sin, because he has been born of God" (NKJV).

The issue is perhaps best addressed in two steps. First, John introduces the topic in 1 John 3:4 not with the expression "the one who sins" but with a fuller expression, "everyone who makes a practice of sinning" (ὁ ποιῶν τὴν ἁμαρτίαν, also 3:8; cf. John 8:34), which he contrasts with "practices righteousness" (ὁ ποιῶν τὴν δικαιοσύνην, 3:7, 10, introduced already in 2:29). That is, John does not have in mind discrete acts of sin, but what might be called a person's lifestyle or character of life, the way one "walks." One walks either in darkness or in light (1:6–7; 2:9, 11). John's use of the present continuous tense of ἁμαρτάνω in 3:6, 9 simply abbreviates this fuller mode of expression.

Second, it is also apparent that in 1 John 3:4–10 John is not speaking in the abstract; his allusion to the deceivers in 3:7 (cf. 2:26) points to the presence of a rival party. John has already alluded to some who boast of having fellowship with God while they walk in darkness (they do not "*practice* the truth," 1:6; cf. John 3:21) and do not keep his commandments (1 John 2:4), yet claim that they have no sin and have not sinned (1:8, 10). John's first readers no doubt know whom he is talking about and the kind of lives these people lead. They also know the distinctive example of John and the kind of life they have been nurtured in "from the beginning." This is the "old" commandment to love one another (2:7), in imitation of God's love for us in sending his Son to be our propitiation, and of Christ's love in laying down his life for his brethren. John writes to establish with absolute clarity just who, in this situation, is to be believed and followed. Who is it that is born of God? "If you know that he is righteous, you may be sure that everyone who practices righteousness has been born of him" (2:29). Who is it that is righteous? "Whoever practices righteousness is righteous, as [Christ] is righteous" (3:7). Righteousness is revealed by doing right, by being Christlike.

John's teaching contradicts the idea that the only thing differentiating a Christian from a non-Christian is that one has her sins forgiven. Whoever is justified is also born of God and now has God's seed abiding in her and hence cannot turn back to a life of sin. If she goes on sinning, "mak[ing] a practice of sin" (1 John 3:4), if she does not abide or remain in him, then she has not been born of God and never really knew Christ. John's declaration that the one born of God does not sin (5:18a) does not mean that the process of sanctification is short-circuited or that perfection is attained in this life. But it does mean that the one who is born of God is forever kept by Christ from the Devil's grasp and *will* practice righteousness (5:18b–c).

Eschatology

Inaugurated Eschatology

Some critics have sought to establish a conflict between the eschatologies of the Fourth Gospel and 1 John by depicting the Gospel as "realized" and 1 John as "futuristic." First John receives this designation largely on the basis of 2:28; 3:1–2; and 4:17, which show a vibrant expectation of Christ's future coming and the final judgment. Yet in 1 John (as also in the Gospel), the events still awaited are simply the outworking of what has already been inaugurated by the great, epochal events of the incarnation, suffering, death, resurrection/ascension, and present session of the Lord Jesus Christ: "the darkness is passing away and the true light is already shining" (2:8; see also 2:17–18; 3:14; 5:11–13). While the emphases of the Gospel and the letters may differ according to their genres and situations, they both exemplify the same harmonious eschatology that is "inaugurated" yet not fully "realized."

Antichrist

Perhaps the most distinguishing feature of the eschatology of 1–2 John is their use of the terms "antichrist" and "antichrists"—according to our present knowledge, for the first time in literature:

- "Children, it is the last hour, and as you have heard that antichrist is coming, so now many antichrists have come. Therefore we know that it is the last hour. They went out from us. . . . Who is the liar but he who denies that Jesus is the Christ? This is the antichrist, he who denies the Father and the Son" (1 John 2:18–19, 22).
- "By this you know the Spirit of God: every spirit that confesses that Jesus Christ has come in the flesh is from God, and every spirit that does not confess Jesus is not from God. This is the spirit of the antichrist, which you heard was coming and now is in the world already" (1 John 4:2–3).
- "For many deceivers have gone out into the world, those who do not confess the coming of Jesus Christ in the flesh. Such a one is the deceiver and the antichrist" (2 John 7).

The *anti* prefix could mean "opposed to" or "instead of," that is, counterfeit or false. The latter meaning (which would likely entail the former as well) is probably the emphasis here. The indirect way in which John refers to a coming Antichrist ("you have heard that antichrist is coming") has led some to claim that he did not himself believe the report he mentions.[24] But John's pronounced affirmation of a spirit of antichrist already at work in the world (1 John 4:3) strongly suggests that the work

[24] B. B. Warfield, "Antichrist," *The Expository Times* 32 (1921): 358–60, reprinted in John E. Meeter, ed., *Selected Shorter Writings of Benjamin B. Warfield*, vol. 1 (Phillipsburg, NJ: P&R, 1970), 356–62. This is tied to a view of the progress of Christianity that seems to rule out the possibility of a future eruption of evil such as the Antichrist expectation assumes.

of this spirit would culminate in a final Antichrist figure. Thus, John must be affirming the future coming of such a figure, though perhaps he does not agree with the views about this figure expressed by others (perhaps by the antichrists themselves). He is simply more interested at this point in affirming that many "antichrists" have already come, namely, those who do not confess the coming of Jesus as the Christ or the coming of Jesus Christ in the flesh.

Jesus himself had warned that many false prophets and "false Christs" (ψευδόχριστοι) would come (see Matt. 24:5, 11, 24), and in John's Gospel he even hinted at a particular individual: "I have come in my Father's name, and you do not receive me. If another [ἄλλος] comes in his own name, you will receive him" (John 5:43).[25] Paul had spoken of an individual "man of lawlessness" to come, who would seek to be recognized as an object of worship (2 Thess. 2:3–4). In the Revelation of John, two "beasts" arise to lead astray those who dwell on earth (Revelation 13).

Interpreters have long struggled to understand how these and several other scriptural predictions about future, climactic manifestations of forces opposed to God might fit together. But the descriptions of the "mystery of lawlessness" already at work mentioned by Paul (2 Thess. 2:7), the "spirit of the antichrist" in the world already mentioned by John (1 John 4:3), and possibly the second beast in Revelation 13 seem to depict very much the same diabolical spiritual influences that always afflict God's people throughout the inter-advent era in anticipation of the final conflict. This spirit/mystery/beast deceives the world into believing what is false (1 John 4:1; 2 John 7; 2 Thess. 2:11; Rev. 13:14). Therefore, it is appropriate that John labels these Asian false teachers "antichrists," for they have been anointed with a false and deceiving spirit. John's language of "anointing" (χρῖσμα) in 1 John 2:20, 27 probably denotes an ironic wordplay. Contrasting with the falsely anointed "antichrists" are those who have received the anointing from "the Holy One," whose anointing teaches them about everything. Because they are anointed, they could be called "christs." Thus, there is one Christ and there are many "christs," just as there is also one Antichrist and there are many antichrists. The spirit of the Antichrist inspires the opponents to deny that Jesus is the Christ, who has come in the flesh, by the water and by the blood. But it is the Holy Spirit who anoints true believers, teaches them all things (John 14:26; 16:13), and glorifies Jesus (John 16:14).

Select Bibliography

Please see the bibliography at the end of this chapter, after 3 John.

---

[25] A number of Patristic writers understood this verse as a direct prediction of the Antichrist. For the developments of the Antichrist idea in the second century and beyond, see C. E. Hill, "Antichrist from the Tribe of Dan," *JTS* 46 (1995): 99–117.

2 JOHN

Introduction

The epistle known as 2 John emerges from the same controversy that lies behind 1 John, one generated by the coming of deceivers, antichrists who spread a false teaching about Jesus Christ. Together with 3 John, this epistle illustrates the message of 1 John by establishing the importance of the two poles of true doctrine and love of the brethren. In 2 John the major concern is confession of the true teaching about Jesus; in 3 John it is loving treatment of the brethren, though in both epistles both themes are intertwined. The short letter 2 John stands in the canon of New Testament Scripture as a perpetual reminder to the church that she is in the last days, even the last hour (1 John 2:18), and will have to confront destructive teaching that falsely claims to be Christian (cf. 2 Tim. 4:3–4). The church must be vigilant in her understanding and defense of the truth, and offer no support to those who would corrupt her witness to Jesus Christ, the true Son of God.

Background Issues

Authorship

Internal indications of style and setting point to the common authorship of 1, 2, and 3 John, and strongly connect these works with the Fourth Gospel as well. Early Christian tradition predominantly supports this and identifies the author as the apostle John.[26] Doubts never surfaced about 1 John in the early church. Origen in the early third century is the first to report uncertainty about the genuineness of 2 and 3 John (*Comm. Jo.* 5; see Eusebius, *Hist. eccl.* 6.25.10). Origen apparently did not share this uncertainty, nor did his student Dionysius of Alexandria (*Hist. eccl.* 7.25.16). Eusebius of Caesarea in the early fourth century hinted that 2 and 3 John, each of which identifies its author as "the elder," might have been written by some John other than the apostle, though he did not explicitly suggest, as he did for the Revelation, that this John might have been a certain "John the elder" mentioned earlier by Papias of Hierapolis (Eusebius, *Hist. eccl.* 2.25.3; 3.39.6).[27] The connection was made, however, by some known to Jerome in about 392 (*On Illustrious Men* 9, 18). In spite of this, apostolic authorship was maintained by most, and even those who accepted a different authorship did not necessarily exclude these letters from the canon (e.g., the *Decretum Gelasianum* of the late fifth or early sixth century). In the end, the main tradition best satisfies the evidence, the tradition that connects all the epistles and the Gospel, as well as the Revelation, with the writing activity of John the son of Zebedee. (See the chapters on John, 1 John, and Revelation.)

The author's self-designation "the elder" (ὁ πρεσβύτερος) in 2–3 John is certainly

---

[26] For more on the reception history, see Hill, *Johannine Corpus in the Early Church*, 459–64.

[27] Papias is the only writer known to have had firsthand knowledge of this elder, and Papias does not connect him with the authorship of any New Testament book.

of interest. It is likely that he means it more in the sense of "the elderly one" (much as Paul called himself "Paul the aged," Παῦλος πρεσβύτης, in Philem. 9 KJV) than as a reference to church office per se, particularly if the author is an apostle. This is not because an apostle could not call himself an elder (Peter does so in 1 Pet. 5:1), but because the title "the elder" would not have distinguished him from a number of others who bore that title even in a single local church, where there would have been a plurality of elders (Acts 14:23; Titus 1:5). Church tradition in Asia Minor, extending in this case very early,[28] testifies that John the apostle lived to be a very old man, dying around the year 100 in the early reign of Trajan. By the last decade of the first century John's advanced age would have been a reminder to others of his presence at "the beginning" with Jesus. It is perhaps also referenced in John 21:23, which mentions the rumor spread abroad that the beloved disciple would not die before the Lord returned. The author may have mentioned the rumor and clarified the Lord's actual words because his advanced age was feeding speculation at the time that the return of Christ had to be imminent. Identifying himself to his readers in 2–3 John as ὁ πρεσβύτερος would be a subtle and modestly self-effacing, yet no-less-unmistakable, way of referencing his identity and authority.

Audience

The letter is addressed to "the elect lady and her children." At least since Clement of Alexandria some interpreters have sought to identify the elect lady with an individual. But this gets quite complicated and clumsy when it is said that not only the author but everyone who loves the truth also loves this lady (cf. 3 John 1), when the elder encourages her to "love one another" (2 John 5), and when greetings at the end of the epistle are delivered from "the children of your elect sister" (2 John 13) but not from the sister herself. Thus, most scholars recognize that "the elect lady" designates a church, and "her children" are the individual members, or perhaps the individual house churches within a city or region. This also makes sense of the fact that the addressees are in the plural in verses 8, 10, and 12.

Structure and Outline

Unlike 1 John, 2 John (and, later, 3 John) shows the elements of a typical ancient letter, with clear greeting, body, and closing sections.[29]

I. Greeting (vv. 1–3)
II. Walking in Truth (vv. 4–7)
III. Warning and Exhortation (vv. 8–11)
IV. Closing (vv. 12–13)

[28] See Irenaeus, *Haer.* 2.22.5, 3.3.4, who is apparently dependent upon both Polycarp and, through Papias's book, other Asian elders.

[29] The original section markers in Codex Vaticanus (the earliest we have) divide 2 John into three paragraphs: 1–3, 4–8, and 9–13. A later system added by another reader of the manuscript divided it into two numbered sections: 1–11 and 12–13. The two systems put together anticipate the outline here given, except that Vaticanus has a break between vv. 8 and 9, not between 7 and 8. But clearly, John begins his warning (βλέπετε) in v. 8. There are no paragraph divisions in Codex Sinaiticus.

Message and Theology

Greeting (2 John 1–3)

"Because of the truth that abides in us and will be with us forever" (v. 2) expresses John's confidence that the truth will prevail through this current crisis and will always stand to sustain God's people. His confidence has been echoed by the confessing church time and time again in its long history, as it was expressed in Luther's words at the time of the Reformation:

> Let goods and kindred go,
> This mortal life also;
> The body they may kill:
> God's truth abideth still,
> His kingdom is forever.

And as long as the everlasting truth abides, so long will the church also enjoy "grace, mercy, and peace" from the Father and the Son (v. 3).

Walking in Truth (2 John 4–7)

Verses 4–6 exhibit the intertwining of three pillars of the faith: truth (understood here to be primarily a reference to right belief), love, and obedience to God's commandments. Each is involved in the others, for right belief and love are also the commandments of God (see 1 John 3:23); so to obey God is to love and to believe the truth. But also, if we love God, we will keep his commandments and believe the truth; if we walk in the truth, we will love one another and God, and will obey him.

That John in verse 5 does not say "that *you* love one another" but "that *we* love one another" may also point ahead to the main motive of the letter. Since John has already affirmed his tender love for this church, the reiteration of Jesus's love command (John 13:34–35) may have been an exhortation that they reciprocate John's love by receiving his authority and affirming his teaching, as opposed to the wicked deception of the false teachers. This would form a contrast to the example of Diotrephes in 3 John (on which, see below), who spurns the apostle and his teaching.

The last clause in 2 John 6 is often translated "that you walk in love" (NIV) or "that you follow love" (RSV). But the word "love" is not in the text; the Greek says "that you walk in it" (ἵνα ἐν αὐτῇ περιπατῆτε). In verse 4 the phrase "walking in" has been completed with "truth" (a word John uses five times in the first four verses), and this could be what John means here in verse 6, forming an *inclusio*.[30] This also might be supported by the fact that the next verse seems to supply the reason for "walking" this way: "For [ὅτι] many deceivers have gone out into the world, those

[30] Or, the two ends of a chiastic arrangement with v. 5 and most of v. 6 forming the inner elements:

a Walking in truth, a commandment we received from the Father (v. 4)
  b Another commandment, one we have had from the beginning (v. 5a)
    c "That we love one another" (v. 5b)
    c' "And this is love, that we walk according to his commandments" (v. 6a–b).
  b' "This is the commandment . . . you heard from the beginning" (v. 6c),
a' that we walk in it (truth) (v. 6d).

who do not confess the coming of Jesus Christ in the flesh. Such a one is the deceiver and the antichrist" (2 John 7). That is, the members (the lady's children) who were found to be walking in the truth in verse 4 have not succumbed to the teaching of the antichrists but are maintaining the truth.

Verse 7 states the reason why the apostle has praised his readers' devotion to the truth, and it prepares for his warning that will come in the next section: many deceivers have gone out into the world, those who will not confess that Jesus Christ has come in the flesh (or will not confess Jesus as Christ coming in the flesh). The use of the present tense ("coming," ἐρχόμενον) makes it possible that the subject is the second coming of Christ (present for future) instead of his first. Some commentators favor this option because in 1 John, where the subject is definitely Christ's first coming, John uses the perfect tense in 4:2 and the aorist in 5:6. But (1) it is not uncommon for John to say the same thing with slightly varying language; (2) the present participle can certainly still be used to refer to the past coming of Jesus, just as in English ("the coming of Jesus Christ in the flesh" or "Jesus (as) Christ coming in the flesh"); and (3) while it is likely that the deceivers also deny a future coming of Jesus Christ in the flesh, it is not likely that such a view would be detached from the denial that he has already come in the flesh. And since we know that his latter denial is the chief issue in 1 John, it seems best to assume that it is the same problem treated here. As in 1 John, the elder here links this teaching with "the deceiver and the antichrist" (probably not two separate persons but two names for one [2 John 7]), thus reminding the first readers and all subsequent readers that we are living in "the last hour" (1 John 2:18).

Warning and Exhortation (2 John 8–11)

In verses 8–11 there is a double warning: John first instructs the believers to take care of themselves (2 John 8–9), and then admonishes that they do nothing to encourage the deceivers (vv. 10–11). He forthrightly warns his readers, "Watch yourselves, so that you may not lose what we have worked for,[31] but may win a full reward" (v. 8). This is reminiscent of what Christ says to the church at Sardis: "Wake up, and strengthen what remains and is about to die, for I have not found your works complete in the sight of my God" (Rev. 3:2). As 2 John 9 goes on to show, John's warning is aimed at preventing anyone "go[ing] on ahead" and not abiding in "the teaching of Christ"; such a person "does not have God," while the one who abides in the doctrine "has both the Father and the Son." This statement reiterates what John says in 1 John 2:23, again showing the similarity of the situations of both epistles.

Finally, John warns them not to receive one of these deceivers into the house or give him any greeting, stating that the one who merely greets a deceiver "takes part in his wicked works" (2 John 11). The "house" could be the personal home of a church member or it may be the house church where the assembly gathers. The latter would seem most likely, because the directives are given in the plural: "comes

[31] See John 4:36; 6:27; 1 Cor. 3:8, 14; etc.

to you [pl.] . . . do not receive [pl.] . . . or give him any greeting" (lit. "say [pl.] the greeting") (v. 10). And so, it is an injunction against the church supporting in any way the spreading of false doctrine about Christ. Still, the principle would seem to apply to many other situations outside the official ministry of a local church. What does John's prohibition mean for a denomination? For a seminary? What does it say to an individual lay Christian or a Christian family?

John will not have Christians supporting or encouraging the ministry of those who do not teach the true doctrine about Christ. He is of course not speaking about a host of minor disagreements in theology or practice between Christians who confess the truth about Jesus. Elsewhere New Testament writers enjoin toleration of minor differences: "Who are you to pass judgment on the servant of another? It is before his own master that he stands or falls. And he will be upheld, for the Lord is able to make him stand" (Rom. 14:4). John's prohibition in 2 John concerns a fundamental christological heresy: a denial of Christ's true humanity, a denial of his true incarnation. This is why it is imperative for the church to identify and publicly hold forth what are the clear "essentials" of Christian faith and for it not to bind the conscience in those areas where Scripture allows godly minds to differ. This it has historically done by closely studying the confessional norms explicitly taught in Scripture and then setting forth its collective understanding in secondary confessional literature.

Closing (2 John 12–13)

John closes his epistle by expressing his hope to come and see the church face-to-face, and then by passing on the greetings of the church where he is residing.

Select Bibliography

Please see the bibliography at the end of this chapter, after 3 John.

---

3 JOHN

Introduction

Through a real-life situation involving the hubris of a local church leader named Diotrephes, 3 John illustrates one of the key problems addressed more fully in 1 John, namely, hatred of the brethren. Diotrephes shows open contempt for John, rebuffs a delegation sent by John, and ejects from the church those who wanted to receive the delegation. This short letter stands in the New Testament as a living reminder to the church that in these last days, as the apostle Paul predicted,

> people will be lovers of self, lovers of money, proud, arrogant, abusive, disobedient to their parents, ungrateful, unholy, heartless, unappeasable, slanderous, without self-control, brutal, not loving good, treacherous, reckless, swollen with conceit, lovers of pleasure rather than lovers of God, having the appearance of godliness, but denying its power. (2 Tim. 3:2–5)

Third John shows such attitudes surfacing even within the church, even among self-styled leaders in the church. It lays out a blueprint for identifying and dealing with such eruptions in the inter-advent age.

Background Issues

Author

Like 2 John, 3 John comes from one who calls himself "the elder." (On this title, see the "Background" sections to 1 John and 2 John.)

There are many theories as to the relationship between the author and Diotrephes, and their relative ranks and actions. Raymond Brown thinks that Diotrephes is host of a Johannine house church, while the presbyter is "a member of the Johannine School of witnesses to the tradition. Thus the two men have different roles and one is not structurally inferior to the other."[32] This, however, is hard to square with the elder's clear expectation that Diotrephes ought to "acknowledge" him, that is, acknowledge his person and accept what he has written (3 John 9). In none of the six basic options Brown outlines for understanding the conflict is the apostolic identity of John taken seriously. Yet such an identity for the author is all but required when we consider the authority with which he writes.

The so-called "Johannine School of witnesses to the tradition," which Brown invokes, has never been found in historical sources, and if it ever existed, it is completely unclear what sort of recognition a member of such a group could expect from Christians in other congregations. Those who held the office of elder in a given church would not normally have had "cross-congregational" authority, as "the elder" of 2–3 John obviously has, addressing and exhorting as he does at least one other church (and maybe more) besides the one from which he writes, and sending emissaries who represent him to that church. He expects the Christian recipients of his letter to "receive" him, that is, not only to give him a hearing but to acquiesce to his instructions and his witness implicitly. And if the author is not an apostle, the questions of how and why an anonymous elder's extremely brief and somewhat enigmatic letters end up in a collection of authoritative apostolic writings accepted far and wide among Christian churches as Scripture are great mysteries.

Audience

Unlike 2 John, which is addressed in a general way to a church or group of churches, 3 John is addressed to an individual, a church leader named Gaius. The references in

[32] Brown, *Epistles of John*, 738.

verse 3 to Gaius "walking in the truth" and in verse 4 to the author's joy in hearing that his children "are walking in the truth" show a close tie to 2 John, where the author rejoices to find some members of a church "walking in the truth." The two situations may well be linked, as may also be suggested by the elder's reference in verse 9 to something he has previously written "to the church"—most likely at least including 2 John.[33] Gaius appears to be a member of the church addressed, or of one of the churches addressed, in 2 John.

Structure and Outline

Like 2 John but unlike 1 John, 3 John shares the typical form of an ancient letter. Its structure may be viewed as follows:[34]

- a Greeting (vv. 1–2)
  - b The faithfulness of Gaius (vv. 3–4)
    - c Faithful treatment of the missionaries (vv. 5–8)
  - b' The faithlessness of Diotrephes (vv. 9–11)
- a' Commendation and closing (vv. 12–15)

Message and Theology

Greeting (3 John 1–2)

On the self-designation "the elder," see the "Introduction" section to 2 John. The elder affirms his love for Gaius and prays for Gaius's welfare.

The Faithfulness of Gaius (3 John 3–4)

The elder already knows it is well with Gaius's soul (3 John 2); John's messengers bear witness to Gaius's "truth" and to his walking "in the truth" (v. 3). John refers to Gaius and evidently many other Christians in the region as "my children" (v. 4), which is, again, not something an ordinary elder of a particular congregation would normally have done.

Faithful Treatment of the Missionaries (3 John 5–8)

Gaius is specifically commended for receiving "these brothers," emissaries from John who were strangers to Gaius. John again testifies to the worthiness of these assistants, and others like them (probably also the person carrying the present epistle), that they went out "for the sake of the name" (probably the name of God; cf. 3 John 6, "worthy of God" and Ignatius, *Phild.* 10.2) and were not supported by "the Gentiles." To support them, he says, is to be a fellow worker for the truth. This principle is very much applicable today. Groups of churches show they are fellow workers with the truth when they together support those whose ministry of the Word takes them to distant places.

[33] And possibly the Gospel. See the hypothesis outlined above in the section on 1 John, "Background Issues," "Date of Writing."
[34] Codex Vaticanus has but one paragraph division, where v. 11 begins; Sinaiticus has none.

Warning about Diotrephes (3 John 9–11)

John speaks of something he has written "to the church" (suggested above as being 2 John and possibly John's Gospel), and it is evidently in regard to the arrival of this writing that Diotrephes has shown his rebellious attitude. Since his rejection of John is also connected with his rejection of "the brothers" (3 John 10; cf. vv. 3, 5), it is likely that the brothers were bearing this writing of John's. Their report to John must be the basis of his knowledge of Diotrephes's actions.

John describes Diotrephes as loving to have first place (φιλοπρωτεύων) over others. His attitude and behavior are much like that of the Pharisees criticized by Jesus in Matthew 23:6, 13. Some years before John wrote, Peter had exhorted the elders of Asia Minor not to be domineering over those in their charge but to be examples to the flock (1 Pet. 5:3). Paul too had instructed Timothy and Titus that the bishop or elder must not be arrogant or quick-tempered but must be, among other things, hospitable, upright, holy, and self-controlled (1 Tim. 3:1–7; Titus 1:7–8; and see his dire warning to the Ephesian elders in Acts 20:29–31). Diotrephes instead has arrogantly domineered the flock, showing neither hospitality nor self-control. Whether Diotrephes holds an office in the church or is simply in charge of the house where the church meets, his loving to "put himself first" is a warning to those who bear, or aspire to bear, any kind of authority in the church today.

Diotrephes does not receive John (οὐκ ἐπιδέχεται ἡμᾶς). In effect, then, he has not received Jesus, who told his disciples, "Truly, truly, I say to you, whoever receives the one I send receives me, and whoever receives me receives the one who sent me" (John 13:20); and "the one who rejects you rejects me" (Luke 10:16; cf. 9:52–53).

There are many today who reject John and other apostles of Jesus when they disparage or ignore the writings that bear the apostles' teaching. Though they might deny it, their rejection of the apostolic word is a rejection of Jesus himself.

Diotrephes's actions extend beyond his effrontery to John and his messengers. He has taken it upon himself to cast out (ἐκβάλλει) of the church those in the congregation who wanted to receive the messengers. Here John uses the same word he used in John 9:34–35 to describe what the Pharisees did to the blind man healed by Jesus, who was cast out of the synagogue (cf. Matt. 23:13).

We are not told on what basis Diotrephes does not "acknowledge" John, beyond his desire to lord it over others in the church. But since it involves his rejection of what John has written, this suggests that Diotrephes might have objections to the teaching contained in that writing. This makes it likely, though not certain, that Diotrephes's loyalty has shifted to the side of the "deceiver[s] and antichrist[s]" of 2 John 7.

In light of the seriousness of Diotrephes's offenses, John's restrained response, "So if I come, I will bring up what he is doing" (3 John 10), has surprised some interpreters. "The measures he takes," says C. H. Dodd, "are tentative. . . . The language which he uses . . . suggests that the Presbyter is not too sure of his ground."[35]

---

[35] C. H. Dodd, *The Johannine Epistles*, MNTC 16 (New York: Harper, 1946), 165.

But there is no tentativeness in John's tone when he lists Diotrephes's offenses. The reserve in John's "measures" may instead reflect his hope that Diotrephes might yet repent when confronted by him. John was no stranger to the transforming work of the Spirit. Whether or not true spiritual change ever occurred for Diotrephes, we may draw great encouragement from the fact that transformation did happen with John himself. The Synoptic Gospels inform us that as a young man John the son of Zebedee was also afflicted with a love of having first place (Matt. 20:20–28) and a quick, retributive temper (Luke 9:54). But through the miracle of new birth (John 3:3, 5; 1 John 2:29) and the "seed" of God (the Holy Spirit) abiding within him (1 John 3:9), the "Son of Thunder" (Mark 3:17) in time became the "Apostle of the Love of God." John's life was proof of the power of God.

Commendation and Closing (3 John 12–14)

Demetrius is almost certainly the bearer of the letter. John's final commendation of Demetrius, "We also add our testimony, and you know that our testimony is true" (3 John 12), is reminiscent of what he writes at the end of the Gospel: "This is the disciple who is bearing witness about these things, and who has written these things, and we know that his testimony is true" (John 21:24). An allusion to this authentication of the Gospel would be fitting in a setting in which John's testimony has been challenged by the likes of Diotrephes.

The epistle closes much as 2 John did, with reference to the elder's desire to see the recipient face-to-face, and then adds a final exchange of greetings to and from "the friends" (3 John 15).

Select Bibliography for 1–3 John

Baugh, S. M. *A First John Reader: Intermediate Greek Reading Notes and Grammar.* Phillipsburg, NJ: P&R, 1999.

Brooke, Alan England. *A Critical and Exegetical Commentary on the Johannine Epistles.* ICC. Edinburgh: T&T Clark, 1912.

Brown, Raymond E. *The Epistles of John.* AB 30. New York: Doubleday, 1982.

Bruce, F. F. *The Epistles of John: Introduction, Exposition, and Notes.* Grand Rapids, MI: Eerdmans, 1966.

Burge, Gary M. *The Letters of John.* NIVAC. Grand Rapids, MI: Zondervan, 1996.

Carson, D. A., and Douglas J. Moo. *An Introduction to the New Testament.* 2nd ed. Grand Rapids, MI: Zondervan, 2005.

Culy, Martin M. *1, 2, 3 John: A Handbook on the Greek Text.* Waco, TX: Baylor University Press, 2004.

Dodd, C. H. *The Johannine Epistles.* MNTC 16. New York: Harper, 1946.

Grayston, Kenneth. *The Johannine Epistles.* NCB. Grand Rapids, MI: Eerdmans, 1984.

Hengel, Martin. *The Johannine Question.* London: SCM; Philadelphia: Trinity Press International, 1989.

Hill, C. E. "Cerinthus: Gnostic or Chiliast? A New Solution to an Old Problem." *Journal of Early Christian Studies* 8 (2000): 135–72.

———. *The Johannine Corpus in the Early Church*. Oxford: Oxford University Press, 2004.

Kistemaker, Simon. *Exposition of James, Epistles of John, Peter, and Jude*. NTC. Grand Rapids, MI: Baker, 1996.

Klauk, Hans-Josef. *Ancient Letters and the New Testament: A Guide to Context and Exegesis*. Translated by Daniel P. Bailey. Waco, TX: Baylor University Press, 2006.

Köstenberger, Andreas J. *A Theology of John's Gospel and Letters: The Word, the Christ, the Son of God*. Grand Rapids, MI: Zondervan, 2009.

Kruse, Colin G. *The Letters of John*. PNTC. Grand Rapids, MI: Eerdmans, 2000.

Kysar, Robert. *I, II, III John*. ACNT. Minneapolis: Augsburg, 1986.

Lieu, Judith M. *I, II, and III John: A Commentary*. NTL. Louisville: Westminster John Knox, 2008.

Marshall, I. Howard. *The Epistles of John*. NICNT. Grand Rapids, MI: Eerdmans, 1978.

Painter, J. *1, 2, and 3 John*. SP 18. Collegeville, MN: Liturgical, 2002.

———. *John, Witness and Theologian*. London: SPCK, 1975.

———. "The 'Opponents' in 1 John." *NTS* 32 (1986): 48–71.

Schnackenburg, Rudolf. *The Johannine Epistles: Introduction and Commentary*. Translated by Reginald and Ilse Fuller. New York: Crossroad, 1992.

Schuchard, Bruce G. *1–3 John*. ConcC. St. Louis, MO: Concordia, 2013.

Smalley, Stephen S. *1, 2, 3 John*. WBC 51. Waco, TX: Word, 1984.

Stott, John R. W. *The Epistles of John*. TNTC. Grand Rapids, MI: Eerdmans, 1964.

Strecker, Georg. *The Johannine Letters: A Commentary on 1, 2, and 3 John*. Translated by Linda M. Maloney. Hermeneia. Minneapolis: Fortress, 1996.

Thompson, Marianne Meye. *1–3 John*. IVPNTC. Downers Grove, IL: InterVarsity Press, 1992.

Wahlde, Urban C. von. *The Gospel and Letters of John*. 3 vols. ECC. Grand Rapids, MI: Eerdmans, 2010.

Westcott, Brook Foss. *The Epistles of St. John: The Greek Text with Notes*. 3rd ed. Cambridge: Macmillan, 1892. Repr., Grand Rapids, MI: Eerdmans, 1950.

Witherington, Ben, III. *Letters and Homilies for Hellenized Christians*. Vol. 1, *A Socio-Rhetorical Commentary on Titus, 1–2 Timothy and 1–3 John*. Downers Grove, IL: IVP Academic, 2006.

Yarbrough, R. *1–3 John*. BECNT. Grand Rapids, MI: Baker Academic, 2008.

24

Jude

Simon J. Kistemaker

Introduction

Jude, one of the smallest books in the New Testament, is a close competitor with 2 Peter (and 2–3 John) for the "most neglected book in the New Testament."[1] The neglect of Jude may be due in part to its focus on less-popular themes, such as false teaching, ungodliness, and God's judgment on sin. In addition, its use of apocryphal literature like 1 Enoch and the Assumption of Moses has caused some concern throughout the history of the church. As a result, Jude, like 2 Peter, also experienced a difficult journey into the New Testament canon.

Regardless, God has preserved this short letter for a reason, namely, because it offers a clarion call to the church to "contend for the faith that was once for all delivered to the saints" (Jude 3) in the midst of false teachers who seek to destroy and divide the body of Christ. Moreover, it contains some of the most encouraging statements about the love and mercy of God (vv. 2, 21–22) and his sustaining grace (vv. 24–25). Thus, Jude is a reminder that God's justice and God's love are not mutually exclusive attributes, but can and do exist side by side. Indeed, it is only when one understands God's righteous judgment on sin that the grace and mercy of Christ can be fully appreciated. In the end, the heart of Jude is pastoral; he is concerned about the spiritual health of believers whose faith is endangered.

Background Issues

Relationship to 2 Peter

The parallelism between Jude and 2 Peter is obvious, for twenty of the twenty-five verses in Jude are similar to those in 2 Peter. Also Peter's order of presentation is

[1] Douglas J. Rowston, "The Most Neglected Book in the New Testament," *NTS* 21 (1975): 554–63.

close to that of Jude. By way of example, table 10 shows a close parallel in wording between 2 Peter 2:1–18 and Jude 4–18.

2 Peter 2	Jude
Master (v. 1)	Master (v. 4)
Judgment (v. 4)	Judgment (v. 6)
Example (v. 6)	Example (v. 7)
Defiling passion (v. 10)	Defile the flesh (v. 8)
Glorious ones (v. 10)	Glorious ones (v. 8)
Destroyed (v. 12)	Destroyed (v. 10)
Feast (v. 13)	Feast (v. 12)
Balaam (v. 15)	Balaam (v. 11)
Gloom . . . reserved (v. 17)	Gloom . . . reserved (v. 13)
Loud boasts (v. 18)	Harsh things (v. 15)

Table 10

These similarities raise the question of whether the two authors borrowed from the other. That is, did Jude write first and Peter then use his document, or did Jude depend on 2 Peter to write his letter? There is, however, a third option. Both Peter and Jude may have used a common source—a text that warned against the insidious influence of false teachers entering the church—as their base for composing their individual works.[2] While "the church fathers generally held that Jude borrowed from 2 Peter," most modern scholars today suggest that 2 Peter borrowed from Jude.[3] Though there are certainly some considerations in favor of the latter view (especially if one holds a late date for 2 Peter), one should not too quickly dismiss the possibility that Jude copied from 2 Peter. Along with having solid Patristic support, this position accounts for the fact that Jude 17–18 seems to be quoting another (earlier, apostolic) source: "But you must remember, beloved, the predictions of the apostles of our Lord Jesus Christ. They said to you, 'In the last time there will be scoffers.'" Given that there is evidence supporting both views, it appears that the priority of one or the other will remain a matter of discussion.

Authorship

The author identifies himself as a servant of Jesus Christ and a brother of James (Jude 1). The James here is likely the brother of Jesus, as well as the leader of the Jerusalem church (Acts 12:17; 15:13; 21:18) and author of the epistle that bears his name.[4] Thus, the author of Jude is also a brother of Jesus, though he does not

[2] Michael Green, *2 Peter and Jude* (Grand Rapids, MI: Eerdmans, 1987), 24.
[3] D. A. Carson and Douglas J. Moo, *An Introduction to the New Testament*, 2nd ed. (Grand Rapids, MI: Zondervan, 2005), 656.
[4] Douglas J. Moo, *The Letter of James* (Grand Rapids, MI: Eerdmans, 2000), 9–22.

explicitly mention this fact. Instead, probably for the sake of humility, he places the emphasis on his status as a "servant" of Christ. Some have suggested that "Judas the son of James" (Luke 6:16; Acts 1:13; cf. John 14:22), one of the twelve disciples, may have written this letter.[5] But this individual is clearly the *son* of James, not the brother, and therefore unlikely to be the author. Moreover, if the author were one of the Twelve, we would expect the author to identify himself as an apostle (cf. 2 Pet. 1:1), but he does not.

We have few historical details about Jude the brother of Jesus. Apparently, he was one of four brothers of Jesus (Matt. 13:55; Mark 6:3), was likely not a believer during Jesus's lifetime (Mark 3:21, 31; John 7:5), and was probably converted just after the resurrection (Acts 1:14). The Greek of his epistle comes from a native of Galilee who was bilingual.[6] Eusebius reports that the grandsons of Jude were summoned before the Roman emperor Domitian in AD 96 and summarily dismissed as poverty-stricken farmers because of their calloused hands.[7] Regardless of the accuracy of this story, it does suggest that Jude's name was well known in some circles of the early church.

Date

Dating the letter of Jude is largely connected to its relationship with 2 Peter. If 2 Peter is dependent upon Jude, then that places Jude sometime before the mid-60s (given my argument above that 2 Peter was written by the apostle Peter), although we do not know exactly when. Richard Bauckham indicates that Jude "might very plausibly be dated in the 50's, and nothing requires a later date."[8] So this option is certainly a possibility. On the other hand, if Jude copied from 2 Peter, then that places the date for Jude no earlier than the mid-60s and possibly even in the 70s or 80s.

Another factor in the dating of Jude is identifying his opponents in the letter. Unfortunately, Jude does not give us a detailed description of the teaching of his adversaries. Some have suggested that the opponents in Jude must be the same as in 2 Peter, given their literary relationship.[9] However, Jude's use of Peter (or vice versa) does not mean they have the same audience or heresy in mind—any more than Luke's use of Mark meant they both had the same audience in mind.[10] They were written at different times and different circumstances. In addition, there is no mention of the denial of the second coming in Jude, a theme that dominates 2 Peter. Others have suggested that Jude is writing against Gnosticism, or some form of early proto-Gnosticism.[11] However, in addition to the fact that Gnostic cosmology or the rejection of the physical body is absent from Jude, the early date for Jude makes even incipient Gnosticism a rather unlikely opponent.

Once again, there seems to be too little information to identify Jude's opponents

[5] John Calvin, *Commentaries on the Catholic Epistles* (Grand Rapids, MI: Eerdmans, 1948), 428–29.
[6] Green, *2 Peter and Jude*, 50.
[7] Eusebius, *Hist. eccl.* 3.19.1, 3.20.6; and Josephus, *Ant.* 20.200.
[8] Richard Bauckham, *Jude, 2 Peter*, WBC 50 (Waco TX: Word, 1983), 13.
[9] J. N. D. Kelly, *A Commentary on the Epistles of Peter and of Jude* (New York: Harper & Row, 1969), 229.
[10] Gene L. Green, *Jude and 2 Peter*, BECNT (Grand Rapids, MI: Baker Academic, 2008), 23.
[11] Kelly, *Epistles of Peter and of Jude*, 231.

with any known group—at least not in such a way that could affect dating. What we can observe, however, is that the core error of these opponents is *antinomianism*. Jude regularly describes their behavior as "ungodly" (vv. 4, 15, 18) and highlights their immoral behavior (vv. 8, 10–13, 16). And this godlessness seems built upon an earlier and more foundational error, namely, that these men "pervert the grace of God into sensuality" (v. 4). It appears that their immoral behavior stems from a misunderstanding of the gospel of grace—perhaps implying that they have distorted the teachings of some of Paul's letters.

Canonicity

Despite the lack of attention from the early church fathers—no doubt due, in part, to its small size—Jude's canonical journey is more positive than we might expect. It was included in our earliest canonical list, the second-century Muratorian Fragment; it was regarded as Scripture by Tertullian;[12] Clement of Alexandria wrote a commentary on it;[13] Origen regarded it as canonical;[14] and Eusebius viewed it as part of the Catholic Epistles because it was a book "used publicly with the rest in most churches."[15]

Not surprisingly, one of the nagging issues with Jude's canonical status was his uses of 1 Enoch (Jude 14–15) and the Assumption of Moses (Jude 9). The use of these noncanonical writings still troubles some today. However, the critical fact that should be observed is that Jude never cites either of these books in a manner that would indicate he regards them as Scripture (typically done by calling a book γραφή, or by introducing it with "it is written"). Apparently, Jude understands these writings to contain some true traditions, which he feels free to employ, but this does not necessitate that he view them as inspired or scriptural. Indeed, biblical authors often cite other sources to make their point without implying that they deserve canonical status (e.g., Josh. 10:13; 2 Kings 15:26, 36; Luke 1:1; Acts 17:28; 1 Cor. 15:33).

Structure and Outline

Outline

- I. Greeting (vv. 1–2)
- II. Purpose for Writing (vv. 3–4)
- III. Examples from History (vv. 5–7)
  - A. Unbelieving Israel (v. 5)
  - B. Evil angels (v. 6)
  - C. Sodom and Gomorrah (v. 7)
- IV. Application and Examples (vv. 8–11)
  - A. Godless men (v. 8)
  - B. Michael and Satan (vv. 9–10)
  - C. Cain, Balaam, and Korah (v. 11)

---

[12] *Cult. fem.* 1.3.1–3.
[13] *Hist. eccl.* 6.14.1.
[14] *Hom. Jos.* 7.1; *Hom. Gen.* 6.115–16.
[15] *Hist. eccl.* 2.23.25 (trans. Kirsopp Lake, LCL).

V. Descriptions (vv. 12–16)
  A. Contemporaries (vv. 12–13)
  B. Saints and sinners (vv. 14–15)
  C. Grumblers (v. 16)
VI. Exhortations to Believers (vv. 17–23)
  A. Remember the gospel (vv. 17–18)
  B. Avoid heretics (v. 19)
  C. Persevere and pray (vv. 20–21)
  D. Show mercy (vv. 22–23)
VII. Doxology (vv. 24–25)

Arrangement

How does Jude arrange his rather short epistle? After the greeting and stating the purpose of his writing, Jude begins his exposition by taking examples from Israel's history and applying them to the life and learning of his readers. These examples were well known to the readers familiar with the Scriptures of the Old Testament and even from the Apocrypha (vv. 14–15).

After the greeting (vv. 1–2), Jude states why he is writing his letter and what he intends to say (vv. 3–4). Next, he writes a long section of warnings against false teachers (vv. 4–19). In this segment he gives examples, such as "certain people [who] have crept in unnoticed" (v. 4), and intruders that are introduced by the pronoun *these*, as in "these dreamers" (v. 8 NKJV) and "these (people)" (vv. 10, 12, 14, 16, and 19).[16] He surveys, chronologically, angels not keeping their God-given positions of authority (v. 6), Sodom and Gomorrah (v. 7), and the archangel Michael in dispute with the Devil about the body of Moses (v. 9). He mentions in succession Cain, Balaam, and Korah (v. 11), described in metaphorical terms: "waterless clouds, swept along by winds; fruitless trees in late autumn, twice dead, uprooted; wild waves of the sea, casting up the foam of their own shame; wandering stars, for whom the gloom of utter darkness has been reserved forever" (vv. 12–13). This description is followed by a reference to Enoch and the coming of the Lord in judgment (vv. 14–16). The epistle's descriptive summary message is expressed in two segments, the introduction (vv. 3–4) and the conclusion (vv. 20–23).

Message and Theology

Jude's message may not be popular in our world today, but it is greatly needed. It can be divided into three main themes: (1) antinomianism, (2) judgment on sin, and (3) the glory of Christ.

Antinomianism

Like 2 Peter, Jude is dealing with false teachers bent on a licentious and immoral lifestyle. Jude's colorful description of them captures the depth of their ungodliness.

[16] Bauckham, *Jude, 2 Peter*, 4.

They are "unreasoning animals" (v. 10), those who "walked in the way of Cain" (v. 11), "hidden reefs" (v. 12), and "shepherds feeding themselves" (v. 12). In addition, the metaphors Jude uses from nature are descriptive: (1) Clouds expected to water the parched land are carried along by the wind and fail to provide even a drop or water (v. 12). As human beings, plants, animals, and insects suffer in the drought, so Christians endure hardship when they are deprived of spiritual nourishment. (2) The reference to barren fruit trees (v. 12) hints at the parable of the fig tree that produces no fruit for three years and therefore should be cut down (Luke 13:6--9). (3) The picture of wild waves of the sea with froth and foam is a reference to sinful human behavior that results in thorough shame (Jude 13). (4) Jude's description of wandering stars refers to shooting stars that lose their light and end up in utter darkness (v. 13).

While these descriptions in many ways sound like the false teachers in 2 Peter, Jude reveals the distinctive motive for this ungodliness, namely, that its practitioners "pervert the grace of our God into sensuality and deny our only Master and Lord, Jesus Christ" (v. 4). Apparently, these men have taken the doctrine of salvation by grace alone—perhaps a doctrine they have heard (or read) from Paul—and erroneously concluded that God does not require holy living. In essence, they reject the lordship of Christ over their lives ("they deny our only Master and Lord"), thinking they can follow Christ and live however they want.

Simply put, their error is *antinomianism*—a rejection of the applicability of God's holy law to the life of the believer. Apparently this error was common enough in the early church that Paul even spent an entire chapter (Romans 6) refuting it. Nonetheless, the belief persisted in various places and still persists today. Of course, modern manifestations of antinomianism are rarely as bold and audacious as Jude's opponents. Instead, antinomianism today is often more subtle; it is accomplished simply by ignoring or downplaying the law rather than openly violating it.

Jude, however, reminds us that holiness and godliness flow naturally from those who know and love the person of Christ. Thus, he encourages his audience, "Keep yourselves in the love of God" (v. 21). Indeed, a life of ungodliness and licentiousness simply makes one subject to judgment—a theme that Jude addresses next.

Judgment on Sin

Jude makes it clear that the persistent ungodliness exemplified by these false teachers will not go unpunished. Like 2 Peter, Jude demonstrates his point by taking the reader on a historical tour of how God has judged sin in the past: after the exodus, God destroyed those in the desert who did not believe (v. 5); angels lost positions of authority and are chained, awaiting judgment (v. 6); Sodom and Gomorrah fell into immorality and faced a penalty of eternal fire (v. 7). If God judged sin in these past instances, then he will judge these false teachers in the present. Jude employs the writing of 1 Enoch to bolster his point: "Behold, the Lord comes with ten thousands of his holy ones, to execute judgment on all and to convict all the ungodly of all their deeds of ungodliness" (quoted in Jude 14–15).

In a world that does not believe that God cares much about sin, a world that assumes he would never punish anyone, the book of Jude becomes essential reading. This tiny letter offers a critical reminder that God's future judgment on sin is very real. And the only escape is the "mercy of our Lord Jesus Christ that leads to eternal life" (v. 21).

The Glory of Christ

Jude addresses the false teaching not only negatively, by exposing antinomianism and warning about the coming judgment on sin, but also positively, by directing his readers back to Christ. Throughout this brief epistle he refers to Jesus Christ six times (vv. 1 [2x], 4, 17, 21, 25). Readers should know that Jesus Christ is their only Master and Lord (v. 4); he grants mercy that leads to life eternal (v. 21); and to him belong glory, majesty, dominion, and authority (v. 25). "Jesus Christ is thus described in a way that puts him on an equal footing with God," notes I. Howard Marshall.[17] The basic message Jude conveys to his readers is to focus attention on Jesus, who amid all of life's vicissitudes and diabolical perversions is urging them to remain true to the Word of God.

In the last two verses of his brief epistle, Jude presents a hymn of praise that is unique in its wording and structure. It is addressed to "the only God our Savior" and channeled through the glory, majesty, and authority of "Jesus Christ our Lord" (v. 25). A doxology that countless pastors use as a parting blessing to the congregation, it is an echo of Isaiah's wording,

> You keep him in perfect peace
> whose mind is stayed on you. (Isa. 26:3)

Indeed, it affirms the doctrine of the perseverance of the saints, which Jude expressed in verse 1: "To those who are called, beloved in God the Father and *kept* for Jesus Christ." Thus, both the greeting and the doxology refer to this doctrine, forming a literary *inclusio* around the theme of perseverance.

Select Bibliography for 2 Peter and Jude

Bauckham, Richard. *Jude, 2 Peter*. WBC 50. Waco TX: Word, 1983.

Bigg, Charles. *Epistles of St. Peter and St. Jude*. Edinburgh: T&T Clark, 1961.

Blum, Edwin A. *Jude*. In *Expositor's Bible Commentary*. Vol. 12, *Hebrews through Revelation*. Edited by Frank E. Gaebelein et al. Grand Rapids, MI: Zondervan, 1981.

———. *1, 2 Peter*. In *Expositor's Bible Commentary*. Vol. 12, *Hebrews through Revelation*. Edited by Frank E. Gaebelein et al. Grand Rapids, MI: Zondervan, 1981.

Calvin, John. *2 Peter, Jude*. Translated by John Owen. Calvin's Commentaries. Grand Rapids, MI: Eerdmans, 1948.

---

[17] I. Howard Marshall, *New Testament Theology: Many Witnesses, One Gospel* (Downers Grove, IL: InterVarsity Press, 2004), 665.

Davids, Peter H. *2 Peter and Jude: A Handbook on the Greek Text*. Waco TX: Baylor University Press, 2011.

Donelson, Lewis R. *1 & 2 Peter and Jude*. Louisville: Westminster John Knox, 2010.

Dunker, Gary. *2 Peter and Jude: Contend for the Faith*. St. Louis, MO: Concordia, 2008.

Gardner, Paul. *2 Peter and Jude*. Fern: Christian Focus, 1998.

Green, Michael. *2 Peter and Jude*. Grand Rapids, MI: Eerdmans, 1987.

Guthrie, Donald. *New Testament Introduction*. Downers Grove, IL: InterVarsity Press, 1990.

Harink, Douglas. *1 & 2 Peter*. Grand Rapids, MI: Brazos, 2009.

Helm, David R. *1 & 2 Peter and Jude: Sharing Christ's Sufferings*. Wheaton, IL: Crossway, 2008.

Johnston, Mark G. *2 Peter & Jude*. Carlisle PA: Banner of Truth, 2005.

Keating, Daniel A. *First and Second Peter, Jude*. Grand Rapids, MI: Baker Academic, 2011.

Kistemaker, Simon. *Exposition of the Epistle of Jude*. NTC. Grand Rapids, MI: Baker. 1987.

———. *Exposition of the Epistles of Peter*. NTC. Grand Rapids, MI: Baker, 1987.

Kruger, Michael J. "The Authenticity of 2 Peter." *JETS* 42 (1999): 645–71.

Luther, Martin. *Commentary on the Epistles of Peter and Jude*. Grand Rapids, MI: Kregel, 1982.

Mayor, Joseph B. *The Epistle of St. Jude and the Second Epistle of St. Peter: Greek Text with Introduction and Notes*. Grand Rapids, MI: Baker, 1965.

Neyrey, Jerome H. *2 Peter, Jude: A New Translation with Introduction and Commentary*. New York: Doubleday, 1993.

Osborne, Grant R. *James, 1 & 2 Peter, Jude*. Carol Stream, IL: Tyndale, 2011.

Schreiner, Thomas. *1, 2 Peter, Jude*. NAC 37. Nashville: Broadman & Holman, 2003.

Sproul, R. C. *1–2 Peter*. St. Andrews Expositional Commentary. Wheaton, IL: Crossway, 2011.

25

Revelation

Charles E. Hill

Introduction

The "Revelation of Jesus Christ" portrays in dramatic fashion the paradoxical present rule of Jesus Christ as King of all the kings of the world, his ultimate triumph, and the salvation of his people through tribulation. As monumental as this is, it is not all. In the course of reexperiencing the visions John saw on Patmos, John's audience witnesses not only the salvation of man, God's image, but also the reclamation of the heavens, the earth, and the subterranean regions (i.e., the sea, the abyss, hades, fountains of water), the domains of man's dominion as originally given in Genesis 1–3. Revelation presents to us a great Serpent, a woman who brings forth a male child who is to rule the earth, and a final restoration of the tree of life. The symbolism of the book ranges through the entire Old Testament canonical Scriptures and drives us back to the very beginning for some of its most elemental imagery.

Thus Revelation presents to God's people the grand denouement, the conclusion, the tying-up of the great drama of salvation begun in the first three chapters of the Bible. It reveals how the seed of the woman crushes the head of the Serpent and completes the new creation. Its canonical order as the last book in our Bible, then, is entirely appropriate. Genesis and Revelation are not only literally but also thematically the bookends of the Bible.

Revelation is not just about the future. It is also about the past and very much about the present—perhaps primarily about the present. For it was written to be read and heard in the present age (Rev. 1:3; 21:7); it provides an essential component for the church's understanding of life in this world between the two comings of Christ.

Purpose

One's understanding of the purpose of the book of Revelation is interrelated with the assessment of its overall meaning. Those who believe the book is mainly about the final seven or so years of history see its purpose as focusing on the needs and experiences of the church in those terminal years. In this view, Revelation primarily serves to inform Christians of what will happen once the future events it depicts are set into motion.

Others see the relevance of the book of Revelation as virtually limited to the immediate first-century and second-century Roman situation. These interpreters tend to view Revelation as primarily a political document, a fiery protest against the violent imperialism of first-century Rome, written to fortify Christians of that day for the possibility of greater oppression. A variation of this highly contextualized approach, however, recognizes an ongoing relevance to the protest. The purpose of Revelation in this view is "to counter the Roman imperial view of the world . . . by opening the world to divine transcendence"[1] and by showing "God's ultimate triumph over all evil and his establishment of his eternal kingdom."[2]

While this modification is certainly helpful, the purpose of Revelation must be both broader and more specific. It is broader in that the symbols, while occasioned by the first-century Roman context, seem to transcend that context and remain relevant to later manifestations of the dragon and his campaign against the church. The purpose is more specific in that Revelation is not simply interested in asserting divine transcendence in a general way, nor even in advancing the sovereign claims of Israel's God in the way that several contemporary Jewish apocalypses do. It is interested in asserting *the lordship of Jesus Christ*, the Lord's Christ, the Lamb of God, and his ultimate victory. God's long-awaited Messiah has come. He died and, behold, he is alive forevermore, and he holds the keys of death and hades (Rev. 1:18).

For these reasons it seems best to view Revelation as oriented not primarily to the past (the preterist approach) or to the future (the futurist approach), though it is linked vitally to both, but to the present life of the church—to the entire span of the time between the first and second comings of Jesus. The initial statement of the book, that it is to show "his servants the things that must soon take place" (1:1), is looking not to the imminent arrival of the end of the world, but to events and forces that will immediately affect the first readers and will continue to be relevant to God's people until the end. The book's purpose is not only to assure us that Christ is certainly "coming with the clouds, and every eye will see him," but also to assure us that in the meantime, Jesus Christ is "ruler of kings on earth" (1:5) in whatever time or place we live.

Revelation delivers to the distressed churches of Asia Minor and to the church in all ages, the triumphant assurance that behind the scenes of history and despite the vicissitudes of history, the kingdom of God is in power, and Jesus Christ the

[1] Richard J. Bauckham, *The Theology of the Book of Revelation* (Cambridge: Cambridge University Press, 1993), 8.
[2] Ibid., 9.

King of all kings is on his Father's throne executing his sovereign judgment over the world. Though to the fleshly eye the events of history may often seem to say the opposite, though the church of Jesus Christ might seem despised and defeated, it is Jesus Christ who rules the kings of the earth, and his purposes are patiently being worked out here below.

Background Issues

Authorship

The author gives his name as "John" and by the mere use of this name assumes that readers in seven named churches throughout a hundred-mile radius from Patmos will have no confusion about who he is. Though *John* was a common Hebrew name, there is only one Christian leader known by that Hebrew name who is attested as having ministered in Gentile Asia Minor at this time and who had the stature (1) to address authoritatively seven named churches distributed throughout the region, and (2) to be recognized by the unembellished use of his Hebrew name, John. That person is the John the son of Zebedee, one of the apostles of Jesus.

This corresponds to the fact that, as far as we can tell, the churches addressed in the book understood the author to be John the apostle. The first definite identification is found in Justin's *Dialogue with Trypho* 8, written ca. AD 160 in Rome. But Justin is reporting a dialogue that took place perhaps twenty years earlier in Ephesus, and his attribution of Revelation to John, "one of the apostles of Christ," is likely based on local knowledge. The same attribution is made by Irenaeus, a native of Smyrna (*Haer.* 5.30.3). Irenaeus grew up in Smyrna in the 130s and 140s and sat under the teaching of Polycarp, a man who, Irenaeus reports, had known the apostle John. Attribution to the same apostle is made by Hegesippus,[3] Clement of Alexandria,[4] the Muratorian Fragment, Hippolytus,[5] Tertullian,[6] Origen,[7] and others.

Aside from the bizarre claim that Revelation was falsely written in John's name by his contemporary "the heretic Cerinthus,"[8] the first reasoned argument against apostolic authorship came in the mid–third century. Amid controversy over a millenarian interpretation of Revelation, Dionysius, bishop of Alexandria, argued on stylistic grounds that Revelation could not have been written by the author of John's Gospel. What Dionysius surprisingly failed to consider were the differing circumstances of writing and the very different type of writing represented by the book of Revelation. Moreover, there are still many stylistic and thematic similarities between Revelation and the rest of the Johannine corpus sufficient to render a confident positive verdict on identity of authorship.

[3] See Eusebius, *Hist. eccl.* 3.18.1. On the identification of the source as Hegesippus, see H. J. Lawlor, *Eusebiana: Essays on the* Ecclesiastical History *of Eusebius Pamphili, ca 264–349 A.D. Bishop of Caesarea* (Amsterdam: Philo, 1973), 50ff.
[4] Eusebius, *Hist. eccl.* 3.23.1–2, 5.
[5] *Antichr.* 36, 50.
[6] *Praescr.* 32; *Marc.* 4.2, 5.
[7] *Commentarium in evangelium Matthaei* 16:6.
[8] Eusebius, *Hist. eccl.* 3.28.2; 7.25.1–2. Even here the "John" assumed in the alleged pseudonym is the apostle, not some other John.

Date and Redemptive Historical Setting

Irenaeus testifies that John's apocalypse "was seen no very long time since, but almost in our day, towards the end of Domitian's reign,"[9] which spanned AD 81–96. This is also the view of Hegesippus (*Hist. eccl.* 3.23.1–2, 5), writing probably just prior to Irenaeus, and of Clement of Alexandria (ca. 190) writing just after. The Muratorian Fragment seems to date Revelation earlier, to the time of Nero, but this is hard to trust, as the author apparently places its writing prior to the letters of Paul. Of these early Christian sources, the most important is surely Irenaeus.

From Revelation itself, two factors will be cited here as supporting a date of writing after the destruction of Jerusalem and the temple. First, in light of the parallels between the judgments of the seals in Revelation 6 and the judgments mentioned by Jesus in his Olivet Discourse (see below), it seems significant that the only parts of the discourse that are absent from the seals are those that concern the fall of Jerusalem.[10] This would make sense if Jerusalem had already fallen by the time John wrote. Second, Revelation 11:1–2 seems to presuppose the previous destruction of Jerusalem because, while the "holy city" is to be trampled for "forty-two months" (a symbol for the inter-advent age), the "temple of God and the altar and those who worship there" are protected. If this concerns the Second Temple of Jesus's day (as some preterists hold), the prophecy failed.[11] But the reference seems to be to the church as the temple of God ("God's temple in heaven," 11:19; cf. 1 Cor. 3:16–17; Eph. 2:20–22; 1 Pet. 2:4–10) and therefore would make the most sense if written well after the earthly temple had been destroyed.

Form and Genre

Revelation relates to a variety of literary forms. It is an "apocalyptic" prophecy, employing symbolic visions and extended symbolic narratives. It takes over much of its imagery from the Old Testament prophets and interprets that imagery in light of the coming of Jesus Christ. Chapters 2 and 3 also use the epistolary form, and in fact the entire book is an epistle addressed to seven churches in Asia Minor (1:4, 11). Because there were more than seven churches in Asia Minor at the time, it is probable that seven were chosen as a symbol of universalism, making the book relevant for all churches.

The word *apocalyptic* was coined from the book of Revelation (ἀποκάλυψις) itself in the nineteenth century, after the rediscovery of a number of Jewish and early Christian works that had certain characteristics in common with the book of Revelation. Other books commonly placed in this "genre" include 1–2 Enoch, Jubilees, 4 Ezra, 2 Baruch, 3 Baruch, Ascension of Isaiah, and the Shepherd of Hermas. Characteristics of such writings include heavy use of visual symbolism, the appearance of heavenly visitors, otherworldly journeys, depictions of the end of the world or of

---

[9] *Haer.* 5.30.3 (*ANF* 1:559–60).

[10] G. R. Beasley-Murray, *Revelation*, NCB (Grand Rapids, MI: Eerdmans, 1974), 129.

[11] As is argued by, e.g., J. Christian Wilson, "The Problem of the Domitianic Date of Revelation," *NTS* 39 (1993): 587–605.

postmortem existence, stark dualism (ethical or metaphysical or both), periodization of history, and use of pseudepigraphy.

Revelation, however, is not simply another member of the genre, conforming to type. Significantly, while all the noncanonical Jewish apocalypses are pseudonymous, John speaks in his own name, to his own generation, as someone known to his original audience: "I, John, your brother . . ." (Rev. 1:9). Second, since he is not speaking pseudonymously, he also is not writing prophecy "after the fact" (*vaticinium ex eventu*). John explicitly calls his own work a prophecy (Rev. 1:3; 22:10, 18) and "the word of God" (1:2), and he records God's own testimony, "These words are trustworthy and true" (21:5; cf. 22:6). Perhaps most importantly, Revelation's particular Christian, redemptive-historical perspective sets it apart from all contemporary Jewish apocalypses. The paramount thing is that God's Messiah has now come! He freed us from our sins by his blood (1:5) and is seated at the right hand of God, where he has received dominion. This fundamental fact is not always adequately appreciated by those who would like to read the book alongside contemporary Jewish apocalypses. In Revelation, what scholars might call traditional or even stock apocalyptic elements—such as the two witnesses, the restoration of God's people, the messianic kingdom, and judgment on God's enemies—are rearranged and reinterpreted according to the truths of Christianity already revealed to the church and known to Christians.

Approaches to Revelation

It is customary to distinguish four major approaches to the interpretation of Revelation: historicist, preterist, futurist, and idealist.

In a historicist approach, the events portrayed symbolically in Revelation unfold virtually in chronological order in the events of ecclesiastical and political history. This was the approach assumed by almost all the early Protestant Reformers. For them the Antichrist was the pope or the papacy (as for many Roman Catholics it was Luther). This approach is virtually unknown today, largely owing to the number of failed, conflicting proposals for historical fulfillments and the restricted scope assumed for the scene of the historical drama (invariably Western Europe). Still, historicists had a strong sense of the providence of God guiding history and looked for the relevance of the prophecy to the church in their day.

The preterist approach views the book as concerned solely with events of its own era, an era that is now past. Werner Georg Kümmel, for example, says, "The Apocalypse is a book of its time, written out of its time and for its time, not for the distant generations of the future or even of the end-time."[12] Some preterists see Revelation as depicting God's judgment upon unfaithful Israel and hence as mainly fulfilled in the events of the war concluded in AD 70. This naturally necessitates a time of writing prior to that date, which is, for several reasons, not the most likely. Many non-preterists also believe preterism makes the book irrelevant for all readers after that cataclysmic event. This may not technically be true (many Old Testament

[12] Werner Georg Kümmel, *Introduction to the New Testament* (London: SCM, 1965), 324.

prophecies remain Scripture even after they are fulfilled); but in any case, the main problems for preterism are exegetical, as we shall see below. On the positive side, preterist interpreters often explore helpful Old Testament backgrounds and seek to illuminate John's contemporary situation.

The futurist approach is surely the most familiar to Christians today, because of extensive efforts at popularization. While first developed by Jesuits, who used it to rebut the Protestant contention that the pope was the Antichrist,[13] futurism was adopted by Edward Irving, J. N. Darby, and other premillenarians in the nineteenth century and is now a staple of American evangelicalism. Futurism holds that after the first few chapters of Revelation, the book concerns only events of the very last years of history. Critics often say this renders Revelation meaningless for all but the last generation of human beings. This too may not technically be true. (Would the same criticism apply to all matters that the Bible places in our future?) But the dispensationalist form of futurism, with its idea of a rapture of the church seven (or three and a half) years before the end, means that not even the church will be around to witness most of the events of the book. Futurism, particularly dispensationalism, also tends to take the book in a linear and literal sense. As we shall see, there are real problems for such an approach to this highly symbolic book.

The idealist approach views Revelation as having to do with ideas, principles, theological conceptions, and historical conditions that are relevant in every age. The strength of this view is its recognition of the application of Revelation to every phase of the church's historical existence since Christ's first coming. While the idealist approach helpfully avoids interpretations that will be outdated or proved wrong by unfolding historical events, and it presents the book as always relevant, it can run the risk of losing the focus on redemptive history and the uniqueness of Christ.

Each of these general approaches has something to offer the faithful interpreter. The idealist approach may prove the most useful of the four, if it can avoid ahistorical abstraction and remain firmly grounded in the book's christological emphasis, allowing also for a climactic future fulfillment of the events surrounding Christ's return.

Hermeneutical Factors

There are some important hermeneutical factors to be considered for interpreting Revelation. While they do not, by any means, clarify everything, they can help establish some firm ground.

Self-Interpreted Symbols

First of all, Revelation interprets some of its symbolism for us: the stars and the lampstands in 1:20 (the angels of the churches and the churches themselves); the harlot in 17:18 (the great city that has dominion over the kings of the earth); the fine linen in 19:8 (the righteous deeds of the saints).

---

[13] Ernest R. Sandeen, *The Roots of Fundamentalism: British and American Millenarianism 1800–1930* (Grand Rapids, MI: Baker, 1978), 37, 39.

The Symbolic Nature of the Visions

Then, too, it is important to recognize that visions are a particular mode of prophetic revelation. Whereas other kinds of verbal prophecy may also make use of nonliteral speech, visions are almost by definition clothed in symbolism. This is emphasized by the typical interaction in apocalyptic or visionary literature between the vision and the interpretation of the vision usually given by an interpreting angel, as in Daniel.

The symbolic nature of the visions may be indicated in the very first verse. Revelation 1:1 says that Christ, by sending an angel (or messenger),"made . . . known" his revelation to John. The verb used, σημαίνω, can simply mean "signify" or "indicate," but can also be used with a more concrete sense: "to show by a sign" or "give a signal" (cf. John 12:33; 18:32; 21:19). This suggests that the visions are in sign form when John receives them.

The relevance of this may be seen, for instance, in the vision of the locust plague in Revelation 9. In the view of some interpreters, the locusts John describes are some form of modern or futuristic military aircraft. Knowledge of such weaponry would have been outside John's frame of reference, so, viewing them from a first-century cultural context, John might have described them as locusts. This supposes, however, that John was carried forward in time and allowed to witness the actual historical event, like a reporter on the scene, and it supposes that it is John who decides to portray what he has seen with the term "locusts" (Rev. 9:3, 7). On the contrary, the symbolic nature of the visions themselves would suggest that it is not John who puts the objects into symbol form; they are presented to him in symbol form.

Thus, when John says he saw a lamb, he saw a lamb. When he says he saw a prostitute sitting on a seven-headed beast, he saw a prostitute sitting on a seven-headed beast. Each object, to be sure, is a symbol to be interpreted. But the objects are in symbolic form, not in the form of historical persons or events, when he sees them.[14]

This has other repercussions as well. One has to keep in mind the possibility that any individual detail of the descriptions of a symbol belongs really to the symbol itself, not in any concrete, transferrable way to the reality it is symbolizing. For example, in 9:7–9 there is a long and detailed description of the locusts. These details (crowns of gold, faces like humans, hair like women's hair, teeth like lion's teeth, etc.) may simply be for the sake of building up the image of monstrous, hideous, hellish beings or influences and may not correspond in a one-to-one way to some nonsymbolic referent.

The Principle of Recapitulation

The third-century commentator Victorinus of Pettau is the first we know of who explicitly noted this phenomenon in Revelation. He wrote:

> We must not regard the order of what is said, because frequently the Holy Spirit, when He has traversed even to the end of the last times, returns again to the

[14] See G. K. Beale, *The Book of Revelation: A Commentary on the Greek Text*, NIGTC (Grand Rapids, MI: Eerdmans, 1999), 52–53.

> same times, and fills up what He had before failed to say. Nor must we look for order in the Apocalypse; but we must follow the meaning of those things which are prophesied.[15]

Revelation presents several pictures of the same realities—in particular, the arrival of the end of history. We are brought to the brink of the last judgment with the sixth seal in 6:12–17, the seventh trumpet in 11:15–19, the great harvest in 14:14–20, the seventh bowl in 16:17–21, the return of Christ in 19:17–21, and the end of the millennium in 20:11–15. This prevents us from assuming that everything in the book happens in chronological succession.

Prolific Use of Old Testament Imagery

It is hard to imagine understanding much of anything in Revelation apart from a deep and expansive knowledge of the Old Testament sources of Revelation's imagery. Revelation seems to be particularly indebted to Daniel, Ezekiel, Jeremiah, Psalms, and Genesis. Recognizing, for instance, that Jesus appears in the first vision as the glorified Son of Man from Daniel 7:9–14, with even some characteristics of the Ancient of Days from that same vision, amplifies for us the fact that Jesus Christ has been given dominion over all peoples, nations, and languages, as prophesied in that passage.

Eschatological Context[16]

It is an important but too-little-recognized fact that in antiquity, individual and global eschatology usually belonged to an integrated complex of related beliefs. In both Jewish and Christian eschatology, what one believed about the future life of the individual (including the "intermediate state," that is, what happens to the person between bodily death and bodily resurrection) was linked to what one believed about the cosmos God had made. The mainstream eschatology of first-century Jews, as expressed in Pharisaic and apocalyptic sources,[17] held that when righteous people died, their spirits (or souls) rested in *sheol* or hades, perceived to be a region situated in the lower parts of the earth. There they would wait in peaceful anticipation until the time of resurrection before they could enter the presence of God. The only human beings exempted from this postmortem existence in hades were men like Enoch and Elijah, who had been translated alive to paradise, who would have to return to earth one day to die. The most common expectation (again, excepting Sadducees and some Hellenistic Jews) was that God would soon establish, probably through the agency of one or more messianic figures, a golden age of righteousness on earth for the benefit of the Jewish nation. This age (there was disagreement as to its duration) would be followed by a general resurrection and last judgment. In

[15] *Commentary on Revelation* 7 (*ANF* 7:352); cf. 11.

[16] For more on this topic, see Charles E. Hill, Regnum Caelorum*: Patterns of Millennial Thought in Early Christianity* (Grand Rapids, MI: Eerdmans, 2001).

[17] There were exceptions: the Sadducees scoffed at any kind of postmortem existence (Matt. 22:23; Acts 23:8; Josephus, *Ant.* 18.16; *J.W.* 2.165), and some Jewish thinkers who assimilated Hellenistic ideas may have anticipated some sort of heavenly afterlife, but it was typically disconnected from the hope of a bodily resurrection (Philo; 4 Maccabees).

this eschatology, an intermediate state for the soul in the subterranean hades kept all eschatological emphasis on the future, when God would intervene for Israel, and later raise and judge the dead.

The coming of Jesus the Messiah brought the profoundest of changes to this common eschatological complex or "system." The Messiah did not mount a military offensive against the Roman oppressor but took on the greatest of God's enemies. Sin could not conquer this Messiah (John 8:46). Satan could not touch him (John 14:30). Death and hades could not hold him (Acts 2:24, 31). The general resurrection unexpectedly began when Christ the firstfruits rose from the dead (1 Cor. 15:23). The anticipated kingdom of God arrived in principle with Jesus's earthly ministry (Matt. 12:28) and commenced in power when he was enthroned at God's right hand in the heavenly sanctuary, from which he poured out the promised Holy Spirit upon his followers (Acts. 1:6–8). For them, eternal life begins not in a far-distant future, but already in the present (John 5:24–25), for they know the power of his resurrection. Even before departing from his disciples, Jesus promised he would come to them and take them to the place where he was going (John 14:2–3). He spoke words to the penitent thief that would have been unthinkable to apocalyptic-minded fellow Jews who waited for the kingdom: "Today you will be with me in Paradise" (Luke 23:43). Since the ascension of Christ, the apostle Paul can say that to be away from the body is to be at home with the Lord (2 Cor. 5:8). Now the *heavenly* Jerusalem is populated with "the assembly of the firstborn who are enrolled in heaven . . . the spirits of the righteous made perfect" (Heb. 12:23).

Christ's enthronement at the Father's right hand signifies no mere "shadow kingdom" or kingdom in abeyance. It powerfully commenced the messianic kingdom promised in Psalm 110:1 (Acts 2:29–36; etc.). This kingdom was to be characterized by the Messiah's ruling not over a completely pacified realm, but "in the midst of your enemies" (Ps. 110:2). He would conquer, rule, and judge until "the day of his wrath," when he would utterly shatter his opposition (Ps. 110:5–7). When believers die in the Lord henceforth, they join Christ in his heavenly kingdom (Luke 23:42–43; 2 Tim. 4:18; 2 Pet. 1:10–11; Rev. 3:21; 20:4). What the New Testament expects when Christ returns from heaven is the full harvest of resurrection, the judgment, and eternal new heavens and new earth. The "interim" kingdom of the Messiah has now been revealed to be *the present reign* of Jesus Christ from heaven.

Early Christianity after the New Testament remained, by and large, true to this New Testament hope. But at times and in some quarters of the church, that hope suffered relapse back into pre-Christian forms. One of the chief issues in ongoing Jewish-Christian interactions was the church's claim that it, as the true Israel, was the true heir of all the blessings promised in the Hebrew Scriptures. This general claim would at times be allowed to accommodate itself to the Jewish understanding of those blessings. In Papias, in the early thought of Justin, and in the late thought of both Irenaeus and Tertullian, the literalistic and earth-centered interpretation of the Messiah's interim kingdom was incorporated; the beneficiary of the kingdom was simply shifted from Israel to the church.[18] Contributing to this reversal in Irenaeus and Tertullian was the battle against Gnostics who denigrated the material world and its Creator. The chiliastic eschatology held attraction because it emphasized the goodness and bounty of God's created order. In this reconfigured version of the Christian hope, Old Testament prophetic passages that in the New Testament had been seen as symbolic or figurative representations of the heavenly or eternal state were reapplied to this earthly kingdom.

Demonstrating the Jewish source of this earthly eschatology is the fact that it came paired with the pre-Christian understanding of the intermediate state of the righteous. Papias, Justin, Irenaeus, and Tertullian, at just the points where they advocated an earthly kingdom (now associated with John's millennium), also advocated the retrogressive view that the souls of the righteous did not ascend to heaven to be with Christ, but remained in hades to await the resurrection.[19] The only people who were spared this fate were those few who had not died[20] or, through Tertullian's creative ingenuity, the Christian martyrs alone.

While chiliasm never became the majority view of the church, it did take centuries for it to fade out in some places. On the other hand, from the beginning, many—including most of the Apostolic Fathers, the late Justin, Clement, Hippolytus, Origen, Cyprian, and others—maintained with various emphases the essential New Testament understanding of Christ's inaugurated heavenly reign and its attendant heavenly hope for the departed.[21]

For our purposes here, it is paramount to note that Revelation not only fully conforms to the general New Testament hope of Christ's present heavenly kingship and the saints' heavenly rest in his presence; it also contributes lavishly to that hope. Revelation's manifold, vibrant depictions of the saints in heaven during the present age[22] set the book clearly apart from the chiliastic eschatology (Jewish and early Christian) and positively contribute to the New Testament's inaugurated eschatology of Christ's kingdom. Its manifold, vibrant depictions of Christ's present heavenly reign[23] do the same. Revelation 20:4–6, which does not in fact mention a reign *on earth*, is most naturally interpreted as another picture of the heavenly life of Christ and his saints in the inter-advent period. (More on this later.)

Structure and Outline

Recognizing the prominent role of sevens in the book, many interpreters have attempted to apply an overall heptadic structure to the book of Revelation.[24] Others have seen various forms of chiastic structure.[25] In my view, the simplest and clearest

[18] See Hill, *Regnum Caelorum*, 11–44.
[19] Justin, *Dial.* 80; Irenaeus, *Haer.* 5.31; Tertullian, *An.* 55.2–4.
[20] Hill, *Regnum Caelorum*, 22–23.
[21] Ibid., 75–207.
[22] See Rev. 2:7, 27; 3:4–5, 11–12, 21–22; 6:9–11; 7:9, 13–14; 18:20; cf. 12:12; 19:8, 14; etc.
[23] E.g., Rev. 1:5, 13–16; 2:26–27; 3:21; 5:5, 9–10; 7:17; 12:5; 17:14; 19:11–16; etc.
[24] E.g., Michael Wilcock, *I Saw Heaven Opened: The Message of Revelation*, BST (Downers Grove, IL: InterVarsity Press, 1975).
[25] E.g., Elizabeth S. Fiorenza, *The Book of Revelation: Justice and Judgment* (Philadelphia: Fortress, 1985), 175–76.

way the book seems to structure itself is by its four main visions, beginning at 1:9; 4:1; 17:1; and 21:9.[26]

Four Visions

Whereas many other scenes in the book of Revelation could also be labeled visions, these four are literarily set off from the rest by the use of four elements that only they have in common. In each there is

- an inaugurator of the vision (either the risen Christ or one of the bowl angels),
- mention of John being "in the Spirit,"
- some kind of verbal introduction to the content of the vision,
- mention of John or others instinctively falling down to worship.

I. First Vision: The Son of Man (1:9–3:22)
   A. Introduced by the voice of the risen Christ (1:10)
   B. In the Spirit on the Lord's Day on the island of Patmos (1:10)
   C. "Write what you see in a book and send it to the seven churches" (1:11); "write therefore the things that you have seen, those that are and those that are to take place after this" (1:19)
   D. John falls down at Christ's feet as though dead (1:17)

II. Second Vision: The Lamb Inaugurates His Heavenly Reign (4:1–16:21)
   A. Introduced by the voice of the risen Christ (ref. back to 1:10)
   B. In the Spirit, called up to heaven (4:2)
   C. "I will show you what must take place after this" (4:1)
   D. The twenty-four elders fall down to worship (4:10; 5:8, 14 [19:4]); all in heaven, earth, and sea worship (5:13)

III. Third Vision: The Judgment of the Harlot (17:1–21:8)
   A. Introduced by one of the seven bowl angels (17:1–2)
   B. Carried away in the Spirit into a wilderness (17:3)
   C. "Come, I will show you the judgment of the great prostitute" (17:1–2)
   D. John falls down to worship the angel (19:10)

IV. Fourth Vision: The Descent of the Bride (21:9–22:8)
   A. Introduced by one of the seven bowl angels (21:9)
   B. Carried away in the Spirit to a great, high mountain (21:10)
   C. "Come, I will show you the Bride, the wife of the Lamb" (21:9)
   D. John falls down to worship at the feet of the angel (22:8)

These repeated elements are prominent enough that even hearers of the book might well be able to mark the transitions as it is being read. The third and fourth visions are linked as thematic opposites—the harlot Babylon and the pure bride New Jerusalem. Each of the four major visions except the last is accompanied by an "outflow" or "aftermath" section, in which various aspects or consequences of the

[26] Irenaeus shows that he is aware of at least the first two visions (*Haer.* 4.20.11). The significance of the four main visions for determining the structure of Revelation is recognized in some form by George Eldon Ladd, *A Commentary on the Revelation of John* (Grand Rapids, MI: Eerdmans, 1972), 14–17; Christopher R. Smith, "The Structure of the Book of Revelation in Light of Apocalyptic Literary Conventions," *NovT* 36 (1994): 373–93. Smith, however, has to posit some rearrangement of the material to make it fit his scheme.

foundational visions are worked out. This leaves a chiasm of seven elements (four visions and three aftermaths), flanked by prologue and epilogue:

- **a** Prologue (1:1–8)
  - **b** Vision (1:9–20)
    - **c** Aftermath (2:1–3:22)
      - **d** Vision (4:1–5:14)
        - **e** Aftermath (6:1–16:21)
      - **d'** Vision (17:1–19:10)
    - **c'** Aftermath (19:11–21:8)
  - **b'** Vision (21:9–22:5)
- **a'** Epilogue (22:6–21)

An overall outline of the book of Revelation now follows:

Outline

- I. Prologue (1:1–8)
  - A. The revelation (1:1–3)
  - B. Trinitarian salutation (1:4–8)
- II. First Vision: The Son of Man (1:9–3:22)
  - A. The revealer: the glorified Christ (1:9–20)
  - B. Aftermath: Christ's words to the seven churches (2:1–3:22)
    1. Ephesus: strong in teaching, weak in love (2:1–7)
    2. Smyrna: faithful unto death (2:8–11)
    3. Pergamum: holding firm but beginning to compromise (2:12–17)
    4. Thyatira: full of good works but tolerant of false faith (2:18–28)
    5. Sardis: at the point of spiritual death (3:1–6)
    6. Philadelphia: keeping the Word (3:7–13)
    7. Laodicea: lukewarm and nauseating (3:14–22)
- III. Second Vision: The Lamb Reigns from the Heavenly Throne Room (4:1–16:21)
  - A. John in the heavenly throne room (4:1–5:14)
    1. Worship of the Creator (4:1–11)
    2. Worship of the Redeemer (5:1–14)
  - B. Aftermath: Messiah's reign (6:1–16:21)
    1. The seven seals (6:1–8:5)
       - a. The six seals (6:1–17)
       - b. *Interlude* (7:1–17)
         - i. The 144,000 (7:1–8)
         - ii. The innumerable multitude (7:9–17)
       - c. The seventh seal (8:1–5)
    2. The seven trumpets (8:6–11:19)
       - a. The six trumpets (8:6–9:21)
       - b. *Interlude* (10:1–11:14)
         - i. The angel and the little book (10:1–11)
         - ii. The measuring stick and the two witnesses (11:1–14)
       - c. The seventh trumpet (11:15–19)
    3. *Interlude* (12:1–14:20)

a. The dragon, the woman, and her seed (12:1–17)
b. The two beasts (13:1–18)
c. Seven signs of assurance (14:1–20)
4. The seven bowls (15:1–16:21)

IV. Third Vision: The Judgment of Babylon (17:1–21:8)
A. Babylon the great (17:1–19:10)
1. The mystery of Babylon (17:1–18)
2. The fall of Babylon (18:1–19:10)
a. Earthly mourning (18:1–24)
b. Heavenly rejoicing (19:1–10)
B. Aftermath: The judgment of the rest of God's enemies (19:11–21:8)
1. The judgment of the beasts (19:11–21)
2. The judgment of Satan (20:1–10)
3. The judgment of death and hades (opening of Lamb's Book of Life) (20:11–15)
4. The heritage of the just and the unjust (21:1–8)

V. Fourth Vision: The New Jerusalem (21:9–22:5[8])[27]
A. Its gates and foundations (21:9–14)
B. Its measurements and materials (21:15–21)
C. Its light and life (21:22–22:5)

VI. Epilogue (22:6[9]–21)

The central and largest part of the book, then, is the aftermath of the second foundational vision, the throne-room vision, where the exalted Lamb of God receives the kingdom from God the Father. This central part contains the three series of sevens: seals, trumpets, and bowls. The connection and compatibility of seals, trumpets, and bowls in this vision is seen in that the seals belong to the scroll held by the Lamb in Revelation 5:7–10, and both trumpets and bowls are implements of the worship in the heavenly temple, the setting of the second vision.

Revelation uses many other structuring devices in major and minor ways throughout the book. Clearly, there is a repetition of the number seven in all kinds of ways, and some of the series of sevens, such as the trumpet and bowl judgments in particular, show a number of parallels. Material often occurs in either compact or extended chiastic arrangements. As just one example of the latter, one may observe a chiastic appearance and disappearance of God's enemies:

a Death and hades (1:18; 6:8)
b Satan (the dragon, the ancient Serpent) (2:9, 13, 24; 3:9; 12:3–6)
c Beasts from sea and land (11:7; 13:1–18)
d Babylon the prostitute (14:8)
d' Babylon destroyed (17:1–19:10)
c' Beasts destroyed (19:11–21)
b' Satan bound, released, and finally destroyed (20:1–10)
a' Death and hades destroyed (20:13–14)[28]

[27] Rev. 22:6–9 belongs to both the vision and the epilogue, an overlap (Bauckham, *Theology of the Book of Revelation*, 57).
[28] The main presentations of the dragon, the beasts, and Babylon come in chaps. 12–17, and they meet their ruin in reverse order (Craig R. Koester, *Revelation: A New Translation with Introduction and Commentary*, AB 38A [New Haven, CT:

Message and Theology

The aim here will be to present a brief explanation of the flow of the book, emphasizing, (1) the structure and its major shifts, in order to facilitate a grasp of the book as a whole, and (2) passages whose interpretation will seem to have a large impact on the overall interpretation of the book.

From the First Vision: The Glorified Son of Man (Rev. 1:9–3:22)

In the book's inaugural vision, Christ appears to John as "one like a son of man" (Rev. 1:13), whose appearance recalls various elements of the Son of Man vision of Daniel 7:9–14. This already communicates that Christ, the divine Son of Man, has appeared before the Ancient of Days and has received universal dominion (Dan. 7:13–14; Matt. 28:19). That he walks in the midst of the churches and holds in his right hand the seven stars (the angels of the seven churches) portrays him unmistakably as the Lord of the churches who can both save (he holds the keys of death and hades) and discipline his church.

There is no formal break between Revelation 1 and Revelation 2 (the vision proper and what I am here calling the "aftermath"). But Jesus's speech continues in his command for John to write particular messages to each of the angels of the churches. The introduction to each message depends on the description of Christ from chapter 1; each reference except the last (Laodicea) comes from the first vision itself, wherein John saw Jesus as the exalted Son of Man (the last reflects John's salutation in Rev. 1:5–6). The letters to the angels are, then, an *exposition* of the first vision of Christ. Christ has appeared in a form appropriate to the message he has for the churches in their particular situations. The messages are based on the vision.

Each letter follows the same basic sevenfold pattern, which is modified according to the particular message:

1. *Address.* "To the angel of the church in ______ write:"
2. *Identification of sender.* All begin with τάδε λέγει ("thus says") and then continue (except Laodicea) with a reference to Christ as revealed in the first vision.
3. *Commendations.* All begin with Jesus saying οἶδα ("I know") and then something about the church that is usually commendable. To Laodicea there is no commendation, and with Laodicea and Sardis the οἶδα is followed by something negative.
4. *Complaints.* The usual form is ἀλλὰ ἔχω κατὰ σοῦ ὅτι ("but I have this [or "a few things"] against you," 2:4, 14, 20). Against Smyrna and Philadelphia there is no complaint. With Sardis the complaint takes the place of the commendation, which is appended later, and with Laodicea the complaints entirely replace the commendations.
5. *Challenges.* The form is an imperative, or imperatives.
6. *Warning.* This usually includes a "but if not" challenge (εἰ δὲ μή). We should probably consider the refrain "he who has an ear to hear, let him hear what

Yale University Press, 2014], 114, 750). But since death and hades also meet their end in 20:14, they may be added to the list of God's enemies, and the chiastic presentation across the expanse of the entire book may be seen to include them as well.

the Spirit says to the churches" as part of the warning, though in the last four letters it comes after the promise to conquerors.

7. *Promise to the conquerors*. The promises to those who conquer have to do with blessings to be known not only in the new heavens and new earth, after the last judgment, but first and foremost in the present heavenly realm, where Christ now reigns with his heavenly assessors. The conquerors then are Christians who have gone to their rewards in heaven.

Christ's messages to the churches might be encapsulated in the following summary ways:

- *Ephesus*. Strong in truth but weak in love
- *Smyrna*. Faithful unto death
- *Pergamum*. Holding firm but beginning to compromise
- *Thyatira*. Full of good works but tolerant of false faith
- *Sardis*. At the point of spiritual death
- *Philadelphia*. Keeping the word
- *Laodicea*. Lukewarm and nauseating

Rather than standing for different epochs of the church, the seven churches, their situations, and Christ's responses to them are best seen as having perennial application to the varied particular situations of the church in every age.

From the Second Vision: The Lamb Reigns from the Heavenly Throne Room (Rev. 4:1–16:21)

This second major vision, the vision of the Lamb taking up his reign from the heavenly sanctuary/throne room, is the source for all that happens up to the end of Revelation 16. The things which "must take place after this" (4:1) will include depictions of judgments and tribulations in three series of sevens (seals, trumpets, bowls) and will show us several pictures of the judgment of the last day.

Immediately in the Spirit again and transported to heaven, John beholds the heavenly worship. The scene is centered on a throne and the One who sits upon it. Most of what John sees, including the rainbow, the twenty-four elders (probably representing, in some way, the heavenly church, signified by the twelve patriarchs and the twelve apostles—cf. Rev. 21:12, 14), the seven spirits of God (signifying the Holy Spirit, 1:4), the four living creatures, and the sea of glass, recalls Old Testament accounts of heavenly visions.[29] Chapter 4 represents the worship of God Almighty as Creator (4:11); chapter 5 represents the worship of Christ as Redeemer (5:9).

Chapter 5 records something *new* in heaven. When the Lamb takes the scroll from the hand of him who sits on the throne, that must depict a state of things conceivable only since the incarnation, death, resurrection, and ascension of Jesus, the Lamb of God, slain for sinners. And indeed this is the effect of the bursts of praise heard in the

[29] See, e.g., Ex. 24:9–10; Isa. 6; Ezek. 1:5–21; 10:2, 20.

new song of the four living creatures and the twenty-four elders in verses 9–10, the innumerable angels in verse 12, and the voice of all creation in verse 13.

The scroll sealed with seven seals is obviously a symbol of great importance. John weeps when no one in heaven or on earth or under the earth is able to open the scroll or look into it. Only the Lamb, who has conquered by being slain, is worthy to break its seals and to reveal its contents. The significance of the scroll, however, has been understood in many ways.[30] The view taken here is that it represents the great book that is referred to several other times in the prophecy, the climactic and all-important book, the book so closely associated with the Lamb that it is said to be his possession: the Lamb's Book of Life.[31] The elect were chosen before the foundation of the world; but in order for their redemption to be accomplished, in order for the book to be opened and their names revealed at the great white throne judgment in Revelation 20:15, the Lamb of God must be slain to take away their sins.

Identifying the scroll as the Lamb's Book of Life can have implications for understanding what is being depicted when its seals are broken in chapter 6. The breaking of the seals represents not what is *contained* in the scroll,[32] but what must take place *leading up to* the actual opening of that Book of Life and the revelation of the names of the redeemed, who are the Lamb's inheritance. Before that day comes, there will be, as Jesus warned his disciples from the Mount of Olives, wars, rumors of wars, earthquakes and famines in many places, and persecution. Thus the connections between the seals and the Olivet Discourse, noted by many scholars, make a great deal of sense.

The Seven Seals (Rev. 6:1–8:5)

Coming to the seals in chapter 6, we are faced with a major interpretative question. Do the judgments connected with the four horsemen depict events reserved for the final years before the world's end? Or have these events already happened in the first century or centuries of the church? Or, do they describe conditions that will prevail throughout the inter-advent age?

Many have observed close parallels between what happens when these seals are broken and the predictions made by Jesus in the Olivet Discourse (Matt. 24–25; Mark 13; Luke 21). As Beasley-Murray says, "There is ground for believing that the content of the seven seals, as distinct from their form, reproduces the essential features of that discourse."[33] Beasley-Murray sets out R. H. Charles's summary, keyed to Mark's version of the discourse (see table 11).

---

[30] Bauckham argues forcefully that the scroll of chap. 5 is the "little scroll" in the hand of the angel in 10:2, 8, and that its content is what is revealed from chap. 10 on, the real content of the book of Revelation (cf. 1:1); everything prior to this is thus preparatory (*Theology of the Book of Revelation*, 80–84; Bauckham, *The Climax of Prophecy: Studies on the Book of Revelation* [Edinburgh: T&T Clark, 1993], 243–66). Beale, *Book of Revelation*, 340, says that the scroll "represents authority in executing the divine plan of judgment and redemption." David Aune, *Revelation*, 3 vols., WBC 52 (Dallas: Word, 1997–1998), 1:374, thinks the scroll and its contents "include the entire eschatological scenario extending from 6:1 through 22:9." Ladd, *Revelation of John*, 81, believes that "the contents of the scroll consist of the material in Revelation 7:1–22:21 . . . that complex of events, both redemptive and judicial, which will accompany the end of this world and the introduction of the world to come."

[31] Rev. 3:5; 13:8; 17:8; 20:12, 15; 21:27.

[32] So also Ladd, *Revelation of John*, 109, though he understands the contents of the scroll differently.

[33] Beasley-Murray, *Revelation*, 129.

Mark 13:7ff., 24f.	Revelation 6
Wars	Wars
International strife	International strife
Earthquakes	Famine
Famines	Pestilence (= death and hades)
Persecutions	Persecutions
Eclipses of sun and moon, falling of stars, shaking of the powers of heaven	Earthquakes, eclipse of sun, ensanguining of moon, falling of stars, men calling on rocks to fall on them, shaking of the powers of heaven

Table 11

Two points then may be made. First, as Beasley-Murray observes, the only parts of the discourse that do not find parallels in the seals and the later visions of Revelation are those that concern the fall of Jerusalem. "Since the fall of Jerusalem lies in the past, it is understandable that John should omit mention of it at this point."[34] Second, the parallels with the Olivet Discourse suggest that these conditions will characterize the entire interim period between Jesus's departure from earth and his second coming. This is because the "signs" Jesus gives in the Olivet Discourse—the wars, rumors of wars, famines and earthquakes, and the persecutions—are not signs that his coming will immediately follow. Rather, they are conditions that characterize the interim, before "the end" (Rev. 2:26) comes. Jesus tells his disciples not to be alarmed when these things happen, for "the end is not yet" and "all these are but the beginning of the birth pains" (Matt. 24:6, 8). This, again, agrees with the idea that the events signified in the breaking of the seals are things that must take place before the scroll is fully opened and the names written in it are revealed on the day of judgment.

With the breaking of the sixth seal the universe collapses, depicting what must be a fearful vision of the end of world history: "For the great day of their wrath has come, and who can stand?" (Rev. 6:17; see 16:14, "the great day of God the Almighty"). Here too we have a strong parallel in the Olivet Discourse (Mark 13:24–27). Some view the predictions of the Gospels and of Revelation as hyperbolic prophetic language describing the fall of Jerusalem in AD 70. But the universalistic language of "kings of the earth and . . . generals . . . and everyone, slave and free" (Rev. 6:15) suggests not a particular judgment on apostate Jews of the first century but a general judgment on the world.[35]

Another hermeneutically significant point thus follows from the meaning of the sixth seal. The fact that already in chapter 6 we have come to the brink of the consummation anticipates the conclusion that there is a principle of *recapitulation*

[34] Ibid., 130.

[35] Jesus predicts a similar response of Jews at the coming travail of Jerusalem in Luke 23:27–30 (see David Chilton, *The Days of Vengeance: An Exposition of the Book of Revelation* [Fort Worth: Dominion, 1987], 199). But Rev. 6:15–17 universalizes this well-known (see Isa. 2:10, 19; Hos. 10:8) cry of agony.

at work in the book of Revelation. The order in which the symbolic events are seen in John's visions does not necessarily correspond to the order in which their historical referents unfold in history. Instead, the same conditions, events, entities, or time periods may be seen repeatedly in John's visions, under various aspects.[36]

Between the sixth and the seventh seals there is an interlude consisting of two visions of encouragement. The 144,000 sealed from "every tribe of the sons of Israel" (Rev. 7:1–8, esp. v. 4) seems impossible to be taken literally and is probably a symbolic representation of the true, spiritual Israel, the church, protected during its sojourn on earth. The innumerable multitude John sees in Rev. 7:9–17 depicts the same chosen people, who have come faithfully through the great tribulation of the present age (7:14), now in heaven and there shown to be from every nation, tribe, people, and tongue (7:9).

The Six Trumpets (Rev. 8:6–9:21)

The breaking of the seventh seal in 8:1 leads directly to the next heptad of divine judgments, marked by seven trumpets blasts. While trumpets (either rams horns or forged instruments) were used for various purposes in ancient Israel, they were customarily to be blown by the priests (first appointed in Num. 10:8; cf. Josh. 6:4ff.). The trumpets in Revelation are given to the seven angels who stand before the Lord in his heavenly temple (whose priestly character is emphasized in 15:5–6), and the blowing of the trumpets is closely associated with the offering of incense and the hurling down of a burning censer from the heavenly altar. These trumpets are *temple vessels* and signify that John is still in the heavenly sanctuary/throne room, from which flows all that happens in Revelation 4–16 (see above).

There are significant parallels with the trumpets blown at the battle of Jericho (Joshua 6). But the Old Testament text that forms the closest comparison with the setting of Revelation 8 in the heavenly temple is 2 Chronicles 29:20–36, where Hezekiah reconsecrates the temple in Jerusalem. After the sin offering was made (2 Chron. 29:20–24),

> the Levites stood with the instruments of David, and the priests with the trumpets. Then Hezekiah commanded that the burnt offering be offered on the altar. And when the burnt offering began, the song to the LORD began also, and the trumpets, accompanied by the instruments of David king of Israel. The whole assembly worshiped, and the singers sang, and the trumpeters sounded. All this continued until the burnt offering was finished. (2 Chron. 29:26–28)

The priestly trumpeters blew their trumpets as part of a temple service inaugurated by a great sacrifice for sin. So in Revelation, all is set in motion by the appearance of a Lamb slain (5:6), whose blood ransoms people for God. This one great, con-

[36] G. B. Caird, *A Commentary on the Revelation of St. John the Divine*, HNTC (New York: Harper & Row, 1966), 106, says: "The unity of John's book, then, is neither chronological nor arithmetical, but artistic, like that of a musical theme with variations, each variation adding something new to the significance of the whole composition. This is the only view which does adequate justice to the double fact that each new series of visions both recapitulates and develops the themes already stated in what had gone before."

quering sacrifice is followed by many more conquering sacrifices, those slain for the Word of God and their testimony, whose souls lay under the altar in 6:9–11. Their prayers, and the prayers of all the saints (8:3–4), burn as incense before the throne. A new song is sung in 5:9–10 in praise of the slain Lamb; a new song is sung in 14:3 by the 144,000 redeemed from the earth (who also seem to have harps); and one is sung just before the pouring out of the bowls of wrath is commenced in 15:3–4. The portrayal of the portentous judgments in Revelation as belonging to one age-long service of heavenly worship is a cause for reflection.

The notion of the last trumpet sounding at the time of Christ's second coming, to announce his coming and to gather the saints, is already familiar from the teaching of both Jesus and Paul (Matt. 24:31; 1 Cor. 15:52; 1 Thess. 4:16). It is reflected in the seventh trumpet in Revelation as well, for we are told in 10:7 that "in the days of the trumpet call to be sounded by the seventh angel, the mystery of God would be fulfilled, just as he announced to his servants the prophets." The sounding of the seventh trumpet in 11:15 will again bring us to the last judgment and will signal, as it were, Christ's "coronation anthem."

All of the judgments, of course, affect humanity, but the first four fall directly onto four aspects of the nonhuman creation—the earth, the sea, the rivers and fountains, and the visible heavens—all the realms of man's original dominion (Gen. 1:26–29; 2:10). "The ground" (the *adamah* from which Adam was taken) was cursed along with Adam (Gen. 3:17–19), and Paul perceives that the entire creation (ἡ κτίσις) was subjected to futility and bondage to decay, for man's sin (Rom. 8:19–23).

The fifth and sixth judgments fall directly on unbelieving humanity (Rev. 9:1–21). God's just judgment will ultimately effect a *new* heaven and a *new* earth, and a *new* humanity to fill them.

That the trumpet judgments follow upon the hearing of the prayers of the saints suggests a difference between the trumpets and the seals. The seal judgments, seen in the light of Jesus's predictions of the Olivet Discourse, signify afflictions that, though they affect all mankind, have to do with the tribulations the church will experience throughout the inter-advent era as it brings the Gospel to all nations. The trumpet judgments assure us that God, in his sovereign administration of world history, will continually bring partial (note the thirds in Rev. 8:7, 10, 11, 12)[37] judgment upon the unbelieving world[38] on behalf of the saints and in response to their prayers for deliverance.

No matter how we interpret the significance of the trumpet judgments, an important point is made about them at the end of the account in 9:20–21. Isaiah 26:9 says,

> For when your judgments are in the earth,
> the inhabitants of the world learn righteousness.

[37] "It is beyond question that in his description of the seals, the trumpets, and the bowls John has deliberately presented a crescendo of divine judgment; for the horsemen ravage a quarter of the earth, the trumpeters a third, and the bowls usher in the last plagues which bring total destruction" (ibid. 104).

[38] Note as well the parallels between the first five trumpet judgments and the plagues on the idolatry of Egypt at the time of the exodus (Exodus 7–12).

Even natural disasters and other judgments of God that fall from time to time are a mercy to those who survive them, for these events teach God's righteousness and his displeasure with human sin. They ought to have the effect of leading people to repentance (Luke 13:1–5). But after witnessing these judgments under their symbolic forms, John is compelled to write the incriminating words, "The rest of mankind, who were not killed by these plagues, did not repent" (Rev. 9:20).

Interlude (Rev. 10:1–11:14)

As was the case with the seven seals, so also with the seven trumpets, between the sixth and the seventh in the series two unnumbered episodes intervene.[39] Their interposition is evidently meant to convey the sense of delay before the end arrives (Rev. 10:6) and to encourage the saints. John is first met by a mighty angel who delivers him a little scroll to eat (cf. Jer. 15:16; Ezek. 2:9–3:3, 11), signifying bittersweet prophecies he is yet to utter "about many peoples and nations and languages and kings" (Rev. 10:11).

Then in a complex vision, John is told to measure the temple of God and the altar and those who worship there, but is instructed not to measure the court outside the temple, for it is given over to trampling by the nations, who will trample the holy city for forty-two months (Rev. 11:1–2). John is then introduced to Christ's two witnesses, who will prophesy for the same period of time (expressed as 1,260 days). These prophet-witnesses will be able to consume all their enemies with God's plagues *until* their testimony is completed, at which time a beast that ascends from the pit will conquer and kill them, much to the world's joy (11:5–10). Like their Lord, the witnesses will rise from death and be taken to heaven in a cloud (11:11–12).

Both major symbols in this complex vision of 11:1–14—the temple that is protected from destruction and the two witnesses who testify—are meaningful symbols of the church. Some interpreters see the temple as the literal stone-and-mortar temple in Jerusalem in the first century, destroyed in AD 70. But the point of John's being told not to measure the "temple of God and the altar and those who worship there" (11:1) is that this temple and its worshipers are to be protected and preserved, even while the outer court and city are trampled underfoot by the nations. Others see the temple as a literal stone-and-mortar temple to be rebuilt in Jerusalem in the last days. The connection with "God's temple in heaven" at the end of the account of the seventh trumpet in 11:19 and with "his dwelling, that is, those that dwell in heaven" in 13:6, suggests, however, that the reference in 11:1 must be to the church in its spiritual, heavenly identity or essence (Heb. 12:22–23; 13:10). The outer court and the city that are trampled are most likely the church on earth, still subject to opposition and persecution.[40]

[39] The intervening episodes are closely tied to the series of trumpets by the three "woes" announced after the fourth trumpet (8:13). The first woe is declared to have occurred after the fifth trumpet (9:12); the third woe is declared just before the seventh trumpet; but the second woe is declared not after the sixth trumpet but instead after the second episode that intervenes between the sixth and seventh trumpets.

[40] See Caird, *Commentary on the Revelation*, 132; Bauckham, *Climax of Prophecy*, 266–73.

Many early commentators in the church (both chiliastic and non-chiliastic) understood the two witnesses to be two eschatological individuals who would return from the past, most often Enoch and Elijah. Many premillennial interpreters still take such a view.[41] This view comes over from certain strands of Jewish apocalypticism, wherein, according to its understanding of Malachi 4:5–6, Elijah (and perhaps others) had to return in person from paradise to earth in order to restore a righteousness that would introduce the messianic kingdom.[42] But Jesus interpreted Malachi's prophecy differently. Elijah had already come in the person of John the Baptist and had fulfilled his restorative ministry of witnessing to the Christ (John 1:6–8, 15, 19, etc.). In keeping with this, Revelation seems to attribute to the church, under the symbolic figure of the two witnesses, the continuation of John's Elijah-like witnessing ministry. The powers given to the two witnesses recall the ministries of both Elijah and Moses, as would follow from Malachi 5:4–5 and from these two prophets' appearance with Jesus on the mount of transfiguration (Matt. 17:1–13 and pars.). These ministries emphasize their prophetic function, but their further identity as "the two olive trees" (Rev. 11:4, royal Zerubbabel and Joshua the high priest from Zechariah 3–4) and "the two lampstands" (Rev. 11:4, lampstands already used as symbols of the churches in 1:20) also mark the church's priestly and kingly functions. As Christ's representative in the world, the ideal church bears his messianic offices of prophet, priest, and king.

The Seventh Trumpet (Rev. 11:15–19)

With the sound of the seventh trumpet the chorus of heaven rejoices: "The kingdom of the world has become the kingdom of our Lord and of his Christ, and he shall reign for ever and ever" (Rev. 11:15). The twenty-four elders fall on their faces and worship, proclaiming that God has taken his great power and has reigned. This is an announcement of the eschatological reign of all eternity after every foe has been obliterated (cf. 1 Cor. 15:20–28). The universality of the picture of judgment in Revelation 11:18 makes it hard to construe this as a reference to the destruction of Jerusalem in AD 70, or to a partial, preliminary judgment executed at the beginning of an earthly millennial kingdom, which would then need to be repeated at its conclusion.[43] Nor does any thousand-year reign intervene here between the time when the righteous dead are rewarded and the time when the wicked dead are destroyed; these happen at the same "time," the "time [ὁ καιρός] for the dead to be judged" (11:18). Thus, the seventh and "last trumpet" (cf. Matt. 24:31; 1 Cor. 15:52; 1 Thess. 4:16) brings us again to the end of the age, to the time of the final judgment and the dawn of the eternal kingdom.

[41] Others, mainly preterists, have related them to the Law and the Prophets, or to the line of Old Testament prophets who culminated in John the Baptist.

[42] 2 Bar. 13:3; 4 Ezra 6:26–28. See Hill, *Regnum Caelorum*, 228–32.

[43] Even Ladd, *Revelation of John*, 161, who follows a historic premillennial approach, concedes that "the perspective here employed in the establishment of God's Kingdom does not distinguish between the millennial reign of Christ and God's reign in the age to come."

The Major Interlude (Rev. 12:1–14:20)

Between the series of the seven trumpets (signifying partial judgments throughout history) and that of the seven bowls (signifying the final intensification of these judgments near the end), there is a major interlude section consisting of three parts. The first of these takes us back to the beginning of the era with the birth and ascension of Christ, and the last ends with another symbolic depiction of the final judgment, this time as a great harvest of the earth. Each of the three sections then portrays the inter-advent era and its conditions with respect to the church and its enemies, presenting it as a time of struggle but protection.

The dragon, the woman, and her seed (Rev. 12:1–17). The "great sign [σημεῖον]" of the dragon, the woman, and her child (Rev. 12:1–17) presents perhaps some of the most obvious symbolism of the Revelation and seems to give us a hermeneutical key for much of the book. First, as to the imagery and plot themselves, it is reasonably claimed that there are strong structural parallels with popular pagan myths with which John's readers would have been familiar.[44] An evil dragon (Python for Greeks, Set for Egyptians) is out to kill a pregnant woman/goddess (Leto or Isis) before her son (Apollo or Horus) can kill the dragon. As political/religious propaganda, the Roman emperor at times portrayed himself as the conquering god in this drama. If this widespread myth was recognized by John's readers, it may have carried the resulting connotation that Jesus, not the emperor or any of the pagan gods, was ultimate ruler of the universe.

But while the vision may access the *form* of a culturally familiar myth, John makes it clear that both the characters and the overall plot of this portentous vision derive from the Hebrew Scriptures and from the eternal gospel now come to light in Jesus Christ. The great red dragon, he tells us explicitly, is "the devil and Satan, the deceiver of the whole world" (Rev. 12:9). The child "is to rule all the nations with a rod of iron" (12:5), a clear allusion to Yahweh's anointed King and Son in Psalm 2:9 and a description already applied to the risen Jesus in Revelation 2:27. The woman clothed with the sun is a complex image, ultimately originating from Eve, whose seed is to crush the Serpent's head (Gen. 3:15). But she is also Zion/Jerusalem (Isa. 66:6–9; Gal. 4:26), the messianic community, the corporate mother of the Messiah and of individual believers (Gal. 4:31). "By the 'woman then clothed with the sun,'" wrote Hippolytus in the early third century, "he meant most manifestly the Church, endued with the Father's word, whose brightness is above the sun."[45] Before the dragon can devour him, the male child is caught up to God and to his throne, an obvious reference to Jesus's ascension.

Besides rendering in wonderful, symbolic form the birth of the Messiah, Satan's failed attempt to destroy him, and his victorious accession to God's throne in heaven, this episode seems to provide the solution to an important hermeneutical question.

[44] Ben Witherington III, *Revelation* (Cambridge: Cambridge University Press, 2003), 164–66, citing the work of Adela Yarbro Collins, *The Combat Myth in the Book of Revelation* (Missoula, MT: Scholars, 1976).

[45] *On Christ and Antichrist*, 61. Victorinus, *Comm. Apoc.*, says that the woman is "the ancient Church of fathers, and prophets, and saints, and apostles."

For it clearly associates the commencement of the three-and-a-half-year period with the time of Christ's ascension.[46] The crucial implication is that this period (forty-two months; 1,260 days; time, and times, and half a time) cannot be projected forward to begin only in the final calendar years of the world,[47] nor can it have begun and ended in the war for control of Jerusalem in the first century. It is a figure for the entire inter-advent age, the age of the paradoxical present reign of Christ. During this period, on the one hand, the beast is allowed to exercise his authority (Rev. 13:5), and the earthly church (the holy city) is subject to trampling (11:2). But, on the other hand, the church (the two witnesses) bears faithful and divinely empowered witness (11:3) and is divinely protected from the flood that pours from the dragon's mouth (12:6, 13–17).

This counterintuitive presentation also accurately reflects the character of the inter-advent age as exhibited elsewhere in the book. The paradox of triumph in tribulation, salvation in suffering, for the church reaches a poignant crescendo in 12:10–12:

> And I heard a loud voice in heaven, saying, "Now the salvation and the power and the kingdom of our God and the authority of his Christ have come, for the accuser of our brothers has been thrown down, who accuses them day and night before our God. And they have conquered him by the blood of the Lamb and by the word of their testimony, for they loved not their lives even unto death. Therefore, rejoice, O heavens and you who dwell in them! But woe to you, O earth and sea, for the devil has come down to you in great wrath, because he knows that his time is short!"

Christ is on his Father's throne (also 2:26–27; 3:21), and his kingdom and authority have come! This results in Satan's violent overthrow and decisive banishment from heaven (Luke 10:18; John 12:31). But it does not mean peace and plenty for Jesus's followers who are still on earth. Christ's kingdom during this age is one in which he rules in the midst of his foes (Ps. 110:2), and in the conquest, his servants prove faithful even to the cost of their lives. The time of Christ's mediatorial reign from heaven and the time of the dragon's wrath on earth paradoxically coincide.

The two beasts (Rev. 13:1–18). Flowing from the words of the heavenly voice in Revelation 12:12, earth and sea are to experience woe even in the wake of Christ's victorious ascension. In the following section (Revelation 13) John sees beasts rising first from the sea and then from the earth. Some interpret the beasts solely with respect to persons, institutions, and events belonging to the Greco-Roman situation

---

[46] First Kings 17 and James 5:17 provide one part of the Old Testament background for the symbolism of the three and a half years. In the days of Ahab and Elijah (cf. Rev. 11:6) the faithful remnant were persecuted but miraculously preserved. The expression "time, times, and half a time" appeared first in Dan. 7:25; 12:7 as the time of the anti-Christian "little horn" of the fourth beast. It has been proposed as well that this is in effect the remainder of the seventieth week from Dan. 9:24–27. Since Christ caused sacrifice and offering to cease in the middle of the seventieth week (9:27), the last half of the week becomes a symbol for the gospel age.

[47] It is probably to avoid this critical implication that Ladd tries so resolutely to disassociate this vision of Rev. 12:1–6 from its obvious historical referent, the birth and the victorious ascension of Jesus of Nazareth (*Revelation of John*, 166–71); e.g., "It is not at all clear that the birth of the Messiah (vs. 2) is meant to represent the birth of the historical Jesus, or that his catching up to heaven is his ascension" (ibid., 167). John F. Walvoord, *The Revelation of Jesus Christ* (Chicago: Moody Press, 1966), 191, concedes that this verse is a reference to Jesus's ascension, but then claims that "there is obviously a tremendous time lapse between verses 5 and 6," so that the three and a half years does not begin until near the end of world history.

at the time of writing.[48] Others limit the application to the end of world history. Once again, however, if we follow the interpretative leads mentioned so far, we are encouraged to view the images themselves painted into bold Danielic outlines with the unmistakable colors of John's historical situation, yet as capable of new "impersonations" throughout the inter-advent age, finally culminating in a climactic manifestation at the end.

The first beast seems to represent tyrannical, totalitarian military/political power arrayed against the church, power that at times grows more virulent and at other times recedes (this will become clearer in Revelation 17). In John's day and for many decades to come, Roman governmental authority promoted and at times compelled worship of the emperor. The second beast represents the deceptive, propagandistic, prophetic/religious apparatus that serves to legitimate the anti-Christian state and carry out its wishes. The immediate embodiment of this second beast may have been the Roman aristocracy, the pagan priesthood, and those of "the synagogue of Satan" (Rev. 2:9; 3:9) who aided Rome in the persecution of Christians. The descriptions justify the view that the sea beast is a blasphemous parody of Christ,[49] and the earth beast (or false prophet, as he is later called) is a blasphemous parody of the Holy Spirit (the "spirit of the antichrist," 1 John 4:3). This false spirit may be the animating power behind a multitude of human tools—false prophets, apostles, demagogues, and opinion-makers—throughout history. With the dragon the two beasts then form an unholy anti-Trinity.

The mark of the beast in Revelation 13:16–18 fills out a picture of totalitarian rule; no one is able to buy or sell without the mark on forehead or hand. Many have sought an interpretation of the 666 by means of "gematria," the practice of manipulating numbers derived from the numerical equivalents of the (Hebrew, Greek, or Latin) letters that make up someone's name (α = 1, β = 2, etc.). Ancient fascination with such puzzles (e.g., Barn. 9.7–8) gives the searches an initial plausibility. On this approach, the best suggestion is probably the name and title "Nero Caesar," but this works only if one begins with the Greek (not the Latin) spelling, then transliterates the Greek letters into Hebrew using one alternative of the Hebrew spelling of Caesar, and then adds together the numerical significance of the Hebrew letters![50] If this is accepted, it may mean that the final incarnation of the beast will have the character of the infamous, Christian-persecuting emperor. Yet, as Irenaeus said, "If it were necessary that his name should be distinctly revealed in this present time, it would have been announced by him who beheld the apocalyptic vision."[51] The phrase ἀριθμὸς ἀνθρώπου may refer not to "the number of a man" but to "the number of man,"

[48] Bauckham, *Theology of the Book of Revelation*, 35–36; Steven J. Friesen, *Imperial Cults and the Apocalypse of John: Reading Revelation in the Ruins* (Oxford: Oxford University Press, 2001), 202–4, thinks the sea beast is the Roman imperial authority and the earth beast is the local aristocracy which promoted worship of the Roman emperors.

[49] See the list of parallels between Christ and the beast in Beale, *Revelation: A Shorter Commentary* (Grand Rapids, MI: Eerdmans, 2015), 271.

[50] But even if accepted, this would not establish the date of the prophecy as the time of Nero's reign, for even by the end of the first century the specter of Nero was already functioning as a type and could be applied to some future power who exhibited Nero-like qualities (see Friesen, *Imperial Cults*, 136–37; Koester, *Revelation*, 570–71).

[51] *Haer*. 5.30.3 (*ANF* 1:550).

for man was created on the sixth day, and six hundred, sixty, and six could signify an exponential intensification (6 + [6 x 10] + [6 x 10 x 10]) of human corruption.[52] The number is said to be placed on the right hand or the forehead. It is thus the antithesis of the seal of God mentioned in 7:3, which the elect wear on their forehead, and of the Lamb's name and his Father's in 14:1, written on the foreheads of the 144,000. If the seal of the elect is not a visible mark (see 2 Cor. 1:22; Eph. 1:13; 4:30), there is no compelling reason why the seal of the beast worshipers need be visible,[53] though there is also nothing preventing it from manifesting itself in some sort of tangible way at a given time and place.[54] The question the church should always be asking is What in our day and culture would sell us out to the beast?

Seven signs of assurance (Rev. 14:1–20). In Revelation 14 the major interlude between the trumpets and the bowls continues with seven tokens of assurance, following in quick succession. First, there is a vision of the Lamb and his 144,000 followers on Mount Zion. This is the heavenly Zion (*pace* Ladd and many others), as verses 2–3 make plain (cf. Heb. 12:22), and it gives us another aspect of the life of the departed saints in heaven during the inter-advent age.[55] They are the heavenly antithesis of the beast worshipers, having on their foreheads not the mark of the beast but the name of the Lamb and the name of his Father. They represent the spiritually chaste (contrast Rev. 2:22; 14:8; 17:2) firstfruits, worshiping with harps and singing a new song before the throne.

Then follow three angels with three messages for those who dwell on earth (14:6–12). The first proclaims an eternal gospel, the second foretells the fall of Babylon the great (the first mention of Babylon in the book), and the third announces the dreadful doom of those who worship the beast and its image and receive its mark. Another heavenly voice pronounces a beatitude on those "who die in the Lord from now on" (14:13). In contrast to the worshipers of the beast, who have no rest (14:11), the Christian faithful enjoy rest from their labors (6:11). As the author of Hebrews says, "There remains a Sabbath rest for the people of God" (Heb. 4:9).

The interlude of Revelation 12–14 is brought to a close with a double picture of the last judgment (the third), this time under the figure of a great harvest (a frequent biblical metaphor for judgment, Matt. 13:36–43; Mark 4:29; etc.). Revelation 14:14–16 appears to depict Christ (one like a Son of Man) gathering the *faithful* into the Father's barns. The gory image of the treading of the winepress in 14:17–20 invokes Old Testament prophetic depictions (Isa. 63:2–3; Joel 3:13) of the wrath of God overtaking the *wicked*.

The Seven Bowls (Rev. 15:1–16:21)

The end of chapter 14 has again brought us to the consummation of world history. Christ the King has come back in judgment to reap the harvest of the world. As

[52] It is sometimes observed that the Greek letters in the name Jesus add up to 888.
[53] "The 'forehead' represents ideological commitment and the 'hand' the practical outworking of that commitment" (Beale, *Revelation: A Shorter Commentary*, 283).
[54] Such as, perhaps, the *libellus*, a certificate signifying that one had offered sacrifice to the emperor, used in the third century.
[55] Cf. Rev. 6:9–11; 7:9–17; 12:12; 13:6; 14:13; 15:2–4; etc.

chapter 15 begins, John's visions once again take us back chronologically to a point in the inter-advent period—perhaps very near or at its close—to behold a heavenly scene and one last series of judgments on the earth. Structurally, John's mention of "another sign [σημεῖον] in heaven" in Revelation 15:1 brings the hearers back to 12:1 ("a great [σημεῖον] appeared"), to the point where he broke off from the seven trumpets with a long interlude.

Before the solemn judgments are recounted, John receives another glimpse of departed saints engaging in heavenly worship in the present age. Here they are described as conquerors—in the language of the letters to the seven churches—who have conquered the beast, its image, and the number of its name. They stand beside the sea of glass (see 4:6). Again they are provided with harps and song (14:2–3), the song of Moses and the song of the Lamb.

Bowls, like trumpets, are temple vessels (see Num. 28:7, 9, 14, 31, etc.). The bowl judgments, too, have their origin in the heavenly worship to which John was introduced in Revelation 4–5, at the commencement of the second major vision. John announces that with these seven plagues, "which are the last, . . . the wrath of God is finished" (15:1). Whereas the first four bowl judgments parallel the first four trumpet judgments, in that they are poured out on the inanimate creation, the bowl judgments are more comprehensive in their destructive effects.[56] There are no limitations by fourths or thirds. As with the trumpets, so with bowls, the dire judgments on evil deeds do not elicit repentance from those who commit them, but instead the judged only curse the name of God (16:9, 11, 21). Again, this demonstrates both the hardness of human hearts and the justice of God's judgments. The perfect justice of God's judgments is, in fact, a recurrent theme of the presentation in chapters 15–16. It is sung in the song of Moses and the song of the Lamb in 15:3; it is proclaimed by the angel of water after the third bowl is poured out into the rivers and fountains in 16:5–6; it is echoed by the altar (probably, by metonymy, the martyrs of 6:9) in 16:7.

In the account of the sixth bowl, the dragon, the beast, and the false prophet pour forth foul spirits who go abroad to deceive the kings of the earth for battle at a place called, in Hebrew, Armageddon. This is the first mention of a battle that will come back into view in 17:14; 19:17–21; and 20:7–10. The mission to deceive the kings of the earth into battle finds a parallel at the end of the millennium, when Satan deceives the nations into attacking the saints.

There is no interlude between the sixth and seventh bowls, perhaps accenting the sense that the end has come with no more delay. Instead, the consummation of God's wrath follows immediately, accompanied by a shout from the throne, "It is done!" (16:17). Babylon has made all nations drink the wine of her impure passion (14:8; 17:2; 18:3), so God fittingly makes her drink the cup of the fury of his wrath! The creation comes apart (16:20–21) in another (the fourth) description of the great day of judgment, recalling the first description in 6:12–17 at the opening of the sixth seal.

[56] So maintains Irenaeus, *Haer*. 4.30.4 (*ANF* 1:504): "The nations receive the same plagues universally, as Egypt did particularly."

This brings the cycle of judgments flowing from John's vision of the heavenly throne room to a close.

From the Third Vision: The Judgment of Babylon 17:1–21:8

Babylon the Great (Rev. 17:1–19:10)

The mystery of Babylon (Rev. 17:1–18). At this point begins the third major vision of the book. One of the seven bowl angels approaches John and tells him to "come" and he will be shown the judgment of the great harlot Babylon. John is then carried away in the Spirit into a wilderness to see a woman sitting on a scarlet beast full of blasphemous names. This third major vision will have an antithetical parallel in the fourth and last vision, beginning in Revelation 21:9, in which John is shown another woman/city, the pure and spotless bride of Christ, the New Jerusalem. This third vision will narrate in order the demise of all God's enemies (reversing the order in which they were introduced in the book). The vision focuses first on Babylon and her destruction (17:1–19:10). Then the aftermath section depicts the ruin of the beast and false prophet (19:11–21), then the dragon (20:1–11), and finally, death and hades (20:11–15). Then John appends a section on the heritage of the just and the unjust (21:1–8).

Babylon is certainly in some aspects a counterfoil of the church, the holy city Jerusalem. But the point of the antithesis does not seem to be that it is an *institutional* false church. She is portrayed as the mirror *opposite* of the bride in her purity and devotion to her husband. If the false church signifies any kind of religion, it appears to be a religion of idolatrous, hedonistic, sensual materialism. Emphasized in chapter 17 are her connections with the sea beast, the self-deifying, persecuting power.

Some interpreters identify Babylon with Jerusalem,[57] and many others with Rome. Certainly in John's context Babylon has to do with Rome, which is even called Babylon in 1 Peter 5:13 (note the seven mountains on which she is seated in Rev. 17:9). The cast of this image does not have to do with Rome's military/political power (which belongs more to the sea beast image), and therefore the name Babylon was apparently not chosen because Rome was the destroyer of the Second Temple in Jerusalem, as Babylon was destroyer of the first. Rather, "Babylon" refers to Roman culture in its commercialistic, materialistic, sensualistic, and religious wantonness. She is depicted as a prostitute, who indeed has an unholy alliance with the persecuting beast, who satiates her with the blood of the saints. Today it does not seem possible to identify Babylon with a single city; a more likely referent would be any *culture* of seductive, idolatrous hedonism that feeds off of or benefits from anti-Christianity and the oppression of God's people.

[57]This gains some plausibility from a comparison of Rev. 18:24 with Luke 11:50–51. But the universality of Rev. 18:24 ("all who have been slain on earth") connects it more closely with Jeremiah's description of Old Testament Babylon in Jer. 51:49 ("the slain of all the earth"). In other words, this was part of the image of Old Testament Babylon, applied now to its New Testament counterpart. Likewise, Rev. 17:1, "who is seated on many waters," hardly refers to historical Jerusalem or to historical Rome; rather, it too is part of the Babylon image, for Babylon is the city that dwells by many waters (Jer. 51:13). Finally, Rev. 17:18, "the woman that you saw is the great city that has dominion over the kings of the earth," is not an easy fit for Jerusalem, but can only mean Rome in John's context.

New information about the sea beast is also added in chapter 17. The beast "was, and is not, and is about to rise from the bottomless pit and go to destruction" (17:8). Yet we are also told that it has seven heads; "five . . . have fallen, *one is*, and the other has not yet come" (17:10). So we have a beast who *is* and who *isn't*! It existed as John wrote but not in its most malevolent form. No matter how we seek to identify the seven heads (as Roman emperors or as a succession of world empires or as something else), it is the eighth head which is the climactic, most vicious manifestation, which reappears from the pits of hell (17:11). The destruction of the eighth head is apparently the destruction of the beast itself. This form was yet future to John and is yet future to us, but it is proleptically present in a succession of oppressive regimes throughout Christian history.

The fall of Babylon (Rev. 18:1–19:10). Having seen an arresting and repulsive picture of Babylon, and having heard the prediction in Revelation 17:16–18 of her destruction at the hands of the beast and its ten royal horns, we are now (18:1–19:10) presented with a long series of laments and rejoicings over the prostitute's demise.

A series of pronouncements and earthly laments (Rev. 18:1–24). Much of the language of this section reflects Old Testament denunciations of corrupt and idolatrous nation states. Especially prominent are allusions to Jeremiah's great denunciation of Babylon in Jeremiah 50–51 (see also Isa. 13:19–22 [Babylon]; 34:8–15 [Edom]; Zeph. 2:14 [Nineveh]; Ezek. 27:25ff.; 28:1ff. [Tyre]). What God did with Old Testament Babylon lies behind the picture here. Babylon was God's instrument of judgment on the ancient idolatrous nations, even on Israel. But Babylon's pride and bloodthirst led it to overstep the bounds God had set for it. Babylon herself, therefore, was judged and destroyed by God. So New Testament Babylon (decadent, idolatrous Roman culture and its later incarnations) will be judged for its highly contagious decadence and its participation in the oppression of the saints (Rev. 18:20, 24; 19:2).

In Revelation 11, the earth dwellers rejoiced and made merry over the killing of the two prophets (picturing the temporary silencing of the church's witness); now they grieve over the killing of Babylon. The whoring kings of the earth (18:9–10), the merchants of the land (18:11–17a), and the merchants of the sea (18:17b–19) all send up bitter laments at her demise.

The relationship of Babylon and the beast(s) to the church is played out repeatedly in the imagery of Revelation. A decadent, hedonistic culture hates Christianity; a totalitarian, self-deifying state also hates Christianity. The two forces feed off each other and for a time are effectively in league with each other against the Christians. Eventually the totalitarian beast will devour even its partner, the inherently weak narcissistic culture. It then turns its force against the church for a climactic confrontation ("battle"). It is at this point that God intervenes and Christ returns.

A series of heavenly rejoicings: the hallelujah choruses (Rev. 19:1–10). The judgment of the great prostitute is the occasion for earth to mourn but for heaven to rejoice. Instead of laments, now is heard a series of heavenly hallelujahs in 19:1–10: first from a great multitude in heaven (19:1–3), then from the twenty-four elders and the four living creatures (19:4), then from the throne—perhaps meaning Christ or the saints (19:5)—then from a heavenly multitude again (19:6–8). The last of these is a hallelujah for God's reign and for the marriage of the Lamb, leading into a pronouncement of blessing on those who are invited to it. This is then followed (19:9–10) by the angel's authentication ("These are the true words of God") and John's strange, aborted worship, signifying the close of the third vision proper and a transition to its aftermath (see "Introduction").

It seems that the destruction of Babylon is the occasion for the marriage of the Lamb and his bride: "for the marriage of the Lamb has come [ἦλθεν]" (19:7). This does not give the impression that the marriage is still a thousand years off into the future. The definite chronological placement of the marriage in 21:2, 9–10 as *following* both the millennium and the last judgment then suggests that the destruction of Babylon comes near the end of the millennium rather than at its beginning—another indication that the millennial period is coincident with the present age.

Aftermath: The Judgment of the Rest of God's Enemies (Rev. 19:11–21:8)

The stated subject of the third vision, the judgment of Babylon, comes to an end at Revelation 19:10 (see above). In a temporal sense, the destruction of Babylon must bring us to a point very near the close of the age. The demise of the rest of God's enemies will now be recounted in three main scenes. It is reasonable to assume that each of these scenes culminates at the close of the age as well.

This aftermath of the third vision, then, records the destruction of the beast and false prophet, with their host (19:11–21); Satan, with Gog and Magog (20:1–10); and finally, death and hades, with those whom they have swallowed up (20:11–15). Each scene thus culminates with a portrayal of God's final judgment on humanity (the fifth, sixth, and seventh of the book's portrayals), as relating to each of the enemies. Besides this, each scene also portrays other important aspects of the judging and ruling activities of God and Christ.

The judgment of the beast and the false prophet (Rev. 19:11–21)

The coming of Christ (Rev. 19:11–16). On a white horse, riding forth from heaven, Christ is represented as a great warrior whose garments are stained with blood. He comes to judge, leading the armies of heaven. Some see this not as a depiction of Christ's second coming, but as the conquest of the gospel throughout the age.[58] One important factor pointing decisively to the first interpretation, however, is that Christ *slays with the sword* that comes out of his mouth (19:15, 21), an obvious reference to the judging activity of his Word (he is called "The Word of God" in 19:13). This is evidently not a symbol for the spiritual conquest of the ungodly by turning them

[58] E.g., Henry Barclay Swete, *The Apocalypse of St John: The Greek Text with Introduction Notes and Indices* (London: Macmillan, 1911), 250–59; Chilton, *Days of Vengeance*, 480–92.

to faith; the birds feast on the flesh of those slain by the sword. Rather the sword of Christ's mouth strikes in judgment, as Jesus said in John 12:48: "The one who rejects me and does not receive my words has a judge; the word that I have spoken will judge him on the last day." Paul applies the metaphor specifically to the defeat of the man of lawlessness (2 Thess. 2:8), and Jesus in Revelation uses it to threaten temporal judgment on the church at Pergamum (2:16).

The last battle (Rev. 19:17–21). John records the final lot of the rebellious beast and false prophet, the definitive result of their futile gathering of the kings of the earth to make war against Christ and his army. The lake of fire that burns with sulfur, which is also the second death (Rev. 20:6, 14; 21:8), is their final abode (19:20). This fiery lake, we shall soon see, will also be the fate of the Devil (20:10), of death and hades (20:14), and of those whose names are not found written in the Book of Life (20:15; 21:8). This was all foreshadowed in Jesus's solemn forewarning in Matthew 25:41, "Depart from me, you cursed, into the eternal fire prepared for the devil and his angels."

The judgment of Satan (Rev. 20:1–10)

The binding of Satan and the reign of Christ and his saints (Rev. 20:1–6). The next ten verses have of course been the cause of a voluminous output of exegetical and theological literature (normally a good thing) and a high level of acrimonious discord among Christians (not a good thing). Because the passage has been and continues to be the focus of so much debate, an excursus on a number of key factors in its interpretation is appended at the end of this essay.[59] Here, the attempt will be made simply to set the narrative of the passage within the flow of the book and explain its basic meaning.

In the structure of Revelation (as we are viewing it), 20:1–10 is not set off as a central section of the book, but has its place in the story of how Christ's reign brings about the ultimate defeat of God's enemies. The devouring of Babylon by her own allies has been told; the vanquishing of the land and sea beasts by the returning King and his army has been related. Before the destruction of the last enemy, death, is documented, John is shown the ruin of "the dragon, that ancient serpent, who is the devil and Satan" (20:2). The destruction of Satan takes place in two stages: first he is bound for a thousand years while Christ and his saints reign (20:1–6); then he is released and destroyed (20:7–10). The binding of Satan arrests his attempt to deceive the nations (20:3). The focus of this deception, however, as 20:8 makes clear, is not simply to entice into sin but to gather the nations for battle against the saints.

The description "that ancient serpent" immediately recalls the first appearance of the Devil in Scripture, in Paradise (Genesis 3). In Revelation 12 we have already heard part of the story of his ultimate defeat at the hands of the woman's seed. There the accuser was definitively cast out of heaven, signifying that his accusations against

[59] See also Hill, *Regnum Caelorum*, 220–48, 260–68, and the commentaries of Beale, Hendriksen, Hughes, Johnson, Kistemaker, Morris, and others in the bibliography following this chapter.

the saints are henceforth, for all time, "thrown out of court." Here in chapter 20 the deceiver is bound in the depths of the earth, signifying that until the end of history Christ thwarts his ability to deceive the nations into gathering for the final battle against the church.

Despite common assumptions of the contrary, the scene in 20:4–6 is not earth but heaven; there is nothing that points convincingly to earth, but several things clearly indicate heaven. Heaven is where the *souls* of the saints, who were faithful unto death (6:9; 12:11–12) and did not worship the beast (15:2), live (2:10–11) and reign with Christ (3:21; 12:10–12), and serve him as priests (7:15) during his reign in the present age. This reign is depicted in many places throughout the book of Revelation, and throughout the New Testament, but only here is it described as lasting a thousand years. This is most probably to signify that it fulfills the ideal reign of the second Adam (see the excursus at the end of this chapter). The "first resurrection" enjoyed by the saints (20:5) is not a resurrection of the body (which would then come a thousand years before that of the wicked), but refers to the rising of the souls to heaven, where Christ is. That the second death would have no power over those who, having conquered, join Christ in heaven was indicated in the letter to the church in Smyrna (2:11; 20:6).

The final defeat of Satan (Rev. 20:7–10). When the thousand years are ended, Satan is released and goes forth to deceive the nations, now given the names Gog and Magog from Ezekiel's prophecy (38:2; 39:1), to gather them together for battle. This is evidently the same battle mentioned earlier (Rev. 11:7; 13:7; 16:14; 19:19). Just when it looks the worst for "the camp of the saints and the beloved city" (20:9), fire falls from heaven and consumes the diabolical foes. The Devil is at last thrown into the lake of fire and sulfur, where he joins the beast and false prophet in eternal torment. Again, this is best seen as the same climactic confrontation with evil that is portrayed in 19:11–21 with Christ's return (see the excursus).

The judgment of death and hades: the last judgment (Rev. 20:11–15). Now John sees a great white throne and him who sits upon it. Here the last judgment is depicted as a court scene, with charges, acquittals, and condemnations. Once again, "books" figure in John's visions. Written in "the books" are the deeds of the dead, "what they had done" (Rev. 20:12). Written in the single "book of life" are the names of those redeemed by the blood of the Lamb. The book once sealed with seven seals is at last unrolled and its precious contents made public.

Paul wrote that the last enemy to be destroyed in Christ's subjugating reign would be death (1 Cor. 15:26). Death and hades had already suffered defeat, for their keys had been held by the victorious Son of Man since the time of his resurrection (Rev. 1:18). Now they are emptied and thrown into the lake of fire, there to join the beast and false prophet, the Devil, and those whose names are not in the Book of Life.

The heritage of the just and the unjust (Rev. 21:1–8). Before the fourth main vision can come to a close, it is natural that John, having witnessed the solemn scene of the great white throne judgment, would be shown his first extended glimpse of eternity. "Then I saw a new heaven and a new earth. . . . And I saw the holy city, new Jerusalem, coming down out of heaven from God" (Rev. 21:1–2).

New Jerusalem is prepared as a bride adorned for her husband, in stark contrast to Babylon the great, mother of harlots, who held temporary dominion over the kings of the old earth. The significance of the descent of the holy Jerusalem is given in verse 3. The book of Revelation contains a host of beautiful, comforting passages, but there is none more beautiful than this:

> Behold, the dwelling place of God is with man. He will dwell with them, and they will be his people, and God himself will be with them as their God. He will wipe away every tear from their eyes, and death shall be no more, neither shall there be mourning, nor crying, nor pain anymore, for the former [first] things have passed away.

God's promise that he will be our God and that we will be his people is the essence of the covenant promise, the source and basis of the intimate fellowship experienced by his people here on earth ever since it was first uttered to Abraham (see Gen. 17:7–8; Ex. 20:2; Lev. 26:11f.; Deut. 5:2–6; Jer. 24:7; 30:22; 31:33; 32:38; Ezek. 11:20; 37:26f.; Zech. 8:8; 13:9; Matt. 13:17; Rom. 4:22; 2 Cor. 6:16). No longer is sin any hindrance to this divine fellowship, which now blossoms eternally in consummate perfection. As always, it is the divine initiative that is set forth here: "He will dwell with them, and they will be his people, and God himself will be with them as their God" (Rev. 21:3).

Paralleling the conclusion of the vision of Babylon's destruction (19:9) comes another "authentication" in 21:5, this time not from the angel, but from him who sat upon the throne: "Write this down, for these words are trustworthy and true."

The heritages of the righteous and the wicked are now contrasted in chiastic parallel: the conquerors shall drink from the fountain of the water of life and be sons of God; the cowardly and faithless shall have as their heritage "the lake that burns with fire and sulfur, which is the second death" (21:8).

a The water of life (21:6)
    b The conquerors (21:7)
    b' The wicked (21:8)
a' The lake of fire (21:8)

From the Fourth Vision: The New Jerusalem, the Bride of the Lamb (Rev. 21:9–22:5)

John now receives his fourth and final major vision. Again he is approached by one of the bowl angels and told the subject of this vision: "Come, I will show you the Bride, the wife of the Lamb" (Rev. 21:9). Again he is carried away "in the Spirit" (21:10), this time to a great, high mountain, and is shown the holy city Jerusalem coming down out of heaven from God. This fourth vision forms a kind of doublet with 21:1–8, which concluded the third vision by introducing the New Jerusalem as the reward and heritage of the saints, the place where God will dwell eternally with his people. Now John is shown the eternal city in more detail, as an extended contrast to the prostitute Babylon. In particular, he is shown

- its gates and foundations (Rev. 21:12–14),
- its measurements and materials (21:15–21),
- its light and life (21:22–22:5).

In this last section there is another chiastic arrangement:

a No night, for the Lord is its light (21:22–26)
  b Nothing unclean, but only those written in the Lamb's Book of Life (21:27)
    c The river of the water of life (22:1–2a)
    c' The tree of life (22:2b)
  b' Nothing accursed, but God's servants worshiping at his throne (22:3–4)
a' No night, for the Lord is its light (22:5)

The cubic dimensions of the city mentioned in 21:16 already recall the fact that the Most Holy Place in the Old Testament tabernacle was cubic in shape. Now the staggering implication is drawn that in this city there is no temple because "its temple is the Lord God the Almighty and the Lamb" (21:22). The absence of a temple in the New Jerusalem signifies a fellowship even more intimate and close, and a complete sanctification of the redeemed creation.

The city is also paradise restored. Parts of this picture reflect Ezekiel's vision of the ideal temple and the river that flowed from the temple (Ezek. 47:1, 7, 12; on the river, see Gen. 2:10; Ps. 46:4; John 4:10, 14; 7:37–39 and note its connections with the Spirit). With no temple in the city, the water flows fittingly from "the throne of God and of the Lamb" (Rev. 22:1). In the city is also the tree of life, which occupied the garden in Genesis. Adam and Eve were denied access to this tree when they sinned. Now, as Jesus has already promised to the conquerors at Ephesus (2:7), the redeemed freely partake of it, and its ever-blooming leaves are for the healing of the nations.

Revelation 22:6–9 forms a transition, both closing the fourth vision (with an authentication and another instance of prostration) and opening the epilogue by repeating some elements of the prologue.

Epilogue (Rev. 22:6[9]–21)

The final section ties the book together with several parallels with the prologue. These include

- sending an angel to show God's servants what must soon take place (Rev. 1:1–2; 22:6, 16),
- blessing on those who hear or read and keep the words of this prophecy (1:3; 22:7),

- nearness of the application of the words of the prophecy (1:1, 3; 22:10),
- Christ coming for judgment (1:7; "soon," 22:7, 12, 20),
- Alpha and Omega, first and last (1:8, 17, of "the Lord God"; 22:13, of Christ).

The epilogue contains a repetition of blessings but pronounces, in a documentary clause, dreadful curses on those who might dare to add to or subtract from the words of the prophecy of the book. After a final promise and a prayer for the Lord's return (22:20), this most marvelous book ends with John's own benediction, which extends far beyond the seven historical churches in Asia to encompass *all* who read, and hear, and keep what is written therein (1:3): "The grace of the Lord Jesus be with all. Amen" (22:21).

Excursus: Exegetical Factors in the Interpretation of Revelation 20:1–10

Eschatological Context

As mentioned in this chapter's introduction, the eschatological context is a crucial starting point for discussion of the millennium. The New Testament documents a major shift from the common Jewish eschatology of the day, and this is due to the supremely important fact of the coming of the Messiah. Revelation's abundant teaching on the present heavenly reign of Messiah Jesus, and the present heavenly blessedness of those who have died in him, places it squarely within the trajectory of the semi-realized, non-chiliastic eschatology of the rest of the New Testament.

Also indicative of this shift is that the most common features of the earthly kingdom as we know them from Jewish apocalyptic sources are entirely absent. Gone from Revelation 20:4–6 is any mention of the return of the lost tribes, a restoration of earthly Jerusalem, the dominion of Israel over the nations, or the fantastic abundance of the earth's produce.[60]

Recapitulation

If the binding of Satan and the rule of the saints in Revelation 20:1–10 are interpreted as following directly upon the return of Christ at the end of chapter 19, then we certainly have a premillennial return of Christ. But in Revelation we have seen that John repeatedly presents us with a vision of the last day and then returns to a point near the beginning of the inter-advent era (recapitulation).[61] A prime example would be the shift from chapter 11 to chapter 12.

Several elements in the passage point in this direction, such as the battle with the enemies called Gog and Magog. In Ezekiel 38–39 Gog and Magog are destroyed, and then the birds feast on their flesh. But in Revelation, the order is seemingly reversed: the feast of the birds is mentioned at the end of chapter 19

[60] See Hill, *Regnum Caelorum*, 235–42.

[61] Two excellent sources on recapitulation in Revelation 20 are R. F. White, "Reexamining the Evidence for Recapitulation in Rev 20:1–10," *WTJ* 51 (1989): 319–44; and Beale, *Book of Revelation*, 974–83.

and the defeat of Gog and Magog is not described until 20:7–10. This is a problem for a chronologically sequential reading of Revelation.[62] If, however, Revelation 19:11–21 and 20:7–10 are simply focusing on different aspects of the same events, then Revelation is consistent with Ezekiel's presentation. In Revelation 19:11–21 the subject is the demise of the beast and the false prophet; in 20:7–10 it is the demise of Satan.

In 11:7 and 13:7 the beast is said to "make war" on the saints, and the word for "war" (πόλεμος) occurs without the article. When the article is used in 16:14; 19:19; and 20:8, "the war" (or "the battle," as in 16:14, the "battle on the great day of God the Almighty") must refer to the same war, indicating that the war at the end of the millennium in 20:8 is the same one that occurs at Jesus's return to earth in 19:19.

Another problem for a sequential reading is that everyone seems to be dead at the end of chapter 19 ("all men," 19:18; "the rest," 19:21). Why, then, does Satan at once have to be bound (20:1–3) so as not to deceive the nations? There are no nations left for him to deceive. And how, then, is the millennial earth populated, if all God's enemies are gone and the righteous have been given their resurrected bodies? And if these problems could be solved, how are there hordes of hostile nations again present at the end of the millennium attacking the saints, in view of the fact that Jesus Christ has personally been ruling the millennial earth with an iron rod? For these and other reasons it seems best to read 19:11–21 and 20:7–10 as chronologically parallel.

What Is the Binding of Satan?

A third major factor in the interpretation of the millennium is the question of how to understand the binding of Satan. For many, the notion that Satan could be "bound" (Rev. 20:2) in the present age is impossible and unthinkable. One only has to glance at the daily headlines for proof of his current diabolical activities. And Peter states that the Devil even now prowls around seeking whom he may devour (1 Pet. 5:8–9). Yet a consideration of the monumental significance of Jesus's defeat of Satan through his cross and resurrection[63] must elicit the joyful affirmation that Satan has most certainly been bound by these events. Hebrews 2:14 says that Christ has "destroy[ed] the one who has the power of death, that is, the devil." If we can affirm that Christ has destroyed the Devil, how can we protest the idea that he has bound him?

The text of Revelation 20:1–3 in fact does not say that Satan's activities are completely arrested for the millennium. Rather, he is bound "that he might not deceive the nations any longer" (20:3). It is rightly observed that, despite the undeniable evidence of satanic deception in our world, Satan cannot, since the first coming of Christ, prevent the spread of the gospel to the nations. But verse 8 makes it clear that the point of the binding of Satan in this passage is to prevent

[62] J. Webb Mealy, *After the Thousand Years: Resurrection and Judgment in Revelation 20*, JSNTSup 70 (Sheffield: Sheffield Academic, 1992), 187, has to conclude that Gog and Magog join battle against Christ "in confrontations on two entirely separate occasions, in two entirely different contexts" separated by a thousand years.

[63] See Matt. 12:29; Luke 10:17–18; John 12:31; 16:11; Col. 2:15; Heb. 2:14–15; 2 Thess. 2:6–7; 1 John 3:8.

his deceiving the nations into assembling for a climactic attack on the saints. No matter the scale of Satan's crimes and delusions, every believer and every true church is living proof that the ancient Serpent has not been able to amass the forces of unbelief into a united front to exterminate the followers of the Lamb.

The same thing is taught in 12:6, 13–17, where Satan is cast down from heaven and, despite his deadly intentions, is prevented from destroying the woman. Again, it is said of the beast in 17:8 that he "was and is not and is to come." Evidently the "is not" means that when John wrote, the persecuting beast was being prevented from exercising its final campaign of terror.

Who Reigns with Christ, and What Is the First Resurrection?

It appears that those who sat on thrones (Rev. 20:4a) and those who had been beheaded for their testimony and had not worshiped the beast (20:4b) are the same group. In any case, the description of the latter as "souls" is significant and would naturally indicate that they are participating in the reign of Christ in a disembodied state before the bodily resurrection. The description is almost identical to that of 6:9–10, where the *souls* slain for the Word of God and for their testimony are now in heaven before the resurrection (recall Matt. 10:28, "Do not fear those who kill the body but cannot kill the soul").

Some interpreters understand the word ἔζησαν in Revelation 20:4 ("they lived" or "they came to life") as necessarily indicating that the martyrs "came to life" *bodily* at this point, so that the "first resurrection" mentioned in verse 5 is understood as a bodily resurrection. This, however, reads a lot into the text. The souls were obviously "alive" when John first saw them. Thus, the aorist ἔζησαν in verse 4 is better translated simply as "they lived," instead of ingressively as "they came to life." This is clear as well from 15:2, where, at a time indisputably before the return of Christ and the bodily resurrection of the saints, those who have conquered the beast and its image and the number of its name already stand in heaven. Also relevant is Luke 20:38, where Jesus says that the patriarchs are now alive, before the resurrection (see also 1 Pet. 4:6). On the other hand, understanding "the first resurrection" (Rev. 20:5) as the bodily resurrection of the just, a thousand years before the bodily resurrection of the unjust, would force a temporal division seen nowhere else in Scripture.[64] The first resurrection might be understood as "rising" to spiritual life in conversion (as in John 5:24–25; Eph. 2:6),[65] but the context suggests that the focus here is on that phase of the new life in Christ that believers enjoy when they "die in the Lord" (Rev. 14:13), when they conquer the beast (15:2) and rise to heaven.[66]

Meredith Kline pointed out that "first" and "second" in Revelation denote not just chronological order but qualitative difference, for sometimes "first" is contrasted not with "second" but with "new," as in 21:1 ("the first heaven and the first earth" and "a new heaven and a new earth").[67] The blessedness of the

[64] Compare the presentations in Dan. 12:2; John 5:28–29; Acts 24:15; Rev. 11:18.
[65] Norman Shepherd, "The Resurrections of Revelation 20," *WTJ* 37 (1974): 34–43.
[66] For extensive treatment, see Beale, *Book of Revelation*, 1002–12.
[67] Meredith G. Kline, "The First Resurrection," *WTJ* 37 (1975): 366–75.

"first resurrection" belongs to the present order of things, anticipatory to the consummate bodily resurrection. Yet it also belongs to the "already" of Christ's firstfruits resurrection and enables the saints' participation with him in heavenly life, serving him as priests and kings (20:6).

The Symbolism of the Thousand Years (Adam Christology)

The symbolism of a thousand years probably is more than simply that it is the perfect number ten, cubed. It probably has to do with an Adam christology that we also see in Paul (Rom. 5:12–21; 1 Cor. 15:21–28, 45–49) and Hebrews (2:5–18). In Jewish apocalyptic thought, a thousand years represented the ideal or intended lifespan and dominion of Adam.[68] Adam fell seventy years short of attaining that ideal due to his sin. This popular conception is taken over in John's vision to designate the reign of the last Adam. Now the Serpent is paid back. He is bound for the period of rule under the ideal Adam, who conquered the Devil through death and resurrection. (The same theology as found in Heb. 2:5–18, where the Devil is depicted as destroyed.)

Revelation 20 thus brings us back to the prelapsarian world of Genesis 1–3 and to a restored paradise.[69] When Jesus promised the thief on the cross entry that day into paradise (Luke 23:42–43), and when he promised paradise and the tree of life to the faithful conquerors of the Ephesian church (Rev. 2:7), he was promising continued fellowship with him after death, in his heavenly kingdom, which is paradise indeed.

[68] Going back at least to Jub. 4:30; 23:150; then in the first century AD, 2 Bar. 17:2, then Genesis Rabbah 19:8; Numbers Rabbah 5:4; 23:13; and in early Christianity, Irenaeus, *Haer.* 5.23.2, 28.3.

[69] Note the reference in Rev. 20:2 to "that ancient serpent" and the mention of his deception in 20:3, and compare Gen. 3:13; John 8:44; 2 Cor. 11:3; 1 Tim. 2:14.

Select Bibliography

Aune, David E. *Revelation.* 3 vols. WBC 52. Dallas: Word, 1997–1998.

Bauckham, Richard. *The Climax of Prophecy: Studies on the Book of Revelation.* Edinburgh: T&T Clark, 1993.

———. *The Theology of the Book of Revelation.* Cambridge: Cambridge University Press, 1993.

Beale, G. K. *The Book of Revelation: A Commentary on the Greek Text.* NIGTC. Grand Rapids, MI: Eerdmans, 1999.

———. *Revelation: A Shorter Commentary.* Grand Rapids, MI: Eerdmans, 2015.

Beasley-Murray, G. R. *Revelation.* NCB. Grand Rapids, MI: Eerdmans, 1974.

Caird, G. B. *A Commentary on the Revelation of St. John the Divine.* HNTC. New York: Harper & Row, 1966.

Charles, R. H. *A Critical and Exegetical Commentary on the Revelation of St. John.* 2 vols. ICC. Edinburgh: T&T Clark, 1920.

Chilton, David. *The Days of Vengeance: An Exposition of the Book of Revelation.* Fort Worth, TX: Dominion, 1987.

Collins, Adela Yarbro. *The Combat Myth in the Book of Revelation*. Missoula, MT: Scholars, 1976.
Fee, Gordon D. *Revelation*. New Covenant Commentary. Eugene, OR: Cascade, 2011.
Fiorenza, Elizabeth S. *The Book of Revelation: Justice and Judgment*. Philadelphia: Fortress, 1985.
Ford, J. Massyngberde. *Revelation*. AYB 38. New York: Doubleday, 1975.
Friesen, Steven J. *Imperial Cults and the Apocalypse of John: Reading Revelation in the Ruins*. Oxford: Oxford University Press, 2001.
Hendriksen, William. *More Than Conquerors: An Interpretation of the Book of Revelation*. Grand Rapids, MI: Baker, 1982.
Hill, Charles E. "The Lamb Slain: The Meaning of the Death of Christ in the Book of Revelation." In *The Glory of the Atonement: Biblical, Historical, and Practical Perspectives: Essays in Honor of Roger Nicole*, edited by Charles E. Hill and Frank A. James III, 190–208. Downers Grove, IL: InterVarsity Press, 2004.
———. Regnum Caelorum*: Patterns of Millennial Thought in Early Christianity*. Grand Rapids, MI: Eerdmans, 2001.
Hughes, Philip Edgcumbe. *The Book of Revelation: A Commentary*. Grand Rapids, MI: Eerdmans, 1990.
Johnson, Dennis E. *Triumph of the Lamb: A Commentary on Revelation*. Phillipsburg, NJ: P&R, 2001.
Kistemaker, Simon. *Revelation*. NTC. Grand Rapids, MI: Baker, 2002.
Kline, Meredith G. "The First Resurrection." *WTJ* 37 (1975): 366–75.
———. "The First Resurrection: A Reaffirmation." *WTJ* 39 (1976): 110–19.
Koester, Craig R. *Revelation: A New Translation with Introduction and Commentary*. AB 38A. New Haven, CT: Yale University Press, 2014.
Kovacs, J., and C. Rowland. *Revelation*. Blackwell Bible Commentaries. Oxford: Blackwell, 2004.
Kümmel, W. G. *Introduction to the New Testament*. London: SCM, 1965.
Ladd, George Eldon. *A Commentary on the Revelation of John*. Grand Rapids, MI: Eerdmans, 1972.
Mealy, J. Webb. *After the Thousand Years: Resurrection and Judgment in Revelation 20*. JSNTSup 70. Sheffield: Sheffield Academic, 1992.
Michaels, J. R. "The First Resurrection: A Response." *WTJ* 39 (1976): 100–109.
———. *Interpreting the Book of Revelation*. Grand Rapids, MI: Baker, 1992.
Morris, Leon. *Revelation*. 2nd ed. TNTC. Grand Rapids, MI: Eerdmans, 1990.
Osborne, Grant R. *Revelation*. BECNT. Grand Rapids, MI: Baker Academic, 2002.
Shepherd, Norman. "The Resurrections of Revelation 20." *WTJ* 37 (1974): 34–43.
Swete, Henry Barclay. *The Apocalypse of St John: The Greek Text with Introduction, Notes and Indices*. London: Macmillan, 1911.
Walvoord, John F. *The Revelation of Jesus Christ*. Chicago: Moody Press, 1966.
White, R. F. "Reexamining the Evidence for Recapitulation in Rev 20:1–10." *WTJ* 51 (1989): 319–44.
Wilcock, Michael. *I Saw Heaven Opened: The Message of Revelation*. BST. Downers Grove, IL: InterVarsity Press, 1975.
Wilson, J. Christian. "The Problem of the Domitianic Date of Revelation." *NTS* 39 (1993): 587–605.
Witherington, Ben, III. *Revelation*. Cambridge: Cambridge University Press, 2003.

Appendix A

The New Testament Canon

Michael J. Kruger

One of the most fundamental questions in any study of the New Testament is Why these twenty-seven books and no others? It is one thing to examine the individual books of the New Testament; it is quite another to ask how these individual books came to be viewed as a single collection and why that collection should be regarded as normative. While most Christians take the final collection of New Testament books for granted, critical scholars do not. Ever since Johann Semler offered one of the earliest critiques of the New Testament canon, *Treatise on the Free Investigation of the Canon* (1771–1775), modern scholars have been quick to point out the problems and challenges presented by the origins of the New Testament. What about the fact that early Christians disagreed over which books to include? What do we make of the abundance of apocryphal books and so-called lost Gospels? And are there books within the New Testament itself that are forged in the name of apostles?

While these questions are difficult and complicated, they require an answer. After all, if we cannot justify the boundaries of the canon, then on what basis could we discuss the *content* of the canon? If there is no such thing as a New Testament, then there certainly can be no New Testament theology. Thus, the purpose of this appendix is to provide a brief overview of how Christians have historically accounted for this twenty-seven-book canon.

The Self-Authenticating Model of Canon

So where do we turn for guidance about how to authenticate canonical books? Or put differently, what standard will we use to determine whether a book is divinely given or not? Many answers have been given to this question. Some have suggested that we should turn to the proclamations of the church (Roman Catholics); others have suggested that we turn to our own experience (existentialists); and others have suggested that we should look to the historical evidences (evidentialists).[1] While there are elements of truth in each of these positions, they ultimately ground the authority of the canon in something outside of it. But, as Herman Ridderbos has observed, "Problems arise whenever the Scriptures are no longer regarded as the exclusive principle of canonicity, when something else is substituted."[2]

It is for this reason that the Reformers, and even the church fathers before them,[3] grounded the authority of the canon in the only place it could be grounded, its own authority. They affirmed what might be called a *self-authenticating* canon.[4] This simply means that the canon, because it is God's Word, is the only place to turn for guidance about how the authority of that Word should be established. Because the canon is the highest possible authority, it must set the terms for its own validation. While this may seem circular to some, it is inevitable when one is dealing with *ultimate* authorities like the canon. For an ultimate authority to be ultimate, it has to be the standard for its own authentication.[5]

When we consider Scripture's own teaching about itself, we recognize three "attributes of canonicity"—characteristics that distinguish canonical books from all other books.[6] These attributes are

1. *Divine qualities*. Canonical books bear the "marks" of divinity.
2. *Apostolic origins*. Canonical books are the result of the redemptive-historical activity of the apostles.
3. *Corporate reception*. Canonical books are recognized by the church as a whole.

The remainder of this appendix is devoted to these three attributes.

Divine Qualities

If canonical books are the product of the Holy Spirit's activities, then we might expect that they would bear evidence of that activity. As Richard Muller has noted, "There must be some evidence or imprint of the divine work of producing Scripture in the Scriptures themselves."[7] Just as the natural world bears evidence of being from God (Ps. 19:1; Rom. 1:20), how much more would we expect special revelation to bear evidence of being from God? John Murray makes this precise argument: "If the heavens declare the glory of God and therefore bear witness to their divine creator,

[1] For more discussion of various canonical models, see Michael J. Kruger, *Canon Revisited: Establishing the Origins and Authority of the New Testament Books* (Wheaton, IL: Crossway, 2012), 27–87.
[2] Herman N. Ridderbos, *Redemptive History and the New Testament Scripture* (Phillipsburg, NJ: P&R, 1988), 7.
[3] E.g., Augustine, *Conf.* 6.5, 11.3. See discussion in F. H. Klooster, "Internal Testimony of the Holy Spirit," in *Evangelical Dictionary of Theology*, ed. Walter A. Elwell (Grand Rapids, MI: Baker, 1984), 564–65.
[4] John Calvin, *Institutes of the Christian Religion*, ed. John T. McNeill, trans. Ford Lewis Battles (Philadelphia: Westminster Press, 1960), 1.7.4–5; Francis Turretin, *Institutes of Elenctic Theology*, ed. James T. Dennison Jr., trans. George Musgrave Giger, 3 vols. (Phillipsburg, NJ: P&R, 1992–1997), 1:89; Herman Bavinck, *Reformed Dogmatics*, vol. 1, *Prolegomena*, ed. John Bolt, trans. John Vriend (Grand Rapids, MI: Baker Academic, 2003), 452.
[5] William Alston, "Knowledge of God," in *Faith, Reason, and Skepticism*, ed. Marcus Hester (Philadelphia: Temple University Press, 1992), 42.
[6] For more detail on these attributes, see discussion in Kruger, *Canon Revisited*, 88–122.
[7] Richard A. Muller, *Post-Reformation Reformed Dogmatics*, vol. 2, *Holy Scripture* (Grand Rapids, MI: Baker, 1993), 270.

the Scripture as God's handiwork must also bear the imprints of his authorship."[8] Calvin agrees, "Indeed, Scripture exhibits fully as clear evidence of its own truth as white and black things do of their color, or sweet and bitter things do of their taste."[9] The Westminster Confession of Faith acknowledges this same principle when it declares that Scripture "doth abundantly *evidence itself* to be the Word of God."[10] Even the early church fathers recognized the divine qualities of Scripture. Origen, for instance, argued, "If anyone ponders over the prophetic sayings . . . it is certain that in the very act of reading and diligently studying them his mind and feelings will be touched by a divine breath and he will recognize the words he is reading are not utterances of man but the language of God."[11]

But what, in particular, are these divine qualities that identify a book as being from God? First would be Scripture's *beauty and excellency*. Since the Scriptures are from God, then they bear the excellencies of God himself. The psalmist picks up on these qualities of Scripture when he says "The law of the LORD is perfect" (Ps. 19:7), "The commandment of the LORD is pure" (Ps. 19:8), and

> How sweet are your words to my taste,
> sweeter than honey to my mouth! (Ps. 119:103)

Second is the *power* or *efficacy* of Scripture. The divine origins of a canonical book are evident not just from what it says, but also from what it does. Scripture brings wisdom (Ps. 119:98), enlightenment (Ps. 119:105), joy (Ps. 119:111), understanding (Ps. 119:144), peace (Ps. 119:50), the conviction of sin (Heb. 4:12–13), and more. Third is the *unity and harmony* of Scripture. There is an amazing consistency among all the canonical books, both doctrinally and historically. This sort of unity, spanning thousands of years and over forty authors, is a mark of divine origins.

Of course, this raises a natural question. If these divine qualities are genuinely present within the canonical books, then why don't more people recognize them? If these qualities are there, then why do so many people reject the Bible? The answer is that the noetic effects of sin have darkened people's minds and understanding so that they cannot recognize the divine character of Scripture (Rom. 3:10–11; 1 Cor. 2:14). The Reformers argued that a person must have the *internal testimony of the Holy Spirit* to open his or her eyes.[12] This testimony is not some private revelation whereby God reveals which books are canonical, but rather the operation of the Spirit by which a person is enabled to see the qualities of Scripture that are objectively there. Jesus made a similar point when he declared, "My sheep [i.e., those with the

---

[8] John Murray, "The Attestation of Scripture," in *The Infallible Word* (Philadelphia: P&R, 1946), 46. Similar arguments can be found in Turretin, *Institutes of Elenctic Theology*, 1:63; John Owen, "The Divine Original: Authority, Self-Evidencing Light, and Power of the Scriptures," in *The Works of John Owen*, ed. William H. Goold, vol. 16 (Edinburgh: Banner of Truth, 1988), 297–421.

[9] *Institutes* 1.7.2.

[10] WCF 1.5, emphasis added.

[11] *Princ.* 4.1.6. English translation from Origen, *On First Principles*, trans. G. W. Butterworth (Gloucester, MA: P. Smith, 1973).

[12] *Institutes* 1.7.4–5; 3.1.1–3; 3.2.15, 33–36. For more, see Bernard Ramm, *The Witness of the Spirit* (Grand Rapids, MI: Eerdmans, 1959); Alvin Plantinga, *Warranted Christian Belief* (New York: Oxford University Press, 2000), 241–89; R. C. Sproul, "The Internal Testimony of the Holy Spirit," in *Inerrancy*, ed. Norman Geisler (Grand Rapids, MI: Zondervan, 1980), 337–54; and John M. Frame, "The Spirit and the Scriptures," in *Hermeneutics, Authority, and Canon*, ed. D. A. Carson and John D. Woodbridge (Grand Rapids, MI: Zondervan, 1986), 217–35.

Spirit] hear my voice, and I know them, and they follow me" (John 10:27). Likewise, he declared of his sheep that "a stranger they will not follow, but they will flee from him, for they do not know the voice of strangers" (John 10:5). Thus, God's Word is rightly recognized by those who have the Holy Spirit in them.

While some might regard the appeal to divine qualities as merely a form of subjectivism, the Reformers were careful to demonstrate that this is not the case. A subjective/existential model of canon grounds the authority of the canon in an experience of the Spirit, whereas the Reformers grounded the authority of the canon on the *objective qualities* it contains. The Spirit is the means by which one recognizes the canon's authority, but not the ground for the canon's authority. Thus, for the Reformers, the objective qualities of Scripture and the testimony of the Holy Spirit function together; they are not to be unduly separated. As Herman Bavinck observes, "Scripture and the testimony of the Holy Spirit relate to each other as objective truth and subjective assurance . . . as the light and the human eye."[13]

Apostolic Origins

Canonical books are marked not only by their internal qualities, but also by their unique historical origins, namely, they are the product of the redemptive-historical activity of the apostles. In short, canonical books are apostolic books.

While Christ himself fully and completely accomplished redemption, he appointed apostles to be those authoritative agents by which the message of redemption would be transmitted, preserved, and guarded.[14] Thus, Christ gave the apostles special authority to speak on his behalf: "The one who hears you hears me, and the one who rejects you rejects me" (Luke 10:16). Similarly, in John 20:21, Jesus declares to the apostles, "As the Father has sent me, even so I am sending you." Peter also tells us that the apostles were "chosen by God as witnesses . . . to preach to the people and to testify that [Christ] is the one appointed by God to be judge of the living and the dead" (Acts 10:41–42). The apostles were God's eschatological "ministers of a new covenant" (2 Cor. 3:6).

Of course, the apostles originally delivered this message of redemption orally, through teaching, preaching, and verbal instruction.[15] But it was not long before the apostolic message was written down in books. Since these books would have borne the same authority as the apostles' oral teaching (2 Thess. 2:15), and thus the author-

[13] Bavinck, *Reformed Dogmatics*, 1:598.

[14] Ridderbos, *Redemptive History and the New Testament Scripture*, 12–14; Geerhardus Vos, *Biblical Theology* (Grand Rapids, MI: Eerdmans, 1954), 303.

[15] For more on oral tradition, see S. Byrskog, *Story as History—History as Story: The Gospel Tradition in the Context of Ancient Oral History* (Leiden: Brill, 2002); Richard Bauckham, *Jesus and the Eyewitnesses: The Gospels as Eyewitness Testimony* (Grand Rapids, MI: Eerdmans, 2006); James D. G. Dunn, *Jesus Remembered* (Grand Rapids, MI: Eerdmans, 2003); Henry Wansbrough, ed., *Jesus and the Oral Gospel Tradition* (Edinburgh: T&T Clark, 2004); Werner H. Kelber, *The Oral and Written Gospel: The Hermeneutics of Speaking and Writing in the Synoptic Tradition, Mark, Paul, and Q* (Philadelphia: Fortress, 1983); Birger Gerhardsson, *Memory and Manuscript with Tradition and Transmission in Early Christianity*, rev. ed. (Grand Rapids, MI: Eerdmans, 1998); K. E. Bailey, "Informal Controlled Oral Tradition and the Synoptic Gospels," *Them* 20 (1995): 4–11; Jan M. Vansina, *Oral Tradition as History* (Madison, WI: University of Wisconsin Press, 1985); Richard A. Horsley, Jonathan A. Draper, and John Miles Foley, eds., *Performing the Gospel: Orality, Memory, and Mark* (Minneapolis: Fortress, 2006); and, most recently, Werner H. Kelber and Samuel Byrskog, eds., *Jesus in Memory: Traditions in Oral and Scribal Perspectives* (Waco, TX: Baylor University Press, 2009).

ity of Christ himself, it is not difficult to see why they would have been regarded by early Christians as foundational documents for the life and ministry of the church. In this sense, the church would not have needed to wait until the fourth century to have a collection of authoritative books; they would have had such a collection even in the first century, owing to the activities of the apostles.

In order for a book to be regarded as "apostolic" by early Christians, there would have been some historical reason to think that it contained reliable, authentic apostolic teaching. Obviously, if a book was written directly by an apostle (as most New Testament books were), then it would have been quite natural to regard its contents as apostolic. But, a document could contain apostolic material in other ways. If it was written by someone who received material directly from the apostles themselves, and was thus written in a time when the apostles were presiding over the transmission of their tradition, then a document could also have been regarded as apostolic. This appears to be the case with books like Luke, which claims to transmit apostolic teaching (Luke 1:2), and Hebrews, where the author makes a very similar claim (Heb. 2:3). Ridderbos makes this very point when he says that the apostolicity of a book is determined by "whether its content embodies the foundational apostolic tradition, *not* whether it was written by the hand of the apostle."[16]

The earliest church recognized the distinctive, foundational, and one-time role of the apostles as the deliverers of the message of redemption.[17] Indeed, the connection between canonical books and the apostles was so well established that books were often rejected precisely because they had no connection to the redemptive-historical epoch of the apostles. The second-century Muratorian Fragment, for example, rejects the Shepherd of Hermas because it was written "very recently, in our own times."[18] In other words, because of its late date the Shepherd had no potential of being an apostolic book and therefore should not be regarded as canonical.

Of course, the apostolic nature of the New Testament has been rejected by much of modern scholarship. Some critical scholars are convinced that many of the New Testament writings are forgeries—such as the Pastoral Epistles, Colossians, Ephesians, 2 Peter, and Jude—and were not written by apostles at all.[19] However, this scholarly "consensus" does not necessitate that the authenticity of the New Testament be abandoned. For one thing, many evangelical scholars have offered able defenses of these books, though their arguments cannot be repeated here.[20] When their arguments are considered, the supposed "consensus" around this issue evaporates. Second, the higher critical methodologies used to demonstrate that these books are forgeries are problematic in their own right. Not only are they built upon

[16] Ridderbos, *Redemptive History and the New Testament Scripture*, 32.

[17] Ignatius, *Rom.* 4.4; 1 Clem. 47.1–3; 42.1–2; 5.2; Tertullian, *Marc.* 4.2.

[18] Line 74.

[19] For general discussions of the critical positions, see Bart D. Ehrman, *Forgery and Counterforgery: The Use of Literary Deceit in Early Christian Polemics* (New York: Oxford University Press, 2012).

[20] Defenses of traditional authorship can be found in the major New Testament introductions; e.g., D. A. Carson and Douglas J. Moo, *An Introduction to the New Testament*, 2nd ed. (Grand Rapids, MI: Zondervan, 2005); Donald Guthrie, *New Testament Introduction* (Downers Grove, IL: InterVarsity Press, 1990); and Andreas J. Köstenberger, L. Scott Kellum, and Charles L. Quarles, *The Cradle, the Cross, and the Crown: An Introduction to the New Testament* (Nashville: B&H Academic, 2009).

non-Christian, Enlightenment assumptions,[21] but they have been rightly criticized for being highly subjective and inconclusive.[22] Third, there are other means of verifying the apostolic authorship of these books, namely, the existence of divine qualities in them (as discussed above) and the corporate reception of these books by the church (as will be discussed below).

Corporate Reception

Now that we have examined two attributes of canonicity, divine qualities and apostolic origins, we turn our attention to the third attribute, the corporate reception of these books by the church. If canonical books really do contain divine qualities and derive from the apostles, and the church really does possess the Holy Spirit, then we would expect those books to be rightly recognized by the corporate church. This does not mean we should expect absolute unity in the church regarding the canon—there would still be groups or factions that disagree—but it does mean that the church, as a whole and throughout the ages, would form a general consensus around these books.

The corporate reception of canonical books flows naturally from the *internal testimony of the Holy Spirit*, discussed above. If that testimony is efficacious in convincing individuals that these books are from God, how much more might we expect it to be efficacious in convincing the church as a whole? After all, the Scriptures are not so much the possession of individual Christians, but the possession of God's corporate, covenant people (Rom. 3:2).[23]

If so, then we have reason to think that the church's corporate reception of a book is a reliable indicator of its canonicity. C. Stephen Evans appeals to this same biblical logic:

> It seems highly plausible, then, that if God is going to see that an authorized revelation is given, he will also see that this revelation is recognized. . . . On this view, then, the fact that the church recognized the books of the New Testament as canonical is itself a powerful reason to believe that these books are indeed the revelation God intended humans to have.[24]

Roger Nicole agrees and argues that we can know which books are in the canon by appealing to "the witness of the Holy Spirit given corporately to God's people and made manifest by a nearly unanimous acceptance of the New Testament canon in the Christian churches."[25]

It is here that we recognize the proper relationship between the church and the canon. The church can inform our understanding of which books are canonical not

[21] Plantinga, *Warranted Christian Belief*, 374–421; C. Stephen Evans, *The Historical Christ and the Jesus of Faith: The Incarnational Narrative as History* (New York: Oxford University Press, 1996), 170–202; William P. Alston, "Historical Criticism of the Synoptic Gospels," in *"Behind" the Text: History and Biblical Interpretation*, ed. Craig Bartholomew (Grand Rapids, MI: Zondervan, 2003), 151–80.

[22] C. Stephen Evans, "Canonicity, Apostolicity, and Biblical Authority: Some Kierkegaardian Reflections," in *Canon and Biblical Interpretation*, ed. Craig Bartholomew et al. (Carlisle: Paternoster, 2006), 147–66.

[23] For a fuller argument on this point, see Kruger, *Canon Revisited*, 103–8.

[24] Evans, "Canonicity, Apostolicity, and Biblical Authority," 155. J. W. Wenham, *Christ and the Bible* (Downers Grove, IL: InterVarsity Press, 1972), 162–63, makes a very similar argument.

[25] Roger Nicole, "The Canon of the New Testament," *JETS* 40 (1997): 199–206.

because the church stands as an authority over the canon, but because the church, which is filled with the Holy Spirit, naturally and inevitably responds to the divine qualities of the canon. Thus, the church's reception of the canonical books does not demonstrate that the church creates the canon, but demonstrates that the canon is powerful enough to elicit a corporate response from the church. As an analogy, the church functions more like a thermometer than a thermostat. While both deal with the temperature in the room, the latter determines it and the former responds to it. Similarly, the church doesn't determine the canon, but responds to the canon.

While the church eventually reached a broad consensus on all twenty-seven books, critics are quick to point out that this did not happen instantaneously. Not only was there no complete consensus until about the fourth century, but up to that point there was substantial dissent and disagreement over these books. Indeed, it is this complex and erratic canonical history that has led some to reject this third attribute of canonicity. We should put no stock in the church's corporate reception of these books, it is argued, because the path to consensus was too tumultuous. If these books are really from God, then why did it take the church so long to recognize them? If the Spirit is really at work in the church, why were there disagreements? Such concerns have led critics to argue that the church's consensus means nothing; it was probably just the result of some theological faction imposing its preferred set of books onto the rest of the church.

In response to this particular objection, we shall argue that the critics overplay the amount of disagreement and dissent regarding the canon. While it is true that the canonical journey for particular books was not always predictable or smooth, a substantial amount of historical evidence suggests that there was a widespread consensus around a canonical "core" of books from a very early time. This core would include the four Gospels, thirteen epistles of Paul, Acts, 1 Peter, 1–2 John, Hebrews, and Revelation. If so, then there is no reason to doubt that the church's reception of these books is a meaningful indicator of their canonicity.

In the remainder of this appendix, we shall briefly survey the reception of these core books up to the end of the second century (ca. AD 200).

The New Testament

Evidence for the canonicity of books begins as early as the New Testament writings themselves. In 2 Peter 3:16, Peter regards Paul's letters as bearing the same authority as "the other Scriptures" of the Old Testament. It is noteworthy that Peter mentions plural letters, suggesting that his audience would have been familiar with a collection of these letters already in circulation. The idea that Paul's letters might be regarded as Scripture is not mentioned by Peter as if it were an innovation or an unprecedented idea; on the contrary, he mentions it offhandedly, with no indication whatsoever that his audience might be unaware of (or opposed to) such a development. And if Paul's letters are regarded as Scripture, the implications for *other* apostolic letters are inescapable: they too would be regarded as Scripture.

In a similar fashion, 1 Timothy 5:18 appears to cite the Gospel of Luke as Scripture: "For the Scripture [ἡ γραφή] says, 'You shall not muzzle an ox when it treads out the grain,' and, 'The laborer deserves his wages.'" While the first citation comes from Deuteronomy 25:4, the second is identical to the words of Jesus in Luke 10:7. Although one might suggest that Paul is citing teachings of Jesus from oral tradition, the fact that he refers to this text as "Scripture" suggests that we are dealing with a *written* source.[26] While it is always possible that Paul is referring to an unknown written source (like Q[27]), it seems more reasonable to explain the citation on the basis of known texts rather than unknown. Which is more likely: that a well-known apostle like Paul cites a Gospel as Scripture that is later forgotten, or that he cites a Gospel as Scripture that later is received by the church and is attributed to his traveling companion Luke? Historical considerations would push us toward the latter.

It should also be observed that the New Testament writings often present themselves as authoritative books. Paul regularly asks that his letters be read publicly to the church (2 Cor. 10:9; Col. 4:16; 1 Thess. 5:27), and the author of Revelation assumes the same will be done with his book (Rev. 1:3). Such a practice closely parallels how the Old Testament was read publicly in the synagogue (Luke 4:17–20; Acts 13:15; 15:21; 1 Tim. 4:13), suggesting that these New Testament books would also have been viewed as Scripture. This public reading of New Testament books as Scripture is confirmed a short time later by Justin Martyr, who tells us that the Gospels were read in worship right alongside the Old Testament writings.[28]

The Apostolic Fathers

As we move into the early second century, we see that a number of Patristic writers, known as the Apostolic Fathers, appear to have received New Testament books as Scripture.[29] For the sake of brevity, we will only mention a few of the texts here.

The epistle known as 1 Clement (ca. AD 95) affirms the authority of Paul's writings: "Take up the epistle of that blessed apostle, Paul. . . . To be sure, he sent you a letter in the Spirit [πνευματικῶς] concerning himself and Cephas and Apollos."[30] Here, the author not only refers his audience to the book of 1 Corinthians, but fully affirms that Paul wrote the letter "in the Spirit," a likely nod to its inspired status.[31] Ignatius, bishop of Antioch (ca. AD 110), also spoke of Paul's letters: ". . . Paul, who

[26] I. Howard Marshall, *A Critical and Exegetical Commentary on the Pastoral Epistles*, ICC (Edinburgh: T&T Clark, 1999), 616.
[27] Anthony T. Hanson, *The Pastoral Epistles*, NCBC (Grand Rapids, MI: Eerdmans, 1982), 102.
[28] *1 Apol.* 47.3.
[29] For more on this subject, see Andrew Gregory and Christopher Tuckett, eds., *The Reception of the New Testament in the Apostolic Fathers* (Oxford: Oxford University Press, 2005); Gregory and Tuckett, eds., *Trajectories through the New Testament and the Apostolic Fathers* (Oxford: Oxford University Press, 2005); D. A. Hagner, "The Sayings of Jesus in the Apostolic Fathers and Justin Martyr," in *Gospel Perspectives: The Jesus Tradition Outside the Gospels*, ed. D. Wenham (Sheffield: JSOT, 1985), 233–68; and A Committee of the Oxford Society of Historical Theology, ed., *The New Testament in the Apostolic Fathers* (Oxford: Clarendon, 1905).
[30] 1 Clem. 47.1–3. English translation from B. D. Ehrman, *The Apostolic Fathers*, 2 vols. (Cambridge, MA: Harvard University Press, 2003).
[31] Other translations offer a similar appraisal of this phrase: *The Apostolic Fathers*, trans. Kirsopp Lake, 2 vols. (London: William Hienemann, 1919), says that Paul wrote with "true inspiration"; and Alexander Roberts and James Donaldson, eds., *The Ante-Nicene Fathers* (Peabody, MA: Hendrickson, 1885), say that Paul wrote "under the inspiration of the Spirit."

was sanctified, who gained a good report, who was right blessed, in whose footsteps may I be found when I shall attain to God, who in *every epistle* makes mention of you in Christ Jesus."[32] Here Ignatius appears to know of a collection of Paul's letters, though it is unclear how many. Given Ignatius's very high regard for the authority of the apostles, there is little doubt that he viewed these letters as bearing the highest possible authority: the authority of Christ himself.[33]

The Epistle of Barnabas, written ca. AD 130, declares, "As it is written, 'Many are called, but few are chosen.'"[34] The fact that this citation is nearly a word-for-word match with Matthew 22:14 has led most scholars to regard it as a citation of Matthew's Gospel.[35] If so, it is noteworthy that Barnabas introduces this citation with the formulaic "it is written"—an indication that he regarded it as Scripture. Papias, bishop of Hierapolis (writing ca. AD 125), indicates that both Mark and Matthew are well known: "The Elder used to say: Mark became Peter's interpreter and wrote accurately all that he remembered. . . . Matthew collected the oracles [τὰ λόγια] in the Hebrew language [Ἑβραΐδι διαλέκτω], and each interpreted them as best he could."[36] The fact that Papias associates both these Gospels with apostles suggests that he viewed them as authoritative sources for the life of Jesus.

Other Second-Century Sources

While the Apostolic Fathers offer only a shadowy glimpse into the canon, things get much clearer as we move further into the second century. We already mentioned above that Justin Martyr appears to receive all four Gospels and places them on par with the Old Testament Scriptures.[37] Irenaeus, well-known bishop of Lyons (writing ca. 170–180), provides extensive information about the New Testament canon. He clearly regards the following books as Scripture: the four Gospels, Acts, the entire Pauline collection (minus Philemon), Hebrews, James, 1 Peter, 1–2 John, and Revelation.[38] Irenaeus is so certain about the Gospels that he suggests their fourfold nature is built into the very structure of creation.[39] Our earliest canonical list, the Muratorian Fragment, dates from about the same time period as Irenaeus.[40] That fragment affirms the canonicity of the four Gospels, Acts, the thirteen epistles of Paul, 1–2 John (and possibly 3 John), Jude, and Revelation. Clement of Alexandria, writing at the end of the second century, received the four Gospels, Acts, all thirteen epistles of Paul, the book of Hebrews, 1 Peter, 1–2 John, Jude, and Revelation.[41]

[32] Ignatius, *Eph*. 12.2, emphasis added.

[33] C. E. Hill, "Ignatius and the Apostolate," in *Studia Patristica*, vol. 36 (Leuven: Peeters, 2001), 226–48.

[34] Barn. 4.14.

[35] E.g., W.-D. Köhler, *Die Rezeption des Matthäusevangeliums in der Zeit vor Irenäus*, WUNT 24 (Tübingen: Mohr, 1987), 113; James Carleton Paget, "The *Epistle of Barnabas* and the Writings That Later Formed the New Testament," in Gregory and Tuckett, *Reception of the New Testament in the Apostolic Fathers*, 229–49.

[36] Eusebius, *Hist. eccl*. 3.39.15–16.

[37] See more detailed discussion in Kruger, *Canon Revisited*, 225–28.

[38] See discussion in Graham Stanton, *Jesus and Gospel* (Cambridge: Cambridge University Press, 2004), 105–6; and Bruce M. Metzger, *The Canon of the New Testament: Its Origin, Development, and Significance* (Oxford: Clarendon, 1987), 154–55.

[39] *Haer*. 3.11.8.

[40] For a defense of the second-century date, see J. Verheyden, "The Canon Muratori: A Matter of Dispute," in *The Biblical Canons*, ed. J.-M. Auwers and H. J. de Jonge (Leuven: Leuven University Press, 2003), 487–556.

[41] Metzger, *Canon of the New Testament*, 135.

By the time we reach the end of the second century, the evidence coalesces into a clear picture. Not only are New Testament books regarded as canonical at a very early time (even the first century), but there is a widespread commitment to a "core" New Testament by AD 200. This means that most of the ongoing disputes and disagreements over books pertain mainly to only a handful of smaller books like 2 Peter, James, and 3 John. Thus, the critical claim that the canon is in complete disarray until the fourth century simply proves to be untrue.

Conclusion

This appendix has been devoted to the question of whether we can know we have the right books in the New Testament canon. When we consider the Scripture's own internal explanation for its origins, we discover that canonical books bear three attributes: divine qualities, apostolic origins, and corporate reception.

Some have objected to the concept of divine qualities by equating it with subjectivism. But we saw that this is a misunderstanding of the Reformers' argument. The divine qualities are *objective* attributes of Scripture—they are really there. Sure, one has to have the Spirit to see them rightly, but that is not the same as subjectivism. Others have objected to the apostolic origins of the New Testament by claiming that many of the books were forgeries, written by later authors pretending to be apostles. However, we observed that numerous scholars have offered able historical defenses of the authorship of these books, pointing out that much of the evidence for these forgeries tends to be inconclusive at best. And still others have objected to the corporate reception of these books, contending that the eventual consensus of the church is meaningless, given its rocky beginnings. While acknowledging that the canonical process was not always pristine, we examined the historical development of the canon and showed that it was not nearly as chaotic as the critics claim. Not only were books regarded as Scripture very early, but there was a "core" New Testament canon in place by the end of the second century.

In the end, these three attributes of canonicity—divine qualities, apostolic origins, and corporate reception—provide a threefold confirmation that the twenty-seven books we possess in our New Testaments are precisely the ones God intended us to have.

Select Bibliography

Aland, K. *The Problem of the New Testament Canon*. London: Mowbray, 1962.

Allert, Craig D. *A High View of Scripture? The Authority of the Bible and the Formation of the New Testament Canon*. Grand Rapids, MI: Baker Academic, 2007.

Alston, William. "Knowledge of God." In *Faith, Reason, and Skepticism*, edited by Marcus Hester, 6–49. Philadelphia: Temple University Press, 1992.

Barton, J. *The Spirit and the Letter: Studies in the Biblical Canon*. London: SPCK, 1997.

Bruce, F. F. *The Canon of Scripture*. Downers Grove, IL: InterVarsity Press, 1988.
Childs, B. S. *The New Testament as Canon: An Introduction*. London: SCM, 1984.
Ehrman, Bart D. *Forgery and Counterforgery: The Use of Literary Deceit in Early Christian Polemics*. New York: Oxford University Press, 2012.
———. *Lost Christianities: The Battles for Scripture and the Faiths We Never Knew*. New York: Oxford University Press, 2002.
———. *Lost Scriptures: Books That Did Not Make It into the New Testament*. New York: Oxford University Press, 2003.
Evans, C. Stephen. "Canonicity, Apostolicity, and Biblical Authority: Some Kierkegaardian Reflections." In *Canon and Biblical Interpretation*, edited by Craig Bartholomew, et al., 147–66. Carlisle: Paternoster, 2006.
———. *The Historical Christ and the Jesus of Faith: The Incarnational Narrative as History*. New York: Oxford University Press, 1996.
Frame, John M. *The Doctrine of the Word of God*. Phillipsburg, NJ: P&R, 2010.
———. "The Spirit and the Scriptures." In *Hermeneutics, Authority, and Canon*, edited by D. A. Carson and John D. Woodbridge, 217–35. Grand Rapids, MI: Zondervan, 1986.
Gamble, H. Y. *Books and Readers in the Early Church*. New Haven, CT: Yale University Press, 1995.
———. "The Canon of the New Testament." In *The New Testament and Its Modern Interpreters*, edited by Eldon J. Epp and George W. MacRae, 201–43. Philadelphia: Fortress, 1989.
Harnack, Adolf von. *Origin of the New Testament and the Most Important Consequences of a New Creation*. London: Williams & Northgate, 1925.
Hill, Charles E. *The Johannine Corpus in the Early Church*. Oxford: Oxford University Press, 2004.
———. *Who Chose the Gospels? Probing the Great Gospel Conspiracy*. Oxford: Oxford University Press, 2010.
Köstenberger, Andreas J., and Michael J. Kruger. *The Heresy of Orthodoxy: How Modern Culture's Fascination with Diversity Has Reshaped Our Understanding of Early Christianity*. Wheaton, IL: Crossway, 2010.
Kruger, Michael J. *Canon Revisited: Establishing the Origins and Authority of the New Testament Books*. Wheaton, IL: Crossway, 2012.
———. *The Question of Canon: Challenging the Status Quo in the New Testament Debate*. Downers Grove, IL: IVP Academic, 2013.
McDonald, Lee Martin. *The Biblical Canon: Its Origin, Transmission, and Authority*. Peabody, MA: Hendrickson, 2007.
McDonald, Lee M., and James A. Sanders, eds. *The Canon Debate*. Peabody, MA: Hendrickson, 2002.
Metzger, Bruce M. *The Canon of the New Testament: Its Origin, Development, and Significance*. Oxford: Clarendon, 1987.
Murray, John. "The Attestation of Scripture." In *The Infallible Word: A Symposium by Members of the Faculty of Westminster Theological Seminary*, edited by N. B. Stonehouse and Paul Woolley, 1–54. Philadelphia: Presbyterian and Reformed, 1946.
Owen, John. "The Divine Original: Authority, Self-Evidencing Light, and Power of the Scriptures." In *The Works of John Owen*. Vol. 16, *The Church and the Bible*, 297–421. Edinburgh: Banner of Truth, 1988.

Plantinga, Alvin. *Warranted Christian Belief*. New York: Oxford University Press, 2000.

Ridderbos, Herman N. *Redemptive History and the New Testament Scripture*. Phillipsburg, NJ: P&R, 1988.

Sproul, R. C. "The Internal Testimony of the Holy Spirit." In *Inerrancy*, edited by Norman L. Geisler, 337–54. Grand Rapids, MI: Zondervan, 1980.

Appendix B

The New Testament Text

An Introduction to New Testament Textual Criticism

Charles E. Hill

Textual criticism attempts to identify all changes made in the textual tradition and, as far as is possible, to restore the text to its original or earliest attainable form. This appendix will offer (1) a short essay on the character and history of the New Testament text, (2) a concise refresher on the practice of textual criticism, (3) a list of textual groupings of New Testament manuscripts, and (4) an indication of some of the main tools now available for the study of the text of the New Testament.

The Character and History of the New Testament Text

Character

Variation between hand-copied manuscripts was a simple fact of life for readers in antiquity. Readers of all kinds of books often sought the opportunity to compare their copies with other good copies and make corrections where they judged necessary.[1] The only way to ensure that a book would have no "textual evolution" at all, and therefore no need for textual criticism, was to keep that book from ever being copied, or even read (because readers marked up their texts too).

Christians, generally speaking, wanted the copying of their books to proliferate, so the introduction of scribal changes to the text was to some extent inevitable. The levels of actual discrepancy could vary considerably, depending upon many factors,

[1] See G. E. Houston, "Papyrological Evidence for Book Collections and Libraries in the Roman Empire," in *Ancient Literacies: The Culture of Reading in Greece and Rome*, ed. W. A. Johnson and H. N. Parker (Oxford: Oxford University Press, 2009), 233–67, at 252–54.

including the textual tradition behind the manuscript being copied, the skill and attentiveness of the scribe making the copy, the external circumstances under which the scribe operated, and the intentions of the scribe or the commissioner of the copy. Evidence from literary sources shows that Christian leaders were concerned to ensure the faithful reproduction of their books.[2] And it is now clear that there is sometimes a qualitative difference between copies made in controlled settings for public use by churches and copies made by individuals for private use.[3]

By the middle of the third century, Origen could write,

> The differences among the manuscripts [of the Gospels] have become great, either through the negligence of some copyists or through the perverse audacity of others; they either neglect to check over what they have transcribed, or, in the process of checking, they lengthen or shorten, as they please.[4]

Today textual scholars estimate that there may be three hundred thousand to four hundred thousand variants scattered throughout our over fifty-five hundred Greek New Testament manuscripts.[5] But by far most of these either are meaningless scribal errors—variant spellings, switched word order, and the like that make absolutely no difference to the interpretation of the text—or are caused by inadvertent skipping of letters, words, or lines and thus are easily spotted and corrected. More meaningful textual variations, such as the pericope of the woman taken in adultery in John 7:53–8:11 or the longer ending of Mark, are much less common, though they are the ones that garner the most attention. Fortunately, a very large store of manuscripts enables us to see clearly where these more significant deviations occur and then study and correct them. Often one scribe's error early in the textual transmission became the occasion for later scribes within that scribal tradition to seek to correct the error in different ways, resulting in a profusion of new variants.

The claims of sensationalists notwithstanding, however, textual critics have never believed that a text very close to the original was out of reach. Even Origen's comment above, at first so alarming, assumes that he is able to tell which manuscripts preserve the original reading at a given point and which ones have suffered scribal corruptions at that point. Origen is consternated by the work of certain scribes, but he is not in despair about locating the original text. When early scholars like Origen met variants in the text, they either rejected the wrong reading and justified the right one or, if they were undecided on the original reading, were content to find meaning in a plurality of viable options.

[2] See Michael J. Kruger, "Early Christian Attitudes toward the Reproduction of Texts," in *The Early Text of the New Testament*, ed. Charles E. Hill and Michael J. Kruger (Oxford: Oxford University Press, 2012), 63–80.

[3] Scott D. Charlesworth, "Public and Private: Second- and Third-Century Gospel Manuscripts," in *Jewish and Christian Scripture as Artifact and Canon*, ed. Craig A. Evans and H. Daniel Zacharias (London: T&T Clark, 2009), 148–75; Charlesworth, "Indicators of 'Catholicity' in Early Gospel Manuscripts," in Hill and Kruger, *The Early Text of the New Testament*, 37–48; Larry Hurtado, *The Earliest Christian Artifacts: Manuscripts and Christian Origins* (Grand Rapids, MI: Eerdmans, 2006), 155–89.

[4] Origen, *Commentary on Matthew* xv.14, GCS *Origenes* x.387.28–388.7, ed. Erich Klostermann, cited by Bruce M. Metzger and Bart D. Ehrman, *The Text of the New Testament: Its Transmission, Corruption, and Restoration*, 4th ed. (Oxford: Oxford University Press, 2005), 200.

[5] Bart D. Ehrman and Daniel B. Wallace, "The Textual Reliability of the New Testament: A Dialogue," in *The Reliability of the New Testament: Bart D. Ehrman and Daniel B. Wallace in Dialogue*, ed. Robert B. Stewart (Minneapolis: Fortress, 2011), 13–60, at 21, 28.

The variations in the transcription of books can be classed as unintentional or intentional (Origen's "negligence" and "perverse audacity"). Though we can make this clear distinction conceptually, it is not always obvious which cause best explains a given deviation. And, to temper Origen's statement a bit, we should not assume that even all *intentional* changes on the part of a scribe were done from perverse motives (see below).

Factors Tending against the Preservation of the Text

As was mentioned, the most significant factor for the multiplication of errors is simply the number of times (generations) a text was copied, without correction from earlier or better parts of the tradition (see below).

"Negligence": unintentional changes. Even the best scribes were prone to mistakes of various kinds. Similarities between letter forms (for instance the letters Σ [written like a C], O, Θ, or M, ΛΛ, A) or sounds (readers typically read aloud and probably even copyists did so when copying) resulted in accidental confusion. Fatigue or inattentiveness could cause scribes to misspell, omit, or invert the order of letters or words. In the simple act of looking back and forth from exemplar to copy (*parablepsis*), the scribe's eyes might inadvertently skip backward or forward to the same or a similar set of letters, thus producing either a repetition (*dittography*) or an omission (*haplography*) of material.

"Audacity": intentional changes. It may seem counterintuitive that scribes who believed the text was sacred or inspired[6] would venture to change the text intentionally. But any scribe who held the text in such high regard would think he was copying a "perfect" text. If he encountered something that did not seem to meet that standard, he may well have concluded that a previous scribe had created the dissonance and that the text needed to be "restored." In other cases, scribes used to "professional" standards of textual reproduction may have made minor changes in the attempt to make the text smoother and more readable.[7]

Some changes were apparently made because of theological or pastoral concerns. In Luke 2:41–43, the references to Jesus's "parents" are replaced in some manuscripts by "Joseph and Mary," presumably in order to avoid the conclusion that Jesus was their child by natural birth. Some critics[8] have capitalized on this phenomenon of theologically motivated changes, but several points should be remembered: (1) Many of the examples cited could also be explained as unintentional. (2) It cannot be assumed

[6] Some scholars assert that the majority of errors entered the New Testament textual tradition before the books of the New Testament were considered Scripture or sacred. But as Ferguson says, "There is no time in Christian history after the writing of the four gospels when one can find evidence of their not being accepted as scripture" (Everett Ferguson, "Factors Leading to the Selection and Closure of the New Testament Canon: A Survey of Some Recent Studies," in *The Canon Debate*, ed. Lee Martin McDonald and James A. Sanders [Peabody, MA: Hendrickson, 2002], 295–320, at 303).

[7] See P. Rodgers, "The Text of the New Testament and Its Witnesses before 200 A.D.: Observations on P90 (P. Oxy. 3523)," in *The New Testament Text in Early Christianity: Proceedings of the Lille Colloquium, July 2000*, ed. C.-B. Amphoux and J. K. Elliott (Lausanne: Éditions du Zèbre, 2003), 83–91, at 90.

[8] See Bart D. Ehrman, *The Orthodox Corruption of Scripture: The Effect of Early Christological Controversies on the Text of the New Testament* (New York: Oxford University Press, 1993); Ehrman, *Misquoting Jesus: The Story behind Who Changed the Bible and Why* (San Francisco: HarperCollins, 2006).

that the more theologically significant reading is automatically secondary; "nontheological" errors occurred too. (3) No *systematic* attempt at doctrinal "correction" can be traced through any single New Testament manuscript, let alone through the whole tradition; instances are usually fairly isolated within the manuscripts. (4) In any case, a large textual tradition makes it easy to spot such secondary, "theological" readings, evaluate them, and restore the original text.

Factors Tending toward the Preservation of the Text

Counteracting these factors are several others that have worked together to preserve for us the texts we have today.

A great cloud of witnesses. The church has been blessed with a remarkably vast and ever-expanding store of hand-copied Greek manuscripts. Many textual critics have seen this as assuring us that all the original readings are somewhere to be found in our textual tradition. This is the conclusion reached not only by Benjamin B. Warfield in 1893, but also by such notable textual critics of the current generation as Kurt and Barbara Aland, Eldon J. Epp, and J. K. Elliott.[9] Practically speaking, this means that if the original reading is not printed in the main text of our critical editions, it is contained in the apparatus. There are a handful of places in which a plausible argument can be made that the original reading is nowhere present in our textual tradition and that we have a need for "conjectural emendation" of the text.[10] In at least many of these cases it may simply be that the original reading does not satisfy our preconceived notions of what the original must have looked like. In any case, these instances are extremely few, and it is still true that "virtually all of the New Testament variants are preserved somewhere in our extant manuscript tradition."[11]

An increasing cloud of early witnesses. Not only do we have an abundance of manuscripts, but new discoveries are giving us access to some very early ones. It is now estimated that over 40 percent of the New Testament is represented in manuscripts of the second or early third century—an amazing fact, by comparison with other books of antiquity. The discovery of sometimes quite extensive papyrus fragments copied prior to the great fourth-century majuscules has been a great boon to textual criticism. While not all these early manuscripts are of superior quality, they have confirmed the essential correctness of the approach of textual critics and their high estimation of Codex Vaticanus and the Alexandrian tradition in general.

---

[9] Kurt Aland and Barbara Aland, *The Text of the New Testament* (Grand Rapids, MI: Eerdmans, 1989), 296; Eldon Jay Epp, "Textual Criticism," in *The New Testament and Its Modern Interpreters*, ed. Eldon Jay Epp and George W. MacRae (Atlanta: Scholars, 1989), 91; also J. Keith Elliott, "Thoroughgoing Eclecticism in New Testament Textual Criticism," in *The Text of the New Testament in Contemporary Research: Essays on the* Status Quaestionis, ed. Bart D. Ehrman and Michael W. Holmes, SD 46 (Grand Rapids, MI: Eerdmans, 1995), 321–35, at 322.

[10] See Michael Holmes, "Text and Transmission in the Second Century," in Stewart, *Textual Reliability of the New Testament*, 61–79; Holmes, "What Text Is Being Edited? The Editing of the New Testament," in *Editing the Bible: Assessing the Task Past and Present*, ed. John S. Kloppenborg and Judith H. Newman (Atlanta: SBL, 2012), 91–122, at 112, who cites Westcott and Hort's opinion that there are some sixty-five places in the entire New Testament where emendation may be necessary.

[11] Eldon Jay Epp, "The Significance of the Papyri for Determining the Nature of the New Testament Text in the Second Century: A Dynamic View of Textual Transmission," in *The Gospel Traditions in the Second Century*, ed. W. L. Petersen (Notre Dame: University of Notre Dame Press, 1989), 101.

Longevity and continual use of manuscripts. Contrary to what is sometimes asserted, the last "generation" of a text was not typically discarded as soon as a new copy was made from it. We now know that books copied onto papyrus could be in use for two hundred or more years.[12] This means that at the time when our earliest extant New Testament manuscripts were being copied, many churches must have possessed copies that were already very old, perhaps in some cases even the originals.

An abundance of versions and quotations. Besides Greek New Testament manuscripts, we have a large number of manuscripts of New Testament books translated into various languages. The early Latin and Coptic translations in particular were quite literal and "wooden," allowing us good access to the underlying Greek. Moreover, it is often stated that if all our Greek New Testament manuscripts were somehow to vanish, we would be able to construct practically the entire New Testament from the quotations made by the early church fathers.[13]

The tenacity of the tradition. One of the characteristics of the New Testament textual tradition is its "tenacity"—that is, "the stubborn resistance of readings and text types to change."[14] Examples that the Alands give include the ending of Romans, the *pericope adulterae* (John 7:53–8:11), and "the practice of concluding the gospel of Mark at 16:8," which continued to be done in some manuscripts for centuries even while Mark 16:9–20 was considered canonical. The Alands say:

> The very plurality of New Testament text types can be explained only by the tenacity of the New Testament textual tradition. Some 10 to 20 percent of the Greek manuscripts have preserved faithfully the different text types of their various exemplars, even in the latest period when the dominance of the Byzantine Imperial text became so thoroughly pervasive. This is what makes it possible to retrace the original text of the New Testament through a broad range of witnesses.[15]

The practice of textual criticism. Finally, we have a means of testing and verifying the text by the careful and judicious application of text-critical procedures. Naturally, these procedures are not infallible; they are continually being refined, and experts employ them with some variation in their results. But they do provide another somewhat objective grid by which to test the data. They are summarized in "The Practice of New Testament Textual Criticism," below.

Textual criticism can deliver a text that takes us very close to the originals, but cannot deliver certainty about every text-critical problem. A measure of uncertainty remains concerning a small amount of text, but in terms of meaning, the stakes are surprisingly small. While some wish to magnify the remaining difficulties, the Alands state matter-of-factly, "When we compare the variations found in the New Testament manuscripts they appear to be quite innocuous, especially since an extensive

[12] Houston, "Papyrological Evidence," 248, 250, 251; Craig A. Evans, "How Long Were Late Antique Books in Use? Possible Implications for New Testament Textual Criticism," *BBR* 25 (2015): 23–37.
[13] Metzger and Ehrman, *Text of the New Testament*, 126.
[14] Aland and Aland, *Text of the New Testament*, 69.
[15] Ibid., 69–70.

manuscript tradition provides a means of control and correction."[16] If somehow we were forced to accept the *least likely* set of variants in the textual tradition, the essential gospel message of the New Testament would not be affected, and no crucial Christian doctrine would be in jeopardy.[17] In fact, it is typically the "least orthodox" reading that is accepted by modern textual critics as original, because it is deemed to be the "most difficult" reading; the *less likely* reading often appears more "orthodox." And in every case of a theologically significant text-critical "dilemma" posed by Bart Ehrman (e.g.: Is Jesus "compassionate" or "angry" in Mark 1:41? Did Jesus die "by the grace of God" or "without God" [i.e., "forsaken"] at Heb. 2:9?), each "alternative" is affirmed elsewhere in the New Testament. The well-known Trinitarian statement added in a few late manuscripts at 1 John 5:7–8 is, of course, by no means necessary for establishing the doctrine of the Trinity.

History of Textual Criticism

Early Attempts to Standardize the New Testament Text

What we now call "textual criticism," a process of comparing manuscripts in order to determine the original reading, was thus probably practiced on a small scale throughout the early period by scribes and Christian scholars who had access to multiple copies of a New Testament work. The scribes responsible for $\mathfrak{p}^{46}$ (Paul) and $\mathfrak{p}^{66}$ (John) appear to have made corrections to their copies by comparison with a second exemplar. Some scholars have theorized that there was already a major attempt by about the middle or the end of the second century to produce a standardized edition or "recension" of New Testament books. Yet our present evidence does not point in this direction.

For generations it was thought that the excellent texts of Sinaiticus (א) and Vaticanus (B) were the result of a late third- or early fourth-century recension in Alexandria. But the discovery of $\mathfrak{p}^{75}$ (containing most of Luke and John), written in the late second or early third century, has debunked this notion. The text of $\mathfrak{p}^{75}$ is exceptionally close to the corresponding text in the mid-fourth-century Codex Vaticanus, making two conclusions necessary. First, we must suppose that these manuscripts had a very early, common ancestor and, second, that this line of transmission was executed with remarkable consistency. Gordon Fee argues that this tradition did not stem from an intentional attempt to standardize the text (a recension). Rather, echoing Hort's judgment about Vaticanus from a century earlier, Fee claims, "These MSS seem to represent a 'relatively pure'[18] form of preservation of a 'relatively pure' line of descent from the original text."[19] There is now much to justify Westcott and Hort's high opinion of what they called the "Neutral" text and to identify this text with a copying tradi-

[16] Ibid., 291.
[17] Daniel B. Wallace, "Challenges in New Testament Textual Criticism for the Twenty-First Century," *JETS* 52 (2009): 79–100, at 92–94. Wallace traces this assertion to Johann Albrecht Bengel in the eighteenth century and notes its continual affirmation by many others since. Wallace's own formulation is "no viable variant affects any cardinal doctrine" (ibid., 93n59).
[18] Hort's words, describing the textual tradition of Vaticanus (B).
[19] Gordon D. Fee, "The Myth of Early Textual Recension in Alexandria," in Eldon J. Epp and Gordon D. Fee, *Studies in the Theory and Method of New Testament Textual Criticism* (Grand Rapids, MI: Eerdmans, 1993), 247–73, at 272. Fee's chapter was originally published in Richard N. Longenecker and Merrill C. Tenney, *New Dimensions in New Testament Study* (Grand Rapids, MI: Zondervan, 1974), 19–45.

tion that stretches back at least well into the second century.[20] Today $\mathfrak{P}^{75}$ is joined by an increasing number of early papyri in attesting this early, stricter line of copying.[21]

Westcott and Hort believed that the Byzantine text originated in a recension undertaken at Antioch near the end of the third century.[22] Many now regard this text instead as a slowly developing tradition that combined elements from earlier types of texts.[23] After Jerome's revised Latin translation of the Bible (the Vulgate) took hold in the West, and the reproduction of Greek manuscripts was virtually confined to the East, it was this Syrian or Byzantine text that came to prevail in the Greek-speaking churches, supplanting even the earlier Alexandrian form. When the Renaissance and Reformation brought a return to the Greek sources, it was predominantly a Byzantine form of the Greek text that could be found in the libraries and monasteries of Europe.

Modern Attempts to Standardize the New Testament Text

Erasmus and the *textus receptus*. Thus, it was a form of the Byzantine text that appeared in the first printed edition of the New Testament in Greek, published by the great scholar Erasmus of Rotterdam in March 1516. This edition was based on a mere seven Greek manuscripts copied in the eleventh, twelfth, and fifteenth centuries, none of which contained the full New Testament. In 1633 the brothers Elzevir in Leiden published a slightly revised edition of Erasmus's text, which they introduced in these words: "You have here, then, a text now received by all (*textum ergo habes, nunc ab omnibus receptum*), in which we give nothing altered or corrupted." This is the origin of the term *textus receptus*. Through some 160 subsequent editions and minor revisions, the "received text" remained virtually the same. "Yet, its textual basis is essentially a handful of late and haphazardly collected minuscule manuscripts, and in a dozen passages its rendering is supported by no known Greek witness."[24]

The nineteenth century and the rise of the uncials. It was not until 1831 that a break was made with the *textus receptus*, when Karl Lachman published a text based on older majuscule (or uncial) manuscripts. The subsequent work of nineteenth-century scholars such as Samuel Prideaux Tregelles (1813–1875), Constantin von Tischendorf (1815–1874), and B. F. Westcott (1825–1901) and F. J. A. Hort (1828–1892) then ended the dominance of the *textus receptus* and transformed the science of New Testament textual criticism.

The magnificent fourth-century Codex Sinaiticus (א) that Tischendorf discovered in the St. Catherine monastery on Mount Sinai in 1844 became the basis for his edition of the New Testament. Tischendorf was unable to take into account the other

---

[20] Bruce M. Metzger, *A Textual Commentary on the Greek New Testament*, 2nd ed. (Stuttgart: Deutsche Bibelgesellschaft, 1994), 5*, regards it as dating to "early in the second century."

[21] See Hill and Kruger, *The Early Text of the New Testament.*

[22] B. F. Westcott and F. J. A. Hort, *Introduction to the New Testament in the Original Greek* (New York: Harper and Brothers, 1882; repr., Peabody, MA: Hendrickson, 1988), 138–39. They find this form of text in such writers as Theodore of Mopsuestia, Basil the Great, and Chrysostom (ibid., 91–92, 137–39; Aland and Aland, *Text of the New Testament*, 65; Metzger and Ehrman, *Text of the New Testament*, 279).

[23] Metzger and Ehrman, *Text of the New Testament*, 279.

[24] Ibid., 152.

great fourth-century majuscule soon rediscovered in the Vatican Library in Rome and called Codex Vaticanus (B). Westcott and Hort considered Vaticanus the best preserved "Neutral" copy of the originals, and it became the basis for their edition of the New Testament published in 1881. Textual critics continue to recognize the high quality of both codices. Westcott and Hort also put great stock in some of the early versions, particularly the Old Latin and the Old Syriac, each probably begun before the end of the second century and translated directly from Greek manuscripts. The two Cambridge scholars were also intrigued by the unusual, fifth-century, bilingual Codex Bezae Cantabrigiensis (D^{ea}), the chief representative of what has been called the "Western" text. Though D^{ea} itself was produced in the fifth century, Westcott and Hort ascribed its basic text to the second and its group of unique interpolations to the fourth.[25]

Westcott and Hort divided the New Testament manuscripts then available into three basic types denominated by region—Alexandrian, Syrian (later known as Byzantine), and Western—and called B a form of a "Neutral" text, a tradition they thought was undisturbed by any conscious attempt to reform the text. Thus, despite vigorous protests from those who defended the traditional *textus receptus*, the nineteenth century advanced the three great uncial codices Sinaiticus, Vaticanus, and Bezae to a place of prominence in New Testament textual criticism.

The twentieth century and the papyrus discoveries. During the nineteenth century hardly any early papyrus manuscripts of the New Testament were known, and only nine were known by the beginning of the twentieth. At the time of writing this appendix (December 2015), 131 portions of New Testament text written on papyrus have been published, of which about sixty to sixty-five date from before the middle of the fourth century and thus predate the great uncial manuscripts mentioned above. About half of these early papyri have come from a single archaeological site, the ancient rubbish heaps of Oxyrhynchus, Egypt. For much of the twentieth century it looked as if the early papyri represented a looser attitude toward copying in the early church. Increasingly, however, it is becoming clear that the less well-copied manuscripts are in the minority. Somewhere between two-thirds and three-fourths of the early papyri are well-copied examples of the "Neutral," or "Proto-Alexandrian," or "B-Cluster" text, showing a consistent line of copying from the various points in the second century, from which our records begin.[26]

The Practice of New Testament Textual Criticism

A simple and basic rule, sometimes called "Bengel's first rule," summarizes the ideal: "Choose the reading which best explains the origin of the others."[27] Establishing a

[25] For a recent assessment of the so-called "Western non-interpolations," so prized by Westcott and Hort, see Metzger, *Textual Commentary*, 6*, 164–66.

[26] See Hill and Kruger, "Introduction," in *The Early Text of the New Testament*.

[27] Metzger and Ehrman, *Text of the New Testament*, 300; Aland and Aland, *Text of the New Testament*, 280–81, rule 8. Eldon Jay Epp, "Traditional 'Canons' of New Testament Textual Criticism: Their Value, Validity, and Viability—or Lack Thereof," in *The Textual History of the Greek New Testament: Changing Views in Contemporary Research*, ed. Klaus Wachtel and Michael W. Holmes (Atlanta: SBL, 2011), 79–127, at 93–96, makes this rule a separate category for textual criticism.

reasonable explanation for the rise of the alternative reading(s) is perhaps the surest way to the original reading, particularly if the text arrived at by these means is attested in manuscripts known to preserve a generally more reliable text.

In all text-critical work, there are three broad areas to investigate: external evidence and the two subdivisions of internal evidence, transcriptional probability and intrinsic probability. The approach taken here is in line with the method called "Reasoned Eclecticism," popularized by the manuals of Metzger (Metzger and Ehrman)[28] and Aland and Aland.[29] It is called "eclectic" because it is not based upon a single manuscript or textual tradition[30] or on a small selection of manuscripts from different text types, but seeks the original in the entire textual tradition, as much as is possible or practicable. It generally begins with the external evidence,[31] following Hort's dictum, "Knowledge of documents should precede final judgement upon readings."[32]

External Evidence

The Date of the Witnesses

A reading that has support in an earlier manuscript or type of text should normally be given more weight than one that occurs only in a later manuscript. Because even early manuscripts suffered corruptions, however, this rule is hardly infallible.

Quality of the Manuscript or Group

An oft-cited adage is that "witnesses are to be weighed rather than counted." That is, a reading that occurs in the *majority* of manuscripts, if that majority simply represents one textual tradition, may not be as significant as a reading attested in an earlier or more trustworthy manuscript or textual cluster.[33] Most scholars believe that the Alexandrian tradition (and particularly $\mathfrak{p}^{75}$, B, and א) preserved the text most accurately. The Western tradition, while faithfully preserving many early readings, was more prone to paraphrasing and harmonization.[34] Some see the Western texts not as a cohesive text type but as simply the product of a looser attitude toward copying. It should be noted that there are no manuscripts of the Catholic Epistles or Revelation that are said to be Western—only manuscripts of the Gospels, Acts, and Paul.[35] The Byzantine tradition, while displaying a relatively

[28] Metzger and Ehrman, *Text of the New Testament*, 300–343.

[29] Aland and Aland, *Text of the New Testament*, 280–81. See now the updated evaluation of the criteria in Epp, "'Canons' of New Testament Textual Criticism."

[30] In this way reasoned eclecticism differs from the majority text or Byzantine text theory, which virtually limits consideration to this one large segment of the tradition.

[31] In this way reasoned eclecticism differs from what is called "Rigorous (or Thoroughgoing, or Consistent) Eclecticism," advocated by George D. Kilpatrick and J. K. Elliott, which highly prioritizes intrinsic factors over external ones. For concise defenses of the three major approaches, see David Alan Black, ed., *Rethinking New Testament Textual Criticism* (Grand Rapids, MI: Baker Academic, 2002).

[32] Westcott and Hort, *Introduction to the New Testament in the Original Greek*, 31.

[33] Metzger and Ehrman, *Text of the New Testament*, 212. Some today discount the whole idea of text types, but the fact remains that some groups of manuscripts have definite textual traits, and other groups have other textual traits. Epp, "Significance of the Papyri," 71–103, prefers "textual cluster," "textual group," or "textual constellation" to the more rigidly conceived "text type."

[34] Metzger and Ehrman, *Text of the New Testament*, 308.

[35] Ibid., 277n9.

great consistency, is characterized by the conflation of earlier readings, stylistic smoothing, greater explicitness, and harmonization.[36] Typically, a reading supported by Alexandrian and Western witnesses is best, but in Paul, the combination of B D G could be strictly Western, because in Paul, B is thought to have a Western element.

Geographical Distribution

Attestation in multiple geographical regions will normally mean that a reading goes back to a period before the text was widely distributed. The search for geographical representation of readings is complicated, however, by the fact that we seldom know where the manuscripts were actually written. Whatever significance we give to the names attached to text types (Alexandrian or Egyptian; Western; Byzantine [or Syrian]; Caesarean), more confidence comes from the versional representation (obviously, Latin in the West, Coptic in Egypt, Syriac in Syria, etc.) and from Patristic citations, because we usually have a good idea of the geographical locations of the fathers.

Procedurally, one first notes which reading or readings have support in the *earliest* texts, versions, or Patristic witnesses. Then, if such a reading has support from multiple geographic regions (that is, text types/clusters, versions, or fathers), particularly if these include Alexandrian witnesses, we have a presumption that this reading is original. If a reading has only late and Byzantine witnesses, it is almost certainly secondary. In any case, only preliminary conclusions should be drawn from the external evidence before moving to the internal evidence.

Transcriptional Probabilities

Investigating transcriptional probabilities is asking what the *scribe* is most likely to have done in the transcription or copying process.

Lectio Difficilior, ***the More Difficult Reading***

One consideration is whether a reading would have been the more difficult to the scribe. The idea is that (if the change was intentional) a scribe is more likely to have altered a difficult reading to make it easier than the reverse. This rule may be especially useful if the surface meaning of a reading seems erroneous or difficult, but "mature consideration" shows it to be correct. "The characteristic of most scribal emendations," says Metzger, "is their superficiality."[37] Clearly, this rule has limits, for at some point a difficult reading becomes an impossible one. It should not be the sole reason for adopting a particular reading.[38]

---

[36] Ibid., 279–80. Aland and Aland, *Text of the New Testament*, 64, say it was "polished stylistically, edited ecclesiastically, and expanded devotionally."

[37] Metzger and Ehrman, *Text of the New Testament*, 303.

[38] Aland and Aland, *Text of the New Testament*, 281, no. 10.

Lectio Brevior/Longior, *the Shorter or the Longer Reading?*

It used to be thought that scribes were more prone to add material than to omit it. This rule, subject to many exceptions,[39] has in fact been challenged by James Royse and others. Royse studied the singular readings (variants that occur in only a single manuscript) of the earliest witnesses and found that it was more common for a scribe to omit what seemed superfluous than it was to add material. Royse's formulation would be this:

> In general the longer reading is to be preferred, except where:
>
> a) the longer reading appears, on external grounds to be late; or
> b) the longer reading may have arisen from harmonization to the immediate context, to parallels, or to general usage; or
> c) the longer reading may have arisen from an attempt at grammatical improvement.[40]

What we should probably take away from this debate is a keen awareness that scribes could add or omit words, or could substitute similar words. *In any case, the scribe's apparent motivation was to increase clarity or ease of reading.* In effect, then, "the longer versus the shorter reading" boils down to another form of the aforementioned *lectio difficilior* principle.

The Reading That Is Disharmonious Compared with a Parallel

A reading that is disharmonious when compared with a parallel is, too, essentially a species of the *lectio difficilior* principle. Harmonization of the text of one Gospel to the parallel text in another (particularly Mark or Luke to Matthew) is one of the most frequent causes of variation in the Gospels, particularly in the Western and Byzantine traditions. The possibility must always be considered, however, that in rare cases the harmonious reading was original and the disharmonious reading is simply an error.

It should be kept in mind that the *lectio difficilior* rule is valid only if the change was conscious and intentional on the part of the scribe. In making determinations, text critics must consider closely the phenomenon of the scribe's unintentionally skipping material between the same or similar letters, and must also realize that some "difficult but intelligible" readings could have been created inadvertently.

Intrinsic Probabilities[41]

A different standard asks what the *author* was more likely to have written. In general, it should be expected that the original reading will

1. make good sense in the immediate context;
2. conform to, or at least not contravene, any established stylistic or vocabulary traits of the author;

[39] See Metzger and Ehrman, *Text of the New Testament*, 166–67.

[40] James R. Royse, *Scribal Habits in Early Greek New Testament Papyri*, NTTSD 36 (Leiden: Brill, 2008), 735. See the extended discussion of Epp, "'Canons' of New Testament Textual Criticism," 106–16.

[41] Metzger and Ehrman, *Text of the New Testament*, 314; Epp, "'Canons' of New Testament Textual Criticism," 116–22.

3. conform to the known theology of the author;
4. where there is an option, likely conform to Semitic forms of expression.

It must be emphasized that all these criteria are rules of thumb and cannot be applied in a wooden way. Often two or more of them will conflict; for example, a reading that best accords with an author's style or theology may be the "easier" reading. Such cases call for wisdom and sound judgment based on intimate familiarity with the author's writing and with the textual tradition. For all their attention to method, textual critics often stress that text criticism is an art as much as it is a science.[42] This is meant not to unleash the critic's inner Van Gogh, but to insist that an informed and sanctified common sense ought to prevail over rigid adherence to any set of predetermined principles.[43]

Textual Groupings of New Testament Manuscripts

The following list is intended to assist the student in forming judgments on the external evidence:[44]

Byzantine or "A-Group" Witnesses

- *Gospels*: p^{42} p^{84} A E F G H K P S V W (in Matthew and Luke 8:13–24:53) Π (partially in Luke and John) Ψ Ω and most minuscules
- *Acts*: p$^{74?}$ H^{a} L^{ap} P^{a} 049 and most minuscules
- *Epistles*: p^{64} p$^{74?}$ L^{ap} 049 and most minuscules
- *Revelation*: 046 051 052 and many minuscules

Alexandrian or "B-Group" Witnesses

Early Alexandrian

- *All Portions*: p^{1} p^{4} p^{8} p^{10} p^{13} p^{15} p^{16} p^{20} p^{23} p^{28} p^{35} p^{39} p^{40} p^{45} (in Luke and Acts) p^{46} p^{49} p^{52} p^{53} p^{62} p$^{64/67}$ p^{65} p^{66} p^{71} p^{75} p^{86} p^{91} p^{92} א B Sahidic (in part), Clement of Alexandria, Origen (in part)

Later Alexandrian

- *Gospels*: p^{3} p^{44} p^{55} p^{60} (C) L T W (in Luke 1:1–8:12 and in John) (X) Z Δ (in Mark) Ξ Ψ (in Mark; partially in Luke and John) 33 579 892 11241 Bohairic
- *Acts*: p^{33+58} p^{50} p^{56} p^{57} A (C) Ψ 33 81 104 326
- *Paul*: p^{11} p^{14} p^{31} p^{34} p$^{61?}$ A (C) H^{p} I Ψ 33 81 104 326 1739
- *Catholics*: A (C) Ψ 33 81 104 326 1739
- *Revelation*: p^{43} A (C) 1006 1611 1854 2053 2344; less good p^{47} א

[42] Metzger and Ehrman, *Text of the New Testament*, 305.

[43] To this point, ponder the words of A. E. Housman: "To be a textual critic requires aptitude for thinking and willingness to think; and though it also requires other things, those things are supplements and cannot be substitutes. Knowledge is good, method is good, but one thing beyond all other is necessary; and that is to have a head, not a pumpkin, on your shoulders, and brains, not pudding, in your head" (*Selected Prose*, ed. John Carter [Cambridge: Cambridge University Press, 1961], 150).

[44] It is a compilation based on Metzger, *Textual Commentary*, 15*–16*; Metzger and Ehrman, *Text of the New Testament*, 306–13; and Epp, "Significance of the Papyri."

Caesarean or "C-Group" Witnesses[45]

- *Pre-Caesarean*: Origen at Caesarea, $\mathfrak{p}^{25?}$ $\mathfrak{p}^{37?}$ $\mathfrak{p}^{45}$ (most of Mark) W (in Mark 5:31–16:20) fam. 1, fam. 13, 28; many Greek Lectionaries
- *Caesarean*: $\mathfrak{p}^{36}$ Θ, 565 700, Eusebius, Old Armenian; Old Georgian

Western or "D-Group" Witnesses

- *Gospels*: $\mathfrak{p}^{19}$ $\mathfrak{p}^{21}$ $\mathfrak{p}^{37?}$ $\mathfrak{p}^{69?}$ א (in John 1:1–8:38) D W (in Mark 1:1–5:30) 0171, Old Latin; syr^{s} and syr^{c} (in part), early Greek and Latin fathers, Diatessaron
- *Acts*: $\mathfrak{p}^{29?}$ $\mathfrak{p}^{38}$ $\mathfrak{p}^{41}$ $\mathfrak{p}^{48}$ D 383 614 1739 syr$^{h\ mg}$ syr^{palms} cop^{G67}, early Latin fathers, Ephraem's commentary (in Armenian)
- *Paul*: the Greek-Latin bilinguals D^{p} E^{p} F^{p} G^{p}; Greek fathers to end of third century; Old Latin (it) and early Latin fathers; Syrian fathers to about AD 450
- *Catholics*: None
- *Revelation*: None

Tools for the Study of New Testament Textual Criticism

Editions

Aland, B., K. Aland, K. Karavidopoulos, C. M. Martini, and B. M. Metzger, eds. *Novum Testamentum Graece*. 28th ed. Stuttgart: Deutsche Bibelgesellschaft, 2012.

———. In collaboration with the Institute for New Testament Textual Research, Münster/Westphalia. *The Greek New Testament*. 4th ed. Stuttgart: Deutsche Bibelgesellschaft, 1993. 11th printing, 2006.

Holmes, Michael W., ed. *The Greek New Testament: SBL Edition*. Atlanta: SBL; Bellingham, WA: Logos Bible Software, 2010.

Institute for New Testament Textual Research. *Novum Testamentum Graecum. Editio Critica Maior*. Vol. 4, *Catholic Letters*. Edited by Barbara Aland, Kurt Aland, Gerd Mink, Holger Strutwolf, and Klaus Wachtel. Four fascicles, each in two parts, have been published: (1) James, (2) the Petrine Epistles, (3) 1 John, (4) 2 and 3 John and Jude.

Websites

Center for the Study of New Testament Manuscripts, http://www.csntm.org

Evangelical Textual Criticism blog, http://evangelicaltextualcriticism.blogspot.com

Institut für Neutestamentliche Textforschung, http://egora.uni-muenster.de/intf/index_en.shtml

TC: A Journal of Biblical Text Criticism, http://rosetta.reltech.org/TC/v19/index.html

Handbooks and Studies

Aland, Kurt, and Barbara Aland. *The Text of the New Testament: An Introduction to the Critical Editions and to the Theory and Practice of Modern Textual Criticism*. 2nd ed. Grand Rapids, MI: Eerdmans, 1995.

Black, David Alan, ed. *Rethinking New Testament Textual Criticism*. Grand Rapids, MI: Baker Academic, 2002.

Comfort, Philip W. *Encountering the Manuscripts: An Introduction to New Testament Paleography and Textual Criticism*. Nashville: B&H Academic, 2005.

[45] Perceived as a mixture of Alexandrian and Western; Aland and Aland, *Text of the New Testament*, deny it as a text type.

———. *New Testament Text and Translation Commentary*. Carol Stream, IL: Tyndale, 2008.

Comfort, Philip W., and David P. Barrett. *The Text of the Earliest New Testament Greek Manuscripts*. Wheaton, IL: Tyndale, 2001.

Ehrman, Bart D. *Misquoting Jesus: The Story behind Who Changed the Bible and Why*. San Francisco: HarperCollins, 2006.

Ehrman, Bart D., and Michael W. Holmes, eds. *The Text of the New Testament in Contemporary Research: Essays on the* Status Quaestionis. SD 46. Grand Rapids, MI: Eerdmans, 1995.

———, eds. *The Text of the New Testament in Contemporary Research: Essays on the* Status Quaestionis. 2nd ed. NTTSD 42. Leiden: Brill, 2013.

Greenlee, J. Harold. *Introduction to New Testament Textual Criticism*. Grand Rapids, MI: Eerdmans, 1977.

Hill, Charles E., and Michael J. Kruger. *The Early Text of the New Testament*. Oxford: Oxford University Press, 2012.

Hurtado, Larry. *The Earliest Christian Artifacts: Manuscripts and Christian Origins*. Grand Rapids, MI: Eerdmans, 2006.

Metzger, Bruce M. *A Textual Commentary on the Greek New Testament*. 2nd ed. Stuttgart: Deutsche Bibelgesellschaft, 1994.

Metzger, Bruce M., and Bart D. Ehrman. *The Text of the New Testament*. 4th ed. Oxford: Oxford University Press, 2005.

Parker, David C. *An Introduction to the New Testament Manuscripts and Their Texts*. Cambridge: Cambridge University Press, 2008.

Stewart, Robert, ed. *The Reliability of the New Testament: Bart Ehrman and Daniel Wallace in Dialogue*. Minneapolis: Fortress, 2011.

Swanson, Reuben J. *New Testament Greek Manuscripts: Variant Readings Arranged in Horizontal Lines against Codex Vaticanus: Galatians*. Wheaton, IL: Tyndale, 1999. There are eight other volumes in this work: the four Gospels, Acts, Romans, and 1 and 2 Corinthians.

Wachtel, Klaus, and Michael W. Holmes, eds. *The Textual History of the Greek New Testament: Changing Views in Contemporary Research*. Atlanta: SBL, 2011.

Wasserman, Tommy. "The Implications of Textual Criticism for Understanding the 'Original Text.'" In *Mark and Matthew I: Comparative Readings: Understanding the Earliest Gospels in Their First-Century Settings*, edited by Eve-Marie Becker and Anders Runesson, 77–96. WUNT 271. Tübingen: Mohr Siebeck, 2011.

Westcott, B. F., and F. J. A. Hort. *Introduction to the New Testament in the Original Greek*. New York: Harper and Brothers, 1882. Repr., Peabody, MA: Hendrickson, 1988.

Appendix C

The Synoptic Problem

Guy Prentiss Waters

Even a casual survey of the four canonical Gospels will compel the reader to conclude that Matthew, Mark, and Luke are very similar to one another and different from John. Because of these similarities, Matthew, Mark, and Luke have been termed the Synoptic Gospels. These three Gospels, however, are not uniform. They show differences of content and arrangement.[1] This blend of similarity and difference raises the question of the Synoptic Gospels' relationships with one another. In other words, do the Synoptic Gospels exist in a relationship of literary dependence upon one another? If so, which Gospel(s) are dependent upon which Gospel(s)?

In the eighteenth century, the New Testament scholar J. J. Griesbach coined the phrase "the synoptic problem" to describe this question, and the difficulties that students of the Gospels have experienced in attempting to answer it. While the synoptic problem has been the subject of considerable attention among biblical scholars in the last two and a half centuries, the questions it attempts to answer have been before the church for much longer.[2] Already in the second century, Irenaeus of Lyons was attempting to account for the unity and diversity represented in the four Gospels.[3] By the late fourth century, Augustine of Hippo influentially argued that Matthew wrote first, then Mark (with Matthew's Gospel before him), and then Luke (with Mark's and Matthew's Gospels before him).[4]

It would be inaccurate, however, to characterize efforts to address the relationships

[1] By "difference" I do not mean "contradiction." I simply refer to the fact that a certain Gospel may include material that another Gospel omits, and vice versa; that accounts of the same events in one or more Gospels may have differences of wording or detail; and that the same pericopes may appear in different order in different Gospels. None of these phenomena necessarily requires the conclusion that the Gospels are mutually contradictory.

[2] For a recent and thorough survey of the modern phase of the discussion, see David L. Dungan, *A History of the Synoptic Problem: The Canon, the Text, the Composition, and the Interpretation of the Gospels* (New York: Doubleday, 1999).

[3] See *Haer.* 3.11.8.

[4] See *Harmony of the Gospels* 1.2 (*NPNF*[1]).

among the Synoptics as an unbroken and consonant conversation, steadily progressing toward univocal academic consensus. On the contrary, the current state of discussion is fragmented and marked by serious disagreement. No small part of this disagreement is due to the fact that the evidence of the Synoptic Gospels has eluded the explanatory power of any single literary theory of origins.[5] That is to say, many such theories can explain a significant proportion of the evidence, but no literary theory has proved capable of explaining all the evidence.

Before we survey this discussion, it may help to pause to reflect on what is and is not at stake. The Gospels in their final form are the inspired and inerrant Word of God. This fact has two implications for our study. First, it is certainly possible that the Evangelists employed predecessor documents in the production of the four Gospels. But neither the existence nor the purported contents of these hypothetical documents can be determinative of the meaning of the canonical Gospels.[6] It is Scripture that must interpret Scripture.[7] Second, it is equally possible that one Gospel writer consulted another Gospel, or more than one, in the production of his own work. Luke's prefatory comments to his Gospel are certainly suggestive of such a state of affairs (Luke 1:1–4).[8] But no Gospel writer would have made use of another Gospel writer in order to correct the other's work or to express disagreement with it. This is so because, while each Gospel was authored by different human writers, all four Gospels were written by inspiration of the Holy Spirit (see John 14:25–26). The Spirit is the divine author of each Gospel, and the Spirit cannot contradict himself.

In what follows, we will survey the major attempts to answer the question of how the Synoptic Gospels are related to one another. I will offer both the strengths and weaknesses of each of the views surveyed. In the course of this survey, I will argue that no literary theory of Gospel origins sufficiently explains all the evidence, and that the origins of the Gospels are better explained by a combination of both written and oral transmission.

Although dozens of positions have been argued in modern scholarship, we may classify the major proposals under three headings. First, there are proposals that understand the Synoptic Gospels to depend on either a single earlier, lost Gospel or multiple lost (written) fragments. Second, there are proposals that understand the Synoptic Gospels to have developed in dependence upon one another. These proposals may or may not make recourse to additional and lost written or oral sources.

---

[5] In passing, we may also note how various theories of synoptic origins have been yoked to contemporary theories of the historical Jesus, as, for instance, the two-source hypothesis was yoked in the nineteenth century to liberal historical Jesus scholarship (cf. Colin Brown, "Quest for the Historical Jesus," *DJG*[2], 727).

[6] Brevard Childs has made a similar point, *The New Testament as Canon* (Philadelphia: Fortress, 1985), 43. As Richard Muller has noted, the interpretative canon that hypothetical predecessor documents may determine the meaning of a biblical book is a distinguishing feature of the historical-critical exegesis of the modern period ("Biblical Interpretation in the 16th and 17th Centuries," in *Historical Handbook of Major Biblical Interpreters*, ed. Donald K. McKim, 127–28 [Downers Grove, IL: InterVarsity Press, 1998]).

[7] Compare WCF 1.9: "The infallible rule of interpretation of Scripture is the Scripture itself: and therefore, when there is a question about the true and full sense of any Scripture (which is not manifold, but one), it must be searched and known by other places that speak more clearly."

[8] Cf. Scot McKnight, *Interpreting the Synoptic Gospels* (Grand Rapids, MI: Baker, 1988), 34–35. Compare the way in which the Fathers represent John as a supplemental Gospel: Clement of Alexandria, cited by Eusebius, *Hist. eccl.* 6.14.7; and Eusebius himself, *Hist. eccl.* 3.24.7f.

Third, there are proposals that understand the Synoptic Gospels primarily as the end product of a process of oral transmission.[9]

Dependence on Lost Written Source(s)

The first set of proposals explaining the origins of the Gospels argues that the Gospel authors depended on an earlier written source or sources.[10] In the nineteenth century, G. E. Lessing and J. G. Eichhorn proposed that the Gospels emerged from a no-longer-extant "Ur-Gospel."[11] Historical justification for this hypothetical document was found in statements of the second-century father Papias and quoted by the fourth-century historian Eusebius.[12] Lessing inferred from these statements that Matthew "first . . . translated the Hebrew Ur-Gospel into Greek" and that Mark and Luke soon followed suit.[13] The differences among the three Synoptic Gospels may be accounted for by the fact that each Evangelist "use[d] . . . different Greek recensions."[14] The meaning of Papias's statements, however, is vigorously debated, and few scholars have followed Lessing's reading.[15]

This family of proposals has included a few twentieth-century proponents.[16] For the most part, however, scholars have not been persuaded that a lost and hypothetical Ur-Gospel is capable of explaining the similarities and differences among the Synoptic Gospels, whether that Ur-Gospel were Hebrew, Aramaic, or even Greek. Papias's statements aside, the absence of any explicit mention of such a document in antiquity at the very least raises grave doubts about its existence.[17]

Interdependence

The second and arguably majority view within New Testament scholarship today is a family of proposals arguing for the Synoptic Gospels' "interdependence," that is, "that two of the evangelists used one or more of the other gospels in constructing their own."[18] Before we explore the varieties of proposals included within this family, it may help to summarize a twofold line of evidence that has pointed scholars in this direction. Proponents of these views have argued that the broad similarities of order and wording in the Synoptic Gospels require a relationship of literary dependence among them.[19] With respect to order, the Gospels evidence similarities that go well

[9] Compare the similar categorizations in D. A. Carson and Douglas J. Moo, *Introduction to the New Testament*, 2nd ed. (Grand Rapids, MI: Eerdmans, 2005), 88–103; A. D. Baum, "Synoptic Problem," in *DJG*², 912–98.

[10] For what follows, I am dependent upon the discussion of Baum, "Synoptic Problem," 913.

[11] Ibid. Baum notes that, for Lessing, this Ur-Gospel was composed in Hebrew; for Eichhorn, in Aramaic.

[12] See *Hist. eccl.* 3.39.14–16.

[13] Baum, "Synoptic Problem," 913.

[14] Robert Stein, "Synoptic Problem," *DJG*, 786.

[15] On the statements of Papias and the complexities of their interpretation, see, representatively, the discussion at Carson and Moo, *Introduction to the New Testament*, 142–46.

[16] For example, C. C. Torrey and X. Léon-Dufour (Carson and Moo, *Introduction to the New Testament*, 90, 90n25). Baum includes S. Hultgren and G. Baltes as contemporary proponents belonging within this family.

[17] Carson and Moo, *Introduction to the New Testament*, 91.

[18] Ibid.

[19] For a considerably more detailed and nuanced summarization of the evidence, see the eight points given by E. P. Sanders and Margaret Davies, *Studying the Synoptic Gospels* (London: SCM; Philadelphia: Trinity Press International, 1989), 53–54. Compare the recent survey of Baum, "Synoptic Problem," 911–12. For important dissents to accounting for these data in terms of literary dependence, see Eta Linnemann, *Is There a Synoptic Problem? Rethinking the Literary Dependence of the First Three Gospels*, trans. Robert W. Yarbrough (Grand Rapids, MI: Baker, 1992); and F. David Farnell, "The Case for

beyond "putting the outstanding events in their natural order: the birth and baptism at the beginning and the death and resurrection at the end."[20] Mark and Luke, according to John Wenham, have an "identity of order of seventy-two pericopes," while Matthew and Mark have "long parallel sequences . . . broken up by three major dislocations, which makes the idea of an underlying memorised sequence look even less probable in their case."[21] With respect to wording, Craig Blomberg reports the estimate that "of the 661 verses in Mark, 500 recur in Matthew in parallel form and 350 recur in Luke."[22] Furthermore, "there are another 235 verses common to Matthew and Luke that are not found in Mark."[23] These verbal parallels extend not only to "Jesus' teachings," but also to the "narrative descriptions of what Christ did."[24]

To many scholars, these patterns have suggested a relationship of literary interdependence among the Synoptic Gospels. What is the nature of that interdependence? Which Gospel(s) are said to evidence such interdependence upon other Gospel(s)? There have been two broad sets of proposals in answer to this question. The first asserts Matthean priority. That is to say, Matthew's Gospel is a literary ancestor of Mark and Luke. The second asserts Markan priority; Mark's Gospel preceded Matthew's and Luke's Gospels. Neither set of proposals excludes the possibility of contributions from other literary sources. As we shall see, such hypothetical sources figure importantly in many of the proposals that we are about to survey. Even so, while such sources may be said to have contributed to the final canonical product of the later Gospels, proponents do not understand them to have played as formative a role as either Matthew or Mark played in the production of the later Gospels.

Matthean Priority

Although Matthean priority is a minority position within contemporary New Testament scholarship, it has a venerable pedigree. Augustine argued for a form of it in the fourth century. As noted earlier, he claimed that Matthew wrote first, then Mark wrote with Matthew before him, and then Luke wrote with Mark before him. In the eighteenth century, Griesbach advocated an alternate form of Matthean priority. He argued that Matthew wrote first, then Luke wrote with Matthew before him, and then Mark wrote with Matthew and Luke before him. In the twentieth century, William Farmer revived the Griesbach hypothesis.[25]

Griesbach's hypothesis argues that when Matthew, Mark, and Luke agree, Mark "usually" serves as the "middle term." This is so "because [Mark] was third and conflated Matthew and Luke."[26] The hypothesis can also account for the "Matthew-

---

the Independence View of Gospel Origins," in *Three Views on the Origins of the Synoptic Gospels*, ed. Robert L. Thomas (Grand Rapids, MI: Kregel, 2002), 226–309.

[20] John Wenham, *Redating Matthew, Mark and Luke: A Fresh Assault on the Synoptic Problem* (Downers Grove, IL: InterVarsity Press, 1992), 9.

[21] Ibid., 9, 10.

[22] Craig L. Blomberg, *Jesus and the Gospels: An Introduction and Survey*, 2nd ed. (Nashville: B&H, 2009), 97.

[23] Ibid., 98.

[24] Ibid.

[25] See W. R. Farmer, *The Synoptic Problem: A Critical Analysis* (New York: Macmillan, 1964). For a recent and brief statement of this position, see William R. Farmer, "The Case for the Two-Gospel Hypothesis," in *Rethinking the Synoptic Problem*, ed. David Alan Black and David R. Beck (Grand Rapids, MI: Baker Academic, 2001), 97–135.

[26] Sanders and Davies, *Studying the Synoptic Gospels*, 87.

Mark agreements against Luke, Mark-Luke agreements against Matthew and even Matthew-Luke agreements against Mark."[27] This latter category of data (Matthew and Luke against Mark) is especially important. Markan prioritists, as we shall see, frequently invoke an additional source(s) to explain it. The Griesbach hypothesis, however, is able to do so solely on the basis of the three canonical Gospels.

While the Griesbach hypothesis has far-reaching explanatory power, not all its explanations have been deemed equally compelling. Robert Stein, a Markan prioritist, argues that Markan priority better explains Mark-Luke agreements against Matthew, and Mark-Matthew agreements against Luke.[28] Grant Osborne, also a Markan prioritist, has argued that it is improbable that Mark, who is said to have written last, would have omitted "the infancy narratives [or] the Sermon on the Mount."[29] Furthermore, when Matthew and Mark have parallel accounts, Mark's is invariably the longer of the two. Is it not counterintuitive, Osborne notes, that the longer account is said to be the later of the two?[30]

Markan Priority

Of New Testament scholars who hold to interdependence among the Synoptic Gospels, the majority viewpoint is some form of Markan priority. There is more diversity in this family of proposals than in the family of Matthean priority. Proponents within this family argue both that Mark is the middle term between Matthew and Luke, and that Matthew and Luke have borrowed from Mark, who wrote his Gospel first. This is true not only with respect to the wording of the Gospels, but also with respect to the ordering of the Gospels' pericopes. There are, furthermore, "substantial [verbal] agreements between Matthew and Mark against Luke, and between Mark and Luke against Matthew, but relatively few agreements between Matthew and Luke against Mark."[31] This same phenomenon is true, Robert Stein has argued, of "agreements in order."[32] That is to say, such "agreement between Matthew and Luke begins where Mark begins and ends where Mark ends."[33]

Some recent Markan prioritists, such as Mark Goodacre and Francis Watson, have argued that Mark is prior to both Matthew and Luke, that Luke had independent access to "oral traditions of the Jesus story," and that "Luke is the interpreter of Matthew."[34] Both the Synoptic Gospels and lost oral traditions suffice to explain the formation of Mark, Matthew, and Luke. Most Markan prioritists, however, espouse what has been called the "two-source hypothesis." This hypothesis also recognizes

[27] Stein, "Synoptic Problem," 786. See Stein's discussion for elaboration of each of these points. Compare Sanders and Davies, *Studying the Synoptic Gospels*, 87.

[28] Stein, "Synoptic Problem," 787. See his discussion of the evidence at ibid., 789.

[29] Grant R. Osborne, "Response [to William R. Farmer]," in Black and Beck, *Rethinking the Synoptic Problem*, 142.

[30] Ibid.

[31] Sanders and Davies, *Studying the Synoptic Gospels*, 54.

[32] Stein, "Synoptic Problem," 788–89.

[33] Sanders and Davies, *Studying the Synoptic Gospels*, 54; McKnight, *Interpreting the Synoptic Gospels*, 34.

[34] The first quotation is that of Baum, "Synoptic Problem," *DJG*², 916, summarizing Mark Goodacre, *The Case against Q: Studies in Markan Priority and the Synoptic Problem* (Harrisburg, PA: Trinity Press International, 2002). The second quotation is that of Francis Watson, *Gospel Writing: A Canonical Perspective* (Grand Rapids, MI: Eerdmans, 2013), 119. Back of both Goodacre and Watson is the work of Michael Goulder, *Luke: A New Paradigm*, 2 vols., JSNTSup 20 (Sheffield: JSOT, 1989).

that Mark alone is unable to account for all of Matthew and Luke. Matthew and Luke share "approximately 200 verses" that do not appear in Mark.[35] But two-source hypothesists ascribe this so-called double tradition to a lost source, "Q," whose name comes from the German word for "source" (*Quelle*).[36] On this hypothesis, Mark did not consult Q in composing his Gospel, but Matthew and Luke consulted Mark and Q (two sources) in composing their Gospels.

The two-source hypothesis has won the acceptance that it has in modern scholarship because of its ability to explain much of the evidence of the Synoptic Gospels. In addition to what we have noted above, scholars argue on literary grounds that there are compelling reasons to posit Mark as the first Gospel, and Matthew and Luke as subsequent and dependent productions.[37] Even so, the two-source hypothesis faces at least two grave difficulties. The first concerns Q. Scholars have long debated the nature, contours, and development of Q. Is it a written source, a body of oral tradition, or a combination of the two? Is it strictly a sayings source, or does it also contain narrative? Was Q coextensive with the double tradition (Matthew-Luke overlaps) or was it larger or smaller? Did Q undergo multiple recensions? Inasmuch as these fundamental questions admit of no universally accepted answers, and it is a purely hypothetical source, scholars have sharply questioned whether Q even existed, much less contributed to the formation of the canonical Gospels.[38] Would not a simpler solution, some critics argue, be to posit Luke's use of Matthew to account for the double-tradition material?

A second problem for the two-source hypothesis is its inability to explain all the data of the Gospels.[39] Particularly troublesome is the "evidence which counts against the independence of Matthew and Luke."[40] Such evidence includes "the minor agreements between Matthew and Luke against Mark in the triple tradition."[41] There are also "five principal instances of a Mark-Q overlap," suggesting that Mark and Q are not the independent sources that the two-source hypothesis posits them to be.[42] Finally, there is the body of evidence, which we have discussed above, which Griesbach argued demonstrates Matthean priority.[43]

Proponents of the two-source hypothesis have not been without answers to these and other challenges to Markan priority. Responses have often followed at least two lines. The first line posits additional hypothetical sources. To account for the presence of material unique to Matthew and Luke—that is, material unaccounted for by Mark and Q—B. F. Streeter proposed two sources, "M" and "L," respectively.[44]

---

[35] Sanders and Davies, *Studying the Synoptic Gospels*, 54.

[36] For recent, brief, and accessible surveys of scholarship concerning "Q," see G. N. Stanton, "Q," *DJG*, 644–50; and G. N. Stanton and N. Perrin, "Q," *DJG*^{2}, 711–18. For a thorough discussion of the subject, see James M. Robinson, Paul Hoffmann, and John Kloppenborg, *The Critical Edition of Q* (Minneapolis: Fortress, 2000).

[37] See Blomberg, *Jesus and the Gospels*, 99–101.

[38] See especially the essays in Mark Goodacre and Nicholas Perrin, eds., *Questioning Q: A Multidimensional Critique* (Downers Grove, IL: InterVarsity Press, 2004), and Watson, *Gospel Writing*, 117–55. For criticism of Q from the perspective of understanding the formation of the Gospels in terms of oral transmission, see James D. G. Dunn, "Altering the Default Setting: Re-envisaging the Early Transmission of the Jesus Tradition," *NTS* 49 (2003): 139–75.

[39] What follows is dependent upon the discussion of Sanders and Davies, *Studying the Synoptic Gospels*, 67–92.

[40] Ibid., 67.

[41] Ibid.

[42] Ibid., 78.

[43] For a discussion of which, see ibid., 84–92.

[44] B. F. Streeter, *The Four Gospels: A Study of Origins* (London: Macmillan, 1924).

The second line of response posits multiple editions of Mark and Luke.[45] Whatever explanatory power they may have, the layering of such proposals upon the two-source hypothesis quickly renders that hypothesis unwieldy. The network of interactions and dependencies among hypothetical sources and lost earlier editions of the canonical Gospels is positively labyrinthine.[46]

But the Ptolemaic intricacy of two-source proposals is not unique to this particular theory. The trajectory of literary solutions to the problem of the origins of the Synoptic Gospels has been one of increasing complexity, not simplicity.[47] This is partly owing to the fact that no single literary theory has emerged that can simply and adequately account for the similarities and differences among the Synoptic Gospels. It is also partly due to a frequently unarticulated but patently operative presupposition in such literary theories: "For everything there is a [written] source."[48] But what if the transmission and adaptation of written sources is not the only way in which the Synoptic Gospels came into being?

Oral Transmission

A third way to explain the formation of the Synoptic Gospels is in terms of oral transmission. The question has rightly been posed whether the modes of transmission posited by the literary theories surveyed above provide plausible explanations of the emergence of the Synoptic Gospels in first-century Jewish culture, a "predominantly oral culture."[49] To affirm the essential orality of first-century Judaism is not necessarily to deny the literacy of some or even many Jews.[50] Nor is it to deny the possibility of literary methods playing some role in the formation of the Synoptic Gospels (cf. Luke 1:1–3). It is to say that oral transmission is a way of explaining the emergence of the Synoptics that is contextually and historically satisfying.

There is, however, no single theory of oral transmission. In the nineteenth century, J. C. L. Gieseler theorized that the "apostles unintentionally created an oral Ur-Gospel," which lay back of the Synoptic Gospels, each of whose authors independently accessed this oral Ur-Gospel in the composition of his respective work.[51] The dominant theory of oral transmission throughout much of the twentieth century, however, has been form criticism, of which Rudolf Bultmann and Martin Dibelius are two of the earliest and best-known proponents.[52] Although there are often significant

[45] Streeter posited a "proto-Luke," which Luke "wrote . . . before seeing a copy of Mark, and then [Luke] revised and expanded it considerably after reading Mark" (Blomberg, *Jesus and the Gospels*, 103–4). Other scholars have posited not only a "proto-Mark" but also a "deutero-Mark," that is, a prior and subsequent edition of the Gospel in the form that we presently have it.

[46] See, for instance, the proposal of F. C. Grant, charted in Sanders and Davies, *Studying the Synoptic Gospels*, 103.

[47] See, for example, the proposals of M.-E. Boismard, discussed in ibid., 105–11; and of David Burkett, *Rethinking the Gospel Sources: From Proto-Mark to Mark* (New York: T&T Clark, 2004), and Burkett, *Rethinking the Gospel Sources*, vol. 2, *The Unity or Plurality of Q*, SBLECL 1 (Atlanta: SBL, 2009).

[48] So, rightly, Sanders and Davies, *Studying the Synoptic Gospels*, 119.

[49] Dunn, "Altering the Default Setting," 149.

[50] On this question in recent scholarship, see the discussion at P. R. Eddy, "Orality and Oral Transmission," *DJG*², 644–45.

[51] Baum, "Synoptic Problem," 914. For the development of this oral Ur-Gospel hypothesis through the nineteenth and into the twentieth centuries, see ibid., 914–15.

[52] On form criticism, see the surveys of Craig L. Blomberg, "Form Criticism," *DJG*, 243–50; Blomberg, *Jesus and the Gospels*, 92–97; N. Perrin, "Form Criticism," *DJG*², 288–94; and see the seminal treatments of Rudolf Bultmann, *The History of the Synoptic Tradition* (New York: Harper & Row, 1963); Martin Dibelius, *From Tradition to Gospel* (New York: Scribner, 1935).

differences among form critics, there is a common understanding of the way in which the Synoptic Gospels came into existence. Form critics argue that Jesus's words for the most part "circulated in small independent units."[53] These small units were transmitted in accordance with what were thought to be particular laws of tradition. This traditional material existed in discrete "forms," what Blomberg has described as "almost a 'mini-genre,'" each of which possessed a certain *Sitz-im-Leben* ("place in life") "in the history of the early church."[54] In other words, each form played a certain function in the life of the church. These functions included preaching, defending the faith against opponents, and exhorting the community of believers.

Form criticism has serious liabilities. First, form critics failed to achieve unanimity concerning some major methodological questions: What precisely were the laws of tradition? As it developed, did the tradition become more or less historical? Precisely how many forms were there? Second, form criticism maintains that the tradition about Jesus's words and deeds was transmitted in "small, individual units."[55] But as C. H. Dodd and, more recently, J. D. G. Dunn have argued, the Gospels share a common narrative that surely was in existence "already in the pre-written Gospel stage."[56] Third, form criticism functionally denies the role that the New Testament assigns to eyewitnesses as those who witnessed and passed down the words and deeds of Jesus. Form criticism, rather, posits an impersonal and communal mechanism of transmission.[57] Fourth, form critics generally maintain that the tradition about Jesus was "significantly distorted during the period of oral tradition."[58] But there is nothing in the mechanics of oral transmission per se to require such skepticism about the historical merits of what we have in the Synoptic Gospels.[59] Furthermore, the so-called "criteria of authenticity" by which form critics claimed to be able to discern earlier from later layers of tradition have been subjected to withering criticism.[60]

Form criticism has hardly been the sole way of explaining the origins of the Synoptic Gospels in terms of oral transmission. Two broad sets of recent proposals merit mention. The first is that of Ken Bailey, followed and developed by Dunn.[61] Both Bailey and Dunn have argued that the Gospels are the end product of a process of oral transmission. Bailey and Dunn regard that process to have been not only communal but, as such, structured. For Bailey and Dunn, "the community itself functions as an informal custodian over the tradition" by ensuring that the tradition is transmitted in accordance with "shared communal norms of faithfulness to the tradition."[62] For

[53] Carson and Moo, *Introduction to the New Testament*, 80.
[54] Blomberg, *Jesus and the Gospels*, 92.
[55] Dunn, "Altering the Default Setting," 174.
[56] Ibid. See also C. H. Dodd, *New Testament Studies* (Manchester: Manchester University Press, 1953), 1–11.
[57] See the discussion in Bauckham, *Jesus and the Eyewitnesses*, 290–318.
[58] Blomberg, "Form Criticism," 246.
[59] See the helpful discussion in ibid.
[60] See the brief discussion in Perrin, "Form Criticism," 292; and, at greater length, Stanley E. Porter, *The Criteria for Authenticity in Historical-Jesus Research: Previous Discussion and New Proposals*, JSNTSup 191 (Sheffield: Sheffield Academic, 2000).
[61] Ken E. Bailey, "Informal Controlled Oral Tradition and the Synoptic Gospels," *AJT* 5 (1991): 34–54. See Dunn, "Altering the Default Setting," 155–56; and, further, Dunn, *Jesus Remembered* (Grand Rapids, MI: Eerdmans, 2003), 173–254. Dunn stresses, however, that he understands his proposal to complement and not to replace "the two-document hypothesis" ("Altering the Default Setting," 158).
[62] Eddy, "Orality and Oral Transmission," 645. Compare Dunn, "Altering the Default Setting," 151–53.

Dunn, at least, this model offers not only structure but also flexibility.[63] "Variation" is, he argues, "the hallmark of oral tradition."[64]

It is unclear from Dunn's discussion, however, how his articulation of variation and flexibility in this tradition can sustain the historical integrity of the Gospels as reliable accounts of the words and deeds of Jesus.[65] A similar model that is better able to sustain the historical trustworthiness of the Synoptic Gospels has been proposed by Birger Gerhardsson.[66] In accounting for the development of the Synoptics, Gerhardsson has appealed to the model of the rabbi and his disciples. In such a context, the rabbi's words were committed to memory, and his disciples "were viewed as an authoritative circle of leadership which carefully safeguarded the traditions."[67] Critics have questioned the suitability of this analogy and have argued that the Gospels evidence more diversity than this model would appear to permit.[68] Neither objection is insuperable, however, and Gerhardsson has proposed a viable and historically credible model to account for the way in which Jesus's words and deeds were reliably transmitted to the church through his apostles.[69] Richard Bauckham's recent work has rightly and commendably stressed that the "transmission process of the Jesus traditions [was] a formal controlled tradition in which the eyewitnesses played an important part."[70] In its emphasis upon the role of the eyewitnesses in the formation of the Gospels, it provides a salutary complement to such proposals as those of Gerhardsson.

Conclusion

The question of the process by which the Synoptic Gospels came into being is one that has occupied students of the Gospels for centuries. The intensification of interest in this question in the last two centuries has yielded a diversity of proposals and a lack of consensus. Even so, we may draw this survey of the so-called synoptic problem to a close with two concluding reflections.

First, both oral transmission and literary transmission likely contributed to the formation of the Synoptic Gospels. On the one hand, the apostles conserved and oversaw the handing down of the teachings and actions of Jesus that they had eye-witnessed and committed to memory.[71] The account of Jesus's ministry that we possess in the Gospels, therefore, was not subject to the vagaries of an ungoverned and anonymous process of transmission. On the other hand, Luke indicates that, in drafting his Gospel, he has accessed existing accounts of Jesus's ministry (Luke 1:1–4).

[63] Dunn, "Altering the Default Setting," 154.
[64] Ibid., 173.
[65] Referencing the differences in the synoptic accounts in Mark 9:14–27 and parallels and Mark 16:1–8 and parallels, Dunn asks "whether such evidence [ought not be] explained in terms of *oral* tradition—that is, as *retellings* of a familiar story, with variations dependent on the teller's foibles and the community's perceived interests" ("Altering the Default Setting," 162, emphasis his; cf. Dunn's comments on 170).
[66] Birger Gerhardsson, *The Reliability of the Gospel Tradition* (Peabody, MA: Hendrickson, 2001). We should note that Gerhardsson does not hold to as high an understanding of the historical reliability of the Gospels as I defend here (cf. Sanders and Davies, *Studying the Synoptic Gospels*, 130).
[67] Blomberg, "Form Criticism," *DJG*, 247.
[68] So Sanders and Davies, *Studying the Synoptic Gospels*, 129–30.
[69] Carson and Moo, *Introduction to the New Testament*, 85. Note Bauckham's sympathetic but not uncritical remarks in *Jesus and the Eyewitnesses*, esp. 94, 249–52.
[70] Bauckham, *Jesus and the Eyewitnesses*, 264.
[71] Ibid., 280–87.

Luke's words expressly indicate that he has consulted eyewitnesses, and may indicate that he has consulted written sources. Even though no literary proposal has presented itself that satisfactorily accounts for all the data, this deficit in no way militates against the possibility of literary transmission playing a role in the formation of the Synoptic Gospels.[72]

Second, the Gospels are not only historically reliable but also inerrant books. Whether they are the end product of oral transmission, literary transmission, or a combination of the two, the Gospels faithfully and unerringly preserve the words and deeds of Jesus Christ. We may affirm this point because Jesus promised the apostles who would impose the four Gospels upon the church, "The Holy Spirit . . . will teach you all things and bring to your remembrance all that I have said to you" (John 14:26). We may infer from this promise that Jesus asserted a keen divine interest in and oversight of the steps leading up to the composition of the Gospels. By whatever process the Gospels came into being, we know that this process unfolded under divine, providential superintendence.[73] Crowning and following this preparative, providential work was the Spirit's activity in producing the text of the Gospels through human authors. The Spirit so worked "within the [Gospel] writers in their entire work of writing, with the design and effect of rendering the written product the divinely trustworthy Word of God."[74] For all our uncertainties regarding the way in which the Gospels came into existence, we may rejoice that the God of providence minutely ordered, governed, and directed that process. And we glory in the unshakable certainty that the Gospels are the very Word of God.

Select Bibliography

Aland, Kurt. *Synopsis of the Four Gospels*. Rev. ed. Stuttgart: Deutsche Bibelgesellschaft; New York: United Bible Societies, 1985.

———. *Synopsis Quattuor Evangeliorum*. 15th ed. Stuttgart: Deutsche Bibelgesellschaft, 1985.

Bauckham, Richard. *Jesus and the Eyewitnesses*. Grand Rapids, MI: Eerdmans, 2006.

Baum, A. D. "Synoptic Problem." In *Dictionary of Jesus and the Gospels*. 2nd ed., edited by Joel B. Green, Jeannine K. Brown, and Nicholas Perrin, 911–19. Downers Grove, IL: IVP Academic, 2013.

Black, David Alan, and David R. Beck, eds. *Rethinking the Synoptic Problem*. Grand Rapids, MI: Baker Academic, 2001.

Blomberg, Craig L. *Jesus and the Gospels: An Introduction and Survey*. 2nd ed. Nashville: B&H, 2009.

[72] Cf. Ibid., 287–89.

[73] On divine superintendence with respect to the authorship of Scripture generally, see the classic treatment of A. A. Hodge and B. B. Warfield, "Inspiration," *The Presbyterian Review* 6 (1881): 225–60.

[74] B. B. Warfield, *Selected Shorter Writings of Benjamin B. Warfield*, ed. John E. Meeter, vol. 2 (Phillipsburg, NJ: P&R, 1973), 615.

Gerhardsson, Birger. *The Reliability of the Gospel Tradition*. Peabody, MA: Hendrickson, 2001.

Goodacre, Mark, and Nicholas Perrin. *Questioning Q: A Multidimensional Critique*. Downers Grove, IL: InterVarsity Press, 2004.

Linnemann, Eta. *Is There a Synoptic Problem? Rethinking the Literary Dependence of the First Three Gospels*. Translated by Robert W. Yarbrough. Grand Rapids, MI: Baker, 1992.

McKnight, Scot. *Interpreting the Synoptic Gospels*. Grand Rapids, MI: Baker, 1988.

Sanders, E. P., and Margaret Davies. *Studying the Synoptic Gospels*. London: SCM; Philadelphia: Trinity Press International, 1989.

Stein, Robert. "Synoptic Problem." In *Dictionary of Jesus and the Gospels*, edited by Joel B. Green, Scot McKnight, and I. Howard Marshall, 784–92. Downers Grove, IL: InterVarsity Press, 1992.

Thomas, Robert L., ed. *Three Views on the Origins of the Synoptic Gospels*. Grand Rapids, MI: Kregel, 2002.

Watson, Francis. *Gospel Writing: A Canonical Perspective*. Grand Rapids, MI: Eerdmans, 2013.

Wenham, John. *Redating Matthew, Mark and Luke: A Fresh Assault on the Synoptic Problem*. Downers Grove, IL: InterVarsity Press, 1992.

Appendix D

The Use of the Old Testament in the New Testament

Trusting the New Testament's Hermeneutics

Robert J. Cara

Introduction

Commenting on Jesus's return from Egypt as a child, Matthew states, "This was to fulfill what the Lord had spoken by the prophet, 'Out of Egypt I called my son'" (Matt. 2:15 with Hos. 11:1). As this one verse conveniently shows, the New Testament writers believed that the Old Testament, among other things, speaks about the Lord Jesus Christ.

This verse also shows that the New Testament writers sometimes used a hermeneutical methodology ("typology") that is not well understood by many modern readers. On the surface, "out of Egypt I called my son" in Hosea is not predictive and is referring to God's bringing Israel out of Egypt; at a deeper level, however, one can see the connections to Jesus.[1]

The above quote is just one of 317 direct quotes of the Old Testament in the New Testament.[2] In addition, there are many "allusions" and "echoes," which are less-defined categories. I define an allusion as a short reference or partial quote the

[1] Once one is aware of the connections between Israel and "son" (e.g., Ex. 4:22–23) and between the Messiah and "son" (Ps. 2:7; 2 Sam. 7:14), along with the associated federal-headship assumptions, plus the understanding that the exodus was the prototypical redemptive event in the Old Testament, then the connection of Jesus to Hos. 11:1 is much clearer.

[2] This exact number is debated to some degree, but scholars do not disagree significantly. This number comes from Barbara Aland et al., eds., *The Greek New Testament*, 5th ed. (Stuttgart: United Bible Societies, 2014), 860–63. All of these quotes are from the traditional Protestant/Jewish Old Testament canon.

source of which the author assumes some readers will recognize. An echo is even less defined and is a more subtle reference or partial quote than is an allusion.[3] According to the editors of the United Bible Society's *Greek New Testament*, the New Testament includes 2,310 Old Testament "allusions and verbal parallels," which, in my nomenclature, are allusions and echoes.[4] In addition to these specific quotes, allusions, and echoes, the New Testament sometimes simply comments about the Old Testament as a whole. For example, Jesus states about the Scriptures, "It is they that bear witness about me" (John 5:39).[5]

The use of the Old Testament in the New Testament is a large and important topic for a variety of interrelated reasons.[6] (1) Part of the New Testament writers' claim that Jesus is the Christ comes from their understanding of Old Testament texts. (2) Some scholars, probably overstating the case, see it as the key to understanding the theology of the New Testament.[7] (3) The hermeneutics of the New Testament writers are shown by their use of the Old Testament, which then has implications for our reading of the Bible. (4) This issue is part of the battleground between conservative and critical/liberal scholars as to the reliability of the Bible; that is, critical/liberal scholars see the New Testament writers as mistakenly interpreting the Old Testament at many points. (5) There has been much discussion as to the hermeneutical methods employed by the New Testament writers as compared to and contrasted with other first-century Jewish and Greco-Roman groups. (6) Simply the large number of direct (317) and indirect references (2,310) of the Old Testament in the New speaks to its importance.

Expanding on reason 3 above, the New Testament writers have multifaceted hermeneutical methodologies for using the Old Testament. By evaluating the New Testament's hermeneutical use of the Old, we are given various methodological patterns of how to interpret the Bible, both the Old and New Testaments. In fact, my own primary method of justifying a hermeneutical method is to argue that the Bible itself uses it. For example, I believe that the same moral law may be used in multiple ways, the so-called three uses of the law. Why? The New Testament has

[3] This is the substance of Richard B. Hays's definitions. For him, "*allusion* is used of obvious intertextual references, *echo* of subtler ones" (*Echoes of Scripture in the Letters of Paul* [New Haven, CT: Yale University Press, 1989], 29, emphasis his). Although I like Hays's definitions, I have serious concerns about many of his exegetical conclusions and also about his hermeneutics of using "echo."

[4] *The Greek New Testament*, 864–82. Although the UBS *Greek New Testament* does include allusions/verbal-parallels from apocryphal sources, I have adjusted the number above so that it includes only New Testament allusions/verbal-parallels from the traditional Protestant/Jewish Old Testament canon.

[5] In the same context, Jesus also notes about "Moses . . . [that] he wrote of me" (John 5:46). Paul comments that "all Scripture . . . is profitable for teaching, for reproof, for correction, and for training in righteousness" (2 Tim. 3:16).

[6] Standard treatments of this topic from a variety of perspectives include Hans Hübner, "New Testament, OT Quotations in the," trans. Siegfried S. Schatzmann, *ABD*, 4:1096–1104; G. K. Beale, *Handbook on the New Testament Use of the Old Testament: Exegesis and Interpretation* (Grand Rapids, MI: Baker Academic, 2012); Peter R. Rodgers, *Exploring the Old Testament in the New* (Eugene, OR: Resource, 2012); Richard Longenecker, *Biblical Exegesis in the Apostolic Period*, Biblical and Theological Classics Library 5 (Carlisle: Paternoster, 1995); Walter C. Kaiser Jr., *The Uses of the Old Testament in the New* (Eugene, OR: Wipf & Stock, 2001); Walter C. Kaiser Jr., Darrell L. Bock, and Peter Enns, *Three Views on the New Testament Use of the Old Testament* (Grand Rapids, MI: Zondervan, 2008). Special notice should be given to the excellent multiauthored work that covers every Old Testament quote and clear allusion in the New Testament, G. K. Beale and D. A. Carson, eds., *Commentary of the New Testament Use of the Old Testament* (Grand Rapids, MI: Baker Academic, 2007).

[7] E. Earle Ellis says, "The NT's understanding and exposition of the OT lies at the heart of its theology, and it is primarily expressed within the framework of typological interpretation" (foreword to *Typos: The Typological Interpretation of the Old Testament in the New*, by Leonhard Goppelt, trans. Donald H. Madvig [Eugene, OR: Wipf & Stock, 2002], xx).

examples of using the same Old Testament law in multiple ways.[8] I interpret every psalm as in some sense referring to both Christ and Christians. Why? Because the New Testament interprets the Psalms this way.[9] I believe that exemplary exegesis, although often abused, is sometimes legitimate because the Bible uses this hermeneutical method.[10]

Given all the interesting and important aspects of the use of the Old Testament in the New, multiple books are needed to adequately cover them. My goal for this brief essay is very truncated. Noting that many do not agree that all of the New Testament's hermeneutics are trustworthy, *I simply want to encourage and reinforce the reader's trust in the New Testament's hermeneutical patterns, especially as they relate to Christ in the Old Testament.* Although I will not be giving a catalog of hermeneutical patterns, I hope for the reader in principle to desire to use all of the New Testament's patterns to see more fully and more often the glories of Christ from the Old Testament.

To encourage and reinforce trust, first, I will argue that the hermeneutical patterns that the New Testament writers use to exegete Christ in the Old Testament should be our hermeneutical guide. Second, I will present some of the New Testament's statements about Christ in the Old Testament to confirm that the New Testament writers truly believe that the Old Testament speaks of Christ. Third, I will give a broad-brush defense of typology.

Hermeneutical Guide?

The whole Bible is full of hermeneutical information to aid us in its interpretation. It is not *just* when a New Testament writer uses the Old or an Old Testament writer uses a previous Old Testament text that we learn hermeneutics.[11] However, it truly is easier to see the hermeneutical methodology in these cases.

As all note, many verses in the Old Testament are used in a straightforward way by the New Testament writers. For example, to show that God gives grace to the appropriately humble, James quotes the proverb that God "gives grace to the humble" (James 4:6 // Prov. 3:34). Other passages, such as those dealing with typology, are not as straightforward and have created controversy.

I am firmly convinced of the following three points concerning a biblical writer's

[8] Paul uses the Ten Commandments in different ways. He uses "do not covet" and "do not commit adultery" sometimes as second use (Rom. 7:7; 2:22 with 3:20) and sometimes as third use (Rom. 13:9). He uses "do not commit adultery" in 1 Tim. 1:10 probably as first use. I am using the same numbering scheme as the Formula of Concord, epitome 6.

[9] Ps. 34:8 // 1 Pet. 2:3 and Ps. 34:12–16 // 1 Pet. 3:10–12 are applied to Christians. Ps. 34:20 // John 19:36 is applied to Christ. Ps. 118:6 // Heb. 13:6 is applied to Christians. Ps. 118:22 // Luke 20:17; Acts 4:11; 1 Pet. 2:7 is applied to Christ. And likewise Ps. 118:25–26 // Matt. 21:9; 23:39 is applied to Christ. Interestingly, Ps. 69:9 (Heb. 69:10) is used in Rom. 15:1–4 to refer to Christ, but then Paul uses Christ's actions as a motive and example for Christians to follow. I see some psalms as primarily about Christ and secondarily about believers, and other psalms, the converse. For a good discussion of the nuanced way Christ is in every psalm, see Richard P. Belcher Jr., *The Messiah and the Psalms: Preaching Christ from All the Psalms* (Fearn: Mentor, 2001).

[10] For instances where humans are used as examples, see Mark 2:25–28; Luke 17:32; 1 Cor. 10:1–13; 11:1; Phil. 4:9; Hebrews 11; James 5:16–18. For instances where Christ is used as an example, see John 13:15; Rom. 15:1–4; 2 Cor. 8:8–10; 10:1; Eph. 5:2, 25; Phil. 2:3–8; 1 Tim. 6:12–13; 1 Pet. 4:1, 12–13.

[11] I often use the term "intra-biblical exegesis" to include Old Testament writers' using previous Old Testament texts; New Testament writers' using Old Testament texts; and New Testament writers' using New Testament texts, e.g., 1 Tim. 5:18. For some, the term "intertexuality" is used, but this usually has postmodern connotations that I do not approve of.

use of a previous biblical passage: (1) The writer properly elucidates at least a portion of the true meaning of that passage. (2) The writer's hermeneutical methodology to elucidate that meaning is proper and infallible for that situation. (3) The writer's hermeneutical methodology is an infallible hermeneutical guide for Christians today as they read other similar passages in the Bible.[12]

Allow me to add three caveats to the above. First, we are not in every instance sure of the biblical writers' complete hermeneutical methodology. Second, our application of biblical writers' hermeneutical methodologies to other appropriate biblical passages is not always correct. Third, I do believe that we can learn aspects of hermeneutics from general revelation to aid us in reading the Bible, but this is a fallible aid, not an infallible aid.[13] But to reiterate and given the caveats, *the biblical writers' hermeneutics are an infallible guide for modern Christians.*[14]

There are two general groups that do not agree that the hermeneutics of the biblical writers provide a hermeneutical guide for us today. The first comprises liberal/critical scholars who simply do not accept that the Old Testament points toward Christ.[15] Since they agree that this is part of the New Testament hermeneutic, and they consider it objectively wrong, these scholars deny that the biblical writers provide us with a proper hermeneutical guide.

The second group is more puzzling to me. It consists of scholars who are broadly evangelical and accept the New Testament statements about Christ but do not agree that the New Testament writers always followed a proper hermeneutic. Or to state their view another way, the meaning that the New Testament writers attribute to the Old Testament text is not always correct, and consequently, the hermeneutic to obtain that meaning is suspect as well. Hence, they argue that modern Christians should *not* follow *all* of the biblical writers' hermeneutical patterns, although we should follow some of the patterns.

Many follow Richard Longenecker with his somewhat famous "no" and "yes" answer. At the end of his book comparing New Testament exegesis to various Jewish methods, he states:

> Can we reproduce the exegesis of the New Testament? I suggest that we must answer both "No" and "Yes." Where that exegesis is based upon a revelatory stance, where it evidences itself to be merely cultural, or where it shows itself to be circumstantial or *ad hominem* in nature, "No." Where, however, it treats the Old Testament in more literal fashion, following the course of what we speak of today as historico-grammatical exegesis, "Yes." Our commitment as Christians

[12] Beale agrees: "Can we reproduce the exegesis of the NT? Yes" (*Handbook on the New Testament Use of the Old Testament*, 26). Concerning typological examples, Patrick Fairbairn notes that the manner in which the Old Testament types were introduced by the New Testament was to give examples. Hence, this leads one to conclude that these examples were "adapted to the occasion, and taken from a vast storehouse, where many more are to be found" (*The Typology of Scripture*, 2 vols. [Grand Rapids, MI: Zondervan, n.d.], 1:22).

[13] For example, the structure and genre of Near Eastern suzerain-vassal treaties add depth to our understanding of the structure of Deuteronomy.

[14] So also, for example, Fairbairn, "On the supposition of the authors of the New Testament being inspired teachers, the character of these citations is of the gravest importance . . . as [they] furnish in those [hermeneutical] principles an infallible direction for the general interpretation of ancient Scripture" (*The Typology of Scripture*, 1:363).

[15] "There is no evidence for an uninterrupted continuity from the OT to the specific theological statements of the NT writers" (Hübner, "New Testament, OT Quotations in the," 4:1096).

> is to the reproduction of the apostolic faith and doctrine, and not necessarily to the specific apostolic exegetical practices.[16]

Peter Enns explicitly agrees with Longenecker that we should not imitate the "exegetical method" of the Old Testament, but Enns does want to imitate the New Testament "hermeneutical goal," which relates to the death and resurrection of Christ.[17] Similarly, Paul Ellingworth, while discussing the hermeneutics of the book of Hebrews, states that "it is important for the modern reader . . . no[t] to assimilate the letter's creative use of the OT to the original meaning of the OT texts to which [the author of Hebrews] refers."[18]

To those who follow Longenecker, Moisés Silva has a good response. "If we refuse to pattern our exegesis after that of the apostles, we are in practice denying the authoritative character of their scriptural interpretation—and to do so is to strike at the very heart of the Christian faith."[19] Of course, this brief essay does not allow the space to defend all of the New Testament's hermeneutical uses of the Old Testament.[20] In the section "Justification of Typology," below, however, I will lay out a broad defense and required presuppositions for agreeing that the Old Testament truly speaks of Christ in typology.

Christ in the Old Testament

Clearly, the New Testament writers believe that the Old Testament speaks of Christ. There are many overarching statements in the New Testament to the effect that the Old Testament, broadly considered, speaks of Christ. In addition, many specific Old Testament texts are cited in the New Testament to show a specific aspect of Christ's person and work.

Examples of overarching statements include the following:

> Do not think that I [Jesus] have come to abolish the Law or the Prophets; I have not come to abolish them but to fulfill them. (Matt. 5:17)

> Beginning with Moses and all the Prophets, [Jesus] interpreted to them in all the Scriptures the things concerning himself. (Luke 24:27; also see 24:46)

> You search the Scriptures . . . ; and it is they that bear witness about me [Jesus]. (John 5:39; also see 5:46; 20:9)

> [Paul was] saying nothing but what the prophets and Moses said would come to pass: that the Christ must suffer and that, by being the first to rise from the dead, he would proclaim light both to our people and to the Gentiles. (Acts 26:22–23; also see 10:43; 28:23)

[16] *Biblical Exegesis in the Apostolic Period*, 219, emphasis his.

[17] "Apostolic Hermeneutics," *WTJ* 65 (2003): 263–87. Enns calls his method a "christotelic hermeneutic" (*Inspiration and Incarnation: Evangelicals and the Problem of the Old Testament* [Grand Rapids, MI: Baker Academic, 2005], 158).

[18] Paul Ellingworth, *The Epistle to the Hebrews: A Commentary on the Greek Text*, NIGTC (Grand Rapids, MI: Eerdmans, 1993), 63.

[19] Moisés Silva, "The New Testament Use of the Old Testament: Form and Authority," in *Scripture and Truth*, ed. D. A. Carson and John D. Woodbridge (Grand Rapids, MI: Eerdmans, 1992), 147–65, esp. 164.

[20] For a defense of the New Testament's use of the Old Testament, see Kaiser, *The Uses of the Old Testament in the New*; and Beale, *Handbook on the New Testament Use of the Old Testament*.

> [Paul was] set apart for the gospel of God, which he promised beforehand through his prophets in the holy Scriptures, concerning his Son. (Rom. 1:1–2; also see 3:21; 10:6–8; 16:25–26)

> Christ died for our sins in accordance with the Scriptures, that he was buried, that he was raised on the third day in accordance with the Scriptures. (1 Cor. 15:3–4)

> For all the promises of God find their Yes in [Christ]. (2 Cor. 1:20; also see 3:14)

> And the Scripture, foreseeing that God would justify the Gentiles by faith, preached the gospel beforehand to Abraham. (Gal. 3:8)

> Concerning this salvation, the prophets who prophesied about the grace that was to be yours searched and inquired carefully, inquiring what person or time the Spirit of Christ in them was indicating when he predicted the sufferings of Christ and the subsequent glories. (1 Pet. 1:10–11; also see 1:25)

Examples of specific texts related to Christ are numerous. Below are five somewhat different types of examples. The first is related to Herod and the Wise Men. The Matthew pericope simply informs the reader that Micah predicted the coming of a great ruler from Bethlehem, and this matches Jesus's historical birthplace. The second relates to Jesus's prediction after the Passover that his disciples will leave him as he goes through his arrest, trial, and crucifixion, and also relates to Jesus's claim that he is the "shepherd" whom God the Father will strike. The third is Paul's confirming evidence that Gentiles will glorify God by following Christ. The fourth is Paul's assertion that the Old Testament Passover lamb actually means something greater than a lamb; it is related to Christ. The fifth is part of the author of Hebrews's argument that even though Jesus is not of the Levitical priesthood lineage, he is still a proper Priest. This is so for several reasons, but the quote relates to Christ's living forever, which was foreshadowed by Melchizedek.

> Now after Jesus was born in Bethlehem . . . [Herod] inquired of [the chief priests and scribes] where the Christ was to be born. They told him, "In Bethlehem of Judea, for so it is written by the prophet:
>
> "'And you, O Bethlehem, in the land of Judah;
> . . . from you shall come a ruler
> who will shepherd my people Israel.'" (Matt. 2:1, 4–6 // Mic. 5:2 [Hebrew 5:1]; also see John 7:40–42)

> You will all fall away because of me [Jesus] this night. For it is written, "I [God the Father] will strike the shepherd, and the sheep of the flock will be scattered." (Matt. 26:31 // Zech. 13:7)

> The Gentiles [will] glorify God for his mercy. As it is written, . . .
>
> "The root of Jesse will come,
> even he who arises to rule the Gentiles;
> in him will the Gentiles hope." (Rom. 15:9, 12 // Isa. 11:10)

> For Christ, our Passover lamb, has been sacrificed. (1 Cor. 5:7; cf. Ex. 12:21, etc.)

> Another priest arises in the likeness of Melchizedek, who has become a priest, not on the basis of a legal requirement concerning bodily descent, but by the power of an indestructible life. For it is witnessed of him,
>
> "You are a priest forever,
> after the order of Melchizedek." (Heb. 7:15–17 // Ps. 110:4)

Hermeneutically speaking, the first example above, related to Bethlehem, is very straightforward. The second and third examples, Jesus's prediction and Paul's confirmation of Gentiles, are reasonably straightforward hermeneutically. The fourth, concerning the lamb, is a clear example of typology. The fifth example, using Melchizedek, is the most complicated of these examples, and it involves several hermeneutical assumptions, including typology.[21]

Justification of Typology

As has been noted, typology is not the only hermeneutical pattern by which one sees Christ in the Old Testament.[22] Also, I note that analogy, typology, and predictive prophecy are all on a continuum, and hard and fast distinctions blur the reality.[23] However, because of its importance in helping Christians to read the Old Testament and its controversial nature in the scholarly world, I will include a very brief definition of typology and the presuppositions necessary to affirm it. (Note, typology relates to more than Christ; for example, it relates also to the church. However, for purposes of this essay, I will discuss typology in relation to Christ.)

Goppelt defines typology as "historical facts—persons, actions, events, and institutions—. . . that are considered to be divinely ordained representations or types of future realities that will be even greater and more complete."[24] Most definitions of typology include this combination of historical correspondence and escalation.[25] For example, the Old Testament kingly office is a historical office that "escalates" to the perfect messianic King.

As many of the New Testament quotes above show, the New Testament writers believed that the Old Testament as a whole and various specific texts include Christ as part of the Old Testament meaning. Of course, the New Testament writers believed that many of the Old Testament texts became clearer once Christ historically appeared (Heb. 8:5), but nevertheless, Christ was part of the intended meaning of

[21] In addition to a typological hermeneutic, other hermeneutical assumptions in Hebrews 7 include the following: arguments from silence may be proper (7:3); changes in priesthood require a change in law (7:12), which is then related to a change in covenant in Hebrews 8–9; perfection is the goal, and the Levitical priesthood was not perfect (7:11); and Psalm 110 is later than the Mosaic law, which justifies that a changed and better priesthood was coming.

[22] Language in the Westminster Standards on Old Testament patterns related to Christ include "promises, prophecies, sacrifices, circumcision, the paschal lamb, and other types and ordinances" (WCF 7.5); "promises, types, and sacrifices" (WCF 8.6); "ceremonial laws, containing several typical ordinances . . . prefiguring Christ, his graces, actions, sufferings, and benefits" (WCF 19.3); and "[God] brought them out of their bondage in Egypt, so he delivereth us from our spiritual thraldom" (WLC 101).

[23] One proof of the continuum is that the New Testament writers sometimes use the same introductory quote formula for direct prophecy fulfillments (e.g., Matt. 8:17) and indirect typological fulfillments (e.g., Matt. 2:14–15). See the discussion in Beale, *Handbook on the New Testament Use of the Old Testament*, 58–59.

[24] *Typos*, 17–18.

[25] So also Fairbairn, *The Typology of Scripture*, 1:3; and Beale, *Handbook on the New Testament Use of the Old Testament*, 14.

the Old Testament.[26] To be sure, it is *not* that the New Testament writers believed that the "original meaning" of the Old Testament was devoid of Christ, and only after seeing Christ in the New Testament is a reader able to look back into the Old Testament to apply texts to him that may originally have applied to others.[27]

So how do we justify the typological hermeneutic of the New Testament? The following is a broad-brush outline of that justification. First, my primary argument: I believe that the ultimate justification for concluding that the Old Testament truly speaks of Christ is that the New Testament says so. Connected to this is that the Holy Spirit aids us in seeing Christ in the Old Testament (2 Cor. 3:14–18). The following are several secondary arguments.

The New Testament writers believe that God is the ultimate author of Scripture, and the human authors are secondary (Matt. 2:15; Heb. 10:15; 2 Pet. 1:21).[28] Because God is speaking, we partially understand a text relative to what we know about him, as we would understand any text relative to our understanding of the author.[29] Hence, God's omniscience comes into play. Related to this is that the original intention of Old Testament passages includes going beyond the original audience. Paul states, "The words 'it was counted to him' were not written for [Abraham's] sake alone, but for ours also" (Rom. 4:23–24). "For whatever was written [in Scripture] in former days was written for our instruction" (Rom. 15:4). Having God as the ultimate author allows that Old Testament texts may have broader meanings imbedded in them that later reading audiences may understand more fully. Also, it eliminates defining the original meaning as solely what is in the mind of the human author.[30]

In addition to God's being the author, typological interpretation is founded on God's providential control of people and events.[31] "Now these things [Old Testament historical events in the wilderness] happened to them as an example, but they were written down for our instruction" (1 Cor. 10:11). Concerning Joseph and the evil committed against him, "God meant it for good" (Gen. 50:20). God is able to intentionally use history so that Adam; the ebbs and flow of the Israelite kingly, priestly, and prophetic offices; the technicalities of Old Testament worship; the vari-

---

[26] After quoting several Old Testament verses to show that the Old Testament spoke of the Trinity, the Belgic Confession 9 notes, "That which appears to us somewhat obscure in the Old Testament is very plain in the New."

[27] Lane G. Tipton, who agrees with me concerning Christ in the Old Testament, points out the potential dangers of advocating a two-reading strategy. The first reading is a historical-grammatical reading based on the human author's historical context. The second looks again at the passage from a New Testament christological standpoint. Tipton sees the danger as not admitting that Christ was part of the original historical meaning, which would then invalidate the apostles' exegesis and deny the reality of God being the author who progressively revealed Scripture. See "The Gospel and Redemptive-Historical Hermeneutics," in *Confident of Better Things: Essays Commemorating Seventy-Five Years of the Orthodox Presbyterian Church*, ed. John R. Muether and Danny E. Olinger (Willow Grove, PA: Committee for the Historian of the Orthodox Presbyterian Church, 2011), 185–213.

[28] See the classic article by B. B. Warfield, "'It Says:' 'Scripture Says:' 'God Says,'" in *The Inspiration and Authority of the Bible*, ed. Samuel G. Craig (Phillipsburg, NJ: Presbyterian and Reformed, 1948), 299–348.

[29] Vern Sheridan Poythress, "Divine Meaning of Scripture," *WTJ* 48 (1986): 241–79, esp. 250.

[30] "There is no truth in the assertion that the intent of the secondary [human] authors, determined by the grammatico-historical method, always exhausts the sense of Scripture, and represents in all its fulness the meaning of the Holy Spirit [primary author]" (Louis Berkhof, *Principles of Biblical Interpretation: Sacred Hermeneutics* [Grand Rapids, MI: Baker, 1950], 60).

[31] E. Earle Ellis comments, "Typological exegesis assumes a divine sovereignty over history, an assumption that admittedly not everyone is prepared to accept" (foreword to Goppelt, *Typos*, xv). Ellis says elsewhere, "The rationale of NT typological exegesis is . . . [God's] Lordship in moulding and using history to reveal and illumine His purpose" (*Paul's Use of the Old Testament* [Grand Rapids, MI: Baker, 1981], 127–28).

ous judgments/destructions ("Remember Lot's wife," Luke 17:32); and so on will perfectly match aspects of the person and work of Christ.

Further, consider that God has revealed himself through covenants. That is, he has been revealing himself progressively in redemptive history and progressively in special revelation.[32] Many of the covenants explicitly include a forward-looking component. Abraham is told that he will be the "father of a multitude of nations" (Gen. 17:4). David is told that his son's kingdom will be established forever (2 Sam. 7:13; Acts 2:30). As the critical scholar Gerhard von Rad argues, the Old Testament itself often indicates that virtually every event is "pregnant with the future and points beyond itself to something yet to come."[33] This unfolding toward a perfect fulfillment culminating in the new heavens and new earth dovetails well with the "escalating" character of typology.

Finally, even when the New Testament writer quotes only one Old Testament verse, it appears that often he is referring to the "total context."[34] That is, the larger context of the Old Testament book, not simply the verse in question, is assumed by the New Testament writer. This challenges the view that the New Testament writers cite the Old Testament without respecting its context, a practice pejoratively termed "proof texting." In the critical-scholarly world, each of these views has many adherents. I believe that the New Testament writers often do imply broader contexts with their quotes (e.g., the Matt. 26:31 quote of Zech. 13:7 implies Zech. 9:9 and 12:10). This broader-context aspect adds occasionally to our understanding of typology.

In sum, typological interpretations are justified because (1) the New Testament says so, and (2) the triune God who wrote Scripture and controls the universe has unfolded his redemption and revelation in an organic and escalating manner.

Conclusion

Some today argue that the New Testament writers used various indefensible hermeneutical patterns to exegete Christ in the Old Testament; and therefore, we should not use these patterns.

I have attempted to remind us that God, through the New Testament writers, has declared that Christ is "in" the Old Testament. Further, God is the author of the Old Testament and controls all history. Finally, the redemptive-historical plan of God dovetails well with one of the most controversial of the New Testament hermeneutical patterns, typology. Therefore, *we should trust the New Testament hermeneutical patterns and use them when reading the Old Testament to further enhance our love for and devotion to Christ.*

There are many hermeneutical patterns about Christ that I have barely touched

---

[32] The classic redemptive-historical work is by Geerhardus Vos, *Biblical Theology: Old and New Testaments* (Carlisle, PA: Banner of Truth, 1975). Also see his prolonged discussion "The Covenant of Grace," in *Reformed Dogmatics*, vol. 2, *Anthropology*, trans. and ed. Richard B. Gaffin Jr. (Bellingham, WA: Lexham, 2014), 76–137.

[33] Gerhard von Rad, *Old Testament Theology*, trans. D. M. G. Stalker, 2 vols. (New York: Harper & Row, 1961–1965), 2:363–87, esp. 372.

[34] C. H. Dodd, *According to the Scriptures: The Sub-Structure of New Testament Theology* (London: Nisbet, 1952), 126. Dodd's book also proposes that the New Testament church had "testimony books" that contained various Old Testament quotes (pp. 28–60). I am not convinced.

upon, if at all. Other authors in this volume provide patterns and examples as they expound the various books of the Bible.[35] My aim here is not to present a catalog of patterns, but to encourage and reinforce our trust of Scripture, even its hermeneutics. May we all be further spurred on to see Christ in all of Scripture.

Select Bibliography

Beale, G. K. *Handbook on the New Testament Use of the Old Testament: Exegesis and Interpretation*. Grand Rapids, MI: Baker Academic, 2012.

Beale, G. K., and D. A. Carson, eds. *Commentary of the New Testament Use of the Old Testament*. Grand Rapids, MI: Baker Academic, 2007.

Dodd, C. H. *According to the Scriptures: The Sub-Structure of New Testament Theology*. London: Nisbet, 1952.

Ellis, E. Earle. *Paul's Use of the Old Testament*. Grand Rapids, MI: Baker, 1981.

Fairbairn, Patrick. *The Typology of Scripture*. 2 vols. Grand Rapids, MI: Zondervan, n.d.

Goppelt, Leonhard. *Typos: The Typological Interpretation of the Old Testament in the New*. Translated by Donald H. Madvig. Eugene, OR: Wipf & Stock, 2002.

Greidanus, Sidney. *Preaching Christ from the Old Testament: A Contemporary Hermeneutical Method*. Grand Rapids, MI: Eerdmans, 1999.

Hübner, Hans. "New Testament, OT Quotations in the." Translated by Siegfried S. Schatzmann. In *ABD*, 4:1096–1104.

Johnson, Dennis E. *Him We Proclaim: Preaching Christ from All the Scriptures*. Phillipsburg, NJ: P&R, 2007.

Kaiser, Walter C., Jr. *The Uses of the Old Testament in the New*. Eugene, OR: Wipf & Stock, 2001.

Kaiser, Walter C., Jr., Darrell L. Bock, and Peter Enns. *Three Views on the New Testament Use of the Old Testament*. Grand Rapids, MI: Zondervan, 2008.

Longenecker, Richard. *Biblical Exegesis in the Apostolic Period*. Biblical and Theological Classics Library 5. Carlisle: Paternoster, 1995.

Moyise, Steve. *The Old Testament in the New: An Introduction*. London: T&T Clark, 2001.

Poythress, Vern Sheridan. "Divine Meaning of Scripture." *WTJ* 48 (1986): 241–79.

———. *The Shadow of Christ in the Law of Moses*. Phillipsburg, NJ: P&R, 1991.

Rodgers, Peter R. *Exploring the Old Testament in the New*. Eugene, OR: Resource, 2012.

Silva, Moisés. "Old Testament in Paul." *DPL*, 630–42.

---

[35] For further reading, see Sidney Greidanus, *Preaching Christ from the Old Testament: A Contemporary Hermeneutical Method* (Grand Rapids, MI: Eerdmans, 1999); Dennis E. Johnson, *Him We Proclaim: Preaching Christ from All the Scriptures* (Phillipsburg, NJ: P&R, 2007); and Vern S. Poythress, *The Shadow of Christ in the Law of Moses* (Phillipsburg, NJ: P&R, 1991).

Appendix E

Scripture Versions Cited

Scripture quotations in this volume, unless otherwise indicated, are from the ESV® Bible (The Holy Bible, English Standard Version®), copyright © 2001 by Crossway, a publishing ministry of Good News Publishers. Used by permission. All rights reserved.

Other Scripture versions cited include the following:

ASV American Standard Version

HCSB The Holman Christian Standard Bible®. Copyright © 1999, 2000, 2002, 2003, 2009 by Holman Bible Publishers. Used by permission.

JB The Jerusalem Bible. Copyright © 1966, 1967, 1968 by Darton, Longman & Todd Ltd. and Doubleday & Co., Inc.

KJV King James Version

NAB New American Bible, copyright © 1970 by the Confraternity of Christian Doctrine, Washington, DC, and used by permission. All rights reserved.

NASB The New American Standard Bible®. Copyright © The Lockman Foundation 1960, 1962, 1963, 1968, 1971, 1972, 1973, 1975, 1977, 1995. Used by permission.

NEB The New English Bible © The Delegates of the Oxford University Press and The Syndics of the Cambridge University Press, 1961, 1970.

NET The NET Bible® copyright ©1996–2006 by Biblical Studies Press, L.L.C. www.netbible.org. All rights reserved. Quoted by permission.

NIV The Holy Bible, New International Version®, NIV®. Copyright © 1973, 1978, 1984 by Biblica, Inc.™ Used by permission. All rights reserved worldwide.

NIV 2011 The Holy Bible, New International Version®, NIV®. Copyright © 1973, 1978, 1984, 2011 by Biblica, Inc.™ Used by permission. All rights reserved worldwide.

NJB The New Jerusalem Bible. Copyright © 1985 by Darton, Longman & Todd Ltd. and Les Éditions du Cerf.

NKJV The New King James Version. Copyright © 1982, Thomas Nelson, Inc. Used by permission.

NLT The Holy Bible, New Living Translation, copyright © 1996, 2004, 2007, 2013 by Tyndale House Foundation. Used by permission of Tyndale House Publishers, Inc., Carol Stream, IL 60188. All rights reserved.

NRSV The New Revised Standard Version. Copyright © 1989 by the Division of Christian Education of the National Council of the Churches of Christ in the USA. Published by Thomas Nelson, Inc. Used by permission of the National Council of the Churches of Christ in the USA.

RSV The Revised Standard Version. Copyright ©1946, 1952, 1971, 1973 by the Division of Christian Education of the National Council of the Churches of Christ in the USA.

TEV Good News Bible in Today's English Version—Second Edition, Copyright ©1992 by American Bible Society. Used by permission.

TNIV The Holy Bible, Today's New International Version. TNIV®. Copyright © 2001, 2005 by International Bible Society. Used by permission of Zondervan. All rights reserved.

Contributors

William B. Barcley (PhD, Boston University) is the senior pastor of Sovereign Grace Presbyterian Church in Charlotte, North Carolina, and served as professor of New Testament at RTS-Jackson 2001–2007. Dr. Barcley's research interests are in Paul's letters and the church in the New Testament. He is the author of *Gospel Clarity: Challenging the New Perspective on Paul* (Evangelical Press, 2010), *The Secret of Contentment* (P&R, 2010), and *1 & 2 Timothy* (Evangelical Press, 2006).

Robert J. Cara (PhD, Westminster Theological Seminary) is the Hugh and Sallie Reaves Professor of New Testament at RTS-Charlotte and the provost and chief academic officer for the RTS institution. Dr. Cara's research interests are in Paul's letters and Luke-Acts. He is the author of *A Study Commentary on 1 and 2 Thessalonians* (Evangelical Press, 2009).

Benjamin Gladd (PhD, Wheaton College) is assistant professor of New Testament at RTS-Jackson. Dr. Gladd's research interests are in biblical theology, eschatology, and the use of the Old Testament in the New Testament. He is the coauthor (with Greg Beale) of *Hidden but Now Revealed: A Biblical Theology of Divine Mystery* (InterVarsity Press, 2014) and the author of *Revealing the Mysterion: The Use of Mystery in Daniel and Second Temple Judaism with Its Bearing on First Corinthians* (de Gruyter, 2008).

Charles E. Hill (PhD, Cambridge University) is the John R. Richardson Professor of New Testament and Early Christianity at RTS-Orlando. Dr. Hill's research interests are in Johannine literature and the origins of the New Testament. He is the author of *The Johannine Corpus in the Early Church* (Oxford, 2004) and *Who Chose the Gospels? Probing the Great Gospel Conspiracy* (Oxford, 2010).

Reggie M. Kidd (PhD, Duke University) is professor emeritus of New Testament at RTS-Orlando, having taught there since 1990. Dr. Kidd's research interests are in Pauline Epistles and Christian worship. He is the author of *With One Voice: Discovering Christ's Song in Our Worship* (Baker, 2005) and *Wealth and Beneficence in the Pastoral Epistles: A Bourgeois Form of Early Christianity?* (Scholars, 1990).

Simon J. Kistemaker (ThD, Free University of Amsterdam) is professor of New Testament emeritus at RTS-Orlando and has served as a professor at RTS since 1971.

Dr. Kistemaker's research interests are in the life and ministry of Jesus, and the use of Psalms in the book of Hebrews. He is the author of numerous volumes in the award-winning New Testament Commentary series, with William Hendriksen (Baker, 2002).

Michael J. Kruger (PhD, University of Edinburgh) is the president and Samuel C. Patterson Professor of New Testament and Early Christianity at RTS-Charlotte. Dr. Kruger's research interests are in the origins of the New Testament canon and the transmission of the New Testament text. He is the author of *Canon Revisited: Establishing the Origins and Authority of the New Testament Books* (Crossway, 2012) and *The Question of Canon: Challenging the Status Quo in the New Testament Debate* (IVP Academic, 2013).

Bruce A. Lowe (PhD, University of Queensland; PhD, Macquarie University) is assistant professor of New Testament at RTS-Atlanta. Dr. Lowe's current research interests include the Greco-Roman background to Paul, particularly as it relates to faith. He is the author of numerous academic articles and scholarly papers in the field of New Testament studies.

Guy Prentiss Waters (PhD, Duke University) is the James M. Baird Jr. Professor of New Testament at RTS-Jackson. Dr. Waters's research interests are in the theology of Paul and the use of Scripture in the New Testament. He is the author of *How Jesus Runs the Church* (P&R, 2011) and *Justification and the New Perspectives on Paul* (P&R, 2004).

General Index

Scripture Index

Indexed references to whole books of the Bible are limited to books other than the main focus of each chapter.

1 Corinthians